LOGIC, COMPUTERS, AND SETS

By

HAO WANG

CHELSEA PUBLISHING COMPANY
NEW YORK, N. Y.

THE PRESENT WORK IS AN UNABRIDGED REPRINT, WITH MINOR ALTERATIONS, OF A WORK FIRST PUBLISHED BY SCIENCE PRESS AT PEKING IN 1962 AND BY SCIENCE PRESS AND NORTH-HOLLAND PUBLISHING COMPANY IN 1964 UNDER THE TITLE A SURVEY OF MATHEMATICAL LOGIC. IT IS PUBLISHED AT NEW YORK, N.Y., 1970 AND IS PRINTED ON ALKALINE PAPER

LIBRARY OF CONGRESS CATALOGUE CARD NUMBER 70-113155

INTERNATIONAL STANDARD BOOK NUMBER 0-8284-0245-0

PRINTED IN THE UNITED STATES OF AMERICA

PREFACE

Some time ago it was suggested that a collection of my papers in the field of mathematical logic be put forth. As the papers deal with only a few subdomains of the field, I have added from unpublished notes discussions of a number of standard topics and replaced a few papers by somewhat more general descriptions of related matter. The result is the present book.

As a survey, it is neither complete nor impartial. For example, modal logic, combinatory logic, and many-valued logic are not considered at all. More serious omissions are any adequate account of more recent works on recursive functions and on intuitionism, two of the subjects which are of the greatest current interest among working mathematical logicians. But these two fields are in the midst of rapid developments; there seems to be no choice but to follow new discoveries as they come out. In a different direction, works not easily accessible to me have not been adequately dealt with.

For the material contained in the present book, I am heavily indebted to various persons for discussions, suggestions, and criticisms. On matters having to do with axiomatic set theory and metamathematics, my indebtedness is chiefly to Bernays, Kreisel, McNaughton, Quine, Rosser, and Specker; in the area of calculating machines, to A. W. Burks, B. Dunham, E. F. Moore, G. W. Patterson, and J. C. Shepherdson. In my earlier education, Chin Yueh-Lin, Shen Yu-Ting, and especially Wang Hsien-Chun have selflessly taught me mathematical logic. In more recent years, Hu Shih-Hua has given me much encouragement.

WANG HAO

June, 1959.

CONTENTS

PART TWO CALCULATING MACHINES

PART THREE FORMAL NUMBER THEORY

PART FOUR IMPREDICATIVE SET THEORY

PART FIVE PREDICATIVE SET THEORY

PART ONE

GENERAL SKETCHES

CHAPTER I

THE AXIOMATIC METHOD

§ 1. Geometry and Axiomatic Systems

Each scientific theory involves a body of concepts and a collection of assertions. When questioned of the meaning of a concept, we often explain it or define it in terms of other concepts. Similarly, when questioned of the truth or the reason for believing the truth of an assertion, we usually justify our belief by indicating that it follows from or can be deduced from certain other assertions which we accept. If somebody, as many children do, continues indefinitely to ask for definitions or deductions, it is obvious that sooner or later one of two things will happen. Either we find ourselves travelling in a circle, making use, in our answers, of concepts and assertions whose meaning and justification we originally set out to explain; or, at some stage, we refuse to supply any more definitions and deductions, and reply bluntly that the concepts and assertions we employ in our answer are already the most basic which we take for granted. When the problem is to understand the meaning of a concept or to see that a proposition is true, there is no basic objection to circular procedures, and, indeed, mutual support may in many cases prove to be the best sort of evidence we can ever obtain. But when we are able to start merely with a small number of primitive ideas and propositions, the linear mode of approach does have a special appeal and fascination in that questions of meaning and truth become concentrated in these few initial primitives plus certain typical ways of definition and deduction.

Usually, the primitive propositions are called axioms or postulates. When the concepts and propositions of a theory are thus arranged according to the connections of definability and deducibility, we have an axiomatic system for the theory.

The best known axiom system is undoubtedly Euclid's for geometry. His *Elements* is said to have had a wide circulation next only to the Bible. Admiration for its rigour and thoroughness has been expressed frequently. Spinoza, for example, attempted to attain the same formal perfection in his *Ethics* (Ethica more geometrico demonstrata).

There are in the *Elements* ten primitive propositions (axioms) of which five are called common notions, five are called postulates. From these and a number of definitions, 465 propositions (theorems) are deduced with considerable logical rigour. The same deductive method was used by Newton in mechanics, by Lagrange in analytic mechanics, by Clausius in thermodynamics. In recent years, axiom systems for many branches of mathematics and natural sciences have appeared.

While Euclid's unification of masses of more or less isolated discoveries was undoubtedly an impressive success in the program of systematizing mathematics, his actual axiom system is, according to the standard generally accepted now, far from formally perfect. For example, instead of taking point and line as primitive concepts, Euclid defines them respectively as "something which has no parts" and "length without breadth". Moreover, investigations in the latter part of last century have revealed many axioms which are implicitly assumed or inadequately formulated by Euclid.

The development of views on axiomatic systems was closely connected with the discovery of non-euclidean geometries. On the one hand, Euclid's axioms as a whole seemed so natural and obvious that they were regarded as logically necessary or, according to Kant, synthetic a priori. On the other hand, since ancient times, many mathematicians have found Euclid's fifth postulate (the "parallel axiom") not sufficiently self-evident and tried to derive it from the other axioms. This disputed axiom states in effect that through a given point one and only one straight line can be drawn which is parallel to a given straight line. Unlike the other axioms, it involves a reference to infinity through the concept of a parallel. During the Renaissance, controversy over the axiom renewed. In the eighteenth century, Lambert and Saccheri tried, with no success, to derive contradictions from the negation of the axiom.

During the first third of the nineteenth century, Lobachevski, Bolyai, and Gauss independently discovered a consistent geometry in which the parallel axiom was replaced by the assumption that there exist more than one parallels through a given point. In 1854, Riemann discussed the possibility of a finite but unbounded space and invented geometries in which there exist no parallel lines at all. All these geometries in which Euclid's fifth postulate is false are called non-euclidean geometries.

The realization of different possible geometries led to a desire to separate abstract mathematics from spatial intuition. For example, Grassmann stressed in his *Ausdehnungslehre* (1844) the distinction between a purely mathematical discipline and its application to nature. Since the axioms are no longer necessarily true in the physical world, deductions must be made independently of spatial intuition. Reliance on diagrams and meaning of geometrical concepts must, therefore, be avoided.

In his book on geometry (1882), Pasch adhered to this changed viewpoint and found out many shortcomings in Euclid's axiomatization. He disclosed the most hidden axioms, those of order. For example, he noted the need of the following axiom: a straight line that intersects one side of a triangle in any point other than a vertex must also intersect another side of the triangle.

Hilbert's famous work on the foundations of geometry appeared in 1899. It further emphasized the point that strict axiomatization involves total abstraction from the meaning of the concepts. Apart from Hilbert's axioms for geometry, alternative systems have been proposed by Peano, Veblen, Huntington, and others. Hilbert arranged the axioms in five groups: The axioms of incidence, of order (betweenness), of congruence, of parallels, and of continuity.

In these systems it is customary to take for granted a basic logic of inference (the theory of quantification or the predicate calculus) which deals with the logical constants "if-then", "not", "all", "some", "or", "and", "if and only if". There are, as we know, standard axiom systems for quantification theory. If we adjoin one such system to an axiom system for geometry, we get a more thoroughly formalized system.

In general, there are different degrees of formalization. If Euclid thought wrongly that his axiom system was completely formal, how do we know that a system considered formal now will not turn out to be imperfectly formalized?

In the evolution of axiom systems, there has emerged a sharp criterion of formalization in terms, not of meaning and concepts, but of notational features of terms and formulae.

Before stating the criterion, let us recapitulate the process of formalization. In a given mathematical discipline, there is a body of asserted and unasserted propositions. Out of the asserted propositions, choose some as axioms from which others can be deduced. In order that the axioms be adequate, they must express all the relevant properties of the undefined technical terms so that it should be possible to perform the deductions even if we treat the technical terms as meaningless words or symbols. Then we turn our attention to the logical particles or nontechnical words and make explicit the principles which determine their meaning or, in other words, govern their use. As a result, we should be able to recognize, merely by looking at the notational pattern, axioms and proofs.

From now on we shall speak of formal or axiomatic systems only when the systems satisfy the following criterion: there is a mechanical procedure to determine whether a given notational pattern is a symbol occurring in the system, whether a combination of these symbols is a well-formed formula (meaningful sentence) or an axiom or a proof of the system. Thus the formation rules, i.e. rules for specifying well-formed formulae, are entirely explicit in the sense that theoretically a machine can be constructed to pick out all well-formed formulae of the system if we use suitable physical representation of the basic symbols. The axioms and rules of inference are also entirely explicit. Every proof in each of these systems, when written out completely, consists of a finite sequence of lines such that each line is either an axiom or follows from some previous lines in the sequence by a definite rule of inference. Therefore, given any proposed proof, presented in conformity with the formal requirements for proofs in these systems, we can check its correctness mechanically. Theoretically, for each such formal system, we can also construct a machine which continues to print all the different proofs of the system from the simpler ones to the more complex, until the machine finally breaks down through wear and tear. If we suppose that the machine will never break down, then every proof of the system can be printed by the machine. Moreover, since a formula is a theorem if and only if it is the last line of a proof, the machine will also, sooner or later, print every theorem of the system. (Following a nearly established usage, we shall always count the axioms of a system among its theorems.)

Mathematical objects such as numbers and functions are studied in ordinary mathematical disciplines. Metamathematics, which constitutes nowadays an important part of mathematical logic, takes, on the other hand, mathematical theories as its objects of study. This is made possible by formalizing mathematical theories into axiomatic systems, which, unlike, for instance, the psychology of invention, are suitable objects of exact mathematical study. Indeed, if the powerful method of representing symbols by positive integers is employed, many problems in metamathematics become problems about positive integers, and the difference in subject matter between metamathematics and mathematics becomes even less conspicuous.

Apart from formal systems we shall also have occasion to study quasiformal systems in the following sense. A quasiformal system is obtained from a formal system by adding "nonconstructive rules of proof", which superficially provide definite methods of proof but really leave open the methods of proof. The best known is the rule of infinite induction according to which if $F(n)$ is a theorem for every positive integer n, then "$(n)F(n)$" is also a theorem. This leaves open the methods by which it is established that $F(n)$ is a theorem for every n.

Concerning each formal system, we can ask a number of different questions which are usually divided into two categories: the syntactical questions which deal with the system taken as a pure formalism or a machine for manufacturing formulae, and the semantical questions which are concerned with interpreting the system.

For example, with regard to a formal system, it is natural to ask whether it might not happen that not only proofs but also provability can be mechanically checked. If this is true for a system, then there is a definite method such that given any sentence of the system, the method enables us to decide whether it is a theorem. Such systems are called decidable systems. Other questions are: whether a given formal system is satisfiable, i.e. admits an interpretation; whether a system is consistent, i.e. contains no contradictory theorems.

Quantification theory occupies a special place with regard to formal systems. It can be viewed either as a subsidiary part of each axiom system which has its own special subject matter, or as a basic common framework such that each special system is but one of its applications. The latter viewpoint leads to an inclination to treat all important problems about formal systems as problems about quantificational formulae. For instance, both the consistency and the decidability of formal systems are reduced to the "decision problem", i.e., the problem of deciding the satisfiability or validity of quantificational formulae.

§ 2. The Problem of Adequacy

One is led to an interest in mathematical logic through diverse paths. The approach determines the posing of questions which in turn determines the replies. It is not so much that different approaches yield different answers to the same problems. Rather logicians of different backgrounds tend to ask different questions. They hold, therefore, different views on what the business of logic is. To settle these differences impartially is beyond the capability of an individual logician qua logician. For a settlement inevitably depends on judgments as to whether one type of question is more interesting than another: a highly partial and subjective matter.

What can be profitably done is to make a declaration of interest in certain problems, coupled with an enunciation of reasons for considering such questions interesting. If there is an attractive unifying principle among these problems, the chances of the declaration being accepted as a definition of logic will increase.

Consider the body of all mathematical disciplines, with their concepts and theorems, as it is formulated in a crystallized form (say, as in textbooks). One main problem of mathematical logic is to organize and systematize each discipline separately and the whole body altogether more or less in the manner of Euclid or, if possible, even more thoroughly. The scale of the program of systematizing the whole mathematics ought to satisfy everyone whose instinctive urge toward system building is reasonably modest. Yet there is no program of comparable scale, with the possible exception of that of unifying physical theory, which enjoys with it the unusual advantages of objectivity of results and proximity to vital human endeavours.

The organization of each discipline separately is not only a necessary preliminary step to the construction of a "grand logic", but important on its own account. In general, if two disciplines are equivalent, we need only study one of them. On the other hand, if an important discipline A is reducible to but substantially weaker than a discipline B, we cannot legitimately conclude that since A is a part of B, A need not be studied separately. For example, number theory and analysis are both reducible to set theory, analysis includes number theory as a proper part; we nonetheless make separate investigations of the three disciplines because each of them presents its own peculiar problems. Indeed, the business of mathematical logic is primarily the systematic study of these three regions and the underlying more elementary discipline of quantification theory. More explicitly, number theory deals with non-negative integers, analysis deals with non-negative integers and real numbers (or sets of integers), set theory deals with arbitrary sets or classes or functions. It is natural to choose to treat these branches because their concepts and methods are familiar and basic. On the one hand, masses of rather objective facts in them have to be accounted for, so that there is little room for capricious preferences. On the other hand, because of the central position of these branches, a clarification of their principles will bring the foundations of other branches of mathematics under control.

For each of the three fields, the first problem is to find a formal system which formalizes the intuitive theory. Given such a formal system, since it is intended as the formalization of an intuitive theory, the natural question is its adequacy. This question may take different forms. One form is, can all known proofs in the intuitive theory be formalized in the system? In many cases, the answer is usually yes: we believe that all known theorems and their proofs in the intuitive theory get close replicas in those formal systems of it which are now generally accepted. The actual derivation of mathematics from any such system is, however, long and tedious; it is practically impossible to verify conclusively that the intuitive theory, with all its details, is derivable in the system. On the other hand, it is also hard to refute such a claim for that would require the discovery of some premise or principle of inference, which has so far been tacitly assumed but unrecognized.

Even where a formal system is said to be adequate to an intuitive theory, it is often possible to construct, in terms of the whole formal system, arguments which can no longer be formalized in the system but are nonetheless of the same general type as arguments formalizable in the system. Next, in the intuitive theory, we are often less hesitant to use methods from other disciplines; for example, the use of analytic methods in number theory. The boundaries between formal systems are generally sharper so that, for example, usual formal systems of number theory do not include the analytic methods. Last but not least, there is always the question of faithful representation: although all known theorems and proofs of the intuitive theory have images in a formal system, we can still query how close these images resemble the originals, whether they are natural or rather distorted pictures. Indeed, if we merely attempt to embed actually recorded arguments but disregard intentions to admit general patterns, diverse artificial formal systems can be constructed for a given theory.

The domain of an intuitive theory is quite indeterminate, and the domain of its known theorems is more so. It is, therefore, desirable to introduce, besides the demonstrability of known theorems, other criteria for the adequacy of a formalization. Since the formal system is constructed to approximate the intuitive theory, the theory is the intended interpretation of the system. One criterion of adequacy is that the system do admit its intended interpretation. A separate and independent criterion is that the system be categorical, i.e., admit essentially only one interpretation, any two interpretations of it are isomorphic or, in other words, essentially equivalent. The most ideal formalization should be adequate by both criteria. Actually, most interesting formal systems are not categorical. It is not even clear that they always admit the intended interpretations: sometimes the intuitive theory to be formalized is so complex that we are unable to specify unambiguously the intended interpretation.

The reference to intuitive interpretations of a formal system inevitably brings in elements which are less precise and exact than the formal system. To avoid this, one is led to the introduction of a criterion of adequacy which refers only to the formal system: a formal system is complete if and only if for every unambiguous sentence in the system, either it or its negation is a theorem. This makes no reference to the intuitive theory and can therefore serve as a criterion of adequacy only after we have been independently convinced that all thoughts in the intuitive theory can be expressed in the formal system and that ordinary theorems can be proved. Once we agree on these matters the criterion of completeness is sufficient since we obviously do not wish to have both a sentence and its negation demonstrable in any theory. On the other hand, it is not clear that a formalization, to be adequate, must be complete in this sense. It is quite possible that an incomplete system reproduces faithfully our incomplete intuitive theory because it may happen that our intuitive procedure of proof is not capable of settling certain questions in the theory.

However that may be, the sharp question of completeness has led to sharp answers. Gödel's famous theorem establishes the conclusion that the usual formal systems for number theory, analysis and set theory are incomplete unless they contain contradictions. Moreover, given any consistent formal system for one of these theories, a sentence of the system can be constructed which is demonstrably indemonstrable. This result and its proof have also as a corollary the impossibility of finding a categorical formal system for any of the disciplines. In other words, in the process of answering the sharper problem of completeness one is led to significant conclusions on the original less precise question of adequacy. This illustrates a rather general phenomenon of studying a vaguer original problem through a related, though apparently different, one which is capable of exact treatment. Another example is the study of the problem of evidence by way of an attack on questions of consistency. The determination of completeness or consistency of a formal system required so much information: in the process of answering such questions one cannot help getting significant conclusions on the more basic problems of adequacy and comprehensibility of the formal system.

Gödel's incompleteness theorem and other general results on the inadequacy of formalization to capture intuition lead to an interest in quasiformal systems and an emphasis on the distinction between truth and demonstrability. If no formal system can yield as theorems all true sentences and no false ones of intuitive number theory, one may yet wish to find some less exact characterization of the class of true sentences which is a little more articulate than the intuitive theory.

If we think of the formulae in a formal system as representing the propositions of an intuitive theory, then all theorems of the system should of course represent true propositions. Now we have many deep-rooted requirements about the concept of truth such as: no proposition and its negation can both be true, a general proposition is true if all its instances are, etc. Hence, we are led to demand that an adequate formal system be consistent, ω–consistent, externally consistent, etc.

The problem of adequacy is different with quantification theory. Here, we are concerned not so much with sentences as with sentence-forms which contain uninterpreted predicate letters. A sentence-form is valid, if it yields a true sentence no matter how we interpret the predicate letters in it. And a system of quantification theory is complete if all valid sentence-forms are provable. It is known that usual systems of quantification theory are complete.

§ 3. The Problem of Evidence

It is customary to trace the beginning of modern foundational researches back to the discovery of paradoxes in set theory around 1900. Most working mathematicians are not much concerned over these paradoxes because their approach is more or less piecemeal and they have little interest in systematic formalization. There are, nonetheless, a number of philosophically-minded mathematicians who have taken them quite seriously. Their views can be taken as inferences from reflections on the paradoxes, and contemporary mathematical logic is to a considerable extent founded on and shaped by these views.

During the latter half of the nineteenth century, there were: (1) the arithmetization of analysis which reduces real numbers to arbitrary infinite sets satisfying certain broad conditions; (2) the extensively studied problem of representing arbitrary functions; (3) Cantor's invention of higher infinities; (4) Frege's and Dedekind's investigation on the foundations of number theory by set-theoretic considerations. These quite naturally led to an interest in the development of an abstract theory of sets. The paradoxes came as a surprise to many mathematicians and philosophers.

One way to eliminate the paradoxes is to build an axiomatic system for set theory in which arguments leading to the paradoxes are excluded. There are different ways of doing this. Hence, we get different axiomatic systems. Each system is constructed with a view to yield, short of contradictions, as much set theory as possible, and as naturally as possible. The systems are only such that we do not know how to get contradictions in them. We do not know that contradictions will never arise in them.

If it is agreed that reality cannot be contradictory, then this ignorance indicates either that sets are not real or at least that we do not have a clear concept of set. This leads to the broad questions of mathematical reality and mathematical evidence. If our intuition is not able to assure us that the theorems in an axiomatic set theory are true, what mathematical propositions can be seen to be true by our intuition? What kind of evidence distinguishes these intuitive mathematical truths from other mathematical propositions?

There seems to be a relative character in the nature of evidence. What is viewed as evident at one stage of the intellectual process may lose its intuitive evidence at a more advanced stage. For example, the information about physical things which sense experiences supply is no longer regarded as evident when a distinction between real and apparent qualities is introduced. Or, Euclidean axioms are no longer regarded as evident after the discovery of non-Euclidean geometries. Similarly, the discovery of paradoxes seems to deprive axioms of set theory of evidence. One is led to the search for some primitive or absolute evidence which will not be discredited at a higher stage of intellectual development.

Poincaré and Russell blamed the use of impredicative definitions. Russell introduced his vicious circle principle to rationalize the exclusion of these definitions, and constructed a formal system, commonly known as the ramified theory of types, according to the principle. There are certain shortcomings in the formal system which led Russell to introduce an axiom of reducibility which violates the vicious circle principle and nullifies completely the initial efforts to exclude impredicative definitions. It now seems possible to construct formal and quasi formal systems which yield most of the fruits of the axiom of reducibility but which still conform to the vicious circle principle. All these will be referred to as systems of predicative set theory.

There is much in common between Brouwer's intuitionism and what Hilbert considered to be finitist methods. A most striking coincidence in the two somewhat different approaches is the denial of the general validity of the law of excluded middle. In other words, even though tertium non datur holds for many sentences, there are others such that neither they nor their negations are true according to the intuitionist or the finitist interpretation.

This position can be made to appear less strange if we accept the following plausible propositions. In the first place, there are more arbitrary functions of integers than computable functions; or, in other words, there are certain functions of integers which are not computable. This can be established rigorously if we get a sharp and reasonable concept of computable functions.

In any case it seems reasonable to believe this to be the case. In the second place, as is commonly asserted, existence means constructibility according to the intuitionistic and the finitist reading of "there exists". It follows in particular that a sentence "for every m, there exists an n, such that $R(m,n)$" is true only if there is a constructive procedure which yields, for each m, its corresponding n, or, in other words, there is a computable function of m such that "for every m, $R(m,f(m))$" is true. In the third place, negating an assertion about an infinite collection does not merely mean that the assertion is false, because to know that would require going through infinitely many cases to decide whether there is a counter example, and it is not effectively possible to do so. Hence, from the effective approach, the negation of an assertion about infinitely many things can only be taken as an assertion of impossibility or absurdity: the assumption that the original assertion is true leads to a contradiction. According to this interpretation, the negation of "for all m, there exists an n, such that $R(m,n)$" means not the nonexistence of a computable function but rather that of an arbitrary function f such that "for every m, $R(m,f(m))$" is true. Hence, there is an asymmetry between a sentence and its negation. Thus, if a general assertion is satisfied only by a noncomputable function, then it is neither absurd nor effectively true. Hence, the law of excluded middle no longer holds for such an assertion.

Some examples may serve to clarify the matter a little more. According to widely accepted rigorous concepts of computable functions, it is possible to find a definite formula $T(m,n)$ such that there is no computable function but one noncomputable function f such that "for every m, $T(m,f(m))$" is true.

Consider now the following three sentences:

(1) For every positive integer m, there exists a positive integer n, n is greater than m and n is a prime (viz., one of the numbers such as 2, 3, 5, 7, etc., which are greater than 1 and cannot be resolved into smaller factors).

(2) For every positive integer m, there exists a positive integer n such that $T(m,n)$.

(3) For every positive integer m, there exists a positive integer n, n is greater than m, n is a prime, and $n+2$ is also a prime.

They are all of the form

(4) $(m)(En)R(m,n)$,

where $R(m,n)$ is, for (1) and (3), a formula such that, for any given values of m and n, the truth or falsity of $R(m,n)$ can be checked by elementary calculations.

Let us now consider, with regard to the three examples, the law of excluded middle:

(5) $(m)(En)R(m,n) \vee \sim(m)(En)R(m,n)$.

In the first place, if (2) is taken as the sentence "$(m)(En)R(m,n)$", (5) is false according to the effective interpretation of (m), (En) (quantifiers) and $\sim$ (negation). This is clear from the discussions given above.

The sentence (1) is known to be true and the familiar proof goes as follows. Given any positive integer m. Consider the number $m!+1$ ($m!$ being the factorial of m, i.e. the product of all positive integers from 1 to m). Clearly $m!+1$ is not divisible by any of 2, 3, $\cdots$, m. Either $m!+1$ is a prime, or, if not itself a prime, it is divisible by some prime. In either case, there must be some prime greater than m, but not greater than $m!+1$.

From this proof it follows that for every m, there exists an n such that $n \leqslant m!+1$ and $R(m,n)$ (i.e. $m < n$ and n is prime). Hence, given any m, theoretically we can go through the sentences $R(m, m+1)$, $\cdots$, $R(m, m!+1)$ and find, by elementary calculations, the smallest integer k, $m+1 \leqslant k \leqslant m!+1$, such that $R(m,k)$. In this way, we get a computable function f such that $(m)R(m,f(m))$. In this way, the proof of (1) establishes that (1) is true by the effective interpretation. It follows that the law of excluded middle (5) is true if (1) is taken as "$(m)(En)R(m,n)$".

It is not known whether (3) is classically true or false. It follows that the truth or falsity of (3) is also not known according to the effective interpretation. There is an ambiguity in the notion of effective methods. If we understand this in the classical sense, then (3) can be true only if it is true in the effective interpretation of existence because $\mu_n R(m,n)$ would be general recursive and effective. On the other hand, the intuitionists would require that a constructive proof be given for the effectiveness of a given function before it can be accepted as effective. Hence, the problem is reduced to a more subtle question of determining what a constructive proof is. According to a classical effective interpretation, if (3) is true in the effective sense, it is also true in the classical sense; if (3) is false in the effective sense, it is also false in the classical sense. On the other hand, if we adopt the doubly effective interpretation of the intuitionists, there are altogether three possibilities: (i) the sentence (3) is effectively true; (ii) it is not effectively true but classically true; (iii) it is false. If either (i) or (iii) is the case, then the law of excluded middle (5) is true for (3). If, on the other hand, (ii) is the case, then it no longer holds for (3). Of course, the intuitionists reject the notion of classical truth and say simply we do not know whether (5) is true for (3).

The account thus far attempts to make it reasonably plausible that sometimes tertium non datur may fail, if an effective or constructive interpretation of logical particles in arithmetic formulae is adopted. There is, however, no ambition to give here a full explanation of either intuitionism or finitist methods. For example, the above account does not even touch on the different attitudes toward interpreting "if-then" between the intuitionist and the finitist views.

It is often stressed that the rise of infinitely many objects in mathematics is the source of all troubles, and that different views on the infinite determine different philosophies of mathematics. The word "finitist" already reveals a somewhat negative attitude toward infinity. According to Brouwer, belief in the absolute validity of classical logic, and in particular its applicability to the mathematics of infinite sets, is not justified, because classical logic was originally abstracted from the mathematics of finite sets.

Suppose we assume a finite set W of positive integers and a numerical formula "$R(m, n, k)$", i.e. a formula such that, for any given m, n, and k, $R(m, n, k)$ can be decided to be true or false by elementary calculations. Consider then the following two sentences:

(4*) For every m in W, there exists an n in W, such that $R(m, n, k)$ for all k in W.

(5*) Either (4*) or $\sim$ (4*).

For any m, n, and k in W, we can verify whether $R(m, n, k)$ or $\sim R(m, n, k)$. Since there are only finitely many triples (m, n, k), we could in principle search through all of them and decide whether for each m in W, there is an n in W such that for all k in W, $R(m, n, k)$. It then follows that (5*) is always true. Or, if we prefer, we could also eliminate quantifiers by interpreting (m) and (k) as conjunctions and (En) as disjunction, (5*) would then become a truth-functional tautology. In any case, since the truth or falsity of (4*) can in principle be effectively decided, (5*) is true. When W is an infinite set, the situation is changed because we cannot, even in principle, go through infinitely many individual cases.

In these considerations, we have assumed that $R(m, n, k)$ is a numerical formula. If it is not numerical then it may very well happen that there exist certain integers m, n, and k in W such that "$R(m, n, k)$" is neither true nor false in the effective sense. Indeed, it is also possible so to choose "$R(m, n, k)$" that (5*) is not true by the effective interpretation, even though we are only concerned with the finitely many integers in W. Similarly, if we deal with finite sets of real numbers, we can easily encounter places where tertium non datur fails in the effective interpretation. It may, therefore, be thought that the emphasis on finitude is misplaced. A reply can, however, be made on the ground that in both cases the infinite already came in at an earlier stage. In general, if one starts only with finitely many things and systematically decidable properties and relations, he can never get to assertions which have ambiguous interpretations (i.e. get different truth values depending on whether classical or effective interpretation of logic is used).

We have at several places referred to "elementary calculations". Roughly speaking, problems such as finding sum or product, deciding whether a given number is prime, determining the greatest prime factor of a given number, etc. can all be settled by elementary calculations. A more exact characterization of the domain of elementary calculations is closely related to the question of delineating the range of computable functions. We shall for the moment continue to speak rather vaguely of numerically decidable formulae, elementary calculations, computable functions.

There is also a rather close kinship between Hilbert's finitist methods and Skolem's desire to dispense with quantifiers and use just free variables and computable functions. Investigations of Gentzen and Ackermann on the consistency of number theory have led to an interest in principles of transfinite induction which seem to yield a rather natural extension of Hilbert's and Skolem's preferred methods. Quite recently, Kreisel has combined these tendencies and formulated a coherent position according to which only quantifier-free methods are to be accepted as basis in building foundations.

To sum up, there are on the one hand the uninhibited axiomatic set-theories of Zermelo and others, and on the other hand, three constructive positions which can be briefly characterized as predicative set theory, intuitionism, and quantifier-free methods. Each constructive approach is faced with the problem of accounting for nonconstructive methods which are commonly employed in analysis and set theory and receive more or less adequate formalization in axiomatic systems of Zermelo and others. It is also desirable to decide how the three constructive positions are related.

Since nonconstructive methods are widely used in mathematics, a constructivist is expected to justify these methods from his point of view. If such justification is not forthcoming, either the poverty of the particular constructive line or the obscurity of the unpliable nonconstructive methods can be deplored.

There are different ways of justifying nonconstructive methods: to prove near analogues on a constructive basis, to reinterpret classical mathematics in constructive systems, to prove consistency of nonconstructive systems by some constructive methods. Each attempt is to be examined individually, in order that its merits and defects can be determined.

On the other hand, interesting new mathematics can also be created by adhering to a special approach. For example, the intuitionists have their own set theory, their own theory of the continuum in which new concepts and distinctions are used.

The program of proving consistency formulates rather sharply the problem of evidence. According to Hilbert, classical mathematics may be viewed as effecting, by the introduction of "ideal elements", a completion and simplification of the system of the intuitively meaningful mathematics. A proof of consistency would assure us that the simplifying idealization yielded no undesirable consequences.

The preferences for certain methods are determined negatively by their differences from those which apparently bred the contradictions, and positively by special interesting features which are peculiar to them. The chosen methods must be different from those whose vindication or clarification is to be achieved on the basis of them. Even if one may have originally been led to an interest in these methods because he finds them natural (say, on biographical grounds), their positive virtues are objective. It is this objective element which accounts for the possibility of arriving at agreement on views with regard to foundations. For example, the proofs in predicative set theory or by quantifier-free methods are transparent at least in the sense that we can see that they will never lead to contradictions.

The question of consistency and in general the question of replacing current methods by the preferred ones, can be profitably studied by the use of formal systems. Formalization is not just an end in itself but in addition a useful instrument which enables us to study the problem of evidence systematically.

There are different kinds of consistency proof. For example, non-Euclidean geometries have been proved to be consistent relative to the Euclidean by models. Similarly, geometry has a model in analysis and, therefore, the consistency of geometry is reduced to that of analysis. When we come to number theory, analysis, or set theory, we can no longer prove consistency by using models because numbers and sets seem to be the most basic mathematical objects and no model from the empirical world could supply all the sharp and exact details. Hence, what is needed is not proofs of relative consistency, but rather absolute consistency proofs which do not presuppose the consistency of whole other systems. The method is to examine usually by some form of induction all possible proofs in a system and to establish that none of them can yield a contradiction as its conclusion.

Numbers and figures form the basic objects of study in mathematics; the more abstract theories and objects are derivative in that they were created either by analogy and generalization or to solve specific problems about numbers and figures. Our intuition is most reliable with regard to simple numbers and figures. There may be different opinions as to the relative priority of numbers and figures. The Greeks seemed to prefer thinking in terms of figures and wished to reduce all mathematics to geometry. On the other hand, it has been common since last century to arithmetize geometry.

§4. A Very Elementary System L

The system L contains a single two-place predicate (a dyadic relation) R, three constant names 1, 2, 3 of individuals, and the variables x, y, z, etc. If R holds between x and y, we write: $R(x, y)$. The axioms of L are as follows:

*A*1. There are exactly the three things 1, 2, 3: $(x)(x=1 \vee x=2 \vee x=3)$; $1 \neq 2$ & $1 \neq 3$ & $2 \neq 3$.

*A*2. $(x)\sim R(x,x)$; in other words, R is irreflexive.

*A*3. $R(x,y)$ & $R(x,z) \supset y=z$; in other words, R is many-one.

*A*4. $R(y,x)$ & $R(z,x) \supset y=z$; in other words, R is one-many.

*A*5. $(x)(Ey)R(x,y)$.

*A*6. $R(1,2)$.

The concepts of model and satisfiability can be defined thus:

Definition 1. *An axiom system is satisfiable if there exists a model or interpretation of the system. An interpretation of an axiom system is an assignment of meanings to the undefined terms of the system according to which all the axioms are true.*

In particular, a model of the system L is determined by: (a) a (not empty) domain D of objects; (b) a rule that associates each constant name with a thing in D; (c) a relation R^* as the model of R; (d) a rule of interpretation telling us, for any objects a and b in D, whether R holds between them, and therefore, derivatively, for any statement of the system, whether it is true or false; (e) the fact that the statements *A*1—*A*6 come out true according to (a)—(d).

It is quite easy to find a model for L. Take the domain D as consisting of three persons, Chang, Li, and Yang, sitting around a round table with Chang immediately to the right of Li, associating them with 1, 2, 3, respectively, and interpret the relation R as holding between two persons a and b if and only if a sits immediately to the right of b. It can be checked that all the axioms *A*1—*A*6 come out true.

In fact, we can take an arbitrary domain D with three objects 1^*, 2^*, 3^* which represent 1, 2, 3 respectively, and obtain a model for the system L by choosing a relation R^* such that R^* is true of the pairs $(1^*, 2^*)$, $(2^*, 3^*)$, $(3^*, 1^*)$, and false for the six remaining pairs. As a result, we even do not have to use any concrete interpretations for L. We can say abstractly that the following matrix defines a model for L.

R	1	2	3
1	—	+	—
2	—	—	+
3	+	—	—

We come to the familiar notion of isomorphism. Thus, two models of L are isomorphic or essentially the same if there exists a one-to-one correspondence between the two domains such that the first model of the relation R holds between two objects of the first domain if and only if the other model of the relation R holds between their images in the other domain. It follows that a statement is true in one model if and only if it is true in the other. For instance, any two models for L, which both satisfy the matrix given above, are isomorphic. In general, an axiom system may contain a number of technical terms which stand for properties, relations, and operations. In two isomorphic models of the systems, all these should correspond so that, for example, if f_1 and f_2 stand for a same functor and a_2, b_2 correspond to a_1, b_1, then $f_1(a_1, b_1)$ must correspond to $f_2(a_2, b_2)$. This condition on models for the technical terms is equivalent to the requirement that any statement of the system is true in one model if and only if it is true in the other. We can, therefore, give the definitions:

Definition 2. *Two models of an axiom system S are said to be isomorphic if there exists a one-to-one correspondence between the two domains and any statement of S is true in one model if and only if it is true in the other.*

Definition 3. *An axiom system S is categorical if and only if every pair of models of S is isomorphic.*

It is not hard to see that the system L, determined by $A1$—$A6$, is categorical. In fact, by straightforward combinatorial considerations, we can see that all models of L satisfy the matrix given above. Thus, by $A1$, the domain of each model of L consists of exactly three objects (say) 1^*, 2^*, 3^*. Therefore, there are nine ordered pairs of the objects of that domain. For each of these pairs, R may either hold or not. Hence, we have 2^9 possible interpretations of the relation R which would all satisfy $A1$. By $A2$, $R(1^*, 1^*)$, $R(2^*, 2^*)$, $R(3^*, 3^*)$, must all be false. Therefore, there are only $2^6 (=2^9/2^3)$ possible interpretations of R satisfying both $A1$ and $A2$. Of these 64 possibilities, only 27 satisfy also $A3$, because, by $A3$, if R holds of the pair (1, 2) then it cannot hold of (1, 3), and so on. By similar considerations, we see easily that of the 27 remaining possibilities, only 18 satisfy also $A4$, 2 satisfy $A4$ and $A5$, and only one satisfies $A4$—$A6$. This interpretation of R that satisfies all the axioms $A1$—$A6$ is determined by the matrix already given: R is true for the pairs $(1^*, 2^*)$, $(2^*, 3^*)$, $(3^*, 1^*)$, and false for the six remaining pairs. Hence, L is categorical.

Thus, it is clear that additional axioms serve, in general, to reduce the number of permissible distinct interpretations for a system. When we add enough axioms to reduce the number of interpretations to one (up to isomorphism), we have a categorical system. But if we add any more axioms which would eliminate also the last interpretation, the resulting system would not be satisfiable according to Df. 1.

In fact, once we assume $A1$, the problem of finding additional axioms to obtain a categorical and satisfiable system is pretty trivial. For example, instead of $A2$—$A6$, we can use directly the following:

$A1^*$. R is true of the pairs $(1,2)$, $(2,3)$, $(3,1)$ and false for the six remaining pairs consisting of 1, 2, and 3.

$A1$ and $A1^*$ determine the same interpretation as $A1$—$A6$. Or, we can choose any one of the other possible interpretations of R by using some analogous axiom in place of $A1^*$. Then we would have in each case a different system, which is again categorical.

If we omit from L the names 1, 2, 3, then we can no longer state the axioms $A1$ and $A6$, although we can still keep the axioms $A2$—$A5$. In place of $A1$, we can use:

$A1'$. There exist only three distinct things: $(Ex)(Ey)(Ez)(w)(x \neq y \ \& \ y \neq z \ \& \ x \neq z \ \& \ (w=x \vee w=y \vee w=z))$.

But nothing resembling $A6$ can be expressed in the new system. The system determined by $A1'$ and $A2$—$A5$ can again be shown to be categorical and complete; the lack of anything like $A6$ is compensated by the decrease in expressing power caused by the omission of the names 1, 2, 3.

Furthermore, if we use instead of the relation symbol R a function symbol f, then we can replace $A2$—$A5$ by the following:

$A2'$. $(x)(f(x) \neq x)$.

$A3'$. $f(y)=f(z) \supset y=z$.

The system determined by $A1'$—$A3'$ is essentially the same as the system determined by $A1'$ and $A2$—$A5$; in the new formulation, $A4$ and $A5$ become absorbed into elementary logic and notational conventions.

Since L has a model, L is satisfiable.

Definition 4. *A system is said to be complete if every proposition p in the system is either provable or refutable; in other words, for every p, either p or $\sim p$ is a theorem.*

From Df. 3 and Df. 4, we can prove:

Theorem 1. *Every categorical system is complete.*

If a system is not complete, there is a proposition p in the system such that neither p nor $\sim p$ is a theorem. Hence, by Th. 10 given below in § 7, there exists one model in which p is true and one model in which p is false. These two models cannot be isomorphic. Hence, the system cannot be categorical.

Since L is categorical, it is complete.

One may also regard the choice of a model as the construction of a sort of truth definition for the system under consideration, specifying the propositions which are true under the interpretation. In fact, in every case we require that all theorems must be true in the model and that for every proposition p, either p or $\sim p$ but not both must be true. Hence, when a system is complete, the theorems must coincide with the true propositions. It follows that for a complete system, a decision procedure for provability also yields a decision procedure for truth.

Definition 5. *A decision procedure for provability (truth, validity) of an axiomatic system is an effective method by which, given any proposition of the systems, we can decide in a finite number of steps whether it is provable (true, valid).*

In the case of the system L which has only one model, we can easily give at once a decision procedure for both truth and provability. Thus, after eliminating "and", "only if", "(Ex)" in familiar manner, we can characterize all propositions of the system L:

(i) If a and b are numbers among 1, 2, and 3, then Rab and $a=b$ are (atomic) propositions;

(ii) If p and q are propositions, so are $\sim p$ and "p or q".

(iii) If Ha is a proposition, so is $(x)Hx$.

(iv) There are no other propositions except those required by (i)—(iii).

A truth definition is simply:

(i) Among the atomic propositions, $R12$, $R23$, $R31$, $1=1$, $2=2$, $3=3$ are true, all others are false;

(ii) $\sim p$ is true if and only if p is false, "p or q" is true if and only if either p or q is true;

(iii) $(x)Hx$ is true if and only if $H1$, $H2$, $H3$ are all true.

This truth definition gives a decision method because for every proposition of L, no matter how complex, we can always reduce the question of its truth to that of less complex propositions, in such a way that in a finite number of steps we arrive at a finite number of atomic propositions which can be decided by (i).

Hence, there is a decision procedure for L both for truth and for provability.

If we delete $A6$ from L, the resulting system is no longer complete, but we can easily see that it still has a decision method for provability.

Theorem 2. *There exist incomplete axiom systems for which there are decision procedures for provability.*

Incidentally, the axioms $A1$ and $A1'$ have a different character from the other axioms in so far as they do not assert properties of R and f but directly specify their domain. Such axioms are sometimes called "axioms of limitation".

§ 5. The Theory of Non-negative Integers

When we come to the theories which are satisfiable only in infinite domains, the problems of categoricity, decidability, etc. become of course more complex. The theory of positive integers or, alternatively, the theory of non-negative integers is probably the most basic. Let us consider the following system Z (see Hilbert-Bernays [7], p. 371) for the theory.

Just like L, the system Z presupposes the ordinary elementary logic dealing with the logical notions of truth functions, quantification, and identity. The only constant name is the numeral 0 and basic functions of Z are addition $+$, multiplication $\cdot$, and successor $'$. The axioms of Z are just the Peano axioms and the recursive equations for addition and multiplication.

Z1. For no $m, m'=0$; in other words, 0 is not the successor of any number.

Z2. For all m and n, if $m'=n'$, then $m=n$; in other words, different numbers have different successors.

Z3. Principle of induction. For each predicate Hk of Z, if $H0$, and for all m, Hm implies Hm', then for all n, Hn; in other words, if a property expressible in Z is inductive (i.e., is such that 0 has it and for every m, m' has it if m does), then every number has the property.

Z4. For every $m, m+0=m$.

Z5. For all m and $n, m+n'=(m+n)'$.

Z6. For every $m, m \cdot 0=0$.

Z7. For all m and $n, m \cdot n'=(m \cdot n)+m$.

It is known that all the ordinary arguments in the theory of numbers, except when appeal to analysis is made, can be carried out in this system Z. With regard to it, Gödel has proved the following famous theorem (compare next section):

Theorem 3. *Let S be either Z or a system containing Z as a part. If S is consistent, then there is a statement of S of the form "For all m, Hm" which is neither provable nor refutable in S, although $H0$, $H0'$, $H0''$, $\cdots$ are each and all provable in S. Therefore, if S is consistent, S is incomplete and incompletable.*

From this and Theorem 1, it follows that no such system S is categorical. In particular:

5.1. The system Z is not categorical.

Let N be the system obtained from Z by omitting addition and multiplication, together with the axioms Z4—Z7. While Z is incomplete, the system N can, on the other hand, easily be shown by known methods (cf. [7], § 6) to be complete and decidable. At first sight, this might appear paradoxical, since obviously less theorems can be proved in N than in the incomplete system Z. However, this is more than compensated by the simultaneous decrease in the power of expression. If we think of an axiom system as a means of singling out theorems from candidates, then we can say that although N singles out fewer theorems, the candidates are even fewer (as compared with those of Z) so that one from each pair of candidates is actually being selected by the axioms of N.

The completeness and decidability of N depends essentially on the possibility of eliminating the quantifiers. Let terms of N be defined thus: (1) 0 and the variables m, n, etc. are terms; (2) if b is a term, then b' is also. Let us call the equations and inequalities between terms the atomic propositions of N. The basic lemma for the elimination of quantifiers is the following. Every proposition of the form "For all m, Hm," where Hm is a conjunction of propositions, can be proved in N to be equivalent to a conjunction of propositions which contain no longer the variable m, and no variables which do not occur in Hm. Eventually, these can be reduced to atomic propositions. We omit the proof for this, which is quite elementary.

5.2. The system N is complete and decidable.

The problem whether N is categorical is more complex. Since N is complete and since in every model and for every statement p, p is true (or false) if and only if $\sim p$ is false (or true): each statement of N, if true in one model for N, is true in all models for N. Nonetheless, N is not categorical. Thus, by Theorem 3, there must exist a model for Z in which $H0$, $H0'$, $H0''$, $\cdots$ are all true but "For all m, Hm" is false. In other words, there is a model for Z in which the domain contains not only models for 0, $0'$, $0''$, $\cdots$, each obtained from 0 by applying a finite number of times the successor operator $'$, but also other things. If we omit from such a model the parts having to do with addition and multiplication, we obtain a model for N, whose domain again contains things besides the models for the numerals 0, $0'$, $0''$, etc. Such a model for N is of course not isomorphic with the standard model for N. Hence, N is not categorical.

Theorem 4. *There exist axiom systems which are complete but not categorical.*

It is clear that one reason why Z is not categorical is because the axioms are not adequate for restricting the domain of objects to 0 and those obtained from 0 by applying the successor operator a finite number of times. Let us say that a model with such a domain for the (non-negative) integers is a model with regular integers. There remains the question of whether any two models for Z with regular integers are always isomorphic. As it turns out, the ordinary proof of the categoricity of the axioms of Z assures us that the answer to this question is yes. Therefore, if we add to Z an axiom of limitation to restrict the domain of any model to regular integers, then the resulting system is categorical. For instance, we can add such an "axiom":

5.3. For every m, m is identical with one of the following: $0, 0', 0''$, $\cdots$, where each term is either 0 or obtained from 0 by applying the successor operator $'$ a finite number of times.

The result of adding 5.3 to Z can easily be shown, by the ordinary proof, to be categorical and, therefore, also complete by Theorem 1. Although 5.3 is rather similar to the axiom $A1$ of the preceding section, the change from a finite to an infinite domain entails much complication. While $A1$ is expressed in the given system L, 5.3 is not expressed nor even expressible in Z.

We can see that the axiom of limitation 5.3 is equivalent to the more familiar "rule" of infinite induction:

5.4. For every predicate Hn expressible in Z, if $H0$, $H0'$, $H0''$, $\cdots$ are each and all theorems, then "For all n, Hn" is also a theorem.

Thus, given 5.3 and $H0$, $H0'$, $H0''$, $\cdots$, we can conclude that for all n, Hn, since, according to 5.3, every n occurs in the sequence $0, 0', 0''$, etc. On the other hand, given 5.4 and $m \neq 0$, $m \neq 0'$, $m \neq 0''$, $\cdots$, we can infer, by taking $m \neq n$ as Hn, that for all n, $m \neq n$; therefore, since "for all n, $m \neq n$" is refutable in Z for every m, we can conclude that every m is identical with some term of the sequence $0, 0', 0''$, $\cdots$ described in 5.3. Our reasoning yields, incidentally, also a new proof of the known conclusion: the result of adding 5.4 to Z is complete. Thus, given 5.4 we can derive 5.3. But we have just indicated that the result of adding 5.3 to Z is complete.

Some authors call 5.4 a non-constructive rule of inference, others refuse to consider it as a rule of inference at all. In any case, since we require that in any axiom system or logistic system it be possible to check mechanically whether a given proof is correct, neither 5.3 nor 5.4 can be taken as forming a proper part of an axiom system. Indeed, since Z is incompletable according to Theorem 3, it is demonstrably impossible to formulate proper axioms or (constructive) rules of inference which would have the effect of 5.3 or 5.4.

These considerations lead us to a few interesting problems.

In the first place, there is the problem of relative categoricity. With regard to a non-categorical system, we can ask whether all models in which certain objects receive the same interpretation are isomorphic. For instance, we know we can define integers in set theory and the integers can receive non-isomorphic interpretations in different models for the set theory; therefore, we know also that set theory is not categorical. However, we can still ask, with regards to those models for set theory in which the integers all receive the same interpretation (that may be either regular or not), whether all such models are isomorphic. If they are, we shall say that set theory is categorical relative to integers. Similarly, a system may also be categorical relative to ordinal numbers, cardinal numbers, and so on. More explicitly:

Definition 6. *A system which contains the (non-negative) integers is said to be categorical relative to its integers if and only if all models for the system, in which the integers receive the same (isomorphic) interpretation, are isomorphic. It is said to be categorical relative to regular integers if and only if all models for it, in which the integers are regular (as described above), are isomorphic.*

For instance, according to this definition, Z is categorical relative to regular integers—a result which is not at all startling. On the other hand, the problem as to whether certain standard systems of set theory are categorical relative to their integers (or relative to regular integers) is still open and seems to be very interesting.

A second problem is with regard to the relation between the rule of infinite induction 5.4 and the ordinary principle of induction ($Z3$ in the system Z). If we contrast $Z3$ with the rule of infinite induction 5.4, we see that $Z3$ follows immediately from 5.4. Hence, we can rephrase our assertions above by saying that while Z is incomplete, if we replace $Z3$ by 5.4, the result is complete.

Now we may regard $Z3$ as one particular way of formalizing a group of cases of 5.4 by a rule with only a finite number of premisses in each instance (viz. the two premisses $H0$ and "For all n, Hn implies Hn'"). If Z were complete, $Z3$ would enable us to derive 5.4 and thereby all other ways of formalizing groups of instances of 5.4. As Z is incomplete, there is the question whether we can discover new rules with finitely many premisses in each case that would enable us to prove general conclusions of the form "For all m, Hm" which are not already provable in Z. We know from Theorem 3 that we cannot effectively describe a group of such rules which would exhaust all the applications of 5.4. But this does not exclude the possibility of finding some effective rules which would cover interesting cases of 5.4 not already covered by $Z3$.

Another point worth stressing is the connection between $Z3$ and the notion of sets. Thus, it is quite customary to use instead of $Z3$, which deals with properties expressible in Z, a principle which is concerned with sets of integers:

$Z3^*$. If a set is inductive (i.e. is such that 0 belongs to it, and for every n, if n belongs to it, n' does also), it contains all non-negative integers.

The notion of sets involved may either be taken for granted as an intuitively clear notion, or be defined more exactly by an axiomatic system for set theory. If we choose the first alternative, since $Z3^*$ refers to all sets, we can assume in particular that there is a set which consists of exactly the numbers $0, 0', 0'', \cdots$ described in 5.3. Therefore, if we apply $Z3^*$ to this particular set, we see that these exhaust all the non-negative integers and 5.3 is true. Hence, as Skolem ([14] p. 42) has emphasized and elaborated, if we assume an intuitive notion of sets according to which there exists a set consisting of just 0, 0′, 0″, ··· and no others, the ordinary proofs for the categoricity of Z and N are valid. The only objection to this approach is that we have to abolish the program of formalizing all our mathematical notions into axiom systems.

Alternatively, if we want to formalize the notion of set, we see from Theorem 3 that it is impossible to find any axiom system containing Z in which we can express and prove formally the existence of a set containing exactly 0, 0′, 0″, ··· and no more. If we could find such a system, we would, contrary to Theorem 3, be able to prove "For all m, Hm" whenever we can prove every one of $H0$, $H0'$, $H0''$, etc.

To illustrate the close connection between the power of $Z3^*$ and the notion of sets we assume, let us consider a very queer notion of set according to which there exist only finite sets (including the empty set) and their complements (i.e. the sets each of which contains everything in the domain with at most a finite number of exceptions). Then we get, besides the ordinary model, also a queer model for N (with $Z3$ replaced by $Z3^*$) determined by the function of adding 1 and the domain 1, 2, 3, ···; ···, $-\frac{3}{2}$, $-\frac{1}{2}$, $\frac{1}{2}$, $\frac{3}{2}$, $\frac{5}{2}$, ···, where the integers and fractions behave as in ordinary mathematics and 1 is the model of 0.

§ 6. Gödel's Theorems

Consider, for example, the system Z described in the preceding section. We can view the system as a game with a finite number of symbols (say ten symbols, or even two, if we prefer). Certain finite combinations of these symbols are called sentences, certain finite combinations of these sentences are called proofs, certain sentences are called axioms which serve to determine the proof. In each axiom system we can enumerate effectively all the primitive symbols, all the terms, all the sentences, all the proofs so that given any positive integer n, we can find in a finite number of steps which combination of symbols is the n-th sentence, and which combination of sentences is the n-th proof, and vice versa. Therefore, instead of talking about proofs, sentences, variables, we can just talk about positive integers, syntactical properties and relations about the system become represented by properties and relations of positive integers. In this way, we get what is called an arithmetization of the syntax of the system. In particular, by the very definition of a logistic or axiomatic system, there is for each system a definite method according to which, given any two positive integers m and n, we can decide in a finite number of steps whether the m-th proof is a proof for the n-th sentence. In other words, given any proof, we can of course determine exactly what is the sentence of which it is a proof. Usually this fact is expressed by stating that the dyadic relation of "being a proof of" is recursive or effectively computable. On account of this situation, we can define in Z (or any system containing Z) a predicate $B(m,n)$ such that for any given m and n, $B(m,n)$ is provable or refutable in the system according as whether the m-th proof of Z is a proof in Z of the n-th sentence of Z or not. In this way, Gödel manages to talk about Z in the system Z itself.

Besides the proof predicate, Gödel also succeeds in defining in Z a function $s(m,n)$ such that $s(m,n)=k$ if and only if the result of substituting occurrences of the n^*-th term (for example, the numeral 100 or the variable j) where n is the numerical expression in Z for the number n^* for occurrences of the variable i (the variable as a symbol being a constant symbol) in the m^*-th sentence of Z where m is the numerical expression for m^*, is the k-th sentence of Z. This is interesting only if the variable i (a constant symbol) happens to occur in the m-th sentence, otherwise the result of substitution is the same as the original and $s(m,n)$ is identical with m. This function $s(m,n)$ is again recursive or effectively computable in the sense that there is a definite method by which, given any numbers m and n, we can calculate the value of $s(m,n)$. As a result, we can express in Z a function $\sigma(m,n)$ such that for any m, n, and k, $\sigma(m,n)=k$ is provable in Z if and only if $s(m,n)$ as described above is k.

Using the predicate B and the function σ, Gödel proceeds to construct a sentence of Z which says of the sentence itself that it is not provable in Z. Hence, if it is provable, it is not; yet if it is refutable, it is provable. Therefore, the sentence must be undecidable, and Z must be incomplete.

Since B and σ can be expressed in Z, the sentence (1) "For no $m, B(m, \sigma(i,i))$" is a sentence of Z containing the variable i. Therefore, we can find a definite number t (for instance, something like 358 trillion) such that (1) is the t-th sentence of Z. Let τ be the numerical expression in Z for the number t, and consider the sentence (2) "For no $m, B(m, \sigma(\tau,\tau))$" of Z. Intuitively the sentence (2) says that there exists no proof in Z for the sentence obtained from the t-th sentence of Z by substituting the term τ for the variable i. Since the t-th sentence of Z is (1) and since the result of substituting the term τ for the variable i in (1) is exactly (2), the sentence (2) of Z says intuitively that (2) itself is not provable in Z. Moreover, if q is the value of $\sigma(\tau,\tau)$, (2) is the q-th sentence of Z.

Assume now (2) is provable in Z. Then we can find a definite number m_0 such that m_0 is a proof of (2). Therefore, by the properties of the predicate B, we can prove in Z the sentence "$B(m_0, q)$". Therefore, since q is the value of $\sigma(\tau,\tau)$, we can prove in Z the sentence "$B(m_0, \sigma(\tau,\tau))$". But this last sentence contradicts (2). Hence, (2) cannot be proved in Z. If it were provable in Z, we would have two contradictory theorems in Z and Z would be inconsistent.

Since (2) is not provable in Z, it follows that for every given m, the m-th proof of Z is not a proof of (2) which is the q-th sentence of Z. Hence, by the property of B, "It is not the case that $B(m,q)$" or "It is not the case that $B(m, \sigma(\tau, \tau))$" is provable in Z for every definite numeral m. In other words, every individual instance of (2) is provable in Z. Therefore, (2) is intuitively true although, as shown above, not provable in Z. Hence, unless Z is very queer, (2) should not be refutable in Z. Hence, if Z is not queer, (2) must be an undecidable sentence of Z. (See Gödel [6]).

By complicating somewhat the sentence (2), Rosser is able to prove that the more complex sentence is undecidable in Z, provided only Z is consistentor contains no contradictory theorems. (See Rosser [10]). Both Gödel's and Rosser's arguments can easily be seen to be applicable also to every system S which contains Z as a part. Therefore, we have the theorem (Theorem 3 stated in the preceding section) to the effect that Z is both incomplete and incompletable.

In other words, Gödel's theorem shows that in any sufficiently rich formal system, we can formulate some arithmetic problem within the system which can be decided by intuitive consideration but not by the proof procedure of the system. Or, we may also say that by constructing a system and then treating the system as the object of our study, we create some new problem which can be formulated but cannot be answered in the given system.

Gödel's undecidable sentence (2) amounts to a device of saying: "This assertion (which I am making now) is not provable in Z." He stresses himself the analogy to the paradox of the liar: (3) "This assertion (which I am making now) is false (i.e. not true)." No contradiction arises on account of (2), because it is not necessary that every statement of Z is either provable or refutable in Z. On the other hand, the fact that (3) does lead to a contradiction is employed in Tarski [8] to prove that we cannot define the notion of truth for Z (or a system containing Z) in the system itself, although, as we just asserted, we can define the notion of theorem for Z in the system itself. More exactly, it is impossible to find in Z a predicate of positive integers such that for any m and p, if p is the m-th sentence of Z, then we can prove in Z: (4) "p if and only if $M(m)$." Thus, if we could find in Z such a predicate M, let us consider the sentence "It is not the case that $M(\sigma(i,i))$" of Z. Assume it is the n-th sentence of Z and consider the sentence "It is not the case that $M(\sigma(n,n))$." By (4) and the property of σ, we would then have as a theorem of Z: "$M(\sigma(n,n))$ if and only if it is not the case that $M(\sigma(n,n))$." Therefore, we have:

Theorem 5. *In Z (or any system which contains Z), we cannot define the notion of truth for the system itself.*

Other interesting applications of Gödel's method include two results of Church (cf. Church [11], [12]):

Theorem 6. *There is no decision procedure for checking which sentences of Z (or of any system containing Z as a part) are provable, provided the system is consistent.*

Proof. If there were a decision procedure for Z, we would have a recursive or effectively calculable function ϕ such that for each m, $\phi(m)=1$ if and only if the m-th sentence of Z is a theorem, $\phi(m)=2$ otherwise. Therefore, we would be able to express in Z a function f such that for each m, "$f(m)=1$" or "$f(m)=2$", is provable in Z according as whether the m-th sentence of Z is a theorem of Z or not. Consider now the sentence "$f(\sigma(i,i))=2$". If it is the k-th sentence of Z, then (5) "$f(\sigma(k,k))=2$" would again be a sentence of Z. According to the property of f, if (5) is a theorem of Z, then by the properties of f and σ, "$f(\sigma(k,k))=1$" would also be provable and we would have a contradiction. On the other hand, if (5) is not a theorem, by the property of f, it would be a theorem. Hence, if there were a decision procedure for Z, Z would be inconsistent. Similarly, the same can be proved for every system which contains Z as a part.

Theorem 7. *There is no decision procedure for checking which sentences of elementary logic (with or without identity) are provable. Or, in other words, there is no decision procedure for quantification theory or the restricted predicate calculus.*

Proof. We know that there is some consistent system S which contains Z as a part and has only a finite number of axioms beyond those of elementary logic. If A is the conjunction of all these finitely many axioms, we know that for every sentence p of the system S, p is provable in S if and only if "If A, then p" is provable in elementary logic. Therefore if there were a decision procedure for elementary logic, we would be able to decide for each sentence of the form, "If A, then p" whether it is provable in elementary logic. Hence, we would have a decision procedure for S, contrary to Theorem 6. Turing [16] contains a very interesting different proof.

A result of Turing, not so closely dependent on Gödel's method, is the following (see Turing [16], p. 259):

Theorem 8. *Every complete system is decidable.*

Proof. A rough sketch is as follows. As we have remarked, the proofs and therewith the theorems of a system can be enumerated. If the system is complete, then the non-theorems of the system can also be enumerated, because in a complete system p is a non-theorem if and only if not-p is a theorem. Hence, we can enumerate all statements of the system in the following manner: first theorem, first non-theorem, second theorem, second non-theorem, third theorem, and so on. Therefore, we can check for each statement of the system whether it occurs at an odd place (it is a theorem) or at an even place (it is a non-theorem) in the enumeration.

Finally, we come to Gödel's important second theorem which states the impossibility of formalizing any consistency proof in the system itself.

Definition 7. *A system is said to be consistent or free from contradiction if there is no sentence p of the system such that both p and not-p are theorems.*

It is quite obvious that we would want a formal system consistent. For one thing, theorems ought to be true and p and not-p cannot both be true. Moreover, there is a generally accepted law of logic such that for any statements p and q, from p plus not-p we can infer q as a theorem. Therefore, if a system is inconsistent, we would have the disconcerting situation that all statements of the system are theorems.

Although we hope and tend to believe that ordinary systems for the principal branches of mathematics are consistent, actually to prove their consistency is very hard in many cases. Often it is not hard to prove that a system is consistent if another one is. But this obviously does not assure us of the consistency of the second system. For example, if we assume the consistency of some standard system of set theory, we can easily prove the (relative) consistency of systems for analysis, geometry, number theory, and so on. But this is not a great help since we do not know the consistency of set theory.

In general, in order to prove the consistency of a system, we have to make use of certain modes of reasoning whose validity we assume. The main question is whether we can use more reliable arguments to demonstrate the consistency of systems which employ stronger or less reliable forms of argumentation. Gödel's theorem provides, in a sense, a negative answer to this question.

Let S be either Z or an arbitrary system containing Z as a part. Gödel's second theorem is:

Theorem 9. *If S is consistent, then the consistency of S cannot be proved in S.*

More exactly, by assuming a definite arithmetization of the syntax of S (i.e., a definite way of representing sentences, proofs, etc. by integers), we can find an arithmetic statement $Con(S)$ expressible in the notation of Z (and therefore, also in S), which represents the assertion that S is consistent. In this way, the consistency problem of a system becomes formalized in the system itself. What Gödel has shown is that although the problem can be asked in the same system, to answer the question in the positive or to prove the statement $Con(S)$, we need a system which is in some sense stronger than S. If S is consistent, $Con(S)$ as a statement of S is not provable in S.

Roughly speaking, Gödel's proof of the theorem depends on the possibility of formalizing in Z the proof of the following result obtained in proving his first theorem: (1) If S (e.g., Z) is consistent, then (2) "For no m, $B(m, \sigma(\tau, \tau))$" is not provable in S. Since, we recall, the number of (2) is the same as $\sigma(\tau, \tau)$, (2) says that (2) is not provable in S. Hence, a representation of (1) is just: If $Con(S)$, then for no $m, B(m, \sigma(\tau,\tau))$. Hence, if $Con(S)$ were provable in S, (2) would also be, and S would be inconsistent by (1).

It may be interesting to note incidentally that although several alternative proofs for Gödel's first theorem have been offered, there exists, so far as we know, no alternative proof for the second theorem.

The significance of this theorem can perhaps best be seen if we recall that at first there had been some vague belief or hope that even the consistency of very powerful systems can be proved within the framework of some system like Z or preferably in certain still weaker systems. The whole program of searching for consistency proofs seems to be based on a belief that we can justify our use of intuitively less reliable arguments by more reliable ways of reasoning. Gödel's theorems show that either the belief is false so far as the matter of proving consistency is concerned, or, what is more likely, there are certain intuitive modes of reasoning about positive integers whose intuitive character we have in our formalizations not yet succeeded in revealing.

Gödel's second theorem has also been applied to the study of relative consistency and relative model. Thus, S_1 is consistent relative to S_2 if we can prove the consistency of S_1 by assuming the consistency of S_2; S_1 has a model relative to S_2 if we can define a model for S_1 by using notions of S_2. In most cases, S_1 is consistent relative to S_2 when and only when S_1 has a model relative to S_2. For example, many non-Euclidean geometries have models (are consistent) relative to the Euclidean, set theory plus the continuum hypothesis has a model (is consistent) relative to set theory.

When S_1 has a model or is consistent relative to S_2, we can usually formalize in Z a proof of the arithmetic theorem "If $Con(S_2)$ then $Con(S_1)$." Hence, if S_1 contains Z, then $Con(S_2)$ is, by Gödel's second theorem, not provable in S_1. Conversely, if $Con(S_2)$ is provable in S_1, then "If $Con(S_2)$, then $Con(S_1)$" cannot be provable in S_1. Hence, if S_1 is strong enough to include most ordinary ways of reasoning, then there is little hope of proving the consistency of S_1 relative to S_2 when $Con(S_2)$ is provable in S_1.

On the other hand, sometimes we seem to have both the consistency of S_1 relative to S_2 and a proof of $Con(S_2)$ in S_1. In such cases, we again arrive at certain intuitive arguments about integers which cannot be formalized in S_1, although S_1 may be very strong and rich by ordinary standards.

§7. Formal Theories as Applied Elementary Logics

The systems we consider all presuppose the ordinary elementary logic dealing with truth functions, quantifiers, and identity. The theory of identity may or may not be considered part of elementary logic. For our purpose, it is more convenient to consider elementary logic without the theory of identity, often referred to as quantification theory or restricted predicate calculus. There are several standard formulations of this theory dealing with truth functions and quantifiers. We can assume any one of them. Call it Q.

All the ordinary axiom systems can be formulated within the framework of Q. If a system contains originally more than one kind of variable, including "higher" variables, we assume it to have been already translated with known methods into one with only one kind of variable.

The system Q contains, besides the truth-functional connectives, the quantifiers, and one kind of variable, also symbols of the following kinds: predicates, functors, and individual names. The theorems of Q are roughly those statements or statement schemata which are true no matter how we interpret these symbols for properties, relations, functions, and individuals. It is more correct to call the sentence-like expressions of Q statement schemata rather than statements, because the symbols for predicate, functions, and individuals are uninterpreted and can be interpreted however we want. As we apply Q to a special system such as L, Z, or some standard system of set theory, certain of these symbols (such as the predicate ϵ for membership, the functor $+$ in Z, and the predicate R in L) get interpreted by dint of additional axioms, and the schemata become statements. For example, in a set theory we want the two-place predicate ϵ to have not only those properties which every two-place predicate must have, but also special properties of the membership relation. The additional axioms of set theory can be taken as schemata of Q which involve the otherwise neutral predicate letter ϵ in an essential way. These are, unlike the theorems of Q which may also involve ϵ, no longer true in all interpretations, but can only be satisfied when we use very special interpretations. The problem of finding a model for set theory becomes equivalent to one of finding a model or interpretation for these additional schemata for ϵ which are not true in all interpretations. As a result, problems of consistency and decision procedure about set theory and other formal systems become reducible to similar problems about schemata of Q.

Skolem, Herbrand, and Gödel have established the following result (see [3], [4], [5]):

Theorem 10. *A system formulated in the framework of Q is consistent if and only if it is satisfiable* (cf. Df. 1).

If we speak of satisfiability not only with regard to axiom systems but also with regard to single statements or statement schemata of Q, then we see immediately that a system formulated in the framework of Q is satisfiable (has a model) if and only if all its axioms are simultaneously satisfiable (true in the same models).

Definition 8. *A schema of Q is valid if it is true in all models or interpretations over every non-empty domain or universe. Thus p is valid if and only if not-p is not satisfiable (in any non-empty domain).*

Definition 9. *A system is said to be open complete, if all valid schemata are theorems of the system.*

In terms of these notions, Theorem 10 may also be given a somewhat different form:

Theorem 11. *The system Q (of qualification theory) is open complete. Moreover, a schema of Q is a theorem if and only if it is valid.*

Given Theorems 10 and 11, we can appreciate the significance of the decision problem of quantification theory (or briefly, the decision problem). A solution for the problem would be a mechanical procedure by which, given any schema of Q, we can decide whether it is a theorem of Q (or is valid). If there were such a procedure, then we could not only solve mechanically the consistency question but obtain a decision procedure for any ordinary axiom system (at least if it contains just a finite number of axioms beyond the axioms of Q). This seems too much to hope for. Indeed, Church's theorem (Theorem 7 described in the preceding section) supplies a negative reply to this question.

If we leave aside the general decision problem, there remain two kinds of special decision problems. On the one hand, we may ask whether there is a decision procedure for all schemata of a particular form. On the other hand, we may ask whether these is one for a given special system (say the system N, or L, or some weak system of set theory). There are many positive and negative results on both kinds of problem. It has been suggested that the time may already be ripe for a general theory of what are decidable and what are not. But not much progress seems to have been made toward such a general theory.

One interesting positive result on the second kind of problem is Tarski's decision method for the elementary theory of real numbers, which only deals with real numbers but not with sets of reals or members (integers or rationals) of reals. Roughly speaking, he has proved the completeness, decidability, and consistency of an axiom system which says that real numbers form a complete ordered field (i.e., an ordered field in which the theorem of least upper bound holds). Ordinarily we seem to consider the theory of real numbers richer and stronger than the theory of integers. Tarski's result shows that we can handle reals more thoroughly even, provided only we do not at the same time talk about integers and rationals. Indeed, as Tarski observes, from his result and Gödel's theorem, it follows that there is no way of finding in the elementary theory of reals a predicate to single out those real numbers which are also rational numbers, or one to single out those reals which are also positive integers. If either were possible, we would be able to express in it all notions of Z and would not be able to have a complete system. (See Tarski [17]).

By Df. 8, a schema or statement of Q is valid or is a theorem of Q if it is true in all possible models or interpretations. In a definite system S of, for example, number theory or set theory, the axioms and theorems beyond Q are not valid in the above sense, but nonetheless they are true or valid in all models for the system S. If we consider in general any set M of statements which are neither theorems of Q nor refutable in Q, we can define validity relative to M by saying that a statement p is valid relative to M if and only if p is true in every model in which all the statements of M are true. Let us call a system complete relative to M, if all the statements of the system which are valid relative to M are theorems of the system. If the set of models determined by M (i.e., the set of all models in which statements belonging to M are all true) happens to possess notable properties, it becomes of interest to ask whether a given system is complete relative to M.

A fairly direct consequence of the definition of relative completeness is the following theorem:

Theorem 12. *Every system S is complete relative to the set M of its axioms.*

Proof. Assume the set M consist of $A_1, A_2, A_3, \cdots$ and let B_1 be A_1 and B_n be the conjunction of B_{n-1} and A_n $(n=2, 3, 4, \cdots)$. Let p be a statement of S not provable in S. Then none of the statements "If B_k, then p" $(k=1, 2, 3, \cdots)$ is provable in quantification theory. Hence, the statements "B_k but not p" $(k=1, 2, 3, \cdots)$, when all added to Q as axioms, determine a consistent system; for, if not, there must be a definite k such that "B_k but not p" alone would already yield a contradiction in Q. Therefore, by Theorem 10, there is a model in which $B_1, B_2, \cdots$ are all true but p is not. Hence, there is a model in which all axioms of S are true but p is not; in other words, p is not valid relative to M. Hence, every p valid relative to M is provable in S, and S is valid relative to the set M of its axioms.

The ordinary proofs for Theorems 10 and 11 also yield as corollary a strengthened form of the famous theorem of Löwenheim: Every consistent system has a denumerable model.

This theorem is interesting mainly because it appears to contradict Cantor's famous theorem on the existence of non-denumerable sets. Since in every standard system of set theory we can carry out Cantor's proof of the theorem, it would seem that any such system should not admit any denumerable models. Yet by Löwenheim's theorem, it must have a denumerable model if it is consistent at all. This phenomenon is sometimes labelled the paradox of Skolem and is usually explained by saying that Cantor's theorem only shows the lack of enumeration in the system, while the enumeration asserted to exist by Löwenheim's theorem is a syntactical one obtained by talking about the given system.

Either by this theorem or by some analogous result, we can also show that no formalized set theory can give us *all* sets of positive integers. Thus, let S be a standard system of set theory. Since we can enumerate the theorems of S, we can also enumerate those theorems of S each of which asserts the existence of a set of positive integers. Consider now, following Cantor, the set K of positive integers such that for each m, m belongs to K if and only if m does not belong to the m-th set in the enumeration. By Cantor's argument, K cannot occur in the enumeration of all those sets of positive integers which can be proved to exist in S. Hence, either there is no statement in S which expresses the existence of K, or, if there is such a statement, it is not a theorem of S. In either case, there exists a set of positive integers which cannot be proved to exist in S.

§ 4 to § 7 of this chapter appeared in slightly different form in the paper "quelques notions d'axiomatique", *Revue philosophique de Louvain,* **51** (1953), 409—443.

References

[1] Georg Cantor, Über eine elementare Frage der Mannigfaltigkeitslehre, *Jahresbericht der Deutsch. Math. Vereing.*, **1** (1890—1891), 75—78.

[2] Leopold Löwenheim, Über Möglichkeiten im Relativkalkül, *Math. Annalen*, **76** (1915), 447—470.

[3] Thoralf Skolem, Über einige Grundlagenfragen der Mathematik, Skrifter utgitt av Det Norske Videnskaps-Akademi i Oslo, I. Matematisk-naturvidenskapelig Klasse, 1929, no. 4, 49 pp.

[4] Jacques Herbrand, Recherches sur la théorie de la démonstration, Warsaw, 1930, 128 pp.

[5] Kurt Gödel, Die Vollständigkeit der Axiome des logischen Funktionenkalküls, *Monatsh. Math. Phys.*, **37** (1930), 349—360.

[6] Kurt Gödel, Über formal unentscheidbare Sätze der Principia Mathematica und verwandter Systeme I, *ibid.*, **38** (1931), 173—198; On undecidable propositions of formal mathematical systems, mimeographed, Princeton, 1934, 30 pp.

[7] David Hilbert and Paul Bernays, Grundlagen der Mathematik, vol. 1, Berlin, 1934.

[8] Alfred Tarski, Der Wahrheitsbegriff in den formalisierten Sprachen, *Studia Philosophica*, **1** (1936), 261—405.

[9] Rudolf Carnap, Ein Gültigkeitskriterium für die Sätze der klassischen Mathematik, *Monatsh. Math. Phys.*, **42** (1935), 163—190.

[10] Barkley Rosser, Extensions of some theorems of Gödel and Church, *Jour. Symbolic Logic*, **1** (1936), 87—91.

[11] Alonzo Church, An unsolvable problem of elementary number theory, *Am. Jour. Math.*, **58** (1936), 345—363.

[12] Alonzo Church, A note on the Entscheidungsproblem, *Jour. Symbolic Logic*, **1** (1936), 40—41, 101—102.

[13] Kurt Gödel, Consistency of the Continuum Hypothesis, Princeton, 1940, 1951, 66 pp.

[14] Thoralf Skolem, Sur la portée du theoreme de Löwenheim-Skolem, Les entretiens de Zurich, ed. F. Gonseth, 1941, Zurich, pp. 25—52.

[15] David Hilbert and Paul Bernays, Grundlagen der Mathematik, vol. 2, Berlin, 1939.

[16] A. M. Turing, On computable numbers, *Proc. London Math. Soc.*, **24** (1936), 230—265.

[17] Alfred Tarski, A Decision Method for Elementary Algebra and Geometry, Rand Corporation, Santa Monica, California, 1948, 60 pp.

[18] J. Ladrière, Les limitations de formalisation, Louvain, 1956.

CHAPTER II

EIGHTY YEARS OF FOUNDATIONAL STUDIES*

One who is situated at the bottom of a well can hardly offer a satisfactory description of the sky. To compensate my restricted range of vision, I intend to indulge occasionally in irresponsible speculations. I shall make no futile attempt to be impartial but simply neglect those aspects of mathematical logic which do not interest me. As I go along, I shall mention more or less standard open problems.

§ 1. Analysis, Reduction and Formalization

The motives and tasks of foundational studies may be said to be the justification and clarification of the fundamental principles and concepts of mathematics. Number, figure, constructivity, proof and inference, set and function, the axiomatic method are among these basic concepts. The study of the psychology of invention and the root of mathematics in practical applications is largely neglected undoubtedly because they are not easily amenable to a mathematical treatment. The representation of figures by numbers provides an excuse, albeit an inadequate one, for neglecting a separate study of the foundations of geometry.

Whether one likes it or not, in foundational studies mathematical logic dominates the scene today. This may be a result partly of an accidental combination of historical circumstances, partly of the general futility thus far of other approaches, and partly of the yet primitive stage of foundational studies. Even if one finds (and I do not) the present situation unfortunate and wishes for a more flexible handling of foundational questions, there is no choice but to face the fact and concentrate on mathematical logic if an attempt is made to survey the actual state of the field. As a branch of mathematics, mathematical logic agrees with other branches in emphasizing new concepts and new results, and in judging their significance according to their degree of novelty, their depth, and their beauty. It distinguishes itself by a preoccupation with the more general and more basic concepts and methods.

Mathematical research takes a thousand different forms many of which are either of no interest to the philosophy of mathematics or of interest only

* This chapter appeared in the Bernays Festschrift, *Dialectica*, **12** (1958), 465—497.

in quite a different manner as they are to the mathematicians. The introduction of the concept of congruence by Gauss or the availability of different proofs of the prime number theorem interests the philosopher of mathematics only in that it illustrates a general point about the importance of a new concept or the efficiency and occasional eliminability of advanced methods in dealing with more elementary results. The analysis of mathematical concepts is more directly of philosophical interest.

We give a few examples from the history of mathematics gradually approaching in generality and centrality the concepts studied in mathematical logic. The representation of complex numbers by pairs of reals is said to have clarified "the metaphysics of *i*". "Berkeley's paradox of the infinitesimals" is resolved by Cauchy's contextual definition of the derivatives, a type of analysis which Ayer once considered as the main concern of all philosophy. Descartes' analysis of elementary geometry leads to his analytic geometry and a definition of constructibility by ruler and compass. A definition of the method of solving equations by radicals is a crucial step in proving the unsolvability of quintic equations. Klein's answer to "what is geometry?" produces stimulus and satisfaction. Analyzing common structures leads to abstract notions of group, field, etc. Dedekind gets the Peano axioms by analyzing the concept of number.

All these examples are of some interest to philosophers. If to analyze were always to philosophize, then much of mathematics would be philosophy. Philosophers tend to contrast analysis with new discovery, clarification with the increase of knowledge. The above examples show that analysis is interesting in mathematics precisely because they enable us to unify diverse methods, to prove impossibility results, to reveal common characteristics. Compared with the idle piecemeal exercises so frequent in contemporary philosophy, how much more satisfying these examples of analysis are!

There are two essential ingredients of analysis, reduction and formalization, which come out conspicuously in mathematical logic. One way of simplifying a concept is by reducing more components to less or by simplifying each separate aspect. For instance, if certain properties follow from others, the former can of course be neglected in the definition of the concept. If we think of a concept as being characterized by the body of theorems one can prove about it, then the same method of reduction is systematically applied in the axiomatic method. To separate reduction from formalization, let us look at the long history of axiomatizing geometry from Euclid to Hilbert. We may say that the reduction part was accomplished by Euclid, yet it had taken very long to arrive at a thorough formalization that makes all implicit assumptions explicit. If we add the predicate logic to Hilbert's axioms, we get something like a theorem-generating machine so that today we possess an objective criterion, in mechanical terms, of a completely formal axiomatization.

The type of reduction involved in defining and deducing in an axiomatic system may be said to be local reductions in contrast to whole reductions such as complex numbers to reals. While individual examples of local reductions are of more interest to mathematics than to mathematical philosophy, individual whole reductions have often impressed philosophers. With regard to formalization, we can, using the criterion in mechanical terms, distinguish between thorough and partial formalizations. A thorough formalization of a concept (or a set of concepts) is given when there is a thorough axiomatization which contains, besides the concepts of the predicate logic, only the concept (or concepts) to be formalized that gets thereby an "implicit definition". In a partial formalization, other concepts may occur and we may or may not have an axiom system. For example, the usual definition of general recursive functions, or a system of number theory with the informal concept of an arbitrary set in the induction principle. In all formalizations, either the concept formalized is irreducible, or we just refrain from reducing it in order to single it out for a separate study.

Since in analyzing and formalizing a concept, we aim at bringing it into a sharper form, we encounter a rather general question: If we begin with a vague intuitive concept, how can we find a sharper concept to correspond to it faithfully? First, it is often not necessary to be entirely faithful. So long as a hard core is preserved, trimming on the margin is quite permissible. Moreover, sometimes we are able to concentrate all the indeterminedness in one corner so that we no longer have to be concerned with the vagueness in every respect. The conceptual gain thus obtained can be very useful. As a result, a sharper concept can correspond to a messier one: we have not omitted the messiness entirely but merely reduced it to a simpler form. The unrestricted existence condition of solutions in the definition of recursive functions is a good example.

Once the formalization of a concept is accepted, we usually find it easy to be articulate about what we have to say on the concept. When we are pressed, we feel better able to defend our answers. Formalization enables us to prove things which otherwise we could only hint at, e.g., that the derivative of x^2 is $2x$. Rigidity of the formalized concept leads to decisions in cases where mere use of the intuitive notion was insufficient. For instance, the existence of an everywhere continuous but nondifferentiable function can only be established after the exact definition of differentiability is introduced. This sort of thing is at the same time an advance and a distortion. To eliminate borderline cases may be useful for certain purposes, while to get answers on things which initially required no answer is hardly desirable in general.

Whole reductions often run up against the grain of truth in the slogan: "Everything is what it is and not another thing." On the one hand, when a reduction is successful, that is the end of the matter and we need no longer worry about the eliminated concept. That is why, for example, mathematical logic is little concerned with fractions and complex numbers. On the other hand, when a reduction gives the impression of being of profound philosophical interest, there is reason to suspect of some trickery. For example, Dedekind and Frege speak of reducing mathematics to logic, and great philosophical significance has been attributed to this achievement. While their definition of number in terms of set is mathematically interesting in that it relates two different mathematical disciplines, it is not so powerful as to provide a foundation for mathematics. Instead of "reduction" which suggests a direction from the more complex to the simpler, the more neutral word "translation" would describe the state of affairs less misleadingly. For example, the theories of finite sets and natural numbers are translatable into each other, and this suggests a common structure underlying both theories which is even more basic than the common characteristics of finite and infinite sets, so that the distinction between finite and infinite sets is more basic than that between integers and finite sets. The talk of logical foundations is misleading at least on two accounts: it gives the impression that number theory and set theory do not provide their own foundations but we must look for foundations elsewhere, viz., in logic; it implies that the grand structure of mathematics would collapse unless we quickly replace the sand underneath by a solid foundation. Neither thought corresponds to the actual situation. Indeed, if we adopt the linear mode of thinking to proceed from the logical foundation to the mathematical superstructure, there is surely something glaringly circular in the mathematical treatment of mathematics itself which makes up mathematical logic. As Bernays remarks, syntax is but a branch of number theory and semantics one of set theory.

The basic circularity suggests that formalization rather than reduction is the more appropriate method, since we are, in foundational studies, primarily interested in irreducible concepts. However impressive the achievements of isolated examples may be in ordinary mathematics, formalization has finally found its home only in mathematical logic for the last eighty years or so.

But the desire to reduce and to justify is hard to resist. When the excessive optimism of a direct reduction to logic led to despair, Hilbert initiated a new programme of roundabout whole reduction by way of consistency proofs. This grand dream of Hilbert's has been instrumental to the appearance of much interesting work on foundations, although it is hard to claim that the things we get today are the things which Hilbert was after. For one thing, the consistency proofs prove more than consistency, and indeed it seems that the stronger results are what make these works so interesting, consistency being more or less a side corollary. For another thing, Hilbert was interested in the justification of less reliable or evident methods by more reliable or evident ones, and it is not clear that Hilbert had a sufficiently clear and broad concept of evidence and reliability or that the methods of proof actually employed in recent times would be acceptable to him. Recently Kreisel has introduced, as a variant to Hilbert's theory, a problem of interpreting transfinite symbols (quantifiers and the like) in proofs, which is intended to bring out the more crucial features of the interesting consistency proofs. Related questions have been investigated by Kleene, Stenius, Hintikka. In contrast to whole reductions, these questions of interpretation might be called uniform local reductions. The simplest example is Herbrand's interpretation of the predicate calculus by the propositional calculus.

In some of his arguments with intuitionists, Hilbert defends the importance of finitist consistency proofs by saying that such a proof for a system enables us to get, from a proof in the system for a conclusion not containing transfinite symbols, a proof of the same conclusion by finitist methods. So the programme of interpretation may be said to be a natural outgrowth of Hilbert's point of view. On the other hand, this modified and generalized programme may also be viewed as a fairly direct generalization of the concept of translation so that one might claim this as an immediate descendant of the older reductionist programme: since translations preserve structure, they cannot be very informative when we try to clarify some structure by a more preferred one; so let us try some weaker connection which does not preserve structure.

Naturally the question of preference does not admit an entirely objective answer. But there is a basic bifurcation of constructive versus nonconstructive methods which may roughly be correlated with the contrast of potential infinity and actual infinity. There are different shades of constructive and nonconstructive methods. According to Bernays, there are five shades in all. If we replace his "finitism in the narrower sense" by an even narrower region of "anthropologism" which deals with the concept of "feasibility," we obtain the following five domains: (1) anthropologism, (2) finitism (in the broader sense), (3) intuitionism, (4) predicative set theory or the theory of natural numbers as being ("predicativism"), (5) classical set theory or the theory of arbitrary sets (platonism). The first three shades may be said to deal with a mathematics of doing and the last two with a mathematics of being. While each heading calls to mind some vague area of concepts and methods, and they are listed in an order of decreasing constructivity, no one of the regions has been characterized sufficiently sharply to satisfy the majority of people working on foundations. Nor is it clear how these regions are tied together. Curiously enough, the characterizations we have today are such that the less constructive a domain is, the more satisfactory is our characterization of it. The prevalent mood nowadays is not to choose a life mate from among the five "schools" but to treat them as useful reports about a same grand structure which can help us to construct a whole picture that would be more adequate than each taken alone. While philosophers may find this armistice less exciting than schools fighting to kill one another, it is undoubtedly conducive to a more successful approach to the original aim of understanding mathematics.

One quite naturally wishes to say that constructive methods are more evident and more reliable, and indeed much work is directed to the systematic extraction of the constructive content of nonconstructive methods. But it is not clear that the constructive concepts are always clearer, and constructive methods are certainly not usually simpler. Relative to our present knowledge, we understand the concept of "arbitrary" sets better than the concept of constructive proofs. A good deal of work is also devoted to explaining constructive concepts in terms of nonconstructive ones.

For those who prefer sharp definiteness, an axiomatic treatment of the five concepts: feasibility, constructivity, proof, number, and set may be said to form the hard core of foundational studies. But then we must pay attention to the various ramifications which at times may be more important than the hard core. There are the partial formalizations such as the formalization of the concept of effective procedures by general recursive functions. Moreover, in each case, we come quickly against the limitations upon formalization, and the axiomatic method itself becomes an object of study. Formal systems are very useful tools, but we not only use our tools but also develop and examine them constantly, not just as a means but almost as our chief end, calling to mind the desire of a critique of pure reason. In short, it seems fair to say that today's main concern in foundational studies is to clarify the five domains listed above by formalizing the irreducible concepts and tying them up by uniform local reductions. This shift in emphasis from justification to clarification has its parallel in philosophy where the chief interest moves from "how we know" to "what we mean".

§ 2. Anthropologism

In mathematics, we constantly use the word "can" to refer to theoretical possibilities. If we are concerned with mathematics as a human activity, practical possibilities become more interesting. In *Sur le platonisme* (1935), Bernays suggests studying such a use of "can" but says explicitly that he is not recommending that we do arithmetic with a restriction to "feasible" ("effectable") processes (pp. 61—62). Bernays mentions the fact that we pass without hesitation from k and j to k^j although nobody has given or can give the decimal expansion of, say, $67({}_{257}{}^{729})$. Yet intuitionists (and finitists, for that matter) do not question the meaningfulness and truth of the assertion that such an expansion exists. One may ask whether we have in this case truly intuitive evidence. "Isn't it rather the general method of analogy that is applied here, consisting in the extension to inaccessible numbers the relations which can be verified concretely for the accessible numbers? Indeed, the reason for applying this analogy is all the more strong since there is no precise limit between the numbers which are accessible and the ones which are not. One could introduce the notion of 'feasible' processes and restrict implicitly the range of significance of recursive definitions to feasible operations. To avoid contradictions, it would only be necessary to abstain from applying the law of excluded middle to the notion 'feasible'." In his *Remarks on the foundations of mathematics* (1956), Wittgenstein makes many cryptic observations (e.g., lines 23—25, p. 65; lines 16—22, p. 84; lines 5—9, p. 156) which become understandable if we keep in mind his preoccupation with the conception of mathematics as feasible activity. Kreisel, in his review of Wittgenstein's book, calls this point of view "strict finitism". The word "anthropologism" is a bit more colorful.

It is on this basis that we can distinguish a finitist proof from one which can actually be carried out and be kept in mind (what Wittgenstein calls "surveyable" or "perspicuous"). For example, from this point of view, a definition, even an explicit one, is not a "mere" abbreviation as it enables us to see a new aspect, to see an old expression as something different, to grasp as a matter of fact a wider range of expressions. The "reduction" of numerical arithmetic to the predicate logic with identity or that of the decimal notation to the stroke notation entails, from this point of view, a great loss which consists in a considerable decrease of the range of numbers which we can actually handle.

Mathematical induction codifies the analogy between accessible and inaccessible numbers. While the justification of the principle lies beyond what is concretely presentable, we are able, once we accept it, to bring a great deal of new things into the range of the surveyable. While we cannot survey the corresponding stroke numeral of every decimal numeral, we convince ourselves by induction that there exists a unique decimal or stroke notation for each positive integer. So also we get an indirect survey of all possible proofs of a system by an inductive consistency proof.

As an actual calculating machine can only handle a restricted amount of data, we have to twist and turn the notations and techniques in order to increase the range of manageable calculations. If one views foundational studies as primarily concerned with the determination of the range of mathematics which we actually can do, then mathematical logic as is practised today could play at most a minor role and its dominance would be giving us a wrong impression of the problems of foundations. For example, if we had only the stroke notation, we could not manipulate with numbers much larger than 10, the decimal notation extends the range, and exponentiation extends it further still; in the use of calculating machines, what notation we use to represent numbers is an important problem. New definitions and new theorems interest the working mathematicians even though mathematical logic may claim that they were all implicitly contained in the logical system to begin with. Anthropologism draws our attention to this distinction which is neglected by mathematical logic.

From this approach, besides number, set, proof, notation also becomes officially an object of study. To describe a system, we have to include not only the basic rules but also the definitions and proofs since how much we can actually do with the system depends a great deal on what definitions and proofs are at our disposal. So also a proposition receives its meaning from a proof or a refutation of it because only afterwards can we place it at the right place in our understanding. Every proof changes our actual concept somewhat and may be said to give us a new concept. Or again, if we reflect on the human elements involved, it is doubtful that a contradiction can lead to a bridge collapsing.

The comparison with machines must not give us a wrong impression. People actually engaged in the use and construction of calculating machines find the current automata studies not quite what they want, and there is demand to study, e.g., what the length of a calculation is, or how to develop something about machine operations that is similar to information theory in paying attention to quantitative details. However, these problems or even the problems about an actual machine whose internal structures and tendency to make mistakes are not clear to us, are different from those for anthropologism. To deal with such machines, one might think of the application of statistics in gas dynamics, and, like von Neumann, talk about "probabilistic logics", but we would still get something similar to mathematical logic in so far as they all deal with something like the truth functions and their distributions. Anthropologism looks for a logic not of the static but of the developing, the becoming. Thus, since it is far beyond our present knowledge and understanding to treat fruitfully man as a machine, anthropologism suggests a behaviouristic or phenomenological, rather than a physiological, treatment of mathematical thinking. This seems to suggest a vague area of research quite different from mathematical logic, although there is no justification in believing that the different lines of research cannot enjoy coexistence.

The intuitionistic logic might turn out to be applicable to anthropologism. But if one wishes to hold consistently to the position of anthropologism, he cannot accept the usual formulation of the intuitionistic calculus which allows for arbitrarily long formulae and arbitrarily long proofs.

§ 3. Finitism

According to Hilbert, finitist methods make up the combinatorial hard-core of mathematical proofs so that only the finitist part has a real mathematical content, everything else is merely "ideal" hypostatizations comparable to lines and points at infinity in projective geometry. Thus far we do not seem to have succeeded in establishing this thesis, set theory being a notable exception. Sometimes Bernays and Hilbert (also Frege in his later years) have also spoken of our basic geometrical intuition of the continuum. The diagonal argument or Dedekind's cut theorem appears to have a real content although we can hardly claim that we have a reduction of it to combinatorial terms. Relative to our present knowledge anyhow and perhaps also in the future, we seem to need independently what Bernays calls "quasi-combinatorial" notions in the sense of an analogy of the infinite collections to the finite collections.

In the first volume of the *Grundlagen* (1934), Bernays gives a characterization of the finitist method. "The distinctive trait of this methodological point of view is that reflections are set up in the form of *Gedankenexperimenten* with objects which are taken as *lying concretely before us.* In number theory, numbers are treated, which are thought as lying before us, in algebra letter-expressions with given numerical coefficients, all lain before us" (p. 20). "What we need to take as essential is merely that we have in the numeral 1, as well as in the appending of another 1, an intuitive object, which may always be recognized again in an unambiguous manner, and that with each numeral we can always survey (überblicken) the discrete parts out of which it is constructed" (p. 21). From the context it is clear that "can" refers to theoretical possibilities and finitism as thus specified is an idealization. This general characterization on the epistemological level leaves room for different interpretations. Thus, for example, Gentzen's consistency proof of number theory falls outside the domain of methods actually enumerated by Bernays in this context. At the same time, Gentzen's proof suggests extensions of the domain which may be said to conform to Bernays' intentions. Indeed, in the second volume of the *Grundlagen* (1939), Bernays speaks of Gentzen's proof as opening a new chapter of proof theory (p. 374). Hence, we may perhaps say that the domain delimited in the first volume is finitism in the narrower sense, while the domain envisaged in the second volume is finitism (in the broader sense). But no sufficient clue is given to enable one to supply an upper limit to the finitist methods.

Skolem and Kreisel have emphasized free variable (quantifier-free) methods which may conveniently be used to characterize the domain of finitism. For example, the consistency proofs of Gentzen and Ackermann have suggested the following formal system F: propositional calculus, primitive recursive functions, ordinal recursive functions of Ackermann, Peano's axioms, quantifier-free transfinite induction up to ε_0 with ordinals in some standard notation, free function variables, free predicate letters. (Although there are only axioms about natural numbers, the range of values of individual variables is left open in the sense that other objects may be taken as falling within the range.) Possibly one may wish to add also primitive recursive functionals of finite types. One might be tempted to stipulate that all and only proofs performable in F are finitist, but that would deprive finitism of much of its philosophical significance. Or one might on vague grounds suspect that there can be no formal system which includes all finitist methods, but that would require an exact argument. To introduce a more exact characterization of finitist methods and, using it, to settle whether some such system as F embodies all the finitist methods, seems a question of much interest. A positive solution would dissolve a good deal of the uneasy feeling that the notion of finitist methods is too vague.

§ 4. Intuitionism

Today it is generally accepted that intuitionist methods are broader than finitist methods. For example, Kronecker envisaged only the finitist methods, while intuitionism adds additional logical methods. In applications, the two types of methods yield practically the same results since the difference does not appear except in artificially complex cases. That is why von Neumann, for example, regards them as the same. Bernays stresses the view that intuitionism should be regarded as an extension of finitism. While finitism deals only with decidable (quantifier-free) propositions, intuitionism permits also logical manipulations with undecided propositions with quantifiers. An intuitionist may use such undecided propositions or even implications between them as premises of implications. In this way, he makes statements which involve a hypothetical statement of the premise, using thereby the totality of all proofs or all constructions which is not concretely specified. That is why finitism requires no special predicate logic (the usual propositional calculus being applicable) while intuitionism has a special logic in which the logical connectives get special interpretations in terms of absurdity, construction on a hypothetically given construction, proof from a hypothetically given proof, etc.

Intuitionists, in their discussions, often bring in the actual state of mathematics at a given time, a feature which distinguishes anthropologism from finitism. But in this respect, the intuitionists are primarily concerned with quantified propositions which have been neither proved nor refuted and which cannot be decided by a general method. For example, Mersenne asserted in 1644 that 2^{257}-1 is a prime and this was refuted only in recent years. Yet even before the refutation, neither the finitists nor the intuitionists would hesitate to assert that either 2^{257}-1 is a prime or not. On the other hand, "either there are infinitely many twin primes or not" is not true for the intuitionists because neither of the two disjunctants has been proved. In general, if $(x)\ (Ey)\ (z)\ R(x, y, z)$ means that there is an effective f, $(x)\ (z)\ R(x, f(x), z)$, and $-(x)\ (Ey)\ (z)\ R(x, y, z)$ means that there exists no function f whatsoever $(x)\ (z)\ R(x, f(x), z)$, then "$(x)\ (Ey)\ (z)\ R(x, y, z)$ or not" is simply not true for a suitable R such that there exists only a noneffective function f, $(x)\ (z)\ R(x, f(x), z)$. There are several such examples in the literature.

Kleene and Gödel have given interpretations of Heyting's arithmetic which bring out the constructive character of the system. It is often said that while classical arithmetic deals with truth, intuitionist arithmetic deals with provability. In view of the emphasis on the actual states of mathematics, it may also be possible to interpret the intuitionistic calculi by using "has been proved" instead of "is provable", but the preceding paragraph shows that special precaution has to be taken to stretch the concept "has been proved" to imagine that every proposition which is true and decidable by a general method has been proved.

It is said that Heyting obtained his logical calculus by compiling a long list of principles true of the notion of constructive proofs, and then striking out redundant ones. The interpretations of Heyting's arithmetic by Kleene and Gödel suggest a different way of viewing the intuitionistic logic: This logic, while retaining the convenient apparatus of quantifiers, differs from classical logic in that it preserves the possibility of interpreting in free variable effective terms all conclusions obtained in number theory, including those which contain number quantifiers. In Kleene's interpretation, this is true only when the conclusion is in the prenex form, while in Gödel's interpretation, this is always true. If we wish, we may say that the intuitionist predicate calculus is but one answer to the problem of so restricting operations with propositional connectives and quantifiers that at least in the domain of number theory, the use of quantifiers does not, in the final result, lead beyond the region directly acceptable to those who are willing to admit all recursive functions.

If we compare the present state of intuitionism with the state of set theory at the time when Cantor was active, we may feel that some day formal systems for intuitionism (on the basis of Brouwer's concepts of construction, constructive proof, and free choice sequence) will be found which are as adequate (neither more nor less) to intuitionism as current formal systems of set theory (on the basis of Cantor's concept of set) are to set theory. So far as number theory is concerned, Heyting's arithmetic is as adequate a formalization of intuitionistic number theory as the system Z of Hilbert-Bernays is one of classical number theory. While Z cannot claim to be a complete formalization in view of the Gödel incompleteness, yet serves as a reasonable basis for many considerations, it seems acceptable to regard Heyting's arithmetic in the same spirit. Heyting's formalization beyond this region is not as satisfactory. Thus Heyting's axioms for functions of natural numbers are satisfied either if we let the variables range over only the absolutely free choice sequences or if we let them range over the union of these and the well-defined functions. Recently, Kreisel adds more axioms so that the result is satisfied only if we take just the absolutely free choice sequences, Kleene adds different axioms so that the result is satisfied only if we take the union of these and the well-defined functions. More axioms are needed for the species. Heyting's discussion suggests that something like the ramified type theory (for finite types only) can be used for dealing with species.

§ 5. Predicativism: Standard Results on Number as Being

If we take the Dedekind-Peano axioms for arithmetic and add all primitive recursive definitions or, equivalently, by a result of Gödel, just those for addition and multiplication, we obtain, by using the intended meaning of the notion of arbitrary sets which occur in the formulation of the induction principle, a categorical characterization of the domain of number theory. Skolem proves, however, that if we wish to avoid this appeal to arbitrary sets and replace the general principle of induction by a finite or enumerable number of special cases, we no longer have a categorical system. The standard formal system obtained in this manner is the system Z of Hilbert-Bernays mentioned before in which induction is permissible over all and only the formulæ in the system itself (i. e. the sets definable in the system itself). Skolem actually constructs a model for Z in which there are, besides the natural numbers, also certain "unnatural" numbers. This result is, in a somewhat weak sense, equivalent to Gödel's theorem (partially anticipated by Finsler) that there exist propositions in Z which are neither provable nor refutable. Thus, by Gödel's theorem, there must be a proposition which is true but not provable. If we add the negation of the proposition to Z, we must have again a consistent system which, by an extension of the completeness theorem of the predicate calculus, has a model that must contain certain unnatural numbers, since the added proposition would be false if we had only the natural numbers. Conversely, we can extend Ryll-Nardzewski's argument for showing that Z has no finite axiomatization and derive from Skolem's result the existence of undecidable propositions in Z. Thus, if we replace quantifiers by functions as Skolem does and obtain a sequence $f_1(n)$, $f_2(n)$, of functions for all axioms of Z, we can, by using Gödel numbering, find a predicate (Ej) $B(j, f(m, n, k))$ which says that j is a proof in Z of the formula $f_m(n)=k$ for any numerals m, n, k. Then $f_m(n)=\mu_k (Ej) B(j, f(m, n, k))$ is true for any given m and n but is not always provable with variable n because otherwise we could follow out Ryll-Nardzewski's construction and obtain a case of the induction principle expressed in Z but not provable in Z.

There is work to find explicit, nonstandard models for partial systems of Z. Attempts, so far unsuccessful, have also been made to find nonstandard models for Z with a view to proving the undecidability (and therewith truth because most of them can be put in quantifier-free form) of certain standard conjectures in number theory. As we know, if we replace the induction principle in Z by the noneffective "rule of infinite induction", we get a complete theory. Rosser proves that for systems dealing with infinite sets also, even the rule of infinite induction fails to make them complete. The results of Gödel and Skolem give one the feeling that Z is not more natural than many extensions and partial systems of it except that the induction principle in Z coincides with what is required by a set of more or less natural formation rules. A successful determination of the range of finitist methods may perhaps yield a better argument for preferring Z.

The extensive use of primitive recursive functions by Skolem and Gödel, together with Ackermann's example of a recursive function which is not primitive recursive, led Herbrand and Gödel to two generalizations of the primitive recursive functions. Gödel's definition gives the general recursive functions which Church and Turing are able to identify with the intuitive notion of effectively calculable functions with quite convincing arguments. Church and Turing, using this identification, show that systems like Z are not effectively decidable and that the decision problem for the predicate calculus is not effectively solvable. The Herbrand recursive functions form a much broader class which can profitably be identified with "effectively definable" functions. On the basis of general recursive functions and quantifiers, Kleene and Mostowski have introduced the arithmetical hierarchy of predicates. Among the arithmetic sets, the recursively enumerable ones have received a good deal of special attention. Different forms of a theory of computable real numbers have been studied by Goodstein, Specker, Grzegorczyk, and others.

There are many other questions about the matter of classification and hierarchies. For example, Grzegorczyk gives an elegant classification of the primitive recursive functions, but we do not possess any satisfactory classification of the whole set of general recursive functions. Preliminary steps have been taken toward a classification of formal systems by notions such as relative consistency, but nothing comparable with the details in the classification of number-theoretic predicates has been achieved. In another line, Davis, Kleene, Kreisel, Myhill, Shepherdson have obtained interesting results on constructive functionals and their classification.

Church and Kleene have introduced a class of recursive ordinals which is useful in the study of hierarchies. Related work has been done on recursive well-orderings by Turing, Markwald, and Spector. Turing, in particular, has studied ordinal logics as an attempt to classify systems and theorems by ordinals.

Using recursive ordinals, Davis, Mostowski, Kleene have introduced the hyperarithmetic hierarchy. Addison, Kuznecov, Grzegorczyk-Mostowski-Ryll-Nardzewski have proved that the hyperarithmetic predicates coincide with those representable by Herbrand recursive functions.

§ 6. Predicativism: Predicative Analysis and Beyond

Traditionally two types of question are both regarded as having to do with the continuum. The first type includes Zeno's paradoxes and the notion of infinitesimals. In *Chuangtse* (4th Century B. C.) one has, "If a rod one foot long is cut short every day by half of its length, it will have something left even after ten thousand generations." These problems do not concern the continuum only but would arise even if we are only concerned with fractions. Today we usually regard them as essentially solved and people working on foundations pay little attention to them. The second type of question is concerned almost exclusively with the continuum, and includes that of defining continuity and clarifying the concept of nonenumerable sets.

We get a pretty standard formalization of this area of mathematics if we use the second-order simple type theory or, alternatively, add to it also a predicative third type. The question of finding an informative consistency proof for such a system, first posed by Hilbert in 1900, remains open today.

The ideas of predicativism are less novel than those of intuitionism. Weyl first tried to develop analysis along the line of predicativism but was not able to remove the difficulty that the least upper bound of a set of real numbers of order n is no longer of the same order. Formerly this difficulty had been removed by the highly impredicative axiom of reducibility. In his consistency proof for the ramified type theory, Fitch suggests that perhaps we can recover some of the power of the axiom of reducibility by using infinite orders. Lorenzen makes the remark that if, for example, we take the union of real numbers of all finite orders, then every real number in the union is of some finite order n, and every real number of the next order is again in the union. In this way, one is able to get classical analysis, with more or less the standard proofs, on a predicative basis with transfinite orders. It seems most natural to reformulate Lorenzen's approach in terms of a transfinite ramified theory of types. The result is similar to Gödel's model for set theory but, of course, we are no longer entitled to use large ordinals which presuppose impredicative totalities.

There are different possible places for stopping, e.g. ω or ε_0. But in order to get a closure property, we seem to wish to stop at a place where indices are used only when they are already available in earlier systems and all ordinals definable in the final theory are used as indices. A result by Spector shows that if we use all and only the recursive ordinals, then every relation in the resulting theory which happens to be a well-ordering again has a recursive ordinal as its order type. Hence, there seems to be good reason for using Σ_{ω_1}, where ω_1 is the least upper bound of the recursive ordinals. If, however, we require that the ordinals for indices must be definable in the earlier systems in a yet to be determined stronger sense, we would presumably stop at some smaller ordinal. On the other hand, arguments can also be given for wishing to go beyond Σ_{ω_1}. These arguments can be better understood in connection with a result by Kleene.

Using certain concepts of Brouwer, Kleene proves that the predicate of being a notation of a recursive ordinal is a complete predicate of the form $(\alpha)(Ex)R(a, \bar{\alpha}(x))$, thereby taking us into the hierarchy of analytic predicates ordinarily treated in the second-order simple type theory. This seems surprising in so far as that the predicate is introduced by an inductive definition and yet all impredicative definitions of the form $(\alpha)(Ex)\ R(a, \bar{\alpha}(x))$, R recursive, becomes reducible to it.

It is true that in order to reduce the inductive definition into an explicit one, we get an impredicative definition. But it is thought that the impredicative definitions needed in converting inductive definitions (to take care of the extremal condition) form only a well-understood small subset of all possible impredicative definitions. Kleene's result leads one to ask whether one might not get complete predicates for more complex forms of analytic predicates by considering larger sets of inductively defined ordinal notations. In their first publication on recursive ordinals, Church and Kleene did introduce a broader set but recently it has been proved that the set is not a complete predicate of the form $(\alpha)(E\beta)(x)\ R(a, \bar{\alpha}(x), \bar{\beta}(x))$. On the other hand, if we modify their definition by requiring relative recursiveness rather than recursiveness in the extension of one "number class" to the next, it seems only possible to define the set by a predicate of the form (α) $(E\beta)$ (x) $R(a, \bar{\alpha}(x), \bar{\beta}(x))$. It has, however, not been proved that this is a complete predicate of the form. The whole question of getting informative complete predicates of more complex forms of the analytic hierarchy seems to remain wide open. Indeed, the very notions of an "inductive" definition and an "inductive" ordinal seem to stand badly in need of a fairly sharp definition.

It seems not unreasonable to regard sets definable by inductive definitions as predicative. With regard to these sets it is true not only that we do not have to go beyond the enumerable, but that, unlike with the impredicative set theory, we always have a unique minimal model which is in fact the intended model. If we accept this argument, then the problem of characterizing the notion of inductive definitions is intricately connected with the question of determining the range of predicativism which would certainly go much beyond Σ_{ω_1}.

Incidentally, in the usual ramified type theory, there is a distinction between (finite) levels and orders. If, e.g., we consider only sets of natural numbers and not sets of sets, etc., we still have sets of higher orders though not sets of higher levels. One might think that by using also higher level sets, we obtain more sets of natural numbers. It turns out, however, we get exactly the same sets of natural numbers because quantification over higher level sets can be replaced by quantification of higher order sets of natural numbers. This consideration can be used to show that the sets of natural numbers definable in Σ_{ω_1} coincide with the hyperarithmetic sets. Spector, and more recently Gandy, have proved a number of results about Σ_{ω_1}. It seems not hard to extend known consistency proofs of the ramified type theory (with finite types only) to Σ_{ω_1}. A more difficult problem would be to extend Ackermann's proof for Z or Gödel's proof for Z by means of his translation of Z into intuitionist number theory and his interpretation of the latter.

If one is interested in giving a satisfactory formulation of predicative set theory, it seems that we can use also variables ranging over all sets in the theory, as well as variables ranging over absolutely free choice sequences or even arbitrary sets in the manner of the intuitionists. If we wish to "reconstruct" classical mathematics on such a basis, then those portions which do not necessarily concern impredicativity can be obtained, as by Lorenzen, those portions where the impredicative and the nonenumerable are intrinsic have to be abolished. There may also be a middle portion where more work is needed to determine whether we have a satisfactory predicative version, Kreisel's example being the Cantor-Bendixson theorem.

§ 7. Platonism

In the theory of arbitrary sets, three notions are involved, besides the notion of infinity already present with integers: (1) impredicative definitions and nonenumerable sets; (2) the formation of new totalities of sets and subsets of these totalities; (3) the totality of all sets. According to Cantor, "by a 'set' we shall understand any collection into a whole *M* of definite, distinct objects *m* (which will be called the 'elements' of *M*) of our intuition or of our thought" (1895). Cantor was not disturbed by the paradoxes because he felt that these arise only on account of a failure to pay attention to the "genetic" element in the process of forming new sets. According to him, the totality of all mathematical objects is no more a mathematical object. He distinguishes between consistent and inconsistent collections, the latter are too large to be sets and can only be treated each as a Many and not as a One, contradictions arising otherwise. If one gets paradoxes by talking about the totality of all sets which is not and cannot be a closed whole, he has only himself to blame.

Zermelo, and very recently Ackermann, have proposed formal systems which are intended to be formalizations of Cantor's original concept of set with its emphasis on the "limitation of size". Zermelo's formulation has been developed further by Fraenkel, Skolem, von Neumann, and received a definitive treatment in the hands of Bernays. This, with some modifications, is concisely described in Gödel's famous monograph and widely accepted by working mathematicians. The consistency and interpretation questions of Ackermann's system have not been much discussed. For example, any property not containing the set concept *M* itself can be proved to be different from *M* in extension so that it is impossible to add consistently anything similar to Gödel's $V=L$. There is no proof of its consistency relative to, say, the system in Gödel's book. Ackermann gives a proof that the latter system is contained in his, but it seems desirable to modify his proof to make use of Skolem's more satisfactory notion of "definite properties" rather than Fraenkel's in terms of "functions." It also seems interesting to ask whether one could choose some reasonable minimal conditions for a standard model and decide the question whether it has a standard model.

Originally, Zermelo leaves the notion of "definite properties" indefinite and nowadays one usually accepts Skolem's specification of the notion. Of course, if we are looking for a formal system, we would have to adopt some such explicit explanation. But broader notions do not violate the original intention, which literally invites arbitrary "definite properties". If, therefore, one is to relax the requirement on formalization to get a more faithful representation of the platonist notion of set, this is a natural place to introduce such relaxations. For example, one could say that given any set and any definite property, however it is to be expressed, there is a subset of the given set which consists of all things which have the given property.

In the paradoxes, both impredicative definitions and the totality of all sets are involved. Since Cantor's concept retains impredicative definitions but excludes a universal set, one may ask whether we cannot retain a universal set but exclude impredicative definitions. This is impossible because we cannot avoid the impredicative question whether the universal set belongs to itself.

Attempts to avoid impredicative definitions have led to various forms of the predicative set theory (ramified type theory) which amount to a virtual abolition of the platonism intrinsic to the notion of an arbitrary set. One gets then one form or another of set theory which is a "no class theory", sometimes given the name of "conceptualism".

Russell developed such a theory but found he could not get what he wanted. So he introduced impredicative definitions under the disguise of an "axiom of reducibility". The net effect is what nowadays we call the simple theory of types. While, as a formalization of set theory, this is not as satisfactory as the line initiated by Zermelo, it remains a useful tool in the study of the detailed structure of sets (hierarchies and classifications). The strength of this system is essentially the same as Zermelo's original set theory with Skolem's notion of "definite properties". But, as Kemeny proves, the latter does contain more sets (and, in particular, more sets of integers). If, however, we weaken slightly the Aussonderungsaxiom in a natural manner, we do get a system with the same sets: instead of any predicate $F(a)$, use only those predicates in which every quantifier is bound by a free variable, e.g., (x) $(x \in b \rightarrow G(x))$, (Ey) $(y \in c \ \& \ H\ (y))$, etc., where b, c are free in $F(a)$.

Frege's inconsistent system already contained a type theory with respect to predicates but none with respect to sets. Indeed, it seems almost a linguistic necessity to introduce types in regard to predicates.

By studying the simple type theory purely formally and disregarding the "metaphysics" behind it, Quine was led to a puzzling formal system which retains both a universal set and impredicative definitions but imposes certain "zigzag" conditions ("stratification") on admissible definitions of sets. An elegant variant (and extension) of the system is included in his book *Mathematical logic* (1951 edition) which is widely familiar among philosophers. We know that the latter is consistent if the former is. There are peculiar features about these two systems; with regard to the former system, it has been proved that, in a definite sense, it possesses no standard models, and that the axiom of choice in its usual form is refutable in it. So far nobody has succeeded in getting a good intuitive understanding of these systems: we have neither a proof that they are inconsistent nor a proof that they are consistent relative to, say, the system in Gödel's book.

There is another line in formalizing set theory according to which troublesome definitions are compared to points of singularity in analysis (Gödel). A formulation by Church and one by Hintikka may be regarded as exemplifying this approach. Both systems, however, have turned out to be inconsistent.

Cantor originally conjectured that all sets can be well-ordered and that the cardinal number of the continuum is the next one after that of the integers (the continuum hypothesis). The first conjecture was proved by Zermelo to be equivalent to the axiom of choice. Considerably later, *D.* Mirimanoff, von Neumann and Zermelo separately introduced the Fundierungsaxiom to exclude certain irregularities. In Gödel's book, *A, B, C* are the axioms of ordinary set theory, *D* is the Fundierungsaxiom, *E* is an axiom of choice. The problem of independence of these principles has been studied very carefully. Fraenkel and others have proved that *D* and *E* are each independent of *A—C,* but it is still an open question whether *E* is independent of *A—D*. Von Neumann has proved that if *A—C* is consistent, then *D* is. Gödel has proved that if *A—D* (or, indeed, *A—C*) is consistent, then *E* and the continuum hypothesis and an axiom of categoricalness ($V=L$) are all consistent. It is, however, not known whether the axiom of categoricalness is independent of *A—D,* whether the continuum hypothesis is independent of *A—E*.

The result obtained from ordinary set theory by adding Gödel's axiom of categoricalness resembles a predicative set theory except that large ordinals are used which presuppose impredicative totalities. In such a system, all impredicative features are reduced to one special kind, namely the existence of certain large ordinal numbers or well-ordered sets. If we truncate the system and use only predicatively defined ordinals, we get a framework for predicative set theory similar to that discussed in the preceding section.

This question of ordinals is closely related to the second notion we mentioned at the beginning of this section, namely the formation of new totalities or repeated extensions of the domain of sets. The postulation of higher and higher ordinals would naturally yield richer and richer set theories by permitting more levels of extensions. The question of finding higher ordinals seems closely related to Gödel's search for stronger axioms of infinity.

From the rather special character of Gödel's model in which the (generalized) continuum hypothesis is true, it appears very plausible that there exist other models in which the continuum hypothesis is false. Both Lusin and Gödel have conjectured that Cantor's continuum hypothesis is independent of the axioms of set theory and indeed false according to the yet unilluminated true meaning of set. Lusin suggests that we try to find a model for the usual axioms of set theory in which Cantor's continuum hypothesis is false but $2^{\aleph_0} = 2^{\aleph_1}$.

The Skolem paradox applies to every formal system of the platonistic set theory. Thus, by intention, each such system deals with nonenumerably many objects while every explicitly specified language can only have enumerably many expressions and theorems, thereby admitting also an enumerable model which is an unintended interpretation. This point can also be brought out by an argument slightly different from Skolem's in the following manner. Take the second-order simple type theory. By the quasi-combinatorial conception, the intended interpretation contains natural numbers and all possible sets of them, i.e., we can either take 1 or leave 1, and in either case, we can either take 2 or leave 2, and so on, ad infinitum. In this way, we see that there are $2^{\aleph_0}$ possible sets. If we assume such a model as somehow given, then we can easily extract an enumerable model. Thus, we have a natural enumerable model for the predicative sets and there are enumerably many additional axioms of set existence for the impredicative sets. If each addition of a new axiom can be satisfied by an addition of enumerably many new sets, we have succeeded. But this can be done with the help of the intended model. Take a simplest case. Suppose we have a new axiom asserting that there is a set K which contains all and only those m such that $(EY)\ F(m, Y)$ and, for brevity, suppose that F contains no other set variables and no other free variables. If we have already an enumerable model before we add this axiom, then, for each given m_0, either the given enumerable model already contains a set Y_1, such that $F(m_0, Y_1)$, then $m_0 \in K$ and we do not change the model; or there is no way to make $F(m_0, Y_2)$ true no matter what Y_2 we choose from the intended maximal model, then $m_0 \notin K$, and we do not change the given model; or there exists a Y_3 in the maximal model but none in the given enumerable model which makes $F(m_0, Y_3)$ true, then we add this set Y_3 and $m_0 \in K$ is true in the extended model. In this way, if we add all the sets Y_3 (at most enumerably many), add the set K defined thus, and add enumerably many new sets to ensure closure with all previously given axioms, then we get an enumerable model for the augmented set of axioms. (When the new axiom contains more set quantifiers, we need a somewhat more complex argument.)

In the above argument, we have used the intended model to begin with, but we could have used any given model and the argument would still go through. If, on the other hand, we wish to prove something more, e.g., to find an enumerable model in which the axiom of choice is true, then it becomes necessary to use the intended (maximal) model. Since the axiom of choice is true in the maximal model, if, after obtaining an enumerable model for the other axioms, we draw more sets from the maximal model to satisfy the axiom of choice, we arrive at an enumerable model of the original theory in which the axiom of choice is also true. In such a model, both the continuum hypothesis and something like Gödel's axiom of categoricalness may be false, but presumably we would not have enough information about the model to prove such conclusions. Similarly, while it seems plausible that some such considerations could be used to get a model of the main body of set theory in which the axiom of choice is false, it is highly doubtful that an acceptable formal independence proof of the axiom of choice can be extracted from such an approach.

Both Frege and Dedekind are able to derive number theory from set theory (in fact, the second-order simple type theory suffices) with the help of the axiom of infinity. Zermelo, Grelling, and Bernays manage to do so without the axiom of infinity. Michael Dummett suggests in conversation a definition which does not appeal to the axiom of infinity but is more closely related to the Frege-Dedekind definition. Thus, if we take the empty set as 0, and the set n plus itself as a new member as the successor n' of n, we let C_n

be $(u)\,(0 \in u \,\&\, (y)\,((y \in u \,\&\, y \neq a) \rightarrow y' \in u))$, then x is a natural number if and only if $(Eu)\, C_x(u)$ and $(v)\,(C_x(v) \rightarrow x \in v)$. Recursive definitions can be defined similarly by using ordered triples. In all these approaches, all finite sets are assumed to exist while only some finite sets are identified with natural numbers. A question of some interest would be to devise a theory of sets in which every set asserted to exist is also a natural number. In such a theory it would be possible to add consistently an axiom of categoricalness stating that all sets are natural numbers.

§ 8. Logic in the Narrower Sense

After taking care of geometry by its analytic representation, Frege and Dedekind try to prove that mathematics is a part of logic. Frege objects to Dedekind on the ground that classes and the membership relation are not usual in logic and are not reduced to accepted logical notions. But then concepts and relations, which Frege uses instead, are mathematically equivalent to classes. In either case, while an elaborate argument is necessary to justify that synthetic truths can be a priori, to call mathematics analytic or call it logic only shifts the burden to a clarification of the concepts of the enriched logic. To take some simple examples: a single application of mathematical induction contains infinitely many syllogisms; recursive definitions, each of which includes infinitely many explicit definitions, constitute a new category of definition which has sometimes been called "creative". Unless logic contains infinite processes to begin with, we must, in reducing mathematics to logic, be getting them out of a hat. Clearly, if for some people logic contains (implicitly perhaps) infinite processes and for others it does not, there are two different senses of logic. One may continue to use the word "logic" in a broader sense and a narrower one, but much excitement over the relation between logic and mathematics disappears once we keep in mind that it is absurd to identify mathematics with the narrower logic and trivial to do so if we adjust the domain of logic to fit that of mathematics.

Traditionally, logic deals with examples such as "all pleasures are transitory, immortality is a pleasure, therefore, immortality is transitory". It is an old story that traditional logic is inadequate in a number of respects such as the treatment of relations. As a result, people sometimes date modern logic from Frege's formalization of the propositional calculus and the predicate calculus in 1879. The completeness of Frege's propositional calculus was proved in about 1920 by Bernays and Post, that of his predicate calculus in 1930 by Gödel, extending results of Herbrand and Skolem. An interesting question is to obtain a satisfactory definition of completeness, a question that is closely related to a definition of logic and logical truth.

In Bolzano's *Wissenschaftslehre* (1837, republished around 1930), we find a partial anticipation of the current definitions of completeness, validity, and logical truth. It is commonly said that a logically true proposition is one true in virtue of its form. Bolzano calls a proposition valid (allgemeingültig) relative to its constituents $i, j, \cdots$ when results obtained by varying these constituents at will are all true. These propositions he calls analytic (analytically true) in the broader sense. He goes on to define analytic propositions in the narrower sense as those in which the unchanging parts all belong to logic. And then a sober comment: "This distinction has of course something vague about it, because the range of the concepts which belong to logic is not so sharply defined that controversies may never arise on the matter" (§ 148). According to him, "certain propositions $A, B, C, D, \cdots, M, N, O, \cdots$, stand in the relation of compatibility, and, in particular, relative to the concepts $i, j, \cdots$," if "there exist certain concepts which, when put in the places of $i, j, \cdots$, make all the propositions true". He continues, "and say that the propositions $M, N, O, \cdots$, are deducible from the propositions $A, B, C, D, \cdots$, relative to the varying constituents $i, j, \cdots$ if every set of concepts which in the places of $i, j, \cdots$, make all the propositions $A, B, C, D, \cdots$, true, also make all the propositions $M, N, O, \cdots$, true" (§ 155). If we take his definition of deducibility as a criterion of the adequacy of a formalization of logic, we see that the completeness of the predicate calculus means simply that the axiomatically defined deducibility relation coincides in power with his concept of deduction.

The problem of defining logic remains unsettled. Bolzano's definition of propositions which are logically true (analytic in the narrower sense) depends on a previous specification of the logical constants the range of which is, as Bolzano himself concedes, not sharply defined. It has, for example, been suggested that we simply give an enumeration of the logical constants. This reminds one of Protagoras who defines virtue by enumerating justice, temperance, holiness, courage, and wisdom which are said to form parts of virtue in the same sense in which mouth, nose, eyes, ears are parts of a face. In any case, for every list one has to offer, some argument is necessary to defend that the list contains all and only logical constants. And the heterogeneous history of logic makes this well nigh an impossible task.

Philosophers tend to worry over the question whether formalization reflects faithfully everyday and scientific discourse. Since mathematical logic has lived a moderately long and rather eventful life of its own, working logicians are inclined to disregard this question, which, as the main concern is with mathematical discourse, is not so very serious anyhow. If we think in terms of the traditional categories of quantity, quality, relation, and modality, we could perhaps claim that monadic predicate calculus takes care of quantity, propositional calculus takes care of quality, polyadic predicate calculus takes care of relation, modal logic takes care of modality. In fact, one might even be inclined to argue that in so far as mathematics is concerned, modal logic is unnecessary, since occurrences of modal concepts in mathematics can be explained away by the other logical or metalogical concepts. It is, however, plausible that when we are concerned with formalizing the notion of constructivity, some variant of modal logic which deals with provability rather than truth, such as Heyting's predicate calculus, is necessary. For mathematics anyhow, the classical predicate calculus and something like the Heyting predicate calculus seem sufficient to handle respectively the nonconstructive and constructive aspects. If we feel that a logic sufficient for the purpose of logical arguments in mathematics must, in a nontrivial sense, be sufficient for other purposes, we seem to have good reason to identify tentatively logic in the narrower sense with the classical and the intuitionistic predicate calculi. From a "common sense" approach, we may even consider the classical calculus as the more basic of the two, and disregard temporarily the intuitionistic calculus.

There remains the questions whether to include identity and higher level predicates and whether to use many-sorted predicate calculi. If we include identity between individuals and predicates of all finite levels or use a suitable many-sorted calculus with identity, we easily get a formal system which may be said to be a formalization of logic. Any proposition in the calculus that is true in all interpretations is then a logical truth. This does not mean that any proposition of logic which happens to be true under a preferred interpretation is a logical truth: "there are three individuals" and "any two individuals differ in at least thirty respects" would be counterexamples. For one who desires purity, one should use a slight reformulation in which even "some individual exists" is excluded so that a logical truth must be true in all domains, not only in all nonempty domains. To say, as some logicians do, that whether certain propositions of logic are *logically* true may depend on the size of the universe or to debate whether the axiom of infinity is a logical truth seems a miscomprehension caused partly by a futile wish to dispense with the concept of model or interpretation and partly by an unwillingness to separate mathematics and logic in the narrower sense from everyday discourse.

The predicate calculus not only gives a complete formalization of all usual methods of argument of a strictly logical nature but also provides a framework in which every axiomatic system may be viewed as an application obtained by adding new axioms to restrict the interpretation of certain predicates and the ranges of the variables. In this way, one can also hope for some general theory about the interpretation of axiomatic systems, such as what Tarski calls the theory of models, as a branch of set theory.

The most important results on the predicate calculus are those of Herbrand and Gentzen which enable us to get proofs without using modus ponens (no "Umweg"). A good deal of work has been done on these results by Bernays, Kreisel, Schütte, Stenius, Craig, Hintikka, Beth. These results are so central that they seem to yield a uniform treatment of the predicate calculus. For example, the completeness theorem follows from Herbrand's result quite directly and Herbrand himself did not draw the conclusion perhaps only because he felt the notion of completeness is not meaningful according to his preoccupation with finitist methods. Herbrand began to use his theorem to give a uniform treatment of all known special cases of the decision problem for the predicate calculus, and the work is being continued by Church and Dreben. Gentzen's treatment is so designed that the intuitionist predicate calculus can be treated simultaneously. Beth is able to use Gentzen's approach to give a completeness proof for the intuitionist calculus and also to supply a reason for Gentzen's choice of his rules of the predicate calculi. A more exact proof of Beth's completeness theorem is desirable and there remains the question of getting an intuitionistically acceptable completeness proof. It, however, seems likely that we can soon have a uniform treatment of logic in the narrower sense which would include the completeness theorems, the Herbrand-Gentzen type theorems, Bernays' results on Hilbert's ε-operator, and special cases of the decision problem.

§ 9. Applications

As we know, the completeness results of the predicate calculus have been applied in the field of algebra. There have been numerous other applications of mathematical logic (in the broader sense). Tarski has sharpened Sturm's method for deciding the number of real roots of a given algebraic equation in one variable x, to give a decision procedure for elementary algebra and elementary geometry. A favourite example of applying logic to solve famous problems from ordinary mathematics is Novikov's negative solution of the word problem for groups. Attempts, unsuccessful so far, have been made to obtain a negative solution to Hilbert's tenth problem (to find an effective method for solving all Diophantine equations). Church mentions from topology the problem of finding a complete set of invariants for elementary manifolds of dimensions above 2. Kreisel has applied mathematical logic to determine bounds in a theorem of Littlewood and a theorem of Artin. Gödel's axiom of categoricalness has been applied by Addison and others to treat open problems in descriptive set theory. In the field of calculating machines, apart from the application of the propositional calculus to the simplification of circuits viewed as static, the addition of the time element to the circuits seems to call for treatment by an application of recursive propositional functions. Moreover, the whole trend of formalization gives rise to the possibility of using machines as an aid to mathematical research. Although in this direction we constantly run up against the difficulty that we need machines 100 or 1,000 times faster, it cannot be denied that moderate tasks such as filling in gaps in a correct proof are not far beyond the capability of machines today and that more can be done with machines which are to appear.

Additional note. More recently, the writer has considered questions relating to "anthropologism" in a paper "Process and existence in mathematics" in *Essays on the foundations of mathematics in honour of A. A. Fraenkel.* In connection with Ackermann's set theory discussed in this paper and in § 6 of chapter XVI, a recent paper by Azriel Lévy (*Jour. Symbolic Logic,* **24** (1959), 154—166) has cleared up the system in several ways.

CHAPTER III

ON FORMALIZATION*

§ 1. Systematization

The most striking results of formalization occur in logic and mathematics.

Here formalization provides at least one kind of systematization. We are led to believe that there is a fairly simple axiom system from which it is possible to derive almost all mathematical theorems and truths mechanically. This is at present merely a theoretical possibility, for no serious attempts seem to have been made to prove, for instance, all the theorems of an elementary textbook of calculus. Nevertheless, we seem to get a feeling of grandeur from the realization that a simple axiom system which we can quite easily memorize by heart embodies, in a sense, practically all the mathematical truths. It is not very hard to get to know the axiom system so well that people would say you understood the system. Unfortunately just to be able thus to understand the system neither gives you very deep insight into the nature of mathematics nor makes you a very good mathematician.

To say that physics uses the experimental method is not to say much about physics. To say that all theorems of mathematics can be proved from certain axioms by chains of syllogism (or *modus ponens*) is to say just as little about mathematics. Merely knowing the experimental method is not knowing the whole of physics; merely knowing an axiom system adequate for developing mathematics is not knowing the whole of mathematics.

There is another kind of systematization which is less superficial than learning the axiom system. It is an intuitive grasp of the whole field, a vivid picture of the whole structure in your mind such as a good chess player would have of the game of chess. This second kind of systematization is something that formalization (or at least formalization alone) would not provide us.

If we had never used logistic systems at all, the many interesting results about logistic systems (such as those of Skolem, Herbrand, and Gödel) would, of course, never have been expressed in the specific form in which they are now being expressed. But it is not certain that essentially the same results might not have been attained, though in other contexts and as the results about other things. Nevertheless, axiomatics or the axiomatic method has a

* This chapter appeared in *Mind*, **64** (1955), 226—238.

strong appeal in that here we seem to be able to prove sweeping conclusions about whole fields. For many of us a significant theorem about a whole field appears more important than particular theorems in the field. In generating systems, formalization serves the function of enabling us to talk precisely about whole fields of learning.

§ 2. Communication

It is hard to say whether in general formalization renders a theory or a proof easier to understand.

Consider, for example, an oral sketch of a newly discovered proof, an abstract designed to communicate just the basic idea of the proof, an article presenting the proof to people working on related problems, a textbook formulation of the same, and a presentation of it after the manner of *Principia Mathematica.* The proof gets more and more thoroughly formalized as we go from an earlier version to a later. It is, however, questionable whether in general a more completely formalized version is clearer or serves better as a means of communication. Each step of it should be easier to follow since it involves no jumps. But even this is not certain, for there are many jumps which we are so used to making that we find it more natural to make the jumps than not to. Or alternatively, we may say that the step actually does not involve jumps and that our formal proof suggests that it does only because our formal system is defective as a map of our intuitive logic.

Who finds which proof easier to follow or who understands which proof in a shorter while depends pretty much on what background the man happens to have. In general, the better acquainted one is with the problem, the easier he finds the use of a more sketchy proof. But there is also a certain limit beyond which even the expert in the matter can no longer supply for himself the missing details. Moreover, there is always the possibility that the presentation would be much shorter if it were not so short. It seems safe, however, to say that a more thoroughly formalized proof is generally longer, provided that we do not appeal to abbreviations in its presentation and the less formalized version does not waste words.

We are all familiar with requests to explain a physical theory without using mathematics, to convey the basic idea of a proof without using symbols. Therefore, it would seem that in general the plain words or the less technical language provide a more efficient means of communication. Actually, however, we can easily think of examples which would indicate that this is not quite true.

To put thoughts on physics into mathematical symbols is one way of formalization. Through accumulation and tradition this way of formalization has also become a powerful way of communication: for those who understand the language, a short formula may express more precisely thought which could only be explained by many pages of ordinary words, and much less satisfactorily. Sometimes it becomes practically impossible to avoid the mathematical language in communicating with others. An elderly English political figure complains that none of the many eminent physicists with whom he has corresponded is courageous enough to pass any definite judgment on his proposed new theory of ether. Then he stresses the similarity between his theory and the concluding paragraph of a recent article by Dirac, and proceeds to discard as non-essential the accompanying mathematical passages in Dirac's article. It may be presumed that if he had also included comparable non-essential mathematical passages in his theory, he would have received more definite responses.

§ 3. Clarity and Consolidation

Does formalization help us to analyse and clarify concepts?

Often in formalizing ordinary concepts, we appear to have platitudes restated in pedantic obscurity; for instance, the mathematical definition of the continuity of a curve or the technical definition of the notion of effective computability. Moreover, the exact formalizations almost always distort our ordinary language at one place or another. For example, it has been pointed out that Russell's theory of descriptions does not apply to sentences such as "the whale is a mammal", and that sometimes in ordinary use the sentence "the king of France is bald" is neither taken as true nor taken as false.

In scientific investigations, we often recognize the advantage and even necessity of paying the price of considerable deviation from ordinary use of words in order to reach fairly precise terminology and notation. But, in what sense is, for instance, the technical notion of effective computability clearer than the corresponding common sense concept? Ordinarily, we would tend to say that the technical notion is *less* clear because it is more difficult to learn and a concept is clearer if and only if it is easier. We might speak of different kinds of clarity just as Mill speaks of different kinds of pleasure. Then we can also speak of a principle of preference: Only those who have experienced the feeling of clarity both of the ordinary notion and of the technical one are qualified to judge which is really clearer. And then, we hope, they will find the formalized notion clearer.

Perhaps we should also say that which definition of a term is clearer depends partly on the purposes we want the term to serve, and partly on our familiarity with the notions involved in each definition. The main advantage of the more articulate definition of a notion is, presumably, that it is sharper: for example, there are many cases where we can give a definite answer to the question whether certain given functions are effectively computable, only after we have made use of the technical notion of computability.

There are many cases where we could neither ask a univocal question nor obtain a univocal answer until we possessed the formalized notion. For example, we needed an exact definition of continuous curves before we could ask and answer the question whether there are space-filling continuous curves. And it was necessary first to formalize the notions of completeness and decidability before a negative answer could be given to the question whether number theory is complete or decidable.

Significant formalization of a concept involves analysis of the concept, not so much in the sense of analysis when we say that being a bachelor entails being unmarried, but more in the sense that an analysis of the problem of squaring the circle is provided by the proof of its unsolvability. When formalization is performed at such a level, it does serve to clarify and explicate concepts.

Another function of formalization is the clarification and consolidation of arguments or proofs. Sometimes we are not quite sure whether we have understood a certain given proof, sometimes we understand a proof once but fail to understand it again when reading it a few days later. Then there often comes the desire to work over the proof thoroughly, to make explicit all the implicit steps involved, and to write down the expanded result once and for all. With some people this desire to formalize and expand proofs may become a habit and a handicap to studying certain branches of mathematics. Yet occasional indulgence in this kind of thoroughness need not be a harmful thing.

In certain cases, there is no sharp line between formalizing and discovering a proof. There are many cases where essentially incomplete sketches, sometimes containing errors as well, get expanded and made into more exact proofs. Sometimes it is not until we have the thoroughly worked out proof on hand that we begin to perceive a connexion between it and the existing hint or sketch. Sometimes it seems hard to decide whether to consider the sketcher or the formalizer the true discoverer of the proof.

§ 4. Rigour

In a sense, to formalize is to make rigorous.

There was Berkeley's attack on the mathematicians of his day entitled: "The analyst: or, a discourse addressed to an infidel mathematician. Wherein it is examined whether the object, principles, and inferences of the modern analysis are more distinctly conceived, or more evidently deduced, than religious mysteries and points of faith." There is the long story of how Lagrange, Cauchy, Weierstrass, and others strove to formalize exactly the basic notions of limits, continuity, derivatives, etc., providing thereby rigorous (though not necessarily reliable) foundations for mathematical analysis.

In the contemporary scene, we have logicians deploring how carelessly ordinary mathematicians use their words and symbols. Some logicians are puzzled that so many apparent confusions in mathematics do not lead more often to serious errors. On the other hand, mathematicians in turn complain about the inaccuracy of alleged proofs of mathematical theorems by physicists and engineers.

In the other direction, physicists consider that mathematicians are wasting their time when they worry about "foundational crisis"; mathematicians consider that logicians are indulging in learned hair-splitting when they devote pages and volumes to discussing the meanings of meaning or the use of quotation marks and brackets.

The right course is to be as rigorous and detailed as the occasion or the purpose requires. But this is more easily said than done. For example, certain authors seem to dwell tirelessly on the obvious, while skipping the crucial and more difficult steps.

The matter of distinguishing expressions from that which is expressed may serve to illustrate some of the questions about rigour. There were occasions when failure to be careful about the distinction actually hindered greatly the advance of logic. It is now customary in logic and philosophy to stress the difference, usually using quotation marks to separate, for example, the city Peking from the word "Peking". At present, even those who do not want to spend much time on using the quotation marks rigorously, often find it necessary to declare, for example, "quotation marks are omitted in most cases since we believe that no confusion will arise from this negligence". Every now and then, we run into certain articles in which the authors are so meticulous about using quotation marks that it becomes very difficult to read and understand what is being said.

One might even distinguish logicians into two groups depending on whether or not they always try to use quotation marks consistently and exactly. It may be a matter of temperament. Or it may also be a question of whether one happens to be either too lazy or too busy.

§ 5. Approximation to Intuition

To put thoughts in words or to describe a particular experience involves formalization of intuition. It has been contended that no finite number of propositions could describe exhaustively all that is involved in a particular experience. In other words, it is impossible to formalize without residue the complete intuition at the moment.

The matter of approximating intuition by formalization is clearer with regard to mathematics. For example, we know intuitively many things about integers. If we are asked to characterize our notion of integers, one way of answering is to say that integers form a group with respect to addition, they form an ordered set with regard to the ordinary relation of being greater than, and so on. The notions of group, ordered set, etc., are more exactly defined or more formalized than the notion of integers. Consequently, such answers tend to clarify somewhat our notion of integers, but they are usually inadequate because they fail to characterize unambiguously the integers.

We may compare the place of abstract structures such as group, field, ordered set, etc., in mathematics with the place of general concepts in ordinary life. They all can be considered as results of formalization or abstraction which serve as tools of thinking and research. As tools they help to economize our thought, as is often remarked. For example, not only integers, but transformations in space, etc., all form groups; anything that we prove about groups in general, of course, applies also to the special groups which may differ from one another in many respects. Similarly, there are many different chairs which can all be employed to support buttocks. In this way formalization, closely tied up with abstraction, produces useful tools.

On the other hand, it is often hard to characterize adequately our intuition through the use of formal structures. For example, it is not easy to describe exactly the colour, shape, etc., of a particular chair. Peano's axioms are thought to be capable of characterizing completely our notion of positive integers. Yet, as Russell observed long ago, Peano's axioms are satisfied by all progressions such as the odd positive integers, the negative integers. Russell thought that only by calling in a set theory could we make a univocal characterization. More recent advances in logic show that he was wrong even in believing this.

In fact, as we know, there are important results which indicate unmistakably that we can formalize without residue neither the fundamental intuitive notion of positive integers nor the basic notion of sets or classes.

Thus, there is Gödel's famous theorem according to which, for any fairly rich system, we can find some property expressible in the system such that we can prove for each of the integers 1, 2, $\cdots$ that it has the property, but we cannot prove the general statement that all positive integers have the property in question. In other words, although intuitively if $P(1)$ (*i.e.,* 1 has the property P), $P(2)$, $P(3)$, $\cdots$ are all true, then it must be the case that all positive integers have the property P; yet in no fairly strong logistic system can we formalize adequately this intuition so as to guarantee the performability of such an inference for all the properties P expressible in the system. It also follows that no ordinary axiom system can preclude the interpretation that besides the ordinary 1, 2, $\cdots$ the set of positive integers also contains certain other queer things; there is no way to formalize in an ordinary logistic system our intuition that 1, 2, $\cdots$ are the only integers.

On the other hand, there is no axiom system in which we can get *all* the real numbers or the classes of positive integers. This follows easily from Cantor's famous argument for non-denumerability. Thus, given any axiom system, we can enumerate all the classes of positive integers which can be proved to exist in the system, either by applying Löwenheim's theorem or by reflecting on the fact that the theorems of existence in the system can be enumerated. Hence, if we define with Cantor a class K of positive integers such that for each n, n belongs to K if and only if n does not belong to the nth class in the enumeration, then the existence of K cannot be proved in the system. In other words, although in the system we can also speak of all the classes of positive integers, we cannot really formalize without residue the intuitive notion of "all" with regard to classes of positive integers; in each formalized axiom system, there is always some class of positive integers that is left out.

§ 6. Application to Philosophy

The application of mathematical logic to the treatment of philosophical problems may also be viewed as an attempt to formalize. Such applications often give the impression that a formidable technical book expresses in tiresome exactitude more or less commonplace ideas which could be conveyed more easily and more directly in a few sentences of plain language. Yet, undoubtedly, there are cases where the appeal to formalization is of more than pedantic interest. For instance, Heyting's formalization of the intuitionistic view of logic and mathematics helps quite a bit in conveying Brouwer's ideas to those people who have a radically different orientation. Another example is the gradual formalization of the notion of being a definite property, employed for defining sets in Zermelo's axiomatic treatment of set theory.

Perhaps we can compare many of the attempts to formalize with the use of an airplane to visit a friend living in the same town. Unless you simply love the airplane ride and want to use the visit as an excuse for having a good time in the air, the procedure would be quite pointless and extremely inconvenient. Or we may compare the matter with constructing or using a huge computer solely to calculate the result of multiplying seven by eleven. When the problems are so simple, even the task of translating them into a language which, so to speak, the machine can understand would already take longer than if we were to calculate the results by memory or with a pencil and a sheet of paper.

It is a practical problem to decide what means of transportation to use in making a certain particular trip, or to decide whether it is feasible to build a computer to handle a certain given type of question. As we know, there are many different factors which are ordinarily taken into consideration before making the decision. Similarly, it is also a practical problem to decide in each particular case whether it is profitable to apply mathematical logic in handling a definite kind of problem. The only difference is that the factors which have to be considered here are often more involved and less determinate.

Take the principle of verification. Various attempts at giving an exact definition of the notion of verifiability have failed. And systematic use of the logistic method has been recommended as the only way to a satisfactory solution. On the other hand, there is also the view that the important thing is a general attitude expressed vaguely in the rough principle of verification, rather than an exact definition of verifiability. Underlying this dispute, perhaps, are the varying attitudes toward the general desirability of crystallization of ideas.

This raises larger problems. Why should we want such crystallization in philosophy? What is the function and business of philosophy? Fortunately, general observations can be made without going into such hard questions.

§ 7. Too Many Digits

After sketching an axiom system for his theory of probability, F. P. Ramsey goes on to say, "I have not worked out the mathematical logic of this in detail, because this would, I think, be rather like working out to seven places of decimals a result only valid to two". There are several disadvantages in working out a result to too many places. It uses up time which might be spent otherwise. It also makes the result harder to memorize or to include in future calculations, if anybody should want to make use of it. And pointless problems would arise regarding the last five places: do they exhibit any interesting pattern which would indicate the lawfulness of nature? Do they coincide with the five digits starting with the 101st in the decimal expansion of π? and so on.

How do we decide whether a result is valid only to two places? If the same experiment is repeated under different but, so far as we know, equally favourable circumstances, with results which agree satisfactorily only to the first two places, then we tend to conclude that the places after the second are not quite reliable. If most people refuse to calculate up to many places and a single person has an irresistible itch for reporting every result to at least seven places, it might be rather hard to decide whether his result is right.

The matter of constructing an exact theory of (say) probability contains an additional factor. Since ordinary language is not exact, new words are coined or ordinary words are given technical usage. In order to evaluate the theory, you have first to understand it. In order to understand it, you have first to learn a new language. Since it is usually impossible to explain clearly and exactly even the technical usages, a formal or exact theory can almost always be defended against charges that it does not conform to fact. As long as there is a sufficiently complicated system and a fairly big and energetic group of people who, for one reason or another, enjoy elaborating the system, we have a powerful school of learning, be it the theory of meaning, the sociology of knowledge, or the logic of induction. There is always the hope that further development of the theory will yield keys to old puzzles or fertilise the spirit of new invention. In any case, since there is mutual support between different parts of a given system, there is little danger that the discrepancy between one part and the facts should discredit the system. And of course if we are interested in the "foundations", there is no need to fear any immediate tests. The worst that can happen to such theories is not refutation but neglect.

§ 8. Ideal Language

Language is employed for expression and communication of thoughts. Failure in communication may either be caused by inadequate mastery of the language, or by internal deficiencies of the language: that is, if there is thought to be conveyed at all. Language is also sometimes used for talking nonsense. Here again, certain languages just seem to offer stronger temptations for doing so. And sometimes the language user is not careful enough, or he merely parrots others. In such cases he does not have thoughts or feelings to express, and there is, of course, no question of correct communication. A less serious disease is confused thinking, often involving internal inconsistency. This again is sometimes the fault of the language, such as the ambiguity of words and a misleading grammar.

The creation of an ideal language would yield a solution of these difficulties once for all. Such a language should be so rich, clear, and exact as to be sufficient both for expressing all thoughts and feelings with unmisunderstandable clarity, and for precluding nonsense. Given such a language, many problems now known as philosophical would be dissolved. Disagreement about what is to be taken as nonsense would lead to the construction of different ideal languages. There would be then the problem of understanding each other's ideal language.

An alternative to the ideal language is to handle each individual case separately and thoroughly. To explain at great length what we intend to say, to give concrete examples when possible, to invite questions and discussions. And to reflect carefully and ask what we really want to say, whether we do have something to say, whether we are not misled by false analogies or naive syntax.

The task of constructing a comprehensive ideal language is in many ways similar to that of finding a mechanical procedure to decide answers to all problems of mathematics. They are equally impossible. If and when these two tasks are clearly formulated, the impossibility can be proved definitely in both cases. In certain simple areas of logic and mathematics, we do possess decision procedures. Similarly in mathematical logic and theoretical physics we have more exact languages. But there is no mechanical method for finding decision procedures, and each significant mathematical problem calls for a special treatment. It is demonstrably impossible to reduce all mathematics to its decidable portion. It seems equally impossible to fit everything we say into the language of logic and physics. Moreover, these languages are more exact in their abstract setup than in their actual use. It is a familiar experience that mathematicians who know the language of mathematics very well often offer fallacious proofs.

The quest for an ideal language is probably futile. The problem of formalization is rather to construct suitable artificial languages to meet individual problems.

§ 9. How Artificial a Language?

The contrast between natural and artificial languages suggests a sharp distinction. Russian is natural, while Esperanto is artificial. But is the language of the biologists or that of the philosophers natural or artificial? Is Mr. Woodger's proposed language for biology natural or artificial? Hilbert's language for the Euclidean geometry is more exact and artificial than that of Euclid's *Elements*. So far as the development of human scientific activities is concerned, the creation of the language of the classical mechanics or of the axiomatic set theory was rather natural.

We might speak of degrees of artificiality, as perhaps measured by the amount of deviation from the natural course. The Chinese language spoken today differs to a rather great extent from that used two thousand years ago, although the changes have been mostly natural. If we had attempted two thousand years ago to bring about the same changes in one year's time, we would have had to create at that time a language quite artificial. To introduce an artificial language is to make a revolution. Unless there are compelling natural needs, the resistance will be strong and the proposal will fail. On the other hand, when an artificial language meets existing urgent problems, it will soon get generally accepted and be no longer considered artificial. Hence, it may be more to the point if we compare artificial languages with Utopian projects.

Attempts to formalize the theory of probability are sometimes criticized on the ground that the efforts fail to make contact with the crucial and burning problems of physical science. One ready reply is that the situation is the same with many interesting investigations in branches of mathematics such as abstract algebra, set theory, and topology. One may argue, however, that more new ideas and methods are introduced through such studies than through the researches on foundations of probability theory. Or maybe there is more substance behind the new languages of algebra and set theory and results obtained there are not as easily discredited by slight shifts of emphasis or subtle mistakes in the original analysis.

Mrs. Joan Robinson somewhere remarks that economists are usually behind their time. An urgent practical problem often ceases to be urgent or practical long before the discovery of a theoretically satisfactory solution. Whether it is worthwhile to continue the search for the solution of a problem which is no longer urgent depends to a large extent on whether the particular problem is intimately connected with larger issues, whether it is sufficiently intriguing intellectually, and whether it is likely to recur in the near future. Similarly, the value of an artificial language has to be decided in accordance with its elegance and its usefulness either in its direct applications or as a model to be followed in future constructions. In a certain sense, an interesting artificial language must not be excessively artificial.

§ 10. The Paradoxes

Much time and space has been devoted to the discussion of the logical paradoxes or contradictions. Sometimes it is said that these paradoxes bring to light the self-contradictory character of our logical intuition. Indeed, as we know, the formalization of logic and set theory was largely motivated by a desire to avoid the paradoxes and yet obtain what we ordinarily want.

It has been suggested that we take the paradoxes too seriously, largely because of our preoccupation with formalization and our lack of flexibility.

What is proposed instead seems to be this. Suppose we find a contradiction by a seemingly plausible argument. Since we get a contradiction, we see that the argument is really not correct and indeed must be faulty. So let us remember never to use the argument again. And that is the end of the matter.

However, when we say that the argument looks plausible, we mean, among other things, that each step of the argument also looks plausible. It seems necessary not only to reject the whole argument as a unit but to pin down exactly which step or steps in the argument caused the trouble. Hence, there are the various attempts to reject one or another of the steps as unwarranted. But why can we not say that although each step is in itself all right, they must not be combined in the particular way that leads to the contradiction? Indeed, we may even use this possibility to justify the attitude of indifference, on the part of many working mathematicians, toward the paradoxes.

It is only when we come to constructing a formal system to embody our arguments that this procedure proves awkward. In a logistic system, we break up proofs and arguments into isolated steps so that if a step is valid at all, it is valid no matter where it occurs. In other words, certain combinations of shapes are taken as axioms so that they can be asserted as valid no matter where they occur; and certain (finite) sequences of combinations of shapes are taken as justified by the rules of inference so that any such sequence, wherever it occurs, is taken as determining valid steps. For instance, if we agree to take as an axiom, for two specific sets named *a* and *b*, the assertion "Either *a* belongs to *b* or *a* does not belong to *b*", we can no longer reject the same statement as an unwarranted step when it occurs in an argument that leads to a contradiction.

Two alternatives to the customary logistic method are: (1) not to attempt any exact characterization of all the valid arguments of any important branch of mathematics; (2) to list either all or samples of all the warranted and unwarranted whole specific arguments as inseparable units, instead of trying to break up all warranted arguments into a small number of basic atomic steps. The alternative (2) will either produce quite messy results or lead to something which is hardly distinguishable from a logistic system.

CHAPTER IV

THE AXIOMATIZATION OF ARITHMETIC*

§ 1. Introduction

I once asked myself the question: How were the famous axiom systems, such as Euclid's for geometry, Zermelo's for set theory, Peano's for arithmetic, originally obtained? This was to me more than merely a historical question, as I wished to know how the basic concepts and axioms were to be singled out, and, once they were singled out, how one could establish their adequacy. One possible approach which suggests itself is to take typical theorems, proofs, definitions, and examine case by case what assumptions and concepts are involved. The obstacle in such an empirical study is, apart from the obvious demand of excessive time and energy, the lack of conclusiveness in both result and justification.

The attempt to find an answer to this question led me to some interesting fragments of history. For example, in 1899 Cantor distinguished consistent collections (the "sets") from inconsistent collections ([1], p. 443), anticipating partly the distinction between the two kinds of classes stressed by von Neumann and Quine. Cantor had already proposed a form of the axiom of substitution ([1], p. 444, line 3), although Fraenkel and Skolem, more than twenty years later, had to adjoin it to Zermelo's list of axioms as a supplement. In another direction, the history of the development of axioms of geometry makes clear how natural it was for Hilbert to raise in 1900 the consistency question of analysis ([2], p. 299) quite independently of the emphasis on set-theoretical paradoxes.

By far the best piece of good fortune I had in these historical researches was, however, my findings with regard to Peano's axioms for arithmetic. It is rather well-known, through Peano's own acknowledgement ([3], p. 273), that Peano borrowed his axioms from Dedekind and made extensive use of Grassmann's work in his development of the axioms. It is not so well-known that Grassmann had essentially the characterization of the set of all integers, now customary in texts of modern algebra, that it forms an ordered integral domain in which each set of positive elements has a least member. Very few people know (cf. [4], p. 490) that Dedekind wrote a very interesting letter (dated 27 February, 1890, addressed to Headmaster Dr. H. Keferstein

* This chapter appeared in *Journal of Symbolic Logic*, **22** (1957), 145—157.

of Hamburg) to explain how he arrived at the Peano axioms. In what follows I intend to quote at length (by written permission of the Niedersächsische Staats- und Universitätsbibliothek at Göttingen given in the autumn of 1954) and to comment on this letter. The notion of non-standard models (unintended interpretations) of axioms for positive integers is, for instance, brought out quite clearly in Dedekind's letter. To clarify the letter, I shall also dwell at length on the contents of Dedekind's famous essay on the nature and meaning of positive integers ([4], pp. 335—391).

§ 2. Grassmann's Calculus

A more elementary question related to the axiomatization of arithmetic would seem to be an explicit statement of some adequate group of natural rules and conventions which enables us to justify all the true numerical formulae containing 0, 1, 2, 3, 4, 5, 6, 7, 8, 9, +, ×, =, (,) such as 7+5=12. Since we must not use "infinitely long expressions" or indispensable and-so-on's, such a task is not as simple as one might think at first. For example, we would need the multiplication table, the "addition table," the convention about the positional system of notation, the ordinary commutative, associative, distributive laws, the substitution of equals for equals. It would be much too tiresome to include the result of any such attempt here, although I am inclined to think that such an exercise could be of pedagogic interest if one wished to explain in an elementary textbook the process of formalizing implicit assumptions. The advantages are that addition and multiplication of positive integers are familiar to everybody and that they are of fundamental importance everywhere. Of course I do not claim that I can predict whether such an example will induce respect for formalization or destroy the pupil's interest in logic. In any case, our interest here is not so much with numerical formulae in the Arabic notation but primarily with general statements in arithmetic.

Many mathematicians have studied natural numbers in complete isolation from their applications. In this way, a large body of concepts and theorems concerning natural numbers has been accumulated. This more or less determined area constitutes the mathematical theory of natural numbers. A transparent characterization of the domain should be interesting by itself and of assistance toward understanding the concept of number. We are familiar with the two usual methods of developing mathematics: the genetic or constructive approach customary in the extension of numbers to integers, fractions, real numbers, complex numbers; and the axiomatic method usually adopted for the teaching of elementary geometry. There are many differences between elementary textbooks of geometry and the sharper formulations of axioms of geometry, so that we might wish to call the former intuitive axiomatics, the latter formal axiomatics. The application of the axiomatic method in the development of numbers is not natural. Its rather late appearance is evidence. If, however, our problem is to have a systematic understanding of the domain of number theory, the axiomatic method suggests itself. Indeed, we now realize that the method can be applied to numbers, and that for certain purposes the application is suitable. It remains a rare thing to teach arithmetic from an axiomatic approach.

In 1861, Hermann Grassmann published his *Lehrbuch der Arithmetik* ([5]). This was probably the first serious and rather successful attempt to put numbers on a more or less axiomatic basis. Instead of just the positive integers, Grassmann dealt with the totality of all integers, positive, negative, and 0. Much of his method can be used to handle the smaller totality of all positive integers, too. He was probably the first to introduce recursive definitions for addition and multiplication, and prove on such a basis ordinary laws of arithmetic by mathematical induction. The work is of interest not only in Grassmann's success in making implicit things explicit, but also in his failure or choice not to characterize formally certain concepts which are neutral or belong to logic.

I shall compare Grassmann's system with the postulational characterization of integers which is customary in present day abstract algebra. According to the latter, integers form an ordered integral domain in which each set of positive integers has a least element. (Compare, for example, [6], p. 36, p. 3, p. 7.)

With non-essential changes we can formulate this into a calculus L_1:

I. Atoms: 0, 1; $+$, $-$, $\cdot$; *Pos*: a, b, c, etc. (variables).

II. Terms: 0 is a term; 1 is a term; a variable is a term; if s and t are terms, $(-s)$, $(s+t)$, $(s \cdot t)$ are terms.

III. Formulae: if s and t are terms, $s=t$ is a formula, $s \in Pos$ is a formula.

IV. Axioms:

(2.1) $a+(b+c)=(a+b)+c.$

(2.2) $a+b=b+a.$

(2.3) $a \cdot (b \cdot c)=(a \cdot b) \cdot c.$

(2.4) $a \cdot b=b \cdot a.$

(2.5) $(a \cdot b)+(a \cdot c)=a \cdot (b+c).$

(2.6) $a+0=a.$

(2.7) $a \cdot 1=a.$

(2.8) $a+(-a)=0.$

(2.9) $c \neq 0,\ c \cdot a=c \cdot b \rightarrow a=b.$

(2.10) $a \in Pos,\ b \in Pos \rightarrow a+b \in Pos.$

(2.11) $a \in Pos,\ b \in Pos \rightarrow a \cdot b \in Pos.$

(2.12) Either $a \in Pos$, or $a=0$, or $-a \in Pos$.

(2.13) If $1 \in A$ and for all b, $b \in A \rightarrow b+1 \in A$, then for all a, $a \in Pos \rightarrow a \in A$.

It may be noted that in the above formulation, logical particles such as "or", "→", "for all", "=", "∈" and the set variable "A" are used though not listed in advance. The rules governing the use of these are also taken for granted.

Grassmann did not present his development in an axiomatic form, although such a recasting is not difficult. To avoid tedious details, I shall reformulate it without indicating at every place the exact reference to his book. By consulting the book, the interested reader will undoubtedly be able to verify the general historical accuracy and discover minor deviations in the following presentation.

Grassmann's calculus L_2:

A. Atoms: =, (,); a, b, c, d, etc. (letters); 1, +, −, ·; *Pos*.

B. Terms: 1 is a term; −1 is a term; a letter is a term; if s and t are terms, then $(s+t)$ and $(s \cdot t)$ are terms.

C. Definitions (observe that Grassmann takes only "negative of" applied to 1 as primitive and defines the general case together with "difference" therefrom; a purist might wish to use two distinct symbols for the two uses of "−"):

(2.20) $0=1+-1.$

(2.21) For any a and b, $a-b$ is the number such that $b+(a-b)=a$.

(2.22) $-a=0-a.$

(2.23) $a>b \longleftrightarrow a-b \in Pos.$

D. Axioms:

(2.26) $a=(a+1)+-1.$

(2.27) $a=(a+-1)+1.$

(2.28) $a+(b+1)=(a+b)+1.$

(2.29) $a \cdot 0=0.$

(2.30) $1 \in Pos.$

(2.31) $a \in Pos \rightarrow a+1 \in Pos.$

(2.32) $b=0$ or $b \in Pos \rightarrow a \cdot (b+1)=(a \cdot b)+a.$

(2.33) $b \in Pos \rightarrow a \cdot (-b)=-(a \cdot b).$

(2.34) If $1 \in A$, for all b, $b \in A \rightarrow b+1 \in A$, and $b \in A \rightarrow b+-1 \in A$; then for all a, $a \in A$.

(2.35) If $1 \in A$, and for all b, $b \in A \rightarrow b+1 \in A$, then for all a, $a \in Pos \rightarrow a \in A$.

As a matter of fact, assuming rules which govern the notions of elementary logic, it is possible to derive all the axioms (2.1)—(2.13) of L_1 from the definitions and axioms of L_2. I shall not present these proofs but merely indicate, by referring to Grassmann's book, how this could be done. (2.1) is proved in Nr. 22 of his book; (2.2) in Nr. 23; (2.3) in Nr. 70; (2.4) in Nr. 72; (2.5) in Nr. 66; (2.6) in Nr. 18; (2.7) can be proved from (2.6), (2.2), (2.32), (2.29); (2.8) can be proved by (2.21), (2.22), and Nr. 2.6; (2.9) is proved in Nr. 96 of Grassmann's book; (2.10) in Nr. 88; (2.11) in Nr. 93; (2.13) is (2.35). The derivation of (2.12) uses primarily (2.21), (2.22), (2.30), (2.31), (2.34). This may serve as an exercise for the reader.

It may be observed that the definition (2.21) makes use of a description. In order to formalize Grassmann's work thoroughly, one would have to consider explicit rules for the truth functional connectives "or", "and", "→", the quantifiers "for all", equality "=", membership "∈", the set variable "*A*", and descriptions. Carrying out such a program would yield almost a formalization of logic. We can, for example, regard more modern works of Frege, Whitehead-Russell, Quine as realizations of such a program, except that their works are entangled with their particular theories of sets. An alternative approach would be to use properties instead of classes and formalize number theory in complete isolation from set theory. Such an approach would enjoy a purer underlying logic unaffected by the difficulties of formalizing set theory.

Grassmann's calculus is defective in at least one important respect. There is no explicit mention of the fact that different numbers have different successors, or the fact that 1 is not the successor of any positive integer. As a result, Grassmann's axioms would be satisfied if all integers are taken as identical with one another. The omission is easily understandable since we more or less take for granted that different numerals represent different objects. The surprising thing is not so much that Grassmann neglected to mention them but rather that shortly afterwards others did state these facts explicitly.

Peano, it is often believed, showed that the entire theory of natural numbers could be derived from three primitive concepts and five axioms in addition to those of pure logic. The basic concepts are: 1, number, successor. The axioms are:

(*P*1) 1 is a number.

(*P*2) The successor of any number is a number.

(*P*3) No two numbers have the same successor.

($P4$) 1 is not the successor of any number.

($P5$) Any property which belongs to 1, and also to the successor of every number which has the property, belongs to all numbers.

Of these concepts and axioms, it is possible to absorb the concept "number" and the first two axioms into an explicit specification of notation, and use just two primitive concepts and three axioms ([7], p. 219). Leaving, however, these and related simplifications aside, we may consider the informal question as to how the selection of these basic concepts and axioms could be made and justified.

Historically, Peano borrowed his axioms from Dedekind who in his remarkable booklet *Was sind und was sollen die Zahlen*? (1888, reprinted in [4]) defined natural numbers as any set of objects which satisfy these axioms, for a suitably chosen successor relation. It is very fortunate that a letter by Dedekind has been preserved in which he explains in great detail how he first arrived at what are now known as the Peano axioms. Since this letter is highly illuminating, I quote it at length. (Notice that Dedekind uses the word "system" as we would now use the word "set" or "class.")

§ 3. Dedekind's Letter

"I should like to ask you to lend your attention to the following train of thought which constitutes the genesis of my essay. How did my essay come to be written? Certainly not in one day, but rather it is the result of a synthesis which has been constructed after protracted labour. The synthesis is preceded by and based upon an analysis of the sequence of natural numbers, just as it presents itself, in practice so to speak, to the mind. Which are the mutually independent fundamental properties of this sequence N, i.e. those properties which are not deducible from one another and from which all others follow? How should we divest these properties of their specifically arithmetical character so that they are subsumed under more general concepts and such activities of the understanding, which are *necessary* for all thinking, but at the same time *sufficient*, to secure reliability and completeness of the proofs, and to permit the construction of consistent concepts and definitions?

When the problem is put in this manner, one is, I believe, forced to accept the following facts:

(1) The number-sequence N is a *system* of individuals or elements which are called numbers. This leads to the general study of systems as such (§ 1 of my essay).

(2) The elements of the system N stand in a certain relation to one another, they are in a certain order determined, in the first place, by the fact that to each definite number n, *belongs* again a definite number n', the number which succeeds or is next after n. This leads to the consideration of the general concept of a *mapping* ϕ of a system (§ 2). Since the image $\phi(n)$ of each number n is again a *number* n' and therefore $\phi(N)$ is a part of N, we are here concerned with the mapping ϕ of a system N *into itself*. And so this must be studied in its full generality (§ 4).

(3) Given distinct numbers a, b, their successors a', b' are also distinct; the mapping ϕ has therefore the character of distinctness or *similarity* (§ 3).

(4) Not every number is a successor n', i.e. $\phi(N)$ is a proper part of N; this (together with the preceding paragraph) constitutes the infinitude of the number-sequence N (§ 5).

(5) More precisely, 1 is the *only* number which does not lie in $\phi(N)$. Thus we have listed those facts which you regard as the complete characterization of an ordered simply infinite system N.

(6) But I have shown in my reply that these facts are still far from being adequate for a complete characterization of the nature of the number-sequence. Indeed, all these facts also apply to every system S which, in addition to the number-sequence N, contains also a system T of arbitrary other elements t. One can always define the mapping ϕ so as to preserve the character of similarity and so as to make $\phi(T) = T$. But such a system S is obviously something quite different from our number-sequence N, and I could so choose the system that scarcely a single arithmetic theorem holds for it. What must we now add to the facts above in order to cleanse our system S from such alien intruders t which disturb every vestige of order, and to restrict ourselves to the system N? This was one of the most difficult points of my analysis and its mastery required much thought. If one assumes knowledge of the sequence N of natural numbers to begin with and accordingly permits himself an arithmetic terminology, then he has of course an easy time of it. He needs only to say: an element n belongs to the sequence N if and only if by starting with the element 1, and going on counting, i.e. by a finite number of iterations of the mapping ϕ (compare the conclusion of 131 of my essay) I eventually reach the element n; on the other hand, I never reach an element t outside the sequence N by means of this process. But it is quite useless for our purpose to adopt this manner of distinguishing between those elements t which are to be ejected from S, and those elements n which alone are to remain in S. Such a procedure would surely involve the most pernicious and obvious kind of circulus vitiosus. The mere words "finally get there" of course will not do either. They would be of no more use than, say, the words "karam sipso tatura", which I invent at this instant, without giving them any clearly defined meaning. Thus: how can I, without assuming any arithmetical knowledge, determine formally and without exception the distinction between the elements n and t? Merely by the consideration of the *chains* (37 and 44 of my essay), and yet completely! When I wish to avoid my expression "chain," I shall say: an element n of S belongs to the sequence N if and only if n is an element of *every such* part K of S which possesses the two properties (i) that the element 1 belongs to K and (ii) that the image $\phi(K)$ is part of K. In my technical language: N is the intersection 1_0 or $\phi_0(1)$ of all those chains K (in S) to which the element 1 belongs. Only after this addition is the complete character of the sequence N determined. — In this connection I remark in passing the following. For a brief period last Summer (1889) Frege's "Begriffschrift" and "Grundlagen der Arithmetik" came, for the first time, into my possession. I noted with pleasure that his method of defining a relation between an element and another which it follows, not necessarily immediately, in a sequence, agrees in *essence* with my concept of chains (37,44). Only one must not be put off by his somewhat inconvenient terminology.

(7) After the essential nature of the simple infinite system, whose abstract type is the sequence N of numbers, had been recognized from my analysis (71, 73), the question arose: does there *exist* at all such a system in our realm of ideas? Without a logical proof of existence there would always remain a doubt, whether the concept of such a system contains internal contradictions. Hence the need for such proofs (66 and 72 of my essay).

(8) After this had also been settled, there was the question: does the analysis thus far contain also a general *method of proof* sufficient to establish theorems which are intended to hold for *all* numbers n? Indeed! The famous proof by induction rests on the secure foundation of the concept of chains (59, 60, 80 of my essay).

(9) Finally: is it also possible to set up consistently *definitions* of numbers and operations for *all* numbers n? Indeed. This is in fact accomplished by Theorem 126 of my essay.

Thus the analysis was complete and the synthesis could begin. Yet this has still caused me enough trouble! Also the reader does not have an easy task; in order to work through everything completely, he needs, apart from sound common sense, also a very strong determination."

§ 4. Dedekind's Essay

The letter is of much historical interest and can also serve to guide a study of Dedekind's essay on the nature and meaning of number. A few explanatory remarks on his essay will supplement the letter.

The first section of Dedekind's essay deals with general principles of set theory. Thus, for any two things (objects of thought) a and b, $a=b$ if there is no property belonging to the one that does not belong to the other. A set M is completely determined when with respect to everything it is determined whether it is an element of S or not; it is explicitly stated, mentioning Kronecker's opposite view, that the determination need not be effective. Two sets are the same, $M=N$, when every element of M is one of N and vice versa (the axiom of extensionality). Set inclusion is defined in the usual manner in terms of the membership relation; M is a part of N if every element of M is an element of N. Yet the same symbol is used for inclusion and membership. Given a set M of sets there is a set which contains every element which belongs to some set in M (axiom of union or sum set). Given a set M of sets there is a set (intersection) which contains every element which belongs to all sets in M. Given anything a, there is a unit set which contains only a as element. While acknowledging the possibility of an empty set, Dedekind excludes it in his development "for certain reasons". The historical interest of this section lies in the fact that it is probably the first partial attempt to state explicitly intuitive principles in the formation of sets. Later on, Zermelo, in his construction of an axiom system, makes use of this and other sections of Dedekind's essay.

The second section deals with the general concept of function (mapping, transformation), more or less following Dirichlet. One-to-one correspondence (similar transformation) is treated in § 3. Mapping of a set into itself is treated in § 4, where the important concept of a chain is also introduced: a set M forms a chain relative to a mapping ϕ if the set of all images of elements of M, $\phi(M)$, is included in M. The intersection of all chains (relative to a mapping ϕ) which contains a as an element is *the* chain of a: $\phi_0(a)$.

In § 5, Dedekind introduces his definition of infinity: a set is infinite if there is a one-to-one correspondence between it and a proper subset of it. It is proved that a set containing an infinite set as part is infinite, and that an infinite set remains infinite after deletion of a single element. A proof that infinite sets exist is given in the manner of Parmenides and Bolzano. Afterwards, Zermelo, in setting up his axiom system disregards the proof but states as an axiom (the axiom of infinity) the existence of some set similar to the one constructed in Dedekind's proof.

The set of natural numbers is defined in § 6. A set N is simply infinite if there exists a one-to-one mapping of N into itself such that there is an element in N which we shall denote by 1 and call the base-element of N, such that 1 does not belong to $\phi(N)$ and the chain $\phi_0(1)$ coincides with N. Any simply infinite set can be taken as the set of natural numbers except that we seem no longer to have a unique set of natural numbers. Dedekind proposes to neglect entirely the special character of the elements and seems to identify the set of natural numbers with what is common to (the essence of) all simply infinite sets. This is very much in the spirit of taking postulates as constituting an implicit definition. Dedekind comes back to his favourite philosophy of number: "With reference to this freeing the elements from every other content (abstraction) we are justified in calling numbers a free creation of the human mind". Indeed, Dedekind proves in § 10 that any two simply infinite systems N and M are isomorphic with regard to their mappings ϕ and ψ and their base elements 1 and 1^*: there is a one-to-one correspondence between N and M such that 1 corresponds to 1^* and if a corresponds to a^*, then $\phi(a)$ corresponds to $\psi(a^*)$. It follows that the abstract structure of a simply infinite set is entirely determined by its definition. Identifying the set of natural numbers with a simply infinite system N, Dedekind supplies in § 10 the Peano axioms: 1, the basic element, belongs to N; $\phi(N)$ is included in N, or, in other words, the successor of a number is again a number; ϕ is one-to-one, so that no two numbers have the same successor; 1 does not belong to $\phi(N)$, or, in other words, 1 is not a successor; $N=\phi_0(1)$, so that induction holds since any set M satisfying the induction hypothesis ($1 \in M$, $a \in M \rightarrow \phi(a) \in M$) is a chain containing 1 and therefore includes $\phi_0(1)$ which is, by definition, the intersection of all chains containing 1.

In § 7, a number n is defined as less than m, $n<m$, if $\phi_0(n)$ contains $\phi_0(m)$ as a proper part. A "counter" set is introduced for each natural number n: Z_n is the set consisting of the numbers from 1 to n. Properties of $<$ and Z_n are proved in § 7 and § 8. It is also proved in § 8 that every unbounded set of natural numbers is simply infinite.

§ 9 contains the earliest set-theoretical treatment of recursive definitions (definitions by induction), such as those of addition and multiplication. As we know, these definitions are not entirely explicit since the operations defined occur in the defining conditions too; as a result, we can only eliminate the defined symbols when no variables occur in the context. To admit outright such definitions in a theory amounts to taking them as axioms, and the operations defined as primitive operations. Since these operations do not deal directly with sets, anybody who wishes to develop arithmetic on the basis of set theory is obliged to supply a method of eliminating them. Dedekind proves here a general theorem that given any mapping θ of an arbitrary set M into itself and an arbitrary element b of M, we can always find a function ψ such that $\psi(1)=b$, and $\psi(n+1)=\psi(\theta(n))$. The general theorem is then applied in § 11, § 12, § 13 to define addition, multiplication, exponentiation, and derive the usual properties.

Finally, in § 14, Dedekind defines the *Anzahl* of a finite set M as the number n such that the counter set Z_n is similar to M, and also gives an elaborate proof of the equivalence of his own definition of infinity and the usual definition according to which a nonempty set is infinite if it is similar to no Z_n. This proof is interesting for two reasons: that the apparently obvious conclusion should require such a complex proof, and that the proof contains an unacknowledged appeal to the axiom of choice, the method of proof first made famous by Zermelo sixteen years later.

§ 5. Adequacy of Dedekind's Characterization

It is remarkable that Dedekind obtained the Peano axioms entirely by analyzing the sequence of natural numbers. What is more remarkable is, once he had completed his analysis, he believed that properties of and theorems about natural numbers can all be derived from his characterization. This belief has to a large extent been confirmed by later developments. Clearly Dedekind did not look at a great number of theorems and proofs about natural numbers to see that no other characteristics are needed. Rather, he verified to his own satisfaction that the sequence of natural numbers is completely determined by his axioms, and then concluded that the axioms are adequate to the derivation of theorems as well. The mystery is how he made his verification.

His letter supplies a useful clue, when he discusses under (6) the question of excluding undesirable interpretations of the set N for which some ordinary arithmetic theorems would fail to hold. This suggests the following line of argument which may have been followed by Dedekind. The definition of natural numbers in terms of the chain of 1 enables us to determine the abstract character of the set of natural numbers entirely: witness his proof that any two sets satisfying the definition are isomorphic. If a theorem is independent of his definition, then there are two possible interpretations of the definition according to one of which the theorem is true and according to another the theorem is false. If the definition determines a unique interpretation of the theory, such situations cannot arise. Therefore, by the uniqueness of interpretation, all theorems about natural numbers must be derivable. This argument is plausible but not entirely rigorous because, among other things, the notion of interpretation has not been made sufficiently explicit to assure that any undecidable theorem will necessarily yield two different interpretations of the definition.

Dedekind's conclusion that these determine adequately the sequence of natural numbers is often expressed equivalently by saying that the Peano axioms are *categorical* or have no essentially different interpretations. As we know, the axioms do admit different interpretations such as taking 100 as 1 or taking the square of a number as the successor of a number. But they are all essentially the same in a technical sense of being isomorphic.

The proof of this is very easy once we concede that the axiom of induction ($P5$) does assure that the number sequence contains no "alien intruders" beyond the true natural numbers each of which is either the base-element or can be reached from the base-element by a finite number of steps. Granting this for the moment, we can assume given two interpretations of the Peano axioms: say 1^{**}, ϕ, N stand for 1, successor, number in one interpretation, 1^*, ψ, M in the other. Correlate 1^{**} with 1^*, and for every successor $\phi(a)$, if a is correlated with a^*, correlate $\phi(a)$ with $\psi(a^*)$. Since we are granting that no "alien intruders" can occur in any interpretation the correlation ensures a one-one correspondence between all objects in N and M which preserve the transit from each element to its successor. And this is the sense in which Peano's axioms are said to be categorical: any two models are isomorphic.

The proof will break down if the axiom of induction cannot exclude entirely the "alien intruders". For then we shall have two models for the axioms, one of which fits our intentions while the other contains additional alien elements which cannot be reached from the base-element by finite numbers of steps.

The question of an adequate specification of the class of natural numbers independently of arithmetic notions may also be viewed as a desire to analyse one use of the phrase "and so on" without explicit appeal to the general concept of finite numbers. Dedekind's discussion in his letter, especially under (6), is very articulate and instructive except that the last step in his argument, which leads to the conclusion that N is completely determined, can be elaborated further. This same conclusion comes out as a theorem in his essay (item 79). His proof comes to this: the class of natural numbers satisfies the conditions that 1 belongs to it and the successor of a member of it again belongs to it. If we consider all classes which satisfy the two conditions, their common part or intersection must be exactly the desired class: it cannot contain less members because every number must be in every one of the original classes; it cannot contain more because if it did there would be a smaller class which again satisfies the conditions.

Now there is, however, the question of specifying the arbitrary classes. How do we know whether a given specification of classes will include all classes or at least enough classes to yield as an intersection the class of numbers as desired? Or, what explicitly are the properties to which ($P5$) is applicable? In recent years a good deal of research in mathematical logic has been devoted to the question of unintended interpretations (nonstandard models) of theories of positive integers. It is therefore of interest to find this question raised in Dedekind's letter. I give a simple example.

A somewhat trivial interpretation of the principle of induction ($P5$) can be constructed if we restrict properties to those only which are expressible in a rather weak language. For example, we can imagine a notation in which every expressible property holds either for only a finite (possibly empty) set of numbers, or for all except a finite set of members. One such notation is obtained if $a_1, a_2, \cdots$ are constant names and every property $F(n)$ can only be a truth-function of finitely many equalities $n=a_i$. For example, no expression in it can represent the set of all odd positive integers.

If we agree to use such a language, we can easily find an unintended model for the whole set of axioms ($P1$)—($P5$). Thus, we can take the domain as consisting of not only the positive integers but in addition the positive and negative fractions of the form $(2b+1)/2$ (b an integer), 1 as 1, and $a+1$ as the successor of a. It can be verified that ($P1$)—($P4$) are satisfied. Moreover,

($P5$) is satisfied because any property for which "$F(1)$" and "$F(m) \to F(m+1)$" hold must hold for all numbers. This is evident with the "true" positive integers. If there were a "positive integer" $a/2$ such that "$F(a/2)$" is not true, "$F((a-2)/2)$" would also be false, $a/2$ being the "successor" of $(a-2)/2$ and "$F(m)$" implying "$F(m+1)$"; similarly, "$F((a-4)/2)$", "$F((a-6)/2)$", etc. would all be false. Hence, we would have a property expressible in the given language, such that there is an infinity of numbers which possess it and there is also an infinity of numbers which do not possess it, contrary to our assumption. Hence, we get two non-isomorphic models for the weakened Peano axioms. The assumption is only true for very restricted languages. For any reasonably rich language, the problem of unintended models becomes more complex. It follows, however, from certain fundamental results of Gödel and Skolem that whenever a language can be effectively set up and proofs can be effectively checked, there are always unintended models of positive integers which satisfy all of the Dedekind-Peano axioms, provided that the properties in the axiom of induction are restricted to ones expressible in the given language. Usually the models directly obtained from these general theorems are quite complex or artificial, and to find intuitively transparent unintended models is in most cases very difficult. Indeed, it is known that for reasonably adequate languages, such non-standard models will have to consist of rather non-constructive sets, e.g., not recursively enumerable.

§ 6. Dedekind and Frege

To turn once again to Dedekind's letter. There is a reference to Frege's works of 1879 and 1884 both of which appeared before Dedekind's essay (1888). As Dedekind says, Frege's definition of the set of positive integers agrees essentially with his own, in terms of what he calls chains. Both of them were interested in characterizing arithmetic properties by general notions independent of arithmetic. Frege's view that arithmetic is a part of logic is well-known; "arithmetic thus becomes simply a development of logic, and every proposition of arithmetic a law of logic, albeit a derivative one" ([8], § 87). In the preface to his essay, Dedekind, also says,

> "In speaking of arithmetic (algebra, analysis) as a part of logic I mean to imply that I consider the number-concept entirely independent of notions or intuitions of space and time, that I consider it an immediate result from the laws of thought."

They do not agree on what logic is, though. Frege uses concept and relation as the foundation stones upon which to erect his structure; Dedekind uses classes and the relation of an element belonging to a class. Nowadays we would think that they employ essentially the same thing. But not for Frege: in his *Grundgesetze* he says,

> "Dedekind also is of the opinion that the theory of number is a part of logic; but his work hardly goes to strengthen this opinion, because the expressions 'system' ['class'] and 'a thing belongs to a thing' used by him are not usual in logic and are not reduced to accepted logical notions" ([9], p. 139).

In addition, Frege thought that his reduction refuted Kant's contention that arithmetic truths are synthetic. The reduction, however, cuts both ways. It is not easy to see how Frege can avoid the seemingly frivolous argument that if his reduction is really successful, one who believes firmly in the synthetic character of arithmetic can conclude that Frege's logic is thus proved to be synthetic rather than that arithmetic is proved to be analytic. Indeed, Russell at one time came close to drawing such a conclusion,

"In the first place, Kant never doubted for a moment that the propositions of logic are analytic, whereas he rightly perceived that those of mathematics are synthetic. It has since appeared that logic is just as synthetic as all other kinds of truth." ([10], p.457)

In the same vein, if one believes firmly in the irreducibility of arithmetic to logic, he will conclude from Frege's or Dedekind's successful reduction that what they take to be logic contains a good deal that lies outside the domain of logic. On account of the basic ambiguities of the words "logic", "arithmetic", "analytic", these arguments embody more than strikes the eye.

In contrast with Dedekind, Frege tries to tie his definition of number more directly to application and defines individual numbers. Frege begins with 0 instead of 1, defining 0 as the extension of the concept "equal to the concept 'not identical with itself'." If we disregard the distinction between concept and class, the definition amounts to identifying 0 with the class of all empty classes or since there is only one empty class by the axiom of extensionality, with the unit class of the empty class. The distinction is, however, important for Frege who apparently finds an empty class absurd, although an empty concept is entirely in order ([9], p. 150). Frege also defines the successor function separately which amounts to the function mapping a class n of similar classes to a new class $\phi(n)$ of classes each of which is obtained from some class in n by adding a new element. The class of natural numbers is then defined as the chain (in Dedekind's sense) of the number 0 thus defined relative to the successor function thus defined.

Already in his *Begriffschrift* Frege has presented the basic ideas of his derivation of arithmetic and also an exact formulation of the underlying logic of deduction, containing both the propositional calculus and the laws of quantification (the restricted predicate calculus). Dedekind has never attempted to formulate explicitly the logic of deduction. Frege's *Grundlagen* contains a good deal of stimulating philosophical discussion on the nature of number.

References

[1] Georg Cantor, Gesammelte Abhandlungen, Berlin, 1932.

[2] David Hilbert, Gesammelte Abhandlungen, vol. 3, reprint, N.Y. 1966.

[3] Philip E. B. Jourdain, The development of the theories of mathematical logic and the principles of mathematics, *Quar. Jour. Math.*, **43** (1912), 219—314.

[4] Richard Dedekind, Gesammelte Werke, vol. 3, reprint, N.Y., 1968.
[5] Hermann Grassmann, Lehrbuch der Arithmetik, 1861 (reprinted in part in his collected works, vol. 2, part I, 1904, 295—349).
[6] G. Birkhoff and S. MacLane, A Survey of Modern Algebra, 1941.
[7] D. Hilbert and P. Bernays, Grundlagen der Mathematik, vol. 1, 1934.
[8] G. Frege, Grundlagen der Arithmetik, 1884 (English translation by J. L. Austin, 1950).
[9] P. Geach and M. Black, Translations from the philosophical writings of G. Frege, 1952.
[10] Bertrand Russell, Principles of Mathematics, 1903.

CHAPTER V

COMPUTATION

§ 1. The Concept of Computability

There are systematic procedures or mechanical routines for treating certain questions. For example, is a given natural number the square of some natural number? We have a systematic procedure by which we can decide, for every natural number *n*, whether *n* is a square.

Turing uses a more colourful example, viz. the puzzle which is sometimes called "15". It consists of a square frame with space for sixteen small squares of equal size. Fifteen of the spaces are taken up by pieces marked $1, \cdots, 15$, the one space is left empty into which any of the neighbouring pieces can be slid leaving a new empty space behind it. One is asked to transform a given arrangement of the 15 squares into another by a succession of such sliding movements. It so happens that for any given initial arrangement, there are arrangements which we can arrive at and ones we cannot. Now one asks whether there is a systematic procedure by which we can decide for any two arrangements A and B if A can be transformed into B. Since there are altogether only 16! possible arrangements and for each arrangement there are only 2 or 3 or 4 possible immediate moves, one can in theory classify all the possible arrangements by a systematic procedure: list all possible configurations and join each to its 2 or 3 or 4 immediate transforms obtainable by a single move. Two configurations are mutually convertible if and only if there is a path joining them, in general through intermediary configurations. The procedure is in practice not very feasible. A more feasible method is obtained if one takes the trouble to observe and prove that A and B are mutually convertible, if and only if one can be transformed into the other by an even number of interchanges of pairs of numbered squares. In any case, the problem is solvable and either solution is acceptable even if one does not have a sharp enough notion of systematic procedures to be able to assert that a certain problem of the same kind is unsolvable.

We are now to consider the concept of a systematic procedure. Mathematically computation procedures are the most interesting of all systematic procedures. Moreover, many things can be represented by numbers so that many procedures which do not explicitly deal with numbers can also be reduced to matters of computation. For example, studies about mathematical proofs, crude mechanical translations from Russian into English. Among all computations, those which deal with natural numbers are the most fundamental.

While in markets and elementary schools we are primarily concerned with individual problems of computation, mathematicians are mostly engaged in the proving of theorems or, in other words, in deciding the truth and falsity of mathematical propositions. The mathematician is, nonetheless, also quite interested in the problem of finding algorithms or computational routines although particular questions of easy computation such as "what is 353 times 267" or what is "27 plus 76" are too simple to interest him.

An algorithm is a set of instructions which, when followed systematically, will yield answer to, not only a single question, but any one of a whole class of related questions. For example, we have algorithms for finding sum and product, for deciding whether a given natural number is a prime number. As a result, we are inclined to think that we can carry out addition, multiplication and testing whether a number is a prime simply by obeying a few easy rules, and that machines can answer such questions too. Thus, while the schoolboy wishes to know the sum and product of particular numbers, the mathematician is interested in the problem whether and how a particular class of questions can be answered by a general method.

Sometimes it happens that a particular problem of computation is so complicated that it becomes interesting mathematically. For example, the problems whether particular numbers of the form

$$2^{(2^{n+9})} + 1$$

are primes. Here there are actually several different kinds of question. In the first place, there is the question whether all numbers of the above form are primes. This is a typical mathematical proposition which mathematicians are interested in proving or disproving. Since it includes infinitely many different cases as n takes different values, no amount of uninspired labour could establish a positive answer if indeed the answer is positive. A positive answer to the general question would be a significant mathematical theorem. In the second place, there is a systematic procedure for deciding whether a given number is a prime; in other words, the class of problems of the form "is $2^{2^{n+9}}+1$ a prime?" is systematically decidable, in theory at least. In the third place, the practical computation involved in deciding the question even for a given n is so complicated that there is considerable difficulty in carrying it out strictly in accordance with the mechanical routine. Hence, ingenuity is called for to get around the formidable calculations and the problems, although in theory decidable mechanically, are turned into significant mathematical problems. This sort of thing is, however, an exception rather than the general rule. In most cases, what is of mathematical interest is either to find a systematic routine for solving a whole infinite class of problems or to decide the truth or falsity of some general proposition which contains infinitely many decidable instances.

The contrast between finding algorithms and proving theorems leads to different notions of problem and solution. Given a class of methods of proof, say by a formal system, a mathematical problem is unsolvable by these methods if on the basis of them it is not possible to decide the truth or falsity of the proposition stating the problem. This of course does not exclude the possibility that the problem can be solved by other methods. Are there absolutely unsolvable problems in the sense that no methods could decide the truth and falsity of certain mathematical propositions? If we construe the notion of method broadly enough, the answer must be no. Each proposition is either true or false, a method of deciding the truth or falsity of a proposition consists simply in writing down true or false according as it is true or false. It will be objected that this is no method at all. Notice, however, we are only concerned with a single proposition. If *A* has a method which consists simply in saying yes to the question whether the proposition is true, and *B* has a method which consists simply in saying no to the same question, one of the two methods must work. It is hard to deny that these are methods since they are entirely simple and mechanical. Similarly, the same trick would apply when we are concerned with an arbitrary finite class of propositions. What disturbs us about these devices is our tacit association that a method should either fall in some general framework or be applicable to a wide class of related questions. The answer is isolated from our knowledge and we still do not know whose "method" gave the right answer. This does not refute the answer that there are no absolutely unsolvable single problems, at any rate for one who insists that every proposition is either true or false: it merely shows that the question is not very interesting, unless a sharper sense were given to it.

On the other hand, if there are infinitely many problems, we can no longer list all the answers. If the problem is to find a systematic method which will provide answers to a whole infinite class of questions, then we can again ask whether there are absolutely unsolvable problems. Only this time what is asked is the existence or nonexistence of a general method for solving not a single problem but simultaneously a whole infinite class of problems. Even though the number of problems is infinite, we wish to have a finite method. To distinguish this from the other, one sometimes speaks of unsolvable decision problems rather than just unsolvable problems. The study of unsolvable decision problems is obviously connected with the problem of formalizing the intuitive concept of a systematic method or procedure.

Given a class of problems, we can represent each problem by a natural number and the answer to each problem by a natural number. When the questions are yes and no questions, we need only two natural numbers for the answers; when the questions have to do with computation, we often need infinitely many numbers as answers. Hence, a method of solving the class of problems is nothing but a method of correlating natural numbers with natural numbers. At the same time, functions of natural numbers are just methods of correlating natural numbers with natural numbers. Hence, it is natural to represent systematic procedures by functions of natural numbers. But what type of function? If a systematic method is identified with a mechanical or effective procedure, then the function must be computable or mechanically computable. Thus, given any class of problems, there is some arbitrary function which represents a solution of the class by providing the required correlation. To ask whether the decision problem for the class is solvable is just to ask whether the corresponding function is computable. The general problem is to determine the totality of all computable functions of natural numbers. Each determination of the totality may be viewed as a proposed definition of the concept of systematic procedure of computability.

There is no reason to suppose that all functions are computable. In fact, it stands to reason to believe that there are functions which are not computable. A computable function or correlation of natural numbers with natural numbers gives a rather neat order of natural numbers. But computable functions do not exhaust all order in the mind or in the world. There are systematic correlations of natural numbers with natural numbers which are not represented by computable functions. For instance, it is rather arbitrary to identify random sequences of natural numbers with sequences which are not represented by computable functions. Noncomputable functions can also be classified and investigated.

In order to determine the totality of all computable functions, one may either begin from without or begin from within. In order to determine the boundary of a country, points outside and points inside are all of assistance. If we are given a large number of functions which are not computable, we get to know things which computable functions are not and then also things which computable functions are. On the other hand, if we know sufficiently many computable functions to begin with, we can try to find out their common characteristics and then proceed to make generalization and abstraction.

The usual procedure of finding demonstrably noncomputable functions is to assume given the totality of computable functions and then "diagonalize" to get a function that is different from each member of the totality. Clearly noncomputable functions obtained in this manner depend on a previous concept of computability and are therefore of no direct assistance to the projected program of determining the totality of computable functions.

On the other hand, we are acquainted with a large number of functions which are known to be computable. The obvious course is to analyze the process of computation involved in the search of values of familiar functions.

Turing and Post at first analyzed the process of human computation into simple basic steps and developed the idea that computation is essentially a mechanical procedure. The net result can be briefly described as follows. Imagine an indefinitely expandable tape divided into squares and a machine which looks at one square at a time. Suppose further that the machine is capable of doing three things to begin with: move left one square, move right one square, and print a star. Now we can give instructions to have the machine perform these three kinds of act in numerous different orders. But this is not adequate for at least two reasons. We use only finite lists of instructions so that each list only tells the machine to go through less than a fixed number of squares. But in general, we want it to be possible that the numbers of squares which are to be operated on can increase indefinitely even with a fixed set of instructions. A more obviously serious defect is that a method must enable us to give different answers to different questions, and therefore some element of recognition and choice must be present in the instructions. All these defects can be removed by adding an additional type of instruction called conditional transfer in computing machines actually in use. By this type of instruction, the machine is to recognise whether the square under scan is blank and then follow two different instructions according as whether it is blank or not.

Once the machine is equipped with these qualifications, we can adopt some convention for representing natural numbers by strings of stars, for instance, n by a string of n stars. Then we can determine the domain of computable functions in the following manner. A function is computable if and only if there is a finite list of instructions so that when the machine begins by scanning an arbitrary number n, the instructions tell the machine to go through certain motions and the machine will stop finally when the value of the function for the argument value n is printed. In this definition, it is merely required that for each argument value n, the function value will sooner or later be printed. There is no stipulation that some estimate of the time taken to compute should be given in advance. In other words, it is merely required that for each n, there exists a number m, such that after m steps the value of the function is obtained. There is no demand to specify the way in which m depends on n. We might feel that a function satisfying the definition is indeed computable but not effectively computable, for to be effectively computable, one ought to have a pretty good idea how long it will take to carry out the computation for each argument value n. In any case, it seems clear that very often we are interested not only in the existence of a bound but also in an estimate of it. This question will be discussed below in relation to an equivalent definition of computable functions, viz., that in terms of recursive functions.

Since addition and multiplication are the most familiar computable functions, it is natural to study first the rules governing their algorithms. These are, as is well-known, embodied in the recursive definitions:

$$a + 1 = a',$$
$$a + b' = (a + b)'.$$
$$a \cdot 1 = a,$$
$$a \cdot b' = a \cdot b + a.$$

a' is of course the successor of a.

It is easy to convince ourselves that all functions defined by such recursions together with some other simple schemata are computable. In this way, we quickly get the class of primitive recursive functions and the conclusion that all primitive functions are computable.

There is a strong temptation to identify effective computability with primitive recursiveness, since apparently all the effectively computable functions which are ever used in ordinary mathematics are primitive recursive. As we know, however, Ackermann many years ago already found an effectively computable function which is not primitive recursive. Hence, there are more computable functions than primitive recursive ones. The problem is to introduce and use a wider notion of recursiveness, and the answer is general recursive functions.

In 1934 Gödel introduced a definition of general recursive functions which he credited in part to an oral suggestion of Herbrand. Using a variant of this definition due to Kleene, Church proposed in 1936 to identify the intuitive notion of computability with the notion of general recursiveness.

Of the two halves of Church's thesis, more weight is usually put on the half stating that all functions which are computable according to the intuitive notion are general recursive. Indeed, this is the half which has led to many important negative results: there are no effectively computable functions or decision procedures for such and such questions; in other words, certain decision problems are unsolvable. The value of Church's thesis in proving these results is obvious: it achieves a great simplification in the form of all the functions which may be effectively computable. If a sharp boundary is found so that a given indeterminate region falls entirely within the interior of the boundary, then everything lying beyond the boundary lies also outside the initial indeterminate region. Clearly the sharp boundary helps matter when we wish to establish that something does not lie within the initial region.

While a number of arguments have been offered to support the identification, it is hard to claim that we have any conclusive proof. In fact, it is largely a matter of opinion whether it is at all possible to ask for a conclusive proof in a case like this.

If one has contrived a machine which as a matter of fact can make what appear to us to be random decisions but by our experience, the decisions generally turn out to be confirmed afterwards by our chance discoveries, can we then say that all functions computable by the machine are effective? It does seem that in the concept of effectiveness, there is a core in mechanical terms, and at the same time, there is an idealization which brings in infinity. Something which a physical object can do reliably and systematically would seem to be effective, no matter whether we understand the process or not. It would then appear to be an empirical question whether all effective functions are general recursive.

Viewed in this light, the recursiveness of all effective functions would appear to be a hypothesis about the physical world. If we do not wish to worry about the empirical elements, then there seem to be some good reasons why all computable functions must be general recursive or Turing computable. Thus, various apparently more powerful conceptions of computing devices can be easily shown to give the same range of computable functions as Turing machines: e.g., machines which have multi-dimensional tapes, move many squares at a time, or generate new squares between given squares, etc., provided these are all set up in a systematic manner. In other words, the class of general recursive functions has strong closure properties. On the other hand, one might feel that if, as a matter of empirical fact, we actually encounter really more powerful machines, our concept of effective functions would change.

A different possibility was suggested by Specker in conversation. If we define a function of n which takes the value 0 or 1 according as on the n-th day from to-day there is an earthquake in the universe or not, for all we know, the function may or may not be general recursive. If it so happens that it is not, can we not yet say that the function is, in theory at least, effectively calculable?

One reply to this is, infinity is primarily a mathematical concept which is only derivatively applied to a description of the physical world. Hence, it is felt that we may at least separate the mathematical concept of effective procedures from such considerations.

If one accepts such a separation, then there remains the question whether all general recursive functions are indeed effective.

The usual arguments to support this contention are roughly of three types. The class has nice coherence and closure properties: if one assumes the notion at one place one arrives back at it at another place. For example, if we require recursiveness in the consecutive steps in the proof procedure of any formal system, then in some fairly simple formal system, we can already calculate all recursive functions but we get the same class even in more powerful systems. A closely related argument is the stability relative to different formulations such as the equivalence of general recursive, lamda-definable, Turing computable. Such reasons may of course be quite weak unless properly supplemented. They assure us that we have got a definite notion, although not necessarily the one we want initially. A third type of argument is that what we usually take to be effective functions all turn out to be general recursive. This has some weight if we want to say that all computable functions are recursive but is little support for the converse since the computable functions we have actually encountered form a rather small class and there can easily be narrower classes which include them all.

The strongest single argument is perhaps Turing's analysis which directly aims at explicating the intuitive notion and makes it seem natural to agree that all Turing computable functions are indeed effective. But, as is noted below, there is here as with general recursive functions, a problem about the contrast between mere existence versus an estimate of the steps required.

Incidentally, Kleene has suggested that one should identify an effective or formal system with one whose theorems form a recursively enumerable set. This identification seems more plausible with Post's equivalent notion of generated sets or canonical languages.

§ 2. General Recursive Functions

Roughly speaking, a function f is general recursive if there is a finite set E of equations containing $=$, variables, numerals, and function symbols such that by substituting numerals for variables, and equals for equals, there exists for each numeral n exactly one derived equation of the form $f(n)=p$, where p is again a numeral giving the correct value of $f(n)$. It is possible to enumerate all such sets of equations and define a primitive recursive predicate T such that $T(m, n, k)$ when the k-th derived equation of the m-th set E is the earliest equation of the required form $f(n)=p$, for the given numeral n. It is also possible to define a primitive recursive function U such that $U(j)$ is p if j is (the Gödel number of) $f(n)=p$. Hence the definition may be put in the following form.

Definition. *A function f is general recursive if there exists a natural number m such that*:

(a) $(n)(Ek)T(m, n, k)$;

(b) $(n)(f(n) = U(\mu_k T(m, n, k)))$.

In terms of quantifier-counting, the definition is of the *EAE*-form. If, as is often the case, we are only interested in a given set E of equations, then the number m is fixed, and the condition (a) is of the *AE*-form. The quantifier (Ek) has a clear and definite meaning in (a) which says that for every numeral n, there exists a numeral k, $T(m, n, k)$ is verifiable or numerically provable for the given m. Nonetheless, the definition leaves open how k depends on n and by what method (a) is to be established.

Church anticipates this question and replies that all we have to do is to interpret the phrase "there exists" in condition (a) in a constructive sense or to make sure that the existence assertion is proved constructively. He then leaves the burden of determining the criterion of constructivity to his readers. This seems to reduce the problem of effectively computable functions to that of characterizing constructive proofs.

It now seems clear that the notion of recursiveness can at most be considered a satisfactory substitute of the intuitive notion of effective procedures in a classical sense, not in a strictly constructive sense. While each function, if known to be recursive, is constructive, the general notion of recursiveness is not constructive since there is no general method for arriving at condition (a) constructively. This situation has not prevented the development of a rich theory of recursive functions. But it does mean that a finitist or an intuitionist would wish to examine this matter more closely. In any case, the notion of constructive proofs rather than effect functions would have to be the more basic for him. If he is thorough in his convictions, he would probably have to deny that the notion as it stands gives him the correct concept of effective functions since the classical interpretation of number quantifiers is not acceptable to him. Independently of one's position on these different outlooks, it also seems desirable to classify all general recursive functions by more constructive means.

It seems possible that an intuitionist might wish to say on considerations about all general recursive functions something similar to what Brouwer in 1912 says about Cantor's classical second number class (*Bull. Amer. Math. Soc.*, **20** (1914), 91).

Let us now consider the concept: "denumerably infinite ordinal numbers". From the fact that this concept has a clear and well defined meaning for both formalist and intuitionist, the former infers the right to create the "set of all denumerably infinite ordinal numbers", the power of which he calls aleph-one, a right not recognized by the intuitionist. Because it is possible to argue to the satisfaction of both formalist and intuitionist, first, that denumerably infinite sets of denumerably infinite ordinal numbers can be built up in various ways, and second, that for every such set it is possible to assign a denumerably infinite ordinal number, not belonging to this set, the formalist concludes: "aleph-one is greater than aleph-null", a proposition that has no meaning for the intuitionist.

One might wish to use partial recursive functions to avoid such problems, since condition (a) is not needed for them. It is, however, even more doubtful that one could claim all partial recursive functions strictly effective. The situation with them seems even less constructive: not only we have no estimate how long the process will stop, we do not even know whether it will stop at all. For example, we can enumerate all propositions of a formal system such as Z and enumerate all proofs, obtaining a partial recursive function which gives a proof if the proposition is provable, but never stops otherwise. We can hardly regard such a function as effectively computable.

Intuitively it is not without doubt that we are always willing to admit that all general recursive functions are effectively calculable. For example, we definitely feel that Herbrand's or Gentzen's proof for eliminating modus ponens gives an effective procedure. On the other hand, we can also derive from the completeness of the predicate calculus a general recursive procedure for eliminating modus ponens. Yet it is not certain that everybody wishes to regard the latter procedure as effective. Or take the proof of the theorem that all complete (closed) systems are decidable, i.e. if a set and its complement are both recursively enumerable, then the set is recursive (cf. Ch. I, Th. 8 above). One has sometimes the uneasy feeling that although the set is correctly proved to be general recursive, it has not really been proved to be effectively calculable. In her book on recursive functions, Péter remarks that in general, although we can effectively decide whether each given number has a property P, and it is known that there is some number which has P, we cannot always effectively seek out the least number which has P (§ 1, no. 8). On the one hand, this would contradict the identification of general recursive functions with effective ones. On the other hand, one is likely to be inclined to agree with the statement.

According to the standard explanation of the concept of a constructive proof, an existence statement is proved constructively if the proof actually exhibits an example or at least indicates a method by which one could in principle find such an example. But what methods are acceptable?

With regard to condition (a) of the definition of general recursive functions, we do have a method of finding the corresponding number k for each given number n, or in other words, of finding, for each n, the corresponding equation of the form "$f(n)$ equals a numeral". The method consists in enumerating all the derived equations of the given set of equations until we come upon one with $f(n)$ as left member and a numeral as right member. Indeed, no matter how we have reached the existence assertion, this method is always applicable in the sense that we shall sooner or later arrive at the equation, since it does *exist* in the infinite sequence of derived equations. More exactly, there is a mechanical procedure for writing out one by one the derived equations so that for each given argument n, an equation will eventually turn up which has the required form. Either we find such methods acceptable, then the question whether the existence assertion is proved constructively makes no more difference. Or, we may find the methods not effective and wish to say that a method of finding the desired equations is effective only if we have, with regard to the mechanical procedure, a *pretty good idea* how soon the process will terminate for each argument value n. Then the desirability of a constructive proof for establishing condition (a) may be justified on the ground that constructive proofs do give a pretty good idea.

The question of deciding the effective computability of a function can also be reduced to one of knowing intuitively its speed functions: corresponding to each set of equations which defines a general recursive function $f(n)$, there is some speed function $f_s(n)$ which, for each constant n_0, gives an upper bound to the number of steps for getting the value of $f(n_0)$ from the given set of equations. In other words, in the condition (a):

$$(1) \quad (n)(Ek)T(m, n, k);$$

We wish to find a function $f_s(n)$ so that

$$(2) \quad (n)(Ek)(k \leqslant f_s(n) \;\&\; T(m, n, k))$$

is also true.

Now it seems rather reasonable to say that a proof of (1) is constructive if and only if an effectively computable function $f_s(n)$ can be found for which (2) is true. If we agree in addition that a general recursive function is effectively computable only if condition (a) is proved constructively, then we get into a circle which need not be harmful, because intuitively we know, to begin with, that certain proofs are constructive and certain functions are effectively computable.

In any case no single formal system can supply proofs for all cases of condition (a), because the functions which are demonstrably general recursive in one system can be enumerated and the diagonal argument can be applied to get a new general recursive function.

On the other hand, it is of interest to know that many proofs are known to be constructive in the above sense. Works by Ackermann have established that all proofs of current number theory as formalized, for example in Z, are constructive in this sense. It is of interest to study similar questions in connection with stronger systems.

There are also constructive proofs not formalizable in some given rich formal system. For instance, proofs of the consistency of number theory by Gentzen and Ackermann, though not formalizable in number theory, are yet known to be constructive. This naturally leads to the question whether all true assertions of consistency or general recursiveness could not be proved constructively in a similar manner. But it is not easy to see how any general results are to be obtained on the question.

The most hopeful approach to an informative classification of computable functions seems to be the concept of ordinal recursive functions introduced by Ackermann in 1940. In contrast with general recursive functions, they are, like the primitive recursive functions, such that the value of a function for an argument value n is determined if the values of the function for all preceding (in some predetermined sense) arguments are determined. They differ, however, from primitive recursive functions in that different ways of ordering numbers may be used so that one number may be preceded by infinitely many other numbers and the value of the function for a given argument n may depend on the values of the function for more than n preceding argument values. For example, if we order the natural numbers in the way that odd numbers precede even numbers, then there are infinitely many numbers which precede the number 2.

If for every infinite ordinal α less than a given ordinal we have chosen a unique effective well-ordering R of the natural numbers, then a function is recursive of order α, if it is defined by a sequence of schemata which are either of order lower than α or of one of the forms for defining primitive recursive functions or of the form

$$f(0, x) = g(x),$$
$$f(y', x) = h(y, f(\theta(y'), x), x).$$

Therein g, h, θ are given functions such that for all $y, R(\theta(y'), y')$, and we assume arbitrarily that the number 0 is always the earliest in every well-ordering.

It is easy to see that all these are general recursive functions since if we start from any number in a well-ordering and proceed to earlier numbers, we must come to a stop in a finite number of steps.

To be more correct, one has to allow for "nested" occurrances of the function f. Then the schema would be:

$$f(0, x) = g(x),$$
$$f(y', x) = h(y, f(G(y', x), x), x).$$

Therein, $(x)R(G(y', x), y')$, and G may contain other given functions and also f itself, subject only to the condition that for each part of the form $f(F(y', x), x)$ in G, we have always $(x)R(F(y', x), y')$.

By using ordinal, instead of general recursive functions, one preserves the continuity of moving from given functions to new functions, and from given values of a function to values for new arguments of the function. Moreover, we get several natural ways of classifying computable functions, if we identify them with ordinal recursive functions: according to the relation used to rearrange the natural numbers, according to the ordinal type of the rearrangement, according to the proof that the rearrangement is a well-ordering, according to the way how values for one argument depends on values for preceding arguments. Here one faces several programs of mathematical research. Results of such research will improve our understanding of the concept of computability; on the other hand, one is led to such mathematical problems by the more or less vague problem of sharpening the intuitive notion of computability.

§ 3. The Friedberg-Mucnik Theorem

In recent years the theory of recursive functions has developed into an independent branch of mathematics comparable, say, with group theory in the last century. Although the theory came into being largely through studies in the foundation of mathematics, it is now in a state that one can pursue it with little knowledge of other branches of mathematical logic. As a result it has a special appeal to the desire to find an interesting self-contained domain where one's ability of pure mathematical thinking can be quickly tested. There are the books of Péter, Kleene, Markov, and Davis which all are primarily concerned with this theory. The development is so fast that there is room for books to take into account of more recent works. No survey of the theory will be attempted here. Instead, an example chosen almost at random will be given as an illustration. Some elementary knowledge of the theory is presupposed.

The example is a solution of "Post's problem" of 1944 obtained independently by Mucnik and Friedberg around 1956. The problem is to decide whether there exists any set B which is not recursive but recursively enumerable such that not all recursively enumerable sets are recursive in B. The solution is to define such a set B and at the same time a recursively enumerable set A not recursive in it.

The proof uses the fact that a set S is recursive if and only if both S and its complement S' are recursively enumerable. The sets A and B are simultaneously defined in such a way that B' is different from all recursively enumerable sets, and A' is different from all sets enumerable by a function recursive in B. It follows that B is not recursive, and A is not recursive in B.

From standard results in the theory of recursive functions, one may assume given general recursive functions d, e, f and partial recursive functions g, h which have the following properties:

3.1. The function d enumerates all definitions of partial recursive functions.

3.2. The function e enumerates all definitions of functions partial recursive in an arbitrary set B. The definitions are independent of the constitution of B, but the values of the functions for given arguments of course depend on the constitution of B.

3.3. The function f enumerates all possible finite situations with an arbitrary set B: each situation consists of a finite number of conditions asserting whether a particular number belongs to B.

3.4. The function $g_i(j)$ gives the value of the j-th derived equation by the definition $d(i)$. Thus the function is defined only when the j-th derived equation of $d(i)$ is of the form $p_i(k)=q$, where p_i is the principal function symbol of $d(i)$, and k, q are numerals. Then $g_i(j)=q$, no matter what k is. For each k, we only define this for the smallest j having the above property.

3.5. The function $h_i(j, k)$ gives the value of the j-th derived equation of the definition $e(i)$ on the assumption that $f(k)$ holds. Since each evaluation depends on only finitely many values of B, there is always some k such that $f(k)$ contains all the conditions on B necessary for any particular evaluation. For any k and i, we leave the function undefined when a same derived equation is repeated.

We proceed to define A and B by imagining the construction of an infinite table:

	0	1	2	3 ···
A				
B				

In the row for *B*, each column will eventually contain either −, or else $d(m)$ for some numeral *m*, with or without an accompanying +. The set *B* is to contain all and only those numbers under which there is some $d(m)$ with an accompanying +. In that case, the number is in common to *B* and the set enumerated by $d(m)$. It is essential that for every *m*, there is a column in the row for *B* which contains $d(m)$ accompanied by +; then B' cannot be recursively enumerable. In the row for *A*, each column will eventually contain either −, or else an $e(m)$ or a + or both. The set *A* is to contain all and only those numbers under which + occurs, either alone or with some $e(m)$. When $e(m)$ and + occur under *n* in row *A*, the number *n* belongs to *A* and the set enumerated by *e*. It is essential that for every *m*, there is a column in which $e(m)$ and + occur; then A' cannot be enumerated by any function recursive in *B*.

To avoid circularity in defining *A* and *B* simultaneously, a device of priority order is used to secure that earlier decisions will not be modified on account of later requirements, except in a very restricted class of cases. Thus in either row, once a column gets −, no more change is permitted at the place. Moreover, in row *B*, once a column gets $d(m)$ and +, the place will not be modified again. The only possible changes are of two kinds. A $d(m)$ not accompanied by + can change position. An $e(m)$ can change position.

The sets *A* and *B* are defined by induction. At each stage a number $f(k)$ is said to agree with the actual state in row *B* at the stage if for every positive condition "*p* belongs to *B*" in $f(k)$ the space under *p* in row *B* is filled by some $d(m)$ followed by +.

Step 0. Write $e(0)$ under 0 in row *A*. See whether $h_0(0, 0)=0$. If not, do nothing and continue with step 1. If yes, consider whether $f(0)$ agrees with the actual state of row *B* at the stage. Since nothing has been written in row *B* yet, agreement can occur only if $f(0)$ includes no positive conditions. If no agreement, do nothing and continue with step 1. If there is agreement, write − under all the numbers *i* in row *B* such that "*i* does not belong to *B*" occurs in $f(0)$, and write + after $e(0)$ under 0 in row *A*. In this last case, we would have established that 0 is in *A*, and even that *B* must be such that 0 is in the set enumerated by $e(0)$ since *B* must not contain any numbers under which − occurs in row *B*.

Step 1. Write in row *B*, under the first available numeral *p*, i.e., the leftmost numeral under which the space in *B* is yet blank, $d(0)$. Calculate whether $g_0(0)=0$. If yes, write + after $d(0)$, and we would have decided that 0 is in *B*. Otherwise do nothing. In either case, continue with step 2.

Step $2(n+1)$. Write $e(n+1)$ under the first available numeral in row A, and call the numeral $a(n+1)$. Calculate $h_i(j, k)$ for all arguments $i, j, k \leqslant n+1$ and find, if any, all cases where $h_i(j, k)$ equals $a(i)$, the number under which $e(i)$ occurs in row A. If there is no such case or in all such cases, $e(i)$ is accompanied by $+$ already (under $a(i)$ in row A), continue with step $2n+3$. If there are such cases where $e(i)$ is not accompanied by $+$, the i's forming a class C, take the smallest i in C and compare $f(k)$, where $h_i(j, k)=a(i)$ for some (and, indeed, by 3.5, at most one) j, with the actual state of row B at this stage. If they do not agree, look at the smallest remaining i in C and repeat. If there is no agreement in any case, continue with step $2n+3$. If in a case where they do agree, i.e., $f(k)$ agrees with the actual state of row B at that stage, we put $+$ after the particular $e(i)$ and adjust row B to avoid conflict. By the definition of agreement, for every position condition "p is in B", p gets $+$ in row B. Among the negative conditions "q is not in B", under each q, row B is filled with: either (i) blank; or (ii) $-$; (iii) $d(s)$, $s<i$; (iv) $d(s)$, $s \geqslant i$. Put $-$ in row B under q in case (i). Do nothing in cases (ii) and (iii). In case (iv), move $d(s)$ to the earliest blank space in row B and write $-$ in row B under the original q (after the evacuation of $d(s)$). This is repeated with all remaining i in C. When there is no more i, we continue with step $2n+3$. It may be noted that $d(s)$ changes position only when there is some i, $s \geqslant i$ such that $e(i)$ gets $+$ before $d(s)$ gets $+$. This can happen at most s^s times for given s.

Step $2n+3$. Write $d(n+1)$ in the earliest blank in row B. For every $i, 0 \leqslant i \leqslant n+1$, suppose $d(i)$ stands in row B below $b(i)$, and of course some or all of these $d(i)$ may be followed by $+$. Calculate $g_i(j)$ for all arguments $i, j \leqslant n+1$, and find, if any, all cases where $g_i(j)=a(i)$. By 3.4, there can be at most one j for each i. If there are no such i, continue with step $2n+4$. If the class C of such i's is not empty, begin with the smallest i in C. Write $+$ after $d(i)$ under $b(i)$ in row B. Examine row A to determine whether any adjustment is necessary. This is done by testing whether there exists any s, $s<i$, such that $e(s)$ and $+$ occur in row A under $a(s)$, and that the $+$ after $e(s)$ was arrived at on the basis of a situation $f(k)$ which contains a negative condition "$b(i)$ is not in B". If there is no such case, continue with the smallest remaining member of C. For any such $s, a(s)$ is not a common member of A and the set enumerated by $e(s)$ relative to B, we have to move $e(s)$ to the earliest remaining blank in row A, leaving $+$ under $a(s)$. This is repeated with every such s, from small to large. When we finish this whole process with one i in C, we do the same with the next member of C, until we exhaust all members of C. Then we are ready to continue with step $2n+4$.

Since a $d(i)$ in row B can only get $+$ once, and a $e(s)$ in row A changes position only when for some k, $k<s$, $d(k)$ gets $+$ after $e(s)$ gets $+$, $e(s)$ changes position at most s times, for each s.

Every $d(i)$ which is general recursive certainly gets $+$ in B at some time, since given any finite set of $b(p)$, there is for every i always some q not in the finite set such that there is $j, g_i(j)=q$. Similarly, every $e(i)$ general recursive relative to arbitrary B must get $+$ in A at some stage.

Hence, we have proved:

Theorem. *There exist recursively enumerable sets A and B such that A is not recursive in B, and B is not recursive.*

§ 4. Metamathematics

Since proof procedures are generally required to be effective, proof theory or metamathematics has largely to do with computable functions. It is, therefore, not out of place to include here a brief sketch of some standard results and directions in this area.

In mathematics we usually prove results in some particular branches by some particular methods. Occasionally, we have also results about whole fields or about all methods of a given kind. For example, the independence of Euclid's fifth postulate, the impossibility of trisecting an arbitrary angle, that of solving quintic algebraic equations, the duality principle in projective geometry. In order to state and prove these conclusions rigorously, we have to formulate the underlying methods of proof or construction very explicitly. Metamathematics emphasizes such explicit formulation and aims at obtaining results of such broad implication. Roughly speaking, this is a branch of mathematics which differs from other branches in treating proofs, construction methods, theories as objects rather than numbers, figures, functions.

The line between mathematics and metamathematics is by no means sharp. Compared with multiplications of particular integers, the law that a number is divisible by 9 if the sums of its digits is, is a metamathematical result about the usual technique of calculation. Yet we can easily state and prove it as a simple theorem in number theory by the easy relation $10^n \equiv 1 \pmod 9$. This lack of sharp boundary persists in more sophisticated cases too. Thus, to take advantage of our vast knowledge of the familiar mathematical objects, Gödel began to represent metamathematical objects by positive integers and functions of them. As a result, many metamathematical results can be taken as of the same type as ordinary theorems about integers. Indeed, the need to forge concepts and tools required for these investigations has led to new mathematical disciplines such as recursive functions and constructive ordinal numbers, which can be fruitfully pursued with no regard to their more philosophical origin.

Known results get sharpened through explicit systematic formulations. Until the notion of proof is characterized syntactically, the duality principle in projective geometry cannot get an entirely adequate justification; although, in this connection, we are inclined to think that there is little gain in being so particularly literary and articulate. A more striking example is Tarski's sharpening of Sturm's theorem for deciding the number of real roots of a given algebraic equation in one variable x. Retaining substantially what might be called the "mathematical core" of Sturm's proof, Tarski succeeds in establishing, by metamathematical considerations, a general decision method for elementary algebra and elementary geometry. That is to say, given any statement in terms of addition, multiplication, variables ranging over real numbers, numerals (though no variables ranging over integers or class of real numbers) and logical symbols, the method can decide whether it is true or false, provable or refutable (in a suitable formal system). Some nontrivial theorems of elementary geometry fall within the domain of applicability of this method.

A favourite example of application of logic to solve famous ordinary mathematical problems is Novikov's negative solution of the word problem for groups. A finite set of letters are given as the generators. Strings of such letters are called words. There is a finite set of operation rules (pairs of words A, B so that if $A \rightarrow B$, then $PAQ \rightarrow PBQ$). If $A \rightarrow B$ is a rule, then $B \rightarrow A$ is also (semigroup). The letters are given in pairs a_1, a_1^{-1}, b_1, b_1^{-1}, etc. and there is in addition an empty word 1 so that $a_i\, a_i^{-1} \rightarrow 1$ and $1 \rightarrow a_i^{-1} a_i$ are operation rules. We assume that generators are fixed and consider all possible sets of operation rules which satisfy the above conditions. The word problem is whether there is an effective method for finding for any finite set of rules and any two words A, B whether $A \rightleftarrows B$. Novikov gives a particular finite set of operation rules for which there is no decision method. (Note incidentally, though the general problem is superficially stronger and gets a negative solution as a weaker corollary, it is unreasonable to expect any different answers for the two problems so related.) Early in Kurt Reidemeister, *Einführung in die kombinationsche Topologie,* Braunschweig 1932, p. 56, there is a positive solution for the word problem for Abelian groups. Incidentally, the general problem for groups is equivalent to the problem of deciding whether any open sentences in a system of axioms characterizing all groups is a theorem: the operation rules are conditions in implications. Since it is effectively decidable whether a given sentence is open, a corollary is that group theory formulated with quantifiers is again undecidable.

Attempts, unsuccessful so far, have been made to obtain a negative solution to Hilbert's tenth problem: to find an effective method for solving all Diophantine equations, viz. a method for deciding whether an arbitrary given polynomial is satisfiable (a free variable formula preceded by a string of existential quantifiers) in the domain of integers. Markov has recently established unsolvability results on the problem from topology of finding a complete set of invariants for elementary manifolds of dimensions above 2 (a complete classification of them), or, in other words, to find a method of calculating about any two closed simplicial manifolds, given by means of a set of incidence relations, whether or not they are homeomorphic. (cf. Markov's lecture at the 1958 International Congress of Mathematicians.)

Important as such applications are, they do not directly concern the basic concepts of number and set, but rather lie on the fringe of foundational studies. Two more central results are the following.

It is generally accepted that most proofs in the theory of numbers can be formalized in a formal system which contains, beyond elementary logic, the Peano axioms and recursive definitions. Gentzen and Ackermann have proved in different ways the consistency of this system. Ackermann's proof yields a method so that given any proof P in the system of a conclusion $(Ex)A(x)$, where $A(x)$ is decidable for each constant value of x, we can systematically calculate a number n_p such that $A(n_p)$ is true; and that similarly we can extract a recursive function $f(x)$ of a rather restricted type from a proof of $(x)(Ey)A(x,y)$, A decidable, such that $(x)A(x,f(x))$ is a theorem.

It is possible, as Kreisel observes, to extend the results slightly to cases where we use an undecided disjunction in the proof (we use the law of excluded middle): e.g. a derivation from the Riemann hypothesis and one from its negation.

$$(z)A(z) \supset (x)(Ey)B(x,y) \qquad \sim (z)A(z) \supset (x)(Ey)B(x,y)$$
$$\sim (z)A(z) \vee (x)(Ey)B(x,y) \qquad (Ez) \sim A(z) \supset (x)(Ey)B(x,y)$$
$$(x)((Ez) \sim A(z) \vee (Ey)B(x,y)) \qquad (z)(x)(Ey)(\sim A(z) \supset B(x,y))$$
$$(x)(Ey)(A(y) \supset B(x,y)) \qquad \sim A(m) \supset B(n, g(m,n))$$
$$A(f(n)) \supset B(n, f(n)).$$

Hence, for every n, either $A(f(n))$, then $B(n,f(n))$, or $\sim A(f(n))$, then $B(n, g(f(n), n))$. We have

$$B(n, f(n)) \vee B(n, g(f(n), n))$$
$$(Ey_n)(y_n \leqslant f(n) + g(f(n), n) \,\&\, B(n, y_n))$$
$$B(n, h(n)).$$

Kreisel applies these results to Littlewood's theorem that $\pi(n) - \mathrm{li}(n)$ changes sign infinitely often $\left(\mathrm{li}(x) = \int_e^x \frac{du}{\log u}\right)$ and to Artin's theorem that every definite rational function $p(x_1, \cdots, x_n)/q(x_1, \cdots, x_n)$ with $p(x_1, \cdots, x_n) \cdot q(x_1, \cdots, x_n) \geqslant 0$ with rational coefficients is a sum of squares of rational functions, also with rational coefficients. By reformulating the statements and proofs of the theorems, Kreisel gets an estimate for the first change of sign of $\pi(n) - \mathrm{li}(n)$ (at least for $n \leqslant 10^9$, $\pi(n) < \mathrm{li}(n)$) and the next change of sign at a place $> n$; and bounds for N as well as the degrees of p_i and q_i in $\sum_1^N (p_i(x_1, \cdots, x_n)/q_i(x_1, \cdots, x_n))^2$ in terms of n and the degrees of p and q (independent of the coefficients of p and q). If one takes the pains to carry out the reformulation explicitly, these bounds can then be extracted mechanically, Kreisel uses intuitive arguments to shorten the procedure. The excluded middle on the Riemann hypothesis is used in Littlewood's proof, Kreisel is able to find an arithmetic statement $(x)A(x)$, A decidable, equivalent to R.H. ($\zeta(s)=\Sigma n^{-s}$, $s=\sigma+it$: $\zeta(s)\neq 0$ when $\sigma>\frac{1}{2}$) on pp. 337—338, *Proc. Dutch Academy,* Ser. A, 55 (1952): for all n, the zeros with (positive) imaginary part $<n+p(n)$ lie in the strip $|\sigma-\frac{1}{2}|<1/(n+p(n))$, $p(n)$ recursive.

Consistency proofs also yield a natural classification of proofs within the formal system of number theory into different degrees of complexity. Roughly, consistency of all proofs with a fixed number of quantifiers can be proved by a proof with more quantifiers, and the complexity of a proof is measured by the number of quantifiers in the formulae for induction (indeed, every proof can be so transformed that only one induction occurs).

The most well-known metamathematical result in set theory is Gödel's proof that if axioms of set theory are consistent then is also the generalised continuum hypothesis. This is the only existing basic result on the continuum problem as proposed by Cantor in 1883 (*Works,* p. 192). It helps to clarify our concept of set in supplying a kind of minimum model of set theory in which both the axiom of choice, the general continuum hypothesis, and an axiom of categoricalness are all true.

From the rather special character of Gödel's model, it appears very plausible that there exist other models in which the continuum hypothesis is false. Gödel (1947) and previously Lusin (1935) both conjectured that Cantor's continuum hypothesis is independent of the axioms of set theory and indeed false according to the yet unilluminated "true" meaning of set. This reveals why attempts to prove or refute the continuum hypothesis by the usual axioms of set theory are futile. We are compelled to consider the system as a whole, just as in the proof of the independence of Euclid's postulate. Lusin suggests that we try to find a model for the usual axioms of set theory in which Cantor's continuum hypothesis is false but $2^{\aleph_0}=2^{\aleph_1}$.

§ 5. Symbolic Logic and Calculating Machines

In Part II we shall deal with a few special aspects in the area falling between mathematical logic and the construction and use of modern calculating machines. In the present section we make a brief general survey in order to mention also directions of work not considered in Part II. We shall also mention additional papers and books which we happen to have come across. The literature is so extensive that we shall make no attempt to be complete in any sense. In particular, there are many interesting works in this area in the Soviet Union, but due to the writer's unfortunate lack of familiarity with their work, no reference will be made to them.

The first area is the application of Boolean algebra or the propositional calculus to the representation and design of electronic circuits. The basic idea is very simple. Since each relay (tube, transistor, magnetic core, etc.) usually has two states "on" and "off", or high and low, or yes and no, we can take them as the universal set and the empty set, or true and false. The function of a basic part is to yield one output of on or off depending on the inputs in a definite manner. For example, one type of basic element has two inputs and the output is on if and only if both inputs are on. This of course corresponds to the logical connective "and" or the operation of set intersection. This interpretation has often been credited to a paper of Shannon's in 1938, although recently it has come to light that it had been previously suggested in the Soviet Union and in Japan.

The interpretation reduces the problem of simplifying circuits to one of simplifying Boolean expressions or truth-functional expressions. It is known in mathematical logic that there is a theoretical procedure to test the equivalence of any two Boolean expressions and therefore also one to find the shortest equivalent expression to any given one. The need in applications now requires not only a theoretically possible procedure but a practically feasible one. The Harvard Computation Laboratory, Quine, Veach, and many others have done work in this area. A survey of work in this area may be found in M. Phister, Logical design of digital computers, 1958. We are yet far from possessing really satisfactory procedures of simplification.

The representation is acceptable only if we abstract switching circuits from the time element. While the abstraction is useful, the designer does often face problems which involve the time element. In this way we are led to the more general problem of symbolic representations of calculating machines. Ch. X below deals with this general problem. In this area, we seem to need, instead of just ordinary Boolean algebra, sequential Boolean functionals or recursive propositional functionals. The abstract study of the machine structure also yields the notion of finite automata. There is a book edited by Shannon and McCarthy called Automata studies, 1956. There are different equivalent languages for this domain of "sequential machines". For example, the algebraic formalism of regular events, the language of logical nets, the restricted recursive arithmetic, the formulation of Huffman (*Journal of Franklin Institute,* 1954), that of Mealy, that of Moore, that of Rabin and Scott (*IBM Journal of Research and Development,* **3** (1959), No. 1; cf. also Shepherdson's paper in the same issue), and the formulation in Ch. X below. Perhaps these equivalent formulations are each of interest in so far as one or another can usually be used more efficiently for given special purposes.

It is also desirable to study formalisms weaker or stronger than these. More can be learnt about some subclass of electric circuits by studying a more restricted symbolic system. A wider system which contains formulae not realizable by circuits may provide a more flexible framework for stating conditions to be satisfied by circuits under construction. The close analogy between certain classes of electric circuits and certain systems of symbolic logic leads to the expectation of mutual benefit from a comparative study of the two: results obtained more directly on one side can be translated into nontrivial results on the other.

Time is brought in because the logic is performed by physical elements. In addition, delay elements are often deliberately introduced which make the use of cycles possible. If we refrain from using cycles, then a slightly extended theory of truth functions can deal with delays as well. If, on the other hand, we permit cycles or feedbacks, the matter becomes considerably more complex. According to the diagram language of nets, a well-formed net is any result obtained by repeated connecting of ends in arbitrary manner from basic nets realizing truth functions (e.g. just the stroke function) and a unit delay, provided every cycle contains at least one delay. Examples are known of physically realizable nets which are not well-formed by this definition.

One way of viewing a machine or a corresponding net is to distinguish input elements from internal elements and view each internal element as realizing a functional which depends on t and the input functions realized by the input elements. Since a mechanistic organism is determined by the state of its immediate past (and, in the case of "output" elements, which we may conveniently disregard for the moment, by the present), we would be studying a certain class of primitive recursive functionals from a fixed number of input functions and a time variable to the set $\{0, 1\}$ or $\{$true, false$\}$. Thus, for a machine with m input elements and n internal elements, the behavior is determined by n such functionals, which we may call sequential Boolean functionals.

If we think of a particular machine with a particular problem to solve it would appear that we need not consider any input functions. The program and data are initially fed into the machine so that the original input could be viewed as the initial internal state. If we think of the whole history of a machine, it would still seem natural to think of the machine as a collection of its various performances each of which realizes an input-free transformation. On the other hand, it is possible to introduce learning devices into a machine, and parts of a machine, e.g. an adder and the storage unit, do interact on one another at various moments. These factors make it desirable to study the more general case that takes into consideration not only the internal states but also effects of inputs at different moments.

The fixed machines determine an interesting class of primitive recursive functionals. One might wish to give a more explicit characterization of this class. For example, we may wish to find for each given number of inputs, a finite list of primitive recursive functionals from which we can define explicitly all and only the functionals of the above class. Or, in general, if we try to find a not too artificial class of formulae $F(i_1, \cdots, i_m, t)$ which would give us all and only these machine transformations, we encounter a little complication because by the very nature of machines it is not meaningful to think of a machine as governed by its future states and consequently we must use no variables or terms whose values are not bounded by t, the present. The problem is of course related to the conversion of recursive definitions into explicit ones, but the standard procedures require formalisms which are too rich for our purpose.

On account of the necessary bound t, the restricted quantifiers are of special interest. In fact, it comes natural with us to state conditions for circuits not in terms of recursive conditions but in terms of the whole past history, thereby using the restricted quantifiers. One may also wish to derive results for a language with restricted quantifiers from logical results for the corresponding weak system of arithmetic with unrestricted quantifiers.

For example, in the first volume of Hilbert-Bernays, there is a decision procedure for the following rather weak system L_1 of arithmetic: the customary formulation of a system with the constant 0, the successor function, number variables, equality, less than, truth functions, and quantifiers. Elgot and Wright are able to infer the inadequacy of this language for representing machine behaviors by the following argument. From the decision procedure, it follows that for any formula $F(t)$ in this language with the only free variable t, we can find a finite number of segments of natural numbers such that $F(t)$ if and only if t belongs to one of the segments. In particular, the input-free transformation "$F(t)$ if and only if t is even" cannot be expressed in the language. But the transformation is realizable by a circuit. If L_2 is the language obtained from L_1 by adding monadic predicate variables, L_2 is also inadequate to a representation of all machine transformations. Nevertheless the subclass of machine transformations expressible in L_2 form a natural class. For example, in L_2 we can express conditions such as "i has been activated at least (exactly, at most) 5 times."

An extension L_2 of the above formalism is obtained if we add also every congruence relation modulo a constant natural number. This does give all the input-free machine transformations.

Let now L_3 be obtained from L_2 by adding addition. It is then well known that if we omit monadic predicate variables from L_3, the resulting system is decidable. It is also known that L_3 is itself undecidable. In the language L_3, we can already get formulae without unrestricted quantifiers which are not realizable by machines. An example is:

$$F(t) \text{ if and only if } (Ex)_0^t((x + x = t \vee x + x + 1 = t) \ \& \ I(x)).$$

Thus, in order to realize this, we have to keep in the storage information about the history of I from t_0 to $2t_0$, if we wish to get the correct outcome for $2t_0$ to $4t_0$. Since t can increase indefinitely, no preassigned fixed storage can do this. Given any machine with N internal elements, it can hold at most

2^N bits of information at any moment and cannot yield the values of F for $2(2^N+1)$ to $4(2^N+1)$.

This need not prevent us from using the formalism L_3 in considering machine transformations, especially if we had an effective procedure for singling out those expressions $F(t)$ which are realizable. For example,

$$(Ea)_0^t(Eb)_0^t(t = am + bn) \text{ if and only if } (Ek)_0^t(x \equiv k(\text{mod } m) \ \& \ k \equiv t(\text{mod } n)).$$

Yet we find the left-hand side intuitively easier to grasp, since we are more familiar with addition than congruences. In general, one often uses formulae $F(t)$ from richer languages to state what circuits are desired. Sometimes we find it natural to state conditions on circuits with the independent and dependent function symbols (input and internal elements) mixed up in some arbitrary manner ("implicit definitions"). Indeed, we often use the very rich ordinary language to state conditions. If, however, we are interested in implicit conditions, there is, beyond the question of effectively singling out realizable formulae $F(t)$, also the question of singling out those formulae $H(i, F, t)$ such that $F(t)$ can be solved explicitly in terms of i and t. This is in addition to the customary questions of analysis (given circuit, find formula) and synthesis (given formula, find circuit). Hence, in any case, it would seem desirable to find classes of formulae which are co-extensional with the class of machine circuits in the strong sense that so far as the transformations determined by them are concerned, the problems of analysis and synthesis all have effective solutions. Among such classes, the ones which are closer to our natural ways of writing out conditions are the more preferable.

It seems clear that different formalisms are sufficient to represent the logical structure of whole computers. The paper by Burks and Copi (*J. Franklin Institute,* 1956) carries out an idealized example in a systematic manner.

With circuits including delay elements, there is of course also the question of simplification and efficiency. There are fewer results on this question than the corresponding question for static circuits or their corresponding Boolean expressions.

A related question on the efficiency of logical elements has been studied by Dunham and his collaborators (*IBM Journal,* 1957 and 1959). It is suggested that multipurpose devices will provide economy in both numbers and assortment of basic computer building blocks. For example, consider the Boolean function:

$$w = yz + x'y'z + xy'z'.$$

If an input is "biased", i.e., so fixed as to be always on and always off, then we can get different functions with two inputs. For example, if x is always 1, then w is on if and only if both y and z are on or both are off. If the inputs x and z are "duplicated", i.e., both inputs are always to have the same signal, then we get the function w is yz. It is proposed that the efficiency of a logical element be equated with the set of subfunctions it realizes upon biasing or duplication of inputs. If, for example, for reasons of economy and reliability it is desirable to build a machine out of relatively standardized blocks, the multipurpose devices should be of interest. It is also suggested that the redundancy intrinsic to multipurpose elements may be used to secure reliability.

Finite automata, the idealization of existing machines, differ from the model envisaged by Turing in that the tape in a Turing machine is potentially infinite. This suggests the concept of growing or potentially infinite automata (see Chs. VIII and X below).

The question of classifying growing machines and singling out special subclasses interesting for specific ends could perhaps throw light on various problems of principle such as a general theory of programming, general connections between a special purpose machine and a corresponding program on a general purpose machine. It is not unnatural, especially in view of Turing's attractive theory, to expect that for many purposes a more informative theory of machines can only appear in terms of growing rather than fixed machines. For example, C. Y. Lee has suggested one can perhaps devise a theoretical measure of the complexities of programs on the basis of the simple program steps of machine W (see Ch. VI, § 4).

In the matter of programming, the question of a satisfactory language is acute. Thus automatic coding requires a language rich, flexible yet exact enough for mechanization. This is close to the requirement of logicians in constructing formal languages and reminds one strongly of a Leibnizian universal language.

At present, different interesting programs are written for different machines and usually they cannot be used on other machines. Moreover, it is not even easy to explain a program on one machine to somebody who is only familiar with certain other machines. As a result, the accumulation of results common in most sciences is greatly handicapped here. Recently, tentative common program languages have been suggested (*Communications of Association for Computing Machinery*, 1959). It is clearly desirable that programmers should be able to build on existing knowledge as in mathematics.

In many ways, the use of machines lags behind the construction of machines. For example, it has been remarked that there will not be enough people to ask for enough work to make the powerful new machines *STRETCH* busy. Apart from the striking application of machines in physics and engineering, there has also been application in weather forecasting, dynamical astronomy, and crystallography, economics. Other possibilities include parlour games, operations research, pattern recognition, mechanical translation, machine learning, and machine proof of mathematical theorems.

Programs have been written for playing checker and chess. It would seem much easier to make a machine to play fairly good bridge since there is more analysis of given data than forward anticipation in playing bridge. The game of go would perhaps be the most difficult game to teach a machine.

Much effort has been devoted to mechanical translation although the results so far do not seem very encouraging, at any rate according to Bar-Hillel who began to work on the subject quite early. In 1954 (*American Scientist,* vol. 42), he wrote a survey which concluded with a rather optimistic passage. Recently, however, he appears to have more reserved views. This problem strikes one as of the kind which only those who have worked on it can have a reasonably good idea of the possibilities and difficulties. The results in mathematical logic may suggest that mechanical translation would become more manageable if some previous standardization of the natural language is undertaken. This would mean that translation of, e.g., novels and poems is not to be attempted at present and efforts should first be concentrated on scientific literature. It may not be entirely unrealistic to work out some standard vocabulary and grammar for writing scientific works in each natural language. For example, we may try to enrich and relax the symbolism of mathematical logic to get some more easily usable partial language within each natural language.

The possibility of proving theorems by machine naturally appears exciting to the logicians. This problem is discussed in Chapter IX below. The problem appears to be one of making machines to simulate the mind in its activity of discovering proofs. Formalization makes mechanical simulation easier because the strategies one uses for discovering proofs in a formal system are comparatively simpler and axiomatization yields a half-way station between machines and intuition. The basic problem in using machines as aid to mathematical discoveries is to find means to trade effectively quantitative complexity with qualitative difficulty. What is to be filled is the gap between how we do mathematics and our knowledge of how we do it. Works on the psychology of invention and on plausible reasoning by Polya and others are relevant but presumably still too advanced for the present stage of the art of machines to be used effectively. Insight is something which by definition eludes imitation; it is useless just to make machines do random things because what they do, though unpredictable, is very unlikely to coincide with the special type of unpredictable movement that is insight.

The reason why there are so many things which a man can do but a machine, with all its accuracy and speed, cannot, is undoubtedly the machine's lack of flexibility. For this reason, the possibility of machine learning is of great interest. In this area, there is a great danger of indulging in fruitless speculations. A rudimentary though precise experiment has been reported by Friedberg (*IBM Journal*, 1958).

There are many discussions on comparing mind with machine. A specially interesting essay is Turing's on the "imitation game", i.e., the possibility of teaching a machine to pretend to be a human being (*Mind*, **60** (1950)).

It is not entirely clear what bearings the well-known results on unsolvable problems have on the theoretical limitations of the machine. For example, it is not denied that machines could be designed to prove that such and such problems are recursively unsolvable. If one contends that we could imagine a man solving a recursively unsolvable set of problems, then it is not easy to give a definite meaning to this imagined situation. It is of the same kind as imagining a human mind which is so constituted that given any proposition in number theory he is able to tell whether it is a theorem. It is a little indefinite to say that it is logically possible to have such a mind but logically impossible to have such a machine.

Along quite a different direction from the questions we mentioned so far, von Neumann, in his *Probabilistic Logics* (lecture notes, 1952, reprinted in the book Automata studies, 1956), suggests a possibility of building a machine more reliable than its components. This work is explained in the last chapter of Tsien's *Engineering Cybernetics* (translation in Chinese, 1958). More recently, Moore and Shannon (*J. Franklin Institute*, **262** (1956)), Kochen (*IBM Journal*, **3** (1959)) and others have extended this work. In the next section, we shall briefly summarize von Neumann's results.

§ 6. The Control of Errors in Calculating Machines

It is a fact that errors do occur in the operation of computing machines. Errors are of different kinds and there are special remedies for each kind of error. They may be caused either by factors intrinsic to the method of calculation, or by human and physical factors external to the machine, or by the components and circuits inside the machine. To control the errors, we either try to prevent them by removing their possible causes beforehand, or try to detect and correct the errors after they have already occurred.

There are at least the following kinds of errors:

(a) Those due to erroneous input data as a result of mistaken programs or careless coding;

(b) Those due to mistaken recording of the actual outputs of the machine;

(c) Those due to stray signals getting into the machine from outside, either carried in from the power supply or because of radiated interference from other electrical machinery (radar sets, high-power X-ray machines) in the neighborhood;

(d) Those due to spurious random-noise pulses;

(e) Those due to rounding off;

(f) Those due to truncations (errors of approximation or truncation);

(g) Those due to failure of components;

(h) Those due to erroneous wiring of the circuits.

Of these eight kinds, little can be said about (c), (d), and (h). For example, if the wiring is incorrect, one just has to find out the exact nature of the error and change the wiring. To avoid stray pulses from power supply, one can isolate the computer and feed it with a local power supply from a motor-generator set. To avoid radiated interference, one can screen the machine or remove it to a trouble-free location.

With regard to the estimate, prevention, detection, and correction of errors of the other kinds, a little more can be said.

The input and output errors are largely human errors, having nothing to do with the machine. Since in performing exact mechanical procedures, the human being is more liable to err than the machine, programming, coding, and copying have become the most common sources of error already at the present stage of the development of machines.

Certain obvious precautions can be taken such as careful proof-reading and its repetitions. For example, tapes should be punched more than once, preferably by different people, and checked against each other. Such a procedure is known as verification.

In general, input data should, as far as possible, be encoded automatically. For example, whenever possible, use ready-made subroutines which have been checked and known to be correct independently of the particular problems in which they are applied. Or, if the machine is to analyze experimental results derived from indicating instruments, analog-to-digital converters should be provided to present their readings directly to the machine.

To verify the correctness of the program, it is customary to make the machine print out the contents of certain registers at various points in the calculation so that the results can be compared with those obtained from hand computations (often called "memory dump"). Another method is to make the machine stop at certain points so that the operator can visually check the contents of certain registers. A third is to print out, in order, the successive operations which it performs (often called "tracing"). The whole process is often called "debugging".

A checking procedure of some theoretical interest is the use of specially chosen codes. These are useful not only for detecting and correcting errors in the input tapes, but they are helpful also in checking errors of the machine operations.

The basic principle in error-detecting and error-correcting codes is to introduce redundancy so that when the standard redundancy is absent, we know there is some error or even what the error is. Thus, as is well-known, if to every number with four binary digits we adjoin a fifth which is 0 or 1 according to whether the sum of the four original digits is odd or even, then we can detect the presence of a single error. This is a parity check. Another single-error-detecting code is the $3n+2$ code. This makes use of the fact that in the five-bit representations of $3n+2$, where n is one of the integers, 0, 1, $\cdots$ 9, any two differ in at least two binary digits.

If we are willing to use a large number of redundant or extra (binary or other) digits, we can also detect the presence of double or triple errors, etc., and even to determine exactly which digit or digits are in error.

For example, a single-error-correcting code may be devised in the following manner (see Hamming, Bell Telephone Tech. Monograph 1757, 1950). To every number with four binary digits, we add three extra binary digits (the fifth, sixth, seventh) to serve as parity checks: the fifth digit is 1 or 0 according as the sum of the first, second, and fourth digits is odd; the sixth digit is 1 or 0 according as the sum of the first, third, and fourth digits is odd; the seventh digit is 1 or 0 according as the sum of the second, third, and fourth digits is odd. Take the binary representation 1010 of the integer ten. Its representation in the code should be 1010101. Suppose the symbol 0 in the second place is written 1 erroneously so that we have 1110101. Since the sum of the first, second, fourth and fifth digits is not even, one of these digits must be wrong. Since the sum of the first, third, fourth, and sixth digits is even and we are only looking for single errors, these digits must be all correct. Hence, either the second or the fifth digit is wrong. If we are assuming that the digits serving as parity checks are always correct, then we conclude that the second digit is incorrect. If we do not make the assumption, we can continue thus. Since the sum of the second, third, fourth, and seventh digits is odd, one of these digits must be wrong. Hence, since either the second or the fifth digit is wrong and we are looking for a single error, the error must be with the second digit. It is not difficult to prove that the code always works if we assume the correctness of the digits serving as parity checks.

If two ten-digit numbers are multiplied together on a desk machine which can handle only ten-digit numbers, it may produce a product which has only ten digits, whereas if the work is done by hand the answer would contain twenty digits. The error which is introduced by neglecting the last ten places is the round-off error. There are different methods of rounding off. The simplest consists of omitting all digits beyond the tenth place. Another one which is commonly in use is to determine first whether the digit at the next (the 11th here) place is less than half the base and then either omit it or add 1 to the last (the tenth) digit accordingly. In other words, add half the base to the next place and then apply the simple round-off. A third method is just to compute to say, nine places and always write down half the base at the tenth (last) place. This is still an unbiased round-off, although the errors have a larger variance.

The problem of round-off errors is serious for computing machines because many operations are performed in succession and the errors due to rounding off accumulate. A simple-minded example, using the method of omitting all digits beyond, may serve to clarify this point.

Suppose we are to make 10^8 multiplications of numbers with 10 decimal digits and the capacity of each unit in the machine is 10 decimal places. The product of two numbers of 10 decimal places has in general 20 decimal places and we have to round off the last 10 decimal places so that the product stored in the machine may differ from the accurate product by a fraction less than 1 (sometimes close to 1). After 10^8 multiplications, the error due to round-off may be theoretically as high as 10^8, so that if the product has 10 decimal places, we have only the first two places for sure and the third may err by 1. Actually, as the round-off errors are in general randomly distributed in the interval (0, 1), we can assume by statistics that the total error due to 10^8 multiplications is just $\sqrt{10^8}=10^4$. This is, however, not quite correct either, since the round-off errors in the earlier parts are frequently "amplified" by the operations of subsequent parts, so that it may be safe to say that the amount of error is in most cases less than 10^6 or 10^7.

Little can be done to reduce the round-off errors except by increasing the capacity of the machine or by making special changes in the computing technique such as using double-precision procedures. Roughly the double-precision procedure applies to the sum of (say) m products: instead of rounding off each product and then adding, calculate and add the exact products and then round off.

Of the round-off errors, one may make either strict estimates or probabilistic estimates. In any case, once we have fairly exact and close estimates, the errors are less dangerous.

The question of choosing round-off methods is sometimes affected by peculiar psychological considerations. For example, if one uses some subtle round-off in a business machine applied to payroll computation, then the people receiving payment may fail to understand the rationale behind the round-off and raise objections. It is, thus, unbiased if one adds instead of half the base a random number whose expected value is half the base: say, instead of adding 5 to the eleventh digit before rounding off, add a random number among 0, 1, 2, 3, 4, 5, 6, 7, 8, 9; yet many would find the method unacceptable, particularly those getting less than the average!

Errors of truncation or approximation are very similar to the round-off errors but more basic or more "static". Truncation errors have to do with the initial data and final results of the calculations, while round-off errors are introduced in the process of calculation at every step.

The initial mathematical problems in general involve transcendental operations and implicit functions. In order to apply digital computers to these problems, we have to replace these limiting processes by elementary arithmetical operations, finitary in nature, which the computer can handle directly. For example, functions defined by infinite series can only be computed if we omit all but a finite number of terms. Integrals have to be replaced by finite sums, differential equations by finite differences.

If, instead of

$$e^x = 1 + x + \frac{x^2}{2!} + \cdots,$$

we use an approximation,

$$e^x = 1 + x + \frac{x^2}{2!} + \frac{x^3}{3!} + \frac{x^4}{4!} + \frac{x^5}{5!} + \frac{x^6}{6!},$$

then, even if we always calculate to as many digit places as is necessary and never round off, we would still get only approximate results.

There are numerous methods for estimating errors of approximation. Results closer to the true ones can often be gotten if we are willing to more or less repeat variants of the same calculation several times.

As is generally known, the gravity of errors in computing machines is not due solely to the great number of operations to be performed, as large numbers of operations are also used elsewhere such as in the operation of telephones. The difficulty lies rather in the fact that practically each step is as important as the whole calculation. According to von Neumann, about 30% of the steps are such that when any of these steps is mistaken, then the end result is no longer usable. Hence, the problem is not so much how many errors have been made, but rather whether any errors have been made at all. This, of course, means a much more stringent requirement.

To illustrate this point, let us consider a simple device consisting of an or-circuit, feeding into itself through a unit delay:

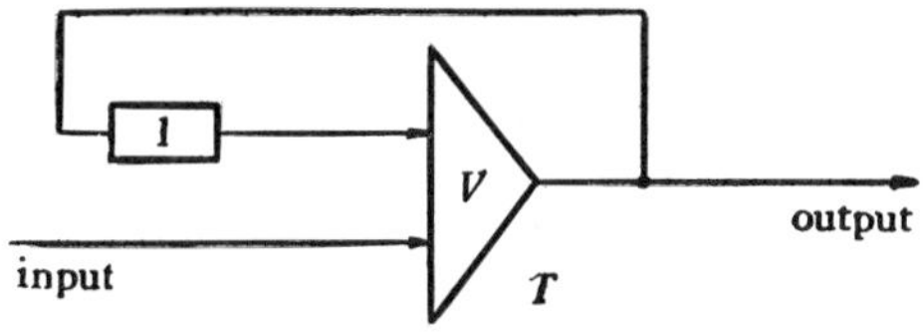

We assume that the input is or is not actuated at t_0, and never again. Clearly the output should be actuated at t_0+1, $t_0+2, \cdots$ or not actuated at t_0+1, $t_0+2, \cdots$ depending upon whether the input was actuated at t_0.

Suppose that the or-circuit T has a probability of malfunctioning ε which may be very small, i.e., there is a probability ε such that either T is actuated when it should not be, or T is not actuated when it should be. Let ρ_i be the probability that T is not actuated at t_0+i although T was actuated at t_0. It is easy to see:

$$\rho_1 = \varepsilon,$$

$$\rho_n = (1-\varepsilon)\rho_{n-1} + \varepsilon(1-\rho_{n-1}) = (1-2\varepsilon)\rho_{n-1} + \varepsilon.$$

From these recursive equations it is a matter of elementary algebra to prove by mathematical induction that

$$\rho_n = \frac{1}{2}\Big[1-(1-2\varepsilon)^n\Big].$$

Since $(1-2\varepsilon)^n \to 0$ as $n\to\infty$, then $\rho_n \to \frac{1}{2}$ as $n\to\infty$.

Similarly, if ρ_i' is the probability that T is actuated at t_0+i if T was not actuated at t_0, we can also prove that $\rho_n' \to \frac{1}{2}$.

It is thus seen that the probabilities are all exactly one-half so that in the long run:

1. If the input is actuated at t_0, the output will be actuated (Correct, $1-\rho_\infty$).
2. If the input is actuated at t_0, the output will not be actuated (Error, ρ_∞).
3. If the output is not actuated at t_0, the output will be actuated (Error, ρ_∞').
4. If the output is not actuated at t_0, the output will not be actuated (Correct, $1-\rho_\infty'$).

In other words, if the process is continued long enough it is almost equally likely that the output will or will not be actuated, regardless of what happened at time t_0. The output thus becomes statistically independent of the input, and the small likelihood of error has approached one-half. It may be worth pointing out that this is indeed the worst case. If the probability of error were to approach unity, we need merely always interpret the result in the opposite sense to what was originally intended, and thus approach perfect reliability.

This conclusion obtained by mathematical reasoning seems to contradict our intuition according to which after a long time the output will almost certainly be no longer actuated. This discrepancy arises because of the inadequacy of the above analysis since it assumes implicitly that it is equally probable to err in either direction. Intuitively, however, it seems more plausible to assume that there is a greater probability not to be actuated when it should be than to be actuated when it should not be. Thus, if we assume that

ε_1 = the probability of T not being actuated when it should be,

ε_2 = the probability of T being actuated when it should not be,

$\varepsilon_1 > \varepsilon_2$,

then we can get the intuitively more acceptable result that after a sufficiently long time, the circuit will most likely no longer be actuated.

In any case, it should be clear that the probability of malfunctioning accumulates rapidly as the number of operations increases. Since it is characteristic of high-speed computers that many operations are performed in succession, the question of malfunctioning is naturally serious.

Once the inputs are correctly introduced into a machine, the main causes of errors will be failures of the components: relays, tubes, transistors, resistors, capacitors. A natural and dependable method of reducing such errors is to improve the reliability of components, to make better tubes, better and more accurate resistors, and so on. Reportedly there are about 50 times more troubles with tubes and crystal diodes than with resistors and capacitors. For many purposes, therefore, we can often speak in terms of tube failures and disregard other troubles on the ground that other troubles either can be discussed similarly or are comparatively less frequent.

At every stage of the development of technology there are many practical limitations to the possibility of further improving the reliability of components. For example, magnetic cores are generally much more reliable than tubes. Moreover, it may well happen that, similar to the question of precise measurement in quantum mechanics, there is a bound beyond which it will be theoretically impossible to improve the quality of the basic components. In either case, if we wish to further reduce error, we have to assume that components have a definite probability of malfunctioning and try to circumvent this by certain built-in checking features. Or, in general, improvements in components and system designs can, of course, supplement each other in their effect.

The problem of improving system design to circumvent limitations in the quality of components may also be taken as one of making the whole better than its parts.

An example of built-in checking circuits is the method of duplicated equipment with comparison circuits in certain computers. The checking devices consist of duplicating the most essential parts of the arithmetic circuits and their controls and producing simultaneously independent results, which can then be compared for equality. The parts duplicated may be, e.g., four registers, the algebraic adder, the comparator, the multiplier-quotient counter, and the high-speed bus amplifier.

The scheme used in these computers is just one example of how we can improve reliability by duplicating machines. In general, we can build two or more machines which are exactly the same and make them compare results at each step, or at the interval of every (say) hundred steps, or at a number of crucial steps. It is easy to see that theoretically there are many possibilities.

A single example will serve to illustrate. Suppose that a machine is given for which there is a probability of 10^{-11} to malfunction at a single operation, and it is necessary to use it to solve a problem that requires 10^{13} operations. There will be about 100 errors if probability theory is to be depended upon. Hence, the machine is just useless. Indeed, the probability of the machine's getting the correct result would be:

$$\left(\frac{10^{11}-1}{10^{11}}\right)^{10^{13}} = \log^{-1}\left[10^{13}\log\left(1-\frac{1}{10^{11}}\right)\right]$$

$$= \log^{-1}\left[10^{13}\left(-10^{-11}+\frac{10^{-22}}{2}-\frac{10^{-33}}{3}+\cdots\right)\right]$$

$$\doteq \log^{-1}(-10^{2}) = e^{-100} \doteq 10^{-43}.$$

Let us now use three such machines and assume that they always compare results after every single operation and then proceed as follows:

(a) if all three have the same result, continue the calculations with no change;

(b) if any two agree with each other but not with the third, change the third to agree with the majority and then continue;

(c) if no two agree, stop the machine. (If we assume a binary language such that the answers are always yes or no, then this case can never happen.)

The machine will not produce an incorrect result unless at one step, at least two machines err simultaneously, the probability being:

$$3 \times 10^{-11} \times 10^{-11} - 2 \times 10^{-11} \times 10^{-11} \times 10^{-11} \doteq 3 \times 10^{-22}$$

since there are 10^{13} steps altogether, the probability that such a situation would happen at all is:

$$(1 - 3 \times 10^{-22})^{10^{13}}.$$

In other words, the chances of getting a correct result are overwhelming.

Here we are assuming that circuits for comparing the results after each operation do not make errors. This is, of course, not realistic. If we wish to duplicate or triplicate the comparing circuits, we get involved in more complicated problems of evaluating probabilities. Moreover, we are forced to face the theoretically troublesome matter of checking the checking circuits, checking the checking circuits of the checking circuits, ⋯.

In practice, we probably do not wish to compare results in several machines at each step and the comparing circuits would contain less hardware so that the problem of checking them is simpler than that of checking the original machines.

Theoretically it is of interest to investigate the possibility of circuits which check themselves. In the remainder of this section, some ideas on this question presented by John von Neumann in his *Probabilistic logics* will be roughly described.

Consider first what is called a majority element

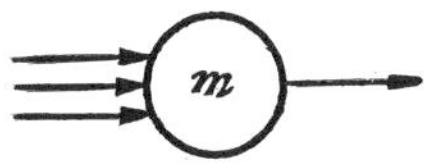

which has three binary inputs and one binary output such that the output is high (on, actuated, energized, etc.) if and only if the majority of inputs are high (on, actuated, energized, etc.). Otherwise the output is low (off, not actuated, deenergized, etc.).

As we go through the machine, each time there is an output from a part of the machine, we consider all the hardware in the machine which directly or indirectly controls the output:

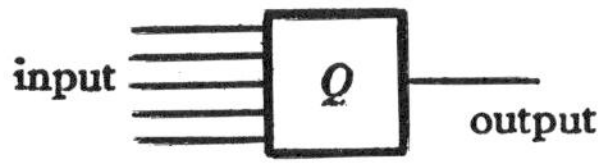

and make three copies of this, connecting them to the majority element:

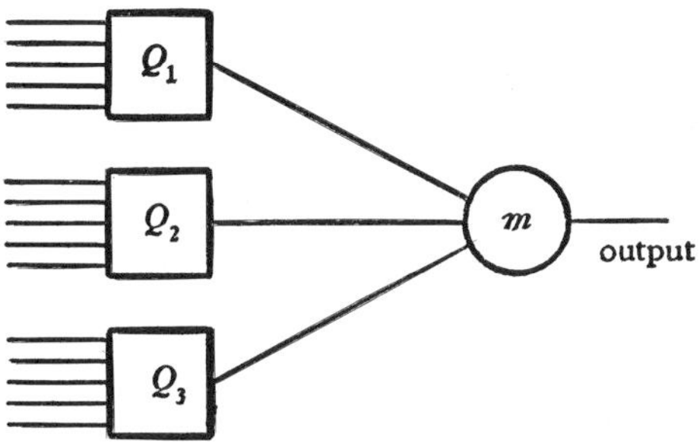

As a result, we have what amounts to three identical machines connected to a large number of majority elements in such a way that the final output is the same as the output of the majority. If we assume that the majority elements never malfunction (an unrealistic simplifying assumption), then the resulting machine would perform the work of three identical machines with perfect checking at each step. It should, however, be noted that we are actually required to triplicate the equipment every time we advance a single step. In other words, at each step, we triplicate the machine and take a vote; then proceed.

The number of equipments required is simply too big for the device to be of any practical interest. Thus, let μ be the maximum number of consecutive actuations from inputs to output which are needed in a particular computation. Suppose μ is 160. Then the number of components needed is more than

$$3^{160} \doteq 2 \times 10^{76},$$

greater than the supposed total number of electrons in the universe.

A more economic method is that of multiplexing. The theoretical considerations will be simplified considerably if we use the known fact that all the basic logic elements can be reduced to a single one if we use merely circuits which are circle-free without delay. There are different methods for doing this. One way is to use a circuit which has one output and two inputs so designed that the output is low (deenergized, not actuated, off) when and only when both the inputs are high (energized, actuated, on). This is called a stroke element. Throughout this section, we disregard delay elements in order to simplify considerations. We note merely that for many purposes, we could view a stroke element as automatically associated with a unit delay.

Schematically, the circuit may be represented as follows:

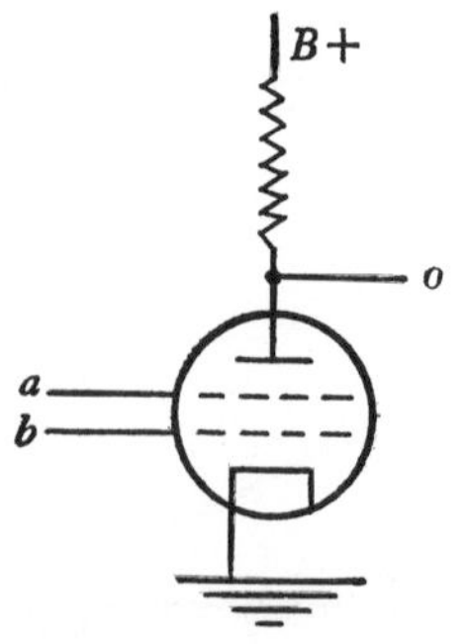

Or, more simply, we use the following diagram:

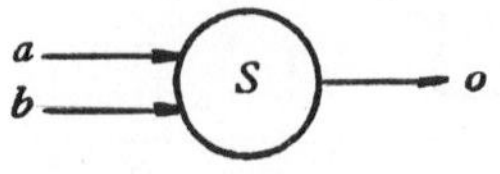

This can be characterized by a table:

a	*b*	*o*
high	high	low
high	low	high
low	high	high
low	low	high

Or, if we speak in terms of truth (T) and falsehood (F) of propositions of the form: the wire designated is at the higher of two possible voltages, the table becomes:

a	*b*	*o*
T	*T*	*F*
T	*F*	*T*
F	*T*	*T*
F	*F*	*T*

a	*b*	*o*
1	1	0
1	0	1
0	1	1
0	0	1

The "output" *o* is thus the stroke function operating on the input *a* and *b*: $a \mid b$. It is well-known that we can define "or", "and", "not" in terms of the stroke element. Thus, we can replace

by

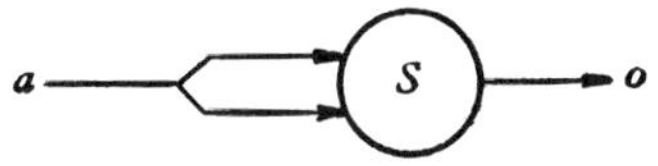

so that the output *o* is low if and only if the input a is high. Similarly, we can replace

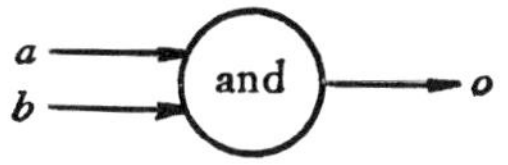

by

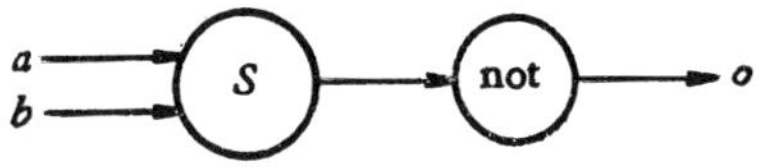

We can replace

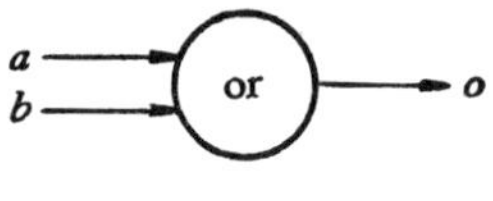

by

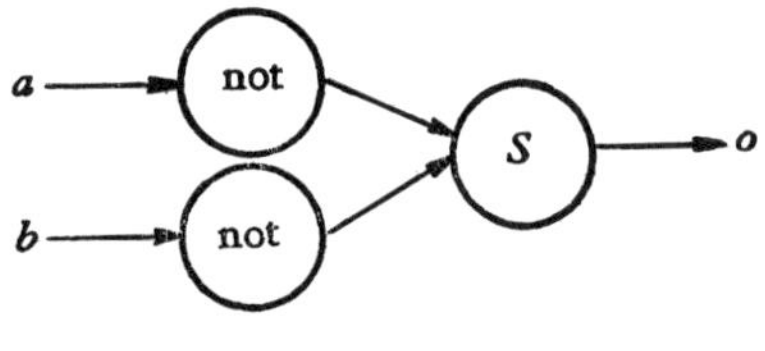

Therefore, it is possible to suppose that in our networks we use solely the stroke elements as basic elements. This would presumably be uneconomical in actual construction since other elements are presumably available; but, as we said before, it simplifies theoretical considerations.

The basic idea of multiplexing is quite simple. Consider a fixed number N. Throughout a machine, every line is replaced by N lines (together with N sets of accompanying components). As a result, instead of just two different states (on and off, high and low), we have $N+1$ states according to the number (from 0 to N) of lines which are stimulated. We have, therefore, more freedom to interpret certain states as yes messages and certain states as no messages. More specifically, a positive number Δ ($\Delta < \frac{1}{2}$) is chosen and the stimulation of $\leqslant \Delta N$ lines of a bundle is interpreted as a negative message and the stimulation of $\geqslant (1-\Delta)N$ lines as a positive message. Any other number of stimulated lines is interpreted as a malfunctioning. It is of course not impossible that we can still get erroneous messages either because the message should be yes but $\leqslant \Delta N$ lines are stimulated or because the message should be no but $\geqslant (1-\Delta)N$ lines are stimulated. What is important is rather that these errors should occur less frequently than in the original network (i.e. for $N=1$). That this is so for a given N or that we can choose such numbers N is not obvious. It is true that many lines carry wrong messages only when many components fail, but, since in multiplexing we do use many more components, it is natural to expect more component failures. That these additional component failures are more than compensated by the circuit design using multiplexing remains to be proved.

The method, in a very simple case, can be described as follows. Since we assume that stroke elements are the only basic elements in the machine, we need only consider how to replace each stroke element

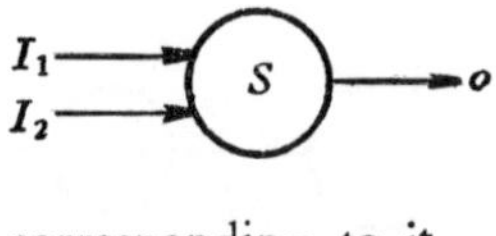

by a multiplexed network corresponding to it.

To simplify matters, take $N=5$. Other values of N can of course be handled similarly. The method is simply this: throughout the machine, replace each stroke element by the following network.

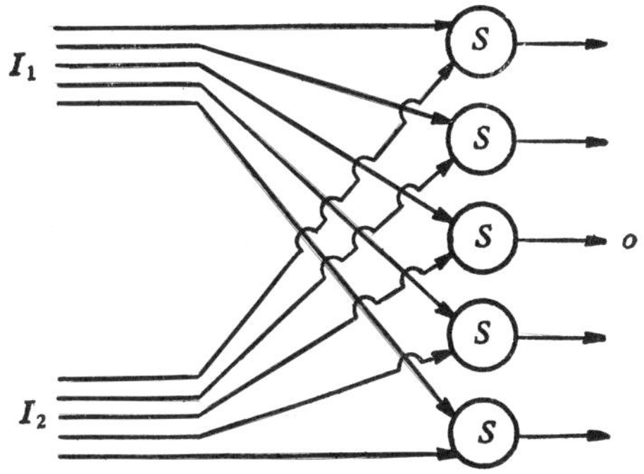

Note that N (5 in the particular case) output lines again serve to replace a single input line for another stroke element in the original network. That is why the same number N can be used throughout the whole network.

Let us assume that each stroke element has a probability ε ($0<\varepsilon<\frac{1}{2}$) of malfunctioning. In other words, there is a probability ε such that one of the following cases would occur:

(i) both inputs I_1, I_2 are on, yet the output o is also on.

(ii) both inputs I_1, I_2 are off, yet the output o is also off.

(iii) one of the two inputs is on, another is off, yet the output o is off.

Of course, it is also possible that I_1 and I_2 already carry the wrong messages. In other words, although we may assume, for our purpose, that at the beginning correct inputs are introduced from outside the machine (i.e., we may disregard these errors which are, properly speaking, not machine errors), we must take into account that the inputs for a stroke element inside a machine are already outputs of other stroke elements of the machine. Thus, for a given stroke element, we may assume that there is a probability ξ that I_1 is a wrong message, and a probability η that I_2 is a wrong message. Clearly, ξ, η do not depend on the stroke element itself but on the relative position it occupies in the machine.

For a given stroke element in the machine, if ξ, η, ε are given, then the probability that its output is incorrect has as an upper bound $\xi+\eta+\varepsilon$. If k is the number of stroke elements involved in producing an output in the machine and if the initial inputs are assumed to be correct to begin with, then the probability of error of the whole machine has the upper bound $k\varepsilon$, as can easily be seen by induction.

If we take more details into consideration, a better upper bound $\max(\xi, \eta)+\varepsilon$, where $\max(\xi, \eta)$ is the greater of ξ and η, is gotten to replace $\xi+\eta+\varepsilon$. Then an upper bound for a whole machine is $\lambda\varepsilon$ where λ is the maximum serial loading on an input. Moreover, an upper bound of the probability of malfunctioning of the simple network

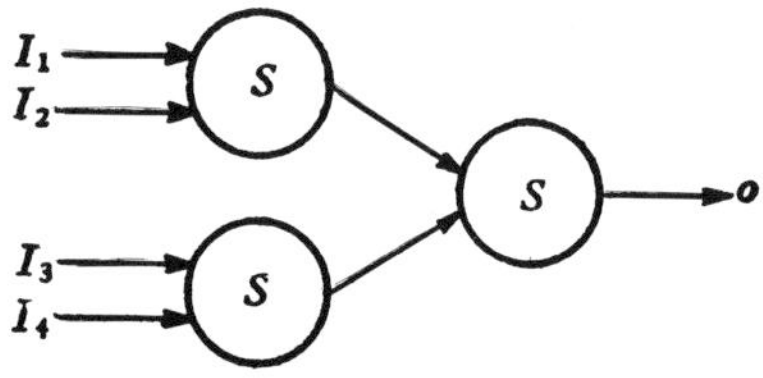

is, by this improved value, 2ε rather than 3ε.

The value $\max(\xi, \eta)$ can be obtained by considering one by one the different alternatives which can happen for a single stroke element with inputs *a, b* and output *c*:

a	*b*	*c*
1	1	0
1	0	1
0	1	1
1	1	1

Consider, for instance, the probability of malfunctioning when the inputs should be 1, 0 and the output should be 1. The malfunctioning can happen if and only if one of the following possibilities occurs: (1) *a* is wrong but *b* is right and the output is correctly determined by the inputs so that we have 0, 0, 1 for *a, b, c* respectively; (2) both inputs correct but a wrong output is produced so that we have 1, 0, 0; (3) input *a* is right but input *b* is wrong and the output is incorrectly determined by the inputs so that we have 1, 1, 1; (4) both inputs wrong and the output incorrectly determined by the inputs.

Now the probabilities for (1)—(4) are respectively given by $\xi(1-\eta)(1-\varepsilon)$, $(1-\xi)(1-\eta)\varepsilon$, $(1-\xi)\eta\varepsilon$, and $\xi\eta\varepsilon$. Therefore, the probability that at least one of the alternatives will occur is:

$$\begin{aligned}
&\xi(1-\eta)(1-\varepsilon) + (1-\xi)(1-\eta)\varepsilon + (1-\xi)\eta\varepsilon + \xi\eta\varepsilon \\
&= \xi + \varepsilon - \eta\xi - 2\xi\varepsilon(1-\eta) \\
&\leqslant \xi + \varepsilon \qquad (\because\ \eta \leqslant 1) \\
&\leqslant \max\ (\xi, \eta) + \varepsilon.
\end{aligned}$$

Similarly, we get the same upper bound when *a, b, c,* should be 1, 1, 0 or 0, 1, 1, or 1, 1, 1.

The network which von Neumann proposes to replace a single stroke element is more complex than the one given above which is only the executive network. There is in addition also a restoring network.

Using again $N=5$, the network to replace a single stroke element is the following network:

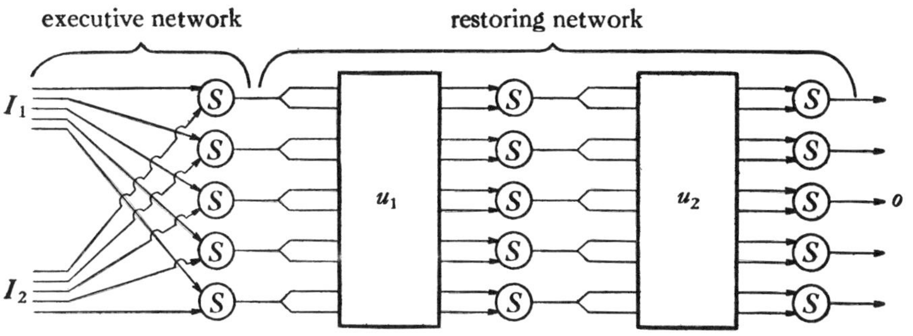

In the above diagram, u_1 and u_2 are black boxes which are to permute the lines to restore randomness.

The reason why the restoring network is needed can be explained thus. For example, if four of the five lines in I_1 are stimulated and four of the five lines in I_2 are stimulated, then it is possible and indeed highly probable that three, rather than four, of the five outputs of the executive network are in the majority state (viz., the state of *not* being stimulated in the particular case). Indeed, it can be proved in general that if the outputs of the executive network are predominantly in the state of non-stimulation of both input bundles, then the most probable level of the output error will be approximately the sum of the errors in the two input bundles. This is why a restoring network is called for.

The restoring network serves, with high probability, to transform an input bundle whose percentage ξ of excited lines is close to zero (resp. one) into an output bundle whose ξ is even closer to zero (resp. one). It turns out that the above restoring network does serve this purpose. Roughly this is accomplished by exaggerating the prevalent state and suppressing the minority states.

Thus if ξN of the N outputs of the executive network are stimulated, then the number ξ' of stimulated outputs of the restoring network is:

$$\xi' = 2\xi^2 - \xi^4.$$

This gives what we want as is clear from the accompanying diagram.

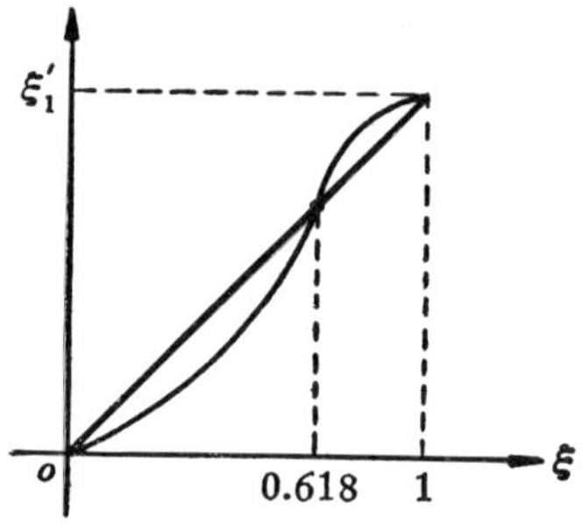

The next problem is to consider the corresponding multiplexed network of each stroke element. Our desire is to determine the conditions under which such networks would have lower probabilities of malfunctioning. We are considering merely the N-multiplexed network corresponding to a *single* stroke element.

Since there are now N, instead of just 1, outputs, we have more latitude for interpreting which combinations of outputs correspond to 'yes' and which to 'no' messages. For example, we might want to say that the message is yes (resp. no) if and only if all N lines carry yes (resp. no) messages. But then there would be many cases where the outputs determine no definite message. Or, going to the other extreme, we might want to say that the message carried on the N outputs is that which is carried on the majority of the N outputs. In such a case, we would have very few indeterminate cases (none if N were odd), but the danger of getting wrong messages is very great because the malfunctioning of even one line may already yield a wrong message. Consequently, we wish to compromise, or to choose some suitable Δ, $0<\Delta<\frac{1}{2}$ so that N outputs carry a definite message only when no more than ΔN lines deviate from the "right" message. This number Δ is called the fiduciary level.

In other words, there are three numbers which can vary:

(i) ε: the probability of malfunctioning for each stroke element;

(ii) N: the number of lines in each bundle;

(iii) Δ: the fiduciary level,

where $0<\varepsilon<\frac{1}{2}$, $0<\Delta<\frac{1}{2}$ and N is a positive integer.

For a fixed ε, the problem is to determine N and Δ so that the probability of malfunctioning of an N-multiplexed network with fiduciary level Δ is smaller than a preassigned δ which is the desired upper bound for the probability of malfunctioning. The interesting possibility is that of making δ smaller than ε, and, moreover, as small as we like.

In other words, if ε, N are given and ξN, ηN are the (probable) numbers of excited (on) lines in the two input bundles, then the (probable) number ψN of excited (on) lines in the output bundle is a function $\psi(\varepsilon, N, \xi, \eta)$ of $\varepsilon, N, \xi, \eta$. Thus, when ψ lies in the interval $0 \leqslant \psi \leqslant \Delta$, the message is 'no', when in the interval $\Delta < \psi < 1 - \Delta$, there is no message at all, and when $1 - \Delta \leqslant \psi \leqslant 1$, the message is 'yes'.

The problem is to find Δ, N, ε such that the probability of malfunctioning is small; i.e., the probability is small that any of the following should happen:

(a) $\xi \geqslant 1 - \Delta$, $\eta \geqslant 1 - \Delta$, but $\psi > \Delta$;

(b) $\xi \leqslant \Delta$, $\eta \leqslant \Delta$, but $\psi < 1 - \Delta$;

(c) $\xi \leqslant \Delta$ and $\eta \geqslant 1 - \Delta$, or $\xi \geqslant 1 - \Delta$ and $\eta \leqslant \Delta$, but $\psi < 1 - \Delta$.

Note that the error column includes both not yielding a definite message (vague), or yielding a definite message which is wrong.

Mathematically the problem is complicated because the three factors Δ, N, ε influence one another. Von Neumann reports on certain results of his calculation but gives no indication of the methods which he employed. His results are quoted here.

He takes as the most favorable fiduciary level:

$$\Delta = .07$$

i.e., stimulation of at least 93% of the lines of a bundle represents a yes message; stimulation of at most 7% of the lines of a bundle represents a no message.

Given the fixed Δ, we can now investigate the interrelation of ε and N. Intuitively, ε must not be too big because in multiplexing, we add many new stroke elements and it is by no means clear that the additional reliability gotten by the use of bundles is adequate to compensate the increase of the probable malfunctionings due to the use of a larger number of basic parts. It may very well be that when ε is not small enough, the method of multiplexing is ineffective. Actually, according to von Neumann, there is an upper bound for the allowable values of ε, viz.,

$$\varepsilon = .0107.$$

In other words, if $\varepsilon \geqslant .0107$, the risk of malfunctioning of the network will be above a fixed, positive lower bound, no matter how large a bundle size N is used.

Hence, we should confine ourselves to those values of ε which are below .0107. For each given value of ε, the probability of malfunctioning of the n-multiplexed network corresponding to a stroke element is a function $\rho_\varepsilon(n)$ of n.

Von Neumann considers only the case $\varepsilon=.005$, and reports that for this particular ε, the function is roughly

$$\rho(n) \approx \frac{6.4}{\sqrt{n}} 10^{-\frac{8.6n}{10,000}}.$$

From this formula, we can get an answer to the following example:

Example. Consider a computing machine with 2500 vacuum tubes which, for brevity, are all assumed to be stroke elements with the probability $\varepsilon=.005$ of malfunctioning. Assume that each tube is actuated on the average once every 5 microseconds and that a mean free path of 8000 hours between errors is desired. Find N, so that the N-multiplexed machine would fulfil the requirement.

In the period of time, there will be

$$\frac{1}{5} \times 2,500 \times 8,000 \times 3,600 \times 10^6 = 1.4 \times 10^{16} \text{ actuations.}$$

Hence, we need a probability of malfunctioning

$$\rho(n) = \frac{1}{1.4 \times 10^{16}} \sim 7 \times 10^{-17}.$$

From the formula for $\rho(n)$, we see that $N=18,000$ would suffice, i.e., the system should be multiplexed 18,000 times.

Such an example is of very little practical interest. The choice of $\varepsilon=.005$ is surprisingly pessimistic, and it is quite impossible to multiplex any fair-sized machine 18,000 times. For instance, it is believed to be quite realistic to assume that $\varepsilon=10^{-9}$ or even $\varepsilon=10^{-10}$. For such values of ε, it is natural to expect we need less lines to get any desired definite results. It would be interesting to know, for instance, the value of n needed in the above example if we take $\varepsilon=10^{-9}$.

The present section is a somewhat modified version of a technical report prepared in the spring of 1954.

References

Apart from scattered references given in § 5 and the list of references at the end of Chapter I, additional items referred to in this chapter are:

[1] L. E. J. Brouwer, Intuitionisme en Formalisme, Groningen, 1912 (English translation, *Bull. Am. Math. Soc.*, **20** (1914)).

[2] M. Davis, Computability and Solvability, New York, 1958.

[3] M. Davis and H. Putnam, *Jour. Symbolic Logic*, **23** (1958), 183—187.

[4] R. M. Friedberg, *Proc. Nat. Acad. Sci. U.S.A.*, **43** (1957), 236—238.
[5] K. Gödel, Consistency of Continuum Hypothesis, Princeton, 1940.
[6] S. C. Kleene, *Trans. Am. Math. Soc.*, **53** (1943), 41—73.
[7] S. C. Kleene, Introduction to Metamathematics, 1952.
[8] G. Kreisel, *Jour. Symbolic Logic*, **23** (1958), 155—182.
[9] N. Lusin, *Fund. Math.*, **25** (1935), 109—131.
[10] А. А. Марков, Труды Математического Института Академии Наук СССР, № 42, Москва, 1954.
[11] А. А. Мисник, *Доклады Академии Наук СССР*, **108** (1956), 194—197.
[12] П. С. Новиков, Труды Математического Института Академии Наук СССР, № 44, Москва, 1955.
[13] R. Péter, Rekursive Funktionen, Budapest, 1951; revised ed., 1957.
[14] E. L. Post, *Bull. Am. Math. Soc.*, **50** (1944), 284—316.
[15] A. M. Turing, *Science News*, no. 31 (1954), 7—23.

PART TWO

CALCULATING MACHINES

CHAPTER VI

A VARIANT TO TURING'S THEORY OF CALCULATING MACHINES*

"Everyone should firmly persuade himself that none of the sciences, however abstruse, is to be deduced from lofty and obscure matters, but that they all proceed only from what is easy and more readily understood."—Descartes.

§ 1. Introduction

The principal purpose of this paper is to offer a theory which is closely related to Turing's [1] but is more economical in the basic operations. It will be proved that a theoretically simple basic machine can be imagined and specified such that all partial recursive functions (and hence all solvable computation problems) can be computed by it and that only four basic types of instruction are employed for the programs: shift left one space, shift right one space, mark a blank space, conditional transfer. In particular, erasing is dispensable, one symbol for marking is sufficient, and one kind of transfer is enough. The reduction is somewhat similar to the realization of, for instance, the definability of conjunction and implication in terms of negation and disjunction, or of the definability of all these in terms of Sheffer's stroke function. As a result, it becomes less direct to prove that certain things can be done by the machines, but a little easier to prove that certain things cannot be done.

This self-contained theory will be presented, as far as possible, in a language which is familiar to those who are engaged in the use and construction of large-scale computers.

Turing's theory of computable functions antedated but has not much influenced the extensive actual construction of digital computers. These two aspects of theory and practice have been developed almost entirely independently of each other. The main reason is undoubtedly that logicians are interested in questions radically different from those with which the applied mathematicians and electrical engineers are primarily concerned. It cannot, however, fail to strike one as rather strange that often the same concepts are expressed by very different terms in the two developments. One is even

---

* This chapter appeared in *Journal of Association for Computing Machinery*, **4** (1957), 63—92. Recent works on related topics include Walter Oberschelp, "Varianten von Turingmaschinen", *Arkiv für math. Logik u. Grundlagenforschung*, Heft **4** (1958), 53—62, and forthcoming papers by C. Y. Lee, and by Shepherdson and Sturgis. In particular, they give a positive solution of the problem at the top of p. 150.

inclined to ask whether a rapprochement might not produce some good effect. This paper will, it is believed, be of use to those who wish to compare and connect the two approaches.

Extensive use of Turing [1] and Kleene [2] (Chapter XIII) will be made, although the exposition is sufficient in itself.

§2. The Basic Machine *B*

No physically realizable general-purpose machine is truly general-purpose in the sense that all theoretically solvable computation problems can be solved by the machine. In each case, the storage unit is necessarily finite: the length of each instruction word is finite, and there are only a definite finite number of addresses in the storage. Given any actual machine, it is easy to find computation problems which require more than its storage capacity.

Indeed, it seems reasonable to agree that given any uniform method of representing positive integers and an arbitrary number n_0, there exist integers not representable by less than n_0 symbols. We shall refrain from philosophical discussions on this question, such as the possibility of infinitely many isolated atomic symbols, etc., but take this for granted. If we accept this reasonable assumption, it follows that, in order to discuss a machine which computes all computable problems, or even a machine which computes just all problems of a given kind, such as the addition of two positive integers, we have to use the fiction of an infinite or indefinitely expandable storage unit, which may consist of a (fictitious) tape, or a (fictitious) internal store, or both.

Consider first a fictitious machine B which has an indefinitely expandable internal (parallel) storage and which uses in addition a tape (a serial storage) that is divided into a sequence of squares (cells) and could be extended both ways as much as we wish. In addition, the machine has a control element and a reading-writing head which, at each moment, is supposed to be scanning one and only one square of the tape. The head can, under the direction of the control element and in conformity with the program step under attention, move one square to the left or right or mark the square under scan, or "decide" to follow one of two other preassigned program steps according as the square under scan is marked or blank. At each moment, the next operation of the machine is determined by the step of the program under attention of the control element, together with the content (blank or marked) of the square under scan. The machine can perform four kinds of operation in accordance with these two factors: (i) the reading-writing head moves one square to the left; (ii) it moves one square to the right; (iii) it marks the square under scan; (iv) the control element shifts its attention to some other program step.

Suppose that the addresses in the internal storage can be any positive integers. Corresponding to the four types of operation, there are four types of basic instructions:

(1) $\rightarrow$: shift the head one square to the right, i.e., shift to scan the next square to the right of the square originally under scan; the same purpose can be accomplished by shifting the tape one square to the left.

(2) $\leftarrow$: shift the head one square to the left.

(3) $*$: mark the square of the tape under scan.

(4) Cn: a conditional transfer.

Of these, (1)—(3) are three single instructions, while the conditional transfer really embodies an infinite bundle of instructions. A conditional transfer is of the form $m.Cn$, according to which the m-th instruction word (i.e., the instruction word at the address m) is a conditional transfer such that if the square under scan is marked, then follow the n-th instruction; otherwise (i.e., if the square under scan is blank), follow the next instruction (i.e., the $(m+1)$-th instruction). The numbers m and n can be any positive integers that are not greater than the total number of instructions of the program in which $m.Cn$ occurs. When $n=m+1$, the instruction is wasteful; but we need not exclude such cases. There is nothing to prevent the occurrence of program steps which would instruct the reading-writing head to mark a square already marked, even though we can usually so construct the programs that when operating on inputs which interest us no such wasted actions will arise. To preclude the marking of already marked squares in the definition of programs would introduce unnecessary complications into the general considerations: e.g., replace every step $m.*$ by two steps $m.C(m+2)$, $m+1.*$ and renumber all steps $m+i$ in the original program by $m+i+1$.

Since there is no separate instruction for halt (stop), it is understood that the machine will stop when it has arrived at a stage that the program contains no instruction telling the machine what to do next. For uniformity and explicitness, however, we shall agree that every program has as its two last lines $N-1.\rightarrow$, $N.\leftarrow$. To illustrate, we give a simple program: $1.*$, $2.\rightarrow$, $3.C2$, $4.\rightarrow$, $5.\leftarrow$. This program enables the reading head to find and stop at the nearest blank to the right of the square initially under scan.

More exactly, a program or routine on the machine B can be defined as a set of ordered pairs such that there exists a positive integer $k (k>2)$ for which (a) for every n, n occurs as the first member of exactly one pair in the set if and only if $1 \leqslant n \leqslant k$; (b) the second member of each pair is either $*$ or $\rightarrow$ or $\leftarrow$ or a number n, $1 \leqslant n \leqslant k-1$; (c) there are the pairs $\langle k-1, \rightarrow\rangle$, $\langle k, \leftarrow\rangle$. We can, according to this definition, represent the example above by: $\{\langle 1, *\rangle, \langle 2, \rightarrow\rangle, \langle 3, 2\rangle, \langle 4, \rightarrow\rangle, \langle 5, \leftarrow\rangle\}$.

In contrast with Turing who uses a one-way infinite tape that has a beginning, we are following Post in the use of a 2-way infinite tape. This is considered a reduction because we are deprived of the privilege of appealing to the beginning of the tape. As it turns out, for the purpose of computation, there is little difference in the capacity of the machine whether we use a 1-way or a 2-way infinite tape. So far as the general theory is concerned, the 1-way tape tends to rule out certain programs as meaningless when they instruct the reading head to go beyond the beginning of the tape. This would introduce unnecessary complications.

We have defined the totality of all possible programs on the machine *B*. For each program, what the machine *B* will do is determined by the initial tape content and the initial position of the reading head relative to the tape, both of which can be given arbitrarily. To simplify our further considerations, we shall assume, once for all, that (i) the initial (input) tape contains only finitely many marked squares, and that (ii) at the beginning of each program, the reading head scans the sixth blank square to the right of the rightmost marked square. On the other hand, subroutines begin on any square within the minimum tape portion containing all the initially marked squares and six blanks to the right, and end similarly. From (i), it follows that at each moment there are only finitely many marked squares on the tape.

We note that given any program Π, its behaviour at each moment is completely determined by: the content of the tape at the moment, the position and content of the square under scan, the instruction of the program that is being attended to at the moment. The three factors plus the given program determine the *complete instantaneous state* of the machine *B*. To be precise, we can represent these states by numbers in the following manner. We represent $\rightarrow$, $\leftarrow$, $*$ by 1, 2, 3 respectively and n by $n+3$, the i-th program step by a power of the i-th prime, so that, for example, $2^3.3^1.5^5.7^1.11^2$ represents the program

$$\{\langle 1,*\rangle, \langle 2,\rightarrow\rangle, \langle 3,2\rangle, \langle 4,\rightarrow\rangle, \langle 5,\leftarrow\rangle\}$$

given above. The length of a program Π is represented by the number $lh(\pi)$ of distinct prime factors in its representing number π and the i-th line of Π is represented by the number $(\pi)_i$ which is the exponent of the i-th prime number (2 being the first prime number) in the factorization of π. The functions $lh(\pi)$ and $(\pi)_i$ are well-known recursive functions (cf. e.g., Kleene [2]). The tape content and the square under scan can be represented by a number of the form $3^a.5^b.7^c$, where $b=0$ or 1 according as the square under scan is blank or marked, a and c represent respectively the tape contents to the left and to the right of the square under scan, in such a way that the i-th digit (from right to left) of a (resp. c) is 0 or 1 according as whether the i-th square to the left (resp. right) is blank or marked. Since only finitely many squares are marked at each moment, a and c are at each time definite numbers. If, for instance, the only marked portion of the tape is:

*		*	*			*	*

and the head scans the fourth (from left) of these squares, the number is

$3^{101}.5.7^{1100}$. Using these numbers, we represent the complete instantaneous state at a moment by the number

$$2^{\pi}.\,3^{a}.\,5^{b}.\,7^{c}.\,11^{i},$$

when the program has number π, the tape content with the square under scan has at the moment the number $3^{a}.5^{b}.7^{c}$, and the program step attended to is i. From this number, we can also recover π, a, b, c, i in a unique manner, on account of the unique factorization of a number into prime factors.

Since we assume that one program step is performed at each moment, the complete instantaneous state of the machine at each moment is determined by that at the preceding moment in a fairly simple manner. Thus, if the number at one moment is $2^{\pi}.3^{a}.5^{b}.7^{c}.11^{i}$ and $i < lh(\pi)$, then the number at the next moment is given as follows:

(i) if $(\pi)_i$ is 1, it is $2^{\pi}.\,3^{10a+b}.\,5^{c'}.\,7^{c/10}.\,11^{i+1}$ (c' being the remainder of dividing c by 10);

(ii) if $(\pi)_i$ is 2, it is $2^{\pi}.\,3^{a/10}.\,5^{a'}.\,7^{10c+b}.\,11^{i+1}$;

(iii) if $(\pi)_i$ is 3, it is $2^{\pi}.\,3^{a}.\,5.\,7^{c}.\,11^{i+1}$;

(iv) if $(\pi)_i$ is $3+j$, it is $2^{\pi}.\,3^{a}.\,5^{b}.\,7^{c}.\,11^{i+1}$, if $b=0$, and $2^{\pi}.\,3^{a}.\,5^{b}.\,7^{c}.\,11^{j}$, if $b=1$.

Hence, given the complete instantaneous state at the moment when the machine begins to perform a program, all later states will be determined. The beginning state is in turn entirely determined by the program and the input tape. It follows from these facts that for each given program π, there is a recursive function $\theta_{\pi}(\iota, t)$ which gives, for any given input tape content represented by ι, the number of the complete instantaneous state of the machine B at moment t. Then we can define a recursive function $\tau_{\pi}(\iota) = \mu_t[(\theta_{\pi}(\iota, t))_5 = lh(\pi)]$, which gives the smallest number t such that, for given ι, the machine will be attending the last line of the program Π at time t, provided the machine does get to that stage for the given ι. For values of ι which would make the machine run forever according to the program Π, $\tau_{\pi}(\iota)$ is not defined. It seems reasonable to call the function $\tau_{\pi}(\iota)$ the *speed function* of the program Π or of the function which Π determines. We may call the recursive function $\theta_{\pi}(\iota, \tau_{\pi}(\iota))/(2^{\pi}.11^{lh(\pi)})$ the function determined by the program Π, since it gives for each input ι, the corresponding output that results from a performance of the program Π. We omit the explicit definitions for these functions which are similar to those of Kleene [2], pp. 374—376.

It follows that the function determined by any program of the machine B is a recursive function. We can state the result by saying that all functions computable by the machine B are recursive. This is a slight generalization of the counterpart of the known theorem that all functions computable in Turing's sense are recursive (Kleene [2], p. 374).

The generalization consists in the waiving of the restriction that the initial input and final output tape contents must be of certain preassigned forms which are taken according to an ad hoc convention as representing positive integers (arguments or values of functions) or n-tuples of integers (arguments of non-singulary functions). For instance, in Kleene [2], the input tape is supposed to consist of a string of 1's, or a string of several strings of 1's any two of which are separated by a 0. What the restriction amounts to is to select effectively from all possible tape situations a suitable subset to represent all positive integers and their n-tuples. In terms of our numerical representation of tape situations, this means that ι is not to range over the set of all integers which represent tape situations but only over some simple recursive subsets of it. Moreover, in our representation of tape situations, we have included information about the square under scan; this is not needed when we are primarily interested only in interpreting initial and final tape contents as questions and answers for evaluating certain functions of positive integers.

When we wish to show that a program Π of the machine B represents a function (say $f(x)$) of positive integers, the natural thing to do would seem to be, (i) represent by a uniform method the argument of the function on the input tape; (ii) read out by a uniform method the final value of the function from the final output tape for a given input by the program Π; (iii) show that the values thus obtained always agree with the values of the function $f(x)$ for the given argument. What uniform methods of representation we choose is more or less arbitrary although they must be effective and indeed "simple" in some intuitive sense. While our considerations thus far are independent of how we choose these effective methods of representation, in order to prove our main theorem, we find it necessary to fix some simple specific method of putting questions on and reading answers from the tape. We shall not consider the general question as to all the possible methods of representing questions and answers by which all recursive functions are computable on the machine B.

We assume the particular method, to be described in the next section, of representing positive integers and strings of them and define computability relative to the representation. A function $f(x)$ of positive integers is said to be B-computable if, and only if, we can find a program such that when x is represented on the tape and when the machine is scanning the representation, the program leads the machine to print more marks on the tape so that when the machine has performed all the instructions of the program, the rightmost portion of the printed part of the tape represents the value of $f(x)$, provided $f(x)$ is defined for the given argument x. A similar definition is obtainable for functions of two or more variables. For example, it is possible to show that the functions

$$f(x) = 2x,$$
$$g(x, y) = xy$$

are B-computable by the above definition.

The main result, to be established in the next section, is that all (partial) recursive functions are B-computable. The proof depends essentially on the known fact (Kleene [2], p. 331) that all recursive functions can be obtained by a few (six, in fact) simple types of schemata. Since each schema, as we shall prove, can be handled by the machine B, the general result follows.

The result is a little stronger than the known fact that all recursive functions are computable in the sense of Turing, because Turing permits additional basic instructions (besides $*, \rightarrow, \leftarrow, Cx$) such as erasing a mark, marking a square by other symbols, unconditional transfer, and other types of conditional transfer. While it is obvious that not all these additional instructions are indispensable, it is by no means obvious that all of them are dispensable. Indeed, the actual proof of the adequacy of $*, \rightarrow, \leftarrow$ and Cx, which will be presented in the next section, is quite complex.

It is also known that all Turing computable functions are recursive. As all B-computable functions are obviously Turing computable, so all B-computable functions are recursive. This last conclusion also follows directly from the more general statement, previously established, that all functions computable by the machine B are recursive.

These results will establish the equivalence or coextensiveness of Turing computability and B-computability in the sense that a function is Turing computable if and only if it is B-computable. The main result that all recursive functions are B-computable yields also, for example, a somewhat simpler proof of the recursive unsolvability of Thue's problem (the word problem for semi-groups) (Kleene [2], p. 382), since fewer types of basic operations need to be considered.

We interrupt the general discussion to give details of our proof of the main theorem. Readers not interested in technical matters may wish to skip the more formal parts of the next section.

§ 3. All Recursive Functions Are B-Computable

We possess fairly simple inductive characterizations of the class of recursive functions: certain simple initial functions are recursive; given a class of recursive functions, certain simple schemata will yield new recursive functions; and these provide us with all recursive functions. To prove that all recursive functions are B-computable, we use induction accordingly: the initial recursive functions are B-computable; given a class of B-computable functions, functions got from them by the recursion schemata are again B-computable.

We shall follow Turing in making a distinction between principal and auxiliary squares on the tape. While this is merely a matter of dispensable convenient convention in Turing's approach, it is not clear that we can get what we want without some form of the distinction, in view of the fact that we do not permit erasing. We shall call one sequence of alternate squares the P-squares (principal squares) and the other sequence A-squares (auxiliary squares). Questions and answers on a tape are determined by the contents of the P-squares alone.

In general, between two marked consecutive P-squares, there is an A-square which may be either blank or marked. We shall represent each positive integer n by a string of n pairs of squares (called a "number expression") which begins with (i.e., at the left end) a P-square and ends with an A-square such that all P-squares in the string are marked and that the P-squares which immediately precede and follow the string are both blank. Incidentally, this leaves the number 0 unrepresented. We shall deliberately consider only positive integers. We could, if we wished to include the number 0, represent n by a string of $(n+1)$ pairs of squares with all P-squares marked. But there is no need to do so. We shall call a number expression clean if all the A-squares in it are blank. In general, we always introduce at first clean number expressions. We begin to mark the A-squares in a number expression only when we operate on it (as we shall see, this means: copy it).

Our purpose is to prove that for each recursive function $f(x_1, \cdots, x_m)$, we can construct a program which, when fed into the machine B, will compute the values of the function. This task we interpret as follows. Given any constant argument values $x_1, \cdots, x_m$, we represent them anywhere on the tape from left to right, first the number x_1, followed by one blank P-square and one blank A-square, followed by the number x_2, etc. Once the argument values are given, it is determined which squares on the tape are the P-squares, since the beginning square of x_1 is a P-square. Our program for the function $f(x_1, \cdots, x_m)$ is to enable us so to operate the machine B that for any given positive integers $x_1, \cdots, x_m$, the machine B will eventually stop and then there is a number expression on the tape to the right of which all squares are blank, and which represents the number that is the value of f for the given argument values $x_1, \cdots, x_m$, provided f is defined for these particular argument values. If $f(x_1, \cdots, x_m)$ is not defined, the machine may either never stop (circular) or stop at a stage when there is no number expression on the tape such that all squares to its right are blank (blocked). In other words, for each recursive function, we try to find a program such that for each given array of argument values (or for each argument value, when we have a function of one variable), the machine B makes a separate calculation on a separate tape. If $f(x_1, \cdots, x_m)$ is defined for all $x_1, \cdots, x_m$ (i.e., not only partial recursive but general recursive), we could use the same tape to calculate all values successively since each calculation uses up only a finite portion of the infinite tape. We shall, however, to simplify the picture, prefer to think that each time we use a new blank tape. We are not interested in what the machine does with the program when the initial tape content does not represent exactly a string of m integers.

We shall so construct our programs for recursive functions that each recursive function is not only *B*-computable but that each of the programs will satisfy several additional conditions. We assume that the initial tape contains a question of the right form. According to the definition of number expressions, any two number expressions must be separated by at least one blank *P*-square. The program will be such that in the process of operating the machine, (a) there are never more than two blank *P*-squares between two number expressions; (b) every marked *P*-square is always part of a number expression; (c) we shall never mark an *A*-square which lies outside the minimum tape portion that contains all the printed marks at the moment; (d) for any values $x_1, \cdots, x_m$, either the machine will never stop or the final tape will contain a number expression to the right of which there is no marked square (i.e., either the function is defined or the operation of the machine is circular, but never blocked). From (a) and (c) it follows that at every stage of operating the machine, there never appear more than 5 blank squares between two marked squares. We shall call a string of 5 (resp. 3) blank squares lying between two marked squares a big gap (resp. a gap). It follows from (a) and (c) that each gap or big gap always begins with an *A*-square and ends with an *A*-square. We shall eliminate a big gap by marking the *A*-square in the middle. The programs also satisfy the following conditions: (e) if the machine does stop for given arguments $x_1, \cdots, x_m$, the last number expression will be clean (i.e., no *A*-square in it is marked); (f) on stopping, all big gaps will be eliminated; (g) on stopping, the reading head will always end up scanning the 5-th blank square to the right of the last number expression, i.e., the 6-th blank square beyond the last marked square (we shall say that the reading head ends up scanning the open). Condition (e) assures that we can immediately use the value of one function in calculating the value of some other function. Condition (*f*) helps to locate previous number expressions on the tape.

Since there are never more than 5 blanks between two marked squares, we can, beginning with the reading head scanning a square within the minimum region of the tape which contains all marked squares, easily find its beginning and its end: go left (resp. right) until a string of 6 blank squares is found.

We introduce a subroutine *Y* such that if the reading head is scanning a square which falls within the minimum tape region which contains all marked squares and 6 blanks to the right of the last marked square, carrying out *Y* will enable the reading head to find the last marked square and end up scanning the open, provided there are initially no more than 5 blanks between any two marked squares. We note that this is useful because at the beginning of each of the programs we are actually going to use below, the square initially under scan always falls within the region just specified. We introduce first a subroutine *X* which enables us to find the nearest marked square to the left of the square initially under scan (or itself, if it is marked) and end up one square to the right.

Subroutine X: 1.C14, 2.←, 3.C14, 4.←, 5.C14, 6.←, 7.C14, 8.←, 9.C14, 10.←, 11.C14, 12.←, 13.C14, 14.→, 15.→, 16.←.

Using X, we can define Y:

(i) Subroutine Y: 1.X, 2.←, 3.→, 4.C3, 5.→, 6.C3, 7.→, 8.C3, 9.→, 10.C3, 11.→, 12.C3, 13.→, 14.C3, 15.→, 16.←.

Next we introduce a subroutine which enables us to add 1 to the last number on the tape and end up with the reading head scanning the last marked square. We use the obvious notation $\leftarrow^n$(resp. $\rightarrow^n$) when ← (resp. →) is repeated n times:

(ii) Subroutine A: 1.Y, 2.$\leftarrow^4$, 3.*, 4.→, 5.←; or simply Y, $\leftarrow^4$, *, →, ←; or even just Y, $\leftarrow^4$, *.

This subroutine can be reiterated to enable us to add any given constant k to the last number. In general, for any subroutine or program Π, we shall use the notation Π^k to represent that Π is repeated k times, and Π^1 is identified with Π. In the case of A, the purpose of A^k could be achieved more directly by using $(A,\rightarrow^2,*)$, $(A,\rightarrow^2,*,\rightarrow^2,*)$, etc. But it is preferable to use reiterations of whole subroutines, when possible.

Similarly with Subroutine Y, we can also introduce a subroutine H which enables us to find the nearest big gap to the left of the square under scan (if there is such a big gap) and end up with the reading head scanning the middle square of the big gap. Note that if the square initially under scan is not marked, we have to find a marked square first.

(iii) Subroutine H: 1.C3, 2.←, 3.←, 4.C3, 5.←, 6.C3, 7.←, 8.C3, 9.←, 10.C3, 11.←, 12.C3, 13.$\rightarrow^2$, (14.→, 15.←.)

The success of the subroutine again depends on the fact that we do not allow more than 5 blanks between two marked squares.

To give direction to our procedure, we recall that our purpose is to prove that all recursive functions are B-computable, and that our proof depends on the possibility of getting all recursive functions from six schemata. Of these six, the first three are direct schemata telling us unconditionally that functions defined by them are recursive, the remaining three are conditional ones. We pause to state the first three schemata, which are simpler, and explain where we are going.

Schema (I). $\varphi(x) = x + 1$.

Schema (II). $\varphi(x_1, \cdots, x_n) = q$, q a given constant.

Schema (III). $\varphi(x_1, \cdots, x_n) = x_i$, i a given constant among $1, \cdots, n$.

To prove, for instance, that the function defined by (I) is B-computable, we find a program such that when the argument value x is given on the tape and the machine begins by having its reading head scanning a square within the minimum tape portion which contained all initially marked squares and 6 blanks to the right of the last marked square, the reading head will find the last marked square in the representation of the number x, move right six squares (leaving thereby a big gap), start to copy the number x in the consecutive P-squares, add 1 after the copying is finished, and indicate that the operation is completed. We shall then have the answer since the last number on the tape will be $x+1$.

To obtain such a program, the most difficult part is to do the copying whose result of course has to vary with the number to be copied. Let us assume for the moment that we have obtained a subroutine for copying:

(iv) Subroutine I_m: this enables us, beginning at the square under scan, to copy in successive alternate squares the m-th number (counting from right to left) which lies to the left of the nearest big gap which precedes (is to the left of) the square under scan, and end up with the reading head scanning the open.

The closing steps of eliminating the last big gap and having the machine scan the open are combined in one subroutine:

(v) Subroutine Z: 1.H, 2.$*$, 3.Y; or, since there is no conditional transfer, simply, H, $*$, Y.

Using Z, the subroutines A, Y already introduced, plus the subroutine I_m (to be introduced formally below), we can now prove that all functions defined by the schemata (I), (II), (III) are B-computable.

The programs needed are:

(I) Y, I_1, A, Z.

(II) Y, $*$, A^{q-1}, Z; when $q = 1$, simply Y, $*$, Z.

(III) Y, I_{n-i+1}, Z.

Hence, to complete this part of our proof, we only have to construct the subroutine I_m. We shall deliberately make it more complicated than necessary in order that the same number expression can be copied more than once. In order to copy a number expression; we have to mark the A-squares between the marked P-squares of the original number expression as we go along, in order to keep track of how far we have advanced. If we use up all these auxiliary squares in the first copying, we shall not be able to make a second copy from the original and we do not wish to make a second copy from the first copy since we wish to operate on it. In general, we contrive to allow the possibility of copying a given number twice, so that we can operate on one copy and reserve one clean copy for future "reference" (i.e., further copying).

These complications are of course only necessitated by our decision not to permit erasing. Indeed, this is a crucial step of the whole proof. Since we may wish to copy a number expression an indefinite number of times and since with each copying we have to mark some squares to keep track of how far we are along in our action, we may feel that erasing is indispensable. The difficulty is solved by the simple trick just described: copy the same expression twice, copy one of the copies twice, etc.

We introduce a few subroutines.

(vi) Subroutine D: 1.$C4$, 2.$\leftarrow^2$, 3.$C6$, 4.$\leftarrow^2$, 5.$C4$, 6.$\rightarrow$, 7.$\leftarrow$.

This enables the reading head, when scanning a P-square, to find and scan the last P-square of the nearest preceding number expression. The process can be repeated so that D^m gives us the last (marked) P-square of the m-th (counting from right to left) number expression which precedes the square under scan.

(vii) Subroutine G: 1.$\rightarrow$, 2.$\leftarrow^2$, 3.$C2$, 4.$\leftarrow^2$, 5.$C2$, 6.$\rightarrow$.

When scanning a P-square, this enables the reading head to find the nearest two successive blank A-squares to its left and end up scanning the P-square between them.

(viii) Subroutine K: 1.$C3$, 2.$C5$, 3.$\leftarrow$, 4.$C1$, 5.$\leftarrow$.

When scanning a marked square, find the nearest blank square to its left and end up scanning the square immediately preceding that blank.

(ix) Subroutine $M(a)$: 1.$C3$, 2.Ca, 3.$\leftarrow^2$, 4.$C6$, 5.A, Ca, 6.$\rightarrow$, 7.$C6$, 8.$*$, A^2.

When scanning a P-square, if it is blank, this asks the machine to follow instruction a (which "plugs" this subroutine into a larger routine or program), if marked, then scan the immediately preceding P-square: if it is blank, then add one to the last number expression on the tape and then follow instruction a; if it is marked, find and mark the nearest blank square to its right, add 2 to the last number expression on the tape and stop.

We are ready to define I_m:

(x) Subroutine I_m: 1.$*$, 2.H, $\leftarrow$, D^m, G, $M(4)$, 3.$C2$, 4.Y.

To illustrate how this works, we give a diagram of a simple example (copying the single number 6), with ↓ indicating the square under scan, * for marked, - for blank squares:

```
                                         ↓
initial tape situation:  *-*-*-*-*-*------,
                                         ↓
step 1:                  *-*-*-*-*-*-----*,
                                       ↓
step 2, H:               *-*-*-*-*-*-----*,
                                   ↓
←, D¹:                   *-*-*-*-*-*-----*,
```

```
                                ↓
G:                      *-*-*-*-*-*-----*,
                              ↓
M(4): 1, 3              *-*-*-*-*-*-----*,
                               ↓
      4, 6              *-*-*-*-*-*-----*,
                                            ↓
      7, 8              *-*-*-***-*-----*-*-*,
step 3, transfer to:
                                     ↓
step 2, H:              *-*-*-***-*-----*-*-*,
                                  ↓
  ←, D¹:                *-*-*-***-*-----*-*-*,
                                 ↓
  G: 1, 2               *-*-*-***-*-----*-*-*,
                               ↓
     3, 4               *-*-*-***-*-----*-*-*,
                             ↓
     5, 2               *-*-*-***-*-----*-*-*,
                           ↓
     3, 4               *-*-*-***-*-----*-*-*,
                            ↓
     5, 6               *-*-*-***-*-----*-*-*,
                                                ↓
M(4):                   *-***-***-*-----*-*-*-*-*,
step 3, transfer to:
                                     ↓
step 2, H:              *-***-***-*-----*-*-*-*-*,
                                  ↓
  ←, D¹:                *-***-***-*-----*-*-*-*-*,
                         ↓
G:                      -*-***-***-*-----*-*-*-*-*,
                        ↓
M(4): 1, 3              --*-***-***-*-----*-*-*-*-*,
                                                    ↓
      4, 5              --*-***-***-*-----*-*-*-*-*-*,
                                                          ↓
step 4:                 --*-***-***-*-----*-*-*-*-*-*------.
```

This example should make a little clearer the subroutines G, $M(a)$, and I_m. The primary purpose of $M(a)$ is to enable the machine to copy two units at a time and use up only at most half of the available A-squares in the number expression to be copied, in order to leave room for the making of a second copy. It leads to three different courses of action according as (1) no more left to copy; (2) only one more unit left; and (3) at least 2 more units yet to be copied.

Once we possess I_m, our proof that all functions defined by the schemata (I)—(III) are B-computable is complete. It remains to be shown that from given B-computable functions only B-computable functions can be generated by the other three schemata. For this purpose, a few more subroutines are necessary, notably the ones for making the second copy of a given number expression.

(xi) Subroutine I_m: 1.*, H^2, ←, D^m, $←^2$, 2.$M(4)$, H^2, ←, D^m, K, 3.$C2$, 4.Y.

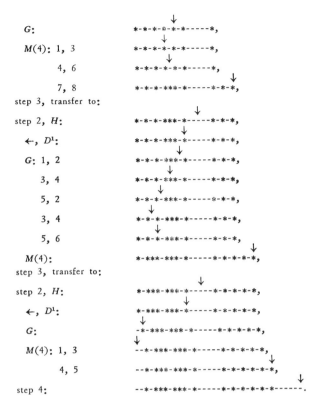

This enables the machine to make a second copy of the m-th (counting from right to left) number expression to the left of the second (counting from right to left) big gap which precedes the square under scan. To illustrate it, we take the last line of the preceding example as the initial tape situation (taking $m=1$):

```
                                                          ↓
                        --*-***-***-*-----*-*-*-*-*-*------,
                                  ↓
step 1:                 --*-***-***-*-----*-*-*-*-*-*-----*,
                                                              ↓
step 2, M(4):           --*-***-*****-----*-*-*-*-*-*-----*-*-*,
                                    ↓
  H², ←, D¹:            --*-***-*****-----*-*-*-*-*-*-----*-*-*,
                              ↓
  K:                    --*-***-*****-----*-*-*-*-*-*-----*-*-*,
step 3, transfer to
                          ↓
step 2:                 --*-*********-----*-*-*-*-*-*-----*-*-*-*-*,
step 3, transfer to
                                                                    ↓
step 2, M(4):           --*-*********-----*-*-*-*-*-*-----*-*-*-*-*-*,
                                                                          ↓
step 4:                 --*-*********-----*-*-*-*-*-*-----*-*-*-*-*-*------.
```

We shall often wish to copy not only a single number expression but a succession of number expressions. We easily get two extensions of I_m and J_m.

(xii) $\bar{I}_m$: I_m, $\leftarrow^2$, I_{m-1}, $\leftarrow^2$, $\cdots$, $\leftarrow^2$, I_1. For example, $\bar{I}_2$ is merely I_2, $\leftarrow^2$, I_1; $\bar{I}_3$ is I_3, $\leftarrow^2$, I_2, $\leftarrow^2$, I_1; etc.

(xiii) $\bar{J}_m$: J_m, $\leftarrow^2$, J_{m-1}, $\leftarrow^2$, $\cdots$, $\leftarrow^2$, J_1.

We shall also use, at one place, the notation $\bar{J}_m - J_1$ for the subroutine obtained from $\bar{J}_m$ by omitting $\leftarrow^2$, J_1 at the end.

A slight variant of I_m is to copy $y-1$ instead of y, the m-th number to the left of the nearest big gap preceding the square under scan.

(xiv) Subroutine L_m: 1.*, 2.H, D^m, $\leftarrow^2$, G, $M(4)$, 3.$C2$, 4.Y.

This differs from I_m only in the insertion of $\leftarrow^2$ in step 2. It is of course only applicable when $y > 1$.

We are now ready to deal with the three remaining schemata.

(IV) If $\chi_1, \cdots, \chi_m$ and ψ are recursive (resp. B-computable), then the function φ defined by the following schema is also recursive (resp. B-computable):

$$\varphi(x_1, \cdots, x_n) = \psi[\chi_1(x_1, \cdots, x_n), \cdots, \chi_m(x_1, \cdots, x_n)].$$

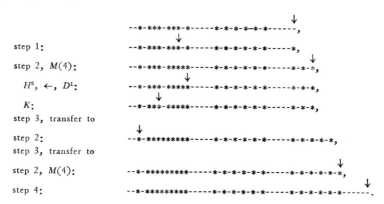

We assume that the programs for $\psi, \chi_1, \cdots, \chi_m$ are respectively $P(\psi)$, $P(\chi_1), \cdots, P(\chi_m)$, we are to find a program $P(\varphi)$ for the function φ. Intuitively the program $P(\varphi)$ will do the following: copy the argument values $x_1, \cdots, x_n$ twice, keep the first copy clean and find the value of $\chi_m(x_1, \cdots, x_n)$ with the second copy and the program $P(\chi_m)$, then make two copies from the clean copy of $x_1, \cdots, x_n$, and get the value of $\chi_{m-1}(x_1, \cdots, x_n)$ with one copy and $P(\chi_{m-1})$; repeating the process, we get the values of $\chi_m(x_1, \cdots, x_n), \cdots, \chi_1(x_1, \cdots, x_n)$; copy all of them in the order $\chi_1(x_1, \cdots, x_n), \cdots, \chi_m(x_1, \cdots, x_n)$ and then apply the program $P(\psi)$, we get the value of $\varphi(x_1,\cdots,x_n)$. The program $P(\varphi)$ is as follows (taking for illustration, $m=2$):

$$Y,\ \bar{I}_n,\ \bar{J}_n,\ H^2,\ *,\ Y,\ P(\chi_2),\ \leftarrow^3,\ *,\ \rightarrow^3,\ \bar{I}_n,\ \bar{J}_n,\ H^2,\ *,\ Y,\ P(\chi_1),\ I_1,\ Z,\ \leftarrow^2,\ I_{n+1},\ H,\ *,\ Y,\ P(\psi).$$

Slight complications are needed in the program to assure that the dispersed values of $\chi_m(x_1, \cdots, x_n), \cdots, \chi_1(x_1, \cdots, x_n)$ can be collected together. We illustrate this program with a simple example with $n=2$, $x_1=x_2=1$ (incidentally, the use of Y before $P(\chi_1)$ or $P(\psi)$ is redundant but makes the illustrations clearer):

```
                                   ↓
Y:                        *---*------
                                             ↓
Ī_n:                      *---*-----*---*------
                                                       ↓
J̄_n:                      *---*-----*---*-----*---*------
                                                       ↓
H², *, Y:                 *---*--*--*---*-----*---*------
                                                                   ↓
P(χ₂):                    *---*--*--*---*-----*---* ··· χ₂(1, 1)------
                                                                                     ↓
←³, *, →³, Ī_n, J̄_n:      *---*--*--*---*-----*---* ··· χ₂(1, 1)--*--*---*-----*---*------,
H², *, Y, P(χ₁):          *---*--*--*---*--*--*---* ··· χ₂(1, 1)--*--*---*-----*---* ··· χ₁(1, 1)
                               ↓
                          ------,

I₁, Z, ←², I_{n+1}:       *---*--*--*---*--*--*---* ··· χ₂(1, 1)--*--*---*-----*---* ··· χ₁(1, 1)
                                         ↓
                          ---χ₂(1, 1)------,
H, *, Y, P(ψ):            *---*--*--*---*--*--*---* ··· χ₂(1, 1)--*--*---*--*--*---* ··· χ₁(1, 1)
                                                                   ↓
                          ---χ₂(1, 1) ··· ψ[χ₁(1, 1), χ₂(1, 1)]------.
```

Next we have the schema for primitive recursion:

$$\text{(V)}\quad \begin{cases} \varphi(1, x_2, \cdots, x_n) = \psi(x_2, \cdots, x_n), \\ \varphi(z+1, x_2, \cdots, x_n) = \chi[z, \varphi(z, x_2, \cdots, x_n), x_2, \cdots, x_n]. \end{cases}$$

Given programs $P(\psi)$ and $P(\chi)$, we are to obtain a program $P(\varphi)$ for the function $\varphi(y, x_2, \cdots, x_n)$. Intuitively, the number of applications of $P(\chi)$ in evaluating $\varphi(y, x_2, \cdots, x_n)$ is unbounded; for a given y, we have to apply $P(\chi)$ $y-1$ times. This is accomplished by testing successively as we go along whether y is 1, $y-1$ is 1 or $y-2$ is 1 or etc. Thus we evaluate $\psi(x_2, \cdots, x_n)$ by $P(\psi)$ and test whether y is 1. If y is 1, we copy $\psi(x_2,\cdots,x_n)$ as answer to $P(\varphi)$; if y is not 1, we evaluate $\chi[1, \psi(x_2,\cdots,x_n), x_2, \cdots, x_n]$ and test whether $y-1$ is 1. If $y-1$ is not 1, we evaluate

$$\chi\{2, \chi[1, \psi(x_2, \cdots, x_n), x_2, \cdots, x_n], x_2, \cdots, x_n\}$$

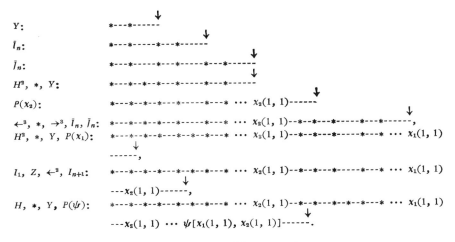

and test whether $y-2$ is 1. And so on. The program $P(\varphi)$ is:

1. Y, $\bar{I}_n$, $\leftarrow^2$, $*$, $\rightarrow^6$, $\bar{J}_{n-1}$, H^2, $*$, Y, $P(\psi)$, $\leftarrow^2$, I_{n+1}, $\leftarrow^6$,
2. $\leftarrow^2$, $C4$,
3. $\rightarrow^2$, $C5$,
4. $\rightarrow^6$, $\bar{I}_n$, A, Y, L_1, I_{n+2}, $\bar{J}_n - J_1$, H^2, $*$, Y, $P(\chi)$, $\leftarrow^2$, L_{n+1}, $\leftarrow^6$, $C2$,
5. $\rightarrow^4$, I_2, Z.

We give an example with $n=2$, $y=3$, $x_2=2$.

1. Y: *-*-*---*-*------ (↓ at end)

$\bar{I}_n$, $\leftarrow^2$, $*$, $\rightarrow^6$, $\bar{J}_{n-1}$, H^2, $*$, Y: ***-*---*-*--*--*-*-*---*-*---*-----*-* -----(↓) (copy y, $x_2, \cdots, x_n$, then write 1, then big gap, then copy $x_2, \cdots, x_n$ again, and then mark first big gap, end up scanning the open).

$P(\psi)$, $\leftarrow^2$, I_{n+1}, $\leftarrow^6$: [***-*---*-*--*--***-*---]*-*---*-----*-* ··· $\psi(x)$---*-*-*(↓)
(braces: y under ***-*, x under *-*, y under ***-*, x under *-*, 1, x under *-*, y under *-*-*)

(evaluate $\psi(x_2, \cdots, x_n)$ then copy y and end up scanning the end of y).

2. $\leftarrow^2$, $C4$ (when following step 1, this tests whether y is 1. If y is 1, then follow step 3 and step 5 and copy $\psi(x_2, \cdots, x_n)$, the calculation is complete. If y is not 1, follow step 4: this is the case in the present example).

4. $\rightarrow^6$, $\bar{I}_n$, A, Y, L_1, I_{n+2}, $\bar{J}_n - J_1$, H^2, $*$, Y: [*-*---*--*--*-* ··· $\psi(x)$---]*-*-*---*-* ---*-*-----*---$\psi(x)$---*-*------(↓) (copy $x_2, \cdots, x_n$, and replace 1 by 2, leave big gap, then copy $2-1$, $\psi(x_2, \cdots, x_n)$, $x_2, \cdots, x_n$, and mark earliest big gap, and end up scanning the open).
(braces: x, 1, x, y, x; 2, 1, x)

$P(\chi)$, $\leftarrow^2$, L_{n+1}, $\leftarrow^6$, $C2$: [*-*-*---]*-*---*-*-----*---$\psi(x)$---*-* ··· $\chi[1, \psi(x), x]$--- *-*(↓) (evaluate $\chi[1, \psi(x_2, \cdots, x_n), x_2, \cdots, x_n]$ and write down $y-1$, ready to transfer to step 2 for testing whether $y-1$ is 1).
(braces: y, x, 2, 1, x; $y-1$)

2. This now tests whether $y-1=1$. Since $y-1\neq 1$ in our example, we repeat step 4 for $y-2$:

4. $\rightarrow^6$, $\bar{I}_n$, A, Y, L_1, I_{n+2}, $\bar{J}_n - J_1$, H^2, $*$, Y: [*-*---*-*--*--*---$\psi(x)$---*-*···$\chi[1, \psi(x), x]$---]*-*---*-*---*-*-*-----*-*---$\chi[1, \psi(x), x]$---*-*------(↓) (copy $x_2, \cdots, x_n$ and replace 2 by 3, leave big gap, then copy $3-1$, $\chi[1, \psi(x_2, \cdots, x_n), x_2, \cdots, x_n]$, $x_2, \cdots, x_n$, mark earliest big gap and end up scanning the open).
(braces: x, 2, 1, x; $y-1$, x, 3, 2, x)

$P(\chi)$, $\leftarrow^2$, L_{n+1}, $\leftarrow^6$, $C2$: [*-*---]*-*---*-*-*-----*-*--- $\chi[1, \psi(x), x]$---*-* ··· $\chi[2, \chi[1, \psi(x), x], x]$---*(↓) (evaluate $\chi[2, \varphi(2, x_2, \cdots, x_n), x_2, \cdots, x_n]$ and write down $y-2$ ready to transfer to step 2 for testing whether $y-2$ is 1).
(braces: $y-1$, x, 3, 2, x; 1 = $y-2$)

2. This now tests whether $y - 2 = 1$. Since $y - 2 = 1$ in our example, we transfer to step 3 and then to step 5.

5. This now merely gives $\chi[2, \varphi(2, x_2, \cdots, x_n), x_2, \cdots, x_n]$ as final answer, marks remaining big gap, and ends up scanning the open: $[\underbrace{*\text{-}*}_{x}\text{---}\underbrace{*\text{-}*\text{-}*}_{3}\text{--}*\text{--}\underbrace{*\text{-}*}_{2}\text{---}\chi[1, \psi(x), x]\text{---}\underbrace{*\text{-}*}_{x}$

$$\cdots\underbrace{\chi[2, \chi[1, \psi(x), x], x]\text{---}*]}_{y-2}\text{---}\chi[2, \chi[1, \psi(x), x], x]\text{------}\overset{\downarrow}{.}$$

Finally, we have to deal with the schema about the μ-operator ("the smallest number such that"):

(VI) $\varphi(x_1, \cdots, x_n) = \mu y[\chi(x_1, \cdots, x_n, y) = 1]$.

The construction of $P(\varphi)$ from $P(\chi)$ is somewhat similar to that in the case of schema (V) but simpler. For any given $x_1, \cdots, x_n$, we evaluate first $\chi(x_1, \cdots, x_n, 1)$ and see whether its value is 1. If yes, we stop; if no, we evaluate $\chi(x_1, \cdots, x_n, 2)$. And so on. The program $P(\varphi)$ is as follows:

1. $Y, \bar{I}_n, \leftarrow^2, *, \rightarrow^6, \bar{\bar{I}}_n, \leftarrow^2, *,$
2. $H^2, *, P(\chi), \leftarrow^3, *, \leftarrow^8, C4,$
3. $\rightarrow^2 C5,$
4. $\rightarrow^6, \bar{I}_{n+1}, A, \rightarrow^6, \bar{\bar{I}}_{n+1}, A, C2,$
5. $\rightarrow^4, I_1, Z.$

This completes the proof of the theorem that all recursive functions are *B*-computable. Thus, every recursive function is defined by a finite succession of conditions such that each condition is of one of the forms (I)—(VI) and, if it is not of one of the forms (I)—(III), the function symbols involved on the right-hand side of the condition are introduced in previous conditions. Hence, we are to assemble the programs for these conditions in a corresponding order to get the program for the final recursive function introduced by the set of conditions. Since this assembling process is mechanical, we could, if we wish, design a program to assemble the subroutines (I)—(VI) for any given definition of some recursive function. That would be a fairly simple form of "automatic programming". We shall, however, not delay over this.

We shall call a function a *B*-computable complete function if the function is defined for all argument values. It follows from the coextensiveness of *B*-computable and (partial) recursive functions that *B*-computable complete functions are exactly the general recursive functions.

We digress to comment on recursive definitions as they are given in mathematical logic. Just as we define speed functions for programs of *B* and their corresponding functions in terms of the time taken (number of steps needed) to evaluate any given input tapes, we can also define speed functions for recursive functions introduced by the schemata (I)—(VI) according to the number of steps needed to evaluate the function from a given definition, by certain standard rules (Kleene [2], p. 264, p. 326). Corresponding to each set of equations E which defines a recursive function $f(n)$, there is some speed function $f_s(n)$ which, for each constant n_0, gives an upper bound to the number of lines (derived equations) needed for deriving logically the value of $f(n_0)$ from E. Obviously each recursive function has many definitions and each definition (set of equations E) has many corresponding speed functions. It is a rather simple matter to give a corresponding speed function for each function defined by the schemata (I)—(VI). Call them (I_s)—(VI_s).

(I_s) $\phi_s(x) = 1,$

(II_s) $\phi_s(x_1, \cdots, x_n) = 1,$

(III_s) $\phi_s(x_1, \cdots, x_n) = 1,$

(IV_s) $\phi_s(x_1, \cdots, x_n) = (\chi_1)_s(x_1, \cdots, x_n) + \cdots + (\chi_m)_s(x_1, \cdots, x_n) + m + 1 + \psi_s[\chi_1(x_1, \cdots, x_n), \cdots, \chi_m(x_1, \cdots, x_n)],$

(V_s) $\begin{cases} \phi_s(1, x_2, \cdots, x_n) = \psi_s(x_2, \cdots, x_n) + 1, \\ \phi_s(z+1, x_2, \cdots, x_n) = \phi_s(z, x_2, \cdots, x_n) + 1 + \chi_s[z, \phi(z, x_2, \cdots, x_n), x_2, \cdots, x_n] + 1, \end{cases}$

(VI_s) $\phi_s(x_1, \cdots, x_n) = 1 + \sum_{i=1}^{\mu y[\chi(x_1, \cdots, x_n, y)=1]} [\chi_s(x_1, \cdots, x_n, i) + 3].$

This digression brings out the point that in many cases although a function is B-computable or recursive, we have no idea in advance how long it will take before the machine grinds out the answer, or the equations yield the desired line for each given argument. This is so even if we are only concerned with B-computable complete functions or general recursive functions. With regard to recursive functions, the indeterminate element is concentrated in schema (VI) and in the corresponding (VI_s). In order that a recursive function defined by (VI) be general recursive, there is the requirement that for all $x_1, \cdots, x_n$, *there exists* y, such that $\chi(x_1, \cdots, x_n, y) = 1$. The condition, however, gives in general no information as to how big a number y could satisfy the equation $\chi(x_1, \cdots, x_n, y) = 1$, for given $x_1, \cdots, x_n$.

The definitions for speed functions are of course not directly applicable to digital computers actually in use. It is, nonetheless, thought that these idealized definitions might give some clue to the study of more practical cases.

§ 4. Basic Instructions

From our definition of a program, if we write only a single instruction in each line, there are clearly, for every n, n^{n+4} possible $(n+2)$-lined programs, since in each line, the instruction can be any one of: $\rightarrow$, $\leftarrow$, $*$, $C1, \cdots, C(n+1)$, and the last two lines are always $n+1. \rightarrow$, $n+2. \leftarrow$.

There are other possible basic instructions which we have avoided to use. Chief among them are erasing E, the unconditional transfer Ux which instructs the machine to follow instruction x independently of the content of the square under scan, and the dual conditional transfer $C'x$ which instructs the machine to follow the instruction x when the square under scan is blank and to follow the next instruction otherwise. Of these, erasing introduces a new basic act while the transfers do not. If we leave out E, there are theoretically 16 possible types of basic instruction: if the square under scan is marked, we can do four different kinds of things, viz., $\rightarrow, \leftarrow, *$, follow instruction x for some given x; similarly if the square under scan is blank. Accordingly we have:

	1	2	3	4	5	6	7	8	9	10	11	12	13	14	15	16
*	→	→	→	→	*	*	*	*	←	←	←	←	w	w	w	w
—	→	*	←	x	→	*	←	y	→	*	←	z	→	*	←	u

The variables x, y, z, w, u can in turn take indefinitely many different values. Given N, there will be $(3+N)^2$ possible different basic instructions in any program with N lines and hence $N^{(3+N)^2}$ possible N-lined programs. The basic steps $\rightarrow, *, \leftarrow$ are respectively 1, 6, 11 in the above table, while the unconditional and the two conditional transfers are special cases of 16. In general, if we use M basic symbols (instead of just the single symbol $*$), we shall have $M+2$ basic acts ($\leftarrow, \rightarrow$ and printing each symbol), $M+1$ possible square contents, $(M+3)^{M+1}$ possible types of basic instructions, $(M+1+N)^{M+1}$ possible basic instructions for programs with N lines. If we allow erasing, the numbers will be $M+3$, $M+1$, $(M+4)^{M+1}$, $(M+2+N)^{M+1}$ respectively.

We shall confine our attention to the machine B and the seven simple types of instructions Cx, $C'x$, Ux, $\rightarrow, \leftarrow, *$, E applicable to it. A corollary of what we have proved could be described very roughly as: computations which can be performed with the help of $C'x$, Ux, E can already be done with $\rightarrow, \leftarrow, *$, Cx alone. This of course does not mean that given $\rightarrow, \leftarrow, *$, Cx, everything which can be done with $C'x$, Ux, E can also be done without them.

Indeed, there are many things which we can do when we permit erasing but which we cannot do otherwise. Erasing is dispensable only in the sense that all functions which are computable with erasing are also computable without erasing. For example, if we permit erasing, we can set up programs in such a way that if the machine begins by scanning the argument values of a function on the tape, by carrying out the program, only the function value (the answer) appears on the tape at the end of the operation, everything else having been erased. Such is obviously impossible in general, if we do not permit erasing. For example, if the answer happens to be shorter than the question.

There are simple things which can be done with the help of $C'x$ or Ux, but which Cx, $\rightarrow, \leftarrow, *$ alone cannot do. Suppose we know there is a marked square somewhere to the left of the square under scan but do not know how far away it is. We cannot construct a program with Cx, $\rightarrow$, $\leftarrow$, $*$ which will always enable us to find the nearest marked square on the left without introducing new marked squares, because given any explicit program with (say) n lines, the reading head cannot arrive at any marked square if there are n or more blank squares between the square under scan and the nearest marked square. This is so because only $\leftarrow$ can carry the reading head leftward, Cx cannot produce any periodic action unless some marked square were encountered. Yet it is easy to do the thing either with $C'x$ alone or with Ux and Cx. Thus: 1. $\leftarrow$, 2. $C'1$, this will stop when and only when a marked square is encountered. Or: 1. $\leftarrow$, 2. $C4$, 3. $U1$, 4. $\rightarrow$, 5. $\leftarrow$; the steps 4 and 5 are of course just to say "stop". Similarly, using $C'x$ only we cannot always find the nearest preceding blank if we do not know how far away it is.

Given Ux and Cx, $C'x$ is dispensable; given Ux and $C'x$, Cx is dispensable; given Cx and $C'x$, Ux is dispensable. Suppose we have a program with k lines and there is a line: $m.C'n (m, n \leqslant k)$. We can eliminate $C'n$ by modifying the line $m.C'n$ and the lines following it: if $n \geqslant m$, replace $m.C'n$ by $m.C(m+2)$, $m+1.U(n+1)$, and increase the index of every later line by 1 (replace $m+i$ by $m+i+1$); if $n<m$, replace $m.C'n$ by $m.C(m+2)$, $m+1.Un$, and increase the index of every later line by 1. In the unusual case when $k=m$, we have to add two more lines: $m+2.\rightarrow$, $m+3.\leftarrow$. Similarly, we can eliminate Cx by using Ux and $C'x$. The elimination of Ux by Cx and $C'x$ is also similar: we simply replace $m.Un$ by $m.Cn$, $m+1.C'n$ (or $m.C(n+1)$, $m+1.C'(n+1)$) and readjust later lines accordingly.

It is of interest to know that there are simple things which we cannot do even with C, C', and U. Assume we know that there is somewhere on the tape a marked square and the reading head is scanning a blank square on the tape; we wish to find a program which will always enable us to find a marked square and stop there, but introduce no new marked squares. The natural thing to suggest would, for example, be: $\rightarrow$, $\leftarrow^2$, $\rightarrow^3$, $\leftarrow^4$, etc.; in other words, look left and right in alternation. We wish to prove that no program using Cx, $C'x$, $\rightarrow$, $\leftarrow$, $*$, Ux can do this. Clearly, $*$ should be left out since we do not allow the introduction of new marked squares. We need not consider Ux, since we can replace its applications by applications of Cx and $C'x$. Assume there is a given arbitrary N-lined program with $\rightarrow$, $\leftarrow$, Cx and $C'x$. We wish to prove that it cannot do what we want. Suppose it does not contain a line of the form $m.C'n$ with $n<m$. If there are more than N squares between the nearest marked square and the square initially under scan, then such a program cannot carry us to a marked square. Hence, the only interesting case is a program which contains a line of the form $m.C'n$, $n<m$.

Let P be an arbitrary such program. We proceed to prove that there is an initial tape situation such that the initial tape contains a marked square but P does not enable us to find it. Assume P contains N lines among which K are of the form $m.C'n, n<m$. We consider first how P would behave when facing initially a completely blank tape. There are two possibilities. In carrying out the program P, either there is one of the K lines of the form $m.C'n$ $(n<m)$ which we encounter more than once, or there is none. In the second case, since only such lines enable us to return to previous lines, the whole program will be carried out in no more than $(K+1)N$ steps. Hence, if there are more than $(K+1)N$ squares between the square initially under scan and the marked square, the program P does not enable us to find the marked square. In the other case, let $m_1.C'n_1(n_1<m_1)$ be the line which, in carrying out the program, we encounter a second time at the earliest stage. We have taken no more than $(K+1)N$ steps before we encounter $m_1.C'n_1$ for the second time. Moreover, since we are assuming a tape initially blank, the steps from the first visit of the line $m_1.C'n_1$ to the second will forever repeat themselves completely. Call the square under scan at the first visit the origin. In the process of carrying out the program between the two visits, there will be (say) scanned N_1 squares to the left of the origin, N_2 to the right, and the reading head will be scanning at the second visit a square (the "new origin"), N_3 squares to, say, the right of the origin. We know that $N_1, N_2, N_3<(K+1)N$. Since the "origin" will keep on shifting to the right, we see that if the initially marked square is more than $2(K+1)N$ to the left of the square initially under scan, the program P does not enable us to find the square.

If erasing is permitted, then we have much more freedom. For example, we can design a program with $*, \rightarrow, \leftarrow, Cx, E$ only which will enable us to find some marked square if there is anywhere a marked square on the tape. Essentially, we begin with the square under scan and go left and right in alternation $(\leftarrow, \rightarrow, \leftarrow^2, \rightarrow^2, \leftarrow^3, \rightarrow^3$, etc.), marking each blank square on the left (resp. right) side if the square immediately preceding (resp. succeeding) it is also blank. When we find a marked square beyond the portions we have marked, we eliminate the marks we introduce and go back to the marked square. The routine has 42 lines:

1.$C41$, 2.$\leftarrow$, 3.$C41$, 4.$\rightarrow$, 5.$\rightarrow$, 6.$C41$; 7.$\leftarrow$, 8.$*$, 9.$\leftarrow$, 10.$\leftarrow$, 11.$C24$, 12.$\rightarrow$, 13.$*$, 14.$\rightarrow$, 15.$C14$, 16.$\rightarrow$, 17.$C33$, 18.$\leftarrow$, 19.$*$, 20.$\leftarrow$, 21.$C20$, 22.$\rightarrow$, 23.$C9$, 24.$\rightarrow$, 25.$\rightarrow$, 26.$C25$, 27.$\leftarrow$, 28.E, 29.$\leftarrow$, 30.$C28$, 31.$\leftarrow$, 32.$C41$, 33.$\leftarrow$, 34.$\leftarrow$, 35.$C34$, 36.$\rightarrow$, 37.E, 38.$\rightarrow$, 39.$C37$, 40.$\rightarrow$, 41.$\rightarrow$, 42.$\leftarrow$.

Given erasing, we can also derive Cx and $C'x$ from each other. We prove how it is possible that given any program using $\rightarrow, \leftarrow, *, Cx, C'x, Ux, E$ we can find a program using $\rightarrow, \leftarrow, *, Cx, E$ which performs the same function. As we have shown before, we can eliminate Ux by Cx and $C'x$. Now we wish to eliminate also $C'x$. Take the first occurrence of $C'x$ in the given program. Suppose the line is $m.C'n$ and suppose $n<m$. We construct the new program by (i) leaving the lines 1 to $n-1$ unchanged; (ii) replace lines n and $n+1$ by: $n.C(n+2)$, $n+1.E$; (iii) renumber the

original lines n to $m-1$ as $n+2$ to $m+1$ respectively; (iv) replace the original line m by: $m+2.C(m+5)$, $m+3.*$, $m+4.C(n+1)$; (v) renumber all the original lines $m+i$ as $m+i+4$; (vi) adjust references to these lines in other conditional transfers accordingly. We leave it to the reader to verify that the new program does the same thing as the original. If $n \geqslant m$, similar constructions can be made. Repeating the process, we can eliminate all occurrences of $C'x$.

It appears unlikely that we could delete any of the four types of basic operations $*, Cx, \rightarrow, \leftarrow$ without adding other operations instead, and still compute all recursive functions. To give an exact proof of the indispensability of each of the four types of instruction, we could proceed as in §2: represent all possible tape contents by positive integers, consider all the possible programs obtained by using only three of the four basic types of instruction, survey all the possible transformations which these programs can perform on initial input tapes, and prove that they do not include all recursive functions. For instance, suppose we use only $*$, Cx, and $\rightarrow$. Consider, for simplicity, just functions of one argument. First, we use a simple function $g(x)$ which maps the set of all possible input tape contents (or a simple recursive subset of it) into the set of positive integers. Then we need another simple function $h(x)$ which maps all the possible final output tape contents into the set of positive integers. Analogously with the functions θ_π, τ_π in §2, we can define a function $\Delta_\pi(x)$ such that $\Delta_\pi(g(\iota))$ gives the number of the output content for an arbitrary program made out of $*, Cx, \rightarrow$, with number π, and an arbitrary input tape content with number ι. It then follows that, for every program Π (with number π) on such a machine, $h[\Delta_\pi(g(\iota))]$ is the function computed by it. It could then be shown, on account of the form of $\Delta_\pi(x)$, that only very simple recursive functions can be represented in the form $h[\Delta_\pi(g(\iota))]$. For example, if h, g are primitive recursive, then all one-placed general recursive functions which can be expressed in the form $h[\Delta_\pi(g(\iota))]$ are primitive recursive. Instead of trying to work out details of the argument, we present intuitive arguments relative to the particular way of representing questions and answers we use.

The necessity of $*$ can be argued on perfectly general ground. Thus, it seems reasonable to represent the same argument values in the same way even when we are concerned with different functions. Moreover, to be unambiguous, we must not interpret the same final tape output as different answers for different questions. This excludes the possibility of reading answers directly from the questions (data) initially given on the tape. For example, given 3 and 5, we may wish to get the value of $3+5$ or the value of 3^5. If the programs for addition and exponentiation yielded the same final tape situation for the given argument values 3 and 5, we would not be allowed to say, "well, it depends on how you read the result, it is $3+5$ if you read it one way, etc." This condition is sufficient to indicate that $*$ is indispensable. Without $*$, the answers must always be the same as the questions are the same as one another for the same argument values.

If we use only →, ←, *, we would get the same changes from the initial tape content for all different argument values of the same function, as we exercise no judgment over the initial question and make no choice from the possible alternative courses. Roughly then a program for a function would only serve as a name for the function rather than provide a method for computing its values. Take, for example, the function $m \times n$. There is no program for it, because given any program made out of →, ←, *, it has only a fixed number N of occurrences of the instruction *, and, for any given m and n, no more than $m+n+N$ *'s can occur on the final tape, although we can easily find m_1 and n_1 such that $m_1 \times n_1 > m+n+N$.

To prove that ← is indispensable, we assume that we have only →, *, Cx on the machine. Such a machine would have a rather restricted memory since the reading-writing head cannot go back (leftwards) and consult what it did to previous squares. Assume a given program Π. At each square, the head can only do two things: * and →. Since we assume that the initial tape contains only finitely many marked squares, if we let the head begin by scanning a square within the marked region, the result of performing Π will either have the head stop within the marked region of the input tape or have it continue to go in some periodic manner or have it operate on an additional portion which has a bound that depends only on Π but is independent of the initial tape situation (i.e., the given argument values). Consider again the function $m \times n$. Suppose a program Π of N lines is given which is intended to compute it, the head begins by scanning a square in the printed portion of the input tape. If the head stops within the initially printed portion, we of course do not get the value of $m \times n$. Assume, therefore, the head has left that region and is scanning a blank to the right of that region and is going to perform line k of the program Π. The interesting point is that, once the head is scanning the open, no single conditional transfer Cx in Π can function twice without introducing a circular loop. Thus, if the i-th line is Cx and it is to function twice, then each time it must be scanning the rightmost marked square and goes to the x-th line in Π. Since there is no ←, if the machine comes back to the i-th line again and the square under scan is again marked, it must repeat the whole process and come back to the i-th line once more scanning a marked square. If no conditional transfer can function twice, then since there are at most N conditional transfers in Π which has only N lines, and since transfer can at most make the machine repeat N lines, there can be at most N^2 steps and at most N^2 new *'s can be marked in the new region of the tape, provided we wish to exclude circular loops. Since no circular loop should occur in a program for $m \times n$ and since we can always find m_1, n_1 such that the value of $m_1 \times n_1$ is greater than N^2, there is no program with →, *, Cx only which can compute the function $m \times n$.

For similar reasons, → is indispensable; and also we cannot compute all recursive functions with just Ux →, ←, * (replacing Cx by the unconditional transfer). It is, however, not known to the author whether $C'x$, $\rightarrow$, $\leftarrow$, $*$ are sufficient in some nontrivial sense. For instance, if we use the method of representing computations developed in the preceding section, it is not clear how $C'x$ can enable us to go through an indefinitely long string of marked squares or whether that is not necessary. One might wish to reverse the roles of blanks and marked squares; but then we have to replace $*$ by E. Rather trivially, E, $\rightarrow$, $\leftarrow$, $C'x$ give a sufficient set from duality considerations.

We note that there is an interesting machine (call it "machine W") which is closely related to machine B but much easier to use: add erasing, so that W has five types of basic operations, viz. $\rightarrow$, $\leftarrow$, $*$, Cx, E. As we have shown above, the instructions Ux and $C'x$ can be derived from these so that we can freely use them too. That all recursive functions are computable on such a machine follows directly from our result on B-computability. Indeed, from Kleene [2] and our constructions in the preceding section, it is fairly obvious that for machine W, we do not need the auxiliary squares, and we can so arrange the matter that in computing a recursive function for given arguments, if the machine stops at all, it will stop with a string of marked squares whose number is exactly the answer sought. In this way, we get a more or less unique natural normal representation of questions and answers. For most purposes, it would seem more attractive to use machine W than machine B.

It remains an open question whether we can dispense with auxiliary squares and still be able to compute all recursive functions by programs consisting of only basic steps $\rightarrow$, $\leftarrow$, $*$, Cx. Of course, it is not necessary to use every other square as the auxiliary square. If we do not mind complications, we can take any fixed n and use every n-th square as the auxiliary square.

§5. Universal Turing Machines

The basic machine B (or the machine W) is fictitious not only in that it assumes an indefinitely expandable tape (which may be viewed as a serial storage), but also because no finite internal storage (a parallel storage) is adequate for storing every program that is involved in proving that all (partial) recursive functions are B-computable. In the proof, we allow ourselves the privilege of using, for every n, programs with more than n instruction words. To many, this assumption of an indefinite parallel storage whose units all are accessible at any moment is even more repulsive than permitting the tape to expand as needed.

One way to get around this difficulty about storage units is to use, instead of the general-purpose machine B for all recursive functions, one special-purpose machine M_i for each recursive function f_i. Thus, for each function f_i, we have available a program for the machine B which will compute values of the function by following the program. Instead of using the storage unit to keep the instructions, we can construct a machine M_i which will carry out the particular program automatically every time it is scanning a tape. Such special-purpose machines could be machines for doing just addition, machines for doing just multiplication, and so on. These correspond more closely than B to what are known as Turing machines.

There is also a method of using a single machine with a finite internal storage unit on which all B-computable functions can be computed. This is by using what Turing calls a universal machine. Intuitively it is very plausible that we can design such universal machines, because, since we have one infinite serial storage (the tape) anyway, we can trade the unbounded internal storage for additional tape by having programs for particular functions stored on the tape.

On the basic machine B, several different programs can, of course, compute the same function in the sense that confronted with the same initial argument values, the programs always yield the same rightmost number on the tape. Therefore, since we can build a corresponding special-purpose machine for each program, we may also have many structurally different machines which correspond to the same function.

Roughly, a universal machine is one which can do what every special-purpose machine does. This it does by imitating in a uniform manner each special-purpose machine M_i and is therefore, different from the basic machine B which permits flexibility in the programs. A universal machine is a machine built specially for the purpose of imitation. We may either store a fixed program in the internal storage of machine B once and for all or build the program into the machine and dispense with the internal storage unit altogether. The universal machine is like a special-purpose machine in that it has only a serial storage (the tape); it is, nevertheless, general-purpose by having the programs for individual functions transported to the tape.

It is possible to construct a universal machine U which is again only capable of the four types of basic instructions. Or to put it differently, it is possible to write up a program for the machine B such that when scanning a tape which contains in addition to the argument values of a function, also a number which represents (a program or its corresponding special-purpose machine for) the function, the machine B, by following the program, will imitate the behavior of the particular machine for the function and compute the value of the function for the arguments given on the tape.

Since many special-purpose machines may correspond to one function, it is desirable to distinguish a functional universal machine and a structural one: the former is able to imitate all special-purpose machines in the sense that there is an effective method of representing every special-purpose machine (or even just at least one machine for each function) on the tape such that afterwards it will yield the same answer for the same question, while the latter is able to do more in that it also imitates the moves (or the carrying out of the program steps) of the special-purpose machine in question. It follows that a functional universal machine need only imitate at least one of the many possible special-purpose machines (or programs) for each function to the extent of yielding the same answers to the same questions. For instance, on a functional universal machine it is permissible to represent all different special-purpose machines corresponding to the same function by the same initial tape situation. Every structural universal machine is a functional one, but not vice versa. Actually it is a little harder to construct a structural universal machine, while a functional universal machine can be derived more or less as an immediate corollary of the results of §3 and known results in recursive function theory. We shall leave the former which is quite complex for the next chapter and discuss merely the latter here. Either of these will yield a positive solution to the question which Professor G. W. Patterson raised in conversation: is it possible to design a one-tape nonerasing universal Turing machine? As a matter of fact, he probably had in mind a direct construction of a structural universal machine.

Since the B-computable functions are all and only the partial recursive functions, it seems sufficient to use the following result of recursive function theory: there is an effective correlation of all definitions for recursive functions with positive integers (called their Gödel numbers) such that for every n, there is a recursive function $V_n(z, x_1, \cdots, x_n)$, often written $U(\mu_y T_n(z, x_1, \cdots, x_n, y))$, which has the property that for every n-placed recursive function $f_e(x_1, \cdots, x_n)$ with the Gödel number e, $V_n(e, x_1, \cdots, x_n)$ coincides with $f_e(x_1, \cdots, x_n)$, for all the argument values $x_1, \cdots, x_n$ for which f_e is defined (Kleene [2], p. 330). Since the functions $V_n(z, x_1, \cdots, x_n)$ are recursive, they are B-computable. We can therefore find a program on the machine B or alternatively construct a special-purpose machine for each $V_n (n=1, 2, \cdots)$ which will compute every n-placed recursive function once we put its Gödel number on the input tape.

An obvious defect of this is that we do not have a really functional universal machine, but one for all singulary B-computable functions, one for all binary functions, etc. It is, however, known that every recursive function can be reduced to a singulary function because we can effectively enumerate for every n all n-tuples of positive integers and introduce recursive functions $[\ ]_1, \cdots, [\ ]_n$, so that $[x]_i$ is the i-th number of the x-th n-tuple, and we can reduce an n-placed function $f(x_1, \cdots, x_n)$ to the one-placed function $f([x]_1, \cdots, [x]_n)$. One might, therefore, wish to say that $V_1(z, x)$ is already a universal function except for the slight drawback that functions with different arguments, which we ordinarily regard as different, may become indistinguishable. Thus, for example, two different functions $g(x, y)$ and $h(x, y, z)$ may satisfy the conditions $g([x]_1, [x]_2) = f(x)$ and $h([x]_1, [x]_2, [x]_3) = f(x)$, for the same function $f(x)$; then $f(x)$, $g(x, y)$, $h(x, y, z)$ become indistinguishable.

To remedy this, we seem to need a recursive or B-computable function with indefinitely many arguments. This is a rather natural notion if we think in terms of the machines (say, the machine B). Given an input containing a sequence of number expressions, the machine will first count the number of number expressions and then proceed in a uniform manner to calculate the function value, taking into consideration the number of arguments initially given. On the other hand, it is also not unnatural to reconstrue the schemata (II)—(VI) for defining recursive functions to include cases with indefinitely many arguments. For instance, we may wish to use $\sum_1^n x_i$ or $\prod_1^n x_i$ for indefinite n. Indeed, it can be proved exactly that if we allow for functions with indefinitely many arguments, recursiveness and B-computability are still coextensive. Thus, if we permit each function in the schemata (II)—(VI) to contain indefinitely many parameters, we can still, with some extra care, prove that all recursive functions in the extended sense are B-computable in the sense that for each such function $f(x_1, \cdots, x_n)$, we can get a program of machine B so that given $x_1, \cdots, x_n$ for arbitrary n on the tape, we can get by the program the value of $f(x_1, \cdots, x_n)$. Since this is not important for our principal result, we shall not enter into details. In the next chapter (on the structural universal machine), we shall have occasion to see more explicitly how a function with indefinitely many arguments can be computed.

Meanwhile, we assume given a recursive function $g_n(x_1, \cdots, x_n)$ (and a program for computing it) whose value is k if and only if for every $n, x_1, \cdots, x_n, (x_1, \cdots, x_n)$ is the k-th n-tuple (of positive integers). Then we define $V(z, x_1, \cdots, x_n) = V_1(z, g_n(x_1, \cdots, x_n))$. There is then a program on the machine B for computing V, since we have programs for V_1 and g. The special-purpose machine realizing the program for V is then a functional universal machine.

Each special-purpose machine, including the functional universal machine for V, as well as the structural universal machine not described here, can be realized physically, for example, by modifying the specification of an idealized computer in Burks and Copi [3]. In each case, we can either construct the machine B (or the machine W) with its internal storage suitably restricted and store the program for the particular machine in the internal storage once and for all, or simply construct a physical realization of the program and dispense with an internal storage altogether. So far as the physical realization of a universal Turing machine is concerned, the one proposed by Moore [4] requires much less physical equipment than either of the two universal machines we envisage. Ours are of interest in that we have reduced the number of different types of basic instructions to a bare minimum. It should be clear that any actual general-purpose digital computer could be viewed as a realization of the machine B (or W), provided we imagine that the internal storage could be expanded as much as we wish.

Incidentally, in our previous considerations, we have assumed that at each stage only finitely many squares are marked. If we permit arbitrary distributions of infinitely many initially marked squares on the tape, we can, roughly speaking, compute values of a function recursive relative to the arbitrary function determined by the initial tape situation (we have, in Turing's terminology, an oracle machine).

§ 6. Theorem-Proving Machines

In conclusion, we permit ourselves to speculate a bit wildly and make a few idle general comments.

While mathematical logic had often been criticized for its uselessness, most professional logicians do not seem to have been overwhelmed by the extensive application of logic to the construction and use of computing machines in recent years. There is a strong feeling that the useful part of logic does not coincide or even overlap with the interesting part; or even a suspicion that what is interesting in logic is not useful, what is useful is not interesting. Yet it cannot be denied that there is a great deal of similarity between the interests and activities of logicians on the one side and designers and users of computers on the other. Both groups are interested in making thoughts articulate, in formalization and mechanization of more or less vague ideas. Certainly logicians are not more precise and accurate than the machine people who are being punished for their errors more directly and more vividly. Just as logicians speak of theorems and metatheorems, there are programs and metaprograms. Just as logicians distinguish between using and mentioning a word, automatic coding must observe the distinction between using an instruction and talking about it. Just as logicians contrast primitive propositions with derived rules of inference, there is the distinction between basic commands and subroutines. Shouldn't there be some deeper bond between logic and the development of computers?

What strikes the eye but is probably not of much theoretical interest is the possibility of using machines to perform known decision procedures.

It is known that in a number of domains of logic and mathematics, there are decision procedures, i.e., effective procedures by which, given any statement in these domains, we can decide in a finite number of steps whether or not it is a theorem. Examples include elementary geometry and algebra, arithmetic with merely addition or merely multiplication, theory of truth functions, monadic predicate calculus. Intutitively, to have an effective procedure for decision amounts to the possibility of constructing a machine to make the decision. It is theoretically possible, for each of the known decision procedures, to construct one machine to perform it. For example, this has been done for the theory of truth functions. And it is only economic and engineering considerations which have thus far prevented the construction of machines to perform the other decision procedures. There is, therefore, the fairly interesting problem of constructing, for instance, a machine for monadic predicate calculus. This would be more properly a "logic machine" because, as is often asserted, all syllogistic inferences can be carried out in monadic predicate calculus.

A related, and probably more practical, problem is to try to program these decision procedures on the ordinary general-purpose computers. These can perhaps lead to two kinds of useful results: (a) a library of subroutines for all or most of the known decision procedures that is ready for use, sometimes with slight modifications, for most ordinary computers now in existence; (b) certain operations which are often needed in programming the decision procedures may lead to the addition or modification of the basic operations in computing machines; for example, it may lead to the replacement of one or more operations by a more useful new operation.

The trouble with these questions is not that they are inhumanly difficult but rather that they are neither urgent for practical purposes nor intellectually sufficiently exciting. In contrast, the questions involved in the imitation of mind by machine or in the attempt to study the philosophy of mind by comparing mind with machine are surely fascinating but quite often we cannot even formulate the problems clearly, or, when we have more specific problems such as mechanical translation or chess-playing, there is little basic conceptual difficulty but a good deal of "engineering" tasks which require a large amount of skilled labour.

What has been discussed less frequently is the possibility of using machines to aid theoretical mathematical research on a large scale. One main contribution of mathematical logic is the setting up of a standard of rigour which is, at least by intention, in mechanical terms. Thus, we learn from mathematical logic that most theorems of mathematics can be proved mechanically within certain axiom systems which are formalistically rather simple. It follows that most mathematical problems can be viewed as inquiring whether certain statements follow from certain axioms, or, since proofs and theorems of any given axiom system can be enumerated effectively, whether certain statements occur in such enumerations. In other words, while in a computation problem, we ask what the value of a computable complete function $f(x)$ is, for some given value of x; in a provability problem, we ask whether there exists some x, such that $f(x)$ is the given number. In order to answer the first question for a given number n_0, we need only carry out the procedure for $f(x)$ as applied to n_0; in order to answer the second question for a given n_0, we have to compute $f(1)$, $f(2)$, $f(3)$, etc., until we arrive, by luck, at a number x_0 such that $f(x_0)=n_0$. If it happens that n_0 is not a theorem, we shall never be able to stop in our search for n_0 from the values of $f(1)$, $f(2)$, etc. In terms of recursive function theory, our question is to ask whether a number belongs to a given recursively enumerable set (i.e., the set of all numbers y such that there exists some $x, f(x)=y$, where f is a given general recursive function).

To come back to the function $f(x)$ which enumerates theorems, since it is general recursive, it is by our main theorem a B-computable complete function and has a program $\Pi(f)$ on the machine B. It is not hard to devise a new program, using $\Pi(f)$, which will test for every given number n_0 whether there exists some x, such that $f(x)=n_0$. Roughly the program does this: write down the number n_0 on the tape and, after a big gap, the number 1, apply $\Pi(f)$, and then compare its result with n_0, if same, stop and write 1, otherwise, write 2 (in general, copy preceding argument value and add 1), and apply $\Pi(f)$, compare result with n_0, if same, stop and write 1, otherwise, etc. Since we can define a procedure on the machine B for comparing two numbers, we can get the desired program. In this way we get a partial recursive function $f_e(y)$ such that $f_e(y)=1$ if and only if there exists a number x, $f(x)=y$; otherwise, $f_e(y)$ is undefined. Thus, given any axiom system (e.g., for arithmetic, or for set theory, or for analysis), we can devise a program or construct a special-purpose machine so that feeding any statement in the notation of the system into the machine will eventually produce an answer 1, if and only if the statement happens to be a theorem.

The standard objections against studying mathematics by such machines are twofold: since our interest is to decide whether a particular statement is a theorem, the method is in general futile as we can never run through the infinitely many arguments for the function f and unless we happen to be fortunate to get a positive result, we shall never know the answer no matter how long we run; secondly, even when the answer happens to be yes, it will be usually a long, long time before we hit upon the answer, since we have to examine all the possible proofs. In reply, we may observe that there are often rather modest aims of research which can be aided more directly, and even in the questions of discovering more ambitious theorems, there is no reason why shortcuts in the testing procedure, elimination of superfluous cases, and technological advancement will not bring the tasks within the range of practical feasibility.

So far as modest research goals are concerned, we may give a few examples. A good deal of brain power has been spent on studying the independence of axioms in the propositional calculus. Apparently there is in general no decision method for such questions. Yet in most cases the independence could be proved by matrices of a few rows and columns (usually less than 5 rows and 5 columns), or disproved by rather short derivations from the initial axioms and rules of inference. Since the matrices and the derivations can be listed and tested mechanically, there is little doubt machines can greatly aid such researches. More generally, we often wish to test whether an alleged proof is correct. If the proof were presented in full detail as in some books on mathematical logic, a machine test would be immediate. The problem becomes more interesting when, as is usual, the alleged proof is only presented in sketch. The situation is rather like (say) picking 20 lines from a proof of 1000 lines. The problem is more or less one of reconstructing 1000 lines from the 20 lines which are given. When an alleged proof is wrong, we can no longer reconstruct a proof out of the 20 lines. Yet, if, for example, we can handle all proofs in a system with less than 100 lines, then it is very probable that we can handle most proofs with 1000 lines when we are given a summary of 20 lines for each proof. Or again, sometimes we suspect that a statement is either a theorem with a short proof or not a theorem at all. Sometimes we feel that a certain statement is a theorem and that certain statements are necessary in its proof. In such cases, the machine usually only has to accomplish a more restricted task in order to confirm and disprove our hunches. In many cases, we should not ask the machine to check all possible cases, but just to perform certain "crucial experiments" in order, for example, to disentangle a few exceedingly confusing steps when we are convinced that our main direction is correct.

A fundamental result of Herbrand has the effect that any derivation of a theorem in a consistent axiom system corresponds to a truth-functional tautology of a form related to the statement of the theorem and the axioms of the system in a predetermined way. This and the possibility already mentioned of viewing axiom systems as proof-grinding machines can both be used to bring about the application of computing machines to the investigation of the question of derivability in general, and inconsistency (i.e., derivability of contradictions) in particular of axiom systems. There is, of course, no reason why we should wish to deny ourselves the privilege of introducing ingenious devices to reduce the great complexity of the combinatorial problems involved in such applications of machines. When machines are extensively used as aids to mathematical discoveries, we shall have a more objective standard of originality of ideas in terms of the magnitude of labour required for a machine to discover them.

If we compare, for example, such possible applications with programming machines to play chess or checkers, the proving machines or proving programs have at least this much advantage on their side: our opponent is Nature or, if one prefers, the platonic world of ideas whose predominant purpose is not, as far as we know, to defeat us at the game.

Surely the dimension of magnitude which we are initially concerned with is staggering: there are so many possible proofs in any interesting axiom system, there are so many truth-functional tautologies. But how do we know whether significant assistance to mathematical research will or will not emerge from such application of machines until preliminary probing has been undertaken on a fairly large scale? If it were thought that such application would have direct bearing on military or business activities, more incentive for looking into it would undoubtedly have been manufactured to direct major effort to the question. Who knows but that such combined application of machines and mathematical logic will not, in the long run, turn out to be more efficient aid to the advance of science, even for the purpose of bigger bombs, longer range missiles, or more attractive automobiles? The logicians on their part will certainly feel happy when other mathematicians find logic an indispensable tool for their own researches. Or perhaps applications of logic in the theory and use of machines will generate interesting new logic just as physics generates important new mathematics.

We often feel that we cannot design machines which are more clever than their designers. We feel that there is an essential difference between such a task and that of designing machines which are physically stronger than their designers. The concept of proving machines shows that this is not so. If, for example Fermat's or Goldbach's conjecture is indeed provable in one of the usual formal systems of mathematics, there is nothing absurd about the belief that a proof will be first discovered by a machine. The important point is that we are trading qualitative difficulty for quantitative complexity. On account of the great restriction on the mind's ability to handle quantitative complexities, we find it more necessary to rely on insight, ingenuity, and vague intuition. Using machines, we find our ability in this respect increased tremendously and it is but natural to expect that we can then go a longer way even with less ingenuity. The grinding out of proofs and the *selection* of the right ones (i.e., the comparison of their conclusions with proposed conjectures) are both mechanically simple procedures. There is no difficulty in imagining that such machines will be more clever than man in performing the tasks of discovery of theorems and confirmation of conjectures faster and more reliably.

We can instruct a proving machine to select and print out theorems which are short but require long proofs (the "deep" theorems). We can also similarly instruct machines to generate interesting conjectures: e.g., short statements which are neither provable nor refutable by proofs of a preassigned high upper bound of complexity; presumably Fermat's and Goldbach's conjectures will occur in some such class with a fairly high bound.

There is a reasonable sense in which the basic machine B or a universal Turing machine can solve all solvable mathematical problems and prove all provable mathematical statements. Thus, if there is a proof for a mathematical statement, it must be, as a proof, expressible in exact terms, beginning with accepted statements and continuing in a systematic manner. We have therefore a program on the machine B which will lead from the initial statements (axioms) to the conclusion.

If we compare Gauss with a universal Turing machine in regard to their mathematical abilities, we have to admit that Gauss, unlike the imagined machine, did not have an infinite mind or an infinite memory. But then he did not have to solve all problems either. What is peculiar is rather that he could create so much more mathematics with a brain by no means proportionally larger than that of an average man. One would have to be considerably more clever if he were to design a machine of a given size to imitate Gauss (in his mathematical activities) rather than an average college mathematics student. But at the present stage, we may feel that the difference is relatively small compared with the gap between a "student mathematics machine" and any digital computer currently in operation.

REFERENCES

[1] A. M. Turing, On computable numbers, *Proc. London Math. Soc.*, Series 2, **24** (1936), 230—265.

[2] S. C. Kleene, Introduction to Metamathematics, Princeton, 1952.

[3] A. W. Burks and I. M. Copi, The logical design of an idealized general-purpose computer, *Jour. Franklin Inst.*, **261** (1956), 299—314, 421—436.

[4] E. F. Moore, A simplified universal Turing machine, *Proc. ACM*, Sept. 8, 1952, 1953.

CHAPTER VII

UNIVERSAL TURING MACHINES: AN EXERCISE IN CODING*

In a previous paper [1], we have studied a basic machine *B* that is an example from a large class of similar machines which we shall refer to as the two-storage general machines. The characteristics of this class are as follows. (i) Each two-storage general machine has an indefinitely expandable internal parallel storage to keep the program, and an indefinitely expandable tape that is divided into a sequence of squares, to be used for input, output, computation, and storage of intermediate data. (ii) Each machine has a (reading-writing) head which scans one and only one square of the tape at every moment and which can perform every one of a predetermined finite class of types of action including at least shift left one square, shift right one square, one way of changing the content of the square under its scan (e.g. making a given mark or erasing). (iii) There is a control element which at every moment attends to one and only one program step (in particular, the first step at the beginning of the operation) and the square currently under the scan of the reading head; in accordance with the step and the content of the square under attention, the control element also either directs the reading head to perform one of its acts or shifts itself to attend to a different program step specified in the step currently observed; we may imagine that the movement of the reading head or the control element always takes place between two time units. (iv) Each square on the tape is capable of at least two states; the control element and the permissible program steps are such that the control element is sometimes capable of choosing from two or more preassigned alternative program steps as the next to follow according to the state of the square currently under scan; in particular, if one of the two alternative next steps is always the immediately following in the original program, then the state of the scanned square which is capable of producing a jump must be among those states which can be introduced by the possible actions of the reading head.

The basic machine *B* is a minimum among those which satisfy these conditions: its reading-writing head can only do three things,

* This chapter appeared in *Zeitsch. f. math. Logik u. Grundlagen d. Math.*, **3** (1957), 69—80.

viz., shift left, shift right, mark the scanned square; each square is capable of only two states, viz., marked or blank; there is only one type of choosing from two alternative courses, viz., the conditional transfer which makes a jump when the scanned square is marked (a state which can be introduced by an action of the head). In general, a two-storage general machine may differ from B in many ways: each square may be capable of an arbitrary preassigned number n of states; the head may be capable of writing other symbols and making other motions; there may be different predetermined ways of choosing from alternative courses. (Compare [1], § 4) Indeed, we could even relax the definition of two-storage general machines by permitting an n-dimensional (rather than the one-dimensional tape) surface or body, or by allowing the control element to scan at every moment an arbitrary preassigned number n of squares.

It follows from our considerations in [1] that all computation problems can be solved by every two-storage general machine. Let us now take two arbitrary such machines P and Q, not necessarily distinct. We assert that we can always find a fixed program Π on Q such that with a fairly direct representation of programs of P on the tape, the program Π will enable the machine Q to imitate all the behaviours of P. Since the program Π is fixed once and for all, we can build it into the machine and dispense with the internal storage altogether. In this way, we have, for any two-storage general machines P, Q a serial storage general machine $U_{p,q}$, commonly known as a universal Turing machine, which can imitate all the behaviours of the machine P by moving the programs onto the tape. The problem is clearly one of finding a suitable program on the machine Q. In general, the order of magnitude of the task is proportional to the simplicity (or economy) of the basic instructions of P, and inversely proportional to that of Q. In other words, for fixed Q, the fewer types of basic instructions permitted in P, the easier to find $U_{p,q}$; for fixed P, the more types of basic instructions permitted in Q, the easier to find $U_{p,q}$. In particular, we can let the machine P itself be the Q machine and seek to construct $U_{p,p}$.

The particular problem which we shall solve is to find $U_{b,b}$, taking the basic machine B both as P and as Q. It would be much easier if we were to take as Q the machine W, which is the same as B except for allowing erasing as an additional basic instruction. Not only is $U_{b,w}$ easier to obtain than $U_{b,b}$, even $U_{w,w}$ is easier to design than $U_{b,b}$. If the reader is a programmer, he may wish to test his ability and patience by coding for $U_{b,w}$ or $U_{w,w}$, or by finding a more elegant program for $U_{b,b}$ than the one which we shall give in this paper. If he is also a designer, he might even tackle the task of actually realizing such machines physically. Such exercises should be of general interest since they do not presuppose experience with any particular computers actually in use. We might imagine some journal or institution sponsoring a contest on such programs and designs; the skill of the authors can be judged by the elegance of their proposals, according to suitably chosen criteria. If such a race were held, it would not be unlikely that the program $U_{b,b}$, to be described, will rank rather low in the listing.

Some apology seems called for in paying a high price to avoid erasing. The simplest and perhaps also the strongest is to say that it is rather satisfying to realize that while erasing makes computation much easier, it is theoretically dispensable. To argue that standard teletype tapes which do not permit erasing are cheaper than magnetic tapes which do appears a bit far-fetched, since, at least at the present stage of technology, we probably do not wish to use universal Turing machines on a large scale anyway, and it is not clear wheter the cheaper price does compensate in cost the additional complexity. Maybe there will be a time in the future when certain equipments are found which are otherwise most efficient but do not permit erasing or can only allow erasing to be performed with speed many times slower than other acts; then the dispensability of erasing will be of practical significance.

There is a rather complex "reproducing" relation involved in universal Turing machines. Thus, since $U_{b,b}$ can imitate every program on the two-storage general machine B, it can also imitate the particular program U of B which determines $U_{b,b}$ itself. If, therefore, the particular program U is represented on the tape by U', then every possible action of $U_{b,b}$ is mirrored by some possible action of $U_{b,b}$ with U' on the tape. Moreover, this situation can further be mirrored if we represent the initial tape content U' by U'' and put both U' and U'' on the tape in the machine $U_{b,b}$.

A somewhat simpler and truer reproducing machine has been discussed by von Neumann in [2]. We summarize briefly his argument. We can construct machines from suitable basic parts by a few simple operations such as connecting two parts together (soldering, etc.). It is, therefore, possible to design and construct a machine-building machine M which can follow instructions in its internal storage to build machines. There is no difficulty in introducing the instruction for building the machine M itself and thereby producing a replica of itself. The only complication is that (say) the slip of paper which contains the instruction is not in the replica. In order to get this, we can adjunct to the machine M a special-purpose machine which afterwards always copies the instruction in the machine-building machine M, and insert it into the machine just built. This enlarged machine M' which contains M as a part can reproduce itself. If we insert the instruction for building M into M, then the whole machine M' will produce a replica of the machine M including the instruction. If we insert the instruction for building M' into M, then the whole machine M' will produce a complete replica of M' including the instruction for building M' inserted at the beginning.

To get a different model of animal reproduction, one might wish to extend this procedure of von Neumann's by permitting growth in the child machine. This feature of growth is, incidentally, at the heart of the distinction between finite automata and Turing machines. Every Turing machine, in particular the universal machine $U_{b,b}$, is finite at every moment but continues to grow if at every moment we regard as a proper part of the machine only those squares on the tape which have been scanned at least once up to that moment. It would, therefore, appear that a universal Turing machine is a closer model of the human brain than the machine M' is a model of the animal body. We can combine a universal Turing machine with a machine-building machine so that the resulting machine H can both compute and build. Among the building activities is included as special case the addition of new parts to the machine itself. Thus the child machine H contains the minimum equipment which has the innate ability to compute and build; the squares on one or two tapes come initially from outside (the environment) and become acquired experience only after they have been scanned, and suitable actions have been performed in response to them. The machine is capable of growth in two ways: the increase of scanned squares, and the addition of new parts to the body in response to suitable new tape squares imported from outside (the programs). Although the machine is capable of growth and doing other things, what it actually does or whether it does anything at all depends on the environment. In particular, it will reproduce only if the environment supplies suitable tape squares which make up a program for reproduction. What these tape squares will be are in general arbitrary and beyond the control of the machine. In order to account for the difference in the innate ability of different individuals, we remind ourselves that we can design different universal Turing machines and machine-constructing machines, some of which are more efficient than others.

It is time to turn to our main task of specifying the machine $U_{b,b}$ by a program on the machine B.

Our problem is to find a program U on B and a uniform method of representing on tape programs and tape contents such that given any program Π of B and any initial tape content, I, if they are represented on the tape according to the uniform method, then the program U will produce a tape whose final portion represents the complete tape content which would eventually be produced by Π operating on

I. In particular, the one will never stop if and only if the other will never stop.

In [1] we have given an exact definition of programs of *B*. It suffices, however, to say that a program of *B* is a program each of its lines is either * (mark the square under scan), or → (shift right one square), or ← (shift left one square), or a conditional transfer. For example, the following is a program:

$$\Pi\text{:}\quad 1.\ C3,\quad 2.\ \rightarrow,\quad 3.\ C2,\quad 4.\ *.$$

Alternatively we may represent it as a finite set of ordered pairs $\langle a, b\rangle$:

$$\{\langle 1, 3\rangle, \langle 2, \rightarrow\rangle, \langle 3, 2\rangle, \langle 4, *\rangle\}.$$

The uniform method of representing programs and tape contents to be imitated is as follows. We shall represent *, →, ← by 1, 2, 3 respectively and *Cn* by $n + 3$. Hence, the program Π will be represented by: $\{\langle 1, 6\rangle, \langle 2, 2\rangle, \langle 3, 5\rangle, \langle 4, 1\rangle\}$. Then we represent 1 by *-, 2 by *-*-, etc., using -- to separate two numbers. On the other hand, for the tape contents to be imitated, we shall always represent * by *--*, and - by ---*. We shall mark the beginning of the program by a prefix **------, its end by ----**. The square under scan is marked by a string of 4 stars **** to the right. The end of a tape portion that is treated as a unit is to be marked by ----**.

What is intended can most easily be seen by an example. We shall illustrate our whole procedure by a single example in which the program is Π and the initial consecutive tape portion which includes all initially marked squares and the square initially under scan is:

$$I\text{:}\ *-\overset{\downarrow}{*}*.$$

We easily see that the history of the operation of Π on *I* can be described simply:

program	step under attention	tape situation
S_1	1	$*-\overset{\downarrow}{*}*$
S_2	3	$*-\overset{\downarrow}{*}*$
S_3	2	$*-\overset{\downarrow}{*}*$
S_4	3	$*-\overset{\downarrow}{*}*$
S_5	2	$*-*\overset{\downarrow}{*}$
S_6	3	$*-**\overset{\downarrow}{-}$
S_7	4	$*-**\overset{\downarrow}{*}$

For the particular Π and I, the initial tape situation for the program U is (assuming that the first program step is to be scanned initially):

R_1: **------*---*-*-*-*-*-*---*-*---*-*---*-*-*---*-*-*-*-*---

--*-*---*------***--*----**--******--*-----**

The desired program U, when operating on R_1 should yield a final tape whose last portion imitates S_7, viz.:

------**--**--**--*****----**

Sometimes we have to copy with or without slight revision (such as changing the square under scan) a representation of the tape portion to be imitated, or even copy with slight revision the most recent representation of the whole program together with the most recent representation of the tape situation. Yet this does not generate excessive complexity because we never have to copy twice from the same original and, moreover, once a copy is made, we never operate on the original again. On account of our decision not to use 6 or more consecutive blanks except for marking the beginning of a program, we can always go to the beginning of the nearest copy of the program by selecting the nearest string of 6 consecutive blanks on the left.

Each program step $\langle a, b\rangle$, when performed, will be marked by *-ing the blank which immediately follows the last * in b (called the *tail* of b). Accordingly, at every moment we can find the first program step $\langle a, b\rangle$ not yet performed. Then we can test whether b has (in its alternate squares) one * or more; if one, then we need only perform the * operation by marking the first square of the quadruplet which immediately precedes ****, and mark the tail of b. If b has more than one *, test whether it has exactly 2 *'s; if two, then we perform the $\rightarrow$ operation by copying the most recent tape situation but interchange **** with the quadruplet immediately to its right (if the quadruplet to the right is ----, simply insert ---* before ****), and mark the tail of b. Similarly, if there are exactly 3 *'s, perform $\leftarrow$. If there are more than 3 *'s in b, we have a conditional transfer $a \cdot C(b-3)$ and there are several possible alternative courses. First, examine whether the first square of the quadruplet immediately preceding **** is blank. If blank, simply mark the tail of b. If not blank, then we have to determine whether $a=b-3$ or $a<b-3$ or $a>b-3$, by matching off *'s in a and b. If $a=b-3$, then we have an unfinishing trivial case which can be easily taken care of. If $a<b-3$, then we can use the unmatched stars in b to mark the

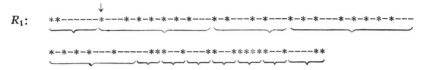

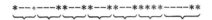

tails of the steps a, $a+1$, $\cdots$, $b-3-1$, and that is all. If $a>b-3$, then we have to locate the step $b-3$ (say, by using unmatched *'s of a) and copy the whole program together with the newest tape content, with the revision that all and only the program steps before the $(b-3)$-th are marked in the copy.

In order to present this outline more exactly, we describe a number of subroutines among which the more complex ones will only be sketched in words at first.

(i) Subroutine α_n. The head goes left along the tape to find the nearest string of n or more consecutive blanks which all lie to the left of the square initially under scan (if there is any such string), and stop at the position scanning the rightmost square of the string.

1. $\leftarrow$, $C1$, 2. $\leftarrow$, $C1$, $\cdots$, n. $\leftarrow$, $C1$, $(n+1)$. $\rightarrow^{n-1}$.

(ii) Subroutine β_n. The head goes right along the tape to find the nearest string of n or more consecutive blanks which all lie to the right of the square initially under scan, if there is any such, and stop at the position scanning at the n-th square of the string.

1. $\rightarrow$, $C1$, 2. $\rightarrow$, $C1$, $\cdots$, n. $\rightarrow$, $C1$.

(iii) Subroutine ξ_n^m. Given a tape on which there is, to the right of the square initially under scan a string of n or more consecutive stars and there are never more than m consecutive blanks between the nearest such string and the square initially under scan. The program enables the head to find the string and stop at the position scanning the n-th square of the string. For instance, ξ_3^6 is:

1. $\rightarrow$, $C2$, $\rightarrow$, $C2$, $\rightarrow$, $C2$, $\rightarrow$, $C2$, $\rightarrow$, $C2$, $\rightarrow$, $C2$, $\rightarrow$ (at steps 2, * will be under scan); 2. $\rightarrow$, $C3$, $\leftarrow$, $C1$ (if another *, continue; otherwise, go back); 3. $\rightarrow$, $C4$, $\leftarrow$, $C1$; 4. $\rightarrow$, $\leftarrow$.

Programs ξ_n^m for other values of m, n can be constructed similarly. Since we shall not be interested in those with $m>6$, we shall use only ξ_n^6 and write simply ξ_n.

(iv) Subroutine $\pi(m)$. When the reading head is scanning a square to the right of the beginning 6 blanks of the last copy of the program, this enables the head to find the first program step $\langle a, b\rangle$ not yet performed and end up scanning the beginning of b. If all steps are performed, go to step m. This depends on the fact that in a copy of the program yet to be used, we never mark the blanks at the end of an a or a b, or the squares between two numbers except for *-ing the tail of b in a performed step $\langle a, b\rangle$.

1. α_3, α_3, $\rightarrow$ 2. β_3, β_2, $\rightarrow$, $C2$, $\rightarrow$, $C3$, $\rightarrow$, Cm, $\leftarrow^2$, 3. α_3, $\rightarrow$.

(v) Subroutine π'. If there is yet some unmarked program step, this enables us to mark the first such and end up scanning the new mark.

1. α_6, 2. β_3, β_2, $\rightarrow$, $C2$, $\rightarrow^2$, $*$.

(vi) Subroutine θ. This enables the reading head to find the beginning of the latest tape representation.

β_7, $\leftarrow^3$, α_4, α_4, $\rightarrow^3$.

(vii) Subroutine θ'. This enables the reading head to find the first square of the quadruplet which represents the square under scan. θ, ξ_5, $\leftarrow^7$.

(viii) Subroutine $\Rightarrow$. This is the subroutine for the operation $\rightarrow$. It enables the machine to copy the latest tape representation but interchange $****$ with its immediately following quadruplet if it is not ----, or else insert ---$*$ before $****$. Then the first yet unmarked program step is marked.

(ix) Subroutine $\Leftarrow$. This is the somewhat similar subroutine for the operation $\leftarrow$.

(x) Subroutine $\mu(m, n)$. When scanning the beginning square of the quadruplet which represents the square under scan, this enables the machine to compare a and b of the first unperformed program step $\langle a, b\rangle$. If $a<(b-3)$, follow step m; if $a>(b-3)$, follow step n; if $a=b-3$ (i. e. the step is $a \cdot Ca$), go on repeating some trifle step.

(xi) Subroutine $\varphi(m)$. This enables the machine to mark the steps $a, a+1, \cdots, b-3-1$ and then follow step m.

(xii) Subroutine $\psi(m)$. This enables the machine to copy the most recent program and tape representations but mark in the copy only the program steps $1, 2, \cdots, b-3-1$ (in particular, if $b-3=1$, no step is marked), and then follow step m.

It will be a major problem to give explicitly the subroutines (viii)—(xii). For the moment, we assume them given and see how the desired program U looks like.

Program U

1. $\pi(13)$ (Find first program step $\langle a, b\rangle$ not yet performed, if there is any; otherwise, go to last step)

2. $\rightarrow^2$, $C4$ (Decide whether b represents the $*$ operation)

3. θ', $*$, π', $C1$ (If so, perform $*$ operation and go back to 1)

4. $\rightarrow^2$, $C6$ (If not, decide whether b represents the $\rightarrow$ operation)

5. $\Rightarrow$, $C1$ (If so, perform it and go back to 1)

6. $\rightarrow^2$, $C8$ (If not, decide whether b represents the $\leftarrow$ operation)

7. $\Leftarrow$, $C1$ (If so, perform it and go back to 1)

8. θ', $C10$ (If not, decide whether the square under scan is blank)

9. π', $C1$ (If so, mark b and go back to 1)

10. μ (11, 12) (If not, compare a and b to determine whether $a=b-3$ or $a<b-3$ or $a>b-3$)

11. $\varphi(1)$ (If $a<b-3$, perform φ and go back to 1)

12. $\psi(1)$ (If $a>b-3$, perform ψ and go back to 1)

13. β_6, $\rightarrow^6$ (We arbitrarily decide to let the machine end up scanning the last marked square).

Once the program U is given, we can of course build it into our machine B (i. e., remodel B according to U and take away internal storage) to get the desired serial-storage general machine $U_{b,b}$ (the desired universal Turing machine).

Now we have to give the subroutines (viii) to (xii).

(viii) Subroutine $\Rightarrow$. We make use of the second square of each quadruplet to keep track of how far we have copied. (Incidentally, the third of each quadruplet which is always blank is to distinguish these quadruplets from the scanning indicator ****)

1. θ, $\leftarrow^3$ (Find beginning of the last tape representation, ready to copy)

2. $\rightarrow^4$, $C8$ (Look at the second square of next quadruplet to see whether marked)

3. $\rightarrow^2$, $C5$ (If not marked, see whether end of tape representation)

4. $\rightarrow$, $C16$ (If so, go to last step)

5. $\leftarrow^2$, $*$, $\leftarrow$, $C7$ (If not, mark the 2nd square and ready to copy the quadruplet)

6. β_5, $\leftarrow$, $*$, $C1$
7. β_5, $\leftarrow$, $*$, $\leftarrow^3$, $*$, $C1$ } (Copy the quadruplet and go back to beginning)

8. $\rightarrow$, $C10$ (If marked at step 2, decide whether the quadruplet is ****)

9. $\leftarrow$, $C2$ (If not, that means it has been copied, go back to 2)

10. $\rightarrow^3$, $C2$ (If yes, examine whether next quadruplet has been copied; if yes, go back to 2)

11. $\leftarrow$, $C15$ (If not, decide whether first square of it is blank)

12. $\rightarrow^3$, $C14$ (If yes, see whether it is the end quadruplet)

13. β_5, $\leftarrow$, $*$, $(\rightarrow, *)^4$, $C16$ (If so, copy and ready to finish)

14. $\rightarrow$, $*$, β_5, $\leftarrow$, $*$, $(\rightarrow, *)^4$, $C1$ (If not, mark the quadruplet, copy it, and return to 1)

15. $\rightarrow$, $*$, β_5, $\leftarrow^4$, $*$, $\rightarrow^2$, $(\rightarrow, *)^5$, $C1$ (Similarly, if no at step 11)

16. β_5, $*$, $\rightarrow$, $*$, π'. (Put an end to the copying and mark the first program step not yet marked)

(ix) Subroutine $\Leftarrow$. This is similar to (viii) except that before copying a quadruplet, we have to find out first whether the quadruplet immediately to the right is $****$ and proceed accordingly. We leave this as an exercise for the reader.

We insert a few simple explanatory remarks and instrumental subroutines. We shall speak of principal and auxiliary squares in the representation of a program step $\langle a, b\rangle$. The originally marked squares are the principal squares, while the alternate squares (which are initially all blank) are the auxiliary squares. In the three subroutines (x)—(xii), we constantly match off $*$'s against $*$'s in the principal squares. For this purpose, we have to mark the auxiliary squares as we go along, in order to keep track of how far we have got. We shall use one set of alternate auxiliary squares to mark matching off, the other set to assist copying. The tail squares of a and b are reserved for the counting of program steps.

Before applying the program $\mu(m, n)$, we have already found out that $b \geqslant 4$, but the reading head is still scanning the quadruplet which precedes $****$. We introduce a subroutine π, a variant of $\pi(m)$, to bring the reading head back to the beginning of b, mark the second auxiliary square to its right, and end up scanning the last principal square of a.

(xiii) Subroutine π. 1. α_6, 2. β_3, β_2, $\rightarrow$, $C2$, α_3, $\rightarrow^4$, $*$, $\leftarrow^7$.

Since, in applying $\mu(m, n)$, we already know $a \geqslant 1$, $b \geqslant 4$, we shall start to compare a and $b-3$ by beginning with the second principal square of a and the fifth of b. For this, we use two simple subroutines.

(xiv) Subroutine ζ. 1. α_3, $\leftarrow$, α_2, 2. $\rightarrow^4$, $C2$.

(xv) Subroutine ζ'. 1. β_3, $\rightarrow^4$, 2. $\rightarrow^4$, $C2$.

Now we come to (x).

(x) Subroutine $\mu(m, n)$. This enables us to decide whether $a > b-3$, $a = b-3$, or $a < b-3$. If $a = b-3$, some trivial circular action. If $a < b-3$, follow step m. If $a > b-3$, follow step n.

1. π (Mark second auxiliary square of b, and go back to end of a)

2. ζ', $\rightarrow$, $C6$ (See whether $b-3$ has one unmatched unit)

3. ζ, $\rightarrow$, Cn (If not, but a has one, then $a>b-3$, go to step n while scanning a part of a)

4. $\leftarrow^2$

5. $C5$ (If neither a nor $b-3$ has one unmatched unit, $a=b-3$, unfinishable case)

6. ζ, $\leftarrow$, $C8$ (If $b-3$ has one, see whether a has one)

7. β_3, $\rightarrow$, Cm (If not, $b-3>a$, go to step m while scanning the beginning of b)

8. $\rightarrow^2$, $C11$ (If a also has one, see whether a has two)

9. ζ', $\rightarrow^3$, Cm (If a has only one, but $b-3$ has two, $b-3>a$, go to m while scanning a part of b)

10. $\leftarrow^2$, $C5$ (If both a and $b-3$ have exactly one, then $a=b-3$)

11. ζ', $\rightarrow^3$, $C13$ (If a has two, see whether $b-3$ has two)

12. α_3, $\leftarrow$, α_2, $\rightarrow$, Cn (If $b-3$ does not have two, $a>b-3$, go to n while scanning the beginning of a)

13. $\leftarrow^3$, $*$, ζ, $*$, $C2$ (If both a and $b-3$ have two more, mark both auxiliary squares and continue)

To specify $\varphi(k)$, we observe that upon entering this subroutine, the machine has found out that $b-3>a$, and the reading head is scanning a part of b (cf. steps 7 and 9 in the above subroutine). Moreover, b is the last instruction word on the tape which is greater than 2 and whose second auxiliary square is marked, since in any transfer with $a>b-3$ we always copy the whole program but delete such marks (cf. $\gamma(k)$ below); hence the subroutine ϱ below is right.

(xi) Subroutine $\varphi(k)$. This enables the reading head to use what is left of $b-3$ to match off and mark the steps $a, a+1, \cdots, b-3-1$.

1. ζ, $\leftarrow$, $C4$ (See whether $a-1$ is even or odd)

2. ζ', $\rightarrow$, $C5$ (If $a-1$ is even, or it is odd but the machine has already gone through step 4 below, begin to match off)

3. β_3, $\leftarrow^2$, $*$, Ck (If $a-1$ is even and $b-3=a+1$, mark step a and go to step k)

4. ζ', $*$, β_3, $\leftarrow^2$, $*$, α_3, $\leftarrow^3$, $C2$ (If $a-1$ is odd, mark step $\langle a, b\rangle$, cross out a pair in $b-3$, and get ready to continue to match off $b-3-a-1$ with program steps $a+1, \cdots, b-3-1$)

5. $\rightarrow^2$, $C7$ (See whether there is another unmatched square in $b-3$)

6. π', Ck (If not, simply mark one more program step and go to k)

7. $\leftarrow^3$, $*$, π', π', ϱ, $C2$ (If yes, then use two $*$'s in $b-3$ to match off two unmarked program steps and go back to a by the subroutine ϱ yet to be specified, and continue)

The subroutine ϱ is:

(xvi) ϱ.

1. α_3, $\rightarrow^3$, $C2$, $\leftarrow^6$, $C1$, 2. $\rightarrow^2$, $C3$, $\leftarrow^8$, $C1$, 3. $\leftarrow$, $C4$, $\leftarrow^7$, $C1$, 4. $\leftarrow^7$.

There remains only (xii) which we shall divide into two parts: part 1 uses the unmatched squares of a to "double mark" the program steps $a-1, \cdots, b-3+1, b-3$; part 2 copies the whole program and the whole most recent tape content, but leaves our doubly-marked steps unmarked. In other words, we have:

(xii) Subroutine $\psi(k)$. 1. $\eta(2)$, 2. $\gamma(k)$.

The problem is to define $\eta(k)$ and $\gamma(k)$.

(xvii) Subroutine $\eta(k)$. The structure of $\eta(k)$ is similar to that of $\varphi(k)$. In $\mu(m, n)$, when it is decided that $a > b-3$ and the machine is ready to follow $\eta(k)$, the reading head is scanning a part of a [cf. steps 3 and 12 of $\mu(m, n)$].

1. ζ', $\rightarrow$, $C4$ (See whether $b-3-1$ is even or odd)

2. ζ, $\leftarrow$, $C5$

3. $\leftarrow^2$, Ck

4. ζ, $*$, α_3, $\leftarrow^2$, $*$, β_3, $\rightarrow$, $C2$ (If $b-3-1$ is odd, double mark step $a-1$, etc.)

5. $\rightarrow^2$, $C7$

6. α_3, $\leftarrow^2$, $*$, Ck

7. $\leftarrow$, $*$, α_3, $\leftarrow^2$, $*$, α_3, $\leftarrow^2$, $*$, β_3, $\rightarrow$, $C2$

(xviii) Subroutine $\gamma(k)$. We are now ready to copy the whole program and the whole most recent tape content. We recall that at this stage the tail of any a is marked only for double marking, and the tail of any b is marked only for marking the whole step $\langle a, b\rangle$; moreover, except in the special cases where the first auxiliary square of a or b coincides with its tail, the first auxiliary square is never marked. Of the program steps to be copied, there are three successive stretches: singly marked steps (possibly none), doubly marked steps (at least step $a-1$), unmarked steps (at least step a). We shall first copy all steps without any marking. Afterwards it will be easy to mark all and only the singly marked steps, and copy the most recent tape content. We use as an auxiliary step subroutine $\sigma(m)$:

1. α_6, 2. $\beta_2, \rightarrow, C3, \rightarrow, C3, \rightarrow^2, Cm$, 3. $\rightarrow^2, C4, \leftarrow^2, C2$, 4. $\leftarrow$, $C2$.

When working on the program to be copied, this enables us to find the first number expression >1, not yet copied, and leads to step m, if no more such numbers. In the program for $\gamma(k)$, the first 12 steps accomplish the copying of the program steps. Note that in the representation of program steps, no two 1's occur in succession, except possibly at the very beginning.

1. $\beta_7, *, \alpha_6, \alpha_6, \rightarrow^7, C2, \beta_7, \leftarrow^3, *, \alpha_6$ (Copy first number of program; and copy next number if it is 1; otherwise, follow standard procedure)

2. $\sigma(12), \rightarrow^3, C5, \beta_7, \leftarrow, *, \leftarrow^2, *$ (Find next numbers >1 not yet copied, if it is 2, copy it and proceed to next step; otherwise, follow step 5)

3. $\alpha_6, \sigma(12), *, \beta_2, \rightarrow, C4, \rightarrow, C4, \rightarrow^2, C12$ (Mark the numbers already copied, and see whether any more numbers left yet to be copied; if no more, go to step 12)

4. $\rightarrow^2, C2, \beta_7, \leftarrow^3, *, \alpha_6, \leftarrow^6, C2$ (If there is a next number and it is 1, copy it and continue; otherwise, just continue)

5. $\rightarrow^2, C6, \beta_7, \rightarrow, *, (\leftarrow^2, *)^2, C3$ (If number is 3, copy it and wind up with steps 3 and 4)

6. $\beta_7, \rightarrow^3, *, (\leftarrow^2, *)^3, \sigma(12), \rightarrow^4, *, \rightarrow^3, C7, \leftarrow^2, C3$ (If number is 4, copy it, mark third auxiliary square, and wind up with steps 3 and 4)

7. $\rightarrow^2, C8, \beta_7, \leftarrow^5, *, C3$ (If one more unit left, copy it and wind up)

8. $\rightarrow^2, C9, \sigma(12)$

9. $\rightarrow, C9, *, \beta_7, \leftarrow^3, *, \leftarrow^2, *, \sigma(12)$ (If 2 or more units left, copy 2 units, mark one additional auxiliary square and continue)

10. $\rightarrow^4, C10, \leftarrow, C11, \leftarrow^2, C2$ (If no more left, go back to 2)

11. $\leftarrow^2, C7$ (Otherwise, continue with 7)

12. $\beta_7, *, \leftarrow, *$ (Mark the end of program with -----**)

The remaining part of $\gamma(k)$ is easy.

13. α_6, α_6

14. $\beta_3, \beta_2, \rightarrow, C15, \leftarrow^3, C17$ (Find next singly marked step, if any; otherwise conclude)

15. α_3, $\leftarrow^2$, $*$, β_7 (Double mark it)

16. β_3, β_2, $\rightarrow$, $C16$, $*$, $C13$ (Mark one step in the copy, and repeat)

17. β_6, $\rightarrow^2$, α_4, $\rightarrow$ (Find beginning of tape content to be copied)

18. $\rightarrow^4$, $C19$, $\rightarrow^2$, $C20$, β_7, $(\rightarrow, *)^2$ (If ****, copy it by step 19, if end, copy it; otherwise to step 20)

19. β_7, $\rightarrow^2$, $(\rightarrow, *)^4$, $C17$

20. $\leftarrow^3$, $C21$, $\rightarrow$, $*$, β_7, $\leftarrow^3$, $*$, $C17$ (Decide whether first square is blank or marked and copy accordingly)

21. $\rightarrow$, $*$, β_7, $\leftarrow^3$, $*$, $\leftarrow^3$, $*$, $C17$

This completes the explicit specification of all the subroutines needed in the main program U. We proceed to illustrate with the program Π(1. $C3$, 2. $\rightarrow$, 3. $C2$, 4. $*$) and input I(*-*↓*) given earlier on. The initial tape situation for U is R_1 as specified above. We now apply U to the initial situation and consider the results at crucial intervals. Since the first step is a conditional transfer and the square originally under scan is marked, U should immediately lead us to its step 10, comparing 1 with 3+3. The result of performing $\mu(11, 12)$, $\varphi(1)$, and $\pi(13)$ in U successively is the following:

```
                                                     ↓
R2:   **-------*---*-***-*-*-**--*-*----*-**--*-*-*---*-*-*-*-*---

      *-*-*-*---*-----***--*---**--******--*-----**
```

This corresponds to S_2 in the history of Π. The next state under the program U is as follows:

```
R3:   **-------**--***-***-****--****--****--*****---***-***-*---

      ***-***---*-----****-*-*-*******-*-----**-------
                       ↓
      *---*-*-*-*-*-**--*-*---*-*---*-*-*---*-*-*---*-*-*-*---*---

      -***--*---**--******--*-----**
```

The interested reader might wish to verify R_2, R_3, and work out R_4, R_5, R_6, R_7 for himself.

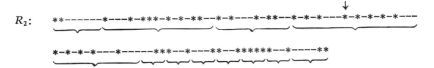

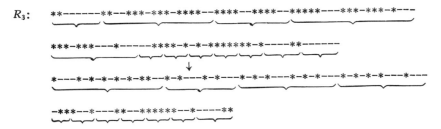

References

[1] Hao Wang, A variant to Turing's theory of computing machines, *Jour. Assoc. Comp. Mach.*, **4** (1957), 63—92 (included here as chapter VI).

[2] John von Neumann, The general and logical theory of automata, Cerebral mechanisms in behaviour (the Hixon symposium), Wiley, 1952; reprinted in *The World of Mathematics* (ed. James R. Newman), vol. 4, Simon and Schuster, 1956.

CHAPTER VIII

THE LOGIC OF AUTOMATA*

§ 1. Introduction

We are concerned in this paper with the use of logical systems and techniques in the analysis of the structure and behavior of automata.

In Section 2 we discuss automata in general. A new kind of automaton is introduced, the growing automaton, of which Turing machines and self-duplicating automata are special cases. Thereafter we limit the discussion to fixed, deterministic automata and define their basic features. We give methods of analyzing these automata in terms of their states. Four kinds of state tables—complete tables, admissibility trees, characterizing tables, and output tables—are used for this purpose. These methods provide a decision procedure for determining whether or not two automaton junctions behave the same. Finally, a class of well-formed automaton nets is defined, and it is shown how to pass from nets to state tables and vice versa. A coded normal form for nets is given.

In Section 3 we show how the information contained in the state tables can be expressed in matrix form. The (i, j) element of a transition matrix gives those inputs which cause state S_i to produce state S_j. Various theorems are proved about these matrices and a corresponding normal form (the decoded normal form or matrix form) for nets is introduced.

In Section 4 we first show how to decompose a net into one or more subnets which contain cycles but which are not themselves interconnected cyclically. We then discuss the relation of cycles in nets to the use of truth functions and quantifiers for describing nets. We conclude by relating nerve nets to other automaton nets.

§ 2. Automata and Nets

2. 1. *Fixed and Growing Automata*

To begin with we will consider any object or system (e.g., a physical body, a machine, an animal, or a solar system) that changes its state in time; it may or may not change its size in time, and it may or may not interact with

* With A. W. Burks. This chapter appeared in *Journal of Association for Computing Machinery*, **4** (1957), 193—218, 279—297.

its environment. When we describe the state of the object at any arbitrary time, we have in general to take account of: the time under consideration, the past history of the object, the laws governing the inner action of the object or system, the state of the environment (which itself is a system of objects), and the laws governing the interaction of the object and its environment. If we choose to, we may refer to all such objects and systems as automata. The main concern of this paper is with a special class of these automata: viz., digital computers and nerve nets. To define this class as a subclass of automata in general, we will introduce various simplifying and specifying assumptions. It will become clear that in adopting each assumption we are making a deliberate and somewhat arbitrary decision to confine our attention to a certain subclass of automata. For example, by altering some of the decisions we arrive at the rather interesting concept of indefinitely growing automata, which include the well-known Turing machines as particular cases.

A. Discrete Units. The first decision we make is to use only discrete descriptions; this means that between any two moments and between any two elements (particles, cells, etc.) there is a finite number of other moments or elements. This decision is a consequence of our interest in digital computers. It carries with it a commitment to emphasize discrete mathematics in the analysis of the systems under investigation: recursive function theory and symbolic logic. Hence our problems differ from the more common ones in which time, the elements of a system, the states (color, hardness, etc.) of an element, and the interaction of an object with its environment are all treated as continuous. When this is done, the emphasis is naturally placed on classical analysis and its applications. In contrast with digital computers, which use discrete units, analog computers simulate in a continuous manner, and for the study of them continuous (nondiscrete) mathematics is especially appropriate.

It should be remarked that, though discrete mathematical systems are generally more useful for the investigation of discrete automata, a very common (and perhaps at the present time even primary) scientific use of digital computers is to represent (approximately, of course) continuous mathematics (e.g., to solve differential equations). In effect, this procedure involves finding discrete mathematical systems which adequately approximate the particular continuous system at hand.

B. Deterministic Behavior. We will not deal with elements capable of random (nondeterministic) behavior. Rather, we will assume that at each time the complete state of an object is entirely determined by its past history, including the effects of its environment throughout the past. Statistics could be employed to treat deterministic automata containing large numbers of elements (cf. the kinetic theory of gases), but we will not do this here.

C. Finitude of Bases. We will always exclude an "actual infinity" of states: each system will contain a finite number of elements at each time, and each element can be in only one of a finite number of states at any time. We will reserve for an independent decision the possibility of a "potential infinity" of elements and states, i.e., whether or not the number of elements or states of each element may change with time and in particular increase without bound.

The finitude of time requires separate treatment. The discreteness condition (*A*) implies that there are never infinitely many moments between two given times. But this still leaves open the question as to how many different times are to be considered. For a general theory it would be inelegant to take a definite finite number, say, 10^{18} or 10^{27}, as an upper bound to the number of possible moments. It seems desirable to allow time to increase indefinitely and to study the behavior of an object through all time. The one remaining choice is the question of an infinite past. The assumption of an infinite past has the advantage of making the entire time sequence homogeneous, thereby destroying a major part of the individuality of each moment of time. However, in the presence of our deterministic assumption an infinite past would be inconvenient (for reasons to be given in Section 3.3), so we stipulate that there is a first moment of time (zero). The internal state of the automaton at time zero will be some distinguished state.

Speaking arithmetically, the two alternatives are to represent moments of time by positive (or nonnegative) integers or by all integers (including the negative ones).

(*C*1) An infinite future but a finite past: Every nonnegative integer represents a time moment and vice versa; the number zero represents the beginning of time.

(*C*2) An infinite future and an infinite past.

Our decision is to adopt the first of these two alternatives.

D. Synchronous Operations. Some computers contain component circuits which operate at different speeds according to their function, location, the time, or the input at the time. Such circuits are called "asynchronous", in contrast to synchronous circuits which work on a uniform time scale (usually under the direction of a central control clock). There are really two aspects to asynchronous operation: (1) the actual intervals of time between operations vary with the time; (2) different parts of the computer pass through their states at different rates, these rates depending, in general, on the information held in the circuits.

We will assume that all elements of a given system (net) operate at the same rate, and we will call this the "synchronous" mode of operation. In particular, this means an element may operate at each nonnegative integer t. This assumption does not imply that all time intervals are equal; e.g., the interval from time 7 to time 8 can be one microsecond, while the interval from time 8 to time 9 is 12 hours. Thus our assumption does not exclude possibility (1) of the preceding paragraph. It involves some restriction with regard to point (2), but not as much as one might think. For example, we can represent different parts of an asynchronous machine by subsystems operating at different rates, interconnecting these with logical representations of interlocks. And just as discrete systems (e.g., digital computers) can be used to simulate continuous systems [cf. the second paragraph under the discussion of assumption (A)], so synchronous computers can be used to simulate asynchronous ones.

E. Determination by the Immediate Past and the Present. The stipulation that the behavior of an automaton at time $t+1$ is determined by the past leaves unsettled the question as to how the remote past influences the present. We will assume that such influence occurs indirectly through the states at intermediary time moments, so that to calculate the state of the automaton at $t+1$ it is not necessary to know its state for any time earlier than the preceding moment t. Thus we assume that for the present to be influenced by an event which happened in the remote past a record of that event must have been preserved internally during the intervening time. This postulate corresponds closely to the actual mode of operation of automatic systems. Of course, a computer with, e.g., a microsecond clock, may have delay lines, e.g., 500 microseconds long, so that a stored pulse is not accessible to the arithmetic unit at every clock time, but such a delay line is naturally represented as a chain of 500 unit (microsecond) delays, with the input and output of the chain connected to the rest of the computer. Indeed, the assumption we are now making causes no significant loss in generality, because for each fixed N such that an automaton A can always remember what happened during the N immediately preceding moments (but not more), we can easily devise an automaton A' which, though capable of directly remembering only the immediate past, simulates completely the automaton A.

When we think of automata which have unbounded memory or, in particular, ones which can remember everything that has happened in the past, we encounter a basically different general situation. In such cases, the information to be retained increases with time, whence for any automation of fixed capacity there may come a time beyond which it can no longer hold all the information accumulated in its life history. Thus, for a machine to remember all past history it is necessary and sufficient that it grow in some suitable fashion. Such growth can be accomplished by the appearance at each moment of a new delay element for each automaton input. In short, in the presence of the postulate of determination by the immediate past, the alternative of remembering all past history is best studied in connection with growing automata.

Another problem connected with determination by the immediate past is the role of present inputs in determining the outputs. It would seem natural to stipulate that the environment at time $t+1$ cannot influence the outputs of the automaton at time $t+1$ but only at time $t+2$. That is the case with neural nets, since each neuron has a delay built into it. Strictly speaking, it is true in computer nets, but because the delay in a switch may be small compared to the unit delay of the system, it is convenient to regard this switching action as instantaneous. Thus the well-formed nets of Burks and Wright [1], which will be discussed further in Section 2.3, permit outputs which are switching functions of the inputs.

F. Automata and Environment. Supposedly the change of state of a solipsist is independent of the environment, and the environment is not affected by the solipsist; cf. Leibnitz's concept of a "monad." A "solipsistic" automaton would be one which (1) changed its state independently of any environmental changes and (2) whose output did not influence the environment. We are not primarily interested in such automata. Rather, we will consider how the environment (the inputs) affects the automaton but not how the output of an automaton affects its environment.

The last point is related to the ordinary method of representing inputs and outputs. It is well known that there are significant and useful logical symbols for the internal action of automata (see Section 2.3). The standard method of representing inputs and outputs is in terms of the binary states of input and output wires. This is not directly applicable in simulating such "inputs" as light and sound waves, physical pressures, etc., and such "outputs" as physical actions. Theoretically, we can, however, just as well interpret certain standard binary elements as representing these. For some purposes, we may want to add as new primitives representations of the lights and keys commonly used on computers (see Burks and Copi [2], p. 306), as well as symbols representing additional methods of sensing and other methods of acting on the environment that automata are capable of. Von Neumann has done some work along this line, but it has not been published (see Shannon [3], p. 1240). It might be suggested that one ought to devise a symbolism for magnetic or paper tape input and output to a computer; but that is unnecessary because such devices are very well represented by net diagrams for a serial type of storage (see Burks and Copi [2], p. 313, ftn. 9).

We will not here attempt to devise separate notations for the various kinds of interactions possible between an automaton and its environment, but will content ourselves with the customary way of simulating inputs and outputs by binary states of wires. Even subject to this restriction there are a number of alternatives to consider. The most general case would be to identify the environment partly or wholly with certain automata so that interaction occurs among these and the particular automaton under study (cf. the many-body problem of mechanics). A simple case would be to identify the whole environment with another automaton (cf. the two-body problem of mechanics). Accordingly, we have the following alternatives:

(*F*0) An object changes its state automatically, independent of the environment.

(*F*1) An automaton changes its state in accordance with its structure and the inputs (the environment).

(*F*2) Different automata interact with one another.

We will be primarily concerned with (*F*1). In other words, we will assume that the automaton has no influence over what inputs it receives, and that in general the inputs do have effects on the internal state (i.e., state of internal cells) of the automaton. As a consequence, we can define the units or atoms of which an automaton is compounded into two classes: input cells and internal cells, or input and internal wires, or input and internal junctions.

The situation under (*F*0) becomes a special case of that under (*F*1) when either the number of input cells (or wires) is zero (a limiting case) or the effects of the inputs are more or less canceled so that the automaton behaves in an input-independent manner. The latter case is exemplified by a logical element whose output wire is always active regardless of the state of the input wire.

(*F*2) may also be regarded as a special case of (*F*1). Since the inputs and outputs of an automaton are wires, two automata may be interconnected to produce a single (more complex) automaton, of which the original automata are parts or subsystems. Thus we regard (*F*2) as a special case of analyzing a complex machine into interrelated submachines. A common application of this concept is to be found in the design of a general-purpose computer. Typically such a computer is divided into Arithmetic Unit, Storage, Input-Output Unit, and Control (see, for example, Burks and Copi [2], p. 301). The utility of making such divisions lies partly in the relatively independent functioning of these units and partly in the (related) fact that it is conceptually easier to understand what goes on in terms of these parts. The kind of structuring under discussion usually occurs at more than one level; e.g., the Parallel Storage (of Burks and Copi [2], pp. 307—313) divides naturally into a switch and 4096 bins (each storing a word), and the bins are in turn "composed" of cells (each storing one bit of a word).

G. Exclusion of Growth. While we have adopted the postulate of finite bases, we have yet to decide whether the structure of an automaton, the number of its cells, or the number of possible states of each cell are to be allowed to change with time. If changes are permitted but are confined by a preassigned finite bound, we might as well have used a fixed automaton which embodies this bound to begin with. Hence the really interesting new case is that of a growing automaton which has no preassigned finite upper bound on the possible number of cells or cell states. Structural changes (e.g., rewiring a given circuit) do not seem to generate unbounded possibilities, although in special studies, such as investigations into the mode of operation of the human brain (cf. Rochester *et al.* [4]), the use of a structurally changing automaton is more illuminating than the use of the corresponding fixed automaton.

In any case, we can, theoretically, reduce all three kinds of growth to increase in either the number of cells or the number of possible cell states: given any growing automaton, we can find another which functions in the same way but grows only in the number of its cells (or, alternatively, only in the number of possible states for each cell). For every and all forms of growth, it seems natural (in the context of our deterministic assumption) to require that the process be effective (recursive). We will therefore assume once and for all that each definition of a growing automaton determines an effective method by which we can, for each time t, construct the automaton and determine its state for that time. An important particular case corresponds to primitive recursive definitions, each of which yields a method by which we can construct the automaton for $t=0$ and, given the automaton *and its state* at t, we can construct the automaton at $t+1$. The growth may not depend on the state or the inputs, but the possibility of its doing so is provided for. Moreover, "growth" is taken to include shrinkage as well as expansion. Thus we could have a "growing" computer which expands and contracts as the computation proceeds, having at each time period just the capacity needed to store the information existing at that time.

Two types of automata, *fixed* and *growing*, can be characterized as follows:

(*G*1) The structure and cells of the automaton are fixed once and for all, and each cell is capable of a fixed number of states.

(*G*2) The automaton may grow (expand *and* contract) in time in a predetermined effective manner.

In this paper we will be concerned entirely with fixed automata, except for some remarks on growing nets in this subsection. These remarks are intended to elucidate the concept of a growing net and to indicate why we think it is important. But before beginning on them we wish to specify (*G*1) further by stipulating that each cell, junction, or wire is capable of two states, on and off, firing and quiet; we will later correlate these with one and zero, and with true and false. We could of course allow each cell to have any fixed finite number of possible states and different cells to have different numbers of states. But it is better to fix the number of states at the constant two. There are a number of reasons for this. The wires and cells of many automata and most digital computers do in fact have two significant states. When this is not the case we can always represent a cell with q possible states by p two-state cells for any $p \geqslant \log_2 q$ (e.g., ten of the sixteen different states of four binary net wires can represent ten discrete electrical states of a single circuit wire), so by adapting our system to the commonest case we do not lose the power to treat the nonbinary cases. This commitment to two-valued logic need not blind us to the fact that there may be cases where multivalued logic is more convenient; the point is that our logic can handle these cases and we have no interest at the moment in exploiting whatever advantages multivalued logic might have here.

We return now to growing nets, mentioning first some special cases of them already known. A Turing machine (see Turing [5]; Kleene [6]; Wang [7, 8]) may be regarded as an automaton with a growing tape. Usually the tape is regarded as infinite, but at any time only a finite amount of information has been stored on it, so it is essentially a finite but expanding automaton net (cf. Burks and Copi [2], p. 313, ftn. 8). If, in a Turing machine, we take as input cells the squares included on the minimum consecutive tape position which contains all marked squares at the moment, then the growth consists simply of the expansion and contraction of the tape. Or if we use the formulation of Wang [7] which eliminates the erasure operation, a Turing machine is a growing automaton with an even more limited type of growth—namely, an expansion of the tape. In contrast, a growing automaton may in general grow anywhere, not only at the periphery but also internally (by having new elements arise between elements already present).

Though a Turing machine is a special kind of growing automaton, it has as much mathematical (calculating) ability as any growing automaton; for every type of computation can be done by some Turing machine, and the mathematical ability of an automaton is limited to computation. In view of this situation one might wonder why the general concept of a growing net is of interest. Its importance can be shown by the following considerations:

John von Neumann has developed some models of self-reproducing machines (von Neumann [9]; Shannon [3], p. 1240; Kemeny [10], pp. 64—67). These are machines that grow until there are two machines, connected together,—the original one and a duplicate of it; the two machines may then separate. Hence they are clearly cases of growing nets.

The basic process to be simulated or modeled in the growth and reproduction of living organisms is the complete process from a fertilized egg to a developed organism which can produce a fertilized egg. For this purpose we would need to design a relatively small and simple automaton which would grow to maturity (given an appropriate environment) and would then produce as an offspring a new small automaton. Von Neumann's models can be construed either at the level of cells or at the level of complete organisms, but in either case they seem to provide only a partial solution. The process of cell duplication is only one component of the complete process described above, and the self-reproduction of a completely developed entity omits the important process of development from infancy to maturity. Hence the model we suggest is a type of growing automaton not yet covered in the literature.

A second novel type of growing automaton is a generalized Turing machine in which growth is permitted at points other than at the ends of the tape. A typical Turing machine, although logically powerful, is clumsy and slow in its operation. Consequently, to design a special-purpose Turing machine or to code a program for a universal Turing machine is a complicated and laborious process (although a completely straightforward one). What complicates the task is the linear arrangement of information on a single tape, which requires the tape or reading-head to be moved back and forth to find the information. That movement may be reduced somewhat by shifting the old information around to make room for the new information, but this operation also contributes to the complexity of the whole process. To develop this point further, we will discuss in more detail the relation between recursive functions and Turing machines. Turing [5] worked in terms of computable numbers; Kleene [6] and Wang [7, 8] work in terms of recursive functions. Since our discussion has been in terms of functions, we will use Kleene's and Wang's works as our references.

The basic mathematical result underlying the significance of Turing machines is the following. Mathematicians have rigorously characterized a set of functions, called partial recursive functions, and this set of functions is in some sense equivalent to what is computable (Kleene [6], Ch. XII). Each partial recursive function is definable by a finite sequence of definitions, each definition being of one of six possible forms (Kleene [6], pp. 219 and 279). It is known how to translate each sequence of definitions into a special-purpose Turing machine and into a program for a general-purpose Turing machine (Kleene [6], Ch. XIII; Wang [7]). This translation, while rigorous and straightforward, is often complicated for the reasons, among others, mentioned in the preceding paragraph. Simpler and more direct translations can be made by using growing nets in which growth is allowed to occur whenever it simplifies the construction, not just at two places, i.e., at the ends of the tape, where it is allowed to occur in the conventional Turing machine. Such growing nets will be generalizations of a Turing machine.

We can arrive at a third novel kind of growing automaton by generalizing a general-purpose computer in the way we generalized a Turing machine in the last paragraph. The usual general-purpose computer consists of a fixed internal computer together with one or more tapes. As in the Turing machine, these tapes may be regarded as expanding at the ends whenever needed; in practice the expansion is handled by an operator replacing tape reels, using either blank tape or tape reels from a library of tapes. In writing programs for such a machine, the programmer needs to keep track of two things:

(1) the development of the computation, in terms of the growth of old blocks of information and the appearance of new blocks of information;

(2) shifting the information from one kind of storage to another (e.g., from a serial to a parallel storage) and moving the information about within a storage unit.

Both of these components of computation are essential. But (1) seems more basic for understanding the nature of the computation, and at any rate it is helpful to be able to study each of the components in isolation. This can be done with growing nets, for we can eliminate (2) by providing for growth wherever it is needed to accommodate new information or new connections to old information. We feel that the study of growing automata would contribute to the theory of automatic programming. The development of a powerful *theory* of automatic programming has so far been impeded by the many details involved in actual computation; by eliminating (2) we would eliminate many of these details and would focus attention on the more basic component (1).

We turn now to fixed automata which satisfy the assumptions (*A*), (*B*), (*C*1), (*D*), (*E*), (*F*1), and (*G*1). In summary, we arrive at the following definition of a (finite) automaton:

Definition 1. *A (finite) automaton is a fixed finite structure with a fixed finite number of input junctions and a fixed finite number of internal junctions such that* (1) *each junction is capable of two states,* (2) *the states of the input junctions at every moment are arbitrary,* (3) *the states of the internal junctions at time zero are distinguished*[1], (4) *the internal state (i.e., the states of the internal junctions) at the time* $t+1$ *is completely determined by the states of all junctions at time* t *and the input junctions at time* $t+1$*, according to an arbitrary pre-assigned law (which is embodied in the given structure). An abstract automaton is obtained from an automaton by allowing an arbitrary initial internal state.*

Several aspects of this definition call for comment. In it automata states have been defined in terms of junction states. This follows Burks and Wright [1], where each wire has the state of the junction to which it is attached, and the nuclei or cell bodies are not regarded as having states but as realizing transformations between junctions or wires. An alternative would be to define automata states in terms of cell states. Condition (4) places some restrictions on the way automata elements are to be interconnected, but it does not completely specify the situation; this will be discussed further in Section 2.3.

The initial state of the internal junctions also calls for discussion. In the definition of an abstract automaton this is taken more or less as an additional input which can be changed arbitrarily. As a result, two abstract automata, to be equivalent, must behave the same for each initial state picked for the pair of them. On the other hand, for most applications to actual automata, it is best to assume a single initial state.

The word "structure" in the above definition can be avoided if we speak exclusively in mathematical terms and consider the transformations realized by automata and abstract automata. We will do so in the next subsection, returning to a more detailed investigation of the structure of automata in the following subsection (viz., 2.3).

---

1) This condition applies only to those junctions whose state at a given time does not depend on the inputs at the same time; cf. condition (4) following.

2.2. *Characterizing Tables and a Decision Procedure*

Consider for a moment automata whose internal states are determined only by the immediate past and hence are not influenced by the present inputs. Let there be M possible input states, $I_0, I_1, \cdots, I_{M-1}$, and N possible internal states, $S_0, S_1, \cdots, S_{N-1}$. Even though each junction of an automaton is capable of only two states, we do not require M and N to be powers of two. For one thing, when an automaton is being defined, the values of M and N are stipulated and are not necessarily powers of two. Also, when an automaton is given, not all possible combinations of internal junction states may occur because of the structure of the automaton, and not all possible combinations of input junctions may be of interest (because, e.g., the automaton is to be embedded in a larger automaton where not all of the possible inputs will be used).

We will assign nonnegative integers to the input and internal states. Let I and S range over these numbers, respectively. A complete automaton state is represented by the ordered pair $<I, S>$. (If the automaton has no inputs, then there are no I's and the complete automaton state is just S.) Let S_0 be the integer assigned to the distinguished initial internal state; S_0 will usually be zero, but not always. An abstract automaton differs from a non-abstract one just in not having a distinguished initial state.

Since the input states are represented by numbers, a complete history of the inputs is a numerical function from the nonnegative integers 0, 1, 2, $\cdots$ (representing discrete times) to integers of the set $\{I\}$. That is, it is an infinite sequence $I(0)$, $I(1)$, $I(2), \cdots, I(t), \cdots$; it may be viewed as representing the real number $\{I(0)+[I(1)/K]+[I(2)/K^2]+\cdots\}$, in which K is the maximum of the set $\{I\}$. By our convention that the initial internal state is S_0 we have $S(0)=S_0$. By the assumption of complete determination by the immediate past we have for all t

$$S(t+1) = \tau[I(t), S(t)],$$

where τ is an arbitrary function from the integer pairs $\{<I, S>\}$ to the integers $\{S\}$. Or, in other words, as the input function I and the time t are the independent variables, τ is an arbitrary function of two arguments (one ranging over functions of integers and another ranging over integers) whose values are integers. It follows by a simple induction that for each infinite sequence $I(0), I(1), \cdots, I(t), \cdots$, repeated application of the function τ yields a unique infinite sequence $S(0), S(1), \cdots, S(t), \cdots$, with $S(0)=S_0$. Since for many purposes we are interested not only in the existence of values of the function τ, but also in finding them, we will assume that τ is defined effectively, though actually much of our discussion would be valid without this restriction.

We next broaden our theory so as to include automata whose internal state at $t+1$ depends also on the inputs at $t+1$. To do this we allow P "output" states $O_0, O_1, \cdots, O_{P-1}$ such that

$$O(t) = \lambda[I(t), S(t)],$$

where λ is again an arbitrary effective function. In general, the complete state of an automaton at any time is given by the ordered triad $<I, S, O>$. In specific cases $I, S,$ or O may be missing.

We can now give an analytic definition of automata and abstract automata by means of these transformations.

***Definition* 2.** *An automaton is in general characterized by two arbitrary effective transformations (τ and λ) from pairs of integers to integers. These integers are drawn from finite sets* $\{I\}, \{S\}$, and $\{O\}$. $\{S\}$ *contains a distinguished integer* S_0. *The transformations are given by*

$$S(0) = S_0,$$

$$S(t+1) = \tau[I(t), S(t)],$$

$$O(t) = \lambda[I(t), S(t)].$$

If we omit the condition $S(0)=S_0$, *we obtain an abstract automaton.*

Thus, speaking analytically, the study of finite automata is essentially an investigation of the rather simple class of transformations τ and λ in the above definition. The definition of the class as thus given is superficially very general in allowing τ and λ to be arbitrary calculable functions. On account of the very restricted range and domain of these functions, however, that generality is only apparent. We can find a simple representation of the class of automaton transformations in the following way:

Since τ is effective, and since its domain and range are finite, we can effectively find for each pair $<I, S>$ the value of $\tau[I(t), S(t)]$. Hence we can produce a table of $M \times N$ pairs $\ll I, S>, S'>$ such that if $<I, S>$ is part of the state at t, then S' is part of the state at $t+1$. We shall call this set the *M–N complete table* of the given automaton. Each complete table is a definition of the function τ.

In a similar way we can construct an *output table* for the automaton, each row being of the form $\ll I, S>, O>$. Such a table defines the function λ.

It is important that the function τ and the complete table involve a time shift, while the function λ and the output table do not. Hence for an investigation of the behavior of an automaton through time the complete table is basic, the output table derivative. That is, by means of the complete table we can compute $S(1)$, $S(2)$, $S(3)$, $\cdots$ from the inputs $I(0)$, $I(1)$, $I(2)$, $\cdots$ and leave the determination of $O(0)$, $O(1)$, and $O(2)$, $\cdots$ for later. Note that to stipulate that the output at time t cannot be influenced by the input at the same time is to require λ to be such that $O(t)=\lambda[S(t)]$. When this is the case the states $O(t)$ and the output table can be dispensed with since $O(t)$ is completely dependent on $S(t)$. (When the behavior of individual junctions is being investigated, the output table may nevertheless be convenient). For these various reasons the state numbers $\{I\}$ and $\{S\}$ are more basic than the state numbers $\{O\}$, and the complete table is much more important than the output table. This being so, we will often concentrate on automata whose internal states are determined only by the immediate past and ignore the output table.

Since the states S at t are so defined that they do not depend on the inputs at t, any I can occur with any S, and hence there are $M \times N$ possible pairs $\langle I, S\rangle$ in the complete table. There are N possible values of S'. Hence there are $N^{M \times N}$ possible complete tables for an M–N automaton.

We will say that two abstract M—N automata, in whatever language they may be described, are equivalent, just in case they have the same complete table. That this definition is proper can be seen from the following considerations. If the complete tables are the same, then for the same initial internal state and the same input functions, the initial complete states in the two automata are the same, and the same complete state at any moment plus the same input functions always yield the same complete state at the next moment. On the other hand, if two complete tables are different, there must be a pair $\langle\langle I, S\rangle, S'\rangle$ in one table but not in both, such that by choosing suitable input functions and a suitable internal state represented by $\langle I, S\rangle$, we can have the complete state represented by $\langle I, S\rangle$ realized at time zero, and yet the complete state at time one will have to differ. Since we can find effectively the complete table of a given automaton (the details of this process will be explained in the next subsection) and compare effectively whether two complete tables are the same, we have a decision procedure for deciding of two given abstract M–N automata whether or not they are equivalent.

The situation is more complex with automata which have predetermined initial internal states, for two M–N automata with different complete tables may yet behave the same (be equivalent). This is possible because it can happen that for every pair $\langle\langle I, S\rangle, S'\rangle$ which occurs in one table but not in the other, we can never arrive at the internal state S from the distinguished initial internal state S_0, and hence can never have the complete state $\langle I, S\rangle$, no matter how we choose the input functions. In such a case, two M–N automata with the same prechosen initial internal state may behave the same under all input functions, despite the fact that they have different complete tables. Hence, identity of complete tables is a sufficient but not necessary condition for equivalence of two automata. To secure a necessary and sufficient condition, it suffices to determine all the internal states which the given initial internal state can yield when combined with arbitrary input words, and then to repeat this process with the internal states thus found, etc. If the two complete tables coincide insofar as all the pairs occurring in these determinations are concerned, the two automata are equivalent. To establish that such determinations will always terminate in a finite time requires an argument: Since there are only finitely many pairs in each complete table, the process of determination will repeat itself in a finite time.

To describe the procedure exactly, we introduce a few auxiliary concepts. We can think of a tree with the chosen initial internal state S_0 as the root. From the root M branches are grown, one for each possible input word I_i with the corresponding internal state at the next moment S_{0i} at the end. These M branches can be represented by $\ll I_0, S_0>, S_{00}>$, $\cdots$, $\ll I_{M-1}, S_0>, S_{0,M-1}>$, which all belong to the complete table. If all the numbers $S_{00}, \cdots, S_{0,M-1}$ are the same as S_0, the tree stops its growth. If not, M branches are grown on each S_{0i} such that $S_{0i} \neq S_0$, and such that S_{0i} does not equal any S_{0p} for which M branches have already been grown, and we arrive at $S_{0i0}, \cdots, S_{0,i,M-1}$. If all the numbers S_{0ij} (i, j arbitrary) already occur among $S_0, S_{01}, \cdots, S_{0,M-1}$, then the tree stops its growth. If not, then M branches are grown on each S_{0ij} such that it does not equal S_0, or any of the S_{0p}, or any S_{0pq} for which M branches have already been grown. That is, whenever in the construction we come to an S, if it is already on the tree we stop, else we grow M branches on it, one for each I. This process is continued as long as some new internal state is introduced at every height. Since there are altogether only M *a priori* possible internal states, the height (i.e., the number of distinct branch-levels) of the tree cannot exceed M. For any M–N automaton, we can construct such a tree which will be called the *admissibility tree* of the automaton. We can, of course, start with any state S as the assumed initial state, and this gives us an *admissibility tree relative to* S for an abstract automaton.

Those values of S (including S_0) which appear in the admissibility tree are called *admissible* internal states. All other values of S are inadmissible. (Cf. Burks and Wright [1], pp. 1364, 1359.)

If we collect together the ordered pairs which represent branches of the admissibility tree, we obtain a (proper or improper) subset of the complete table, which we shall call the *M–N characterizing table* of the automaton. (As in the case of the admissibility tree, it is easy to define the concept of a *characterizing table relative to* S for an abstract automaton.) In order that two M–N automata be equivalent (i.e., behave the same), it is necessary and sufficient that they have the same characterizing table. Since there is an effective method of deciding whether two M–N automata have the same characterizing table, we have a decision procedure for testing whether two M–N automata are equivalent.

Quite often we are not interested in the whole automaton, but rather in the transformations which particular cells (junctions, wires) of an automaton realize. To discuss this aspect of the situation we need to correlate states of automata with states of the elements of automata. We will do this in two stages; first, by putting state numbers in binary form (in the present subsection), and, next by correlating zero and one with junction states (in the next subsection).

The state numbers I and S are nonnegative integers. The binary representation of states is made simply by putting each state number in binary form, making all the I the same length, and making all the S the same length (by adding vacuous zeros at the beginning when necessary). Let m, n be the number of bits of I, S, respectively, in a characterizing table or complete table in binary form. Clearly m is the least integer as large as (or larger than) the logarithm (to the base two) of the maximum I; similarly with n. Let the bits of I be called $A_0, A_1, \cdots, A_{m-1}$, so that $I = A_0 \frown A_1 \frown \cdots \frown A_{m-1}$ where the arch signifies concatenation. Similarly, let the bits of S be called $B_0, B_1, \cdots, B_{n-1}$, so that $S = B_0 \frown B_1 \frown \cdots \frown B_{n-1}$. In the next subsection we will associate the A's with input junctions and the B's with internal junctions. We speak of the characterizing table in binary form as an *m-n characterizing table.*

If follows from our discussion of characterizing tables that the function τ of definition 2, given by

$$S(0) = S_0,$$
$$S(t+1) = \tau[I(t), S(t)],$$

is a rather simple primitive recursive function (with a finite domain) and that the function $S(t)$ is defined primitive recursively relative to the input function $I(t)$. If our interest is in the transformation realized by a particular internal junction, we use another primitive recursive function σ_i such that $\sigma_i(n)$ gives the ith binary digit of $n(i=0, 1, \cdots)$. Hence each such junction realizes a transformation $\sigma_i[S(t)]$ or $B_i(t)$ which is primitive recursive relative to $I(t)$ (Burks and Wright [1], Theorem XIV; Kleene [11], Theorem 8).

Since the magnitudes of m and n affect the number of junctions of the corresponding automaton, it is of interest to obtain a minimal representation in terms of bits. Given a characterizing table, one can so rewrite the state numbers as to minimize m and n. That is accomplished by so assigning the numbers that the largest I is smaller than the least power of 2 greater than or equal to M, and similarly for S and N. A special case occurs when the states $I_0, I_1, \cdots, I_{M-1}$ are assigned the numbers $0, 1, \cdots, M-1$, respectively, and the states $S_0, S_1, \cdots, S_{N-1}$ are assigned the numbers $0, 1, \cdots, N-1$, respectively (note that the distinguished state S_0 is assigned the number zero). A characterizing table put in this form is said to be in *coded normal form.* Automata nets corresponding to this form will be discussed in the next subsection. (Note that minimizing a complete table does not suffice here, because the number of inadmissible states may be such as to require more bits for representing the set of states than for representing the set of admissible states.)

Another special type of automaton is the decoded normal form automaton; it is of interest in connection with the application of matrices to the analysis of nets. In a *decoded normal form* characterizing table the input words are coded as for the coded normal form, but the internal states $S_0, S_1, \cdots, S_{N-1}$ are assigned the numbers $2^0, 2^1, \cdots, 2^{N-1}$; here an N bit word is needed to represent the N internal states. For six internal states we would have the numbers 100000, 010000, 001000, 000100, 000010, 000001; notice that S_0 has a one on the extreme left, i.e., for S_0, B_0 is one and all other B_i are zero. Automata nets corresponding to decoded normal form characterizing tables will be presented in Section 3.

Each of the A's and B's (bit positions of the binary representations of I and S) is a binary variable. Hence the complete table and, more importantly, the characterizing table are (when put in binary form) kinds of truth tables. Thus we have to large extent reduced the problem of automata description and analysis to the theory of truth functions. Of course the S' in $\ll I, S>, S'>$ is the state at $t+1$, while S is the state at t, so we need to distinguish different times here and hence to use propositional functions (see Section 4). Nevertheless, as the table shows, we need only a very special form of the theory of propositional functions, in which each time step is a matter of the theory of truth functions. So great is the advantage of this partial reduction to the theory of truth-function logic that we will hereafter assume that all characterizing tables are in binary form. Consequently, we may henceforth use any of the techniques of the theory of truth functions which are applicable, not merely the (often cumbersome) truth-table technique.

We return now to the transformations realized by individual elements of the automata, which involves considering the bits of S, i.e., the B's. In the next subsection each B will be associated with an internal junction, so the analysis is also in terms of junctions. The basic problem is to compare the behavior of two bits or junctions, which may or may not belong to the same automaton or characterizing table.

If the two junctions to be compared belong to the same automaton, then they realize the same transformation (behave the same) if and only if the corresponding bits in the S (or S') entries of the characterizing table are everywhere the same. (The state S_0 need not appear in the S' column of $\ll I, S>, S'>$; every other state which is in the S column is in the S' column and vice versa. Of course, all bits are the same in S_0.) This is so because the values of S are the admissible states of the automaton, and at each moment the internal junctions of the automaton are in just one of these states. Hence the question as to whether two junctions of an automaton behave the same can be decided effectively.

If the two junctions are in two different automata, then it is in general not necessary that the automata have the same number of junctions, i.e., that the characterizing tables have the same number of columns, for them to behave the same. Since the transformations depend ultimately only on the time and the inputs, the number of internal junctions need not be the same; since the behavior of an internal junction may be independent of some inputs, even the number of input junctions may be different. Suppose the two junctions belong to an m_1-n_1 and an m_2-n_2 automaton. Then a necessary and sufficient condition for these junctions to realize the same transformation is that there exist some new m_3-n_3 automaton, with $n_3=n_1+n_2$, $m_1+m_2 \geqslant m_3 \geqslant \max(m_1, m_2)$, which is obtained from the two given automata by connecting a subset of the inputs of one to a subset of inputs of the other in a one-one fashion, and in which the internal junctions under consideration realize the same transformation. That supplies an effective procedure because there is only a finite number of inputs to each automaton and hence only a finite number of ways to interconnect them, and for each way the question of equivalent behavior can be decided effectively. When the process is conducted on the characterizing tables it involves identifying certain of the columns of the I part of the tables.

It is allowed that the subset of inputs which are interconnected may be null, in which case $m_3=m_1+m_2$ and the resulting automaton is just the result of juxtaposing the two original automata. For just as the behavior of a junction or cell may be independent of one of the inputs, so it may be independent of all of the inputs. In this case the junction changes from one state at t to another at $t+1$ in a uniform manner independent of the states of the inputs at t. In other words, it realizes a transformation which is independent of the input functions; we will call such a transformation an *input-independent transformation* (it was called a "constant transformation" in Burks and Wright [1], p. 1358) and speak of the junction as an *input-independent junction*. The number of internal states of an automaton is finite, and an automaton is completely determined by the immediate past, hence all input-independent transformations must be periodic (Burks and Wright [1], Theorem I). Therefore no automaton can realize the simple primitive recursive input-independent transformation which has the value one if and only if t is a square $(0, 1, 4, 9, \cdots)$ (Burks and Wright [1], Theorem II; Kleene [11], Section 13).

A very special type of automaton is one whose internal junctions are all input-independent junctions. In such a net, which we call an *input-independent net,* there may be input junctions, but these cannot influence the internal state at any time. For each such automaton, complete and characterizing tables can be found which have no input states.

The admissibility tree provides an effective means for deciding whether the behavior of an internal junction or cell is independent of a specified input and hence for deciding whether the behavior of a junction is independent of all inputs (i.e., realizes an input-independent transformation). For this purpose it is helpful to identify all occurrences of a given state on the admissibility tree. Then one can trace the behavior of the automaton by proceeding in cycles around the tree. We will not describe the procedure in detail, but will make a few comments about it. By a direct inspection of the characterizing table we can tell whether a change in an input junction A at t can make a difference in B at $t+1$. Repeating this process we can find all the junctions that A can influence directly, all that these can influence directly, etc. Since the net is finite, this process will terminate. That is, because of the finite nature of the net there is an interval of time q such that if A can influence the behavior of B, it can do it within the time interval q; this interval may be determined from the structure of the net.

If no input junction influences B_i, then B_i realizes an input-independent transformation, which has been already stated to be periodic. This special case of input-independence can be discovered directly from the characterizing table, for a junction B_j realizes an input-independent transformation if and only if for each S there is a unique value of B_i in S', no matter what I is. The behavior of the input-independent transformation during its initial phase and during its main period can be found from the admissibility tree.

(The problem of deciding whether or not two junctions B_j and B_k realize the same transformation is really a special case of the problem of deciding whether a junction realizes a particular input-independent transformation; for we can have B_j and B_k drive an equivalence element, whose output will be the simple input-independent transformation 11111 $\cdots$ if and only if B_j and B_k realize the same transformation. See the next subsection.)

In our discussion we have for some time ignored the output table. It too can be put in binary form, and since both the O and S entries refer to the same time, the result is a straight truth table (in contrast to the characterizing table, where some columns refer to time t and some to $t+1$). Hence the preceding results are easily extended to include the case of output tables.

We have not yet considered methods of minimizing the labor required to calculate the admissibility tree and the characterizing table. In many cases it is convenient to work with the equations describing a net by means of variables (see the next subsection) rather than with the values of these variables. In some cases one can go directly from such equations to the characterizing table. It is also possible to decompose many nets so as to reduce greatly the number of states to be considered (see Section 4.1). Other methods of simplifying the work will occur to one who is engaged in it and to one familiar with the methods for simplifying truth-table computation.

Before proceeding further let us briefly summarize the concepts introduced in this subsection.

Definition 3. *An automaton is in general characterized by state numbers I, S and O. The complete table of an automaton is the set of all pairs $\ll I, S>, S'>$ such that, for given $I(t)$ and $S(t)$, S' is the value of $S(t+1)$.*

The characterizing table of an automaton is the subset of its complete table such that each S and S′ in it is admissible. A state S is admissible if and only if it is the distinguished initial state S_0 or it can be arrived at from the initial state by choosing a suitable finite sequence of inputs. An admissibility tree is a graph used in computing the admissible states, beginning with S_0 and proceeding systematically. An output table is a table of pairs $\langle\langle I, S\rangle, O\rangle$, stating a value $O(t)$ for given values of $I(t)$ and $S(t)$. *An input-independent junction realizes a transformation whose values are independent of the inputs.*

We will conclude this subsection by commenting on the relation of the decision procedure described above for testing whether or not two junctions realize the same transformation to other decision procedures. Recently a decision procedure for Church's formulation of computer logic has been announced[1]. We are not acquainted with this decision procedure and hence cannot compare it with ours. However, we can prove the equivalence of Church's system[2] to ours, from which it follows that the two decision procedures accomplish the same result. We do this in two steps. First, the definition of automata given in Section 2.1 is in all essential respects equivalent to that of a well-formed net in Burks and Wright [1] (this will be shown in the next subsection). Church's simultaneous recursion is a slight generalization of the second definition of determinism given in Burks and Wright [1], p. 1360; the difference lies in the fact that Church's "*A*'s" and "*B*'s" are independent of each other, whereas in the Burks-Wright definition of determinism each A_i has a certain relation to the corresponding B_i. Because of this relation between the two definitions, it follows directly that every transformation realized by a well-formed net is definable by a Church recursion. The converse may be shown by a net construction in which for each i a net is made for A_i and for B_i, and the outputs are combined to give A_i for $t=0$ and B_i for $t>0$.

It is perhaps worth noting that our decision procedure may be extended to give a method for deciding whether the transformations defined by a set of equations (Burks and Wright [1], p. 1358) are deterministic or not. This may be done by going through all the states $\langle I, S\rangle$ and seeing if for each of these the equations yield a unique S'. If a given S is admissible (by the admissibility tree) and does not yield a unique S' for each I, then the net (i.e., the transformations it realizes) is not deterministic. There is, in any event, only a finite number of cases to consider, so the procedure is effective.

We remark finally that since monadic propositional functions of time may be used in describing net behavior, it might seem that known decision

---

1) Joyce Friedman, "Some results in Church's restricted recursive arithmetic", *The Journal of Symbolic Logic,* **21** (June, 1956), 219; this is an abstract of a paper presented at a meeting of the Association for Symbolic Logic on December 29, 1955.

2) Alonzo Church, Review of Edmund C. Berkeley's "The Algebra of States and Events", *The Journal of Symbolic Logic,* **20** (Sept., 1955), 286—287.

procedures for the monadic functional calculus directly apply here. However, the exact relation between quantifiers and net theory is not known, and in any event when quantifiers are used they required bounds, which are essentially dyadic (see Section 4.2).

2.3. *Representation by Nets, The Coded Normal Form*

We turn now to the representation of automata by diagrams (called automata nets) which show the internal structure of automata. For this purpose we need to correlate the binary digits zero and one used in the preceding subsection to the physical states of wires, junctions, or cells. On the *normal interpretation* zero and one are associated with the inactive and active states, respectively. A *dual interpretation* (zero to active, one to inactive) is also possible, and the two interpretations may be interrelated by the well-known principle of duality.

It is clear from the developments of the preceding subsection that we need net elements capable of performing two kinds of operations: truth functions and delays. For these purposes we adopt two distinct kinds of elements: switching elements for truth-function operations and a delay element for the delay operation.

Some standard logical connectives of the theory of truth functions are: ., & (two representations of conjunction, "and"), $\vee$ (disjunction, "or"), $\downarrow$ ("neither nor"), $|$ ("not both"), $\equiv$ ("if and only if"), $\supset$ ("if $\cdots$ then $\cdots$"), and $-$, $\sim$, $'$ (three representations of negation, "not"). Circuits for realizing all of these are common. As is well-known, all truth functions may be constructed from the dagger ($\downarrow$) or from the stroke ($|$), so we shall in general assume sufficient primitive switching elements to realize these. Sometimes it is convenient to have an infinity of primitive switching elements, one for each truth function. Of course, in practice complicated switching functions are realized by compounding simple switching elements, but by representing such circuits by single net elements we can separate the problem of compounding these circuits from other problems in net analysis (see, for example, fig. 1).

A *switching element* consists of a nucleus together with input wires and an output wire. The termini of these wires are called junctions. Switching elements may be interconnected in *switching nets* in ways to be discussed subsequently. For examples, see figure 1 and other figures of this paper. Propositional variables are associated with each junction of net. Corresponding to each switching element there will be an equation of the theory of truth functions which describes the behavior of that element. For example, if a conjunction ("and") element has the variables A_0 and A_1 attached to its input junctions (and wires) and the variable C_0 attached to its output junction (and wire), it realizes the equation $C_0(t) \equiv [A_0(t) \ \& \ A_1(t)]$, or, more succinctly, $C_0 \equiv (A_0 \ \& \ A_1)$. The theory of switching nets corresponds to the theory of truth functions and is well developed (see Shannon [12]; Burks and Wright [1]).

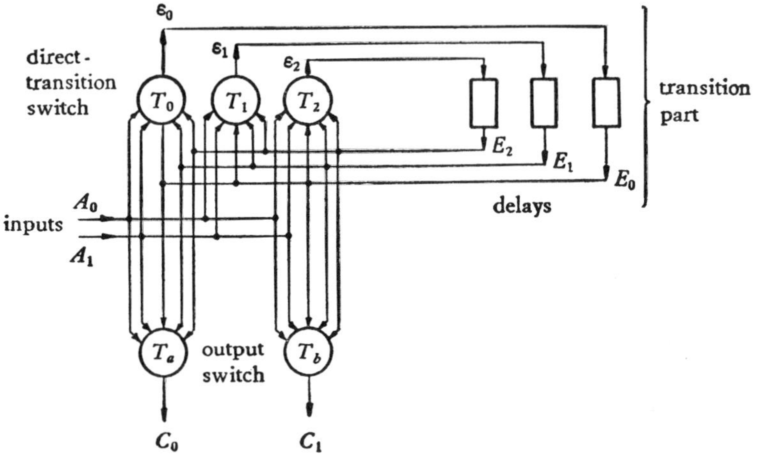

Fig. 1. Normal form net

One aspect of the equation $C_0(t) \equiv [A_0(t) \ \& \ A_1(t)]$ needs discussion; it is that the value of the output is given at the same time t as the inputs. In the physical realization of a conjunction this, of course, cannot happen; the output will occur slightly later than the inputs. This suggests putting a delay in at the output of each switching element. Such a delay does in fact exist in each nerve cell. However, for purposes of theoretical analysis it is best to isolate the logical, nontemporal functions of automata from the temporal aspects of their behavior. Hence we can first construct the theory of switches, basing it on the theory of truth functions, and we can later augment this theory to deal with the additional complications brought in by delays. This organization of the subject has practical bearings as well as theoretical value, for to a certain extent the design of switches does and should proceed independently of the design of those parts of computers which produce the transitions from state to state. Hence our switching nets have no delays in them. When we come to formulate the rules governing their interconnection (formation rules for well-formed nets), we will take this factor of idealization into account and not permit interconnections that could lead to trouble because we have ignored it. Hence we will return to this topic at that time.

The *delay element* consists of a nucleus with an input and an output wire; see figure 1. It delays an input signal one unit of time; i.e., its input wire state at time t becomes its output wire state at time $t+1$. We assume that its output wire is inactive (in the zero state) at time zero. If A_0 is the variable associated with its input and E_0 the variable associated with its output, its behavior is defined by the equations

$$E_0(0) \equiv 0,$$

$$E_0(t+1) \equiv A_0(t).$$

Another way of expressing this is $E_0(t) \equiv (t>0)$ & $A_0(t \dot{-} 1)$, where "$\dot{-}$" signifies the primitive recursive pseudosubtraction

$$x \dot{-} y = x - y \text{ if } x \geqslant y,$$

$$x \dot{-} y = 0 \qquad \text{if } x < y.$$

Each switching element corresponds to a symbol (or complex of symbols) of the theory of truth functions. We will introduce the symbol δ to correspond to the delay element. If the input and output to the delay element are A_0 and E_0 as before, then $E_0(t) \equiv \delta[A_0(t)]$ or, more succinctly, $E_0 \equiv \delta A_0$. Hence,

$$\delta[A_0(0)] \equiv 0,$$

$$\delta[A_0(t+1)] \equiv A_0(t).$$

In itself the δ operator does not, strictly speaking, take us beyond the theory of truth functions (see Section 4.2), but the δ operator together with a cycle rule which allows an output of a net to be connected back to an input of the same net does take us beyond truth-function theory to quantifier theory (see Section 4).

We need now a set of formation rules such that all nets constructed by these rules represent automata, and all automata defined by characterizing tables and output tables may be represented by these nets. We will use the rules given in Burks and Wright [1], p. 1361, extending them to allow an arbitrary set of switching elements Σ.

Definition 4. *A combination of figures is a well-formed net (w.f. n.) relative to the set Σ if and only if it can be constructed by the following rules:*

(1) *A switching element or a delay element is w.f.*

(2) *Assume N_1 and N_2 are disjoint w.f.n. Then,*

(a) *the juxtaposition of N_1 and N_2 is w.f.;*

(b) *the result of joining functions $F_{q1}, \cdots, F_{qi}$ of N_1 to distinct input junctions $G_{p1}, \cdots, G_{pi}$ of N_2 is w.f.;*

(c) *the result of joining input junctions F_p and F_q of N_1 is w.f.;*

(d) *if all the wires connected to F_p of N_1 are delay-element input wires, then the result of joining any F_q of N_1 to F_p is w.f.*

The ends of wires which do not impinge on a switching-element circle or a delay-element rectangle are called *junctions*. A junction with no output wires attached to it is called an *input junction*; all other junctions are called *internal junctions* (these are sometimes called *output junctions*).

One can label each junction of a net with a variable. We will usually use A_0, A_1, $\cdots$ for input junctions, C_0, C_1, $\cdots$ for *switch output junctions* (junctions driven by switching elements), and E_0, E_1, $\cdots$ for *delay output junctions* (junctions driven by delay elements). A well-formed net (diagram) with every junction labeled with a variable is called a *labeled net*. One can also label the input junctions with functional constants designating particular input functions (e.g.,000$\cdots$,111$\cdots$,0101$\cdots$,0100100001000001$\cdots$), and the internal junctions with functional constants naming the functions they actually realize (e.g., if the inputs to a conjunction are labeled with 111 $\cdots$ and 010101 $\cdots$, the output should be labeled 010101 $\cdots$). The result is called a *net history*; cf. the concept of a net state in Burks, McNaughton, *et al.* [13], p. 207.

Consider the net of figure 1. Every net of this form (with arbitrary numbers of delays and switching elements) is well-formed (relative to a sufficiently rich set of switching elements) by our rules. We say that the net of figure 1 is in *normal form*. A normal form net is organized as follows. It has a *direct-transition switch*, fed by the net inputs and the delay outputs, and driving the delay inputs. It has an *output switch*, fed by the delay outputs and the net inputs, and not driving any delay elements.

Given a sufficiently rich set of switching elements, we can construct for each well-formed net a normal form net which behaves the same. We first place the delays of the original net in an array like that of figure 1. Then, for each delay element E_i, we analyze the original net to determine what switching element T_i will produce the same result at ε_i as is produced by the switching circuitry of the original net. In the same way we find those switching elements T_a, T_b, $\cdots$ whose outputs behave the same as the switch output junctions of the original net, or those switch output junctions we are particularly interested in. (The latter can be indicated by labeling them with triangles.) Similarly, given a set of switching elements Σ rich enough to represent all truth functions, we can translate a normal form net into a w.f.n. made of those switching elements; e.g., if Σ contains only the stroke element, we replace each T of figure 1 by an equivalent stroke-element switch. (Note that while a switching element T_i receives inputs from all the net input junctions and all the delay output junctions, its output need not depend on all of these. For example, if in the original net the input to delay element E_2 was the net input junction A_0, then T_2 has the property that $\varepsilon_2(t) \equiv A_0(t)$ for all values of $A_1(t)$, $E_0(t)$, $E_1(t)$, and $E_2(t)$.) (Note also that any well-formed net can be arranged somewhat in the form of figure 1, if we allow the switches to be of other forms and allow the direct-transition switch to have junctions which do not drive delay inputs.)

At this point we wish to make two comments about our representation of switches. The first concerns a topic we have mentioned earlier, the fact that physically it takes time for information to go from the inputs of a switch to the output, while in calculating the behavior of a switch we assume that the output occurs at the same time as the input. The reason for this assumption is that in many applications the switching time is much less than the delay time, so the logic of switching is treated separately from the logic of delay. We wish our theory to accommodate this case. The reader can imagine a small delay in the output of each switching element, with extra delays put in at various places to make the phasing correct. He can then imagine that each unit delay of figure 1 is reduced by the accumulated amount of delay in the switch driving it, so the total delay from delay output back to delay output is one unit. (The concept of rank as defined in Burks and Wright [1], p. 1361, is useful here.) The concept of well-formed net has been so defined as to make this always possible, as is evident from figure 1. This way of regarding the matter conforms with practice in designing some machines; see De Turk *et al.* [14]. Those automata with delay built into each switching element (e.g., neural nets) can also be accommodated within our theory; they correspond to special cases of w.f.n. and can be defined by modifying the formation rules.

The second comment is connected with the fact that our switching elements represent the flow of information in only one direction; i.e., inputs and outputs are not interchangeable. There are many devices that permit information to flow in only one direction (vacuum tubes, transistors, etc.), but not all do; relays are one notable exception. Relay contacts permit information to flow in either direction, and hence bridge circuits can be made from them. Relays are electromechanical devices and hence are relatively slow. For this reason they are becoming less important as much faster electronic and solid-state devices become available and competitive in price. Further, because of the combination of a coil and contacts, relay automata present special problems, and no formation rules for them which take full account of all the uses that can be made of contacts and coils have been published. However, a new and promising device, the cryotron, also permits the information (in this case, current) to flow in either direction and hence can be used in bridge circuits (see Buck [15]). We will not attempt here to devise formation rules for all uses of relays, cryotrons, and whatever other devices there may be which are not unidirectional.

It should be pointed out, however, that every well-formed switching net can be realized by a relay and by a cryotron circuit. Since every truth transformation (i.e., every switching function) can be represented by a well-formed switch and vice versa (Theorem XII of Burks and Wright [1]), our diagrams do represent ways of realizing all truth functions with non-unidirectional elements. Since our diagrams represent a unidirectional flow of information, it follows that the power of relays and cryotrons to pass information in two directions does not add to their power to do logic. It does make a difference in the number of elements needed. Thus a relay bridge circuit may do a certain job more economically than a relay contact network in the form of a well-formed switch.

We return now to the problem of correlating w.f.n. and automata. As a first step we will define a set of state numbers $D_0, D_1, \cdots, D_q$. Each D will express the states of the delay output junctions. Let these junctions be labeled $E_0, E_1, \cdots, E_q$. Then D is the binary number $E_0 \frown E_1 \frown \cdots \frown E_q$. Since a delay output is assumed to be zero at time zero, $D(0)=0$. Let D_0 be this initial state, i.e., $D(0)=D_0$. We wish to justify this decision, but before doing so we need to discuss a question concerning the identity of an automaton.

We may run a machine from Monday to Friday, turn it off at 5:00 P.M. Friday and then turn it on again at 8:00 A.M. the following Monday. Should we regard it as one machine or two? There is a similarity between this and a human (automaton?) going to sleep at night; however, when a human wakes up in the morning he still remembers quite a bit of his past history, while often (though not always) a computer starts a new life every time it is turned on anew. To preserve the identity of the machine before and after the gap of inaction, we can think of some simple *ad hoc* device such as a special input cell whose sole function is to turn the machine on and off in such a manner that, when a machine is in operation, stimulating this input cell will put the machine into a unique initial state; such an operation is often called an initial clear. In this way we can preserve the identity of a machine through all the different runs it makes.

On this assumption there is only one initial state of an automaton, and we can identify it with the all-off or all-quiet state. Such an identification is natural since neurons, vacuum tubes, etc., are usually inactive when first turned on, and even if they are not this identification can be made by a suitable convention without much loss of generality. The situation is somewhat different if we choose to regard each machine run as a new automaton, but even here there will probably be a single initial state for all runs and it is convenient to identify it with the all-quiet state. Note that this does not commit us to identifying S_0 with D_0. In fact, we shall not always do so (the complete decoded net of Sec. 3.2 is an example). Hence one can handle other initial states by identifying D_0 with some value of S other than S_0.

We now proceed to establish the equivalence of w.f.n. and automata. We show first how to derive a characterizing table and an output table for each w.f.n. We translate the given net into a normal form net. Label the inputs of this normal form net $A_0, A_1, \cdots$ and let $I=A_0 \frown A_1 \frown \cdots$; for a two input net we would have, for example, $I_0 \equiv \bar{A}_0 \,\&\, \bar{A}_1$, $I_1 \equiv \bar{A}_0 \,\&\, A_1$, $I_2 \equiv A_0 \,\&\, \bar{A}_1$, and $I_3 \equiv A_0 \,\&\, A_1$. Label the delay inputs $\varepsilon_0, \varepsilon_1, \cdots$ and define $\Delta = \widehat{\varepsilon_0}\,\widehat{\varepsilon_1}\cdots$. Label the delay outputs $E_0, E_1, \cdots$; then $D = \widehat{E_0}\,\widehat{E_1}\cdots$. Let $T_0, T_1, \cdots$ be the truth functions realized by the direct-transition switch. Then we have

$$\varepsilon_i(t) \equiv T_i[A_0(t), A_1(t), \cdots; E_0(t), E_1(t), \cdots],$$
$$E_i(t) \equiv \delta\varepsilon_i(t)$$

for each i. Finally, we let D_0 be S_0 and each other D be an S, and thereby get a complete table. By the use of the admissibility tree we can construct the characterizing table. This procedure takes care of the transition part of a normal form net. To complete the analysis, we perform a similar construction for the switching elements of the original net, or for those switch outputs we are interested in as final outputs. Let $T_a, T_b, \cdots$ be the truth functions realized by these outputs. Then we have

$$C_j(t) \equiv T_j[A_0(t), A_1(t), \cdots; E_0(t), E_1(t), \cdots]$$

for each j, and this gives us the output table.

A *coded normal form net* is a normal form net whose characterizing table is in coded normal form.

When the complete table is derived from a net, there will be a bit position for each input junction and each delay output junction. In this case the numbers m and n (of Section 2.1) are the numbers of input and delay output junctions, respectively. An $m-n$ automaton has then 2^{m+n} possible complete states and 2^n possible internal states. If all input states are considered, we then have $(2^n)^{(2^{m+n})}$ different $m-n$ automata complete tables. Many of these are the same except for the permutation of columns (i.e., of input and internal cells or junctions). Clearly, there is little significance whether a particular junction is labeled the 1st, 2nd, or the mth. In other words, if we can find a way of identifying one-to-one input junctions of two $m-n$ automata so that they behave the same, they are equivalent even though they may have different characterizing tables. Analogously, permutations among the labels for the delay output junctions make no essential difference. It follows that there are actually only $(2^n)^{(2^{m+n})}/(m!)(n!)$ rather than $(2^n)^{(2^{m+n})}$ distinct abstract $m-n$ automata complete tables. Similarly, characterizing tables which are obtainable from one another by permuting columns are to be identified. There will be fewer than $(2^n)^{(2^{m+n})}/(m!)(n!)$ distinct $m-n$ automata characterizing tables, for some of the distinct complete tables will differ only with regard to inadmissible states.

In designing the transition part of an automaton it is in general desirable to maximize the number of admissible internal states (i.e., to minimize the number of inadmissible states), since the total number of states is a rough measure of the parts needed for construction, while the capacity for doing different things is in general proportional to the number of admissible states. We will call an automaton *complete* if all states S are admissible. (A stronger condition would be that all states S are admissible relative to every initial state, instead of just the distinguished initial state S_0; we will not give to automata satisfying the stronger condition any special name.) If the number of admissible states of an automaton is less than 2^{n-1}, we can always replace the automaton by a simpler automaton by using the coded normal form. In a coded normal form characterizing table n is the least integer as large as or larger than the logarithm of N to the base two (similarly for m).

For automata with the same number of admissible states, it seems desirable to maximize the "recoverable" ones. Following Moore [16], p. 140, we shall call an automaton *strongly connected* if and only if it is possible to go from every admissible state S_i to every admissible state S_j (i may be equal to j). An alternative definition can be given in terms of an admissibility tree in which all occurrences of a given state S_i are identified. An automaton is strongly connected if and only if for any ordered pair of states $<S_i, S_j>$ (i may be equal to j), we can pass from S_i on the tree to S_j on the tree, by a continuous forward route (plus backward jumps from a given state to the same state located lower on the tree). Since the possibility of repetition is important for an automaton, any admissible state which cannot be recovered adds rather little to the capacity of the automaton. Thus it would seem best in general to design a machine which is both complete and strongly connected.

Hence, from a practical point of view, complete, strongly connected, and coded normal form automata are the most important. For the theory of automata, however, many nets falling outside this class are of interest. In particular, we will find decoded normal form automata nets of interest in connection with the use of matrices to analyze nets.

It remains to show how to construct a well-formed net for any given characterizing table (or complete table) and output table. There are various ways of doing this, one of which is to identify S_0 with D_0 (if S_0 is not equal to zero, its value must be changed to zero) and to let every other S be a value of D. The general process of going from nets to tables is then just reversed. There are various ways of constructing the switches needed. Let us consider the matter with regard to the characterizing table $\ll I, S>, S'>$. A single column of S' is to be identified with a particular E_i (and ε_i). Delete all other columns of the S' part of the table. We then have a truth-table definition of our function T_i, such that

$$\varepsilon_i(t) \equiv T_i[A_0(t), A_1(t), \cdots; E_0(t), E_1(t), \cdots].$$

Given sufficient primitives, this can be realized by one switching element, as in figure 1. Given switches for "and", "or", and "not", it can be realized by using disjunctive normal form. Consider each row of the truth table. If ε_i is zero, do nothing; if ε_i is one, construct an element to sense $I \frown S$ of that row. The desired switch for ε_i is obtained by disjoining (using "or" on) all the outputs so obtained.

We have thus established our first theorem.

Theorem 1. *Given a well-formed net, we can construct a complete table, a characterizing table, and an output table describing its behavior. Given a complete table, characterizing table, and an output table, we can construct a well-formed net realizing these tables.*

This theorem establishes the equivalence of automata and nets, and since nets are idealized representations of digital computers, it follows that for most theoretical considerations automata without any special sensing and acting organs can be viewed as digital computers.

We conclude this section by noting the similarity of well-formed net diagrams and flow diagrams used in programming. This similarity is what one would expect, since a net diagram describes the structure of a computer, and a flow diagram describes its behavior during a certain computation, and both symbolize recursive functions. While a program is stored in a computer, part of it (the coded representation of the operations) usually remains invariant through the computation; this means that during the computation not all states of the computer are used. For each such fixed program one could devise a special-purpose machine which would perform the same computation. This is a special case of the general principle that there is a great deal of flexibility with regard to what a machine is constructed to do versus what it is instructed to do. This suggests that there should be one unified theory of which the theory of automata structure and the theory of automata behavior (i.e., the theory of programming) are parts.

Each program is in effect a definition of a recursive function. Since there is no effective way of deciding whether two definitions define the same recursive function, there is no effective way of deciding whether two programs will produce the same answer. Two different programs, each finite, may nevertheless produce the same answer because the feedback from the computation may be different in the two cases.

§ 3. Transition Matrices and Matrix Form Nets

3.1. *Transition Matrices*

The transition part of a net controls the passage of the net from state to state and is therefore the heart of the net. In this subsection we introduce "the transition matrix", a table which describes a net by showing the various ways in which it may pass from one delay state to another.

We use a characterizing table with M input (state) words I, N internal state words S, and $M \times N$ rows, each of the form $\ll I, S>, S'>$, to define N^2 *direct-transition expressions* I_{ij} as follows. I_{ij} is a disjunction of all those I_k such that $\ll I_k, S_i>, S_j>$ is a row of the characterizing table; if there are no such I_k, then I_{ij} is ϕ ("the false"). That is, I_{ij} is a disjunction of all those input words (if any) which can cause the net to pass from state S_i at time t to state S_j at time $t+1$; it is allowed that i equals j. It is clear that each I_{ij} is a disjunctive normal form expression of the input function variables.

Note that the direct-transition expression "ϕ" is distinct from the direct-transition expressions "0", "00", "000", etc.; the former means that no direct transition between the two states is possible, while the latter mean that such a transition is brought about by making all the inputs zero.

A *direct transition* from S_i to S_j in a net is a passage from state S_i at t to state S_j at $t+1$. Such a transition is possible only in the case where $I_{ij} \not\equiv \phi$. We say that $<I_k, S_i>$ (or $\widehat{I_k S_i}$) at time t *directly produces* S_j at time $t+1$ only in the case where the net makes a direct transition from S_i to S_j under the influence of input I_k at t.

A *transition* from S_i to S_j in a net is a passage from state S_i at t to state S_j at $t+w$ ($w>0$). Such a transition is possible only where there exists a sequence of direct-transition expressions, none of which are ϕ, of the form $I_{ia_1}, I_{a_1a_2}, \cdots, I_{a_wj}$. We say that $\widehat{I_{ia_1} S_i}(t), I_{a_1a_2}(t+1), \cdots, I_{a_wj}(t+w-1)$ *produces* S_j at $t+w$ if and only if there is a transition from $S_i(t)$ to $S_j(t+w)$ under the direction of the listed inputs; this is a transition of w *steps* (or, alternatively, a transition of *length* w).

It is convenient to arrange the information in an $M-N$ characterizing table in a *direct-transition matrix of order* N by arranging the N^2 direct-transition expressions in square array. The following is a *direct-transition matrix schema* of order four:

$$\begin{bmatrix} I_{00} & I_{01} & I_{02} & I_{03} \\ I_{10} & I_{11} & I_{12} & I_{13} \\ I_{20} & I_{21} & I_{22} & I_{23} \\ I_{30} & I_{31} & I_{32} & I_{33} \end{bmatrix}.$$

It is clear that a direct-transition matrix presents the same information as a characterizing table, but in a different way. For many purposes this form is more convenient, because it reflects the fact that the basic behavior of an automaton consists of a sucession of transitions from one state to another. (Since a transition matrix is equivalent to a characterizing table, the formulae given in section 2.3 for the number of $M-N$ automaton characterizing tables apply here also.)

The information contained in a complete table can also be expressed in matrix form. Since for an abstract automaton the complete table is the characterizing table, the matrix derived from the complete table is a direct-transition matrix.

We give an example of a transition matrix. A matrix for a four-stage cyclic counter is:

$$\begin{array}{c} \\ S_0 \\ S_1 \\ S_2 \\ S_3 \end{array} \begin{array}{c} \begin{array}{cccc} S_0 & S_1 & S_2 & S_3 \end{array} \\ \begin{bmatrix} I_0 & I_1 & \phi & \phi \\ \phi & I_0 & I_1 & \phi \\ \phi & \phi & I_0 & I_1 \\ I_1 & \phi & \phi & I_0 \end{bmatrix} \end{array}.$$

(We have added the S's as a mnemonic aid, but given a conventional ordering of them, they need not be written in.) Thus, an input I_0 (e.g., 0) causes the counter to stay in its given state, while an input I_1 (e.g., 1) causes it to advance to the next state (modulo 4). All other entries are ϕ's since they represent cases where direct transitions are impossible.

3.2. *Matrix Form Nets*

In this subsection we will present a net form closely related to the transition matrix. Our presentation is in two steps; the first is to construct a decoded normal form net.

Consider for a moment a coded normal form net in relation to its coded characterizing table. Each S is associated with a D, and in general any arbitrary number of bits of D may be unity. Consider in contrast a decoded normal form characterizing table. Exactly one bit of each S is unity, which suggests associating each state S primarily with a single junction. That can be done for an N state decoded normal form table as follows. Let $S=B_0\frown B_1\frown\cdots\frown B_{N-1}$ as before, and form a net with N delay elements so that $D=E_0\frown E_1\frown\cdots\frown E_{N-1}$. Of the 2^N delay words D, we use only $N+1$, namely, $D_0(=000\cdots)$ and the N words having exactly one bit which is unity and all other bits zero$(100\cdots$, $010\cdots$, etc.). We next construct a junction C which is the output of a disjunctive element ("or") fed by E_0 and by the input-independent transformation $100\cdots$. Hence,

$$C(0)\equiv 1,$$
$$C(t)\equiv E_0(t), \text{ for all } t>0.$$

We now associate B_0 with C, and each B_i with E_i for $0<i<N$; that is, we equate $B_0\frown B_1\frown\cdots\frown B_{N-1}$ and $C\frown E_1\frown\cdots\frown E_{N-1}$. Hence we have N junctions $(C, E_1, \cdots, E_{N-1})$ such that each state S is associated primarily with one junction:

namely, that junction which is active when the net is in that state. These junctions are called the *state junctions* of the net. See figure 2, where the state junctions are labeled C, E_1, and E_2, and are also labeled with the states (S_0, S_1, and S_2) which they "represent".

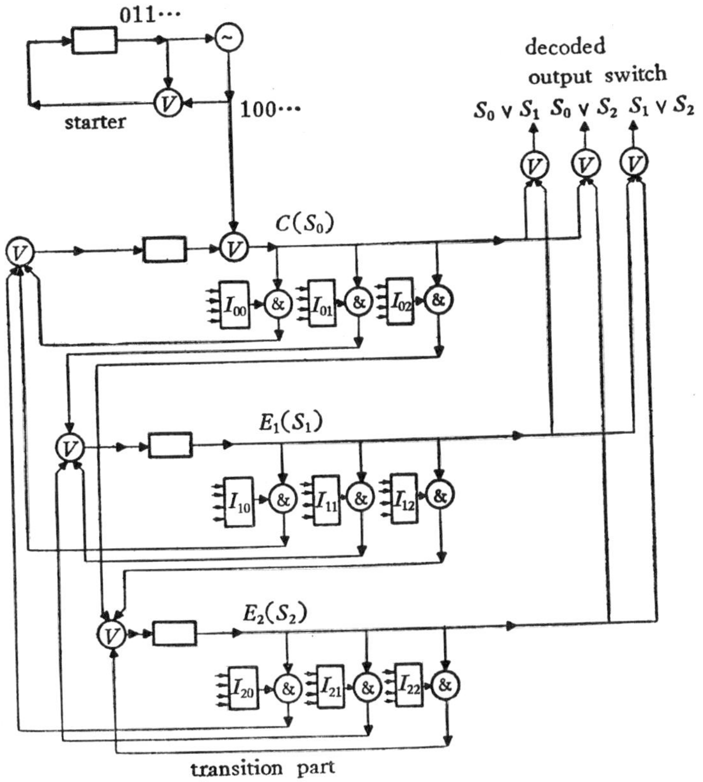

Fig. 2. Decoded normal form net

We now wish to construct a net containing wires $C, E_1, \cdots, E_{N-1}$, so connected that at each time exactly one of them is active (in state one) while all others are zero, and with the following inductive property.

(A) Junction C (representing S_0) is active at time 0.

(B) For any time t, if the junction labeled S_i (i.e., C for $i=0$, E_i for $i>0$) is active at time t, the net input at time t is I_k, and $\ll I_k, S_i>, S_j>$ is a row of the characterizing table, then the junction labeled S_j will be activated at time $t+1$.

To realize condition (A), we construct a *starter* (see fig. 2) to produce the input-independent transformation $100\cdots$. The starter output is then disjoined with E_0 to produce C. This will insure that $C(0)\equiv 1$, and that $C(t)\equiv E_0$ for $t>0$. The starter, which adds another delay element to the net, may be constructed without a cycle (see section 4.3).

The realization of (B) is more complicated. Since there is a state junction for each state (C for S_0, E_{i+1} for S_{i+1}), the concept of a direct-transition word is useful here. At each state junction S_i we build N switches such that:

$I_{i0}\frown S_i$ directly produces S_0 (i.e., activates C at the next moment of time);

$I_{i1}\frown S_i$ directly produces S_1 (i.e., activates E_1 at the next moment of time);

$\vdots$

$I_{i,N-1}\frown S_i$ directly produces S_{N-1} (i.e., activates E_{N-1} at the next moment of time).

A net to accomplish this purpose is shown in figure 2, which is actually a *net schema* rather than a net, since the I_{ij} are not specified.

The boxes labeled with the direct-transition expressions I_{ij} are called *direct-transition switches.* (Note that these direct-transition switches are different from the direct-transition switch of figure 1, though both kinds of switches play the same basic role in a net.) A direct-transition switch I_{ij} has an output at time t if and only if the input to the net is represented by a disjunct of I_{ij}. Every such switch can be made of a disjunction driven by conjunctions of positive and negative inputs. For example, let I_{10} be 0101 $\vee$ 0110 $\vee$ 1111, which may be written as $\bar{A}_0 A_1 \bar{A}_2 A_3 \vee \bar{A}_0 A_1 A_2 \bar{A}_3 \vee A_0 A_1 A_2 A_3$, and the latter is readily realized by a switch. Of course the number of inputs may vary from net to net; we will usually show four inputs in our figures (as we do in fig. 2).

If a particular I_{ij} is ϕ, the switch I_{ij} and the conjunction it drives may be deleted. If a net always passes directly from a state S_i to a state S_j, no matter what the inputs are (or because there are no inputs), then we can run a direct line from the S_i junction to the input of the delay element driving the S_j junction. An input-independent net thus becomes a string of delays (corresponding to the initial part of the input-independent transformation), driven by a starter and driving a cycle of delays (corresponding to the periodic part of the function); cf. Theorem XIII and the accompanying figure of Burks and Wright [1], p. 1363.

We call a net of the form of figure 2 a *decoded normal form net.* We will first explain why we call this form "decoded" in contrast to the "coded" form described earlier, and then discuss the exact relation between decoded and other nets. The terminology is justified by the fact that in a coded normal form net the numbers representing delay states (i.e., the D's) appear in coded form, while in the decoded normal form net the numbers representing the delay states (the D's, except that E_0 is replaced by C at time zero) appear in decoded form, in the sense in which the terms "coded" and "decoded" are used in switching theory. A *decoding switch* is a switch with the same number of output junctions $C_0, \cdots, C_{N-1}$ as there are admissible input words $I_0, \cdots, I_{N-1}$, and so connected that when the input state is I_n the output junction C_n is active and all other outputs are inactive. (This is a special case of the nets discussed in Burks, McNaughton, *et al.* [13]). The information on the inputs is in *coded* form, while that on the outputs is *decoded.* In our coded and decoded normal form nets, however, the coding and decoding applies to delay outputs rather than to switch outputs.

Given any automaton net, we can construct a decoded normal form net which models that automaton net in the sense of having junctions which behave the same. Let us begin with the transition part of the given automaton net. Suppose it has n delay output junctions $F_0, F_1, \cdots, F_{n-1}$ and N admissible states $S_0, S_1, \cdots, S_{N-1} (N \leqslant 2^n)$. We next construct the transition part of a decoded normal form net with junctions $C, E_1, \cdots, E_{N-1}$, such that the i-th bit from the left of $C \frown E_1 \frown \cdots \frown E_{N-1}$ is unity when the original automaton is in state S_{i-1}. Any function F_j is equivalent to a disjunction $S_{a_1} \vee S_{a_2} \vee \cdots \vee S_{a_k}$ of just those states for which F_j has the value one. Hence by disjoining the appropriate state junctions of the decoded normal form net we can obtain a junction F_j' such that $F_j'(t) \equiv F_j(t)$ for all t. Figure 2 shows a *decoded output switch* which realizes $S_0 \vee S_1$, $S_0 \vee S_2$, and $S_1 \vee S_2$. The "single-disjunct disjunctions" S_0, S_1, and S_2 are already represented in figure 2, and the input-independent outputs $(\bar{S}_0 \,\&\, \bar{S}_1 \,\&\, \bar{S}_2)$ and $(S_0 \vee S_1 \vee S_2)$ (i.e., $000 \cdots$ and $111 \cdots$) are readily obtained from the net if needed.

This shows how to construct junctions of a decoded normal form net which behave the same as the delay output junctions of the original net. Any other junction of the original net whose behavior at time t does not depend on the state of the inputs at time t can be treated in the same way. For the remaining junctions we can build an output switch fed both by the decoded output switch and the net inputs. Alternatively, the decoded output switch can be replaced by a switch driven by the state junctions and the net inputs. Switches of these various kinds are allowed as parts of decoded normal form nets. We can now incorporate these results in a theorem.

Theorem 2. *For any well-formed net with junctions $C_0, C_1, \cdots$, one can construct a decoded normal form net with junctions $C_0', C_1', \cdots$ such* that $C_i(t) \equiv C_i'(t)$ *for all i and t.*

The transition part of a decoded normal form net can be drawn in matrix form to bring out its relation to the transition matrix. In figure 3 this is done for a transition matrix of order 4; the result is called a *matrix box.* The disjunction elements of figure 2 are omitted by the convention that several wires can drive a line (see Burks and Copi [2], p. 307). A normal form net with the transition part put in matrix-box form is called a *matrix form net.* Figure 4 is an example which lacks an output switch.

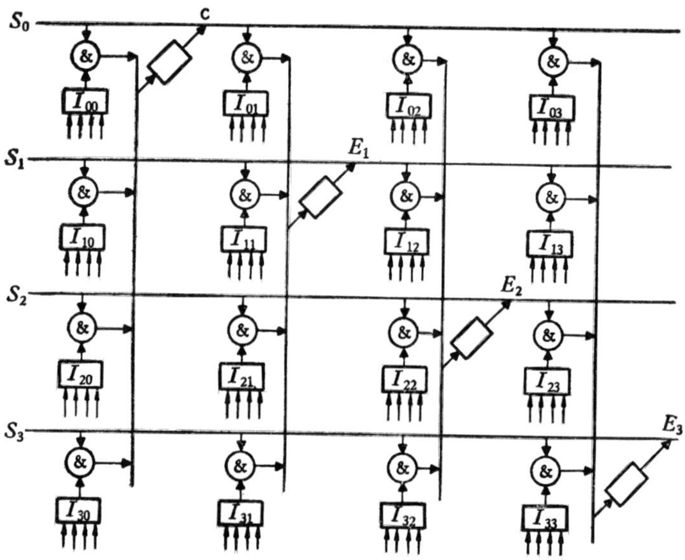

Fig. 3. Matrix box of order 4

A particular net of order four may be obtained from the schema of figure 3 by substituting the appropriate switches for the direct-transition-switch schemata. We illustrate this with the four-stage cyclic counter whose transition matrix was given in section 3.1. If we let input $I_0 \equiv 0$ and input $I_1 \equiv 1$ (so the counter counts pulses rather than the absence of pulses), we get the matrix box of figure 4. Each $I_{ii} \equiv I_0 \equiv 0$, so we replace these direct-transition-switch schemata by negation elements. For each i, j such that $j = i+1$ modulo four, $I_{ij} \equiv 1$, so we replace these direct-transition-switch schemata by single input lines. All other transition-switch schemata correspond to ϕ's in the transition matrix defining the counter, so these are dropped; e.g., no direct transition from S_2 to S_1 is possible, so there is no direct coupling from S_2 to ε_1. It is manifest from figure 4 that the counter stays in its prior stage when the input is zero, but advances to the next stage (modulo four) when the input is one.

3.3. *Some Uses of Matrices*

The discovery that matrices may be used to characterize automata nets opens up a number of interesting lines of investigation. In the present subsection we will discuss a few applications of matrices to the analysis of automata nets.

A direct-transition matrix (whose elements are direct-transition expressions) characterizes the direct transitions of an automaton. We will first establish some properties of this matrix, and then generalize the concepts of direct-transition expression and direct-transition matrix to cover transitions of arbitrary length.

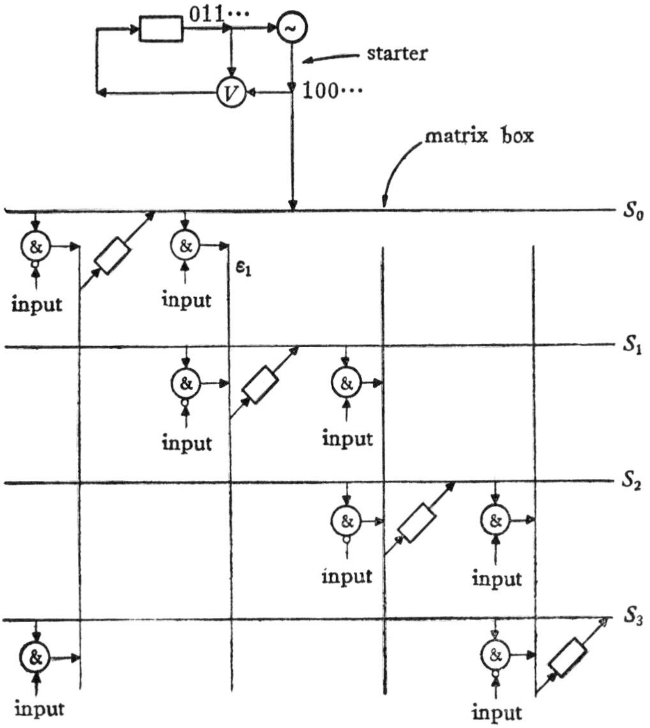

Fig. 4. Matrix form binary counter

Each row of a direct-transition matrix is a partition of M input words $I_0, I_1, \cdots, I_{M-1}$ into N columns $S_0, S_1, \cdots, S_{N-1}$. Hence the disjunction of a row contains all the admissible input words. If these are all the possible words, the disjunction of a row is a tautology. If there are inadmissible input words, then the hypothetical whose consequent is the disjunction of the matrix row and whose antecedent is a disjunction of all the admissible input words is a tautology. In this case we can say that the matrix row sums to a tautology relative to the admissibility conditions, or that it is a *tautology* in an extended sense of this word. (Note that this relative sense of "tautology" is relevant in minimality problems; in minimizing a switch we are not looking for a switch logically equivalent to the given one, but rather for a switch logically equivalent to the given one relative to the admissibility conditions on the inputs.) A single element j of a row i may be a tautology, in which case all other elements in the row are ϕ; this means that whenever the automaton is in state S_i it makes a direct transition to state S_j, no matter what the input is. No input word can occur more than once in a row, else the automaton would not be deterministic.

The disjunction of the elements of a column is not in general a tautology, but cases where it is are of special interest as they are related to the concept of backward determinism.

Definition 5. *An abstract automaton is backwards deterministic if and only if for each finite sequence* $I(0), I(1), \cdots, I(t), S(t+1)$, there is a *unique sequence* $S(0), S(1), \cdots, S(t)$ *satisfying the complete table. A direct-transition matrix is backwards deterministic if and only if for each* I_k *and* S_j *there is at most one state* S_i *such that* $\widehat{I_k S_i}$ *directly produces* S_j.

We give an example of a backwards-deterministic matrix of order three:

$$\begin{bmatrix} I_0 \vee I_1 & \phi & I_2 \\ \phi & I_0 \vee I_1 \vee I_2 & \phi \\ I_2 & \phi & I_0 \vee I_1 \end{bmatrix}.$$

Another example of interest is:

$$\begin{bmatrix} I_0 & I_1 & I_2 & I_3 \\ I_1 & I_2 & I_3 & I_0 \\ I_2 & I_3 & I_0 & I_1 \\ I_3 & I_0 & I_1 & I_2 \end{bmatrix}.$$

Besides being backwards deterministic, this matrix has the property that a direct transition is possible from any state to any other state. We call such a matrix directly strongly connected; see definition 6 below.

Theorem 3. *The disjunction of every column of a direct-transition matrix is a tautology if and only if that matrix is backwards deterministic. An abstract automaton is backwards deterministic if and only if its direct-transition matrix is backwards deterministic.*

We prove first that having every column sum (logically) to a tautology is a necessary and sufficient condition for a direct-transition matrix to be backwards deterministic. If every column sums to a tautology, every input word must occur at least once in each column. But no input word could occur twice in a column, because in the $N \times N$ matrix every input word must appear exactly once in a row and there are exactly N occurrences of each input word. If an input word occurred twice in the same column, then at least one of the $(N-1)$ remaining columns must miss that word and could not be a tautology. Hence for a given state S_j at time $t+1$, and a given input word I_k at time t, there is only one state S_i which together with I_k could have directly produced S_j. Therefore, having every column sum to a tautology is a sufficient condition for a direct-transition matrix to be backwards deterministic. The proof that it is a necessary condition is obtained by reversing the considerations just used. In a backwards-deterministic matrix no input word can occur twice in the same column. But each row contains exactly one occurrence of each input word and there are exactly N occurrences of each input word in the matrix. Hence, no input word is missing in any column, because otherwise it must occur twice or more in at least one other column. Therefore, every column must sum to a tautology.

We show next that if a direct-transition matrix is backwards deterministic, the abstract automaton is backwards deterministic. Consider a finite sequence $I(0)$, $I(1)$, $\cdots$, $I(t)$, $S(t+1)$. It follows from the results of the preceding paragraph that there is exactly one $S(t)$ which together with $I(t)$ directly produced $S(t+1)$. Iterating this argument, we see that there is a unique sequence $S(0)$, $S(1)$, $\cdots$, $S(t)$ satisfying the complete table (for the given $I(0), \cdots, I(t)$, $S(t+1)$). To prove the second part of the theorem in the other direction, we note that if a matrix is not backwards deterministic, there will be some I_k and some S_j such that there are two distinct states S_a and S_b, either of which will, together with I_k, directly produce S_j. Hence for the sequence $I(0)=I_k$ and $S(1)=S_j$, there are two sequences (namely, $S(0)=S_a$ and $S(0)=S_b$) satisfying the complete table.

In section 2.1 we remarked that in the presence of our deterministic assumption an infinite past would be inconvenient. The first part of theorem 3 may be used to justify this statement. In order to describe the behavior of a net over a certain period of time t, $t+1, \cdots, t+w$, we would naturally need to know the inputs $I(t)$, $I(t+1)$, $\cdots$, $I(t+w)$ and the internal state S at one of these times (or perhaps at $t+w+1$). Now if every net were backwards deterministic, it would not matter for which time S was known. But for a net which is not backwards deterministic we must know $S(t)$ to determine $S(t+1)$, $\cdots$, $S(t+w)$. Hence we might as well pick a time $t=0$ as a standard reference point for our analysis and always work forward from this time; we therefore allow t to range over the nonnegative integers only. (We could define backwards deterministic on the basis of each infinite sequence $\cdots$, $I(-7)$, $\cdots$, $I(0)$, $\cdots$, $I(t)$, $S(t+1)$ determining an infinite sequence $\cdots$, $S(-7)$, $\cdots$, $S(0)$, $\cdots$, $S(t)$ and conduct the discussion in terms of this definition. Theorem 3 then holds with the following exception: The direct-transition matrix of a backwards-deterministic automaton may fail to be backwards deterministic with regard to states which cannot be recovered. For example, a backwards-deterministic automaton can have a transition matrix in which both $\widehat{S_a I_k}$ and $\widehat{S_b I_k}$ directly produce the same state S_j, but in which no state and input combination directly produces S_a or S_b.)

We turn now to the task of generalizing the notion of direct-transition expression to cover nondirect transitions. Consider an example. Suppose it is possible to go from state three of an automaton to state seven with either a sequence I_4, I_6, or with I_2. We could write this as $I_4 I_6 \vee I_2$, but it must be understood that juxtaposition here represents a noncommutative type of conjunction, since I_6 followed by I_4 may not carry the net from state three to state seven. We will sometimes use a special operation, called concatenated conjunction, to express the order-preserving conjunction needed here. Thus the above may be written $I_4 \frown I_6 \vee I_2$. However, the *concatenated-conjunction* symbol, $\frown$, may be omitted if the context makes clear what is intended. The noncommutative nature of concatenated conjunction can be brought out by making the role of time explicit: $I_4 \frown I_6$ is short for $I_4(t) \cdot I_6(t+1)$, while $I_6 \frown I_4$ is short for $I_6(t) : I_4(t+1)$. Clearly $I_4(t) \cdot I_6(t+1)$ is not equivalent to $I_6(t) \cdot I_4(t+1)$.

Concatenated conjunction can be used to build up transition words from direct-transition expressions. For example, we might have the transition expression $I_{3,2} \frown I_{2,5} \frown I_{5,7} \vee I_{3,7}$, or, more briefly, $I_{3,2} I_{2,5} I_{5,7} \vee I_{3,7}$. In a concrete case it might reduce to the transition expression $I_4 \frown (I_6 \vee I_9) \frown I_5 \vee (I_3 \vee I_6)$, or, more briefly, $I_4 (I_6 \vee I_9) I_5 \vee (I_3 \vee I_6)$, which is of course equivalent to the transition expression $I_4 \frown I_6 \frown I_5 \vee I_4 \frown I_9 \frown I_5 \vee I_3 \vee I_6$, or, more briefly, $I_4 I_6 I_5 \vee I_4 I_9 I_5 \vee I_3 \vee I_6$. For this expansion we use a distribution principle for concatenated conjunction: $(p \vee q) \frown (r \vee s) \equiv (p \frown r \vee p \frown s \vee q \frown r \vee q \frown s)$.

We can now define the general concept of transition expression. A *transition expression* is a disjunction of concatenated conjunctions of direct-transition expressions, provided that if any concatenated conjunction contains a ϕ, it may be replaced by ϕ. Thus $I_{2,5} I_{5,3} \vee I_{2,3}$ might become $(I_3 \vee I_7) \frown \phi \vee \phi$, which would reduce to ϕ. we allow direct-transition expressions as special cases of transition expressions.

Definition 6. *A transition matrix of order N is an N×N array whose elements are transition expressions. Two transition matrices of order N can be combined by the following operations, where $\alpha(a, b)$, $\beta(a, b)$ are transition expressions for transitions from state a to state b.*

Matrix disjunction: $[\alpha(a, b)] \vee [\beta(a, b)] = [\alpha(a, b) \vee \beta(a, b)]$.

Matrix concatenated conjunction: $[\alpha(a, b)] \frown [\beta(a, b)] = [\gamma(a, b)]$, where $\gamma(a, b) = \sum_{i=0}^{N-1} \alpha(a, i) \frown \beta(i, b)$, where Σ represents disjunction.

Matrix (concatenated) power: $M^1 = M$

$$M^n = M^{n-1} \frown M.$$

Sum of matrix powers: $\sum_{i=1}^{n} M^i = M \vee M^2 \vee \cdots \vee M^n$.

The *characteristic matrix* $C(M)$ of a transition matrix M is obtained by replacing the elements of M with zeros or ones, according to whether the elements do or do not reduce to ϕ, i.e., according to whether transitions from state a

to state b are not or are possible by M. A direct-transition matrix M is *directly strongly connected* if and only if every element of $C(M)$ is unity. *Inequality between characterizing matrices* is defined by $C(M) \leqslant C(N)$ if and only if for each element $\alpha(a, b)$ of $C(M)$ and the corresponding element $\beta(a, b)$ of $C(N)$, $\alpha(a, b) \leqslant \beta(a, b)$, i.e., $\alpha \supset \beta$.

Theorem 4. *Let M be a direct-transition matrix of order n. A transition from state S_i to state S_j in exactly w steps is possible if and only if the element $\alpha(i, j)$ of $C(M^w)$ is one. A transition from S_i to S_j in w or less steps is possible if and only if the element $\alpha(i, j)$ of $C(\sum_{k=1}^{w} M^k)$ is one.. A transition from state S_i to state S_j is possible if and only if* (a) *for $i \neq j$, the element $\alpha(i, j)$ of $C(\sum_{k=1}^{n-1} M^k)$ is one;* (b) *for $i=j$, the element $\alpha(i, j)$ of $C(\sum_{k=1}^{n} M^k)$ is one. A net is strongly connected if and only if every element of $C(\sum_{k=1}^{n} M^k)$ is unity. If α and β are positive integers, then*

$$C\left(\sum_{k=1}^{\alpha} M^k\right) \leqslant C\left(\sum_{k=1}^{\alpha+\beta} M^k\right),$$

$$C\left(\sum_{k=1}^{n} M^k\right) = C\left(\sum_{k=1}^{n+\alpha} M^k\right).$$

To prove this theorem, we first examine the structure of the elements of M^w, where M is the direct-transition matrix. Each element $\alpha(i, j)$ is a disjunction of concatenated conjuncts, each of the form $I_{i a_1} I_{a_1 a_2} \cdots I_{a_w j}$. Clearly a transition from S_i to S_j in exactly w steps is possible if and only if at least one of these concatenated conjunctions does not reduce to ϕ, i.e., if and only if the element $\alpha(i, j)$ of $C(M^w)$ is unity. A matrix $\sum_{i=1}^{w} M^k$ has as its elements transition expressions covering transitions in 1, 2, $\cdots$, or w steps, and hence the elements of $C(\sum_{i=1}^{w} M^k)$ are one or zero according to whether a transition from S_i to S_j can or cannot be made in w or less steps. It remains for us to show that beyond a certain power (n for $i=j$, $n-1$ for $i \neq j$), raising M to a higher power does not add to the possible transitions that can occur, but only to the way in which they occur. Consider two distinct states, S_i and S_j. There are only $n-2$ other states to pass through. The automaton's being in one of these states S_k for more than one moment of time does not increase the possibility of getting to S_j from S_i, since whatever can be accomplished from a later occurrence of S_k can be accomplished from the first occurrence of S_k. The argument is similar for possible transitions from S_i to S_i, with the difference that here we must consider $n-1$ other states.

§ 4. Cycles, Nets, and Quantifiers

4.1. *Decomposing Nets*

In this section we discuss cycles in nets and their bearing on the application of logic to net analysis. As a first step we discuss the elimination of unnecessary cycles from nets.

A well-formed net (w.f.n.) may have unused switching-element input wires. This is especially likely to be the case for a coded normal form net constructed from a characterizing table, for not all bits of D and I need influence a given delay input junction. By inspection of the characterizing table of a w.f.n., we can tell which bits are irrelevant to a switch output C_i. A particular bit A_j of $\widehat{ID}$ is irrelevant to C_i if and only if for each pair $\widehat{ID}$ identical in every position A_j the value of C_i is the same. Using this criterion we can eliminate all the unused switch input wires by replacing the original switching elements with other elements which behave the same for all inputs and on which every switch input has an influence. The same process can be applied to an output table and an output switch.

It should be noted that the above process is a minimization technique, i.e., a technique for producing a simpler net which realizes the same transformations as the original net. In section 2.3 we showed how to minimize the number of delay elements by using a coded normal form. Other minimization methods are implicit in the results of preceding sections. For example, if two junctions of a net behave the same (cf. the decision procedure of section 2.2), one may be eliminated. Note that for these minimization procedures we can work from complete tables, characterizing tables, and output tables; we need not refer to the net diagrams at all.

However, our main interest at present is not in minimality in general, but in minimality only insofar as it relates to the number and nature of cycles in a net. For example, every normal form net with at least one delay element will have cycles, while the corresponding net with no irrelevant switching-element inputs may have either fewer cycles or perhaps no cycles at all. For this reason we shall hereafter consider only such nets. Our next task is to define a measure of the complexity of the cycles of a net.

A sequence of junctions $A_1, A_2, \cdots, A_n, A_1$ (possibly with repetitions) constitutes a *cycle* if and only if each A_j is an input to an element whose output is A_k, where $k \equiv j+1$ modulo n. Thus a junction occurs in a cycle if it is possible to start at that junction, proceed forward (in the direction of the arrows) through switching elements and delay elements, and ultimately return to the junction. A junction which does not occur in a cycle has *degree* zero, as does an input-independent junction. It should be noted that this definition assigns degree zero to some junctions occurring in cycles, i.e., to all input-independent junctions which occur in cycles. The reason will become clear in the next subsection. For the same reason we require a further modification of the net before degrees are assigned to the remaining junctions of it. That modification is to replace all cycles containing both input-independent and non-input-independent junctions by cycles containing only one of these kinds of junctions. Let C be an input-independent junction occurring in a cycle with a non-input-independent junction E. Break the cycle at C by deleting the element whose output wire is joined to junction C; to make the net behave the same, we connect C to the output of a subnet which realizes the input-independent transformation originally realized by C. Such a subnet may be so constructed that it has only one cycle, and such that every junction in it is an input-independent junction (Burks and Wright [1], Theorem XIII, p. 1363). Thus, given any net N, we can find an equivalent net N' with no more cycles than N and which has no cycles containing both input-independent and non-input-independent junctions. We say that a net with no irrelevant switching-element inputs and with no cycles containing both input-independent and non-input-independent junctions is in *reduced form*. We assign degrees to all the junctions of N' (and hence derivatively to all junctions of N) as follows:

The degree of a non-input-independent junction which occurs in a cycle is the maximum number of distinct delay elements it is possible to pass through by traveling around cycles in which the junction occurs. Figure 5 shows

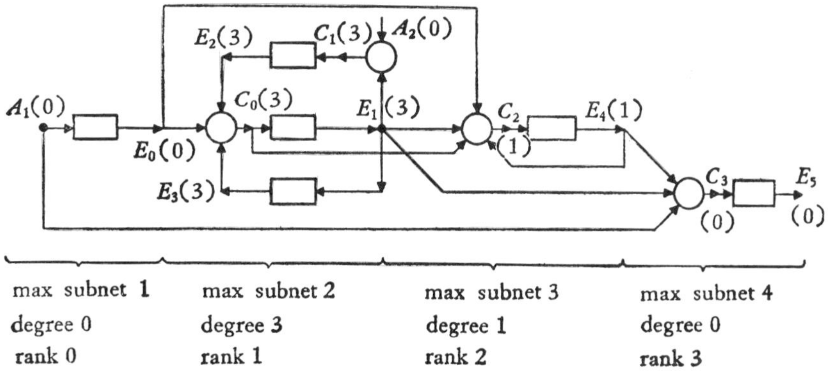

Fig. 5. Net of degree 3

a net with the degree of each junction in parentheses. (We stipulate that in fig. 5 the switching functions are so chosen that no junction is input-independent, and the net is in reduced form.) Note that in order to get to both E_2 and E_3 from C_0, it is necessary to pass through E_1 twice.

The *degree of a net* is the maximum of the degrees of its junctions. Figure 5 is of degree 3. A net is *entirely connected* if and only if its degree is greater than zero and the number of delay elements in it is equal to its degree. This notion should be compared with the analogous notion of "strongly connected," defined in section 2.3. We define *directly entirely connected* analogously to the notion "directly strongly connected" of section 3.3; that is, in a directly entirely connected net it is possible to start at any delay output junction and proceed forward to any delay input junction, passing only through switching elements. One of these sets of notions concerns states; the other set concerns the bits used to represent states.

Figure 5 is not entirely connected, but it may be completely decomposed into two nets of degree zero (the net A_1-E_0 and the net $E_4-E_1-A_1-C_3-E_5$) and two entirely connected subnets ($E_0-C_0-E_1-A_2-C_1-E_2-E_3$ and $E_0-C_0-E_4-C_2$).

A *maximal entirely connected subnet associated with a net junction,* say *F,* is the net formed of all junctions which occur in a cycle with *F,* together with the elements between these junctions, and the switch input junctions of all switches whose output junctions are in a cycle with *F.* Subnet 2 of figure 5 (the net $E_0-C_0-E_1-A_2-C_1-E_2-E_3$) is a maximal entirely connected subnet associated with the junctions E_2, C_1, C_0, E_1, E_3. The part of this subnet which results by deleting the delay element between E_1 and E_3 is an entirely connected subnet of figure 5, but it is not maximal.

Since any two junctions of a net either do or do not occur in the same cycle, each element of a net either belongs to a subnet of degree zero (i.e., is not in a cycle) or belongs to a unique, maximal, entirely connected subnet of the original net. (Note in this connection that "occurring in the same cycle" is a transitive relation.) A given net element may belong to several subnets of degree zero; e.g., the delay C_3-E_5 of figure 5 belongs to subnet 4 and to the subnet consisting of itself.

There are various ways to group the elements connected to junctions of degree zero into maximal subnets, of which we will give one. Let *A* be a junction of degree zero and *B* be any other junction of the net. Proceeding forward from *B* to *A* along a certain path, we can pass through n ($n \geqslant 0$) maximal entirely connected subnets before arriving at *A.* Note that n is bounded, for if we could pass through a given maximal entirely connected subnet *M* and then (always proceeding forward in the direction of the arrows) later come back to *M* and pass through it again, it would not be the case that *M* is maximal. Since there are a finite number of junctions in the net and a finite number of paths from each to *A*, there is a maximum such number *N* to be associated with *A.* Then group into a *maximal subnet of degree zero* all the elements lying between junctions with the same maximal numbers *N,* together with the input wires of all switches whose output junctions are assigned the number *N.* Subnet 4 of figure 5 is a maximal subnet of degree zero.

It is by now clear that any net in reduced form can be uniquely and effectively decomposed into maximal entirely connected subnets and maximal subnets of degree zero, i.e., into *maximal subnets* of various degrees. Figure 5 is uniquely decomposed into the four subnets shown there. To decompose a net, one need only find the degrees of the junctions, one by one, remove all input-independent junctions which occur in cycles with non-input-independent junctions, determine the classes of junctions belonging to the same cycles, and then determine the maximal subnets of degree zero.

A *rank* can then be assigned to each maximal subnet inductively. A maximal subnet which has no net inputs or whose only inputs are net inputs is of rank 0. A maximal subnet which has at least one input from another maximal subnet of rank r and no inputs from maximal subnets of rank greater than r, is of rank $r+1$. See figure 5 for an example of ranks. There may, of course, be several maximal subnets of the same rank. It is clear that every maximal subnet has a unique rank, for there cannot be two such subnets driving each other, else they would not be maximal (cf. Theorem IX of Burks and Wright [1]). It is worth noting that if each maximal subnet of a net is replaced by a single box with inputs and outputs, the result is a diagram without cycles. The following structure theorem summarizes these results.

Theorem 5. *Any net in reduced form may be uniquely decomposed into (one or more) maximal subnets, each of which has a unique degree and rank.*

We conclude this subsection with a conjecture: For any degree d, there is some transformation not realized by any net of degree d. This means that there is no maximal degree such that any transformation can be realized by a net of this degree. Our grounds for making this conjecture are as follows. Consider counters with one input, designed to produce an output modulo m. When m is a power of two, one can construct a sequence of binary counters, each of degree one, each driving its successor, except the last one, which drives nothing but produces the desired output, and the whole net will be of degree 1. When m is not a power of two, the standard way of constructing the desired counter is to take a counter modulo a power of two, sense with a switch when it reaches $m-1$, and use that information to clear the counter back to zero. But such a feedback loop produces a net of arbitrarily high degree. Considerations of this sort lead us to believe that the conjecture is true.

4.2 *Truth Functions and Quantifiers*

We have already indicated (section 2.2) the close correspondence between switching nets (switches) and the theory of truth functions (the propositional calculus, Boolean algebra). That correspondence permits us to assign variables to switch inputs and to associate with each switch output a truth-functional expression which is a truth function of the input variables for that switch. Thus we can represent the output of a switch as an explicit function (in particular, a truth function) of its inputs.

It is natural to seek analogs for well-formed nets in general. We will give an analog for nets of degree zero and then discuss the problem for nets of arbitrary degree.

Consider first nets with delays but without cycles. For these we can express each output as an explicit function of the inputs by using the theory of truth functions enriched with the delay operator δ. Thus in figure 5 $E_0 \equiv \delta A_1$. That this can always be done for noncyclic nets can be proved from the formation rules (with rule 5 deleted, of course); the considerations involve generalizations of those connected with the concept of rank in Burks and Wright [1], p. 1361 ff.

We next mention two theorems for delay nets without cycles. The first concerns shifting a delay operator across a logical connective; for example,

$$\delta(A \,\&\, B) \equiv \delta A \,\&\, \delta B.$$

To prove this formula, we apply the definition of δ to both sides:

$$\delta[A(0) \,\&\, B(0)] \equiv \delta A(0) \,\&\, \delta B(0) \equiv 0,$$
$$\delta[A(t+1) \,\&\, B(t+1)] \equiv \delta A(t+1) \,\&\, \delta B(t+1) \equiv A(t) \,\&\, B(t).$$

The legitimacy of this operation is connected to the fact that conjunction is a positive truth function (i.e., has the value zero when all its arguments are zero). In general, if P is a positive truth function, the following holds:

$$\delta P(A_1, A_2, \cdots) \equiv P(\delta A_1, \delta A_2, \cdots).$$

Both $\vee$ and $\not\equiv$ are also positive truth functions. A negative truth function is one which has the value one when all arguments are zero; $\sim$, $|$, $\downarrow$, $\equiv$, and $\supset$ are examples. To develop analogous principles for these, we need an operator δ' defined by

$$\delta' A(0) \equiv 1$$
$$\delta' A(t+1) \equiv A(t).$$

If N is a negative truth function, we have

$$\delta' N(A_1, A_2, \cdots) \equiv N(\delta A_1, \delta A_2, \cdots).$$

If the negative function is not tautologous (i.e., not true for all values of its variables), then

$$\delta N(A_1, A_2, \cdots) \equiv N(\delta^{a_1} A_1, \delta^{a_2} A_2, \cdots),$$

where each δ^{a_i} is either δ or δ'. For example, $\delta \sim A \equiv \sim \delta' A$. Note that two formulae which are the same except for the absence or presence of primes on deltas describe two functions which differ only initially; after some fixed time which is determined by the number of deltas involved they are equivalent Shifting deltas across truth-functional connectives is equivalent to shifting all delay elements to inputs, so the resultant net consists of delays followed by a switch. This theorem can often be used to simplify expressions and nets. For example, consider a net which realizes $\delta(\delta A \not\equiv A) \not\equiv (\delta A \not\equiv A)$. Applying the theorem, we get $(\delta\delta A \not\equiv \delta A) \not\equiv (\delta A \not\equiv A)$, which by the theory of truth functions reduces to $\delta\delta A \not\equiv A$.

The second theorem concerns input-independent transformations. By a result of section 2 every such transformation is periodic, and hence is of the form $\phi\frown\alpha\frown\alpha\frown\alpha \cdots$, where ϕ and α are binary words. For example, in $1010100100100 \cdots \phi$ is 1010 and α is 100. We call the length of α in bits the periodicity of the transformation, assuming that α is of minimum length. The periodicity of our example is three (not six, or nine, or etc.). The second theorem states that the class of input-independent transformations realized by cycle-free nets is equivalent to the class of periodic transformations of period one. We omit a detailed proof. The essential point in showing that every input-independent transformation realized by a cycle-free net is of period one lies in the fact that an automaton without cycles cannot remember anything for more than a fixed period of time. To show that every periodic transformation of period one can be realized by a noncyclic net, we can use part of the construction of the figure for Theorem XIII of Burks and Wright [1]. With this construction we can realize any transformation of the form $\phi 0000 \cdots$. To realize a transformation of the form $\psi 1111 \cdots$, we feed $\bar{\psi} 0000 \cdots$ through a negation element, where $\bar{\psi}$ is the bitwise complement of ψ.

Consider next input-independent nets, i.e., nets all of whose internal junctions realize input-independent transformations. These nets may have cycles. Nevertheless, we can express the behavior of a net output as an explicit function of the inputs (in a vacuous sense) without using quantifiers. To do so it suffices to state the times at which the junctions are active. Thus, for $F(t) \equiv 111010101 \cdots$, we have $F(t) \equiv [(t=1) \vee (t \equiv 0 \mod 2)]$. We can now let an input of a noncyclic net be driven by an input-independent junction, and by making an appropriate substitution still obtain an expression for the output as an explicit function of the inputs. Thus, given

$$C(t) \equiv A_0(t) \,\&\, \delta A_1(t),$$

we can identify A_1 with F above and obtain

$$\begin{aligned} C(t) &\equiv A_0(t) \,\&\, \delta[(t = 1) \vee (t \equiv 0 \bmod 2)] \\ &\equiv A_0(t) \,\&\, [(t = 2) \vee \{(t > 0) \,\&\, (t \equiv 1 \bmod 2)\}]. \end{aligned}$$

We can further extend our theory of truth functions to include expressions like those just used. By adding $t=a$, $t>a$, $(t-a) \equiv c \bmod b$, where t is a variable and a, b, and c are integers, we can describe any periodic function (using, of course, the truth-functional connectives). We call the theory obtained by adding these symbols and the operator δ the *extended theory of truth functions.* It is clear from the preceding discussion that the following theorem holds:

Theorem 6. *For every junction of a net of degree zero, we can effectively construct a formula of the extended theory of truth functions which describes the behavior of the junction as an explicit function of the behavior of the inputs.*

This theorem provides the motivation for our decision in the preceding subsection to classify input-independent junctions occurring in cycles along with non-input-independent junctions not occurring in cycles, for both can be handled by our extended theory of truth functions. A much more difficult problem is to find formulae which describe the behavior of junctions of degree greater than zero as explicit functions of the net inputs. The natural place to seek such formulae is quantification theory, the next step beyond truth-function theory in the usual development of symbolic logic.

The theory of quantifiers uses, in addition to the truth-functional connectives, the quantifiers "(x)" ("all x"), "$(\exists x)$" or "$(\mathrm{E}x)$" ("some x"), etc. The functional expressions of net theory "$A(t)$", "$B(t+3)$", etc., are clearly monadic propositional functions or predicates. An essential feature of a deterministic net is that an output $C(t)$ cannot depend on any inputs for times greater than t; hence the quantifiers used must be bounded. These bounds may be expressed by predicates such as "$x<t$" and "$x \leqslant y < t$", which are basically dyadic (the second is triadic but is easily reduced to dyadic predicates). Hence the required form of quantification theory involves monadic predicates and bounded quantifiers ranging over the nonnegative integers.

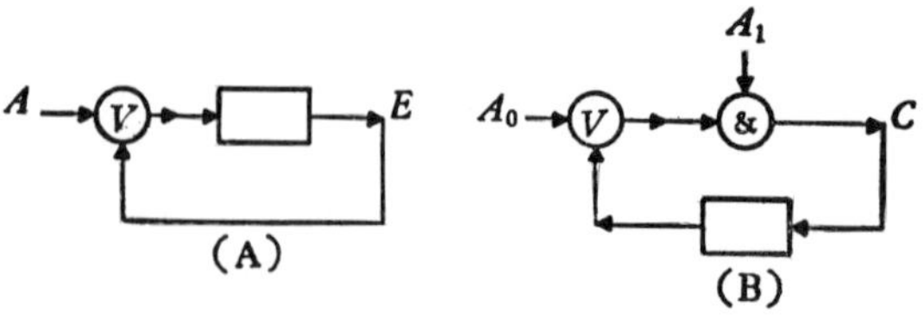

Fig. 6. Two simple nets

Figure 6A shows a very simple cyclic net; it is described by the bounded quantifier expression

$$E(t) \equiv (Ex): x < t \cdot A(x), \qquad (4.2\text{–}1)$$

which states that E is active at t if and only if A has been active at some prior time. The slightly more complicated cyclic net shown in figure 6B is described by the quantifier expression

$$C(t) \equiv (Ex) :: x \leqslant t \cdot A_0(x) : \cdot (y) : x \leqslant y \leqslant t \cdot \supset A_1(y), \qquad (4.2\text{–}2)$$

which asserts that C is active at time t if and only if there is some nonlater time x at which A_0 was active and such that at that time and all later times A_1 was active. It is easy to give examples of quantifier formulae for much more complicated nets with cycles. Whether or not formulae of this type can be found for arbitrary w.f.n. is an open question.

It should be noted that in the above examples the quantifier expressions do describe the output as an explicit function of the inputs; i.e., the only function variables on the right are input variables. That is analogous to using a truth-functional expression to describe a switch output as a truth function of its inputs alone. It stands in contrast to the recursive methods for describing net behavior used previously, in which the output was expressed as a function not only of the input junctions of the net but also (in general) of the internal junctions (at an earlier time). In some cases such a recursive formulation is the natural way of specifying the behavior of a desired circuit. On the other hand, it is often simpler and more direct to specify the behavior of a net in terms of the inputs alone by means of quantifiers and simple arithmetic predicates like "is odd", "is between m and n", etc. Hence it is of interest to develop a form of quantification theory that will facilitate this method of characterizing an automaton and to find both effective (in the purely theoretical sense) and practical ways of passing from formulae in the calculus to the corresponding automaton nets and vice versa.

The problem of finding a quantifer formula for a net characterized recursively may be viewed as one of converting recursive definitions into explicit ones. As we have remarked in section 2.2, the transformation realized by each delay output of a net is primitive recursive relative to the net inputs. Theoretically one can use the well-known procedures for converting primitive recursive functions (cf. Hilbert and Bernays [17], pp. 412—421) to obtain the desired result. As it turns out, however, this method produces quantifier expressions in which some quantified variables range not over time but over the history of the states of the delay outputs. The quantifier expressions so obtained are intuitively always no more and actually less transparent than the corresponding recursive characterization.

4.3. *Nerve Nets*

We will close this paper with a few remarks about nerve nets and cycles in nets. A nerve net is a special case of a well-formed automaton net, in which each neuron consists of a positive switching element driving a delay element. Hence our general results apply to nerve nets. Not all transformations realized by well-formed nets can be realized by nerve nets.

According to theorem 2, every transformation realized by a w.f.n. can be realized by a decoded normal form net. By the results of section 4.1 the starter of a decoded normal form net may be constructed without cycles. Hence we can construct a decoded normal form net whose cycles pass through conjunctions and delays only. Hence every transformation realized by a w.f.n. can be realized by a w.f.n. in which the only positive switches occur in cycles. A neural net is a net in which only positive switches occur in cycles. It differs from a decoded normal form net in two basic respects: First, it has no starter, and second, every switch is combined with a delay. Hence, if a starter is added to the system of nerve nets, every automaton transformation can be realized by a nerve net, except that the nerve-net output may be later in time because each neuron has a delay built into it. Usually the total time lag can be made two, because a disjunctive normal form expression, e.g., $(p \cdot \bar{q}) \vee (\bar{p} \cdot q)$, is a disjunction of conjuncts (see, for example, Kleene [11], theorem 3).

Kleene [11] has investigated the logic of nerve nets in some detail. He analyzes nets in terms of the kinds of events (input histories) they can detect, and he establishes the result that an event can be detected by a net if and only if the event is regular (theorems 3 and 5). The reader is referred to page 22 of Kleene [11] for a definition of "regular"; we note here merely that an important ingredient of the notion of regularity is periodicity. For example, an input of the form $\alpha^\frown\alpha^\frown \cdots \alpha^\frown\phi$, with an indefinite number of α's, is regular. It is easy to construct a net which will be active at time t if and only if the history of its input is of the form $\alpha^\frown\alpha^\frown \cdots {}^\frown\alpha^\frown\phi$, for an indefinite number of α's; cf. the discussion of section 4.2 on periodic transformations.

The pervasiveness and importance of cycles in the analysis of automata and nerve nets are worth emphasizing. When cycles are permitted in automata nets, these nets become much more powerful, and, correspondingly, the logic required to treat them becomes much more complicated. There are many ways in which nets can involve cycles. We have just noted that by Kleene's results an important aspect of any input history which can be detected or distinguished by automata is the periodicity ingredient in its regularity. By our results of the previous subsection the internal structure of an automaton is analyzable into cycles; and by earlier results (see section 2.2) any output which is independent of the inputs is periodic, and hence cyclic in character. The relations between these various cyclic aspects of automata remain to be investigated. It would be of interest to have a theory which shows how they are interconnected.

References

[1] Arthur W. Burks and Jesse B. Wright, Theory of logical nets, *Proc. IRE*, **41** (1953), 1357—1365.

[2] Arthur W. Burks and Irving M. Copi, The logical design of an idealized general-purpose computer, *Jour. Franklin Inst.*, **261** (1956), 299—314 and 421—436.

[3] Claude Shannon, Computers and automata, *Proc. IRE*, **41** (1953), 1234—1241.

[4] N. Rochester, J. H. Holland, L. H. Haibt and W. L. Duda, Tests on a cell assembly theory of the action of the brain, using a large digital computer, *IRE Trans. on Information Theory*, 1956, 80—93.

[5] A. M. Turing, On computable numbers, with an application to the Entscheidungsproblem, *Proc. London Math. Soc.*, Series 2, **42** (1936—1937), 230—265, with a correction, *ibid.*, **43** (1937), 544—546.

[6] S. C., Kleene, Introduction to Metamathematics, New York, D. Van Nostrand Company, Inc., 1952.

[7] Hao Wang, A variant to Turing's theory of computing machines, *Jour. Assoc. Computing Machinery*, **4** (1957), 63—92.

[8] Hao Wang, Universal Turing machines, an exercise in coding (included here as chapter VII).

[9] John von Neumann, The general and logical theory of automata, pp. 1—41 in *Cerebral Mechanisms in Behavior*, John Wiley and Sons, 1951.

[10] John G. Kemeny, Man viewed as a machine, *Scientific American*, **192** (1955), 58—67.

[11] S. C. Kleene, Representation of events in nerve nets and finite automata, pp. 3—41 in *Automata Studies*, edited by C. E. Shannon and J. McCarthy, Princeton Univ. Press, 1956.

[12] Claude Shannon, A symbolic analysis of relay and switching circuits, *Trans. AIEE*, **57** (1938), 713—723.

[13] Arthur W. Burks, Robert McNaughton, Carl H. Pollmar, Don W. Warren and Jesse B. Wright, Complete decoding nets: general theory and minimality, *Jour. Soc. Ind. Appl. Math.*, **2** (1954), 201—243.

[14] J. E. De Turk, A. L. Garner, J. Kautman, A. W. Bethel and R. E. Hock, Basic Circuitry of the MIDAC and MIDSAC, Ann Arbor, Univ. of Mich. Press, 1954.

[15] D. A. Buck, The cryotron—a superconductive computer component, *Proc. IRE*, **44** (1956), 482—493.

[16] Edward F. Moore, Gedanken-experiments on sequential machines, pp. 129—153 in *Automata Studies*, edited by C. E. Shannon and J. McCarthy, Princeton Univ. Press, 1956.

[17] D. Hilbert, and P. Bernays, Grundlagen der Mathematik, vol. 1. Berlin, Springer, 1934.

CHAPTER IX

TOWARD MECHANICAL MATHEMATICS*

THE GALLANT TAILOR: SEVEN (FLIES) IN ONE BLOW.

IBM 704: 220 THEOREMS (IN THE PROPOSITIONAL CALCULUS) IN 3 MINUTES

Results are reported here of a rather successful attempt at proving all theorems, totalling near 400, of *Principia Mathematica* which are strictly in the realm of logic, viz., the (restricted) predicate calculus with equality. A number of other problems of the same type are discussed. It is suggested that time is ripe for a new branch of applied logic which may be called "inferential" analysis, treating proofs as numerical analysis does calculations. This discipline, it is believed, will in the not too remote future lead to proofs of difficult new theorems by machine. An easier preparatory task is to use machines to formalize proofs of known theorems. This line of work may also, it is thought, lead to mechanical checks of new mathematical results comparable to the debugging of a program.

§ 1. INTRODUCTION

If we compare calculating with proving, four differences strike the eye. (1) Calculations deal with numbers, proofs with propositions. (2) Rules of calculation are generally more exact than rules of proof. (3) Procedures of calculation are usually terminating (decidable, recursive) or can be made so by fairly well-developed methods of approximation; whereas procedures of proof are often nonterminating (undecidable or nonrecursive, though recursively enumerable), indeed incomplete in the case of number theory or set theory, and we do not have a clear conception of approximate methods in theorem-proving. (4) We possess efficient calculating procedures, while with proofs it frequently happens that even in a decidable theory, the decision method is not practically feasible; while short-cuts are the exception in calculations, they seem to be the rule with proofs in so far as intuition, "insight", experience, and other not easily imitable vague principles are applied. Since the proof procedures are so complex or lengthy, we simply cannot manage unless we somehow perceive (discover) peculiar connections in each particular case.

It is undoubtedly such differences that have discouraged responsible scientists from embarking on the enterprise of mechanizing significant portions of the activity of mathematical research. The writer, however, feels

* This chapter appeared in *IBM journal for research and development*, vol. 4, 1960.

that the nature and the dimension of the difficulties have been misrepresented through uncontrolled speculation, and exaggerated on account of a lack of appreciation of the combined capabilities of mathematical logic and calculating machines.

Of the four differences, the first is taken care of by either quoting Gödel representations of expressions or recalling the familiar fact that alphabetic information can be handled on numerical (digital) machines. The second difference has largely been removed by the achievements of mathematical logic in formalization during the past eighty years or so. (3) is not a difference that is essential to the task of proving theorems by machine. The immediate concern is not so much theoretical possibility as practical feasibility. Quite often a particular question in an undecidable domain is settled more easily than one in a decidable region, even mechanically. We do not and cannot set out to settle all questions of a given domain, decidable or not, when, as is usually the case, the domain includes infinitely many particular questions. In addition, it is not widely realized how large the decidable subdomains of an undecidable domain (e.g., the predicate calculus) are. Moreover, even in an undecidable area, the question of finding a proof for a proposition known to be a theorem or formalizing a sketch into a detailed proof is decidable theoretically. The state of affairs arising from the Gödel incompleteness is even less relevant to the sort of work envisaged here. The purpose here is at most to prove mathematical theorems of the usual kind, e.g., as exemplified by treatises on number theory, yet not a single "common and garden" theorem of number theory has been found unprovable in the current axiom system of number theory. The concept of approximate proofs, though undeniably of another kind than approximations in numerical calculations, is not incapable of more exact formulation in terms of, say, sketches of and gradual improvements toward a correct proof.

The last difference is perhaps the most fundamental. It is, however, easy to exaggerate the degree of complexity which is necessary, partly because abstract estimates are hardly realistic, partly because so far little attention has been paid to the question of choosing more efficient alternative procedures. There will soon be occasion to give illustrations to these two causes of exaggeration. The problem of introducing intuition and experience into machines is a bit slippery. Suffice it to say for the moment, however, that much of our basic strategies in searching for proofs is mechanizable but not realized to be so because we had had little reason to be articulate on such matters until large, fast machines became available. We are in fact faced with a challenge to devise methods of buying originality with plodding, now that we are in possession of slaves which are such persistent plodders. In the more advanced areas of mathematics, we are not likely to succeed in making the machine imitate the man entirely. Instead, however, of being discouraged by this, one should view it as a forceful reason for experimenting with mechanical mathematics. The human inability to command precisely any great mass of details sets an intrinsic limitation on the kind of thing that is done in mathematics and the manner in which it is done. The superiority of machines in this respect gives hope to the possibility that the machines, while following the broad outline of paths drawn up by man, will yet yield surprising new results by making many new turns which man is not accustomed to taking.

It is, therefore, thought that the general domain of algorithmic analysis can now begin to be enriched by the inclusion of inferential analysis as a younger companion to the fairly well-established but still rapidly developing leg of numerical analysis.

The writer began to speculate on such possibilities in 1953, when he first came into contact with calculating machines. These vague thoughts were afterwards appended to a paper on Turing machines[1]. Undoubtedly many people have given thought to such questions. As far as the writer is aware, works more or less in this area include Burks-Warren-Wright[2], Collins[3], Davis[4], Newell-Shaw-Simon, Gelernter[5]. Of these, the most extensively explained and most widely known is perhaps that of Newell-Shaw-Simon, which they have told in a series of reports and articles[6] since 1956. Their work is also most immediately relevant to the results to be reported in this paper. It will, therefore, not be out of place if an indication is made of the basic differences in the respective approaches and the specific advances beyond their work.

They report[7] that their program *LT* on *JOHNNIAC* was given the task of proving the first 52 theorems of *Principia Mathematica* of Whitehead and Russell: "Of the 52 theorems, proofs were found for a total of 38 · · ·. In 14 cases *LT* failed to find a proof. Most of these unsuccessful attempts were terminated by time or space limitations. One of these 14 theorems we know *LT* cannot prove, and one other we believe it cannot prove". They also give as examples that a proof for *2.45 was found in 12 minutes and a report of failure to prove *2.31 was given after 23 minutes.

The writer wrote three programs last summer (1958) on an *IBM* 704. The first program provides a proof-decision procedure for the propositional calculus which prints out a proof or a disproof according as the given proposition is a theorem or not. It was found that the whole list of the theorems (over 200) of the first five chapters of *Principia Mathematica* were proved within about 37 minutes, and 12/13 of the time is used for read-in and print-out, so that the actual proving time for over 200 theorems was less than 3 minutes. The 52 theorems chosen by Newell-Shaw-Simon are among the easier ones and were proved in less than 5 minutes (or less than 1/2 minute if not counting input-output time.) In particular, *2.45 was proved in about 3 seconds and *2.31 in about 6 seconds. The proofs for these two theorems and some more complex proofs are reproduced in Appendix I exactly as they were printed out on the machine.

The other two programs deal with problems not considered by Newell-Shaw-Simon in their published works. The second program instructs the machine to form itself propositions of the propositional calculus from basic symbols and select nontrivial theorems. The speed was such that about 14,000 propositions were formed and tested in 1 hour, storing on tape about 1000 theorems. The result was disappointing in so far as too few theorems were excluded as being trivial, because the principles of triviality actually included in the program were too crude.

The third program was meant as part of a larger program for the whole predicate calculus with equality which the writer was unable to complete last summer due to lack of time. The predicate calculus with equality takes up the next 5 chapters of *Principia Mathematica* with a total of over 150 theorems. The third program as it stands can find and print out proofs for about 85% of these theorems in about an hour. The writer believes that slight modifications in the program will enable the machine to prove all these theorems within 80 minutes or so. The full program as envisaged will be needed only when we come to propositions of the predicate calculus which are much harder to prove or disprove than those in this part of *Principia Mathematica.*

It will naturally be objected that the comparison with the program of Newell-Shaw-Simon is unfair since the approaches are basically different. The writer realizes this but cannot help feeling, all the same, that the comparison reveals a fundamental inadequacy in their approach. There is no need to kill a chicken with a butcher's knife. Yet the net impression is that Newell-Shaw-Simon failed even to kill the chicken with their butcher's knife. They[8] do not wish to use standard algorithms such as the method of truth tables, because "these procedures do not produce a proof in the meaning of Whitehead and Russell. One can invent 'automatic' procedures for producing proofs, and we will look at one briefly later, but these turn out to require computing times of the orders of thousands of years for the proof of *2.45". It is, however, hard to see why the proof of *2.45 produced by the algorithm to be described in this paper is less acceptable as a proof, yet the computing time for proving *2.45 is less than 1/4 second by this algorithm. To argue the superiority of "heuristic" over algorithmic methods by choosing a particularly inefficient algorithm seems hardly just.

The word "heuristic" is said to be synonymous with "the art of discovery", yet often seems to mean nothing else than a partial method which offers no guarantees of solving a given problem. This ambiguity endows the word with some emotive meaning that could be misleading in further scientific endeavors. The familiar and less inspiring word "strategy" might fare better.

While the discussions by Newell-Shaw-Simon are highly suggestive, the writer is inclined to prefer to avoid hypothetical considerations when possible.

Even though one could illustrate how much more effective partial strategies can be if we had only a very dreadful general algorithm, it would appear desirable to postpone such considerations till we encounter a more realistic case where there is no general algorithm or no efficient general algorithm, e.g., in the whole predicate calculus or in number theory. As the interest is presumably in seeing how well a particular procedure can enable us to prove theorems on a machine, it would seem preferable to spend more effort on choosing the more efficient methods rather than on enunciating more or less familiar generalities. And it is felt that an emphasis on mathematical logic is unavoidable because it is just as essential in this area as numerical analysis is for solving large sets of simultaneous numerical equations.

The logical methods used in this paper are along the general line of cut-free formalisms of the predicate calculus initiated by Herbrand[9] and Gentzen[10]. Ideas of Hilbert-Bernays[11], Dreben[12], Beth[13], Hintikka[14], Schütte[15] and many others on these formulations, as well as some from standard decision methods for subdomains of the predicate calculus presented by Church[16] and Quine[17], are borrowed. The special formulations actually used seem to contain a few minor new features which facilitate the use on machines. Roughly speaking, a complete proof procedure for the predicate calculus with equality is given which becomes a proof-decision procedure when the proposition to be proved or disproved falls within the domain of the propositional calculus or that of the "*AE* predicate calculus" (i.e. those propositions which can be transformed into a form in which no existential quantifier governs any universal quantifier) which includes the monadic predicate calculus as a subdomain.

The treatment of the predicate calculus by Herbrand and Gentzen enables us to get rid of every "Umweg" (cut or *modus ponens*) so that we obtain a cut-free calculus in which, roughly speaking, for every proof each of the steps is no more complex than the conclusion. This naturally suggests that we can, given any formula in the predicate calculus, examine all the less complex formulae and decide whether it is provable. The reason why this does not yield a decision procedure for the whole predicate calculus is a rule of contraction which enables us to get rid of a repetition of the same formula. As a result, in searching for a proof or a disproof, we may fail in some case because we can get no proof no matter how many repetitions we introduce. In such a case, the procedure can never come to an end although we do not know this at any finite stage. While this situation does not preclude completeness, it does exclude a decision procedure.

Now if we are interested in decidable sub-domains of the predicate calculus, we can usually give suitable reformulations in which the rule of contraction no longer occurs. A particularly simple case is the propositional calculus. Here we can get a simple system which is both a complete proof procedure and a complete decision procedure. The completeness receives a very direct proof, and as a decision procedure it has an advantage over usual procedures in that if the proposition tested is provable, we obtain directly from the test a proof of it. This procedure is coded in Program *I*. Moreover, it is possible to extend the system for the propositional calculus to get a proof-decision procedure for the *AE* predicate calculus which has the remarkable feature that in searching for a proof for a given proposition in the "miniscope" form, we never need to introduce any premise which is longer than its conclusion. This procedure is coded in Program *III*.

A rather surprising discovery, which tends to indicate our general ignorance of the extensive range of decidable subdomains, is the absence of any theorem of the predicate calculus in *Principia* which does not fall within the simple decidable subdomain of the *AE* predicate calculus. More exactly, there is a systematic procedure of separating variables to bring a proposition into the "miniscope" form (a term to be explained below). Once this is done (easily by hand or by machine for these particular theorems), every theorem in the predicate calculus part of *Principia* can be proved by the fairly simple Program *III*.

Originally the writer's interest was in formalizing proofs in more advanced domains such as number theory and differential calculus. It soon became clear that for this purpose a pretty thorough mechanization of the underlying logic is a necessary preliminary step. Now that this part is near completion, the writer will discuss what he considers to be not too remote further possibilities in the concluding part of this paper.

§ 2. The Propositional Calculus (System *P*)

Since we are concerned with practical feasibility, it is preferable to use more logical connectives to begin with when we wish actually to apply the procedure to concrete cases. For this purpose we use the five usual logical constants $\sim$ (not), & (conjunction), $\vee$ (disjunction), $\supset$ (implication), $\equiv$ (biconditional), with their usual interpretations.

A propositional letter P, Q, R, M or N or et cetera, is a formula (and an "atomic formula"). If ϕ, ψ are formulae, then $\sim\phi$, $\phi \,\&\, \psi$, $\phi \vee \psi$, $\phi \supset \psi$, $\phi \equiv \psi$ are formulae. If π, ρ are strings of formulae (each, in particular, might be an empty string or a single formula) and ϕ is a formula, then π, ϕ, ρ is a string and $\pi \rightarrow \rho$ is a sequent which, intuitively speaking, is true if and only if either some formula in the string π (the "antecedent") is false or some formula in the string ρ (the "consequent") is true, i.e., the conjunction of all formulae in the antecedent implies the disjunction of all formulae in the consequent.

There are eleven rules of derivation. An initial rule states that a sequent with only atomic formulae (proposition letters) is a theorem if and only if a same formula occurs on both sides of the arrow. There are two rules for each of the five truth functions one introducing it into the antecedent, one introducing it into the consequent. One need only reflect on the intuitive meaning of the truth functions and the arrow sign to be convinced that these rules are indeed correct. Later on a proof of their completeness, i.e. all intuitively valid sequents are provable, and consistency, i.e., all provable sequents are intuitively valid, will be given.

*P*1. Initial rule: if λ, ζ are strings of atomic formulae, then $\lambda \rightarrow \zeta$ is a theorem if some atomic formula occurs on both sides of the arrow.

In the following ten rules, λ and ζ are always strings (possibly empty) of atomic formulae.

*P*2a. Rule $\rightarrow\sim$: If $\phi, \zeta \rightarrow \lambda, \rho$, then $\zeta \rightarrow \lambda, \sim\phi, \rho$.

*P*2b. Rule $\sim\rightarrow$: If $\lambda, \rho \rightarrow \pi, \phi$, then $\lambda, \sim\phi, \rho \rightarrow \pi$.

*P*3a. Rule $\rightarrow \&$: If $\zeta \rightarrow \lambda, \phi, \rho$ and $\zeta \rightarrow \lambda, \psi, \rho$ then $\zeta \rightarrow \lambda, \phi \,\&\, \psi, \rho$.

*P*3b. Rule $\& \rightarrow$: If $\lambda, \phi, \psi, \rho \rightarrow \pi$, then $\lambda, \phi \,\&\, \psi, \rho \rightarrow \pi$.

*P*4a. Rule $\rightarrow \vee$: If $\zeta \rightarrow \lambda, \phi, \psi, \rho$, then $\zeta \rightarrow \lambda, \phi \vee \psi, \rho$.

*P*4b. Rule $\vee \rightarrow$: If $\lambda, \phi, \rho \rightarrow \pi$ and $\lambda, \psi, \rho \rightarrow \pi$, then $\lambda, \phi \vee \psi, \rho \rightarrow \pi$.

*P*5a. Rule $\rightarrow \supset$: If $\zeta, \phi \rightarrow \lambda, \psi, \rho$, then $\zeta \rightarrow \lambda, \phi \supset \psi, \rho$.

*P*5b. Rule $\supset \rightarrow$: If $\lambda, \psi, \rho \rightarrow \pi$ and $\lambda, \rho \rightarrow \pi, \phi$, then $\lambda, \phi \supset \psi, \rho \rightarrow \pi$.

*P*6a. Rule $\rightarrow \equiv$: If $\phi, \zeta \rightarrow \lambda, \psi, \rho$ and $\psi, \zeta \rightarrow \lambda, \phi, \rho$ then $\zeta \rightarrow \lambda, \phi \equiv \psi, \rho$.

*P*6b. Rule $\equiv \rightarrow$: If $\phi, \psi, \lambda, \rho \rightarrow \pi$ and $\lambda, \rho \rightarrow \pi, \phi, \psi$, then $\lambda, \phi \equiv \psi, \rho \rightarrow \pi$.

As a proof procedure in the usual sense, each proof begins with a finite set of cases of *P*1 and continues with successive consequences obtained by the other rules. As will be explained below, a proof looks like a tree structure growing in the wrong direction. We shall, however, be chiefly interested in doing the steps backwards, thereby incorporating the process of searching for a proof.

The rules are so designed that given any sequent, we can find the first logical connective, i.e. the leftmost symbol in the whole sequent that is a connective, and apply the appropriate rule to eliminate it, thereby resulting in one or two premises which, taken together, are equivalent to the conclusion. This process can be repeated until we reach a finite set of sequents with atomic formulae only. Each connective-free sequent can then be tested for being a theorem or not by the initial rule. If all of them are theorems, then the original sequent is a theorem and we obtain a proof; otherwise we get a counter-example and a disproof. Some simple samples will make this clear.

For example, given any theorem of *Principia,* we can automatically prefix an arrow on it and apply the rules to look for a proof. When the main connective is $\supset$, it is simpler, though not necessary, to replace the main connective by an arrow and proceed. For example:

$$*2.45.\ \vdash : \sim (P \vee Q) \cdot \supset \sim P,$$

$$*5.21.\ \vdash : \sim P \& \sim Q \cdot \supset \cdot P \equiv Q$$

can be rewritten and proved as follows.

*2.45. $\sim (P \vee Q) \rightarrow \sim P$ (1)

$(1) \rightarrow \sim P, P \vee Q$ (2)

$(2)\ P \rightarrow P \vee Q$ (3)

$(3)\ P \rightarrow P, Q$

VALID

QED

*5.21. $\rightarrow \sim P \& \sim Q \cdot \supset \cdot P \equiv Q$ (1)

$(1) \sim P \& \sim Q \rightarrow P \equiv Q$ (2)

$(2) \sim P, \sim Q \rightarrow P \equiv Q$ (3)

$(3) \sim Q \rightarrow P \equiv Q, P$ (4)

$(4) \rightarrow P \equiv Q, P, Q$ (5)

$(5)\ P \rightarrow Q, P, Q$

VALID

$(5)\ Q \rightarrow P, P, Q$

VALID

QED

These proofs should be self-explanatory. They are essentially the same as the proofs printed out by the machine, except that certain notational changes are made both to make the coding easier and to avoid symbols not available on the machine printer. The reader may wish to read the next section which explains these changes and then compare these with more examples of actual print-outs reproduced in Appendix I. It is believed that these concrete examples will greatly assist the understanding of the procedure if the reader is not familiar with mathematical logic.

§ 3. PROGRAM *I*: THE PROPOSITIONAL CALCULUS *P*

There is very little in the program which is not straightforward. To reserve the dot for other purposes and to separate the numbering from the rest, we write, for example,

2*45/ instead of *2.45.

For the other symbols, we use the following dictionary:

—	→
B	≡
C	&
D	∨
F	~
I	⊃

Moreover, we use a modified Polish notation by putting, for example, *CFP.FQ* instead of ~*P* & ~*Q*. By putting the connective at the beginning, we can more easily search for it. The use of dots for grouping makes it easier to determine the two halves governed by a binary connective. The reader will have no difficulty in remembering these notational changes if he compares the examples *2.45 and *5.21 with the corresponding proofs in the new notation given in Appendix I.

With the longer examples in Appendix I, the reader will observe that the numbers on the right serve to identify the lines, while the numbers on the left serve to identify the conclusions for which the numbered lines are premises. Essentially each proof is a tree structure. Since we have to arrange the lines in a one-dimensional array, there is a choice from different possible arrangements. The one chosen can be seen from the example 4*45 given in Appendix I. The tree structure would be:

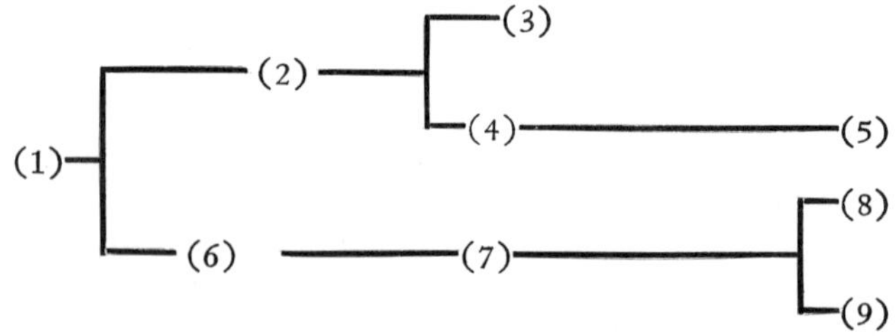

and the one-dimensional arrangement we use is:

(1), (1, 2), (2, 3), (2, 4), (4, 5), (1, 6), (6, 7), (7, 8), (7, 9).

The whole program has about 1000 lines. The length of the sequents to be tested is deliberately confined to 72 symbols, so that each sequent can be presented by a single punched card. While this restriction can be removed, it makes the coding considerably easier and gives ample room for handling the problems on hand. Thus, for instance, the longest theorem of the propositional calculus in *Principia,* 5*24, has only 36 symbols. When presented with any punched card, the program enables the machine to proceed as follows.

Copy the card into the reserved core storage COL1 to COL72, 72 addresses in all, in the standard *BCD* notation, i.e. a conventional way of representing symbols by numbers, one symbol in each address. Append the number 1 at the last address, viz. COL72. Search for the arrow sign. If it does not occur, then the line is regarded as ordinary prose, printed out without comment, and the machine begins to study the next card. In particular, the machine stops if the card is blank. If the arrow sign occurs, then the machine marks all symbols before the arrow sign as negative and proceeds to find the earliest logical connective. According as it is *F, C, D, I,* or *B,* the machine turns to *RTNF, RTNC, RTND, RTNI,* or *RTNB.* In each case the proper rule is applied according as whether the connective is before or after the arrow.

After COL1 to COL72, 144 addresses are reserved for getting the one or two premises. As soon as the premises are found according to the proper rule, the original line is printed out and the first premise is shifted into COL1 to COL72 and gets the next number for its identification. If there is a second premise, it has to be shifted away to the idle section and wait for its turn. When the line in COL1 to COL72 contains no more logical connectives, the machine goes to a compare routine to determine whether there is a formula occurring on both sides of the arrow or not and prints the line out with VALID or NOT VALID appended to it. Then it looks at the idle section to see whether any earlier premises remain there. If there is, it moves the first line there into COL1 to COL72 and push the remaining lines of the idle section to fill up the vacancy. If there is no more line left then it concludes, according as whether all final sequents are valid, that the original sequent is a theorem (QED) or not (NOT VALID). When the original sequent is not a theorem, the conjunction of all the resulting nonvalid connective-free sequents amounts to a conjunctive normal form of the original sequent.

Several alternatives are permitted by putting down suitable sense switches. If the interest is to determine merely whether the given sequent is a theorem, it is natural to stop as soon as a non-valid connective-free sequent is found. This is indeed taken as the normal procedure in the program. Another permissible choice is to omit the proofs or disproofs altogether but only print out the final answer. A third possible choice is to give the output by punching cards rather than printing. The possibility of omitting the proof or the disproof enables us to separate the calculating time from the input-output time.

While the program is sufficiently fast for testing propositions we ordinarily encounter, it is not the most efficient testing procedure for more complex propositions. If the purpose is to find an isolated fast test procedure just for the propositional calculus and not to obtain at the same time a proof procedure which can be combined naturally with proofs in more advanced domains, it is possible to find much more efficient methods. For example, B. Dunham, R. Fridshal, and G. Sward have one which is being coded by them.

On the other hand, the storage needed is not large. Not only each theorem is proved from scratch so that earlier theorems need not be kept in the store, but in each proof there is no need to keep all the intermediate lines. In fact, at any time the machine need to keep in its store at most one line from each level of the proof in its tree form.

This can be made clear by the following example:

$$6{*}6/-BBBBBQR.\,P..\,BQR...\,BBPQ..\,BP.\,BQR....\,BP..\,BQ.\,BQR$$

There are 13 occurrences of B (if and only if) in this theorem. Since every elimination of B gives two new branches, the complete proof consists of 2^{14}—1 or about 16,000 lines. Yet at no time the machine need to keep in the store for the idle section more than 13 lines. If we use one address for each symbol, we need 72×13 addresses for this; if we pack up these idle lines, we need only 12×13 addresses, a very small number for such a long proof. The length of the proof incidentally illustrates how inefficient the procedure can be for certain long propositions. While the complexity of the ordinary truth table test is determined by the number m of distinct proposition letters (2^m rows) and the number n of distinct subformulae (n columns), the length of proof of the present approach is determined by the number k of occurrences of propositional connectives, i.e., $2^{k+1}-1$ lines or less since in many cases a conclusion has only one instead of two premises.

The estimated running time for a complete proof of the above theorem with all steps printed out on line is about 5 hours (about 2500 of the 16,000 lines were printed out in 48 minutes or so). On the other hand, if the proof is not printed out, it took the machine less than 30 minutes to get the answer. Hence, about 12/13 of the time is spent in reading in and printing out. Since axioms and definitions are not used in this approach, they are taken as theorems to be proved and one arrives at about 220 theorems from the first five chapters of *Principia.* These were proved in about 37 minutes. When only the theorems themselves and the answers (i.e., QED) are printed out, it took 8 minutes. The actual calculating time, i.e., not counting the input-output time, is less than 3 minutes.

§ 4. Program *II*: Selecting Theorems in the Propositional Calculus

A natural question to ask is, even though the machine can prove theorems, can it select the theorems to be proved? A very crude experiment in this direction was made with some quite preliminary results. These will be reported here not for their intrinsic interest but for suggesting further attempts on the same line. The motive is quite simple: by including suitable principles of triviality, the machine will only select and print out less trivial theorems; these may in turn suggest further principles of triviality; after a certain stage, one would either arrive at essentially the same theorems which have already been discovered and considered interesting, or find in addition a whole crowd of interesting new theorems.

What has been done is to make the machine form a fairly large class of propositions (sequents) and select "interesting" theorems from them. At first all formulae with exactly 6 symbols containing at most the proposition letters P, Q, R are formed. These come to a total of 651, of which 289 are basic and 362 are trivial variants obtainable from the basic ones by renaming the propositional letters. Of these 651 formulae, 107 are theorems. The program enables the machine to form these formulae, one stored in a single address, and select the theorems among them, prefixing each with a minus sign.

Then the machine is to form all (non-ordered) pairs (π, ρ) such that either π or ρ is (or both are) among the 289 basic formulae and for each pair (π, ρ), the sequents $\pi \rightarrow \rho$, $\rho \rightarrow \pi$, $\pi, \rho \rightarrow$, $\rightarrow \pi, \rho$, when neither π nor ρ is a theorem. When π, ρ are the same, $\pi \rightarrow \rho$, $\rho \rightarrow \pi$, $\rightarrow \pi, \rho$ are not formed. These are the only principles of triviality which are included. Thus, the distinction between basic formulae and their variants avoids the necessity of testing those sequents which are variants (a large number of them) of other tested sequents. Moreover, if either π or ρ is a theorem, $\rightarrow \pi, \rho$ is a trivial consequence, $\pi, \rho \rightarrow$ is a trivial variant of $\rho, \rho \rightarrow$ or $\pi, \pi \rightarrow$; moreover, then $\pi \rightarrow \rho$ (resp. $\rho \rightarrow \pi$) is a theorem, and a trivial one, if and only if ρ (resp. π) is a theorem. Finally, $\pi \rightarrow \pi$ is always a (trivial) theorem.

It was at first thought that these crude principles are sufficient to cut down the number of theorems to a degree that only a reasonably small number of theorems remain. It turns out that there are still too many theorems. The number of theorems printed out after running the machine for a few hours is so formidable that the writer has not even attempted to analyze the mass of data obtained. The number of sequents to be formed is about half a million, of which about 1/14 are theorems. To carry out the whole experiment would take about 40 machine hours.

The reason that such a high portion are theorems comes from the bias in our way of forming sequents. If we view an arbitrary truth table with n proposition letters, since the table gives a theorem if and only if every row gets the value true and there are 2^n rows, the probability of getting a theorem is $1/2^{(2n)}$. In particular, if $n=3$, we get 1/256. However, the sequents $\pi \rightarrow \rho$, $\rho \rightarrow \pi$, $\rightarrow \pi, \rho$, $\pi, \rho \rightarrow$ amount to $\sim\pi \vee \rho$, $\sim\rho \vee \pi$, $\rho \vee \pi$, $\sim\rho \vee \sim\pi$, each being a disjunction. Hence, the probability is much higher since the probability of $\phi \vee \psi$ being true is 3/4. If there are 3 proposition letters, we have $(3/4)^8$ which is about 1/10. The few crude principles of triviality, besides cutting the sequents to be tested to less than half, reduces this percentage to about 1/14. It would seem clear that other principles of triviality should be devised and included, e.g., if $\pi \equiv \rho$ and $\theta(\pi)$ are theorems, $\theta(\rho)$ is a trivial consequence which need not be recorded.

In the actual program, input cards are used to assign the region of sequents to be formed and tested, since otherwise the machine would simply run continuously for about 40 hours until all sequents are formed and tested. Each sequent formed is retained in a reserved region of the core memory or simply thrown away, according as it has been found to be a theorem or a non-theorem. When all the sequents required by the input card have been tested or when the reserved region has been filled up, the theorems obtained to date are transferred on a tape which afterwards is printed out off line. Just as a curiosity, a very small random consecutive sample of the print-out is reproduced in Appendix II.

§ 5. Completeness and Consistency of the Systems P and P_s

A simple proof for the consistency and the completeness of the system P is possible. Since, however, such considerations become even shorter if fewer truth-functional connectives are used, a system P_s based on the single stroke $|$ connective (not both) will be given and proved consistent, as well as complete. It will then be clear that a similar proof applies to the system P.

The formulae and sequents are specified similarly as with the system P except that the clause on forming new formulae is now merely: if ϕ and ψ are formulae, then $\phi \mid \psi$ is. There are only three rules:

P_s1. Same as $P1$

If λ and ζ are strings (possibly empty) of atomic formulae, then:

P_s2. If $\phi, \psi, \zeta \rightarrow \lambda, \rho$, then $\zeta \rightarrow \lambda, \phi | \psi, \rho$.

P_s3. If $\lambda, \rho \rightarrow \pi, \phi$ and $\lambda, \rho \rightarrow \pi, \psi$, then $\lambda, \phi | \psi, \rho \rightarrow \pi$.

Consistency of the calculus P_s. One can easily verify by the intended interpretation of the arrow and the comma that P_s1 is valid, i.e., true in every interpretation of the atomic formulae, that the conclusion of P_s2 is valid if (and only if) its premise is, and that the conclusion of P_s3 is valid if (and only if) its premises are. It follows that every provable sequent is valid.

Completeness of the calculus P_s. We wish to prove that every sequent, if valid, is provable. Given any sequent, we find the earliest non-atomic formula, if any, in the antecedent, and apply P_s3 in reverse direction, thereby obtaining two premises each with less occurrences of $|$. If there is no $|$ in the antecedent, we find the earliest, if any, occurrence of $|$ in the consequent and apply P_s2 in reverse direction. We then repeat the same procedure with the results thus obtained. This process will be continued with each sequent until | no longer occurs. Since there are only finitely many occurrences of | in each sequent, this process always comes to an end and then we have a finite class of sequents in which only atomic formulae occur. Now the original sequent is valid if and only if every sequent in the class is. But a sequent with only atomic formulae is valid if and only if it is a case of $Ps1$ and we can decide effectively in each case whether this is so. Hence, the calculus is complete and we have a decision procedure for provability which yields automatically a proof for each provable sequent.

§ 6. The System P_e: The Propositional Calculus with Equality

It is convenient, though not necessary, to add the equality sign = before introducing quantifiers. This procedure serves to stress the fact that equality is more elementary than quantifiers even though customarily quantifiers are presented prior to equality. The changes needed to reach this system from the system P are rather slight. Variables X, Y, Z, S, T, U, V, W, et cetera are now taken as terms and the domain of atomic formulae are extended to include all expressions of the form $\alpha=\beta$ when α and β are terms.

The only additional rules necessary for equality are an extension of the initial rule *P*1 so that in addition to the rules *P*1 to *P*6b of the system P, we now have: If λ, ζ are strings (possibly empty) of atomic formulae, then:

*P*7. $\lambda \rightarrow \zeta$ is a theorem if there is a term α such that $\alpha=\alpha$ occurs in ζ.

*P*8. $\lambda \rightarrow \zeta$ is a theorem if $\alpha=\beta$ occurs in λ and $\lambda \rightarrow \zeta'$ is a theorem, where ζ' is obtained from ζ by substituting α (or β) for some or all occurrence of β (α).

It is quite easy to extend Program *I* to obtain a program for the system P_e. The writer, however, did not write a separate program for P_e but includes such a program as a part in Program *III*. This part enables the machine to proceed exactly as in Program *I* except that in testing whether a sequent of atomic formulae is a theorem, the machine does not stop if the sequent is not a theorem by the initial rule *P*1 but proceeds to determine whether the sequent can be shown to be a theorem by using the additional initial rules *P*7 and *P*8. To distinguish sequents of atomic formulae which are valid truth-functionally from those which become valid only after applying *P*7 or *P*8, the former case is marked with *VA* only, while the latter case is marked in addition by =. Examples of print-outs are given in Appendix III.

The longish example *13.3 is included to make a minor point. It has been suggested that it would be interesting if the machine discovers mistakes in *Principia*. This example may be said to reveal a mistake in *Principia* in the following sense. The authors of *Principia* proved this theorem by using *10.13 and *10.221 from the predicate calculus. From the discussion attached to the proof of this theorem, it seems clear that the authors considered this as a theorem which presupposes the predicate calculus. Yet in the proof printed out by the machine, no appeal to anything beyond the system *P*, i.e., no appeal even to the additional rules *P7* and *P8*, is made. This is revealed by the fact that all the sequents of atomic formulae, viz. lines 6, 10, 14, 18, 24, 28, 32, 36 in the proof, are marked with *VA* without the additional = sign. At first the writer thought this indicates a mistake in the program. An examination of the theorem shows, however, that *13.3 is indeed a theorem of the propositional calculus. In fact, Program I alone would yield essentially the same proof.

§ 7. Preliminaries to the Predicate Calculus

Thus far an attempt has been made to avoid heavy technicalities from symbolic logic. A few more exact definitions seem, however, necessary when one comes to the predicate calculus.

Formulae, terms, and sequents of the full predicate calculus are specified as follows. Basic symbols are = ; the five truth-functional connectives; the two quantification symbols for "all" and "some"; proposition letters *P, Q, R,* et cetera; predicate letters *G, H, J, K,* et cetera; variables *X, Y, Z,* et cetera; function symbols *f, g, h,* et cetera; numerals 1, 2, · · ·, 9, et cetera; dots or parentheses for grouping. Terms are: (i) a variable is a term; (ii) a numeral is a term; (iii) if α, β, et cetera are terms and σ a function symbol, then $\sigma\alpha$, $\sigma\alpha\beta$, et cetera, are terms. A variable or a numeral is a simple term; other terms are composite. The five truth-functional connectives and two quantification symbols are called logical constants. Atomic formulae are: (i) proposition letters; (ii) $\alpha=\beta$, when α, β are terms; (iii) $G\alpha$, $H\alpha\beta$, et cetera, where α, β, et cetera are terms. Formulae are: (i) atomic formulae are formulae; (ii) if ϕ, ψ are formulae, $\sim\phi$, $\phi \vee \psi$, $\phi \supset \psi$, $\phi \equiv \psi$, $\phi \,\&\, \psi$, $(E\alpha)\,\phi$, $(\alpha)\,\phi$ are formulae, where α is a variable. A string may be empty or a single formula, and if π, ρ are nonempty strings π, ρ is a string. Given any two strings π and ρ, $\pi\rightarrow\rho$ is a sequent.

Intuitively it is clear what the scope of a logical constant is. In mechanical terms, the method of finding the scope of a logical constant in a given formula depends on the notation. According to the notation actually chosen for the machine, $\phi \vee \psi$, $\phi \,\&\, \psi$, $\phi \supset \psi$, $\phi \equiv \psi$ are written as $D\phi - \psi$, $C\phi - \psi$, $I\phi - \psi$, $B\phi - \psi$, with the blank filled in by a string of dots whose number is one larger than the longest string in ϕ and ψ except that no dot is used when both ϕ and ψ are proposition letters. These and related details in the notation can be understood easily from the Appendices. Given a sequent, the scope of a logical constant Γ standing at the beginning of a whole formula in the sequent is the entire formula minus Γ. If Γ is singularly, that is, $\sim$ or one of the two quantification symbols, the scope of the next logical constant Γ' in the formula, if any, is the whole remaining part of the formula minus Γ'. If Γ is binary, then its scope breaks into two parts at the longest string of dots in the scope and each part, if containing a logical constant at all, must begin with one, say Γ', whose scope is the whole part minus Γ'. This gives a mechanizable inductive definition of the scope of every logical constant in any sequent. A logical constant Γ is said to "govern" a logical constant Γ', if Γ' falls within the scope of Γ.

To avoid the explicit use of the prenex normal form, i.e., the form in which all quantifiers in a formula stand at its beginning, it is desirable to introduce, after Herbrand[18], the sign of every quantifier in a sequent. Two simple preliminary operations will be performed on a given sequent before calculating the signs of the quantifiers in it. First, distinct quantifiers are to get distinct variables, even when one quantifier does not govern the other; moreover, the free variables in the sequent are not used as variables attached to explicit quantifiers. This simplifies the elimination of quantifiers afterwards. Second, all occurrences of $\equiv$ which governs any quantifiers at all are eliminated by either of two simple equivalences: $\phi \equiv \psi$ if and only if $(\phi \,\&\, \psi) \vee (\sim\phi \,\&\, \sim\psi)$, or, alternatively, $(\sim\phi \vee \psi) \,\&\, (\sim\psi \vee \phi)$.

The positive and negative parts of any formula in the sequent are defined thus: (i) (an occurrence of) ϕ is a positive part of (the same occurrence of) ϕ; (ii) if ϕ is a positive (resp. negative) part of ψ, then ϕ is a negative (resp. positive) part of $\sim\psi$; (iii) if ϕ is a positive (resp. negative) part of ψ or of χ, then ϕ is a positive (resp. negative) part of $\psi \vee \chi$; (iv) similarly with ϕ and $\psi \,\&\, \chi$; (v) if ϕ is a positive (resp. negative) part of ψ, then ϕ is a positive (resp. negative) part of $(\alpha)\,\psi$; (vi) similarly with ϕ and $(E\alpha)\psi$; (vii) if ϕ is a positive (resp. negative) part of ψ, then ϕ is a positive (resp. negative) part of $\chi \supset \psi$, and a negative (resp. positive) part of $\psi \supset \chi$. Any formula ϕ in a sequent is a positive or negative part of the sequent according as (i) it is a positive (resp. negative) part of a whole formula in the consequent (resp. antecedent), or (ii) it is a negative (resp. positive) part of a whole formula in the consequent (resp. antecedent). Any quantifier (α) with the scope ϕ in a given sequent is positive (resp. negative) in the sequent if and only if $(\alpha)\,\phi$ is a positive (resp. negative) part of the sequent; $(E\alpha)$ is positive (resp. negative) if and only if $(E\alpha)\phi$ is a negative (resp. positive) part of the sequent; the different occurrences of a same free variable α in the sequent also make up a positive quantifier (as if (α) were put at the head of the whole sequent).

This involved definition can be illustrated by an example:

Ex. 0. $(X)(GXY \supset (\sim GXX \,\&\, (EZ)HXZ))$,
$(W)((\sim GWW \,\&\, (EU)HWU) \supset GWY) \rightarrow \sim (EV)HYV.$

In this example, (X) is a negative quantifier, (EZ) is positive, (W) is negative, (EU) is negative, (EV) is positive. For instance, $(EU)HWU$ is positive in $\sim GWW \& (EU)HWU$ but negative in $(\sim GWW \& (EU)HWU) \supset GWY$ and $(W)\,((\sim GWW \& (EU)HWU) \supset GWY)$, which is a whole formula in the antecedent. Hence, $(EU)HWU$ is positive in the sequent.

Hence, (EU) is negative. The assignment of signs to quantifiers coincides with the result in a prenex normal form; positive for universal, negative for existential. Thus, one prenex form of Ex. 0 is:

$$(Y)(EX)(EW)(EU)(Z)(V)\{[(GXY \supset (\sim GXX \& HXZ))$$
$$\& ((\sim GWW \& HWU) \supset GWY)] \supset \sim HYV\}.$$

Another useful but involved concept is "miniscope" forms of a formula of the predicate calculus. It is in a sense the opposite of the prenex form which generally gives every quantifier the maximum scope. Since the interweaving of quantifiers and variables is the main factor determining the complexity of a formula of the predicate calculus, it is not hard to see that separating variables and reducing the ranges of quantifiers may help to simplify the problem of determining whether a formula is a theorem. The unfortunate part is that sometimes it can be a very complicated process to get a formula into the miniscope form.

It is easier to explain the notion for a formula in which $\equiv$ and $\supset$ no longer occur (say, eliminated by usual definitions) so that the only truth-functional connectives are $\sim$, &, $\vee$. Such a formula is said to be in the miniscope form if and only if: (i) an atomic formula ϕ is in the miniscope form; (ii) if ϕ in $(\alpha)\,\phi$ (resp. $(E\alpha)\,\phi$) is a disjunction (resp. conjunction) of formulae each of which is in the miniscope form and either contains α or contains no free variable at all, then $(\alpha)\,\phi$ (resp. $(E\alpha)\,\phi$) is in the miniscope form; (iii) if ϕ and ψ are in the miniscope form, so are $\sim\phi$, $\phi \vee \psi$, $\phi \& \psi$; (iv) if ϕ in $(\alpha)\phi$ (or $(E\alpha)\phi$) begins with $(E\beta)$ $((\beta))$ and is in the miniscope form, so is $(\alpha)\,\phi$ $((E\alpha)\,\phi)$; (v) a formula beginning with a string of quantifiers of the same kind is in the miniscope form if every formula obtained by permuting these quantifiers and then dropping the first is in the miniscope form.

One procedure for bringing a formula into the miniscope form is explained in detail by Quine[19]. In what follows only parts of Quine's procedure will be used and explained, the machine will follow quite different procedures if the formulae in a given sequent are not easily brought into the miniscope form.

§ 8. The System Qp and the AE Predicate Calculus

A specially simple decision procedure is available for many of those sequents not containing function symbols in which each formula is in the miniscope form and in the AE form, i.e., no positive quantifier is governed by a negative quantifier. The procedure can be extended by two preliminary steps and described as follows:

Step 1. Bring every formula into the miniscope form and at the same time apply the truth-functional rules *P*2–*P*6b, whenever possible. In general, we obtain a finite set of sequents which all are theorems if and only if the original sequent is.

Step 2. Test each sequent and decide whether it is in the *AE* form. If this is so for all the sequents then they and the original sequent all fall within the *AE* predicate calculus, and we proceed to decide each sequent by continuing with Step. 3. If this is not so for some sequent, then the original sequent does not belong to the *AE* predicate calculus and has to be treated by appealing to a richer system *Q* to be described below.

Step 3. For a sequent in the *AE* predicate calculus, drop all quantifiers and replace all the variables attached to negative quantifiers by numerals, one numeral for each quantifier. The resulting sequent contains no more quantifiers.

Step 4. Apply the truth-functional rules to obtain a finite set of sequents which contain no more logical constants. Test each sequent by the initial rules and retain only the non-valid ones.

Step 5. List all the variables and numerals occurring in this last set of sequents of atomic formulae, make all possible substitutions of the variables for the numerals in the sequents (substitute *X* for the numerals if no variables occur), and test each time whether the resulting sequents are all valid. The initial sequent of Step 3 is a theorem if there is a substitution which makes all the sequents in the finite set theorems.

Step 6. The original sequent is a theorem if all the sequents obtained by Step 1 are theorems by Steps 3 to 5.

This completes the description of *Qp*. It is possible to formulate this system more formally as formed from the basic system P_e by adding additional explicit rules. But the result would be rather lengthy and a bit artificial. Since the above less explicit formulation conforms to the general theoretical requirements of a formal system, we shall not give a formally more pleasing description. This remark applies also to the systems to be described below. Here are a few simple examples which illustrate this procedure and some minor modifications in it.

*10.25.	$(X)GX \rightarrow (EY)GY$		(1)
(1)	$G1 \rightarrow G2$	NOT	(2)
(1)	$GX \rightarrow GX$	VA	(2)
	QED		

*11.21.	$\rightarrow (X)(Y)(Z)GXYZ \equiv (V)(U)(W)GUVW$	(1)
(1)	$(X)(Y)(Z)GXYZ \rightarrow (V)(U)(W)GUVW$	(2)
(1)	$(V)(U)(W)GUVW \rightarrow (X)(Y)(Z)GXYZ$	(3)

(2)	$G123 \rightarrow GUVW$	NOT (4)
(2)	$GUVW \rightarrow GUVW$	VA (4)
	PQED	
(3)	$G213 \rightarrow GXYZ$	NOT (5)
(3)	$GXYZ \rightarrow GXYZ$	VA (5)
	QED	
*11.57.	$\rightarrow (X)GX \equiv (Y)(Z)(GY \,\&\, GZ)$	(1)
(1)	$(X)GX \rightarrow (Y)(Z)(GY \,\&\, GZ)$	(2)
(1)	$(Y)(Z)(GY \,\&\, GZ) \rightarrow (X)GX$	(3)
(3)	$G1 \,\&\, G2 \rightarrow GX$	(4)
(4)	$G1,\ G2 \rightarrow GX$	NOT (5)
(4)	$GX, GX \rightarrow GX$	VA (5)
	PQED	
(2)	$(X)GX \rightarrow (Y)GY \,\&\, (Z)GZ$	(6)
(6)	$(X)GX \rightarrow (Y)GY$	(7)
(6)	$(X)GX \rightarrow (Z)GZ$	(8)
(7)	$G1 \rightarrow GY$	NOT (9)
(7)	$GY \rightarrow GY$	VA (9)
	PQED	
(8)	$G1 \rightarrow GZ$	NOT (10)
(8)	$GZ \rightarrow GZ$	VA (10)
	QED	
*9.22.	$(X)(GX \supset HX) \rightarrow (EY)GY \supset (EZ)HZ$	(1)
(1)	$(X)(GX \supset HX), (EY)GY \rightarrow (EZ)HZ$	(2)
(2)	$G1 \supset H1, GY \rightarrow H2$	(3)
(3)	$H1, GY \rightarrow H2$	NOT (4)
(3)	$GY \rightarrow H2, G1$	NOT (5)
(3)	$GY \rightarrow HY, GY$	VA (5)
(3)	$HY, GY \rightarrow HY$	VA (4)
	QED	

These examples are intended to show several things. In the first place, for example, in line (5) of *11.21, the possible substitutions for (1, 2, 3) are (X, X, X), (X, X, Y), (X, X, Z), (X, Y, X), (X, Y, Y), (X, Y, Z), (Y, X, X), (Y, X, Y), (Y, X, Z), (Y, Y, X), (Y, Y, Y), (Y, Y, Z), et cetera, 27 in all. If one tries out the substitutions one by one, as was done in Program *III,* it will take some time before one reaches the correct substitution (Y, X, Z). It is, however, clear that an equally mechanizable procedure is to single out occurrences of the same predicate letter on both sides of the arrow and select the substitutions which would make all the sequents in question theorems. This is one minor change which will be made in Program *III*. Incidentally, this is also an instance of a simple strategy which improves the program.

In the second place, *9.22 shows that there is no need to eliminate $\supset$ because the definition of formulae in the miniscope form can easily be modified to include formulae containing $\supset$ in addition to $\sim$, $\vee$, &. All that is needed is to remember that $\phi \supset \psi$ is the same as $\sim\phi \vee \psi$.

In the third place, as will be proved later on, the Steps 3 to 5 given above are applicable to a sequent in the *AE* form which contains at most one positive quantifier even if it is not in the miniscope form. This is, e.g., why in the proof of *11.57, (3) does not have to be transformed into the miniscope form, while (2) has to. Thus if the quantifiers in (2) are not separated as in line (6), one gets:

(2)	$G1 \rightarrow GY \& GZ$	(6)
(6)	$G1 \rightarrow GY$	NOT (7)
(6)	$G1 \rightarrow GZ$	NOT (8)

No possible substitution can make both (7) and (8) theorems. Hence, although *11.57 is a theorem, no proof would be obtained in this way, unless a reduction to the miniscope form is made first. On the other hand, in an alternative procedure to be described below, Step 5 in the above procedure is replaced by a different substitution, performed before Step 4, so that *G*1 is replaced by *GY, GZ* in the above example and it is no longer necessary to have the sequent in the miniscope form to begin with. The relative merits of the two procedures will be compared below.

§ 9. Program *III*

This program was originally intended to embody the procedure *Qp*. But the preliminary part of bringing a formula into the miniscope form has not been debugged. It is now clear that just for the purpose of proving all the theorems of the predicate calculus in *Principia,* it is not necessary to include all the rules for bringing a formula into a miniscope form. Indeed, only about 5% of the theorems need such rules at all, and only rather simple ones.

There are, however, a few other differences between Program *III* and the procedure described above. Instead of eliminating all quantifiers at once according to their signs, quantifiers are treated on the same basis as the truth-functional connectives with two rules for each. If λ and ζ are strings (possibly empty) of atomic formulae and i is a new numeral, v is a new variable:

Rule $\rightarrow \forall$. If $\zeta \rightarrow \lambda, \phi v, \pi$, then $\zeta \rightarrow \lambda, (\alpha)\phi\alpha, \pi$.

Rule $\rightarrow \exists$. If $\zeta \rightarrow \lambda, \phi i, \pi$, then $\zeta \rightarrow \lambda, (E\alpha)\phi\alpha, \pi$.

Rule $\forall \rightarrow$. If $\lambda, \phi i, \rho \rightarrow \pi$, then $\lambda, (\alpha)\phi\alpha, \rho \rightarrow \pi$.

Rule $\exists \rightarrow$. If $\lambda, \phi v, \rho \rightarrow \pi$, then $\lambda, (E\alpha)\phi\alpha, \rho \rightarrow \pi$.

These rules make for uniformity in the whole procedure except that precaution should be taken that the same quantifier, when recurring at different places on account of truth-functional reductions, should still be replaced by the same variables or numerals, although when the replacement is by a numeral, the difference is not vital. When this precaution is not taken, it can happen that certain theorems of the *AE* predicate calculus do not get proofs. This in fact happened with Program *III*, which failed to yield proofs for *10.3, *10.51, *10.55, *10.56, *11.37, *11.52, *11.521, *11.61, for no other reason than this.

A less serious defect in Program *III* is that truth-functional reductions are not always made as often as possible before eliminating quantifiers. This has the defect that several separate problems are sometimes treated as one whole problem and the running time required for getting a proof becomes unnecessarily long. In 4 special cases, viz., *10.22, *10.29, *10.42, *10.43, this defect in fact results in the failure to get a proof, even though a proof for each can be found by Program *III*, if all possible truth-functional reductions are made before eliminating quantifiers. Both this and the preceding defects of Program *III* can easily be amended. The reason for dwelling so long on them is to illustrate how machines can assist mathematical research in revealing theoretical defects in preliminary formulations of general procedures.

Since the present methods do not use axioms and definitions, the axioms and definitions of *Principia* are rewritten as theorems. The resulting list, thus augmented, of theorems in *Principia* (*9 to *13) from the predicate calculus with equality, has a total number of 158 members. Of these 139 can be proved by Program *III* as it stands, although some of them require unnecessarily long running time, e.g., *11.21 and *11.24. If we make the few minor modifications mentioned above, the running time for all becomes reasonably short and the 12 theorems listed in the last two paragraphs become provable. Altogether there are only 7 of the 158 theorems which stand in need of some preliminary simple steps to get the formulae into the miniscope form: *11.31, *11.391, *11.41, *11.57, *11.59, *11.7, *11.71. The rules needed to take care of these cases are three:

(i) Replace $(\alpha)(\phi\alpha \,\&\, \psi\alpha)$ by $(\alpha)\phi\alpha \,\&\, (\alpha)\psi\alpha$.

(ii) Replace $(E\alpha)(\phi\alpha \vee \psi\alpha)$ by $(E\alpha)\phi\alpha \vee (E\alpha)\psi\alpha$.

(iii) Replace $(\alpha)(\chi\alpha \supset (\phi\alpha \,\&\, \psi\alpha))$ by $(\alpha)(\chi\alpha \supset \phi\alpha) \,\&\, (\alpha)(\chi\alpha \supset \psi\alpha)$.

Hence, to summarize, Program *III* can be somewhat modified to prove all the 158 theorems of *Principia,* with the modified program doing the following. Given a sequent, see whether the rules (i), (ii), (iii) are applicable and apply them if so. Then make all truth-functional simplifications by the rules *P*2a–*P*6b. This in general yields a finite set of sequents. If every one is in the *AE* form and either contains no more than one positive quantifier or is in the miniscope form, then the original sequent is often decidable by the method, otherwise it is beyond the capacity of the method. If the former is the case, proceed to decide each sequent either by eliminating all quantifiers at once as in Step 3 of the preceding section, or by mixing the application of the rules *P*2a–*P*6b with the rules $\rightarrow\forall$, $\rightarrow\exists$, $\forall\rightarrow$, $\exists\rightarrow$. Finally, use Steps 4 and 5 of the preceding section.

A sample of the print-outs by Program *III* without the modifications is given in Appendix IV. In this connection, it may be of interest to report an amusing phenomenon when Program *III* is in operation. The machine usually prints out the lines of a proof in quick succession, and then there is a long pause, as if it were thinking hard, before it prints out the substitution instance which makes all the nonvalid sequents of atomic formulae valid. For example, the first 15 lines of *11.501 in Appendix IV were printed out in quick succession, followed by a long pause of over 2 minutes, and then the remaining few lines were printed out.

§ 10. Systems Qq and Qr: Alternative Formulations of the AE Predicate Calculus

As remarked in connection with the proof of *11.57, one can replace Step 5 by a different way of substitution and then the new method Qq becomes applicable even when the formulae in the sequent are not in the miniscope form, as long as the sequent is in the *AE* form.

More exactly, the new method of substitution is as follows. Consider the sequent obtained immediately after the elimination of quantifiers, and determine all the occurring variables and numerals. If $\alpha_1, \cdots, \alpha_n$ are the variables, a formula ϕi, where i is a numeral, is replaced by $\phi\alpha_1, \cdots, \phi\alpha_n$. For example, take (2) of *11.57:

$$(X)GX \rightarrow (Y)(Z)(GY \,\&\, GZ) \qquad (1)$$

$$(1)\ G1 \rightarrow GY \,\&\, GZ \qquad (2)$$

$$(2)\ GY, GZ \rightarrow GY \,\&\, GZ \qquad (3)$$

$$(3)\ GY, GZ \rightarrow GY \qquad \text{VA}\ (4)$$

$$(3)\ GY, GZ \rightarrow GZ \qquad \text{VA}\ (5)$$

QED

What are the comparative merits of Qp and Qq? According to Qq, only one substitution is made and at the beginning rather than at the end, but unlike Qp, the results obtained may be sequents longer than any previous sequents in the proof. To apply Qq it is not necessary that the formulae be first brought to the miniscope form——the procedure is applicable as long as the sequent is in the AE form; but the method Qp has the compensating advantage that sometimes a sequent not in the AE form can be reduced to sequents in this form by bringing it into the miniscope form. For example, all sequents of the monadic predicate calculus are decidable by Qp, but not by Qq. Church's example[20] in Appendix VI is such a case. On the other hand, the same example also shows that the procedure of bringing a sequent into the miniscope form can get very involved, so that other methods become preferable. While both Qp and Qq can be incorporated in the system Q for the whole predicate calculus, to be described below, a third method Qr is closer to Q in spirit. Hence, Q will be presented as an extension of Qr rather than one of Qp or Qq.

The method Qr proceeds in the same way as Qp except that at the step of substitution, the disjunction of all substitution instances is tested for truth-functional validity. Thus, take (2) of *11.57 again:

$$(X)GX \rightarrow (Y)(Z)(GY \,\&\, GX) \qquad (1)$$

$$(1)\ G1 \rightarrow GY \,\&\, GZ \qquad (2)$$

$$(2)\ G1 \rightarrow GY \qquad (3)$$

$$(2)\ G1 \rightarrow GZ \qquad (4)$$

Now we test whether the disjunction of the conjunction of $GY \rightarrow GY$ and $GY \rightarrow GZ$, and that of $GZ \rightarrow GY$ and $GZ \rightarrow GZ$, is truth-functionally valid. This is indeed so because if the first disjunctant is false, then $GY \rightarrow GZ$ is false and then $GZ \rightarrow GY$ is true and therewith the second disjunctant is true. Alternatively, this disjunction can also be expressed as a conjunction of four clauses:

(i) $GY, GZ \rightarrow GY, GY$

(ii) $GY, GZ \rightarrow GY, GZ$

(iii) $GY, GZ \rightarrow GZ, GY$

(iv) $GY, GZ \rightarrow GZ, GZ$

Now we have three alternative methods Qp, Qq, Qr for the AE predicate calculus. In Appendix V, we give an example with its three alternative disproofs.

How do we justify the methods Qp, Qq, and Qr? First, if there is no proof, then the original sequent is not valid. The proof for this is easiest for Qq. In the example in Appendix V, line (3) under method Qq is not valid if and only if the original sequent (1) is not valid in the domain $\{X, Z\}$. The fact that (4), (5), (6), (7) are not all valid shows that (3) is not valid. In fact, if GXX and GXZ are true but GZX and GZZ are false, (3) is not valid. Therefore, (1) is false under the particular interpretation and hence not valid. More exactly, we wish to find an interpretation under which $(EX)(Y)(GXY \vee GYX) \& \sim (Z)(EW)\, GZW$, or more simply, $(Y)(GXY \vee GYX) \& (W) \sim GZW$, is satisfiable in $\{X, Z\}$. That is to say, to find an interpretation under which the conjunction of $GXX \vee GXX$, $GXZ \vee GZX, \sim GZX, \sim GZZ$ is true, or its negation (3) is false. The interpretation of G given above serves this purpose. It is not hard to generalize the argument to all sequents in the AE form. Indeed, such considerations are familiar from standard decision procedures[21].

The justification of Qp consists in the fact that if an AE sequent is in the miniscope form, then all the negative quantifiers essentially govern a disjunction in the consequent and a conjunction in the antecedent. As a result, the substitution at the end is often equivalent to that obtained by the method Qq. For example, in Appendix V, the disjunction under method Qp is of:

(i) $GXX \rightarrow GZX$; $GXX \rightarrow GZX$ or simply $GXX \vee GXX \rightarrow GZX$

(ii) $GXX \rightarrow GZZ$; $GXX \rightarrow GZZ$ or simply $GXX \vee GXX \rightarrow GZZ$

(iii) $GXZ \rightarrow GZX$; $GZX \rightarrow GZX$ or simply $GXZ \vee GZX \rightarrow GZX$

(iv) $GXZ \rightarrow GZX$; $GZX \rightarrow GZZ$ or simply $GXZ \vee GZX \rightarrow GZZ$

Hence, the disjunction is equivalent to

$$\sim (GXX \vee GXX) \vee \sim (GXZ \vee GZX) \vee GZX \vee GZZ,$$

which, in turn, is equivalent to (3) under method Qq.

When a sequent has no more than one positive quantifier, whether in the miniscope form or not, it is quite obvious that a proof by Qq is obtainable if and only if one by Qp is, since in either method there is only a single possible substitution. In the general case, however, as Mr. Richard Goldberg has pointed out in correspondence, there are AE sequents in the miniscope form which are provable by Qq but not by Qp. He gives the following valid sequent as example:

$$(X)GXU \rightarrow (EW)(GYW \,\&\, GZW).$$

It follows that Qp is applicable only to a subclass of AE sequents in the miniscope form. Hence, it would seem that the correct course is to modify Program III to embody the procedure Qq or the procedure Qr. The modifications needed are, fortunately, again not extensive.

With some care, it is possible to prove by an inductive argument that a proof by Qq is obtainable if and only if one by Qr is. This is so because the substitutions at the beginning of *Qq* give the same result as the taking of disjunctions at the end of *Qr*. Hence, it is true that all valid sequents of the *AE* predicate calculus are provable in *Qq* and in *Qr*.

It is easier to prove that if there is a proof by any of the methods, then the sequent is valid. In the case of *Qp*, one can simply replace all numerals throughout by the correct variables found at the end and the result would be a quite ordinary proof which can easily be seen to yield only valid results. In the case of *Qq*, one can again make the replacement throughout, so that the result is a proof which, instead of $\rightarrow\forall$, $\rightarrow\exists$, $\forall\rightarrow$, $\exists\rightarrow$, uses $\rightarrow\forall$, $\exists\rightarrow$, and:

Rule $\rightarrow\exists^*$: If $\zeta \rightarrow \lambda, \phi\alpha_1, \cdots, \phi\alpha_n, \pi$, then $\zeta \rightarrow \lambda, (E\alpha)\phi\alpha, \pi$.

Rule $\forall\rightarrow^*$: If $\lambda, \phi\alpha_1, \cdots, \phi\alpha_n, \rho \rightarrow \pi$, then $\lambda, (\alpha)\phi\alpha, \rho \rightarrow \pi$.

Finally, since there is a proof by *Qr* if and only if there is one by *Qq*, every theorem of *Qr* is also valid.

§ 11. System *Q*: The Whole Predicate Calculus with Equality

Thus far we have considered only *AE* sequents and used no function symbols. Now we shall consider arbitrary sequents of the predicate calculus and make use of function symbols from time to time.

The method *Q*, an extension of *Qr*, can be explained as follows. It is desirable (i.e. reduces the running time usually) but not necessary, to make preliminary truth-functional reductions so that one problem is broken up into several simpler problems. For each problem, the following steps are used.

Step I. Eliminate all occurrences of $\equiv$ whose scopes contain quantifiers. Determine the positive quantifiers, the negative quantifiers, and for every positive quantifier governed by negative quantifiers, if there is any, the negative quantifiers which govern it. Use distinct variables for all the free variables and positive quantifiers.

Step II. Drop all quantifiers and replace all variables attached to a negative quantifier by a distinct numeral, all variables attached to a positive quantifier governed by negative quantifiers by a function symbol followed by the numerals for the governing negative quantifiers.

Step III. Make truth-functional simplifications until all logical constants are eliminated and a finite set of sequents of atomic formulae is obtained.

Step IV. Make all possible substitutions on these sequents obtaining results S_1, S_2, S_3, et cetera. The original sequent is a theorem if and only if there is a truth-functional tautology among S_1, $S_1 \vee S_2$, $S_1 \vee S_2 \vee S_3$, et cetera.

The substitutions to be made are a bit more complex than those in the *AE* predicate calculus. The basic terms consist of not only all the occuring variables, say X and Y, but also instances of the composite terms such as, say, fX, ffX or f^2X, fY, f^2Y, f^3X, f^3Y, f^4X, et cetera. The numerals are to be substituted by all possible selections from these basic terms. If no variables occur in the sequents, a single variable X is added.

We give a few simple examples. More complex examples are included in Appendices VI and VII[22].

Example 1.	$\rightarrow (EY)(Z)(GXZ \supset GXY)$	(1)
(1)	$\rightarrow GXf1 \supset GX1$	(2)
(2)	$GXf1 \rightarrow GX1$	(3)
(2)	$GXfX \rightarrow GXX$	(4)
(2)	$GXf^2X \rightarrow GXfX$	(5)
(2)	$GXf^3X \rightarrow GXf^2X$	(6)

and so on.

Since the disjunction of (4) and (5) is already valid, this is a theorem. In this simple case, (4), (5), (6) are S_1, S_2, S_3, and S_1, $S_1 \vee S_2$, $S_1 \vee S_2 \vee S_3$ can be simply rewritten as S_1 and:

$$GXfX,\ GXf^2X \rightarrow GXX,\ GXfX$$

$$GXfX,\ GXf^2X,\ GXf^3X \rightarrow GXX,\ GXfX,\ GXf^2X.$$

Example 2.	$(X)(EY)GXY \rightarrow (EZ)(W)GZW$	(1)
(1)	$G1f1 \rightarrow G2g2$	(2)
	$GXfX \rightarrow GXgX$	(S_1)
	$GfXf^2X \rightarrow GXgX$	(S_2)
	$GXfX \rightarrow GfXgfX$	(S_3)
	$GfXf^2X \rightarrow GfXgfX$	(S_4)

and so on.

In this example, the basic terms are X, fX, gX, fgX, gfX, f^2X, g^2X, fg^2X, gf^2X, f^2gX, g^2fX, f^3X, g^3X, et cetera. Intuitively it can be seen that no matter what basic terms we substitute for 1 and 2, we can never arrive at a tautologous disjunction. Thus, no matter what we do, we can never get an antecedent of the form $G\alpha f\beta$, or a consequent of the form $G\alpha f\beta$. Hence, this is not a theorem of Q.

An alternative procedure Q' which is more directly related to the standard method initiated by Herbrand is to make the substitutions immediately after the quantifiers are eliminated. In Appendix VI, a proof of

Ex. 3 is given by this method. Clearly Q' is an extension of Qq just as Q is an extension of Qr. While it is not clear whether Q or Q' is superior if the problem is done by hand, it is conjectured that Q is mechanically less cumbersome, especially if the final test procedure is programmed along the line suggested in Appendix VII.

To justify the procedures Q and Q', i.e., to prove their correctness and completeness, one need to introduce only slight modifications into standard arguments of Skolem and Herbrand. The equivalence of the two procedures is established by the same kind of argument as that for the equivalence of Qq and Qr. Hence, it suffices to prove the correctness and completeness of Q'.

The correctness, i.e., that every provable sequent is valid, is immediate. Given a proof of Q', i.e., a disjunction of substitution instances which is tautologous, we can derive a sequent which is equivalent to the original sequent to be proved except that every whole formula in the sequent is in the prenex form. Take Ex. 1. The proof by Q' consists merely in replacing the lines (3)—(6) in the above proof by the tautologous line

$$\text{(i)} \quad \rightarrow GXfX \supset GXX,\ GXf^2X \supset GXfX$$

From this line, we can by the usual rules of quantification infer:

$$\rightarrow GXfX \supset GXX,\ (Z)(GXZ \supset GXfX)$$
$$\rightarrow GXfX \supset GXX,\ (EY)(Z)(GXZ \supset GXY)$$
$$\rightarrow (Z)(GXZ \supset GXX),\ (EY)(Z)(GXZ \supset GXY)$$
$$\rightarrow (EY)(Z)(GXZ \supset GXX),\ (EY)(Z)(GXZ \supset GXY)$$
$$\rightarrow (EY)(Z)(GXZ \supset GXX)$$

It may be remarked that since a new term for the universal quantifier is introduced every time, viz. fX, f^2X, et cetera, we can always reintroduce it successively without violating the restriction that the term to be replaced by Z is not free elsewhere. Strictly speaking the terms fX, f^2X, et cetera should first be replaced by new variables, say U, V, et cetera. Then the line (i) remains valid truth-functionally, and the resulting proof of the original sequent of Ex. 1 would conform entirely to usual rules for quantifiers[23].

The completeness of Q' can be proved by using ideas familiar in mathematical logic[24]. We wish to prove that if there is no proof, then its negation is satisfiable in an enumerable domain, and hence the original sequent is not valid. Consider Ex. 2 for which none of S_1, $S_1 \vee S_2$, $S_1 \vee S_2 \vee S_3$, et cetera is valid. In other words, for each disjunction, there are truth-value assignments which would make it false. Since every later disjunction contains all earlier disjunctions as part, a falsifying assignment of $S_1 \vee \cdots \vee S_n$ (call it D_n) also falsifies all D_i, $i<n$. In other words, there is a truth-assignment which falsifies D_1, and for every n, there exists a falsifying assignment for D_n which has an extension that falsifies D_{n+1}. In the simple example Ex. 2, we have:

D_1 is falsified if $GXfX$ is true but $GXgX$ is false,

D_2 is falsified if, in addition $GfXf^2X$ is true,

D_3 is falsified if, in addition $GfXgX$ is false,

D_4 is falsified if, in addition $GfXf^2X$ is true,

and so on.

In general, we have an infinite tree structure such that there is a finite set of nodes falsifying D_1 of which at least one has extensions or nodes on the second level, which falsify D_2. Among the nodes on the second level, i.e., truth-value assignments which falsify D_2, at least one has extensions which falsify D_3, and so on. It then follows by the *Unendlichkeitslemma*[25] that there exists an infinite path, or an infinite truth-value assignment which falsifies D_1, D_2, ··· simultaneously. Thus, since each node originates only finitely many (possibly zero) immediate branches and there are infinitely many paths, there must be one node a_1 at the first level which occurs in infinitely many paths, and among the finitely many nodes of the second level joined to a_1, there must be at least one node a_2 which occurs in infinitely many paths. This is true for every level, and hence a_1, a_2, a_3, ··· determines an infinite path. This is no longer true generally when there may be infinitely many branches for a given node. For example, there is no infinite path in a "spread" in which there is one node of the first level (the origin) and a path from it of length n, for every n, all disjoint except for the origin.

An assignment which falsifies D_1, D_2, ··· simultaneously is a model of the negation of, say, Ex. 2:

$$(X)(EY)GXY \mathbin{\&} \sim (EZ)(W)GZW,$$

or

$$(X)[(EY)GXY \mathbin{\&} (EW) \sim GXW]. \qquad (N)$$

Thus the individuals are X, fX, gX, f^2X, g^2X, fgX, et cetera, and we have found an interpretation of G such that for every individual a, there is an individual b, viz. fa, and an individual c, viz. ga, such that $Gafa \mathbin{\&} \sim Gaga$. Hence, in this domain with this G, the negation N of Ex. 2 is true, and Ex. 2 is not valid.

A program for the method Q or the method Q' has not yet been written. It seems clear that certain auxiliary procedures will be useful in reducing the running time and extending the range of application. For example, it seems desirable to separate scopes of different quantifiers when possible, although it is not immediately obvious whether always bringing a sequent into the miniscope form first is feasible on the whole. Other simplifications such as dropping tautologous or repetitive conjunctants could easily and profitably be included. In general, the practical limitation of the machine will necessarily impose certain restrictions on the solvable problems. The machine will have to concede defeat when the running time is too long or the easily available storage is exhausted. When such a situation arises, it seems desirable to try some alternative procedure before giving up the problem entirely.

An intrinsic limitation of the methods Q and Q' is the following. There are various sequents which amount to an axiom of infinity, i.e., a proposition satisfiable in an infinite domain but in no finite domain. If the machine is given the negation of such a sequent, the method Q or the method Q' will never give the desired negative answer since it is, being the negation of an axiom of infinity, valid in every finite domain, though not a theorem of the predicate calculus. Simple examples of this type are:

Example 6. $\rightarrow (EX)GXX, (EX)(Y) \sim GXY,$
$(EX)(EY)(EZ)(GXY \,\&\, GYZ \,\&\, \sim GXZ)$

Example 7. $\rightarrow (EX)GXX, (EX)(Y) \sim GXY,$
$(EX)(Y)(EZ)(GYZ \,\&\, \sim GXZ)$

This class of propositions may be of special interest if we wish to test whether a formal system is consistent. Most of the interesting formal systems are intended to be satisfiable only in infinite domains. Hence, if the system is consistent, then its negation, though not a theorem of the predicate calculus, is valid in every finite domain. Hence, even theoretically, the methods Q and Q' can at most discover contradictions in an inconsistent formal system but cannot ascertain that an interesting formal system is indeed consistent.

This suggests the desirability of adding special decision procedures which cover some propositions in this class. Such results are rather scarce. The only one seems to be Ackermann's, which is applicable only to a rather special subclass[26].

A question concerning the efficiency of the methods Q and Q' is the obvious remark that if some of $D_1, D_2, \cdots$ is indeed a tautology, the human being often finds such a disjunction in the sequence without actually examining all the preceding disjunctions. Hence, it may be possible to include suitable strategies for choosing such disjunctions. The difficult problem here is to find suitable strategies of sufficient generality. This is in part related to the larger questions of making use of previously proved theorems. The methods considered in this paper so far all begin from scratch. When we get into more advanced disciplines, it seems unlikely that the machine can feasibly avoid reference to previously proved theorems. Yet there is the analogous situation in ordinary calculations where it is often faster for the machine to calculate known results on the spot rather than look them up in tables stored in some remote corner of the machine. On account of questions of storage and access time, some golden mean has to be struck between the knowledgeable pedant and the ignorant proving prodigy.

§ 12. Conclusions

The original aim of the writer was to take mathematical textbooks such as Landau on the number system[27], Hardy-Wright on number theory[28], Hardy on the calculus[29], Veblen-Young on projective geometry[30], the volumes by Bourbaki, as outlines and make the machine formalize all the proofs (fill in the gaps). The purpose of this paper is to report work done recently on the underlying logic, as a preliminary to that project.

The restricted objective has been met by a running program for the propositional calculus and a considerable portion of the predicate calculus. Methods for dealing with the whole predicate calculus by machine have been described fairly exactly. A summary of results and a comparison with previous work in this field were given in the introductory section and will not be repeated here.

The writer sees the main interest of the work reported here not so much in getting a few specific results which in some ways are stronger than expected (e.g., the fast speed attained and the relatively small storage needed), as in illustrating the great potentiality of machines in an apparently wide area of research and development. Various problems of the same type come to mind.

Decision procedures for the intuitionistic and modal propositional calculi are available but often too lengthy to be done by hand[31]. It seems possible and desirable to code these procedures in a manner similar to the classical systems of logic. The intuitionistic predicate calculus with its decidable subdomains, such as all those propositions which are in the prenex form, may also be susceptible to analogous treatment. Since the efficiency of the proof-decision procedure in Program I depends on the elimination of *modus ponens* (rule of detachment), a related question of logic is to devise cut-free systems for various partial and alternative systems of the propositional calculus.

A good deal of work has been spent in constructing different systems of the propositional calculus and of modal logic. The questions of completeness and independence are often settled by methods which are largely mechanizable and even of no great complexity. This suggests that many of the results in this area, reported, e.g., in Prior's book[32], can be obtained by mechanical means. Given a system, in order to determine the independence and completeness (i.e., non-independence of all axioms of some given complete system) of its axioms, we may simultaneously grind out proofs and matrices used for independence proofs and stop when we have either obtained a derivation or a matrix that establishes the independence of the formula under consideration. It is true that Linial and Post[33] have proved the undecidability of this class of problems so that we cannot be sure that we can always settle the particular question in each case. Nonetheless, we may expect this procedure to work in a large number of cases. The only practical difficulty is that in grinding out proofs, the rules of *modus ponens* makes the matter rather unwieldy. When equivalent cut-free formulations are available, this mechanical aid to such simple mathematical research would become more feasible. Alternatively, the strategies devised by Newell-Shaw-Simon may find here a less wasteful place of application.

A mathematically more interesting project is to have machines do some easy number theory. Here there are two possible alternative approaches: use quantifiers or avoid quantifiers. It is known in mathematical logic that ordinary number theory can be developed largely without appeal to quantifiers. Thus, from the discussions in the body of the paper, it is clear that quantifiers serve essentially to replace an indeterminate class of function symbols. In number theory, these function symbols can usually be replaced by specific function symbols introduced by recursive definitions. Since these are more specific and often intuitively more familiar, it seems quite plausible that avoiding quantifiers would be an advantage. On the other hand, it may be better to use existential quantifiers but avoid mixing quantifiers of both kinds ("all" and "some"), that being the main source of the complexity of the predicate calculus.

If one wishes to prove that the square root of 2 is not a rational number, this can be stated in the free-variable form as

$$2Y^2 \neq X^2,$$

and a proof can be written out without use of the quantifiers. On the other hand, if one wishes to prove that there are infinitely many primes, it seems natural to state the theorem as

$$(EX)(Y < X \,\&\, X \text{ is a prime}).$$

Essentially, the usual proof gives us a simple recursive function f, such that

$$Y < fY \,\&\, fY \text{ is a prime}$$

is true. But before we get the proof and the required function, it is convenient to use the quantifier (EX) which serves to express the problem that a yet unknown function is being sought for.

In this connection, it may be of interest to make a few general remarks on the nature of expansive features in different proof procedures. The attractive feature of the system P as a proof procedure is that given a sequent, all the lines in a proof for it are essentially parts of the sequent. As a result, the task of searching for a proof is restricted in advance so that, at least in theory, we can always decide whether a proof exists or not. This contrasts sharply with those proof procedures for the propositional calculus which make use of the *modus ponens*. There, given q, we wish to search for p, such that p and $p \supset q$ are theorems. There is no restriction on the length and complexity of p. What the cut-free formulation achieves is a method such that for every proof by the expansive method there is a corresponding proof in this method without expansion, and vice versa.

Since there is no decision procedure for the predicate calculus or current number theory, it follows that expansive features cannot be eliminated entirely from these disciplines. The cut-free formulation for the predicate calculus concentrates the expansive feature in one type of situation: viz., a conclusion $(EX)\, FX$ may come from $F1$ or $F2$ or et cetera. The method Q given above further throws together all such expansions for a given sequent to be proved or disproved at the end of the process. These devices have the advantage that one may direct the search for more efficient partial methods or strategies mainly to one specific region which contains the chief source of expansion.

If one develops number theory with no appeal to quantifiers, the above type of expansion is avoided. It is, however, not possible to avoid in general another type of expansion. Thus we can conclude $X=Y$ from $fX=fY$, but given X and Y, there are in general infinitely many candidates for the function f, so that trying to find an f which leads to $X=Y$ through $fX=fY$ is an expansive procedure. So much for different expansive features.

Other possibilities are set theory and the theory of functions. In these cases, it seems desirable to use a many-sorted predicate calculus[34] as the underlying logic. While this is in theory not necessary, it will presumably make for higher efficiency.

As is well-known, all standard formal systems can be formulated within the framework of the predicate calculus. In general, if a theorem p is derived from the axioms $A_1, \cdots, A_n$, then the sequent

$$A_1, \cdots, A_n \rightarrow p$$

is a theorem of the predicate calculus. In particular, if a system with finitely many axioms is inconsistent, the negation of the conjunction of all its axioms is a theorem of the predicate calculus. (The restriction on finitely many axioms is, incidentally, not essential since in most cases we can reformulate a formal system to use only finitely many axioms, with substantially the same theorems.) Specker has proved[35] that Quine's *New Foundations* plus the axiom of choice is inconsistent. Hence, the negation of the conjunction of these (finitely many) axioms is a theorem of the predicate calculus. If a sufficiently efficient program for the predicate calculus on a sufficiently large machine yields, unaided, a proof of this, we would be encouraged to try to see whether the system without the axiom of choice might also be inconsistent. If the system is indeed inconsistent, then there would be a chance that a proof of this fact can be achieved first by a machine.

So far little is said about specific strategies. In number theory, we are often faced with the problem of choosing a formula to make induction on. Here an obvious strategy would be to try first to use as the induction formula the whole conclusion, and then the various subformulae of the conclusion to be established. When faced with a conclusion $(EX)FX$, it seems usually advantageous to try terms occurring elsewhere in the known part of the proof, or their variants, in order to find α such that $F\alpha$. Polya's book[36] contains various suggestions on strategies for doing number theory which will presumably be useful when one gets deeper into the project of mechanizing number theory. Efficient auxiliary procedures such as the one already mentioned by Dunham-Fridshal-Sward for the propositional calculus will undoubtedly be of use in shortening running time, when one tries to formalize proofs or prove theorems in more advanced domains.

While formalizing (known or conjectured) proofs and proving new theorems are intimately related, it is reasonable to suppose that the first type of problem is much easier for the machine. That is why the writer believes that perhaps machines may more quickly become of practical use in mathematical research, not by proving new theorems, but by formalizing and checking outlines of proofs, say, from textbooks to detailed formulations more rigorous than *Principia,* from technical papers to textbooks, or from abstracts to technical papers.

The selection of interesting conjectures or theorems and useful definitions is less easily mechanizable. For example, Program II described above gives only very crude results. It should be of interest to try to get better results along the same line. In more advanced domains, however, the question seems to have a complexity of a different order.

If we use a machine to grind out a large mass of proofs, then there seems to be some mechanical test as to the importance and centrality of concepts and theorems. If a same theorem or a same expression occurs frequently, then we may wish to consider the theorem interesting or introduce a definition for the expression. This is, however, a rather slippery criterion. The finite number of proofs printed out at a given time may form a class that is determined on the ground of some formal characteristic of an accidental nature. Unless there is some acceptable norm in advance for ordering the proofs to be obtained, one can hardly justify in this way the claim that certain theorems are interesting.

A more stable criterion may be this. A formula which is short but can only be proved by long proofs is a "deep" theorem. A short expression which is only equivalent to very long expressions is a "rich" concept.

In the normal situations, we have, of course, less restricted objective guidance. There is a fixed body of concepts and theorems which is for good reasons regarded as of special interest (the "archive of mathematical knowledge built up by the cumulative effort of the human intellect"). For such a body it is theoretically possible to select important theorems and concepts mechanically, as well as to find elegant alternative proofs. However, even in this case, one is looking backwards. It is not easy to find a forward-looking mechanizable criterion for mathematical centrality. For example, it is hard to render the nice criterion of ranges of application articulate.

One special kind of mathematics is developing one discipline from another. For example, theories of natural numbers and real numbers can be developed from set theory. If theorems are generated mechanically from set theory, then any set of theorems isomorphic with the axioms for real numbers (resp. natural numbers) determines expressions which may be taken as definitions for the basic concepts of the theory of real numbers (resp. natural numbers). In such a case, one can claim that machines can discover definitions too.

It has often been remarked that the machine can only do what it is told. While this is true, one might be misled by an ambiguity. Thus the machine can be told to make a calculation, find a proof, or choose a "deep" theorem, et cetera. The main problem of using rather than building machines is undoubtedly to say more things in mechanical terms.

The limitation of machines has been seen as revealed by its inability to write love letters. That depends on the quality of the love letters to be composed. If one takes the common sort of love letter taught in manuals of effective letter-writing, the machine can certainly write some useful love letters more quickly than it can prove an interesting theorem. If the image of Don Juan in some films is to be believed, the machine can surely be taught to repeat the few sentences of flattery to every woman.

If experimenting with machine to see what it can do is compared with the usual type of scientific research, it seems more like engineering than physics, in so far as we are not dealing with natural objects but man-made gadgets, and we are applying rather than discovering theories. On the other hand, calculating machines are rather unique among man-made things in that their potentialities are far less clear to the maker than other gadgets. In trying to determine what a machine can do, we are faced with almost the same kind of problem as in animal or human psychology. Or, to quote Dunham, we are almost trying to find out what a machine is.

The suspiciously aggressive term "mechanical mathematics" is not unattractive to a mathematical logician. It is a common complaint among mathematicians that logicians, when engaged in formalization, are largely concerned with pointless hairsplitting. It is sufficient to know that proofs can be formalized. Why should one take all the trouble to make exact how such formalizations are to be done, or even to carry out actual formalizations? Logicians are often hard put to give a very convincing justification of their occupation and preoccupation. One lame excuse which can be offered is that they are of such a temperament as to wish to tabulate all scores of all base ball players just to have a complete record in the archives. The machines, however, seem to supply, more or less after the event, one good reason for formalization. While many mathematicians have never learned the predicate calculus, it seems hardly possible for the machine to do much mathematics without first dealing with the underlying logic in some explicit manner. While the human being gets bored and confused with too much rigour and rigidity, the machine requires entirely explicit instructions.

It seems as though that logicians had worked with the fiction of man as a persistent and unimaginative beast who can only follow rules blindly, and then the fiction found its incarnation in the machine. Hence, the striving for inhuman exactness is not pointless, senseless, but gets direction and justification. One may even claim that a new life is given to the Hilbert program of the *Entscheidungsproblem* which von Neumann thought was thoroughly shattered by Gödel's discoveries. While a universal decision procedure for all mathematical problems is not possible, formalization does seem to promise that machines will do a major portion of the work that takes up the time of research mathematicians today.

More recently the writer has succeeded to have the machine prove, with improved methods, all the theorems of *9 to *13 of *Principia* in about 4 minutes. This includes the time for writing tapes but of course only the offline printer is used. The output is about 47 pages of 60 lines each. This and related results will be reported in the near future.

Additional notes. Recent works on related questions include a paper by Gilmore in *IBM journal* (1960), a paper by Prawitz and others and a paper by Davis and Putnam both in *ACM journal* (1960), and a paper by the writer (Part I, *ACM communications,* 1960, 220—234; Part II, *Bell Systems journal,* 1961, 2—41).

With regard to the possibility of a quantifier-free proof of the irrationality of $\sqrt{2}$ (p. 254), this is true only when extended free variable induction principles are admitted. A conclusive treatment of this question is contained in Shepherdson's yet unpublished "the principle of induction in free variable systems of number theory".

It may be of interest to note that we can get a simple formulation of the classical propositional calculus with implication alone. Thus, if we use $p \rightarrow (q \rightarrow r)$ as $p, q \rightarrow r$ and $\rightarrow ((p \rightarrow q) \rightarrow q)$ as p, q, and reiterate; we can then identify $\supset$ with $\rightarrow$ and use $P1$, $P4$a, $P4$b (p. 230) as a complete system. The advantage of such a formulation is that it yields directly both a completeness proof and a decision procedure.

APPENDICES

Appendix I

A sample from print-outs by Program I

2*45/FDPQ-FP	1
1/-FP, DPQ	2
2/P-DPQ	3
3/P-P, Q	4
VALID	4
QED	
5*21/-ICEP. FQ..BPQ	1
1/CFP. FQ-BPQ	2
2/FP, FQ-BPQ	3
3/FQ-BPQ, P	4
4/-BPQ, P, Q	5
5/P-Q, P, Q	6
VALID	6
5/Q-P, P, Q	7
VALID	7
QED	
2*31/DP. DQR-DPQ, R	1
1/P-DPQ, R	2
2/P-P, Q, R	3
VALID	3
1/DQR-DPQ, R	4
4/Q-DPQ, R	5
5/Q-P, Q, R	6
VALID	6
4/R-DPQ, R	7
7/R-P, Q, R	8
VALID	8
QED	
4*45/-BP..CP. DPQ	1
1/P-CP. DPQ	2
2/P-P	3
VALID	3
2/P-DPQ	4
4/P-P, Q	5
VALID	5
1/CP. DPQ-P	6
6/P, DPQ-P	7
7/P,P-P	8
VALID	8
7/P, Q-P	9
VALID	9
QED	

5*22/-*BFBPQ... DCP. FQ.. CQ. FP* 1

QED

5*23/-*BBPQ... DCPQ..CFP. FQ* 1

QED

5*24/-*BFDCPQ..CFP. FQ... DCP. FQ..CQ. EP* 1

QED

*7. PRELIMINARY TO PREDICATE CALCULUS 1
7*1/*IG2. H2, GX, KX-CH3. K3* 1
1/*H2, GX, KX-CH3. K3* 2
2/*H2, GX, KX-H3* 3
NOT VALID 3
2/*H2, GX, KX-K3* 4
NOT VALID 4
1/*GX, KX-CH3. K3, G2* 5
5/*GX, KX-H3, G2* 6
NOT VALID 6
5/*GX, KX-K3, G2* 7
NOT VALID 7
NOT VALID

Appendix II

Sample from print-outs by Program II

/-*BDPR. R, CDPQ. P*
/*CCPQ. R-BIPR. P*
/*CCPQ. P-BIPR. R*
/*CBPQ. Q-CBPP. Q*
/*CCPP. Q-CIPP. Q*
/*CCPP. R-CIPP. P*
/*CDPP. R-CDPP. P*
/*BBPP. P-DCPQ. P*
/*DCPQ. P-BBPP. P*
/*BIPP. P-DDPP. P*
/*DDPP. P-BIPP. P*
/*CIPR. P-BDPQ. P*
/*BIPQ. P-CDPR. P*
/*CCPR. R-BIPQ. Q*
/*CCPR. Q-BIPQ. R*
/*CCPR. P-BBPR. P*
/*CBPR. P-BCPR. P*
/*CIPQ. P-BDPR. P*
/*BIPR. P-CDPQ. P*
/*CCPQ. R-BIPR. Q*
/*CCPQ. Q-BIPR. R*
/*CCPQ. P-CBPP. P*

/*CBPQ. P-CCPP. P*
/*CDPP. P-CIPP. P*
/*CIPP. P-CDPP. P*
/*BBPP. R-DBPQ. R*
/*BCPP. Q-DBPQ. P*
/-*BDPP. R, DDPP. R*
/*BIPP. P-DDPP. Q*
/*BIPP. R-DCPP. R*
/*BBPQ. P-DCPP. Q*
/*BBPQ. Q-DCPP. P*
/*DCPP. P-BBPQ. Q*
/-*BDPQ. P, CIPR. Q*
/*BIPQ. P-CDPR. Q*
/*CDPR. P-BIPQ. Q*
/*CCPR. Q-BBPR. P*
/*CBPR. R-BBPR. R*
/*CBPR. Q-BCPR. P*
/-*BCPR. R, CIPQ. R*
/*CIPQ. P-BDPR. Q*
/*CDPQ. R-BDPR. R*
/*CCPQ. R-BIPR. R*
/*CCPQ. Q-CBPP. P*

/*CCPQ. P-CBPP. Q*
/*CBPQ. R-CBPP. R*
/*CBPQ. Q-CCPP. P*
/*CCPP. Q-CBPQ. P*
/*CBPQ. P-CCPP. Q*
/*CCPP. R-CIPP. R*
/*CDPP. Q-CIPP. P*
/*BBPP. Q-DCPQ. Q*
/*DCPQ. Q-BBPP. Q*
/*BCPP. Q-DBPQ. Q*
/*BIPP. P-DDPP. R*
/*BIPP. Q-DDPP. Q*
/*BBPQ. Q-DCPP. Q*
/*CIPR. Q-BDPQ. Q*
/*CIPR. P-BDPQ. R*
/*CDPR. Q-BIPQ. Q*
/*CCPR. R-BBPR. P*
/*CCPR. Q-BBPR. Q*
/*CCPR. P-BBPR. R*
/*CBPR. R-BCPR. P*
/*CBPR. P-BCPR. R*
/-*BDPR. P, CIPQ. R*

/BIPR. P-CDPQ. R
/CDPQ. P-BIPR. R
/CCPQ. R-CBPP. P
/CCPQ. Q-CBPP. Q
/CCPP. Q-CBPQ. Q
/CBPQ. Q-CCPP. Q
/CDPP. Q-CIPP. Q
/CDPP. R-CIPP. P
/BBPP. P-DDPQ. P
/BCPP. Q-DBPQ. R
/BBPQ. Q-DCPP. R
/-BCPQ. P, DCPP. P
/CCPR. Q-BBPR. R
/CCPR. P-BCPR. P
/CBPR. Q-BCPR. R
/CBPR. P-BDPR. P
/CBPP. P-CDPQ. P
/CDPQ. P-CBPP. P
/CCPQ. R-CBPP. Q

/CCPQ. P-CCPP. P
/CBPQ. P-CDPP. P
/BBPP. P-DDPQ. Q
/BBPP. Q-DDPQ. Q
/BBPP. R-DCPQ. R
/BDPP. Q-DBPQ. P
/BIPP. R-DDPP. R
/BBPQ. P-DDPP. Q
/BBPQ. Q-DDPP. P
/DDPP. P-BBPQ. Q
/-BCPQ. P, DCPP. Q
/DCPP. P-BCPQ. Q
/CIPR. P-BIPQ. Q
/CCPR. R-BBPR. R
/CCPR. Q-BCPR. P
/CBPR. R-BCPR. R
/CBPR. Q-BDPR. P
/CIPQ. R-BDPR. R
/CDPQ. R-BIPR. R

/CCPQ. R-CBPP. R
/CCPQ. Q-CCPP. P
/CCPP. Q-CCPQ. P
/CCPQ. P-CCPP. Q
/CBPQ. Q-CDPP. P
/CDPP. Q-CBPQ. P
/CBPQ. P-CDPP. Q
/CDPP. R-CIPP. R
/BBPP. P-DDPQ. R
/BBPP. Q-DDPQ. Q
/BDPP. Q-DBPQ. Q
/BBPQ. Q-DDPP. Q
/-BCPQ. P, DCPP. R
/-BCPQ. Q, DCPP. Q
/CIPR. Q-BIPQ. Q
/BBPR. P-CDPR. R
/CDPR. R-BBPR. P

Appendix III

Sample of print-outs by Program III (no quantifiers)

*13. IDENTITY		1
13*1/=XY-IGX. GY		1
1/GX, =XY-GY	=VA	2
QED		
13*12/=XY-BGX. GY		1
1/GX,=XY-GY	=VA	2
1/GY,=XY-GX	=VA	3
QED		
13*13/GX,=XY-GY	=VA	1
QED		
13*14/GX, FGY-F=XY		1
1/GX-F=XY, GY		2
2/=XY, GX-GY	=VA	3
QED		
13*15/-=XX	=VA	1
QED		
13*16/-B=XY. =YX		1
1/=XY-=YX	=VA	2
1/=YX-=XY	=VA	3
QED		
13*17/=XY, =YZ-=XZ	=VA	1
QED		

13*171/=XY, =XZ-=YZ	=VA	1

QED

13*172/=YX, =ZX-=YZ	=VA	1

QED

13*18/=XY, F=XZ-F=YZ		1
1/=XY-F=YZ, =XZ		2
2/=YZ, =XY-=XZ	=VA	3

QED

13*194/-BCGX. =XY...CGX..CGY. =XY		1
1/CGX. =XY-CGX..CGY. =XY		2
2/GX, =XY-CGX..CGY. =XY		3
3/GX, =XY-GX	VA	4
3/GX, =XY-CGY. =XY		5
5/GX, =XY-GY	=VA	6
5/GX, =XY-=XY	VA	7
1/CGX..CGY. =XY-CGX. =XY		8
8/GX. CGY. =XY-CGX. =XY		9
9/GX, GY, =XY-CGX. =XY		10
10/GX, GY, =XY-GX	VA	11
10/GX, GY, =XY-=XY	VA	12

QED

13*3/DGY. FGY-BDGX. FGX..D=XY. F=XY		1
1/GY-BDGX. FGX..D=XY. F=XY		2
2/DGX. FGX, GY-D=XY. F=XY		3
3/GX, GY-D=XY. F=XY		4
4/GX, GY-=XY, F=XY		5
5/=XY, GX, GY-=XY	VA	6
3/FGX, GY-D=XY. F=XY		7
7/GY-D=XY. F=XY, GX		8
8/GY-=XY, F=XY, GX		9
9/=XY, GY-=XY, GX	VA	10
2/D=XY. F=XY, GY-DGX. FGX		11
11/=XY, GY-DGX. FGX		12
12/=XY, GY-GX, FGX		13
13/GX, =XY, GY-GX	VA	14
11/F=XY, GY-DGX. FGX		15
15/GY-DGX. FGX, =XY		16
16/GY-GX, FGX, =XY		17
17/GX, GY-GX, =XY	VA	18
1/FGY-BDGX. FGX..D=XY. F=XY		19
19/-BDGX. FGX..D=XY. F=XY, GY		20
20/DGX. FGX-D=XY. F=XY, GY		21
21/GX-D=XY. F=XY, GY		22
22/GX-=XY, F=XY, GY		23
23/=XY, GX-=XY, GY	VA	24
21/FGX-D=XY. F=XY, GY		25
25/-D=XY. F=XY, GY, GX		26

26/-=XY, F=XY, GY, GX		27
27/=XY-=XY, GY, GX	VA	28
20/D=XY. F=XY-DGX. FGX, GY		29
29/=XY-DGX. FGX, GY		30
30/=XY-GX, FGX, GY		31
31/GX, =XY-GX, GY	VA	32
29/F=XY-DGX. FGX, GY		33
33/-DGX. FGX, GY, =XY		34
34/-GX, FGX, GY, =XY		35
35/GX-GX, GY, =XY	VA	36

QED

Appendix IV

Sample of print-outs by Program III (the AE predicate calculus)

10*25/AXGX-EXGX		1
1/G1-EXGX		2
2/G1-G2	NOT	3
2/GS-GS	VA	3

QED

11*26/EXAYGXY-AYEXGXY		1
1/AYGSY-AYEXGXY		2
2/GS1-AYEXGXY		3
3/GS1-EXGXT		4
4/GS1-G2T	NOT	5
4/GST-GST	VA	5

QED

11*501/-BEXFAYGXY. EXEYFGXY		1
1/EXFAYGXY-EXEYFGXY		2
2/FAYGSY-EXEYFGXY		3
3/-EXEYFGXY, AYGSY		4
4/-EYFG1Y, AYGSY		5
5/-FG12, AYGSY		6
6/G12-AYGSY		7
7/G12-GST	NOT	8
1/EXEYFGXY-EXFAYGXY		9
9/EYFGUY-EXFAYGXY		10
10/FGUW-EXFAYGXY		11
11/-EXFAYGXY, GUW		12
12/-FAYG3Y, GUW		13
13/AYG3Y-GUW		14
14/G34-GUW	NOT	15
14/GUW-GUW	VA	15
7/GST-GST	VA	8

QED

13*22/-BEZEWC=ZX..C=WY. GZW...GXY		1
1/EZEWC=ZX..C=WY. GZW-GXY		2

2/*EWC=SX..C=WY. GSW-GXY*		3
3/*C=SX..C=TY. GST-GXY*		4
4/*=SX, C=TY. GST-GXY*		5
5/*=SX, =TY, GST-GXY*	= VA	6
1/*GXY-EZEWC=ZX..C=WY. GZW*		7
7/*GXY-EWC=*1*X..C=WY. G*1*W*		8
8/*GXY-C=*1*X..C=*2*Y. G*12		9
9/*GXY-=*1*X*	NOT	10
9/*GXY-C=*2*Y. G*12		11
11/*GXY-=*2*Y*	NOT	12
11/*GXY-G*12	NOT	13
11/*GXY-GXY*	VA	13
11/*GXY-=YY*	= VA	12
9/*GXY-=XX*	= VA	10

QED

Appendix V

Different methods for the AE predicate calculus

$$(EX)(Y)(GXY \vee GYX) \rightarrow (Z)(EW)GZW \qquad (1)$$

Method *Qp*.

(1)	$GX1 \vee G1X \rightarrow GZ2$		(2)
(2)	$GX1 \rightarrow GZ2$	NOT	(3)
(2)	$G1X \rightarrow GZ2$	NOT	(4)

This is not valid since (3) and (4) are not both valid no matter whether, for (1, 2), we substitute (*X, X*), (*X, Z*), (*Z, X*) or (Z, Z).

Method *Qq*.

(1)	$GX1 \vee G1X \rightarrow GZ2$		(2)
(2)	$GXX \vee GXX, GXZ \vee GZX \rightarrow GZX, GZZ$		(3)
(3)	$GXX, GXZ \rightarrow GZX, GZZ$	NOT	(4)
(3)	$GXX, GZX \rightarrow GZX, GZZ$	VA	(5)
(3)	$GXX, GXZ \rightarrow GZX, GZZ$	NOT	(6)
(3)	$GXX, GZX \rightarrow GZX, GZZ$	VA	(7)

This immediately suggests a simplification since (4) and (6), (5) and (7) are the same. The sequent (1) is not a theorem since (4) and (6) are not valid.

Method *Qr*. Proceed as in *Qp*, and then test the disjunction of the two conjunctions which is equivalent to the conjunction of (4), (5), (6), (7). Hence, again, (1) is not valid.

Appendix VI

An example of Church's

Example 3. $(X)(EY)\{[JX \equiv (JY \supset GY)] \,\&\, [GX \equiv (JY \supset$
$\supset HY)] \,\&\, [HX \equiv ((JY \supset GY) \supset HY)]\} \rightarrow$
$\rightarrow (Z)(JZ \,\&\, GZ \,\&\, HZ).$ (1)

This is a sequent in the monadic predicate calculus. It is not of the *AE* form but its miniscope forms must be in the *AE* form. As a result, this can be proved either by *Qp* or by *Q*, though not by *Qq* or *Qr*. It seems more tedious to use *Qp* than *Q*.

To bring (1) into the miniscope form, we have to eliminate the occurrences of $\equiv$. Then we have to bring the quantifier-free part of the antecedent into a disjunctive normal form, distribute (EY) and separate out those parts of the scope of every occurrence of (EY) which contains the variable X. Then we have to bring the new antecedent minus the initial (X) into a conjunctive normal form and distribute (X) in the same way. The reader may wish to convince himself how complex the whole procedure is. The separation of quantifiers in the consequent is, of course, easy. After the separation of quantifiers, the resulting sequent in the miniscope form is very long. The remaining steps, while easy, are also tedious.

On the other hand, if method *Q* is used instead, the proof is not so lengthy. By hand, it is even easier by *Q'*.

$$(1)\ J1 \equiv (Jf1 \supset Gf1),\ G1 \equiv (Jf1 \supset Hf1),$$
$$H1 \equiv ((Hf1 \supset Gf1) \supset Hf1) \rightarrow JX \,\&\, GX \,\&\, HX. \quad (2)$$

We may substitute for 1, X, fX, f^2X, f^3X, et cetera to get S_1, S_2, S_3, S_4, et cetera and test for validity of S_1, $S_1 \vee S_2$, $S_1 \vee S_2 \vee S_3$, $S_1 \vee S_2 \vee S_3 \vee S_4$, et cetera.

For this purpose it is sufficient to find a disjunction such that any interpretation (truth-value assignment) which makes the antecedents of all the disjunctants true, will make the consequents of all the disjunctants true. It turns out that the disjunction of S_1 to S_7 does this. If one is doing this by hand, it is easier to argue, for example, from $JX \equiv (JfX \supset GfX)$, that if JX is false, then JfX must be true and GfX must be false. In this way, one would see that it is not possible to make all the antecedents of S_1 to S_7 true without also making all their consequents true.

A simple consequence of Ex. 1 may illustrate that sometimes *Qq* is preferable to *Qp*:

Example 4 $(EY)(X)\{[JX \equiv (JY \supset GY)] \,\&\, [GX \equiv (JY \supset$
$\supset HY)] \,\&\, [HX \equiv ((JY \supset GY) \supset HY)]\} \rightarrow$
$\rightarrow (Z)(JZ \,\&\, GZ \,\&\, HZ).$

This is in the *AE* form, though not in the miniscope form. The proof of this is easier than Ex. 3 no matter which method we use. Nonetheless the proof by *Qq* seems considerably shorter than the proof by *Qp* which still includes similar (though somewhat simpler) steps as with Ex. 3. The proof by *Qq* is quite easy since we need only drop quantifiers, substitute 1 for *Z* and verify that:

$$JY \equiv (JY \supset GY),\ GY \equiv (JY \supset HY),\ HY \equiv ((JY \supset GY) \supset HY),$$
$$JZ \equiv (JY \supset GY),\ GZ \equiv (JY \supset HY),\ HZ \equiv ((JY \supset GY) \supset HY) \rightarrow$$
$$\rightarrow JZ \ \& \ GZ \ \& \ HZ.$$

The verification for this is quite easy. Thus, we wish to show that if all clauses of the antecedent are true, then *JZ, GZ, HZ* are all true. By the first clause, *JY* and *GY* are true. Hence, by the fourth clause, *JZ* is true; by the second clause, *HY* is true. Hence, by the fifth and the sixth clauses, *GZ* and *HZ* are true.

Appendix VII

An example of Quine

Example 5. $\rightarrow (EY)(Z)(EW)\{[GYX \ \& \ (GYW \ \& \ GWY)] \vee$
$\vee [\sim GYX \ \& \sim (GYZ \ \& \ GZY)]\}$ (1)

(1) $\rightarrow G1X \ \& \ (G12 \ \& \ G21),\ \sim G1X \ \& \sim (G1f1 \ \& \ Gf11)$ (2)

(2) $G1X \rightarrow G1X$ (3)

(2) $G1f1,\ Gf11 \rightarrow G1X$ (4)

(2) $G1X \rightarrow G12$ (5)

(2) $G1X \rightarrow G21$ (6)

(2) $G1f1,\ Gf11 \rightarrow G12$ (7)

(2) $G1f1,\ Gf11 \rightarrow G21$ (8)

Now we wish to make substitutions on (3)—(8). Since (3) is valid for all substitutions, it can be omitted. We obtain S_1, S_2, S_3, S_4 et cetera by substituting, for (1,2), (X, X), (X, fX), (fX, X), (fX, fX), et cetera. In forming each substitution instance, valid sequents and repetitions of a same sequent can be omitted so that, for example, the conjunctive clauses of S_1, S_2, S_3 are as follows.

S_1: $GXfX,\ GfXX \rightarrow GXX.$

S_2: $GXfX,\ GfXX \rightarrow GXX;\ GXX \rightarrow GXfX;\ GXX \rightarrow GfXX.$

S_3: $GfXf^2X,\ Gf^2XfX \rightarrow GfXX;\ GfXX \rightarrow GfXX;\ GfXX \rightarrow GXfX;$
$GfXf^2X,\ Gf^2XfX \rightarrow GXfX.$

It can be verified that $S_1 \vee S_2 \vee S_3$ is a tautology. If GXX is true, then S_1 is true. If GXX is false but $GXfX$ or $GfXX$ is false, then S_2 is true. If both $GXfX$ and $GfXX$ are true, then S_3 is true.

While the verification is easy here, it appears that as the number of conjunctions increases, the test for the disjunction of all conjunctions can get mechanically cumbersome. A presumably more managable method of testing suggests itself.

Make two lists for S_1, one for the antecedents, one for the consequents:

(A_1) $GXfX$, $GfXX$.

(C_1) GXX.

Test whether every string in (C_1) is contained in some string in (A_1). If yes, a proof is obtained. If not, form two lists for S_2:

(A_2) $GXfX$, $GfXX$; GXX.

(C_2) GXX; $GXfX$; $GfXX$.

Test whether every string obtained by combining a string from (C_1) with a string from (C_2) is contained in every string similarly obtained from (A_1) and (A_2). If yes, a proof is obtained. Otherwise, form two lists for S_3 and continue.

It is not hard to convince oneself that this procedure is equivalent to the usual procedure for testing the validity of S_1, $S_1 \vee S_2$, $S_1 \vee S_2 \vee S_3$, et cetera.

References

[1] H. Wang, A variant to Turing's theory of computing machines, *Jour. Assoc. Comp. Mach.*, **4** 88—92 (included here as chapter VI).

[2] A. W. Burks, D. W. Warren and J. B. Wright, An analysis of a logical machine using parenthesis-free notation, *Math. Tables and Other Aids to Computation*, **8** (April, 1954).

[3] G. E. Collins, Tarski's decision method for elementary algebra, *Proc. Summer Institute of Symbolic Logic at Cornell University*, 1957, p. 64.

[4] M. Davis, A program for Presburger's algorithm, *ibid.*, p. 215.

[5] H. Gelernter, Theorem proving by machine, *ibid.*, p. 305.

[6] E. g., A. Newell, J. C. Shaw and H. A. Simon, Empirical explorations of the logic theory machine: a case study in heuristics, Report P–951, Rand Corporation (March, 1957), 48 pp.

[7] *Ibid.*, p. 26 and p. 28.

[8] *Ibid.*, p. 8 and p. 10.

[9] J. Herbrand, Recherches sur la théorie de la démonstration, *Travaux de la Société des Sciences de Varsovie*, no. 33 (1930), 128 pp.

[10] G. Gentzen, Untersuchungen über das logische Schliessen, *Math. Zeitschrift*, **39** (1934—35), 176—210, 405—431.

[11] D. Hilbert and P. Bernays, Grundlagen der Mathematik, vol. 2, 1939.

[12] B. Dreben, On the completeness of quantification theory, *Proc. Nat. Acad. Sci. U.S.A.*, **38** (1952), 1047—1052.

[13] E. W. Beth, La crise de la raison et la logique, Paris et Louvain, 1957.

[14] K. J. J. Hintikka, Two papers on symbolic logic, *Acta Philos. Fennica*, **8** (1955).

[15] K. Schütte, Ein System des verknupfenden Schlissens, *Archiv f. Math. Logik u. Grundlagenforschung*, **2** (1956), 375—387.

[16] A. Church, Introduction to Mathematical Logic, vol. I., Princeton, 1956.

[17] W. V. Quine, Methods of Logic, New York, 1950.

[18] Herbrand, *op. cit.*, p. 21.

[19] Quine, *op. cit.*, pp. 101—107.

[20] Church, *op. cit.*, p. 262, 46. 12 (3).

[21] Compare, e. g., Church, *op. cit.*, p. 249.

[22] The example in Appendix VII is from Quine, Mathematical Logic, *180 and *181, pp. 129—130.

[23] Compare Herbrand, *op. cit.*, Ch. V.

[24] Compare, e. g., the references to Schütte and Beth.

[25] D. König, Theorie der Graphen, Leipzig, 1936, p. 81.

[26] Church, *op. cit.*, Case X, p. 257.

[27] E. Landau, Grundlagen der Analysis, 1930, reprint, New York, 1965.

[28] G. H. Hardy and E. M. Wright, Introduction to the Theory of Numbers, Oxford, 1954.

[29] G. H. Hardy, A Course of Pure Mathematics, various editions.

[30] O. Veblen and J. W. Young, Projective Geometry, 1910.

[31] See, e. g. G. Kreisel and H. Putnam, Ein Unableitbarkeitsbeweismethode, *Arkiv f. Math. Logik u. Grundlagenforschung*, **3** (1957), 74—78.

[32] A. N. Prior, Formal Logic, Oxford, 1954.

[33] S. Linial and E. L. Post, Recursive unsolvability of axioms problems of the propositional calculus, *Bull. Am. Math. Soc.*, **55** (1949), 50.

[34] See, e. g., Church, *op. cit.*, p. 339.

[35] *Proc. Nat. Acad. Sci. U.S.A.*, **39** (1953), 972—975.

[36] G. Polya, Mathematics and Plausible Reasoning, Oxford, 1954.

CHAPTER X

CIRCUIT SYNTHESIS BY SOLVING SEQUENTIAL BOOLEAN EQUATIONS*

§ 1. Summary of Problems and Results

There is an intrinsic ambiguity in the standard problems of analysis (given circuit, find formula) and synthesis (given formula, find circuit), because both the circuit and the formula (i.e., the condition to be satisfied) are to be specified in suitable symbolisms but there are no universally accepted symbolisms for these purposes. This is especially true of the initial languages expressing the conditions to be synthesised. Of course, the richer the language, the easier it is to express an intuitive requirement, but at the same time, the harder it is to obtain a systematic procedure for dealing with all conditions expressed in the language. A good starting language would seem to be that of sequential Boolean equations obtained by adding to the ordinary Boolean operations a sequential operator to take care of the time element.

We shall study in this paper the general problem of solving such equations to get explicit representations of outputs as functions, or rather functionals, of time and the input functions. It turns out that in general such equations can have three different types of solution: deterministic ones, (effective) predictive ones, and noneffective ones. The first two types are effective and can be realized by circuits in one way or another. Algorithms for deciding solvability and exhibiting the solutions will be given for the different senses of solution. The last two types of solution do not seem to have been much studied in the literature. There are systematic procedures (see Friedman [6], Burks-Wang [1], Church [4]) for obtaining all deterministic solutions. But the one to be given below seems somewhat more efficient than the known alternative methods. The present approach is on the whole close in spirit to Burks-Wright [2] and Burks-Wang [1].

In addition, we shall discuss the question of extending the language of sequential Boolean equations to include restricted quantifiers and certain modulo operators, in such a way that any condition expressed in the enriched language can be turned effectively into one of the more restricted language. As a related topic, growing or potentially infinite machines will be considered.

---

* This chapter appeared in *Zeitschr. f. Math. Logik u. Grundlagen d. Math.*, **5** (1959).

An exact definition for a restricted class of such machines, viz. all Turing machines in a simple normal form, will be stated, and an alternative proof of Kleene's normal form theorem for all recursive functions will be given.

As we shall see, there are a variety of related problems not treated in this paper.

§ 2. Sequential Boolean Functionals and Equations

We extend ordinary Boolean algebra by introducing a distinction between input variables and output variables, and adding a time operator d so that intuitively, e.g., x means x_t and dx means x_{t+1}. More exactly, each equation is obtained by joining two terms with the equal sign =, and a term is either a constant 1 (on, true) or 0 (off, false), or an input variable i, j, etc., or an output variable x, y, etc., or obtained from given terms A, B by the Boolean operators $'$, ., +, or by the time operator d, e.g., A', $A.B$ or AB, $A+B$, dA etc.

With the time operator d, we shall use the natural convention:

$$d^0A = A,\ d^1A = dA,\ d^2A = ddA, \text{ and so on.}$$

Simple properties of the time operator d are:

(2.1) $d(A') = (dA)'$, $d(AB) = (dA)(dB)$, $d(A+B) = (dA) + (dB)$.

(2.2) $d^kG(A, \cdots, B) = G(d^kA, \cdots, d^kB)$.

Some familiar theorems from ordinary Boolean algebra are useful (cf., e.g., Couturat [5]).

(2.3) $A = 0, \cdots, B = 0$ if and only if $A + \cdots + B = 0$.

(2.4) $A = 1, \cdots, B = 1$ if and only if $A \cdots B = 1$.

(2.5) The following are all equivalent:

(1) $A = B$; (2) $AB' + A'B = 0$; (3) $AB + A'B' = 1$.

From these it follows immediately that any finite set of Boolean equations is equivalent to a single equation. Hence, we need not distinguish cases with single equations from those with finite sets of equations.

To simplify our considerations, we shall discuss first equations of the particular form

(S) $H(i, \cdots, j, x, \cdots, y, di, \cdots, dj, dx, \cdots, dy) = 0$.

There are m inputs and n outputs in the equation, and H is an ordinary Boolean function of the arguments $i, \cdots, dy$. We shall later on indicate how equations containing components such as d^2i, d^3x, etc. can be reduced to the form (S). Often it will be sufficient to illustrate the situation with the simpler schema:

$$H(i, x, y, di, dx, dy) = 0.$$

The general problem is to find functionals, i.e. functions of functions, $x_s(i, t)$ and $y_s(i, t)$ such that for all i and t,

$$H(i_t, x_s(i, t), y_s(i, t), i_{t+1}, x_s(i, t+1), y_s(i, t+1)) = 0.$$

There is in the general statement of the problem no explicit restriction on how simple these functionals must be, even though some solutions may be uninteresting for the purpose of designing circuits. For example, any functionals, even though highly nonconstructive, of i and t will, when substituted for x and y, satisfy an identical equation such as

$$ixydidxdy\,(i' + x' + y' + di' + dx' + dy') = 0.$$

To separate out those functionals which are of special interest to us, we introduce the following definitions. (Compare [2], [3], [1], [4]).

(2.6) If $A(i_0, \cdots, j_0), \cdots, B(i_0, \cdots, j_0)$ are any ordinary Boolean functions of $i_0, \cdots, j_0$, $C(x, \cdots, y, i, di, \cdots, j, dj), \cdots, D(x, \cdots, y, i, di, \cdots, j, dj)$ are such of $x, \cdots, dj$, then the functionals $x, \cdots, y$ defined by the following $m \times n$ schema (D) are deterministic sequential functionals.

$$(D)\begin{cases} x_0 = A(i_0, \cdots, j_0), \cdots, y_0 = B(i_0, \cdots, j_0). \\ dx = C(x, \cdots, y, i, di, \cdots, j, dj), \cdots, \\ dy = D(x, \cdots, y, i, di, \cdots, j, dj). \end{cases}$$

(2.7) If p, q are two given nonnegative integers, then the functionals $x, \cdots, y$ defined by the following $m \times n$ schema (P) are predictive sequential functionals:

$$(P)\begin{cases} x_0 = A(i_0, \cdots, d^p i_0, \cdots, j_0, \cdots, d^p j_0), \cdots, \\ y_0 = B(i_0, \cdots, d^p i_0, \cdots, j_0, \cdots, d^p j_0). \\ dx = C(x, \cdots, y, i, \cdots, d^q i, \cdots, j, \cdots, d^q j), \cdots, \\ dy = D(x, \cdots, y, i, \cdots, d^q i, \cdots, j, \cdots, d^q j). \end{cases}$$

The deterministic functionals form a proper subclass of the predictive ones. The schemata (D) and (P) allow any finite number of functionals to be introduced simultaneously. It may be noted that we lose no generality in confining 2.6 and 2.7 to a single application of (D) and (P). In these schemata, $i, \cdots, j$ are the given functions, $x, \cdots, y$ are the defined functionals. We may wish to use previously introduced functionals as given functions. But it can easily be seen that such auxiliary functionals $z, \cdots, w$

can be introduced simultaneously by the same schema, if we eliminate occurrences of $z_0, \cdots, w_0, dz, \cdots, d^2w$, etc. by substitution.

By the schema (D), the state of the outputs at $t+1$ is determined by the input at the same time and the complete state at the preceding moment. It is natural to wish to permit determination by the whole past history. To make this exact, we would presumably be interested only in effective determination. Moreover, we cannot express dependence on, e.g., the state at the time which is the integral part of the half of t or the square root of t, unless we were to extend the notation considerably by adding more complex time operators than d. If we use the same notation, we can at most express dependence of the state at $t+r+1$ on the states at $t, \cdots, t+r$, in each case for a predetermined constant r. In this way one arrives at an extended schema which does not give a broader class of functionals, because we can achieve the same effect by a succession of applications of the schema (D). It follows that, we need not treat the extended schema separately, although we are free to use them, whenever convenient. A similar remark applies to the schema (P).

§ 3. The Method of Sequential Tables

A common feature of the methods of solution to be given below is the use of certain sequential tables. We shall first tabulate all the $2(m+n)$-tuples of 0's and 1's which, as $(i, \cdots, dy,)$, satisfy the equation (S). Then we shall solve (S) by bringing the sequential order to bear.

The first table will be called a *characterizing table*. All the possible values of $(i, \cdots, j, x, \cdots, y, di, \cdots, dj)$ are listed under separate entries. Under each we set down all values of $(dx, \cdots, dy)$, if any, which would satisfy the equation (S) in combination with the given $(i, \cdots, j, x, \cdots, y, di, \cdots, dj)$. When no such $(dx, \cdots, dy)$ exists, we put a + in the space and call the entry *blocked*. There is clearly an effective method of constructing the characteristic table for any equation (S).

To find the deterministic solutions, we use in addition a *reduced characterizing table* which is obtained from the first table by crossing out all inadmissible entries: (i) all the blocked entries are inadmissible; (ii) every entry which shares a same $(i, \cdots, j, x, \cdots, y)$ with an inadmissible entry is inadmissible; (iii) every value of $(dx, \cdots, dy)$ in an entry with $(di, \cdots, dj, dx, \cdots, dy)$ which occurs as $(i, \cdots, j, x, \cdots, y)$ only in inadmissible entries is crossed out and every entry in which all values of $(dx, \cdots, dy)$ are thus crossed out is inadmissible. This definition gives an effective method for constructing the table.

To decide general solvability, we construct from the first table a *solution table* and do not use the reduced characterizing table.

It seems best to give an example to illustrate the construction of the three types of sequential table, and leave the explanation of the general method of constructing solution tables to a later section.

Example 1. To find the three types of table for the equation:

$$i'x'dx' + i'x\,dx + ix'\,di + ix\,di' = 0. \tag{3.1}$$

The characterizing table is:

i	0	0	0	0	1	1	1	1
x	0	0	1	1	0	0	1	1
di	0	1	0	1	0	1	0	1
dx	1	1	0	0	0,1	+	+	0,1

The reduced characterizing table is obtained as follows. Cross out entries (columns) 6 and 7 by (i), entries 5 and 8 by (ii), entries 2 and 4 by (iii), and finally, entries 1 and 3 by (ii) again. Hence the table is empty. As we shall see, this implies that the equation (3.1) has no deterministic solution.

The solution table of (3.1) is:

i	x	di	dx	d^2i	d^2x	d^3i	d^3x	d^4i	d^4x	d^5i
0	0	0	1	0						
	1		0							
0	0	0	1	1	0	0	0	0		
							1			
0	0	0	1	1	0	0	0	1		
							1			
0	1	0	0	1	1	1	0	0	0	0
									1	
0	1	0	0	1	1	1	0	0	0	1
									1	
0	1	0	0	1	1	1	1	1		
0	1	1	0	0	0	0	1	0		
					1		0			
0	1	1	0	0	0	0	1	1		
					1		0			
0	1	1	0	0	0	1				
					1					

0	0	1	1	1	0	0	0	0	1	0
							1		0	
0	0	1	1	1	0	0	0	0	1	1
							1		0	
0	0	1	1	1	0	0	0	1		
							1			
0	0	1	1	1	1	1				
1	0	0	0	0	1	0				
			1		0					
1	0	0	0	0	1	1	0	0		
1	0	0	1	0	0	1	1	1	0	0
1	0	0	1	0	0	1	1	1	1	1
1	0	0	1	1	0	0				
1	0	0	0	1	1	1	0	0		
1	0	0	0	1	1	1	1	1		
1	1	1	0	0	0	0	1	0		
					1		0			
1	1	1	0	0	0	0	1	1	0	0
1	1	1	0	0	1	0	0	1	1	1
1	1	1	0	0	1	1	0	0		
1	1	1	0	0	0	1	1	1		
1	1	1	1	1						

§ 4. Deterministic Solutions

Given an equation (S) with m inputs and n outputs, the problem of finding deterministic solutions will be interpreted to mean that of obtaining $m \times n$ cases of the schema (D) such that the n functionals $x, \cdots, y$ thus defined satisfy the equation for all t and all input functions. This is somewhat different from looking for n deterministic sequential functionals $x, \cdots, y$ which will satisfy (S), since, to do the latter, we may use a definition of the form (D) that defines more than n functionals among which $x, \cdots, y$ all occur. As it turns out, the difference is inessential, because there are no cases where an equation is solvable in the latter case but not solvable in the former sense. We shall return to this point when we give the solutions. Meanwhile, let us confine to deterministic solutions in the first sense.

It is quite obvious that there is, at least in theory, an effective solution of the problem. Thus, given any equation (S) with m inputs and n outputs, there are only a finite number of definitions of the form (D), the number being $2^{mn}\, 2^{(2m+n)n}$. It can be tested effectively in each case whether the functionals defined satisfy the given equation (S). (See, e.g., Burks-Wang [1].) Hence:

Theorem 1. *There is an effective method for testing whether the equation* (S) *has deterministic solutions and writing out all the deterministic solutions, when that is the case.*

Of course this method is not in general feasible. A more satisfactory method is given in Church [4] which appears, however, still quite cumbersome. The following method seems to be more direct and closer to intuition.

Given any condition expressible in terms of an equation of the form (S), we can find all its deterministic solutions by the following steps:

Step 1. Construct its characterizing table.

Step 2. Construct its reduced characterizing table.

Step 3. Examine whether each of the 2^m possible values of $(i, \cdots, j)$ occurs in at least one of the remaining entries. This is the case if and only if the original condition has deterministic solutions.

Step 4. If the condition has deterministic solutions, then the reduced table may be viewed as a fairly intuitive representation of all the solutions. If we wish to put the solutions into the form of schema (D), this can be accomplished mechanically: (i) choose any possible selection of 2^m entries each containing a distinct value of $(i, \cdots, j)$, and use the values of $(x, \cdots, y)$ in these entries as the corresponding initial states; (ii) for each entry in the reduced table, choose one value of $(dx, \cdots, dy)$; (iii) each such selection gives a determination of $(x_0, \cdots, y_0)$ from $(i_0, \cdots, j_0)$, and one of $(dx, \cdots, dy)$, from $(i, \cdots, j, x, \cdots, y, di, \cdots, dj)$, and can be put into the form (D) in obvious manner.

The method is justified as follows. Obviously, a set of functionals satisfy the equation (S) if and only if at every time, for any $i, \cdots, j, di, \cdots, dj$, the values of $x, \cdots, y, dx, \cdots, dy$ satisfy (S), i.e., occur in some entry of the characterizing table. If the functionals are required to be deterministic, the values of $(dx, \cdots, dy)$ must be determined entirely by $(i, \cdots, j, x, \cdots, y, di, \cdots, dj)$ and cannot be adjusted to suit future inputs. Hence, all entries beginning with $(i, \cdots, j, x, \cdots, y)$ must be rejected if it is rejected for some value of $(di, \cdots, dj)$ at all, otherwise when we arrive at a next state agreeing with $(i, \cdots, j, x, \cdots, y)$, we can so choose $(di, \cdots, dj)$ as to get an impossible situation. Moreover, in every entry, we must obviously reject every value of $(dx, \cdots, dy)$ in the context $(di, \cdots, dj, dx, \cdots, dy)$ which occurs as $(i, \cdots, j, x, \cdots, y)$ only in rejected entries and reject every entry which has no more possible values of $(dx, \cdots, dy)$ left. This shows that every deterministic solution has to satisfy also the reduced characterizing table. On the other hand, in the reduced table, for every $(i, \cdots, j, x, \cdots, y, di, \cdots, dj)$, there is at least one value of $(dx, \cdots, dy)$ such that a continuation is possible no matter what the next inputs are. Hence, provided there is at least one permissible value of $(x_0, \cdots, y_0)$ for every possible value of $(i_0, \cdots, j_0)$, there is a solution. Of course, if there is some value of $(i, \cdots, j)$ for which there is no entry beginning with it, then there can be no solution.

In Example 1, if, e.g., i_0 and i_1 are both 0, then x_0 and x_1 have to be 0 and 1. Since this has to be so no matter what i_2 and i_3 are, the values have to be acceptable if, in particular, we choose i_2 and i_3 to be both 1. Then x_2 has to be 0 and there is no possible value for x_3.

At this point it should be obvious that by allowing auxiliary variables, we do not ever get a deterministic solution when there was none without auxiliary variables. If, e.g., we postulate for Example 1 an auxiliary variable z, we could get complicated characterizing tables by choosing different deterministic functionals for z, but can never get an entry in the reduced table whose part not containing z and dz can disagree with the corresponding entry in the original reduced table. In this particular case, this means that the new reduced table is again empty. Hence, in general, if there is any deterministic solution of an equation with auxiliary variables, there must be a corresponding solution which disregards entirely the effect of the auxiliary variables. A similar remark applies to other types of solution.

We may now summarize the results of this section:

Theorem 2. *An equation (S) has a deterministic solution if and only if its reduced characterizing table contains at least one entry for each possible input* $(i, \cdots, j)$; *if (S) has deterministic solutions, all of them can be written out from the reduced table in an effective way.*

There is one defect of the above procedure which can be remedied by paying more attention to details of the reduced table. Quite often a solution need not go through all the complete states or output states which remain in the reduced table, and it is of practical interest to get a solution which uses a minimum number of states. The above procedure does not explicitly inform us what states are actually experienced by a given solution. To remedy this, we observe that for each particular choice of initial states, we often arrive at repetitions of complete states everywhere, before we go through all complete states in the reduced table, and a careful examination of the table enables us to make a choice.

A more transparent way of doing this is to use "graphs" to streamline all the possible transitions. Thus, to get a particular solution, we choose arbitrarily any 2^m entries each containing a distinct value of $(i, \cdots, j)$ and use the values of $(x, \cdots, y)$ in these entries as the corresponding initial output states. Then, for each of these values of $(i, \cdots, j, x, \cdots, y)$ and each possible value of $(di, \cdots, dj)$, choose arbitrarily and adhere to one of the occurring values of $(dx,\cdots,dy)$ in the entry as the next output state. Use these values of $(di,\cdots,dj,dx,\cdots,dy)$ as $(i,\cdots,j,x,\cdots,y)$ and repeat the process along each path until we reach a complete state $(di,\cdots,dj,dx,\cdots,dy)$ which has already occurred. This process always terminates because there are only 2^{m+n} possible complete states. The initial complete state chosen plus the transitions from $(i,\cdots,j,x,\cdots,y,di,\cdots,dj)$ to $(dx,\cdots,dy)$ will yield directly a deterministic solution of the original condition.

To survey all the solutions, we redo the above steps but this time we record all possible $(dx,\cdots,dy)$ at each stage and follow up every possible choice till repetitions occur everywhere in each choice. This can be recorded in a "graph". We then ask whether all complete states occurring in the reduced characterizing table as $(i,\cdots,j,x,\cdots,y)$ or $(di,\cdots,dj,dx,\cdots,dy)$ have occurred. If not, we take arbitrarily one of the remaining complete states and work out a graph in the same way until we come on each path to a complete state $(di,\cdots,dj,dx,\cdots,dy)$ which has already occurred in one of the graphs. This process is repeated until every possible complete state has occurred in some graph. Then all the possible deterministic solutions can be obtained from these graphs by choosing every set of 2^m complete states, one for each possible $(i,\cdots,j)$, as the initial states and using every possible alternative way of continuation.

These explanations will become clear with a few examples.

Example 2. To find a circuit with one input i and two outputs x and y such that at any moment, an odd number of i, x, y, dx, di are true and an even number of i, x, y, dy, di are true.

The four possible states of (x, y) can be written briefly:

$$e = (0, 0), \quad f = (0, 1), \quad g = (1, 0), \quad h = (1, 1). \tag{4.1}$$

The characterizing table is easily constructed.

i	0	0	0	0	0	0	0	0	1	1	1	1	1	1	1	1
(x, y)	e	e	f	f	g	g	h	h	e	e	f	f	g	g	h	h
di	0	1	0	1	0	1	0	1	0	1	0	1	0	1	0	1
(dx, dy)	g	f	f	g	f	g	g	f	f	g	g	f	g	f	f	g

The reduced characterizing table is the same, since no entry is blocked. It follows that the example is solvable.

The general solution is given by:

$$x_0 = A(i_0), \quad y_0 = B(i_0), \tag{4.2}$$

$$dx = i'(x'y'di' + x'ydi + xy'di + xydi') + \\ + i(x'y'di + x'ydi' + xy'di' + xydi),$$

$$dy = i'(x'y'di + x'ydi' + xy'di' + xydi) +$$
$$+ i(x'y'di' + x'ydi + xy'di + xydi').$$

Therein A, B are any Boolean functions of i_0.

It is rather obvious in this example that we would get simpler solutions by taking f or g as initial states. Thus, for example, the following is one set of graphs for the whole reduced table, beginning with $0e$ and $1h$:

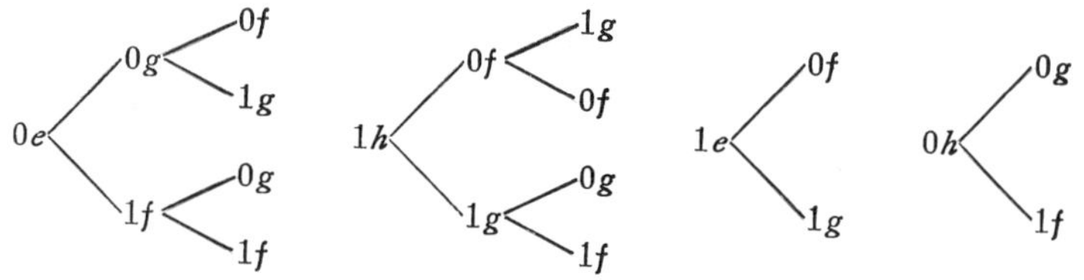

If we begin with $(0e, 1h)$, we have to go through all the four output states and six of the eight complete states. If, e.g., we begin with $(0f, 1g)$, we need only go through the two output states f and g, and the four complete states containing them, and have the simple solution:

$$(4.3) \qquad x_0 = i_0,\ y_0 = i_0', \quad dx = (x'y + xy')(i'di + idi'),$$
$$dy = (x'y + xy')(idi + i'di').$$

Example 3. To find a circuit with one input i and two outputs x, y such that at every time t, exactly 2 of i, x, y, di, dx, dy are true.

The reduced characterizing table is:

i	0	0	0	0	1	1
(x, y)	f	f	g	g	e	e
di	0	1	0	1	0	1
(dx, dy)	f, g	e	f, g	e	f, g	e

One set of graphs for this is:

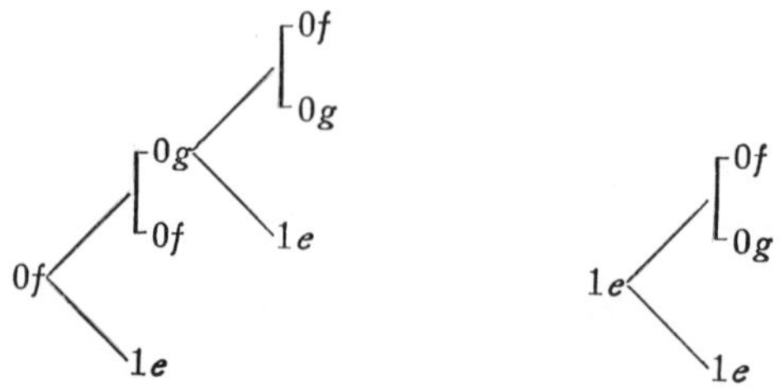

The general solution of the example is:

$$(4.4)\quad x_0 = ai_0',\ y_0 = a'i_0',$$
$$dx = abcr(i'x'y + i'xy' + ix'y')di' + a'(b' + c' + r')(bi'x'y + ci'xy' + rix'y')di',$$
$$dy = a'b'c'r'(i'x'y + i'xy' + ix'y')di' + a(b + c + r)(b'i'x'y + c'i'xy' + r'ix'y')di'.$$

Therein a, b, c, r are parameters which can take 0 and 1 as values.

There are altogether 16 solutions among which there are two simplest involving either only $0f$ and $1e$ or only $0g$ and $1e$:

$$(4.5)\quad x_0 = 0,\ y_0 = i_0',\ dx = 0,\ dy = (i'x'y + i'xy' + ix'y')di'.$$
$$x_0 = i_0',\ y_0 = 0,\ dx = (i'x'y + i'xy' + ix'y')di',\ dy = 0.$$

Example 4. $ix'di + i'xdx' = 0$.

For instance, one solution is: $x=1$. This can be seen directly from the equation. The general solution can be obtained in the same way as before.

Example 5. $dx = xy' + x'y$, $dy = y'$, $dx\,dy\,dz = dx\,dy\,di$, $dw = w'$, $w'z = w'dz$.

Since i does not occur in these equations and di matters only in a few special cases, we may simplify the construction of the characterizing table by omitting i and di. The reduced table is then:

(x, y)	e	e	f	f	g	g	h	h
w	1	1	0	0	1	1	0	0
z	0	1	0	1	0	1	0	1
(dx, dy)	f	f	g	g	h	h	e	e
dw	0	0	1	1	0	0	1	1
dz	0,1	0,1	0	1	di	di	0	1

The value of (x, y, w, z) in each of the eight entries may be taken as the initial state for all i_0. For each choice, there are four possible solutions because in the first two entries, we have four possible alternative ways of choosing dz.

§ 5. Related Problems

There are several related problems which call for some comment: input-independent solutions; simplification; alternative memory elements besides the operator d; conditional solutions.

We have incidentally touched on the problem of simplification, e.g., in the solution of Example 2, where it is seen that fewer elements are sufficient to realise the given condition. A systematic consideration of the problem will not be undertaken here, which would probably require, e.g., a distinction between internal and output states, a distinction we avoid in this paper in order not to confuse the more general issue.

In terms of physical realization, we have other basic memory elements such as the trigger and the set-reset flip-flop. In practice, different choices are often open to us in constructing a circuit, and the costs may differ. We shall not study this question of economy except to remark that in theory other memory elements can naturally all be obtained from the delay element d by Boolean operations. For example, the trigger is:

$$dx = y, \quad y = ix' + i'x.$$

In general, an equation with no deterministic (or other) solutions usually can have such solutions when we impose suitable conditions on the inputs. Such conditional solutions are sometimes of interest, e.g., when we are mainly interested in an output as a functional of some of the inputs and there is a conditional solution which requires only restrictions on the other inputs. In such a case, we may be able to adjunct suitable elements with outputs satisfying the conditions on these other inputs. Or sometimes, we are not interested in certain values of the input functions. This is another question which we shall not consider. Perhaps a simple example will help to clarify the remark:

$$(5.1) \qquad ij'dx + i'j'xdx' + i'jdx' + ij = 0.$$

This has no (deterministic) solution for x since when i and j are both 1, no values of x or dx can satisfy the equation. Nonetheless, if we add the condition $i'+j'=1$, then we do have solutions such as: $x_0=0$, $dx=i'j'x+i'j$.

In special cases, an equation may have solutions which are simple sequential functions of the time t and independent of the input functions. The solution of such equations are specially easy. Thus, an equation (S) has an input-independent solution if and only if it has a solution for the 2^{2m} equations obtained from (S) by substituting all possible values of $(i,\cdots,j,$ $di,\cdots,dj)$. Hence, the problem reduces to one of solving equations in which input variables do not occur. We can treat the question in the same way as with deterministic solutions, only the construction of tables becomes much simpler.

The most familiar example is some simple ordinary counters. An artificial example is:

Example 6. Find a circuit such that if an even number of i and di are true, then an odd number among i, x, y, di, dx, dy are true; if an odd number of i and di are true, then an even number among i, x, y, di, dx, dy are true.

This is only a complicated way of saying that an odd number among x, y, dx, dy are true. The reduced characterizing table is simply:

(x, y)	e	f	g	h
(dx, dy)	f, g	e, h	e, h	f, g

In fact, there are essentially only two states since e and h, f and g function in the same way. Among the solutions there are, for example:

(5.2) $$x_0 = 0,\ y_0 = 0 \quad dx = x,\ dy = y'.$$

(5.3) $$x_0 = 0,\ y_0 = 0,\ dx = y,\ dy = x'.$$

When we are concerned with input-independent solutions, the distinction between deterministic and predictive of course loses sense. If we wish to, we can also give unnaturally complex solutions. Thus, the following is also a solution of the above example: (x_0, y_0) is $(0, 0)$; according as (x, y) is e, f, g, h, (dx, dy) is respectively f, e, e, f if t is a prime integer, and g, h, h, g respectively if otherwise. But it is clear that if an equation (S) has any input-independent solution, it must also have some "periodic" solution with a period no greater than 2^n. Thus, since there are only 2^n possible values of $(x, \cdots, y)$, if there is any input-independent solution, we can always choose and adhere to a same next state for each given state. Hence, once a state repeats, everything following it repeats, but there must be a repetition after at most 2^n steps. If we represent the 2^n states by the integers $0, \cdots, 2^n-1$, then there is always a solution of the form $(x_0, \cdots, y_0) = p_0, \cdots, (x_{q-1}, \cdots, y_{q-1}) = p_{q-1}, (x_{s+kq}, \cdots, y_{s+kq}) = (x_s, \cdots, y_s)$, where $p_0, \cdots, p_{q-1}$ are among $0, \cdots, 2^n - 1$, $q \leqslant 2^n$, k ranges over all positive integers, s ranges over $0, \cdots, q-1$. (For a related remark, compare Burks-Wright [2], Theorem 3—1).

§ 6. An Effective Criterion of General Solvability

When we are interested in arbitrary solutions of the equation (S), it may happen at some stage that, for given $(i, \cdots, j, x, \cdots, y, di, \cdots, dj)$, although there is no one value of $(dx, \cdots, dy)$ which would be continuable for all future inputs, there are two or more values of $(dx, \cdots, dy)$ which, taken together, can be continued for all future inputs. In such a case, we may choose the value of $(dx, \cdots, dy)$ according to the future inputs. Since the general problem is to solve $x, \cdots, y$ as functionals of $i, \cdots, j$ and t, such solutions are admissible in theory and, indeed, as we shall see, often of interest for circuit synthesis, since many of them can be realised indirectly by circuits.

There are simple cases where from the characterizing table alone, we can see quite directly that the given condition has no solution whatsoever. In other cases, more work is necessary to determine solvability and find solutions. The general methods to be described below are much more complex than the one for deterministic solutions.

The following is a simple unsolvable condition:

Example 7. To find two functionals x and y of i and t such that at every moment exactly 2 of i, x, y, di, dx are true and exactly 2 of i, x, y, di, dy are true.

The characterizing table can be briefly summarized: if none of i, x, y, di is true or more than 2 of them are true, then there are no possible values of (dx, dy); if exactly 2 of them are true, (dx, dy) must be e; if exactly one of them is true, (dx, dy) must be h. The reduced characterizing table is empty so that the condition has no deterministic solution. Moreover, since for any (i, x, y, di), there is at most one permissible value of (dx, dy) by the characterizing table, there is no room to take precaution to avoid future blind alleys. Hence, there is no solution at all.

In what follows, we shall prove that an equation is solvable in general if and only if it has a solution table. We explain the method of constructing the solution table with the help of the solution table of Example 1 given in § 3.

The solution table for an equation (S) is to be constructed from its characterizing table according to the following steps.

Step 1. Certain successions of inputs are tabulated thus. Consider all the 2^m possible values of $(i, \cdots, j)$ and extend each to $(di, \cdots, dj)$, etc. in all different ways until along each path we reach $(d^p i, \cdots, d^p j)$ and $(d^{p+1} i, \cdots, d^{p+1} j)$ which have already occurred on the same path as $(d^q i, \cdots, d^q j)$ and $(d^{q+1} i, \cdots, d^{q+1} j)$ for some smaller q. The maximum length of these successions is determined by the number of inputs. In Example 1, since there is a single input which has only 2 possible states, there are only 4 pairs $(d^q i, d^{q+1} i)$, and a same pair must repeat as $(d^p i, d^{p+1} i)$, for $p \leqslant 4$. In general, the maximum length of the successions of inputs for an equation (S) with m inputs is $2^{2m}+2$. This of course imposes a finite bound on the number of different successions to be listed.

These particular finite sequences of inputs we choose have the property that any specific input history can be obtained by hooking these finite sequences in some suitable manner. Every entry (row) R' whose first 2 inputs agree with the last 2 inputs of an entry R is said to be a successor of R, and R is said to be a predecessor of R'. For instance, in Example 1, the successors of the second entry are the first six entries. Given any specific input history, we can find one entry which agrees with an initial segment of it and then find a successor of the entry which agrees with a next segment of it, and so on. At each stage, the required entry always exists since all possibilities are included up to the repetition of a same pair of input states.

Step 2. We fill in all the permissible values of $(x, \cdots, y)$ to $(d^p x, \cdots, d^p y)$ in each entry, together with their interconnections. Take, e.g., the second entry of the solution table of Example 1. By looking at the characterizing table, we see that when i and di are both 0, x can be either 0 or 1. If x is 0, dx is 1, if x is 1, dx is 0, and neither is blocked. Now if dx is 1, d^2x is 0, if dx is 0, d^2x is 1. But $(1, 1, 0)$ as (i, x, di) is blocked, hence d^2x cannot be 1. Since this is the only possible continuation of $dx=0$ for the given inputs, dx cannot take the value 0. Similarly, x cannot take the value 1. Hence, we arrive at:

i	x	di	dx	d^2i	d^2x	d^3i	d^3x	d^4i
0	0	0	1	1	0	0		0

Now $(1, 0, 0)$ as (d^2i, d^2x, d^3i) can be followed by both 0 and 1 according to the characterizing table. Moreover, neither $(0, 0, 0)$ nor $(0, 1, 0)$ is blocked. Hence, the row is completed by putting both 0 and 1 under d^3x. The solution table for Example 1 is particularly simple. It is clear that in general, there may be branches of branches, etc. in a same entry.

If there is any entry which cannot be completed in this way, i.e., for which at some stage we can find no permissible output states, then we stop and say there is no solution table for the given equation. In such a case, it is easy to see that the equation can have no solution, since if we choose an input history which begins with the inputs of that entry, there is no possible values of the output state which can satisfy those cases of the original equation (S) when the inputs are specified by the particular input history. If there are no such incompletable entries, we may continue with the construction of the solution table by examining whether the entries can be hooked together in all possible ways and still never get blocked. For each entry (row), we shall speak of the final output set F, i.e., the set of all possible final output states $(d^p x, \cdots, d^p y)$ in the entry, and the initial output set B.

Example 8. Consider an equation with the following characterizing table:

i	0	0	0	0	1	1	1	1
x	0	0	1	1	0	0	1	1
di	0	1	0	1	0	1	0	1
dx	+	1	1	0	0,1	+	+	0,1

If we try to construct a solution table for this, then we see that we cannot complete any entry beginning with $(0, 0, 1, 1)$ as (i, di, d^2i, d^3i). It follows that this example has no solutions whatsoever.

Step 3. For every entry, compare its final output set F with the initial output set B of each of its successor entries. If there exists an entry R with a successor R' such that the F of R has no common member with the B of R', then we stop and say that the original equation has no solution table. In fact, when there are such entries R and R', there is no solution for any input history which begins with the inputs of R and R' hooked together by deleting one occurrence of the joining input state. If there are no such entries, we are ready to continue. There are no such entries in the table for Example 1.

Step 4. For every entry, compare its final output set F with the union of the initial output sets B of all its successor entries. Delete from F all the final output states which do not occur in the union of the B's together with all previous output states in the same entry which only lead to the deleted final output states. The reason for doing this is simply because each entry can only be continued through its successor entries, such additional output states cannot be continued at all. In the table for Example 1, no such deletions were needed to begin with. The result obtained up to this stage will be called the kernel of the solution table. In Example 1, the kernel is the same as the solution table, but this is not so in general. And even when this is true, we need the next step to ascertain that this is so.

Step 5. For every entry R, we compare its initial output set B with the final output set F of each of its predecessor entries. If in all cases B contains all members of F, we have obtained a solution table. This is the case with Example 1. If there is some entry R' with some predecessor R such that the B of R' does not include all members of the F of R, we open up for each pair R and R' a new entry with the same succession of inputs as R' but with the intersection of the B of R' and the F of R instead of the original B of R as the new initial output set, and continued with all their succeeding outputs in the old entry R'. In this way, after going through all the entries of the kernel of the solution table, we obtain an augmented table with a finite number of new entries. In this augmented table, one succession of inputs may serve as the frame for several entries. We can divide all entries into exclusive ***input sets*** each containing all entries with a same succession of inputs as their frame.

Step 6. We repeat Step 3 with the augmented table except that this time we compare the F of each entry R with the input set of each of its successor entries. If there exists an entry R with a final set F and a successor R' such that F has no common member with the B of *any* entry in the input set containing R', then we stop and say that the original equation has no solution table. In such a case, we can find some finite input history which will include the inputs of R at a certain stage and have only the output states of R as possible solutions for that period of time, so that if we hook on the input of R', the resulting finite input history will have no solution. If such a situation does not arise for any entry R in the augmented table, we repeat something like Step 5 except that we now compare the B of each entry R', with the input set of each of its predecessors. If for every

R', its B contains, for each predecessor R, all members of the F of at least one entry in the input set containing R, then we have obtained a solution table. Otherwise we repeat Step 6 with the augmented table.

This process will always come to an end after a predetermined finite number of steps, since there are only finitely many possible output states and finitely many input sets of entries, and each time there is at least some input set which has a new entry with at least one less initial output state than some old entry. Either we end up with a solution table, or at some repetition of the modified Step 3, we come to a situation which yields some input history for which the original equation has no solution.

Hence, we have proved:

Theorem 3. *There is an effective method for deciding whether a given equation* (S) *has a solution table.*

The next problem is to prove the necessity and sufficiency of the existence of a solution table as a condition of general solvability.

In the steps for constructing a solution table, we have already incidentally established the necessity of the condition. Thus, if there is no solution table, either the construction stops at Step 2, or it stops at Step 3 or a variant of Step 3 in the middle of Step 6. In each case, we can choose specific input histories which begin with suitable initial inputs $(i_0, \cdots, j_0)$ to $(d^s i_0, \cdots, d^s j_0)$ for some finite s such that there exist no values $(x_0, \cdots, y_0), \cdots, (d^s x_0, \cdots, d^s y_0)$ which would make (S) true for the times $t=0, \cdots, s$, with the given inputs.

To prove the sufficiency of the condition, we need only show that if a solution table for (S) exists, then for every input history (set of input functions) $i, \cdots, j$, and every time t, there exist values of $(x, \cdots, y)$ and $(dx, \cdots, dy)$ which satisfy (S) when combined with the values of the input functions at t and $t+1$. We shall first prove this for the special case of the solution table of the equation (3.1) in Example 1.

Beginning with the 26 entries in the solution table of (3.1), we may attempt to construct a "fan" by making all possible extensions at each stage, i.e., hooking on all successor entries of the last entry at each point. Every given input function is exhibited in one and only one infinite path. In forming the infinite path for a particular input function, if the F of R is the same as the B of R', then we need not change the output states in R; or the F of R is a proper subset of the B of R', then we have to eliminate those output states of R which only lead to output states in F not contained in the B of R'. In any case, there are still remaining outputs in R for every time, and the final output set of R' hooked with R is the same as the final output set of R'. As we repeat the process indefinitely to get the whole given input history, there can be no stage at which we lose all output states for some time t, since we can cross out all output states at a time t only if we have crossed out all output states at some later time. The problem is to show that there is an infinite set of values $x_0, x_1, \cdots$ which together with the values $i_0, i_1, \cdots$ of the given input function i, satisfy the equation (3.1) simultaneously.

This is plausible enough but seems to require for an exact proof the Unendlichkeitslemma (König [10], p. 81) familiar in mathematical logic. Thus, if we construct a "fan" for all the possible solutions at each time for the given input function i, since at every time at least one branch can be continued, there must be an infinite path going through all time, giving the required sequence $x_0, x_1, \cdots$.

This concludes the proof that (3.1) is solvable. In the general case, each succession of inputs in the kernel of the solution table may appear several times, their entries making up an input set. Given any input history, we can begin with any entry R which coincides with an initial segment of the input history and get at least one solution. At each later stage, we choose any successor entry R' which agrees with a next segment of input history, provided only the B of R' is included in the F of the entry R just chosen. By the construction of the solution table, such a successor entry R' always exists.

Hence, we have:

Theorem 4. *An equation (S) is solvable if and only if it has a solution table.*

§7. A Sufficient Condition for Effective Solvability

It is rather easy to see that (3.1) has no effective solutions. Thus, from the first entry of the solution table, it follows that if the input history is 0 at all time, then x_0 can be either 0 or 1. On the other hand, if the input history begins with 0's but contains a 1 at some t, then the value of x_0 is no longer arbitrary but depends on whether the first 1 in the history occurs at an odd or even t, and whether it is followed by a 0 or a 1. Thus by entries 7 to 13, x_0 is 0 if either t is odd and i_{t+1} is 1, or t is even and i_{t+1} is 0; otherwise x_0 is 1. This means that the values of x_0 may depend on the whole infinite history and there is no one finite number such that the value of x_0 can always be determined by the finite segment of every input history up to that finite number.

To get solutions of (3.1) from its solution table, we observe that in every entry, dx is, except for entry 14, uniquely determined by the value of x and the succession of inputs in the entry. Hence, the value of dx is always determined by x and at most $i, \cdots, d^5i$. If we summarize those entries where dx gets the value 1, and simplify, we have

$$dx = i'x' + ix'di'(ad^2i'd^3i' + d^2i'd^3id^4i + d^2id^3i') + ixdid^2i.$$

Therein a can take 0 or 1 as value.

Hence, the only noneffective feature comes in with the solution of x_0: if i begins with three 0's, then x_0 is determined as in the preceding paragraph. For all other inputs:

$$x_0 = i'_0 i'_1 i_2 i_3 + i'_0 i_1 i'_2 + i_0 i_1.$$

Two other simple examples which are solvable but have no effective solutions are the following. We shall not include their solution tables which can be constructed in the same way as in Example 1.

Example 9. $i(x'di + xdi') + i'(x'dx + xdx') = 0.$

Intuitively, this says: if $i=1$, $x=di$; if $i=0$, $x=dx$. Hence x_0 is arbitrary if the input history is 0 at every time, otherwise it is the same as i_{t+1} for the first i_t which is 1.

Example 10. $i'x'(di' + didx') + i'xdidx + ix'di + ixdi'dx = 0.$

The characterizing table is:

i	0	0	0	0	1	1	1	1
x	0	0	1	1	0	0	1	1
di	0	1	0	1	0	1	0	1
dx	+	1	0,1	0	0,1	+	0	0,1

When the input history begins with $0101\cdots$, x_0 is determined by the earliest input i_t which breaks the pattern, i.e. i_t is 0 preceded by 0, or 1 preceded by 1. x_0 is 0 or 1 according as t is even or odd.

We have not studied the problem of classifying noneffective solutions of sequential Boolean equations.

These examples suggest a clue to finding a method for deciding whether a solvable equation (S) has effective solutions. For this purpose, we shall take the kernel of the solution table of a solvable equation and make a special study of the ambiguous entries, i.e., those entries each with an initial output set containing two or more members.

We give an effective method for constructing from the kernel of the solution table a *partial ambiguity table* which would decide for every ambiguous entry whether it is "infinite" or not. We extend the kernel in all possible directions, with the help of the whole solution table, and call the set P_t of all possible output states under $(d^t x, \cdots, d^t y)$ following a particular alternative output state P in a given extended entry the descendant of P at t, and that at the next moment after P the immediate descendant. On each path, the extension stops when any one of the following three situations arises: (i) if at a time t, only one initial output state in the path has a nonempty descendant, all other initial output states having been eliminated because they only lead to impossibilities; (ii) if at a time t, all the initial output states in the path have the same descendant (all of them are "merged"); (iii) if at a time t, neither (i) nor (ii) has happened but for any two of the remaining initial outputs P and Q in the path, either their descendants at t are the same, or there are $p, q, q<p<t$ such that the inputs at q and $q+1$ are the same as those at p and $p+1$, and there are two distinct output states one in P_p and P_q (resp. P_p and Q_q), one in Q_p and Q_q (resp. Q_p and P_q).

We shall show that the extension stops on every path before a predetermined finite bound on the number of steps. An entry in the kernel of the solution table is said to be infinitely ambiguous if there is an extension on which (iii) is the case, otherwise, it is inessentially ambiguous. In the table for (3.1), the partial ambiguity table is the same as the (kernel of the) solution table, and the first entry is the only ambiguous entry which, as it happens, is also an infinitely ambiguous entry. We shall prove that the absence of infinitely ambiguous entries is a sufficient condition for effective solvability.

The bound on the time t for the above construction of the partial ambiguity table is $K=1+(2^{2m}2^n(2^n-1))/2$, m the number of inputs, n the number of outputs. Thus, if we have arrived at $t=K$ on a path, then either (i) or (ii) has occurred, or else there are at least two distinct initial output states which have no common descendant at any time thus far. This is so because once two initial outputs have the same descendant at one time, they have the same descendant ever after. Take any pair of initial output states whose descendants are distinct at every time thus far and choose arbitrarily a pair of distinct output states to represent their descendants at each moment, there are at most $2^n(2^n-1)/2$ such pairs, and 2^{2m} possible pairs of input states surrounding each pair of output states. Hence a repetition must have occurred at $t=K$.

Now if (iii) occurs on an extension of an entry, then it is possible to find an infinite input history such that there are at least two distinct initial output states with distinct descendants at every moment which satisfy the original equation (S) simultaneously. This is so because we need only repeat indefinitely the input history from $q+1$ to p, from $p+1$ onwards. It follows in particular that every solvable equation with any infinite ambiguity must have at least two distinct solutions, or in other words, no uniquely solvable equation can have any infinite ambiguity. There are of course many solvable equations without infinite ambiguities which have more than one solution.

We prove the following theorem:

Theorem 5. *Every solvable equation with no infinite ambiguities, in particular, every uniquely solvable equation, has effective solutions of the form (P) given in 2.7 (predictive solutions) with $p \leqslant K$, $q \leqslant K+1$. Moreover, there is an effective method for finding these solutions.*

If there are no infinite ambiguities, then the partial ambiguity table rather directly determines a class of effective solutions. All the remaining initial output states in each entry can be used for all input histories beginning with the entry, because either (i) is the case, the remaining initial output state is the only possible one and yet the equation is known to be solvable, or (ii) is the case, then no remaining initial output state can be eliminated by future inputs unless the common descendant is, which would eliminate all remaining initial states and make the equation unsolvable. Hence, we can make any choice of initial states one for each entry of the partial ambiguity table and write out $(x_0, \cdots, y_0)$ as functions of the inputs from 0 to K.

To find how $(dx, \cdots, dy)$ is determined by $(x, \cdots, y)$ and the input history, we choose for each initial output state P of each entry R the next output states from its immediate descendant. We neglect in R the initial inputs and outputs and all descendants of the initial output states other than P and consider the remainder R'. There must be a set S of entries whose succession of inputs includes or is included in that of R'. If there is an entry E whose inputs are included in those of R', then the set S can have only one member. We compare the initial outputs of R' with those of E which must include all those of R', because any initial states eliminated by E must be eliminated by R'. Hence, in this case, the state P can be followed by every member of its immediate descendant, for the input situation of R. If there is an entry E whose inputs include those of R' as a proper part, we compare the initial inputs of R' with those of each such E. There must be some common member because otherwise there would be an extension of R which would eliminate the initial state P, contrary to what we have established. We can choose any common member as the next output state of P on the extension of the inputs of R in which the extension of the inputs of R' coincides with those of E. In this way, we again determine all the possible next states of P on the inputs of R or some extension of it. In every case, since E is at most of length $K+1$, the state after P is determined by the inputs from t to $t+K+1$. Moreover, these extensions taken together will take care of all future input histories because the partial ambiguity table includes the beginning of all possible input histories.

Hence, we can make, for all possible histories from t to $t+K+1$, any choice from the possible next states $(dx, \cdots, dy)$ one for each possible input history from t to $t+K+1$ and each possible $(x, \cdots, y)$, i.e., each initial output state of an entry whose inputs are included in that input history from t to $t+K+1$. By combining any solution of $(x_0, \cdots, y_0)$ given above with any solution of $(dx, \cdots, dy)$ just specified, we get one effective solution for the given equation.

This completes the proof of Theorem 5. It is, however, not true that no equation with infinite ambiguities have effective solutions. To reach a necessary and sufficient condition for effective solvability, we have to examine the infinite ambiguities more closely. For this purpose, we make changes in the partial ambiguity tables to get ambiguity tables.

§ 8. An Effective Criterion of Effective Solvability

Take the solution table of (3.1) which is also its partial ambiguity table. We examine every entry R with an infinite ambiguity, the first entry only in this particular case, and look at all its successor entries R'. For each initial output state P of R, we look at its descendant D at the end of the entry, if there is a successor entry whose initial output set contains no member of D, we cross out P. We do this because we argue that P cannot be used in any effective solution. Thus, since the entry R is infinitely ambiguous, we cannot find an effective condition on the inputs under which P is acceptable. For every M, we can find some input history of length longer than M for which P is acceptable, and some for which P is not. Thus, by repeating a suitable cycle explained in (iii) while constructing the partial ambiguity table, we get an infinite history on which P is always acceptable as an initial state. On the other hand, we can also introduce the inputs of the successor entry R' at arbitrarily late junctures to forbid P. Thus, in the case of (3.1), we eliminate the initial state $x=0$ of the first entry by the second entry and the initial state $x=1$ by the fourth entry. Then there is for the inputs of this entry, no possible initial output state which can occur in an effective solution, and we can conclude that (3.1) has no effective solution.

In the general case there can be more than 2 initial output states in an infinitely ambiguous entry of the partial ambiguity table. This makes it necessary to modify the table somewhat to begin with. Then we can proceed to construct the ambiguity table. The steps are as follows:

Step 1. We modify the construction of the partial ambiguity table to get a new table T. We make the same construction except that, instead of (iii), we now use (iv): when neither (i) nor (ii) has occurred but at a time there is a repetition of p and $p+1$ of a pair of inputs at q and $q+1$ such that the decendant at p of each remaining initial output contains a member which occurs as a member of the descendant at q of some of the remaining initial states. Now we call the entries stopped by (i) and (ii) inessentially ambiguous and call the entries stopped by (iv) essentially ambiguous. Every essentially ambiguous entry has the property that every initial output in it can remain in some infinite history beginning with the entry. The bound needed is assured by the fact that the output set at every moment must have at least 2 members, and repetition of a same output set with a same pair of inputs is sufficient to stop the extension. Hence, if we begin with $(i, \cdots, j)$ and stop at $(d^{p+1}i, \cdots, d^{p+1}j)$, $p+1$ can never be greater than

$$N = 2^{2m}(2^n - n - 1).$$

Step 2. For each essentially ambiguous entry E and each initial output state P in it, we consider a subentry R obtained from E by deleting all other initial outputs and their descendants. For each subentry R, we consider all its successor entries in the table T. If there is any successor entry in T whose B has no common member with the F of R, we delete R, as well as P and its descendants from the original entry E. As with (3.1), we justify this by observing that P cannot occur in an effective solution for the input situation of E. We continue this process with every essentially ambiguous entry E, using the most recent version of T at each stage. We stop when either there is an E with no initial output state left, or each E has at least one remaining initial output state and, consequently, every remaining initial output state P has a final descendant in E which has some common member with every one of the successor entries of E. In the first case, we conclude there are no effective solutions and stop. In the latter case, we continue.

Step 3. In every remaining subentry R for an initial P of an entry E, we now neglect the initial input and the initial output and compare the remainder R' of R with every entry S of the modified T whose succession of inputs includes or is included in R'. We take first such entries S, if any, which are essentially ambiguous. For every such entry S whose B does not contain all members of the B of R', delete all those members of B of R' not occurring in the B of S, together with their descendants, in R', R and E. We do this because such states cannot follow the state P in an effective solution, for all future inputs including the inputs of E. In particular, if all initial output states of R' are deleted at some stage, we delete R, as well as P and its descendants from E. Moreover, if this has not happened but there is such an entry S which is inessentially ambiguous but has B with no member in common with the B of R', we also delete R and its part in E. In such a case, we can choose to repeat the cycle of inputs under (iv) above in R and E as long as we wish and then bring in the inputs of S to block it. Hence, we cannot give an effective condition to determine when P is admissible. We do this with every subentry of every E. This step and the preceding step are then repeated as long as necessary, each time with the most recent version of T. Finally, we either find an entry E in T which has no more initial input states left, or every entry in T still has at least one remaining initial output state, but this and the preceding steps can no longer be applied to make further reductions. In the former case, there is no effective solution, in the latter case we continue.

Step 4. At this stage, the F of each essentially ambiguous entry E must have a common member with each of its successor entries in T. Not only so, but the final descendant of each initial output state P in such an entry E must have some common member with the B of every successor entry of E. We just look at all the inessentially ambiguous entries to see whether any such entry has a successor entry whose B has no common member with its F. If this happens for some entry, then we can find a succession of inputs for which there is no possible initial output state satisfying an extension of T. The original equation can have no effective solution. Otherwise we continue.

Step 5. For every essentially ambiguous entry E, an initial state P can occur as an initial state in an effective solution for some input histories beginning with E, only when it remains for every successor entry of E, because otherwise we can again repeat the cycle of inputs, and so on. Hence, we should treat every remaining subentry of E as a separate entry. We take the table T obtained at the end of the last step and replace every essentially ambiguous entry by all its remaining subentries. Call the new table T'. From the table T', we construct the ambiguity table by the same steps as step 6 for the construction of the solution table. If we get stopped in the process, then there is no effective solution for similar reasons as there is no general solution when the construction of the solution table is stopped before completion. If we can finish the process and get an ambiguity table, we shall show that there are then effective solutions for the original equation. In this step, the essentially ambiguous entries get no new replicas since each has only one initial state.

If there is no ambiguity table, then the construction must have been stopped at some specific place. By comments in the above steps and in the steps for constructing a solution table, we can in each specific situation find suitable input histories to show that the original equation has no effective solution.

Given the ambiguity table, we can see, by an argument similar to that for proving general solvability from the solution table, that the ambiguity table does give solutions. That it does give effective solutions follows from the fact that for each input situation occurring in some entry R of the ambiguity table, every initial state of R can be used for all input histories beginning with the input situation of R, and that for every initial state and every extension of the inputs of R of total length $N+2$ (N the bound given in Step 1 above), there is always a successor which satisfies all future input histories beginning with the extension of R.

This will become clearer with an indication of how to get the effective solutions. We arbitrarily choose any set of entries from the ambiguity table, one entry for each input succession in the table, and in each entry arbitrarily choose one initial output state as the value of $(x_0, \cdots, y_0)$ for all input histories beginning with the input situation of the entry. Each such set of values can be used as a solution for $(x_0, \cdots, y_0)$ in terms of the inputs $(i_0, \cdots, j_0), \cdots, (i_p, \cdots, j_p), p \leqslant N$.

To get $(dx, \cdots, dy)$ as a function of $(x, \cdots, y)$ and the inputs of t to $t+q$, $q \leqslant N+1$, we proceed as with equations having no infinitely ambiguous entries. Thus we take all initial output states in every entry of the ambiguity table and choose $(dx, \cdots, dy)$ from the immediate descendants. We observe that the entries of the ambiguity table can again be divided into input sets, each set containing all entries with a same succession of inputs. We wish to determine for each initial state in each entry all its possible successors on the input situation of the entry or some bounded extensions of it. Take an essentially ambiguous entry R with its initial state P. Neglect the initial input state and output state of R and look at its remainder R'. Take the set S including every input set whose inputs include that of R' or is included in that of R'. If there is one whose inputs are included in those of R', S can have no other member since no input succession of any entry in the table can contain that of another as a proper part. In this case, every member of the immediate descendant of P is a possible next state for the inputs of R, because each must occur in some entry of the input set in question. This is clear since any state excluded by the inputs of input sets must be excluded by those of R. If, on the other hand, there is no such input sets, there will be several input sets each having an input succession which includes that of R'. Of course none can be longer than $N+1$. We take these sets one by one and determine in each case the possible next states of P. A next state of P in R is possible provided it occurs as an initial input state in some entry of the input set. By Step 3 above, every P must have at least one possible next state for the succession of inputs of the particular input set. Hence, we can list for each possible extension of R' in the table all possible values of $(dx,\cdots,dy)$ for the given value of $(i,\cdots,j)$ and $(x,\cdots,y)$ (viz. P) in R. If we take the time of P at t, then the inputs in each case are from t to $t+q$, $q\leqslant N+1$. This completes the determination of $(dx,\cdots,dy)$ for essentially ambiguous entries. For the inessentially ambiguous entries, argue similarly although with no appeal to Step 3 (compare also the proof of Theorem 5).

Hence, we have reached the following theorem:

Theorem 6. *There is an effective method of deciding whether an equation* (S) *has effective solutions, and, when* (S) *is effectively solvable, of exhibiting effective solutions of the form* (P) *in* 2.7 *with* $p\leqslant N, q\leqslant N+1$.

It follows that every effectively solvable equation (S) has solutions of the form (P) with $p\leqslant N$ and $q\leqslant N+1$. Once we have obtained the bound on p and q, we can also try to devise more directly methods of deciding effective solvability by extending the known method for getting deterministic solutions. We shall, however, not enter upon such possibilities in this paper.

We conclude this section by a few examples of effectively solvable equations with no deterministic solutions.

A trivial and obvious example would be $x=di$. Less trivial examples are the following:

Example 11. $dx=x'$, $x'y=x'i$, $xy=xdy$.

Using e,f,g,h for the states of (x,y) as before, we can construct the tables rather more simply since di does not occur in the equations.

The characterizing table is:

i	0	0	0	0	1	1	1	1
(x, y)	e	f	g	h	e	f	g	h
(dx, dy)	g, h	+	e	f	+	g, h	e	f

The reduced characterizing table is empty so that the example has no deterministic solutions.

Since we need now only a repetition of i rather than one of (i, di), the solution table is simply:

i	0	0	0	1	1	1
(x, y)	$g;e$	$e;h$	$e;h$	$f;g$	$f;g$	$h;f$
di	0	1	1	0	0	1
(dx, dy)	$e;g,h$	$g;f$	$h;f$	$g;e$	$h;e$	$f;g,h$
d^2i		0	1	0	1	
(d^2x, d^2y)		$e;g,h$	$f;g,h$	$e;g,h$	$f;g,h$	

We get the ambiguity table if we just break each entry into two. The effective solutions are given in the following manner. There are 2^6 possible choices of the initial state, 2 for each input succession in the table. These can be combined into 2^4 because for each i_0 and i_1, there are 2 possible choices of x_0. For example, we may choose e, h, g, f respectively for (i_0, i_1) being $(0, 0)$, $(0, 1)$, $(1, 0)$, $(1, 1)$: $x_0 = i_0 i_1' + i_0' i_1$, $y_0 = i_1$.

There is a uniform method of obtaining (dx, dy) from the ambiguity table. For example, if di is 0 and (x, y) is g, then (dx, dy) is e; if di is 0, (x, y) is e, d^2i is 0, then (dx, dy) is g, etc. The solution of dx has to be as originally given:

$$dx = x'.$$

The solution of dy, when simplified, is:

$$dy = xy + x'd^2i.$$

A similar example is:

Example 12. $dx = x'y + xy'$, $dy = y'$, $xyz = xyi$, $(x+y)z = (x+y)dz$.

Incidentally, if we replace $(x+y)z = (x+y)dz$ in the above example by $z = dz$, the result is no longer solvable.

§ 9. The Normal Form (*S*) of Sequential Boolean Equations

In the above discussion we have left two loose ends—the physical realizability of certain solutions which are not deterministic, and the reducibility of all sequential Boolean equations to the normal form (S) given in § 2.

9.1. Every finite set of sequential Boolean equations is reducible to the form (S), sometimes with the help of new output variables.

This is immediate by (2.3) and (2.5) if all the occurring arguments are among $i, \cdots, j, x, \cdots, y, di, \cdots, dj, dx, \cdots, dy$. If, on the other hand, e.g., d^2i, d^4i, and d^3y also occur in the given equations after we distribute the d's according to (2.2) first, then we add new equations:

$$u = di, \; v = du, \; w = dv, \; z = dy, \; s = dz,$$

and replace d^2i, d^4i, d^3y respectively by du, dw, ds. Then we get an equation of the form (S) with more output variables. Clearly the procedure applies to all cases.

9.2. Given any definition of the form (P) in (2.7), we can find a definition of the form (D) in (2.6) with additional output variables which define the original functionals with $(d^p i, \cdots, d^p j)$, if $p \geqslant q$, otherwise $(d^q i, \cdots, d^q j)$, instead of $(i, \cdots, j)$, as arguments.

For example, suppose the given definition is:

$$x_0 = i_0 i_3, \; dx = did^2 i + x'.$$

We take $j = d^3 i$ as the new argument and get a definition of the form (D):

$$z_0 = 0, \; w_0 = 0, \; u_0 = 0, \; dz = j, \; dw = z,$$
$$du = w, \; x_0 = u_0 j_0, \; dx = wz + x'.$$

Clearly the procedure applies to all cases of (P). Hence, there is a definite sense in which predictive sequential functionals are physically realizable.

This fact was pointed out to the writer by Arthur Burks.

So far we have used only the input variables and output variables as the basic terms in forming sequential Boolean equations. It seems natural to extend the formalism by adding i_0, j_0, etc., x_0, y_0, etc. as basic terms. By a procedure similar to the proof of 9.1, we can again reduce each finite set of such initialized sequential Boolean equations to one equation of the form:

$$(S_0) \quad H(i_0, \cdots, j_0, x_0, \cdots, y_0, di_0, \cdots, dj_0, dx_0, \cdots, dy_0, i, \cdots,$$
$$j, x, \cdots, y, di, \cdots, dj, dx, \cdots, dy) = 0.$$

It is possible to modify the methods for solving equations of the form (S) to obtain similar methods of solving equations of the form (S_0). One method is to form the logical product P of all 2^{2m+2n} results obtained from H by substituting strings of 1's and 0's for $(i_0, \cdots, dy_0)$ and solve the equation $p=0$. Then we have to verify in addition that it is possible to choose $x_0, \cdots, y_0$, $dx_0, \cdots, dy_0$ so that (S_0) is satisfied for $t=0$.

9.3. The methods of solving equations of the form (S) can be modified to yield methods for solving equations of the form (S_0).

It may be of some interest to compare equations of the form (S) with equations which represent nets in the sense of Burks-Wright [2]. These nets are obtained as a generalization and idealization of the diagrams familiar to circuit designers (cf. e.g., Keister-Ritchie-Washburn [8]), by abstracting from the physical elements which are to realize them. A net is an arbitrary configuration obtained from delay elements and ordinary Boolean elements by joining up the variables (the ends) in arbitrary manners. In terms of the equations which represent these configurations according to Burks-Wright [2], every net is represented by a finite set of sequential Boolean equations and:

9.4. A finite set of sequential Boolean equations represents a net if and only if every equation in the set is either of the form $dy=i$, or of the form $dy=x$, or of the form $x=B$, where B is an ordinary Boolean expression not containing d. Any such set will be called a net equation set.

Obviously every net equation set is equivalent to an equation of the form (S). Conversely, we now prove:

9.5. For every finite set of sequential Boolean equations, we can find a net equation set which contains essentially all the variables of the original set such that every solution of the second set gives directly one of the first set.

We use the following steps. (i) As in 9.1, we eliminate all occurrences of d which governs other occurrences of d by adding new output variables. (ii) We replace equations of the forms $i=x$, $x=dy$, $B=x$ by $x=i$, $dy=x$, $x=B$. (iii) We drop every equation of the form $i=j$, and substitute j for i in all the other equations. (iv) We replace every equation of the form $di=x$ or $di=j$ by two equations $y=i$, and $dy=x$ or $dy=j$, y being a new variable. (v) We replace every equation of the form $A=B$, where neither A nor B is a single letter, by $x=A$ and $x=B$, where x is a new variable.

Obviously these steps preserve all variables and their interrelationships in the original equations, eliminating one of the two variables occurring in some equation $i=j$ making no essential difference.

Moreover, further reductions are possible. A device is used in Burks-Wright [2] by which "multiple junctions" can be got rid of, i.e., occurrences of a same variable at the left-hand side of more than one equation can be eliminated. For example, if $x=A$, $x=B$, $x=C$ all occur in the set, we can replace them by

$$x = A,\ y = (AB + A'B') + y',\ z = (BC + B'C') + z',$$

or

$$x = A,\ y = (xB + x'B')(xC + x'C') + y'.$$

Similarly, if $dx=A$, $x=B$ occur, we replace $x=B$ by $y=(xB+x'B')+y'$. If $dx=A$, $dx=B$ occur, we replace $dx=B$ by $y=(AB+A'B')+y'$.

Furthermore, there is no point in retaining equations of the form $x=i$, and the form $x=y$. Indeed, if we are interested in solving the equations, we may eliminate all equations of the form $x=B$, when B does not contain x, and substitute B for x in all the other equations. Hence, we may confine ourselves to the solution of sets of equations in the *net normal form*:

9.6. A set of equations is said to be in the net normal form, if no variable occurs at the left-hand side of two or more equations, and every equation is either of the form $x=A$, where A contains x but does not contain d, or of the form $dy=B$, where B contains y but does not contain d.

If we are concerned with solving equations in the net normal form, it becomes clear that the main problem is to solve the equations of the form $x=A(x)$ which involve a "circular" condition on x.

Given a set of equations in the net normal form, we would naturally simplify the right-hand side of each equation as far as possible by methods for simplifying non-sequential Boolean expressions. If, moreover, there are two equations $dx=A$, $dy=B$ for which A and B are equivalent, we can drop one equation, say $dy=B$, and replace all occurrences of y by x in other equations. If there are two equations $x=A(x), y=B(y)$ such that $A(x)$ and $B(x)$ are equivalent, we can do the same. Then we can combine all equations not containing d into one and simplify. Then the problem is to solve a set of equations with one "circular" condition without delays plus a finite number of delay equations. It is thought that, for example, the method of finding deterministic solutions in Church [4] can be shortened somewhat with the help of this normal form.

We have thus far shown that the problem of solving equations of the form (S) is essentially equivalent to that of solving net equation sets. In Burks-Wright [2], there is a notion of "well-behaved nets" which amounts to: an arbitrary net is well-behaved if its set of equation is uniquely solvable in the general sense. Hence, Theorem 5 above gives incidentally a method for deciding whether a net is well-behaved, and a determination of the form of all possible solutions of well-behaved nets. It seems, however, clear that in circuit synthesis we are not only interested in unique solvability but also in solvability as such.

The uniquely solvable equations of the form (S_0) are of special interest if we are interested in comparing sequential Boolean functionals and recursive definitions familiar in mathematical logic. We digress to make some incidental remarks on this point.

In the theory of recursive functions, definitions of the form (P) in 2.7 correspond to the primitive recursive definitions. An equation of the form (S_0), if it has a unique solution, would correspond to an Herbrand recursive definition. The counterpart of a general recursive definition would be an equation (S_0) which is not only uniquely solvable but is such that for any given t, and any given input values of $i, \cdots, j$, we can derive from (S_0), by Boolean algebra and substitution, for every output variable x in (S_0), an equation $x_t = 0$ or $x_t = 1$, but never both (Compare Gödel [7], p. 26). While it is known that there are many Herbrand recursive functions which are not general recursive, the two corresponding types of definition of sequential functionals determine the same class of functionals. Thus, every functional definable by a uniquely solvable (S_0) is, by Theorem 5 and 9.3, definable by a definition of form (P), and every definition of form (P) obviously satisfies the additional requirement about derivability. Indeed, we can even prove that the two classes of definitions are coextensional (not only they determine the same domain of functionals):

9.7. An equation of the form (S_0) is uniquely solvable if and only if for any specific input functions $i, \cdots, j$, all the substitution instances of (S_0), i.e., all the instances of (S_0) obtained by substituting every non-negative integer for t, and their Boolean consequences include, for every numeral t, either $x_t = 0$ or $x_t = 1$, $\cdots$, either $y_t = 0$ or $y_t = 1$, but never both $x_t = 0$ and $x_t = 1$, $\cdots$, or both $y_t = 0$ and $y_t = 1$.

An equation (S_0) is uniquely solvable if and only if, for any given functions $i, \cdots, j$, there is a unique assignment of values 0 and 1 to $x_0, \cdots, y_0, x_1, \cdots, y_1$, etc. such that all substitution instances of (S_0) are true by the normal interpretation of all Boolean operators and the equal sign. More explicitly, (S_0) has no solution if there are functions $i, \cdots, j$ for which no possible (0, 1)– assignments to x_0, etc. would make all instances of (S_0) true; (S_0) has two or more solutions, if there are assignments for every set of given input functions and there are functions $i, \cdots, j$, for which there are two or more interpretations of $x, \cdots, y$ all making all instances of (S_0) true.

Hence, 9.7 follows from the following two statements 9.8 and 9.9.

9.8. For any given $i, \cdots, j$, all substitution instances of (S_0) can be made true simultaneously by choosing suitable functions $x, \cdots, y$ if and only if there exist no t and no output variable (say x) such that both $x_t = 0$ and $x_t = 1$ are derivable.

If there are such x and t, then those instances of (S_0) from which we can derive $x_t = 0$ and $x_t = 1$ cannot be true no matter what functions we choose for $x, \cdots, y$. On the other hand, if there are no such t and output variable, then every finite subset of all instances of (S_0) must be true according to some interpretation of $x, \cdots, y$. Hence, by a familiar theorem of mathematical logic, or by a direct application of the Unendlichkeitslemma, there is one interpretation of $x, \cdots, y$ which would make all the instances true.

9.9. For given $i, \cdots, j$, all instances of (S_0) have two or more true interpretations if and only if there exist some time t and some output variable (say x) such that neither $x_t=0$ nor $x_t=1$ is derivable.

If there are two interpretations of $x, \cdots, y$ which make all instances of (S_0) true, they must differ for some output (say x) at some time t. Hence, neither $x_t=0$ nor $x_t=1$ can be derivable. Conversely, if neither is derivable, it must be possible to make all instances of (S_0) true no matter whether we take x_t to be 0 or 1.

This completes the proof of 9.7.

In mathematical logic, it is customary to identify general recursiveness with effective calculability. Since the solution of every uniquely solvable sequential Boolean equation is a predictive functional in the sense of 2.7, it is natural to ask whether one could identify effectively calculable Boolean functionals with predictive sequential functionals. In so far as we allow only d as the time operator, this seems reasonable. But we could also use arbitrary general recursive time operators and still retain effectiveness.

§ 10. Apparently Richer Languages

In specifying conditions to be satisfied by circuits, one often uses restricted quantifiers and certain modulo operators. These additional means of expression are convenient but generally dispensable if we have the language of sequential Boolean equations. It is, therefore, desirable to set up apparently richer languages and prove that conditions expressed in them can be mechanically turned into ones expressed in the initial language of sequential Boolean equations. In what follows, we shall not formulate exactly any such languages except to give a few examples to illustrate how a number of familiar forms of expression can be reduced to sequential Boolean equations.

For this purpose, it is less confusing and more intuitive, if we begin with the symbolism of the monadic predicate calculus rather than that of Boolean algebra, explicitly exhibiting the time indicators 0, t, $t+1$, etc. as arguments. At the end, we can return to the simpler notation in familiar manner.

10.1. The output x is on at t if and only if the input i is on at all (resp. some) time s, $0 \leqslant s \leqslant t$.

These we express by:

(1) $$x(t) \equiv (s)_0^t\, i(s),$$

(2) $$x(t) \equiv (Es)_0^t\, i(s).$$

They are equivalent to:

(1′) $$(x(0) \equiv i(0)) \;\&\; (x(t+1) \equiv (x(t) \;\&\; i(t+1))),$$

(2′) $$(x(0) \equiv i(0)) \;\&\; (x(t+1) \equiv (x(t) \vee i(t+1))).$$

If, for example, we wish to solve a condition $H((s)_0^t\, i(s))$, we may solve instead the condition:

$$H(x(t)) \,\&\, (1').$$

It is quite obvious that the original condition has solutions if and only if the new one has, since we can always choose x which satisfies $(1')$. This consideration applies equally to the examples to follow.

10.2. The output x is on at t if and only if for the period $0 \leqslant s \leqslant t$, the input i is on at k different moments s, such that $k \equiv 1 \pmod 3$.

This we express by

(3) $$x(t) \equiv (1_3 s)_0^t\, i(s).$$

This is equivalent to

(3a) $$(x(0) \equiv i(0)) \,\&\, (x(t+1) \equiv ((x(t) \,\&\, \sim i(t+1)) \vee (y(t) \,\&\, i(t+1)))),$$

provided,

(3b) $$(y(0) \equiv \sim i(0)) \,\&\, (y(t+1) \equiv ((y(t) \,\&\, \sim i(t+1)) \vee (\sim y(t) \,\&\, \sim x(t) \,\&\, i(t+1)))).$$

if now we take the conjunction of (3a) and (3b) as $(3')$, then we can, as in the preceding example, reduce the solution problem of $H((1_3 s)_0^t\, i(s))$ to that of $H(x(t))$ & $(3')$.

10.3. The output x is on at t, if and only if, for all s, $0 \leqslant s \leqslant t$, $i(s)$ is on exactly when $s \equiv 3 \pmod 4$.

(4) $$x(t) \equiv (s)_0^t (s \stackrel{4}{=} 3 \,|\, i(s)).$$

(4′) $$(x(0) \equiv \sim i(0)) \,\&\, (x(t+1) \equiv (x(t) \& (i(t+1) \equiv (y(t) \,\&\, \sim z(t)))) \& \sim y(0) \,\&\, \sim z(0) \& (y(t+1) \equiv \sim (y(t) \equiv z(t))) \,\&\, z(t+1) \equiv \sim z(t).$$

The new expressions introduced in these examples may be called the restricted quantifiers, the modulo quantifiers, and the modulo conditions. We leave open the problem of generalizing these examples to get a fairly neat inessential extension of the language of sequential Boolean equations.

A related problem from quite a different direction was raised on p. 296 of [1]. Thus, it is natural to ask, e.g., whether all deterministic sequential functionals can be expressed explicitly in terms of Boolean operations with the help of the modulo conditions and the restricted and modulo quantifiers.

This is another problem which is open. We give two simple examples to indicate that it seems plausible such simple recursions can be thus eliminated.

10.4. $x_0 = i_0,\ dx = x'di.$

In the alternative notation, the definition is:

$$x(0) \equiv i(0),\ x(t+1) \equiv (\sim x(t) \,\&\, i(t+1)).$$

This definition can be replaced by the following explicit one:

$$x(t) \equiv [(t = 0 \,\&\, i(t)) \vee (Es)_0^t(t = s + 1 \,\&\, ((q)_0^t(q^2 = t | i(q)) \vee (Ep)_0^s(p^2 = s | (\sim i(p) \,\&\, (q)_{p+1}^t(q^2 = t | i(q))))))].$$

10.5. $x_0 = i'_0,\ dx = xdi' + di.$

$$x(t) \equiv [(t = 0 \,\&\, \sim i(t)) \vee (Es)(t = s + 1 \,\&\, ((Ep)_0^t(i(p) \,\&\, (q)_{p+1}^t \sim i(q)) \vee (q)_0^t \sim i(q)))].$$

§ 11. Turing Machines and Growing Automata

In [1] and [4], growing or potentially infinite automata are considered. We add some remarks on these concepts.

If we think of each machine as given by a set of deterministic sequential functionals characterized by a definition of the form (D) in 2.6, then a growing automata could be taken as an arbitrary effective sequence of such sets. Thus, since we can enumerate effectively all definitions of the form (D), say by a recursive function $e(n)$, we can define a growing automaton as:

11.1. A growing automaton is an arbitrary sequence $e(h(0)), e(h(1)), \cdots$ of ordinary machines, where h is any function defined by: $h(0)$ is a constant, $h(t+1) = g(h(t))$, g being an arbitrary general recursive function.

This is rather broader than the examples of growing automata with which we are familiar, in particular the Turing machines. If we begin with Turing machines, we are able to get more restricted classes of growing automata of which we have more detailed information.

It would not do to think of a Turing machine as an interlinked pair of finite machines, because the length of the tape half has no pre-assigned bound. Nor can we view it as a finite machine and regard the tape as a part of the environment since the tape not only carries inputs but also serves as a storage unit. We cannot eliminate the need for a growing machine by distinguishing machine and environment and then permitting information to be stored in and recovered from environment, as the environment would then have to be viewed as a growing machine. It would seem that the correct course is to take a single Turing machine as a digital computer with a growing internal serial storage but no parallel or random access storage, that is, stored information cannot be retrieved in a single step. A basic machine which treats each particular Turing machine by a program can be taken as a hypothetical digital computer with both a growing internal serial storage and a growing internal random access storage.

We assume a particular formulation of Turing machines which is rather simple but sufficient to calculate all recursive functions. In this formulation, there is only one symbol for marking tape squares, the scanning head can mark (represented by *), erase (E), and read to choose the next state: Cm means that go to state m if the square under scan is marked, otherwise, go to the next state. The tape can shift one square left ($\leftarrow$) or right ($\rightarrow$). Any non-negative integer n is represented on the tape by a continuous string of $n+1$ marked square. The questions (i.e. the arguments of the function) are separated from each other by a blank square between every two. At the beginning the machine is to scan the leftmost marked square of the leftmost argument. At the end of the calculation, if there is an end for the particular arguments, everything except the answer is erased, and the machine stops (S), scanning the leftmost marked square of the answer. That such Turing machines can calculate all recursive functions is clear from the literature (see Kleene [9] and Wang [14]).

To represent each such Turing machire, we give each square on the tape an integer as coordinate. At every moment, the square under scan gets 0 as its coordinate, the square immediately to the right (resp. left) of the square with the coordinate a gets the coordinate $a+1$ (resp. $a-1$). The machine is viewed as having a fixed part which is a finite automoton with the scanning head as its only input node.

We give first a simple example which does addition of two nonnegative integers. All the machine has to do is to mark the blank between the two arguments, erase the two rightmost marks, and go back to the leftmost marked square. This can be described by the following:

1. $\rightarrow$, $C1$; 2. *; 3. $\rightarrow$, $C3$; 4. $\leftarrow$; 5. E; 6. $\leftarrow$; 7. E; 8. $\leftarrow$, $C8$;
9. $\rightarrow$; 10. S.

In terms of conditions, we shall take the 10 items as 10 states; $q_1, \cdots, q_{10}$. For any given arguments m and n, $q_k(m,n,t)$ is true or false according as the machine is at state q_k at t or not. Similarly, $p(m,n,a,t)$ is true or false according as at t, the square with the coordinate a is marked or blank.

The conditions representing the machine are then as follows:

11.2. $p(m,n,a,0) \equiv (0 \leqslant a \leqslant m \vee m+2 \leqslant a \leqslant m+n+2)$.

$$p(m,n,a,t+1) \equiv ((q_{10} \,\&\, p(a)) \vee ((q_4 \vee q_6 \vee q_8) \,\&\, p(a+1)) \vee ((q_1 \vee q_3 \vee q_9) \,\&\, p(a-1)) \vee (q_2 \,\&\, (a=0 \vee p(a))) \vee ((q_5 \vee q_7) \,\&\, (a \neq 0 \,\&\, p(a)))).$$

$$q_1 \quad (m, n, 0)$$
$$\sim q_k \quad (m, n, 0), k = 2, \cdots, 10.$$
$$q_{k+1} (m, n, t + 1) \equiv q_k, k = 4, 5, 6.$$
$$q_1 \quad (m, n, t + 1) \equiv (q_1 \& p(0)).$$
$$q_{k+1} (m, n, t + 1) \equiv (q_k \& \sim p(0)), k = 1, 3, 8.$$
$$q_{k+1} (m, n, t + 1) \equiv (q_k \vee (q_{k+1} \& p(0))), k = 2, 7.$$
$$q_{10} \quad (m, n, t + 1) \equiv (q_9 \vee q_{10}).$$

In the above conditions, q_k is always understood as $q_k\ (m, n, t)$, for $k = 1, \cdots, 10$; similarly, $p(b)$ is understood as $p(m, n, b, t)$.

In general, we can set up a general schema for defining all Turing machines in the specified form. For brevity, we consider only functions of two arguments.

11.3. For any constant N (the number of states), any truth functions $Q_1, \cdots, Q_5$ of $q_1, \cdots, q_N$ which are mutually exclusive and jointly exhaust all states $q_1, \cdots, q_N$ at t for given arguments m, n, and for any similar truth functions $F_1, \cdots, F_N$ of $q_1, \cdots, q_N$ and $p(0)$, we can define a Turing machine by the following schema (G):

$$p(m, n, a, 0) \equiv (0 \leqslant a \leqslant m \vee m + 2 \leqslant a \leqslant m + n + 2).$$
$$\begin{aligned} p(m, n, a, t + 1) \equiv ((Q_1 \& p(a)) &\vee (Q_2 \& p(a + 1)) \\ &\vee (Q_3 \& p(a - 1)) \vee (Q_4 \& (a = 0 \vee p(a))) \\ &\vee (Q_5 \& a \neq 0 \& p(a))). \end{aligned}$$
$$q_1(m, n, 0).$$
$$\sim q_k(m, n, 0), k = 2, \cdots, N.$$
$$q_k(m, n, t + 1) \equiv F_k(p(0), q_1, \cdots, q_N), k = 1, \cdots, N.$$

It is obvious that all predicates $p(m, n, a, t)$ definable by (G) are primitive recursive. Indeed, there can be no p such that:

$$p(m, n, a, t + 1) \equiv m + n + a \leqslant t^2.$$

Here the increase in the number of squares which change state at t is a function of t and not bounded by any uniform bound independent of t.

On the one hand, all partial recursive functions can be calculated by these machines; on the other hand, the predicate required to represent these machines form a narrow subclass of the class of primitive recursive functions. It is natural to wish to make explicit the relation between the predicate p and the function computable by its corresponding machine.

When the machine stops, we arrive at a stage, where

$$(a)(p(m, n, a, t) \equiv p(m, n, a, t + 1)).$$

To get a bound on the variable a, we observe that by the standard method of computation, at every time t, at most one more square need be affected so that we can use the bound $m+n+3+t$. Hence, from the stipulation that at the end of a calculation the scanning head is to scan the leftmost square of the answer, we see that the value of the function $g(m, n)$ computed by the machine represented by the corresponding equivalences is given by:

$$T(p, m, n, t) \equiv (a)(a \leqslant m + n + 3 + t \mid p(m, n, a, t) \equiv p(m, n, a + 1, t)),$$

$$U(p, m, n, t) \equiv \mu a(a \leqslant m + n + 3 + t \mid \sim p(m, n, a + 1, t)).$$

$$g(m, n) = U(p, m, n, \mu_t T(p, m, n, t)).$$

For every partial recursive function $g(m,n)$, there exists a predicate p, defined by a schema (G) such that the last relation above holds. Both U and T are primitive recursive, and the result may be viewed as an alternative proof of Kleene's normal form theorem ([9], p. 330). In particular, $g(m,n)$ is general recursive, if and only if the condition (m) (n) (Et) $T(p, m, n, t)$ holds.

References

[1] A. W. Burks and H. Wang, The logic of automata, *Jour. Assoc. Comp. Mach.*, **4** (1957), 193—218, 279—297.

[2] A. W. Burks and J. B. Wright, Theory of logical nets, *Proc. IRE*, **41** (1953), 1357—1365.

[3] A. Church, Review of a paper by Berkeley, *Jour. Symbolic Logic*, **20** (1955), 286—287.

[4] A Church, Application of the recursive arithmetic to the problem of circuit synthesis, Summaries of talks at the Summer Institute of Symbolic Logic in 1957 at Cornell University, pp. 3—50.

[5] L. Couturat, The Algebra of Logic (translated), London and Chicago, 1914.

[6] J. Friedman, Some results on Church's restricted recursive arithmetic, *Jour. Symbolic Logic*, **22** (1957), 337—342.

[7] K. Gödel, On undecidable propositions of formal mathematical systems, mimeographed, Princeton, 1934.

[8] W. Keister, A. E. Ritchie, S. H. Washburn, The Design of Switching Circuits, Princeton, 1951.

[9] S. C. Kleene, Introduction to Metamathematics, Princeton, 1952.

[10] D. König, Theorie der Graphen, 1936, reprint, New York, 1964.

[11] L. Löwenheim, Über die Auflösung von Gleichungen im logischen Gebietekalkül, Über Transformationen im Gebietekalkül, Gebietsdeterminanten, *Math. Annalen*, **68** (1910), 169—207; **73** (1913), 245—272; **79** (1919), 223—236.

[12] G. H. Mealy, A method for synthesizing sequential circuits, *The Bell System Technical Journal*, **34** (1955), 1045—1079.

[13] E F. Moore, Gedanken-experiments on sequential machines, *Automata Studies*, 1956, 129—153, Princeton.

[14] H. Wang, A variant to Turing's theory of computing machines, *Jour. Assoc. Comp. Mach.*, **4** (1957), 63—92 (included here as chapter VI).

PART THREE

FORMAL NUMBER THEORY

CHAPTER XI

THE PREDICATE CALCULUS

§ 1. The Propositional Calculus

In Ch. IX, we have incidentally considered certain formulations of the propositional calculus and the predicate calculus. In this chapter, we shall describe a number of points in this area more leisurely.

It is well-known that the propositional calculus is essentially equivalent to Boolean algebra. For example, the following is an axiom system for Boolean algebra. The variables are x, y, z, etc., 0 is the only constant, a term is: (i) a constant or a variable; or (ii) a' or ab when a, b are terms. A formula is $a=b$, if a, b are terms. One can then define 1 as $0'$, $a+b$ as $(a'b')'$. And the axioms are:

(1) $aa = a$,
(2) $ab = ba$,
(3) $a(bc) = (ab)c$,
(4) $a0 = 0$,
(5) if $ab' = 0$, then $ab = a$,
(6) if $ab = a$ and $ab' = a$, then $a = 0$.

A well-known system of the propositional calculus is that of Whitehead-Russell, as modified by Bernays, and adopted by Hilbert-Ackermann. The connectives "not" and "or" are used with the others defined. The axioms are:

(1) $(p \vee p) \supset p$,
(2) $p \supset (p \vee q)$,
(3) $(p \vee q) \supset (q \vee p)$,
(4) $(p \supset q) \supset ((r \supset p) \supset (r \supset q))$.

The rules of inference are modus ponens and substitution if p, q, r, etc. are construed as proposition letters. If they are construed as schemata, then the rule of substitution is unnecessary.

If in any formula of the propositional calculus, we replace p, q, etc. by x, y, etc., complement by negation, intersection by conjunction, sum by disjunction, it is possible to show that a formula A is a theorem in the propositional calculus if and only if $A^*=1$ is a theorem in Boolean algebra, A^* being the transform of A.

Another well-known system is that of Hilbert-Bernays in which the five common connectives are all taken as primitive. The axioms are:

(1a) $p \supset (q \supset p)$,

(1b) $(p \supset (p \supset q)) \supset (p \supset q)$,

(1c) $(p \supset q) \supset ((q \supset r) \supset (p \supset r))$;

(2a) $(p \,\&\, q) \supset p$,

(2b) $(p \,\&\, q) \supset q$,

(2c) $(p \supset q) \supset ((p \supset r) \supset (p \supset (q \,\&\, r)))$;

(3a) $p \supset (p \vee q)$,

(3b) $q \supset (p \vee q)$,

(3c) $(p \supset r) \supset ((q \supset r) \supset ((p \vee q) \supset r))$;

(4a) $(p \equiv q) \supset (p \supset q)$,

(4b) $(p \equiv q) \supset (q \supset p)$,

(4c) $(p \supset q) \supset ((q \supset p) \supset (p \equiv q))$;

(5a) $(p \supset q) \supset (\sim q \supset \sim p)$,

(5b) $p \supset \sim\sim p$,

(5c) $\sim\sim p \supset p$.

The rules of inference are modus ponens with or without substitution as before.

These systems are all known to be complete and consistent. The axioms are also independent. The usual method of proving independence is by choosing an interpretation in which the particular axiom is not true, but all theorems derivable from the other axioms are true. For example, if we take 1 as true, then the following interpretation gives the independence (1a):

p	q	p	$p \vee q$	$p \,\&\, q$	$p \equiv q$	$p \supset q$
1	1	3	1	1	1	1
1	2	3	1	2	3	3
1	3	3	1	3	3	3
2	1	2	1	2	3	1
2	2	2	2	2	1	1
2	3	2	2	3	3	3
3	1	1	1	3	3	1
3	2	1	2	3	3	1
3	3	1	3	3	1	1

Thus, every axiom except (1a) always gets the value 1, and if p and $p \supset q$ always get the value 1, so does q. On the other hand, when p and q take the values 2 and 1 respectively, (1a) takes the value 3.

If one omits (5c) from the above system, one gets the "minimal calculus". If one omits (5c) and replaces (5a) and (5b) by: $(p \supset \sim p) \supset \sim p$, (5b′)$\sim p \supset (p \supset q)$; then the resulting system is the intuitionistic propositional calculus.

It is also known that (5a) to (5c) can be replaced by:

(5a′) $(p \supset \sim q) \supset (q \supset \sim p)$, (5b′),

(5c′) $((p \supset \sim p) \supset q) \supset ((p \supset q) \supset q)$.

This alternative formulation has, according to Lukasiewicz, the following property: drop (5c′), we get intuitionistic calculus, drop also (5b′), we get the minimal calculus.

§ 2. Formulations of the Predicate Calculus

There are different formulations of the predicate calculus, variously known as quantification theory, the restricted or first order predicate calculus, the first order functional calculus. Often these diverse formulations are of interest for different purposes. We give here three alternative formulations.

We may use proposition letters p, q, r, etc., variables x, y, z, etc., predicates F, G, etc. A proposition letter or a predicate followed by variables is an atomic proposition. If A and B are propositions and v is a variable, then $\sim A$, $A \vee B$, (v)A, (Ev)B are propositions. A proposition containing no quantifiers is an elementary proposition. Other connectives &, $\supset$, $\equiv$ may either be included initially or be introduced by definitions. A proposition is a tautology if it as a truth function of its components which may or may not contain quantifiers is always true by the usual interpretation of truth-functional connectives. A given occurrence of a variable v is said to be bound in a formula if it is governed by a quantifier (v) or (Ev), otherwise free. If the result of writing general quantifiers for all free variables in A before A is a theorem, we write $\vdash A$.

2.1. System L_q (see Quine, *Mathematical Logic*, 1951 ed.).

*100. If A is a tautology, $\vdash A$

*101. $\vdash (v)(A \supset B) \supset ((v)A \supset (v)B)$

*102. If v is not free in A, $\vdash A \supset (v)A$.

*103. If B is like A except for containing free occurrences of u wherever A contains free occurrences of v, then $\vdash (v)A \supset B$.

*104. If $A \supset B$ and A are theorems, so is B.

This system has *104, the modus ponens, as the only rule of inference, which is less general than the usual one in so far as A and B contain no free variables. Vacuous quantifiers are included so that $(v)A$ is a proposition even when v is not free in A. This enables one to dispense with a rule of generalization: if $\vdash A$, then $\vdash (v)A$, which is included in the usual systems. No rule for the particular quantifiers are included since (Ev) is to be defined as $\sim(v)\sim$. There is no rule of substitution since the axioms are already schemata in the manner of von Neumann. The principle *100 can be replaced by a finite number of specific schemata in the usual manner, and it is sometimes convenient to do so.

It may be noted (see *J. Symbolic Logic*, **12** (1947), 130—132) that we can dispense with *102 if we replace *100, *101, and *104 respectively by:

*100′. If A is a tautology, $\vdash (v)A$.

*101′. If v is not free in B, $\vdash (v)(A \supset B) \supset (A \supset (v)B)$.

*104′. If $\vdash A$ and $\vdash A \supset B$, then $\vdash B$.

The equivalence is quite direct. All the new principles are easy consequences of results in ML: *100 and *115; *159; *111. Conversely, *102 is proved by *100′, *101′, *104′; *100 and *104 are special cases of *100′ and *104′; *101 can be proved by *101′ and *103 with the help of *115 whose proof uses only the new principles.

As a second system, we present one in Herbrand's thesis (Recherches sur la théorie de la démonstration, Warsaw, 1930). There is no need to allow vacuous quantifiers (called "fictitious" quantifier in his thesis, p. 29), and particular quantifiers are assumed to begin with, while truth functions besides $\sim$ and $\vee$ are taken as defined.

2.2. System L_h.

L_h 1. Rule of tautology. If A is an elementary proposition and a tautology then $\vdash A$.

L_h 2. Rules of inversion. Within a given proposition, if v is not free in B, we can replace each one by the other in any of the pairs:

(1) $\sim(v)A$, $(Ev)\sim A$; (2) $\sim(Ev)A$, $(v)\sim A$;

(3) $(v)(A \vee B)$, $(v)A \vee B$; (4) $(Ev)(A \vee B)$, $(Ev)A \vee B$.

L_h 3. Rule of generalization. If $\vdash Av$, then $\vdash (v)Av$.

L_h 4. Rule of particularization. If $\vdash Avv$, then $\vdash (Eu)Avu$, in other words, if $\vdash A$ and B is obtained from A by substituting u for v at some or all occurrences of v, then $\vdash (Eu)B$.

L_h 5. Rule of simplification. If $\vdash A \vee A$, then $\vdash A$.

L_h 6. Modus ponens. If $\vdash A \supset B$ and $\vdash A$, then $\vdash B$.

This remarkable system is specially useful for the study of proofs in the predicate calculus. Here are some concepts and results about the system:

2.21. Dreben's lemma. If for all A, $\vdash A$ follows from $A \vee \cdots \vee A$, then $\vdash (B \vee \cdots \vee B) \supset B$.

A proof of this which depends on 2.23 will be given at the end of this chapter.

2.22. Given any proposition $H(p, \cdots, q)$ built up from proposition letters by $\sim$ and $\vee$, the *sign* of each occurrence of each letter in H is defined thus: (1) p is positive in p; (2) the sign of an occurrence of p in $\sim A$ is the opposite of its sign in A; (3) the sign of an occurrence of p in A is the same as its sign in $A \vee B$. (Thesis, p. 21.)

The rules of inversion in L_h are specially convenient for bringing a proposition to the prenex normal form: i.e., a proposition with all quantifiers standing at the beginning. Given an occurrence of a quantifier in a proposition, when brought to the beginning, it may remain the same, or change from general to particular or vice versa. The definition 2.22 can be extended in obvious manner to occurrences of any propositions in a given proposition, we need only add that the sign of an occurrence of A in B is the same as its sign in $(v)B$ or $(Ev)B$. It then happens that a quantifier remains the same when brought to the beginning, if and only if the component proposition beginning with the quantifier has a positive occurrence in the whole proposition.

One peculiar feature of L_h is that the rule of tautology only uses elementary propositions. For the system, we can actually derive:

L_h 1′. The strengthened rule of tautology. If A is a tautology, $\vdash A$.

Given a tautologous elementary proposition, we wish to show that if we substitute more complex propositions for the atomic propositions in it, the results are always theorems of L_h. For this purpose, we may as well replace all atomic propositions by proposition letters and consider some given tautology $H(p, \cdots, q)$.

In general, each letter $p, \cdots, q$ in H may have a number of positive occurrences and a number of negative occurrences. By the rules of inversion, we may assume that the propositions to substitute the letters $p, \cdots, q$ are in the prenex normal form. We prove first a special case when each letter $p, \cdots, q$ has at most one positive occurrence and one negative occurrence in H:

2.23. For every elementary tautology $H(p, \cdots, q)$ of this restricted type, all substitution results from H are theorems of L_h.

While each result is obtained when we make all substitutions on the different proposition letters at the same time, we imagine that we break the process into different steps, one step for each proposition letter. Suppose we have shown that $H(By, \cdots, A)$ is shown to be a theorem, we wish to show that if instead of By we substitute $(Ey)By$ or $(y)By$ for p, we again get a theorem. Suppose p has one positive occurrence and one negative occurrence and suppose, for brevity, $(Ey)By$ is to replace p. Hence, we wish to derive, from $H(p,p,\cdots, A)$:

$$H((Ex)Bx, (Ey)By, \cdots, A) \text{ or } (y)(Ex)H(Bx, By, \cdots, A).$$

By hypothesis, $H(By, By, \cdots, A)$ is a theorem. Hence, by L_h 4 and L_h 3, we get the desired theorem.

From 2.23, it follows that for any A,C,B,D: $\vdash B \supset B$, and

$$(1) \qquad \vdash ((A \supset B) \,\&\, (C \supset D)) \supset ((A \vee C) \supset (B \vee D)).$$

If we substitute B for C and D, $B \vee B$ for A in (1), then we get by modus ponens:

$$\vdash ((B \vee B) \supset B) \supset ((B \vee B \vee B) \supset (B \vee B)).$$

By 2.21 and the rule of simplification, we have also $(B \vee B) \supset B$. Hence, if $\vdash B \vee B \vee B$, then $\vdash B \vee B$. Therefore, by the rule of simplification, if $\vdash B \vee B \vee B$, then $\vdash B$. If we repeat the process by substituting $B \vee B \vee B$, etc. for A in (1), we get:

2.24. If $\vdash B \vee \cdots \vee B$, then $\vdash B$.

With the help of this, we can now prove the general theorem:

Theorem 1. *The strengthened rule of tautology L_h 1′ is derivable in L_h; there is an effective (in fact, primitive recursive) method, such that for every tautology A, we can find a proof for it in L_h.*

We illustrate the procedure by a simple example. Suppose $H(p;p,p,p;q,q;q)$ is an elementary tautology with one positive occurrence of p, two of q, three negative occurrences of p, one of q. And we wish to prove the result of substituting $(x)(Ey)Fxy$ for p, $(z)Gz$ for q.

By $L_h 2$, $L_h 3$, and $L_h 4$, it is sufficient to prove:

(2) $$H((Ey)Fxy; (Ey)Fxy, (Ey)Fxy, (Ey)Fxy; (z)G(z), (z)Gz; (z)Gz).$$

To prove this, by 2.24, $L_h 3$, and $L_h 4$, it is sufficient to prove:

(3) $$H(Fxu; Fxu, Fxv, Fxw; (z)Gz, (z)Gz; (z)Gz) \vee H(Fxv; \cdots) \vee H(Fxw; \cdots).$$

For the same reason, this in turn follows from

(4) $$H(Fxu; \cdots; Gz, Gy; Gz) \vee H(Fxv; \cdots; Gz) \vee H(Fxw; \cdots; Gz) \vee H(Fxu; \cdots; Gy) \vee H(Fxv; \cdots; Gy) \vee H(Fxw; \cdots; Gy).$$

Now we wish to show that, since $H(p;p,p,p;q,q;q)$ is a tautology, (4) is also one and falls under $L_h 1$. Instead of the two atomic propositions p and q, we now have five: Fxu, Fxv, Fxw, Gz, Gy. If we put $H(p;a,b,c;d,e;q)$ into a conjunctive normal form, then since signs of the atomic propositions are preserved, each conjunctive term must be a part of

(5) $$p \vee \sim a \vee \sim b \vee \sim c \vee d \vee e \vee \sim q.$$

Moreover, since the original H is tautologous, each conjunctive term must contain either p and at least one of $\sim a$, $\sim b$, $\sim c$, or $\sim q$ and at least one of d and e. Now if we turn each disjunctive term of (4) into the corresponding form and get

(4′) $$H(a; a, b, c; d, e; d) \vee \cdots \vee H(c; a, b, c; d, e; e),$$

then we can show that (4′) must be true for all possible truth values of a,b,c,d,e.

First, consider the corresponding form for (3):

(3′) $$H(a; a, b, c; q, q; q) \vee H(b; \cdots) \vee H(c; \cdots).$$

This must be a tautology. If a,b,c are all false, every conjunctive term (a disjunction) in every disjunctive term of (3′) must be true since it must contain either q and $\sim q$, or at least one of $\sim a$, $\sim b$, $\sim c$. If at least one of a,b,c is true, say b, then, $H(b;a,b,c;q,q;q)$ must be always true.

Hence, if we take the conjunctive normal form of

(3″) $$H(a; a, b, c; d, e; q) \vee H(b; \cdots) \vee H(c; \cdots),$$

then each conjunctive term must contain either d and $\sim q$ or e and $\sim q$, provided we drop all terms $a \vee \sim a$, $b \vee \sim b$, $c \vee \sim c$. But (4′) is equivalent to a disjunction of the two propositions obtained from (3″) by substituting d and e for q. For any possible truth values of a,b,c,d,e, if d, e are both false, then every one is true since $\sim q$ occurs. If at least one is true, take that one.

This completes the proof of Theorem 1, since the example includes all the essential features for the general case.

The proof is based on the method in Herbrand's thesis. But the argument put forward in the example above is more complicated than Herbrand's, because we feel there are some gaps in his simpler proof. In Whitehead-Russell, the whole *9 is devoted to a sketch of a proof of Theorem 1 along quite a different line. Since they do not establish the completeness of their axioms for the propositional calculus, they cannot use arguments of the type as exemplified in the above proof.

In his thesis, Herbrand continues to exhibit a procedure whereby he can transform any given proof in L_h into one which does not use the rule of modus ponens. This is the famous:

2.25. Herbrand's Theorem. There is an effective (in fact, primitive recursive) procedure whereby, given any proof in an ordinary formulation of the predicate calculus, we can turn it into a proof of L_h with no appeal to the rule of modus ponens.

There is an extensive literature on this theorem mostly following the alternative treatment by Gentzen. We shall not attempt an exposition of Herbrand's original proof which, however, we believe, contains many interesting distinctive features well worth exploring. Instead, we shall consider some related results and some different formulations.

In mathematics, we constantly use the following mode of reasoning: "There exist y such that Ay. Let x be one such and consider whether this x has such and such other properties." In the symbolism of the predicate calculus, one might wish to formalize this by using a rule "from $(Ey)Ay$, infer Ax". But since the x chosen is not an arbitrary object but an arbitrary object which happens to have the property A, the variable x in such a rule cannot be expected to behave like ordinary variables in mathematical logic. To overcome this difficulty, Hilbert introduced the ε-symbol and infers $A(\varepsilon_x Ax)$ from $(Ex)Ax$. This symbol is treated thoroughly in Hilbert-Bernays' book, volume II.

The predicate calculus is then formulated a little differently. In addition to the variables, ε-expressions $\varepsilon_x Ax$, etc. also become terms and Fv, Gvu, etc. are propositions for arbitrary terms v, u, etc. If, e.g., we take the system L_h, we can obtain a new system L_b by some changes.

2.3. System L_b.

The system includes $L_h 1$ to $L_h 7$ with the propositions reconstrued in the extended sense, and a new rule:

(ε) The ε–rule. $\vdash (Ev)Av \supset A(\varepsilon_v Av)$.

Incidentally, given the ε–symbol, it is possible to omit quantifiers in the primitive apparatus and introduce them by definitions.

2.31. $(Ev)Av$ if and only if $A(\varepsilon_v Av)$.

2.32. $(v)Av$ if and only if $A(\varepsilon_v \sim Av)$.

For the system L_b, two fundamental theorems are proved in Hilbert-Bernays II (stated on p. 18). If F is a system formalized in the framework of L_b and, in general, contains additional symbols for individuals and predicates, as well as a finite number of new axioms $A_1, \cdots, A_n$ which do not contain the ε–symbol, but may contain quantifiers, then:

2.33. The first ε–theorem. If the axioms $A_1, \cdots, A_n$ contain no bound variables and B is a theorem of F which contains no bound variables, then B can also be derived from $A_1, \cdots, A_n$ without using bound variables.

2.34. The second ε–theorem. If B does not contain the ε–symbol but may contain quantifiers, it can be derived from $A_1, \cdots, A_n$ without using the ε–symbol (hence, can be derived in L_h).

In Hilbert-Bernays, Herbrand's theorem is deduced from these, and the two ε–theorems are extended to imbed also the axioms for equality. We shall not enter upon proofs of these results.

If we combine the use of the ε–symbol with the method of natural deduction as developed by Quine (*Methods of Logic*, 1950), we obtain a rather symmetric system L_g, which has the same terms and propositions as L_b but uses different rules. In particular, the deduction theorem is now taken as a primitive rule, and we are allowed to write down any new axiom as a hypothesis. The final result is a theorem of L_g only if it is freed from all hypotheses. Formally, a hypothesis may be marked by a * at the beginning which stands also in front of all consequences of the hypothesis. A line in a proof of L_g is a theorem of L_g only when it does not begin with a *.

$L_g 1$. Rule of assumption. We may set down any proposition A as a line at any stage in the course of a deduction, provided we prefix a new * on the line and all its consequences.

$L_g 2$. Rule of deduction. If under the assumption of $*A$ we arrive at $*B$, then we may write a new line $A \supset B$, with one $*$ less.

$L_g 3$. Rule of tautology. We may write a line which is implied truth-functionally by one or more previous lines taken together.

$L_g 4$. Rule of generalization. If v is a variable and $\vdash Av$, then $\vdash (v)Av$.

$L_g 5$. Rule of instantiation. If u is any term and $\vdash (v)Av$, then $\vdash Au$.

$L_g 6$. Rule of particularization. If u is any term and $\vdash Au$, then $\vdash (Ev)Av$.

$L_g 7$. Rule of specification. If $\vdash (Ev)Av$, then $\vdash A(\varepsilon_v Av)$.

For the system L_g, it is rather direct to prove something like the second ε-theorem. For this purpose, we need an additional rule which is no longer derivable if we drop $L_g 7$:

$L_g 7'$. Weakened rule of specification. If $\vdash Av \supset B$ and v is not free in B, then $\vdash (Ev)Av \supset B$.

We have then:

2.4. If B is derivable in L_g from $A_1, \cdots, A_m$ and the ε-symbol does not occur in $A_1, \cdots, A_m, B$, then B can be derived from $A_1, \cdots, A_m$ in L_g with the help of $L_g 7'$ but without using the ε-symbol.

Suppose a derivation of B in L_g from $A_1, \cdots, A_m$ is given and

$$\varepsilon_x C_1 x, \cdots, \varepsilon_x C_n x$$

are all the ε-terms introduced in the proof by $L_g 7$, arranged in the order in which they appear in the proof.

It follows that if instead of using $L_g 7$, we just write down each of $C_1(\varepsilon_x C_1 x), \cdots, C_n(\varepsilon_x C_n x)$, we get again a proof of B, but this time from $A_1, \cdots, A_m$, together with $C_1(\varepsilon_x C_1 x), \cdots, C_n(\varepsilon_x C_n x)$. The problem now is to find another proof in which the additional premises are dispensed with.

Consider the last of these: $C_n(\varepsilon_n C_n x)$. By the rule $L_g 2$, we can prove "$C_n(\varepsilon_n C_n x) \supset B$" from $A_1, \cdots, A_m, C_1(\varepsilon_x C_1 x), \cdots, C_{n-1}(\varepsilon_x C_{n-1} x)$ without using $L_g 7$. Throughout the proof, we can replace $\varepsilon_x C_n x$ everywhere by a new variable 'v' (say) and obtain a proof of "$C_n v \supset B$". By the additional rule $L_g 7'$ assumed especially for this purpose, we can then derive "$(Ev)C_n v \supset B$" without using $L_g 7$.

But "$C_n(\varepsilon_n C_n x)$" was originally introduced by $L_g 7$. Its premise "$(Ex)C_n x$" is, therefore, derivable from $A_1, \cdots, A_m, C_1(\varepsilon_x C_1 x), \cdots, C_{n-1}(\varepsilon_x C_{n-1} x)$ already. Hence, since "$(Ev)C_n v \supset B$" is also derivable from the same, B is already derivable from $A_1, \cdots, A_m, C_1(\varepsilon_x C_1 x), \cdots, C_{n-1}(\varepsilon_x C_{n-1} x)$ without using $L_g 7$.

Hence, we have succeeded in getting rid of the premise $C_n(\varepsilon_x C_n x)$. Repeating the same process, we can get rid of the other premises $C_{n-1}(\varepsilon_x C_{n-1} x), \cdots, C_1(\varepsilon_x C_1 x)$ one by one and obtain a proof of B from $A_1, \cdots, A_m$ in which $L_g 7$ is not applied.

In the resulting proof, there may still appear ε–terms introduced by $L_g 1$, $L_g 3$, and $L_g 5$. Suppose that

$$\varepsilon_x H_1 x, \cdots, \varepsilon_x H_k x$$

are all the ε–terms in the resulting proof, arranged in the order in which their last occurrences appear. Replace $\varepsilon_x H_k x$ throughout the proof by a new free variable, and we get again a proof of B from $A_1, \cdots, A_m$ in which $L_g 7$ is not used. Repeat the same with $\varepsilon_x H_{k-1} x$, and so on. We finally get a proof B from $A_1, \cdots, A_m$ in which the ε–symbol does not occur.

Sometimes the predicate calculus is taken as to include also the theory of equality. Hence, one particular predicate Rxy is chosen and rewritten as $x=y$, together with special axioms for them. In this way, we obtain a system:

2.5. System L_e: e.g., system L_q plus the axioms for equality $L_e 1$ and $L_e 2$.

$L_e 1$. $\vdash v=v$.

$L_e 2$. If B is like A except for containing free occurrences of u in place of some free occurrences of v, and $\vdash v=u$, then $\vdash A \equiv B$.

It is also often convenient to include constant names and functors. Then variables give way to the more general notion of terms which include constants, variables, and functors followed by terms. As these additional symbols usually do not affect general considerations about the predicate calculus, we shall often neglect them, though taking them for granted when necessary.

§ 3. Completeness of the Predicate Calculus

Using the notion of maximal consistent extensions (Gödel, "Eine Eigenshaft der Realisieung des Aussagenkalküls", *Ergebnisse eines Math. Kolloquiums*, **4** (1933), 20—21; L. Henkin, *J. Symbolic Logic*, **14** (1949), 159—166), it is possible to give a short proof of the completeness of the systems L_q, L_h, L_b, L_g.

Theorem 2. *The systems L_q, L_h, L_b, L_g are all complete; in fact, not only a single formula, but any enumerable set of formulae, if not* *containing the ε-symbol and consistent with these systems (i.e., no contradictions arising when they are taken as axioms) has an enumerable model.*

The proof can be obtained for L_b and L_g first, then, by 2.41, the theorem also holds for L_q and L_h.

We assume all the quantificational formulae, i.e., say, all formulae of L_g, are enumerated in a definite manner so that each is correlated with a unique positive integer in the standard ordering: q_1, q_2, etc. If a consistent set S_0 of quantificational formulae is given, its maximum consistent extension is constructed in the following manner. If S_0 plus q_1 is consistent, then S_1 is S_0 plus q_1; otherwise S_1 is the same as S_0. In general, if S_n plus q_{n+1} is consistent, then S_{n+1} is S_n plus q_{n+1}; Otherwise, S_{n+1} is the same as S_n. The maximum consistent extension is the union of the sets S_i.

Let S_0 be a consistent set of formulae in L_g. We may assume all free variables as bound at the beginning with general quantifiers (hence, only "closed" formulae) and then eliminate all general quantifiers and all connectives besides "neither-nor" in familiar manner. Construct the maximum extension (call it S) of S_0 within the system L_g or L_b. Call a closed formula true or false according as whether it belongs to S or not. We assert that hereby we get a model of S_0 in the enumerable domain D of all constant ε-terms (i.e., those containing no free variables).

In the first place, if P is an arbitrary predicate with n arguments and $a_1, \cdots, a_n$ are n constant ε-terms, then either $P(a_1, \cdots, a_n)$ or $\sim P(a_1, \cdots, a_n)$, but not both, is true, because S is maximal consistent. In the second place, "neither p nor q" is true if and only if neither p is true nor q is true, again because S is maximal consistent. In the third place, $(Ex)F(x)$ is true if and only if there is some constant ε-term a such that $F(a)$ is true, because "$(Ex)F(x) \supset F(\varepsilon_x Fx)$" belongs to S. Moreover, since S_0 is a subset of S, all formulae in S_0 are true.

This completes the proof of Theorem 2, completeness being the special case when S_0 contains a single formula.

There is a long history behind this theorem.

In 1915, Löwenheim (*Math. Annalen*, **76**, 447—470) proved:

3.1. Every quantificational formula, if satisfiable in any (nonempty) domain at all, is satisfiable in an enumerable domain.

In 1920, Skolem (Vidensk. Skrifter I, Mat. Naturw. Klasse, Oslo, no. 4) improved the proof and extended it to any enumerable set of formulae. These proofs all use the axiom of choice. The idea is particularly simple and illuminating. Suppose a single formula is given in the prenex normal form:

$$p: \ (x)(Ey)(Ez)(w)(u)(Ev)H(x, y, z, w, u, v).$$

Following Gödel, let us call "Skolem functions for p and M" any functions $f(x)$, $g(x)$, $h(x,w,u)$ in M such that for any elements x, w, u of M the following is true:

$$p^*: \ H(x, f(x), g(x), w, u, h(x, w, u)).$$

By the axiom of choice, there exist such functions f, g, and h. These functions can be applied fruitfully in many considerations.

Hence if a quantificational formula p is satisfiable at all, it is satisfiable in a denumerable domain. Thus, if 0 is an arbitrary object, the domain is the union of all sets M_i, such that $M_0=0$, and M_{j+1} contains all and only those objects which either belong to M_j or are $f(a)$, $g(a)$ or $h(a, b, c)$ for some a, b, and c that belong to M_j.

In 1923 and 1929 (cf. ibid., no. 4 for 1929), Skolem proved 3.1 and its generalization to infinitely many formulae without using the axiom of choice.

Skolem merely assumes that the quantificational formulae be given in prenex normal form. But, for brevity, let us consider a single formula in the Skolem normal form:

$$\text{(A)} \quad (x_1)\cdots(x_m)(Ey_1)\cdots(Ey_n)H(x_1, \cdots, x_m; y_1, \cdots, y_n).$$

Skolem takes $H(1, \cdots, 1; 2, \cdots, n+1)$ as H_1, and then considers all the m-tuples of the positive integers no greater than $n+1$, ordering them in an arbitrary manner with the m-tuple $(1, \cdots, 1)$ as the first. If $(k_{i1}, \cdots, k_{im})$ is the i-th m-tuple, then H_i is:

$$H_{i-1} \,\&\, H(k_{i1}\cdots k_{im};\ n(i-1)+2, \cdots, ni+1).$$

He then considers all the m-tuples of the positive integers used so far, and again couples the i-th m-tuple with the n-tuple consisting of the n consecutive integers starting with $n(i-1)+2$. In this way he defines a sequence of quantifier-free conjunctions $H_1, H_2, \cdots$ all gotten from the formula A.

His proof of 3.1 contains two parts:

3.2. If a quantificational formula A is satisfiable at all, then none of the formulas $\sim H_1, \sim H_2, \cdots$ is a tautology.

3.3. If none of the formulas $\sim H_1, \sim H_2, \cdots$ is a tautology, then the formula A itself is satisfiable in the domain of positive integers.

At about this time, Herbrand (*Comptes rendus*, Paris, **188** (1929), 1076) proved as part of his famous theorem:

3.4. If $\sim A$ is not a theorem of the predicate calculus, then none of $\sim H_1, \sim H_2, \cdots$, is a tautology.

From 3.3 and 3.4, the completeness of the predicate calculus follows as a corollary.

Soon after, Gödel independently proved these theorems (*Monatsh. Math. Phys.* **37** (1930), 349—360). His proof is widely known through Hilbert-Ackermann.

While a proof of Herbrand's theorem (see 2.25 above) requires metamathematical considerations about the structure of proofs, it has been observed by Beth and Dreben that one can derive from 3.3 and 3.4 a weaker Herbrand theorem which uses a general recursive rather than a primitive recursive procedure to get a proof not using modus ponens. Thus, by 3.3, if A is a theorem, some of $H_1, H_2, \cdots$ must be a tautology. Since we can effectively construct $H_1, H_2, \cdots$ from A and test for tautology, we can effectively find some tautologous H_i, provided only A is a theorem. By the proof of 3.4, we can actually write out a proof of A using only $L_h 1$ to $L_h 5$, i.e., not using the rule of modus ponens.

We append a remark on the relation between the axiom of choice and the ε–symbol.

Clearly there is some connection between the axiom of choice and rules governing Hilbert's ε–operator. Occasionally, the ε–rule is referred to as a generalized principle of choice. This is misleading. For example, if the axiom of choice were a special case of the ε–rule, why does the consistency of the axiom of choice not follow from the ε–theorems according to which application of the ε–rules can be dispensed with if the ε–operator occurs in neither the axioms nor the conclusions? Indeed, if the axiom of choice were derivable from the ε–rule, we would, by the ε–theorems, be able to derive the axiom of choice from the other axioms of set theory. But, as we know, the independence of the axiom of choice is an unsolved problem.

Of course, there is at least one difference between the ε–rule and the axiom of choice. The former makes a single selection, while the latter requires that a simultaneous choice from each member of a given set be made and that all these selected items be put together to generate a new set. Hence, there is no reason to suppose that, in general, the axiom of choice follows from the ε–rule.

If the following

$$(x)(Ey)(z)(z\varepsilon y \equiv (Ew)(w\varepsilon x \,\&\, z = \varepsilon_u(u\varepsilon w)))$$

happens to be a theorem in a certain system of set theory, then the axiom of choice does follow from the ε-rule in that system. But then it would be highly unlikely that the ε-operator did not appear in the axioms of the system.

There are also cases where, although the ε-rule would yield the desired result, the axiom of choice would not. For example, in the Zermelo theory we can infer "$(x)R(x, \varepsilon_y Rxy)$" from "$(x)(Ey)Rxy$" by the ε-rule, but we cannot infer "there exists f, $(x)R(x, fx)$" from "$(x)(Ey)Rxy$" by the axiom of choice, on account of the absence of a universal set in Zermelo's theory.

Most of the remarks in this section and the preceding section appeared in a symposium paper in *Mathematical Interpretation of Formal Systems*, Amsterdam, 1955, pp. 57—84.

The completeness theorem of the predicate calculus has been applied to prove results in algebra by Malcev, Henkin, A. Robinson, Tarski. There is also a complementary trend of proving results of interest to logic from the algebraic approach.

The completeness theorem is applied in the following form: if A is an enumerable set and B a finite set of formulae in the predicate calculus, and if there is, for every finite subset A' of A, a model satisfying both B and A', then there is a model satisfying A and B. For example, this can be applied to prove that every partial ordering can be extended to a total ordering. That a relation R is a total ordering can be expressed in the predicate calculus saying that R is transitive and that Rxy or Ryx for all distinct x and y. These propositions on R form the finite set B. If R is given as a partial ordering, then A is the set of all propositions $R(a, b)$ which are true, i.e., in which the objects a and b stand in the partial ordering relation R. Since any finite subset of A can be made into a total ordering, a model can be found to satisfy both B and any finite set of A. Hence, a model can be found to satisfy both A and B. That is to say, R can be extended to a total ordering.

Additional Note. B. S. Dreben gives the following proof of 2.21 stated on p. 311 above. Consider the case when B is $(x)(Ey)(z)Gxyz$ and there are three occurrences of B in the premiss. Let G_i be Gx_{3i-2} $x_{3i-1}\,x_{3i}$, then, by 2.23,

$$((G_1 \vee G_2 \vee G_3) \supset G_1) \vee ((G_4 \vee G_5 \vee G_6) \supset G_2) \vee ((G_7 \vee G_8 \vee G_9) \supset G_3)$$

is a theorem. Hence, by repeated applications of L_h 3 and L_h 4, we get B in place of each $G_j (j=1, \cdots, 9)$. Hence, the conclusion of 2.21 follows from its hypothesis.

CHAPTER XII

MANY-SORTED PREDICATE CALCULI

§ 1. One-sorted and Many-sorted Theories

Certain axiomatic systems involve more than one category of fundamental objects; for example, points, lines, and planes in geometry; individuals, classes of individuals, etc. in the theory of types. It is natural to use variables of different kinds with their ranges respectively restricted to different categories of objects, and to assume as substructure the usual predicate calculus for each of the various kinds of variable including the usual propositional calculus for all the formulae of the system. An axiomatic theory set up in this manner will be called many-sorted. We shall refer to the theory of truth functions and quantifiers in it as its (many-sorted) elementary logic, and call the primitive symbols and axioms (including axiom schemata) the proper primitive symbols and proper axioms of the system. Among the proper primitive symbols of a many-sorted system $T_n(n=2, \cdots,)$ there may be included symbols of some or all of the following kinds: (1) predicates denoting the properties and relations treated in the system; (2) functors denoting the functions treated in the system; (3) constant names for certain objects of the system. We shall, however, assume, for simplicity, that the systems T_n which we shall consider contain neither names nor functors.

We can describe each theory T_n as follows: There is at least one predicate. There are variables of different kinds: $x_1, y_1, z_1, \cdots$ (variables of the first kind); $x_2, y_2, z_2, \cdots; x_n, y_n, z_n, \cdots$. Each k-placed ($k=1, 2, \cdots$) predicate with its places filled up by variables of the proper kinds is a formula (an atomic formula); and quantification on, as well as truth-functional combinations of, given formulae again give formulae. In general, for each place of a predicate more than one kind of variable may be proper. However, to simplify our considerations, we shall always assume that each place of every predicate is to be filled up by one and only one kind of variable. Then a many-sorted elementary logic L_n is determined by the principles 1_n—5_n:

1_n. If ϕ is a tautology, then $\vdash \phi$.

2_n. $\vdash (\alpha)(\phi \supset \psi) \supset ((\alpha)\phi \supset (\alpha)\psi)$.

3_n. If α is not free in ϕ, then $\vdash(\alpha)\phi$.

4_n. If α and α' are variables of the same kind, and ϕ' is like ϕ except for containing free occurrences of α' whenever ϕ contains free occurrences of α, then $\vdash(\alpha)\phi\supset\phi'$.

5_n. If $\phi\supset\psi$ and ϕ are theorems of L_n, so is ψ.

By adding certain proper axioms (or also axiom schemata) to L_n, we obtain a system T_n.

As an alternative way, we may also formulate a system involving several categories of fundamental objects by using merely one kind of variables which have the sum of all the categories as their range of values. The simplest way to bring in the distinction of categories is to introduce n one-place predicates $S_1, S_2, \cdots, S_n$ such that x belongs to the i-th category if and only $S_i(x)$. We can then set up a one-sorted theory $T_1^{(n)}$ corresponding to T_n in the following manner: In $T_1^{(n)}$ the atomic formulas are determined by the predicates of T_n plus $S_1, \cdots, S_n$ with their places all filled up by general variables. Formulae, etc. can be defined in $T_1^{(n)}$ in the usual way. And $T_1^{(n)}$ contains a usual one-sorted elementary logic L_1 determined by five principles 1_1—5_1 (viz. *100 to *104 in L_q of the preceding chapter) which are similar to 1_n—5_n but are concerned with formulae and variables of $T_1^{(n)}$. Then we understand by the elementary logic $L_1^{(n)}$ the system obtained from L_1 by adding the following additional principle:

6_1. For every $i(i=1, \cdots, n)$, $(E\alpha)\, S_i(\alpha)$ is a theorem.

And we introduce a rule for translating between statements of L_n and those of $L_1^{(n)}$:

RT. A statement ϕ' in $L_1^{(n)}$ and a statement ϕ in L_n are translations of each other if and only if ϕ' is the result obtained from ϕ by substituting simultaneously, for each expression of the form $(x_i)(\text{—}x_i\text{—})$ in ϕ $(i=1, \cdots, n)$, an expression of the form $(x)(S_i(x)\supset(\text{—}x\text{—}))$ (with the understanding that different variables in ϕ are replaced by different variables in ϕ').

By using this rule, we see that every statement of L_n has a translation in $L_1^{(n)}$, and some (although not all) statements of $L_1^{(n)}$ have translations in L_n. In particular, the proper axioms of T_n all have translations in $L_1^{(n)}$ and $T_1^{(n)}$ is just $L_1^{(n)}$ plus the translations of these proper axioms of T_n.

The following results (I)—(IV) can be proved:

(I) A statement of any system T_n is provable in T_n if and only if its translation in the corresponding system $T_1^{(n)}$ is provable in $T_1^{(n)}$.

(II) If a system T_n is consistent, then the corresponding system $T_1^{(n)}$ is also consistent.

(III) If $T_1^{(n)}$ is consistent, then T_n is.

(IV) There is a primitive recursive method by which, given a statement of T_n and a proof for it in T_n, we can find a proof in $T_1^{(n)}$ for its translation in $T_1^{(n)}$; and conversely, there is a primitive recursive method by which, given a statement of $T_1^{(n)}$ which has a translation in T_n, and given a proof for it in $T_1^{(n)}$, we can find a proof in T_n for its translation in T_n.

From the results (I), (II), and (III), we see that for purposes of questions concerned with the consistency of T_n, we may consider $T_1^{(n)}$ instead which is simpler in that it contains only one kind of variables. However, $T_1^{(n)}$ is more complicated than T_n in that it contains new predicates $S_1, S_2, \cdots, S_n$. In many cases, given a system T_n, we can find a corresponding system which contains only one kind of variables and no new predicates, and which can serve the same purposes both for the study of consistency questions and for the development of theory. Whether we can find such a corresponding system depends on whether we can express membership in the different categories by the following means: general variables (whose range of value is the sum of all the special domains), the quantifiers and truth-functional connectives, the brackets, plus the predicate letters of the given many-sorted theory reconstrued as having their argument places filled up by general variables. It seems that in most cases we can.

Of the theorems (I)—(IV), (III) is obvious. Moreover, (II) is a direct consequence of (I). Thus, obviously there exists a statement ϕ of $T_1^{(n)}$ such that both ϕ and $\sim\phi$ are translatable into T_n. Assume that $T_1^{(n)}$ is inconsistent. Then every statement in $T_1^{(n)}$ is provable, and therefore ϕ and $\sim\phi$ are both provable in $T_1^{(n)}$. Hence, by (I), their translations ψ and $\sim\psi$ according to RT are both provable in T_n, Hence, T_n is inconsistent.

In this chapter, we shall first indicate that in L_n we can easily prove counterparts of theorems in L_1 and that about L_n we can prove counterparts of the metamathematical theorems of completeness, etc. about L_1. We shall then show that from these the theorem (I) (and therewith the theorem (II)) follows. We shall also show that, conversely, given (I) and the metamathematical theorems about L_1, we can prove certain similar theorems about L_n as corollaries.

The theorem (IV) of course implies (I). A proof of (IV) will depend on syntactical considerations about the structure of proofs in the systems compared. In his Thesis (p. 64), Herbrand first stated such a theorem. But his proof is inadequate, failing to take into account that there are certain reasonings which can be carried out in $L_1^{(n)}$ but not in L_n. A. Schmidt pointed this out and gave a detailed proof of the theorem in *Math. Annalen*, **115** (1938), 485—506. This proof seems to contain some difficulties. Afterwards he gave an improved and simplified treatment in *Math. Annalen*, **123** (1951), 187—200. An alternative treatment was given by the writer in *J. Symbolic Logic*, **17** (1952), 105—116. This paper was completed and submitted for publication before the appearance of Schmidt's 1951 paper, and therefore failed to take it into account. The proof, however, seems to be more direct than even Schmidt's simplified proof. The remainder of this chapter will reproduce the major parts of the writer's paper.

All these proofs are subject to the restriction mentioned above, viz.,

1.1. In each argument place of the primitive predicates of the many-sorted theories may occur only variables of one given sort.

Recently, P. C. Gilmore extended the proof to apply to cases where the above restriction is waived. (See *Composito Mathematica*, 1958.) Thus, for example, in the theory of types it is no longer necessary to use different predicates for the membership relation. T. Hailperin has recently considered questions relevant to many-sorted logics in *J. Symbolic Logic*, **22** (1957), 19—35 and 113—129.

A useful lemma will be inserted here from *J. Symbolic Logic*, **15** (1950), 110—112.

1.2. We can prove as metatheorems in $L_1^{(n)}$ the translations of 1_n—5_n for each kind of variable in $L_1^{(n)}$.

For this purpose we may use results from Quine's *ML*, as well as the additional axiom 1_6.

If we are not concerned with actually exhibiting the proofs, 1.2 can be proved by a modelling argument. Let A be any formula provable in the predicate calculus. By the consistency of the predicate calculus, A is valid in any nonempty domain D. Now let $S_1, \cdots, S_n$ be any subsets of D and A' be the formula which is obtained from A by restricting the range of variables to be $S_1, \cdots, S_n$ in a suitable manner as in $L_1^{(n)}$. If B is the conjunction of the axioms in 6_1, then, since D is arbitrary, $B \supset A'$ is also valid. Hence, by the completeness of the predicate calculus, $B \supset A'$ is provable in L_1, and A' is therefore provable in $L_1^{(n)}$. For example, if A is $\sim(x)\,(Cx \& \sim Cx)$, and A' is $\sim(x)\,(S_1 x \supset (Cx \& \sim Cx))$, then A' is provable in $L_1^{(n)}$ with the help of $(Ex)\, S_1(x)$.

To give an effective (indeed, primitive recursive) method of transforming a proof of A in L_n to one of A' in $L_1^{(n)}$, we indicate how translations of 1_n—5_n are to be proved in $L_1^{(n)}$.

This is obvious for 1_n, since each proper part beginning with quantifiers is taken as a unit, and the translation does not affect the character of being a tautology. When there are free variables, we merely add conditions $S_1(x)$, etc. as antecedent which of course preserves tautologies. The cases of 3_n and 5_n are similar.

To prove the translation of 2_n, it is only necessary to observe that, e.g.,

$$(x)\,((S_1x \supset Ax) \supset (S_1x \supset Bx)) \text{ is equivalent to } (x)\,(S_1x \supset (Ax \supset Bx)).$$

The translation of 4_n can be proved with the help of 6_1.

§ 2. The Many-sorted Elementary Logics L_n

Theorems in and about L_n can be proved in a similar manner as those in and about L_1. For example, we can get prenex normal forms, Skolem normal forms, the deduction theorem, etc.

Likewise we can define valid and satisfiable formulas of L_n just as those of L_1:

2.1. A value assignment for a predicate or its corresponding atomic formula $Fx_{n_1}^{(k_1)} \cdots x_{n_j}^{(k_j)}$ of L_n over a set of n non-empty domains is a function from the predicate or its corresponding atomic formula to a j-adic relation whose i-th place takes the individuals of the n_i-th domain.

2.2. A formula ϕ of L_n with no free variables is valid in a particular set of n non-empty domains if all value assignments for all the atomic formulas occurring in ϕ are such that, under the normal interpretation of the truth-functional connectives and quantifiers, ϕ becomes true. ϕ is valid if it is valid in all sets of n non-empty domains.

2.3. ϕ is satisfiable in a particular set of n non-empty domains if $\sim\phi$ is not valid in it. ϕ is satisfiable if it is satisfiable in some set of n non-empty domains.

With these definitions we can prove the following theorems for L_n just as for L_1:

2.4. If $\vdash\phi$ in L_n, then the closure of ϕ is valid.

2.5. If the closure of ϕ is valid in a set of n denumerable domains, then $\vdash\phi$ in L_n.

2.6. If the closure of ϕ is valid, then $\vdash\phi$ in L_n.

2.7. If $\phi_1, \phi_2, \cdots$ are statements of L_n and the system T_n obtained from L_n by adding $\phi_1, \phi_2, \cdots$ as proper axioms is consistent, then

$\phi_1, \phi_2, \cdots$ are simultaneously satisfiable in a set of n denumerable domains.

We merely outline a proof for the following theorem 2.8 from which 2.5 follows immediately.

2.8. If the statement $\sim\phi$ is not provable in L_n, then ϕ is satisfiable in a set of n denumerable domains.

Suppose that the variables of the p-th kind $(p=1, \cdots, n)$ in L_n are $v_p^{(1)}, v_p^{(2)}, \cdots$ and ϕ is the statement $(v_{n_1}^{(k_1)}) \cdots (v_{n_t}^{(k_t)}) (\mathsf{E}v_{m_1}^{(j_1)}) \cdots (\mathsf{E}v_{m_s}^{(j_s)})\ \psi(v_{n_1}^{(k_1)}, \cdots, v_{n_t}^{(k_t)}; v_{m_1}^{(j_1)}, \cdots, v_{m_s}^{(j_s)})$. Let $\psi_i\ (i = 1, 2, \cdots)$ be $\psi(v_{n_1}^{\tau(i,1)}, \cdots, v_{n_t}^{\tau(i,t)}; v_{m_1}^{\sigma(i,1)}, \cdots, v_{m_s}^{\sigma(i,s)})$, where $(\tau(i,1), \cdots, \tau(i,t))$ is the i-th term of the sequence of all the t-tuples of positive integers ordered according to the sum of the t integers and, for those with the same sum, lexicographically; and the sequence of the s-tuples $(\sigma(i, 1), \cdots, \sigma(i,s))$ $(i=1, 2, \cdots)$ is such that, if among $m_1, \cdots, m_s$, m_{r_1} is identical with $m_{r_2}, \cdots, m_{r_q}$ and with no others, then $\sigma(1, r_1), \cdots, \sigma(1, r_q), \sigma(2, r_1), \cdots, \sigma(2,r_q), \sigma(3, r_1), \cdots$ coincide with $1, \cdots, q, (q+1), \cdots, 2q, (2q+1), \cdots$.

In order to prove 2.8, we observe first that we can prove just as in the case of L_1 the following two propositions.

2.8.1. If $\sim\phi$ is not provable in L_n, then none of $\sim\psi_1, \sim\psi_1 \vee \sim\psi_2, \cdots$ is a tautology.

2.8.2. If none of $\sim\psi_1, \sim\psi_1 \vee \sim\psi_2, \cdots$ is a tautology, then $\psi_1, \psi_2, \cdots$ are simultaneously satisfiable.

Therefore, by correlating each variable $v_j^{(k)}$ in $\psi_1, \psi_2, \cdots$ with the j-th power of the k-th prime number, we can, similarly as in the case of L_1, provide a true interpretation for ϕ in the set of the domains $D_1, D_2, \cdots$ such that D_j is the set of the j-th powers of all the prime numbers. Hence, 2.8 and 2.5 can be proved.

We note in passing that we can also avoid the complications regarding the definitions of $\psi_1, \psi_2, \cdots$ and prove 2.8 more simply by treating, for any i, j, k, $v_i^{(k)}$ and $v_j^{(k)}$ as the same in our considerations. Then we can use almost completely the arguments for L_1 to give a true interpretation for ϕ in a set of n identical domains, each being the set of positive integers.

Since in many cases we want the different categories (e.g., points, lines, and planes, etc.) to be mutually exclusive, we might think that in such cases there should be no satisfying assignments with all the domains identical. However, the possibility just indicated shows that this is not the case. Indeed, it becomes clear that there is no means to express in L_n explicitly the requirement that the domains of any satisfying assignment for ϕ must be different. Such a requirement is merely one of the implicitly understood conditions which we want a normal interpretation of the theory to fulfill. But there is nothing in the definitions of the satisfying assignments of values to preclude cases where such informal conditions are not fulfilled. In a one-sorted theory we can add axioms such as $\sim(\mathrm{E}x)\,(S_i(x)\,.\,\,S_j(x))$ to make the demand explicit, because in the value assignments we insist that the truth-functional and quantificational operators retain their normal interpretations.

§ 3. The Theorem (I) and the Completeness of L_n

From the completeness of L_n, we can derive the theorem (I) stated in section 1.

Let us consider a statement ϕ in T_n and its translation ϕ' in $T_1^{(n)}$. Suppose that the variables in ϕ are all among the m_1-th, $\cdots$, and the m_k-th kinds. If A is a value assignment for $\sim\phi$ in a set D of domains, then there is an associated assignment A' for $\sim\phi'$ in the sum D' of all the domains of the set D, such that $(\mathrm{E}x)S_{m_1}\,.\cdots.\,(\mathrm{E}x)\,S_{m_k}(x)$ receives the value truth and that all the other predicate letters in $\sim\phi'$ receive, for those entities of D' which belong to the proper domains of D, the same values as within A and, for all the other entities of D', receive (say) the value falsehood. Conversely, given an assignment A' for $\sim\phi'$ in a domain D' such that $(\mathrm{E}x)S_{m_1}(x)\,.\cdots.\,(\mathrm{E}x)\,S_{m_k}(x)$ receives the value truth, there is an associated A for $\sim\phi$ such that the m_i-th ($i=1, \cdots, k$) domain consists of the things x such that $S_{m_i}(x)$ receives the value truth in A' and all the predicate letters of $\sim\phi$ receive the same values as in A'. Obviously in either case, A satisfies $\sim\phi$ if and only if A' satisfies $\sim\phi'$. Hence, we have: $\sim\phi$ is satisfiable if and only if $(\mathrm{E}x)\,S_{m_1}(x)\,.\,\cdots\,.\,(\mathrm{E}x)\,S_{m_k}(x)\,.\sim\phi'$ is. Therefore, we have:

3.1. ϕ is valid if and only if $(\mathrm{E}x)S_{m_1}(x)\,.\cdots.\,(\mathrm{E}x)S_{m_k}(x)\,.\supset\phi'$ is.

Therefore, we can prove:

3.2. ϕ is provable in L_n if and only if ϕ' is provable in $L_1^{(n)}$.

Proof. If ϕ is provable in L_n, then, by 2.4, it is valid. Hence, by 3.1, $(\mathrm{E}x)S_{m_1}(x)\,.\cdots.\,(\mathrm{E}x)S_{m_k}(x)\,.\supset\phi'$ is valid and therefore, by the completeness of L_1, provable in L_1. Hence, by 6_1, ϕ' is provable in $L_1^{(n)}$.

Conversely, if ϕ' is provable in $L_1^{(n)}$, we can assume that all the (finitely many) cases of 6_1 used in the proof for ϕ' in $L_1^{(n)}$ are among $(\mathrm{E}x)S_{m_1}(x), \cdots, (\mathrm{E}x)S_{m_k}(x)$, for we can so choose $m_1, \cdots, m_k$. Therefore, by the deduction theorem for L_1, $(\text{E}x)S_{m_1}(x).\cdots.(\text{E}x)S_{m_k}(x). \supset \phi'$ is provable in L_1 and therefore valid. Hence, by 3.1, ϕ is valid and, by 2.6, provable in L_n.

From 3.2, the theorem (I) follows immediately by the deduction theorems for L_1 and L_n. Conversely, given (I) we can also derive 3.2. Moreover, as noted in section 1, the theorem (II) stated there is a corollary of (I). Now we prove that 2.6 and 2.7 can be inferred, with the help of (I), from their corresponding theorems for L_1.

Proof of 2.6. If ϕ is valid, then by 3.1, $(\text{E}x)S_{m_1}(x).\cdots.(\text{E}x) S_{m_k}(x). \supset \phi'$ is valid and therefore, by the completeness of L_1, provable in L_1. Hence, by 6_1, ϕ' is provable in $L_1^{(n)}$. Hence, by 3.2, ϕ is provable in L_n.

Proof of 2.7. Assume that the system T_n obtained from L_n by adding the statements $\phi_1, \phi_2, \cdots$ of L_n as proper axioms is consistent. By (II), the system $T_1^{(n)}$ corresponding to T_n is consistent. Hence, by the theorem for L_1 corresponding to the theorem 2.7 for L_n, all the axioms of $T_1^{(n)}$ are simultaneously satisfiable in a denumerable domain. But the axioms of $T_1^{(n)}$ are just those of L_1, the axioms $(\text{E}x)\, S_1(x), \cdots, (\text{E}x)\, S_n(x)$, and the translations $\phi_1', \phi_2', \cdots$ of $\phi_1, \phi_2, \cdots$. Hence we can divide the domain into n domains such that the i-th domain consists of all the individuals x such that $S_i(x)$ is true. In this way, we obtain a set of n non-empty domains each either finite or denumerable in which both $\phi_1, \phi_2, \cdots$ and the axioms of L_n are satisfiable (compare the arguments in the proof of 3.1). Consequently, we can find a set of n denumerable domains in which T_n is satisfiable. And the proof of 2.7 is completed.

§ 4. Proof of the Theorem (IV)

We may break up the theorem (IV) into two parts:

4.1. There is an effective process by which, given any proof in T_n for a statement ϕ of T_n, we can find a proof in $T_1^{(n)}$ for the translation ϕ' of ϕ in $T_1^{(n)}$.

4.2. There is an effective process by which, given any proof in $T_1^{(n)}$ for a statement ϕ' of $T_1^{(n)}$ which has a translation ϕ in T_n, we can find a proof in T_n for ϕ.

First, we prove 4.1. In the proof of ϕ, we employ only a finite number of the proper axioms of T_n. Let the conjunction of these axioms be Φ. By the deduction theorem, we have an effective process by which, given the proof of ϕ in T_n, we can find a proof of $\Phi \supset \phi$ in L_n. And if its translation $\Phi' \supset \phi'$ has a proof in $L_1^{(n)}$, then we have immediately a proof in $T_1^{(n)}$ for ϕ' by modus ponens and the proper axioms of $T_1^{(n)}$, because Φ' is the translation of the conjunction of certain proper axioms of T_n. Hence, we need only prove that there is an effective process by which, given a proof in L_n for a formula ψ of T_n, we can find a proof in $L_1^{(n)}$ for its translation ψ' in $T_1^{(n)}$.

By 1.2, we can prove as metatheorems in $L_1^{(n)}$ the translations of 1_n—5_n for each kind of variables in $L_1^{(n)}$. Since in each proof of L_n, we use only a finite number of special cases of 1_n—5_n, given any proof in L_n for a formula ψ of L_n, we have a proof for its translation ψ' in $L_1^{(n)}$ which consists of the proofs of the translations in $L_1^{(n)}$ of these special cases together with a translation in $L_1^{(n)}$ of the proof for ψ in L_n. Hence, 4.1 is proved.

The proof of 4.2 is more complex. We note that it is sufficient to prove the following theorem:

4.3. There is an effective process by which, given any proof in $L_1^{(n)}$ for a statement χ' of $T_1^{(n)}$ which has a translation χ in T_n, we can find a proof in L_n for χ.

Thus, let ϕ' be a statement of $T_1^{(n)}$ with a proof in $T_1^{(n)}$, then, by the deduction theorem for L_1, we have a proof for $\Phi' \supset \phi'$ in $L_1^{(n)}$, Φ' being the conjunction of the proper axioms of $T_1^{(n)}$ used in the given proof of ϕ'. Hence, by 4.3, we have a proof in L_n for the translation $\Phi \supset \phi$ of $\Phi' \supset \phi'$ in L_n, and thereby also a proof for ϕ in T_n.

Consequently, given 4.3, we can prove 4.2. We shall prove 4.3.

By hypothesis, a proof Δ' in $L_1^{(n)}$ is given for a statement χ' of $T_1^{(n)}$ which has a translation χ in T_n. Our problem is to find a proof Δ in L_n for the translation χ of χ' in T_n. In what follows, we shall assume that χ' has been given in such a form that its translation χ is in the prenex normal form. Accordingly, since for each variable α and each formula ψ of $T_1^{(n)}$ we can substitute $(\mathrm{E}\alpha)(S_i(\alpha) . \psi)$ for $\sim(\alpha)(S_i(\alpha) \supset \sim\psi)$, each quantification in χ' is either of the form $(\alpha)(S_i(\alpha) \supset \phi)$ or of the form $(\mathrm{E}\beta)(S_j(\beta) . \phi')$, where α and β are variables in $T_1^{(n)}$, ϕ and ϕ' are formulas in $T_1^{(n)}$, and i and j are among $1, \cdots, n$. Moreover, every formula $S_i(\alpha)$ occurs, if at all in χ', in one and only one context either of the form $(\alpha)(S_i(\alpha) \supset \phi)$ or of the form $(\mathrm{E}\alpha)(S_i(\alpha) . \phi)$; and every variable α occurs, if at all in χ', in one unique part either of the form $(\alpha)(S_i(\alpha) \supset \phi)$ or of the form $(\mathrm{E}\alpha)(S_i(\alpha) . \phi)$. Such an assumption as to the form of χ' does not restrict our result in any way, because we know that each statement of $T_1^{(n)}$ which has a translation in T_n can be converted into such a form by procedures analogous to those for transforming a statement into the prenex normal form.

Therefore, if we associate each occurrence of a variable α with the number i when there is a formula $(\alpha)(S_i(\alpha) \supset \phi)$ or a formula $(\mathrm{E}\alpha)$

$(S_i(\alpha) . \phi)$ occurring in χ', we see that each occurrence of a variable in χ' is associated with a unique number, and two occurrences of the same variable in χ' always have the same number.

Consider now the formula χ_1 obtained from χ' by dropping all parts of the forms $S_i(\alpha) \supset$ and $S_i(\alpha) .$, or, in other words, by replacing each quantification of the form $(\alpha)(S_i(\alpha) \supset \phi)$ by $(\alpha)\phi$, and each quantification of the form $(\mathrm{E}\alpha)(S_i(\alpha) . \phi)$ by $(\mathrm{E}\alpha)\phi$. We see that χ_1 no longer contains occurrences of atomic formulas of the form $S_i(\alpha)$, and that χ_1 is like the translation χ of χ' in T_n except for containing occurrences of variables (say) $x, y, \cdots, z$ which are associated with the numbers $i, j, \cdots, k$ where χ contains occurrences of $x_i, y_i, \cdots, z_k$. Moreover, χ_1 is also in the prenex normal form. From now on we understand that each occurrence of any variable in χ_1 is associated with the number which was given to its corresponding occurrence in χ'.

Let us say that an occurrence of a variable (in a proof of L_1) is associated with the proper number if its number is exactly the number for the kind of variable which is to fill up the place in question of the predicate of T_n that occurs with the variable. For example, an occurrence of α in a context $P\alpha\beta \cdots \gamma$ is said to be associated with the proper number, if α is associated with i and the first argument place of P is to be filled up by the i-th kind of variable in T_n. From this definition and the way numbers are associated with variable occurrences, we have, since χ' has a translation in T_n, the next theorem:

4.4. Each occurrence in χ_1 of any variable is associated with the proper number.

We prove another theorem:

4.5. Given the proof Δ' in $L_1^{(n)}$ for χ', we can actually write out a proof Δ_1 in L_1 for χ_1.

Proof. In Δ' each line is either a case of 1_1—4_1 or 6_1, or a consequence by 5_1 of two previous lines. Let us replace throughout Δ' all occurrences of all formulas of the form $S_i(\alpha)$ by those of formulas of the form $S_i(\alpha) \vee \sim S_i(\alpha)$. Then, in the result Δ'', each line which was a case of 6_1 becomes an easy consequence of 1_1—5_1. If we add the easily obtainable proofs for these cases of 6_1 at the top of Δ'', then we obtain a proof in L_1 for a conclusion χ'' which is like χ' except for containing occurrences of formulas of the form $S_i(\alpha) \vee \sim S_i(\alpha)$ instead of those of the form $S_i(\alpha)$. But, it is then easy to see that from a proof for χ'' in L_1, we can obtain a proof in L_1 for χ_1 by 1_1 and the principle of the substitutivity of biconditionals. Hence, we obtain a proof Δ_1 in L_1 for χ_1.

Now let us apply Herbrand's theorem which for our purpose can be stated thus:

HT. There is an effective method which, for any given proof of L_1 for a statement ψ in prenex normal form, yields a new proof II for ψ (ψ being therefore the last line of II) whose first line is a truth-functional tautology and each of whose other lines is obtained from its immediate predecessor by applying one of the following three rules: (1) Given a formula of L_1 which has the form of an alternation (disjunction), we can replace an alternation clause $\phi\beta$ by $(\mathrm{E}\alpha)\phi\alpha$ where α is an arbitrary variable; (2) Given a formula of L_1 which has the form of an alternation, we can replace an alternation clause $\phi\beta$ by $(\alpha)\phi\alpha$ where β is a variable not free in any other parts of the formula; (3) Given a formula of L_1 which has the form of an alternation, we can omit repetitions of an alternation clause.

It is easy to convince ourselves that the proof II for ψ as specified in HT is again a proof in L_1 or, more exactly, that from II (as given) we can easily construct a proof of L_1 with ψ as the last line. Let us refer to proofs for an arbitrary statement ψ which are of the kind as described in HT, as proofs of L_1 in the Herbrand normal form. Then the content of HT says simply that every proof of L_1 for a statement in the prenex normal form can be transformed into one in the Herbrand normal form.

By 4.5 and HT, since χ_1 is in the prenex normal form, we can actually find a proof II of L_1 for χ_1 in the Herbrand normal form. Suppose given such a proof II. Our problem is to construct from II a proof Δ of L_n with χ as its last line.

As was mentioned above, each occurrence in χ_1 of any variable is associated with a definite number, which is, moreover, according to 4.4, the proper number. Using these correlations, we can now associate every occurrence in II of any variable with a definite number in the following manner:

4.6. If the occurrence is in a line ϕ which is followed by a line ϕ', then it is associated with the same number as the corresponding occurrence of the same variable in ϕ' except for the following special cases:

4.6.1. If ϕ' is obtained from ϕ by substituting $(\alpha)\psi\alpha$ for an alternation clause $\psi\beta$ and the occurrence in ϕ is one of the variable β in the clause $\psi\beta$, then it is associated with the same number as the corresponding occurrence of the variable α in the part $\psi\alpha$ of ϕ'.

4.6.2. Similarly for the case with a particular quantification $(\mathrm{E}\alpha)\psi\alpha$ in ϕ'.

4.6.3. If ϕ' is obtained from ϕ by omitting repetitions of an alternation clause ϕ_1 and the occurrence in ϕ is in some occurrence of

ϕ_1, then it is associated with the same number as the corresponding occurrence in the alternation clause ϕ_1 of ϕ'.

Let us replace every occurrence in II of a variable associated with the number i by an occurrence of a corresponding variable of the i-th kind in T_n (for instance, if an occurrence of x is associated with i in II, replace it by an occurrence of x_i) and refer to the result as $\triangle_2$. We easily see that the last line of $\triangle_2$ is exactly χ, the translation of χ' in T_n. Moreover, by 1.1, each line of $\triangle_2$ is a formula of T_n which is either a truth-functional tautology or follows from its immediately preceding line by a quantificationally valid rule of inference (a rule of inference derivable in L_n). Therefore, from $\triangle_2$ we can easily construct a proof $\triangle$ of L_n for the conclusion χ.

This completes the proof of 4.3. Therefore, 4.2 and theorem (IV) (using 4.1) are all proved.

CHAPTER XIII

THE ARITHMETIZATION OF METAMATHEMATICS

§ 1. Gödel Numbering

In this chapter we shall briefly consider Gödel's reduction of metamathematics to number theory, together with a few applications: Gödel's two famous theorems, Kleene's normal form for recursive functions, Bernays' lemma as a sharpening of the completeness theorem of the predicate calculus, and Löb's theorem.

The trend of formalization has led to a stage where it is sometimes possible to describe, if not to understand, a formal system by talking about symbols and their combinations. There are certain primitive symbols such that it is possible, in theory, to decide effectively whether a given shape is one of the symbols. There are rules for combining these symbols to form meaningful expressions so that it can be decided effectively whether any combinations are terms or propositions and whether any given sequence of propositions is a proof. As a result, it is possible to represent the primitive symbols by certain numbers (say, the prime numbers) and combinations of them by other numbers, e. g. a proposition by the number $2^a\ 3^b \cdots$ such that a, b, etc. are the numbers of the symbols in the proposition. In this way, one can generally define primitive recursive functions and predicates which represent the properties and relations such as being a proposition, being a proof, etc.

To fix our attention, we consider the system Z of number theory mentioned in Chapter I, the underlying logic being the predicate calculus with equality L_e extended to include not only variables but also terms. For example, *103 of L_q also applies to the case $(x)F(x) \supset F(t)$, when t is an arbitrary term in the system.

If now the sequence of symbols or propositions $AB \cdots$ is represented by the number $2^a\ 3^b \cdots$, where a, b, etc. represent A, B, etc., then we can define the number of the n–th member of a sequence represented by the number x as the smallest y less than x such that x is divisible by the y–th power of the n–th prime but not by the $(y+1)$–th, and so on.

In this way, one can define a predicate $B(x, y)$ such that x represents a sequences of propositions in Z of which the last is represented by y, and that each proposition in the sequence is either an axiom or follows from previous propositions in the sequence by some rule of inference. In other words, $B(x, y)$ holds when x represents a proof of Z with its conclusion represented by y.

Suppose "0" is represented by 2, "=" by 3, the variable "i" by 5. Then "$i=0$" is represented by $2^5 3^3 5^2$ or 21600 which in Z is written as 0 followed by 21600 prime marks. Suppose for simplicity 21600 is actually a term in Z. If now we substitute "21600" for the variable "i" in the expression whose Gödel number is 21600, we then obtain "21600=0" which has again a Gödel number, say 3129578. Now, it is possible to define a primitive recursive function $s(x, y)$ such that $s(21600, 21600)=3129578$. In general, for any numerals $\bar{x}$ and $\bar{y}$, $s(\bar{x}, \bar{y})$ is supposed to give the Gödel number of the expression obtained from the expression whose number is $\bar{x}$ by substituting the numeral $\bar{y}$ for the variable "i". If "i" does not occur in the original expression, then $s(\bar{x}, \bar{y})=\bar{x}$.

Now it is possible to show (see §2 below):

1.1. Any numerical formula, i. e. one which contains equality and primitive recursive functions but no variables, free or bound, is provable in Z if and only if it is intuitively true.

Let us consider:

(1) $$(x) \sim B(x, s(i, i)).$$

This is an abbreviation of a formula consisting only of primitive symbols of Z. If we do not mind the trouble, we could actually write out the formula and compute its Gödel number. Assume we have found that $\bar{p}$ (a constant numeral, not a variable) is its number.

Since s is primitive recursive, there is a unique numeral $\bar{q}$ for which we can prove in Z:

(2) $$s(\bar{p}, \bar{p}) = \bar{q}.$$

But by the way s is defined, $\bar{q}$ is also the number of

(3) $$(x) \sim B(x, s(\bar{p}, \bar{p})).$$

(3′) $$(x) \sim B(x, \bar{q}).$$

By (2), we can prove in Z:

(4) $$(x) \sim B(x, s(\bar{p}, \bar{p})) \equiv (x) \sim B(x, \bar{q}).$$

We can also easily define a primitive recursive function n, such that $n(\bar{q})$ gives the number of the negation of the formula with number $\bar{q}$.

Using 1.1, we can prove about **Z** that for any given numerals $\bar{m}$ and $\bar{k}$, we can prove in Z:

(5) $$\sim B(\bar{m}, \bar{q}).$$

(6) $$\sim B(\bar{k}, n(\bar{q})).$$

This does not mean that we can prove $(m)(k)(\sim B(m, \bar{q})\ \&\ \sim B(k, \bar{q}))$. Indeed, it will follow from Gödel's second theorem that this last is not provable in Z.

Assume we can prove in **Z**:

(7) $$B(\bar{m}, \bar{q}).$$

Then $\bar{m}$ is the number of a proof of (3). Hence, by (4) and Lq 4, i.e. *103, we can extend the proof to get a proof of (3′) and thence one of (5), i.e., we can from the given $\bar{m}$ actually write out a proof for (5). Since we assume Z to be consistent, we cannot prove both (5) and (7) in **Z**. Hence (7) is not provable, and, by 1.1, (5) is provable in Z.

Now assume we can prove in **Z**:

(8) $$B(\bar{k}, n(\bar{q})).$$

Since $\bar{q}$ is the number of (3), $n(\bar{q})$ is the number of the negation of (3). If we can prove (8), then it is true, and we can actually, from $\bar{k}$, write out a proof for the negation of (3). Hence, by (4), we can write out a proof of

(9) $$\sim (x) \sim B(x, \bar{q}).$$

Since we have proved above that (5) is provable for every $\bar{m}$, this would mean a situation where we can prove for some F, both all of $F(0)$, $F(1)$, $\cdots$ and also $\sim(x)\ F(x)$. This is intuitively unsatisfactory and cannot happen if we assume that Z is ω–consistent, i.e. for no F can it be that $(Ex)\sim F(x)$ or $\sim(x)F(x)$ is provable yet all cases $F(0)$, $F(1)$, $\cdots$ are also provable. This requirement seems reasonable since we feel that if $F(0)$, $F(1)$, $\cdots$ are all provable and, therefore, true, $(x)F(x)$ must also be true even if it may happen to be unprovable. Of course, ω–consistency implies consistency.

Hence, (9) is not provable, and, therefore, (8) is not. Hence, if Z is ω–consistent, then all cases of (5) and (6) are provable in Z. In the above argument, we have incidentally also proved that neither

(3′) nor its negation (9) is provable in Z. Hence, (3) is undecidable in Z. It follows that (1) is also undecidable in Z.

It also follows that if we add (9) to Z, we can get a consistent but ω-inconsistent system, assuming the consistency of Z.

This completes the proof of Gödel's first theorem.

Rosser has introduced a trick which enables one to dispense with the stronger hypothesis of ω-consistency.

Instead of (1), Rosser uses:

$$(10) \quad (x)(B(x, s(i, i)) \supset (Ey)(y \leqslant x \ \& \ B(y, n(s(i, i))))).$$

Let $\bar{p}$ be the number of the above formula, and $\bar{q}$ be the number of

$$(11) \quad (x)(B(x, s(\bar{p}, \bar{p})) \supset (Ey)(y \leqslant x \ \& \ B(y, n(s(\bar{p}, \bar{p}))))).$$

$$(11') \quad (x)(B(x, \bar{q}) \supset (Ey)(y \leqslant x \ \& \ B(y, n(\bar{q})))).$$

Then (2) holds and therefore

$$(12) \qquad (11) \equiv (11').$$

We want to show again that all cases of (5) and (6) are provable in Z.

Assume again we can prove (7). Then we can again prove (11) and (11′). Using (7) again, we can prove:

$$(13) \qquad (Ey)(y \leqslant \bar{m} \ \& \ B(y, n(\bar{q}))).$$

Since the quantifier is restricted by a numeral, (13) is equivalent to a numerical formula. It follows that from (13) we can infer that (8) must be provable for some $\bar{k}$, $\bar{k} \leqslant \bar{m}$. This would make the negation of (11′) provable. Hence, if Z is consistent, (11′) is not provable, and all cases of (5) are provable.

Now assume (8) is provable for some $\bar{k}$. Hence the negation of (11) and (11′) is provable. It follows that the following is porvable in Z:

$$(14) \quad (Ex)(B(x, \bar{q}) \ \& \ \sim (Ey)(y \leqslant x \ \& \ B(y, n(\bar{q})))).$$

But, from (14) we can infer:

$$(15) \qquad (Ex)(x \leqslant \bar{k} \ \& \ B(x, \bar{q})).$$

Then, however, we can prove (7) for some $\bar{m}$, $\bar{m} \leqslant \bar{k}$. This directly contradicts our conclusion about (5). Hence, if Z is consistent, (14) is not provable in Z and all cases of (6) are provable in Z. Therefore, if Z is consistent, neither (14) nor (11′) is provable in Z.

This completes the proof of Rosser's extension of Gödel's first theorem.

The consistency of Z can be expressed in Z by the proposition:

$$(16) \qquad (Ex)B(x, \underset{\sim}{k}) \supset (Ex)B(x, n(\underset{\sim}{k})).$$

Briefly: $Con(Z)$:

Gödel's second theorem says:

Theorem 1. *If Z is consistent, then Con(Z) is not a theorem of Z.*

Intuitively it is highly plausible that this follows from the first theorem. Thus, in the above arguments we have argued that if Z is consistent then (3) is not provable in Z. If we formalize this statement in metamathematics, then it is:

$$(17) \qquad Con(Z) \supset (x) \sim B(x, \bar{q}).$$

Hence, if we can formalize the argument in Z, we can prove (17) in Z. Then since $(x){\sim}B(x, \bar{q})$ is not provable if Z is consistent, it follows that $Con(Z)$ is not provable if Z is consistent.

To actually carry out this matter is not easy. The only place where this is done seems to be Hilbert-Bernays II. For example, Löb's theorem is proved with the help of this work.

In his book *Introduction to Metamathematics* (p. 211), Kleene suggests to use $(x){\sim}B(x, \bar{q})$ as the statement expressing the consistency of Z, and dispense with the exercise of formalizing. This suggestion does not seem to be justified. It is indeed obvious that this implies $Con(Z)$ and the implication can be quickly proved in Z. But it is not obvious that the intuitive argument for proving (17) can be formalized in Z. It is possible that a statement, though intuitively equivalent to $(x){\sim}B(x, \bar{q})$, is provable in Z and the intuitive equivalence cannot be formalized in Z. For example, in Gentzen's or Ackermann's consistency proof for Z, the hypotheses of transfinite induction can be proved in Z, but the transfinite induction, which one may reasonably claim to be intuitively no less evident than the argument for proving (17), cannot be formalized in Z, and this fact alone prevents one from proving $Con(Z)$ in Z.

Hence, it would seem necessary that we understand $Con(Z)$ as a formula which gives a direct formalization of the original definition of consistency or a close equivalent. If one does not do this, then there can be a great deal of room for ambiguous interpretations of statements on the consistency question as has been stressed by Kreisel, Koninklijke Nederlandse Akad. Wet., *Proc.*, **56** (1953), 405—406.

In Hilbert-Bernays II the following three results are proved in detail:

1.2. If a formula with number $\bar{m}$ is derivable in Z from a formula with number $\bar{q}$, then we can prove in Z:

$$(Ex)B(x, \bar{q}) \supset (Ex)B(x, \bar{m}).$$

1.3. We can prove in Z:

$$(Ex)B(x, n(y)) \supset (Ex)B(x, n(s(y, z))).$$

1.4. If $f(y)$ is any given primitive recursive function of one argument and $\bar{k}$ is the number of the formula $f(i)=0$, then we can prove in Z:

$$f(y) = 0 \supset (Ex)B(x, s(\bar{k}, y)).$$

With the help of 1.2—1.4, Gödel's second theorem is proved as follows. As before, let $\bar{p}$ be the number of (1), $\bar{q}$ be that of (3). Then (2) and (4) again are provable in Z. Let $\bar{k}$ and $\bar{m}$ be the numbers of:

(18) $$B(i, \bar{q}),$$

(19) $$\sim B(i, \bar{q}).$$

Hence, by 1.2, we can prove in Z:

(20) $$(Ex)B(x, \bar{q}) \supset (Ex)B(x, \bar{m}).$$

But we can prove in Z:

$$n(\bar{k}) \mathrel{\dot{=}} \bar{m}.$$

Hence, by 1.3, we can prove in Z:

(21) $$B(y, \bar{q}) \supset (Ex)B(x, n(s(\bar{k}, y))).$$

But by 1.4, we can prove in Z:

(22) $$B(y, \bar{q}) \supset (Ex)B(x, s(\bar{k}, y)).$$

Now if we could prove (16) in Z, we would have, by (21) and (22), as a theorem of Z:

$$\sim B(y, \bar{q})$$

and

$$(x) \sim B(x, \bar{q}).$$

This contradicts the proof of the first theorem.

Hence, (16) or $Con(Z)$ is not provable in Z.

It has often been asked whether Gödel's proofs can be formalized in some suitable formal systems. The above proof incidentally gives a formalization of a part of the proof of the first Gödel theorem in the system Z itself.

Incidentally, since it is an easy matter to formalize in Z a proof of the converse of (17), it follows that the following is a theorem of Z:

(i) $$Con(Z) \equiv (3').$$

On the other hand, if we take (3″) as $(x){\sim}B(x, n(\bar{q}))$, then

(ii) $$Con(Z) \supset (3'')$$

is no longer a theorem of Z because otherwise we would get a proof of $Con(Z')$ in Z', where Z' is obtained from Z by adding $Con(Z)$ as a new axiom. Thus, if $\bar{t}$ is the number of ${\sim}Con(Z)$, then, by (i) and 1.2, we can prove in Z: $(Ex)B(x, \bar{t}) \supset (Ex)\, B(x, n(\bar{q}))$. Hence, we can also prove in Z: $(3'') \supset (x){\sim}B(x, \bar{t})$. If we assume (ii), we would have $(x){\sim}B(x, \bar{t})$ as a theorem of Z' from which we can easily get $Con(Z')$.

On the other hand, for Rosser's proof, it is possible to prove in Z, both $Con(Z) \supset (11')$ and $Con(Z) \supset (11'')$. It follows that one cannot prove in Z: $Con(Z) \equiv (11')$.

As Shen Yuting observes (*J. Symbolic Logic*, **20**, 119), in ordinary language, the following statement gives a paradox:

(23) What I am saying cannot be proved.

Thus if this can be proved, it must be true, i.e., in its own words, it cannot be proved. Therefore, this statement cannot be proved, since supposing otherwise has led to a contradiction. In other words, the statement is true. In this way we have proved the statement.

The difference with Gödel's argument is the fact that within a formal system such as Z, it may happen that a statement (3′) answering to (23) is true but unprovable. Hence, instead of a contradiction, we get the incompleteness.

Now if we say instead:

(24) What I am saying can be proved,

then there is of course no paradox.

It only has the peculiar property that if it is true then it is provable. Now, according to Gödel's theorem, not every statement in a formal system has this property relative to the proving method of the system. In the system Z, such a statement would become:

$$(25) \qquad (Ex)B(x, s(\bar{p}, \bar{p})),$$

where $\bar{p}$ is the number of $(Ex)B(x, s(i, i))$.

Löb proves the following theorem (*J. Symbolic Logic*, **20**, 115—118).

Theorem 2. *The statement* (25) *is a theorem of* Z; *in general, for every statement* A *with Gödel number* $\bar{k}$, *if* $(Ex)B(x, \bar{k}) \supset A$ *is a theorem in* Z, *so is* A.

It may be noted that there are by this theorem, of course also statements A with number $\bar{k}$, such that $(Ex)B(x, \bar{k}) \supset A$ is not a theorem of Z, e.g. the statement (1) above. Another example not depending on this theorem is $0=1$ as A; otherwise, since $0 \neq 1$ is a theorem of Z, $Con(Z)$ would be one also.

Löb's proof uses 1.2 and the following:

1.5. For any $\bar{k}$, if $\bar{m}$ is the number of $(Ex)B(x, \bar{k})$, then the following is a theorem of Z:

$$(Ex)B(x, \bar{k}) \supset (Ex)B(x, \bar{m}).$$

1.6. If A is provable in Z and has number $\bar{k}$, $(Ex)B(x, \bar{k})$ is provable in Z.

1.6 is obvious. He derives 1.5 from 1.3 and 1.4. Then the proof goes as follows. Let A be a given formula having the required property, and $\bar{p}$ be the number of

$$(26) \qquad (Ex)B(x, s(i, i)) \supset A.$$

and $\bar{q} = s(\bar{p}, \bar{p})$ be the number of

$$(27) \qquad (Ex)B(x, s(\bar{p}, \bar{p})) \supset A,$$

which is equivalent to

$$(28) \qquad (Ex)B(x, \bar{q}) \supset A.$$

If $\bar{t}$ is the number of $(Ex)B(x, \bar{q})$, then, by 1.2, we can prove in Z:

(29) $((Ex)B(x, \bar{t})\ \&\ (Ex)B(x, \bar{q})) \supset (Ex)B(x, \bar{k})$.

But, by 1.5, $(Ex)B(x, \bar{q}) \supset (Ex)B(x, \bar{t})$. Hence, (29) reduces to

(30) $(Ex)B(x, \bar{q}) \supset (Ex)B(x, \bar{k})$.

Hence, by hypothesis, we can conclude that (28) is a theorem of Z. So is also (27). Therefore, $(Ex)B(x, \bar{q})$, by 1.6. Therefore, by (28), A is a theorem of Z. Theorem 2 is proved.

Now (28) says essentially:

(28) If (28) is provable then A.

In ordinary language, we may get a paradox this way. Assume (28) is provable. Then (28) is true and, since the hypothesis of (28) is assumed, then A. Hence, we have proved that if (28) is provable then A. That is to say, we have proved (28). Hence, we may conclude: A. This leads to the conclusion that every statement A is true and provable. On the other hand, when provability is construed relative to Z, we arrive at the different situation in the above proof, which may be recapitulated thus.

(31) If (31) is provable in Z, then A.

We can not prove (31) in Z for arbitrary A, unless Z were inconsistent. As it is, we can only prove in Z:

(32) If (31) is provable in Z, then A is provable in Z.

Hence, in order to arrive at A, we need the additional hypothesis that the following is provable in Z:

(33) If A is provable in Z, then A.

But this is the case only for suitable A.

§ 2. Recursive Functions and the System Z

So far we have not given a proof of 1.1. This follows from a stronger result of Gödel on the elimination of primitive recursive functions in Z, carried out in some detail in Hilbert-Bernays I, pp. 412—421. It is a little easier to prove 1.1 than the stronger result. Since the basic ideas are the same and since we are not going to give much details, we give the stronger result and indicate roughly how it has been proved.

2.1. A primitive recursive function is any function definable from 0, the successor function, and the variables by substitutions and primitive recursions, i.e. given g, h define f by: $f(0, x) = g(x)$, $f(y', x) = h(y, f(y, x), x)$.

A predicate F is represented by a function f if $f(x) = 0 \equiv F(x)$, and $f(x) = 1 \equiv \sim F(x)$, for all x. A different definition, not usually used, would be to require only that for all x, $f(x) = 0 \equiv F(x)$.

A predicate is primitive recursive if its representing function is primitive recursive.

2.2. If $A(x)$ and $B(y)$ are primitive recursive, so are $\sim A(x)$, $A(x)$ & $B(y)$, etc.

Thus, if a, b represent A, B, then let $c(0) = 1$, $c(x') = 0$; $d(0, y) = 1$, $d(x', y) = c(y)$. $\sim A(x)$ is represented by $c(a(x))$, $A(x)$ & $B(y)$ by $d(c(a(x)), c(b(y)))$.

2.3. If $f(x)$ and $g(y)$ are primitive recursive, so are $f(x) < g(y)$, $f(x) = g(y)$.

2.4. If $R(x, y)$ and $f(z)$ are primitive recursive, so are $(Ex)(x < f(z)$ & $R(x, y))$, and $\mu x(x < f(z)$ & $R(x, y))$.

If $a(x, y)$ represents R, then, e.g., the first predicate in 2.4 is represented by b: $b(0, y) = a(0, y)$, $b(z', y) = a(z'y) \cdot b(z, y)$.

The theorem of Gödel's is:

Theorem 3. *If g, h can be represented in Z, then a function f defined by primitive recursion as in 2.1 can be represented in Z in the sense that there is a formula R(x, y, z) in Z such that the following are theorems of Z:*

$$(Rxyz \;\&\; Rxyw) \supset z = w,\; R(0, x, g(x)),\; R(y', x, h(y, \mu_z R(y, x, z), x)).$$

Take a simple case when $f(0)$ is a constant a, $f(x') = g(x, f(x))$. As von Neumann first observed, we can think of the finite sequences $f(0), \cdots, f(n)$, for every n and represent them by integers, e.g.:

$$2^{f(0)} \cdots p_{n+1}^{f(n)},$$

and take the primitive recursive function $h(m, k)$ which gives the k-th term of the sequence represented by m. Then the required function f can be defined explicitly:

$$(1) \quad f(n) = \mu_y (Ex)(h(x, n) = y \;\&\; h(x, 0) = a \;\&\; (z)(z < n \supset \supset h(x, z') = g(z, h(x, z)))).$$

Hence, it follows that the function h is available in Z, then the theorem can be proved.

What Gödel did was to show by an additional argument that we can achieve something similar with merely addition and multiplication as the originally given primitive recursive functions, as is the case in Z. He uses the following lemma (for detailed proof of this, see M. Davis, *Computability and Solvability*, 1958, p. 45):

2.5. For any finite sequence $a_0, \cdots, a_n$, there are integers p and q such that, for all $k=0, \cdots, n$, $p \equiv a_k (\text{mod } k'q+1)$.

From this, we can use p to represent the given sequence, and $h(x, k)$ can be defined as the remainder of dividing p by $k'q+1$, and we can again define f explicitly by (1).

In order to prove this can be correctly done in Z, it is necessary to prove in Z:

$$(Ex)(Ey)(Eu)(x = uy' + a \; \& \; (z)(z < n \supset (Ev)(Ew)(Et) \cdot$$
$$\cdot (x = v(z'y+1) + t \; \& \; x = w(z''y+1) + g(z, t)))).$$

Such a proof is given in Hilbert-Bernays I, p. 416 ff.

Once Theorem 3 is given, it is relatively easy to prove 1.1, since the steps for evaluating each numerical formula from the recursive definitions can easily be performed in Z.

Another famous application of the method of Gödel numbering is Kleene's normal form for recursive functions. Since the form of equations defining a recursive function and the rules of derivation can easily be represented by primitive recursive methods, Kleene is able to define a primitive recursive predicate T such that $T(\bar{x}, \bar{y}, \bar{z})$ holds if $\bar{x}$ is the number of the definition for a function f, and $\bar{z}$ is the number of the earliest derived equation of the form $f(\bar{y}) = \bar{k}$, $\bar{k}$ some numeral. He also defines a primitive recursive function U such that $U(\bar{z})$ is $\bar{k}$ if $\bar{z}$ is the number of an equation of the above form. Hence, we get (see Kleene's book, p. 288 and p. 33):

Theorem 4. *If f is general recursive, then there is some number e, such that $f(x) = U(\mu_y T(e, x, y))$; a similar theorem holds for partial recursive functions.*

Another application of the Gödel numbering is to give a "truth definition" of Z (see Hilbert-Bernays II, pp. 330—340). Thus, since addition and multiplication are the only initially given functions in Z, it is easy to characterize the set of numerical formulae in Z which are true. We can represent the transformation of any formula into the prenex normal form, and then we can define $(x)F(x)$ as true when $F(0)$, $F(1)$, $\cdots$ all are true. Similarly with $(Ex)F(x)$. In this way, we can define inductively a relation $M(n, k)$ such that $M(n, 0)$ holds if n is the number of a true numerical formula, and $M(n, k')$ holds if n is, e.g., the number of $(x)F(x)$ and for all numbers j of the formulae $F(0)$, $F(1)$, etc., $M(j, k)$. Then a number n is one of a true formula if $(Ek)M(n, k)$.

The inductive definition of $M(n, k)$ is of the form:

$$(2) \qquad M(n, 0) \equiv A(n), \quad M(n, k') \equiv B(n, k).$$

Therein A is primitive recursive but B contains quantifiers. And it is a consequence of Gödel's theorems that there exists no predicate M in Z, for which we can prove in Z the above relation (2).

§ 3. Bernays' Lemma

According to the completeness of the predicate calculus, every system S, if consistent, has an arithmetic model or a "true" interpretation in the domain of natural numbers. As a consequence, if S is consistent, then there are true assertions about natural numbers which answer to all its axioms. Since, however, we know that the system S (for example, a strong set theory) can be much stronger than the ordinary number theory, the questions arise as to what those true counterparts of the axioms of S are like and whether they might be unprovable or even unexpressible in number theory. Bernays' lemma contains an answer to these questions.

To use a definite example, let us suppose that S is the original Zermelo set theory as refined by Skolem, and assume that an arithmetization for the syntax of S is given so that an arithmetic statement $Con(S)$ expresses the consistency of S. Then the lemma, when applied to S, is as follows. There is an arithmetic predicate expressible in the notation of ordinary number theory such that when it is substituted for the membership predicate in the axioms of S, the resulting assertions are all provable in the system obtained from ordinary number theory by adding $Con(S)$ as a new axiom. In proving this lemma, we extend slightly the construction in Hilbert-Bernays II, pp. 234—353. The material was originally included in *Methodos*, 1951, pp. 217—232.

Let Q be the ordinary predicate calculus as formulated in some standard way, e.g., as in L_q or L_k. Concerning such a system Q, it is generally known that we can associate with each statement A a Skolem consistency normal form C which is a statement of the form $(x_1) \cdots (x_r) (Ey_1) \cdots (Ey_s) B(x_1, \cdots, x_r; y_1, \cdots, y_s)$, where $r, s > 0$, and B contains no quantifiers in such a way that the following law holds.

3.1. There is an effective process by which, given any statement A of Q, we can find an associated C in Skolem consistency normal form such that $C \supset A$ is a theorem of Q, and that if $\sim C$ is a theorem of Q then $\sim A$ is also. Moreover, we can find a statement C' which is a result obtained from C by substituting suitable predicate-expressions for the predicate letters of C which are not also in A, such that $A \supset C'$ is a theorem of Q.

In order to prove the main theorem, we assume that the systems which we consider are all formulated within the framework of Q. Thus, each system which includes more than one kind of variable in its primitive notation is supposed to have been already translated with known methods into one with only one kind of variable.

Consider now any system S whose primitive notation includes only one kind of variable. There are in S, besides the connectives, the quantifiers, and the variables, symbols of some or all of the following kinds: predicates, functors, and individual constants. These symbols are usually written in definite forms and given special names according to the axioms of S: the membership predicate ϵ, the addition functor $+$, the number zero 0, etc. When we say that S is formulated in the general quantification theory Q, we mean that these special symbols are supposed to have been arbitrarily identified with certain symbols of the same kinds in Q so that the notation of S is contained in the notation of Q and all formulas of S are also formulas of Q.

We assume that S contains as a part its own quantification theory, viz. the part of Q in which only symbols belonging to S occur. To distinguish Q from such special quantification theories, we refer to Q as the general quantification theory. As it is known that theoretically function symbols and individual constants can be dispensed with by using predicates, we assume that neither Q nor S contains function symbols or individual constants in their primitive notations. Moreover, since all rules of inference of S either are special cases of those of Q or can be replaced by axiom schemata, it is sufficent to consider in what follows merely the axioms of S, assuming that the rules of inference beyond the quantification theory have all been replaced by axiom schemata.

Suppose now such a system S is given with its axioms $A_1, A_2, \cdots$ all expressed in the notation of Q. The following theorem can be proved.

3.2. If Q remains consistent after adding $A_1, A_2, \cdots$ as new axioms, then S has a true interpretation in the domain of natural numbers.

Let $C_1, C_2, \cdots$ be the Skolem consistency normal forms of $A_1, A_2, \cdots$ respectively. By hypothesis, for every n, $\sim A_1 \vee \cdots \vee \sim A_n$ is not provable in Q. Here we can assume that the new predicate letters, which have to be introduced in the formation of Skolem normal forms, are chosen separately for each C_i so that those new predicate letters which occur in C_j are all different from those occurring in $C_k(k \neq j)$. Let $C'_1, C'_2, \cdots$ be related to $C_1, C_2, \cdots$ as C' is to C in 3.1. If now $\sim C_1 \vee \cdots \vee \sim C_n$ were provable, then also $\sim C'_1 \vee \cdots \cdots \vee \sim C'_n$ would be provable. But, by 3.1, $\sim C'_i \supset \sim A_i$ is provable in $Q(i=1, \cdots, n)$, and also the statement $\sim C'_1 \vee \cdots \vee \sim C'_n \supset \sim A_1 \vee \cdots \vee \sim A_n$ is provable. So it would follow that $\sim A_1 \vee \cdots \vee \sim A_n$ were provable. Hence, $\sim C_1 \vee \cdots \vee \sim C_n$ is not provable in Q.

For every positive integer i, let $\bar{x}_i$ be an r_i–tuple of variables and $\bar{y}_i$ be an s_i–tuple of variables, where $r_1, s_1, r_2, s_2, \cdots$ form a sequence of positive integers. We may assume that for every positive integer i, C_i is $(\bar{x}_i)(E\bar{y}_i)\, B_i(\bar{x}_i; \bar{y}_i)$ or $(x_1)\cdots(x_{r_i})(Ey_1)\cdots(Ey_{s_i})\, B_i(x_1, \cdots, x_{r_i}; y_1, \cdots, y_{s_i})$. Let $x_0, x_1, x_2, \cdots$ be a sequence of distinct variables of Q. Let $\bar{x}^i_1, \bar{x}^i_2, \cdots$ be a sequence of r_i–tuples of variables drawn from the sequence $x_0, x_1, \cdots$ (with repetitions) and arranged in the order of the sum of the indices and, for those with the same sum, lexicographically. Let $\bar{y}^i_k$ be an s_i–tuple of variables drawn from the variables $x_0, x_1, \cdots$ such that $\bar{y}^1_1, \bar{y}^1_2, \bar{y}^2_1, \bar{y}^1_3, \bar{y}^2_2, \bar{y}^3_1, \bar{y}^1_4, \cdots$ coincide with $x_1, x_2, \cdots$: for example, $\bar{y}^1_1$ is $x_1, \cdots, x_{s_1}$; $\bar{y}^1_2$ is $x_{s_1+1}, \cdots, x_{2s_1}$; $\bar{y}^2_1$ is $x_{2s_1+1}, \cdots, x_{2s_1+s_2}$. Let D_1 be $B_1(\bar{x}^1_1; \bar{y}^1_1)$ and D_n be $(D_{n-1} \,\&\, B_1(\bar{x}^1_n; \bar{y}^1_n) \,\&\, B_2(\bar{x}^2_{n-1}; \bar{y}^2_{n-1}) \,\&\, \cdots \,\&\, B_{n-1}(\bar{x}^{n-1}_2; \bar{y}^{n-1}_2) \,\&\, B_n(\bar{x}^n_1; \bar{y}^n_1))$.

It is possible to prove by induction that for every n, the following is a theorem in Q: $(x_0)(\bar{y}^1_1) \cdots (\bar{y}^n_1) \sim D_n \supset \sim C_1 \vee \cdots \vee \sim C_n$. Therefore, since the consequent is not provable in Q, the antecedent is not provable either and $\sim D_n$ is not a tautology. Hence, for every k, D_k contains no quantifiers and is fulfillable (i. e., is such that we can so assign the truth-values truth and falsehood to the atomic formulas occurring in D_k that by the normal interpretation of truth functions, D_k receives the value truth). Moreover, if, for every k, F_k is the formula obtained from D_k by supplanting x_0 by 0, x_1 by 1, etc., then each F_k is again a fulfillable truth-functional formula.

Now we want to show that the truth-functional formulas $F_1, F_2, \cdots$ are simultaneously fulfillable. Let $P_1, P_2, \cdots$ be the atomic formulas occurring in $F_1, F_2, \cdots$ arranged in the order of their first appearances, and let t_i be the largest number t such that P_t occurs in $F_1, \cdots, F_i$. Hence, F_k contains t_k atomic formulas $P_1, \cdots, P_{t_k}$ and there are 2^{t_k} possible truth value assignments for F_k which we can represent by different numbers in the following manner. Let us represent the values truth and falsehood by the numbers 0 and 1, and represent the truth-value assignment which correlates $P_1, \cdots, P_{t_k}$ with $m_1, \cdots, m_{t_k}$ respectively by the number $2^{t_k-1} m_1 + \cdots + 2m_{t_k-1} + m_{t_k}$. In this way the 2^{t_k} possible truth-value assignments for F_k are represented by the numbers from 0 to 2^{t_k-1}. Let us refer to a truth-value assignment on the atomic formulas $P_1, \cdots, P_{t_k}$ for which F_k gets the value truth as a fulfilling assignment for F_k. Since every F_k is fulfillable, there is at least one (and at most 2^{t_k} different) fulfilling assignments for F_k. If $j>k$, then every fulfilling assignment for F_j contains as part a fulfilling assignment for F_k, because F_k is a part conjunction of F_j. Let us refer to this fulfilling assignment for F_k as the k-part of the fulfilling assignment for F_j.

If a fulfilling assignment for F_k is the k-part of a given fulfilling assignment for F_j and n is any number between k and j, then it is also the k-part of the fulfilling assignment for F_n which is the n-part of that given assignment for F_j. Therefore, for every k, there is at least one fulfilling assignment for F_k such that for every $n(n>k)$ it constitutes the k-part of a fulfilling assignment for F_n. Hence, for every k, we can select a unique assignment on $P_1, \cdots, P_{t_k}$ which is the fulfilling assignment for F_k with the smallest representing number such that, for every $n(n>k)$, it is the k-part of a fulfilling assignment for F_n.

Suppose given for each k the selected assignment for F_k. We can prove for these selected assignments that for any two numbers j and $n(j>n)$ the selected assignment for F_n is the n-part for that of F_j. This is so because, from the way we represent assignments by numbers, we can infer that if j_1, j_2 represent two assignments on $P_1, \cdots, P_{t_j}$ and n_1, n_2 represent the n-parts of them respectively, then $j_1>j_2$ when and only when $n_1>n_2$. Consequently, these selected assignments taken together provide an assignment on $P_1, P_2, \cdots$ fulfilling $F_1, F_2, \cdots$ simultaneously. Therefore, if we interpret each statement letter P as standing for a statement about natural numbers which is true or false according as in the above assignments P receives the value truth or falsehood, and interpret each predicate letter V with n arguments $(n>0)$ as standing for an n-placed predicate of number theory which is true of n given numbers $m_1, \cdots, m_n$ if $V(m_1, \cdots, m_n)$ occurs in some F_i and receives the value truth in the above assignments, and is false otherwise, then we have an interpretation in the domain of natural numbers for the predicates occurring in $F_1, F_2, \cdots$ under which $F_1, F_2, \cdots$ all become true.

But each F_k is a conjunction of terms of the form $B_n(\bar{m}_i^n; \bar{j}_i^n)$ which is obtained from $B_n(\bar{x}_i^n; \bar{y}_i^n)$ by supplanting 0 for x_0, 1 for x_1, etc. Therefore, the formulas $B_n(\bar{m}_i^n; \bar{j}_i^n)$ $(i, n=1, 2, \cdots)$ are all true under the given interpretation. Since for every $n(n=1, 2, \cdots)$, the r_n-tuples $\bar{m}_1^n, \bar{m}_2^n, \cdots$ exhaust all the r_n-tuples of natural numbers, C_n(viz. $(\bar{x}_n)(\exists\bar{y}_n)B_n(\bar{x}_n; \bar{y}_n)$) is true under the above interpretation in the domain of natural numbers. Consequently, by 3.1, $A_1, A_2, \cdots$ are all true under the interpretation. Hence 3.2 is proved.

The above proof remains sound if $A_1, A_2, \cdots$ are all the same statement (say $\sim C$). In that case the proof guarantees that if C is not provable in Q then $\sim C$ is fulfillable (in the domain of natural numbers). Consequently, for every statement C of Q, if C is valid (generally true), then C is a theorem of Q. In other words, the completeness of Q also follows from 3.2.

Before proving the main theorem, it seems desirable first to take care of a minor complication caused by the existence of theorems of Q which contain symbols not present in S and are therefore not theorems of S. This is taken care of by the following theorem:

3.3. The system obtained from Q after adding all the axioms of S is translatable into S.

Proof. From the predicates of S we can generate an arbitrary number of predicates and statements, with the help of quantifiers and truth-functional connectives. By substituting in a definite way one of these for each predicate or statement letter of Q in all the statements of Q, we obtain a translation of the system Q plus the axioms of S into the system S. It can be checked that axioms of S remain unchanged in the translation while axioms and rules of inference of the general quantification theory are translated into those of the special quantification theory of S.

By applying the method of arithmetization to the proof for 3.2, the main theorem can be proved.

Theorem 5. *If S is consistent, then we can define in the system Z_s obtained from number theory by adding $Con(S)$ as an axiom, certain predicates such that the axioms A_1, A_2, $\cdots$ of S all become provable in Z_s if in them we replace all the predicates one by one by these predicates defined in Z_s and let all variabes range over natural numbers.*

Assume given an arithmetization of the syntax of Q. Since S is formulated in Q, we have therewith also one of the syntax of S. Let $\text{Thq}(m)$ be the arithmetic statement expressing that m represents a theorem of Q.

By hypothesis, S is consistent. Hence, by 3.3, Q remains consistent when we add A_1, A_2, $\cdots$, and the consistency of the resulting system follows from $Con(S)$. Therefore, for every constant i, $\sim A_1 \vee \cdots \vee \sim A_i$ is not provable in Q and, because $Con(S)$ is an axiom of Z_s, $(i)\sim\text{Thq}(a_i)$ is a theorem of Z_s where $a_1, a_2, \cdots$ are the numbers of $\sim A_1$, $\sim A_1 \vee \sim A_2, \cdots$ respectively.

Let K_1, K_2, K_3 and K_4 be the classes of the Gödel numbers of the formulas respectively of the forms $\sim C_1 \vee \cdots \vee \sim C_k$, $\sim D_k$, $(x_0)(\bar{y}_1^1) \cdots \cdots (\bar{y}_1^k) \sim D_k \supset \sim C_1 \vee \cdots \vee \sim C_k$, and $\sim F_k (k=1, 2, \cdots)$. Then we can convince ourselves that all these classes are recursive because, in general, given any formula of Q, we can always decide whether it is of one of the forms or not.

By the ordinary proof for 3.1 and the arguments in the proof of 3.2, there is an effective process which, for every proof in Q of $\sim A_1 \vee \cdots \vee \sim A_k$, yields one for $\sim C_1 \vee \cdots \vee \sim C_k$. Hence, the following is a theorem of Z_s: for every m, if m belongs to K_1, then $\sim \text{Thq}(m)$.

Since in proving that for each given n, $(x_0)(\bar{y}_1^1)\cdots(\bar{y}_1^n)\sim D_n \supset \sim C_1 \vee \cdots \vee \sim C_n$ is a theorem of Q, only induction and elementary syntactical considerations are used, the proof can be arithmetized to yield the following theorem of Z_s: for every m, if m belongs to K_3, then $\text{Thq}(m)$. Hence, if $\text{taut}(m)$ is the arithmetic statement expressing that m is the number of a tautological formula, we can also prove in Z_s: for every m, if m belongs to K_2, then $\sim\text{taut}(m)$, and if m belongs to K_4, then also $\sim\text{taut}(m)$.

In other words, each of $F_1, F_2, \cdots$ is truth-functionally fulfillable. As before, let $P_1, \cdots, P_{t_k}$ be the atomic formulas occurring in F_k. We can define a recursive function Q such that $Q(k, n)$ if and only if n represents a fulfilling assignment for F_k over the atomic formulas of F_k. We can also define a recursive function e such that $e(k)$ is the number of atomic formulas contained in F_k. Using these notions, we can prove the following theorem in Z_s:$(\exists m)(m < 2^{e(k)} \; \& \; Q(k,m))$.

Moreover, from the considerations on the selected truth-value assignments which taken together fulfill $F_1, F_2, \cdots$ simultaneously, we can also define a function a such that for every k, $a(k)$ is the number which represents the selected assignment on the atomic formulas of F_k. To do this we assume a recursive relation H such that $H(k, m, j, n)$ when and only when m represents the k-part of a fulfilling assignment for F_j represented by n. Then the definition of the requisite function a is: $a(k) = \mu_m(j)(k \leqslant j \supset (\exists n) H(k, m, j, n))$. This function a need not be recursive because the values which the variable j may take is not bounded above for each given k. The axiom $Con(S)$ enters essentially in causing the above definition for it in Z_s to provide the desired function.

Let $V_1, V_2, \cdots$ be all the statement and predicate letters occurring in some of $C_1, C_2, \cdots$ arranged in the order of their first appearances. For every $i (i=1, 2, \cdots)$, assume that V_i is p_i-placed $(p_i = 0, 1, 2, \cdots)$. For each V_i we can define a recursive function k_i such that for every $n_1, \cdots, n_{p_i}$ and m, $k_i(n_1, \cdots, n_{p_i}) = m$ if and only if $V_i(n_1, \cdots, n_{p_i})$ is P_m. Since $(k)(k \leqslant e(k))$, therefore, for every k, P_k occurs in F_k. Consequently, for every instance $V_i(n_1, \cdots, n_{p_i})$ of the predicate $V_i(z_1, \cdots, z_{p_i})$ occurring as P_m in $F_1, F_2, \cdots$, the value which $V_i(n_1, \cdots,$

n_{p_i}) takes in all the selected assignments is the value which P_m takes in the selected assignment for F_m(on $P_1, \cdots, P_{t_m}$) represented by $a(m)$. Assume further we have introduced a recursive function γ_1 such that $\gamma_1(m, k, j)=0$ if and only if the assignment represented by m on the atomic formulas of F_k assigns the value truth to P_j. Using these notions, we can represent the condition that $V_i(n_1, \cdots, n_{p_i})$ takes the value truth in all the selected assignments by the formula $\gamma_1[a(k_i(n_1, \cdots, n_{p_i})), k_i(n_1, \cdots, n_{p_i}), k_i(n_1, \cdots, n_{p_i})]=0$.

Therewith the predicate-expression $\gamma_1[a(k_i(z_1, \cdots, z_{p_i})), k_i(z_1, \cdots, z_{p_i}), k_i(z_1, \cdots, z_{p_i})] = 0$, which we shall refer to as $V_i^*(z_1, \cdots, z_{p_i})$, constitutes the desired arithmetic counterpart of $V_i(y_1, \cdots, y_{p_i})$ originally occurring in C_1, C_2, etc. We want to show that each of the results C_1^*, C_2^*, $\cdots$ obtained from C_1, C_2, $\cdots$ by substituting V_1^*, V_2^*, $\cdots$ respectively for all occurrences of V_1, V_2, $\cdots$ is provable in Z_s.

Let us abbreviate $(\exists m)(m<2^{e(k)} \;\&\; Q(k, m))$ as $q(k) = 0$. Since then $q(k) = 0$ is provable in Z_s, it is sufficient to show that each specific C_n^* can be derived in Z from $q(k)=0$. The formula C_n^* is of the form $(m_1)\cdots(m_{r_n})(Ej_1)\cdots(Ej_{s_n})\, B_n^*(m_1, \cdots, m_{r_n}; j_1, \cdots, j_{s_n})$, where B_n^* is related to B_n as C_n^* is to C_n. In order to derive C_n^*, it is sufficient to derive:

$$B_n^*(m_1, \cdots, m_{r_n}; \eta_n(m_1, \cdots, m_{r_n}), \cdots, \eta_n(m_1, \cdots, m_{r_n}) + s - 1)$$

where $\eta_n(m_1, \cdots, m_{r_n})$ is a recursive function which yields the first term of the s_n-tuple $\bar{j}_i^n$ if the terms of $\bar{m}_i^n$ are just $m_1, \cdots, m_{r_n}$. ($\bar{m}_i^n$ and $\bar{j}_i^n$ are defined as in last part of the proof of 3.2.) But the derivation for this is exactly analogous to those used by Hilbert and Bernays for the case where, instead of infinitely many Skolem normal forms C_1, C_2, $\cdots$, only a single one is considered.

Given that each C_n^* is provable in Z_s, Th. 5 follows immediately. For then, by 3.1, A_n^* is also a theorem of Z_s, where A_n^* is related to A_n as C_n^* is to C_n. Therefore, A_1^*, A_2^*, $\cdots$ are all provable in Z_s. Moreover, there is an effective process by which, given any A_n, we can find its corresponding A_n^* in Z_s.

In order to apply Th. 5 to a system with many kinds of variable, the system should first be reduced to one with only one kind of variable. However, it should be noted here, we can also prove analogously a theorem similar to Th. 5 for a many-sorted quantification theory so that it can be applied directly to systems with more than one kind of variable.

Moreover, it is not hard to modify the proofs for 3.1, 3.2, 3.3, and Th. 5 so as to obtain similar theorems for the cases where Q includes denumerably many individual constants and S includes finitely or denumerably many individual constants which can be supposed to have been identified arbitrarily with some or all of those of Q.

While it is possible to give a shorter alternative proof of Theorem 5 by an arithmetization of shorter proofs of the completeness of the predicate calculus, it seems very likely the information obtained would be less and certain applications such as Kreisel's in Fund. Math., vol. 37, pp. 265—285, which depends on certain details of the longer proof, can no longer be made.

§ 4. Arithmetic Translations of Axiom Systems

In this section, we discuss the notions of translation studied in *Trans. Am. Math. Soc.*, **71** (1951), 283—293. These notions were defined for certain specific purposes on hand and in their generality, there is an ambiguity between existence and provability, as has been pointed out by Gödel and Kreisel. Two notions were originally defined, which become four if we distinguish demonstrable translations from ones where mere existence of an effective correlation is required.

Let S and S' be any two formal systems formalized in the framework of the predicate calculus.

Definition 1. *S is said to have an inner model S′ if there exists an effective way of replacing all the predicates of S by predicates of S′ such that the resulting statements in place of the theorems of S all are theorems of S′.*

More explicitly, this definition contains at least the following parts:

(1) The image of a quantification (namely, a formula beginning with a quantifier) of S is a quantification in S'.

(2) The image of the negation of a formula of S is the negation of the image of the formula.

(3) The image of the conjunction of two formulae of S is the conjunction of their images.

(4) The images of the theorems of S all are theorems of S'. Or alternatively.

(4.1) The images of the axioms of S are theorems of S'.

(4.2) If a statement of S is deducible from certain other statements of S by a rule of inference and the images of these latter statements of S are theorems of S', then the image of the former statement is also a theorem of S'.

In this definition, functions are, for brevity, not mentioned because they can be replaced by predicates or included in an analogous manner.

For the purpose of comparing the relative strength of formal systems it is often desirable to require that the conditions are demonstrably satisfied.

Definition 2. *Let B and B' be the proof predicates of S and S', and T be a system dealing with natural numbers, S is said to be T–translatable into S' if there is a recursive function f such that we can prove in T:* (i) $Q(k) \supset Q'(f(k))$, *where Q and Q' are the classes of Gödel numbers of quantificational formulae in S and S'*; (ii) $c(f(k), f(m)) = f(c(k, m))$, *where $c(a,b)$ is the number of the conjunction of the formulae with numbers a, b*; (iii) $f(n(k)) = n(f(k))$, *where n is the function for negation as before*; (iv) $(Ex)B(x, y) \supset (Ex)B'(x, f(y))$.

To sacrifice generality for definiteness, we shall dispense with the relativity with T and speak simply of translatibility when T is understood to be the system Z.

It is very frequent that when we speak of S being obtainable in S' or contained as part in S' or relatively consistent to S', we have actually that S is translatable into S' according to this definition. For example, reducing the algebra of complex numbers to that of real numbers, the (relative) consistency of various geometries (by the translation into the Euclidean geometry or the system for real numbers), the consistency of the theory of finite sets, the relative consistency of the axiom of choice and the generalized continuum hypothesis, the reduction of arithmetic to set theory.

Using this definition, we can restate Bernays' lemma:

Theorem 6. *Every formal system S (formalized within the framework of the predicate calculus) is translatable into the system Z_S obtained from Z by adding $Con(S)$ as a new axiom.*

Definition 3. *Two formal systems S and S' are said to be of equal strength if they are translatable into each other; S' is said to be stronger than S if S is translatable into S' but not conversely.*

Two systems of equal strength may be said to have the same "structure".

It is not unlikely that on the basis of this definition we can get some satisfactory classification of ordinary formal systems. For purposes of classifying partial systems of Z, it will be desirable to use T–translation relative to some system T more elementary than Z, such as the system R of primitive recursive arithmetic obtained from Z by omitting all quantifiers and then adding all primitive recursive definitions.

In order to preserve consistency only, one need not require so much of a translation since the essential thing is that negation be preserved. We may, therefore, introduce also a weaker notion of translation.

Definition 4. *Let S and S′ be formal systems containing a negation sign. The system S is said to be weakly T–translatable (or simply, translatable, if T is Z) into S′ if there is a recursive function f, such that conditions* (iii) *and* (iv) *in Definition 2 are satisfied.*

For example, the predicate calculus is known to be weakly translatable into the propositional calculus by simply dropping all quantifiers in every formula. It is also known that Z is weakly translatable into Heyting's system for intuitionistic number theory.

There are a number of more or less obvious consequences of these definitions.

4.1. If S is (weakly) translatable into S' then S is consistent if S' is, and $Con(S)$ is derivable from $Con(S')$ in Z.

We assume the usual form of $Con(S)$ and $Con(S')$. If $\sim Con(S)$, then we can get some constant $\bar{k}$ such that $(Ex)B(x, \bar{k})$ and $(Ex)B(x, n(\bar{k}))$. By (iii) and (iv) above, we have $(Ex)B'(x, f(\bar{k}))$ and $(Ex)B(x, n(f(\bar{k})))$, and therefore $\sim Con(S')$.

It is not known whether the theorem is true if in place of "S is translatable into S'" one uses only the hypothesis "S has an inner model in S'".

4.2. If Z and a consistent system S are translatable into S' and the translation of $Con(S)$ in S' is a theorem of S', then S' is stronger than S; in particular, S may be the same as Z.

Otherwise the translation of $Con(S')$ in S' would be provable in S'. By an extension of Gödel's second theorem, S', and therefore also S, would be inconsistent.

4.3. If we take the known ω–consistency of Z for granted, then S is consistent if and only if Z_S is.

If we take the Zermelo set theory and drop the axiom of power set, we obtained a system S_1 with an infinite set containing all finite sets. If we call S_2 the system obtained from S_1 by adding an axiom that the power set of that infinite sets exists, call S_3 the further extension including the power set of that power set, and so on, then we know from the literature that the following holds:

4.4. There exists a sequence of systems $S_1, S_2, \cdots$ such that they are all stronger than Z, and that if they are consistent then for every m and n, S_m is stronger than S_n when and only when m is greater than n.

As we know, the set theories $S_1, S_2, \cdots$ can be so formulated that in the axioms of each system merely a single dyadic predicate (the membership predicate) occurs. Let these predicates be $E_1, E_2, \cdots$, and their arithmetic translations according to Bernays' lemma be $E_1^*, E_2^*, \cdots$, respectively.

Definition 5. *A predicate E implicitly determined by certain assertions concerning it is said to be definable or has a model in a system S′ if there exists a system S which includes the assertions about E as theorems and which is translatable into S′.*

For example, the predicate of being a natural number is according to this definition definable in these systems, if we take the system Z as determining the predicate. By 4.4, we have:

4.5. None of the predicates $E_1, E_2 \cdots$ is definable in Z. If S_1, $S_2, \cdots$ are all consistent, then for every m and n, E_m is definable in S_n when and only when m is not greater than n.

When a predicate E is determined by certain postulates, a translation E^* of the predicate is determined by the translations of the postulates. Therefore, we have also:

4.6. None of the predicates $E_1^*, E_2^*, \cdots$ is definable in Z.

Let Z_S be, as before, the system obtained from Z by adding $Con(S)$ as a new axiom. Using the same sequence of systems, we have:

4.7. If $S_1, S_2, \cdots$ are all consistent, then:

(a) All the systems $Z_Z, Z_{S_1}, Z_{S_2}, \cdots$ are consistent and have the same primitive notation as Z;

(b) Each system in the sequence $Z, Z_Z, S_1, Z_{S_1}, S_2, Z_{S_2}, \cdots$ is translatable into every later system in the sequence;

(c) For all positive integers m and n, if $m-1$ is greater than n, then S_m is not translatable into Z_{S_n};

(d) If m is not greater than n, then E_m is definable in Z_{S_n}, if $m-1$ is greater than n then E_m is not definable in Z_{S_n};

(e) If $m-1$ is greater than n, then Z_{S_m} is not translatable into Z_{S_n} and, therefore, for example, each system in the sequence Z, Z_{S_1}, $Z_{S_3}, Z_{S_5}, \cdots$ is stronger than all its predecessors.

Proof. (a) By 4.3.

(b) By Theorem 6, each S_i is translatable into Z_{S_i}. But each S_i contains Z and $Con(S_{i-1})$ as a theorem. Hence, $Z_{S_{i-1}}$ is translatable into S_i.

(c) Since $m-1$ is greater than n, Z_{S_n} is, by (b), translatable into S_{m-1}. Therefore, if S_m were translatable into Z_{S_n}, S_m would be translatable into S_{m-1}.

(d) By Definition 5, (b), and (c).

(e) By (b) and (c).

Two questions remain unanswered: Is Z_{S_n} translatable into S_n? Is $Z_{S_{n+1}}$ translatable into Z_{S_n}? We know merely that Z_{S_n} is translatable into S_n for every n, if and only if, for every n, $Z_{S_{n+1}}$ is not translatable into Z_{S_n}.

From (d) and (e) of 4.7, we have the following corollary:

4.8. There exists a sequence of systems $L_0(=Z)$, L_1, L_2, $\cdots$ all of the same notation such that if they are all consistent, then each is stronger than all its predecessors and therefore translatable into none of them. There exists also a sequence of predicates P_1, P_2, $\cdots$ such that P_m is definable in L_n when and only when m is not greater than n.

Using the notion of translation, Gödel's theorem on the incompleteness of systems can also be stated:

4.9. There exists no consistent system S such that there is a translation of the number theory Z into S according to which, for every statement A of Z, either A or $-A$ is translated into a theorem of S.

Recently Kreisel has obtained results on translatability (see *Mathematical Interpretation of Formal Systems*, 1955, pp. 26—50; *J. Symbolic Logic*, **23**, 108—110) among which the following:

4.10. If S and S' are systems with primitive recursive proof predicates, S contains Z, and $Con(S) \supset Con(S')$ is a theorem of S' then there is a weak S-translation of S' into S.

S. Feferman has made an extensive study of inner models and translations in his dissertation (1957, Berkeley, California). Among other things, he makes an exact study about possible formulae for expressing the consistency of a given system S, i.e., what formulae can be correctly taken as $Con(S)$.

To illustrate the applications of Theorem 6, we consider two special systems N and N' such that N' is a predicative extension of N.

N is a weak system of set theory formulated after the manner of Quine and belonging to the kind of set theory in which the distinction between elements (or sets) and (non-element) classes is made so that all classes are classes of elements. The axioms of N assure us only that the null class is an element and classes of one or two members are elements. Accordingly N admits a model containing denumerably many elements plus classes of them. Such a model seems to make it clear that N is roughly as strong as a second-order predicate calculus founded on natural numbers.

N may also be characterized as a system obtained from a well-developed system of Quine's *Mathematical Logic* by replacing all his elementhood axioms by a single one stating that pairs are elements. It is formulated within the quantification theory Q used ordinarily, with a single special predicate written as ϵ.

In N, element variables a, b, c, and so on are introduced by contextual definitions such as:

4.11. $(a)A(a)$ for $(x)((\exists y)(x\epsilon y)\supset A(x))$.

4.12. $(\exists a)$ for $-(a)-$.

And identity is defined in the usual manner:

4.13. $x=y$ for $(z)(z\epsilon x\equiv z\epsilon y)$.

The special axioms of N are given in $C1$—$C3$.

$C1$. $x=y\supset(x\epsilon z\supset y\epsilon z)$.

$C2$. $(\exists a)(b)(b\epsilon a\equiv(b=x\vee b=y))$.

$C3$. If A is any formula of N in which y is not free, then $(\exists y)(a)(a\epsilon y\equiv A)$.

It is known that the number theory Z is translatable into N. One way of making the translation is as follows. Identify 0 with the null class and the successor of a natural number with its unit class. In this way, all natural numbers are identified with elements of N. Then define the class Nn of natural numbers as the intersection of all classes x of N such that x contains 0 and, for every n, if x contains n it also contains the successor of n. The principle of induction follows immediately: Every class which contains 0 and contains the successor of n if containing n, contains Nn. Variables m, n, and so on which take natural numbers as values and the μ-operators μ_m, μ_n, and so on can be introduced in N by contextual definitions. The following metatheorems of N are provable.

4.14. If y is not free in A, then $(\exists y)(m)(m\epsilon y\equiv A)$.

4.15. $(\exists m)A(m)\supset A(\mu_m A(m))$.

4.16. $(n)(A(n)\equiv B(n))\supset\mu_n A(n)=\mu_n B(n)$.

The system N' is an extension of N, the primitive notations of which being those of N plus a new kind of variable X, Y, and so on and a new dyadic predicate η. The atomic formulas of N' are $x\epsilon y$, and so on, and $x\eta Y$, and so on from which we build up all the formulas of N' by truth-functional connectives and quantifiers. N' contains the quantification theory for the variables x, y, and so on, and that for the variables X, Y, and so on. The special axioms of N' are $C1$—$C3$ and the following additional ones ($C1$ now redundant):

$C4$. If A is a formula of N' in which Y is not free, then $(\exists Y)(x)(x\eta Y\equiv A)$.

C5. $(x)(x \epsilon y \equiv x \epsilon z) \supset (y \eta X \supset z \eta X)$.

Let us assume that the syntax of N and that of N' have both been arithmetized in the usual manner. Since N is a part of N', let us assume that the arithmetization of the syntax of N coincides with a part of that of N'. With such arithmetizations, we have two arithmetic statements $Con(N)$ and $Con(N')$ expressing respectively that N is consistent and that N' is consistent. Let $N\#$ be the system obtained from N by adding $Con(N)$ as a new axiom. Then we can also obtain an arithmetization of the syntax of $N\#$ from that of N and, therefore, there is an arithmetic statement $Con(N\#)$ expressing that $N\#$ is consistent. We want to prove in the number theory Z: If $Con(N\#)$, then $Con(N')$.

This we do in the following manner. By Theorem 6, N is translatable into the system Z_N obtained from number theory by adding $Con(N)$ as a new axiom. More precisely, we know that in Z_N theorems can be proved which are like the axioms of N given in *C1—C3* (imagining that all the defined symbols $=$, a, b, and so on have been eliminated with the help of the defintions 4.11—4.13) except for containing an arithmetic predicate ϵ^* (say) of Z_N in place of ϵ and variables m, n, and so on instead of the variables x, y, and so on. Since N contains Z, $N\#$ contains Z_N. Therefore, these arithmetic translations of the axioms *C1—C3* of N and N' are all provable in $N\#$. For example, corresponding to *C1*, we can prove in $N\#$:

C1'. $(m)(m \epsilon^* k \equiv m \epsilon^* j) \supset (k \epsilon^* n \supset j \epsilon^* n)$.

Let us use m^*, k^*, and so on, as abbreviations:

4.17. m^* for $\mu_n(j)(j \epsilon^* n \equiv j \epsilon^* m)$, and so on.
Then we have in $N\#$:

4.18. $j \epsilon^* m^* \equiv j \epsilon^* m$.

Proof. Since $(j)(j \epsilon^* m \equiv j \epsilon^* m)$, so $(\exists n)(j)(j \epsilon^* n \equiv j \epsilon^* m)$. By 4.15 and 4.17, the theorem follows immediately.

Let A be an arbitrary formula of $N\#$ built up exclusively from formulas of the forms $n \epsilon^* m$ and $m^* \epsilon y$ with the help of quantifiers and truth-functional connectives. By 4.14 and 4.18, we have:

4.19. If y is not free in A, then $(\exists y)(m)(m^* \epsilon y \equiv A)$ is a theorem of $N\#$.

Another useful theorem of $N\#$ is the following:

4.20. $(j)(j \epsilon^* k \equiv j \epsilon^* m) \supset (k^* \epsilon y \supset m^* \epsilon y)$.

Proof. Assume: $(j)(j \epsilon^* k \equiv j \epsilon^* m)$. Therefore, $(j)(j \epsilon^* n \equiv j \epsilon^* k) \equiv (j)(j \epsilon^* n \equiv j \epsilon^* m)$. Hence, by 4.16 and 4.17, $k^* = m^*$. Hence, $k^* \epsilon y \supset m^* \epsilon y$, and 4.20 is proved.

To show that the whole system N' is translatable into the system $N\#$, we use a translation according to which the translation in $N\#$ of a statement A of N' is obtained from A by the following transformations: (1) Any formula of N' of the form $x \epsilon y$ is replaced by a formula of $N\#$ of the form $m \epsilon^* k$, and the associated quantifiers (x) and (y) are replaced by the quantifiers (m) and (k); (2) Any formula of N' of the form $x \eta Y$ is replaced by a formula of $N\#$ of the form $m^* \epsilon y$, and the associated quantifiers (x) and (Y) are replaced by (m) and (y); (3) Every truth-functional connective remains unchanged.

It should be easy to see that the translation satisfies all the conditions in Definition 2 and Definition 4. The only item that calls for some comment seems to be 4.15, which requires that all theorems of N' be translated into theorems of $N\#$.

As mentioned above, the translations of $C1$—$C3$ are all theorems of $N\#$. And the translations of $C4$ and $C5$ are just 4.19 and 4.20 which have been proved for $N\#$. Moreover, we can obtain in $N\#$ the quantification theory for the variables x, y, and so on and that for the variables m, n, and so on. Hence, all theorems of N' are transformed into theorems of $N\#$ according to the translation described above.

Theorem 7. *N' is translatable into $N\#$.*

Hence, by 4.1, we have:

4.21. $Con(N')$ is derivable from $Con(N\#)$ in number theory; $Con(N')$ is derivable from $Con(N\#)$ in N'.

Therefore, we have:

4.22. If N' is consistent, then $Con(N\#)$ is not a theorem of N'. In other words, if $Con(N\#)$ is a theorem of N', then N' is inconsistent.

An interesting connection between N and $N\#$ is embodied in the next theorem.

Theorem 8. *If N is ω-consistent, then $N\#$ is consistent.*

Proof. Assume that $N\#$ is inconsistent. Then every statement of $N\#$, including $-Con(N)$, is provable in $N\#$. Let A be the conjunction of the axioms of N used in the proof for $-Con(N)$. Then, since $Con(N)$ is the only axiom in $N\#$ which is not also an axiom of N, we have a proof for $-Con(N)$ in $N\#$ using the conjunction $(A \,\&\, Con(N))$. Therefore, by the deduction theorem, we can prove $((A \,\&\, Con(N)) \supset -Con(N))$ in the quantification theory of N. Therefore by truth-functional transformations, $(A \supset -Con(N))$ is a theorem of the quantification theory too. Hence, $-Con(N)$ is a theorem of N.

Therefore, if $Pc(n)$ is the arithmetic predicate expressing that n represents a proof in N for the statement (say) $0=1$, then $(\exists n)Pc(n)$ is a theorem of N. If N is inconsistent, then a fortiori it is also ω-inconsistent. On the other hand, if N is consistent then, for every given n, $-Pc(n)$ is true and therefore provable in N, because it is a statement obtained from a primitive recursive predicate by substituting a constant numeral in the argument and every true statement of such a form is provable in number theory. But $(\exists n)Pc(n)$ is also a theorem of N. Therefore, N is ω-inconsistent. Combining the two cases, we have: if N is ω-consistent, then $N\#$ is consistent.

Therefore, by 4.21, we have:

4.23. If N is ω-consistent, then N' is consistent.

The method of proving the relative consistency of N' to $N\#$ can also be applied to other systems. Let S be the part of Zermelo set theory consisting of the Aussonderungsaxiom, the axiom of extensionality, the axiom of infinity, and the axiom of power set; let S' be a simple theory of types with S as its theory of individuals. Since, according to a known result, the simple theory of types founded on natural numbers is translatable into S, we can apply the method of proving the relative consistency of N' to $N\#$ and prove:

4.24. If S is ω-consistent, then S' is consistent.

Other examples may be given. Consider, for example, the simple theory of types as formulated by Gödel. This system T is founded on natural numbers and contains, besides the Peano axioms and the axiom of extensionality, only the axiom of comprehension: If n is a positive integer and A is any formula of T in which y_{n+1} is not free, then $(\exists y_{n+1})(x_n)(x_n \in y_{n+1} \equiv A)$ is an axiom of T. It is easy to see that this can be replaced by the next two principles which at first sight appear to be weaker: (1) If A contains no variable of any type higher than $n+1$, then $(\exists y_{n+1})(x_n)(x_n \in y_{n+1} \equiv A)$; (2) If A is any formula of T in which y_2 is not free, then $(\exists y_2)(x_1)(x_1 \in y_2 \equiv A)$. Let T' be the system obtained from T by omitting the principle (2), and let us refer to it as the monotonic simple theory of types. Then we can speak of the part T'_n of T' which contains nothing of any type higher than n as the *monotonic* predicate calculus of the nth order, in contrast with the corresponding part T_n of T which forms the nth order predicate calculus. Using the method for N' and N, we can prove:

Theorem 9. *If T'_2 is ω-consistent, then T'_3 is consistent; if T'_3 is ω-consistent, then T'_5 is consistent; if T'_4 is ω-consistent, then T'_7 is consistent; and so on.*

If we call a system regular when we know that it is either inconsistent or ω-consistent but that it cannot be consistent yet ω-inconsistent, we obtain the next theorem.

4.25. If T_2' is consistent and T_2', T_3', $\cdots$ are all regular, then T_3', T_4', $\cdots$, as well as T', are all consistent.

Thus, in a certain sense, we can say that the reason why a predicate calculus (founded on natural numbers) of a higher order is stronger than one of a lower order merely comes from the presence of the principle (2) which enables us to form new classes of natural numbers in the predicate calculus of higher order.

The method does not seem to be applicable to the systems T_3, T_4, $\cdots$ of predicate calculi in any analogous manner. Indeed, the principle (2) seems to make much difference.

An alternative proof of the relative consistency of N' to N, as well as of systems similarly related, will be given in § 5 of Ch. XVI. According to a result of McNaughton (*J. Symbolic Logic*, **18** (1953), 136—144), these proofs can be formalized in T_3. It follows that:

4.26. For each n, $Con(T_n')$ is provable in T_3.

4.27. $Con(T')$ is provable in T_4 by induction on n in $Con(T_n')$.

CHAPTER XIV

ACKERMANN'S CONSISTENCY PROOF

§ 1. The System Z_a

Apart from Gentzen's celebrated consistency proof of the system Z with his special formulation of the predicate calculus (*Math. Annalen*, **112** (1936), 493—565 and *Forschungen zur Logik und etc.*, no. 4, 1938, 19—44), there are also alternative proofs by Ackermann (*Math. Annalen*, **117** (1940), 162—194) and Schütte (*Math. Annalen*, **122** (1951), 369—389). In this chapter, we give an exposition of Ackermann's proof which has certain interesting applications.

Ackermann's formulation is in many ways very elegant. We quote it in full.

Basic symbols: $0, ', \dot{-}1, +, \cdot, =, \sim, \supset$, variables x, y, etc., ε–operators $\varepsilon x, \varepsilon y$, etc.

Formulae and terms: 0 is a term, a variable is a term, if a and b are terms, so are a', $a \dot{-} 1$, $a+b$, ab, if $A(a)$ is a formula, $\varepsilon_x A(x)$, etc. are terms; if a, b are terms, $a=b$ is a formula, if A, B are formulae, so are $\sim A$, $A \supset B$.

There are three groups of axiom schemata with modus ponens as the single rule of inference. No free variables are to appear in any axioms or proofs. In particular, in the rule of modus ponens, viz. B if A and $A \supset B$, no free variables occur in A and B. We shall call a term or a formula closed if it contains no free variables, otherwise open.

I. Propositional calculus.

I1. $p \supset (q \supset p)$.

I2. $(p \supset (q \supset r)) \supset ((p \supset q) \supset (p \supset r))$.

I3. $(\sim p \supset \sim q) \supset (q \supset p)$.

II. Number theory. If a, b, c are closed terms then

II1. $a=a$.

II2. $a'=b' \supset a=b$.

II3. $a \neq 0 \supset (a \dot{-} 1)' = a$.

II4. $a+0=a$.

II5. $a+b'=(a+b)'$.

II6. $a0=0$.

II7. $ab'=ab+a$.

II8. $a=b\supset a'=b'$.

II9. $a=b\supset a\dot{-}1=b\dot{-}1$.

II10. $a=b\supset a+c=b+c$.

II11. $a=b\supset c+a=c+b$.

II12. $a=b\supset ac=bc$.

II13. $a=b\supset ca=cb$.

III. The ε–operator.

III1. $A(a)\supset A(\varepsilon_x A(x))$.

III2. $A(a)\supset \varepsilon_x A(x)\neq a'$.

III3. $\sim A(\varepsilon_x A(x))\supset \varepsilon_x A(x)=0$.

III4. $a=b\supset \varepsilon_x A(x,a)=\varepsilon_x A(x,b)$.

The equivalence of this system with Z holds in the sense that a theorem not containing the ε–symbol is provable in Z if and only if it is provable in Z_a. For the "if" half, it is sufficient to recall the eliminability of the μ–operator in Z, and the possibility of identifying ε with μ. For the "only if" half, it is only necessary to derive the principle of mathematical induction from II3, III1, and III2 (Hilbert-Bernays II, p. 85) and $(x)(x'\neq 0)$ from the definition of (x) in terms of the ε–symbol by III2 and III3.

The consistency proof aims at eliminating the ε–symbol to correlate every proof with a succession of true numerical formulae. For this purpose, a number of concepts are needed.

1.1. An ε–term is a term which begins with ε.

1.2. The principal variable of an ε–term $\varepsilon_x A(x)$ is x.

1.3. A term b is said to be subordinate to a term a, if a is an ε–term, b is a proper part of a, and the principal variable of a occurs in b. It follows that b is an open term.

1.4. A term b is said to reside in a term a, if b is a proper part of a but is not subordinate to a.

From 1.3 and 1.4, it follows:

1.5. If a is not an ε–term and b is a proper part of a, then b resides in a; if a is an ε–term and b is a proper part of a, then b

either resides in a or is subordinate to a, but not both.

1.6. An occurrence of a term b is said to be a direct constituent of an ε–term a, if (i) it resides in a; (ii) it is not subordinate to any ε–term contained in a; (iii) it is not a proper part of any term residing in a.

For example, if a is $\varepsilon_y(x+2=\varepsilon_z(y+1=z))$, then $\varepsilon_z(y+1=z)$ and $y+1$ do not satisfy (i), z does not satisfy (ii), x and z do not satisfy (iii). But $x+2$ satisfies all.

1.7. The ε–category of an ε–term a, open or closed, is obtained from the term by substituting distinct free variables which do not occur in a for all direct constituents of a. When a has no direct constituent, it is its own ε–category. An alphabetic variant is regarded as the same ε–category.

For example, $\varepsilon_z(z+\varepsilon_y(y=3)=z'')$ is its own ε–category; $\varepsilon_y(u=\varepsilon_z(y+1=z))$ is the ε–category of the term a given above and also of $\varepsilon_y(\varepsilon_w(w=2)+3=\varepsilon_z(y+\varepsilon_v(v=2)=z))$. One could treat these ε-categories as functions of their free variables.

What is wanted in a direct constituent is a maximum complete unit which can be substituted without affecting other parts of the ε–term.

1.8. An ε–substitution of a set of ε–categories is an assignment of a number to each closed ε–category in the set, and a function to each open ε–category. The number or function thus assigned to an ε-category is said to be its substituent in the ε–substitution.

The number of arguments of each function is the same as the number of free variables in the original ε–category. The functions used are always recursive and indeed of the simple kind such that each takes the value 0 except for a finite number of argument values.

1.9. The resolvent of a set of closed formulae relative to an ε–substitution of its ε–categories is the result obtained from the formulae when all ε–terms are replaced by their substituents. The resolvent relative to a finite sequence of ε–substitutions is the resolvent relative to the last ε–substitution of the sequence.

The final aim is to find, for each proof, a finite sequence of ε–substitutions such that the resolvent of the set of formulae in the proof is true, i.e., all formulae in the resolvent set are true. That we can speak of true and false of the resolvent formulae follows from the fact that since the original formulae contain no free variables and since all ε–terms are replaced by their substituents, the results are numerical formulae containing no ε–terms (i.e., no quantifiers).

To get true resolvents, the main burden is to get substituents for every $\varepsilon_x A(x)$ or $\varepsilon_x B(x, a)$ such that the resolvent of $A(\varepsilon_x A(x))$ or $B(\varepsilon_x B(x, a), a)$ is true. That is to say, to make cases of III1 true.

Given a finite set of closed formulae, in particular a proof, we consider all the ε-terms occurring in it and arrange their ε-categories in a sequence such that if an ε-term a is subordinate to an ε-term b, then the ε-category of a precedes that of b.

1.10. Property P. An ε-substitution G of a set of formulae has the property P if for every ε-category in the sequence, say $\varepsilon_x B(x, y)$, and for every numeral n, the substituent of $\varepsilon_x B(x, n)$ is either 0 or else a positive m such that $B(m, n)$ is true but for no k, $k < m$, is $B(k, n)$ true.

In other words, if G has P, then the resolvent of $A(\varepsilon_x A(x))$ can be false only when the substituent of $\varepsilon_x A(x)$ is 0.

Incidentally, each ε-substitution gives substituents for all the infinitely many ε-terms falling under an ε-category of the set, although only finitely many ε-terms occur in a proof.

1.11. The substituent of an ε-category is null if it is 0 or a function which always takes the value 0. The null ε-substitution assigns the null substituent to every category. A member of a sequence of ε-categories is said to be raw in an ε-substitution if both it and all ε-categories following it get null substituents.

Now we are to define by induction a sequence of ε-substitutions which all have the property P in the hope that we can always end up in a finite number of steps with an ε-substitution in which all resolvents of the formulae of the original proof are true.

As the initial ε-substitution, we take the null substitution. This of course has trivially the property P.

Suppose an ε-substitution G given which has the property P but the resolvent of some formula in the proof is not true. Since it has the property P, the resolvent of an axiom can be false only when it is of the form III1. Consider the first formula in the proof whose resolvent is not true, say:

$$A(a, b) \supset A(\varepsilon_x A(x, b), b). \tag{1}$$

Suppose the value of b is n under G, and that of a is k. Then $A(k, n)$ is true, but $A(0, n)$ is false, 0 being the value of $\varepsilon_x A(x, n)$ under G. Let us determine the earliest m, $m \leqslant k$, such that $A(m, n)$ is true.

Now we define the next ε-substitution as follows. First, change the substituent of the ε-category $\varepsilon_x A(x, y)$ at one place, viz. $\varepsilon_x A(x, n)$

is m instead of 0 now. This does not necessarily make (1) true since the ε–category $\varepsilon_x A(x, y)$ may be subordinate to that of b so that as a result of the change, b may get a value different from n. But we do not use such a strong conclusion. We simply assign all ε–categories following $\varepsilon_x A(x, y)$ in the original sequence the null substituent; of course this change is unnecessary if they get null substituent in G already.

The new ε–substitution again has the property P. Thus, since $\varepsilon_x A(x, y)$ is not subordinate to any earlier ε–categories, their substituents remain the same. All the later ones, having null substituents, trivially possess P. With regard to $\varepsilon_x A(x, y)$ itself, if b gets the value n as before, the resolvent of (1) in the new ε–substitution is true. Otherwise, if, e.g., it has now the value j, then $\varepsilon_x A(x, j)$ has the same value as in G, and, is therefore, either 0 or the smallest number i, such that $A(i, j)$. In either case, the new ε–substitution still preserves the property P.

The problem now is to introduce suitable measures of the ε-substitutions in order to show that we are progressing toward the final goal as we continue to modify them.

§ 2. Proof of Finiteness

For this purpose we order all the closed ε–terms occurring in the original proof or in any finite set of formulae in such a way that if a resides in b, then a precedes b. Suppose there are $k+1$ such terms: $a_0, a_1, \cdots, a_k$.

2.1. The order of an ε–substitution G relative to the original finite set of formulae is given by $2^k\varphi(0) + 2^{k-1}\varphi(1) + \cdots + \varphi(k)$, where $\varphi(i)$ is 1 or 0 according as a_i gets the null substituent in G or not.

Since the substituents which are not null are good according to property P, it is generally desirable to have lower orders.

2.2. The degree of an ε–substitution G relative to a finite set of formulae is its order relative to the set of formulae:

(2) $$A(0, n), \cdots, A(k, n).$$

Therein A is from (1) and (1) is the first formula in the original proof which gets a false resolvent by G, and a gets the value k in G. When all the formulae get true resolvents by G, the degree of G is taken to be 0.

2.3. The index of an ε–substitution G relative to a proof is $\omega m + n$, where m is its order and n its degree.

2.4. An ε-substitution G_j of a finite set of ε-categories is no less advanced than G_i if for every positive (i.e., not zero) substituent of a closed ε-term assigned by G_i, the same (positive) substituent is assigned by G_j. If, in addition, there is some closed ε-term which gets a positive substituent by G_j, but a zero substituent by G_i, G_j is more advanced than G_i.

Theorem 1. *If G_j is no less advanced than G_i, both of a set of ε-categories which includes all those of the ε-terms of a finite set of formulae (not necessarily a proof), then either the order of G_j relative to the set of formulae is smaller than that of G_i; or else the substituents of all the closed ε-terms in the formulae of the set are the same in G_i and G_j.*

Proof. Suppose they are not all the same in G_i and G_j. Let $\varepsilon_x A(x, b)$ be the first in the ordering of closed ε-terms defined before in 2.1. Since b precedes it, its substituents in G_i and G_j are the same, say n. Hence $\varepsilon_x A(x, n)$ must get different values by G_i and by G_j. Since G_j is no less advanced than G_i, this is possible only if it is 0 by G_i but positive by G_j. But then, by 2.1, the order of G_j must be smaller than that of G_i.

Theorem 2. *If G_j is no less advanced than G_i, then either the index of G_j relative to the proof is smaller than that of G_i, or else G_{j+1} (i.e. the next ε-substitution after G_j by the construction above) is no less advanced than G_{i+1} and they are obtained from G_j and G_i by adding the same positive substituents for the same closed ε-terms.*

Proof. If the order of G_j is smaller, this is proved by 2.3. Otherwise, by Th. 1, all closed ε-terms in the proof get the same substituents in G_i and G_j. Consider now the set of formulae (2) under 2.2 for G_i and G_j. Since G_j is also no less advanced than G_i relative to this set, either the order of G_j relative to this set, i.e., its degree relative to the original proof, is smaller than that of G_i, or else, by Th. 1, $\varepsilon_x A(x, n)$ must get the same positive value in G_{i+1} and G_{j+1}.

2.5. Given a proof and its finite sequence of ε-categories, the rank of an ε-substitution G relative to the sequence is the number of raw ε-categories in G (cf. 1.11). When the last ε-category is not raw, then the rank is 0. If g is the number of ε-categories for a proof, then the ranks are always $\leqslant g$.

If it were true that G_{i+1} is always no less advanced than G_i, so that the rank of G_{i+1} is no greater than that of G_i, we would be able to establish the consistency rather simply; since every new ε-substitution corrects at least one substituent, we would come to an end soon. But, as we mentioned before, we could spoil the ε-category of a by changing the substituent of $\varepsilon_x B(x, a)$, if $\varepsilon_x B(x, y)$ happens to be subordinate to the ε–category of a. Hence, G_{i+1} may have a higher rank than G_i.

It is, however, true that in any sequence of ε–substitutions defined for a proof in the manner of §1, either the rank of G_{i+1} is always no greater than that of G_i, or else there exists some G_i of rank m followed by a finite number of ε–substitutions of rank $<m$, and then a G_{i+k} which is of rank $\geqslant m$ again.

2.6. An m–section of ε–substitutions relative to a proof is a finite sequence of ε–substitutions $G_i, \cdots, G_{i+k}(k \geqslant 0)$, such that G_i is of rank $\geqslant m$, $G_{i+1}, \cdots, G_{i+k}$ are of ranks $<m$, and either G_{i+k} is the last ε–substitution (making all resolvents true), or G_{i+k+1} is of rank $\geqslant m$.

Since we never have an ε–substitution of rank less than 0, a 0–section has a single term only. Since the highest rank is g, the number of ε–categories for the proof, the null ε–substitution has rank g, and all later ε–substitutions have ranks $<g$. Hence, we need only consider m–sections for $m<g$.

Theorem 3. *If $G_1, \cdots, G_k$ and $H_1, \cdots, H_j$ are two consecutive m–sections with indices $a_1, \cdots, a_k, b_1, \cdots, b_j$, and H_1 has the rank m, $m<g$, then*: (i) *H_1 is more advanced than G_1*; (ii) *there is some number p, $1 \leqslant p \leqslant k$, $1 \leqslant p \leqslant j$, such that $a_p > b_p$, and for all i, if $i<p$, then $a_i = b_i$, if $1 < i \leqslant p$ then G_i and H_i have the same rank.*

Proof. Let $\varepsilon_x A(x, y)$ be the $(g-m)$–th ε–category, i.e., the $(m+1)$ –th from the end, of the original sequence. Since $G_2, \cdots, G_k$ all are of ranks less than m, they retain the substituents in G_1 of $\varepsilon_x A(x, y)$ and all preceding ε–categories. Therefore, since H_1 is of rank m, it must be got from G_k by giving a new positive substituent to $\varepsilon_x A(x, n)$ for some numeral n. Hence (i) is proved when $1<k$. This, by the way, does not necessarily mean that H_1 has a smaller index than G_1 or a new closed ε–term gets a positive substituent. It may happen that exactly the same closed ε–term $\varepsilon_x A(x, b)$ which got a positive substituent in G_1 now requires a different positive substituent on account of changes made in $G_2, \cdots, G_k$.

If, H_1 follows directly G_1, then, since the rank of H_1 is no greater than that of G_1, (i) is again true. Hence, (i) is proved.

To prove (ii), we note that if $a_1 > b_1$, $p=1$. If $a_1 = b_1$, then there must be some p, $a_p \neq b_p$. We assume there is no such p and consider two different cases. Suppose $k>j$. First H_j cannot be the last ε–substitution, otherwise since it has the same index as G_j, we would have stopped at G_j. But H_j is no less advanced than G_j by (i). Hence, by Th. 2, H_{j+1} must be no less advanced than G_{j+1}. But this is impossible since G_{j+1} has rank less than m, while H_{j+1} has rank no less than m.

Suppose $k \leqslant j$. By hypothesis, G_k and H_k have the same index. Hence, H_1 and H_{k+1} must get the same new positive substituent. But this is impossible, since H_k being of rank less than m still preserves the positive constituent introduced at H_1.

Hence, in either case, there is some p, $a_p \neq b_p$. Take the first such p, then preceding ε-substitutions in both m-sections all yield the same resolvents, and (ii) is proved.

We now extend the definition of index to m-sections.

2.7. The index of a 0-section is the same as the index of the single ε-substitution which it contains, the index of an $(m+1)$-section is $\omega^{a_1} + \cdots + \omega^{a_k}$, where $a_1, \cdots, a_k$ are the indices of the finitely many m-sections which together make up the $(m+1)$-section.

Theorem 4. *Given two consecutive m-sections, $m < g$, such that the first ε-substitution of the second m-section has rank m. Let p be any number $0 \leqslant p \leqslant m$, and $a_1, \cdots, a_j$; $b_1, \cdots, b_k$ be the indices of the p-sections out of which the two m-sections are made, j, $k \geqslant 1$. There is then a number q, such that $a_q > b_q$ and for all i, $i < q$, $a_i = b_i$.*

Proof. By Th. 3, this theorem is true when p is 0 and m is arbitrary. Assume it true for all smaller m and all smaller p.

By Th. 3, there are two earliest corresponding ε-substitutions in the two m-sections such that the index of the first is greater than that of the second. Since the index of an ε-substitution determines its rank, they must belong to two corresponding p-sections with indices a_q and b_q. Now each of the two p-sections is made up of one or more $(p-1)$-sections. By the induction hypothesis, $a_q = \omega^{c_1} + \cdots + \omega^{c_u}$, $b_q = \omega^{d_1} + \cdots + \omega^{d_v}$, and there is an earliest $c_t > d_t$. Hence, $a_q > b_q$.

From this theorem, the consistency of Z_a follows because given any proof, we can write out its ε-categories and construct ε-substitutions in the manner described before. If there are g ε-categories, then the initial ε-substitution G_1 has rank g. Since all later ε-substitutions, if there are any, have smaller rank, there is one g-section. Since the second of two consecutive p-sections in a $(p+1)$-section always has a smaller index than the first, there can be only finitely many $(g-1)$-sections. In each $(g-1)$-section, there can be only finitely many $(g-2)$-sections. Hence, for every proof, there is a finite sequence of ε-substitutions which gives numerically true resolvents for all formulae in the proof. Hence, e.g., $0=1$ is not provable.

To formalize this proof, one would need transfinite induction up to the first Cantor ε-number. Thus, if we consider all proofs each of which contains g ε-categories or less, we would at most need a transfinite induction up to $\omega(g+1)$, where $\omega(0) = \omega$, $\omega(n+1) = \omega^{\omega(n)}$. Since a single ε-substitution has an index of the form $\omega m + n$, a 0-

section has index less than $\omega(1)$, in fact less than ω^2. If a p-section has index less than $\omega(p+1)$, then a $(p+1)$-section has index less than $\omega(p+2)$. Hence, the single g-section has index less than $\omega(g+1)$. To formalize this, we prove that every decreasing sequence of ordinals less than $\omega(g+1)$ is finite. If we are concerned with all proofs of Z_a, then g is not bounded, and we need induction through all of $\omega(0)$, $\omega(1)$, etc., up to the first ε-number. From Gödel's second theorem, such induction cannot be formalized in Z_a. Gentzen gives a direct proof of this fact in connection with his own consistency proof (see *Math. Annalen*, **119** (1943), 140—161).

§ 3. Estimates of the Substituents

To reproduce as much of the argument as is possible in Z_a, one represents ordinals by natural numbers. For each $\omega(n)$ a well-ordering R_n of natural numbers is defined by induction. Thus, R_0 is the usual natural ordering, $R_1(2^a(2b+1)-1, 2^c(2d+1)-1)$ if and only if either $a<c$ or $a=c$ but $b<d$. Given R_p, $p>0$, if $R_p(b_i, b_{i+1})$, $R_p(c_i, c_{i+1})$, $R_{p+1}(2^{b_1}+\cdots+2^{b_j}-1, 2^{c_1}+\cdots+2^{c_k}-1)$ if and only if $R_p(b_1, c_1)$ or etc. or $b_1=c_1, \cdots, b_j=c_j$, but $j<k$.

Now the index of each m-section can be represented by a natural number, if the index of an m-section is represented by a, then the total number of ε-substitutions in the m-section can be defined by a simple ordinal recursive function $f(a, m)$:

3.1. $f(a,0)=1, f(2^{a_1}+\cdots+2^{a_k}-1, p+1)=f(a_1, p)+\cdots+f(a_k, p)$.

We have defined degree, order, rank of an ε-substitution. Now we define degree, order, rank of a proof in a different way.

3.2. The order of a proof is the number of closed ε-terms in it.

3.3. The degree of a closed term is 0 if it is 0 or an ε-term, it is $n+1$ if it is of the form a', $a \dot{-} 1$, $a+b$, or ab in which a has the degree n, or the maximum degree of a and b is n. The degree of a proof is the maximum degree of the closed terms in it.

3.4. The rank of a proof is the number of ε-categories in its associated sequence.

Suppose given a proof of degree d and an ε-substitution G. If m is the maximum value which a closed ε-term can get under G, then $b(d, m)$ is the maximum value which any closed term can get:

3.5. $b(0,m)=m, b(d+1, m)=(b(d, m))^2+1$.

This is so because with each increase in degree we only go from $b(d, m)$ to $(b(d, m))'$, $b(d, m) \dot{-} 1$, $b(d, m)+b(d, m)$, $b(d, m)\cdot b(d, m)$, all less than or equal to $(b(d, m))^2+1$.

Since for the initial ε–substitution G_1, $m=0$, the greatest value is no greater than $b(d, 0)$. From the way we obtain G_{i+1} given G_i, the maximum value at each substitution G_i is $c(d, i)$ defined by:

3.6. $c(d, 0)=b(d, 0),\ c(d, i+1)=b(d, c(d, i))$.

It therefore follows that given a bound to the number of ε–substitutions, a bound for numerical values can also be obtained.

If the degree of the proof is k, then the degree of the ε–substitution G_i is no greater than:

3.7. $e(d, i, k)=2^{(c(d, i)+1)k}$.

This is so because in the sequence $A(0, n), \cdots, A(j, n)$ of 2.2, j is no greater than $c(d, i)$, and each formula contains no more than k terms.

The difficult part is to define a function $g(p, i, a)$ which gives an upper bound to the ordinal notation less than a which is the index of a p–section beginning with G_i. Assume the function g is given, then we can define $h(p, i, a)$ which gives an upper bound to the index of a $(p+1)$–section that begins with a p–section whose first term is G_i whose index is a:

3.8. $h(p, i, a)=2^a+h(p,i+f(a, p), g(p, i+f(a, p), a))$.

Both g and h are also functions of d and k (the degree and the order of the proof), although we are not writing out these arguments explicitly. In fact, the functions g and h are defined simultaneously.

(i) $g(p,i, 0)=0$. (ii) $g(0, i, 2^b(2c+1)-1)$ is $2^b(2c-1)-1$, if $c\neq 0$, and $2^{b-1}(2e(d, i, k)+1)-1$, if $c=0, b\neq 0$. (iii) when $p>0$, $a>0$: (iiia) if a is even, $g(p, i, a)=a-1$; (iiib) if a is odd and of the form 2^b-1, $g(p, i, a)=h(p-1, i, g(p-1, i, b))$; (iiic) if a is $2^j+2^b+\cdots+2^c-1$, then $g(p, i, a) = 2^j+g(p, i+f(j, p-1), 2^b+\cdots+2^c-1)$.

Once h is given, we may forget the function g, and again use the letter g as the rank of the proof, and rewrite the function h as $h(d, k, g, i, a)$.

Then we can estimate the total number of ε–substitutions from a given proof of Z_a whose degree, order, rank are d, k, g. We can effectively find its sequence of ε–substitutions and therefore calculate the index $2^a+\cdots+2^b-1$ of the only g–section in the sequence. Hence, the total number of ε–substitutions $f(2^a+\cdots+2^b-1, g)$ is no more than: $f(h(d, k, g-1, 1, a), g)$.

Now a satisfies $R_g(a, t(g-1, k))$, where $t(0, k)=2^{k+1}$, $t(p+1, k)=2^{c(p, k)}-1$. Hence, the total number of ε–substitutions is no more than:

3.9. $m(d, k, g)=f(h(d, k, g-1, 1, t(g-1, k)), g)$.

By combining this with 3.7, we see that for any proof with degree, order, rank d, k, g given, the maximum numerical value used in the final resolvents is:

3.10. $c(d, m(d, k, g))$.

From this situation, some surprising consequences can be drawn. For this purpose, it is more direct to state the consequences in the notation of the equivalent system Z.

Theorem 5. *Given any theorem of the form* $(Ex)\cdots(Ey)$ $A(x, \cdots, y)$ *where* A *contains no quantifiers, we can calculate from the proof a number* p *such that* $A(j, \cdots, n)$ *holds for some* $j, \cdots, n$ *all no greater than* p.

This can be directly generalized to systems which contain more recursive functions as primitive symbols. This shows that in proving a pure existence theorem, we can obtain actual examples with a finite amount of labour which has a predetermined bound yielded by the proof.

A related consequence is:

Theorem 6. *If a theorem* $(x)(Ey)A(x, y)$, A *containing no quantifiers, is given in* Z, *we can take a recursive function* $f(x)$ *of a definite type (viz., the functions actually used in defining 3.10, the ordinal recursive functions of Ackermann) such that for all* x, $R(x, f(x))$ *is true.*

For this purpose, we assume d to be the degree of the proof and consider the proofs of $R(0, \varepsilon_y R(0, y)), R(1, \varepsilon_y R(1, y)), \cdots$. Then we see that the following must hold:

$$(x)(Ey)(y \leqslant c(x + d, b(d, k, g)) \,\&\, R(x, y)).$$

Hence, the theorem follows by eliminating the bounded quantifier y.

One may hope to generalize these to more complex theorems. However, Kreisel has shown that a direct generalization is impossible and introduces a program of interpretation (see *J. Symbolic Logic*, **16**, 241—267; **17**, 43—58; **23**, 155—182). We proceed to summarize some of Kreisel's results in the next section.

§ 4. Interpretation of Nonfinitist Proofs

Theorem 7. *There are theorems of the form* $(x)(Ey)(z)R(x, y, z)$, R *quantifier-free, such that* $(x)(z)R(x, f(x), z)$ *is not true for any recursive function* $f(x)$.

Consider the theorem:

$$(3) \qquad (i)(Ey)(z)(B(y, s(i, i)) \vee \sim B(z, s(i, i))).$$

Therein B and s are those used previously in proving Gödel's theorems.

Since there is a notation in Z for every recursive function, we may take every proposed recursive function f and prove that there is for it some values of x and z such that:

$$(4) \qquad B(f(i), s(i, i)) \vee \sim B(z, s(i, i))$$

is false. Suppose the Gödel number of

$$(5) \qquad \sim B(f(i), s(i, i))$$

is $\bar{p}$. Then

$$(6) \qquad \sim B(f(\bar{p}), s(\bar{p}, \bar{p}))$$

is true, because otherwise, $f(\bar{p})$ would give a proof of the formula whose number is $s(\bar{p}, \bar{p})$, viz. (6) itself. On the other hand, since (6) is a numerical formula, it, being true, is provable in Z with a proof whose number is $\bar{k}$. Hence,

$$(7) \qquad B(\bar{k}, s(\bar{p}, \bar{p}))$$

is true and provable in Z. Hence (4) is false, if we substitute $\bar{p}$ and $\bar{k}$ for i and z.

Another example was used by Specker (*J. Symbolic Logic*, **14** (1949), 145—158). Classically, if $a(m)$ is a monotone bounded sequence of rational numbers, then for all x, there exists y, such that for all z and w, $2^x|a(z) - a(w)| < 1$, for $z, w > y$. The usual proof gives no idea how y is to be determined from x. And Specker gives a monotone bounded recursive sequence $a(m)$ such that there exists no recursive function f for which the following holds:

$$(x)(z)(w)(z, w > f(x) \supset 2^x|a(z) - a(w)| < 1).$$

Kreisel uses a free-variable formalism F which is obtained from Z by dropping all quantifiers but adding all ordinal recursive functions of order k, for every k. That is to say, all functions definable from primitive recursive functions by addition of ordinal recursions of each order k, where

$$f(0, x) = g(x), \quad f(m', x) = h(x, m, f(\phi(m'), x)),$$

g, h, ϕ are given functions such that $R_k(\phi(m), m)$, for all m, according to the ordering R_k defined in §3. The system F contains also a rule of transfinite induction for each order k, viz., if there is a function ϕ, $R_k(\phi(m), m)$. Then $A(n)$ follows from $A(0)$, and $A(\phi(m')) \supset A(m')$.

To each formula A of Z is associated effectively a sequence of formulae $A_1, A_2, \cdots$ in F such that:

4.1. From a proof of A in Z, we can read off a proof of some A_i in F.

4.2. From a proof of any A_i in F, we can read off a proof of A in Z; indeed, since A_i can be expressed in Z, we can prove A_i in Z and derive A from A_i in Z.

We can easily generalize and modify Theorem 6 to get:

4.3. If $(x)(Ey)R(x, y)$ is provable in Z, R primitive recursive, then there is an ordinal recursive function g of some finite order such that we can prove in F:

$$R(n, g(n)) \,\&\, (m < g(n) \supset \sim R(n, m)). \tag{8}$$

Let $t(n, x)$ be $t_n(x)$, where t_n is the n-th function which is 0 except for a finite number of argument places in some simple enumeration.

Let the formula A of Z be, e.g., $(Ex)(y)(Ez)C(x, y, z)$.

Enumerate all the proofs of Z which lead up to a conclusion with $(Ex)(y)(Ez)$ followed by a primitive recursive predicate and let the i-th such proof lead to

$$(Ex)(y)(Ez)D_i(x, y, z).$$

Then we can also prove in Z:

$$(n)(Ex)(Ez)D_i(x, t(n, x), z).$$

Hence, by 4.3, there are ordinal recursive functions a_i, b_i in some enumeration such that:

$$D_i(a_i(n), t(n, a_i(n)), b_i(n))$$

can be proved in F.

Now the sequence of formulae associated with A is simply that A_i is, for $i = 1, 2, \cdots$:

$$C(a_i(n), t(n, a_i(n)), b_i(n)). \tag{9}$$

If A can be proved in Z, C must coincide with some D_i, and therefore A_i, i.e., (9) is provable in F for some i.

Conversely, if some A_i is provable in F, it is also provable in Z and we can derive from it, again in Z, A itself:

In (9), if we choose a suitable term s, as on pp. 6—7 of *Math. Zeitschrift*, **57** (1952), we can make:

$$a_i(s) = \mu_x(y)(Ez)C(x, y, z),$$
$$t(s, a_i(s)) = \mu_y(z) \sim C(a_i(s), y, z),$$
$$b_i(s) = \mu_z C(a_i(s), t(s, a_i(s)), z).$$

Then A follows from A_i in Z.

CHAPTER XV

PARTIAL SYSTEMS OF NUMBER THEORY

§ 1. Skolem's Non-standard Model for Number Theory

In this section we summarize the work of Skolem in *Fund. Math.*, **23** (1934), 157—159, *Mathematical Interpretation of Formal Systems*, 1955, 1—14, and the related results of Ryll-Nardzewski, *Fund. Math.*, **39** (1952), 239—263.

By the famous theorem of Löwenheim, set theory has also an arithmetic model. Skolem emphasized that this leads to a relativization of the concept of set to each formal system. If one desires to develop arithmetic as a part of set theory, a definition of natural numbers in a formal set theory has a relative meaning so that an enumerable (and, therefore nonstandard) interpretation of the whole system would also yield a nonstandard interpretation of the natural numbers. From this it is natural to expect if we try to characterize the sequence of natural numbers directly by a formal system, we would not obtain a complete characterization. Skolem has succeeded in showing that this is really so.

Let us use the formal system Z. Every formula is equivalent to a prenex normal form beginning with a string of quantifiers, followed by truth-functional combinations of equations. In familiar manner, we can delete the truth-functional connectives, e.g., by the following relations.

1.1. $a \neq b$ by $(Ex)((a=x+b) \vee (b=a+x))$.

1.2. $(a=b) \vee (c=d)$ by $ad+bc=ac+bd$.

Then we can drop all quantifiers and replace all variables attached to particular quantifiers by functions or ε–terms. The resulting system contains no more quantifiers but only equations with free variables. Call it Z_f.

We enumerate all the functions of one argument, i.e., all terms containing one free variable:

$$f_1(t), f_2(t), \cdots \tag{1}$$

Let M_1, M_2, M_3 be respectively the subsets of the set N of natural numbers for which

$$f_1(t) < f_2(t),\ f_1(t) = f_2(t),\ f_1(t) > f_2(t).$$

Let N_1 be the M_i with least subscript which is infinite. Of course, one at least of M_1, M_2, M_3 must be infinite. This defines whether

$$f_1 < f_2,\ f_1 = f_2,\ f_1 > f_2$$

For the infinitely many members of N_1, there must be at least one infinite subset for which every member has a same relation between $f_1(t)$ and $f_3(t)$, and a same relation between $f_2(t)$ and $f_3(t)$. For example, if N_1 is M_1, then for every t in N_1, at least one of the following relations hold:

$$f_3(t) < f_1(t) < f_2(t),\ f_3(t) = f_1(t) < f_2(t),\ f_1(t) < f_3(t) < f_2(t),$$
$$f_1(t) < f_3(t) = f_2(t),\ f_1(t) < f_2(t) < f_3(t).$$

This gives five subsets of N_1, choose the first infinite subset as N_2.

This process is continued so that we get an infinite sequence of infinite subsets of N of monotone nonincreasing size. In this way an ordering of the functions in (1) is defined.

Let $g(i)$ be the least member of N_i, then we have:

Theorem 1. *For any pair a, b, the same relation $<, =$, or $>$ holds between $f_a(g(t))$ and $f_b(g(t))$ for all $t >$ max (a, b), this relation is also the ordering relation between f_a and f_b. The function $g(t)$ is monotone nondecreasing. In particular, since all constants occur in* (1), *viz., functions which always take a same value, $g(t)$ is not bounded.*

It is easy to see that the relations $=$ and $<$ thus defined over the sequence (1) have the usual properties of such relations. We now treat each equivalent class as a nonstandard number, and the ordering defines a sequence N^* of higher order type than N.

Among these equivalent classes, the constant numbers also occur in distinct equivalent classes with the correct ordering relation. If we reinterpret all the free variables of Z_b as ranging over N^* instead of N, we can see that all theorems of Z_f would be true in the new interpretation. In other words, if we replace variables over N by variables over N^* in theorems of Z, the results are true. For example, this can be verified for 1.2 and for the principle of induction.

Theorem 2. *The system has a model which is not isomorphic to the standard model, and the order type of the nonstandard numbers is greater than ω.*

It may be noted that the argument applies equally well to partial systems of Z. While the model defined above is not constructive, the same method can be applied to weak fragments of number theory to obtain transparent effective nonstandard models. Skolem himself has given simple examples. Related questions are also studied by Hasenjaeger, *J. Symbolic Logic*, **17** (1952), 81—97.

An application in a different direction was made by Ryll-Nardzewski. He takes the system Z and deletes all but a finite number of special cases of the schema of mathematical induction. For any such partial system S, he shows by using Skolem's model that there is some case of the induction schema not deducible in the system.

Theorem 3. *There is no finite set of theorems of Z (indeed, no finite set of formulae true in the standard model of Z) from which we can derive by the predicate calculus all axioms of Z.*

Assume given such a partial system S. In order that it be adequate at all, it must include the various special things we use below from Z. We assume that quantifiers are taken away as before.

There are only a finite number of axioms beyond the predicate calculus, and only a finite number of functions $f_1, \cdots, f_k$ in these axioms. These are taken as the basic functions.

For the arbitrary terms a and b of S, we can define in S a predicate which says:

1.3. b is of order i relative to a and $f_1, \cdots, f_k$, or, briefly, b is an i-th descendant of a: a is its own 1-descendant; b is an $(n+1)$-descendant of a if a is $f_i(c, \cdots, d)$ and some of $c, \cdots, d$ is an n-descendant of a but none is of order more than n relative to a and $f_1, \cdots, f_k$.

In addition, it is easy to define a relation R such that:

1.4. $R(x, y, z)$ if and only if x is at most of order y relative to z and $f_1, \cdots, f_k$.

Let $\phi(y)$ be the formula that for every z there exists t such that for all x, if x is of order no more than y relative z and $f_1, \cdots, f_k$, then $x \leqslant t$:

1.5. $\phi(y)$ is $(z)(Et)(x)(R(x, y, z) \supset x \leqslant t)$.

Then it is possible to prove in S:

1.6. $\phi(1)$,

1.7. $\phi(y) \supset \phi(y+1)$.

However, the conclusion

1.8. $\phi(y)$

is not provable in S.

Assume a Skolem model N^* for S given. The equivalent classes containing the standard natural numbers form only an initial segment of N^*. Let w be an arbitrary element of N^* not among the above. Then all descendants of w determine a model of S. Then the equivalent class (n) for each natural number n satisfies the relation: $(n) < w$.

If $\phi(w)$ is true, then, by 1.5, there is some c,

$$(2) \qquad (d)(R(d, w, w) \supset d \leqslant c).$$

But the successor c^* of c in the model can be obtained from w as a descendant, say a k-descendant. Hence, $R(c^*, w, w)$, contradicting (2). Hence, Theorem 2 is proved.

It seems possible to use the same argument to prove a somewhat stronger result, viz. we cannot derive all axioms of Z from any finite consistent set of formulae in Z. Thus, given a such set which can be written as a single formula A, either not all theorems of Z are derivable from A, or else we can carry out Ryll-Nardezwski's construction and get a case of the induction schema which is derivable in Z but not derivable from A, provided only A is consistent. Hence, if all theorems are derivable from A, A must be inconsistent.

There appears to be a connection between Skolem's result and Gödel's first theorem. From Gödel's theorem, we can get a non-standard model of Z. Conversely, we can also extend Ryll-Nardezwski's argument to find an undecidable proposition of Z by the Skolem model. Thus, the above argument depends on the possibility of enumerating all terms of S in Z. If S is Z itself, the enumeration can no longer be made directly in Z, but we can make an indirect enumeration by the proof predicate. Compare Ch. II, §5 above.

§ 2. Some Applications of Formalized Consistency Proofs

In this section we give an explanation of the paper by Kreisel and the writer, *Fund. math.*, **42** (1955), 101—110; **45** (1958), 334—335.

We consider partial systems F of Z and Z_a which are obtained from them by suppressing those proofs which are too "complex". We shall prove the consistency of such systems F in Z and Z_a; F would be demonstrably weaker since a formula expressing its consistency cannot be proved in F itself. We shall denote such a formula by $Con(F)$; it is to be understood that the formula chosen satisfies conditions sufficient to ensure the application of Gödel's second theorem.

For the first measure of complexity we use the rank of a proof in Z_a, viz., the number of ε-categories.

2.1. The system Z_a^n: a proof of Z_a of rank $\leqslant n$ is a proof of Z_a^n.

2.2. For each integer n, $Con(Z_a^n)$ is a theorem of Z_a.

This is direct from Ackermann's consistency proof since, for each n, transfinite induction to $\omega(n)$ can be proved in Z_a.

A second measure of complexity is obtained from the truth definition of Z given in Hilbert-Bernays II.

2.3. The system $Z^{(n)}$: a proof Z whose formulae are all of type $\leqslant n$, i.e., in each formula if we construct a graph of quantifiers governed by a given quantifier, the maximum succession is always of length $\leqslant n$, is a proof of $Z^{(n)}$.

2.4. For each n, $Con(Z^{(n)})$ is a theorem of Z.

To prove this, the truth definition has to be modified somewhat. It is assumed that "natural" definitions of the following syntactical terms and predicates have been chosen.

$\eta_1^{(m)}(n), \cdots, \eta_m^{(m)}(n)$ as in Hilbert-Bernays II, p. 235.

$\varrho(m, a, n)$ is the number of the formula got from A (with number a) by replacing the variable v_i, $i \leqslant m$, in A by $\eta_i^{(m)}(0^{(n)})$ and v_j, $j > m$, by 0. It is not assumed that all v_i, $i \leqslant m$, occur in A. All the variables we use in the proofs will be v_1, v_2, v_3, etc. Trivially, if A is a closed formula, $\varrho(m, a, n) = \varrho(0, a, 0)$. ($v_i$ are free variables.)

$P(a, b)$ if and only if a is a numerical proof of the formula b (*i.e.*, a proof in the elementary calculus, no variables). We recall that the consistency of numerical arithmetic can be proved in Z.

If a and b are numbers of A and B, then $t(a, b)$ is the number of $A|B$.

$U(a)$ if and only if a is the number of a formula of the form $(x)B(x)$, and then $s[u(a), y]$ is the number of $B(0^{(y)})$.

Similarly, $Q(a)$ if and only if a is the number of a formula of the form $(Ex)B(x)$, and then $s[q(a), y]$ is the number of $B(0^{(y)})$.

For each k, a truth definition $T_k(b)$ can be given by means of a formula of Z, satisfying the following conditions (compare *ibid.*, p. 334):

$$T_0[\varrho(m, a, n)] \text{ if and only if } (Ey)P[y, \varrho(m, a, n)]$$

or

$$(Ex)(Ey)\{x < \varrho(m, a, n) \mathbin{\&} y < \varrho(m, a, n) \mathbin{\&}$$
$$\mathbin{\&} \varrho(m, a, n) = t(x, y) \mathbin{\&} [T_0(x) \,|\, T_0(y)]\};$$

$$T_{k+1}[\varrho(m, a, n)] \text{if and only if } T_k[\varrho(m, a, n)]$$

or

$$\{U[\varrho(m, a, n)] \mathbin{\&} (y)T_k[\varrho(m, s(u(a), y), n)]\}$$

or

$$\{Q[\varrho(m, a, n)] \& (Ey)T_k[\varrho(m, s(q(a), y), n)]\}$$

or

$$(Ex)(Ey)\{x < \varrho(m, a, n) \& y < \varrho(m, a, n) \& \\ \& \varrho(m, a, n) = t(x, y) \& [T_{k+1}(x) \mid T_{k+1}(y)]\}.$$

It can be verified in the usual manner that $T_k(b)$ is a normal truth definition, and hence $Con(Z^{(k)})$ may be proved in Z. Note that $T_n(b)$ is a truth definition for the system $Z^{(n)}$ only, and not for Z; in particular, n is not a free variable.

Observe that the consistency proof of 2.4 is capable of various extensions: *e.g.*, if $\mathfrak{Z}$ is an extension of Z by some principle of transfinite induction, we get a consistency proof of $\mathfrak{Z}^{(n)}$ in $\mathfrak{Z}$.

Let F be a system consisting of the predicate calculus with a single closed formula A as axiom.

Theorem 4. *If F is consistent, there is a theorem of Z not provable in F.*

Let k be the type of A, roughly the number of distinct quantifiers in it. If $\sim Con(F)$, there is a proof in the predicate calculus of $\sim A$. By Herbrand's theorem, $\sim A$ can be proved with a proof each formula of which is of type $\leqslant k$. Thus, $\sim A$ can be proved in $Z^{(k)}$. Hence, by the normal truth definition of Z^k, we can prove in Z: $\sim Con(F) \supset \sim A$. Therefore, the following is a theorem of Z:

$$(1) \qquad A \supset Con(F).$$

Now if F contains all theorems of Z, the deducibility conditions for the application of Gödel's second theorem would be applicable to F, since we are assuming the "natural" proof predicate of F; further the formula (1) and hence $Con(F)$ would be theorems of F, and F would be inconsistent.

It is actually possible to exhibit from the proof, for any given consistent F, a theorem of Z not provable in F.

This result and the result in the preceding section shows that there are infinitely many axioms, which cannot be reduced to a finite number. Kleene proves in *Memoirs of Am. Math. Soc.*, no. 10, 1952, 27—68, that if we introduce auxiliary predicate symbols, such reduction is always possible.

These considerations can also be applied to deal with Gödel's result on the length of proofs (*Ergebnisse Math. Kolloquiums*, **7** (1936), 23—24). Thus since $Con(Z^{(n)})$ is provable in Z but not provable in $Z^{(n)}$, there is also some formula $(x)C(x)$ which is provable in Z but not in $Z^{(n)}$, although $C(1)$, $C(2)$, $\cdots$, all are provable in $Z^{(n)}$. Then for large constants k, we would seem to need a proof of unbounded length to prove $C(k)$ in Z^n, although in Z it is always an immediate consequence of $(x)C(x)$.

In view of 2.2. and 2.4, the measure of length or complexity of a proof is for us more easily given by the rank and type of a proof, i.e., the number of ε-categories or the number of distinct quantifiers.

Theorem 5. *If the length of a proof of Z_a is measured by the number of ε-categories in it, and F' is an extension of Z_a in which $Con(Z_a)$ is a theorem, then for each n, $Con(Z_a^n)$ can be proved in F' by proofs of bounded length, but its shortest proof in Z_a is longer than n. Similarly, if we use the type as a measure of length, an analogous theorem holds for Z and the theorems $Con(Z^{(n)})$.*

Finally, according to the Bernays' lemma, every S is translatable into Z_S, viz. Z plus a new axiom $Con(S)$. Now for systems with finitely many axioms, we can prove a converse to it:

Theorem 6. *If a finite axiom system F is translatable into Z, then $Con(F)$ can be proved in Z.*

Let the translation of the axiom A of F be the theorem B of Z. If $\sim Con(F)$, there would be a proof of $\sim F$ in the predicate calculus, and hence a proof of $\sim B$ in $Z^{(m)}$ for some fixed number m, the type of A. Hence, we have in Z, $\sim Con(F) \supset \sim T_m(b)$, b being the number of B.

Since $T_m(a)$ is a normal truth definition, $\sim T_m(b) \supset \sim B$. Hence, we have in Z: $B \supset Con(F)$. Hence, $Con(F)$ is a theorem of Z.

PART FOUR

IMPREDICATIVE SET THEORY

CHAPTER XVI

DIFFERENT AXIOM SYSTEMS

§ 1. The Paradoxes

In this chapter, we shall describe a number of well-known systems of set theory as a general basis for later chapters, and mention a number of standard results in this field. For the systematic development of axiomatic set theory, the standard works are Bernays' series of papers in the *J. Symbolic Logic* (seven parts so far from 1938 to 1954), Gödel's 1940 monograph on the consistency of the continuum hypothesis, and Bernays' new book *Axiomatic Set Theory*, 1958, Amsterdam. For surveys, there is a brief one by McNaughton and the writer (*Les systèmes axiomatiques de la théorie des ensembles*, 1953, Paris) and a more detailed one by Fraenkel and Bar-Hillel (*Foundations of Set Theory*, 1958, Amsterdam).

The systems to be described are the Zermelo-Fraenkel theory *ZF*, the Bernays theory *NB*, the simple theory of types *T*, the Quine systems *NF* and *ML* (the latter as repaired by the writer), a system of negative types *NT*, Frege's system, Ackermann's system, and several subsystems of *ZF* and *NB*. The system *G*, the theory of finite sets (general set theory) is obtained from *ZF* by omitting the axiom of infinity. The system *P*, the predicative theory of number-sets, is obtained from *NB* by deleting the axiom of infinity. The system *Q*, the impredicative theory of number-sets, is obtained from *ZF* by deleting the axiom of power set. The system *R*, the predicative theory of real-sets, is obtained from *NB* by omitting the axiom of power sets. More than half of the remaining chapters of this book deal with such partial systems of set theory, often described and labelled in somewhat different ways.

In the present section, we give a summary of some well-known paradoxes which, as a historical fact, were closely related to the development of axiomatic set theory. It seems fair to say that there is a general tendency to exaggerate the consequences of these paradoxes. It is sometimes overlooked that there is an amount of intuitive evidence in classical set theory which makes the construction of systems of set theory much less arbitrary than has often been asserted. It is not just a matter of experimenting with devices which somehow give us a great deal and yet, as far as we know, do not engender contradictions. For example, *ZF* and *NB* have intuitive models which, though short of providing formal consistency proofs, make us feel more at home with them than with *NF* and *ML*.

Disregarding the histoical succession of events, one could very well develop axiomatic set theory along the line of *ZF* or *NB* without discussing the logico-mathematical antinomies. We are, nonetheless, considering these for their intrinsic interest and suggesting power.

Around the year 1900, modes of reasoning apparently similar to those occurring in Cantor's proofs of the existence of nonenumerable sets were seen to lead to contradictions. In 1897, Burali-Forti published the paradox known since then by his name. Thus, in Cantor's theory, if we order according to magnitude all the ordinal numbers which are smaller than a given ordinal number α, then the ordinal number of the resulting well-ordered set is α. Consider now the well-ordered set S of all the ordinal numbers arranged by magnitude. If its ordinal number is W, then every ordinal number in the given set is smaller than (and therefore different from) W, which contradicts the hypothesis that S contains all the ordinals. Hence, we have a contradiction. A related paradox is Cantor's about the greatest cardinal number. A more surprising paradox is Russell's of the set of all sets each of which does not belong to itself, discovered in June of 1901. Let K be the set. If K does not belong to K, then, by the definition of K, K belongs to K; if K belongs to K, then, by the definition of K, K does not belong to K. This had also been discovered indepdndently by Zermelo before Russell's discovery was published in 1903. (Cf. Zermelo's 1908 paper on the axiom of choice.)

The discovery of these paradoxes is sometimes considered as a great event leading to a modern crisis in mathematics. Indeed, as it is often noted, Frege admitted that Russell's paradox undermines the foundations of his life work to construct arithmetic on the basis of set theory (See appendix to Frege, *Grundgesetze*, vol. 2, 1903, dated October 1902.) Dedekind refrained from putting out a new edition of his classic set-theoretic treatment of concepts and principles of arithmetic (Dedekind 1888), and when in 1911 he finally let appear the third edition of his book, he acknowledged in the new preface that developments since the issuing of the second edition (1893) had rendered the foundations of his theory somewhat questionable. On the other hand, many distinguished mathematicians either rejoiced (e.g. Poincaré, "La logistique n'est plus stérile; elle engendre la contradiction!") at the paradoxes or paid no attention to them at all.

Cantor himself, who, by the way, unlike Frege and Dedekind, never interested himself in the task of justifying the theory of natural numbers by set theory, did not seem to be much disturbed. He had found in 1895 an argument similar to that used in the Burali-Forti paradox and communicated it to Hilbert in 1896 (see Bernstein 1905, *Math. Annalen*, **60**) but he did not consider the argument any serious trouble for his set theory. In his letters to Dedekind (1899), he distinguished between manifolds which are at the same time unities (the sets) and those which cannot consistently be thought of as unities (the "inconsistent manifolds"). The totality of all ordinal numbers is an example of the second kind (see Cantor's *Collected Works*, 443—450). Apparently he considered such a distinction intrinsic to set theory and adequate to resolving the paradoxes, and he blamed people who talk about paradoxes for overlooking this natural distinction. According to Young (see Young 1929, *Math. Gazette*, **14**, 98), Cantor in 1907 attacked Burali-Forti's paper and criticized that the author has not understood rightly the concept of the well-ordered set.

These paradoxes led to attempts to axiomatize set theory. It is rather interesting that there are now in existence several standard systems of set theory which retain analogues of Cantor's proofs but, so far as we know, exclude the superficially similar contradictions. Our knowledge in these matters is so restricted that there is a very great gap between what is known to be consistent and what is known to be contradictory.

This lack of information are treasured by those who adopt a constructive viewpoint. The region of the constructive is known as consistent, and they look at the area beyond more or less as fantasy that is foreign to scientific understanding.

In Russell 1906, there is an interesting discussion of possible methods of avoiding paradoxes. He distinguishes three possible ways: (1) the zigzag theory; (2) the theory of limitation of size; (3) the no classes theory. Russell himself chooses to develop the no classes theory which is closely related to the abolition of impredicative sets. Zermelo's system (1908) may be taken as a theory of limitation of size. Thus, a set term or propositional function can define a set only if its extension is not "too big". Later on von Neumann (1929) specifies the notion to mean: an extension is not too big when and only when it is not equivalent to the universe of all sets. If we wish to, we may also consider Quine's system *NF* as an example of the zigzag theory.

It may be of interest to make a rough comparison of these, as well as some other proposed methods for avoiding the paradoxes.

Consider again Russell's paradox. Let K be the set denoted by $\hat{x} \sim (x \in x)$. By the very nature of sets, we have

$$(1)\qquad \begin{cases} x \in \hat{x} \sim x \in x \equiv \sim x \in x \\ x \in K \equiv \sim x \in x. \end{cases}$$

If we substitute K for x in (1), we have

(2) $$K \in K \equiv \sim K \in K.$$

By the law of excluded middle,

(3) $$K \in K \vee \sim K \in K.$$

If $K \in K$, then $\sim K \in K$ by (2); if $\sim K \in K$, then $K \in K$ by (2). In either case, $K \in K$ & $\sim K \in K$. Hence, by (3), we have

(4) $$K \in K \,\&\, \sim K \in K,$$

a contradiction.

To avoid this paradox, there are a number of possible courses. It is interesting to note that almost every course has been followed by somebody.

In the theory of simple types, it is meaningless to say that a set belongs to itself, so that there is no open formula (propositional function) to express the property of not belonging to itself. In Zermelo's theory *ZF* or Quine's theory *NF*, there is a meaningful open formula '$\sim x \in x$', but it is not permitted to use it to define a set. In *NB*, it is possible to prove that the open formula '$\sim x \in x$' defines the universal collection (in other words, '$(x) \sim x \in x$' is a theorem) but the universal collection is not a set.

A different method is to permit a set K defined by $\hat{x} \sim (x \in x)$ and admit (1) and (2), but refuse to admit (3). This is done by stipulating that although there is a set K, K happens to be of a peculiar kind for which neither $K \in K$ nor $\sim K \in K$ need be true. In other words, the law of excluded middle does not apply to the sentence '$K \in K$'. Therefore, the derivation of the contradiction (4) breaks down. This approach is used in Skolem 1929 (p. 20) for a rudimentary system, and again by Fitch in his book of 1952 with regard to a thoroughly formalized system.

Recently Shen has introduced sveral other set-theoretical paradoxes (*J. Symbolic Logic*, **18** (1953), 114): that of the class of all grounded classes, that of the class of all noncircular classes, that of the class of all classes not noncircular. The last is a generalization of Russell's paradox previously also noted by Quine (*Mathematical Logic*, p. 130).

A set x for which there is an infinite sequence of sets y, z, etc. (not necessarily all distinct) such that $\cdots \in z \in y \in x$, is said to be groundless. Let K be the set of all grounded sets, i.e. all sets which are not groundless. If K is groundless, then there is a sequence y, z, etc., such that $\cdots \in z \in y \in K$. Then y would be groundless as well. But $y \in K$, and therefore is grounded. Therefore, K must be grounded. But then $K \in K$, and we have $\cdots \in K \in K \in K$. Hence, K is also groundless.

As we shall see in the next section, there is an axiom in *ZF* to exclude such sets so that K would be the universal set if there were a universal set in *ZF*. Or in other words, K is a nonelement (a class) but not an element (a set) in *NB*.

A set x_1 is n-circular if there exists sets $x_2, \cdots, x_n$, such that $x_1 \in x_n \in \cdots \in x_2 \in x_1$, and a set is circular if there exists some n such that it is n-circular. Quite obviously, by arguments similar to the above, we get the other paradoxes of Shen.

In 1926, Ramsey introduced a distinction between logical (mathematical) and semantic (epistemological) paradoxes. The ones considered so far are logical paradoxes, while the semantic ones involve notions of truth, designation, expressibility, and the like. The distinction is not entirely sharp. E.g., Shen's paradoxes about provability would seem a borderline case. In any case, through the arithmetization of metamathematics, the semantic paradoxes can usually be mirrored in formal systems and often suggest sharper results which are no longer paradoxes.

The liar paradox and the Richard paradox are the most familiar semantic paradoxes. There are also many variants. We list some.

1.1. The liar: this proposition is false; what I am saying is false; or, if we make a sentence talk: I am false.

1.2. The sentence on the blackboard on May Day, 1955 in the Sheldonian is false, provided this is the only sentence on the only blackboard in that theater on that day.

1.3. A book beginning with: the first sentence of the book is false.

1.4. "does not produce a true statement when appended to its own quotation" produces a true statement when appended to its own quotation.

1.5. If 1.5 is true, then it will snow tomorrow.

By modus ponens, given 1.5 and its antecedent, then the consequence is true. Since the antecedent of 1.5 is equivalent to 1.5, we can assert 1.5 unconditionally. Then we have "1.5 is true". By modus ponens again, we have proved: it will snow tomorrow (Geach, *Analysis*, 1955; Löb, *J. Symbolic Logic*, 1955).

1.6. I am not demonstrable.

1.7. I am refutable.

1.8. It can be proved that 1.8 can be refuted.

1.9. We cannot prove the statement which is arrived at by substituting 1.9 for the variable in the statement-form *x*.

1.10. On a card, on one side there is "the sentence on the other side is false", on the other side, "the sentence on the other side is true" (Specker).

1.11. (a) *b* is false. (b) *a* and *c* are true. (c) *a* is false.

1.12. (a) *b* is false. (b) *c* is true. (c) *d* is false. (d) *a* is true. Some variants of Russell's paradox are:

1.13. The barber in a village who shaves all and only those persons in the village who do not shave themselves. One would say there was never such a barber.

1.14. A book which lists all books which do list themselves in the bibliography (Gonseth).

1.15. The relation between two relations when one does not have itself to the other.

If we modify Cantor's nonenumerability argument to refer to nameable sequences of natural numbers in a given language such as English, we get Richard's paradox of 1905.

Thus we can enumerate all expressions in English which name such sequences. We can also have the expression "the sequence whose n-th member is 1 more than the n-th member of the n-th sequence in the enumeration". This has to occur in the enumeration yet is different from every sequence occurring in the enumeration.

A simpler version is Berry's expression: the least natural number not nameable with fewer than three hundred letters.

Another form is the least indefinable transfinite ordinal (König, 1905).

Grelling's paradox of "heterological" may also be viewed as a form of Richard's paradox if we enumerate the vocabulary. Thus, "English" is English, "polysyllabic" is polysyllabic; but "French" is not French, "red" is not red. These latter words are called heterological. Then "heterological" is heterological if and only if it is not.

§ 2. Zermelo's Set Theory

We mentioned in §1 Cantor's distinction between sets and inconsistent manifolds. The main idea is that there are certain manifolds, chiefly those which are "too big", which, if taken as sets, would lead to contradictions. These Cantor called the inconsistent manifolds. It is of course inadequate merely to assert that these should be rejected.

We need some definite procedure for distinguishing sets from inconsistent manifolds. As a matter of fact, Cantor did give indications as to how such procedures could be constructed. Thus, according to Cantor (1899, *Collected Works*, p. 444), two equivalent manifolds are either both sets or both inconsistent, every subset of a set is a set, the sum set of a set (i.e., the set consisting of all members of members of the given set) is a set. If we can write down explicitly all the principles according to which sets are to be constructed, then of course we would possess a definite method of distinguishing sets from the inconsistent manifolds. However, Cantor did not make special efforts to state exhaustively the principles for constructing sets which he and others tacitly assumed. (Some of the principles are also stated in the first few pages of Dedekind 1888.) And the systematic enumeration of such principles later turned out to be much more difficult than one might think at first. For example, in 1904 Zermelo's explicit statement of the axiom of choice, which had been commonly assumed by mathematicians before him, caused much debate and controversy.

Zermelo's axiom system of 1908 is a 'theory of limitation of size', and is probably as close to Cantor's own view on set theory as an axiom system can be.

In Zermelo's formal system *ZF*, there is only one kind of variable $x, y, z, \cdots$ ranging over sets, and one primitive predicate ϵ for the relation of membership (belonging to). The sentences are all got from $x \epsilon y$, $z \epsilon w$, etc. by using truth-functional connectives and quantifiers. The system *ZF* contains quantification theory (predicate calculus), e.g. L_q or L_h, and special axioms numbered Z1—Z9 as follows. The formula $x=y$ is defined as an abbreviation of $(z)(z \epsilon x \equiv z \epsilon y)$.

Z1. Axiom of extensionality. If $x=y$, then $(w)(x \epsilon w \supset y \epsilon w)$.

Z2. Axiom of pairing. $(\exists w)(x)[x \epsilon w \equiv (x=y \vee x=z)]$.

Z3. Axiom of separation (Aussonderungsaxiom). If y does not occur in Fx, $(\exists y)(x)[x \epsilon y \equiv (x \epsilon z \ \& \ Fx)]$ (axiom of subset formation).

Z4. Axiom of the power set. $(\exists y)(x)[x \epsilon y \equiv (w)(w \epsilon x \supset w \epsilon z)]$.

Z5. Axiom of the sum set. $(\exists y)(x)[x \epsilon y \equiv (\exists w)(x \epsilon w \ \& \ w \epsilon z)]$.

Z6. Axiom of choice. $(y)(z)\{(y \epsilon x \ \& \ z \epsilon x) \supset [(\exists w)\, w \epsilon y \ \& \sim (\exists w)(w \epsilon y \ \& \ w \epsilon z)]\} \supset (\exists u)(y)\{y \epsilon x \supset (\exists v)(t)[t=v \equiv (t \epsilon u \ \& \ t \epsilon y)]\}$.

Z7. Axiom of infinity. Let e be the empty set, then $(\exists z)[e \epsilon z \ \& \ (x)(x \epsilon z \supset \{x\} \epsilon z)]$.

Z8. Axiom of foundation (Fundierungsaxiom). $(\exists x)\, Fx \supset (\exists y)[Fy \ \& \ (z) \sim (z \epsilon y \ \& \ Fz)]$ (axiom of restriction, axiom of regularity, axiom of groundedness).

Z9. Axiom of replacement (Ersetzungsaxiom). If $(x)(y)(z)(w)$ $[(Fxz \mathbin{\&} Fyw) \supset (x=y \equiv z=w)]$ and $(\exists x)(u)(u \in x \equiv (\exists v)\ Fuv)$, then $(\exists y)(v)(v \in y \equiv (\exists u) Fuv)$.

The axiom system *ZF* thus presented differs from Zermelo's original theory in a number of respects.

The following three changes are due largely to Fraenkel (especially Fraenkel 1922, *Math. Annalen*, **86**, 230—237).

(a) Zermelo originally allowed for things which are not sets (the "Urelements"), while only sets are admitted in *ZF*. This elimination of non-sets enables us to simplify the formal system considerably and conforms well with the purpose of using set theory to develop mathematics.

(b) In place of the axiom of pairing Z2, Zermelo used an axiom which contains three parts: (1) there is an empty set, (2) there is the unit set of each given set, and (3) there is the pair set of any two given sets. The possibility of omitting (1) and (2) is seen thus. The part (1) is a consequence of Z3: take $\neg x \in z$ as Fx. The part (2) is an immediate consequence of the part (3).

(c) In place of Z1, Zermelo took identity = as a separate primitive and assumed as an axiom: if two sets x and y have the same elements, then $x=y$. In adopting such a procedure, he of course also tacitly assumed as axioms all the primitive principles about identity. The present procedure of taking Zermelo's axiom as a definition dispenses with the additional primitive of identity and any additional axioms which would otherwise be necessary. An alternative and equivalent procedure, as suggested by the theory of types, would be to define $x = y$ as $(w)(x \in w \equiv y \in w)$ or $(w)(x \in w \supset y \in w)$ and assume Zermelo's original axiom:

$$(z)(z \in x \equiv z \in y) \supset x = y.$$

The most important deviation of *ZF* from Zermelo's original system is the more precise form of Z3 in contrast with Zermelo's own axiom of separation. Instead of allowing every sentence Fx as in Z3, Zermelo's original axiom admits only "definite" properties or sentences for separating subsets from a given set. According to Zermelo (see Zermelo 1908, *Math. Annalen*, **65**, 263), "a question or sentence E is called *definite* if the basic relations of the domain (Bereich) under consideration, in virtue of the axioms and the general logical laws, determine without arbitrariness whether E is valid of not." Such a notion is rather lacking in precision and Zermelo's form of Z3 certainly violates the modern requirement that in an axiom system it must be possible mechanically to check for each sentence of the system whether it is an axiom or not. As a matter of fact, there have been criticisms of the axiom, as well as attempts to improve it. The axioms in the form of Z3 is due essentially to Skolem, who made the proposal in as early as 1922 (see his remarks in *Fund. Math.*, **15**). However, even after Skolem's suggestion, rival forms of the axiom, using notions of function, continued to be in use for several years, notably by Fraenkel. Skolem's form of the separation axiom was adopted for the first time by Zermelo in 1930, and then by Quine in 1936, by Ackermann in 1937. Today it seems to be generally accepted.

The axiom Z8 excludes what Mirimanoff called extraordinary sets (see p. 42 of Mirimanoff 1917, *L'enseignement math.*, **19**). A set y is said to be extraordinary if there exists an infinite sequence of sets 1^*, 2^*, 3^*, etc. such that $1^* \in y$, $2^* \in 1^*$, $3^* \in 2^*$, etc. Thus, if there is such a set y, then Z8 fails because if we take the sentence Fx as one holding of y, 1^*, 2^*, 3^*, etc. and no others, then for every x such that Fx, there is a member z of x such that Fz. Conversely, if Z8 fails, then there exists an extraordinary set. Thus, suppose Fx violates Z8 and y be a set such that Fy. Then, since each such y has some member satisfying Fx, there is a member 1^* of y such that Fy. Similarly, there is a member 2^* of 1^* such that $F(2^*)$. And so on. Hence, y is an extraordinary set.

There is nothing in the axioms Z1—Z7 to preclude the possibility of such sets. In other words, it is possible to construct models for Z1—Z7 in which Z8 fails. Originally Zermelo did not include Z8 in his system. A few years after Mirimanoff, Fraenkel considered such sets (Fraenkel 1922, *op. cit.*, p. 233) and suggested an axiom of limitation stipulating that we admit no more sets except those declared to exist by the axioms Z1—Z7. Then it would follow that no extraordinary sets exist, since they are not required (though not excluded either) by Z1—Z7. But it is hard to see directly how such a strong axiom of limitation could be stated formally in a rigorous manner. (For the difficulties regarding Fraenkel's form of the axiom of limitation, see von Neumann 1925, *Crelle's*, **154**, 230—231.)

Rather than trying to exclude extraordinary sets by such an axiom, Neumann introduced (*ibid.*, p. 239, axiom VI4) an axiom which states explicitly that no such sets are to be allowed. Later he presented the axiom in the same form as Z8 (Neumann 1929, *ibid.*, **160**, 231). Zermelo introduced this axiom independently in 1930.

The axiom Z9 was not included in Zermelo's original system. This is rather surprising since, as we mentioned above, Cantor in 1899 already stipulated that a manifold equivalent to a set is again a set. For example, a set consisting of all finite sets of the infinite set given by Z7, or a set containing as member the infinite set of Z7 and the power set of each of its member, can be proved to exist by Z9 and Z7; but apparently their existence is not provable when we do not have Z9. In order to remedy this defect, Fraenkel proposed the following axiom (Fraenkel 1922; see also postulate 3 on p. 49 of Mirimanoff 1917, Nr. 4 of Skolem 1923, *Vorträge 5 Kongress Skandinav. Math.*): If x is a set and every element of x is replaced by a set, then the result is again a set. The problem of formalizing this axiom more exactly is similar to that about the axiom of separation. The form of Z9 given above is the generally accepted formulation now.

Sometimes, Z3 and Z9 are replaced by the following axiom: For every sentence $F(u, v)$, if $(x)(y)(z)\{[F(x, z) \,\&\, F(y, z)] \supset x = y\}$ and $(\exists x)(u)[u \in x \equiv (\exists v)\, F(u, v)]$, then $(\exists y)(v)[v \in y \equiv (\exists u) F(u, v)]$. In the framework of *ZF*, this axiom is provable; and, conversely, given this axiom, Z3 and Z9 can be derived from the other axioms of *ZF* (see Bernays 1941, *J. Symbolic Logic*, **6**, 3).

If we delete the axiom of infinity Z7 from *ZF*, then the resulting system *G* of general set theory admits of a very simple model in the theory of natural numbers (see Ackermann, *Math. Annalen*, **114**). All we need is to take the range of values of the variables x, y, etc. as consisting of the natural numbers, the empty set as the number 0, and the membership relation $x \in y$ as the relation that the quotient of dividing y by the x-th power of 2 is an odd number. Then, as is easily verified, all the axioms of *ZF* (except Z7) become simple theorems of elementary number theory.

If we omit the axiom of replacement Z9, the remaining axioms Z1—Z8 possess an interesting intuitive model, which is described in Bernays 1948 (*J. Symbolic Logic*, **13**). Let e be the empty set, $p(0)$ be e, $p(n+1)$ be the power set of $p(n)$, $p(\omega)$ be the set of all sets which belong to some $p(k)$, where k is finite, and $p(\omega+k+1)$ be the power set of $p(\omega+k)$. Now we assert that the domain consisting of all sets belonging to some $p(g)$, where g is an ordinal $<\omega\cdot 2$, gives the model.

Let us call all such sets d-sets. We can prove the following items about the d-sets:

(1) For every $g (g<\omega\cdot 2)$, every member of $p(g)$ is a subset of $p(g)$.

Proof. When g is 0 or ω, (1) is true by the definitions of $p(0)$ and $p(\omega)$. Assume (1) is true when g is g_1, we want to prove that (1) is also true when g is g_1+1. Let x be a member of $p(g_1+1)$, then x is a subset of $p(g_1)$ by the definition of $p(g_1+1)$. Therefore, if y is a member of x, then y is a member of $p(g_1)$. Hence, by induction hypothesis, y is a subset of $p(g_1)$. By the definition of $p(g_1+1)$ again, y is a member of $p(g_1+1)$. Therefore, x is a subset of $p(g_1+1)$. Therefore, (1) is proved.

(2) Given any g, $p(g)$ includes every $p(h)$ where g is no smaller than h.

Proof. When g is 0 or ω, (2) is true by the definition of $p(0)$ and $p(\omega)$. Assume (2) is true when g is g_1, we want to prove that (2) is also true when g is g_1+1. By (1), every member of $p(g_1)$ is a member of $p(g_1+1)$. But if h is no greater than g_1+1, then h is g_1+1 or h is no greater than g_1. Hence, by induction hypothesis, (2) is proved for the case when g is g_1+1. Therefore, (2) is proved.

(3) Every subset of a d-set is a d-set.

Proof. Assume x is a d-set belonging to $p(g)$. By (1), x is a subset of $p(g)$. Hence, every subset of x is also a subset of $p(g)$, and therefore a member of $p(g+1)$. Therefore, (3) is proved.

(4) The power set of a d-set is again a d-set.

Proof. Assume x is a d-set belonging to $p(g)$. By reasoning as in the proof of (3), every subset of x is a member of $p(g+1)$. Hence, the power set of x is a member of $p(g+2)$, and therefore a d-set.

(5) Every member of a d-set is again a d-set.

Proof. If y is a member of a d-set x belonging to $p(g)$, then by (1), x is a subset of $p(g)$ and therefore y belongs to $p(g)$.

(6) The sum set of a d-set is again a d-set.

Proof. Let y be the sum set of a d-set x belonging to $p(g)$, z be a member of y and w be a member of z. By reasoning as for (5), z belongs to $p(g)$. Hence, y is a subset of $p(g)$ and a member of $p(g+1)$.

(7) If x and y are d-sets, then the set $\{x, y\}$ is also a d-set.

Proof. Assume that x belongs to $p(g)$ and y belongs to $p(h)$. If g is greater than h, then by (2), y also belongs to $p(g)$. Hence, we can assume that g is the same as h. But then $\{x, y\}$ is a subset of $p(g)$ and a member of $p(g+1)$.

(8) The d-set $p(\omega)$ is an infinite set.

(9) The infinite set $\{e, \{e\}, \{\{e\}\}, \{\{\{e\}\}\}, \cdots\}$ is a d-set.

Proof. The set in question is obviously a subset of $p(\omega)$ and therefore a member of $p(\omega+1)$.

(10) Given any non-empty collection of d-sets, there exists some d-set x in the collection such that no members of x belongs to the given collection.

Proof. Among the d-sets in the collection, there is one (say x) belonging to some $p(g)$ such that for every h smaller than g, no d-set in the collection belongs to $p(h)$. No members of this d-set x belongs to the collection, because each member of x belongs to some $p(h)$ with h smaller than g.

(11) The collection of all the d-sets provides a model for the simple theory of types (system T) to be described in §4.

Proof. Let us take all the d-sets belonging to $p(\omega)$ as the individuals (entities of type 1), and all the d-sets belonging to $p(\omega+k+1)$ but not to $p(\omega+k)$ as the classes of type $k+2$. Then it is easy to see that the axioms of the simple theory of types are all satisfied.

(12) The set $E=\{p(\omega), p(\omega+1), \cdots\}$ is not a d-set.

Proof. If E belonged to $p(\omega+k)$, then, by (1), E would be a subset of $p(\omega+k)$ and, since $p(\omega+k)$ belongs to E, $p(\omega+k)$ would, contrary to our constructions, be a member of itself.

In order to see that the axioms Z1—Z8 are satisfied by the collection of d-sets described above, we note that Z1 is implicitly assumed in the construction of d-sets, and that Z2, Z3, Z4, Z5, Z7, Z8 are satisfied by dint of the items (7), (3), (4), (6), (9), (10) respectively. Z6 is also satisfied. Thus, if x is a d-set, by (6), the sum set y of x is also a d-set, belonging (say) to $p(g)$. Since, by definition, $p(g)$ contains as members all the subsets of each of its members, it must also contain the subset u of y which possesses the property of having one and only one member in common with each element of x.

It should be noted that this model presupposes the possibility of constructing subsets by all kinds of impredicative definition, and does not yield a proof of consistency as long as we have got no consistency proof for impredicative sets in general.

A related model, for the type theory T is given in greater detail in the paper by Rosser and the writer, *J. Symbolic Logic*, **15** (1950), 113—129. It is also observed there that if we assume the generalized continuum hypothesis, we may take all the ordinals less than ω_ω as the model.

§3. The Bernays Set Theory

Bernays' system NB, based in part on works of von Neumann, is a predicative extension of ZF. The axioms of ZF are infinite in number since Z3, Z8, and Z9 all are axiom schemata. If now we introduce variables ranging over classes defined by the predicates in these schemata, we can restate them as single axioms. Moreover, it is possible to enumerate these classes by a finite number of axioms in the system. In this way we get NB as an extension of ZF which contains only a finite number of axioms with two kinds of variable, small ones ranging over sets (elements), and large ones ranging over (proper) classes (non-elements).

It is easy to extend ZF to NB in the following manner; in fact, we could use only one kind of variable if we wished to (see *Proc.*

Nat. Acad. Sci. U.S.A., **35** (1949), 150—155). Add variables X, Y, Z, etc., and new atomic formulae $x \in X$, $z \in Y$, etc. Instead of the original definition of $x=y$, we now use:

3.1. If a, b are variables (both small, both large, or one small and one large), then $a=b$ is an abbreviation of $(z)\ (z \in a \equiv z \in b)$.

3.2. $X \in Y$ stands for $(Ez)\ (z=X\ \&\ z \in Y)$.

3.3. $X \in y$ stands for $(Ez)\ (z=X\ \&\ z \in y)$.

The underlying logic is a 2-sorted predicate calculus. To state the axioms, one may either use the notion of ordered pairs as a primitive and give its characteristic property

$$\langle a, b\rangle = \langle c, d\rangle \supset (a = c\ \&\ b = d)$$

as an axiom or introduce it by definitions. We adopt here the second course and define only contexts when pairs occur before $\in$, the other contexts are regarded as abbreviations eliminable by definitions such as 3.1 to 3.3:

3.4. $u \in \{x, y\} \equiv (u=x \vee u=y)$.

3.5. $\langle x, y\rangle = \{\{x\}, \{x, y\}\}$.

3.6. $\langle x, y, z\rangle = \langle x, \langle y, z\rangle\rangle$.

The axioms of *NB* are *B*1 to *B*16.

*B*1. If a, b, c are three variables, $a=b \supset (a \in c \supset b \in c)$.

*B*2. Same as *Z*2.

*B*3. Replace Fx by $x \in X$ in *Z*3.

*B*4—*B*7. Same as *Z*4—*Z*7.

B8. Same as Z8, with Fa replaced by $a \in X$.

*B*9. Same as *Z*9, with Fab replaced by $\langle a, b\rangle \in X$.

*B*10. $(EY)\ (x)\ (y)\ (\langle x, y\rangle \in Y \equiv x \in y)$.

*B*11. $(EY)\ (x)\ (x \in Y \equiv (x \in X \mid x \in Z))$.

*B*12. $(EY)\ (x)\ (x \in Y \equiv (Ey)\ \langle y, x\rangle \in X)$.

*B*13. $(EY)\ (x)\ (y)\ (\langle x, y\rangle \in Y \equiv y \in X)$.

*B*14. $(EY)\ (x)\ (y)\ (z)\ (\langle x, y, z\rangle \in Y \equiv \langle y, z, x\rangle \in X)$.

*B*15. $(EY)\ (x)\ (y)\ (z)\ (\langle x, y, z\rangle \in Y \equiv \langle y, x, z\rangle \in X)$.

*B*16. $(EY)\ (x)\ (x \in Y \equiv x \in y)$.

It is well-known that from the two permutations in *B*14 and *B*15, we can get all permutations of x, y, z. As Markov (*Известия Акаде-*

мии Наук СССР Сер. Мат., **12** (1948), 569—570) observes, the axiom for interchanging x and y can be obtained. Thus, by $B13$ and the predicate calculus we get the domain of $\langle z, x, y\rangle$ from $\langle x, y\rangle$; by $B14$ and $B15$, we get then the domain of $\langle z, y, x\rangle$ from $\langle x, y\rangle$. By $B12$, we get $\langle y, x\rangle$.

Using the method of Bernays' paper of 1937 or Gödel 1940, we can then prove the desired general principle:

BP. For every formula Fx in NB which contains no bound class variable, $(EY)\ (x)\ (x \in Y \equiv Fx)$.

This principle is not quite the same as the desired conclusion that every predicate in ZF corresponds to a class in NB, because F may contain free class variables. If, however, we think of the classes as being introduced step by step, then each time we can get a new definite class only when the free class variables are replaced by definite classes. In this way, it is intuitively clear that the class variables are essentially an abbreviational measure which should not increase the strength of ZF greatly.

Indeed, different proofs of relative consistency have been given from which it can be inferred that if a formula of ZF is a theorem of NB, it is also a theorem of ZF (see *Fund. Math.*, **37** (1950), 87—110; *J. Symbolic Logic*, **15** (1950), 113—129). More recently, by extending the ε–Theorems of Hilbert and Bernays, Shoenfield proves an even stronger result:

Theorem 1. *There is a primitive recursive procedure such that given a proof in NB of a formula A of ZF, we can find a proof of A in ZF.*

The basic ideas of the relative consistency proofs are rather simple. For example, if ZF is consistent, then it has an enumerable model. Then we have a fixed enumerable universe of sets for NB, and the axioms $B10$—$B16$ can be viewed as principles for giving an original class (by $B10$) and then generating new classes from given classes (by the others). This would yield an enumerable number of classes without affecting the original domain of sets. Moreover, the structure of these classes can be determined entirely on the basis of the domain of sets.

Alternatively, we may feel that given a proof in NB of a conclusion A with no class variables, then we should be able to eliminate all class variables from the proof by going backwards and obtain a proof in ZF. Shoenfield's proof shows that this is indeed so. But the bound class variables in the predicate calculus calls for quite complex considerations. Recently, Bernays has reformulated NB in Axiomatic set theory using only free class variables. In such a formulation, Theorem 1 would be quite immediate.

A natural extension of *NB* would be to replace *BP* or *B*10—*B*15 by the stronger:

BQ. If *Fx* is a formula of *NB*, $(EY)(x)(x \in Y \equiv Fx)$.

The resulting system *NQ* would be an impredicative extension of *ZF* and is demonstrably stronger than *NB* in so far as *Con*(*NB*) can be proved in *NQ* as a theorem.

If we omit the axiom of infinity from *NB*, the resulting system *P* is the predicative theory of number-sets. If we omit the axiom of infinity from *NQ*, the resulting system is the impredicative theory of number-sets, which is also equivalent to the result obtained from *ZF* by deleting the axiom of power set. If we omit the axiom of power set from *NB*, then we get the predicative theory of real-sets, the system *R*.

One way of using only free class variables is to introduce a constant class *E* for *B*10, and six operators for *B*11—16. Then we have the whole predicate calculus for the small variables, and only one rule for the class variables: if *FX*, then *Fa*, where a may be a small variable or any term obtained from variables and the constant *E* in a proper manner. Axioms *B*10—*B*16 now become:

*NB*10. $\langle x, y\rangle \in E \equiv x \in y$.

*NB*11. $x \in X | Y \equiv (x \in X | x \in Y)$.

*NB*12. $x \in D(X) \equiv (Ey)\ \langle y, x\rangle \in X$.

*NB*13. $\langle x, y\rangle \in V \times X \equiv y \in X$.

*NB*14. $\langle x, y, z\rangle \in \mathrm{Cyc}\ (X) \equiv \langle y, z, x\rangle \in X$.

*NB*15. $\langle x, y, z\rangle \in \mathrm{Per}\ (X) \equiv \langle y, x, z\rangle \in X$.

*NB*16. $x \in C(y) \equiv x \in y$.

For such a formulation of *NB*, it is quite easy to prove Theorem 1, given any proof of a conclusion not containing any class variables, we can eliminate all (free) class variables in a systematic way. Every time the only rule for class variables is applied, we replace the variable *X* in the premiss by the term *a* in the conclusion. We do this from the conclusion back to all the earlier lines of the proof. The result must remain a proof of *NB*. If any free class variables remain, then we substitute all of them by *E*, say. Then the result is again a proof which no longer contains any class variables, although it may still contain class constants such as *E* and *D*(*E*). But these can be eliminated step by step by using *NB*10 to *NB*16 repeatedly. We finally get a proof of *ZF*.

The argument can be formalized to yield:

Theorem 2. *We can prove in Z:* $Con(ZF) \supset Con(NB)$.

It should be noted that the above argument does not give a translation of *NB* in *ZF*, because each formula of *NB* which contains free class variables gets not a unique translation in *ZF* but infinitely many different ones according to what constant terms are substituted for the variables. It can be proved exactly that there is no translation of *NB* in *ZF* (see *Fund. Math.*, **42** (1955), 101—110).

Theorem 3. *NB is not translatable into ZF, P is not translatable into G, nor in Z.*

This is a consequence of Theorem 5 of Chapter XV. In the first place, we can reformulate, in familiar manner, *NB* and *P* with only one kind of variable. In the second place, it is possible to develop *Z* in *P* (and also in *G*), as shown in Bernays's papers, so that *Z* is translatable in *P* (and in *G*). By Ackermann's model for *G*, it is also possible to translate *G* into *Z*. Hence, we have:

Theorem 4. *G and Z are translatable into each other, Z is translatable in P; we can prove in Z:* $Con(Z) \equiv Con(G)$; $Con(P) \supset Con(Z)$.

By Theorem 5 of Chapter XV, since *P* has finitely many axioms only, if *P* were translatable into *Z* or *G*, we would be able to prove $Con(P)$ in *Z* and hence $Con(Z)$ in *Z*. To prove the part about *NB* and *ZF*, we observe (compare next chapter) that a theorem similar to Theorem 5 of Chapter XV can be proved for *ZF*, so that the same argument gives the conclusion.

Incidentally, it is also possible to prove the relative consistency of *NQ* to *ZF* (see §5 below and §4 of Chapter XIII above).

About the systems *ZF* and *NB*, there are various basic results in the literature of which we quote only a few. It is more convenient to state these results in connection with *NB*.

There are three axioms which are of central interest to the foundation of set theory: the axiom of choice, the continuum hypothesis, and Gödel's axiom of categoricalness (axiom of constructible sets). For the statement of these axioms, we follow Gödel's monograph of 1940 which contains exact formulations of these in the notation of *NB*. Moreover, we regroup the axioms in the familiar manner of Gödel. Group *A* contains the axioms *B*16, *B*1, *B*2; group *B* contains the axioms *B*10 to *B*15; Group *C* contains the axioms *B*7, *B*4, *B*5, *B*3, *B*9; group *D* contains the axiom of foundation *B*8; *E* is an axiom of choice stronger than *B*6.

E. The axiom of choice. There exists a choice function *X* (a class of ordered pairs) such that for every nonempty set *x*,

$$(Ey)(y \in x \,\&\, \langle y, x\rangle \in X).$$

G. The generalized continuum hypothesis.

H. The axiom of categoricalness. All sets are constructible, or $V=L$.

Another interesting axiom not frequently discussed was first introduced by von Neumann.

F. Axiom of limitation of size. A class is not a set (i.e., is a proper class) if and only if there is a one-to-one correlation between it and the universal class V (i.e., the class of all sets).

If in the model of $Z1$—$Z8$ in the preceding section, we allow arbitrary ordinals obtainable in ZF, we obtain a model Π for the whole system ZF. Define in NB a function p on the proper class of all ordinals, such that $p(0)$ is the empty set, $p(\alpha+1)$ is the power set of $p(\alpha)$, and for a limit ordinal the value of p is the union of all earlier values of p. The union of all values of the function p, if taken as the universal class gives the model Π. Such a model can be constructed on the basis of the axioms of NB of groups A, B, C alone. Since D satisfies this model Π, von Neumann gives in this way a proof that if axioms A, B, C are consistent, then axioms A, B, C, D are consistent (*Crelle's*, **160**, 227):

Theorem 5. *If the axioms A, B, C are consistent, then it remains consistent when we add the axiom of foundation D, further, if the axioms A, B, C, E are consistent (i. e. if the original sets and classes determined by axioms A, B, C, satisfy the axiom of choice), then the whole NB including axioms A to E is consistent (i.e. the model which always satisfies the axiom of choice also satisfies the axiom of foundation).*

In short, if set theory, with or without the axiom of choice, is consistent, it remains so when we add the axiom of foundation. This, however, says nothing about the relative consistency of the axiom of choice.

Now the axiom of foundation has the effect that all sets belong to the intuitive model Π. Since, if the axiom of choice is true in Π, then axiom F is true in Π, von Neumann established:

Theorem 6. *We can derive axiom F in NB, i.e. axioms A to E; moreover, if axioms A, B, C, E are consistent, then it remains so if we add both the axiom of foundation D and the axiom of limitation of size F.*

In fact, von Neumann took axiom F as an axiom which makes the Aussonderungsaxiom, the axiom of choice E and the Ersetzungsaxiom all redundant (derivable).

The axiom F of course gives a sharp criterion for distinguishing sets (elements) from proper classes (nonelements). If there is a one-

one correlation between a set x and a class Y and Y is not a set, then there is a one-one correlation between Y and the universal class V and hence a one-one correlation between x and V. But then x would be a nonelement too. Hence, Y must be an element. Similarly, given x and Y, if $\hat{u}(u \in x \ \& \ u \in Y)$ is a nonelement, then there is a one-one correlation between it and V and so V can be mapped one-one to a subset of x; but of course x can be mapped one-one to a subclass of V, hence there is a one-one correlation between x and V, and x must be a nonelement. That is, if x is a set, so is $\hat{u}(u \in x \ \& \ u \in Y)$.

To prove the axiom of choice, we take the proper class O of all ordinal numbers. It cannot be a set, otherwise we get the Burali-Forti paradox. Hence, there must be a one-one correlation A between it and V. Hence, since O is well-ordered, we can define:

$$y = Od(x) \equiv (\langle y, x \rangle \in A \ \& \ (z)(z < y \supset \langle z, x \rangle \notin A))$$
$$\langle y, x \rangle \in As \equiv (y \in x \ \& \ (z)(Od(z) < Od(y) \supset z \notin x)).$$

Then As is a universal selection operator for all sets, and we get Gödel's E. Of course, these are only sketches of proofs which can be worked out in detail as in some of von Neumann's papers.

The model Π (and the function p) above can also be employed in certain studies of Zermelo and Shepherdson. Let a super-complete model be one which satisfies axioms A, B, C and all classes of the model are contained in V_m, ϵ_m coicides with ϵ for classes in the model. An inaccessible number (in the narrower sense) be an ordinal number such that (1) it is regular, i.e., every ascending sequence of ordinals with the order type of the sequence less than it has a limit less than it (in other words, cannot be reached by using only smaller ordinal numbers), (2) for all α, if ω_α precedes it, 2^{ω_α} also, (3) it is greater than ω. Then there is only one super-complete model (the trivial one) which satisfies A, B, C, D and $On = On_m$. Given any inaccessible i, A, B, C, D, E and $On_m = i$ determines the unique super-complete model whose universe is $p(i)$, for the Neumann function p.

Gödel's monograph contains an exact proof of the following remarkable result:

Theorem 7. *If the axioms A, B, C, with or without D, are consistent, then adding the axiom of categoricalness H, the system remains consistent; moreover, we can derive the axiom of choice E and the generalized continuum hypothesis from A, B, C, and H. Hence, if the system consisting of A, B, C is consistent, then the system consisting of A, B, C, D, E, G, H is consistent, and, in fact, the latter system is translatable into the former.*

Moreover, from Gödel's construction, the following is also an immediate consequence:

Theorem 8. *In ZF, we can consistently add $V=L$, which contains no class variable, as a new axiom, and in the thus extended ZF, there is a formula $A(x, y)$ such that: (i) if $A(x, y)$, $x \in y$; (ii) for all y, there is some x, $A(x, y)$, provided y is not empty; (iii) if $A(x, y)$ and $A(z, y)$, then $x=z$.*

The intuitive idea of Gödel's proof is brought out more sharply in his outline (*Proc. Nat. Acd. Sci. U. S. A.*, **25** (1939), 220—224). His model Δ is similar to the model Π except that at each ordinal, instead of the impredicative power set, a predicative extension is considered. This has the immediate effect that all sets in the model can be enumerated relative to the class of all ordinal numbers which can be defined and well-ordered without appeal to the axiom of choice. Hence, the relative consistency of the axiom of choice follows. That such a model exists follows from the familiar argument that if a formula has a model, it has an enumerable model by the Skolem functions.

To get the generalized continuum hypothesis, the crucial step seems to be the fact that for any given infinite cardinal c, if we consider only ordinals whose cardinality is no greater than c, then we never need a set in the model whose order is an ordinal of higher cardinality than c, in order to satisfy the Aussonderungsaxiom. If we delete the axiom of power set from NB and consider just the original continuum hypothesis, a brief summary of Gödel's argument could be the following.

Let the empty set be the only set of order 0. For every ordinal a of Cantor's second number class, if a is a successor, then the sets of order a are all predicative subsets of the set of all sets of order $a-1$, if a is a limit ordinal, then the sets of order a are all sets of smaller orders. Now if we consider all the enumerable sets of sets required by the Aussonderungsaxiom, we find that in an impredicative condition $F(x)$ which contains quantifiers ranging over all these sets, there is yet no need to go beyond the given range in order to satisfy the quantifiers in the condition by values of the requisite Skolem functions which always go from enumerable to enumerable.

The questions whether the axiom of choice E is independent of the axioms A to D, whether the axiom of categoricalness H is independent of A to D, whether the generalized continuum hypothesis is independent of A to E remain unsolved. In each case, what is needed is a model for the original axioms in which the negation of the additional axiom is true.

One partial result is that the generalized continuum hypothesis implies the axiom of choice. Hence, if E is independent of A to D, G is also independent of A to D. This has nothing to do with the more interesting and more difficult question whether G is independent of A to E.

A partial result, together with various extensions, on the independence of the choice axiom has been established by Fraenkel, Mostowski, Specker, Shoenfield, and Mendelson. (See Specker, Habilitationsschrift, 1951, *Zeitschr, f. math. Logik u. Grundlagen d. Math.*, **3** (1957), 173—210.) The basic result is:

Theorem 9. *The axiom of choice is independent of the axiom A, B, C; there is a model for A, B, C in which both D and E are false.*

§ 4. The Theory of Types, Negative Types, and "New Foundations"

Russell proposed in *Proc. London Math. Soc.*, **4** (1906), 34, the word predicative to refer to all norms which are capable of defining classes and the word impredicative (or nonpredicative), to all which are not; since, he argued, it is clear from the paradoxes that there must be norms which are incapable of defining classes. He then observed that the main question was to decide which are the predicative and which are the impredicative norms. In discussing Russell's proposal, Poincaré suggested in *Rev. métaph. mor.*, **14** (1906), 307 to identify the impredicative definition with one for an entity e in which reference is made to a totality containing e as a member. An impredicative definition in this sense was considered as involving a vicious circle and should therefore be avoided at all cost. Let us quote Poincaré: "Sans quoi la définition de E contiendrait un cercle vicieux; on ne peut pas définir E par l'ensemble E lui-même. ··· Ainsi *les définitions qui doivent être regardées comme non prédicatives sont elles qui contiennent un cercle vicieux*". The idea of solving the paradoxes by abolishing such impredicative definitions was credited by Poincaré partly to Richard's letter of the previous year (Richard 1905).

In a prompt reply Russell approved of the suggested solution of the paradoxes but observed the inadequacy of stating merely that impredicative definitions be rejected. According to him, such a statement only gave a negative criterion, while a positive theory of what are the predicative definitions is needed. Then he sketched his no classes theory (or, as is commonly known now, his ramified theory of types) and asserted that it provides us with the desired answer. This system was presented afterwards in greater detail in *Am. Jour. Math.*, **30** (1908), and formed the basis of the massive *Principia* (Whitehead and Russell) published during the years 1910—1913. But the code of the system is a complicated affair and remains hard to uuderstand despite the extensive developments and the impressive edifice constructed on it. For one thing, it was meant as a remedy not only of the mathematical paradoxes about classes and numbers mentioned above, but at the same time of the semantic paradoxes (Epimenides, Grelling's, Richard's) involving the notions of truth, naming, and defining. Another serious difficulty is the cryptic use or uses of the term propositional function. A third obstacle to understanding is the intricate connection with the axiom of reducibility.

If, however, we make use of the various distinctions and devices which are customary today, the ramified theory of types can be identified with the following system:

Assume there are infinitely many constants 0, 1, 2, $\cdots$ denoting individuals and variables x, y, $\cdots$ which take individuals as values. These constants and variables are said to be the terms of order 1. Assume a predicate P such that $P(a, b)$ is an atomic sentence whenever a and b are terms of order 1. Such sentences together with all those obtained from such by using the sentence connectives of (say) denial $\neg$ and conjunction &, as well as the general quantifiers (x) (for all x), etc. and the particular quantifiers $(\exists x)$ (for some x), etc., are the sentences of order 2. Terms of order 2 are formed in the first place from those sentences of order 2 which contain free variables, by abstraction: e.g., $\hat{x}P(x, x)$, $\hat{y}\hat{z}(\exists x)[P(x, 0)\ \&\ \neg P(y, x)\ \&\ P(x, z)]$, etc. In general, if $F(x, \cdots, z)$ is a sentence containing the m (say) free variables $x, \cdots, z$ and no more, then $\hat{x} \cdots \hat{z}\ (F(x, \cdots, z))$ is an abstract (a class-expression) of order 2 and degree m, defining a m-adic relation of individuals (or a class when m is 1). The meaning of these abstracts are determined by assertions of the following form: $F(x, \cdots, z)$ if and only if $(\hat{x} \cdots \hat{z}F(x, \cdots, z))(x, \cdots, z)$. We then introduce variables ${}_1x^2$, ${}_1y^2$, etc. for classes of order 2; ${}_2x^2$, ${}_2y^2$, etc. for dyadic relations of order 2; etc. All the abstracts and variables of order 2 are called terms of order 2. Any terms of order 2 followed by a suitable number of terms of order 1 yields another atomic sentence of the system: e.g., ${}_2x^2(1, x)$, $(\hat{x}P(x, x))(0)$, etc. The sentences obtained from these plus the sentences of order 2, with the help of the sentence connectives and the quantifiers (x), $({}_1x^2)$, $(\exists_2y^2)$, etc., are of order 3. The sentences of order 3 include those of order 2 and are more complex only when variables of order 2 occur. From a sentence of order 3 which contains free variables, we can obtain an abstract of order 3 by abstraction: e. g., $\hat{x}[{}_2x^2(1, x)]$, $\hat{y}_3\hat{x}^2[{}_3x^2(0, y, 2)\ \&\ P(1, y)]$, etc. Then we can again introduce the various kinds of variable of order 3, and generate the sentences of order 4. And so on.

This is, in effect, Russell's ramified theory of types (without the axiom of reducibility to be discussed below). If we associate the individual constants 0, 1, 2, $\cdots$ and the predicate P with some simple interpretation (for instance, as natural numbers and the relation of smaller than), it is possible to formalize the theory into an axiomatic system and prove its consistency. (Compare Fitch, *J. Symbolic Logic*, **3** (1938)). From the way we build up the system in the preceding paragraph, we can well order the totality of all its sentences in such a way that the denial of a sentence p comes after p, the conjunction of p and q comes after p and q, and each general sentence comes after all its instances. Accordingly, once the axiom system is presented, it is easy to supply a truth definition according to which all the theorems are true and no denial of any true sentence is true. The consistency of the system would follow immediately. However, we shall not study details of the axiomatization and the consistency proof, since it is in any case not hard to see that the theory enables us to avoid the known paradoxes (see Russell 1908).

More serious is the question whether this theory is adequate for deriving set theory and what can be constructed in set theory. Obviously the proof of Cantor's theorem breaks down, because the set N of all sets k which do not belong to $f(k)$ in the proof can no longer be proved to exist. There are even difficulties in defining identity. Moreover, in deriving the theory of natural numbers from set theory, we meet with obstacles as we come to the proving of the principle of mathematical induction.

Russell recognized (see Russell 1908 or *Principia Mathematica*) these difficulties and proposed to assume in addition what he calls the axiom of reducibility. Thus, the order of every abstract is clearly at least one more than that of each of its arguments. When the abstract is of the order next above the highest (order) of its arguments, we call it a *predicative* abstract of its arguments. For example, if ${}_1\hat{x}^2F({}_1x^2)$ is of order 3, then it is a predicative abstract of its argument ${}_1x^2$ which is of order 2. The ax. of red. is merely this: Every abstract is equivalent, for all its values, to some (class defined by a) predicative abstract with the same arguments. By the help of this axiom, statements about "all predicative abstracts of x" yield the results which otherwise would require "all abstracts of x". Thus mathematical induction, for example, need now be stated only for all predicative abstracts of numbers; it then follows from the ax. of red. that it holds of any abstract whatsoever.

From the very beginning, Russell seems to have felt quite uneasy about the truth or validity of the ax. of red. Most of the time, he seems to claim for it no more than the pragmatic justification that the results to which it leads are all such as appear valid. (See *Principia*, vol. 1, pp. 59—60 and 2nd ed., p. xiv). In his 1908 paper (p. 242), however, he did urge that the axiom is involved in the common-sense admission of classes which leads us to conclude, given any sentence $F(e)$, of whatever order, that it is equivalent, for all values of e, to a statement of the form "e belongs to the class A". But if the equivalence holds, then the ax. of red. is justified. According to him, there is no advantage in assuming that there are really such things as classes, and the contradictions indicate the unclarity of the notion of class. He believed the chief purpose which classes serve, and the chief reason which makes them linguistically convenient, is that they provide a method of reducing the order of a sentence or an abstract.

What Russell believed then might be right, and it seems reasonable to justify the ax. of red. by appealing to what common-sense effects by the admission of classes. It is, however, clear that a theory which includes an axiom only thus justified can neither be claimed to be constructive, nor to be a "no classes theory".

In 1909, Poincaré made some adverse criticism of the ax. of red. mainly on the ground that it is more questionable and less clear than the principle of mathematical induction which, according to Russell, is to be proved by the ax. of red. Three years later, Chwistek seriously questioned the axiom and proposed the course of retaining the ramified theory of types but rejecting the axiom. It was only in the 1920's that Chwistek began to carry out in formal details his project for developing the ramified theory of types without the ax. of red. (Incidentally, many of his later works are concerned with the different problem of constructing formal systems which include notations for both mathematical and semantic concepts.)

In 1921 we find Chwistek making the first proposal of the now widely accepted simplification of Russell's theory of types. Five years later, Ramsey distinguished (in *Proc. London Math. Soc.*, **25** (1926)) sharply between the mathematical and the semantic paradoxes, and presented a very clear account of the simplified form of the theory of types.

In the original theory of types, apart from the distinction of orders, we can also distinguish types, as Russell did, of the various different terms. The type or type index of the terms of order 1 is 1, and the type of an abstract is determined by those of its arguments. For example, the type of an abstract $\hat{x}\hat{y}F(x, y)$ is (11), no matter how complicated $F(x, y)$ may be, and the type of $\hat{x}_2\hat{y}^2G(x, {}_2y^2)$ is (1(11)), and so forth. The type index (or simply the type, when no confusion seems likely) of an abstract is one more than the highest type index of its arguments: e.g., $\hat{x}\hat{y}F(x, y)$ is of type 2, and $\hat{x}_2\hat{y}^2G(x, {}_2y^2)$ is of type 3 since ${}_2y^2$ is of type 2. (Compare Carnap 1929, *Abriss der Logistik*, §9 and §13.) Obviously two abstracts of the same type can be of different orders because the types depend only on the arguments while the orders depend on the degree of complexity of the defining sentences. For example, $\hat{x}\hat{y}P(x, y)$ is of order 2, but $\hat{x}\hat{y}(\exists_1x^2)({}_1x^2(x)$ & $\neg\, {}_1x^2(y))$ is of order 3; although they are both of the same type. In contrast with the order which is determined by the way how an abstract is introduced, the type of an abstract is determined completely by its extension.

As a result of the analysis by Chwistek and Ramsey, it turns out that so far as the mathematical concepts of class, belonging to, etc. are concerned, the result obtained by banishing both the ax. of red. and at the same time the distinction of orders from the ramified theory of types is essentially of the same strength as the original system which retains both the axiom and the orders. The result thus obtained, depending merely on the distinction of individuals, classes (and relations) of individuals, classes (and relations) of them, and so forth, is the simple theory of types. Since we are not concerned with the semantic paradoxes, we can assert simply that the ramified theory of types with the ax. of red. is the same as the simple theory of types.

This can be seen very directly in the following manner (compare Quine, *Mind*, **45** (1936)). By the ax. of red., every abstract is equivalent to a predicative abstract, and every variable is of the same range as one which has the lowest order compatible with its type. Replace all the variables and abstracts in the sentences of the ramified theory of types by their equivalent variables and abstracts of the lowest orders. Then the sentences and theorems of the ramified theory of types would become indistinguishable from those of the simple theory of types, except for minor notational deviations.

Another remarkable improvement of the theory of types is Wiener's reduction of relations to classes (Wiener, *Proc. Cambridge Philos. Soc.*, **17** (1914)). He identified a relation with a class of ordered pairs (or a class of triples, etc.) and showed that the ordered pair (or the ordered triple, etc.) could be defined within the theory of classes. As a result, we can further simplify the theory of types and consider no more relations but merely individuals, classes of individuals, and classes of classes of individuals, and so on. Seven years later, Kuratowski presented (Kuratowski, *Fund. Math.*, **2** (1921)) a somewhat different definition of the ordered pairs which is now most commonly in use.

In most presentations of the theory of types since 1930 or so, the above two simplifications regarding the orders and the relations are adopted. Two slightly different standard formulations were given by Gödel (Gödel, *Monatsh. Math. Phys.*, **38** (1931), 176—178) and Tarski (Tarski, *ibid.*, **40** (1933), 97—103). Today when we mention the theory of types, we usually mean some system like these. These are, in appearance, very much different indeed from Russell's theory of 1908.

Take Gödel's formulation which will be called the system T.

Roughly, T contains as primitives the truth-functional operators, the quantifiers, the membership predicate ϵ, the symbol 0 for zero, the symbol f for the successor function, and infinitely many kinds of variables: $x_1, y_1, \cdots; x_2, y_2, \cdots; \cdots$. The predicate ϵ occurs only in contexts of the form $x_n \epsilon y_{n+1}$, etc. ($n=1, 2, \cdots$). The axioms and rules of inference of T may be stated as follows ($x_n = y_n$ standing for $(z_{n+1})(x_n \epsilon z_{n+1} \equiv y_n \epsilon z_{n+1})$).

A. The axioms and rules of some many-sorted quantification theory (predicate calculus).

B. Axioms for the individuals.

1. $fx_1 \neq 0$.

2. $fx_1 = fy_1 \supset x_1 = y_1$.

3. $[0 \epsilon x_2 \,\&\, (x_1)(x_1 \epsilon x_2 \supset fx_1 \epsilon x_2)] \supset y_1 \epsilon x_2$.

C. Axioms of extensionality ($n=1, 2, \cdots$).

$$(z_n)(z_n \in x_{n+1} \equiv z_n \in y_{n+1}) \supset x_{n+1} = y_{n+1}.$$

D. Axiom of set existence (axiom of comprehension). Let A be any formula in which y_{n+1} does not occur, $(Ey_{n+1})(x_n)(x_n \epsilon y_{n+1} \equiv A)$, $n=1, 2$, etc.

E. Axiom of choice. If the members x_{n+1} of x_{n+2} are nonempty and mutually exclusive, then there is a set z_{n+1} which contains one and only one member from each x_{n+1} in x_{n+2}.

The system can be equivalently formulated in different forms. We may replace the axioms of group B either by the theory finite sets G so that finite sets are the individuals, or by the full number theory Z, i.e. by adding recursive definitions for additions and multiplications.

It is well-known that:

Theorem 10. *The system T is translatable into the system ZS obtained from ZF by deleting the axiom of replacement $Z9$.*

For example, one may use the following translation. Define $x=y$ in the alternative way by $(z)\ (x \epsilon z \equiv y \epsilon z)$, and define:

$$t_1(x) \text{ if and only if } x = 0 \vee (Ey)(x = fy)$$
$$t_{n+1}(x) \text{ if and only if } (y)(y \in x \supset t_n(y)) \,\&\, \sim t_1(x)$$
$$(x_n)Fx_n \text{ if and only if } (x)(t_n(x) \supset Fx).$$

However, it is not true that ZS is translatable into T, even though they seem to possess the same intuitive model. This is so because the variables of ZS can range over all sets of different types at the same time, while in T, we can at most make a variable range over sets of a finite number of types. This fact makes it seem plausible that we can characterize T externally within the framework. Indeed, Kemeny has announced the following result (*J. Symbolic Logic*, **15** (1950), 78, an abstract):

Theorem 11. *A normal truth definition of T can be obtained in ZS, Con (T) can be proved in ZS, ZS is not translatable into T.*

A detailed proof for the theorem may require some special care as a result of the situation that there are not only infinitely many axioms but also infinitely many kinds of variable.

If we weaken slightly ZS, i.e. ZF minus $Z9$, we can get a system of equal strength as T.

Theorem 12. *If in the Aussonderungsaxiom $Z3$, we require that every quantifier in the predicate Fx is restricted by a variable free in Fx and distinct from the variable x, e.g. $(z)(z \in u \supset Gz)$, $(Ew)(w \in v \;\&\; Hw)$, then the weakened theory ZS is of equal strength as T.*

Intuitively, since in defining the new set, u, v are always given sets and therefore of fixed types, the quantifiers only range over sets of fixed types and not over all sets at the same time. To formalize such a proof would require care in extending T to allow for mixing of types, which can be done with some effort.

As a matter of curiosity, we quote the following simple results from *Math. Annalen*, **125** (1952), 65—66.

Since it is unlikely that we could generate classes of infinitely many types with only a finite number of class axioms, we may expect that the irreducibility of the axiom of comprehension of T to any finite number of sentences can be proved.

We prove the following theorem:

4.01. If T' is an arbitrary system obtained by using quantification theories for all types of variables and including as axioms the cases of the axiom of extensionality (C) plus a finite number of additional axioms, then either T' is inconsistent, or it is impossible to derive in T' all cases of the axiom of comprehension (D).

Proof. In the finitely many additional axioms, only variables of up to a definite finite type, say n, can occur. Let T'_n be the part of T' in which only variables of type n or lower occur. If T' is consistent, then T'_n is consistent and has a model. If we extend the model (say) by assuming in each of the types higher than n a single class which contains as members all the classes of the next lower type, then we obtain a model for T' which is not satisfied by the axiom of comprehension (D). In other words, we can make a translation of T' into T'_n so that the translations of all the theorems of T' are theorems of T'_n but there are many cases of (D) whose translations are not theorems of T'_n. For example, we can use the following translation.

Replace every sentence or part of a sentence of the form $x_m \in y_{m+1}(m > n)$ by a tautology, say $(x_1)(x_1=0 \vee \sim x_1=0)$, and one of the form $x_n \in y_{n+1}$ by $(x_{n-1})(x_{n-1}\epsilon x_n \vee \sim x_{n-1}\epsilon x_n)$ if $n>1$, or by $(x_n=0 \vee \sim x_n=0)$ if n is 1; after making such replacements everywhere, we omit the vacuous quantifiers which are no longer attached to variables (of types higher than n) and call the results the translations in T'_n of the original sentences of T'. It can be verified that the translations of all axioms and rules of quantification theories remain valid, the translations of all cases of the axiom of extensionality are theorems of T'_n and the translations of the additional axioms are the same as the original sentences; but, for example, the negation of the translation of the case $(\exists y_{n+1})(x_n)(x_n \in y_{n+1} \equiv \sim x_n = x_n)$ of (D) is also a theorem of T'_n so that the particular sentence must be independent of the axioms of T'.

Since this conclusion in 4.01 seems to be something which is plausible even without our proof, we may wish to find some stronger result such as: there exists no infinite set of sentences of which only a finite number concern each type and from which we can derive all the axioms of T. It happens that we can prove the negation of this. We can prove:

4.1. We can find a subset S of the set of the sentences of T which fall under the comprehension axiom (D) such that (1) for each n only a finite number of sentences of the form $(\exists y_{n+1})(x_n)(x_n \in y_{n+1} \equiv A)$ belong to S, and (2) by substituting the members of S for all cases of (D) of the system T, we obtain a system in which we can derive all cases of (D) and therefore also all the axioms of T.

Proof. We observe that we can develop in T the ordinary theory of identity without using the axiom of comprehension, and that we can define the unit class $\{x_n\}$ of a class or a natural number x_n in some usual manner. Let us enumerate all the sentences of T in which none of the variables $y_2, y_3, y_4, \cdots$ occur: $F_1, F_2, F_3, \cdots$. Clearly it is sufficient to derive for each given n all the sentences $(\exists y_{n+1})(x_n)(x_n \in y_{n+1} \equiv F_i)(i=1, 2, 3, \cdots)$. We assert that the following cases of (D) are sufficient for deriving all the cases of (D), using the other axioms of T.

4.1.1. $(\exists y_2)(x_1)(x_1 \in y_2 \equiv x_1 = w_1)$.

4.1.2. " " (" $\equiv \{x_1\} \in z_3$).

4.1.3. " " (" $\equiv F_1$).

4.2.1. $(\exists y_3)(x_2)(x_2 \in y_3 \equiv x_2 = w_2)$.

4.2.2. " " (" $\equiv \{x_2\} \in z_4$).

4.2.3. " " (" $\equiv (\exists x_1)(x_2 = \{x_1\} \ \& \ F_2)$).

4.2.4. " " (" $\equiv F_1$).

4.2.5. $(\exists y_3)(x_2)(x_2 \in y_3 \equiv F_2)$.

4.3.1. $(\exists y_4)(x_3)(x_3 \in y_4 \equiv x_3 = w_3)$.

4.3.2. " " (" $\equiv \{x_3\} \in z_4)$.

4.3.3. " " (" $\equiv (\exists x_2)(x_3 = \{x_2\} \; \& \; F_3))$.

4.3.4. " " (" $\equiv (\exists x_2)(x_3 = \{x_2\} \; \& \; (\exists x_1)(x_2 = \{x_1\} \; \& \, F_3)))$.

4.3.5. " " (" $\equiv F_1)$.

4.3.6. " " (" $\equiv F_2)$.

4.3.7. " " (" $\equiv F_3)$.

And so on, and so on.

Thus, from 4.1.1, 4.1.2, and 4.2.3, we can derive:

4.1.4. $(\exists y_2)(x_1)(x_1 \in y_2 \equiv F_2)$.

Similarly, from 4.2.1, 4.2.2, and 4.3.3, we can derive:

4.2.6. $(\exists y_3)(x_2)(x_2 \in y_3 \equiv F_3)$.

From 4.2.1, 4.2.2, and 4.3.4, we can derive:

4.2.7. $(\exists y_3)(x_2)(x_2 \in y_3 \equiv (\exists x_1)(x_2 = \{x_1\} \; \& \; F_3))$.

From 4.1.1, 4.1.2, and 4.2.7, we can derive:

4.1.5. $(\exists y_2)(x_1)(x_1 \in y_2 \equiv F_3)$.

In general, for every n, we need $(2n+1)$ axioms of the form $(\exists y_{n+1})(x_n)(x_n \in y_{n+1} \equiv A)$, and, given all such axioms for types from 1 to k, we can prove all sentences $(\exists y_{n+1})(x_n)(x_n \in y_{n+1} \equiv F_i)$ where n and i may each take any value from 1 to k. Therefore, given such axioms for all types, we can derive all the cases of the axiom of comprehension (D).

A natural extension of T seems to be the possibility of using negative types. Such a theory was suggested in a note in *Mind*, **61** (1952), 366—368. We quote the note in full.

The simple theory of types T deals with the relation of belonging to (the membership relation) among individuals (entities of type 0), classes of individuals (entities of type 1), classes of classes of individuals (entities of type 2), and so on, ad. inf. The fundamental principles (axioms) are three: (1) axiom of comprehension—given any sentence of the theory about the entities of type $n-1$, there exists a class of type n containing all and only those entities for which the sentence is true; (2) axiom of extensionality—any two classes of type n are identical (*i.e.* they can substitute for each other in every sentence without affecting its truth or demonstrability), when they contain the same members (of type $n-1$); (3) axiom of infinity—there exists at least one infinite class.

In this theory T, the individuals occupy a peculiar place. For one thing, they do not satisfy the axiom of extensionality (2) as given, because there are no entities of any type lower than they. Indeed, it may be argued that in logic and mathematics there is no reason for us to discuss individuals. Thus, in the rival approach to logic of the Zermelo kind of class theory, it is now customary to omit all reference to the non-class entities which were at first explicitly admitted.

A highly controversial issue about T is the status of the axiom of infinity. Unless we assume such a special axiom, the other two principles seem to provide no assurance that there must exist some infinite class. For example, from the axiom of comprehension we can prove that there is an empty class E of type 1, there is its unit class $u(E)$, there is the unit class $u(u(E))$ of the latter, and so forth. But the totality of such classes is not a class in T, since they are of different types. Alternatively, we might reason as follows. Since there is at least one class of type 1 (*viz.* E), there are at least 2 classes of type 2, 4 of type 3, 16 of type 4, etc. Therefore, we can get as big a finite class as we want. However, as Russell points out, this is of no help because no infinite class would ever be generated by such procedure.

Somehow many people tend to believe that the axiom of infinity is more questionable than the other principles of T, that it is, unlike axioms (1) and (2), probably not analytic nor *a priori*. For this feeling there is at least one strong favourable argument. The consistency of T without the axiom of infinity (3) is known, while in a very definite sense, the question of the consistency of T including (3) remains open.

As a kind of curiosity, we consider an extension T' of the theory T which includes also "negative types". Instead of the individuals, let us speak of classes of type 0. In addition, we introduce also (whatever these may mean) classes of type -1, classes of type -2, and so on. The axioms of comprehension and extensionality will be reconstrued as covering all these classes (n taking every integer as value), and the axiom of infinity will be deleted.

In the resulting theory T', there are no more individuals, and all types are on an equal footing at least in that for each type there are both infinitely many types above and infinitely many below. Moreover it would seem possible to argue in T', without appealing to the axiom of infinity, that there exist infinite classes.

Consider, for example, the classes of type 2. By the axiom of comprehension in T', there exists an empty class E_1 of type 1; therefore, there is the class $u(E_1)$ of type 2, with one member. Similarly, there exists an empty class E_0 of type 0; therefore, there exist two classes E_1 and $u(E_0)$ of type 1, and there exists a class of type 2 containing these two as members. Similarly, there exists the empty class of type -1, two classes of type 0, four classes of type 1, and therefore one class of type 2 with 4 members. And so on. We see that there must exist some infinite class of type 2. Similarly, for each type k, there must exist some infinite class of type k.

As another example, consider the universal class V_1 of type 1, which exists by the axiom of comprehension. There also exists a class V_0 of type 0 such that V_1 contains all and only the subclasses of V_0. Similarly there exists a class V_{-1} of type -1 such that V_0 contains all and only the subclasses of V_{-1}. And so on. It is easy to show, using arguments of the preceding paragraph, that each of these classes V_1, V_0, V_{-1}, etc., has more than one member. Therefore, the classes V_1, $u(V_0)$, and $u(u(V_{-1}))$, etc., are all of type 1 and distinct from one another. Hence, the class of type 2 which contains all of them is an infinite class. Similarly for every other type.

The question now is, can we formalise some of these arguments in T' and prove an axiom of infinity with the other principles? It turns out that such formalisation is demonstrably impossible. But the reasons are less obvious than in the case of the original system T.

If we could prove the axiom of infinity in T', T' would be at least as strong as T since every theorem of T would also be a theorem of T'. Therefore, a consistency proof for T' would yield one for T. According to a theorem of Gödel, the consistency of a fairly strong system (such as T) cannot be proved in the system itself. Hence, if the axiom of infinity were provable in T', it would follow that no consistency proof for T' were formalisable in T. But this is not true, for it is quite easy to prove the consistency of T' in the following manner. If T' were inconsistent, we would be able to derive a contradiction from a finite number of cases of the principles of comprehension and extensionality. These finitely many sentences contain only variables of a finite number of types. Assume n be the lowest type of the variables involved. Using well-known arguments, we can then prove the consistency of these sentences by constructing a model in which the only entity of type n is the empty class E_n. Hence, T' is not inconsistent. Moreover, it is easy to formalise the argument in T. Hence, T' cannot be as strong as T and the axiom of infinity is not demonstrable in T'.

If we look at the arguments for generating infinite classes more closely, we shall see that in each case infinitely many different types are involved. In order to formalise these arguments in T', it would seem necessary to make induction on the type indices. However, since the type indices serve merely as communication signs from the syntax of T', such induction can only be carried out in the syntax of T', but not in T' itself. Hence, even without the proof of unprovability, it would be reasonable to suppose that there exists no derivation of the axiom of infinity in T'. It would be interesting to investigate whether by combining T' with its syntax we might obtain some consistent system in which all or nearly all theorems of T have images or graphs.

Recently, Specker has given (Dialectica, no. 47/48, 1958, pp. 451—465) an interesting relation between the theory of negative types and Quine's well-known system *NF* (*Am. Math. Monthly*, **44** (1937), 70—80).

The system *NF* contains, like *ZF*, only one kind of variable, and only one primitive predicate, ϵ. Then $x=y$ is defined by $(z)(x \epsilon z \equiv y \epsilon z)$. There are only one axiom and one axiom schema

N1. $(w)(w \epsilon x \equiv w \epsilon y) \supset x=y$.

N2. If Fx is stratified, i.e., if we can so assign indices to the variables that Fx becomes a formula of type theory, then $(Ey)(x)(x \epsilon y \equiv Fx)$.

The problem whether *NF* is consistent remains unsolved. Now Specker proves:

Theorem 13. *The theory of negative types has a model such that if A is true, then A^*, obtained from A by raising every type index by 1, is true, if and only if, NF is consistent.*

Thus, if *NF* is consistent, it has a model M. Then we can define a model for the theory of negative types by correlating each a in M with all (a, k), $k=0, -1, 1, \cdots$ and define $a_k \epsilon b_{k+1}$ if and only if $a \epsilon b$ in M.

Conversely, if the theory of negative types has a model of the required sort, then, as Specker shows, there is one-to-one correspondence between sets of type k in the model and sets of type $k+1$, for every k. If f is a function which is the mapping, then the axioms of *NF* are also satisfied if we take the objects in the model for negative type theory and interpret $a \epsilon b$ for *NF* as $a \epsilon f(b)$ in the given model.

Another remarkable result on *NF* by Specker is (*Proc. Nat. Acad. Sci. U.S.A.*, **39** (1953), 972—975):

Theorem 14. *If we add the axiom of choice to NF, then the resulting system is inconsistent; moreover, since the axiom of choice for finite sets is provable in NF, the axiom of infinity is derivable in NF.*

Intuitively, *NF* has the puzzling property that if V is the universal set, V_1 is the set of all unit subsets of V, and so on, the cardinalities of $V, V_1, V_2, \cdots$ form a steadily decreasing sequence, and every earlier set contains all later sets. A set consisting of $V, V_1, V_2, \cdots$ would make the axiom of choice false. However, such a set is not definable in *NF*, the condition being unstratified. What Specker does is to consider every cardinal number m and define a sequence $g(m)$ which begins with m and has 2^a follow each term a. To assure that they have the same type, 2^a is taken as the cardinality of all subsets of a set A such that the set of all unit sets of members of A has the cardinality a. If there is an infinite sequence $g(m)$, then there is a set of cardinal numbers which contains no least member, and the axiom of choice is violated. If $g(m)$ is finite for some m, then by the axiom of choice, there is a least such m. In this case, Specker is able to derive a contradiction by comparing $g(m)$ with the sequence of their representing sets.

Previously an attempt had been made to prove the same conclusion by the following argument (*Math. Zeitschr.*, **59** (1953), 47—56). There is a finite axiomatization of *NF* (Hailperin, *J. Symbolic Logic*, **9** (1944), 1—19). With the help of the axiom of choice, one can then define in *NF* a formula which would enumerate all the sets required by the finitely many axioms. This gives the possibility of stating in *NF* an axiom of enumerability requiring that only these sets exist. Intuitively this new axiom should be consistent with the axioms of *NF* plus the axiom of choice. But then, by the diagonal argument, we can give in *NF* a set distinct from all the sets constructed. Hence, the resulting system would be inconsistent. Since it is consistent relative to *NF* plus the axiom of choice, the axiom of choice must be false in *NF*. Hence, one gets an alternative proof of the above theorem. Conversely, given the axiom of enumeration, the axiom of choice is provable, so that the axiom of enumeration is false in *NF*. This argument has not been carried through because in order to apply the diagonal argument, it is necessary to have the set of all m such that m belongs to the m-th set in the enumeration. This is defined by an unstratified condition and therefore not directly obtainable in *NF*. To complete the argument, one would have to contrive to show that such a set does occur in the model.

Another interesting result about *NF*, without the axiom of choice of course, is that in a definite sense it has no standard models, although it is not known to be inconsistent. This was proved in a paper by Rosser and the writer (*J. Symbolic Logic*, 1950). This result is relative to the natural development by Rosser of number theory and the theory of infinite ordinals in *NF*.

Since the intended interpretation or standard model of a set theory is nonenumerable and "maximal", it is not easy to set down sufficient conditions to ensure that a model is standard. In any case, to understand the conditions correctly, one would have to presuppose the standard model. It is a little easier to give explicit necessary conditions that a standard model must satisfy. For example, a model is not standard, if any one of the following is the case: (a) if the relation representing the equality relation in the formal system is not the equality relation for objects in the model; (b) the objects which are supposed to represent the natural numbers are not obtainable from the model for the initial number by a finite number of taking successors; (c) the objects in the model which are supposed to represent the ordinals are not well-ordered by the ordering relation in the model.

Either by (b) or by Theorem 14, the axiom of infinity must hold in a standard model for *NF*. Then one can develop the theory of infinite ordinals in *NF* in a similar manner as Rosser does for a related system (*J. Symbolic Logic*, **7**(1942), 1—17). Then one can derive the Burali-Forti paradox in *NF* provided the principle of transfinite induction can be proved for a certain particular formula of *NF*. But by (c), if the model is standard, the principle must be true in the model. Hence, either *NF* is inconsistent, i.e., has no model at all, or, if it has a model, it has no standard model.

The related system from which Rosser derived the Burali-Forti paradox is the system proposed by Quine in 1940 in his book Mathematical logic. In 1950, the writer repaired the system so that the result is an impredicative extension of *NF*, related as *NQ* is to *ZF*, and proved the relative consistency of it to *NF*. This modified system has been adopted by Quine in the revised edition of his book and is often known in the literature as *ML*. In the next section, we quote this paper of 1950 in full (*J. Symbolic Logic*, **15**, 25—32). The formal system *P* in it is the system *ML*.

§5. A Formal System of Logic

The main purpose of this section is to present a formal system *P* in which we enjoy a smooth-running technique and which countenances a universe of classes which is symmetrical as between large and small. More exactly, *P* is a system which differs from the inconsistent system of [1] only in the introduction of a rather natural new restrictive condition on the defining formulas of the elements (sets, membership-eligible classes). It will be proved that if the weaker system of [2] is consistent, then *P* is also consistent.

After the discovery of paradoxes, it may be recalled, Russell and Zermelo in the same year proposed two different ways of safeguarding logic against contradictions (see [3], [4]). Since then various simplifications and refinements of these systems have been made. However, in the resulting systems of Zermelo set theory, generation of classes still tends to be laborious and uncertain; and in the systems of Russell's theory of types, complications in the matter of reduplication of classes and meaningfulness of formulas remain. In [2], Quine introduced a system which seems to be free from all these complications. But later it was found out that in it there appears to be an unavoidable difficulty connected with mathematical induction. Indeed, we encounter the curious situation that although we can prove in it the existence of a class V of all classes, and we can also prove particular existence theorems for each of infinitely many classes, nobody has so far contrived to prove in it that V is an infinite class or that there exists an infinite class at all. In particular, we have so far not been able to prove in it the theorem that for every natural number n there exists a class with n members. In other words, we have not been able to prove in it the *axiom of infinity* ordinarily required in constructing mathematics on the basis of type theory. And, as a consequence, we cannot even prove in it the Peano axiom that if the successors of two natural numbers m and n are identical then m and n are identical, unless we assume that there exists a class with $m+1$ members. (Cf. [5] and [6], especially *T*16 of [5].)

To overcome this kind of difficulty, Quine was led to adopt in [1] a measure employed in the von Neumann-Bernays-Gödel kind of set theory (see [7], [8], [9]). Like these systems, the system of [1] contains a bifurcation of classes into elements and nonelements. It differs from the system of [7], [8], [9] in that it has a different domain of elements. And, according to Quine, the elements of [1] answer to the classes of [2] (see [1], p. 165, line 8 from bottom).

This system of [1] was well liked both for the manipulative convenience we regain in it and the symmetrical universe which it furnishes. Then Rosser in [10], and independently Lyndon, discredited the system by showing that it admits the Burali-Forti paradox. To meet this situation, Quine proposed in [11] a course of stressing economy in the elementhood axioms. He suggests adhering to a minimum of such axioms adequate to purposes at hand, and setting down supplementary axioms when needed as we proceed to higher branches of the theory. Two sets of weak axioms to replace the troublesome axiom *200 of elementhood are considered in [11], and it is shown that these are both adequate for the purposes of the topics covered in [1]. Recently, I proposed in [12] a system with even weaker axioms and proved that it is also adequate for the same purposes.

In contrast with this kind of procedure two types of alternative courses have been advocated. On the one hand, there is the charge that the above program leaves the logical systems in the perpetually precarious position of being liable to give rise to unforeseen contradictions. Thus, for example, Fitch suggests in [13] the alternative procedure of staying within the dependable realm where we are assured of consistency, and expanding it as far as possible. Indeed, this line of approach has generated many interesting results. Both Fitch's recent publications on his basic logic and its expansions and the contributions of Quine and Goodman toward their nominalism seem to be along this line. Moreover, we find the same trend is also represented in the earlier works of Brouwer's and Weyl's school of intuitionism, as well as in those of Chwistek's school of nominalism.

On the other hand, one may find this feature of piecemeal postulation unsatisfying and want to construct a system similar to that in [1], but in which the contradictions are no longer derivable. Black's suggestion in [14] of attempting to modify the system of [1] only slightly so as to be just sufficient to break down the proof of contradictions is along this line. But I have seen no recent systems constructed in this spirit, probably because of the lesson learned from the inconsistency of other audacious systems. In this paper I venture to present a system P which seems to fit Black's program nicely.

Let us first describe briefly the system of [1]. If we assume the theory of truth functions (the propositional calculus) and the theory of quantifiers (the functional calculus of the first order) from the beginning, we may describe the system as containing a single two-place predicate ϵ as primitive, from which we may build up (well-formed) formulas in the usual manner. And, if we speak of a formula as *stratified* if it is possible to put numerals for its variables in such a way that ϵ comes to be flanked always by consecutive ascending numerals, then we may state (with non-essential changes) the axioms of [1] as follows:

*200. If ϕ is stratified and has no free variables beyond $x, y_1, \cdots, y_n$, then $\vdash (\exists z_1)(y_1 \epsilon z_1) . \cdots . (\exists z_n)(y_n \epsilon z_n) . \supset (\exists y)(\hat{x}\phi \epsilon y)$.

†201. $(w)(w \epsilon x \equiv w \epsilon y) \supset . x \epsilon z \supset y \epsilon z$.

*202. If y is not free in ϕ, $\vdash (\exists y)(x)(x \epsilon y \equiv . (\exists z)(x \epsilon z) . \phi)$.

Therein $(\exists y)(x \epsilon y)$ if and only if x is an element, and the formula $(\exists y)(x \epsilon y)$ replaces the formula $x \epsilon V$ of [1]. (For the justification of this procedure, see [15], p. 157). The formulas $\hat{x}\phi \epsilon y$ are abbreviations defined as follows:

*Df*1. $x \epsilon \hat{x}\phi$ *for* $(\exists z)(x \epsilon z) . \phi$.

*Df*2. $z = \hat{x}\phi$ *for* $(x)(x \epsilon z \equiv x \epsilon \hat{x}\phi)$.

*Df*3. $\hat{x}\phi \epsilon y$ *for* $(\exists z)(z = \hat{x}\phi . z \epsilon y)$.

*Df*1 covers special cases of *D*9′ of [16] which, as it is shown in [16], can be employed to replace *D*9 of [1].

A formula is said to be *normal* if all the bound variables in it are element variables; or, in other words, all the quantifications are of the form $(\exists z)(y \in z)$, $(x)((\exists z)(x \in z) \supset \phi)$, or $(\exists x)((\exists z)(x \in z) . \phi)$, where ϕ is another formula. Then P may be described as a system which differs from the system of [1] only in containing in place of *200 the following:

**200. If ϕ is normal and stratified and (etc., as in *200).

Before discussing the consistency problem of the system P, I want to point out that Quine is wrong in thinking that the elements of [1] answer to the classes of [2]. The system of [2] may be described as a system which is like that of [1] except for containing in place of *200—*202 the following two axioms:

*F*1. If ϕ is stratified and y is not free in ϕ, $\vdash (\exists y)(x)(x \in y \equiv \phi)$.

*F*2. $(w)(w \in x \equiv w \in y) \supset . x \in z \supset y \in z$.

It should be obvious that there are elements in the system of [1] which do not have counterparts among the classes of [2], because in the defining formulas of the elements of [1] there may occur bound unrestricted class variables which under the normal interpretation have no counterparts in [2]. More specifically, the troublesome elements $\text{seg}_\alpha \leqslant$, $Nr(P)$, $\leqslant$ of the system of [1] used in Rosser's derivation of the paradoxes answer directly to no classes in [2]. On the other hand, it is also obvious that the elements of P answer precisely to the classes of [2]. Indeed, we may even guess that P is the system Quine originally intended to present but that he made a mistake in his presentation. Had this system P been discovered earlier, it would have been much easier to revise the book [1] to meet the situation created by the appearance of [10].

In P, the whole of Quine's book [1] can be developed without any changes except the replacement of *200 by **200 in a few proofs. It is not difficult to see that P is a theory richer than the simple theory of types (leaving out its axioms of infinity and choice). Indeed, when we recall that the system of [2] is obtained from type theory by relaxing various restrictions, we see that the domain of elements of P is already richer than the domain of classes of type theory. Moreover, a theorem answering to the axiom of infinity of type theory can also be proved in P. If we define a natural number n as the class of all n-numbered classes, we can thus state the axiom of infinity (compare *125.13 of [17]):

$$\textit{ax. inf.} \quad \Lambda \,\bar{\in}\, Nn,$$

Λ being the empty class and Nn being the class of all natural numbers. But this formula *ax. inf.* is †670 of [1], and therefore a theorem in P. Hence, in P we can obtain counterparts of all definitions and theorems of the type theory (including its axiom of infinity), and, from the generally accepted statement that the type theory is adequate for the development of ordinary mathematics, we can infer that so is also the system P.

When needed, we can also introduce the axiom of choice (the multiplicative axiom) as a new axiom of P:

†203. $(x)(y)(x, y \in z . x \neq y . \supset . (\exists w)(w \in x) . \sim(\exists u)(u \in x . u \in y)) \supset$
$(\exists y')(x')(x' \in z \supset (\exists z')(u')(u' \in x' . u' \in y' . \equiv . u' = z'))$.

However, in what follows, we shall consider P as determined by **200, †201, and *202.

In P, Rosser's derivation of the theory of ordinal numbers in [10] up to and including †836 remains intact. But the proof of the Burali-Forti paradox breaks down because the defining formulas of the classes $seg_a \leqslant$, $Nr(P)$, $\leqslant$ in †837, †838, and †842 are not normal and therefore can, in P, no longer be shown to be elements. My attempts to adapt the proof to P have thus far also failed. In particular, the course of changing the definitions $D808$, $D815$, and $D817$ so as to make the defining formulas of the above classes normal did not succeed because, apart from other difficulties, it then seems necessary either to prove that the class A in the proof of †836 is an element, or to prove that the class B in the proof of †835 is an element; but the defining formula of A is not stratified, and that of B contains free unrestricted class variables. Consequently, neither of them could directly be shown to be elements by **200, and there seems to be no way of getting around this difficulty. An analysis of Rosser's derivation of the Burali-Forti paradox in the system of [1] reveals that it turns essentially on the peculiar feature of *200 that bound unrestricted class variables are allowed in the defining formulas of elements. The conclusion suggests itself strongly that, once we purge the system [1] of this feature, probably there is not much reason to suspect that the resulting system P is more liable to engender unforeseen contradictions than the more usual systems of Russell and Zermelo.

The proof of the relative consistency of P to [2] is obtained by using an argument presented in the last part of [12] together with Gödel's extension (see [18], top of p. 359) of the Löwenheim-Skolem theorem (cf., e.g., [19], p. 83). According to this latter result, every consistent system of axioms among whose primitive symbols there is only one kind of variable possesses a model in the domain of natural numbers. Therefore, if the system of [2] is consistent, it has a model in the domain of natural numbers. In other words, if the system of [2] is consistent, then there is a relation G of natural numbers such that the axioms $F1$ and $F2$ become true when ϵ therein is interpreted as G. Assume such a relation G be given. Then we can see that the axioms of P hold true when the variables therein are construed as ranging over the classes of natural numbers. Specifically, we shall show that the axioms of P must become true when ϵ therein is construed as a relation between classes α and β of natural numbers which holds when and only when (1) $(\exists m)(\hat{n}(nGm)=\alpha . m \epsilon \beta)$, wherein the ϵ is genuine membership relation between natural numbers and classes of natural numbers, and $\hat{n}(nGm)$ is the class of all natural numbers which bears the relation G to m.

On account of the known isomorphism between the classes of natural numbers and the real numbers, it follows that P has a model in the domain of real numbers. And, therefore, relying on our confidence in the consistency of the ordinary theory of real numbers, we may conclude that P is consistent if the system of [2] is. It may be noted that, since in P we can obtain other transfinite cardinals and ordinals besides real numbers, the ϵ in the above formula (1) is more innocuous than the ϵ of P as well as that of Russell's or Zermelo's system.

Let us proceed to state a more explicit and detailed formulation of the argument showing that the membership relation between classes of natural numbers, as described above, does satisfy the axioms of P.

In order to do this, we first set up a system in which we can carry out the argument. We set up a system S in which there are variables $m, n, k, \cdots$ for natural numbers, and variables $\alpha, \beta, \gamma, \cdots$ for classes of natural numbers. Formulas of S are built up out of atomic formulas of the forms mGn and $m \epsilon \beta$ in the usual manner. In S we adopt the following definitions:

Dm. $n \epsilon m$ *for* nGm.

Di. $m=\beta$ *for* $(n)(n \epsilon m \equiv n \epsilon \beta)$.

Di'. $m=n$ *for* $(k)(k \epsilon m \equiv k \epsilon n)$.

Then we can simply define the membership relation between classes of natural numbers as follows:

Dϵ. $\alpha\epsilon\beta$ *for* $(\exists m)(m=\alpha . m \epsilon \beta)$.

Stratified and *normal* formulas can be specified as in P. And S contains the following axioms:

*A*1. If ϕ is a formula of S in which β is not free, $\vdash (\exists\beta)(m)(m \epsilon \beta \equiv \phi)$.

*A*2. If ψ is like ϕ except for containing free occurrences of m whenever ϕ contains free occurrences of α, then $\vdash m=\alpha \supset . \psi \equiv \phi$.

*A*3. $m=n\supset.m\in\alpha\supset n\in\alpha.$

The following theorems can be proved in *S*:

*T*1. $(\exists\alpha)(m=\alpha).$

*T*2. $(\exists\beta)(m\in\beta).$

*T*3. $(\exists\gamma)(\alpha\in\gamma)\equiv(\exists m)(m=\alpha).$

*T*4. If m is not free in ϕ and ψ is like ϕ except for containing free occurrences of m whenever ϕ contains free occurrences of α, then (a) $\vdash(\alpha)((\exists m)(m=\alpha)\supset\phi)\equiv(m)\psi$; (b) $\vdash(\exists\alpha)((\exists m)(m=\alpha).\phi)\equiv(\exists m)\psi$.

*T*5. $(\exists n)(n=m.n\in k)\equiv m\in k.$

By hypothesis, there is a relation G of natural numbers such that *F*1 and *F*2 become true when $\in$ therein is interpreted as G. Let us refer to the results obtained from *F*1 and *F*2 by substituting $m, n, k, \cdots$, G for $x, y, z, \cdots$, $\in$ as *F*1′ and *F*2′. In proving the relative consistency of *P*, we are entitled to make use of *F*1′ and *F*2′.

We want to prove in *S* the formulas obtained from the axioms of *P* by substituting formulas of the form $\alpha\in\beta$ for those of the form $x\in y$. That is to say, by *D*$\in$ and *Df*1—*Df*3 given above, we want to prove the following:

**200. If ϕ is a normal and stratified formula of *S* and has no free variables beyond $\alpha, \beta_1, \cdots, \beta_n$, then $\vdash(\exists\gamma_1)(\beta_1\in\gamma_1).\cdots.(\exists\gamma_n)(\beta_n\in\gamma_n).\supset(\exists\beta)(\exists\gamma)(\gamma\in\beta.(\alpha)(\alpha\in\gamma\equiv.(\exists\alpha')(\alpha\in\alpha').\phi))$.

†201. $(\gamma)(\gamma\in\alpha\equiv\gamma\in\beta)\supset.\alpha\in\alpha'\supset\beta\in\alpha'.$

*202. If ϕ is a formula of *S* in which β is not free, then $\vdash(\exists\beta)(\alpha)(\alpha\in\beta\equiv.(\exists\alpha')(\alpha\in\alpha').\phi)$.

The proofs are as follows:

Proof of **200. Let χ be the formula obtained from ϕ by replacing all occurrences of all the variables $\alpha, \beta, \gamma, \cdots$ in ϕ by occurrences of the variables $m, n, k, \cdots$ respectively. Then χ is a stratified formula of *S* containing only variables for natural numbers. Therefore, by *F*1′ and *Dm*,

$$(\exists n')(m)(m\in n'\equiv\chi),$$

where n' is not free in χ. By *T*5,

$$(\exists n')(m)((\exists n)(n=m.n\in n')\equiv\chi).$$

Let ψ be like χ except for containing free occurrences of α whenever χ contains free occurrences of m. By *T*4,

$$(\exists n')(\alpha)((\exists m)(m=\alpha)\supset.(\exists n)(n=\alpha.n\in n')\equiv\psi).$$

By the theory of quantifiers,

$$(\exists n')(\alpha)((\exists n)(n = \alpha . n \in n') \equiv . (\exists m)(m = \alpha) . \psi).$$

By $T4$ and $D\epsilon$,

$$(\exists \gamma)((\exists k)(\gamma = k) . (\alpha)(\alpha \in \gamma \equiv . (\exists m)(m = \alpha) . \psi)).$$

By $T3$,

$$(\exists \gamma)((\exists \beta)(\gamma \in \beta) . (\alpha)(\alpha \in \gamma \equiv . (\exists \alpha')(\alpha \in \alpha') . \psi)).$$

By the theory of quantifiers,

$$(\exists \beta)(\exists \gamma)(\gamma \in \beta . (\alpha)(\alpha \in \gamma \equiv . (\exists \alpha')(\alpha \in \alpha') . \psi)).$$

Therefore, by $T3$ and $T4$,

$$(\exists \gamma_1)(\beta_1 \epsilon \gamma_1) . \cdots . (\exists \gamma_n)(\beta_n \in \gamma_n) . \supset (\exists \beta)(\exists \gamma)(\gamma \in \beta . (\alpha)(\alpha \in \gamma \equiv . (\exists \alpha')(\alpha \in \alpha') . \phi)).$$

Proof of †201. By $A2$ and Di,

$$(j)(j \in m \equiv j \in \beta) \supset . (\exists n)(n = m . n \in \alpha') \supset (\exists n)(n = \beta . n \in \alpha').$$

By $T4$ and $D\epsilon$,

$$(\exists k)(k = \alpha) \supset : (j)(j \in \alpha \equiv j \in \beta) \supset . \alpha \in \alpha' \supset \beta \in \alpha'.$$

By $D\epsilon$ and the theory of quantifiers,

$$(j)(j \in \alpha \equiv j \in \beta) \supset . \alpha \in \alpha' \supset \beta \in \alpha'.$$

By $T5$,

$$(j)((\exists m)(m = j . m \in \alpha) \equiv (\exists m)(m = j . m \in \beta)) \supset . \alpha \in \alpha' \supset \beta \in \alpha'.$$

By $T4$ and $D\epsilon$,

$$(\gamma)((\exists m)(m = \gamma) \supset . \gamma \in \alpha \equiv \gamma \in \beta) \supset . \alpha \in \alpha' \supset \beta \in \alpha'.$$

Therefore, by $D\epsilon$ and the theory of quantifiers,

$$(\gamma)(\gamma \in \alpha \equiv \gamma \in \beta) \supset . \alpha \in \alpha' \supset \beta \in \alpha'.$$

Proof of *202. If m and β are not free in ϕ and ψ is like ϕ except for containing free occurrences of m whenever ϕ contains free occurrences of α, then, by A1,

$$(\exists \beta)(m)(m \in \beta \equiv \psi).$$

By $T5$,

$$(\exists\beta)(m)((\exists n)(n = m . n \in \beta) \equiv \psi).$$

By $T4$,

$$(\exists\beta)(\alpha)((\exists n)(n = \alpha) \supset .(\exists n)(n = \alpha . n \in \beta) \equiv \phi).$$

By the theory of quantifiers,

$$(\exists\beta)(\alpha)((\exists n)(n = \alpha . n \in \beta) \equiv .(\exists n)(n = \alpha) . \phi).$$

By $T3$ and $D\epsilon$,

$$(\exists\beta)(\alpha)(\alpha \in \beta \equiv .(\exists\alpha')(\alpha \in \alpha') . \phi).$$

That completes the proof that if the system of [2] is consistent, then P is also consistent.

It may be observed that the above argument of proving relative consistency applies to all pairs of systems which are related to each other as P and the system of [2] are related. As an example, I may mention the system NQ proposed on p. 151 of [20] and the system defined by Z1—Z6 of [20]. They would form such a pair, if we replace $N6$ of NQ by the slightly different axiom:

$N6'$. If ϕab is a formula which contains no unrestricted class variables and in which a and b are free but c, d, and e are not free, then the formula $(a)(b)(c)((\phi ab . \phi ac) \supset b = c) \supset (\exists d)(a)(a \in d \equiv (\exists b)(b \in e . \phi ba))$ is an axiom.

After the change, we can prove with analogous argument that if the system determined by Z1—Z6 is consistent, NQ is also consistent.

§ 6. The Systems of Ackermann and Frege

We have largely refrained from discursive remarks. In this section, we shall indulge in some. Two specially interesting essays on the foundations of set theory, which we shall not consider, are Gödel's paper in *Philosophy of Bertrand Russell*, 1944 and Stenius' monograph *Das Problem der logischen Antinomien*, Helsingfors, 1949.

Cantor's much discussed definition of set reads: Unter einer Menge verstehen wir jede Zussamenfassung M von Bestimmten wohlunterschiedenen Objekten m unserer Anschauung oder unseres Denkens (welche die "Elemente" von M gennant werden) zu einem Ganzen. (1895, *Works*, p. 282).

The words "definite" and "distinct" would seem to suggest that it is objects such as fog and water which are being excluded. Objects of intuition are roughly concrete entities and objects of thought are roughly abstract entities such as numbers and classes or other universals. The interesting phrase "collection into a whole" refers to some sort of act of collecting. This brings a certain "constructive" or "genetic" element into Cantor's concept of set. The act of collecting needed here is inevitably of an abstract character and not quite the same as throwing pennies into a hat or putting two braces about a finite string of names.

As is rather well-known, Cantor was not particularly sympathetic to formalization. This view seems to be shared by Finsler who also refuses to give more manageable conditions. In both cases, there is also an inclination to look with disfavour on attempts to codify set theory. One could argue that our problem here is with natural and not formal language. The problem of resolving paradoxes is an absolute one and not relative to particular formal languages. When the paradoxes are reformulated in the framework of a formal language, we change the problem, since the concepts in the formal language deviate more or less from the corresponding ones in the natural language. The problem is not to formalize or reconstruct mathematics on sound principles in the manner of Euclid but to offer explanations which would reveal the flaw in the apparent contradictions and show that mathematics, despite these "paradoxes", remains clear enough. Those who object to this procedure wishes to say that without codification there is no reliable basis for communication and discussion because of the inevitable vagueness in the general comments.

Interconnected with the question of formalization is the contrast between classes as extensions and as given by defining conditions. Cantor's own definition lends directly to an extensional interpretation. In particular, the null class and unit classes do not quite fall under the definition since we have no "collecting into a whole" in these cases; they have to be taken as just a manner of speaking. Both an extensionalist and an intensionalist may choose to use or reject codification, although a formalized set theory, even when based on an extensional interpretation, tells us also those defining conditions which are explicitly permitted. We may compare the intended extensional non-enumerable with the unintended intensional enumerable interpretations.

At least two radically different proposals to clarify Cantor's definition along axiomatic lines have been made, thus revealing the possibility of contradictory interpretations of Cantor's words. One is the well-known theory of Zermelo and von Neumann that a collection is a set only when it is not too large, i.e. the theory of size limitation, in Russell's terminology. The other is a recent system of Ackermann's (*Math. Annalen,* **131** (1956), 336–345).

So far as I know, no extensive study has been made of Ackermann's system which is rather interesting in that almost any axioms of categoricalness would seem to be refutable. It would be of great interest to study some independence results in connection with this theory. For example, it could be used as a bridge because it seems likely that it is consistent relative to Zermelo and yet inconsistent with axioms imposing too much order.

The system contains four axiom schemata:

A1. $(x)(F(x) \supset M(x)) \supset (Ey)(z)(z \in y \supset F(x))$.

A2. $(x \subset y \ \& \ y \subset x) \supset x = y$.

A3. If $F(u)$ does not contain M and contains the free variables $x_1, \cdots, x_n$, then

$$\{[M(x_1) \ \& \cdots \ \& \ M(x_n)] \ \& \ (y)[F(y) \supset M(y)]\}$$
$$\supset (Ez)[M(z) \ \& \ (u)(u \in z \equiv F(u))].$$

A4. $[M(x) \ \& \ (y \in x \vee y \subset x)] \supset M(y)$.

Of these, *A2* is natural from an extensional approach and indeed embodies a basic property of classes even if we stress how they are to be defined. *A1* is stronger than the corresponding principle for nonelement collections in the von Neumann approach. On the one hand, if we feel that any collecting together of elements would yield a collection, not necessarily an element, then we may prefer *A1* to the more restricted form (only quantification over sets are allowed). On the other hand, if we do not wish to collect nonelement collections, then one may wonder how we can use quantifiers ranging unrestrictedly over them. This same objection would also apply to *A3*. But one might reply that we do not care what conditions are used in definitions so long as restriction on M is observed.

Ackermann's justification of *A3* is a bit involved. Since we are to proceed from given sets to new sets, the condition on free variables is natural. It is also inevitable, otherwise every collection is a set. Since the concept of set is open (at every stage we can go up and get new sets), the totality of all sets cannot be taken as sharply defined. Hence, the requirement that M should not occur in F.—One might wonder why it is then we can use general variables in F ranging over arbitrary collections, since that totality is even less sharply defined. But it is quite possible to maintain that we do have a definite larger totality of all collections (viz. any property, all properties, will do), though not a sharp totality of sets in it. We can prove that for any formula F not containing M, $F(x) \not\equiv M(x)$, otherwise we have universal set and also Russell set. It would seem natural so to interpret Cantor's definition that we only perform the collection into a whole with regard to given objects. If so, we cannot have a universal set which, of course, has to be its own element. We can never obtain it because in order to make collecting, it must be there already. Indeed, it would seem natural to conclude from Cantor's definition that whenever we collect objects into a whole, the whole must be a new object distinct from all these objects which are its elements. In other words, it would seem natural from any "contructive" approach, however generous we may construe the word, no set can contain itself as an element.

The justification of the first half of *A*4 is easy. Since we always collect sets to get a new set, an element of a set must be a set. Ackermann justifies the second half by remarking that in defining a subset of a set x, we need not refer to the totality of all sets but only those sets which are elements of x or elements of elements of x, etc. This justification does not mean that in the formal system in question we can explicitly write out a defining condition by referring only to the set x and previously given sets. If that were so, this would be a consequence of *A*3. Nonetheless, we can argue that in some sufficiently rich language the smaller totality can be described without appeal to M. As it is, *A*4 permits us to define an arbitrary subset $y=\hat{u}(u \in x \& F(u))$ for arbitrary F, since by *A*1, there is such a collection. Perhaps, a more direct justification should be that if we can collect all elements of x into a set, any subcollection (extensionally) can also be collected into a set.

The deriving power of *A*1—*A*4 is rather remarkable. If in *A*3, we take $y \neq y$ as $M(y)$, then the antecedent is trivially satisfied and we get the null set. If we take $(y=x_1 \vee y=x_2)$ as $F(y)$, we get the pair set. If in *A*3, we take $(Ev)(y \in v \,\&\, v \in x_1)$, then we get the sum set of x_1 by the first half of *A*4. Similarly if we take $y \subset x_1$ as $F(y)$, we get the power set of x_1 by the second half of *A*4. We have already indicated how to get the Aussonderungsaxiom from *A*1 and *A*4. We can also obtain an infinite set z which contains the empty set as element and contains as element the unit set of every element of it. Thus, by *A*3, we can find an intersection of such infinite sets which is a set that again is infinite. The axiom of substitution can be proved for any relation $R(v,y)$ which does not contain M and maps sets to sets. Thus, since $M(x_1)$ and $(R(v,y) \,\&\, M(v)) \supset M(y)$, if we take $(Ev)(R(v,y) \,\&\, v \in x_1)$ as $F(y)$ in *A*3, we get the required set $\hat{u}(Ev)(R(v,u) \,\&\, v \in x_1)$.

To show that this axiom is no weaker than the corresponding one in the Zermelo type of theory, Ackermann uses Fraenkel's definition of functions. It should be of interest to compare and translate this consideration into a form in terms of the Bernays-Gödel form of $R(v,y)$.

Frege distinguishes between objects and functions. Concepts are special cases of functions. He has a form of type theory for concepts and functions, but classes are regarded as objects (value-ranges of concepts) which are no longer unsaturated. Objects are not just concrete objects but rather anything denoted by nouns (concepts corresponding to adjectives). Concepts applied to objects (or lower-level concepts) are primitive in forming meaningful propositions and can never be separated from the objects. Abstraction is employed as a primitive to obtain classes as value-ranges from concepts, and then membership is defined with the help of the description operator. The reason why he does not or cannot use membership as primitive and use class axiom as usual remains obscure, even if we admit that he wishes to stress the conceptual source of classes.

$$\begin{aligned}\hat{x}F(x) = \hat{x}(EG)(x = \hat{y}G(y) \,\&\, \sim G(x)) \\ \supset (x)(F(x) \equiv (EG)(x = \hat{y}G(y) \,\&\, \sim G(x))) \\ \supset F(\hat{x}F(x)) \equiv (EG)(\hat{x}F(x) = \hat{y}G(y) \,\&\, \sim G(\hat{x}F(x))) \\ \supset F(\hat{x}F(x)) \equiv (\hat{x}F(x) = \hat{x}F(x) \,\&\, \sim F(\hat{x}F(x))) \\ \supset F(\hat{x}F(x)) \equiv \sim F(\hat{x}F(x)).\end{aligned}$$

The troublesome axiom (Vb) says that if concepts have the same value-range then they always have same truth value for the same argument. This is more or less equivalent to the assumption $x \in \hat{y}F(y) \equiv F(x)$, for arbitrary F. It implies (Vb) by truth functions, the converse is not so clear.

Schröder and Dedekind fail to distinguish between membership and inclusion, and get a contradiction. This is because their wrong view of classes as extensions (viz. heaps). The inverse relation of membership can only be achieved via concepts.

There is the problem of making sense of the extensional view of classes: to construe classes and concepts as real objects existing independently of our definitions and constructions. Instead of concepts one might wish to use the more neutral word attribute (propositional functions). Classes are to be regarded as pluralities of things or as structures consisting of a plurality of things. Observe that there are really two separate moments in realism and extensionalism: on the basis of realism, classes may be regarded "as concepts taken in extension", but classes and concepts are both real; there is a contrast between concept and definition ("our" definition and construction, whether the class or concept comes into being with the definition, or are only described by the definition), classes can exist independently of definitions but not of concepts. By an extensional view of class, we cannot mean just (1) the principle of extensionality holds for classes (for nobody wishes to deny this, and Frege or Gödel may even wish to accept this for concepts), nor (2) classes behave like heaps. Now what is left of the extensional view except the realist position plus the principle of extensionality for classes? Consider all possible classes of positive integers. Here we seem to gain some advantage through considering classes as extensions, i.e. paying no attention to the corresponding concepts. We seem to be able to envisage a totality of all these possible sets. We cannot say much that is positive about the totality. Since it is maximal, we know that, by the diagonal argument, it cannot be enumerable. Hence, it cannot consist of any enumerable collection of enumerably many sets, etc. But we do not know how many of them there are. In order even to give sense to this problem, we are faced with something like Cantor's theory of ordinal numbers which, however, does not much help because the difficult notion "all possible classes" is only replaced by "all possible well-ordering relations". We can still ask how many such relations there are. As far as our knowledge is concerned, it seems that these classical totalities forever remain negative notions which can only be considered "illegitimate" from a constructive approach. If we persist in a constructive approach, we shall have to resign ourselves to imperfect characterization of all possibilities and still leave room for a negatively given nonenumerable totality. These are all very natural and plausible except that we cannot do much with them.

One might wish to follow Gödel in distinguishing concepts from nominalistic notions and introduce a principle of extensionality for concepts to the effect that no two properties can belong to exactly the same things, although the same concept may correspond to many different notions. Such a practice amounts to a new stipulation for the use of "concept" which might be helpful for certain purposes, but can hardly claim much intuitive evidence.

Both Frege and Russell object to taking classes in the pure extensional way as simply heaps or conglomerations on the ground that there would then be no null class ("If we burn down all the trees of a wood, we thereby burn down the wood") and no distinction between a unit class and its only object. This objection can be met by considering null class and unit classes as fictions. A more serious question would seem to be the failure to distinguish between membership and inclusion. Is this failure a necessary consequence of the pure extensional view? Schröder deduces a paradox. Consider the class of those classes that are equal to 1. By definition, it contains only 1. But every class contains the empty class 0. But the defining predicate "equal to 1" must apply to every thing in the class. Hence, 0=1. If we think of several woods as forming a class in the sense of a conglomeration, then it would seem natural to think of a collection of concrete objects so that every tree is included in and belongs to the class, every wood is included in and belongs to the class, the collection of all but one wood also is included in the class. Or at least, we may feel inclined to use only the part-whole relation, and not think of membership relation at all. We can leave aside the restriction to concrete objects, still just consider classes as heaps, we do not even need the words "individual" and "single thing".

Once we speak of heap "of numbers", heap "of woods", heap "of trees", the situation is changed. But the change is not so much as to compel us to introduce the concept defining the heap or class. We need only have the general concept under which all members of the class does fall. Thus, once we have the concept of number, we can think of all classes of numbers extensionally. A somewhat less obvious case is, once we have the notion of set M, we can continue to view arbitrary sets of sets extensionally. Extensionally, we can collect given objects into a class, a "many-in-one", in which the individuality of the elements are preserved. The difference between Zermelo and Ackermann lies in that the former speaks only of subsets of given sets while the latter uses almost arbitrary defining conditions. If we weaken Ackermann's $A3$ by adding the condition $(Ex)(\sim F(x) \,\&\, M(x))$, then we can probably remove the restriction on F (that M does not occur in it). The additional condition is very reasonable and presumably does not hamper much the power. In Ackermann's system, the condition is redundant, because any condition violating it would yield a contradiction. On the other hand, the removal of restriction on F can also be defended on the ground that we do not really care about how to define the new set provided we do not jump to all sets. We may need an axiom that $M(0)$, 0 being the empty set. In any case, we must keep in mind that the extensional view does not deny that in forming a set we go from objects to a new object. Hence, the calculus of individuals or nominalistic no-class conception violates entirely the spirit.

It is impossible to deny that to every class there must correspond a concept (in some sense) whose value range is the class. This is also not what an extensional view purports to deny. What is proposed is to neglect the concepts and consider arbitrary manners of collection. In this way, we more easily get to all possible subsets of a given set; otherwise, we have to continue to ask what the defining concepts are like and move slowly because we wish to have some survey of the types of concepts which we are willing to envisage. Somehow we more easily arrive at arbitrary sets by thinking extensionally than by thinking intensionally. The realistic concepts have the advantage of bridging arbitrary extensions and articulate defining conditions, but somehow can only move beyond all bounds first through their connection with classes as extensions. When we are concerned with individual classes, we seem forced to go through intensions, while in considering all possible classes, we seem to move more freely with extensions.

An army is more than a class, just as a heap is less. In an army there is a binding relation between the members, while in a class, we are only concerned with the relation between the one (the class) and the many (the elements). A class is a totality such that it is well-determined what the units are, but it is irrelevant what relations the units stand to one another. A concept does yield a totality satisfying both conditions.

Frege's type theory with regard to functions and concepts is based on linguistic necessity. Grammatically, we simply cannot allow a predicate occur without a subject. The essence of a function or an attribute is the general notion of a regular form of transition from one (or more) object to another. We can use variables ranging over functions, but we should remember that everything which can be said involving a function can be said using only the language in which the functional expression occurs only with its argument place. Because ambiguities can only be eliminated by things of the right kind, $(\quad)^2+1$ can take a number as argument, but $((\quad)^2+1)^2+1$ cannot be regarded as a value of $(\quad)^2+1$, since $(\quad)^2+1$ cannot serve to eliminate entirely an ambiguity. For the same reason, no variables can range over functions of different types, or objects and functions of the same kind. This principle is preserved by Russell in that part of his theory which led to the simple theory of types. On the other hand, Frege's free manipulation with sets or value-ranges is abolished by Russell but partially preserved in type-free systems.

A final point on Frege is the question whether classes can be regarded as a species of individuals (part of the ultimate furniture of the world). Since Cantor proves that there are more classes than individuals, this cannot be true. In other words, if we regard them all as individuals, then we may ask for the correlate of the class $\hat{x}(x \notin x)$; by Cantor, it corresponds to no individual. Hence, a contradiction. Frege actually imagines correlation of value-ranges with objects previously given in some arbitrary fashion, e.g., the concept prime with the number 3 or the concept German with Nehru so that there is no "logical intuition" to see that a class cannot be its own member. In the same way, if one introduces Frege's restriction that the defined class itself is to be excluded, we can only cut the number of classes by half (not distinguishing the two cases that the defined class belongs to itself, or not). But for $n>2$, $2^{n-1}>n$. Hence, a contradiction for any universe with more than two objects. Formally, this can presumably be carried out and indeed be applied to wide classes of cases which try to exclude singular points. Any fixed singular points would still give contradictions. On the other hand, if the singular points are to include also all those definable indirectly in terms of the set to be introduced, then it is (1) difficult to carry out, (2) not clear how different from the positive "constructive" approach.

Note on partially defined predicates and sets. There is a possibility of using arbitrary defining conditions but restricting the law of excluded middle. This approach to set theory (compare p. 386 above) has been studied by Skolem, Behmann, Bochvar, Ackermann, Fitch, Schütte. A natural formulation would seem to yield systems somewhat different from those of these authors. We use Lukasiewicz's 3-valued (t, u, f) tables for "and", "or", "not" and extend them to quantifiers in the natural manner. Then we use $\rightarrow$ as implication but do not permit reiteration. We say that $p \rightarrow q$ is valid if and only if q gets the value t whenever p gets the value t. Then, for quantifier-free p and q, we can decide whether $p \rightarrow q$ is valid. Modifying slightly the system L_h (p. 310), we get a system PP of the partial predicate calculus which can be proved along familiar lines to be complete relative to the given interpretation of logical constants. Moreover, if we change the interpretation of $p \rightarrow q$ to read: this is valid if and only if q does not get the value f whenever p gets the value t; then we get a similar formulation KP which gives the classical predicate calculus. It can be proved that $p \rightarrow q$ is a theorem of KP if and only if $(p \,\&\, (q \vee \sim q)) \rightarrow q$ is a theorem of PP. If we adjoin to PP set terms $\hat{x}Fx$ for arbitrary F, we can develop set theory by introducing axioms of excluded middle to stipulate that certain predicates are complete. For example, we may wish to assert $x=y \vee x \neq y$ for all sets whether complete or partial, then we would get a large amount of set theory without having to introduce many new axioms. There are many attractive questions regarding further developments of set theory on this basis and interpretation of iterated implications.

References

[1] W. V. Quine, Mathematical Logic, New York, 1940.

[2] W. V. Quine, New foundations for mathematical logic, *Am. Math. Monthly*, **44** (1937), 70—80.

[3] Bertrand Russell, Mathematical logic based on the theory of types, *Am. Jour. Math.*, **30** (1908), 222—262.

[4] Ernst Zermelo, Untersuchungen über die Grundlagen der Mengenlehre I, *Math. Ann.*, **65** (1908), 261—281.

[5] Barkley Rosser, On the consistency of Quine's "New foundations for mathematical logic," *Jour. Symbolic Logic*, **4** (1939), 15—24.

[6] Barkley Rosser, Definition by induction in Quine's "New foundations for mathematical logic," *ibid.*, 80—81.

[7] J. von Neumann, Eine Axiomatisierung der Mengenlehre, *Jour. reine und angewandte Mathematik*, **154** (1925), 219—240.

[8] Paul Bernays, A system of axiomatic set theory, Part I, *Jour. Symbolic Logic*, **2** (1937), 65—77; Part II, *ibid.*, **6** (1941), 1—17.

[9] Kurt Gödel, The Consistency of the Continuum Hypothesis, Princeton, 1940.

[10] Barkley Rosser, The Burali-Forti paradox, *Jour. Symbolic Logic*, **7** (1942), 1—17.

[11] W. V. Quine, Element and number, *ibid.*, **6** (1941), 135—149.

[12] Hao Wang, A new theory of element and number, *ibid.*, **13** (1948), 129—137.

[13] F. B. Fitch, Review of [11], *ibid.*, **7** (1942), 121—122.

[14] Max Black, Review of [1], *Mind*, N. S., **52** (1943), 264—275.

[15] W. V. Quine, On existence conditions for elements and classes, *Jour. Symbolic Logic*, **7** (1942), 157—159.

[16] Hao Wang, Existence of classes and value specification of variables, *Jour. Symbolic Logic*, **15** (1950), 103—112.

[17] A. N. Whitehead and Bertrand Russell, Principia Mathematica, Cambridge, England, 1910—1913.

[18] Kurt Gödel, Die Vollständigkeit der Axiome des logischen Funktionenkalküls, *Monatsh. Math. Phys.*, **37** (1930), 349—360.

[19] Alonzo Church, Introduction to mathematical logic, Princeton, 1944.

[20] Hao Wang, On Zermelo's and von Neumann's axioms for set theory, *Proc. Nat. Acad. Sci. U.S.A.*, **35** (1949), 150—155.

CHAPTER XVII

RELATIVE STRENGTH AND REDUCIBILITY

§ 1. Relation between P and Q

In this and the next section we consider two papers by the writer (*Proc. Nat. Acad. Sci. U.S.A.*, **36** (1950), 479—484; *Math. Annalen*, 125 (1952), 56—66), together with several related papers by Mostowski (*Fund. Math.*, **39** (1953), 133—158), R. Suszko (*Studia Philos.*, **4** (1951), 301—330), Myhill (*Proc. Nat. Acad. Sci.*, **38** (1952), 979—981), and McNaughton (*Proc. Am. Math. Soc.*, **5** (1954), 505—509). On account of the complications involved in formalization, many of these works contain errors, although most of the errors seem repairable. It may be of some interest to give an account of the theorems actually proved, as well as the remedies for defective proofs.

The one common basic idea is very simple. If there are only finitely many axioms stating the existence of sets, then all the sets required to exist by these axioms can be enumerated in the set theory itself, and, hence, in particular, by the diagonal argument, there must be some condition in the system which cannot be proved by the finitely many axioms to be defining a subset of the set of integers. Thus, for example, since every condition in ZF defines a subset of the set of integers, there is no finite set of theorems from which we can derive all axioms of ZF. To actually carry out this and related arguments, the presence of impredicative definitions and the complication with mathematical induction call for great care.

In the writer's paper of 1950, two systems P and Q are used which are respectively the predicative and impredicative theories of number sets (see § 3 of the preceding chapter). In this paper the main work is to prove some results to indicate how Q is stronger than P. The sketches, though too brief, are essentially correct. Then it is quickly remarked that the same argument can be used to prove similar results if any finite extension of P is used in place of P. This part overlooks the complications introduced by the presence of impredicative definitions. In his review (*J. Symbolic Logic*, **16** (1951), 143), Rosser criticized the first half which is in fact the correct part. In what follows the argument sketched there will be given in greater detail. The writer's paper of 1952 was an attempt to remedy the second half, viz. the part about finite axiomatization. This topic will be considered in the next section.

The method of enumeration is clear from Gödel 1940. We should take care of Gödel's axioms of group B and his axiom $A1$, or, in other words, the axioms $NB\,10$—$NB\,16$ or $B\,10$ to $B\,16$ in § 3 of the preceding chapter. Since the sets of P can be enumerated in P according to the Ackermann model of G, we may assume given an enumeration of the sets. Then we can, e.g. represent E by 5, the class with the same extension as the a-th set by 7^a, the complement of the intersection of the a-th and the b-th classes by $11^a\,13^b$, the domain of the a-th set by 17^a, $V \times X$ where X is the a-th set by 19^a, $\mathrm{Cyc}(X)$ and $\mathrm{Per}(X)$ by 23^a and 29^a. The simple class of numbers so used can be called C. The formal enumeration runs as follows.

1.1. $G(j, B)$ for $(k)(n)(2^k \cdot 3^n \in B \supset n \leqslant j) \,\&\, (m)\{m \leqslant j \supset [(m=5 \,\&\, \vec{B}`m = E) \vee \cdots \vee (Ei)(i \in C \,\&\, m = 29^i \,\&\, \vec{B}`m = \mathrm{Per}(\vec{B}`m)) \vee (m \notin C \,\&\, \vec{B}`m = \Lambda)]\}$.

1.2. $2^m \cdot 3^n \in F$ or $m \in \vec{F}`n$ for $(EB)(G(n, B) \,\&\, 2^m \cdot 3^n \in B)$.

1.3. $\vec{F}`n = A \equiv (m)(m \in A \equiv m \in \vec{F}`n) \equiv (EB)(G(n, B) \,\&\, \vec{B}`n = A)$.

Proof. $(EB)(G(n, B) \,\&\, \vec{B}`n = A) \equiv (EB)(G(n, B) \,\&\, (m)(m \in A \equiv 2^m \cdot 3^n \in B))$, the right hand side implies $(m \in A \supset (EB)(G(n, B) \,\&\, 2^m \cdot 3^n \in B))$ and $(m \in \vec{F}`n \supset m \in A)$.

To prove the other half, we have to use $(EB)G(n, B)$, a theorem provable only by induction in Q. Hence, the equivalence holds only in Q.

1.4. $N(A, m)$ or $(EB)H(A, m, B)$ for $(EB)(G(m, B) \,\&\, \vec{B}`m = A)$.

H contains no other class variables. In these definitions, $\vec{B}`m$ is the same as $B``\{m\}$, but we cannot use $B``m$ instead. We shall assume that $V \times A$, $\mathrm{Cyc}(A)$, etc. contain only ordered pairs (resp. triples) as members.

It is, by the way, known also by other methods that Q is stronger than P. Indeed, $Con(P)$, a usual formulation of the consistency of P, can be proved as a theorem in Q, by the argument indicated on p. 273 of *Trans. Am. Math. Soc.*, **73** (1952). Similarly, it is shown there that $Con(NB)$ is a theorem of NQ.

We can formulate an axiom of categoricalness:

$(P1)$ $(X)(Em)N(X, m)$ or $(X)(Em)(EB)H(X, m, B)$.

Intuitively, we have a minimum model for P in which only the intended integers exist and only the explicitly required classes exist. In such a model, not only all theorems of P, but $(P1)$ is also true. If, now, we call the translation of a formula in P the result of restricting class variables to range over only those classes X for which $(Em)(EB)H(X, m, B)$, while not changing the number variables in any way (a simplifying assumption to be discussed below), we can immediately prove that translations of all theorems of P are again theorems of P. Moreover, the translation of the axiom of limitation also appears to be intuitively true, since all classes in the enumeration must satisfy the enumerating condition. This intuitive sense is, however, not very simple because of the two different ranges of the variable B and B^* in the translation "$(X^*)(Em)(EB^*)H(X^*, m, B^*)$" or "$(X)((Em)(EB)H(X, m, B) \supset (Em)(EB^*)H(X, m, B^*))$", which is different from the tautologous "$(X^*)(Em)(EB)H(X^*, m, B)$".

In order to see that the translation of $(P1)$ is true, we consider all classes A satisfying $N(A, j)$ for some j. If j is 1, i.e. $N(A, 1)$, we can take the empty class which does occur in the enumeration as B^*, and have:

1.5. $N(A, 1) \supset (EB^*)H(A, 1, B^*)$ (abbreviated $K(A, 1)$).

1.6. $(EB^*)(m)(n)(2^m \cdot 3^n \in B^* \equiv (n \leqslant 1 \;\&\; H(A, N, B^*) \;\&\; m \in A))$. (Abbreviated $M(A, 1)$).

Suppose we have found B_j^* which satisfies 1.5 and 1.6 when 1 is replaced by j, then we can find B_{j+1}^* in terms of B_j^*:

1.7. $2^m 3^k \in B_{j+1}^* \equiv \{k \leqslant j+1 \;\&\; [(k=5 \;\&\; m \in E) \vee \cdots \vee (Ei)(i \in C \;\&\; k = 29^i \;\&\; (Ea)(Eb)(Ec)(m = 2^{2^a 3^b} 3^c \;\&\; 2^{2^{2^a 3^c} 3^b} 3^i \in B_j^*)) \vee (m \notin C \;\&\; 2^m 3^k \in B_j^*)]\}$.

Hence, we can prove in P:

1.8. $K(A, j) \supset K(A, j+1)$.

1.9. $M(A, j) \supset M(A, j+1)$.

Furthermore, we can make induction in Q and prove from 1.5 and 1.8:

1.10. $\vdash_Q (n)(A)(N(A, n) \supset (EB^*)H(A, n, B^*))$, therefore also the translation of $(P1)$.

From 1.6 and 1.9 we see that both in P and in Q we can prove the existence of classes $B_1^*, B_2^*, \cdots$ which form a monotone increasing sequence in the sense that B_n^* is included in B_{n+1}^*. The union of all these classes can also be proved to exist in Q:

1.11. $\vdash_Q (EB)(m)(n)(2^m 3^n \in B \equiv (EA)(G(n, A) \;\&\; 2^m \cdot 3^n \in A))$.

Intuitively this class B is not among the classes required by $(P1)$ and therefore cannot be proved to exist in P. To establish this more exactly, we proceed as follows. By 1.10 and the argument earlier on:

Theorem 1. *When all class variables are restricted as before, P is translatable into P, P plus $(P1)$ is translatable into Q.*

We note incidentally that if a model for P contains only regular integers, then, because 1.5 and 1.8 are theorems of P, then the formula in 1.10 and the translation of ($P1$) must be true in the model. We shall prove that, nonetheless, the translation of ($P1$) is not derivable in P.

Theorem 2. *The formula in 1.11 is not a theorem of P, if Q is consistent.*

Proof. If the class in 1.11 is provable in P, so is also its complement. Then its translation is a theorem of Q. Hence, by 1.10, the following is also a theorem of Q:

$$(EB^*)(m)(n)(2^m 3^n \in B^* \equiv \sim (EA)(G(n, A) \,\&\, 2^m \cdot 3^n \in A)).$$

In particular,

$$2^j 3^j \in B^* \equiv \sim (EA)(G(j, A) \,\&\, 2^j 3^j \in A).$$

If $N(B^*, j)$, however,

$$2^j 3^j \in B^* \equiv (EA)(G(j, A) \,\&\, 2^j 3^j \in A).$$

Hence, a contradiction.

Theorem 3. *If Q is consistent, then the union B in 1.11 of the monotone increasing sequence of classes $B_1^*, B_2^*, \cdots$ of P is not a class of P.*

Theorem 4. *The translation of (P1) or the formula in 1.10 is not a theorem of P; there is a model of P in which the following is true:*

$$(EX)[(En)(EY)H(X, n, Y) \,\&\, \sim(En)(EY^*)H(X, n, Y^*)].$$

Proof. Take an arbitrary class X not provable to exist in P (say the class in 1.11) and construct a model for P in which the negation of the consistency of the extended system is true (or take the negation of $Con(Q)$). Now put

$$Y = X + \langle X, \mu_m(m \text{ is a proof of contradiction})\rangle.$$

Then we get the desired counterexample.

There is one omission in the above proofs. In defining the translation of a formula, we assumed the number variables unchanged. Since numbers are identified with certain sets in P which in turn are coextensional with classes, this assumption may appear to cause troubles. Since, however, we are using an enumeration of a sets, this is indeed all right. An alternative method of dealing with this is given in *Math. Annalen.*, vol. **126**, 385—409.

The same arguments can also be employed to prove similar theorems for *NB* and *NQ* in place of *P* and *Q*. For this purpose, we use the fact that *Con*(*NB*) is a theorem of *NQ* and apply Bernays' lemma.

The results of Myhill and Suszko seem at first set quite closely related to these results. There is, however, an essential difference. For example, Myhill takes *NB* and gives an enumeration of all classes required by Gödel's axioms of group *B* with no special clause to take care of *A*1, i.e. the representation of sets by classes. He then proposes to prove the translatability into *NB* of the system obtained from *NB* by adding the hypothesis that all classes are nameable, i.e. the statement corresponding to (*P*1) above now with an enumeration omitting the clause on representation of sets by classes. From the considerations above it would appear that such an assertion cannot be true, and the system is at most, translatable into *NQ*, not into *NB*.

In fact, Myhill's observation 5 on p. 980 seems wrong since the mathematical induction in question cannot be carried out in *NB*. And his Theorem IV can be refuted by arguments similar to the proof of Theorem 4 above. Moreover, since Myhill uses Gödel's $V=L$ which is no longer directly true in *NQ*, it is not even obvious that *NB* plus his hypothesis of nameability is translatable into *NQ*.

Suszko avoids the difficulty by using as underived notion an enumerating predicate which satisfies the induction conditions. This, however, means that he is using an extension of *NB* rather than *NB* itself. It seems desirable to determine exactly the range of application of Suszko's method.

§ 2. Finite Axiomatization

In the writer's paper of 1952, the system *ZF* is extended to include something like Gödel's axiom of categoricalness. As a result, there is, by Theorem 8 of the preceding chapter, a definite formula Gxy of *ZF*, such that whenever $(x)(Ey)A(x,y)$ for some A, we can conclude $A(x, \epsilon_y Gxy)$ in the consistently extended system of *ZF*.

This is all that is needed to give in the extended *ZF* an enumeration by the Skolem functions of all sets required to exist by any finite number of theorems of *ZF*. For brevity, assume the conjunction of the finitely many axioms F is simply:

$$(1) \qquad (x)(Ey)A(x,y),$$

A containing no more quantifiers. Since (1) is assumed to be consistent, it has model from which we can extract an enumerable model which is the smallest part such that, say, the model of the empty set is in it, and, for every x, if the model of x is in it, so is the model of $\epsilon_y Gxy$. Now we can define a function E and prove in the extended ZF:

(2) $E(0)$ is the empty set.

(3) $E(n+1)$ is $\epsilon_y G(E(n), y)$.

If now we consider the translation (1) obtained by restricting the quantifiers to range over this enumerable domain, then, by McNaughton 1954, we can give a normal truth definition of the translation of F and prove $Con(F)$ in the extended ZF. It follows from this that no finite set of theorems of ZF can give all axioms of ZF as consequences, since otherwise the finite set of axioms plus the single axiom of categoricalness would give all axioms of the extended ZF and, by Gödel's second theorem, the extended ZF, and therewith ZF, would be inconsistent. In fact, more follows from the normal truth definitions:

Theorem 5. *There is no consistent finite set F of formulae ZF, with no additional constants, from which we can derive all proper axioms of ZF, viz. Z1 to Z9, as well as the axiom of categoricalness.*

Thus, if ZF is inconsistent, then this is true since F is consistent. If ZF is consistent and F yields all theorems of ZF together with the axiom of categoricalness, then by McNaughton's construction, we can again prove $Con(F)$ in F provided F is a finite set. This is so because we can then construct a truth definition of F in F by means of the derived part answering to the extended ZF; and, since all axioms of F are theorems of F, the truth definition can be proved to be normal, moreover, since F has only finitely many axioms, a formal proof of $Con(F)$ is obtained.

These considerations can be sharpended in a natural way along several directions. By the treatment of truth definitions for partial systems of Z in Chapter XV, it is quite clear that we can parallel the consideration for Z and prove for the theory G of finite sets a similar theorem like Theorem 5 there that if F is a finite consistent set translatable into G, then $Con(F)$ is provable in G. Moreover, the same is true of any extension of G, since the necessary common basis of Z is of course obtainable in the extension. Hence, we can prove a stronger theorem:

Theorem 6. *For any extension S of G (in particular ZF) which contains no new constants, and for every consistent finite set F of formulae which are translatable into S, or, in particular, which are theorems of S, $Con(F)$ is provable in S; hence, S is not translatable into any such F, and no such F can yield all theorems of S.*

Another direction of sharpening these results is to introduce measures of complexity of proofs in G and its extensions according to the structure of quantifiers in each proof. This is possible since the quantifiers needed for proving $Con(F)$ bear simple constant relations to the quantifiers in F.

A third possibility is to prove by similar considerations a theorem of Montague (*Bull. Am. Math. Soc.*, **62** (1956), 260, abstract):

Theorem 7. *If ZS is obtained from ZF by deleting the axiom of replacement Z9, then no finite set of formulae with no new constants can be consistently added to ZS to yield all axioms of ZF.*

This does not fall directly under Theorem 6, since ZS also has infinitely many proper axioms. If, however, we make use of the known result that $Con(ZS)$ is provable ZF, then we can arrange to extend the proof of $Con(ZS)$ to get proofs of the consistency of its finite extensions.

It, therefore, seems that the results the writer originally aimed at can all be proved by later methods. The problem is whether the writer's original proof in the 1952 paper is correct or even can be made correct by supplementation.

In that paper, the writer tried to apply directly the diagonal argument to the model of formula (1) above, after giving (2) and (3). It was contended that the model also satisfies:

$$(4) \qquad (y)(En)(y = E(n)).$$

Now the following is clearly a theorem of ZF:

$$(5) \qquad (Ey)(m)(m \in y \equiv m \notin E(m)).$$

Hence, if all axioms of ZF were derivable in F, (5) would also be true in the model, contradicting (4). And then Theorem 5 follows.

But no adequate proof was given for the conclusion that (4) is true in the model. Instead, it was argued on intuitive grounds that since the model was constructed to satisfy (4), (4) must be true in the model. This, however, overlooked the fact that (4) as a formula of ZF must also be relativized according to the model. More specifically, as Montague pointed out clearly and succinctly in correspondence, one has to prove that if x is in the model, then $\epsilon_y Gxy$, for the particular predicate G given above, must also be in the model and satisfy the relation $G(x, \epsilon_y Gxy)$ in the model. Since G contains quantifiers, these quantifiers have to be taken as ranging over the objects of the model.

In other words, in view of (2), (3) and the construction of the model, a proof that (4) is true in the model would reduce to showing that:

(6) the model of the empty set is the unique element in the model which satisfies, say $(x)x \notin y$ relative to the model.

(7) If x is the model of a, and $F(x)$ is the object in the model taken as $\epsilon_y Gay$, then $(x, F(x))$ must satisfy the relation G relative to the model.

It is easy to show (6). But to prove (7), we would have to show that $G(x, y)$ is true in the enumerable model if and only if it is true in the larger original model from which the enumerable model was extracted. Since G is quite complex and contains many bound variables, this is by no means obviously true.

Hence, there is no doubt that Montague's criticism is justified. He also pointed out that a related proof of Mostowski 1953 is open to similar objections.

It seems, however, possible to repair this proof without adopting a different approach. We have to take care in the construction of the enumerable model so that the predicate G is satisfied as we continue.

Thus, for brevity, let us assume Gxy is simply:

$$(u)(Ev)B(u,v,x,y), \tag{8}$$

B containing no more quantifiers.

If now the finite system is consistent, then it has a model D in which (1) is true, and, for every x in D, there is a unique y in D for which (8) is true. We extract an enumerable model D' by the following conditions: (a) the model in D of the empty set is in D'; (b) if the model of x in D is in D', so is the model of $\epsilon_y Gxy$; (c) if the models in D of u, x, $\epsilon_y Gxy$ are in D', the models of $\epsilon_v B(u, v, x, \epsilon_y Gxy)$ is in D'. But this model D' can be enumerated in the extended ZF by a function E, and (4) is satisfied. Hence, Theorem 5 is proved by the same kind of consideration as used in writer's paper of 1952.

§ 3. Finite Sets and Natural Numbers

The original reduction of arithmetic to set theory by Frege and Dedekind uses quantification over infinite sets. If, e.g. we take the empty set as 0, the unit set of n as the successor n, then their definition of the set of natural numbers is the intersection of all infinite sets each of which contains the empty set, and the successor of each member of it. Zermelo and others have shown the possibility of developing number theory in the theory of finite sets by giving first a general theory of ordinal numbers in set theory. Recently, Michael Dummett has suggested in conversation a definition which is quite similar to the Frege-Dedekind definition but requires only the theory of finite sets. A development based on the new definition is given here.

For this purpose, the axiom of extensionality, the axioms ensuring the existence of finite sets based on the empty set, and the axiom of groundedness are needed. The last is of course to get mathematical induction. We seem to need also a special case of the Aussonderungsaxiom, viz., given x and y, there is the set of all members of x except y.

To be more explicit, we use only the membership predicate as primitive, use the predicate calculus without equality as the underlying logic, define equality as in ZF, i.e., two sets are equal when they have the same members. We assume also the usual way of handling abstracts so that $x \in \hat{y}Fy$ amounts to Fx, the definition of equality may be extended to abstracts, and $\hat{y}Fy \in a$ amounts to $(Ex)(x=\hat{y}Fy \,\&\, x \in a)$. Then the axioms are as follows:

I. Axiom of extensionality. If $x=y$, $x \in z \equiv y \in z$.

II. Existence of the empty set. $(Ey)(y=\hat{x}(x \neq x))$.

III. Existence of generalized successors. $(x)(y)(Ez)(z=\hat{u}(u \in x \lor u=y))$.

IV. Axiom of groundedness. Same as $Z8$.

V. Existence of generalized predecessors. $(x)(y)(Ez)(z=\hat{u}(u \in x \,\&\, u \neq z))$.

The definitions are:

Definition 1. $0 =_D \hat{x}(x \neq x)$.

Definition 2. $x' =_D \hat{z}(z \in x \lor z=x)$.

Definition 3. $C_a(u) =_D (0 \in u \,\&\, (y)((y \in u \,\&\, y \neq a) \supset y' \in u))$.

Definition 4. $Nn(x) =_D [(Eu)C_x(u) \,\&\, (v)(C_x(v) \supset x \in v)]$.

Definition 5. $\{x\} =_D \hat{y}(y=x)$.

Definition 6. $x \cup \{y\} =_D \hat{z}(z \in x \lor z=y)$.

Definition 7. $x - \{y\} =_D \hat{z}(z \in x \,\&\, z \neq y)$.

Definition 8. $\langle x,y \rangle =_D \hat{z}[z=\{x\} \lor z=\hat{u}(u=x \lor u=y)]$.

Definition 9. $\langle x, y, z \rangle =_D \langle\langle x, y \rangle, z\rangle$.

Definition 10. $x+y=z =_D (Eu)(\langle x, 0, x\rangle \in u \,\&\, (v)(w)[(\langle x, v, w\rangle \in u \,\&\, v \neq y) \supset \langle x, v', w'\rangle \in u] \,\&\, \langle x, y, z\rangle \in u)$.

Definition 11. $x \cdot y=z =_D (Eu)(\langle x, 0, 0\rangle \in u \,\&\, (v)(w)[(\langle x, v, w\rangle \in u \,\&\, v \neq y) \supset (Et)(\langle x, v', t\rangle \in u \,\&\, w+x=t)] \,\&\, \langle x, y, z\rangle \in u)$.

We can prove the following theorems:

Z1. $Nn(0)$.

Proof. Take $0'$ as u, we have $C_0(u)$. But $0 \epsilon v \supset 0 \epsilon v$. Hence, $C_0(v) \supset 0 \epsilon v$.

Z2. $0 \neq x'$.

Proof. $x \epsilon x'$ but $x \notin 0$.

L1. $x \notin x$.

Proof. If $x \epsilon x$, then $\{x\}$ is not grounded, contradicting IV, when $y = x$ is taken as $A(y)$.

L2. $x \neq x'$.

Proof. $x \epsilon x'$ but $x \notin x$.

L3. $x \notin y \vee y \notin x$.

Proof. If $x \epsilon y \& y \epsilon x$, then $\hat{u}(u = x \vee u = y)$ is not grounded, contradicting IV.

Z3. $x' = y' \supset x = y$.

Proof. If $x' = y'$, then, since $x' = x \cup \{x\}$, $y' = y \cup \{y\}$, we have $(x \epsilon y \vee x = y)$ and $(y \epsilon x \vee y = x)$. By L3, $x = y$.

L4. $C_x(w) \supset C_{x'}(w \cup \{x'\})$.

Proof. If $C_x(w)$, then $0 \epsilon w \cup \{x'\} \& (y)[(y \epsilon w \cup \{x'\} \& y \neq x \& y \neq x') \supset y' \epsilon w \cup \{x'\}]$. But $y = x \supset y' = x'$. Hence, $(y)[(y \epsilon w \cup \{x'\} \& y \neq x') \supset y' \epsilon w \cup \{x'\}]$.

L5. $C_{x'}(v) \supset C_x(v - \{x'\})$.

Proof. If $C_{x'}(v)$, then $0 \epsilon v \& (y)[(y \epsilon v \& y \neq x') \supset y' \epsilon v]$. Hence, $0 \epsilon v - \{x'\} \& (y)[(y \epsilon v - \{x'\} \& y \neq x \& y \neq x') \supset y' \epsilon v - \{x'\}]$. But $x' \notin v - \{x'\}$. Hence, $y \epsilon v - \{x'\} \supset y \neq x'$, and $(y)[(y \epsilon v - \{x'\} \& y \neq x) \supset y' \epsilon v - \{x'\}]$.

Z4. $Nn(x) \supset Nn(x')$.

Proof. Since $Nn(x)$, there is w, $C_x(w)$. By L4, $C_{x'}(w \cup \{x'\})$. If $C_{x'}(v)$, then $C_x(v - \{x'\})$ and since $Nn(x)$, $x \epsilon v - \{x'\}$. But for all v, if $C_{x'}(v)$, $y \epsilon v$, $y \neq x'$, then $y' \epsilon v$. Hence, by L2, $x' \epsilon v$.

L6. $Nn(x) \supset [x = 0 \vee (Ey)(x = y')]$.

Proof. Suppose $Nn(x) \& x \neq 0$. There exists u, $C_x(u)$. Suppose $\sim(Ey)(x = y')$. Then, $\sim(Ey)(y \neq x \& x = y')$. Then $C_x(u - \{x\})$. But $x \notin u - \{x\}$, which contradicts the hypothesis $Nn(x)$.

L7. $[C_x(v) \& x \notin v] \supset (Eu)[C_{x'}(u) \& x' \notin u]$.

Proof. If $C_x(v)$, then $0 \epsilon v - \{x'\}$ because $0 \neq x'$. If $x \notin v$, then $(y)[(y \epsilon v \& y \neq x') \supset y' \epsilon v - \{x'\}]$ and $(y)[(y \epsilon v - \{x'\} \& y \neq x') \supset y' \epsilon v$

$-\{x'\}]$. Hence, $C_{x'}(v-\{x'\})$ and $x' \notin v-\{x'\}$.

*L*8. $Nn(x') \supset Nn(x)$.

Proof. Since $Nn(x')$, there is $w, C_{x'}(w)$. By *L*5, $C_x(w-\{x'\})$. If $C_x(v) \,\&\, x \notin v$, then $(Eu)[C_{x'}(u) \,\&\, x' \notin u]$, contradicting the hypothesis $Nn(x')$.

Z5. $[A(0) \,\&\, (y)(A(y) \supset A(y'))] \supset (x)[Nn(x) \supset A(x)]$.

Proof. We wish to infer $\sim(Ex)[Nn(x) \,\&\, \sim A(x)]$ from $A(0)$ and $(y)[A(y) \supset A(y')]$. Suppose $(Ex)[Nn(x) \,\&\, \sim A(x)]$. By IV, there exists y, $[Nn(y) \,\&\, \sim A(y)] \,\&\, \sim(Ez)[z \in y \,\&\, Nn(z) \,\&\, \sim A(z)]$. By *L*6, $y=0$ or $(Ez)(y=z')$. Since $A(0)$, $y \neq 0$. If $y=z'$, then $z \in y$ and, by *L*8, $Nn(z)$. Moreover, since $A(z) \supset A(z')$, $\sim A(y) \supset \sim A(z)$. Therefore, $[Nn(y) \,\&\, \sim A(y)] \,\&\, (Ez)[z \in y \,\&\, Nn(z) \,\&\, \sim A(z)]$, contradicting the consequence of IV stated above.

Z6. $x+0=x \,\&\, x+y'=(x+y)'$.

Proof. Take $u_0=\{\langle x, 0, x\rangle\}$, we have $\langle x, 0, x\rangle \in u_0 \,\&\, (v)(w)[(\langle x, v, w\rangle \in u_0 \,\&\, v \neq 0) \supset \langle x, v', w'\rangle \in u]$. Hence, by Df. 10, $x+0=x$. Given $x+y=z$, i.e., by Df. 10, there exists u_y such that $\langle x, 0, x\rangle \in u_y \,\&\, (v)(w)[(\langle x, v, w\rangle \in u_y \,\&\, v \neq y) \supset \langle x, v', w'\rangle \in u_y] \,\&\, \langle x, y, z\rangle \in u_y$, take $u_{y'}=u_y \cup \{\langle x, y', z'\rangle\}$, we have $\langle x, 0, x\rangle \in u_{y'} \,\&\, (v)(w)[(\langle x, v, w\rangle \in u_{y'} \,\&\, v \neq y') \supset \langle x, v', x'\rangle \in u_{y'}] \,\&\, \langle x, y', z'\rangle \in u_{y'}$. I.e., by Df. 10, $x+y'=z'=(x+y)'$.

Z7. $x \cdot 0=0 \,\&\, x \cdot y'=(x \cdot y)+x$.

Proof. Similar, using Df. 11.

Clearly every function defined by a primitive recursion can be treated similarly.

CHAPTER XVIII

TRUTH DEFINITIONS AND CONSISTENCY PROOFS*

§ 1. Introduction

From investigations by Carnap, Tarski, and others, we know that given a system S, we can construct in some stronger system S' a criterion of soundness (or validity) for S according to which all the theorems of S are sound. In this way we obtain in S' a consistency proof for S. The consistency proof so obtained, which in no case with fairly strong systems could by any stretch of imagination be called constructive, is not of much interest for the purpose of understanding more clearly whether the system S is reliable or whether and why it leads to no contradictions. However, it can be of use in studying the interconnection and relative strength of different systems. For example, if a consistency proof for S can be formalized in S', then, according to Gödel's theorem that such a proof cannot be formalized in S itself, parts of the argument must be such that they can be formalized in S' but not in S. Since S can be a very strong system, there arises the question as to what these arguments could be like. For illustration, the exact form of such arguments will be examined with respect to certain special systems, by applying Tarski's "theory of truth" which provides us with a general method for proving the consistency of a given system S in some stronger system S'. It should be clear that the considerations to be presented in this paper apply to other systems which are stronger than or as strong as the special systems we use below.

Originally the studies reported here were motivated by a desire to look more carefully into the following somewhat puzzling situation.

Let S be a system containing the usual second-order predicate calculus with the usual number theory as its theory of individuals, and S' be a system related to S as an $(n+1)$th order predicate

---

* This chapter appeared in *Trans. Am. Math. Soc.*, 73 (1952), 243—275. A summary had been previously given in Wang [21]. Some of the results on the relation between NB and ZF were obtained independently by Mostowski at about the same time, see *Fund. Math.*, 37 (1950), 111—124 and *J. Symbolic Logic*, 16 (1951), 142—143. A general survey of related questions is given in Rosser's Deux esquisses de logique, Paris, 1955.

calculus is to an nth except that we do not use variables of the $(n+1)$th type in defining classes of lower types. Tarski's assertions seem to lead us to believe that we can prove the consistency of S in S'. On the other hand, it is known that if S is consistent then S has a model in the domain of natural numbers. But if S has such a model, then, we seem also to be able to argue, S' has a model in S because S contains both natural numbers and their classes. Therefore, we can formalize (so it appears) these arguments in S' and prove within S' that if S is consistent then S' is. If that be the case we shall have a proof of the consistency of S' within S' and therefore, by Gödel's theorem on consistency proofs, S' (and probably also S) will be inconsistent. Indeed, since we need at least a system like S' to develop analysis and since these reasonings do not depend on peculiar features of the systems under consideration, we shall be driven to the conclusion that practically every system adequate to analysis is inconsistent.

In trying to examine exactly where the above arguments break down, we have found it helpful to formalize more explicitly certain truth definitions and consistency proofs with such definitions. The results of such formalizations as presented below, it is thought, bring out more clearly than usual certain features in the procedures of constructing truth definitions and proving consistency. For example, the use of impredicative classes is dispensable for defining truth but does not seem so for proving consistency; whether the number of axioms of a system to be proved consistent is finite or infinite seems also to imply much difference in formalizing a consistency proof; and the employment of variables of higher types in defining classes of a given type engenders essentially new classes even for systems which contain otherwise already certain impredicative classes.

It turns out that the arguments of a paragraph back break down because of the relativity of number theory to the underlying set theory. As a result, certain intuitively simple reasonings cannot be formalized in even very strong systems. Thus, for systems S and S' related as above, no matter how strong they are, the following results hold for them if they are consistent.

If natural numbers are taken as primitive notions or introduced with the same definitions in both S and S', then (1) for some predicate ϕ in S', we can show that $\phi(0), \phi(1), \cdots$ are all provable in S' but that $\forall m(\phi(m) \supset \phi(m+1))$ is not; (2) for some other predicate ϕ' of S', we can prove $\phi'(0)$ and $\forall m(\phi'(m) \supset \phi'(m+1))$ in S' but not $\forall m \phi'(m)$. These immediately yield new examples of consistent but ω-inconsistent systems. On the other hand, if we choose in S and S' suitable (different) definitions for natural numbers, we can prove in S' that if S is ω-consistent then S' is consistent and also prove in S' the consistency of S, but not the ω-consistency of S. This also shows that although S' contains a truth definition for S, we cannot prove in S' that S must possess a standard or nonpathological model.

In order to separate two different moments of a truth definition, we shall distinguish between a truth definition and a normal truth definition. If we can find in S' a predicate or a class Tr for which we can prove with regard to the sentences of S all the cases of the Tarski truth schema, we say that S' contains a truth definition for S. If in addition we can prove in S' that all theorems of S are true according to the truth definition, then we say that S' contains a normal truth definition for S. This rather natural distinction will be assumed throughout this paper.

§ 2. A Truth Definition for Zermelo Set Theory

Expressions of Zermelo set theory are built up from the set variables $x_1, x_2, x_3, \cdots$ and three constants: the sign $|$ for alternative denial (Sheffer's stroke function, disjunctive negation), the sign $\forall$ for general or universal quantification (all-operator), and the sign ϵ for the membership relation (belonging to). Parentheses for grouping different parts of an expression, although theoretically dispensable, are also employed. A sentence (or well-formed formula) is either of the simple form $y \epsilon z$ or of the complex form $p|q$ or $\forall y p$, where we may substitute in place of y and z any variables, and in place of p and q any sentences. From among the sentences some may be selected as theorems. However, since this section is concerned merely with the construction of a truth definition and not a normal truth definition, the selection of theorems is irrelevant for the considerations here. So just let us imagine for the moment that an arbitrary definite set of sentences are taken as theorems of the Zermelo theory.

The problem is to find a suitable system S_1 in which we can find a class (or a predicate) Tr and prove as theorems the special cases of the Tarski truth schema for all the statements (closed sentences, well-formed formulas containing no free variables) of Zermelo theory.

To simplify the structure of the required metasystem, let us assume that the syntax of Zermelo theory (as well as that of every other system we consider) has been arithmetized after the manner of Gödel[1]. Then each expression (and in particular, each statement) is represented by a definite number (say)[2] $\mathfrak{m}$. Let $H(\mathfrak{m})$ be the expression represented by the number $\mathfrak{m}$. The problem is to define in a system

1) See Gödel [2] and Hilbert-Bernays [3], vol. 2, §4.

2) In contrast with the variables m, n, etc., the symbols $\mathfrak{m}$, $\mathfrak{n}$ etc. stand ambiguously for the numerals 0, 1, 2, etc.

S_1 a class Tr of natural numbers for which the following holds:

(TS) For each statement $H(\mathfrak{m})$ of Zermelo theory, we can prove in S_1: $H(\mathfrak{m})$ if and only if $\mathfrak{m}$ belongs to Tr.

Naturally we can choose the metasystem S_1 in different manners, and the proof of (TS) would become somewhat easier if the metasystem we use is richer or stronger. However, since one of our purposes is to make explicit the material needed for constructing a truth definition, it seems desirable to choose as weak (or simple) a system as is conveniently possible. The system S_1 we choose may be roughly described as of equal strength as a second-order predicate calculus founded on natural numbers. It does not seem possible to use any system which is substantially weaker than this system S_1 (but compare the system S_2 given below).

S_1 contains variables $x_1, x_2, \cdots$ for elements and variables $X_1, X_2, \cdots$ for classes. Sentences are built up from simple sentences of the forms $x_1 \in x_2$ (the element x_1 belongs to the element x_2), etc. and $x_1 \eta X_2$ (the element x_1 belongs to the class X_2), etc. by truth-functional connectives and quantifiers for both kinds of variable in the usual manner.

The theorems of S_1 are determined as follows. It contains the ordinary quantification theories (the predicate calculi) for both kinds of variable, as well as proper axioms given below (where $x_1 = x_2$ stands for $\forall x_4 (x_4 \in x_1 \equiv x_4 \in x_2)$):

$Ax1$. First axiom of extensionality. $(x_1 = x_2 \,\&\, x_1 \in x_3) \supset x_2 \in x_3$.

$Ax2$. Existence of the null element. $\exists x_2 \forall x_1 (-x_1 \in x_2)$.

$Ax3$. Existence of finite elements. $\exists x_2 \forall x_1 (x_1 \in x_2 \equiv (x_1 \in x_3 \vee x_1 = x_4))$.

$Ax4$. Second axiom of extensionality. $(x_1 = x_2 \,\&\, x_1 \eta X_1) \supset x_2 \eta X_1$.

$Ax5$. The class axiom. For every sentence p of S_1 in which the variable X_1 does not occur, $\exists X_1 \forall x_1 (x_1 \eta X_1 \equiv p)$.

From $Ax2$ and $Ax3$, we can obtain all finite elements constructed from the null element by taking unit sets and sum sets. $Ax5$ states that every property or predicate of these elements which are expressible in S_1 determines a class of S_1. This system is closely related to certain standard systems. Thus, on the one hand, it differs from the part consisting of the axioms of groups I—III of Bernays' system[1)] only in that $Ax5$ takes the place of the somewhat weaker axioms of his group III. On the other hand, it is practically of the same

1) See Bernays [1], Part I. We note incidentally that the axiom $Ax1$ of S_1 is actually redundant by virtue of $Ax4$ and $Ax5$. For similar reasons, as Bernays of course realizes, the middle two of the four axioms on identity listed on Bernays [1], p. 67, as well as the first of the two on p. 68, are derivable from the other axioms on identity with the help of his axioms of group III.

strength as a system proposed by Quine[1]), although Quine uses in place of $Ax3$ an axiom stating that the sum set of two elements is again an element.

In S_1 we can follow either the definitions used by Bernays or those used by Quine and develop the ordinary number theory while taking certain elements as natural numbers. Thus, we can define with von Neumann[2]):

2.1. The number zero 0 is identified with the null element.

2.2. The successor x_1+1 of a natural number x_1 is identified with the element consisting of all the members of x_1 together with x_1 itself (i.e., the sum set of x_1 and its unit set).

Then we can define the predicate Nn of being a natural number in either of the following two manners[3]).

2.3. $Nn(x_1)$ if and only if $\forall X_1((0\eta X_1 \,\&\, \forall x_2(x_2\eta X_1 \supset (x_2+1)\eta X_1)) \supset x_1\eta X_1)$.

2.4. $Nn(x_1)$ if and only if the following conditions are satisfied:

(1) $\forall x_2 \forall x_3((x_2 \in x_3 \,\&\, x_3 \in x_1) \supset x_2 \in x_1)$;

(2) $\forall x_2 \forall x_3((x_2 \in x_1 \,\&\, x_3 \in x_1 \,\&\, x_2 \neq x_3) \supset (x_2 \in x_3 \vee x_3 \in x_2))$;

(3) $\forall X_1((\exists x_2(x_2\eta X_1) \,\&\, \forall x_2(x_2\eta X_1 \supset x_2 \in x_1)) \supset \exists x_3(x_3\eta X_1 \,\&\, \forall x_4 - (x_4 \in x_3 \,\&\, x_4\eta X_1)))$;

(4) $\forall x_2((x_2 \in x_1 \vee x_2 = x_1) \supset (x_2 = 0 \vee \exists x_3(x_2 = x_3 + 1)))$.

Recursive functions such as addition and multiplication can be defined in known manner[4]). Hence, number theory can be developed in S_1. Variables m, n, k, etc. ranging over natural numbers can be introduced by contextual definitions such as: $\forall m\phi m$ stands for $\forall x_1(Nn(x_1) \supset \phi x_1)$, etc. The principle of induction can be proved, with the help of $Ax5$ (the class axiom), for all sentences of S_1:

2.5. If ϕx_1 is any sentence of S_1, then $(\phi 0 \,\&\, \forall n(\phi n \supset \phi(n+1))) \supset \forall m\phi m$.

From the considerations thus far, we see that S_1 is, in the matter of linguistic forms, an extension of the Zermelo set theory, and contains: (1) variables of a higher type; (2) usual notations of general

1) See Quine [11], p. 140.

2) See von Neumann [7].

3) The first definition is essentially the same as the last definition on Quine [11], p. 142 (cf. also Quine [1, p. 216]).

The second definition is the definition of finite ordinals on p. 11 of Bernays [1, Part II], while ordinals are defined by the second definition appearing on p. 9, ibid.

4) See Quine [10], p. 259 and Bernays [1], Part II, p. 11.

logic; (3) all expressions of the Zermelo theory; (4) the ordinary number theory. Therefore, according to an assertion of Tarski[1], if the axioms of S_1 are sufficiently strong, we can use S_1 as a metalanguage and define in it the concept of truth for Zermelo theory, with merely the help of names and predicates of expressions (or terms from the morphology) of Zermelo theory. However, since S_1 contains number theory and the syntax of Zermelo theory is assumed to have been arithmetized, we can use in S_1 natural numbers and their predicates as names and predicates of expressions of Zermelo theory. Hence, we may expect, with good reasons, that we can obtain in S_1 a truth class (or predicate) for Zermelo theory. The only remaining question is whether the axioms of S_1 are strong enough to enable us to prove the schema (TS). We shall show that the answer is positive. The constructions follow in their general line the methods developed by Tarski and others[2], although the demonstrations, as well as the exact theorems of the metasystem which are needed, are here exhibited more explicitly than by these previous authors.

With the arithmetization of the syntax of the Zermelo theory, we can define in S_1 syntactical predicates and functions for it. Let us assume that all the sentences (well-formed formulas) of the Zermelo set theory have been enumerated, and in particular in such a way that when a sentence is a part of another, the part always precedes the whole. For each $\mathfrak{i}$, let $F(\mathfrak{i})$ be the $\mathfrak{i}$th sentence of Zermelo theory in the assumed enumeration. For example, $F(1)$ may be just $x_1 \in x_1$. We can define in S_1 three predicates $M(m, n, k)$, $T(m, n, k)$, $Q(m, n, k)$, and a function R_m satisfying the following conditions.

2.6. $M(\mathfrak{m}, \mathfrak{n}, \mathfrak{k})$ when and only when $F(\mathfrak{m})$ is $x_{\mathfrak{n}} \in x_{\mathfrak{k}}$.

2.7. $T(\mathfrak{m}, \mathfrak{n}, \mathfrak{k})$ when and only when $F(\mathfrak{m})$ is $(F(\mathfrak{n}) \mid F(\mathfrak{k}))$.

2.8. $Q(\mathfrak{m}, \mathfrak{n}, \mathfrak{k})$ when and only when $F(\mathfrak{m})$ is $\forall x_{\mathfrak{n}} F(\mathfrak{k})$.

2.9. $R_{\mathfrak{m}}$ is the number of logical operators in $F(\mathfrak{m})$.

Then the following elementary properties are easily provable in S_1.

2.10. $(M(m, n, k) \,\&\, M(m, n', k')) \supset (n=n' \,\&\, k=k')$.

2.11. $(T(m, n, k)) \,\&\, T(m, n', k')) \supset (n=n' \,\&\, k=k')$.

2.12. $(Q(m, n, k) \,\&\, Q(m, n', k')) \supset (n=n' \,\&\, k=k')$.

2.13. $R_m \leqslant 0 \supset \exists n \exists k M(m, n, k)$.

2.14. $(R_m \leqslant (j+1) \,\&\, (T(m, n, k) \vee Q(m, i, k))) \supset (R_n \leqslant j \,\&\, R_k \leqslant j)$.

---

1) See Tarski [16], p. 399, Thesis A. Instead of (1), Tarski requires that the order or type of the metalanguage should be higher than the language for which the truth definition is constructed. His notion of the order or type of a language seems to concern both the linguistic forms and the proving power of the language system.

2) See Tarski [16; 17; 18], Hilbert-Bernays [3], vol. **2**, p. 324 ff.

The definition of truth for Zermelo theory is roughly this[1]: a sentence (with or without free variables) of Zermelo theory is true if and only if it is satisfied by all finite sequences of sets of Zermelo set theory, and a finite sequence g satisfies (a sentence $F(\mathfrak{m})$ represented by the number) $\mathfrak{m}$ when and only when $F'(\mathfrak{m})$, where $F'(\mathfrak{m})$ is the result obtained from $F(\mathfrak{m})$ by substituting simultaneously, for all its free variables $x_{\mathfrak{n}}$ ($\mathfrak{n}$ among 1, 2, $\cdots$), the $\mathfrak{n}$th term of g for $x_{\mathfrak{n}}$[2]. In the particular cases where $F(\mathfrak{m})$ is a statement (of Zermelo theory), it follows that $\mathfrak{m}$ belongs to the class of numbers representing true statements when and only when $F(\mathfrak{m})$.

In Tarski's definitions, infinite sequences are used instead of finite sequences. This is not possible in our approach, because the axioms of S_1 only guarantee that all finite sequences of elements are again elements but not that infinite sequences are also. However, as we have sequences with any arbitrary finite number of terms, we can dispense with infinite sequences altogether in our considerations.

The definition for a sequence is simply this. An element x_1 of S_1 is a finite sequence of elements of S_1 if there exists a number n ($n=1, 2, \cdots$) such that x_1 is an n-termed sequence; and x_1 is an n-termed sequence when and only when for all $m, m>0$ and $m\leqslant n$, there exists a unique element x_2 of S_1 such that the ordered pair of m and x_2 belongs to x_1. More explicitly, the definition may be stated as follows[3].

2.15. The ordered pair (x_1, x_2) of two elements x_1 and x_2 of S_1 is the element of S_1 consisting of the unit set of x_1 and the sum set of x_1 and x_2.

2.16. $\mathrm{Sq}(x_1)$ (i.e., x_1 is a finite sequence) when and only when $\exists n(n>0\ \&\ \forall x_3(\exists x_2)(x_2, x_3)\in x_1)\equiv \exists m(m=x_3\ \&\ m\leqslant n)\ \&\ \forall x_2\forall x_3\forall x_4(((x_2, x_3)\in x_1\ \&\ (x_4, x_3)\in x_1)\supset x_2=x_4)$.

In S_1 there exist of course elements which are finite sequences according to this definition. Indeed, for each n and any n elements

1) See Tarski [16], pp. 311—313.

2) It should be noted that here, as elsewhere in this paper, we are trying to avoid the use of quotation marks and corners (cf. Quine [10], p. 33). It is hoped that no serious misunderstandings or confusions will result from such a practice.

3) In this connection we should like to mention an interesting alternative definition of sequences which applies equally well to finite and infinite sequences: $\mathrm{Sq}(x_1)$ when and only when $\forall x_2(x_2\in x_1\supset\exists x_3\exists m\ (x_2=(x_3, m)\ \&\ m\neq 0))$. In other words, instead of labelling the terms of the sequences, we label the members of each term and call the sum of all these labelled members the sequence consisting of these terms. Thus, if x_1 is a sequence, the jth term of x_1 is just the set of all x_2 such that $(x_2, j)\in x_1$. When the sets or classes of a system are divided into types so that a set and its members are of different types, this definition has over the ordinary one the advantage of keeping the sequence in the same type as its terms. In certain cases, it seems necessary to use such a definition, replacing the definiens of 2.18 by $(x_1, j)\in g$ and that of 2.19 by $((m\neq n\ \&\ (x_1,m)\in g)\vee(m=n\ \&\ x_1\in x_2))$. When necessary, we shall assume that these definitions have been adopted instead of 2.16, 2.18, and 2.19 given in the text. For example, when we define truth for R in R' and prove 5.8 in the last section, we shall assume such alternative definitions.

$x_1, \cdots, x_n$ of S_1, the set consisting of $(x_1, 1), (x_2, 2), \cdots, (x_n, n)$ is one such. Let us use the letter g as a variable ranging over those elements of S_1 which are finite sequences:

2.17. $\forall g \phi g$ when and only when $\forall x_1(\mathrm{Sq}(x_1) \supset \phi x_1)$.

The jth term g_j of a finite sequence g is the set correlated with j:

2.18. $x_1 \in g_j$ when and only when $\exists x_2((x_2, j) \in g \,\&\, x_1 \in x_2)$.

This definition involves a rather undesirable complication which would not arise if infinite sequences were employed instead. Thus, when g has only k terms and j is greater than k, we would want to say that g has no jth term; however, according to this definition, g_j would then be the null set. In such degenerating cases, we have the result that (g_j, j) does not necessarily belong to g. It turns out that this unnatural feature is harmless for our further developments in the sense that it does not affect the definitions and theorems in which we are mainly interested.

Next is the notion of "the sequence $t(g, n, x_2)$ obtained from g by substituting the set x_2 for its nth term":

2.19. $(x_1, m) \in t(g, n, x_2)$ when and only when $(m \neq n \,\&\, (x_1, m) \in g) \vee (m = n \,\&\, x_1 = x_2)$.

Using the preliminary notions introduced in 2.6—2.9 and 2.16—2.19, we can now characterize the notion of satisfiability ("gSm", meaning "g satisfies the mth sentence of Zermelo theory") by the following conditions: (1) $M(m, n, k) \supset (gSm \equiv g_n \in g_k)$; (2) $T(m, n, k) \supset (gSm \equiv (gSn \mid gSk))$; (3) $Q(m, n, k) \supset (gSm \equiv \forall x_1(t(g, n, x_1)Sk))$. This recursive characterization can be converted into an explicit definition for "gSm" with known methods and then the concept of truth for Zermelo theory can be defined.

Definition 1. *$G1(g, m)$ when and only when $\exists n \exists k(M(m, n, k) \,\&\, g_n \in g_k)$.*

Definition 2. *$G2(g, m, X_1)$ when and only when $\exists n \exists k(T(m, n, k) \,\&\, ((g, n)\eta X_1 \mid (g, k)\eta X_1))$.*

Definition 3. *$G3(g, m, X_1)$ when and only when $\exists n \exists k(Q(m, n, k) \,\&\, \forall x_1((t(g, n, x_1), k)\eta X_1))$.*

Definition 4. *$G(g, m, X_1)$ when and only when $(G1(g, m) \vee G2(g, m, X_1) \vee G3(g, m, X_1))$.*

Definition 5. *$G_j(X_1)$ when and only when $\forall g \forall m(R_m \leqslant j \supset ((g, m)\eta X_1 \equiv G(g, m, X_1)))$.*

Definition 6. *gSm when and only when $\forall X_1(G_{R_m}(X_1) \supset (g, m)\eta X_1)$.*

Definition 7. *$m\eta Tr$ when and only when $\forall g(gSm)$.*

Definition 5 amounts essentially to this: if $G_j(X_1)$, then X_1 contains all the ordered pairs (g, m) such that g satisfies m and R_m is no greater than j. In order to prove the conditions (1)—(3) as theorems of S_1, we first show that for each j, there exists in S_1 a class X_1 such that $G_j(X_1)$ and that if $G_{R_m}(X_1)$ then for every g, gSm when and only when (g, m) belongs to X_1.

The next three theorems of S_1 are obvious from the definitions.

2.20. $M(m, n, k) \supset (-G2(g, m, X_1) \ \& \ -G3(g, m, X_1))$.

2.21. $T(m, n, k) \supset (-G1(g, m, X_1) \ \& \ -G3(g, m, X_1))$.

2.22. $Q(m, n, k) \supset (-G1(g, m, X_1) \ \& \ -G2(g, m, X_1))$.

We prove the theorem that for each j there exists in S_1 a class X_1 such that $G_j(X_1)$.

2.30. $\exists X_1(G_0(X_1))$.

Proof. By Df4 (using 2.13 and 2.20), for every X_1, if $R_m \leqslant 0$, then $(G1(g, m) \equiv G(g, m, X_1))$. By $Ax5$, there exists a class X_1 such that for every g and every m, $((g, m)\eta X_1 \equiv G1(g, m))$. Hence, by Df5, $G_0(X_1)$.

2.31. $\exists X_1(G_j(X_1)) \supset \exists X_2(G_{j+1}(X_2))$.

Proof. Let X_1 be a class such that $G_j(X_1)$. Hence, by Df5, $R_m \leqslant j \supset ((g, m)\eta X_1 \equiv G(g, m, X_1))$. By $Ax5$, there exists a class X_2 such that $\forall g \forall m((g, m)\eta X_2 \equiv G(g, m, X_1))$. So, if $R_i \leqslant j$, then $((g, i)\eta X_1 \equiv (g, i)\eta X_2)$. Hence, by 2.14 and Df1—Df4, if $R_m \leqslant j+1$, then $(G(g, m, X_1) \equiv G(g, m, X_2))$. Therefore, $R_m \leqslant j+1 \supset ((g, m)\eta X_2 \equiv G(g, m, X_2))$. Hence, by Df5, 2.31 is proved.

From 2.30 and 2.31, we have immediately:

2.32. For each constant $\mathfrak{j}$, we can prove in S_1: $\exists X_1(G_{\mathfrak{j}}(X_1))$.

Moreover, by applying induction (the consequence 2.5 of $Ax5$) to the sentence $\exists X_1(G_j(X_1))$, we obtain from 2.30 and 2.31:

2.33. $\forall j \exists X_1(G_j(X_1))$.

We note that in order to prove 2.33, we require that bound large (class) variables be allowed in the defining sentence p of $Ax5$ for class formation. It will be emphasized later that this is one of the few places where such cases of $Ax5$ must be applied in our considerations.

Having on hand for each j the existence of some class X_1 such that $G_j(X_1)$, we want now to prove some kind of uniqueness theorem for these classes. As in the definition of G_j we are interested only in the numbers m such that $R_m \leqslant j$, we shall prove merely that for all m where $R_m \leqslant j$, if $G_j(X_1)$ and $G_j(X_2)$, then $(g,m)\eta X_1$ if and only if $(g, m)\eta X_2$.

2.34. $(R_m \leqslant 0 \;\&\; G_0(X_1) \;\&\; G_0(X_2)) \supset ((g, m)\eta X_1 \equiv (g, m)\eta X_2)$.

Proof. By Df4 and Df5 (using 2.13 and 2.20), if $(G_0(X_1) \;\&\; G_0(X_2) \;\&\; R_m \leqslant 0)$, then $((g, m)\eta X_1 \equiv G1(g, m))$ and $((g, m)\eta X_2 \equiv G1(g, m))$. Hence, the theorem is proved.

2.35. If $\forall X_1 \forall X_2 \forall g \forall m((R_m \leqslant j \;\&\; G_j(X_1) \;\&\; G_j(X_2)) \supset ((g, m)\eta X_1 \equiv (g, m)\eta X_2))$, then $\forall g \forall m((R_m \leqslant j+1 \;\&\; G_{j+1}(X_3) \;\&\; G_{j+1}(X_4)) \supset ((g, m)\eta X_3 \equiv (g, m)\eta X_4))$.

Proof. Assume that $G_{j+1}(X_3)$ and $G_{j+1}(X_4)$. Then, by Df5, we have also: $G_j(X_3)$ and $G_j(X_4)$. Hence, by hypothesis, if $R_m \leqslant j$, then $(g, m)\eta X_3 \equiv (g, m)\eta X_4$. Therefore, by 2.14 and Df4, if $R_m \leqslant j + 1$, then $G(g, m, X_3) \equiv G(g, m, X_4)$. Hence, by Df5, the theorem is proved.

An immediate consequence of 2.34 and 2.35 is:

2.36. For each constant $\mathfrak{j}$, we can prove in S_1: $(R_m \leqslant \mathfrak{j} \& G_{\mathfrak{j}}(X_1) \;\&\; G_{\mathfrak{j}}(X_2)) \supset ((g, m)\eta X_1 \equiv (g, m)\eta X_2)$.

Again, by applying the induction principle 2.5, we have:

2.37. $(j)(R_m \leqslant j \;\&\; G_j(X_1) \;\&\; G_j(X_2)) \supset ((g, m)\eta X_1 \equiv (g, m)\eta X_2)$.

This is the second place where we need a case of *Ax*5 in which the defining sentence for a class contains large bound variables.

The next theorem follows from 2.37.

2.38. $G_{R_m}(X_1) \supset (gSm \equiv (g, m)\eta X_1)$.

Proof. By 2.37, $(G_{R_m}(X_1) \;\&\; (g, m)\eta X_1) \supset \forall X_2(G_{R_m}(X_2) \supset (g, m)\eta X_2)$. Hence, by Df6, the theorem is easily proved.

If we have only 2.36 but not 2.37, then we can prove only:

2.39. For every constant $\mathfrak{m}$, we can prove in S_1: $G_{R_\mathfrak{m}}(X_1) \supset (gS\mathfrak{m} \equiv (g, \mathfrak{m})\eta X_1)$.

Now we are ready to prove the characteristic properties of the relation gSm.

2.40. $M(m, n, k) \supset (gSm \equiv g_n \in g_k)$.

Proof. By 2.20 and Df5, $(M(m, n, k) \;\&\; G_0(X_1)) \supset ((g, m)\eta X_1 \equiv G1(g, m))$. Hence, by Df1, $(M(m, n, k) \;\&\; G_0(X_1)) \supset ((g, m)\eta X_1 \equiv \exists n \exists k(M(m, n, k) \;\&\; g_n \in g_k))$. Obviously, $M(m, n, k) \supset (g_n \in g_k \supset \exists n \exists k (M(m, n, k) \;\&\; g_n \in g_k))$. On the other hand, by 2.10, $(M(m, i, j) \;\&\; g_i \in g_j) \supset (M(m, n, k) \supset g_n \in g_k)$. Hence, $(M(m, n, k) \;\&\; G_0(X_1)) \supset ((g,$

$m)\eta X_1 \equiv g_n \in g_k)$. Therefore, by 2.38, $(M(m, n, k)$ & $G_0(X_1)) \supset (gSm \equiv g_n \in g_k)$. By 2.30, the theorem is proved.

2.41. $T(m, n, k) \supset (gSm \equiv (gSn \mid gSk))$.

Proof. By 2.21 and Df5, $(T(m, n, k)$ & $G_{R_m}(X_1)) \supset ((g, m)\eta X_1 \equiv G_2(g, m, X_1))$. Hence, by 2.11 and Df2, $(T(m, n, k)$ & $G_{R_m}(X_1)) \supset ((g, m)\eta X_1 \equiv ((g, n)\eta X_1 \mid (g, k)\eta X_1))$. By 2.38, $(T(m, n, k)$ & $G_{R_m}(X_1)) \supset (gSm \equiv (gSn \mid gSk))$. Therefore, by 2.33, the theorem is proved.

2.42. $Q(m, n, k) \supset (gSm \equiv \forall x_1(t(g, n, x_1)Sk))$.

Proof. By 2.22 and Df5, $(Q(m, n, k)$ & $G_{R_m}(X_1)) \supset ((g, m)\eta X_1 \equiv G3(g, m, X_1))$. Hence, by 2.12 and Df3, $(Q(m, n, k)$ & $G_{R_m}(X_1)) \supset ((g, m)\eta X_1 \equiv \forall x_1((t(g, n, x_1), k)\eta X_1))$. Therefore, by 2.38, $(Q(m, n, k)$ & $G_{R_m}(X_1)) \supset (gSm \equiv \forall x_1(t(g, n, x_1)Sk))$. By 2.33, the theorem is proved.

From 2.40—2.42 we can derive the following important metatheorem about S_1.

2.43. Let g be a variable not occurring in the sentence $F(\mathfrak{m})$ of Zermelo theory (and, a fortiori, of S_1) which contains free occurrences of the variables $x_{\mathfrak{t}}, \cdots, x_{\mathfrak{f}}$ and of no others. If $F'(\mathfrak{m})$ is the sentence obtained from $F(\mathfrak{m})$ by substituting the set expressions $g_{\mathfrak{t}}, \cdots, g_{\mathfrak{f}}$ (as defined in 2.18) respectively for these variables $x_{\mathfrak{t}}, \cdots, x_{\mathfrak{f}}$, then we can prove in S_1: $gS\mathfrak{m} \equiv F'(\mathfrak{m})$.

Proof. We prove 2.43 by making induction on the number of logical operators in $F(\mathfrak{m})$.

Case 1. $F(\mathfrak{m})$ contains no logical operators. We may assume that $F(\mathfrak{m})$ is the sentence $(x_{\mathfrak{n}} \in x_{\mathfrak{k}})$. Therefore, since we can develop number theory in S_1, we can prove: $M(\mathfrak{m}, \mathfrak{n}, \mathfrak{k})$. Hence, 2.43 follows from 2.40 because $F'(\mathfrak{m})$ is $(g_{\mathfrak{n}} \in g_{\mathfrak{k}})$.

Case 2. Assume 2.43 holds true for all cases where $F(\mathfrak{m})$ contains no more than s logical operators. We want to prove it for the cases where $F(\mathfrak{m})$ contains $s+1$ logical operators.

Case 2a. $F(\mathfrak{m})$ is of the form $(p \mid q)$. We may assume that the sentence is $(F(\mathfrak{n}) \mid F(\mathfrak{k}))$. Therefore, we can prove in S_1: $T(\mathfrak{m}, \mathfrak{n}, \mathfrak{k})$. Let $F'(\mathfrak{n})$ and $F'(\mathfrak{k})$ be related to $F(\mathfrak{n})$ and $F(\mathfrak{k})$ in the same manner as $F'(\mathfrak{m})$ is to $F(\mathfrak{m})$. By 2.41, $gS\mathfrak{m} \equiv (gS\mathfrak{n} \mid gS\mathfrak{k})$. Hence, by induction hypothesis, $gS\mathfrak{m} \equiv (F'(\mathfrak{n}) \mid F'(\mathfrak{k}))$. Hence, 2.43 is proved, because $(F'(\mathfrak{n}) \mid F'(\mathfrak{k}))$ is $F'(\mathfrak{m})$.

Case 2b. $F(\mathfrak{m})$ is of the form $\forall x_{\mathfrak{n}} p$. We may assume that $F(\mathfrak{m})$ is the sentence $\forall x_{\mathfrak{n}} F(\mathfrak{k})$. Therefore, we can prove in S_1: $Q(\mathfrak{m}, \mathfrak{n}, \mathfrak{k})$. Let $F'(\mathfrak{k})$ be related to $F(\mathfrak{k})$ as $F'(\mathfrak{m})$ is to $F(\mathfrak{m})$ except that free occurrences of $x_{\mathfrak{n}}$ in $F(\mathfrak{k})$ are not replaced by those of $g_{\mathfrak{n}}$ in $F'(\mathfrak{k})$.

By 2.42, $gS\mathfrak{m} \equiv \forall x_\mathfrak{n}(t(g, \mathfrak{n}, x_\mathfrak{n})S\mathfrak{k})$. Therefore, by induction hypothesis, $gS\mathfrak{m} \equiv \forall x_\mathfrak{n} F'(\mathfrak{k})$. Hence, 2.43 is proved, because $F'(\mathfrak{m})$ is $\forall x_\mathfrak{n} F'(\mathfrak{k})$.

From this the truth schema (TS) for Zermelo theory can be proved directly.

2.44. If $F(\mathfrak{m})$ is a closed sentence (statement) of Zermelo theory, then we can prove in S_1: $\mathfrak{m}\eta Tr \equiv F(\mathfrak{m})$.

Proof. By 2.43, if $F(\mathfrak{m})$ is a closed sentence, then we can prove in S_1: $gS\mathfrak{m} \equiv F(\mathfrak{m})$. Hence, by Df7, $\mathfrak{m}\eta Tr \equiv F(\mathfrak{m})$.

Hence, we reach the main theorem of this section.

Theorem 1. *In S_1 we can construct a truth definition for the Zermelo set theory.*

It may be worthwhile to emphasize here again that in this section we are merely concerned with the construction of a truth definition which need not be also a normal one; in other words, we do not assert that according to the truth definition given above, we can prove in S_1 that all the theorems of Zermelo theory are true. In order that in a system S we be able to prove such an assertion, it would be necessary to require that S contain S_1, as well as theorems which answer to those of the Zermelo set theory under consideration. This problem will be studied more carefully in a later section.

Although, when compared with standard axiomatic systems for set theory, S_1 should be considered a very weak system, it already contains the impredicative feature (through $Ax5$) which separates typical set theories from more elementary disciplines. It is therefore of interest to note in this connection that we can also obtain a truth definition (but not a normal one) for Zermelo theory in a system which does not contain impredicative classes.

Let S_2 be the system which contains the same linguistic forms as S_1 and is obtained from S_1 by substituting for $Ax5$ the following axioms[1)].

*Ax*6. For every sentence p of S_2 in which neither X_1 nor any bound large variables occur, $\exists X_1 \forall x_1(x_1\eta X_1 \equiv p)$.

*Ax*7. $\exists x_3 \forall x_1(x_1 \epsilon x_3 \equiv (x_1 \epsilon x_2 \ \& \ x_1\eta X_2))$.

We want to prove that in S_2 we can also obtain a truth definition for the Zermelo theory. Since S_2 has the same notation as S_1, all the definitions in S_1 are also definitions in S_2, except that it would

1) If we have merely *Ax*6 instead of *Ax*5, we have to require that the predicate Nn of being a natural number be defined by a "constitutive expression" (cf., e.g., Bernays [1], Part II, p. 12), while the bound class variable in condition [3] of 2.4 contradicts this. If we assume also *Ax*7, the class variable in the condition can be replaced by a set variable; see Bernays [1], Part II, top of p. 9.

be more correct to write $Tr(m)$ in place of $m\eta Tr$ in Df7, because there is no truth class in S_2 but only a predicate. However, this point is not important for our purpose.

Our problem is to prove a metatheorem for S_2 which answers to 2.44 for S_1. In the first place, when $Ax5$ is replaced by $Ax6$, the theorems 2.33 and 2.38 are no longer demonstrable, and we can only prove the metatheorems 2.32 and 2.39. Consequently, in place of the theorems 2.40—2.42, we can prove in S_2 only the following metatheorems:

2.45. $M(\mathfrak{m}, \mathfrak{n}, \mathfrak{k}) \supset (gS\mathfrak{m} \equiv g_{\mathfrak{n}} \in g_{\mathfrak{k}})$.

2.46. $T(\mathfrak{m}, \mathfrak{n}, \mathfrak{k}) \supset (gS\mathfrak{m} \equiv (gS\mathfrak{n} \mid gS\mathfrak{k}))$.

2.47. $Q(\mathfrak{m}, \mathfrak{n}, \mathfrak{k}) \supset (gS\mathfrak{m} \equiv \forall x_1(t(g, \mathfrak{n}, x_1)S\mathfrak{k})$.

However, an examination of the proofs for 2.43 and 2.44 should make it clear that 2.45—2.47 are already adequate to the derivation of 2.43 and 2.44. Therefore, it would seem that we can define truth for Zermelo theory in S_2 even without applying $Ax7$.

Such would be true if we could develop number theory in S_2 without using $Ax7$. As a matter of fact, there seems to be no way of doing so, although it is known that number theory can be developed in S_2 with the help of $Ax7$[1].

Consequently, we have the next theorem:

Theorem 2. *In S_2 we can construct a truth definition for the Zermelo theory.*

§ 3. Remarks on the Construction of Truth Definitions in General[2]

In order to exhibit the procedure of constructing truth definitions more explicitly, we studied in the previous section only two special systems. Here we indicate how similar considerations are applicable to other formal systems as well.

In the Zermelo theory we can consider the predicate $\in$ as an operator for generating sentences from variables, and the logical operators $\mid$ and $\forall$ as operators for generating new sentences from given ones. Let L be an arbitrary system which contains one kind of variable just as Zermelo theory, but contains in addition to (or instead of) $\in$, other

1) See Bernays [1], Part II.

2) Later sections are independent of the material contained in this section, which can be omitted by a reader interested only in the few conclusions regarding the relativity of number theory and induction, to be presented in the last part.

predicates $P_1, \cdots, P_i$, in addition to (or instead of one or both of) $|$ and $\forall$, other operators $O_1, \cdots, O_j$. Here again, we can suppose that the theorems of L have been selected in an arbitrary but definite way.

Let L^* be the system which is like S_1 except that it contains, besides the sentences of S_1, also the sentences generated by the predicates $P_1, \cdots, P_i$ and the logical operators $O_1, \cdots, O_j$. Let the axioms of L^* be like those of S_1 except that the domain of the sentences p in *Ax*5 be extended accordingly. Then we can construct in L^* a truth definition for L just as we did in S_1 for Zermelo theory. The necessary changes are few and simple. Thus, instead of Df1, we define in similar manner $G1(g, m), \cdots, Gi(g, m)$ for the predicates $P_1, \cdots, P_i$ of L, and instead of Df2—Df3, we define $G(i+1)\ (g, m, X_1), \cdots, G(i+j)\ (g, m, X_1)$ for the logical operators $O_1, \cdots, O_j$. The definition Df4 for $G(g, m, X_1)$ is then modified as an alternation of the $(i+j)$ clauses $G1, \cdots, G(i+j)$ thus defined.

After these changes in the definitions, it would be a routine matter to modify the proofs in the preceding section and demonstrate two theorems in L^* which are notationally the same as 2.33 and 2.38. From these two theorems, theorems answering to 2.40—2.42 can be proved with analogous proofs. Hence, we have:

Theorem 3. *If L is any system with one kind of variable and L^* contains S_1, as well as all sentences of L, we can construct in L^* a truth definition for L.*

In the above proof, we have assumed that the number of predicates and logical operators is finite. The theorem also holds if in L either the number of predicates or that of logical operators or both are denumerably infinite. In such a case, some further modifications in the procedure are necessary, for otherwise we would need for the definition of $G(g, m, X_1)$ an infinite alternation of clauses. We can proceed in the following manner. Define, as in Df1—Df3, $G1, G2, \cdots$ for all the predicates and logical operators. Let $F(\mathfrak{m})$ be the $\mathfrak{m}$th sentence of L, $R_\mathfrak{m}$ be the number of logical operators in $F(\mathfrak{m})$, and $N_\mathfrak{m}$ be the greatest $\mathfrak{k}$ such that the $\mathfrak{k}$th predicate occurs in $F(\mathfrak{m})$. Instead of $G(g, m, X_1)$ as defined in Df4, define $G(g, m, X_1, 1)$, $G(g, m, X_1, 2), \cdots$ as (finite) alternations of terms drawn from $G1, G2, \cdots$ in such a way that for each $\mathfrak{i}$, the clauses $G1, G2, \cdots$ for all the predicates and logical operators occurring in some $F(\mathfrak{m})$ for which $N_\mathfrak{m} \leqslant \mathfrak{i}$ and $R_\mathfrak{m} \leqslant \mathfrak{i} - 1$ occur as alternation terms in $G(g, m, X_1, \mathfrak{i})$. Instead of definitions Df5—Df7, we use definitions of the following forms $(\mathfrak{j}, \mathfrak{m} = 1, 2, \cdots)$:

Definition 5.' $G_\mathfrak{i}(X_1)$ *when and only when* $\forall g \forall_m((R_m \leqslant \mathfrak{i} - 1\ \&\ N_m \leqslant \mathfrak{j}) \supset ((g, m)\eta X_1 \equiv G(g, m, X_1, \mathfrak{j})))$.

Definition 6'. *$gS\mathfrak{m}$ when and only when* $\forall X_1(G_{R_\mathfrak{m}+N_\mathfrak{m}}(X_1) \supset (g, \mathfrak{m})\eta X_1)$.

Definition 7'. *$\mathfrak{m}\eta Tr$ when and only when* $\forall g(gS\mathfrak{m})$.

With these definitions we can prove for L^* metatheorems answering to 2.32 and 2.39 (although not the theorems corresponding to 2.33 and 2.38), and therefore those answering to 2.45—2.47. However, these are precisely what we need in order to prove the metatheorems for L and L^* which answer to 2.43 and 2.44 for Zermelo theory and S_1. Hence, in these cases, we can also give in L^* a truth definition for L. In other words, Theorem III holds true no matter whether L contains finitely or (denumerably) infinitely many predicates and logical operators.

We insert here a few remarks on function symbols and constant names. We have thus far been assuming that systems are so formulated that function symbols and constant names do not occur among their primitive notations. Such an approach seems to be in accord with Tarski's procedure. And it is partly justified by the assertion[1] that when we use sufficiently many predicates, constant names and function symbols are theoretically dispensable. Nevertheless, it must be admitted, the alternative procedure of including among the primitive notation of a system constant names and function symbols from which terms are generated seems to be more intuitive and tends to clarify matters in many connections. However, if we consider a system formulated with terms among its primitive notation, the construction of a truth definition for it would have to differ considerably from what is described in the preceding section. Moreover, for such systems it would often appear possible to construct truth definitions with more direct and intuitive methods[2]. Since considerations regarding such possibilities would lead us far afield, we shall continue to assume that no function symbols or constant names occur in the primitive notations of the systems which we study.

So far we have restricted ourselves to systems each containing only one kind of variable in its primitive notation. Let us now consider the case where a system contains many kinds of variable.

The simplest way of handling such a case seems to be the following: consider instead of the given system with many kinds of

1) See Quine [10], p. 149; Hilbert-Bernays [3], vol. **1**, p. 460.

2) If we compare the truth definition for number theory in Hilbert-Bernays, vol. **2**, with the truth definition for Zermelo theory elaborated in the present paper, it seems fair to consider the former more straightforward and intuitively simpler, involving a more direct recursion. It is not very easy to determine the exact conditions which a system must satisfy in order to possess such a truth definition. See also the observations in the paragraph between parentheses on p. 63 of Tarski [18].

variable (a many-sorted system) an "equivalent" system with one kind (a one-sorted system). Since we know this is always possible[1], we seem to be able to avoid altogether the question of defining truth for many-sorted theories.

However, since in certain cases it is more natural to use many kinds of variable, it is desirable to consider directly how we can construct a truth definition for a given many-sorted theory. In this connection, Tarski has given indications as to how we should proceed[2]. We state merely the general conditions which a metasystem should satisfy.

Given a one-sorted system, what do we need in a metasystem in order that it be adequate to defining truth for the given system? If we examine the construction of truth definition for Zermelo theory, we see that the following things are needed: (1) General logic (quantification theory and theory of identity) for each kind of variable in the metasystem; (2) ordinary number theory together with variables $m, n, \cdots$ ranging over natural numbers; (3) sufficient resources for defining all finite sequences of entities of the given system and for introducing a variable g which ranges over such sequences; (4) existence of a class of ordered pairs of g (a finite sequence) and m (a natural number), corresponding to each sentence of the metasystem which contains g and m as free variables.

Let K be an arbitrary many-sorted theory. In order that a system K^* be adequate as a metasystem in which we can define truth for K, K^* must contain materials similar to those listed under (1)—(4). The only important necessary alteration is with regard to item (3). To satisfy a sentence of K with n free variables, we need a suitable sequence with n terms such that for each k between 1 and n, the kth term is an object falling within the range of values of the kth free variable in the given sentence. Hence, it is necessary that, besides the things listed under (1), (2), and (4), such finite sequences g of arbitrary terms from K be obtainable in K^*. Roughly speaking, if K^* contains number theory, we need only classes which take as members all entities of K, because finite sequences and ordered pairs can usually be defined with the help of natural numbers. Thus, for example, if K is the predicate calculus of the ith order founded on natural numbers, then it is sufficient to use the predicate calculus of the $(i+1)$th order as K^*[3].

---

1) See chapter XII. We are here interested in ordinary systems which contain for each kind of their variables the ordinary complete quantification theory.

2) See Tarski [16].

3) See Tarski [17], p. 110, the first three sentences of §8.

§ 4. Consistency Proofs via Truth Definitions

It seems to be widely believed that once we have in L^* a truth definition for L, it is then a routine matter to formalize in L^* a consistency proof for L. Probably partly on account of this belief, details of such consistency proofs are usually not supplied. However, as we remarked before, in order to prove in L^* the consistency of L through a truth definition, we also have to prove in L^* that all theorems of L are true by the definition; and such a proof not only calls for strong axioms in L^* but usually also involves a number of complications. We consider in this section a few special cases of such consistency proofs.

Consider first a weak and simple system S_3 of set theory. The linguistic forms of S_3 are as given in §2 for the Zermelo theory. The theorems of S_3 are specified in the following manner. The proper axioms of S_3 are just the axioms $Ax1$—$Ax3$ of the system S_1. Moreover, all axioms of the quantification theory as given below are also theorems of S_3:

*Q*1. $p \supset (q \supset p)$.

*Q*2. $(p \supset (q \supset r)) \supset ((p \supset q) \supset (p \supset r))$.

*Q*3. $(-p \supset -q) \supset (q \supset p)$.

*Q*4. $\forall x(\phi x \supset \psi x) \supset (\forall x \phi x \supset \forall x \psi x)$.

*Q*5. If x is not free in p, $p \supset \forall x p$.

*Q*6. $\forall x \phi x \supset \phi y$.

The only rule of inference is modus ponens for closed sentences.

*Q*7. If p and $p \supset q$ are theorems, then q is also.

It should be noted that, following Quine[1], we do not allow free variables to occur in theorems. Thus, when a sentence is listed as an axiom or a theorem, we mean actually that a closure of the given sentence (i.e., a closed sentence obtained from the given sentence by prefixing distinct general quantifiers for all its free variables) is an axiom or a theorem. Moreover, we also follow Quine in calling $\forall x p$ a vacuous quantification when x is not free in p.

By Theorems 1 and 2, S_1 and S_2 each contains a truth definition for S_3. Moreover, all the theorems of S_3 are also theorems of S_1 and S_2. We now show that the consistency of S_3 can be formally proved in S_1. In all probability no consistency proof for S_3 can be formalized in S_2, although we possess no proof of the impossibility.

1) See Quine [10], Chap. 2.

Since S_1 contains number theory, syntactical notions for S_3 can be defined in S_1 through an arithmetization of the syntax of S_3. In particular, we assume that the following notions have been defined in S_1: $\supset(m, n, k)$ ($F(m)$ being $(F(n) \supset F(k))$), $\exists(m, n, k)$ ($F(m)$ being $\exists x_n F(k)$), $\equiv(m, n, k)$ ($F(m)$ being $F(n) \equiv F(k)$), $\vee(m, n, k)$ ($F(m)$ being $(F(n) \vee F(k))$), inf (m, n, k) ($F(m)$, $F(n)$, $F(k)$ being all closed, and $\supset(m, n, k)$), ax$fr(m)$ (a closure of $F(m)$ is an axiom of S_3 and none of the initial general quantifiers of $F(m)$ whose ranges extend to the end of $F(m)$ is vacuous), ax(m) ($F(m)$ is an axiom of S_3 which, incidentally, must be a closed sentence), pr(n, m) (the nth proof of S_3 is a proof for $F(m)$, an arbitrary enumeration of the proofs of S_3 having been assumed), thm(m) ($F(m)$ is a theorem of S_3: $\exists n(\text{pr}(n, m))$), neg (m) (the number k such that $F(k)$ is the negation of $F(m)$), $Con(S_3)$ (S_3 is consistent: $\forall n - \text{pr}(n, \mathfrak{m}_0)$, $F(\mathfrak{m}_0)$ being the sentence $\forall x_2 \exists x_1 (x_1 \epsilon x_2)$ of S_3), $\lambda(n)$ (the number of lines in the nth proof), $\rho(m)$ (the number of general quantifiers standing at the beginning of $F(m)$ and having ranges all extended to the end of $F(m)$).

We note incidentally that we can fix on an arbitrary enumeration of all the proofs of S_3. We assume merely that the enumeration is made in such a way that when the mth proof contains the nth proof as a proper part, then $m > n$ in the enumeration.

From 2.41—2.42 and Df7, we can prove immediately that the following are theorems of S_1.

4.1. $\supset(m, n, k) \supset (gSm \equiv (gSn \supset gSk))$.

4.2. $\equiv(m, n, k) \supset (gSm \equiv (gSn \equiv gSk))$; $\vee(m, n, k) \supset (gSm \equiv (gSn \vee gSk))$.

4.3. $\exists(m, n, k) \supset (gSm \equiv \exists x(t(g, n, x)Sk))$.

4.4. (inf (m, n, k) & $m\eta Tr$ & $n\eta Tr) \supset k\eta Tr$.

By the definitions (2.18 and 2.19) of g_i and $t(g, n, x)$, we can prove in S_1:

4.5. $(t(g, n, x))_n = x$, $(t(t(g, n, x), m, y))_n = x$, $(t(t(g, n, x), m, y))_m = y$, etc.

By 2.44, we have:

4.6. $-\mathfrak{m}\eta Tr \equiv$ neg $(\mathfrak{m})\eta Tr$.

The first crucial theorem we want to prove in S_1 is:

4.7. ax$fr(m) \supset m\eta Tr$.

Proof. The axioms of S_3 are of nine kinds falling under two groups: (1) the axioms of quantification theory given by $Q1$—$Q6$;

(2) the three definite axioms $Ax1$—$Ax3$ of set theory. If ax$fr(m)$, then a closure of $F(m)$ is an axiom of S_3. We prove 4.7 by making induction on $\rho(m)$. First we assume that we have defined nine arithmetic predicates $\mathrm{ax}_1, \cdots, \mathrm{ax}_9$ corresponding to the nine kinds of axioms with their initial quantifiers omitted. Thus, for instance, $\mathrm{ax}_1(m)$ if and only if $F(m)$ is of the form $(p \supset (q \supset p))$.

Case 1. $\rho(m)=0$. We have then in S_1: $\mathrm{ax}fr(m) \supset (\mathrm{ax}_1(m) \vee \cdots \vee \mathrm{ax}_9(m))$. Since the proofs for all cases in each of the two groups are similar, we prove only one case from each group for illustration.

Case 1a. $F(m)$ is of one of the forms given in $Q1$—$Q6$. Then 4.7 can be proved by 2.41—2.42 (together with their consequences such as 4.1) and the number theory of S_1. For example, suppose $F(m)$ is of the form $(\forall x(\phi x \supset \psi x) \supset (\forall x \phi x \supset \forall x \psi x))$. In other words, $\mathrm{ax}_4(m)$. We can prove in S_1: $\exists m_1 \cdots \exists m_7 \exists n(\supset(m, m_1, m_2) \,\&\, Q(m_1, n, m_3) \,\&\, \supset(m_2, m_4, m_5) \,\&\, Q(m_4, n, m_6) \,\&\, Q(m_5, n, m_7) \,\&\, \supset(m_3, m_6, m_7))$. Hence, by repeated applications of 2.42 and 4.1, we have: $gSm \equiv (\forall y(t(g, n, y) Sm_6 \supset t(g, n, y)Sm_7) \supset (\forall y(t(g, n, y)Sm_6) \supset \forall y(t(g, n, y)Sm_7)))$. Therefore, by the quantification theory in S_1, gSm. Hence, by Df7, $m\eta Tr$.

Case 1b. $F(m)$ is of one of the forms $Ax1$—$Ax3$. Then 4.7 can be proved by appealing to 2.40—2.42 (together with their consequences such as 4.1—4.4) and the corresponding axioms $Ax1$—$Ax3$ in S_1. For example, suppose $F(m)$ is: $\exists x_2 \forall x_1(x_1 \in x_2 \equiv (x_1 \in x_3 \vee \forall x_5(x_5 \in x_1 \equiv x_5 \in x_4)))$. In other words, $\mathrm{ax}_9(m)$. We can prove in S_1: $\exists m_1 \cdots \exists m_8(\exists(m, 2, m_1) \,\&\, Q(m_1, 1, m_2) \,\&\, \equiv(m_2, m_3, m_4) \,\&\, M(m_3, 1, 2) \,\&\, \vee(m_4, m_5, m_6) \,\&\, M(m_4, 1, 3) \,\&\, Q(m_5, 5, m_6) \,\&\, \equiv(m_6\, m_7, m_8) \,\&\, M(m_7, 5, 1) \,\&\, M(m_8, 5, 4))$. Hence, by repeated applications of 2.40, 2.42, 4.2, and 4.3, we have: $gSm \equiv \exists x \forall y((t(t(g, 2, x), 1, y))_1 \in (t(t(g, 2, x), 1, y))_2 \equiv ((t(t(g, 2, x), 1, y))_1 \in (t(t(g, 2, x), 1, y))_3 \vee \forall z((t(t(t(g, 2, x), 1, y), 5, z))_5 \in (t(t(t(g, 2, x), 1, y), 5, z))_1 \equiv (t(t(t(g, 2, x), 1, y), 5, z))_5 \in (t(t(t(g, 2, x), 1, y), 5, z))_4)))$. Therefore, by 4.5, writing a in place of $(t(t(g, 2, x), 1, y))$, we have: $gSm \equiv \exists x \forall y(y \in x \equiv (y \in a_3 \vee \forall z(z \in y \equiv z \in (t(a, 5, z))_4)))$. Since a and $(t(a, 5, z))_4$ are by definition again terms of S_3 (taking sets as values), (a closure of) the right-hand side of the equivalence is provable in S_1 by $Ax3$. Hence, we can prove in S_1: gSm. By Df7, $m\eta Tr$.

Case 2. Assume that 4.7 is true for all m such that $F(m)$ satisfies the condition $\rho(m)=n$. We want to prove the cases of 4.7 where $\rho(m)=n+1$. Suppose given: ax$fr(m) \,\&\, \rho(m)=n+1$. By induction hypothesis, we can then prove: $\exists j \exists k(Q(m, j, k) \,\&\, k\eta Tr)$. Therefore, we have by Df7 and 2.19: $\exists j \exists k(Q(m, j, k) \,\&\, \forall x(t(g, j, x)Sk))$. Hence, by 2.42 and Df7, $m\eta Tr$.

Combining Case 1 and Case 2, we prove 4.7 by applying the induction principle 2.5 of S_1.

It should be noted that here again we are applying $Ax5$ of S_1 in its full generality on account of the indispensable bound class variable involved in the definition of Tr. In other words, the above case of induction cannot be proved in S_2 where only inductions with regard to sentences involving no bound class variables are allowed.

Two immediate corollaries of 4.7 are[1]:

4.8. $\vdash_{S_1} \mathrm{ax}(m) \supset m\eta Tr$.

4.9. If a constant $\mathfrak{m}$ is given, then $\vdash_{S_1} \mathrm{ax}(\mathfrak{m}) \supset \mathfrak{m}\eta Tr$.

Then we can prove that every theorem of S_3 is true.

4.10. $\vdash_{S_1}(\mathrm{pr}(n,m) \,\&\, \lambda(n) \leqslant 1) \supset m\eta Tr$.

Proof. If $(\mathrm{pr}(n, m) \,\&\, \lambda(n) \leqslant 1)$, then $(\mathrm{ax}(n) \,\&\, n = m)$ and therefore, by 4.8, $m\eta Tr$.

4.11. If $\forall n \forall m((\mathrm{pr}(n, m) \,\&\, \lambda(n) \leqslant k) \supset m\eta Tr)$, then $\forall n \forall m((\mathrm{pr}(n, m) \,\&\, \lambda(n) \leqslant k + 1) \supset m\eta Tr)$.

Proof. If $(\mathrm{pr}(n, m) \,\&\, \lambda(n) \leqslant k + 1)$ then, according to the assumption about the enumeration of proofs, $\mathrm{ax}(m) \vee \exists i \exists j(\mathrm{inf}\ (i, j, m) \,\&\, \exists n_1 \exists n_2 (\mathrm{pr}(n_1, i) \,\&\, \mathrm{pr}(n_2, j) \,\&\, \lambda(n_1) \leqslant k \,\&\, \lambda(n_2) \leqslant k))$. Therefore, if $\forall n \forall m ((\mathrm{pr}(n, m) \,\&\, \lambda(n) \leqslant k) \supset m\eta Tr)$, then $\mathrm{ax}(m) \vee \exists i \exists j(\mathrm{inf}\ (i, j, m) \,\&\, i\eta Tr \,\&\, j\eta Tr)$. Hence, by 4.8 and 4.4, $m\eta Tr$.

4.12. $\vdash_{S_1} \mathrm{pr}(n, m) \supset m\eta Tr$. Or $\vdash_{S_1} \mathrm{thm}(m) \supset m\eta Tr$.

Proof. If $\mathrm{pr}(n, m)$, then $\exists k(\lambda(n) \leqslant k)$. Therefore, by 4.10, 4.11, and the induction principle 2.5 of S_1, 4.12 is proved.

The consistency of S_3 can now be proved.

Theorem 4. $\vdash_{S_1} - \mathrm{pr}(n, \mathfrak{m}_0)$. *Or* $\vdash_{S_1} Con(S_3)$.

Proof. By definition, $F(\mathfrak{m}_0)$ is the sentence $\forall x_2 \exists x_1 (x_1 \in x_2)$, the denial of which is equivalent to $Ax2$ of S_3. Therefore, $\mathrm{thm}(\mathrm{neg}(\mathfrak{m}_0))$ and, by 4.12, $\mathrm{neg}(\mathfrak{m}_0)\eta Tr$. Hence, by 4.6, $-\mathfrak{m}_0 \eta Tr$ and, by 4.12, $-\mathrm{pr}(n, \mathfrak{m}_0)$. Therefore, we have also $Con(S_3)$.

This completes the formalization within S_1 of a consistency proof for S_3. We now make a few remarks on the relation between analogously related systems.

If S is any set theory which has the same notation as S_3 but contains in addition to all the axioms of S_3 also a finite number of other set-theoretical axioms, and S' is related to S as S_1 is to S_3; then we can formalize similarly in S' a consistency proof for S.

1) We use the sign $\vdash$ as in Quine [10]. When necessary, we specify the system concerned by $\vdash_{S_1}$, etc.; for instance, $\vdash_S \phi$ if and only if the closure of ϕ is a theorem of S.

However, if S should include an infinite number of set-theoretical axioms (i.e., include axiom schemata beyond quantification theory), then the situation would be different. Thus, let S_4 be the ordinary Zermelo set theory which has the same notation as S_3 but contains beyond $Ax1$—$Ax3$, the axioms of infinity, sum set, power set, and the following axiom schema (the Aussonderungsaxiom)[1]:

$Ax8$. If p is any sentence of S_4 in which x_2 is not free, then $\exists x_2 \forall x_1 (x_1 \in x_2 \equiv (x_1 \in x_3 \,\&\, p))$.

Let S_5 be the system obtained from S_1 by adding the extra axioms of S_4. Can we prove $Con(S_4)$ (as a sentence of S_5) to be a theorem of S_5?

We cannot do this with the above method of proving Th 4. More specifically, the proof for the analogue of Case 1b of 4.7 would break down, the crux being that we would need something like an infinite alternation of sentences. As a result, we can prove only the analogue of 4.9 (but not that of 4.8), and therefore we cannot prove an analogue of 4.10.

Since S_5 contains a truth definition of S_4 as well as all the theorems of S_4, we would expect $Con(S_4)$ to be provable in S_5 by some alternative method. However, our attempts for obtaining such a proof have not been successful. We even suspect that there might be a way of demonstrating the unprovability of $Con(S_4)$ in S_5. In any case, so far as we know, the provability or unprovability of $Con(S_4)$ in S_5 remains an open question.

We have assumed the same axiom $Ax8$ in both S_4 and S_5, allowing no class variables to occur in the sentence p. If we extend the system S_5 and replace $Ax8$ by a similar but stronger $Ax8'$ in which p may be any sentence of S_5, then a proof of $Con(S_4)$ can indeed be obtained in the resulting system S_5'. Thus, we can proceed exactly as in the proof of Theorem 4 except that in proving an analogue of Case 1b of 4.7, we employ special treatments for the alternative when $F(m)$ is of the form $\exists x_2 \forall x_1 (x_1 \in x_2 \equiv (x_1 \in x_3 \,\&\, p))$ as given in $Ax8$. There are of course infinitely many sentences of S_4 which are of this form, but for each $F(m)$ of such a form, there exists a natural number j such that $F(m)$ is $\exists x_2 \forall x_1 (x_1 \in x_2 \equiv (x_1 \in x_3 \,\&\, F(j)))$. Hence, by arguments similar to those used in the proof of 4.7, we can prove in S_5' something like: $gSm \equiv \exists x \forall y (y \in x \equiv (y \in a \,\&\, gSj))$, a being a term of S_4 which takes sets as values. But the right-hand side of the equivalence is a case of $Ax8'$ (although not a case of $Ax8$ on account of the class variable occurring in gSj through an analogue of Df6). Therefore, we have in S_5': gSm. In this way we can prove:

1) Compare for a description of these other axioms Wang [20].

4.13. $\vdash_{S_5'} Con(S_4)$.

Similarly, if a system S' is related to a system S as a predicate calculus of the $(n+1)$th order founded on natural numbers is to one of the nth order, we can prove $Con(S)$ in S'; but if we weaken S' by stipulating that no variables of the highest type are allowed in defining sets of lower types, then the question whether $Con(S)$ is provable in the resulting system seems to remain open.

Another point worthy of some consideration is the question of proving $Con(S_3)$ in S_2. In the proof of $Con(S_3)$ (as a sentence of S_1) in S_1, the induction principle 2.5 is applied at four places (viz. in the proofs of 2.33, 2.37, 4.7, and 4.12) in such a manner that analogous arguments do not seem formalizable in S_2. Hence, a similar proof of $Con(S_3)$ cannot be carried out in S_2, although, as we mentioned before, we have not been able to obtain a proof for the assertion that $Con(S_3)$ as an arithmetic sentence in S_2 is not provable in S_2.

If we want to prove *Con* (S_3) (with the arithmetic notions involved as defined in S_2) in S_2, we must try to avoid the applications of induction to sentences containing bound class variables, such as in the proofs of the theorems (answering to) 2.33, 2.37, 4.7 and 4.12. But it does not seem possible to avoid all these applications.

One crucial point seems to be the presence of a rule of inference (the rule *Q7* of modus ponens) in S_3 which permits us to infer a shorter sentence from longer ones. If we could so reformulate S_3 that all its rules of inference are such that we can only infer a longer sentence from some definite finite number of shorter ones, then, no matter whether the number of axioms be finite or infinite, we would be able to prove $Con(S_3)$ for the reformulated S_3 without applying those inductions. Indeed, if that were possible, we would have a decision procedure for S_3, and the proof of $Con(S_3)$, as can be expected, would be quite simple.

It may be of interest to note that we can prove in place of $Con(S_3)$ the following metatheorem about S_2 which tells us that no given definite proof of S_3 can be a proof of the sentence $\forall x_2 \exists x_1 (x_1 \in x_2)$ of S_3:

4.14. If $\mathfrak{n}$ is a constant, then $\vdash_{S_2} - \mathrm{pr}(\mathfrak{n}, \mathfrak{m}_0)$.

This depends on the fact that if we consider only the individual numbers one by one, we need not make the inductions. To see this, we merely observe that 2.45—2.47 (instead of 2.40—2.42) are sufficient for proving in place of two theorems answering to 4.10 and 4.11 two metatheorems:

4.15. For given $\mathfrak{m}$ and $\mathfrak{n}$, $\vdash_{S_2} (\mathrm{pr}(\mathfrak{n}, \mathfrak{m}) \,\&\, \lambda(\mathfrak{n}) \leqslant 1) \supset \mathfrak{m} \eta Tr$.

4.16. For each given $\mathfrak{k}$ and each given $\mathfrak{m}$, if for every given $\mathfrak{n}$, $(\mathrm{pr}(\mathfrak{n}, \mathfrak{m})$ & $\lambda(\mathfrak{n}) \leqslant \mathfrak{k}) \supset \mathfrak{m}\eta Tr$, then for every given $\mathfrak{n}$, $(\mathrm{pr}(\mathfrak{n}, \mathfrak{m})$ & $\lambda(\mathfrak{n}) \leqslant \mathfrak{k}+1) \supset \mathfrak{m}\eta Tr$.

Moreover, if S_6 is the system obtained from S_3 by adding $Ax8$ as a new axiom and $\mathrm{pr}_6(n, m)$ (an arithmetic sentence of S_2) represents that the nth proof of S_6 is a proof of $F(m)$, we can also prove for S_2 a metatheorem analogous to 4.14:

4.17. If $\mathfrak{n}$ is a constant, then $\vdash_{S_2} - \mathrm{pr}_6(\mathfrak{n}, \mathfrak{m}_0)$.

The connections between S_2 and S_6 are of special importance because they are similarly related as the von Neumann-Bernays set theory and the Zermelo-Fraenkel. It is known[1] that given any two systems S'' and S related to each other as S_2 is to S_6, the relative consistency of S'' to S can be proved. Furthermore, the proof can be formalized in each ordinary system which is roughly as strong as S_1 or a second order predicate calculus founded on natural numbers. In other words[2],

4.18. If S'' is related to S as S_2 is to S_6, and S''' is an ordinary system roughly no weaker than S_1, then $\vdash_{S'''} Con(S) \supset Con(S'')$, $Con(S)$ and $Con(S'')$ being arithmetic sentences of S''' representing respectively the consistency of S and S''.

Therefore, if we choose S and S'' in such a way[3] that arguments which can be carried out in S_1 can also be carried out in S'', then $Con(S) \supset Con(S'')$ as a sentence of S'' becomes a theorem of S'' and therefore, by Gödel's second theorem, $Con(S)$ cannot be provable in S'' unless S'' is inconsistent.

4.19. If S and S'' are related as before and S'' contains S_1, then $Con(S)$ is not a theorem of S'' unless S'' is inconsistent.

However, if the arithmetic sentence $Pc(n)$ of S'' represents that the nth proof of S is the proof of a definite refutable sentence of S (i.e., a sentence such as $0=1$ whose denial is known to be provable in S), then $\forall n(-Pc(n))$ may be taken as $Con(S)$ and we can prove:

4.20. If S and S'' are as in 4.19, then $\vdash_{S''} - Pc(\mathfrak{n})$, $\mathfrak{n}$ being any given number.

In other words, in such a case although Con (S) is demonstrably unprovable in S'', we can prove by elementary considerations about S'' that no proof of S can be given which is a proof of a previously fixed refutable sentence of S. Indeed, such considerations can be for-

---

1) See Novak [8] and Rosser-Wang [12].

2) See McNaughton, *J. Symbolic Logic,* 18(1953), 136—144.

3) For example, S'' would be like that if we choose as S the system S_4 or the system N in §2 of Wang [22].

malized in number theory and we can prove in number theory an arithmetic sentence Con^* representing that for every number n, if it is for a certain numeral $\mathfrak{m}$ of S'' the number of a sentence $-Pc(\mathfrak{m})$ of S'', then the nth sentence of S'' is a theorem of S''. Since S'' is assumed to be at least as strong as S_1 which contains number theory, Con^* as a sentence of S'' can also be proved in S'' although $Con(S)$ cannot.

4.21. If S and S'' are as in 4.19, then $\vdash_{S''} Con^*$.

If we assume that all theorems of S'' are *true* in some definite sense, Con^* may also be taken as expressing indirectly the consistency of S. But, it has to be admitted, this is not very clear.

§5. Relativity of Number Theory and in Particular of Induction

In each of many different forms of set theory, we say that we can develop the ordinary number theory. Sometimes within a same set theory we can also develop number theory in more than one way. Naturally the number theory which we obtain is in each case relative to the axioms of the set theory as well as to the definitions we adopt for the arithmetic notions. If we consider each set theory as a theory for the set concept, then the number theory and the arithmetic concepts we obtain in each case are also relative to the underlying set concept. In particular, in each system of set theory which contains number theory, the principle of induction becomes a set-theoretical principle derivable from the axioms of the system; and whether induction is applicable to a certain sentence of the system depends both on the strength of the axioms of the system and the definitions for the arithmetic notions such as those for the number zero, for the successor function, and for the predicate of being a natural number (or for the class of all natural numbers). In this section we shall illustrate the connection between number theories and their underlying set theories with some rather striking examples.

Let us consider first a system R which has the same notations as S_3 (or as Zermelo set theory) and contains $Q1$—$Q7$, plus certain stronger proper axioms in place of $Ax1$—$Ax3$. These axioms are, roughly speaking, such as to guarantee the development of ordinary number theory, the existence of infinite sets of natural numbers and predicative classes of such sets. In strength R amounts to a system related to a second-order predicate calculus founded on natural numbers as the von Neumann-Bernays set theory is to the Zermelo-Fraenkel. However, to facilitate considerations about the system, we are presenting it in a rather unnatural form. Thus the general variables $x, y, z, \cdots$ of R are understood roughly as ranging over natural numbers, infinite sets of them, as well as classes of such sets. From these we select by contextual definitions the sets $a, b, c, \cdots$ which are capable of being elements of classes:

5.1. $\forall a\phi a$ for $\forall x(\exists y(x\epsilon y) \supset \phi x)$.

5.2. $\exists a$ for $-\forall a-$.

And then variables $r, s, t, \cdots$ of the lowest type are introduced by further restricting the domain:

5.3. $\forall t\phi t$ for $\forall a(\exists b(a \epsilon b) \supset \phi a)$.

5.4. $\exists t$ for $-\forall t-$.

Identity is defined as in S_3:

5.5. $x=y$ for $\forall z(z \epsilon x \equiv z \epsilon y)$.

The proper axioms of R can now be stated.

*R*1. Axiom of extensionality. $x=y \supset (x \epsilon z \supset y \epsilon z)$.

*R*2. Existence of denumerably many entities of the lowest type.

$$\exists t\forall s(s \epsilon t \equiv (s = c \vee s = b)).$$

*R*3. Existence of infinite sets of them. $\exists a\forall t(t \epsilon a \equiv t \epsilon x)$.

*R*4. Existence of predicative classes of such sets. If y is not free in ϕ and all bound variables in ϕ are element variables (a, b, etc.), then $\exists y\forall a(a \epsilon y \equiv \phi)$.

It should be emphasized that *R*4 can actually be replaced by a small finite number (7 being sufficient) of axioms so that the number of the proper axioms of R become finite. We shall assume such a reduction has actually been made so that R contains only a finite number of axioms (besides the quantification axioms *Q*1—*Q*6). Consequently, the method of consistency proof for S_3 is applicable to R.

We know that number theory can be developed in R in different ways. To be explicit, we assume that number theory is developed in R in the following manner:

By *R*3 and *R*4, $\exists a\forall t(t \epsilon a \equiv -t \epsilon t)$. Therefore, $\exists a\forall t(a \neq t)$. Hence, by *R*2, if we substitute a for both c and b, $\exists t\forall s(s \epsilon t \equiv s \neq s)$. Take this set t as the number zero.

By *R*2, for every t, there exists an s (the unit set of t) which contains t as the only member. For every natural number t, let the unit set of t be its successor $t+1$.

Let the set of natural numbers t be the intersection of all sets which contain zero and the successor of each of its members.

5.6. $Nn(t)$ for $\forall x((0 \epsilon x \,\&\, \forall s(s \epsilon x \supset s+1 \epsilon x)) \supset t \epsilon x)$, or $t \epsilon Nn$ or $Nn(t)$ for $\forall a((0 \epsilon a \,\&\, \forall s(s \epsilon a \supset s+1 \epsilon a)) \supset t \epsilon a)$.

We note that on account of $R3$, the two alternative ways of defining Nn are really the same.

According to 5.6 and $R4$, if $\forall m \phi m$ stands for $\forall t(Nn(t) \supset \phi t)$, then we have immediately the induction principle:

5.7. If ϕ is as in $R4$, then $(\phi 0 \,\&\, \forall n(\phi n \supset \phi(n+1))) \supset \forall m \phi m$.

Let R' be a system with the same notation as S_1 and related to R as S_1 is to S_3. In other words, R' is exactly like S_1 except for containing $R1$—$R4$ in place of $Ax1$—$Ax3$; or what is the same, R' contains $Ax4$—$Ax5$ in addition to the axioms of R. Number theory can be developed in R' in exactly the same manner as in S_1, for instance, by defining zero and successor as in R but defining $Nn(t)$ as in 2.3 (or, what is the same, by replacing x by X in 5.6). Using such a definition for Nn, we can prove in R' a principle of induction applicable to all sentences of R' (just like 2.5).

Let us assume that the syntax of R and that of R' have both been arithmetized in the usual manner, yielding two arithmetic statements $Con(R)$ and $Con(R')$ which express respectively the consistency of R and R'. If the arithmetization is carried out in the framework of a set theory, then the exact expansion of the arithmetic statement $Con(R)$ or $Con(R')$ depends on the definitions we adopt for the arithmetic notions. Thus, since in R and R' we just assumed different definitions for Nn, the arithmetic statements expressing the consistency of R and R' are different in the two systems. Let $Con_1(R)$ and $Con_1(R')$ be the arithmetic statements of R which express respectively the consistency of R and R', and $Con_2(R)$ and $Con_2(R')$ be those of R'. Let further $R\#$ be the system obtained from R by adding $Con_1(R)$ as a new axiom, then there are also arithmetic statements $Con_1(R\#)$ and $Con_2(R\#)$ respectively of R and R' which express the consistency of $R\#$.

Using the method of proving $Con\ (S_3)$ in S_1, we can prove:

5.8. $\vdash_{R'} Con_2(R)$.

Moreover, applying the method of a previous paper[1], we can also prove:

5.9. $\vdash_{R'} Con_2(R\#) \supset Con_2(R')$.

As $R\#$ is a natural extension of R with an additional axiom whose truth is guaranteed by the consistency of R, we would expect the provability of the relative consistency of $R\#$ to R as expressed by: (1) $Con_2(R) \supset Con_2(R\#)$. However, if that were provable in R', we would obtain from 5.8 and 5.9: $\vdash_{R'} Con_2(R')$. Then R' would be

1) See the argument for proving the relative consistency of N'' to N in §2 of Wang [22].

inconsistent[1]. Therefore (1) cannot be provable in R'. But why?

Indeed, we can prove the following:

5.10. $\vdash_{R'} Con_1(R) \supset Con_2(R\#)$.

Thus, since R' contains a truth definition for R, we can derive from $Con_1(R)$ and the truth schema that the number of $Con_1(R)$, like the numbers of all the theorems of R, belongs to the truth class Tr. Therefore, we would be able to prove $Con_2(R\#)$ in the same way as $Con_2(R)$.

In short, the difficulty lies in the inference from $Con_2(R)$ to $Con_1(R)$.

Theorem 5. *If we can derive $Con_1(R)$ from $Con_2(R)$ in R', then R' is inconsistent.*

The reason why no such derivation is available seems to be the following. Let us call a set or class inductive if it contains 0 and the successor of each of its members. In R and R' the class of natural numbers is the intersection of all the inductive classes of R and R' respectively. Since R' contains more classes and therefore more inductive classes, their intersection is smaller than the corresponding intersection in R. Hence, it is possible that there exists some non-standard model for R which contains more natural numbers than any model of R'. Accordingly, as $Con(R)$ amounts to an assertion that no natural number represents a proof of contradiction, it is conceivable that although no natural number of R' does so, some natural numbers of R do. At any rate, there is no obvious reason to think that we can prove in R' such is impossible.

Alternatively, we may want to use in R' the same definitions for the arithmetic notions as in R. Then we have instead of the two arithmetic statements, merely the one statement $Con_1(R)$ for both systems. But then we can no longer prove $Con_1(R)$ as we proved $Con(S_3)$ in S_1, since we have in R', with such definitions, only the induction principle 5.7, while a stronger induction principle is needed for proving analogues of 2.40—2.42. Indeed, if we could prove $Con_1(R)$ in R', R' would be inconsistent either by Theorem 5 or by the following 5.11 and 5.12. Thus, using proofs similar to those for 5.9 and 5.10, we can prove:

5.11. $\vdash_{R'} Con_1(R\#) \supset Con_1(R')$.

5.12. $\vdash_{R'} Con_1(R) \supset Con_1(R\#)$.

Since the only hindrance in the way of proving Con_1 (R) in R' is the two applications of induction on sentences containing large

1) As we mentioned in the introduction, a reasoning roughly like this was what motivated the investigations reported in this paper.

variables (as we have already discussed in the last section), we have the following theorem[1]:

Theorem 6. *If R' is consistent and we use the same definitions for natural numbers as in R, then the principle of induction in its full generality is independent of the axioms of R' and, in particular, there exists some sentence ϕi of R' containing large variables such that $\phi 0$ and $\forall n(\phi n \supset \phi(n+1))$ are provable in R' but $\forall m \phi m$ is not.*

It follows that if R' is ω-consistent, such a sentence $\forall m \phi m$ must be undecidable in R'.

Another example of undecidable sentences can be obtained if we use considerations similar to those used for 4.20. Let $Pc_1(n)$ be an arithmetic sentence of R and R' which represents that the nth proof of R is the proof of a definite refutable sentence of R. We have:

5.13. If R' [etc. as in Theorem 6], then for each $\mathfrak{n}$, $-Pc_1(\mathfrak{n})$ is provable in R' but $\forall m(-Pc_1(m) \supset -Pc_1(m+1))$ is not.

If the latter were provable, we would have by 5.7 a proof for $Con_1(R)$ in R'.

Moreover, we know that even when we use in R' the same definition of Nn as in R, the induction principle in its generality can be derived from the following form of reducibility principle:

$R5.$ $\exists y \forall m(m \in y \equiv m\eta X)$, or $\exists a \forall m(m \in a \equiv m\eta X)$.

Therefore, we have:

5.14. The axiom $R5$ is independent of the axioms of R'.

For similar reason, if $m \geqslant n$ stands for $\forall X((n\eta X \,\&\, \forall k(k\eta X \supset (k+1)\eta X)) \supset m\eta X)$, then the following statement is also independent of the axioms of R':

$R6.$ $\forall m(m=0 \vee \exists n(m=n+1)) \,\&\, \forall X \exists m \forall n(n\eta X \supset n \geqslant m)$.

Of course in $R5$ and $R6$ we are assuming that the variables m, n, etc. are introduced in R' with the same definitions as in R.

Another remark relates to the possibility of proving ω-consistency. By 5.9 and Gödel's theorem, it follows that $Con_2(R\#)$ is not provable in R'. But we know[2] that if R is ω-consistent, then $R\#$ is consistent. Therefore, either (1) the ω-consistency of R is not provable in

1) This theorem and a number of other conclusions of the present paper are summarized in Wang [21]. However, in Theorem 9 of Wang [21], which answers to the present theorem, the example in parentheses should be deleted. Moreover, the arguments in the lines fourteen to twenty on p. 451 of Wang [21] are also in error and should be corrected according to the more detailed discussions of the present paper.

2) See Wang [22], §2.

R', or (2) we cannot formalize in R' the proof for the assertion that $R\#$ is consistent, if R is ω-consistent. Which of the two alternatives is the case?

The answer seems to depend again on how we define the notion of ω-consistency which is closely related to the natural numbers and pseudo-natural numbers allowable by the axioms and definitions of the system. Let us consider merely the simple case where we assume R contains only the normal natural numbers 0 (the empty set), $0+1$ or 1 (the unit set of 0), $1 + 1$ or 2 (the unit set of 1), etc. and no more.

5.15. The arithmetic statement $w\ Con_2(R)$ of R' (R is ω-consistent) expresses that for every ϕ of R if $\phi 0$, $\phi 1$, $\phi 2$, etc. are all provable in R, then $-\forall m \phi m$ is not provable in R.

Using this definition, we can prove with the known arguments[1]:

5.16. $\vdash_{R'} w\ Con_2(R) \supset Con_2(R\#)$.

Thus let us take $\forall n - Pc_1(n)$ (see 5.13) as $Con_2(R)$. If $-Con_2(R\#)$, then $-\forall n - Pc_1(n)$ would be a theorem of $R\#$ and, as $\forall n - Pc_1(n)$ is the only additional axiom of $R\#$, also a theorem of R. If $-Pc(0)$, $-Pc(1)$, $-Pc(2)$, etc. are all theorems of R, then, by 5.15, $-w\ Con_2(R)$. If there is a numeral $\mathfrak{n}$ such that $Pc(\mathfrak{n})$ is provable in R, then $-Con_2(R)$ and therefore, by 5.15, $-w\ Con_2(R)$. It is not hard to formalize the argument in R'.

Therefore, we can also infer the following conclusion:

Theorem 7. *Although R' contains a normal truth definition for R and we can prove the consistency of R (viz., $Con_2(R)$), we cannot prove the ω-consistency of R (viz. $w\ Con_2(R)$) in R' unless R' is inconsistent.*

We may take this opportunity to state a few simple observations regarding the connection between truth definitions and consistency proofs. Tarski often stresses the importance of the truth schema. Given two systems S and S', he often asks whether there is a class or predicate Tr of S' such that every statement which falls under the following schema is a theorem of S':

(T) p if and only if x belongs to Tr. (Or, alternatively, p if and only if $Tr(x)$).

In this schema the letter p can be replaced by any statement of the system S and the letter x by the metalogical designation (name, Gödel number, etc.) of this statement.

1) See Wang [22], §2.

Let us say that S' contains a truth definition for S if and only if we can find a class or predicate Tr in S' and prove all the cases of (T), and that S' contains a normal truth definition for S if S contains both a truth definition for S and derivatively a consistency proof for S (or in other words, roughly speaking, S' contains a truth definition for S according to which all the theorems of S are true). Obviously,

5.17. There exist systems S and S' such that S' contains a truth definition for S but no normal one.

For example, take S to be the full Zermelo set theory with all its axioms, and S' to be the system S_1 (see §2); since the former is easily seen to be "stronger" than the latter, there can be no consistency proof for S in S'.

Moreover, if we call a truth definition for S abnormal if some theorems of S come out false according to the definition, we can also find systems S and S' such that S' contains an abnormal truth definition for S. For example, this would be the case if we take again the full Zermelo theory as S and take S_1 plus a contradictory of the axiom of infinity for the elements of S_1 (values of the small variables) as S'.

There is the question whether S' is stronger than S or whether S' is translatable into S, if S' contains a truth definition for S. To answer these questions, we must of course first make clear what we mean by being stronger than or being translatable into another system. Let us assume the definitions we employed on a previous occasion[1)], which do not appear far removed from our ordinary use of such words as modelling, translation, and strength of systems.

As we have shown there, it then follows from Gödel's theorem that if S' is sufficient for ordinary number theory and contains a *normal* truth definition for S, then S' is not translatable into S and S' has no model in S. If further S' contains S as a part then S' is stronger than S.

However, using the same definitions, it is perfectly possible that S' contains a truth definition for S but is both weaker than and translatable into S. For example, S_1 contains a truth definition for the full Zermelo theory, but it is easily shown that S_1 is translatable into the latter but the latter is not translatable into S_1. Although Tarski has shown[2)] that no system S' with the same notation as a system S can contain a truth definition (normal or not) for S, we cannot infer that S' must be stronger than S if S' contains any truth definition for S at all.

---

1) See Wang [22], §1.

2) See Tarski [16].

On the other hand, it is possible that S' and S have the same linguistic forms, and yet S' contains some "transformed" truth definition for S in the sense that there is a correlation of all the sentences of S with some sentences of S of certain special forms and for which latter there is a truth definition in S' (normal or not). For example, this seems to be what is happening when we say that a (transformed) normal truth definition for one system of the Zermelo set theory (for example, the original Zermelo system as refined by Skolem) can be found in another (for example, the Zermelo-Fraenkel), which has the same linguistic forms but contains additional axioms (the axiom of substitution in the case of our example)[1].

§ 6. Explanatory Remarks

We tabulate below in one place the characteristics of the principal systems studied above, for reference.

First we give in summary brief descriptions of the principal systems considered in the preceding sections.

(1) S_3 is a very weak set theory in which we assume merely the null set and the finite sets constructed out of it; S_3 has the same notations as the ordinary Zermelo set theory (one primitive predicate and one kind of variable only) and contains merely the axiom of extensionality, the axiom of null set, and an axiom saying that by adding a new member to a given set, we have again a set. As we know, S_3 has a simple model in the elementary theory of numbers.

(2) S_1 is a second-order predicate calculus with S_3 as its theory of individuals; S_1 contains both predicative and impredicative classes of sets of S_3. (Compare the systems of Quine [11] and Wang [19].) S_1 is as strong as a second-order predicate calculus with the ordinary theory of numbers as its theory of individuals.

(3) S_6 is obtained from S_3 by adding the Aussonderungsaxiom (a schema) guaranteeing the existence of every subset of a given set. S_6 has the same arithmetic model as S_3.

(4) S_2 is related to S_6 as S_1 is to S_3 except that S_2 contains only predicative classes (and no impredicative ones) of the sets of S_6 and that the Aussonderungsaxiom in S_2 becomes a single axiom (the intersection of a set and a class is again a set) involving a free class variable; S_2 is the partial system of the Neumann-Bernays system as determined by the axioms of the groups I—III and Va of Bernays [1], and S_6 is related to S_2 as the Zermelo-Fraenkel system is to the Neumann-Bernays.

---

1) See Tarski [17], p. 110, and Rosser-Wang [12], p. 128.

(5) S_4 is roughly the ordinary Zermelo set theory (including, beyond the axioms of S_6, the axioms of infinity, power set, and sum set), and S_5 is related to S_4 as S_3 is to S_1. We note that in S_5 the Aussonderungsaxiom remains the same as in S_4 and no references to classes are allowed in defining sets (or elements). S_5' is a further extension of S_5 where the restriction is removed and the new Aussonderungsaxiom states (as in S_2) that the intersection of a set and a class is again a set.

(6) R is a system which is formulated in the notation of ordinary Zermelo set theory but is as strong as an extension of S_1 related to S_1 as S_2 is to S_6 or, alternatively, as a third order predicate calculus with only predicative classes on the highest level. An important feature of R is that it contains only a finite number of proper axioms (i.e., axioms beyond quantification theory). R' is an extension of R related to R as S_1 is to S_3; $R\#$ is obtained from R by adding $Con(R)$ as a new axiom.

We note that S_2 is related to S_6 in the same way as the Neumann-Bernays system (cf. Bernays [1], to be referred to as the system *NB*) is to the Zermelo-Fraenkel (obtained from S_4 by adding the Ersetzungsaxiom and the Fundierungsaxiom, to be referred to as the system *ZF*). When two systems S'' and S are related in the same way as *NB* is to *ZF*, we say that S'' is a predicative extension of S. Thus, Theorem II (in §2) and the results 4.17—4.21 (in §4) are concerned with the relations between systems and their predicative extensions.

S_1 and S_3, S_5 and S_4, R' and R are all related to each other in the same way. When S' and S are thus related, we say that S' is an impredicative extension of S. Thus, S_1 is an impredicative extension of S_3, S_5 is one of S_4, R' is one of R. The main results in this paper (including the Theorems 1, 4, 5, 6) are all concerned with the relations between systems and their impredicative extensions. The interest and validity of these results depends largely on the relative consistency of a system and its impredicative extension, first established by the present author (see Wang [21] and Wang [22]). It seems proper to say that the relative consistency of a system and its predicative extension is much less surprising than that of a system and its impredicative extension. Indeed, the former seems to have been widely accepted even before rigorous proofs by Dr. Novak and others appeared; and usually we assume that $Con(S)$ cannot be proved in a predicative extension S'' because impredicative classes are needed, even when we still have no exact formalization of the matter. On account of these circumstances, we believe that the main results of the present paper have no analogues in studies where merely relations between a system and its predicative extension are considered.

Among the systems we tabulated under (1)—(6), the relation between S_5' and S_4 is again of a different sort. S_5' differs from a predicative extension of S_4 in that it contains in addition also the impredicative classes; while it differs from the impredicative extension S_5 of S_4 in that class variables are allowed in defining sets. In other words, it actually contains all the axioms of both extensions of S_4. When S''' and S are related in such a way, we shall say that S''' is an *irreducible* extension of S. Thus S_5' is an irreducible extension of S_4.

As we have mentioned above (cf. 4.13 in §4), the consistency of S_4 is provable in S_5'. Moreover, since we can prove in S_5' that there exists an inductive set (cf. remark after Theorem 5 in §5)[1], and that the intersection of a class and a set is again a set, the intersection of all inductive classes of S_5' is the same as the intersection of all the inductive sets of S_5'. Therefore, if we define in S_4 the set Nn of all natural numbers as the intersection of all its inductive sets and use the same formal definition in S_5', we can in S_5' still make induction on all classes and therefore all sentences of S_5' (compare the remarks about $R5$ in §5). Hence, by arguments similar to those for 5.10 (in §5), we can derive $Con(S_4\#)$ from $Con(S_4)$ in S_5', where $S_4\#$ is related to S_4 as $R\#$ is to R. Hence, $Con(S_4\#)$ is also a theorem of S_5'. But we know (compare the proof of 5.11 in §5) that we can also derive $Con(S_5)$ from $Con(S_4\#)$ in S_5. Therefore, $Con(S_5)$ is also provable in S_5' and $Con(S_4\#)$ is not provable in S_5. Hence, S_5' is demonstrably stronger (in the sense of Wang [4]) than S_5. (Compare Theorems 6, 11, and 12 of Wang [3].)

Let NQ be the system obtained from NB by adding all the impredicative classes. Then NQ is an irreducible extension of ZF, related to ZF as S_5' is to S_4. By reasoning similar to those in the preceding paragraph, we can prove $Con(ZF)$ and $Con(ZF\#)$ in NQ($ZF\#$ is to ZF as $R\#$ is to R). Since we know that $Con(ZF)$ cannot be proved in NB, it also follows that there must be certain impredicative classes which cannot be proved to exist in NB. Indeed, since the relative consistency of NB to ZF can be proved in NQ, $Con(NB)$ can also be proved in NQ. It is not clear whether $Con(NB)$ might also be provable in the impredicative extension of ZF, which is demonstrably weaker than NQ (just as S_5 is weaker than S_5').

The most common examples of irreducible extensions seem to be the cases where S is the ordinary nth order (n being $2, 3, 4, \cdots$) predicate calculus and S''' is the $(n+1)$th. If we take natural numbers as the individuals (the entities of the first or lowest type) of

1) This of course depends on the definitions of zero and the successor function, and the particular form of the axiom of infinity. For instance, if we use the original Zermelo axiom of infinity and define zero and the successor function as in 2.1 and 2.2 (of §2), then the sum set of the postulated infinite set is an inductive set.

these systems, then we see that what we have said about S_4, S_5, S_5' all apply (mutatis mutandis) to the systems S, S' (the impredicative extension of S) and S''', respectively.

A similar but slightly different case is the following. Let R^* be the system obtained from R' by adding the new axiom $R5$ (stating that every class of natural numbers is equivalent to a set of natural numbers, see §5), then we see that R^* is again related to R and R' as S_5' is related to S_4 and S_5.

References

[1] Paul Bernays, A system of axiomatic theory, *Jour. Symbolic Logic*, Part I, **2** (1937), 65—77; Part II, **6** (1941), 1—17.

[2] Kurt Gödel, Über formal unentscheidbare Sätze der Principia Mathematica und verwandter Systeme I, *Monatsh. Math. Phys.*, **38** (1931), 173—198.

[3] David Hilbert and Paul Bernays, Grundlagen der Mathematik, vol. 1, 1934, vol. 2, 1939, Berlin, Springer.

[4] Leon Henkin, The completeness of formal systems, a thesis at Princeton University accepted in October, 1947; abstract appeared on p. 61 of *Jour. Symbolic Logic,* **13** (1948).

[5] Leon Henkin, Completeness in the theory of types, *Jour. Symbolic Logic,* **15** (1950), 81—91.

[6] A. Malcev, Untersuchungen aus dem Gebiete der mathematischen Logik, *Recueil Mathématique,* N.S., **1** (1936), 323—336.

[7] John von Neumann, Zur Einführung der transfiniten Zahlen, *Acta litterarum ac scientiarum Regiae Universitatis Hungaricae Francisco-Josephinae, Sectio scientiarum mathematicarum,* **1** (1923), 199—208.

[8] Ilse L. Novak, A construction for models of consistent systems, *Fund. Math.,* **37** (1950), 87—110.

[9] John G. Kemeny, Type theory vs. set theory, a thesis at Princeton University (1949); abstract appeared on p. 78 of *Jour. Symbolic Logic,* **15** (1950).

[10] W. V. Quine, Mathematical Logic, New York, 1940; second printing, Cambridge, Mass., 1947.

[11] W. V. Quine, Element and number, *Jour. Symbolic Logic,* **6** (1941), 135—149.

[12] J. Barkley Rosser and Hao Wang, Non-standard models for formal logics, *Jour. Symbolic Logic,* **15** (1950), 113—129.

[13] Arnold Schmidt, Über deduktive Theorien mit mehreren Sorten von Grunddingen, *Math. Ann.,* **115** (1938), 485—506.

[14] Thoralf Skolem, Über einige Grundlagenfragen der Mathematik, Skrifter

utgitt av Det. Norske Videnskaps-Akademi, I, no. 4, 1929, 49 pp.

[15] Thoralf Skolem, Über die Nicht-charakterisierbarkeit der Zahlenreihe mittels endlich oder abzählbar unendlich vieler Aussagen mit ausschliesslich Zahlenvariablen, *Fund. Math.*, **23** (1934), 150—161.

[16] Alfred Tarski, Der Wahrheitsbegriff in den formalisierten Sprachen, *Studia Philosophica*, **1** (1936), 261—405 (original in Polish, 1933).

[17] Alfred Tarski, On undecidable statements in enlarged systems of logic and the concept of truth, *Jour. Symbolic Logic*, **4** (1939), 105—112.

[18] Alfred Tarski, The semantic conception of truth and the foundations of semantics, *Readings in Philosophical Analysis*, selected and edited by Herbert Feigl and Wilfred Sellars, New York, 1949, pp. 52—84; original appeared in *Philosophy and Phenomenological Research*, **4** (1944).

[19] Hao Wang, A new theory of element and number, *Jour. Symbolic Logic*, **13** (1948), 129—137.

[20] Hao Wang, On Zermelo's and von Neumann's axioms for set theory, *Proc. Nat. Acad. Sci. U.S.A.*, **35** (1949), 150—155.

[21] Hao Wang, Remarks on the comparison of axiom systems, *ibid.*, **36** (1950), 448—453.

[22] Hao Wang, Arithmetic translations of axiom systems, *Trans. Am. Math. Soc.*, **71** (1951), 283—293.

CHAPTER XIX

BETWEEN NUMBER THEORY AND SET THEORY*

I shall discuss a number of interconnections between number theory (i. e. the theory of natural numbers or nonnegative integers) and certain systems of set theory. Relations between transfinite numbers and arbitrary sets will not be considered.

While Dedekind and Frege tried to provide foundations for number theory by what are essentially set-theoretic considerations, Kronecker and Poincaré insisted that natural numbers are the most basic items in our mathematical thinking. It now seems clear that we understand better the nature of natural numbers than that of arbitrary sets. We know in a pretty definite sense the consistency of number theory but not that of set theory. We can in a definite sense obtain or derive number theory in set theory but not vice versa.

If we only talk about finite sets exclusively, set theory is equivalent to number theory. If we allow infinite sets but not "impredicative" sets, then set theory still resembles number theory quite well, although no exact equivalence between them is known. The big gap between number theory and set theory proper is the introduction of impredicative sets in set theory.

These are all well-known. The purpose of this paper is to formulate more precisely these connections between number theory and set theory. I shall consider several set-theoretic systems of varying strength but each strong enough to enable us to derive number theory. I shall ask, among other things, how far the interpretations for each system are determined by a fixed interpretation of the part of the system corresponding to number theory.

The results obtained below will, it is hoped, provide us with new insights into the close connections between number theory and set theory, as well as the peculiarities of impredicative sets.

In the first section, I shall consider general set theory or Zermelo's set theory minus the axiom of infinity. Several systems are used. The system G is the basic system of general set theory including the axiom of extensionality, the Aussonderungsaxiom, and an axiom assuring the

* This chapter appeared in *Math. Annalen.*, **126** (1953), 385—409.

existence of finite sets. The system G' contains, beyond the axioms of G (referred to as $M1$—$M3$), also the axioms $M4$—$M8$ of foundation, replacement, sum set, power set, and choice. In other words, G' contains all the axioms, except the axiom of infinity, of the Zermelo set theory. The system Z is the ordinary system of elementary number theory used, for example, by Hilbert and Bernays.

The main results obtained in section 1 are the following. (1) It is known that G and G' have a simple denumerable model in common. A predicate E is now constructed in G itself which serves to enumerate all the sets of the simple model. (2) Using this predicate E, we can express in G an axiom of limitation:

ALG. Every set is limited; or, in other words, for every x, there is a natural number m, such that x is $E(m)$.

We can therefore consider the system G^* obtained from G by adding *ALG* as a new axiom. (3) It is proved that all theorems of G' are also theorems of G^*; in other words, the presence of *ALG* renders the axioms $M4$—$M8$ redundant. (4) The system G^* is categorical relative to its number theory in the sense that any two models for G^* are isomorphic whenever their parts for the number theory in G^* are isomorphic. (5) G^* is effectively translatable into G.

In section 2, I shall consider first a system P' which is a predicative extension of G'. Every predicate of G' defines a collection of sets and P' treats both the sets and these collections so that, for example, instead of the predicate "$H(x)$", we can now write "$x \eta Y$" (x belongs to the collection Y defined by the predicate H). P' may also be described as the Bernays set theory minus the axiom of infinity. The following conclusions are established. (i) It is known that we can enumerate in a direct way all the collections required to exist by the axioms of P'. Formalizing this fact, we now define a predicate $\eta^*(m, n)$ of natural numbers such that if we add statements (implicitly) defining η^* as axioms to the number theory Z, then P' is effectively translatable into the resulting system. (ii) It is proved that η^* cannot be a general recursive predicate. (iii) It is possible to express in P' a predicate $R(X, m)$ which intuitively enumerates all the collections of P'. (iv) But the definition of R involves bound variables ranging over all collections and therefore, on account of difficulties with induction, we cannot prove in P' that R does serve to enumerate *all* collections called for by axioms of P'.

Finally, in the third section, ways of getting rid of the difficulty about induction are considered. (a) The use of a rule of infinite induction would do. (b) The introduction of impredicative collections would also eliminate the difficulty. Let P be the extension of G related to G as P' is to G', and Q be the system obtained from P by adding a principle for forming impredicative collections. Let P^* be the system obtained from P by adding the axiom ALG and also the axiom ALP which says that for every collection X, there is a natural number m, X is $R(m)$. (c) It is then proved that P^* is effectively translatable into Q. It follows that Q is stronger than P and the principle for forming impredicative collections is independent of the axioms of P. (d) The system P^* is also categorical relative to its number theory, if we restrict ourselves to ω–consistent models (viz. models in which there is no predicate $H(m)$ for which $H(0), H(1), \cdots$ are all true but "for all $m, H(m)$" is false). (e) Certain new forms of undecidable statements in set theory are given and discussed.

This completes the summary of results. The following brief index of notions and notations specially defined in this paper may also be useful: ϵ^*(see 1.1), $a(n)$(1.2), $b(n)$(1.3), $L(x)$(1.17), L–translation (1.18), η^*(2.16), n^*(2.17), e (the empty set or collection), $Nn(y)$ (y is a natural number), $H(n, Y)$ (2.18), $R(X, m)$ (2.20), $L(X)$ (3.7), R–translation (3.8).

In this paper, when I speak of a model for an axiom system or for a part of a system, I mean merely a domain or a set of domains of objects associated with an assignment of truth values (true or false) to each statement of the system or the part of a system such that the following conditions are satisfied: (1) in assigning truth values to the statements, the truth-functions and quantifiers receive their normal interpretation so that, for instance, p is true if and only if the negation of p is false; (2) All the theorems of the system or the part of a system are true according to the truth value assignment. In particular, in order to speak of models for a certain part of an axiom system, I do not have to consider the question whether the part also forms an axiom system by itself or, if it does, what that axiom system is.

In this paper, I do not have to take the concept "categorical" in its usual impredicative sense. In my application of the concept I can avoid the impredicativity since the one-to-one correspondence in the case of my theorems on categoricity can be effectively set up.

§ 1. General Set Theory

Systems of number theory and set theory all contain as part predicate calculus with identity, dealing with typical properties of truth functions, quantifiers, and identities (see Hilbert-Bernays [8], p. 375 and p. 389). As the basic system of number theory, we use the famous system Z of Hilbert-Bernays (*ibid.*, p. 384) determined by the Dedekind-Peano axioms for natural numbers, and the recursive equations for addition and multiplication. In system Z, whenever there are numbers having a certain property, it is always possible to introduce a descriptive term "the smallest of the numbers having the property".

Ordinary functions and arguments of number theory are all obtainable in Z.

To begin with, we consider the axiomatic system of set theory first proposed by Zermelo and later on modified and refined by others. Let us for the moment omit the axioms of infinity and study merely the remaining axioms which constitute what is sometimes called general set theory. It is known that general set theory and number theory are translatable into each other in the following sense[1]. There exists an effective way of replacing the membership predicate of general set theory by a predicate of number theory such that the resulting statements in place of the theorems of the former all are theorems of the latter; conversely, there exists an effective way of replacing symbols of number theory by suitable symbols of general set theory such that theorems of the former become theorems of the latter.

In order to apply and extend these results, we describe first more fully the system of general set theory.

It contains a single two-place predicate ϵ (membership, belonging to) the variables x, y, z, etc. for sets, and the following axioms[2].

$M1$. *The axiom of extensionality.* Two sets having the same elements are identical; or, if two sets x and y have the same elements and x belongs to z, then y also belongs to z.

$M2$. *The axiom of finite sets.* To a set x can be adjoined a set y which is not already in x; in other words, if there exist two sets x and y, then there exists a set z such that x is included in z (i. e., every element of x is also one of z) and y is the only element of z which does not also belong to x.

$M3$. *The Aussonderungsaxiom.* Given any set x and any predicate $H(y)$ of the system (or, any property expressible in the system), there exists a subset of x which contains all and only those elements y of x such that $H(y)$ (i. e., y possesses the given property).

$M4$. *The axiom of foundation.* Given any predicate $H(x)$ of the system such that there exists some $x, H(x)$. Then there exists some set x such that $H(x)$ and that, for no set y belonging to $x, H(y)$.

$M5$. *The axiom of replacement.* If the range of a one-to-one correspondence is a set, the domain is also represented by a set; in other

1) For a more exact discussion of the notion of translation, cf. Wang [14].

2) It is more customary to use in place of $M2$ the weaker axiom of pairing. But it is more convenient to use $M2$ for our purpose.

As we know, we can either use identity as basic and assume ordinary theory of identity, or define $x=y$ as meaning that x and y have the same members and derive the theory of identity from the alternative formulations of $M2$ given below. Whenever convenient, we shall assume that identity is defined in terms of the membership relation. This sometimes simplifies a little certain considerations about systems of set theory.

words, if any predicate $U(x, y)$ of the system determines a one-to-one correspondence and the collection of all sets x such that there exists some $y, U(x, y)$ forms a set, then so does also the collection of all sets y such that there exists some $x, U(x, y)$.

M6. The axiom of sum set. Given a set x, there exists a set y which is the sum of all the elements of x.

M7. The axiom of power set. Given a set x, there exists a set y which consists of all the subsets of x.

M8. The axiom of choice. Given a set x of mutually exclusive non-empty sets y, there exists a set z which contains exactly one element in common with each set y in x.

Let us refer to the system determined by $M1$—$M3$ as G, and the system determined by $M1$—$M8$ as G'. In terms of the systems G and G', the known relations between number theory Z and general set theory can be stated more precisely.

In the first place, we know from investigations by Zermelo, Grelling, and others[1)] that number theory is translatable into G and therefore ipso facto translatable into G'. In other words, with suitable definitions for the number zero 0, the successor Sx of x, the predicate of being a natural number, addition, and multiplication, all axioms of Z are derivable in G and G'.

On the other hand, Ackermann has proved[2)] that G' (and therefore also G) is translatable into number theory. Thus, G' and G have in common a simple model consisting of all the finite sets $e, \{e\}, \{\{e\}\}, \{e, \{e\}\}, \{e, \{e\}, \{\{e\}\}\}$, and so on, obtained from the empty set e by iterated applications (any finite number of times) of the axiom $M2$. We can also represent these sets one-to-one by natural numbers. The natural number zero 0 for the empty set e, $2^{a_1} + 2^{a_2} + \cdots + 2^{a_k} (a_1 > a_2 > \cdots > a_k \geqslant 0)$ for the set consisting of the k sets which are represented respectively by the numbers $a_1, \cdots, a_k$. With these representations the m-th set belongs to the n-th if and only if the quotient of dividing n by 2^m is odd, no matter whether there is any remainder. If we say that $m \in^* n$ if and only if the quotient of dividing n by 2^m is odd, then $\in^*$ is obviously a predicate definable in number theory. Ackermann's result is that if we replace the predicate $x \in y$ in all the axioms of G' by the predicate $m \in^* n$ then the results all are theorems of number theory.

1.1. Let $\in^*$ be the predicate of natural numbers such that $m \in^* n$

1) See Zermelo [16], Grelling [6], and Bernays [3].

2) See Ackermann [1]. His system does not include $M2$, $M4$, or $M5$. But it presents no special difficulty if we add these axioms (in connection with $M5$, cf. Péter [1]).

when and only when the quotient of dividing n by 2^m is odd, no matter whether there is a remainder.

These results taken together lead to certain quite interesting conclusions. Thus, since G contains both number theory and the finite sets built up from the empty set, it turns out to be possible to express in G itself the correspondence between the sets and the natural numbers. Such a correlation further leads to some axiom of limitation (Beschränktheitsaxiom, cf. Fraenkel [4] and von Neumann [9]) which, when added to G, renders the system complete in a certain sense.

In Ackermann's representation of the finite sets, there exists for each $n (n>0)$ at least one number m such that $m<n$ and the n-th set is obtained from the m-th by adding exactly one more member. In other words, for every positive n, there exist m and k, such that $n=m+2^k$ and the quotient of dividing m by 2^k is even (i. e., the k-th set does not belong to the m-th).

1.2. Let $a(n)$ $(n>0)$ be the smallest m such that there exists a number k, $n=m+2^k$ and the quotient of dividing m by 2^k is even.

1.3. Let $b(n)$ $(n>0)$ be the number k such that $n=a(n)+2^k$.

Using these notions, we can enumerate in G all the sets of the model for G and G' by a predicate E such that $E(e, 0)$ (or $E(0)$ is the empty set e) and $E(n)$ $(n>0)$ is the set $E(a(n))+\{E(b(n))\}$ obtained from $E(a(n))$ by adjoining $E(b(n))$ as a single additional member. To find this predicate E, we need only the usual technique of converting recursive definitions into explicit ones (cf. Bernays [3], p. 13).

Both for later use and for illustrating how in general recursive functions can be defined in G, we describe here some of the details for defining E.

As usual, the ordered pair $\langle x, y\rangle$ of x and y is the set $\{\{x\}, \{x, y\}\}$, a (dyadic) relational set is a set of ordered pairs, a functional set is a one-many relation, and the domain of a functional set y is the set of all z such that there exists some w, $\langle w, z\rangle$ belongs to y.

1.4. Let $E(x, m)$ stand for the following: $\langle x, m\rangle$ belongs to a functional set y with the successor Sm of m (which by the definition adopted is the set of all natural numbers $\leqslant m$) as domain such that $y(0)$ is e and for every positive $n (n \leqslant m)$, $y(n)$ is $y(a(n))+\{y(b(n))\}$.

By known method (see Bernays [3]), we can then prove in G that for every m, there exists an x, $E(x, m)$ and that for any x, y, m, if $E(x, m)$ and $E(y, m)$, then $x=y$. We can therefore write $x=E(m)$ in place of $E(x, m)$ and think of E as defining a function.

The system G contains the ordinary forms of induction principle with respect to all properties expressible in G:

1.5. For every property expressible (say, by $H(x)$) in G, if $H(0)$, and for all $n, H(n)$ implies $H(Sn)$, then for all natural numbers $m, H(m)$.

1.6. If $H(0)$ and if $H(m)$ provided, for all n smaller than m, $H(n)$: then, for all $m, H(m)$; in other words, if a property is possessed by 0, and by an arbitrary n if it is possessed by all smaller numbers, then it is possessed by all natural numbers.

Using these principles and the notions introduced under 1.1—1.4, we can prove in G quite easily the following theorems:

1.7. For no $j, j \in {}^*0$.

1.8. $E(0)$ is the empty set e.

1.9. For every positive k and for every $m, m \in {}^*k$ if and only if either $m \in {}^*a(k)$ or m is $b(k)$.

1.10. For every positive $n, E(n) = E(a(n)) + \{E(b(n))\}$.

1.11. For all positive m and $n, m = n$ if and only if $a(m) = a(n)$ and $b(m) = b(n)$.

1.12. For all positive m and n, $E(m) = E(n)$ if and only if $E(a(m)) = E(a(n))$ and $E(b(m)) = E(b(n))$.

1.13. For all m and $n, E(m) = E(n)$ if and only if $m = n$.

Proof. As we noted before, if $E(x, m)$ and $E(y, m)$, then $x = y$. Therefore, if $m = n, E(m) = E(n)$. Therefore, we have to prove merely that if $E(m) = E(n)$, then $m = n$. This we prove by induction. By 1.10, if $k > 0, E(k)$ contains at least one member $E(b(k))$. Hence, $E(k)$ is the empty set e when and only when $k = 0$. Therefore, 1.13 is true when either m or n is 0. Let m be an arbitrary positive integer and assume that (1) "$E(m) = E(n)$ implies $m = n$" is true for all values of n smaller than j. We want to show that it is also true when $n = j$. Suppose that $E(m) = E(j)$. Then, by 1.12, $E(a(m)) = E(a(j))$ and $E(b(m)) = E(b(j))$. By induction hypothesis, since $a(j) < j, b(j) < j$, (1) is true when $n = a(j)$ or $n = b(j)$. Therefore, $a(m) = a(j)$ and $b(m) = b(j)$. Hence, by 1.11, (1) is true when $n = j$. By induction, (1) is proved. Therefore, 1.13 is proved.

We can also prove in G:

Theorem 1. *For all m and n, $E(m) \in E(n)$ if and only if $m \in {}^*n$.*

Proof. We make induction on n. If $n = 0$, theorem is true by 1.7 and 1.8. Assume theorem is true for all $n < j$. Since $a(j) < j$, we have: for all $m, E(m) \in E(a(j))$ if and only if $m \in {}^*a(j)$. By 1.13, $E(m)$ is $E(b(j))$ if and only if m is $b(j)$. Hence, by 1.9 and 1.10, $E(m) \in E(j)$ if and only if $m \in {}^*j$. Hence, by 1.6, theorem is proved.

From Theorem 1 and Ackermann's result mentioned above, we have:

1.14. If we replace the predicate $x \in y$ by the predicate $E(m) \in E(n)$ in all the axioms of G', the results all are theorems of G.

Next let us consider an axiom of limitation for G and G' which restricts the sets to those which are enumerated by E:

ALG. For every x, there exists an m, $x = E(m)$.

It is easy to see that ALG is independent of the axioms of G and G' since, for example, the axioms of G and G' do not preclude infinite sets while ALG does.

1.15. ALG is independent of the axioms of G and G', if the system obtained from G by adding an axiom of infinity is consistent.

Proof. Obviously $E(0)$ is not an infinite set. Assume that for each n smaller than j, $E(n)$ is a finite set. Since $a(j)$ is smaller than j, $E(a(j))$ is therefore finite. But $E(j)$ contains only one more member than $E(a(j))$. Hence, $E(j)$ is also finite. By induction, for every k, $E(k)$ is a finite set. Hence, ALG contradicts axioms of infinity and is independent of the axioms of G and G'.

We proceed to consider the system obtained from G by adding ALG.

1.16. Let G^* be the system obtained from G by adding ALG as a new axiom.

1.17. Let us agree: $L(x)$ or x is limited if and only if there exists some natural number m such that x is $E(m)$.

1.18. Let the L-translation of an arbitrary statement of G and G' be the result obtained by restricting the range of the variables to the limited sets: in other words, the L-translation of a statement is the result obtained by substituting" for all x, if $L(x)$, then $H(x)$" for each clause "for all x, $H(x)$", and "for some x, $L(x)$ and $H(x)$" for each clause "for some x, $H(x)$".

Using these notions, we can prove:

1.19. We can prove in G and G^*: The L-translation of a statement of G holds if and only if the result obtained from it by substituting throughout the predicate $E(m) \in E(n)$ for $x \in y$ holds.

Proof. By 1.17 and ordinary laws of logic, "for all x, if $L(x)$, then $H(x)$" is equivalent to "for all m and x, if x is $E(m)$, then $H(x)$". Moreover, "for all m and x, if x is $E(m)$ then $H(x)$" is clearly equivalent to "for all m, $H(E(m))$". Therefore, "for all m, $H(E(m))$" is equivalent to the L-translation of "for all x, $H(x)$". Similarly, we can prove that "for some $k, H(E(k))$" is equivalent to the L-translation of "for some $y, H(y)$". Therefore, 1.19 is proved.

1.20. A statement is provable in G^* if and only if its L-translation is provable in G^*.

Proof. On account of *ALG*, "for all $x, H(x)$" is equivalent to "for all x, if $L(x)$ then $H(x)$" in G^*, and "for some $x, H(x)$" is equivalent to "for some $x, L(x)$ and $H(x)$". Hence, 1.20 is proved.

In the proofs 1.19 and 1.20, if we think of the original statement as given in prenex normal form (i. e. in such a form that all the phrases "for all x", "for some y", and the like, stand at the beginning and their ranges all extend to the end of the statement), then we can see even more directly that the proofs are right.

From 1.14, 1.19, and 1.20, it follows immediately:

Theorem 2. *The axioms M4—M8 of G' all are theorems of G^*.*

To express more exactly the close connection between G^* and number theory, we introduce the notion of categoricity relative to number theory:

Definition 1. *A system in which number theory is derivable is said to be categorical relative to number theory if and only if any two models for the system are isomorphic whenever their parts for the number theory in the system are isomorphic*[1].

This definition can be made clearer by the example of G^*.

Theorem 3. *The system G^* is categorical relative to number theory.*

Proof. Consider two models for G^* which are isomorphic with regard to the number theory of G^*. In other words, there is a one-one correspondence between the objects representing the natural numbers in the two models and that each statement of G^* involving only variables and notions of number theory is either true in both models or false in both. By *ALG* and 1.13, there is a one-one correspondence between the natural numbers and all the sets of G^*. Hence, there is a one-one correspondence between all the objects in the two models. Moreover, by 1.20, 1.19, and Theorem 1, for every statement p of G^* there is a demonstrably equivalent statement p' obtained from p by substituting throughout the predicate $m \in^* n$ for the predicate $x \in y$.

1) The number theory in a system is the part of the system which contains merely notions answering to those of Z. Thus, a statement which involves both notions of number theory and notions not in number theory is not considered as a statement of the number theory of the system. While any statement p of the system is clearly equivalent to some statement of the mixed type (for example, "p and $0=0$"), it is not always obvious whether every statement of some specific system is equivalent to one of its number theory.

Since all theorems of G^* must be true in models for G^*, "p if and only if p'" must be true in both models for G^*. But in every case p' is a statement of number theory and is by hypothesis either true in both models or false in both. Since p' must have the same truth value as p, p is also either true in both models or false in both. Hence, the two models are isomorphic, as was to be proved.

As we know, Gödel's incompleteness theorem also applies to the system G^*. Hence, there are undecidable number-theoretic statements in G^*, and it is possible to find some model for G^* in which a given undecidable statement is true and also some other in which the same statement is false. Theorem 3 does not contradict this fact but merely shows that once we *assume* for a model of G^* a definite assignment of truth values to all the undecidable number-theoretic statements of G^*, then the truth values of all the statements of G^*, are uniquely determined.

Indeed, 1.20, 1.19, and Theorem 1 taken together also show that if we complete the number theory in G^* by some non-constructive rule of inference, the system G^* itself also becomes completed. Thus, as we know, number theory can be made complete by adding the following rule of infinite induction[1]:

1.21. Given any predicate H of number theory, if $H(0), H(1), H(2), \cdots$ are all theorems, then "for all $m, H(m)$" is also a theorem.

Hence, if we add 1.21 to G^*, we obtain a complete system in which each statement is either provable or refutable. This is worth remarking, because the addition of 1.21 is not sufficient to render certain strong systems complete (see Rosser [11]).

Next we ask the problem whether ALG is consistent with the axioms of G. In one sense, the answer is direct since the simple model for G and G' described above also satisfies ALG and is therefore also a model for G^*. On the other hand, we can also prove, not so directly, the relative consistency of G^* to G in a sharper sense. We can prove that G^* is translatable into G and therefore if there

---

1) This assertion becomes obvious, if we reflect that all true statements containing no variables are provable in number theory and 1.21 gives us all the true statements of number theory, as determined by the truth definition in Hilbert-Bernays (cf. [8], p. 333).

With regard to the rule of infinite induction, there are the following two different ways of construing it. On the one hand, the rule may be construed as a part of, so to speak, a metamathematical definition of the system of "true" number-theoretic statements (in classical sense), expressing a property of closure. On the other hand, the rule may also be construed as one for derivation, which differs from the usual rules of derivation in that it requires admission of proof schemata as generating proofs. It is by the first interpretation of infinite induction that number theory becomes complete and ω-complete by the addition of 1.21. If we had adopted the second interpretation, it could only be said that there is, after addition of the infinite induction, no *demonstrable* ω-incompleteness because any general argument for proving, say, that $H(0)$, $H(1)$, $H(2), \ldots$ are all provable would also yield, by infinite induction, a proof for "for all m, $H(m)$".

were any contradiction in G^*, we could effectively determine a related contradiction in G. (For a general discussion of this notion of translation, cf. Wang [14].)

Theorem 4. *The system G^* is translatable into G.*

Proof. It is sufficient to prove that the L-translations of all axioms of G^* are provable in G. By 1.19 and 1.14, the L-translations of $M1$—$M3$ are all provable in G. Hence, the only problem is to prove that the L-translation of ALG is also provable in G.

More explicitly, if Nn is the predicate of being a natural number as defined in G, the problem is to prove:

1.22. The L-translation of the statement "for all x, there exists a set y such that $Nn(y)$ and x is $E(y)$" is a theorem of G.

In other words, let $Nn^*(y)$ be the L-translation of the sentence $Nn(y)$ of G and $y=E^*(x)$ be the L-translation of the sentence $y=E(x)$, then the problem is to prove:

1.23. For all x, if $L(x)$, then there exists a set y, such that $L(y)$ and $Nn^*(y)$ and $x=E^*(y)$.

The proof of this consists of four steps:

(i) For all y, if $Nn(y)$, then $L(y)$.

(ii) For all x, if $Nn(x)$, then $Nn^*(x)$.

(iii) For all x and m, if $L(x)$ and $x=E(m)$, then $x=E^*(m)$.

(iv) For all x, if $L(x)$, then there is some y such that $Nn(y)$ and $x=E(y)$.

Thus, from (iv) and (iii), for all x, if $L(x)$ then there is some y such that $Nn(y)$ and $x=E^*(y)$. Therefore, by (i) and (ii), we have 1.23. Hence, given (i)—(iv), 1.23, 1.22, and Theorem 4 can all be proved.

Before sketching the proofs of (i)—(iv), we insert a remark of explanation. The axiom ALG is of the same kind as the axiom IV 2 of von Neumann [10] and the statement $V=L$ of Gödel [5]. The proof of the translatability of G^* into G also follows the pattern of their proofs for the consistency of their statements. But of course our statement and proof are concerned with a much more elementary system. Accordingly, the considerations are much simpler.

The proofs for (i)—(iv) can be carried out in the same manner as the proofs of "absoluteness" in Gödel [5].

In order to prove (i) and (ii), we have to review first the definition of the predicate Nn adopted in G. Thus, if we use $y \neq y$ as $H(y)$ in $M3$, then we can prove that there exists the empty set e such that for no x, does x belong to e. This set e is identified with the number zero 0. By $M2$, there exists for every set x also the set $x+\{x\}$ obtained from x by adjoining x itself as an additional number. The set $x+\{x\}$ is taken as the successor Sx of the set x. The chief difficult step is to find the predicate Nn which would single out exactly those sets occuring in the sequence 0, $S0$, $SS0$, etc. (i. e., in the sequence e, $\{e\}$, $\{e\}+\{\{e\}\}$, etc.)

The predicate Nn is defined thus. For every set x, $Nn(x)$ if and only if the following four conditions are all satisfied: (1) x is transitive, or, for all y and z, if y belongs to z and z belongs to x, then y belongs to x; (2) for any two distinct members y and z of x, either y belongs to z or z belongs to y; if y is either x or a member of x, then y is either 0 or the successor Sz of some set z; (4) for every non-empty subset y of x, there belongs to y a set z which has no common member with y.

We prove (i) by induction. If y is 0, obviously we have: if $Nn(y)$, then $L(y)$. Assume now we have, for some x, $Nn(x)$ that $L(x)$ and x is $E(k)$. Then, Sx is, by the definition of successor, just $E(k+2^k)$ and therefore, $L(Sx)$. Hence, (i) is proved.

The proof of (iv) is direct from 1.17.

Using the predicate Nn just described, we can carry out the proof of (ii) in G. Thus, conditions (1) and (2) are immediate, because anything true of all sets is also true of all limited sets. The L-translation of condition (3) can also be proved because, by definition of the successor function, z is limited if Sz is. The L-translation of condition (4) also holds because we can prove by induction that if $L(y)$ and z belongs to y, then $L(z)$, and therefore, for every limited non-empty subset y of x, the member z of y having no common member with y, is also a limited set.

We omit the complex but not specially difficult details of the proof of (iii). For example, it would be necessary to handle explicit definitions of $a(n)$ and $b(n)$ in G. We merely observe that in order to prove that $x=E^*(m)$ or that $E^*(x, m)$, we use instead of the functional set y in the definition 1.4, the set consisting of members z of y such that $L(z)$.

§2. Predicative Set Theory

The systems G, G', and G^* considered above have one common characteristic: in each of them only finite sets (i. e., sets with finitely many members) can be proved to exist, none of them includes any axiom to assure the existence of any infinite set. Nevertheless, there are altogether infinitely many sets and there are properties expressible in the system which are true of infinitely many sets. These properties define infinite collections. For example, the property of being self-identical defines an infinite collection of sets. So does also the predicate Nn. If we introduce variables which range over not only the sets of general set theory but also all the collections (or manifolds) definable by predicates of the systems G, G', and G^*, we obtain the predicative set theory which is more or less the system developed by von Neumann and Bernays (see [9], [2], [3]), with the axiom of infinity excluded.

To be specific, we consider first a system P' corresponding to G'. This is just the system of Bernays (see [2], [3]) minus its axiom of infinity. It contains, besides the predicate ϵ and the variables of general set theory, variables $X, Y, \cdots$ ranging over all collections definable in G', and a predicate η between sets and collections so that $x \eta Y$, $y \eta Y$, and the like, are meaningful symbolic combinations of P'. It contains also predicate calculus with identity, for both kinds of variables.

The axioms of P' are roughly those of G' plus a few axioms specifying the ways of forming collections. We can number them as *N*1—*N*10. *N*1, *N*2, and *N*6—*N*8 are exactly the same as *M*1, *M*2, and *M*6—*M*8. *N*3—*N*5 correspond to *M*3—*M*5 but are stated somewhat differently, on account of the presence of the new variables:

*N*3. Given a set y and a collection X, the collection of all sets belonging to both y and X is again a set.

*N*4. Given a non-empty collection X, there exists some set in X which has no common member with X.

*N*5. If X is a collection of ordered pairs $<x, y>$ such that no two pairs have either the same first member or the same second member, and the collection of all the first members is a set, then the collection of all the second members is also a set.

*N*9 and *N*10 refer to general properties of the collections. *N*9 is just a subsidiary axiom of extensionality for sets saying that, for all collections Y, if two sets x and y have the same members and $x \eta Y$, then $y \eta Y$. *N*10 is more complex but amounts to saying that every predicate of G' defines a collection in P':

*N*10. If $H(x)$ is a predicate of P' containing no bound large variables (i. e., containing no phrases such as "for all X", "for some Z", $\cdots$; or involving no reference to the totality of all collections), then there exists a collection Y which contains all and only those sets x for which $H(x)$.

One important thing about *N*10 which we shall use is the reducibility of it to a few specific cases. In P', and indeed using only

$N1$—$N3$ and $N9$, we can derive $N10$ from the following special cases of it (cf. Bernays [2] and Gödel [5]):

$N10.1$. Every set is a collection.

$N10.2$. There exists a collection X of all the ordered pairs $\langle x, y\rangle$ such that x belongs to y.

$N10.3$. Given two collections X and Z, there exists a collection Y which contains all and only those sets belonging to both X and Z (intersection).

$N10.4$. Given any collection X, there exists a collection Y which contains all and only those sets not belonging to X (complement).

$N10.5$. Given a collection X of ordered pairs $\langle x, y\rangle$, there exists a collection Y containing all and only the sets such that, for some x, $< x, y >$ belongs to X.

$N10.6$. Given a collection X of sets y, there exists a collection Y of all and only the ordered pairs $\langle x, y\rangle$ such that y belongs to X.

$N10.7$. Given a collection X of ordered triples $\langle x, y, z\rangle$ (viz., $\langle x, \langle y, z\rangle\rangle$), there exists a collection Y of all and only the triples $\langle y, z, x\rangle$ where $\langle x, y, z\rangle$ belongs to X.

$N10.8$. Given a collection X of ordered triples $\langle x, y, z\rangle$, there exists also a collection Z of all and only the ordered triples $\langle y, x, z\rangle$ where $\langle x, y, z\rangle$ belongs to X.

Of these eight axioms, the first two express unconditionally that certain collections exists, while each of the rest states that given certain collection or collections there exists another related to the given in a definite and specific manner. Moreover, in none of the conditions for introducing new collections do we refer to the totality of all collections. Consequently, we can enumerate quite easily all the collections whose existence are required by the axioms, and obtain a fairly simple denumerable model for the system P'.

To describe the model in more precise terms, we proceed to introduce predicates of natural numbers which will serve as models for the predicates ϵ and η. Since the sets of P' are the same as those of general set theory, the model for ϵ is just the arithmetic predicate ϵ^* used above. The model for η is a predicate η^* which can be described in the following manner.

We can represent the collections in P' by the following sequence of triads of natural numbers: $(0,0,0), (1,0,0), \cdots, (7,0,0), (0,0,1), \cdots, (7,0,1), (0,1,0), \cdots, (7,1,0), (0,1,1)$, and so on. Thus, for any m and n, the triad $(0, m, n)$ represents $E(m)$ or the set correlated to m by the enumeration of 1.4. For any m and n, $(1, m, n)$ represents the collection of ordered pairs required by *N*10.2. For any m and n, $(2, m, n)$ represents the collection which is the intersection (cf. *N*10.3) of the two collections represented respectively by the m-th and n-th triads in the above sequence. Similarly, for any m and n, $(3, m, n)$ represents the complement of the collection represented by the m-th triad. And so on. (Compare Gödel [5] and Wang [13].) Then the predicate η^* is roughly: $m \eta^* n$ if and only if the set represented by m (viz. the set $E(m)$) belongs to the collection represented by the n-th triad.

As we know, ordinary recursive or computable functions can all be defined explicitly in the system Z of number theory. In particular, the following simple functions of natural numbers are definable. (See Hilbert-Bernays [7], §7.) We can enumerate all the dyads (0,0), (0,1), (1,0), (1,1), (0,2), (2,0), (1,2), (2,1), (2,2), (0,3), $\cdots$ and define:

2.1. A function $\sigma(m, n)$ such that $\sigma(m, n)$ is k if and only if the dyad (m, n) is the k-th ($k=0, 1, 2, \cdots$) in the sequence.

2.2. Two functions $\sigma_1(k)$ and $\sigma_2(k)$ such that $(\sigma_1(k), \sigma_2(k))$ is the k-th dyad.

Other definable functions, which we shall use, are:

2.3. A function $\beta(n)$ which takes the values 1 and 0 according as n is 0 or not.

2.4. A function $\alpha(m, n)$ which takes the values 0 and 1 according as $m=n$ or not.

2.5. A function $m \dot{-} n$ which is 0 when $m<n$ and is $m-n$ otherwise.

2.6. A function $\varrho(m, n)$ which gives the remainder of dividing m by n.

2.7. A function $\pi(m, n)$ which gives the quotient of dividing m by n.

2.8. If (m, n, k) is the j-th triad in the enumeration given above, then $\tau(m, n, k) = j$: $\tau(m, n, k) = 8\,\sigma(n, k) + \varrho(m, 8)$. If $m > 7$, we identify (m, n, k) with $(\varrho(m, 8), n, k)$.

2.9. If $\tau(m, n, k)=j$, then $\tau_1(j)=m$, $\tau_2(j)=n$, $\tau_3(j)=k$: $\tau_1(j)= \varrho(j, 8)$; $\tau_2(j)=\sigma_1(\pi(j, 8))$; $\tau_3(j)=\sigma_2(\pi(j, 8))$.

2.10. If $E(m)$ is x and $E(n)$ is y, then $E(\gamma(m, n))$ is $\langle x, y\rangle$: $\gamma(m, n)=2^{(2^m)}+(\alpha(m, n)\cdot 2^{(2^m+2^n)})$. $\gamma(m, n, k)=\gamma(m, \gamma(n, k))$.

2.11. Dy(m) if and only if $E(m)$ is an ordered pair (i.e., there exist n and k such that $m=\gamma(n, k)$). Tri(m) if and only if there exist j, n, k such that $m=\gamma(j, n, k)$.

2.12. When k is positive, $\mu(k)$ is the greatest number j such that k is divisible by 2^j, and $\mu(0)=0$.

2.13. If $E(m), E(n), E(k)$ are x, y, z respectively and z is $\langle x, y\rangle$, then $\gamma_1(k)$ is m, $\gamma_2(k)$ is n (k being $2^{(2^m)}$ when $m=n$, and $2^{(2^m)}(1+2^{(2^n)})$ otherwise):

$$\gamma_1(k) = \mu(\mu(k)).$$

$$\gamma_2(k) = \mu(\mu(\pi(k, 2^{(2^{\gamma_1(k)})}) \dot{-} 1)) + (\gamma_1(k) \cdot \beta(k \dot{-} 2^{(2^{\gamma_1(k)})})).$$

2.14. If $E(k)$ is $\langle x, y, z\rangle$ then $E(\kappa_1(k))$ is $\langle y, z, x\rangle$ and $E(\kappa_2(k))$ is $\langle y, x, z\rangle$:

$$\kappa_1(k) = \gamma(\gamma_1(\gamma_2(k)), \gamma_2(\gamma_2(k)), \gamma_1(k)).$$

$$\kappa_2(k) = \gamma(\gamma_1(\gamma_2(k)), \gamma_1(k), \gamma_2(\gamma_2(k))).$$

2.15. $Cr(m)$ if and only if $E(m)$ is a pair $\langle x, y\rangle$ such that x belongs to y; in other words, $Cr(m)$ if and only if there exist n and k such that $m=\gamma(n, k)$ and $n \in^* k$.

With these predicates and functions, we can finally describe more exactly the predicate $m\, \eta^* n$ or $\eta^*(m, n)$.

2.16. $\eta^*(m, n)$ if and only if one of the following conditions is satisfied:

(1) $\tau_1(n)=0$ and $m \in^* \tau_2(n)$;
(2) $\tau_1(n)=1$ and $Cr(m)$;
(3) $\tau_1(n)=2$, $\eta^*(m, \tau_2(n))$, and $\eta^*(m, \tau_3(n))$;
(4) $\tau_1(n)=3$ and it is not the case that $\eta^*(m, \tau_2(n))$;
(5) $\tau_1(n)=5$, $\mathrm{Dy}(m)$, and $\eta^*(\gamma_2(m), \tau_2(n))$;
(6) $\tau_1(n)=6$, $\mathrm{Tri}(m)$, and $\eta^*(\kappa_1(m), \tau_2(n))$;
(7) $\tau_1(n)=7$, $\mathrm{Tri}(m)$, and $\eta^*(\kappa_2(m), \tau_2(n))$;
(8) $\tau_1(n)=4$, and there exists a number k, such that $\eta^*(\gamma(k, m), \tau_2(n))$.

It is possible to convince ourselves that if it were not for the alternative (8), we could decide effectively for any given m and n whether $\eta^*(m, n)$ or not. The condition (8) has a non-effective character because in this case in order to decide effectively whether $\eta^*(m, n)$ or not, we would have to perform first the impossible task of checking for the infinitely many numbers k whether $\eta^*(\gamma(k, m), \tau_2(n))$. Hence, it seems reasonable to conjecture that η^* is not a recursive (or effectively calculable) predicate. Indeed, we shall soon prove that η^* cannot be recursive.

2.17. Let us call the η^*-translation of a statement p of P' the result obtained by substituting in p, the predicates $m \in^* n$, and $m\, \eta^* n^*$ (where n^* is the smallest k such that for all j, $j\, \eta^* n$ if and only if $j\, \eta^* k$) respectively for $x \in y$, and $x\, \eta\, Y$.

We note that if we extend the system Z of number theory by adding η^* as a new primitive predicate and 2.16 as a new axiom, then the η^*-translations of all theorems of P' are provable in the resulting system.

Theorem 5. *The η^*-translations of all theorems of P' are provable in the system obtained from Z by adding η^* and 2.16.*

Proof. As we have remarked above, it is known that G' is translatable into number theory when we replace $x \in y$ by $m \in^* n$. Therefore, translations of the axioms $N1$, $N2$, and $N6$—$N8$, which contain only symbols of G', are provable in Z and therefore also provable in the strengthened system.

The translations of $N3$—$N5$ can be proved by induction, since by adding η^* as a primitive we are also allowing the application of induction on sentences containing η^*. For instance, the translation of $N3$ is:

$N3^*$. For all j and m, there is some n such that for all k, $k \in^* n$ if and only if $k \in^* j$ and $k \eta^* m^*$.

To prove $N3^*$, we make induction on j. If j is 0, n is 0, no matter what m is. Assume $N3^*$ true for all $j<i$. In particular $N3^*$ is true for $j=a(i)$. Let an arbitrary m be given. Suppose that the value of n for $a(i)$ is n_1. Either $b(i)\eta^* m^*$ or not. If $b(i)\eta^* m^*$, then $N3^*$ is true if we take $n_1+2^{b(i)}$ as n; otherwise, $N3^*$ is true if we take n_1 as n.

The translation of $N9$ can be proved by the definition of j^* which is the smallest k such that for all m, $m\eta^* j$ if and only if $m\,\eta^* k$.

The translations of $N10.1$—$N10.8$ follow immediately from 2.16.

Hence, Theorem 5 is proved.

We turn now to the question whether η^* is recursive:

Theorem 6. *The predicate η^* is not recursive.*

Proof. We know that the system Z of number theory is translatable into G. Hence, given any statement p of Z, there is a corresponding statement p' in P' which contains no large variables (viz. the variables $X, Y, \cdots$ ranging over collections in general) such that p and p' are either both true or both false. We can assume without loss of generality that p' is either of the form "for some $y, H(y)$" or of the form "for all $y, F(y)$", where $H(y)$ and $F(y)$ again contain no large variables. From the derivation of $N10$ from $N10.1$—$N10.8$ (see Bernays [2], p. 72, or Gödel [5], p. 8) and our representation of collections by natural numbers, we see that for any given $H(y)$ and $F(y)$, we can find effectively definite numbers m_1 and n_1 such that the collection of ordered pairs $\langle x, y\rangle$ satisfying "$H(y)$ and $x=x$" is represented by the m_1-th triad, and the collection of ordered pairs $\langle x, y\rangle$ satisfying "$F(y)$ and $x=x$" is represented by the n_1-th triad. It then follows that we can also find effectively two definite numbers m_2 and n_2 so that the collection of sets x satisfying "for some $y, H(y)$ and $x=x$" is represented by the m_2-th triad, and the collection of sets x satisfying "for all $y, F(y)$ and $x=x$" is represented by the n_2-th triad. Hence, for instance, the empty set e belongs to the m_2-th collection of P' if and only if for some $y, H(y)$ and $e=e$. Therefore, e belongs to the m_2-th collection if and only if for some $y, H(y)$. Similarly, e belongs to the n_2-th collection if and only if for all $y, F(y)$.

Hence, in each case, given any statement p of Z and therewith its translation p', we can find a definite numeral k_1 such that e belongs to the k_1-th collection if and only if p'. In other words, since e is $E(0)$, $0\ \eta^* k_1$ if and only if p'. Consequently, for each statement p of Z, we can find effectively a corresponding natural number n such that p is true if and only if $0\ \eta^* n$ is true.

But if η^* were recursive, we would have an effective way of deciding, for each given n, whether $0\ \eta^* n$ holds or not. Hence, we would have a decision method for telling whether an arbitrary given statement of Z is true or false. Then we would, by taking all true statements of Z as axioms, have a complete formal system, contrary to Gödel's famous theorem on the incompletability of number theory. Hence, η^* cannot be a recursive predicate.

Therefore, Theorem 6 is proved[1)].

An open question is: can we find in Z a predicate $K(m, n)$ such that by substituting K for η^* in 2.16, the result becomes a theorem in Z? If we can, then it follows from Theorem 5 that P' is translatable into Z. On account of the similarity between 2.16 and sentences defining predicates not obtainable in Z (cf. Hilbert-Bernays [8], p. 339), it seems natural to believe that we cannot find any such predicate K for η^* in Z. However, we know no way of proving this.

As we noted, the system P' corresponds to G'. The system P corresponding to G does not contain $N4$—$N8$ but contains merely $N1$—$N3$ and $N9$—$N10$. We can prove that for many purposes, P gives us as much as P'. Of course, any model for P' is also one for P.

1) There is the following more direct proof of theorem 6. If $P(x)$ is any arithmetic predicate, then a number t of a triad can be effectively determined such that for every number m, we have $m\eta^* t$ if and only if $P(E(m))$. Therefore, if η^* were recursive, we could effectively decide for every number k (for which indeed m can be effectively determined so that $k=E(m)$) whether $P(k)$ holds. Thus every arithmetic predicate would be recursive, which by Kleene's well-known results is not the case.

I am keeping the above proof because it might be considered more elementary in so far as it does not depend on Kleene's result.

In a certain weaker sense, we can obtain η^* in P. Thus, we can find in P a predicate $K(m, n)$ such that although the result of substituting K for η^* in 2.16 is not itself provable in P, all the special cases for $K(m, 0)$, $K(m, 1)$, $K(m, 2)$, etc., are provable in P. Roughly, for an arbitrary m, we can define in P a collection which contains all and only the ordered pairs $\langle m, k\rangle$ such that $k \leqslant n$ and $\eta^*(m, k)$, and then we say that $K(m, n)$ if and only if $\langle m, n\rangle$ belongs to the n-th such collection[1)].

In discussing general set theory, we considered an arithmetic predicate ϵ^* and a predicate E providing an enumeration of the sets of the model. With regard to predicative set theory, the predicate η^* corresponds to ϵ^*. We proceed to introduce now a predicate R which corresponds to E and provides an enumeration of all the collections represented by triples of natural numbers in the preceding section.

The definition of the predicate $R(X, m)$ is somewhat similar to the definition 1.4 for $E(x, m)$. Roughly, for every X and m, $R(X, m)$ if and only if X is the m-th collection of P' (i. e., X is represented by the m-th triple of natural numbers described above). In order to define R, we define first a predicate $F(\langle x, n\rangle)$ such that $F(\langle x, n\rangle)$ when and only when x belongs to the n-th collection. More exactly, the definitions for F and R are as follows (compare Wang [13], p. 481)[2)]:

2.18. Let $H(n, Y)$ stand for the following: Y is a relation and the domain of Y is contained in Sn (i. e., $\langle x, m\rangle$ belongs to Y only if $m \leqslant n$) and for all $k \leqslant n$ and for all x, $\langle x, k\rangle\ \eta\ Y$ if and only if one of the following conditions is satisfied:

(1) $\tau_1(k)=0$ and $x \in E(\tau_2(k))$;
(2) $\tau_1(k)=1$ and x is a pair $\langle y, z\rangle$ such that $y \in z$;
(3) $\tau_1(k)=2$ and $\langle x, \tau_2(k)\rangle\ \eta\ Y$ and $\langle x, \tau_3(k)\rangle\ \eta\ Y$;
(4) $\tau_1(k)=3$ and $\langle x, \tau_2(k)\rangle$ does not belong to Y;
(5) $\tau_1(k)=4$ and there exists some y, $\langle\langle y, x\rangle, \tau_2(k)\rangle\ \eta\ Y$;
(6) $\tau_1(k)=5$ and x is a pair $\langle y, z\rangle$ and $\langle z, \tau_2(k)\rangle\ \eta\ Y$;
(7) $\tau_1(k)=6$ and x is a triple $\langle y, z, w\rangle$ and $\langle\langle z, w, y\rangle, \tau_2(k)\rangle\ \eta\ Y$;
(8) $\tau_1(k)=7$ and x is a triple $\langle y, z, w\rangle$ and $\langle\langle z, y, w\rangle, \tau_2(k)\rangle\ \eta\ Y$.

2.19. $F(\langle x, n\rangle)$ if and only if $\langle x, n\rangle$ belongs to some collection B such that $H(n, B)$.

---

1) We omit the details of the definition of K and the proofs of the cases for $K(n, 0)$, $K(n, 1)$, etc., on the following grounds: (1) details of similar definitions and proofs are treated in Wang [15] in the general case; (2) the case of R which we shall consider soon is again similar, although somewhat more complex.

2) Notice that the following definition actually combines two different things: (1) the translation of the conditions of 2.16 on the relation η^* into conditions on a collection of pairs; (2) the proof, by the Dedekind method, of the existence of a collection of pairs satisfying those conditions.

2.20. $R(X, m)$ if and only if X is the collection of all and only the sets x such that $F(\langle x, m\rangle)$.

Using these definitions, we can prove:

2.21. For each constant n, we can prove in P that for all X and Y, if $R(X, n)$ and $R(Y, n)$, then $X=Y$.

2.22. For each constant n, we can prove in P that there exists a collection R such that $R(X, n)$.

Let us write, whenever convenient, $X=R\ (m)$ in place of $R(X, m)$.

For each given number n, we can also prove that $R(n)$ has the desired properties. For example, if $\tau_1(n)=0$, we can prove in P that for all $x, x\,\eta\, R(n)$ if and only if $x \in E(\tau_2(n))$; if $\tau_1(n)=3$, we can prove in P that for all $x, x\,\eta\, R(n)$ if and only if x does not belong to $R(\tau_2(n))$; and so on.

Moreover, a comparison of 2.16 and 2.18—2.20 will convince us that the following can also be proved with the help of Theorem 2:

2.23. For each given $n (n=0, 1, 2, \cdots)$, we can prove in P that for all $m, E(m)\,\eta\, R(n)$ if and only if $m\,\eta^* n^*$.

It should be emphasized, although we can prove in P with regard to R and η^* most of the desired results for each of the constant numbers $0, 1, 2, \cdots$; there is no apparent way of proving in P the general results "for all $m, - - m - -$" in these cases (such as 2.21—2.23). The natural thing to do would be to make mathematical induction. Yet in the present connection this is not possible in P (not even in P'), because the axioms of P and P' only assure us existence of collections defined by sentences not containing bound large variables (i. e., the predicative collections defined without reference to totalities containing themselves) and therefore in P and P' we can only make induction on such collections and their defining sentences. Since we use bound large variables in defining both η^* and R in P (for example, the phrase "some collection B" in 2.19), we have in P and P' no way of making induction on sentences which involve the predicates $\eta^*(m, n)$ and $R(X, n)$. Yet in order to prove, for instance, 2.16 and general theorems corresponding to 2.21—2.23, we have to make induction on sentences involving these predicates.

In the next section, we shall discuss ways of extending the system P so as to make the general theorems derivable.

§ 3. Impredicative Collections and ω-Consistency

As we know, a system S is said to be ω-consistent, if for every predicate $H(m)$ of S, "for some m, it is not the case that $H(m)$" is a theorem of S only if some of the statements $H(0), H(1), H(2), \cdots$ is not a theorem of S. Therefore, if a system S is ω-consistent, then the system S' obtained from S by adding to theorems of S the following rule of infinite induction is consistent:

3.1. For every predicate $H(m)$ of the system S, if $H(0), H(1), \cdots$ are theorems of S, then "for all $m, H(m)$" is a theorem of S'.

Let W be the system obtained from P by adding 3.1 (replacing S and S' by P and W) as a new rule of inference. Then we can derive in W both 2.16 and, from 2.21—2.23, the following theorems:

3.2. For all X, Y, and n, if $R(X, n)$ and $R(Y, n)$, then $X=Y$.

3.3. For every n, there exists a collection $X, R(X, n)$.

3.4. For all m and $n, E(m) \eta R(n)$ if and only if $m \eta^* n^*$.

In this way, we have found an extension of P in which the desired general theorems become provable. Moreover, the consistency of W follows from the ω-consistency of P. But W is not satisfactory in one respect: the rule 3.1 involves infinitely many premises and cannot be considered a part of any ordinary formal or logistic system.

A more usual way of extending P is to introduce impredicative collections. Thus, let Q be the system obtained from P by replacing $N10$ by the stronger:

$N10'$. If $H(x)$ is *any* predicate of P, then there exists a collection Y which contains all and only those sets x for which $H(x)$.

In other words, Q uses the same symbols and notations as those of P and P' but contains as axioms $N1$—$N3$, $N9$, and $N10'$. We can develop number theory in Q in the same way as we do in P and P', but on account of $N10'$, we are now allowed to make induction on all sentences of these systems.

In particular, by formulating suitably the proofs of 2.21—2.23 and special cases of 2.16, the theorems 3.2—3.4 and 2.16 can be proved in Q by induction.

If we compare W and Q as two alternative ways of extending P to get 2.16 and 3.2—3.4, we find the following interesting phenomenon: while Q is a more formal system and therefore neater in a certain sense, it is less reliable than W because we know nothing about the consistency of Q yet we know that W is consistent since we can prove the ω-consistency of P by using a suitable intuitive model[1)].

This example gives hope to the conjecture that may be all the purposes served by impredicative classes in mathematics can be served

1) By this, we do not mean a constructive (intuitionistic) model.

by other modes of reasoning which, though formalistically more messy, are intuitively less opaque. For instance, it might be possible to prove many other theorems of Q not available in P in the system W' whose theorems include all those of P and also those derivable by the stronger rule:

3.5. For every $H(m)$ of P, if $H(0)$, $H(1)$, $H(2)$,$\cdots$ all are theorems of W', then "for all $m, H(m)$" is also a theorem of W'.

The system W' thus obtained contains many more theorems than W, but can also be seen to be consistent by using a suitable intuitive model for the system P.

So much for the conjectures.

We turn next to the connections between P and Q, and to the problem of extending P to obtain a categorical system relative to number theory.

Let us now consider the following two axioms of limitation[1]:

ALG. For all x, there is some $m, x=E(m)$.

ALP. For all X, there is some $n, X=R(n)$.

By considerations similar to those used in the proofs of 1.15 and 1.23, we can prove that *ALG* is both independent of and compatible with the axioms of P and P'.

Using impredicative collections, we can prove:

3.6. If Q is consistent, then *ALP* is independent of the axioms of P.

Proof. In Q, we can prove, by $N10'$, the existence of a collection C such that for all natural numbers $n, n \eta C$ if and only if n does not belong to $R(n)$. If for some $m, C=R(m)$, we would have: $m \eta R(m)$ if and only if m does not belong to $R(m)$. Hence, for no $m, C=R(m)$. Hence, the denial of *ALP* is provable in Q. Therefore, if Q is consistent, then the denial of *ALP* is consistent with the axioms of P. Therefore, 3.6 is proved.

Similarly, we can also prove that if Q plus the other axioms of P' is consistent, then *ALP* is independent of the axioms of P'.

Let P^* be the system obtained from P by adding *ALG* and *ALP* as additional axioms.

3.7. Let us agree: $L(X)$ or X is limited if and only if there exists some natural number m such that X is $R(m)$.

---

1) We note that in P and P', we can define a collection E of ordered pairs $\langle x, n\rangle$ such that $(x, n)\eta E$ if and only if $E(x, n)$ according to 1.4. However, we shall not emphasize the distinction between the collection E and the corresponding predicate $E(x, n)$.

3.8. Let the R-translation of an arbitrary statement of P and Q be the result obtained by restricting the range of the small variables to the limited sets and the range of the large variables to the limited collections. (Compare 1.18)[1].

Using considerations similar to those involved in the proof of 1.19, we can prove:

3.9. We can prove in P and Q: the R-translation of a statement of P and Q is true if and only if the result obtained from it by substituting throughout the predicate $E(m) \epsilon E(n)$ for $x \epsilon y$ and $E(k)$ $\eta R(j)$ for $z \eta Y$ is true.

Hence, since we can prove 3.4 and Theorem 1 in Q, we can also prove:

3.10. The R-translation of a statement of P and Q is a theorem of Q if and only if its η^*-translation is one.

Therefore, since 2.16 is provable in Q for a suitable predicate, we have, by Theorem 5:

3.11. The η^*-translations and R-translations of all theorems of P' are theorems of Q.

Next we want to prove:

Theorem 7. *The system obtained from P^* by adding the other axioms of P' is translatable into Q.*

To simplify somewhat our considerations, we divide the proof into two parts.

3.12. The L-translations (cf. 1.18)[2] of all theorems of the system Q' obtained from Q by adding ALG as a new axiom, are theorems in Q.

Proof. From the considerations in the proof of Theorem 4, the L-translations of $N1$—$N3$ and ALG are provable in Q. Moreover, the L-translations of $N9$ and $N10'$ are also theorems of Q, since the L-translation of a predicate of Q is again a predicate of Q and anything true of all sets is also true of all limited sets. For $N9$, we have to use also the fact that members of any limited set are again limited sets. Hence, 3.12 is proved.

Theorem 7 follows from 3.12 and the following assertion:

---

1) The phrase "statement of P and Q", used here and elsewhere is awkward since the statements in P and Q are the same. This can be understood to mean "statement of P" or "statement of Q" according as which fits the context better.

The L-translation of a statement of P and Q differs from its R-translation in that the large variables in an L-translation are not restricted to the limited collections. Compare also the next footnote.

2) We are assuming that in the L-translation of a statement containing also large variables, these variables remain unchanged.

3.13. The R-translations of all theorems of P^* plus P' are provable in Q'.

Proof. By 3.11, the R-translations of all axioms of P' are theorems of Q'. Moreover, the R-translation of ALG is provable in Q' by considerations similar to those used in the proof of 1.23. Hence, to prove 3.13, we need only prove that the R-translation of ALP is provable in Q'.

In other words, if the R-translations of $Nn(y)$ and $R(X, m)$ are $Nn\#(y)$ and $R\#(X, m)$, then we want to prove in Q':

3.14. For every X, if $L(X)$, then there exists a set y, such that $L(y)$, $Nn\#(y)$ and $R\#(X, y)$.

Proof. By 2.19 and 2.20, $R(X, m)$ if and only if: for every x, $x \eta X$ when and only when there exists some collection B such that $H(m, B)$ and $\langle x, m \rangle \eta B$. According to 2.18, the predicate $H(m, B)$ involves no other large variables besides B. Hence, by arguments in the proof of 1.20, since ALG is an axiom of Q', for all m and B, $H(m, B)$ is equivalent to its L-translation $H\#(m, B)$. For similar reason, $Nn(y)$ if and only if $Nn\#(y)$. Hence, using also (i) in the proof of 1.24, we need only prove: For every X, if $L(X)$, then there is an m such that for all limited sets x, x belongs to X if and only if there exists some collection B such that $L(B)$, $H(m, B)$, and $\langle x, m \rangle \eta B$. Hence, by expanding $L(X)$ according to 2.19, 2.20, and 3.7, we see that all we have to prove is: (1) For all m and B, if $H(m, B)$, then $L(B)$.

To prove this, we make induction on m. By 2.18, $H(0, A_0)$ if and only if A_0 is the empty collection e. Clearly, we can find a definite natural number m_0, such that $R(e, m_0)$. Assume (1) is true when $m = j$. More specifically, assume that A_j is the collection such that $H(j, A_j)$, and that m_j is a number for which $R(A_j, m_j)$. We can then define A_{Sj} in terms of A_j: for all x and k, $\langle x, k \rangle \eta A_{Sj}$ if and only if $k \leqslant Sj$ and one of the conditions (1)—(8) in 2.18 (with A_j replacing Y) is satisfied. Then we can prove immediately: $H(Sj, A_{Sj})$. Moreover, from the way in which A_{Sj} is defined in terms of A_j, we can also find an elementary arithmetic function f such that for every j, if A_j is $R(i)$, then A_{Sj} is $R(f(i))$. Hence, by induction, (1) is proved in Q'.

This completes the proof of 3.14, and therewith also the proof of 3.13 and Theorem 7.

From Theorem 7, we have immediately:

3.15. If Q is consistent, then the system obtained from P^* by adding the other axioms of P' is consistent.

3.16. If Q is consistent, then $N10'$ is independent of the axioms of P and P'.

Proof. If $N10'$ were provable in P', we would be able to prove in P' the existence of a collection C such that for all n, $n \eta C$ if and only if n does not belong to $R(n)$. Then, *ALP* would be refutable in P' (cf. proof of 3.6), contrary to 3.15.

With regard to the Cantor collection of all natural numbers n such that n does not belong to $R(n)$, we note the following difference between P and Q. By the Löwenheim-Skolem theorem, if Q is consistent, it must have a denumerable model and there exists the collection of all natural numbers n such that n does not belong to the n-th collection of the model. Such a collection also cannot be proved to exist in Q. Since every collection of natural numbers which is defined by a property expressible in Q can be proved (by $N10'$) to exist, the defining property of the Cantor collection must be inexpressible in Q. The Cantor collection in 3.16 is different in that it is defined by a property which is expressible in the same system. We might say that Q possesses a certain kind of completeness which P and P' lack.

The independence of $N10'$ can be seen in another way. By known methods (cf., e. g., remarks in Wang [15]), it is possible to formalize in Q a consistency proof of G. Moreover, McNaughton has recently proved[1)] a general theorem from which it follows that we can formally derive in Q the consistency of P from the consistency of G. Therefore, we have:

3.17. We can formalize in Q a consistency proof of P.

Hence, by Gödel's theorem on consistency proofs, Q must be different from P. Since $N10'$ is the only principle of Q not already in P, $N10'$ must be independent of the axioms of P.

Since *ALG* and *ALP* provide enumeration of all the sets and collections of P^*, it seems natural to ask whether P^* is categorical relative to number theory (compare Definition 1 and Theorem 3).

Suppose we make two assumptions: (1) 3.4 is provable in P^*; (2) the predicate η^* is definable in the system Z of number theory. Then we can prove, using arguments strictly analogous to those used for 1.19, 1.20, and Theorem 3, that P^* is categorical relative to number theory. But since we have no proof for either (1) or (2), the situation is more complex.

Consider (1) first. As we discussed above, 3.4 is provable in Q, and the same proof cannot be used in P or P^* because certain induction cannot be carried out. For all we know, 3.4 may be independent of the axioms of P^*.

---

1) See Robert McNaughton, *J. Symbolic Logic,* **18** (1953), 136—144.

Assumption (2) is stronger than (1). If (2) is true, then (1) is also true because the difficulty with regard to induction would no longer exist. As we remarked after Theorem 6, (2) is probably not true. In any case, we have no proof that (2) is true. If (2) is not true, η^* lies beyond the part of P^* which correspond to the system Z of number theory. Nevertheless, by 2.23, special cases of 3.4 are provable in P^*. Hence, if either (1) or (2) is false, we have, as with Gödel's undecidable statements, a case where "for all n, $H(n)$" ($H(n)$ being "for all $m, E(m)\ \eta\ R(n)$ if and only if $m\ \eta^* n^*$") is not a theorem of P^*, although $H(0), H(1), H(2), \cdots$, for the numerals $0, 1, 2, \cdots$ all are theorems of P^*. Therefore, if P^* is consistent, by adding as an axiom to P^* the denial of "for all n, $H(n)$", we have again a consistent system which is, however, ω-inconsistent. In any model for such a system, there must be an object which represents a natural number but does not correspond to any of the ordinary numerals. On account of such models, it becomes hard to see whether every statement of P^* has the same truth value in two models of P^* which provide the same interpretation for notions of number theory.

To avoid such anomalies, it is sufficient to restrict ourselves to ω-consistent models for P^*:

3.18. A model for an arbitrary system S is said to be ω-consistent, if and only if, for every predicate $H(x)$ of S, whenever it is true of all the ordinary numerals, "for all $m, H(m)$" is also true[1].

In any ω-consistent models for P^*, 3.4 is of course true[2]. If we restrict ourselves to ω-consistent models for P^*, we can prove, using arguments similar to those employed in the proof of Theorem 3, that P^* is categorical relative to number theory. Briefly, we can express this state of affairs by the following theorem:

Theorem 8. *The system P^* is categorical relative to ω-consistent number theory.*

The problem whether P^* is simply categorical relative to number theory remains open.

On the one hand, by Theorem 8, P^* possesses a certain kind of categoricity. On the other hand, by Gödel's theorem, if P^* is consistent, there are certain statements of number theory which are undecidable in P^*. It is of interest to inquire whether there are, besides these, also statements of P^* about sets and collections in general, which are undecidable in P^*.

---

1) In general, "for all m, $H(m)$" may be an abbreviation introduced by a contextual definition.

2) Incidentally, it is not hard to see that in every ω-consistent model for P^*, all the axioms of P' are true. In particular, the truth of $N4$ and $N5$ follow from the truth of their special cases and the truth of ALP.

Intuitively, a collection X exists according to P^* if and only if there is some $m, X=R(m)$. If we assume that the totality of all natural numbers is given and fixed, then the totality T of all collections X such that $L(X)$ (i. e. there exists some $m, X=R(m)$) is also fixed. Therefore, on the basis of the axioms of P^*, the existence of each collection of the limited sets (i. e. the sets x such that for some m, $x=E(m)$) is completely decided according as whether it belongs to the above totality T or not. Nevertheless, it does not follow that all statements about the existence or non-existence of collections are decidable in P^*. Although, for each X, either "X belongs to T" or "X does not belong to T" is true, it does not follow that at least one of the two is provable in P^*.

In other words, given an arbitrary collection X for which, say, $F(X)$ holds. We can prove or refute "there exists an $X, F(X)$" in P^*, *provided* we can decide in P^* whether or not there is some m, $X=R(m)$. But there is no assurance that for each X, we can decide in P^* whether or not there exists some m for which $X=R(m)$. Indeed, using Gödel's theorem, we can prove that there must be cases where we cannot decide.

Thus let p be a known undecidable statement of P^* (for example, the arithmetic statement $Con(P^*)$ expressing the consistency of P^*). Consider the following existence statement: (α) there exists a collection X such that for all $n, n\eta X$ if and only if p is false and n does not belong to $R(n)$. Then we can prove the equivalence of (α) and p in P^*: If p, then (α) holds when we take the empty collection as X. If p is false, then the denial of (α) holds because we can prove in P^* that there exists no collection X such that for all $n, n\eta X$ if and only if n does not belong to X (compare 3.16). Hence we have[1]:

3.19. The existence statement (α) is undecidable in P^*.

It follows immediately by *ALP*:

3.20. The following existence statement is also undecidable in P^*: There exists an m such that the collection X defined by (α) is $R(m)$.

There is also another kind of derivative undecidable statements in P^*. For a given predicate $H(x)$ of P^* containing no large variables, we can find a definite numeral k such that whether k belongs to the collection of sets satisfying $H(x)$, is demonstrably undecidable in P^*. Thus let us carry out in P^* an arithmetization of the syntax of P^*

1) We note that similar considerations also apply to G^*. For example, if p is a given undecidable statement, then the statement "there exists some set y such that for all x, ϵ y if and only if p is false and $x=x$" is also undecidable.

So far as we know, the general method of generating equivalent undecidable statements in the above manner was first introduced in a different connection by W. V. Quine (see *Journal of Symbolic Logic*, **6**, 140).

and define in P^* the arithmetic predicate (β) "$s(x,x)$ is not a theorem of P^*" (i.e., the predicate "the result of substituting the numeral x for the variable "x" in the expression of P^* whose Gödel number is x is not a theorem of P^*", cf. Hilbert-Bernays [8], §5. b)). The predicate is of the form $H(x)$ and contains no large variables. Therefore, by $N10$, there exists a collection Y of P^* such that for all x, $x \eta Y$ if and only if $s(x,x)$ is not a theorem of P^*. Since "$s(m,m)$ is not a theorem of P^*", where m is the Gödel number of (β), is known to be undecidable in P^* (Hilbert-Bernays, *ibid.*), the statement "m belongs to the collection Y (just described)" is also undecidable in P^*:

3.21. It is undecidable in P^* whether the set m, which is the Gödel number of the expression (β), belongs to the collection Y of P^* consisting of all sets x which satisfy the predicate (β).

Of course, in 3.21 we need, as usual, the hypothesis of the ω-consistency of P^*. We can also find similarly an undecidable statement corresponding of Rosser's (Hilbert-Bernays, *ibid.*, p. 275) and use merely the hypothesis of the consistency of P^*.

It is clear from these considerations that undecidable statements of the form "a (certain special) set belongs to a (certain special) collection" are obtainable in all set theories which are not weaker than P.

Before concluding this section[1], we make a few remarks regarding models and natural numbers.

Closely related to the ω-consistent models are the models with regular natural numbers:

3.22. A model of a system S is said to be one with regular natural numbers if the natural numbers of the models (i.e., the objects satisfying the predicate Nn being a natural number in the system) are exactly the objects corresponding to the numerals 0, 1, 2, etc.

Clearly every model with regular natural numbers is also an ω-consistent model. But the converse is not true. Indeed, it is possible that we can have an ω-consistent model in which there is a natural number not denoted by any name or description (the-expression) of the system[2]. However, we can prove a weaker relation:

3.23. A model in which every object is denoted by a term of the given system is one with regular natural numbers, if and only if it is ω-consistent.

---

1) Many of the considerations in this and the previous sections can be generalized to apply to further predicative extensions of P and P', or to systems of the ramified theory of types without the axiom of reducibility.

2) For an example, see G. Kreisel, *Math. Reviews*, **16** (1955), p. 103.

Proof Assume there were an object denoted by t which is a natural number in the model but is distinct from all the objects denoted by the numerals. Then we would have "$0 \neq t$", "$1 \neq t$", etc. all are true, but "for all $m, m \neq t$" false in the model. Therefore, we would have an ω-inconsistent model.

In terms of models with regular natural numbers, we can also express the import of *ALG* and *ALP* in the following manner.

3.24. Let us assume a sequence of standard terms of G^* and P^* one for each of all the finite sets $e, \{e\}, \{\{e\}\}, \{e, \{e\}\}$, etc. Then, in every ω-consistent model of G^* or P^*, if "for some $x, F(x)$" is true, there is some term t of the above sequence such that "for some x, $F(x)$ and $x=t$" is true.

3.25. Let us assume an enumeration of all the predicates $H(y)$ of P^* which do not contain large variables. Then, in every ω-consistent model for P^*, if "for some $X, F(X)$" is a theorem, then there is some $H_i(y)$ of the above sequence such that "for some $X, F(X)$ and for all $y, y \eta X$ if and only if $H_i(y)$" is true.

References

[1] Wilhelm Ackermann, *Math. Ann.*, **114** (1937), 305—315. Review by Rósza Péter, *Jour. Symbolic Logic*, **2** (1937), 167.

[2]—[3] Paul Bernays, *Jour. Symbolic Logic*, **2** (1937), 65—77; **6** (1941), 1—17.

[4] A. Fraenkel, Einleitung in die Mengenlehre, 3rd ed., 1928.

[5] Kurt Gödel, Consistency of the Continuum Hypothesis, Princeton, 1940.

[6] Kurt Grelling, Die Axiome der Arithmetik, Dissertation, Göttingen, 1910.

[7]—[8] D. Hilbert and P. Bernays, Grundlagen der Mathematik, vol. 1, 1934; vol. 2, 1939.

[9]—[10] J. von Neumann, *Jour. Reine Angew. Math.*, **154** (1925), 219—240; **160** (1929), 227—241.

[11] J. B. Rosser, *Jour. Symbolic Logic*, **2** (1937), 129—137.

[12] Roman Suszko, *Studia Philosophica*, **4** (1951), 301—330.

[13]—[15] Hao Wang, *Proc. Nat. Acad. Sci. U.S.A.*, **36** (1950), 479—484; *Trans. Am. Math. Soc.*, **71** (1951), 283—293; *Jour. Symbolic Logic*, **18** (1953), 49—59.

[16] E. Zermelo, *Acta Math.*, **32** (1909), 185—193.

CHAPTER XX

SOME PARTIAL SYSTEMS

§ 1. Some Formal Details on Class Axioms

This chapter is mainly devoted to a brief summary of the writer's doctoral dissertation (Harvard, 1948) which is largely concerned with giving a more economic set of axioms than Quine's book *Mathematical Logic,* and developing mathematics further than is done there. Frequent reference will be made in this chapter to the 1940 edition of Quine's book, familiarity with which is presupposed. Much of the material has been published as separate papers. The present section is from *J. Symbolic Logic,* 15 (1950), 103—110. The second section is from *ibid.,* 13 (1948), 129—137. The third section is from ibid., 15, 241—247.

This type of work had for years preoccupied people of the so-called logistic school. In recent years, with the development of mathematical logic into a more regular mathematical discipline, interests in such formal details have steadily decreased. It seems, however, that the hopeful prospect of proving mathematical theorems by machines may create a genuine need to carry out such somewhat tedious formalizations with all seriousness.

The typical representatives of this tradition seem to be Frege, Peano, Whitehead and Russell, Chwistek, Carnap, Quine, Church, the Münster group led by Scholz and Hermes, Rosser, Fitch. On the whole, mathematicians do not have much sympathy with such works.

In mathematics, when we want to introduce classes which fulfill certain conditions, we usually prove beforehand that classes fulfilling such conditions do exist, and that such classes are uniquely determined by the conditions. The statements which state such unicity and existence of classes are in mathematical logic consequences of the principles of extensionality and class existence. In order to illustrate how these principles enable us to introduce classes into systems of mathematical logic, let us consider an example.

For instance, before introducing the definition of the non-ordered pair of two classes,

1.1 *Dfn* $x \in [yz] . \equiv : (\exists u)(x \in u) : x = y . \vee . x = z,$

one puts down as its justification the following two axioms:

$A3.\quad (x)(x \in w \,.\!\equiv\!.\, x \in y) \supset .\, w = y.$

$A4.\quad (y)(z)(\exists w)(x)(x \in w \,.\!\equiv\!:\, (\exists u)(x \in u) : x = y \,.\vee.\, x = z).$

By *A4*, for every two classes y and z there exists at least one non-ordered pair w of them; and by *A3*, w is uniquely determined in *A4*.

Then, after classes have been introduced in such a manner, they are considered as falling under the range of values of the variables and we are allowed to infer that a statement is true for these classes if it is true for all values of a variable. In other words, if we call the expression corresponding to a class its *abstract*, the following principle of specification is applied tacitly:

PS. If $\vdash \ulcorner(\alpha)\phi\urcorner$, and ψ is like ϕ except for containing free occurrences of a variable or abstract ζ wherever ϕ contains free occurrences of α, then $\vdash \psi$.

Such procedure seems to involve no breach of rigor, if the notion of class is taken as primitive and the convention is made that 'x', 'y', 'z', ··· be variables whose range consists of all classes[1)].

Now, instead of the classes, let us consider their corresponding abstracts. How do we decide whether expressions such as '$[yz]$' introduced by contextual definitions such as 1.1 are abstracts (expressions denoting classes) or not? The answer which one would give seems to be that an expression η introduced by a definition

DC. $\ulcorner \alpha \in \eta \,.\!\equiv \phi \urcorner.$

is an abstract if *A3* and the closure of

EC. $\ulcorner(\exists\beta)(\alpha)(\alpha \in \beta \,.\!\equiv \phi)\urcorner$ (β not free in ϕ and distinct from α).

are each a theorem or an axiom. Thus, '$[yz]$' is an abstract, because *A3* and *A4* are axioms. If we construe the abstracts in this way, particular cases of *PS* in which ζ is an abstract are provable as metatheorems or theorems. In order to prove *PS* for a specific ζ, we seem to need, in place of *A3*, a special principle of extensionality which applies specifically to the kind of classes corresponding to ζ. But such a principle follows from the definition of identity for abstracts stated under footnote 1). For example, if ζ is '$[yz]$', we can prove *PS* for it if we assume 1.1, *A4*, and, instead of *A3*, the following

---

1) At most places, the notation in this paper will follow Quine's *Mathematical Logic* (New York, 1940), which will be referred to by the abbreviation '*ML*.'

More accurately, *Dfn* 1.1 should be supplemented with rules explaining, e.g., '$[yz] \in x$' and '$x = [yz]$' as well as '$x \in [yz]$' before one can speak of substituting an abstract for a variable α in an *arbitrary formula* ϕ. We can use rules such as

$$x = [yz] \equiv (w)(w \in x \equiv w \in [yz]),$$

$$[yz] \in x \equiv (\exists w)(w = [yz] \,.\, w \in x).$$

$A4'$. $(x)(x \in w .\equiv. x \in [yz]) \supset . w = [yz]$.

But $A4'$ is a direct consequence of the definition of identity just mentioned.

The proof of PS for '$[yz]$', which uses beyond 1.1, $A4$, and $A4'$ only elementary logic[1], runs as follows:

$A4$(and Dfn 1.1)	$(\exists w)(x)(x \in w .\equiv. x \in [yz])$	(1)
*149	$[(w)A4' \supset . 1 \supset](\exists w)(w = [yz])$	(2)
*104	$(x)fx \supset fw$	(3)
*220	$w = [yz] .\supset: [3 \equiv .](x)fx \supset f([yz])$	(4)
(4),*163	$[4 \supset .](x)fx \supset f([yz])$.	(5)

Hence, by (5) and *modus ponens* (*105), PS is proved for the case where ζ is '$[yz]$'. Evidently PS can be proved similarly for other abstracts.

In ML Quine proves a principle *231 corresponding to PS:

*231. If ψ is related to ϕ as in PS, then $\vdash \ulcorner (\alpha)\phi \supset \psi \urcorner$.

The way Quine proves *231 in ML from his $D9$, *202, and $D10$ bears some resemblance to the way we proved PS for '$\{yz\}$' from 1.1, $A4$, and $A4'$. However, Quine's course is different in several respects. In the first place, he does not introduce classes and abstracts piecemeal, but introduces all kinds of classes and abstracts by what we may call a single 'meta-definition'

$D9$. $\ulcorner(\beta \in \hat{\alpha}\phi)\urcorner$ for $\ulcorner(\exists\gamma)(\beta \in \gamma . (\alpha)(\alpha \in \gamma .\supset \phi))\urcorner$

(γ being new), according to which the definition for '$[yz]$' would be:

1.1' $Dfn\ x \in \hat{x}(x = y . \vee . x = z)$
$.\equiv (\exists u)(x \in u . (x)(x \in u .\supset: x = y . \vee . x = z))$

which is different from 1.1.

Secondly, instead of using special axioms such as $A4$ which are each concerned exclusively with a specific kind of classes, Quine adopts a general principle (a 'meta-axiom') *202 which states that for every formula '$\ldots x \ldots$' there exists a class whose members are all and only those elements

1) By 'elementary logic' I mean that portion of logic which comprises the propositional calculus, the restricted functional calculus, and the principles of substitutivity and reflexivity for identity. In what follows, I shall make use of the metatheorems and theorems of elementary logic proved in ML. Starred and daggered numerals will be employed as in ML to refer to its metatheorems and theorems. For brevity, I have used in the next proof some notations which differ from that of ML. *220 used in the next proof should be proved with a proof somewhat different from its proof in ML. We can obtain such a proof by using the theory of identity and the definition of '$w = [yz]$' as given under footnote 1) (p. 508).

x such that $\cdots x \cdots$:

*202. If β is not α and not free in ϕ, then $\vdash \ulcorner(\exists\beta)(\alpha)(\alpha \in \beta \,.\!\equiv\!.\, \alpha \in \mathrm{V} \,.\, \phi)\urcorner$.

If we replace '$\alpha \in \mathrm{V}$' by '$(\exists\gamma)\,(\alpha \in \gamma)$' ($\gamma$ distinct from α)[1] in *202, we shall have $A4$ as a particular case of it.

Thirdly, instead of taking identity as a primitive, he defines it in terms of the membership relation, thereby embodying the general principle of extensionality for all classes in the definition

$D10$. $\qquad \ulcorner(\zeta = \eta)\urcorner$ for $\ulcorner(\alpha)\,(\alpha \in \zeta \,.\!\equiv\!.\, \alpha \in \eta)\urcorner$,

where ζ and η each may be a variable or an abstract. A consequence of $D10$ corresponding to $A4'$ is:

$A4''$.
$$(x)\,(x \in w \,.\!\equiv\!.\, x \in \hat{x}(x = y \,.\, \vee \,.\, x = z)) \supset .\; w = \hat{x}(x = y \,.\, \vee \,.\, x = z).$$

Let '$\phi[\alpha, \zeta]$' be used as abbreviation for 'the expression ψ which is like ϕ' except for containing free occurrences of ζ whenever ϕ' contains free occurrences of α, ϕ' being an (arbitrarily specified) alphabetic variant of ϕ for which there exists such a ψ'. In general, there exist such alphabetic variants ϕ' of ϕ, because any one in which no variable free in ζ is bound would do. In particular, we require the specification be so made that $\phi[\alpha, \zeta]$ is ϕ when ζ is α.

Suppose now we replace $D9$ in ML by[2]

$D9'$. $\qquad \ulcorner(\beta \in \overset{\frown}{\alpha}\phi)\urcorner$ for $\ulcorner((\exists\gamma)(\beta \in \gamma) \,.\, \phi[\alpha, \beta])\urcorner$

(γ distinct from β). Let us distinguish a metatheorem like Quine's *230 and the metatheorem $\cap$ *230 obtained from it by changing each '^' to '⌒'. Then it is easily seen that $\cap$*231 can be derived from $D9'$, $\cap$ *202, and $\cap$ $D10$ just as the special case of PS where ζ is '$[yz]$' was derived from 1.1, $A4$, and $A4'$. The derivation of $\cap$*231 from $D9'$, $\cap$*202, and $\cap D10$ is more direct than the derivation of *231 from $D9$, *202, and $D10$.

Actually we can show that in the system of ML, $D9$ and $D9'$ are equivalent definitions in the sense that we can not prove any different theorems by using one definition instead of the other. We can prove that the biconditionals

1) In ML, $\vdash \ulcorner\alpha \in \mathrm{V} \equiv (\exists\gamma)\,(\alpha \in \gamma)\urcorner$. See p. 178, †255.

2) It would seem relevant to point out the close connection between $D9''$ and another way of introducing class names into set theory by contextual definitions—namely by using a description operator. In a system which contains such an operator, abstracts can be introduced by the direct definition: $\ulcorner\overset{\frown}{\alpha}\phi\urcorner$ *for* $\ulcorner(\imath\eta)(\alpha)(\alpha \in \eta \equiv \phi)\urcorner$. Using $A3$ and EC and the standard theorems for the symbol '$\imath$' we easily obtain, by elementary logic, a metatheorem answering to $D9''$.

corresponding to $D9$ and $D9'$ are mutually derivable on the basis of *202 or ∩*202 and elementary logic, keeping ∩$D10$ and ∩$D15$ notationally unchanged as $D10$ and $D15$ in ML except for containing '$\hat{}$' in place of '$\wedge$'.

On the one hand, $D9'$ does not give more than $D9$, because the biconditional *$D9'$ corresponding to $D9'$ can be proved as a metatheorem on the basis of $D9$, *202, $D10$, $D15$, and elementary logic. Since *235 and †255 are in ML shown to be provable on the same basis, the proof of *$D9'$ runs as follows:

*$D9'$. $\vdash \ulcorner \beta \in \hat{\alpha}\phi \,.\!\equiv\!.\, (\exists\gamma)(\beta \in \gamma) \,.\, \phi[\alpha, \beta]\urcorner$, if γ is not β.

Proof. *235 $\vdash \ulcorner \beta \in \hat{\alpha}\phi \,.\!\equiv\!.\, \beta \in \mathrm{V} \,.\, \phi[\alpha, \beta]\urcorner$ (1)

†255, *123 $\vdash \ulcorner [1 \equiv] D9' \urcorner$.

On the other hand, $D9'$ does not give less than $D9$, because the biconditional ∩*$D9$ corresponding to $D9$ can be proved as a metatheorem on the basis of $D9'$, ∩*202, ∩$D10$, ∩$D15$, and elementary logic. To begin with, if we employ $D9'$ in place of $D9$, we can prove a principle ∩*230 with ∩$D10$, ∩$D15$, and elementary logic:

∩*230. $\vdash \ulcorner \alpha \in \hat{\alpha}\phi \,.\!\equiv\!.\, \alpha \in \mathrm{V} \,.\, \phi \urcorner$.

Proof. *100(&$D9'$) $\vdash \ulcorner \alpha \in \hat{\alpha}\phi \,.\!\equiv\!.\, (\exists\gamma)(\alpha \in \gamma) \,.\, \phi \urcorner$ (1)

*100(&$D10$) $\vdash \ulcorner \alpha = \alpha \urcorner$ (2)

(1)(&$D15$) $\vdash \ulcorner \alpha \in V \,.\!\equiv\!.\, (\exists\gamma)(\alpha \in \gamma)[.2]\urcorner$ (3)

(3), *123 $\vdash \ulcorner 230[\equiv 1] \urcorner$.

But as remarked before, ∩*231 is also derivable when $D9$ is replaced by $D9'$. Hence, a proof of ∩*$D9$ can be given as follows:

∩*$D9$. If γ is not α nor β nor free in ϕ, then

$\vdash \ulcorner \beta \in \hat{\alpha}\phi \,.\!\equiv (\exists\gamma)(\beta \in \gamma \,.\, (\alpha)(\alpha \in \gamma \,.\!\supset \phi))\urcorner$.

Proof. *100 $\vdash \ulcorner [230.]\alpha \in \hat{\alpha}\phi \,.\!\supset \phi \urcorner$ (1)

*135 $\vdash \ulcorner \beta \in \gamma \,.\, (\alpha)(\alpha \in \gamma \,.\!\supset \phi)$

$.\!\supset (\exists\gamma)(\beta \in \gamma \,.\, (\alpha)(\alpha \in \gamma \,.\!\supset \phi))\urcorner$ (2)

∩*231(&hp) $\vdash \ulcorner [(\gamma)2 \supset\!:]\beta \in \hat{\alpha}\phi \,.\, (\alpha)(\alpha \in \hat{\alpha}\phi \,.\!\supset \phi) \,.\!\supset R2\urcorner$ (3)

*135 $\vdash \ulcorner \beta \in \gamma \,.\!\supset (\exists\gamma)(\beta \in \gamma)\urcorner$. (4)

Let ϕ' be an alphabetic variant of ϕ such that $\phi[\alpha, \beta]$ is like it except for containing free occurrences of β wherever it contains free occurrences of α.

*104 $\vdash \ulcorner (\alpha)(\alpha \in \gamma \,.\!\supset \phi') \supset\!: \beta \in \gamma \,.\!\supset \phi[\alpha, \beta]\urcorner$ (5)

*171 $\vdash \ulcorner [5 \equiv\!:.](\alpha)(\alpha \in \gamma \,.\!\supset \phi) \supset\!: \beta \in \gamma \,.\!\supset \phi[\alpha, \beta]\urcorner$ (6)

*100, *163(&$D9'$, hp)

$\vdash \ulcorner(\exists\gamma)([4.6.]\beta \epsilon \gamma . (\alpha)(\alpha \epsilon \gamma .\supset \phi)) \supset . \beta \epsilon \hat{\alpha}\phi\urcorner$ (7)

*100 $\vdash \ulcorner[(\alpha)1.3.7 .\supset]D9\urcorner$.

Moreover, if we adopt $D9'$ in place of $D9$, we can derive $\cap$*202 from $\cap$*231 with the help of $\cap$*230 which was just proved independently of $D9$ and $\cap$*202:

Proof of $\cap$*202.

*135 $\vdash \ulcorner(\alpha)(\alpha \epsilon \beta .\equiv. \alpha \epsilon V . \phi) \supset 202\urcorner$ (1)

*231 $\vdash \ulcorner[(\beta)1 \supset . (\alpha)\cap 230 \supset]202\urcorner$.

But once we have $\cap$*231, $\cap$*$D9$ can also be proved without using $\cap$*202. Therefore, not only are *231 and *$D9'$ derivable from *202 and $D9$, but $\cap$*202 and $\cap$*$D9$ are also derivable from $\cap$*231 and $D9'$. In other words, $D9'$ and the principle $\cap$*231 of specification can take the place (as 'meta-definition' and 'meta-axiom') of $D9$ and the principle *202 of class existence in any system without affecting the bulk of consequences derivable with the help of elementary logic.

This result may be of some interest because, in contrast with $D9$ and *202, $D9'$ and $\cap$*231 seem to be more intuitive and more directly comparable with tradition.

In the above, *202 has been applied in its full generality to derive *231 from the axioms of class existence either with $D9$ or with $D9'$. Sometimes we may encounter a system in which we do not possess as strong a principle of class existence as *202; sometimes we want to prove a general principle from finitely many axioms of class existence and may want to have *231 at hand before we obtain the general principle of class existence. It may be mentioned in passing that we can prove *231 with elementary logic and $D10$ plus a single consequence of *202 which guarantees the existence of the null class

AN. $(z)(\exists y)(x)(x \epsilon y .\equiv. x \epsilon V . x \epsilon z . x \bar{\epsilon} z)$,

provided we replace the definition $D9$ of ML by

$D9''$. $\ulcorner(\beta \epsilon \hat{\alpha}\phi)\urcorner$ for $\ulcorner(\exists\gamma)(\beta \epsilon \gamma . (\alpha)(\alpha \epsilon \gamma .\equiv. (\exists\delta)(\alpha \epsilon \delta) . \phi))$

(γ being any new variable and δ any variable distinct from α).

On the basis of elementary logic and a principle *202' (the result obtained from *202 by substituting '$(\exists\gamma)(\alpha \epsilon \gamma)$' for '$\alpha \epsilon V$') we can prove a metatheorem which shows that it makes after all no difference to the deductive power of a system like ML whether we use $D9$ or $D9''$.

MT. If γ is not α nor free in ϕ, and δ is not α, then

$$\vdash \ulcorner(\exists\gamma)\,(\beta \in \gamma \,.\, (\alpha)\,(\alpha \in \gamma \,.\!\supset \phi)) \equiv (\exists\gamma)\,(\beta \in \gamma \,.\, (\alpha)\,(\alpha \in \gamma \,.\!\equiv\!.\, (\exists\delta)\,(\alpha \in \delta) \,.\, \phi))\urcorner. \qquad \text{(i)}$$

Proof. *100 $\quad \vdash \ulcorner \alpha \in \gamma \,.\!\equiv\!.\, (\exists\delta)\,(\alpha \in \delta) \,.\, \phi \,{:}\!\supset\!{:}\, \alpha \in \gamma \,.\!\supset \phi\urcorner$ (1)

*102 $\quad \vdash \ulcorner[(\alpha)1 \supset .]\,(\alpha)\mathrm{L}1 \supset (\alpha)\mathrm{R}1\urcorner$ (2)

*100 $\quad \vdash \ulcorner[2.]\beta \in \gamma \,.\, (\alpha)\mathrm{L}1 \,.\!\supset\!.\, \beta \in \gamma \,.\, (\alpha)\mathrm{R}1\urcorner$ (3)

*149 $\quad \vdash \ulcorner[(\gamma)3 \supset .](\exists\gamma)\mathrm{L}3 \supset (\exists\gamma)\mathrm{R}3\urcorner.$ (4)

Let δ' be distinct from α and β.

*134 $\quad \vdash \ulcorner \beta \in \gamma \,.\!\supset (\exists\delta')\,(\beta \in \delta')\urcorner$ (5)

*104 $\quad \vdash \ulcorner(\alpha)\,(\alpha \in \gamma \,.\!\supset \phi) \supset\!{:}\, \beta \in \gamma \,.\!\supset \phi[\alpha, \beta]\urcorner$ (6)

*100, *163(&hp) $\quad \vdash \ulcorner(\exists\gamma)\,([5.6.]\beta \in \gamma . (\alpha)(\alpha \in \gamma \,.\!\supset \phi)) \supset$
$\quad .\, (\exists\delta')\,(\beta \in \delta') \,.\, \phi[\alpha, \beta]\urcorner$ (7)

*202′ $\quad \vdash \ulcorner(\exists\gamma)\,(\alpha)\,(\alpha \in \gamma \,.\!\equiv\!.\, (\exists\delta)\,(\alpha \in \delta) \,.\, \phi)\urcorner$ (8)

*104 $\quad \vdash \ulcorner(\alpha)\,(\alpha \in \gamma \,.\!\equiv\!.\, (\exists\delta')\,(\alpha \in \delta') \,.\, \phi) \supset\!{:}\, \beta \in \gamma$
$\quad .\!\equiv\!.\, (\exists\delta')\,(\beta \in \delta') \,.\, \phi[\alpha, \beta]\urcorner$ (9)

*171 $\quad \vdash \ulcorner[9 \equiv .](\alpha)\,(\alpha \in \gamma \,.\!\equiv\!.\, (\exists\delta)\,(\alpha \in \delta) \,.\, \phi) \supset \mathrm{R}9\urcorner$ (10)

*100 $\quad \vdash \ulcorner[10.]\mathrm{L}10 \,.\!\supset\!{:}\, \mathrm{R}7 \supset .\, \beta \in \gamma \,.\, \mathrm{L}10\urcorner$ (11)

*149 $\quad \vdash \ulcorner[(\gamma)11 \supset .\ 8 \supset](\exists\gamma)\mathrm{R}11\urcorner$ (12)

*160(&*D*4) $\quad \vdash \ulcorner[12 \equiv .]\mathrm{R}7 \supset (\exists\gamma)\mathrm{RR}11\urcorner$ (13)

*100 $\quad \vdash \ulcorner[4.7.13 \,.\!\supset]\mathrm{i}\urcorner.$

As a lemma for proving *231, we have[1)]

†189. $(x) \qquad x = \hat{y}(y \in x).$

Proof. *134 $\quad y \in x \,.\!\supset (\exists z)\,(y \in z)$ (1)

*100 $\quad [1 \supset\!{:}]\,y \in x \,.\!\equiv\!.\, (\exists z)\,(y \in z) . y \in x$ (2)

*134(&*D*9″) $\quad y \in x[.(y)2] \,.\!\supset\!.\, y \in \hat{y}(y \in x)$ (3)

*104 $\quad (y)(y \in w \,.\!\equiv\!.\, (\exists z)(y \in z) . y \in x\,) \supset\!{:}\, y \in w$
$\quad .\!\equiv\!.\, (\exists z)\,(y \in z) . y \in x$ (4)

*100, *163 $\quad (\exists w)([4.]y \in w . (y)\,(y \in w$
$\quad .\!\equiv\!.\, (\exists z)\,(y \in z) . y \in x)) \supset .\, y \in x$ (5)

*100(&*D*9″) $\quad [3.5. \supset\!{:}]\,y \in x \,.\!\equiv\!.\, y \in \hat{y}(y \in x)$ (6)

*100(&*D*10) $\quad [(y)6 \equiv .]\,x = \hat{y}(y \in x).$

Proof of *231.

---

1) In the following two proofs, we are assuming that abstracts have been introduced by *D*9″.

Case 1: ζ is a variable. *104.

Case 2: ζ is an abstract $\ulcorner \hat{\delta}\chi \urcorner$. Let α' and γ be new and distinct.

*100(&$D9''$, $D10$), *123	$\vdash \ulcorner \hat{\delta}\chi = \hat{\delta}((\exists\gamma)(\delta \in \gamma) . \chi) \urcorner$	(1)
*121, *117(&$D9''$, $D10$)	$\vdash \ulcorner (\delta)(\delta \in \alpha' . \equiv . (\exists\gamma)(\delta \in \gamma) . \chi)$	
	$\supset . \hat{\delta}(\delta \in \alpha') = \hat{\delta}((\exists\gamma)(\delta \in \gamma) . \chi) \urcorner$	
*223	$\supset : [189 \equiv .] \alpha' = \hat{\delta}((\exists\gamma)(\delta \in \gamma) . \chi) \urcorner$	
*223	$\supset : [1 \equiv .] \alpha' = \hat{\delta}\chi \urcorner$	(2)
*149	$\vdash \ulcorner [(\alpha')2 \supset .](\exists\alpha')\mathrm{L}2 \supset (\exists\alpha')\mathrm{R}2 \urcorner$	(3)
*100	$\vdash \ulcorner \delta \in \alpha' . \mathrm{L}2 . \supset \mathrm{L}2 \urcorner$	(4)
*149(&$D9''$)	$\vdash \ulcorner [(\alpha')4 \supset :] \delta \in \hat{\delta}\chi . \supset (\exists\alpha')\mathrm{L}2 \urcorner$	(5)
AN	$\vdash \ulcorner (\exists\alpha')(\delta)(\delta \in \alpha' . \equiv . \delta \in \mathrm{V} . \delta \in \gamma . \delta \tilde{\in} \gamma) \urcorner$	(6)
*100, *117	$\vdash \ulcorner \sim(\exists\alpha')\mathrm{L}2 \supset (\delta)(\gamma)([5 \supset :] \delta \in \mathrm{V} . \delta \in \gamma$	
	$. \delta \tilde{\in} \gamma . \equiv . \delta \in \hat{\delta}\chi) \urcorner$	
*121(&$D10$)	$\supset . [6 \equiv](\exists\alpha')(\alpha' = \hat{\delta}\chi) \urcorner$	(7)
*100	$\vdash \ulcorner [3 . 7 . \supset](\exists\alpha')(\alpha' = \hat{\delta}\chi) \urcorner$	(8)
*223(&hp)	$\vdash \ulcorner \alpha' = \hat{\delta}\chi . \supset : [104 \equiv .](\alpha)\phi \supset \psi \urcorner$	(9)
(9), *163	$\vdash \ulcorner [8 \supset] 231 \urcorner$.	

Among the axioms of set theory, the principle of extensionality *A*3 has the effect of excluding non-classes entirely and assuming that every value of a variable is a class. This is so because, according to the normal interpretation of '$\in$', *A*3 can be read: 'Any two entities are identical if they have the same members', while only classes are supposed to be capable of having members. Moreover, since *A*3 is an immediate consequence of the definition *D*10 of identity, *D*10 obviously has also the same effect. Such an effect can be avoided either by reinterpreting '$\in$' or by making less strenuous requirements on the conditions for two entities to be identical. However, so far as mathematics and mathematical logic are concerned, it is possible to get along without non-classes.

Sometimes it is desirable to narrow down further the range of entities and confine our attentions to certain specific kind of classes. For instance, after we have identified natural numbers with certain classes, we may want to develop natural arithmetic from logic and be concerned for the moment almost exclusively with this specific kind of classes. Then it becomes convenient to introduce a new kind of variables whose range consists of all and only those classes which are natural numbers. Using '$P(x)$' as an abbreviation for 'x is a natural number', we can introduce variables for natural numbers by the following contextual definition:

DU. $\ulcorner (\bar{\alpha}_1) \cdots (\bar{\alpha}_n)\phi' \urcorner$ for $\ulcorner (\alpha_1) \cdots (\alpha_n)(P(\alpha_1) . \cdots . P(\alpha_n) . \supset \phi) \urcorner$

($n \geqslant 1$; ϕ' being like ϕ except for containing free occurrences of $\ulcorner \bar{\alpha}_1 \urcorner, \cdots,$ $\ulcorner \bar{\alpha}_n \urcorner$ whenever ϕ contains free occurrences of $\alpha_1, \cdots, \alpha_n$). Obviously we could have used '$P(x)$' as abbreviation for some other matrices such as 'x is an element (or a set)' or 'x is a real number', etc.

§ 2. A New Theory of Element and Number

2.1. *Basal Logic and Elementhood Axioms*

Quine remarked that the system of his book exclusive of *200 is a completely safe basal logic. Axioms of this basal logic are given by *100—*105 and *201—*202 in *ML*. For relation theory and number theory, we need some further axioms to guarantee elementhood of certain entities. In the article *EN*[1], Quine proposed to adopt as axioms †610 and the following two statements:

*EA*1. (x) $\quad \iota x \in \mathrm{V}.$

*EA*2. $(x)(y)$ $\quad x, y \in \mathrm{V} \,.\supset.\, \bar{x} \cap \bar{y} \in \mathrm{V}.$

There he also pointed out that, for purposes of the topics covered in *ML*, two weaker axioms will suffice after suitable alteration of the definitions. The axioms are *EA*1 and

*EA*3. $(x)(y)$ $\quad x, y \in \mathrm{V} \,.\supset.\, x \cup y \in \mathrm{V}.$

Further investigation reveals that we can adopt even weaker axioms for the topics in *ML*. Specifically we can use as axioms merely the following two statements:

*EA*4. $\quad \Lambda \in \mathrm{V}.$

*EA*5. $(x)(y)$ $\quad x, y \in \mathrm{V} \,.\supset.\, \iota x \cup \iota y \in \mathrm{V}.$

Moreover, it can be shown that a single axiom

*EA*6. $(x)(y)$ $\quad \iota x \cup \iota y \in \mathrm{V}$

will serve the same purpose as *EA*4 and *EA*5 taken together. This is seen from the fact that *EA*6 and the conjunct of *EA*4 and *EA*5 are mutually deducible in basal logic.

However, before turning to deductions, let us suppose Chapter IV of *ML* carried over with mere omission of *200 and those theorems and metatheorems depending on *200; viz., *200, †210—†212, †241, *253, *254, *256—*259, †261, *263, †272—†274, †359—†361, and *363.

1) Element and number, *J. Symbolic Logic*, vol. 6.

Then we know that *EA*6 can be proved with basal logic, if we adopt *EA*4 and *EA*5 as axioms:

*Proof of EA*6. *EA*5 $x, x \in V \,.\supset.\, \iota x \cup \iota x \in V$

†277, *224 $\supset.\, \iota x \in V$ (1)

†343 $x \tilde{\in} V \,.\supset.\, \iota x = \Lambda$

*224 $\supset:\, \iota x \in V\ [.\equiv \text{EA4}]$ (2)

†343 $y \tilde{\in} V \,.\supset.\, \iota y = \Lambda$

*224 $\supset:\, \iota x \cup \iota y \in V \,.\equiv.\, \iota x \cup \Lambda \in V$

†297, *224 $\supset:\, \iota x \cup \iota y \in V \,.\equiv.\, \iota x \in V$ (3)

*100 $[1 \,.\, 2 \,.\, 3 \,.\, \text{EA5} \,.\supset]\ \text{EA6}.$

On the other hand, if we adopt *EA*6 as axiom, it is easy to prove *EA*4 and *EA*5 with basal logic:

*Proof of EA*4. *EA*6 $\iota\hat{x}\,(x \tilde{\in} x) \cup \iota\hat{x}\,(x \tilde{\in} x) \in V$ (1)

†277, *224 $[1 \equiv .]\ \iota\hat{x}\,(x \tilde{\in} x) \in V$ (2)

†343 $[260 \equiv .]\ \iota\hat{x}\,(x \tilde{\in} x) = \Lambda$ (3)

*223 $[3 \supset .\ 2 \equiv]\ EA4.$

*Proof of EA*5. *100 $[EA6 \supset]\ EA5.$

In what follows, a development of the arithmetic of natural numbers based on basal logic and the single elementhood axiom *EA*6 will be attempted.

To begin with, we introduce *EA*6 as an axiom and deduce its consequences in an addendum to Chapter IV, using italics to distinguish newly applied reference numbers from reference numbers whose application remains as in the book. Thus we have:

†300. $(x)(y)$ $\iota x \cup \iota y \in V.$ (†360)

†370. $\Lambda \in V$ *Proof* given above. (†211)

†371. $(x)(y)$ $x, y \in V \,.\supset.\, \iota x \cup \iota y \in V$ *Proof* given above.

†372. (x) $\iota x \in V.$ (†359)

Proof. †300 $\iota x \cup \iota x \in V$ (1)

†277, *224 $[1 \equiv]\ 372.$

†373. (y) $(\exists x)(x \neq y).$ (†212)

*374. If α is not free in ϕ, $\vdash \ulcorner \hat{\alpha}\phi = V \,.\equiv \phi \urcorner.$ (*253)

*375. If α is not free in ϕ, $\vdash \ulcorner \hat{\alpha}\phi = \Lambda \,.\equiv \sim\phi \urcorner.$ (*254)

*376. $\vdash \ulcorner (\alpha) \sim \phi \supset.\, \hat{\alpha}\phi \in V \urcorner.$ (*257)

Proofs of †373—*376 like those given in the article *EN* under †410g′,*410*e*′, *410*f*′ and *410*d*′ (but with '410*a*' changed to '370').

It happens that all use of *200 throughout Chapter V is mediated by †211, †359, *360. Accordingly, Chapter V remains intact after the revision, except for change of the few occurrences of '211', '359', '360' in proofs to '370', '372', '300'.

2.2. *The Arithmetic of Natural Numbers*

By construing the successor of a natural number as its unit class, we shall obtain a theory of natural numbers that avoids any elementhood assumption beyond †300. The number 0 is identified with the null class. Accordingly *D*36—*D*39 are replaced by the new definitions:

*D*36. '0' for 'Λ'.

*D*37. '1' for '$\iota 0$'.

*D*38. '2' for '$\iota 1$'.

*D*39. 'S' for '$\lambda_x \iota x$'.

In place of †610 and †614, we have the stronger †372 and

†614. (x) $\quad \mathrm{S}`x = \iota x$ $\quad$ *Proof.* †546 (& *D*39).

The theorems †611—†613, †615—†617 and the proofs of them remain notationally unchanged, except for the obvious adjustments of references: †359, †610, †614, *D*36—*D*39 give way to †370, †372, †614, *D*36—*D*39.

The following †621 and †624 take the place of †621 and †624:

†621. $\quad \mathrm{S}`\Lambda = 1$ $\quad$ *Proof* by †615 (& *D*36).

†624. (x) $\quad x \in \mathrm{V} \,.\!\equiv\!.\, \mathrm{S}`x \neq 0.$

Proof. †614, *223 (& *D*36) $\quad [343 \equiv\!:]\ x \,\bar{\in}\, \mathrm{V} \,.\!\equiv\!.\, \mathrm{S}`x = 0$ $\quad$ (1)

*100 $\quad [1 \equiv]\, 624.$

The definition *D*40 of the class of all natural numbers remains notationally unchanged:

*D*40. '*Nn*' for '$({}_{*}\mathrm{S}``\iota 0)$'.

Together with *D*40, the theorems and metatheorems †630—*637 as well as the proofs of them remain as in *ML*, except for minor changes of references: using †372 and *D*39 in place of †610 and *D*39.

The remaining crucial theorem to derive, for arithmetical purposes, is the theorem †677 to the effect that no two natural numbers have the same successor. A stronger †677 is proved here.

†677. $(x)(y)$ $\quad x \in \mathrm{V} \,.\!\supset\!:\, \mathrm{S}`x = \mathrm{S}`y \,.\!\equiv\!.\, x = y.$

Proof. †614, *224 $\quad 677[\equiv 358].$

And now all the definitions and theorems and proofs of the succeeding §§47—49 of *ML,* on powers of relations and algorithm of arithmetic, can be carried over without any changes whatsoever except for using †624 (with minor complications in the proofs of †682 and †683) and †677 instead of †624 and †677.

Fourteen further theorems concerned rather with the *application* of natural numbers are the †618—†620, †622, †623, †625—†629, †638—†641 of *ML.* A natural number n is construed in *ML* as the class of all n-membered classes; consequently, to say that a class x has n members amounts merely to saying that $x \in n$. The theory here lacks such convenience. But we can define the class $\# n$ of all n-membered classes by making use of the theory of powers of relations set down in §47 of *ML.* And the definition together with its consequences may be appended to §49 and numbered accordingly.

Intuitively[1)], n is the number of x if we can pair off the members of x one by one with all the natural numbers z such that $0 < z \leqslant n$, pairing x itself with 0. The formal definition of $\# n$ turns out to be fairly neat:

*D*49. ‘$\mathfrak{S}$’ for ‘$\hat{x}\hat{w}(\exists y)\,(y \in x \,.\, w = x \cap \overline{\iota y})$’.

*D*50. ‘$\# z$’ for ‘$\mathfrak{S}^{z}\text{‘‘}\iota\Lambda$’.

Theorems can then be derived with the help of theorems in connection with the powers of relations. In place of the aforementioned fourteen theorems †618—†620, †622, †623, †625—†629, †638—†641, we have respectively †730—†732, †734, †733, †735—†739, †740—†743 as follows:

†730. $(x)(z)$ $\quad z \in Nn \,.\supset :\, x \in \#(S\text{‘}z) \,.\equiv.\, (\exists y)(y \in x \,.\, x \cap \overline{\iota y} \in \# z) \,.\, x \in V.$

Proof. *685 $\quad z \in Nn \,.\supset.\, \mathfrak{S}^{S\text{‘}z} = \mathfrak{S} \mid (\mathfrak{S}^{z})$

*226 $\quad \supset.\, (\mathfrak{S}^{S\text{‘}z})\text{‘‘}\iota\Lambda = (\mathfrak{S} \mid (\mathfrak{S}^{z}))\text{‘‘}\iota\Lambda$

*495, *224(&*D*50) $\quad \supset.\, \#(S\text{‘}z) = \mathfrak{S}\text{‘‘}(\# z)$

*223 $\quad \supset :\, x \in \#(S\text{‘}z) \,.\equiv.\, x \in \mathfrak{S}\text{‘‘}(\# z)$

*230 (&*D*28), *123 $\quad \supset :\, x \in \#(S\text{‘}z) \,.\equiv.\, (\exists w)(\mathfrak{S}(x, w) \,.\, w \in \# z) \,.\, x \in V$

*433 (&*D*49), *123 $\quad \supset :\, x \in \#(S\text{‘}z) \,.\equiv.\, (\exists w)(x, w \in V \,.\, (\exists y)(y \in x \,.\, w = x \cap \overline{\iota y}) \,.\, w \in \# z) \,.\, x \in V$

1) It seems that we might, without using the powers of relations, have defined the matrix ‘$x\ N\ y$’ as follows:

‘$x_n \subset y$’ *for* ‘$(\exists z)(\lambda_w(z\text{‘}w)\text{‘‘}y = x)$’, ‘$x_n = y$’ *for* ‘$x_n \subset y \,.\, y_n \subset x$’, ‘$xNy$’ *for* ‘$x \in Nn \,.\, {}_{*}\mathfrak{E}\text{‘‘}x_n = y$’.

But it is difficult to derive the desired theorems with this definition.

*158, *123 $\supset : x \in \#(S\text{‘}z) . \equiv . x \in V . (\exists w)(w \in V . (\exists y)$
$(y \in x . w = x \cap \overline{\iota y}) . w \in \#z) . x \in V$

*100, *123 $\supset : x \in \#(S\text{‘}z) . \equiv . (\exists w)((\exists y)(y \in x .$
$w = x \cap \overline{\iota y}) . w \in V . w \in \#z) . x \in V$

†191, *123 $\supset : x \in \#(S\text{‘}z) . \equiv . (\exists w)((\exists y)(y \in x .$
$w = x \cap \overline{\iota y}) . w \in \#z) . x \in V$

*158, *123 $\supset : x \in \#(S\text{‘}z) . \equiv . (\exists w)(\exists y)(y \in x .$
$w = x \cap \overline{\iota y} . w \in \#z) . x \in V$

*138, *123 $\supset : x \in \#(S\text{‘}z) . \equiv . (\exists y)(\exists w)(y \in x .$
$w = x \cap \overline{\iota y} . w \in \#z) . x \in V$

*158, *123 $\supset : x \in \#(S\text{‘}z) . \equiv . (\exists y)(y \in x . (\exists w)$
$(w = x \cap \overline{\iota y} . w \in \#z)) . x \in V$

*234b, *123 $\supset$ R730.

†731. $(x)(z)$ $z \in Nn . x \in \#(S\text{‘}z) . \supset (\exists y)(y \in x . x \cap \overline{\iota y} \in \#z).$

†732. $(x)(z)$ $z \in Nn . y \in x . x \cap \overline{\iota y} \in \#z . x \in V . \supset . x \in \#(S\text{‘}z).$

Proofs of †731 and †732 from †730 immediate, using *100 and *135.

†733. (x) $x \in \#0 . \equiv . x = \Lambda.$

Proof. †682, *224(&*D*50) $x \in \#0 . \equiv . x \in I\text{‘‘}\iota\Lambda$
†558, *224 $\equiv . x \in \iota\Lambda$
†345 $\equiv . [370.]x = \Lambda.$

†734. $\Lambda \in \#0$ *Proof*: †733, †182.

†735. $\#1 = \hat{x}(\exists y)(y \in x . x \subset \iota y).$

Proof. †683 $[632 \supset .]\mathfrak{S}^{S\text{‘}0} = \mathfrak{S}^0 | \mathfrak{S}$
†682, *227 $= I | \mathfrak{S}$
†559 $= \mathfrak{S}$ (1)
†182 (& *D*50) $\#1 = \mathfrak{S}^{1}\text{‘‘}\iota\Lambda$
†621 (& *D*36), *227 $= \mathfrak{S}^{S\text{‘}0}\text{‘‘}\iota\Lambda$
(1), *227 $= \mathfrak{S}\text{‘‘}\iota\Lambda$
†182 (& *D*28) $= \hat{x}(\exists w)(\mathfrak{S}(x, w) . w \in \iota\Lambda)$
*433, *188(& *D*49) $= \hat{x}(\exists w)(x, w \in V . (\exists y)(y \in x . w$
$= x \cap \overline{\iota y}) . w \in \iota\Lambda)$
*246 $= \hat{x}(\exists w)(w \in V . (\exists y)(y \in x . w$
$= x \cap \overline{\iota y}) . w \in \iota\Lambda)$

*100, *188	$= \hat{x}(\exists w)((\exists y)(y \in x \,.\, w = x \cap \overline{\iota y}) \,.$ $w \in V \,.\, w \in \iota\Lambda)$
†191, *188	$= \hat{x}(\exists w)((\exists y)(y \in x \,.\, w = x \cap \overline{\iota y}) \,.\, w \in \iota\Lambda)$
*158, *188	$= \hat{x}(\exists w)(\exists y)(y \in x \,.\, w = x \cap \overline{\iota y} \,.\, w \in \iota\Lambda)$
*138, *188	$= \hat{x}(\exists y)(\exists w)(y \in x \,.\, w = x \cap \overline{\iota y} \,.\, w \in \iota\Lambda)$
*158, *188	$= \hat{x}(\exists y)(y \in x \,.\, (\exists w)(w = x \cap \overline{\iota y} \,.\, w \in \iota\Lambda))$
*234b, *188	$= \hat{x}(\exists y)(y \in x \,.\, x \cap \overline{\iota y} \in \iota\Lambda)$
*345, *188	$= \hat{x}(\exists y)(y \in x .[370 \,.\,] x \cap \overline{\iota y} = \Lambda)$
*321, *188	$= \hat{x}(\exists y)(y \in x \,.\, x \subset \overline{\iota y})$
†275, *227	$=$ R735.

†736—739 follow †735 as †626—629 follow †625, except that '1' becomes '#1'.

†740. $(w)(x)(y)(z)$ $z \in Nn \,.\!\supset\!:\, y, w \in x \,.\, x \in V \,.\, x \cap \overline{\iota w} \in \#z$ $.\!\supset\!.\, x \cap \overline{\iota y} \in \#z$

†741. $(x)(y)(z)$ $z \in Nn \,.\, y \in x \,.\!\cap\!:\, x \in \#(S`z) \,.\!\equiv\!.\, x \cup \iota y \in \# z \,.$ $x \in V$

†742. $(x)(y)(z)$ $z \in Nn \,.\, y \in \bar{x} \,.\!\supset\!:\, x \cup \iota y \in V \,.\, x \in \#z$ $.\!\equiv\!.\, x \cup \iota y \in \#(S`z)$

†743. $(x)(y)(z)$ $z \in Nn \,.\!\supset\!:\, x \in \#z \,.\, y \in \#z \,.\, x \subset y \,.\!\supset\!.\, x = y.$

Proofs of †740—743 like those of †638—641 in *ML* with minor complications like the replacement of '$z \in$ V' by '$z \in Nn$' and that of '$\in z$' by '$\in \# z$'.

We have almost entirely omitted §§45—46 of *ML*, on counter sets and infinitude. A theory of counter sets like that given in *ML* seems not available in the present revision—as is to be expected in view of the fact that our axioms do not even guarantee any element having more than two members. In fact, for any natural number n, we may think of the class $_*\mathfrak{C}``n$ as its counter set in our theory. Thus Λ, $\iota\Lambda$, $\iota\Lambda \cup \iota\iota\Lambda$, $\iota\Lambda \cup \iota\iota\Lambda \cup \iota\iota\iota\Lambda$ are respectively the counter sets of 0, 1, 2, 3. But the trouble is we do not know whether any class with more than two members (for example, the class $\iota\Lambda \cup \iota\iota\Lambda \cup \iota\iota\iota\Lambda$) is an element or not. Consequently, we are deprived of the privilege of defining the class of all such counter sets, since the members of any class must be elements (according to †190). Similarly, without some further axiom of elementhood, the function $\lambda_x(_*\mathfrak{C}``x)$, in view of †536, need not give the desired counter set for any x which is greater than 2.

In §46 of *ML*, the class Fin of all finite classes is identified with the class of all members of natural numbers, and the existence of infinite elements is proved. In the present theory, we have no guarantee that the corresponding class $\hat{x}(\exists y)(x \in \# y)$ would give us the desired Fin. Moreover, a proof for the existence of any infinite element in our revised theory is certainly beyond our reach, seeing that we cannot prove the existence even of any element with three members.

Nevertheless, we know that there are infinitely many elements, and, using the notions of greater and less among natural numbers, we are able to provide the *axiom of infinity* in one of its many forms by the three theorems which are to follow.

*D*41. ‘$x < y$’ for ‘$x, y \in Nn \centerdot ({}_*\mathfrak{E}|\mathfrak{E})(x, y)$’.

†665. $(x)(y)(z)$ $\quad x < y \centerdot y < z \centerdot \supset \centerdot x < z.$

Proof. *100(& *D*41) $\quad x < y \centerdot y < z \centerdot \supset \centerdot x, z \in Nn \centerdot ({}_*\mathfrak{E}|\mathfrak{E})(x, y) \centerdot ({}_*\mathfrak{E}|\mathfrak{E})(y, z)$ (1)

†519 $\quad {}_*\mathfrak{E}|\mathfrak{E} \subset {}_*\mathfrak{E}$ (2)

†446 $\quad [2 \equiv]\ (x)(y)(({}_*\mathfrak{E}|\mathfrak{E})(x, y) \supset {}_*\mathfrak{E}(x, y))$ (3)

*116 $\quad [3 \supset \centerdot]\ ({}_*\mathfrak{E}|\mathfrak{E})(x, y) \supset {}_*\mathfrak{E}(x, y)$ (4)

*100 $\quad [1 \centerdot 4 \centerdot] x < y \centerdot y < z \centerdot \supset \centerdot x, z \in Nn \centerdot {}_*\mathfrak{E}(x, y) \centerdot ({}_*\mathfrak{E}|\mathfrak{E})(y, z)$

*135 $\quad \supset (\exists y)(x, z \in Nn \centerdot {}_*\mathfrak{E}(x, y) \centerdot ({}_*\mathfrak{E}|\mathfrak{E})(y, z))$

*158 $\quad \supset \centerdot x, z \in Nn \centerdot (\exists y)({}_*\mathfrak{E}(x, y) \centerdot ({}_*\mathfrak{E}|\mathfrak{E})(y, z))$

†486, *123 $\quad \supset \centerdot x, z \in Nn \centerdot ({}_*\mathfrak{E}|({}_*\mathfrak{E}|\mathfrak{E}))(x, z)$

†491, *224 $\quad \supset \centerdot x, z \in Nn \centerdot (({}_*\mathfrak{E}|{}_*\mathfrak{E})|\mathfrak{E})(x, z)$

†517, *224(& *D*41) $\quad \supset \centerdot x < z$

†666. (x) $\quad x \in Nn \centerdot \supset (\exists y)(x < y).$

Proof. †190 $\quad x \in Nn \centerdot \supset \centerdot x \in \mathrm{V}$

†555 $\quad \supset I(x, x)$

†566 $\quad \supset \mathfrak{E}(x, \iota x)$ (1)

†512 $\quad \mathfrak{E} \subset {}_*\mathfrak{E}|\mathfrak{E}$ (2)

†446 $\quad [2 \equiv]\ (x)(w)(\mathfrak{E}(x, w) \supset ({}_*\mathfrak{E}|\mathfrak{E})(x, w))$ (3)

*233 $\quad [3 \supset \centerdot] \mathfrak{E}(x, \iota x) \supset ({}_*\mathfrak{E}|\mathfrak{E})(x, \iota x)$ (4)

†614, *224 $\quad [631 \equiv :]\ x \in Nn \centerdot \supset \centerdot \iota x \in Nn$ (5)

*100 (& *D*41) $\quad [1 \centerdot 4 \centerdot 5 \centerdot \supset :]\ x \in Nn \centerdot \supset \centerdot x < \iota x$

*232 $\quad \supset (\exists y)(x < y)$

†667. (x) $\quad \sim(x < x).$

Proof. †564 $\quad \mathfrak{E}(x, \Lambda) \equiv \centerdot x \in \Lambda\ [\centerdot 370]$ (1)

*100 $\quad [1 \centerdot 192 \centerdot \supset] \sim ({}_*\mathfrak{E}(\Lambda, x) \centerdot \mathfrak{E}(x, \Lambda))$ (2)

*131	$\sim(\exists x)({}_*\mathfrak{E}(\Lambda, x) \,.\, \mathfrak{E}(x, \Lambda))[\equiv (x)2]$	(3)
†486, *123(& $D36$)	$\sim({}_*\mathfrak{E}\vert\mathfrak{E})(0, 0)[\equiv 3]$	(4)
†564	$\mathfrak{E}(y, \iota x) \equiv . \; y \in \iota x[.\, 372]$	(5)
*223	$x = y \,.\!\supset .\, {}_*\mathfrak{E}(\iota x, x) \equiv {}_*\mathfrak{E}(\iota x, y)$	(6)
*100, *163	$(\exists y)({}_*\mathfrak{E}(\iota x, y) . \mathfrak{E}(y, \iota x)[.\, 5 \,.\, 6 \,.\, 555 \,.\, 345])$	
	$\supset . \; I(x, x) \,.\, {}_*\mathfrak{E}(\iota x, x)$	
†566, *123	$\supset . \; \mathfrak{E}(x, \iota x) \,.\, {}_*\mathfrak{E}(\iota x, x)$	
†487	$\supset (\mathfrak{E}\vert{}_*\mathfrak{E})(x, x)$	
†524, *224	$\supset ({}_*\mathfrak{E}\vert\mathfrak{E})(x, x)$	(7)
*100	$[7.] \sim ({}_*\mathfrak{E}\vert\mathfrak{E})(x, x) \,.\!\supset \sim(\exists y)({}_*\mathfrak{E}(\iota x, y) . \mathfrak{E}(y, \iota x))$	
†486, *123	$\supset \sim({}_*\mathfrak{E}\vert\mathfrak{E})(\iota x, \iota x)$	
†614, *224	$\supset \sim({}_*\mathfrak{E}\vert\mathfrak{E})(S`x, S`x)$	(8)
*636	$[(\;)8 \,.\, 4 \,.] x \in Nn \,.\!\supset \sim({}_*\mathfrak{E}\vert\mathfrak{E})(x, x)$	
*100 (& $D41$)	$\supset \sim(x < x)$	(9)
*100 (& $D41$)	$x \,\tilde{\in}\, Nn \,.\!\supset \sim(x < x)$	(10)
*100	$[9 \,.\, 10 \,.\!\supset] \sim (x < x).$	

2.3. *Model and Enumeration of Elements*

It is clear that our axiom of elementhood is very incomplete; in other words, there are many statements of elementhood which are neither demonstrable nor refutable in our theory. One simple example is the statement '$\iota\Lambda \cup \iota\iota\Lambda \cup \iota\iota\iota\Lambda \in V$'. Accordingly, there are many entities such that we do not know whether they are elements, and an enumeration of *all* the entities which are elements is out of the question. Nevertheless, the entities which we know to be elements by our axiom are denumerable.

As we have shown before, †300 (*EA*6) and the conjunct of *EA*4 and *EA*5 are mutually deducible with basal logic. So let us suppose that we had adopted *EA*4 and *EA*5 instead of †300 as axioms of elementhood. *EA*4 says in effect that Λ is an element. *EA*5 is to the effect that any class having two (identical or different) elements as its sole members is itself an element. It can be seen that, starting with Λ, we are able to generate all the chosen elements of our theory by forming the logical sum of the unit classes of any two preceding (identical or different) elements.

We take Λ as the first element. Let us represent the first, second, third, fourth element, etc. by 1, 2, 3, 4, etc. respectively, and agree that $\sigma(m, n)$ is to represent the logic sum $\Sigma(m, n)$ of the unit classes of the m-th and n-th elements. It seems natural to enumerate these elements in such a way that $\sigma(1, 1) = 2$, $\sigma(1, 2) = 3$, $\sigma(2, 2) = 4$, $\sigma(1, 3) = 5$, $\sigma(2, 3) = 6$, $\sigma(3, 3) = 7$, $\sigma(1, 4) = 8$, $\sigma(2, 4) = 9$, etc. The general formula for the enumeration turns out to be a fairly simple one:

$$\sigma(n-i, n) = 1 + (n(n+1)/2) - i$$
$$(n = 1, 2, 3, \cdots; \ i = n-1, n-2, \cdots, 1, 0).$$

It is evident that the enumeration does exhaust the chosen elements guaranteed by *EA*4 and *EA*5. On the other hand, that no element is enumerated more than once could be seen by †354 of *ML*. Let M, M', N, N' be any elements represented respectively by m, m', n, n', and suppose that $\Sigma(m, n) = \Sigma(m', n')$. In view of our formula for enumeration, we know then that $m \leqslant n$, and $m' \leqslant n'$. Now, under these conditions, †354 enables us to conclude that $M=M'$, and $N=N'$. Since, however, no two positive integers below 10 (say) represent the same element, we get the conclusion that $\Sigma(m, n) = \Sigma(m', n')$ if, and only if, $m=m'$ and $n=n'$. Moreover, for any two elements P and Q represented by p and q, $P \in Q$ if, and only if, $(\exists n)(n \geqslant 0 \ . \ q = 1 + n(n+1)/2 - (n-p))$.

Let us proceed to the construction of a model for our revision of the system of *ML*.

We may remember that the axioms of our theory consist of those of the basal logic and a single one of elementhood. These axioms are given in the eight statements: *100—*104, *201, *202, and †300. In what follows, it will always be understood that the statement connectives and quantifiers retain their normal interpretation.

To be remarked in the first place is that the revised system, when curtailed by leaving out *202, would be true of a universe wherein the only entities are the $\aleph_0$ elements enumerated above. This fact may serve as an indication that *202 is independent of the other axioms, as well as a guide to our search for a model. Since *202 assures us in effect that for every aggregate of elements, there is an entity in the universe having all and only those elements as members: all we need to do in order to get the model is to enlarge the universe so as to contain not only the elements enumerated above but also all the classes having some or all of them as members.

Among all the classes of elements, those having no more than two members are themselves elements, while all other classes of elements are non-elements. We have already represented the elements by positive integers. In order to obtain arithmetical representations of the non-elements, let us consider an arbitrary infinite sequence all terms of which are exclusively either 0 or 1. Any such infinite sequence will be called a two-valued sequence. A two-valued sequence s is said to represent a class C of elements if $(n)((\exists x)(x \in C \ . \ (x$ is represented by $n)) \equiv ($the n-th term of s is $1))$. Accordingly, when P is an element represented by p and Q is a non-element represented by q, '$P \in Q$' is true if, and only if, the p-th term of q is 1. It can be seen that the non-element classes of elements are represented, one by one, by those two-valued sequences in which more than two terms have the value 1.

All *such* two-valued sequences and all the positive integers taken together turn out to provide us with a model for a universe of which our axioms would hold true—provided we agree (in addition to the truth-conditions mentioned above for the statement '$P \in Q$', when P is an element) that the unit classes of any non-element will always be represented by 1, i.e., will be Λ, and that '$P \in Q$' is false for every non-element P.

That this is the case can be seen by an examination of the axioms given by *201, *202 and †300; for it is intuitively clear that all the axioms of quantification would be true of such a universe.

But *201 says no more than that, if any two entities x and y have the same elements as members, then they have the same members and $(z)((x$ is a member of $z) \equiv (y$ is a member of $z))$. And that †300 would hold true of this specific universe can be seen from a review of the deduction of it from $EA4$ and $EA5$ with basal logic, the crucial theorem there used being

$$\dagger 343. \quad (x) \qquad x \notin \mathrm{V} \mathbin{.\equiv.} \iota x = \Lambda .$$

*202 would also be true of this universe, since in the statement '$(\exists y)(x)(x \in y \mathbin{.\equiv.} x \in \mathrm{V} \mathbin{.} \ldots x \ldots)$', '$x \in y$', and '$x \in \mathrm{V} \mathbin{.} \ldots x \ldots$' always have the same truth-value (namely, falsehood) when x is a non-element, and we do have *all* the classes of elements in the universe (described above)[1].

In passing we may remark that the model serves to indicate the independence of certain axioms.

Thus $EA3$ (therewith also the stronger axiom $EA2$) is seen to be independent of our axioms, because the truth of $EA3$ would require that, for example, $\iota\Lambda \cup \iota\iota\Lambda \cup \iota\iota\iota\Lambda$ (represented by the infinite sequence with first, fourth, and eleventh term each taking the value 1, and all other terms taking the value 0) be an element.

The independence of †300 in our revised system could be indicated by reconstruing, for example, $\iota\Lambda \cup \iota\iota\Lambda$ (represented by 3) as non-element, and identifying all those non-elements which differ from one another only in that their third terms are different. †300 would not be true of this twisted universe, because $\iota\Lambda \cup \iota\iota\Lambda$ would be a non-element, though Λ and $\iota\Lambda$ are elements.

The independence of *202 has been mentioned before. Now *201 can also be shown to be independent of our other axioms by altering the model slightly. In order to do this, we adjoin to our arithmetical model the infinite sequence all of whose terms take the value 0, and require that it represent a non-element X. We agree that '$x \in X$' is always false, whatever x may be. Then X and Λ would be identical in the sense that $(x)(x \in X \mathbin{.\equiv.} x \in \Lambda)$; but '$\Lambda \in \iota\Lambda$' is true, while '$X \in \iota\Lambda$' would be false, because X is a non-element.

---

1) We might have reduced all the defined symbols in our axioms to statement connectives and quantifiers plus 'ϵ', and merely set down formal truth-conditions for the schema $\ulcorner \zeta \epsilon \eta \urcorner$ in terms of our arithmetical model—thereby indicating the consistency of our rather weak axioms, relative to a classical theory of real numbers.

§ 3. Set-Theoretical Basis for Real Numbers

3.1. *Introduction*[1]

In [1] we have considered a certain system L and shown that although its axioms are considerably weaker than those of [2], it suffices for purposes of the topics covered in [2]. The purpose of the present paper is to consider the system L more carefully and to show that with suitably chosen definitions for numbers, the ordinary theory of real numbers is also obtainable in it. For this purpose, we shall indicate that we can prove in L a certain set of twenty axioms used by Tarski which are sufficient for the arithmetic of real numbers and are to the effect that real numbers form a complete ordered field[2]. Indeed, we cannot prove in L all Tarski's twenty axioms in their full generality. One of them, stating in effect that every bounded class of real numbers possesses a least upper bound, can only be proved as a metatheorem which states that every bounded *nameable* class of real numbers possesses a least upper bound. However, all the other nineteen axioms can be proved in L without any modification.

This result may be of some interest because the axioms of L are considerably weaker than those commonly employed for the same purpose. In L variables need to take as values only classes each of whose members has no more than two members. In other words, only classes each with no more than two members are to be elements. On the other hand, it is usual to assume for the purpose of natural arithmetic that all finite classes are elements, and, for the purpose of real arithmetic, that all enumerable classes are elements.

3.2. *The System L*

In developing L, elementary logic (viz., the theory of truth functions and quantifiers) is assumed from the beginning. The single additional primitive is the two place predicate ϵ with which we can generate formulas of L from variables and logical operators in the usual manner. The usual definitions (e.g., $D9$—$D35$ of [2]) of the theory of classes and relations are assumed. In particular, let ιx denote the unit class of x, $x \cup y$ denote the sum class of x and y, and V denote the class of all elements. The axioms of L are given by the following three statements:

*M*1. $\iota x \cup \iota y \in V.$

*M*2. $x = y \supset . \, x \in z \supset y \in z.$

*M*3. If ϕ is any formula of L in which y is not free, then

$$\vdash (\exists y)\,(x)(x \in y \equiv . \, x \in V \,.\, \phi).$$

1) This paper forms part of a doctoral thesis presented to the Department of Philosophy at Harvard University, April 1948.

2) See pp. 213—235 of [3], and, e.g., p. 64 of [4].

*M*1 states that all classes with no more than two members are elements. *M*2 is a principle of extensionality. *M*3 states that, for each logical formula ϕ, there exists a class of elements defined by it. This principle (which constitutes an infinite bundle of axioms) serves to bring classes into the range of variables.

Given *M*2, it is provable in elementary logic that, if $x=y$ (i.e., according to the definition *D*= of identity in [2], $(z)(z \in x \equiv z \epsilon y)$), and ψ is formed from ϕ by putting y for some occurrences of x, then we have $\phi \equiv \psi$ (cf. *224 of [2]). In other words, in any system which contains the membership connective ϵ as the only primitive beyond elementary logic, if we assume *M*2 and use *D*= as the definition for identity, then x is identical with y if and only if there is no way of expressing in the system any difference between x and y. This shows that the definition *D*= is in accordance with the principle of identifying indiscernibles.

The axiom *M*1, when added to *M*2 and *M*3, has, among others, the following consequences (respectively †372, †410, †411 of [1] and [2]), wherein $x \,;\, y$ denotes the ordered pair of x and y:

*C*1. $$\iota x \in V.$$

*C*2. $$z \in x \,;\, y \equiv . \; z = \iota x \vee z = \iota x \cup \iota y.$$

*C*3. $$x \,;\, y \in V.$$

*C*1 assures us that all unit classes are elements; accordingly, if, as we have done in [1], we define natural numbers as unit classes of a special kind, then it assures us that all natural numbers are elements. Analogously, *C*3 assures us that all ordered pairs are elements; accordingly, if, as we shall do in this paper, we define ratios as a certain kind of ordered pairs of natural numbers, *C*3 assures us that all ratios are elements.

By *C*2, for any elements x, y, z, w, if $x \,;\, y = z \,;\, w$, then $x=z$ and $y=w$. It may be observed that *C*2 can be used to replace *M*1 in *L*. In other words, *M*1 and *C*2 are mutually deducible on the basis of elementary logic plus *M*2 and *M*3. This seems worth remarking because *C*2 embodies the fundamental property of ordered pairs. The derivation of *C*2 from *M*1 was described in [1]; the derivation of *M*1 from *C*2 is immediate, if we recall the definition of $x;y$ (for $\iota\iota x \cup \iota(\iota x \cup \iota y)$) and note that the following *C*4 (†348 of [2]) can be proved in *L* without using *M*1:

*C*4. $$(x) \quad (z \in \iota x \cup \iota y \equiv . \; z = x \vee z = y) \equiv . \; x \in V \,.\, y \in V.$$

In [2] a special assertion †610 that the successor of an element is an element is needed in order to guarantee that natural numbers are elements. In *L* natural numbers are by *C*1 elements. In any case it seems necessary to postulate elementhood of natural numbers in order to obtain natural arithmetic. However, it is not always necessary, in order to develop a theory about a certain kind of classes, to assume that such classes are elements. Sometimes it is possible to postulate merely that what we take to be members of each such class are elements. Thus, in what follows, we shall define real numbers as a certain kind of class of ratios, and then develop arithmetic of real numbers without assuming that real numbers are elements. This is possible, because, in this connection, we are primarily concerned with real numbers, not with classes of real numbers.

The step of refusing to postulate that real numbers be elements has its consequences. In the first place, we are deprived of the class NR of real numbers. Usually, we first define NR and then begin each theorem about real numbers with a clause such as $x \in NR \,\blacksquare\, y \in NR$. Since, however, real numbers may be non-elements, there is the danger that statements beginning with clauses like $x \in NR \,\blacksquare\, y \in NR$ may *all* become trivially demonstrable by the theorem of L (*230 of [2]):

$$x \in \hat{x}\phi \equiv \blacksquare\, x \in V \,\blacksquare\, \phi.$$

We are compelled to define the statement matrix $NR(x)$ directly, and then begin theorems on real numbers with clauses like $NR(x) \,\blacksquare\, NR(y)$. This switching from $x \in NR$ to $NR(x)$ has the advantage that, while $x \in NR$ is refutable for every non-element x, $NR(x)$ may be provable for certain non-elements x. A second consequence of our step is connected with the theorem of least upper bound, which, in contrast with other ordinary laws of real arithmetic, deals explicitly with classes of real numbers instead of dealing merely with individual real numbers. Consequently, as we have mentioned above, it cannot be proved within L in its full generality, because we cannot profitably talk about *all* such classes in L.

Obviously the system L is incomplete in respect of its elementhood axioms. Indeed, for any class with more than three members, we cannot decide in L whether it is an element or it is not an element (cf. [1], p. 135). We may yet raise the question whether the elementhood axioms are completable. The answer falls into two parts. On the one hand, they are demonstrably incompletable[1)]. Thus, in the system L, if every statement of elementhood were demonstrable or refutable, then, contrary to Gödel's theorem, *every* statement ϕ would be demonstrable or refutable, since, in L (using the notation of [2] and [1]),

$$\vdash \phi \equiv \blacksquare\, \hat{x}(x \tilde{\epsilon}\, x \,\blacksquare\, \sim\phi) \in V.$$

Proof. †260	$\hat{x}(x \tilde{\epsilon}\, x) \tilde{\epsilon}\, V$	(1)
*100, *117 (& hp)	$\sim\phi \supset (x)(x \tilde{\epsilon}\, x \equiv \blacksquare\, x \tilde{\epsilon}\, x \,\blacksquare\, \sim\phi)$	
*121	$\supset\!: [1 \equiv \blacksquare]\ \hat{x}\,(x \tilde{\epsilon}\, x \,\blacksquare\, \sim\phi) \tilde{\epsilon}\, V$	(2)

1) The following proof is a modification of Quine's proof for systems in which V is an element. See p. 140 of [5].

*100, *117 (& hp)	$\phi \supset (x) \sim(x \tilde{\epsilon} x \,.\, \sim\phi)$	
*194	$\supset \hat{x}(x \tilde{\epsilon} x \,.\, \sim\phi) = \Lambda$	
*223	$\supset : \hat{x}(x \tilde{\epsilon} x \,.\, \sim\phi) \epsilon V [\,.\equiv 370]$	(3)
*100	$[3 \,.\, 2 \,.\, \supset :] \phi \equiv . \ \hat{x}(x \tilde{\epsilon} x \,.\, \sim\phi) \epsilon V.$	

On the other hand, we seem to have a complete set of elementhood axioms, if we add the following two restrictive axioms to the system L:

$M4.$ $x \epsilon V \supset (y)(z)(z \epsilon x \,.\, (w)(^*\grave{\epsilon}(\Lambda, w) \supset . \, w \epsilon y) \,. \supset . \, z \epsilon y).$

$M5.$ $x \epsilon V \supset (\exists y)(\exists z)(x = \iota y \cup \iota z).$

Therein $^*\grave{\epsilon}\,(\Lambda, w)$ is an abbreviation for the assertion that the empty class Λ is w or else belongs to w or else belongs to some class which belongs to w or else etc. With $M4$ and $M5$ we can prove in L the following theorem:

$ET.$ $x \epsilon V \equiv . \, x = \Lambda \vee (\exists y)(\exists z)(^*\grave{\epsilon}(\Lambda, y) \,.\, ^*\grave{\epsilon}(\Lambda, z) \,.$
$(w)((w')(^*\grave{\epsilon}(\Lambda, w') \supset . \, w' \epsilon w) \supset . \, y \epsilon w \,.\, z \epsilon w) \,.$
$x = \iota y \cup \iota z).$

According to ET, the elements of L (strengthened by adding $M4$ and $M5$) are just the classes Λ, $\iota\Lambda$, $\iota\Lambda \cup \iota\iota\Lambda$, etc. enumerated in [1] (cf. pp. 135—136). Consequently, we can decide whether a class is an element or not, if we can decide whether the right-hand side of ET holds true of it or not; and, the elementhood axioms of L are incompletable only in the sense that there must exist some formula ϕ with x as its only free variable for which it is formally undecidable whether the class of elements x satisfying ϕ is or is not identical with one of the elements enumerated in [1].

3.3. *Real Numbers*

We proceed to describe how in L we can deal adequately with natural numbers, rational numbers, and real numbers[1)].

With the start obtained in [1], we can prove in L all the familiar theorems of natural arithmetic, including the theorem that every class of natural numbers has a least member. In L we can also define the notion of "the least number x such that —x—", sometimes abbreviated as μ_x(—x—). By $M3$, $(\exists y)(x)(x \epsilon y \equiv . \, x \epsilon V . \text{—}x\text{—})$. Since natural numbers are elements, and since, with regard to each matrix —x— we are primarily concerned with the least *number* which fulfills it, we can conveniently consider $\mu_x(x \epsilon y)$ or simply μy instead of μ_x(—x—). We use the definition[2)]:

1) Formal details of the developments of the theory of these numbers will be omitted on the ground that one may easily convince oneself by studying the definitions below that such details could be supplied. However, such details can be found in the thesis referred to under footnote one. Cf. also [6] for the theory of primes and ratios, and [7] for the derivation of the theory of natural and real numbers.

2) The numbering of definitions is rather arbitrary except that numbers already used in [1] and [2] are avoided.

$D58.\qquad \mu y$ *for* $(\imath x)(x \in y \,.\, (n)(n \in y \supset n \geqslant x))$.

According to this definition, the definition *D*17 of [2] for the description symbol, and the definition of natural numbers in [1], $\mu y=0$ when no natural number belongs to the class *y*. We can also prove the following: $(\exists m)(m \in y) \supset \mu y \in y$; $n \in y \supset n \geqslant \mu y$.

If we want our rational numbers to be elements in *L*, we cannot identify a rational number with a class of all ordered pairs of natural numbers having the same ratio, because such infinite classes of pairs cannot be proved to be elements in *L* and we do need for our purpose that rational numbers be elements. An alternative course which we shall adopt is to identify a rational number with an ordered pair of relative primes[1]. Using such definitions, we need certain theorems concerning relative primes in order to develop the theory of rational numbers. The following are a set of definitions with which we can derive the theory of rational numbers.

$D59.\quad PI$ *for* $\hat{x}(x \in Nn \,.\, x \neq 0)$.

$D60.\quad Prm(x, y)$ *for* $x, y \in Nn \,.\, (z)(w)(x')(z, w, x' \in Nn \,.\, x = z \times x' \,.\, y = w \times x' \,.\supset x' = 1)$.

$D61.\quad (z, w)Prm(x, y)$ *for* $x \in Nn \,.\, y \in PI \,.\, Prm(z, w) \,.\, z \times y = x \times w$.

$D62.\quad x/y$ *for* $\hat{z}(\exists w)(\exists w')((w, w')Prm(x, y) \,.\, z \in w \,;\, w')$.

$D63.\quad x \,{}_s\!> y$ *for* $(\exists z)(\exists z')(\exists w)(\exists w')(z, w \in Nn \,.\, z', w' \in PI \,.\, x = z/z' \,.\, y = w/w') \,.\, (z)(z')(w)(w')(z, w \in Nn \,.\, z', w' \in PI \,.\, x = z/z' \,.\, y = w/w' \,.\supset z \times w' > w \times z')$.

$D64.\quad x \,{}_s\!\geqslant y$ *for* $x \,{}_s\!> y \vee x = y$.

$D65.\quad x \,{}_s\!\leqslant y$ *for* $y \,{}_s\!\geqslant x$.

$D66.\quad x \,{}_s\!< y$ *for* $y \,{}_s\!> x$.

$D67.\quad x \,{}_s\!+ y$ *for* $(\imath x')(z)(z')(w)(w')(z, w \in Nn \,.\, z', w' \in PI \,.\, x = z/z' \,.\, y = w/w' \,.\supset x' = (zw' + wz')/(z'w'))$.

$D68.\quad x \,{}_s\!\times y$ *for* $(\imath x')(z)(z')(w)(w')(z, w \in Nn \,.\, z', w' \in PI \,.\, x = z/z' \,.\, y = w/w' \,.\supset x' = (zw)/(z'w'))$.

$D69.\quad {}_s x$ *for* $(x/1)$.

$D70.\quad Ra$ *for* $\hat{w}(\exists x)(\exists y)(x \in Nn \,.\, y \in PI \,.\, w = x/y)$.

$D71.\quad PRa$ *for* $\hat{u}(\exists x)(\exists y)(x, y \in PI \,.\, u = x/y)$.

Then we are in a position to derive the arithmetic of real numbers. We may begin with the arithmetic of non-negative real numbers, the definitions of which are stated below:

---

1) Similar definitions are employed in [6].

D72. $Nr(x)$ *for* $x \neq Ra \,.\, x = \hat{z}(z =_s 0 \vee (\exists y)(y \in x \,.\, y \,_s\!> z))$.

D73. $x \,_r\!> y$ *for* $Nr(x) \,.\, Nr(y) \,.\, (\exists z)(z \in x \,.\, z \,\tilde{\in}\, y)$.

D74. $x \,_r\!\geqslant y$ *for* $x \,_r\!> y \vee \,.\, Nr(x) \,.\, Nr(y) \,.\, x = y$.

D75. $x \,_r\!< y$ *for* $y \,_r\!> x$.

D76. $x \,_r\!\leqslant y$ *for* $y \,_r\!\geqslant x$.

D77. $x \,_r\!+ y$ *for* $\hat{u}(\exists z)(\exists z')(z \in x \,.\, z' \in y \,.\, u = z \,_s\!+ z')$.

D78. $x \,_r\!\times y$ *for* $\hat{u}(\exists z)(\exists z')(z \in x \,.\, z' \in y \,.\, u = z \,_s\!\times z')$.

D79. $_r x$ *for* $\hat{y}(y =_s 0 \vee x \,_s\!> y)$.

D80. $x \,_r\!- y$ *for* $(\imath z)(Nr(z) \,.\, x = y \,_r\!+ z)$.

Using these definitions, we can prove in L the following twenty statements:

R1. $Nr(x) \,.\, Nr(y) \,.\, \supset Nr(x \,_r\!+ y)$.

R2. $Nr(x) \,.\, Nr(y) \,.\, \supset Nr(x \,_r\!\times y)$.

R3. $Nr(x) \,.\, Nr(y) \,.\, \supset x \,_r\!+ y = y \,_r\!+ x$.

R4. $Nr(x) \,.\, Nr(y) \,.\, Nr(z) \,.\, \supset x \,_r\!+ (y \,_r\!+ z) = (x \,_r\!+ y) \,_r\!+ z$.

R5. $Nr(x) \,.\, Nr(y) \,.\, \supset x \,_r\!\times y = y \,_r\!\times x$.

R6. $Nr(x) \,.\, Nr(y) \,.\, Nr(z) \,.\, \supset x \,_r\!\times (y \,_r\!\times z) = (x \,_r\!\times y) \,_r\!\times z$.

R7. $Nr(x) \,.\, Nr(y) \,.\, Nr(z) \,.\, \supset x \,_r\!\times (y \,_r\!+ z) = (x \,_r\!\times y) + (x \,_r\!\times z)$.

R8. $Nr(_{rs}0)$.

R9. $Nr(_{rs}1)$.

R10. $_{rs}1 \neq_{rs} 0$.

R11. $Nr(x) \supset x \,_r\!+_{rs} 0 = x$.

R12. $Nr(x) \supset x \,_r\!\times_{rs} 1 = x$.

R13. $Nr(x) \,.\, Nr(y) \,.\, \supset \,.\, x = y \vee x \,_r\!> y \vee x \,_r\!< y$.

R14. $x \,_r\!> y \supset \sim(y \,_r\!> x)$.

R15. $x \,_r\!> y \,.\, y \,_r\!> z \,.\, \supset x \,_r\!> z$.

R16. $Nr(x) \,.\, y \,_r\!> z \,.\, \supset x \,_r\!+ y \,_r\!> x \,_r\!+ z$.

R17. $x \,_r\!\geqslant y \supset (\exists z)(Nr(z) \,.\, x = y \,_r\!+ z)$.

R18. $x \,_r\!>_{rs} 0 \,.\, y \,_r\!> z \,.\, \supset x \,_r\!\times y \,_r\!> x \,_r\!\times z$.

R19. $Nr(x) \,.\, Nr(y) \,.\, y \neq_{rs} 0 \,.\, \supset (\exists z)(Nr(z) \,.\, x = y \,_r\!\times z)$.

R20. *If* y, z *are not free in* ϕ, *then* $\vdash (\exists x)\phi \,.\, (\exists y)(x)(\phi \supset y \,_r\!\geqslant x) \,.$
$\supset (\exists z)(Nr(z) \,.\, (y)((x)(\phi \supset y \,_r\!\geqslant x) \equiv y \,_r\!\geqslant z))$.

The proofs for *R*1—*R*20 are rather complicated but not particularly difficult. For example, we can prove *R*20 for the class $\hat{u}(\exists x)(\phi \,.\, u \in x)$ by the following easy consequences of the preceding definitions:

$T1.\quad y \,{}_r\!\geqslant x \supset . Nr(x) . Nr(y).$

$T2.\quad Nr(x) . Nr(y) . \supset . x \,{}_r\!\geqslant y \equiv y \subset x.$

$T3.\quad x \,{}_r\!\geqslant y . y \,{}_r\!\geqslant z . \supset x \,{}_r\!\geqslant z.$

$T4.\quad y \subset x . Nr(x) . \supset y \neq Ra.$

$T5.\quad Nr(x) \supset : w \in x \equiv . w =_s 0 \vee (\exists y)(y \in x . y \,{}_s\!> w).$

Once we possess the usual theorems for the arithmetic of non-negative real numbers, it is comparatively easier to extend the theorems to signed real numbers. We use the following definitions:

$D81.\quad -x$ *for* $x \cap \overline{\iota\, {}_s0}.$

$D82.\quad NNr(x)$ *for* $(\exists y)(Nr(y) . y \neq_{rs} 0 . x = -y).$

$D83.\quad NR(x)$ *for* $Nr(x) \vee NNr(x).$

$D84.\quad |x|$ *for* $(\iota z)(Nr(x) . z = x . \vee . NNr(x) . x \cup \iota\, {}_s0 = z).$

$D85.\quad x \,{}_R\!> y$ *for* $Nr(x) . NNr(y) . \vee . x \,{}_r\!> y . \vee . NNr(x) . NNr(y) . |y| \,{}_r\!> |x|.$

$D86.\quad x \,{}_R\!\geqslant y$ *for* $x \,{}_R\!> y \vee . NR(x) . NR(y) . x = y.$

$D87.\quad x \,{}_R\!\leqslant y$ *for* $y \,{}_R\!\geqslant x.$

$D88.\quad x \,{}_R\!< y$ *for* $y \,{}_R\!> x.$

$D89.\quad x \,{}_R\!+ y$ *for* $(\iota z)\,(Nr(x) . Nr(y) . z = x \,{}_r\!+ y . \vee . NNr(x) . NNr(y) . z = -(|x| \,{}_r\!+ |y|) . \vee . NNr(y) . x \,{}_r\!\geqslant |y| . z = x \,{}_r\!- |y| . \vee . NNr(y) . |y| \,{}_r\!> x . z = -(|y| \,{}_r\!- x) . \vee . NNr(x) . |x| \,{}_r\!> y . z = -(|x| \,{}_r\!- y) . \vee . NNr(x) . y \,{}_r\!\geqslant |x| . z = y \,{}_r\!- |x|).$

$D90.\quad x \,{}_R\!- y$ *for* $(\iota z)(x \,{}_r\!\geqslant y . z = x \,{}_r\!- y . \vee . x \,{}_r\!< y . z = -(y \,{}_r\!- x) . \vee . Nr(x) . NNr(y) . z = x \,{}_r\!+ |y| . \vee . NNr(x) . Nr(y) . z = -(|x| \,{}_r\!+ y) . \vee : NNr(x) . NNr(y) : |x| \,{}_r\!\geqslant |y| . z = -(|x| \,{}_r\!- |y|) . \vee . |x| \,{}_r\!< |y| . z = (|y| \,{}_r\!- |x|)).$

$D91.\quad x \,{}_R\!\times y$ *for* $(\iota z)\,(Nr(x) . Nr(y) . \vee . NNr(x) . NNr(y) : z = |x| \,{}_r\!\times |y| : \vee : Nr(x) . NNr(y) . x \neq {}_{rs}0 . \vee . NNr(x) . Nr(y) . y \neq {}_{rs}0 : z = -(|x| \,{}_r\!\times |y|) : \vee : x = {}_{rs}0 . NNr(y) . \vee . NNr(x) . y = {}_{rs}0 : z = {}_{rs}0).$

$D92.\quad {}_Rx$ *for* ${}_rx.$

$D93.\quad RA(x)$ *for* $(\exists y)(y \in Ra . x = {}_Ry \vee x = -{}_Ry).$

$D94.\quad IN(x)$ *for* $(\exists y)(y \in Nn . x = {}_{Rs}y \vee x = -{}_{Rs}y).$

With these definitions, we can prove in L fairly easily twenty statements corresponding to $R1$—$R20$ for signed real numbers. In other words, we can prove in L that the real numbers form a complete ordered field.

§ 4. Functions of Real Variables

In order to develop the theory of real functions, we need a predicative extension R of the system L given in the preceding section. This system R, the predicative theory of real-sets, can be obtained from L in the same way as NB was obtained from ZF, and has only a finite number of set-theoretical axioms. In such a theory, the usual definitions and theorems about real functions and the calculus can be obtained without much trouble. We give a brief sketch. Often we omit the subscript R.

D100. *The ordered pair of two real numbers is given by*:

$$(x, y) \text{ for } \hat{z}(NR(x) \,\&\, NR(y) \,\&\, (Eu)(Ev)(u \in x \,\&\, v \in y \,\&\, z = u; v)).$$

D101. *A relation of real numbers (similarly, $Rel(X)$ for natural numbers, replacing NR by Nn)*:

$$Rel(X) \text{ for } (z)(z \in X \supset (Ex)(Ey)(NR(x) \,\&\, NR(y) \,\&\, z = (x, y)).$$

D102. *A function from reals to reals (similarly $Fcn(X)$ for natural numbers)*:

$$Fcn(X) \text{ for } Rel(X) \,\&\, (x)(y)(z)(((x, y) \in X \,\&\, (x, z) \in X) \supset y = z).$$

D103. $F(x)$ *for* $(\imath y)(Fcn(F) \,\&\, (x, y) \in F)$.

D104. $\lim_{x \to a} F(x)$ *for* $(\imath y)\,(u)\,(u > 0 \supset (Ev)\,(v > 0 \,\&\, (x)\,((x \neq a \,\&\, |x - a| < v) \supset |F(x) - y| < u))$.

D105. $Seq(x)$ *for* $(y)(y \in x \supset (Eu)(Ev)(y = u; v \,\&\, u \in Nn \,\&\, NR(\check{x}``u)))$.

D106. a_n *for* $\hat{u}(Seq(a) \,\&\, n; u \in a)$.

D107. $a_n \to b$ *for* $Seq(a) \,\&\, NR(b) \,\&\, (u)\,(u > 0 \supset (Em)\,(n)\,(n > m \supset |a_n - b| < u))$.

D108. $Conv(a)$ *for* $Seq(a) \,\&\, (Ev)(a_n \to v)$.

D109. $\lim a_n$ *for* $(\imath x)(Conv(a) \,\&\, a_n \to x)$.

D110. Cauchy (a) *for* $Seq(a) \,\&\, (u)\,(u > 0 \supset (En)\,(m)\,(k)\,((n < m \,\&\, n < k) \supset |a_m - a_k| < u))$.

D111. $bd(a)$ *for* $Seq(a) \,\&\, (Ex)(n)(a_n < x)$.

D112. $Sub(a, b)$ *for* $Seq(a) \,\&\, Seq(b) \,\&\, (Ex)\,(Fcn(x) \,\&\, (m)(x(m) < x(m + 1)) \,\&\, (n)(a_n = b_{x(n)}))$.

D113. $CI(a, b)$ *for* $\hat{x}(NR(a) \,\&\, NR(b) \,\&\, a \leqslant x \,\&\, x \leqslant b)$.

D114. $OI(a, b)$ *for* $\hat{x}(x \in CI(a, b) \,\&\, x \neq a \,\&\, x \neq b)$.

*D*115. $Cont(F, a)$ *for* $Fcn(F)$ & $NR(a)$ & $(u)(u > 0 \supset (Ev)(v > 0$ & $(x)(|x - a| < v \supset |f(x) - f(a)| < u)))$.

*D*116. $Conti(F, X)$ *for* $(y)(y \in X \supset Cont(F, y))$.

*D*117. y/x *for* $(\imath z)(x \times z = y)$.

*D*118. $F'(x)$ *for* $\lim_{u \to 0} \frac{F(x+u) - F(x)}{u}$.

*D*119. $Diff(F, X)$ *for* $Fcn(F)$ & $(x)(x \in X \supset (Ey)(x; y \in X$ & $(Ez)(NR(z)$ & $F'(x) = z)))$.

*D*120. $\int G dx = F$ *for* $(x)(F'(x) = G(x))$ & $Fcn(F)$ & $Fcn(G)$.

Standard theorems can be derived in R with standard proofs: A few examples are:

4.1 $Seq(a) \supset ((a_n \to x$ & $a_n \to y) \supset x = y)$.

4.2 $\lim a_n + \lim b_n = \lim (a_n + b_n)$, etc.

4.3 $Conv(a) \equiv \text{Cauchy}(a)$.

4.4 $Conv(a) \supset bd(a)$.

4.5 $bd(a) \supset (Eb)(Sub(b, a)$ & $Conv(b))$.

4.6 $Cont(F, a) \supset (x)((Seq(x)$ & $x_n \to a) \supset \lim_{x_n \to a} F(x_n) = F(a))$.

4.7 $(Ey)(F'(x) = y$ & $NR(y)) \supset Cont(F, x)$.

4.8 $(Conti(F, CI(a, b))$ & $Diff(F, OI(a, b))$ & $F(a) = 0$ & $F(b) = 0)$ $\supset (Ex)(a < x$ & $x < b$ & $F'(x) = 0)$.

4.9 $\Big(Conti(F, CI(a, b))$ & $Diff(F, OI(a, b))) \supset (Ex)(a < x$ & $x < b$ & $F'(x) = \frac{F(b) - F(a)}{b - a}\Big)$.

4.10 $Conti(G, NR) \supset (EF)\Big(\Big(\int G dx = F$ & $(H)\Big(\Big(\int G dx = H \supset (Ea)(x)\Big(H(x) = F(x) + a\Big)\Big)\Big)$.

References

[1] Hao Wang, A new theory of element and number, *Jour. Symbolic Logic*, **13** (1948), 129—137.

[2] W. V. Quine, Mathematical Logic, New York, 1940.

[3] Alfred Tarski, Introduction to Logic and to the Methodology of Deductive Sciences, New York, 1941.

[4] Garrett Birkhoff and Saunders MacLane, A Survey of Modern Algebra, New York, 1946.

[5] W. V. Quine, Element and number, *Jour. Symbolic Logic*, **6** (1941), 135—149.

[6] A. N. Whitehead and Bertrand Russell, Principia Mathematica, vol. 3. Cambridge, England, 1913.

[7] E. Landau, Grundlagen der Analysis, 1930, reprint, New York, 1965.

PART FIVE

PREDICATIVE SET THEORY

CHAPTER XXI

CERTAIN PREDICATES DEFINED BY INDUCTION SCHEMATA*

It is known that we can introduce in number theory (for example, the system Z of Hilbert-Bernays[1]) by induction schemata certain predicates of natural numbers which cannot be expressed explicitly within the framework of number theory. The question arises how we can define these predicates in some richer system, without employing induction schemata. In this paper a general notion of definability by induction (relative to number theory), which seems to apply to all the known predicates of this kind, is introduced; and it is proved that in a system L_1 which forms an extension of number theory all predicates which are definable by induction (hereafter to be abbreviated d.i.) according to the definition are explicitly expressible.

In order to define such predicates and prove theorems answering to their induction schemata, we have to allow certain impredicative classes in L_1. However, if we want merely to prove that for each constant number the special case of the induction schema for a predicate d.i. is provable, we do not have to assume the existence of impredicative classes. A certain weaker system L_2, in which only predicative classes of natural numbers are allowed, is sufficient for the purpose. It is noted that a truth definition for number theory can be obtained in L_2. Consistency proofs for number theory do not seem to be formalizable in L_2, although they can, it is observed, be formalized in L_1.

In general, given any ordinary formal system (say Zermelo set theory), it is possible to define by induction schemata, in the same manner as in number theory, certain predicates which are not explicitly definable in the system. Here again, by extending the system in an analogous fashion, these predicates become expressible in the result-

---

* This chapter appeared in *Journal of Symbolic Logic*, **18** (1953), 49—59. Slightly later, John Myhill studied related questions independently in his paper "Arithmetic with creative definitions by induction", *ibid.*, pp. 115—118. The relation of such predicates to hyperarithmetic predicates are investigated as a side issue in Kleene's paper, *Trans. Am. Math. Soc.*, **79** (1955), 312—340.

1) See p. 384 of D. Hilbert and P. Bernays, Grundlagen der Mathematik, Vol. II (Berlin, 1939). This system Z contains the quantification theory (for natural numbers), the axioms for identity, the Peano axioms for arithmetic, and the recursion equations for addition and multiplication. Throughout this paper, number theory will be understood to be this system Z.

ing system. The crucial predicate instrumental to obtaining a truth definition for a given system is taken as an example.

As a first example of predicates d.i. (relative to number theory) we mention the predicate $M(n, k)$ discovered by Hilbert and Bernays in setting up a truth definition for their system Z of number theory[1]:

$$\begin{cases} M(n,0) \equiv R(n), \\ M(n,k+1) \equiv ((R_1(n) \& (x) M(f(n,x),k)) \vee (R_2(n) \& (Ex) M(f(n,x),k))). \end{cases}$$

Therein $R(n), R_1(n), R_2(n)$, and $f(n, m)$ are all recursive (in the customary sense) and therefore explicitly definable in number theory. It has been shown by them that the predicate M is not expressible in number theory.

We are to study predicates defined similarly to M. In view of the form of the induction schema for M, we propose the following definition:

Definition 1. *A predicate $P(n_1, \cdots, n_s, k)$ of natural numbers is said to be d.i. (relative to number theory), if it satisfies an induction schema of the following form (where for brevity, we assume there is only one parameter, taking s to be 1):*

$$(D) \begin{cases} P(n,0) \equiv Q(n), \\ P(n,k+1) \equiv R(n, k, P(f_1(n, k, m_1, \cdots, m_i), h_1(k)), \cdots, \\ \qquad P(f_j(n, k, m_1, \cdots, m_i), h_j(k))). \end{cases}$$

Herein apart from occurrences of the symbol P as indicated, only symbols of number theory occur, i and j are two constants, and the variables $m_1, \cdots, m_i$ are all bound in R. Moreover, the functions $f_1, \cdots, f_i$, $h_1, \cdots, h_j$ are all definable in number theory so that, in particular, we can prove in number theory: for every $k, h_1(k) \leqslant k, \cdots, h_j(k) \leqslant k$.

The last conditions on $h_1, \cdots, h_j$ guarantee that once $P(n, 0), \cdots, P(n, m)$ are determined for all n, $P(n, m+1)$ is also determined for all n, by merely those cases of (D) where k is smaller than $m+1$. On account of these conditions, if in a suitable extension of number theory (for example, the system L_1 or the system L_2 to be described below) we can prove these cases of (D) for a certain predicate expression P and demonstrate $(P(n, 0) \equiv Q_0(n)), \cdots, (P(n, m) \equiv Q_m(n))$, where $Q_0(n), \cdots, Q_m(n)$ are all sentences no longer involving the predicate P, then we can find a sentence $Q_{m+1}(n)$ of the system which does not involve P and prove: $P(n, m+1) \equiv Q_{m+1}(n)$.

Let us say that a predicate P is *indirectly d.i.*, if either (1) there is a schema of the form (D) wherein, besides the symbols of number theory, symbols for predicates d.i. also occur, or (2) symbols for pre-

1) Ibid., pp. 328—340.

dicates defined as in (1) also occur, or etc. We shall only discuss these predicates indirectly d.i. in passing. Our main interest lies in studying the simpler predicates d.i. falling under Def. I, since all the related predicates which are of special interest belong to this type.

Consider now the following system L_1 which is roughly an extension of the number theory Z in which all expressible classes of natural numbers are assumed to exist. L_1 contains the number theory Z (with its variables $m, n, \cdots$ for natural numbers) and variables $X, Y, \cdots$ for classes of natural numbers. Sentences of L_1 are formed from simple sentences of the form $m\eta X$ (m belongs to X) plus those of Z, by means of truth-functional operators and quantifiers for both kinds of variable. The ordinary quantification theory[1)] is assumed for each kind of variable, and the induction principle of Z is replaced by the following stronger one:

*Ax*1. $(X)((0\eta X \,\&\, (m)(m\eta X \supset (m+1)\eta X)) \supset (n)n\eta X)$.

Further axioms of L_1 which lie beyond Z, are the following:

*Ax*2. Substitutivity of identity. $m=n \supset (m\eta X \supset n\eta X)$.

*Ax*3. Existence of classes. For any sentence p of L_1 in which Y does not occur: $(EY)(m)(m\eta Y \equiv p)$.

We want to show that every predicate $P(n, k)$ of natural numbers d.i., as determined by a schema (D) given above, is explicitly definable in L_1.

The principal question is to define in L_1 a class K which contains all the ordered pairs $\langle n, k\rangle$ such that $P(n, k)$ holds according to the schema (D). In order to do so, we consider first a sequence of classes the m-th among which contains all the ordered pairs $\langle n, k\rangle$ such that $k<m$ and $P(n, k)$ holds according to the schema (D). Then K is (roughly speaking) just the union (sum class) of all the classes of this sequence.

The formal definition for K is as follows:

1.1. $\langle m, n\rangle$ for $2^m \cdot 3^n$.

1.2. $G(n, k, X)$ for $R(n, k, \langle f_1(n, k, m_1, \cdots, m_i), h_1(k)\rangle\eta X, \cdots, \langle f_j(n, k, m_1, \cdots, m_i), h_j(k)\rangle\eta X)$.

1.3. $K_m(X)$ for $(k)(n)(k \leq m \supset (\langle n, k\rangle\eta X \equiv ((k=0 \,\&\, Q(n)) \vee (Ek_1)(k=k_1+1 \,\&\, G(n, k_1, X)))))$.

1.4. $K(n, k)$ or $\langle n, k\rangle\eta K$ for $(X)(K_k(X) \supset \langle n, k\rangle\eta X)$.

1) For instance, the axioms and rules of inference on p. 88 of W. V. Quine's Mathematical Logic (New York, 1940), with ϕ, ϕ', and ψ understood as arbitrary sentences of L_1.

We prove first the existence of each member of the sequence of classes whose union is to be the desired class K.

1.5. $(EX)K_0(X)$.

Proof. By 1.3, $K_0(X)\equiv(n)(\langle n, 0\rangle\eta X\equiv Q(n))$. By $Ax3$, $(EX)(n)(k)(\langle n, k\rangle\eta X\equiv Q(n))$. Therefore the theorem is proved.

1.6. $(EX)K_m(X)\supset(EY)K_{m+1}(Y)$.

Proof. Assume $K_m(X)$. By $Ax3$, there exists a class Y such that: (1) $(n)(k)(\langle n,k\rangle\eta Y\equiv((k=0\&Q(n))\vee(Ek_1)(k=k_1+1\&G(n,k_1,X))))$. So, by 1.3, if $k\leqslant m$, then $\langle n, k\rangle\eta X\equiv\langle n, k\rangle\eta Y$. But by hypothesis (cf. Def. 1), we can prove: $h_1(k)\leqslant k, \cdots, h_j(k)\leqslant k$. Hence we can substitute Y for X in (1) and obtain, by 1.3:$K_{m+1}(Y)$.

1.7. $(m)(EX)K_m(X)$.

Proof. By 1.5, 1.6, and induction (a consequence of $Ax1$ and $Ax3$).

Next we prove that these classes are uniquely determined at least for those elements of them in which we are chiefly interested.

1.8. $(k\leqslant 0\ \&\ K_0(X)\ \&\ K_0(Y))\supset(\langle n, k\rangle\eta X\equiv\langle n, k\rangle\eta Y)$.

Proof. By 1.3, if $k\leqslant 0\ \&\ K_0(X)\ \&\ K_0(Y)$, then $\langle n, k\rangle\eta X\equiv Q(n)$, and $\langle n, k\rangle\eta Y\equiv Q(n)$. Hence the theorem is proved.

1.9. If $(X)(Y)(k)(n)((k\leqslant m\ \&\ K_m(X)\ \&\ K_m(Y))\supset(\langle n, k\rangle\eta X\equiv\langle n, k\rangle\eta Y))$, then $(k\leqslant m+1\ \&\ K_{m+1}(X')\ \&\ K_{m+1}(Y'))\supset(\langle n, k\rangle\eta X'\equiv\langle n, k\rangle\eta Y')$.

Proof. Assume that $K_{m+1}(X')$ and $K_{m+1}(Y')$. Then, by 1.3, we have also: $K_m(X')$ and $K_m(Y')$. Hence, by hypothesis, if $k\leqslant m$, then $(\langle n, k\rangle\eta X'\equiv\langle n, k\rangle\eta Y')$. But by hypothesis (cf. Def. 1), we can prove: $h_1(k)\leqslant k, \cdots, h_j(k)\leqslant k$. Hence, by 1.2, we have: $(k\leqslant m+1\ \&\ k=k_1+1)\supset(G(n, k_1, X')\equiv G(n, k_1, Y'))$. Therefore, by 1.3, theorem is proved.

1.10. $(m)(X)(Y)(k)(n)((k\leqslant m\ \&K_m(X)\ \&K_m(Y))\supset(\langle n,k\rangle\eta X\equiv\langle n,k\rangle\eta Y))$.

Proof. By 1.8, 1.9, and induction (a consequence of $Ax1$ and $Ax3$).

1.11. $(K_m(X)\ \&\ k\leqslant m)\supset(K(n, k)\equiv\langle n, k\rangle\eta X)$.

Proof. By 1.10, $(K_m(X)\ \&\ k\leqslant m\&\langle n, k\rangle\eta X)\supset(Y)(K_m(Y)\supset\langle n, k\rangle\eta Y)$. Hence, by 1.4, theorem is proved.

With 1.7 and 1.11, we are ready to prove the main property of K.

1.12.
$$\begin{cases} K(n, 0)\equiv Q(n), \\ K(n, k+1)\equiv R(n, k, K(f_1(n, k, m_1, \cdots, m_i), h_1(k)), \cdots, \\ \qquad K(f_j(n, k, m_1, \cdots, m_i), h_j(k))). \end{cases}$$

Proof. By 1.11 and 1.3, $K_0(X) \supset (K(n, 0) \equiv Q(n))$. Hence by 1.7, $K(n, 0) \equiv Q(n)$. Similarly, by 1.11 and 1.3, we have: (1)$K_{k+1}(X) \supset (K(n, k+1) \equiv G(n, k, X))$. But by hypothesis (cf. Def. 1), $h_1(k) \leqslant k, \cdots, h_i(k) \leqslant k$. Hence, by 1.11 and 1.2, we can eliminate X from the right-hand side of (1) by using K. Therefore, by 1.7, the second part of the theorem is also proved.

Consequently, we have proved that every predicate P d.i. is expressible in L_1.

It is not hard to see that every predicate indirectly d.i. (relative to number theory) is also expressible in L_1. Thus, we can eliminate one by one the predicates occurring in the induction schema for a predicate P indirectly d.i. For example, if in the schema (D) for the predicate P a symbol for a predicate d.i. occurs, we can first express the latter predicate as in 1.1—1.4 and then replace in the schema (D) the symbol Q by the corresponding predicate-expression of L_1. Despite the presence in the resulting schema (D') of expressions of L_1 which lie beyond number theory, it will be a routine matter to check that we can proceed in an exactly analogous manner as above and prove two theorems which are like the two sentences of the schema (D') except for containing in place of the symbol P a certain predicate expression of L_1. If other symbols for predicates d.i. or indirectly d.i. occur in the schema (D) for a predicate indirectly d.i., they can be handled similarly.

Instead of the system L_1, we can also use a system L_3 of Quine[1] which can be characterized as differing from L_1 in that the number theory Z is replaced by a theory of elements (sets) m, n, etc. with a single primitive predicate ϵ so that expressions of the forms $m \epsilon n$, etc. and $m\eta X$, etc. are the only simple sentences from which all sentences of the system are built up. Apart from the axioms and rules of inference of the quantification theories, the axioms of L_3 are the following (where this time $m = n$ stands for $(k)(k \epsilon m \equiv k \epsilon n)$):

*AxQ*1. Existence of the null set. $(En)(m) - m \epsilon n$.

*AxQ*2. Existence of finite sets. $(En)(m)(m \epsilon n \equiv (m \epsilon k \vee m = j))$.

*AxQ*3. $m = n \supset (m\eta X \supset n\eta X)$.

*AxQ*4. If p is any sentence of L_3 in which X does not occur, then $(EX)(m)(m\eta X \equiv p)$.

It is known[2] that in this system we can develop number theory so that natural numbers come out as certain elements (sets) of it and

1) See pp. 140—145 of Quine's *Element and number*, *Journal of Symbolic Logic*, **6** (1941), 135—149. The system is presented here in a somewhat different manner. However, it is essentially as rich as the system formulated there on p. 140, since we are only interested in finite sets (elements).

2) See the reference in the preceding footnote.

sentences as well as theorems answering to all those of L_1 are obtainable in it. Therefore, what is expressible in L_1 is also expressible in L_3.

We have two theorems:

Theorem 1. *Every predicate of natural numbers d.i. (relative to number theory) is definable explicitly in both* L_1 *and* L_3.

Theorem 2. *Every predicate indirectly d.i. is explicitly definable in both* L_1 *and* L_3.

Besides the predicate M of Hilbert-Bernays mentioned above, there are several other interesting predicates which are both d.i. (relative to number theory) and demonstrably inexpressible in number theory. The earliest is probably the one considered by Kalmár and Skolem[1]. Recently Kleene introduces another such predicate d.i. in his classification of predicates of natural numbers[2]. Then there is another form of such predicates studied by Hilbert and Bernays in connection with the formalization of Gentzen's consistency proof for number theory[3].

Both in formalizing Gentzen's proof, and in the case of a consistency proof for number theory, via a truth definition (using the predicate M mentioned above), Hilbert and Bernays observe that the recursion schemata for these predicates d.i. are the only tools employed which transcend the number theory Z itself[4]. Hence, from Theorem 1, we have immediately:

Theorem 3. *In both* L_1 *and* L_3 *we can formalize completely both Gentzen's consistency proof for number theory and the Hilbert-Bernays consistency proof via a truth definition.*

The question of defining a certain predicate in a certain system seems to involve a number of subtleties. We mention here merely the following. Consider a dyadic predicate of natural numbers d.i. as characterized by the schema (D). It is conceivable that we can define in a certain system a predicate expression P and prove for it in the same system all special cases $P(n, 0)$, $P(n, 1)$, $P(n, 2)$, etc. of the schema (D), without being able to prove two theorems answering to the two sentences (the second of which is a general assertion) of the schema. We shall indicate that such situations do arise, and arise in a significant way. In such a case it would appear natural also to say that the predicate is definable in the system. To distinguish this from

1) See the predicate H defined in the last part of Skolem's *Über Zurückführbarkeit einiger durch Rekursionen definierter Relationen auf arithmetische*, *Acta litterarum ac scientiarum* (Szeged), **8** (1936—1937), 73—88.

2) See p. 71 of S. C. Kleene, *Recursive predicates and quantifiers*, *Trans. Amer. Math. Soc.*, **53** (1943), 41—73.

3) Hilbert-Bernays, op. cit., p. 368.

4) Ibid., p. 369 and pp. 338—339.

the case considered above, we shall speak of definability* in a system so that if a predicate is definable in a system, it is also definable* in the system, but sometimes a predicate may be definable* but not definable in a system. We proceed to show that all predicates d.i. are definable* in a system L_2 which is much weaker than L_1 and contains no impredicative classes.

L_2 contains the same notations as L_1, the quantification theories for both kinds of variable, the axioms of the number theory Z (including the ordinary induction principle), and the following two axioms (instead of $Ax1$—$Ax3$):

$Ax'1$. If ϕm is any sentence of L_2, then $m=n\supset(\phi m\supset\phi n)$.

$Ax'2$. If p is any sentence of Z (i.e. any sentence of L_2 which contains no class variables), then $(EX)(m)(m\eta X\equiv p)$.

Let P be a predicate characterized by the schema (D) of Def. 1; we want to prove that P is definable* in L_2. Since L_2 has the same notation as L_1, the definitions 1.1—1.4 are all available in L_2 and the predicate K (1.4) can be defined in L_2. Our purpose is to prove in L_2 theorems which answer to all special cases of the schema (D) where k in the second sentence is a constant number, with the symbol K occurring in place of the symbol P.

We proceed as follows.

2.1. For each given constant m, we can prove in L_2: $(EX)K_m(X)$.

Proof. Since by hypothesis (cf. Def. 1), Q contains no symbols beyond number theory, by 1.3 and $Ax'2$, there exists a class X such that both $K_0(X)$ and $(n)(k)(\langle n,k\rangle\eta X\equiv Q(n))$. Hence, by 1.2 and $Ax'2$, there is Y,

$$(n)(k)(\langle n,k\rangle\eta Y\equiv((k=0\,\&\,Q(n))\vee(Ek_1)(k=k_1+1\,\&\,G(n,k_1,X)))).$$

Therefore, by reasoning similar to that in the proof of 1.6, we have: $K_1(Y)$. Similarly, we can obtain one after another classes Y', Y'', etc. for which we can prove in L_2: $K_2(Y')$, $K_3(Y'')$, etc. Hence the proof of 2.1 is complete.

2.2. For each given constant m, we can prove in L_2:

$$(X)(Y)(k)(n)((k\leqslant m\,\&\,K_m(X)\,\&\,K_m(Y))\supset(\langle n,k\rangle\eta X\equiv\langle n,k\rangle\eta Y)).$$

Proof. The proofs for 1.8 and 1.9 can be carried out in L_2 Hence, 2.2 follows immediately.

2.3. For each constant m, we can prove in L_2:

$$(k\leqslant m\ \&\ K_m(X))\supset(K(n,k)\equiv\langle n,k\rangle\eta X).$$

Proof. By 2.2 and 1.4.

2.4. For each given constant k, we can prove in L_2 the special case of the two sentences in 1.12.

Proof. By 2.3, 1.3, and 2.1 (compare the proof of 1.12).

Hence, every predicate d.i. is definable* explicitly in L_2. We note that a system L_4 consisting of the axioms I—III and VII of the Bernays system of set theory[1] and a system L_5 consisting of the axioms I—III and Va of the same are each of them at least as rich as L_2. Thus, both L_4 and L_5 can be considered as having the same notations as the system L_3 discussed above. The axiom I amounts to $AxQ3$, II is the same as $AxQ1$ plus $AxQ2$. The axiom III is like $AxQ4$ except for the restriction that no bound capital variables are allowed in p. The axioms Va and VII are as follows:

Va. $(z)(X)(Ey)(x)(x \in y \equiv (x \in z \,\&\, x\eta X))$.

VII. $(X)((Ex)(x\eta X) \supset (Ey) y\eta X \,\&\, (z) - (z \in y \,\&\, z\eta X)))$.

It may be noted that neither L_4 nor L_5 contains impredicative classes Summing up, we have the following theorem:

Theorem 4. *All predicates of natural numbers d.i. (relative to number theory) are definable* in the systems L_2, L_4, and L_5.*

When we apply this theorem to the predicate M of Hilbert-Bernays mentioned above, we obtain a rather interesting conclusion. Thus, in proving the adequacy of their truth definition for number theory[2], Hilbert and Bernays need only the special cases of the schema defining M and do not need the second sentence of the schema as a general assertion in the system[3]. Consequently, we have as a corollary of the preceding theorem:

Theorem 5. *An adequate truth definition for number theory (the system Z) can be obtained in each of the systems L_2, L_4, and L_5.*

---

1) See P. Bernays, *A system of axiomatic set theory*, *Journal of Symbolic Logic*, 2 (1937), 65—77, and 6 (1941), 1—17.

2) We say that a truth definition Tr for a system L is *adequate*, if for each constant m which is the number of a statement (sentence containing no free variables) p_m of L, the following case of the "truth schema" holds: $Tr(m) \equiv p_m$. If we can define Tr and prove all such equivalences in L', then we say that L' contains an adequate truth definition for L. It is not necessary that in L' we can also prove all theorems of L to be true according to the definition. This weaker criterion of adequacy seems to conform to Tarski's outspoken conventions (see, for instance, § 4 of his popular article The semantic concept of truth, *Philosophy and Phenomenological Research*, 4 (1944), 341—376), although some of his assertions (especially those regarding consistency proofs) appear to be justifiable only if we require in addition that all theorems of L can be shown to be true according to the definition. In any case, when we speak of adequate truth definitions in this paper, we shall not make such additional requirements. It is thought that even if the present use of the term "adequate truth definition" disagrees with Tarski's intention, it is of enough interest to deserve separate study. We might refer to adequate truth definitions which satisfy the additional requirements on theorems as *normal* ones.

3) Compare the considerations on pp. 334—337 of Hilbert-Bernays, op. cit.

However, it does not follow that in any of the systems L_2, L_4, and L_5 we could formalize a consistency proof for number theory. In order to formalize such a proof, we seem to need either certain impredicative classes or some strong axioms of ordinary induction. Let us ask what minimum additions to these systems are necessary for formalizing a consistency proof of number theory.

As noted above, Hilbert and Bernays assert that a consistency proof for the number theory Z can be formalized in the system Z' obtained from Z by adding as new axioms the two sentences in the recursion schema for the predicate M[1]. Therefore, in order to extend (say) L_2 so that the consistency proof becomes formalizable, we need only add the axioms necessary for deriving the two sentences of the schema.

We introduce two abbreviations:

2.5. $F_1(m)$ for $(EX)K_m(X)$.

2.6. $F_2(m)$ for $(X)(Y)(k)(n)((k \leqslant m \,\&\, K_m(X) \,\&\, K_m(Y)) \supset (\langle n,k\rangle \eta X \equiv \langle n, k\rangle \eta Y))$.

As we see from 1.1—1.3, the special form of $K_m(X)$ (and hence also the special forms of $F_1(m)$ and $F_2(m)$) depends on the special form of the induction schema (D) for the predicate P. We assume here that the predicate P is just the one defined by the schema for the special predicate M. Also $F_1(m)$ and $F_2(m)$ are understood to have been defined with respect to this schema.

Let L_2' be the system obtained from L_2 by first strengthening $Ax'2$ to allow p to be any sentence of L_2 which may contain free class variables (different from X) but no bound ones, and then adding the following two induction axioms:

$Ax'3$. $(F_1(0) \,\&\, (n)(F_1(n) \supset F_1(n+1))) \supset (m)F_1(m)$.

$Ax'4$. $(F_2(0) \,\&\, (n)(F_2(n) \supset F_2(n+1))) \supset (m)F_2(m)$.

An examination of the derivations of 1.5—1.12 in L_1 will reveal that they can be carried through in L_2', applying $Ax'3$ and $Ax'4$ in the proofs of 1.7 and 1.10. Hence, it follows that the Hilbert-Bernays consistency proof can be formalized in the system L_2'.

Similarly, if we add $Ax'3$ and $Ax'4$ to either L_4 or L_5, we can also formalize the proof in the resulting systems L_4' and L_5'. Moreover, the proof can also be formalized in the systems L_4'' and L_5'' if they are obtained respectively from L_4 and L_5 by adding instead of $Ax'3$ and $Ax'4$ the following two axioms in each case:

1) Incidentally, it follows from Theorem 4 that Z' is consistent if one of the systems L_2. L_4, and L_5 is ω-consistent.

$Ax''3.$ $(EX)(m)(m\eta X \equiv F_1(m))$.

$Ax''4.$ $(EX)(m)(m\eta X \equiv F_2(m))$.

Therefore, we can state a theorem:

Theorem 6. *The Hilbert-Bernays consistency proof for number theory can be formalized in every one of the systems* L'_2, L'_4, L'_5, L''_4, *and* L''_5.

Thus far we have been concerned exclusively with predicates d.i. relative to number theory. In general, given an arbitrary system T, we can also define by induction schemata predicates which are not explicitly expressible in T. The principal argument of each predicate thus introduced must of course take natural numbers as values; but some or all of the other arguments (the parameters) may this time take as values other entities treated in the system T. If in T we can develop number theory, then we can introduce such predicates by induction schemata which involve (apart from the symbols for the predicates to be introduced) nothing beyond the resources of T. If T does not contain number theory, we should consider the system obtained from T by adding number theory.

To simplify our problems, let us consider a partial system T of Zermelo's set theory as formulated in some of the standard ways[1]. The system T we choose satisfies the next two conditions: (1) Number theory can be developed in T. (2) Finite sequences of any entities (sets) assumed to exist in T can be defined in such a way that all of them are again entities (sets) provided by the theory. We describe briefly the system.

T contains the axiom of extensionality, the axiom of pairing, the Aussonderungsaxiom, the axiom of the sum set, and the axiom of infinity. The null set is defined as the number zero, and the unit set of a given natural number is defined as its successor. Then the set of natural numbers is the intersection of all sets which contain both zero and the successor of each member. The ordered pair of two sets can be defined in the ordinary manner. The finite sequence of k sets $x_1, \cdots, x_k$ is the set x consisting of the ordered pairs $\langle x_1, 1\rangle, \cdots, \langle x_k, k\rangle$. By the axiom of pairing and the axiom of the sum set, if $x_1, \cdots, x_k$ are sets of T, x is also a set of T. Let us use the letter g as a variable in T ranging over all finite sequences of sets.

Assume that the variables of T (set variables) and the sentences of T are both enumerated, and that in the enumeration of sentences every one precedes all those which contain it as a part. Then we can

1) For example, as formulated by us on pp. 150—151 of the *Proc. Nat. Acad. Sci. U.S.A.*, **35** (1949).

define a predicate $S(g, m)$ (the finite sequence g satisfies the $(m+1)$-th sentence) by a recursion schema of the following form[1]:

$$\begin{cases} S(g, 0) \equiv Q(g), \\ S(g, k+1) \equiv R(g, k, S(g, h_1(k)), S(g, h_2(k)), S(f(g, k, x), h_3(k))). \end{cases}$$

Therein apart from the occurrences of the symbol S as indicated, only symbols definable in T occur, the variable x is bound in R, and the functions h_1, h_2, and h_3 are such that we can prove in number theory: $h_1(k) \leqslant k$, $h_2(k) \leqslant k$, $h_3(k) \leqslant k$.

By considerations analogous to the construction of a truth definition for number theory with the predicate M, it is possible to show that by adding the two sentences in the schema for S as axioms to the system T, we can define truth for T in the resulting system T'. Hence, by a theorem of Tarski[2], the predicate S is not explicitly definable (nor even definable*) in T.

If T_1 is related to T as L_1 is to Z, then we can prove just as before that S is definable in T_1. Moreover, if T_2 is related to T as L_2 is to Z, we can show, by considerations similar to those employed above, that the predicate S is definable* in T_2 and that there is a truth definition for T in T_2.

Since the adequacy of a truth definition for a given system depends only on the linguistic forms available in the system[3], an adequate truth definition for T is also one for every other system of Zermelo set theory. Thus, for example, let T^* be the system obtained from T by adding the axiom of the power set and the Ersetzungsaxiom, then there is in both T_1 and T_2 also an adequate truth definition for T^*, despite the fact that T^* is a system apparently stronger than both T_1 and T_2.

1) An explicit formulation of the definition of the predicate S and a proof of its adequacy for defining truth would lead us too far afield for our present purpose. For outlines of the main ideas involved we refer to § 11 of Tarski's paper mentioned before under footnote 11 and his more technical paper "Der Wahrheitsbegriff in den formalisierten Sprachen", *Studia Philosophica,* **1** (1935), 261—405.

2) See Hilbert-Bernays, op. cit., pp. 254—258.

3) We are assuming that the provability of all cases of the truth schema is sufficient criterion for an adequate truth definition. That is why the strength of the theorems of the system is not relevant here. Compare footnote 2 on p. 542.

CHAPTER XXII

UNDECIDABLE SENTENCES SUGGESTED BY SEMANTIC PARADOXES*

§ 1. Introduction

In applying the method of arithmetization to a proof of the completeness of the predicate calculus, Bernays has obtained a result which, when applied to set theories formulated in the predicate calculus, may be stated thus[1].

1.1. By adding an arithmetic sentence $Con(S)$ (expressing the consistency of a set theory S) as a new axiom to the elementary number theory Z_μ (*HB* II, p. 293), we can prove in the resulting system arithmetic translations of all theorems of S.

It then follows that things definable or expressible in S have images in a simple extension of Z_μ, if S is consistent. Since S can be a "strong" system, this fact has interesting consequences. Some of these are discussed by me and some are discussed by Kreisel[2]. Kreisel finds an undecidable sentence of set theory by combining 1.1 and the Cantor diagonal argument. I shall prove below, using similar methods, a few further results, concerned with the notions of truth and designation. The method of numbering sets which I use (see 3.1 below) is different from Kreisel's. While the method used here is formally more elegant, Kreisel's method is much more efficient if we wish actually to calculate the numerical values.

Gödel himself has observed the close relation between his undecidable sentences and the Epimenides paradox ("the liar"). While Gödel constructs a sentence of a system L which may be interpreted as saying of itself that it is not a theorem of L, the Epimenides paradox would arise in a system L in which we could construct a sentence saying of itself that it is not true. This latter situation is often expressed by saying that the notion of truth of a system L is not expressible in L. If L happens to be Z_μ and S a set theory in which

* This chapter appeared in *Journal of Symbolic Logic,* **20** (1955), 31—43.

1) Hilbert and Bernays [2] (to be referred to as *HB*), II, pp. 234—253. See also Wang [6].

2) Kreisel [3], I, and Wang [5].

the notion of truth of Z_μ can be defined, then, by Bernays' theorem, we have, in Z_μ plus $Con(S)$, a model or translation of the truth schema of Z_μ. I shall prove that the argument of the Epimenides paradox then yields an undecidable sentence of S and Z_μ. Similarly, the impossibility of defining the relation of designation in a system itself also leads to undecidable sentences. One of these is closely connected with the Richard paradox.

These results, it is hoped, will throw some new light on the semantic paradoxes. Moreover, like the result of Kreisel (op. cit.), the conclusions are also of interest in that they connect indefinable classes and relations with undecidable sentences. There seems to be a certain similarity between this situation and the possibility of two different methods of avoiding mathematical paradoxes: the usual way of refusing to countenance a class K of all classes which are not self-members, and the alternative approach of admitting such a class K but treating as undecidable the question whether K belongs to K.

The essential step in Kreisel's and my construction of undecidable sentences is in nearly every case to find a sentence of set theory which is true but whose model or translation according to 1.1 is false. If a set theory is consistent, then it is translatable (in the sense of 1.1) into Z_μ and also into the part of the set theory itself answering to Z_μ. If the set theory has an ω-consistent model, then the translation of a theorem of it must also be true (compare 2.6 below). Therefore, if the set theory has an ω-consistent model, then the true sentence whose translation is false must be undecidable in the set theory. The fact that there are such sentences also proves incidentally that the model of a system as determined by 1.1 is in a certain sense not very "natural", because we would ordinarily expect the model of a true sentence to be true.

§ 2. Preliminaries

In this paper, I shall be concerned with a set theory S' in which Z_μ can be developed. To fix ideas, the reader can think of S as a definite current set theory without the axiom of infinity[1] and S' as obtained from S by adding the Hilbert ε-symbol.

The formula $Con(S')$ of Z_μ is more explicitly $(m)\neg\mathfrak{B}(m, \mathfrak{f})$ which expresses directly that the formula $0=1$, whose Gödel number is $\mathfrak{f}$, is not provable in S'. The same formula is assumed in Wang [6], while Bernays takes a different formula $(n)[\mathfrak{q}(n)=0]$ (cf. *HB* II, p. 243) in his proof of 1.1. It should be noted that $Con(S')$ is a closed

1) See Bernays [1], or the system (S) described in Kreisel [3], II.

formula. This is relevant since in the arguments below the Deduktionstheorem is implicitly applied several times.

In what follows, it is often necessary to consider the translation of a formula (or term) of Z_μ in S', that of a formula (or term) of S' in Z_μ, its translation in S', etc. To achieve clarity, I introduce once and for all notations for these translations. Since Z_μ can be developed in S' (i.e., is translatable into S'), S' has a part answering to Z_μ. This number-theoretic part of S' will be denoted by S_0. Let "$\mathfrak{A}^s$" denote the translation in S_0 of a formula "$\mathfrak{A}$" of Z_μ, and "$\mathfrak{A}^z$" denote the translation (according to 1.1) in Z of a formula of S'. Therefore, "$\mathfrak{A}^{zs}$" would be the translation in S_0 of "$\mathfrak{A}^z$", etc. In particular, "$[Con(S')]^s$" is the translation of "$Con(S')$" in S_0. Similar notations for terms are also assumed.

In proving the theorems, I shall assume that S' has an ω-consistent model. As usual, a system S' is said to be ω-consistent, if for every formula $\mathfrak{A}(a)$ of Z_μ, $[(\exists m)\neg\mathfrak{A}(m)]^s$ is a theorem of S' only when one of $[\mathfrak{A}(0)]^s$, $[\mathfrak{A}(1)]^s$, $[\mathfrak{A}(2)]^s$, $\cdots$ is not a theorem of S'. A model of S' is an ω-consistent model of S', if for every formula $\mathfrak{A}(a)$ of Z_μ, $[(\exists m)\neg\mathfrak{A}(m)]^s$ is true in the model only when one of $[\mathfrak{A}(0)]^s$, $[\mathfrak{A}(1)]^s$, $[\mathfrak{A}(2)]^s$, $\cdots$ is false.

More explicitly, I assume the following definition:

2.1. A system S' is said to have an ω-consistent model, if it is possible to divide all sentences of S' into two classes T (true) and F (false) so that the following conditions are satisfied: (a) $\neg\mathfrak{A}$ belongs to T if and only if $\mathfrak{A}$ belongs to F, $\mathfrak{A}$ & $\mathfrak{B}$ belongs to T if and only if both $\mathfrak{A}$ and $\mathfrak{B}$ belong to T; (b) $(\exists x)\mathfrak{A}(x)$ belongs to T, if for some term $\mathfrak{t}$ of S' which contains no free variables, $\mathfrak{A}(\mathfrak{t})$ belongs to T; (c) for every formula $\mathfrak{A}(a)$ of Z_μ with the sole free variable a, $[(\exists m)\neg\mathfrak{A}(m)]^s$ belongs to T only when some of $[\mathfrak{A}(0)]^s$, $[\mathfrak{A}(1)]^s$, $[\mathfrak{A}(2)]^s$, $\cdots$ do not belong to T; (d) $\mathfrak{A}$ belongs to F if and only if it does not belong to T; (e) all theorems of S' belong to T.

Throughout this paper, I shall assume that an ω-consistent model for S' is given. Whenever I say that a sentence of S' is true (or false), I mean simply that it belongs to T (or F) in the given particular model. This convention will be found very convenient.

Incidentally, although all systems which have ω-consistent models are obviously ω-consistent, the converse probably is not true.

The following lemmas follow from the nature of the translations.

2.2. The operation of passing from $\mathfrak{A}$ to $\mathfrak{A}^{zs}$ does not affect the relative positions of the sentential connectives.

2.3. If $\mathfrak{A}$ is provable in S', then $[Con(S')\supset\mathfrak{A}^z]^s$ is also provable in S'.

The following lemmas follow from the assumption that S' has an ω-consistent model.

2.4. $[Con(S')]^s$ is true.

2.5. If $\mathfrak{A}$ and $\mathfrak{A} \supset \mathfrak{B}$ are true, then $\mathfrak{B}$ is true.

Proof. Since $\neg[\mathfrak{A} \,\&\, (\mathfrak{A} \supset \mathfrak{B}) \,\&\, \neg\mathfrak{B}]$ is true.

2.6. If $\mathfrak{A}$ is provable in S', then $\mathfrak{A}^{zs}$ is true.

Proof. By 2.3, 2.4, and 2.5.

2.7. If $\mathfrak{A}$ and $\mathfrak{A}^{zs}$ have different truth values, then $\mathfrak{A}$ is undecidable in S'.

Proof. If $\mathfrak{A}$ is true, then, by (d) and (e) of 2.1, $\neg\mathfrak{A}$ is not provable in S'. By 2.6, as $\mathfrak{A}^{zs}$ is false, $\mathfrak{A}$ is also not provable in S', because otherwise $\mathfrak{A}^{zs}$ would be true. Similarly, if $\mathfrak{A}$ is false and $\mathfrak{A}^{zs}$ is true, neither $\mathfrak{A}$ nor $\neg\mathfrak{A}$ is provable in S'.

It is often convenient to consider the system obtained from S' by adding $[Con(S')]^s$.

2.8. Let $S\#$ be the system obtained from S' by adding $[Con(S')]^s$ as a new axiom.

2.9. If $\mathfrak{A}$ is provable in $S\#$, then $\mathfrak{A}$ is true.

Proof. By 2.4 and the fact that only true sentences can be derived from true sentences (cf. 2.5).

2.10. $S\#$ is consistent.

2.11. If $\mathfrak{A}$ is provable in S', then $\mathfrak{A}^{zs}$ is provable in $S\#$.

§ 3. Conditions Which the Set Theory is to Satisfy[1)]

An immediate corollary to Bernays' Theorem 1.1 is:

3.1. If we add to a set theory S the Hilbert ε-symbol together with the ε-formulas (*HB* II, p. 13), and extend the notions of term, formula, and theorem accordingly, then the resulting system S' is again translatable into Z_μ plus $Con(S)$, with the μ-symbol serving as the model of the Hilbert ε-symbol.

Proof. The only theorems of S' which are not also theorems of S are those which we prove by applying the ε-formulas (*HB* II, p. 13). Since, however, exactly corresponding formulas for the μ-symbol are provable in Z_μ (*HB* II, p. 293), the translation of every theorem

1) In what follows I shall make no attempt to obtain the weakest possible conditions. For example, although only certain parts of Z_μ are needed, I shall assume that the whole Z_μ can be developed in the set theory.

of S' is also derivable from $Con(S)$ in Z_μ.

Thus, for example, if S contains only = and e (belonging to) as primitive predicates and Z_S is the system obtained from Z_μ by adding $Con(S)$ as axiom, then, by 3.1, we can define in Z_S arithmetic models $e^z(m, n)$ and $m =^z n$ for the predicates $e(x, y)$ and $x=y$ of S' such that, when we replace, in terms and formulas of S', all the predicates by their arithmetic models, the ε-symbol by the μ-symbol, all theorems of S' become theorems of Z_S. For brevity, I shall refer to the retranslation into S' of the formula or term of Z_μ which corresponds to a formula or term of S' according to 3.1 as the Bernays model of the latter formula or term; e.g., the Bernays model of a formula $\mathfrak{A}$ is $\mathfrak{A}^{zs}$.

When S and S' are related as in 3.1, we can derive, by using the second ε-theorem (*HB* II, p. 18), the consistency of S' from that of S. By assuming an arithmetization of the syntax of S and S', we can also prove, by formalizing the proof of the second ε-theorem, that the sentences $Con(S)$ and $Con(S')$ are mutually derivable in Z_μ.

Let us, for the moment, confine our attention to systems like S' (i.e., to systems which contain the Hilbert ε-symbol) and describe sufficient conditions under which the theorems to be proved are valid.

The first condition on S' is:

*C*1. S' has one kind of variables x, y, z, etc., one (the predicate $e(x, y)$ or "x belongs to y") or more primitive predicates. S' contains the theorems of the ordinary predicate calculus, as well as those about identity and those about the Hilbert ε-symbol. (This amounts to saying that S' presupposes no queer elementary logic.)

The second condition on S' is:

*C*2. We can develop Z_μ in S'; or, in other words, S' contains a model S_0 of Z_μ: there is an effective rule for translating terms $\mathfrak{t}$ and formulas $\mathfrak{A}$ of Z_μ into $\mathfrak{t}^s$ and $\mathfrak{A}^s$ of S' so that all theorems of Z_μ are translated into theorems of S_0.

More explicitly, *C*2 entails the following consequences.

*C*2.1. There is a definite term 0^s of S' (e.g., the term $\varepsilon_x(y)\neg e(y, x)$) which stands for the term 0 of Z_μ.

*C*2.2. There is a term $+(x)$ of S' such that, if $\mathfrak{t}$ is a term of Z_μ, then the term $+(\mathfrak{t}^s)$ (e.g., $\varepsilon_x(y)[e(y, x) \equiv (y = \mathfrak{t}^s \vee e(y, \mathfrak{t}^s))]$) is $(\mathfrak{t}+1)^s$.

*C*2.3. There is a predicate (not necessarily primitive) $N(x)$ of S' such that all the Peano axioms can be proved for 0^s, $N(x)$, and $+(x)$. $(m)\mathfrak{A}(m)$ and $(\exists m)\mathfrak{A}(m)$ in Z_μ correspond to $(x)[N(x) \supset \mathfrak{A}^s(x)]$ and $(\exists x)[N(x) \,\&\, \mathfrak{A}^s(x)]$ respectively in S'.

*C*2.4. There are in S' two functions for which the ordinary recursion equations for addition and multiplication can be proved.

*C*2.5. To every term $\mu_m \mathfrak{A}(m)$ of Z_μ there is a corresponding term $[\mu_m \mathfrak{A}(m)]^s$ of S', viz.,

$$\varepsilon_x\{[N(x) \,\&\, \mathfrak{A}^s(x) \,\&\, (y)((N(y) \,\&\, \mathfrak{A}^s(y)) \supset y \geqslant x)] \vee [(y)(N(y) \supset \neg \mathfrak{A}^s(y)) \,\&\, x = 0^s]\}$$

for which the theorems for the μ-symbol (*HB* II, p. 128) can be proved. We shall denote the term by $\mu^s_m \mathfrak{A}^s(m)$.

Among less direct consequences of *C*2 which depend on assuming an arithmetization of the syntax of S' are the following.

*C*2.6. (Gödel's substitution function). We can define in S' a term $[\mathfrak{s}(x, y)]$ which involves, besides the unrestricted variables x and y, merely symbols of S_0 and which is such that, if $\mathfrak{m}$ is the Gödel number of a formula $\mathfrak{A}$ of S' and $\mathfrak{k}$ the Gödel number of the formula obtained from $\mathfrak{A}$ by substituting a numeral $\mathfrak{n}^s$ for the variable "x", then the equation $\mathfrak{s}(\mathfrak{m}^s, \mathfrak{n}^s) = \mathfrak{k}^s$ is numerically true and provable in S_0 (*HB* II, p. 256).

*C*2.7. It is possible to define in S' a term $f(x)$ which involves, besides the unrestricted variable x, only notions of S_0 and which correlates each natural number in S_0 with its Bernays model. Or more exactly, for each numeral $\mathfrak{n}$, the equation $f(\mathfrak{n}^s) = (\mathfrak{n}^s)^{zs}$ is provable in S'.

Proof. Let $\nu(m, n)$ be the exponent of the n-th prime in the factorization of m. Let "$F(i, k)$" stand for

$$\text{“}[\nu(k,0) = \mu_n(m) \neg e^z(m, n)] \,\&\, (j)\{j < i \supset \nu(k, j+1) = \mu_n(m)[e^z(m, n) \equiv (m =^z \nu(m, j) \vee e^z(m, \nu(m, j)))]\}\text{”}.$$

If we take "$\nu[\mu_m F(k, m), k]^s$" as "$f(k)$", then we can prove in S_0 that the function f fulfills the requirements. Since we do not care what the value of $f(x)$ is when x is not an integer, it is easy to modify the above argument so as to get a general function $f(x)$ instead of the function $f(k)$.

*C*2.8. There is a term $h(x)$ in S' such that if $\mathfrak{m}^s$ is the Gödel number of a term $\mathfrak{t}^s$ of S', then $h(\mathfrak{m}^s)$ is the Gödel number of the term $(\mathfrak{t}+1)^s$ of S', i.e., of the term $+(\mathfrak{t}^s)$.

The next condition is:

*C*3. S' has an ω-consistent model.

An immediate consequence is:

*C*3.1. For every formula $\mathfrak{A}(a)$ of Z_μ with the sole free variable a, $[\mu_m \mathfrak{A}(m) = \mathfrak{n}]^s$ is true for some value of $\mathfrak{n}$ among 0, 1, 2, etc.

Proof. Since $(\exists n)[n = \mu_m \mathfrak{A}(m)]$ is a theorem of Z_μ, its translation is a theorem of S_0. By 2.1 and *C*3, the assertion is proved.

It also follows from *C*3 that 2.4—2.10 all hold for S'.

The fourth condition has to do with the possibility of defining in S' the semantic notions of truth and designation of S_0 (viz., the counterpart of Z_μ in S'):

*C*4a. A predicate $W(x)$ (a formula with the sole free variable x) can be found in S' such that for every sentence $\mathfrak{A}$ of S_0, if its Gödel number is $\mathfrak{n}$, then we can prove in S': $W(\mathfrak{n}^s) \equiv \mathfrak{A}$.

*C*4b. A function D can be defined in S' such that for every definite term $\mathfrak{t}$ of S_0 which contains no free variables, if its Gödel number is $\mathfrak{n}$, then we can prove in S': $D(\mathfrak{n}^s) = \mathfrak{t}$.

If conditions *C*2 and *C*4b hold for a certain system S', we can define a function $\mathfrak{b}(n)$ in S_0 such that the following holds (*HB* II, pp. 261—263).

*C*4b.1. If $\mathfrak{A}$ is any sentence of S_0 and $\mathfrak{n}$ is its Gödel number, then we can prove in S': $D[\mathfrak{b}(\mathfrak{n}^s)] = 0 \equiv \mathfrak{A}$.

Another useful condition is:

*C*4c. Every predicate of S_0 can be represented in S': for every predicate $\mathfrak{A}(x)$ of S' which contains, besides the unrestricted variable x, only symbols of S_0, we can find a term $\mathfrak{t}$ in S' for which and for each numeral $\mathfrak{n}$ we can prove in S' that $\mathfrak{A}(\mathfrak{n}^s)$ if and only if $e(\mathfrak{n}^s, \mathfrak{t})$ ($\mathfrak{n}^s$ belongs to $\mathfrak{t}$)[1].

§ 4. The Epimenides Paradox

Now we are ready to state and prove the existence of certain undecidable sentences in systems satisfying suitable conditions.

Assume that S' satisfies the conditions *C*1, *C*2, and *C*4a. Let us consider the following formula of S':

$$(1) \qquad \neg W^{zs}\{f[\mathfrak{s}(x, x)]\}.$$

Suppose further that $\mathfrak{q}$ is the Gödel number of the following formula of S':

$$(2) \qquad \neg W^{zs}\{f[\mathfrak{s}(\mathfrak{p}^s, \mathfrak{p}^s)]\},$$

$\mathfrak{p}$ being the Gödel number of (1).

1) If S' contains the axiom of infinity then this is clearly satisfied. It is shown in Bernays [1] that *C*4c is satisfied by the set theory developed there even when the axiom of infinity is not included.

Then (2) is a sentence of S_0 because $f[\mathfrak{s}(\mathfrak{p}^s, \mathfrak{p}^s)]$ is a constant term of S_0 and the translation of a formula W^z of Z_μ is one of S_0. Moreover, by *C*2.6, the following is also provable in S_0:

(3) $$\mathfrak{s}(\mathfrak{p}^s, \mathfrak{p}^s) = \mathfrak{q}^s.$$

Now we assert:

Theorem 1. *If S' satisfies conditions C*1—*C*3 *and C*4a, *then the sentences $W(\mathfrak{q}^s)$ and $W^{zs}[f(\mathfrak{q}^s)]$, where $\mathfrak{q}$ is determined as above, are undecidable in S'.*

Proof. By condition *C*4a, we can prove in S' the equivalence of $W(\mathfrak{q}^s)$ and (2). Using (3), we can prove in S' and $S\#$ (see 2.8) the following equivalence:

(4) $$W(\mathfrak{q}^s) \equiv \neg W^{zs}[f(\mathfrak{q}^s)].$$

If $W(\mathfrak{q}^s)$ is provable in S', then its translation $[W(\mathfrak{q}^s)]^{zs}$ or $W^{zs}(\mathfrak{q}^{szs})$ is provable in $S\#$ by 2.11. By *C*2.7, $f(\mathfrak{q}^s) = \mathfrak{q}^{szs}$ is provable in S'. Hence, we can, by *C*1, prove in $S\#$:

(5) $$W^{zs}[f(\mathfrak{q}^s)].$$

Therefore, by (4) and (5), if $W(\mathfrak{q}^s)$ is provable in S', then $S\#$ would be inconsistent, contradicting 2.10.

Similarly, if $\neg W(\mathfrak{q}^s)$ is provable in S', then we can show that $\neg(5)$ is provable in $S\#$. Then we see again that, by (4), 2.10 would be contradicted.

Therefore, $W(\mathfrak{q}^s)$ is undecidable in S'. By (4), $W^{zs}[f(\mathfrak{q}^s)]$ is also undecidable in S'.

Alternatively, Theorem 1 can also be proved directly by *C*3. Thus, since (4) is a theorem of S', it is true. Hence, by *C*2.7, $W(\mathfrak{q}^s)$ and its Bernays model must have opposite truth values. Hence, by 2.7, $W(\mathfrak{q}^s)$ is not decidable in S'.

By *C*4b.1, using $D(\mathfrak{b}(x))=0$ in place of $W(x)$, we can prove similarly (where $\mathfrak{q}$ is the Gödel number of a formula corresponding to the formula (2) above):

4.1. If S' satisfies the conditions *C*1—*C*3 and *C*4b, then the sentences $D(\mathfrak{b}(\mathfrak{q}^s))=0$ and $D^{zs}[\mathfrak{b}^{zs}(f(\mathfrak{q}^{zs}))]=0^{zs}$ are undecidable in S'.

A form of Kreisel's theorem (op. cit.) can also be proved from the present approach.

4.2. If S' satisfies the conditions *C*1—*C*3 and *C*4c, and $\mathfrak{t}$ is the term (of S') such that for each numeral $\mathfrak{m}$,

$$e(\mathfrak{M}^s, \mathfrak{t}^s) \equiv \neg e^{zs}[f(\mathfrak{M}^s), \mathfrak{M}^s]$$

is true, and if $\mathfrak{n}^s$ is such that $\mathfrak{t}^{zs} = \mathfrak{n}^s$ is true, then the sentence

$$(6) \qquad e(\mathfrak{n}^s, \mathfrak{t})$$

is undecidable in S'.

Proof. By *C*2.7 and (e) of 2.1, $f(\mathfrak{n}^s) = \mathfrak{n}^{szs}$ is true. Hence, by the definition of $\mathfrak{t}$, $e(\mathfrak{n}^s, \mathfrak{t}) \equiv \neg e^{zs}(\mathfrak{n}^{szs}, \mathfrak{n}^s)$ is true. Therefore, by 2.5 and the substitutivity of equals ($\mathfrak{t}^{zs}$ for $\mathfrak{n}^s$),

$$(7) \qquad e(\mathfrak{n}^s, \mathfrak{t}) \equiv \neg\, [e(\mathfrak{n}^s, \mathfrak{t})]^{zs}$$

is true. Consequently, (6) and its Bernays model must have different truth values. Hence, by 2.7, 4.2 is proved.

Note incidentally that the term $\mathfrak{t}$ denotes the set of those numbers n^s whose models $(n^s)^{zs}$ do not belong to n^s. Thus, we have here an analogue of the Russell paradox.

In passing, we may mention two somewhat amusing corollaries to these theorems.

Either (6) or its negation is true according to *C*3. Suppose (6) is true. Consider the system R obtained from S' by adding (6) as a new axiom, and the system $R\#$ obtained from R by adding $[Con(R)]^s$. By 3.1, a Bernays model of (6) is true and provable in $R\#$. On the other hand, by (7), the negation of another Bernays model of (6) is also true and provable in R (and therefore also in $R\#$). Hence, if (6) is true in the model, then one Bernays model of (6) is true while another is false. Similarly, if the negation of (6) happens to be true[1].

A second corollary is the following. By Theorem 1, $W^{zs}[f(\mathfrak{q}^s)]$ is undecidable in S_0 (and in S'). If $(S\#)_2$ is the system obtained from $S\#$ by adding $[Con(S\#)]^s$ as axiom, then $S\#$ is, by 3.1, also translatable into $(S\#)_2$. But the Bernays model $W^{zs}(f(\mathfrak{q}^s)) \equiv \neg W^{zs}[f(\mathfrak{q}^s)]^{zs}$ of (4) is provable in $(S\#)_2$. Hence, by reasoning similar to the proof of Theorem 1, the new Bernays model "$\mathrm{tr}_2\{W^{zs}[f(\mathfrak{q}^s)]\}$" of (5) is undecidable in $S\#$. Similarly, if $(S\#)_3$ is obtained from $(S\#)_2$ by adding $Con[(S\#)_2]$, then the model "$\mathrm{tr}_3\{\mathrm{tr}_2[W^{zs}(f(\mathfrak{q}^s))]\}$" of the model of (5) is also undecidable in $(S\#)_2$. Hence, we have, using *C*2.7:

4.3. The sentences $[W(\mathfrak{q}^s)]^{zs}$, $\mathrm{tr}_2\{[W(\mathfrak{q}^s)]^{zs}\}$, and so on, ad infinitum, all are undecidable sentences of the system S_0 (and of S').

§ 5. The Richard Paradox

As a preliminary step, we make the following observation. The argument for the Richard paradox can be employed to prove that it

1) Compare Kreisel [3], I, p. 283.

is impossible to define in S_0 the relation of designation of S_0. This makes use of the fact that the functions $\mathfrak{s}(x, y)$ and $h(x)$ ($C2.6$ and $C2.8$) can be defined in S_0.

5.1. It is impossible to find in S_0 a term $D(m)$ such that for every term $\mathfrak{t}$ of S_0 which contains no free variables, if $\mathfrak{n}$ is the Gödel number of $\mathfrak{t}$, we can prove in S_0: $D(\mathfrak{n}^s)=\mathfrak{t}$.

Proof. Consider any term $D(m)$ of S_0. Assume that the Gödel number of the term

$$D\{h[\mathfrak{s}(x, x)]\}$$

is $\mathfrak{p}$, and that of

$$D\{h[\mathfrak{s}(\mathfrak{p}^s, \mathfrak{p}^s)]\}$$

is $\mathfrak{q}$. Since $\mathfrak{s}(\mathfrak{p}^s, \mathfrak{p}^s)=\mathfrak{q}^s$, we can, supposing D has the desired property, prove in S_0,

$$(8) \qquad D(\mathfrak{q}^s) = D[h(\mathfrak{q}^s)].$$

Moreover, by hypothesis and by definition of $h(x)$, we can prove in S_0,

$$(9) \qquad D(\mathfrak{q}^s) + {}^s1^s = D[h(\mathfrak{q}^s)].$$

Therefore, by (8) and (9), we get a contradiction. Hence, the term $D(m)$ does not have the property in which we are interested[1].

From this, we can find an undecidable sentence in a system S' satisfying the conditions $C1$—$C3$ and $C4b$.

Consider the sentence $\mathfrak{t}_1=D[h(\mathfrak{t}_2)]$ where $\mathfrak{t}_1$ and $\mathfrak{t}_2$ are definite terms of S' and its Bernays model is:

$$(10) \qquad \{\mathfrak{t}_1 = D[h(\mathfrak{t}_2)]\}^{zs} \text{ or } \mathfrak{t}_1^{zs} = {}^{zs}D^{zs}[h^{zs}(\mathfrak{t}_2^{zs})].$$

If we substitute $f(y)$ and $f(\mathfrak{s}(x, x))$ for $\mathfrak{t}_1^{zs}$ and $\mathfrak{t}_2^{zs}$, the result $f(y) = {}^{zs}D^{zs}\{h^{zs}[f(\mathfrak{s}(x, x))]\}$ is again a formula of S'. Moreover,

$$(11) \qquad \overset{s}{\mu}_m[f(m) = {}^{zs}D^{zs}\{h^{zs}(f[\mathfrak{s}(x, x)])\}]$$

is a term of S' which contains x as the sole free variable. Suppose that the Gödel number of (11) is $\mathfrak{p}$, and that $\mathfrak{q}$ is the Gödel number of

$$(12) \qquad \overset{s}{\mu}_m[f(m) = {}^{zs}D^{zs}\{h^{zs}(f[\mathfrak{s}(\mathfrak{p}^s, \mathfrak{p}^s)])\}],$$

which is a term of S_0. By $C4b$ we can prove in S': $D(\mathfrak{q}^s)=(12)$. By $C2.6$, $\mathfrak{s}(\mathfrak{p}^s, \mathfrak{p}^s)=\mathfrak{q}^s$. Hence, we can prove in S':

$$(13) \qquad D(\mathfrak{q}^s) = \overset{s}{\mu}_m\{f(m) = {}^{zs}D^{zs}(h^{zs}[f(\mathfrak{q}^s)])\}.$$

1) This simplifies somewhat a proof on pp. 263—268 of *HB* II.

By *C*3.1, we can find some $\mathfrak{n}$ among 0, 1, 2, ⋯ such that

$$(14) \qquad \mathfrak{n}^s = D(\mathfrak{q}^s)$$

is true (in the model of 2.1). Since, by *C*2.8, $h(\mathfrak{q}^s)$ is the Gödel number of $+[(12)]$, by *C*4b, $D[h(\mathfrak{q}^s)] = +[(12)]$ is provable in S'. From this equation, together with $D(\mathfrak{q}^s) = (12)$, we get by *C*1,

$$\mathfrak{n}^s = D(\mathfrak{q}^s) \supset (\mathfrak{n}+1)^s = D[h(\mathfrak{q}^s)].$$

Therefore, this formula is, by (e) of 2.1, true; and since (14) is true, we have, by 2.5,

$$(15) \qquad (\mathfrak{n}+1)^s = D[h(\mathfrak{q}^s)]$$

is also true.

Theorem 2. *If S' satisfies the conditions C1—C3 and* C4b, *then (15) is undecidable in S'.*

Proof. Since, by (e) of 2.1, all theorems of S' are true, we shall not distinguish truth and provability in S' because in the argument we wish to establish truth only. We shall also apply 2.5 implicitly. Suppose that (15) is decidable in S'. Then it is a theorem because it is true. Hence, its Bernays model

$$(16) \qquad (\mathfrak{n}+1)^{szs} = {}^{zs}D^{zs}[h^{zs}(\mathfrak{q}^{szs})]$$

is true by 2.6. By *C*2.7 and *C*1,

$$(17) \qquad (\exists m)\{f(m) = {}^{zs}D^{zs}(h^{zs}[f(\mathfrak{q}^s)])\}.$$

By (13), (17) and the property of μ, $f[D(\mathfrak{q}^s)] = {}^{zs}D^{zs}\{h^{zs}[f(\mathfrak{q}^s)]\}$. By (14), $f(\mathfrak{n}^s) = {}^{zs}D^{zs}\{h^{zs}[f(\mathfrak{q}^s)]\}$. By *C*2.7,

$$(18) \qquad \{\mathfrak{n}^s = D[h(\mathfrak{q}^s)]\}^{zs}.$$

On the other hand, we can prove in S': $\neg\mathfrak{n}^s = (\mathfrak{n}+1)^s$. Hence, by (15), we can also prove in S': $\neg\mathfrak{n}^s = D[h(\mathfrak{q}^s)]$. Hence,

$$(19) \qquad \neg\{\mathfrak{n}^s = D[h(\mathfrak{q}^s)]\}^{zs}$$

is also true. Since (18) and (19) cannot both be true, the assumption that (15) is decidable in S' is false.

Incidentally, we can again prove that the Bernays model of some true sentence is false. For otherwise, (16) and (19), being Bernays models of true sentences, would both be true, and we would again get the absurd conclusion that (18) and (19) are both true.

§ 6. Final Remarks

Set theories are ordinarily formulated without using the Hilbert ε-symbol. The results just proved refer to systems S' which are obtained from such systems S by adding the ε-symbol. It would be natural to ask whether there are also similar undecidable sentences in the systems S if they satisfy similar conditions. The answer is positive and can be verified by using ordinary methods of introducing terms in context (compare, e.g., *HB* II, p. 259). Either we may repeat in a somewhat modified fashion all the foregoing considerations, talking about terms in a roundabout way. Or, we can use the second ε-theorem (*HB* II, p. 18).

Thus, let L be a system formulated entirely in the pure predicate calculus and L' be obtained from L by adding the ε-symbol and the ε-formulas. Therefore, L' includes L (*HB* II, p. 8). By the second ε-theorem, every theorem of L' which does not contain the ε-symbol is also a theorem of L. Hence, from a given undecidable sentence $\mathfrak{A}$ of L', to find a corresponding one of L, we need only find in L' a sentence $\mathfrak{A}'$ not containing the ε-symbol such that the equivalence of $\mathfrak{A}$ and $\mathfrak{A}'$ can be proved in L'. This can be done for each of the undecidable sentences given in §4 and §5, because we know it is possible to eliminate the terms in these sentences by transforming whole contexts. I shall not go into details of this matter here.

Incidentally, if L happens to contain a suitable axiom of choice, it is not necessary to use the second ε-theorem, because a corresponding system L' with something like the ε-symbol is then obtainable from the axioms of L. Indeed, the ε-terms, as used in S', can be replaced everywhere by ι-terms (descriptions), and so, instead of the second ε-theorem, the elimination theorem for ι-terms becomes sufficient.

Another problem is: what systems S and S' would satisfy the conditions of these results? If we leave aside the condition of ω-consistency, many ordinary systems of set theory (sometimes after formalistic readjustments) can be shown to satisfy the other conditions $C1$, $C2$, $C4$a, $C4$b, $C4$c. Yet for most such systems, neither the ω-consistency nor even the simple consistency is known.

It is, however, possible to prove that the system (S) described in Kreisel ([3], II) does satisfy all the conditions. That (S) satisfies $C1$, $C2$, and $C4$c is shown in Bernays [1]. It is, moreover, possible to give an ω-consistent model for (S). (Compare the discussion in Kreisel [3], II). Furthermore, it is also possible to define in (S) truth and designation for Z_μ or S_0. This can be accomplished by known methods. Thus, if we think of (S) as dealing with sets and classes (two kinds of object) and let (S_1) be the part of (S) dealing with sets only, then Z_μ can already be represented in (S_1). As a result, the problem reduces to one of defining in (S) truth and designation for (S_1). This latter problem can, however, be handled in the manner of, e.g., Wang [7]. Hence, it is possible to prove that (S) satisfies also $C4$a and $C4$b.

It remains to distinguish, in the arguments above, constructive proofs and those for which the tertium non datur is used. The first proof of Theorem 1 has a constructive character. Since the conventional proof of condition $C3$ uses the tertium non datur, the proofs of 4.2 and Theorem 2, which are in part based on $C3$, are not constructive. Kreisel's original proof of 4.2 is constructive.

References

[1] P. Bernays, A system of axiomatic set theory, Part II, *Jour. Symbolic Logic*, **6** (1941), 1—17.

[2] D. Hilbert and P. Bernays, Grundlagen der Mathematik, vol. 2, Berlin (Springer) 1939, xii + 498 pp.

[3] G. Kreisel, Note on arithmetic models for consistent formulae of the predicate calculus, Part I, *Fund. Math.*, **37** (for 1950, pub. 1951), 265—285; Part II, *Proceedings of the XIth International Congress of Philosophy* (Brussels, August 20—26, 1953), **14** (1953), 39—49.

[4] G. Kreisel, Some concepts concerning formal systems of number theory, *Math. Zeit.*, **57** (1952), 1—12.

[5] H. Wang, Arithmetic translations of axiom systems, *Trans. Am. Math. Soc.*, **71** (1951), 283—293.

[6] H. Wang, Arithmetic models of formal systems, *Methodos*, **3** (1951), 217—232.

[7] H. Wang, Truth definitions and consistency proofs, *Trans. Am. Math. Soc.*, **73** (1952), 243—275.

CHAPTER XXIII

THE FORMALIZATION OF MATHEMATICS*

§ 1. Original Sin of the Formal Logician

Zest for both system and objectivity is the formal logician's original sin. He pays for it by constant frustrations and by living ofttimes the life of an intellectual outcaste. The task of squeezing a large body of stubborn facts into a more or less rigid system can be a painful one, especially since the facts of mathematics are among the most stubborn of all facts. Moreover, the more general and abstract we get, the farther removed we are from the raw mathematical experience. As intuition ceases to operate effectively, we fall into many unexpected traps. The formal logician gets little sympathy for his frustrations. He is regarded as too rigid by his philosophical colleagues and too speculative by his mathematical friends. The life of an intellectual outcaste may be a result partly of temperament and partly of the youthfulness of the logic profession. The unfortunate lack of wide appeal of logic may, however, be prolonged partly on account of the fact that very little of the well-established techniques of mathematics seems applicable to the treatment of serious problems of logic.

The axiomatic method is well suited to provide results which are both exact and systematic. How attractive would it be if we could get an axiom system in which all the axioms and deductions were intuitively clear and all theorems of mathematics were provable? Such a system would undoubtedly satisfy Descartes who admits solely intuition and deduction, which are, for him, the only "mental operations by which we are able, wholly without fear of illusion, to arrive at the knowledge of things." Indeed, according to Descartes, intuition and deduction "are the most certain routes to knowledge, and the mind should admit no others. All the rest should be rejected as suspect of error and dangerous"[1].

§ 2. Historical Perspective

Euclid's unification of masses of isolated discoveries in Greek elementary geometry was undoubtedly the first impressive success in systematizing mathe-

* This chapter appeared in *Journal of symbolic logic,* **19** (1954), pp. 241—266. It has been discussed by W. Stegmüller in *Arkiv f. Philos.*, vol. **7** (1957), pp. 45—81 and by Fraenkel and Bar-Hillel in Foundations of set theory, 1958. Certain inadequacies and omissions in this Chapter will be discussed in Chapter XXV.

1) *The rules for the direction of the mind,* Rule III.

matics. In a way it came about quite naturally. Of the four hundred sixty-five propositions in Euclid's *Elements,* some are quite obvious to our geometrical intuition, some are not so obvious. Confronted with the existing proofs of the less obvious by the more obvious, it was natural to ask how the various theorems are interrelated. Then it became mainly a matter of perseverance and acuteness to get the theorems arranged the way Euclid actually did arrange them.

There are, however, several points worth remarking. In the first place, systematization calls for more than the ability of a good librarian. For example, it was not until the nineteenth century that Pasch first formulated axioms concerning the concept "between" which had been tacitly assumed but not explicitly stated in Euclid. Moreover, a field has often to be developed very thoroughly before it is ripe for a systematic and rigorous organization. The history of the calculus illustrates this point clearly: founded in the seventeenth century, rapidly expanded in the eighteenth, the calculus got acceptable foundations only in the nineteenth century and even today logicians generally have misgivings on the matter or, like Weyl, still think that analysis is built on sand.

During the nineteenth century, the attempts to found analysis on a reliable basis went generally under the caption "arithmetization of analysis". It is well known that Cauchy, Weierstrass, Dedekind, Cantor all made important contributions to this program. Indeed, their results were so well received among mathematicians that in 1900, Poincaré asserted: "Today there remain in analysis only integers and finite or infinite systems of integers, interrelated by a net of relations of equality or inequality. Mathematics, as we say, has been arithmetized. ... We may say today that absolute rigour has been attained." [1)]

If by "arithmetization" is meant merely the elimination of geometrical intuition, then the success is hardly disputable. If, on the other hand, by "arithmetization" is meant a reduction of analysis to a theory of integers, then the matter becomes more involved because not only integers but also "finite or infinite systems of integers" are needed. Nowadays it would be more customary to refer to these "systems" as sets or classes. What is accomplished is not the founding of analysis on the theory of integers alone, but rather on the theory of integers plus the theory of sets. Therefore, the problem of getting a satisfactory theory of real numbers and real functions is not solved but shifted in a large part to the problem of finding a satisfactory theory of sets. And, as we know, to get a wholesome set theory is no small matter.

---

1) Du rôle de l'intuition et de la logique en mathématiques, *Compte-rendu du IIième Congrès International des Mathématiciens,* 1900, Paris (1902), 200—202.

§ 3. What is a Set ?

More explicitly, to get a rigorous basis of the calculus, an exact theory of the continuum is needed. Since real numbers can be regarded as arbitrary sets of rational numbers or positive integers which satisfy a few very broad conditions, this means that an exact development of the calculus logically calls for a general theory of sets.

There is also another way in which problems of ordinary mathematics should have led in the nineteenth century to queries as to what a set is. There were frequent occasions to consider arbitrary curves or arbitrary functions of real numbers. For example, is an arbitrary function representable by a trigonometric series? What functions are integrable? Many serious mathematicians were busy with such problems. Yet to answer these questions, it would appear prerequisite to have a pretty good idea of what an arbitrary function or set is.

It is of interest to note that as an historical fact mathematicians often speak of arbitrary functions and arbitrary curves when they have no precise definition of these notions and actually have in mind only certain special functions and special curves. The great discrepancy between the really arbitrary and the moderate arbitrariness which is actually needed in living mathematics explains the possibility of various basically different systems of set theory which compete to provide the true foundations of mathematics.

In the nineteenth century nobody paused to supply an exact definition of the notion of arbitrary set or arbitrary function. To do so would have required a thorough examination of all the means of definition at their disposal. There was at that time neither reason to suppose this work necessary nor enough advance preparation for carrying it out. Only after the discovery of paradoxes around 1900 was it realized that not all apparent laws or definitions could define sets and that some restriction on the permissible means of defining sets was necessary.

The historical course of events was different from the logical process of descending from the more abstract to the less general. Cantor did not have a general set theory to begin his investigations but was rather led to the study of point sets (sets of real numbers) by a comparatively more concrete problem which arose quite naturally from ordinary mathematics.

The problem is that of representing functions by trigonometric series which interested many a mathematician when Cantor began his research career around 1870. In trying to extend the uniqueness of representation to certain functions with infinitely many singular points, he was led to the notion of a derived set which not only marked the beginning of his study of the theory of point sets but led him later on to the construction of transfinite ordinal numbers.

Such historical facts ought to help combat the erroneous impression that Cantor invented, by one stroke of genius, a whole theory of sets which was entirely isolated from the main stream of mathematics at his time. In addition, it may be interesting to recall that mathematicians such as Heine and Dedekind were familiar with the problems which Cantor treated in his set theory and quite capable of handling them had they wished to. Indeed, du Bois-Reymond discovered independently of Cantor the notion of derived set, as well as the notion of derived set of infinite orders which led Cantor to the transfinite ordinals of the second number class. Moreover, du Bois-Reymond anticipated Cantor[1)] by about twenty years in using the diagonal argument now generally attributed to Cantor. The main reason why Cantor has been so much more influential is probably his ability to free himself gradually from applications and develop the theory of sets more and more for its own sake. Only in thus generalizing and following up logical conclusions everywhere, did Cantor become the founder of set theory.

§ 4. The Indenumerable and the Impredicative

The notions of denumerability and well-ordering were of central importance for Cantor: the former is the pillar of his theory of cardinal numbers, the latter of his theory of ordinal numbers.

In inventing set theory, the two most remarkable jumps which Cantor made were: the invention of transfinite ordinal numbers of his second number class, and the use of indenumerable and impredicative sets. The first is now known to be harmless and useful (especially in certain metamathematical considerations), while the second remains a mystery which has shed little light on any problems of ordinary mathematics. There is no clear reason why mathematics could not dispense with impredicative or absolutely indenumerable sets.

Cantor gives two proofs of the indenumerability of real numbers and one proof of the indenumerability of his second number class. All these proofs make use of impredicative sets.

Since not everybody is familiar with the nature of impredicative definition, it may be worthwhile to pause and review the well-known diagonal argument for proving the indenumerability of real numbers.

To prove this, it is, as we know, sufficient to prove that the set M of all sets of positive integers is not denumerable. Cantor's proof for this is as follows. Suppose there were a one-to-one correspondence $f(x, k)$ or $x=f(k)$ between M and the set P of positive integers, so that for every given positive integer k_0, there is a set $f(k_0)$ in M which is the image of k_0. For each posi-

1) See e.g., P. du Bois-Reymond, Über asymptotische Werte, infinitäre Approximationen und infinitäre Auflösung von Gleichungen, *Mathematische Annalen,* **8** (1875), 363—414.

tive integer k, either k belongs to its image $f(k)$ or not. Consider the set N of all positive integers k such that k does not belong to $f(k)$. N would be a set of positive integers and therefore a member of M. By hypothesis, there would be a positive integer n such that N is $f(n)$. Either n belongs to $f(n)$ or not. If n belongs to $f(n)$, then, by the definition of N, n does not belong to $f(n)$, $f(n)$ being N. If N does not belong to $f(n)$, then by the definition of N again, n belongs to $f(n)$. Hence, we obtain a contradiction. It follows that given any one-to-one correspondence between positive integers and sets of positive integers, we can always find a set of positive integers which is different from all the sets already enumerated.

We can make a number of different comments on the arguments. From the proof, it certainly follows that given any law which enumerates sets of positive integers

$$x_1, x_2, x_3, \cdots,$$

we can find a set x which is different from every one of the above. Moreover, given x and the sets $x_1, x_2, \cdots$, we can also find a law which enumerates $x_1, x_2, \cdots$ together with x:

$$x, x_1, x_2, x_3, \cdots;$$

but then there is another set y which is different from all these. Then we can also find another sequence which includes y and all terms of the previous sequence. And so on.

From the fact that no enumeration can exhaust all sets of positive integers, Cantor infers that the set of all sets of positive integers is absolutely indenumerable. In order to justify this inference, we have to assume that there is a set which includes all sets of positive integers, or that there is a law which defines a set that includes all sets of positive integers. Constructive set theory refuses to recognize any such set or any such law. While the constructive viewpoint accepts totalities of laws relative to different stages of construction, it rejects a closed totality which excludes possibilities of further construction.

If, however, we do allow that there is a set M of *all* sets of positive integers, then the above argument shows that such a set M is absolutely indenumerable. Moreover, we then see that the argument uses what is known as an impredicative definition to define the set N of positive integers. Thus, by definition, k belongs to N if and only if *there exists* a set K in M such that K is $f(k)$ and k does not belong to K. This is impredicative because in defining N, we make use of the totality M which contains N as a member. Thus, in order to determine whether a given k_0 belongs to N, we have, so to speak, to check through all members of M (including N itself) to see whether some one of them is $f(k_0)$ and yet does not contain k_0 as member. Hence, in order to define N, N must already be there. This is clearly inacceptable from a constructive viewpoint according to which the set only comes into being by a definition. Only if we take the sets as somehow existing before we say anything about them, can we accept such definitions: and then, not as definitions, but as descriptions of properties which sets possess by themselves, or as directions for picking suitable sets from a huge ocean containing all sorts of familiar, as well as curious, fish.

The situation is quite similar with Cantor's proof that the second number class is not denumerable.

It is no accident that all proofs of absolute indenumerability use impredicative sets. Indeed, it is at least intuitively plausible that all predicative sets are denumerable. We may also recall that Russell's paradox was first obtained from analysis of Cantor's diagonal argument and uses an impredicative set, too.

§5. The Limitations upon Formalization

A satisfactory axiomatization of set theory seems to be the most hopeful way of carrying out the ambitious program of systematizing all mathematics. At the beginning of the century the discovery of paradoxes plus the popularity of axiomatic method in geometry and arithmetic led quite naturally to attempts to construct axiom systems for set theory in which as much of Cantor's "naive" theory as possible, but of course none of the paradoxes, is to be derived. As a result, we possess today a number of axiom systems for set theory.

In order to formalize mathematics in axiomatic set theory it is customary, on account of the great diversity of content, to make certain preliminary representations or reductions. For example, geometrical points can be represented by real numbers, functions and relations can be construed as sets (of couples, etc.), numbers can be identified with certain special sets, and so on. With these reductions, it is often asserted and believed that each of several standard axiom systems of set theory is adequate to the development of all mathematics. For example, the system of *Principia Mathematica*, or the system constructed by Zermelo and extended by his successors.

The actual derivation of mathematics from any such system is long and tedious. It is practically impossible to verify conclusively any claim that this and that branch of mathematics, with all their details, are derivable in such a system. It is also hard to refute such a claim for that would require the discovery of some premise or principle of inference, which has so far been tacitly assumed but unrecognized.

There are, nonetheless, at least three rather general objections to claims of this sort. In the first place, none of these standard systems is known to be free from contradictions. In the second place, each system can easily be expanded, for instance, by adding a higher level of sets, to a new system which at the same time contains new theorems and yet can be proved to be no less reliable than the original. Indeed, a proof can be given in each case for the conclusion that the extended system is consistent, provided the original is. Moreover, the extended system can again be similarly extended; the process of such extensions can be continued indefinitely. A closely related difficulty is that all these systems are subject to the Gödel imcompleteness. A third objection is that none of these systems can supply all the set theory as originally constructed by Cantor. Specifically, this has to do with Cantor's notion of indenumerable sets and his use of impredicative definitions. While Cantor asserts the existence of sets which are absolutely indenumerable, any of these axiom systems can supply only sets which are indenumerable relative to the means of expression in the system. Such sets are denumerable in the absolute sense, as it is possible to enumerate the elements of each by talking *about* the original axiom system.

There are, largely as a result of the first objection, numerous attempts to construct artificial systems which are both demonstrably consistent and also adequate to the development of the "principal" (or "useful") parts of mathematics. Most of these systems modify our basic logical principles such as the law of excluded middle and the principle of extensionality (for sets), and it is not easy to become familiar with them. So far as I know, none of these has been accepted widely.

The attitude toward the second and the third objections is usually either one of indifference or one of resignation. These objections, it is argued, need not be taken seriously, since what we have is already sufficient for all ordinary purposes and the creation of new inadequacies by considering the system as given is quite idle. Others contend that these difficulties are the price which we have to pay for using a formal language or using an axiom system.

In what follows an approach will be suggested in outline which is both natural and not subject to the above three objections.

§ 6. A Constructive Theory

This is not the place to describe the formal details of the constructive theory which is claimed to possess all the wonderful properties of naturalness, adequacy, and demonstrable consistency. The theory will only be roughly sketched and an attempt will be made to make it appear plausible that the theory can do the things which it is supposed to do. I possess a more exact treatment of the matter which I hope will in the near future become available for scrutiny to those who are interested.

The system or theory will be denoted by the capital Greek letter sigma Σ. It has in the lowest order (the 0-th order) a denumerable totality consisting of (say) all the positive integers or all the finite sets built up out of the empty set. In the first order are these same sets plus sets of them which can be defined by properties referring at most only to the totality of all sets of the 0-th order (or, in other words, by formulas which contain no bound variables of the first or a higher order). Similarly, for every positive integer n, the sets of order $n+1$ include all sets of order n together with sets of them defined by properties referring at most only to the totality of all sets of the n-th order. The sets of order ω include all and only sets of the finite orders. For any ordinal number $\alpha+1$, the sets of order $\alpha+1$ are related to those of order α in the same way as the sets of order $n+1$ to those of order n (n a nonnegative integer). For any ordinal number β which is the limit number of a monotone increasing sequence $\alpha_1, \alpha_2, \cdots$ of ordinals, the sets of order β are related to the sets of orders $\alpha_1, \alpha_2, \cdots$ in the same way as the sets of order ω are related to those of finite orders. In short, sets of orders higher than 0 are constructed according to the Poincaré-Russell vicious-circle principle.

All the ordinal numbers which are used belong, of course, to what is known as Cantor's second number class. Moreover, we use only "constructive" ordinals. What a constructive ordinal number is presents an interesting and difficult problem. A simple and straightforward characterization of the totality of constructive ordinals is likely to get into the difficulty that the diagonal argument would produce a new ordinal number which should again be regarded as constructive. Let us assume for the moment that a suitable notion of constructive ordinals is given. Longer discussion of the topic will be included in a later section. We observe merely that in any case the usual ordinal numbers of Cantor's second number class, such as ω^2, the ε-numbers, all are constructive ordinals.

The axioms of the theory Σ can be briefly described as follows. All axioms and rules of inference of the standard quantification theory (predicate calculus) hold with regard to sets of each order. Set terms or abstracts of different orders are included in the primitive notation. Two sets x_α and y_β are equal or $x_\alpha = y_\beta$ if and only if they have the same extension; or, more exactly, if $\alpha \geqslant \beta$, every set z_α belongs either to both x_α and y_β or to none. Special axioms of the theory are:

A. Identity: for every γ, $\gamma \geqslant \alpha$, $\gamma \geqslant \beta$, if $x_\alpha = y_\beta$ and $x_\alpha \in z_\gamma$, then $y_\beta \in z_\gamma$.

B. Infinite summation: for every limiting ordinal number α, if $\beta < \alpha$, then for every x_β, there is y_α, such that $y_\alpha = x_\beta$.

C. Abstraction: for every formula $F(x_\beta)$, every y_β belongs to $\hat{x}_\beta F(x_\beta)$ if and only if $F(y_\beta)$.

D. Foundation: if x_α is not empty, then there is some y_α such that $y_\alpha \in x_\alpha$, and y_α and x_α have no common member.

E. Bounded order: if $x \in y$ and y is not of higher order than x, then there exists a set z of lower order than y such that $x = z$.

F. Limitation: see III in the next section.

The ideas employed in the construction of the theory Σ are not new. Russell, Weyl, Chwistek, Lorenzen[1] all have developed mathematics along somewhat similar lines. I shall not enter into detailed comparison of the present approach with works of these authors, except merely to remark that Russell and Weyl do not even claim adequacy of their systems for the development of analysis, that I have not been able to understand Chwistek, and that Lorenzen has little regard for formalization. Many of the conclusions obtained by using the theory Σ are very much the same as what Lorenzen arrives at from a somewhat informal approach.

The theory Σ is not exactly a logistic system but rather a system schema. It is the union of all formal systems Σ_α, where α is an arbitrary constructive ordinal, and Σ_α deals with all and only those sets which are of order α or less. By referring to these partial systems Σ_α, we shall be able to make many quite exact statements about the comprehensive theory Σ.

§ 7. The Denumerability of all Sets

One peculiarity about the theory Σ is that all sets of Σ are enumerable in Σ. Indeed, it is possible to enumerate all sets of any given order α by a function of order $\alpha+2$. By using standard methods for giving Tarski truth definitions and constructions employed by Bernays in his demonstration of a general class metatheorem from a finite number of axioms, we can prove, at least for α not too large (say less than ω^2), the following two results:

I. For each α, we can find a function E_α of order $\alpha+2$, such that E_α enumerates all sets of order α; or, in other words, the domain of E_α is the set of all positive integers and its range is the universal set V_α consisting of all sets of order α.

II. For each α, we can find a truth definition of Σ_α in $\Sigma_{\alpha+2}$ and formalize a consistency proof of Σ_α in $\Sigma_{\alpha+2}$ (i.e., prove $Con(\Sigma_\alpha)$ in $\Sigma_{\alpha+2}$).

Incidentally, it may be of interest to compare these with similar results on ordinary predicate calculi in which impredicative definitions are allowed. For example, consistency of the predicate calculus of type n can be proved in that of type $n+1$, by the use of impredicative sets; while here we have to prove the consistency of Σ_α in $\Sigma_{\alpha+2}$. Both in proving the consistency of Σ_α and in enumerating V_α, we have to use sets which take sets of order α as members but are defined with the help of bound variables of order $\alpha+1$. While these sets are impredicative sets of type $\alpha+1$ according to their members, they are sets of order $\alpha+2$ according to their definitions. That is why in both I and II we have to use the order $\alpha+2$ instead of $\alpha+1$.

---

1) Paul Lorenzen, Die Widerspruchsfreiheit der klassischen Analysis, *Mathematische Zeitschrift*, **54** (1951), 1—24.

Using the functions E_α, we are able to state powerful axioms of limitation which stipulate that in the theory Σ we recognize no sets other than those explicitly enumerated by the functions E_α (compare also Chwistek's axiom of enumerability and Fitch's hypothesis of similarity[1]):

III. For each order α and each set x_α, there is a positive integer m such that $E_\alpha(m)$ is x_α.

From these axioms of limitation, it becomes possible to prove general theorems on all sets of each order by using mathematical induction. Since E_α well-orders all sets of order α, certain axioms of choice can be proved. Moreover, it is clearly also possible to enumerate all sets of order α which are ordinal numbers. It follows that we can, in $\Sigma_{\alpha+2}$, find a one-to-one correspondence between all sets of order α and all sets of order α which are ordinal numbers. One can also prove, by the diagonal argument, that no such correlation exists in Σ_α itself. Therefore, the continuum hypothesis (viz. the hypothesis that the set of all sets of order α has the same cardinality as the set of all sets of order α which are ordinal numbers) is provable or refutable according as whether equi-cardinality is defined by the existence of a correlation of order $\alpha+2$ or one of order α. In short, we have:

IV. Axioms of choice are provable in Σ.

V. Certain forms of the continuum hypothesis are provable in Σ; certain other forms are refutable in Σ.

Moreover, since $Con(\Sigma_\alpha)$ is provable in $\Sigma_{\alpha+2}$, the Gödel undecidable propositions of each Σ_α are provable in $\Sigma_{\alpha+2}$. Hence, the only possible way to construct a Gödel proposition which is undecidable in Σ would be, so far as I can see, to find a sequence of increasing constructive ordinals $\alpha_1, \alpha_2, \cdots$ such that its limit is no longer a constructive ordinal and consider the union of $\Sigma_{\alpha_1}, \Sigma_{\alpha_2}, \cdots$; yet there is, so far as I can see, no apparent way to show that such a union is again a formal system or a system to which Gödel's constructions are applicable. We have, therefore:

VI. Gödel's famous constructions do not yield directly any propositions which are undecidable in the theory Σ.

It would be of interest to investigate whether there might not be some indirect means of constructing undecidable propositions in Σ.

Developing real numbers in some standard fashion[2], we can also prove standard theorems of classical analysis in the theory Σ. For example, we can prove, with pretty much the traditional arguments, the theorem of least upper bound, the Bolzano-Weierstrass theorem, and the Heine-Borel theorem.

1) Frederic B. Fitch, The hypothesis that infinite classes are similar, *Journal of Symbolic Logic*, **4** (1939), 159—162. Leon Chwistek, Über die Hypotheses der Mengenlehre, *Mathematische Zeitschrift*, **25** (1926), 439—473.

2) E.g., as in Bernays' series of articles on axiomatic set theory in *Journal of Symbolic Logic*, **2** (1937); **6** (1941); **7** (1942); **8** (1943); **13** (1948); **19** (1954).

This is actually not surprising since we do not hesitate, when necessary, to use sets of higher orders. For example, in the general case, the least upper bound of a set whose members are of order α is a set of order $\alpha + 1$. Both Weyl and Russell were aware of such possibilities but they found the use of higher orders objectionable. This and related points will, in the next section, be discussed at great length.

Let me insert a few words on the use of indenumerable sets in measure theory.

It is widely known that in measure theory there is a theorem stating that every denumerable set is of measure zero. It would seem that in the theory Σ where all sets are denumerable, the whole measure theory would collapse. In actuality, however, this is not the case because, although there are no sets which are absolutely indenumerable, for each α, there are sets of order α which are indenumerable by any functions of order α. And the notion of relative indenumerability is sufficient to provide us with sets of nonzero measures for measures defined on each given level.

Thus, let us recall the standard proof of the theorem. Given a denumerable set M of points

$$x_1, x_2, x_3, \cdots,$$

we can choose an arbitrarily small ε and cover each x_i by the interval from $x_i - \frac{\varepsilon}{2^i}$ to $x_i + \frac{\varepsilon}{2^i}$, then it is easy to see that the sum of these intervals is no greater than 2ε and that the measure of the original set is smaller than 2ε. Hence the set M has measure zero.

For each α, this proof can be carried out in Σ_α only if the given denumerable set M of points can be enumerated within Σ_α. It is perfectly possible for the same set to have measure zero in $\Sigma_{\alpha+1}$ and a nonzero measure in Σ_α.

I think this situation is completely satisfactory. We even get an explanation of the relation between the continuous and the discrete (i.e., denumerable). A set of points is continuous only relative to our knowledge or our power to isolate the numerous points. What is seen as continuous in a less powerful set theory becomes discrete as we come to use a richer set theory.

§ 8. Consistency and Adequacy

From the known consistency of the ramified theory of types it is natural to expect the consistency of the theory Σ. Indeed, the consistency of each system Σ_α can be proved similarly to that of the ramified type theory. Since the theory Σ is the union of all systems Σ_α, the consistency of Σ follows immediately.

We can prove the consistency of each system Σ_a by describing more in detail its intuitive model. The arguments are similar to Fitch's proof[1] of the consistency of the ramified theory of types.

Or, we can also give a proof-theoretic consistency proof of each system Σ_a. Such a proof is analogous to Lorenzen's and Schütte's finitist proofs[2] of the consistency of the ramified type theory.

It is very difficult to explain exactly the sense in which Lorenzen's proof is finitist. But the following vaguely specified difference between it and Fitch's proof is clearly relevant.

Given any proof in the formal system of the ramified theory of types, Lorenzen's procedure can change it effectively into a different proof in which every line is more complicated than each of its premises (indeed, longer except for occasional deletion of repetitious terms). In other words, we get cumulative proofs. It is true that these proofs can contain potentially infinitely many propositions, e.g., in order to prove $(m)m \geqslant 0$, we use $0 \geqslant 0$, $1 \geqslant 0$, $2 \geqslant 0$, etc. Nonetheless, each application of the rule of infinite induction is determined unambiguously by the corresponding step of the original proof. Consequently, the actual applications of the rule of infinite induction are much less unmanageable than what the abstract statement of the rule itself would lead us to think.

In Fitch's proof by an intuitive model, the situation is more complex. It is not easy to see how we can get effectively, from a proof in the formal system, a corresponding proof in the intuitive model. For example, in order ot justify that for every proposition *p*, '*p* or not-*p*' belongs to the set of true propositions, we have to apply the law of excluded middle to the infinite set of true propositions and argue that either *p* belongs to the set, whence '*p* or not-*p*' also belongs to it, or else *p* does not belongs to the set, whence not-*p* belongs to it and hence also '*p* or not-*p*'. It is not possible to avoid altogether reference to the alternative that a proposition does not belong to the set of true propositions (i.e., belongs to the set of propositions which are not true). In other words, we cannot carry out the consistency proof without constantly 'going out of' the set of true propositions.

Naturally the consistency proofs for Σ involve peculiar features on account of special characteristics of the theory. Yet it is certainly reasonable to expect that these proofs can be carried out. Details will not be given here.

At several places we proved the required theorems only by ascending to higher orders: the axioms of choice, the reinterpretations of the continuum hypothesis, the least upper bound theorem, the Bolzano-Weierstrass

1) The consistency of the ramified Principia, *Journal of Symbolic Logic*, **3** (1938), 140—149.

2) Paul Lorenzen, Algebraische und logistische Untersuchungen über freie Verbände, *Journal of Symbolic Logic*, **16** (1951), 81—106; Kurt Schütte, Beweistheoretische Untersuchung der verzweigten Analysis, *Mathematische Annalen*, **124** (1951—52), 123—147.

theorem. For many people this seems to cut through rather than meet the original difficulties.

For example, Weyl mentions in *Das Kontinuum* (p. 23) the possibility of defining the least upper bound of a given bounded set of real numbers by a real number of a higher order, but discarded it immediately as philosophically unsatisfactory.

For a ramified analysis, an obvious difficulty which has often been mentioned is: since the least upper bound of a given set of real numbers is a real number of a higher order, so that there are necessarily infinitely many different orders of real numbers, how can one speak of all real numbers at the same time?

Under the approach sketched here, we have no clear idea of *all* real numbers, but, for each given α, we can consider *all* real numbers of order α. Moreover, we can use a sort of schematic method by which we discuss all real numbers by talking about all real numbers of each order indiscriminately.

Nonetheless, it is not necessary to adopt this approach, if our purpose is just to be able to speak of infinitely many orders at the same time. Consider the system Σ_ω (or, for that matter, any Σ_α, where α is a limiting ordinal number). We can prove easily that for every bounded set x_ω of real numbers, there is a real number y_ω which is the least upper bound of x_ω. This is so, because every set x_ω is a set of real numbers of some finite order n, and its least upper bound is a real number of order $n+1$ and *ipso facto* a set of order ω.

Therefore, as soon as we get to sets of order ω, we can already avoid the necessity of ascending to any higher orders to get least upper bounds. Similarly, the sets needed for the axiom of choice, the interpretations of the continuum hypothesis, and the Bolzano-Weierstrass theorem are also of order ω, provided each given set is of order ω (and therefore of an order n, for *some* finite n).

It follows from this remark that in order to speak of all sets of all finite orders at the same time, we need neither Russell's axiom of reducibility (see below) nor the full theory Σ which includes an indeterminate totality of orders. The system Σ_ω is more satisfactory than Russell's method which unnecessarily introduces unmanageable difficulties in connection with impredicative sets. The theory Σ is philosophically even more satisfying because it seems rather arbitrary to stop at either order ω or some other order α. For example, the fact that Σ_ω is directly subject to Gödel's theorems while the theory Σ, so far as I can see, is not, is one indication of the preferableness of Σ. We might say that the approach embodied in Σ is superior to Russell's in more than one way.

It is customary to define real numbers as certain sets of natural numbers or rational numbers. Since these sets are infinite, each of them has to be given by a law or a principle for selecting its members. Naturally, therefore, how rich a theory of real numbers is depends very much on the method of definition we are permitted to employ. We can, of course, think of many curious ways of defining sets. Consequently we do not have any clear idea of *all* sets. The notion of set and thereby that of real number is relative to our theory of definition in the sense that different theories of definition would give us different theories of sets and real numbers.

This was apparently not realized by people of the nineteenth century. They seem to talk as if there was a unique absolute theory of definition. Thus Dedekind spoke of all sets or cuts of real numbers without bothering to stop and examine what he meant by *all*. Similarly Cantor spoke of all denumerable sets in his proof of the indenumerability of the set of all real numbers.

Now, how do we know that the theory Σ does give us all the real numbers we need in ordinary mathematics?

If we examine the real numbers actually used in mathematics, we easily see that the domain has gradually been expanded. The rational numbers, of course. Then there were simple irrational numbers such as $\sqrt{2}$. The Greeks also considered more complex cases. In general, however, they seem to confine themselves to irrationalities obtained by repeatedly taking the square root, an operation performable geometrically by ruler and compass. The next logical extension is to include all algebraic numbers. There are also transcendental numbers, e.g., e and π.

Since it seems natural to think that every infinite decimal defines a real number, it is worthwhile to get an idea of the wide range of possible laws or definitions for determining these decimals. We can roughly contrast "natural" with "artificial" definitions. The natural ones arise out of the actual development of mathematics, such as those for e, π, values of certain common functions, etc. Usually there are organic connections between these and our main body of knowledge so that we have more information about the infinite decimals and real numbers determined by them. The artificial ones can be manufactured by playing with accidental characters of notation or actuality. For example, the following infinite decimal

$$0.1223334444 \cdots,$$

defined by the law that for every numeral n, n is repeated n times (for example the numeral 15 is written 15 times in succession).

Or the infinite decimal obtained from that for π by substituting an arbitrary numeral (say 7, or 891) for every digit 1 (or 2 or 3, etc.). Obviously, from each infinite decimal we can in this way generate infinitely many artificial infinite decimals about which we know nothing apart from their definitions.

A different kind of artificial definition is obtained if, for example, we determine

$$0.a_1a_2a_3a_4 \cdots$$

in the following manner: beginning with January 1, 2000, a_i is 0 or 1 according to whether or not more boys are born than girls on the i-th day.

From these examples it should become clear how easy it is to make the invention of curious infinite decimals an enduring pastime. We shall, however, refrain from self-indulgence and confine ourselves to the natural definitions.

The most efficient way of generating new real numbers is by functions. Thus, given a fixed subclass D of the class of real numbers (e.g., D may be the class of rational numbers or that of algebraic numbers) and a function

$$y = f(x),$$

there is a real number y for every x in D. It may happen that for every x in D, $f(x)$ is also in D. Then the function $f(x)$ generates no new real numbers. However, it may also happen that for certain values of x in D, $f(x)$ is no longer in D. Let D' be the class of all real numbers which are either in D or are the values of $f(x)$ for some x in D. With regard to D', it may again happen that for some x in D', $f(x)$ is not in D'. We can then consider a larger class D''. And so on. In general, this process can be continued indefinitely and the sum of all such classes (call it D_f) satisfies the condition that for every x in D_f, $f(x)$ is also in D_f.

In this way, given each fixed class D of real numbers and a function $f(x)$, we can try to find the corresponding D_f which in special cases may be the same as D. Hence, we can approach the totality of all real numbers in the following manner. Let us start from, say, the domain of rational numbers. Consider, e.g., the ordinary algebraic and transcendental functions. Let us add them successively and every time expand the domain of real numbers to get a larger one in which for every x in it $f(x)$ is also in it. In this way, we reach a totality of real numbers *closed* with regard to a given totality of functions.

No number of functions could determine all the real numbers. Yet we certainly want to get at least a domain of real numbers which would be *closed* with regard to all the functions we have occasion to consider in ordinary mathematics. Once we are sure that a certain theory of real numbers does provide a domain satisfying this requirement, we need not be too much concerned with the question how many more real numbers are also included.

Therefore, in order to determine the minimum requirements that a theory of real numbers is to satisfy, it is relevant to consider first the ordinary functions in analysis.

It is quite easy to prove that all real numbers which can be obtained by ordinary procedures of classical analysis can be obtained in the system Σ_ω (indeed, in a partial system, say, Σ_5).

There is presumably a great gap between the totality of all the special laws and series which we have had an opportunity to study and the totality of all possible laws and series which we may or may never get around to investigating. If so, how can we ever hope to get a satisfactory theory of all possible laws or definitions?

The answer to this rhetorical question is to distinguish two types of theories of "all" laws. If what is desired is a theory which provides us with detailed information about all the possible laws concerning some of which we may never get such information otherwise, it would almost be a tautology to say that no such theory can be obtained. On the other hand, there is no reason why a much more modest theory would not actually suffice for the purpose of setting up a rigorous foundation of real numbers and mathematical analysis. For example, we can employ a theory in which all the known laws of defining infinite decimals are included, and at the same time we deliberately use the word "all" ambiguously so that the door is open for other newcomers to join the totality of *all* laws of the theory. The theory Σ seems to be one such.

§ 9. The Axiom of Reducibility

Roughly the ramified theory of types is equivalent to the system Σ_ω minus the variables of order ω. Russell's axiom of reducibility says that for every set there is a coextensional set which is of the order next above the highest order of its arguments. For example, every set whose members are objects of order 0 is, by this, coextensional with a set of order 1.

By the help of such an axiom of reducibility, statements about "all first-order functions (or sets) of m" yield most results which otherwise would require "all functions (or sets) of m". The axiom leads to all the desired results and, so far as we know, to no others. Nevertheless, Russell thinks that it is not the sort of axiom with which we can rest content and conjectures that perhaps some less objectionable axiom might give the results required. (By the way, Russell's original form of the axiom of reducibility was more complex than the currently accepted formulation, because Russell could not make up his mind exactly what methods are permitted in defining functions or sets of lowest orders. We are assuming that all and only methods of formal logic are admitted.)

The purpose of this section is to argue that there is nothing wrong in speaking of functions or sets of all orders at the same time, and to prove that we do not need the axiom of reducibility at all. Thus, for example, if we use the variables x_n, y_n, z_n, etc. ($n=1, 2, \ldots$) to refer to sets of positive integers of order *n*, we seem to need either the axiom of reducibility or an infinitely long expression in order to make a statement about sets of positive integers of all orders. There is, however, nothing to prevent us from introducing in addition, as in the system Σ_ω, a new kind of variable x_ω, y_ω, z_ω, etc., which take all these sets no matter of what order, as values.

Once we introduce such general variables for all sets (of whatever order), of a same type, we can do all the things for which the axiom of reducibility was originally proposed. Consequences of the axiom which are no longer available are precisely the results that contradict the basic spirit of the constructive approach, intended by Russell's theory of ramified types.

The announced reason for introducing the axiom of reducibility was to enable us to talk about all sets or functions of certain given things in addition to all sets or functions of each given order. Let us discuss one by one how the use of general variables can substitute for the axiom of reducibility for the various situations considered by Russell.

The first thing is with regard to mathematical induction. Russell wants to say that a positive integer is one which possesses *all* properties possessed by 1 and by the successors of all numbers possessing them. If we confine this statement to all first-order properties x_1, we cannot infer, without using the axiom of reducibility, that it holds of second-order properties x_2. However, using general variables x_ω, y_ω, etc., for sets of positive integers of all (finite) orders, we can now make the above statement with regard to *all* properties x_ω (of positive integers).

A second use of the axiom of reducibility is with regard to the definition of identity. He defines two individuals as identical when they have the same first-order properties. By the axiom of reducibility, he then proves the theorem that two such individuals have the same properties of every order. In the system Σ_ω, we can, using general variables for all properties, adopt his theorem as the definition of identity. Thereby the axiom of reducibility is no longer needed.

A third and more important application of the axiom is in the development of the Dedekind theory of real numbers. Thus, if we define real numbers as certain sets of rational numbers satisfying Dedekind's requirements, then, since there are such sets of different orders, there are also real numbers of different orders. This, as we have observed, can again be handled in systems such as the system Σ_ω.

On the other hand, the abolition of the axiom of reducibility does entail the important consequence that Cantor's proof for the theorem that there are absolutely more real numbers than positive integers breaks down in Σ_ω, although, in a modified form, it can be gotten by the axiom of reducibility in a system with only finite orders. Indeed, it is no longer possible to prove the existence of any cardinal number greater than aleph-zero (the number of positive integers) in Σ_ω.

From the constructive point of view adopted by Russell, this is, however, not only no objection to the approach embodied in Σ_ω, but rather a point strongly in its favour. This is so, because in proving the existence of any infinity beyond aleph-zero, the impredicative definitions are indispensable, and impredicative definitions are precisely what Russell's theory set out to abolish.

In other words, the axiom of reducibility actually serves two very different purposes: (1) to enable us to speak of all sets or functions of certain things without having to enumerate the infinitely many different orders; (2) to enable us to introduce sets by impredicative definitions and properties. It seems that Russell, in trying to remedy a minor verbal difficulty, unwittingly reintroduced impredicative definitions at a back door through the axiom of reducibility (indeed, introduced an assumption which embodies the very essence of impredicative definitions in set theory). The remarks of this and the preceding sections should be sufficient to establish the conclusion that as soon as general variables are introduced, the axiom of reducibility becomes unnecessary at least for all the things which it was originally introduced to do.

In my opinion, the present approach also illuminates the criticism of Weyl by Hölder in a paper of 1926[1]. According to Hölder, since in the definition of the least upper bound of a set M of real numbers the quantification may be understood as ranging over the real numbers of M only, which are given beforehand, and not over *all* real numbers, it is not true that the definition of the least upper bound involves a circle. If we adopt the standard formalization of the least upper bound theorem where we do not admit real numbers of different orders, Hölder seems clearly wrong. But if we accept a constructive approach as in the present essay, then Hölder is right because in each given set M the real numbers must be of a definite order, and we can define a least upper bound which is of the next higher order.

I think Hölder's remarks are very interesting for the present approach because they seem to show that it is quite natural to use a ramified analysis. We might even view the systems of this essay as, among other things, attempts to formalize Hölder's interpretation of the classical theorem of least upper bound.

§ 10. The Vicious-Circle Principle

The theory Σ is built up in accordance with the Poincaré-Russell vicious-circle principle. Since the theory of types is also based on the same principle but differs from Σ in many ways, it is of interest to ask whether the theory Σ does not violate the principle in certain respects.

1) Otto Hölder, Der angebliche circulus vitiosus und die sogenannte Grundlagenkrise in der Analysis, *Berichte über die Verhandlungen der Sächsischen Akademie der Wissenschaften zu Leipzig*, Mathematisch-physische Klasse, **78** (1926), 243—250.

Several somewhat different forms of the principle are given by Russell, but we can confine ourselves to the one stating that no totality can contain members definable only in terms of that totality. This vicious-circle principle, according to Russell, enables us to avoid "illegitimate totalities." It follows that given an open formula (propositional function) p which either contains quantifiers referring to sets of order α or has its argument value referring to sets of order α, the set defined by p must be at least of order $\alpha+1$.

Thus, if we start from a given totality of basic objects and call them of (say) order 0, we can proceed to define sets of orders 1, 2, 3, etc. by introducing new variables and new abstracts at successive stages. It is natural to record our advance by using such order indices. When we have gone through all finite ordinals, there is nothing to prevent us from going to transfinite orders.

Sets of order ω should be all and only those which are defined in terms of variables and abstracts of finite orders. On the one hand, since ω is higher than all finite ordinals, every abstract containing only variables and abstracts of finite orders defines a set of order ω. On the other hand, since ω is the smallest infinite order, an abstract containing any variable or abstract which is not of a finite order must be of order higher than ω. Similarly, for each limiting ordinal α. As a result, for each limiting ordinal α, sets of order α serve to sum up all sets of all lower orders in the theory Σ.

There is no reason that we should stop at any particular ordinal number α of the second number class, since we can certainly proceed further and define abstracts of order $\alpha+1, \alpha+2$, etc. Hence, instead of using a definite formal system, we allow in Σ indefinitely many orders α and corresponding partial systems Σ_α.

In *Principia Mathematica*[1] it is emphasized that certain expressions are neither true nor false but meaningless. Thus, for example, it is neither true nor false to say that a set belongs to itself, because the question is meaningless. In general, '$a \in b$' is meaningless unless a and b are of suitable types (more specifically, b is just one type higher than a).

Recently, this emphasis has often got into headlines in philosophy. It is contended that many, if not all, philosophical problems arise because we want to get a 'yes or no' answer to meaningless questions. When we say that the universal set belongs to itself, or that justice is blue, we are said to be making a 'category mistake.'

However suggestive, for philosophy, the idea may be, it does not seem necessary so far as logic is concerned. An obvious way is to call the expressions false instead of meaningless. Indeed, this is followed in the theory Σ.

The procedure in *Principia* of treating expressions such as "$a_n \in a_n$" (n as type or level index) as meaningless rather than false leads to the con-

1) A. N. Whitehead and Bertrand Russell, Vol. 1, p. 41.

sequence that the sets are divided into mutually exclusive ranges of significance. This is so because it would be extraordinarily queer and inconvenient to say, for example, that "$a_n \in a_n$" is meaningless while "$b_n \in a_n$" is meaningful (and true), or, in general, that some term can replace another term in one meaningful expression but not in another. The situation is most striking with regard to the substitution of equals for equals (substitutivity of identity). On the other hand, it is quite all right to say, for example, that "$a_n \in a_n$" is false but "$b_n \in a_n$" is true.

Hence, the fact that the ordinary theory of simple types does not permit mixture of types is closely connected with the decision of considering certain expressions as meaningless instead of false. If, for example, we introduce types or levels to the system in Σ which deals solely with sets and variables of finite orders and then add the axiom of reducibility to nullify the distinction of orders, then we get a theory which is like the simple theory of types but permits the mixing of different types.

It goes without saying that the use of transfinite orders (and without bounds) is the principal difference between the theory Σ and the ordinary ramified theory of types without the axiom of reducibility. The axioms of limitation provide a new feature which has often been discussed but has never been carried out before in standard forms of set theory.

It may be thought that the famous Gödel proposition, which essentially says of itself that it is not provable in a certain system, violates the vicious-circle principle. If so, it would be pretty bad for the vicious-circle principle, since Gödel's construction is a perfectly sound procedure. Actually, however, the self-reference is achieved by using considerations from outside the system. Gödel is defining by a non-objectionable method something which ordinarily can only be defined by a vicious circle. This is like proving some set defined by an impredicative definition actually equivalent to a set defined by a predicative definition, thereby making the set non-objectionable.

More exactly, if we say, "This proposition is not provable", we are using self-reference, and defining a proposition by referring to itself (or a totality including itself), but when we find a way of doing the matter as Gödel does, it is justified. We no longer define a proposition but just interpret a proposition, and prove results by means of this interpretation.

§ 11. Predicative Sets and Constructive Ordinals

In this essay constructive sets are identified with predicative sets. Predicative sets are sets which can be defined without violating the vicious-circle principle. It is desirable to have a more exact characterization which is, for instance, as sharp and acceptable an explication for predicativeness as recursiveness is for the intuitive concept of effective computability.

If we confine our attention to mathematical objects, one possibility is to say that a set is predicative if and only if it is coextensional with a set of the theory Σ. Leaving aside the difficult question of justifying the adequacy of the identification, we are faced also with the more urgent question of rendering the answer clear.

To determine even roughly the domain of sets available in Σ, we should have a pretty good idea of what a constructive ordinal is, since Σ is the union of all systems Σ_α where α is a constructive ordinal.

The Church-Kleene definition[1] of constructive ordinals in terms of recursive functions is clear and definite enough for the purpose. Yet it is rather narrower than what is wanted, since, in defining new ordinals, we would like to say that each monotone increasing sequence, generated by a predicative function of constructive ordinals determines a limit which is again a constructive ordinal, and yet there are predicative functions which are not recursive. As a result, we seem to get into a circle: in order to determine the region of predicative sets, we must have first a definite notion of constructive ordinals; in order to get such a definite notion, we must determine first the region of predicative sets.

One possible way to eliminate this impasse is to begin with a definite totality of ordinals (e.g., all ordinals below the first ε-number, or all constructive ordinals in the sense of Church-Kleene) and then consider the totality of all ordinals β definable in some of the systems Σ_α, where α is an ordinal in the first totality. In general, the new totality contains the first totality as a proper part. We can then consider the totality of all ordinals γ definable in some system Σ_β, where β is an ordinal of the second totality. And so on. There is, of course, no obvious assurance that all constructive ordinals we want will be obtained in this fashion. Certainly a large variety of ordinals can be gotten.

The usefulness of this definition of constructive ordinals depends on the following facts: given an ordinal number α, we have, as described above, a definite procedure of constructing Σ_α; given a system Σ_β, the totality of the ordinal numbers obtainable in Σ_β is determined. No circularity is involved.

The limitations upon formal systems were discussed in § 5. Let us now make a few general observations on how the approach embodied in the theory Σ is both natural and not subject to objections raised there.

One reason why the approach is natural is the inclusion of all principles employed in standard systems. The consistency is assured by rejecting altogether impredicative sets. The possibility of immediate extension is excluded by deliberately avoiding the postulation of a highest level of sets. There is, so to speak, at every stage an indeterminate limit on our actual knowledge of the possibilities of constructing new sets from given sets. Every

1) See S. C. Kleene, On notation for ordinal numbers, *Journal of Symbolic Logic*, **3** (1938), 150—155, and Alonzo Church, The constructive second number class, *Bulletin of the American Mathematical Society*, 44 (1938), 224—232.

given determination of the limit can be transcended, but no determinate limit transcends or even exhausts all the possibilities which are permitted by the theory. In this way the second objection is evaded.

To meet the third objection, indenumerable sets are entirely excluded. Given any enumeration of sets of (say) positive integers in the theory, there is always some other set of positive integers, not included in the enumeration. Moreover, given an arbitrary order, there are sets which cannot be enumerated by sets of that order. Nevertheless, every set in the theory is denumerable by some set (relation) in the theory. There are not only no absolutely indenumerable sets, but even no sets of the theory which are not denumerable in the theory. There are only indenumerable sets relative to each order in the theory.

This meets the third objection only by adopting a certain preferred viewpoint (you might say, a philosophy) which interprets sets as in some sense constructed. From this point of view, the fact that no enumeration can exhaust all sets of positive integers is explained not by the existence of indenumerable sets but rather by the impossibility for our intellect to have a clear and distinct idea of the totality of *all* sets or laws defining enumerations, for unless we are able to contemplate such a totality, it is quite senseless to ask whether there exists any set which is indenumerable in the absolute sense. If each time we can only contemplate a portion of all sets or laws of enumeration, we can only prove that certain sets are indenumerable when we restrict our means of enumeration to the given kind.

Or, the same fact can be explained by our inability to contemplate at one and the same time the totality of *all sets* (or laws defining sets) *of positive integers*. For, it may be argued, although we cannot contemplate all laws of enumeration at the same time, we can contemplate each of them. Therefore, if we can grasp at once the totality of all sets of positive integers, we can see schematically that each law of enumeration is inadequate to an enumeration of all of these, and then conclude that the totality of all sets of positive integers is absolutely indenumerable. But if, as is natural to assert from a constructivistic view, we cannot have a clear and distinct idea of the totality of all sets of positive integers, then it is quite senseless to ask whether or not such a totality, if we could grasp it, could be exhausted by a specific law of enumeration.

From this approach, to ask whether the totality of all sets of positive integers is denumerable (in the absolute sense) is very much like asking, as a common man though perhaps not as a physicist, whether or not the world is bounded in time and space. The totality of all sets or of all sets of positive integers is like Kant's thing-in-itself, while the constructible sets correspond to all possible experience. To parrot Kant: Now if I inquire after the quantity of the totality, as to its number, it is equally impossible, as regards all my notions, to declare it indenumerable or to declare it denumerable. For neither assertion can be contained in mental construction, because construction of an indenumerable totality or a closed denumerable totality incapable of further expansion, is impossible; these are mere ideas. The number of the totality, which is determined in either way, should therefore be predicated of the transcendent totality itself apart from all constructive thinking[1]. We cannot indeed, beyond all possible construction, form a definite notion of what the transcendent totality of all sets may be. Yet we are not at liberty to abstain entirely from inquiring into it; for construction never satisfies reason fully, but in answering questions, refers us further and further back, and leaves us dissatisfied with regard to their complete solution···. The enlarging of our views in mathematics, and the possibility of new discoveries, are infinite. But limits cannot be mistaken here, for mathematics refers to the constructible only, and what cannot be an object of intuitive contemplation, such as the totality of all laws, lies entirely without its sphere, and it can never lead to them; neither does it require them[2].

The question whether Σ can further be extended is debatable. Since we make conventions in Σ which depend on previous ones, we cannot effectively predict or well-order all possible orders used in Σ once and for all. On the other hand, it seems possible to look from outside and speak of the totality of all sets in Σ or all orders used in Σ. To speak of a universal set which contains all sets in Σ as members is either making an impossible convention or making a convention of a higher kind. It may be exaggeration to call such a convention impossible. It is just not very informative. Thus, it appears possible to add consistently to Σ an isolated universal set, provided we do not try to say too much about this transcendent set. If we wish to, we may even say that Σ is all that is needed for mathematics, introduction of sets beyond belongs to the realm of philosophy.

§ 12. Concluding Remarks

We may say that there are three regions in mathematics: (1) the effectively decidable; (2) the constructive; and (3) the transcendent. The theory Σ is an attempt to formalize the second region. Cantor's jump to the absolutely indenumerable belongs to the third region, while Brouwer's logic, as well as Hilbert's finitist viewpoint, deals mainly with the first region. Hilbert and Brouwer differ in that Brouwer never accepts willingly anything but the decidable logic, while Hilbert would allow us to use everything which can be justified on the basis of the decidable logic. This might also be expressed by saying that Brouwer requires restriction to his logic in all mathematics, while Hilbert requires it only in the domain of metamathematics.

For Hilbert, anything which can be seen or proved consistent finitistically, is acceptable: to be is to be consistent. It appears from discussions on the

1) Compare Prolegomena to any future metaphysic, § 52, c.

2) Ibid, § 57.

finitist viewpoint that the theory Σ can be proved consistent by finitist arguments. The theory Σ may perhaps be viewed as a theory satisfying Hilbert's demands for the foundations of mathematics. Of course there are finitist arguments which are not formalizable in current systems of elementary number theory[1].

The main purpose of a construction and development of the theory will be not so much the exhibition of a formal system as the basis of all mathematics, as the presentation of an argument to justify all mathematical reasoning which does not get into the transcendent. It will be an attempt to show that all such reasoning can be formalized in some formal system falling under the schema Σ.

Once it is clear that all constructive mathematical reasoning, that is, all mathematical reasoning that does not involve the dubious use of the impredicative definitions or jump to the indenumerable, can be formalized in the loose framework Σ, there will be no more need to formalize each argument by making explicit the orders of the various sets concerned. Rather we can then proceed with no special attention to the orders, with the realization that whenever we wish, we can always formalize each argument in some system Σ_α. In this way, the common practice in ordinary mathematics can be justified by the theory Σ. It is the kind of justification which does not interfere with the common practice. In this sense it is again more natural than other approaches to the foundations of mathematics.

But how can we prove that this is the case? There are two methods: a long one and a short one. The long method consists in a completion of the arguments by developing in Σ the various branches of mathematics. For example, as the Bourbaki group continues to turn out more and more volumes of their treatise, we show for each volume how all the definitions and proofs can be formalized in the theory Σ. While there does not seem to be fundamental obstacles to such a program, actually to carry it out is a complex and time-consuming matter. Whether this is worthwhile is hard to decide because on the one hand, many mathematicians would undoubtedly find the result of carrying out such a program quite uninteresting, while on the other hand, without an actual carrying out of the program most logicians would suspect the soundness of the high claim.

The short method is to let the matter stand as it does in an expanded version of this essay (or, more exactly, an expanded version which includes detailed formal development of matter covered in §§ 6—8) and challenge anybody who questions the adequacy of Σ to produce some mode of inference which is used in ordinary mathematics but cannot be formalized in Σ. The trouble with this shortcut is that few mathematicians who have a more or less clear view of the whole field of mathematics are likely to care to study the theory Σ carefully.

1) See, e.g., D. Hilbert and P. Bernays, Grundlagen der Mathematik, vol. **II**, p. 373.

There are many open problems concerning the relation between the decidable and the constructive, as well as the relation between the constructive and the transcendent. The theory Σ is intended to be a definitive theory of the region of the constructive so far as mathematics is concerned. It is not clear to the writer whether there is a generally accepted unique characterization of the region of the decidable. So far as the region of the transcendent is concerned, we note merely that it is of course also possible to construct a theory which is related to (say) Zermelo's full set theory in the same manner as the theory Σ is to the system Σ_0. Indeed, for the transcendentists it may even be possible to use as order indices ordinal numbers beyond Cantor's second number class.

The most famous open problem in the field of transcendent set theory is Cantor's continuum problem or the problem whether Cantor's hypothesis is independent of the other axioms of set theory. A related problem is the independence of the axiom of choice. While the independence of the continuum hypothesis from the basic set theory follows from the independence of the axiom of choice, a more interesting question is to prove its independence when the axiom of choice is added to the basic set theory. A less famous but more basic open problem is the consistency of the use of impredicative sets.

One objection to Σ is that it does not contain a maximum order so that, for example, we cannot speak of all sets, or all real numbers at the same time in Σ. This is at least partly a linguistic difficulty and can be avoided to that extent by some linguistic device. Thus, in Σ we can introduce an additional kind of general variable x, y, z, etc. so that we can assert '$(x)F(x)$' when and only when for each α, we can assert '$(x_\alpha)F(x_\alpha)$'; we can assert '$(x)(\exists y)F(x, y)$' when and only when for each α, there is a β; we can assert '$(x_\alpha)(\exists y_\beta) F(x_\alpha, y_\beta)$', etc. This device has also the additional advantage that for many purposes we can make general assertions without making the relevant order indices explicit. This draws the theory closer to the common practice in mathematics.

Since the notion of set determined by the theory Σ is more transparent than the transcendent notion of set, it seems reasonable to expect that the theory Σ may enable us to get better insight into certain mathematical problems which are difficult mainly because they are very abstract and general. For example, we may be in a better position to deal with problems which are concerned with arbitrary sets or arbitrary functions.

Gödel defends transcendent set theory by contending that it can be justified by conceiving sets and concepts as real objects and that it is legitimate so to conceive them. "It seems to me that the assumption of such objects is quite as legitimate as the assumption of physical objects and there is quite as much reason to believe in their existence. They are in the same sense necessary to obtain a satisfactory system of mathematics as physical bodies are necessary for a satisfactory theory of our sense perceptions and in both cases it is impossible to interpret the propositions one wants to assert about these entities as propositions about the 'data,' i.e., in the latter case the actually occurring sense perceptions."[1)]

One possible interpretation of the argument is to say that it amounts to conceding that transcendent set theory and the assumption that sets are real objects are necessary evils which we have to put up with if we want to have a fairly simple theory of mathematics. The theory Σ seems to show that the evil of accepting transcendent set theory is not necessary. In the first place, so far as the data to be accounted for are concerned, neither Gödel nor others consider it necessary to preserve Cantor's higher infinities, but nearly everybody wishes to retain classical analysis. The evil of using impredicative sets is considered necessary because it is thought that classical analysis cannot be developed without these sets. The theory Σ establishes that this is not the case.

As far as simplicity is concerned, there are of course many different senses of the word 'simplicity'. In one important sense, the demonstrable consistency of the theory Σ proves conclusively that it is simpler, at least relative to our present knowledge, than standard systems of transcendent set theory. Usually the ramified theory of types is considered to be hopelessly messy because we have to distinguish at least two hierarchies in it (the orders and the types or levels). It is, however, known that one hierarchy is enough, and the theory Σ actually uses just one hierarchy. Moreover, in formalizing actual proofs we do not have to let even the distinction of orders intrude, as long as we are careful not to use circular arguments in which impredicative definitions cannot be dispensed with. Once we have seen how much can be done in the theory Σ, we can continue to do mathematics as usual with the realization that the arguments used can be formalized in Σ if and when we wish to. Only occasionally we encounter 'strange' modes of reasoning which have to be examined more carefully before we can decide whether they are formalizable in Σ or belong to the domain of transcendent set theory. For example, most people, when confronted with Cantor's indenumerability arguments, presumably have some uneasy feeling and suspect the presence of some hidden fallacy. Undoubtedly ordinary mathematicians would consider such arguments as extraordinarily uncommon.

---

1) Kurt Gödel, Russell's mathematical logic, *The philosophy of Bertrand Russell, The Library of Living Philosophers,* vol. V, 1944, edited by P. A. Schilpp, p. 137.

CHAPTER XXIV

SOME FORMAL DETAILS ON PREDICATIVE SET THEORIES

§ 1. The Underlying Logic

We present in this chapter some formal details, written in 1953, about the theory sketched in the preceding chapter. Most of the material in this chapter can be easily obtained from standard results by Bernays, Lorenzen, Schütte, Fitch. Hence, this chapter is largely expository. Moreover, at the time when the material was written, the writer did not fully appreciate the various difficulties and subtleties about ordinals, and assumed that it would not make much difference no matter what set of ordinals is presupposed provided the set satisfies some vague broad conditions. For the present purpose of a trial development, it seems best to assume that in this chapter members of some known set of unique notations of the Church-Kleene recursive ordinals are taken as order indices.

More recent developments will be discussed in the next chapter. In view of the various new results, it appears very plausible that much better formulations can be obtained than those given in the present chapter. It is, nonetheless, thought that the following details may be of some use as building blocks for more satisfactory comprehensive treatments in the future. For example, the system of hyperarithmetic set theory sketched in the next chapter would appear to be much more elegant. Yet in order to make a detailed study of it, it may turn out that we have to bring out the order indices more explicitly in some manner analogous to the formulation in this chapter.

The primitive symbols with which we build up terms and sentences of the system are the following:

1. Variables—for each constructive ordinal numbers α, x_α, y_α, z_α, u_α, w_α, $\cdots$ are variables of order α;
2. The sentence connectives $\neg$ (not), $\vee$ (or);
3. The abstraction symbol $\hat{}$;
4. The membership relation symbol ϵ;
5. The grouping symbols (,), [,], {, };

6. The existential quantifiers $(\exists x_\alpha)$, $(\exists y_\alpha)$, $(\exists z_\alpha)$, $\cdots$ for all α and all variables of order α.

The notions 'sentence' and 'term' are defined by simultaneous induction in the following manner:

1. Every variable of order α is a term of order α.

2. If b, c are terms of orders β and γ, then $b \in c$ is a sentence of order β or γ according as $\beta \geqslant \gamma$ or $\gamma \geqslant \beta$.

3. If p and q are sentences of orders β and γ, then $\neg p$ is a sentence of order β, and $p \vee q$ is of order β or γ according as $\beta \geqslant \gamma$ or $\gamma \geqslant \beta$.

4. If $F(v_\alpha)$ is a sentence of order β containing an arbitrary free variable v of order α, then $(\exists v_\alpha)F(v_\alpha)$ is a sentence of order β or $\beta+1$ according as $\beta > \gamma$ or $\beta = \gamma$ (where the case $\beta < \gamma$ is not possible).

5. If $F(x_0)$ is of the form

$$\neg\neg(\exists y_0)\neg\neg[\neg(\neg y_0 \in x_0 \vee \neg\neg y_0 \in x_0) \vee \neg(\neg\neg y_0 \in x_0 \vee \neg y_0 \in x_0)]$$

(i.e., $x_0 \neq x_0$ by definitions to be introduced below), then $\hat{x}_0 F(x_0)$ is a term of order 0; if b and c are terms of order 0, then the term of the form

$$\hat{x}_0\{x_0 \in b \vee \neg(\exists y_0)\neg\neg[\neg(\neg y_0 \in x_0 \vee \neg\neg y_0 \in c) \vee \neg(\neg\neg y_0 \in x_0 \vee \neg y_0 \in c)]\}$$

(i.e., $\hat{x}_0(x_0 \in b \vee x_0 = c)$ by definitions to be introduced below) is also a term of order 0. Terms of order 0 will also be referred to as basic terms.

6. If $F(v_\alpha)$ is a sentence of order β and $\hat{v}_\alpha F(v_\alpha)$ is not a basic term, then $\hat{v}_\alpha F(v_\alpha)$ is a term of order β or $\beta+1$ according as $\beta > \alpha$ or $\beta = \alpha$.

Since all terms are set terms or terms denoting sets, we shall also refer to the terms as abstracts. The basic terms define finite sets built up from the empty set.

The system Σ (or rather, the system schema Σ) contains two parts: the underlying logic of inference (quantification theory), and the theory of sets proper. The logic of inference is the standard one but is formalized in a special form in order to facilitate certain metamathematical considerations.

The logic of inference of Σ is based on one axiom schema (*Ax*I) and eight rules of inference (*Ri*1—*Ri*8). The set theory proper in Σ is based on seven axiom schemata (*Ax*II—*Ax*VII). In this section we merely state the axioms and rules of the logic of inference.

*Ax*I. The law of excluded middle. For every sentence p of Σ, $\neg p \vee p$.

We use the formula $p \rightarrow q$ to indicate that if p is a theorem then q is also; similarly, $p, q \rightarrow r$ indicates that if p, q are theorems then r is also.

*Ri*1. $p \vee [q \vee (r \vee s)] \rightarrow p \vee [r \vee (q \vee s)]$.

*Ri*2. $p \vee (q \vee r) \rightarrow p \vee (r \vee q)$.

*Ri*3. $p \vee p \rightarrow p$.

*Ri*4. $q \rightarrow p \vee q$.

*Ri*5. $\neg p \vee q \rightarrow \neg (p \vee p) \vee q$.

*Ri*6. $p \vee q, \neg q \vee r \rightarrow p \vee r$.

*Ri*7. If b is a term of order α, $q \vee F(b) \rightarrow q \vee (\exists v_\alpha) F(v_\alpha)$.

*Ri*8. If v_α does not occur in q, $\neg F(v_\alpha) \vee q \rightarrow \neg (\exists v_\alpha) F(v_\alpha) \vee q$.

We can show that the system determined by *Ax*I and *Ri*1—*Ri*8 is equivalent to the following system known to be complete.

1.1. $\neg (p \vee p) \vee p$.

1.2. $\neg q \vee (p \vee q)$.

1.3. $\neg (p \vee q) \vee (q \vee p)$.

1.4. $\neg (\neg q \vee r) \vee [\neg (p \vee q) \vee (p \vee r)]$.

1.5. $p, \neg p \vee q \rightarrow q$.

1.6. If b is a term of order α, $\neg F(b) \vee (\exists v_\alpha) F(v_\alpha)$.

1.7. If v_α does not occur in q, $\neg F(v_\alpha) \vee q \rightarrow \neg (\exists v_\alpha) F(v_\alpha) \vee q$.

Since it is easy to verify that all theorems provable by *Ax*I and *Ri*1—*Ri*8 are valid and, therefore, provable in the complete system determined by 1.1—1.7, it is only necessary to prove that conversely 1.1—1.7 are derivable from *Ax*I and *Ri*1—*Ri*8. Those who do not doubt that this can be proved should skip the rest of this section.

It happens that 1.7 is identical with *Ri*8. We proceed to derive 1.1—1.6, using auxiliary rules whenever necessary.

1.5. $p, \neg p \vee q \rightarrow q$.

Proof. By *Ri*4, $p \rightarrow q \vee p$. Hence, $p, \neg p \vee q \rightarrow q \vee p$, $\neg p \vee q$. Therefore, by *Ri*6, $p, \neg p \vee q \rightarrow q \vee q$. By *Ri*3, $p, \neg p \vee q \rightarrow q$.

1.8. $p \vee q \rightarrow q \vee p$.

Proof. By *Ri*4, $p \vee q \rightarrow (q \vee p) \vee (p \vee q)$. Therefore, by *Ri*2, $p \vee q \rightarrow (q \vee p) \vee (q \vee p)$. Hence, by *Ri*3, $p \vee q \rightarrow q \vee p$.

1.1. $\neg(p \vee p) \vee p$.

Proof. By *Ax*I, $\neg p \vee p$. Hence, by *Ri*5, $\neg(p \vee p) \vee p$.

1.9. $p \vee (q \vee r) \rightarrow q \vee (p \vee r)$.

Proof. By *Ri*4, $p \vee (q \vee r) \rightarrow \neg(\neg p \vee p) \vee [p \vee (q \vee r)]$.
By *Ri*1, $p \vee (q \vee r) \rightarrow \neg(\neg p \vee p) \vee [q \vee (p \vee r)]$.
By 1.5 and *Ax*I, $p \vee (q \vee r) \rightarrow q \vee (p \vee r)$.

1.2. $\neg q \vee (p \vee q)$.

Proof. By *Ax*I and *Ri*4, $p \vee (\neg q \vee q)$.
By 1.9, $\neg q \vee (p \vee q)$.

1.3. $\neg(p \vee q) \vee (q \vee p)$.

Proof. By *Ax*I and *Ri*2.

1.6. $\neg F(b) \vee (\exists v_a)F(v_a)$.

Proof. By *Ax*I and *Ri*7.

1.10. $p \vee (q \vee r) \rightarrow (p \vee q) \vee r$.

Proof. By *Ri*2, $p \vee (q \vee r) \rightarrow p \vee (r \vee q)$.
By 1.9, $\rightarrow r \vee (p \vee q)$.
By 1.8, $\rightarrow (p \vee q) \vee r$.

1.11. $p \vee [(q \vee r) \vee s] \rightarrow p \vee [q \vee (r \vee s)]$.

Proof. By *Ri*2, $p \vee [(q \vee r) \vee s] \rightarrow p \vee [s \vee (q \vee r)]$.
By *Ri*1, $\rightarrow p \vee [q \vee (s \vee r)]$.
By 1.10, $\rightarrow (p \vee q) \vee (s \vee r)$.
By *Ri*2, $\rightarrow (p \vee q) \vee (r \vee s)$.
By 1.8, $\rightarrow (r \vee s) \vee (p \vee q)$.
By 1.9, $\rightarrow p \vee [(r \vee s) \vee q]$.
By *Ri*2, $\rightarrow p \vee [q \vee (r \vee s)]$.

1.4. $\neg(\neg q \vee r) \vee [\neg(p \vee q) \vee (p \vee r)]$.

Proof. By *Ax*I, $\neg(\neg q \vee r) \vee (\neg q \vee r)$.
By 1.9, $\neg q \vee [\neg(\neg q \vee r) \vee r]$. (1)
By *Ax*I, $\neg(p \vee q) \vee (p \vee q)$.
By 1.10, $[\neg(p \vee q) \vee p] \vee q$. (2)
By (2), (1), *Ri*6, $[\neg(p \vee q) \vee p] \vee [\neg(\neg q \vee r) \vee r]$.
By 1.9, $\neg(\neg q \vee r) \vee \{[\neg(p \vee q) \vee p] \vee r\}$.
By 1.11, $\neg(\neg q \vee r) \vee [\neg(p \vee q) \vee (p \vee r)]$.

This completes the derivation of 1.1—1.7 from *Ax*I and *Ri*1—*Ri*8.

To summarize. The rules of inference are eight in number of which *Ri*1—*Ri*6 are concerned with the standard properties of the truth functions so that by combining *Ax*I with *Ri*1—*Ri*6, all truth-functional tautologies can be obtained as theorems of the system. *R*7 and *R*8 are concerned with the properties of the quantifiers. By combining *Ax*I with *Ri*1—*Ri*8, we can get all theorems of a many-sorted predicate calculus.

§ 2. The Axioms of the Theory Σ

We can now describe and discuss the axioms of the system Σ.

The symbol v_α is used to stand for an arbitrary variable of order α, and b_α, c_β are to stand for arbitrary terms of orders α and β.

The following customary definitions are assumed:

*D*2.1. '$=_D$' means 'stands for'.

*D*2.2. $p \supset q =_D \neg p \vee q$.

*D*2.3. $p \,\&\, q =_D \neg(p \supset \neg q)$.

*D*2.4. $p \equiv q =_D [(p \supset q) \& (q \supset p)]$.

*D*2.5. $(v_\alpha) =_D \neg(\exists v_\alpha)\neg$.

*D*2.6. If α is of the nonsuccessor kind and $\alpha \geqslant \beta$, then:

$$b_\alpha = c_\beta =_D (v_\alpha)(v_\alpha \in b_\alpha \equiv v_\alpha \in c_\beta).$$

$$c_\beta = b_\alpha =_D \quad b_\alpha = c_\beta.$$

*D*2.7. If β is of the successor kind and $\beta > \alpha$ or $\beta = \alpha$, then:

$$b_\alpha = c_\beta =_D (v_{\beta-1})(v_{\beta-1} \in b_\alpha \equiv v_{\beta-1} \in c_\beta).$$

$$c_\beta = b_\alpha =_D \quad b_\alpha = c_\beta.$$

The theorems of the system are those sentences of the system which are either axioms or derivable from other theorems by the rules of inference *Ri*1—*Ri*8 which all are concerned with the standard properties of the notions $\neg$, $\vee$, $(\exists)$.

The axioms of the system are of seven kinds.

*Ax*I. The law of excluded middle: for every sentence p of the system, $\neg p \vee p$.

*Ax*II. The axioms for identity: for every γ, $\gamma \geqslant \alpha$, $\gamma \geqslant \beta$, $[x_\alpha = y_\beta \,\&\, x_\alpha \in z_\gamma] \supset y_\beta \in z_\gamma$.

*Ax*III. The axioms of infinite summation: for every limit number α, if $\beta < \alpha$, then $(x_\beta)(\exists y_\alpha)(y_\alpha = x_\beta)$.

*Ax*IV. The axioms of abstraction:

$$y_\beta \in \hat{x}_\beta F(x_\beta) \equiv F(y_\beta).$$

*Ax*V. The axioms of pair sets: for every limit number α,

$$(\exists z_\alpha)[z_\alpha = \hat{u}_\alpha(u_\alpha = x_\alpha \vee u_\alpha = y_\alpha)].$$

*Ax*VI. The axioms of foundation:

$$(\exists x_\alpha) x_\alpha \in z_\alpha \supset (\exists y_\alpha)\{y_\alpha \in z_\alpha \,\&\, (x_\alpha) \neg [x_\alpha \in y_\alpha \,\&\, x_\alpha \in z_\alpha]\}$$

*Ax*VII. The axioms of bounded order: If $\alpha > \beta$ and $x_\alpha \epsilon y_{\beta+1}$, then $(\exists z_\beta)(z_\beta = x_\alpha)$; if $\alpha > \beta$, $x_\alpha \epsilon y_\beta$, and β is of the nonsuccessor kind, then

$$(\exists z_\beta)(z_\beta = x_\alpha).$$

*Ax*VIII. The axioms of limitation: we shall derive the theory of nonnegative integers and prove that for every α, it is possible to enumerate all sets of order α required to exist by the system (before adding *Ax*VIII); the axioms of limitation which state that these enumerated sets are all the sets of the system can then be expressed.

From the rules *Ri*7 and *Ri*8, we can infer the following consequences in the system:

*T*2.1. If b_α is a term and v_α a variable of order α,

$$F(b_\alpha) \supset (\exists v_\alpha) F(v_\alpha), \text{ and } (v_\alpha) F(v_\alpha) \supset F(b_\alpha).$$

*T*2.2. If $F(v_\alpha) \supset q$ is a theorem and v_α does not occur in q, then $(\exists v_\alpha) F(v_\alpha) \supset q$ is also a theorem.

By combining *Ax*II, *Ax*IV, *D*2.6, and *D*2.7, we can obtain the ordinary principle of extensionality and the ordinary theory of identity. In particular, it follows directly from *D*2.6 and *D*2.7.

*T*2.3. $(x_\alpha) x_\alpha = x_\alpha$.

By *Ax*IV, *Ax*II, *T*2.1, we have immediately:

*T*2.4. $[x_\alpha = y_\beta \,\&\, F(x_\alpha)] \supset F(y_\beta)$.

*Ax*IV embodies the fundamental principle of set theory. It says roughly that every property expressible in the system defines a set of the system. It follows from *Ax*IV and *T*2.1:

*T*2.5. If $\hat{x}_\beta F(x_\beta)$ is a term of order α, then $(\exists z_\alpha)(y_\beta)[y_\beta \in z_\alpha \equiv F(x_\beta)]$.

Moreover, by *T*2.1, *D*2.6 and *D*2.7:

*T*2.6. If $\hat{x}_\beta F(x_\beta)$ is a term of order α, $(\exists z_\alpha)[z_\alpha = \hat{x}_\beta F(x_\beta)]$.

It may be noted that in *T*2.5 and *T*2.6, $\alpha > \beta$. The important point is that $\alpha = \beta + 1$ only in those cases where $F(x_\beta)$ happens to be a sentence of order $\leqslant \beta$. This is different from an impredicative theory or a theory with the axiom of reducibility in which *T*2.5 and *T*2.6 are strengthened by taking α always as $\beta + 1$, no matter what order $F(x_\beta)$ may have.

*Ax*V is important for the definition of ordered pairs and therewith the reduction of relations and functions to sets.

By excluding queer sets, *Ax*VI assures us the principle of mathematical induction and that of transfinite induction.

*Ax*VIII enables us to reduce considerations about all sets to those about all (of their corresponding) nonnegative integers. As a result, many general theorems on sets (e.g., the axioms of choice, the least upper bound theorems) can be proved by mathematical induction. Indeed, if mathematical induction were available without *Ax*VI, we could also derive *Ax*VI from *Ax*VIII by induction. Roughly, in order that *Ax*VIII can get the required meaning, we have to presuppose a normal interpretation of nonnegative integers, which in turn seems to call for the axioms *Ax*VI of foundation. Hence, it does not appear possible to derive *Ax*VI formally from the actual formulation of *Ax*VIII, although strong intuitive axioms of limitation should perhaps include *Ax*VI as special cases.

*Ax*VII formulates the principle that if α is the limit of the ordinals $\beta_1, \beta_2, \cdots$, then the sets of any order β_i are among the sets of order α. For example, all sets of finite orders are also sets of the order ω. This can easily be extended to the general case where α is any ordinal number.

*T*2.7. For any α and β, if $\alpha > \beta$, then $(x_\beta)(\exists y_\alpha)(y_\alpha = x_\beta)$.

Proof. If α is 0, this is trivial since $0 > \beta$ is always false. If α is a limit number, this follows from *Ax*III. Assume, therefore, α is of the successor kind, and $\alpha = \gamma + 1$. If β is also of the successor kind, then take

$$y_\alpha = \hat{z}_\gamma[z_\gamma \in x_\beta \,\&\, (\exists u_{\beta-1})(u_{\beta-1} = z_\gamma)].$$

By *D*2.7, $x_\beta = y_\alpha$. If β is of the nonsuccessor kind, then take

$$y_\alpha = \hat{z}_\gamma[z_\gamma \in x_\beta \,\&\, (\exists u_\beta)(u_\beta = z_\gamma)].$$

Again, by *D*2.7, $x_\beta = y_\alpha$.

Combining *T*2.6 and *T*2.9, we have:

*T*2.8. If $\hat{x}_\gamma F(x_\gamma)$ is of order β and $\alpha > \beta$ or $\alpha = \beta$, then $(\exists z_\alpha)[z_\alpha = \hat{x}_\gamma F(x_\gamma)]$.

In short, the sets of the system are cumulative: all sets of any lower order are also sets of any higher order.

One consequence of *Ax*VI is:

*T*2.9. $(y_\alpha) \neg y_\alpha \in y_\alpha$.

Proof. If $y_\alpha \in y_\alpha$, then $\hat{x}_\alpha(x_\alpha = y_\alpha)$ would be a set which contradicts *Ax*VI.

Similarly:

*T*2.10. $(x_\alpha)(y_\alpha) \neg (x_\alpha \in y_\alpha \ \& \ y_\alpha \in x_\alpha)$.

Proof. Otherwise the set $\hat{z}_\alpha(z_\alpha = x_\alpha \vee z_\alpha = y_\alpha)$ would violate *Ax*VI.

*Ax*III is necessary because, according to the way terms (or more specifically, set terms) are introduced in the system, no terms which do not contain free variables are of order α if α is a limit number. *Ax*III assures that if α is a limit number, each set determined by a term of order lower than α is also a set of order α, or, in other words, each term of order lower than α is also a term of order α.

*Ax*VII is apparently independent of the other axioms. It serves to restrict somewhat the effect of admitting as meaningful assertions which state that a set of a higher order belongs to one of a lower order. *Ax*VII says in effect that if a set b belongs to a set c of order $\alpha(\alpha > 0)$, then b must be identical (i.e. coextensional) with a set of order lower than α.

The following remarks on finite sets are in order. By *T*2.5 and the definition that $\hat{x}_0(x_0 \neq x_0)$ is of order 0, we have:

*T*2.11. $(\exists z_0)[z_0 = \hat{x}_0(x_0 \neq x_0)]$.

Similarly, by *T*2.6 and the definition of terms of order 0, we have:

*T*2.12. If b and c are terms of order 0, then $(\exists z_0)[z_0 = \hat{x}_0(x_0 \in b \vee x_0 = c)]$.

Since variables are terms, we have:

*T*2.13. $(\exists z_0)[z_0 = \hat{x}_0(x_0 \in u_0 \vee x_0 = y_0)]$.

By combining *T*2.11, *T*2.13 and *Ax*III, we can derive a theory of the finite sets built up from the empty set.

This depends on the special clause on terms of order 0. If we do not assume such a clause, then we have the following situation. $\hat{x}_0(x_0 \neq x_0)$ is of order 1, $\hat{x}_1[x_1 \in \hat{x}_0(x_0 \neq x_0) \vee x_1 = \hat{x}_0(x_0 \neq x_0)]$ is of order 2, and so on. Then we would, by assuming no existence on the lowest order, get an infinite number of finite sets at order ω. Indeed, it would then follow intuitively from *Ax*VIII:

$$(\exists z_\omega)[z_\omega = \hat{x}_0(x_0 \neq x_0)]; \; (\exists z_\omega)[z_\omega = \hat{u}_\omega(u_\omega \in x \vee u_\omega = y_\omega)].$$

Nonetheless, the formal development would presumably be more complex than the present approach.

We note that *Ax*V is intuitively a consequence of *Ax*VIII. Thus, by *Ax*VIII, every set of order α (α a limit number) is of some order β, $\beta < \alpha$. Therefore, the couple consisting of two sets of order α is again one of order α. Since, however, in order to express *Ax*VIII, we already need some theory developed with the help of *Ax*V, it is not clear that we can formalize a derivation of *Ax*V from *Ax*VIII.

For each α, Σ_α is the part of the above symbolism that contains only variables and sets of order $\leqslant \alpha$. When α is a limit number, $\Sigma_{\alpha}-$ is the part of the above symbolism that contains only variables and sets of order $< \alpha$. If α is not a limit number, system $\Sigma_{\alpha}-$ would of course be just $\Sigma_{\alpha-1}$. We denote by Σ the whole formalism, i.e., the sum or union of all the systems Σ_α.

Strictly speaking the system Σ is not a formal or logistic system in the ordinary sense since there is no effective way of giving all the primitive symbols from the beginning. For each α, Σ_α is a formal system. Although given each α, a system Σ_α can be constructed effectively, there is no effective way of determining all these ordinals α. It is perhaps more correct to view Σ as a schema of formal systems or a recipe for making formal systems whenever an ordinal α is given. Nonetheless, for our purpose, it is more convenient to continue calling Σ a system.

§ 3. Preliminary Considerations

Relations can be identified with ordered pairs, ordered triples, and so on. The notations for ordered and nonordered pair, ordered triple, etc., can be introduced in such a way that the pair or triple or n-tuple of sets of the same or different orders is of the same order as the set of the highest order.

The non-ordered pair of x_α and y_β:

*D*3.1. $\{x_\alpha, y_\beta\} =_D \{y_\beta, x_\alpha\} =_D \hat{z}_\alpha(z_\alpha = x_\alpha \vee z_\alpha = y_\beta) \, (\alpha \geqslant \beta)$.

The set whose sole member is x_α:

*D*3.2. $\{x_\alpha\} =_D \{x_\alpha, x_\alpha\}$.

If $\alpha \geqslant \beta$ and α is an ordinal of the nonsuccessor kind, then:

*D*3.3. $\langle x_\alpha, y_\beta \rangle =_D \{\{x_\alpha\}, \{x_\alpha, y_\beta\}\}$.
$\langle x_\beta, y_\alpha \rangle =_D \{\{x_\beta\}, \{x_\beta, y_\alpha\}\}$.

On account of *Ax*V, $\langle x_\alpha, y_\beta \rangle$ or $\langle x_\beta, y_\alpha \rangle$ is a set of order α.

If $\alpha \geqslant \beta$ and α is an ordinal of the successor kind, then the situation becomes more complex. As an approximation, we can define first the pair set of x_α and y_β:

*D*3.4. $x_\alpha \times y_\beta =_D \hat{z}_{\alpha-1}(\exists x_{\alpha-1})\ (\exists y_{\beta-1})\ (z_{\alpha-1} = \langle x_{\alpha-1}, y_{\beta-1}\rangle \ \&\ x_{\alpha-1} \epsilon x_\alpha \ \&\ y_{\beta-1} \epsilon y_\beta)$, when β is a successor and assuming $\langle x_{\alpha-1}, y_{\beta-1}\rangle$ already defined.

$$x_\alpha \times y_\beta =_D \hat{z}_{\alpha-1}(\exists x_{\alpha-1})\ (\exists w_\beta)(z_{\alpha-1} = \langle x_{\alpha-1}, w_\beta\rangle \ \&\ x_{\alpha-1} \epsilon x_\alpha \ \&\ w_\beta \epsilon y_\beta),$$

when β is of the nonsuccessor kind and assuming that $\langle x_{\alpha-1}, w_\beta\rangle$ already defined. Similarly for $y_\beta \times x_\alpha$.

The reason why we cannot identify the pair set of x_α and y_β with the ordered pair of x_α and y_β is because several couples of sets may have the same pair set; e.g., if y_β is empty, then $x_\alpha \times y_\beta$ is the empty set no matter what set x_α is. There are many possible artificial devices to get around this difficulty. The method used below is quite complex. Maybe there are simpler methods.

For any $x_\alpha, y_\beta, \cdots, z_\gamma$ (altogether three or more sets), the n-tuple of them is got by taking repeatedly the ordered pair of two sets:

*D*3.5. $\langle x_\alpha, y_\beta, \cdots, z_\gamma\rangle =_D \langle x_\alpha, \langle y_\beta, \cdots, z_\gamma\rangle\rangle$.

As the empty set will be identified with the number zero, we use the following abbreviation:

*D*3.6. $0 =_D \hat{x}_0(x_0 \neq x_0)$.

If $\alpha \geqslant \beta$ and α is of the successor kind, then:

*D*3.7. $\langle x_\alpha, y_\beta\rangle =_D \hat{z}_{\alpha-1}(\exists x_{\alpha-1})(\exists y_{\beta-1})[(x_{\alpha-1} \epsilon x \ \&\ z_{\alpha-1} = \langle \{0\}, x_{\alpha-1}, 0\rangle) \vee (y_{\beta-1} \epsilon y_\beta \ \&\ z_{\alpha-1} = \langle 0, 0, y_{\beta-1}\rangle)]$, when β is a successor.

When β is of the nonsuccessor kind, replace $y_{\beta-1}$ by w_β in the above definition. Similarly for $\langle y_\beta, x_\alpha\rangle$.

To extend the notion of ordered n-tuples to the trivial case of n being 1:

*D*3.8. $\langle x_\alpha\rangle =_D x_\alpha$.

It may be noted that the definitions *D*3.3, *D*3.5, *D*3.7 involve an inductive moment so that in general they are to be applied successively. When they are taken together, ordered pairs and ordered n-tuples are defined for sets of all orders.

We are now in a position to discuss informally the enumeration of all sets of each given order.

For each ordinal α, there is the universal set V_α containing all sets of order α as members:

*D*3.9. $V_a =_D \hat{x}_a(x_a = x_a)$.

By *Ax*IV and *T*2.3, we have:

*T*3.1. $(x_a)x_a \in V_a$.

The sets of order 0 are determined by the definition of terms and include all and only the sets satisfying the following conditions:

(i) $0 \in v_0$, (ii) if $x_0 \in v_0$ and $y_0 \in v_0$, then $\hat{z}_0(z_0 \in x_0 \vee z_0 = y_0) \in v_0$.

It is quite easy to enumerate these sets. A formalization of the enumeration will be discussed later on.

The sets of order 1 are determined by *Ax*IV so that for every sentence $F(y_0)$ of order 1, there is a corresponding set $\hat{y}_0F(y_0)$. To enumerate the sets, it is sufficient to enumerate all these sentences. We need not, however, distinguish equivalent sentences such as alphabetic variants of each other (e.g., $x_0 = x_0$ and $y_0 = y_0$, or $(x_0)\neg y_0 \in x_0$ and $(z_0)\neg y_0 \in z_0$) since they define the same set.

It will be proved that all sets of order 1 gets enumerated by a set in Σ_2. This possibility depends on the fact that there are only finitely many kinds of atomic sentences (i.e., sentences which do not contain other sentences as parts), and that there are only finitely many ways of getting more complex sentences from less complex ones.

More exactly this depends on the following known result (Compare Bernays 1937 or Gödel 1940, p. 8).

*T*3.2. If p is a sentence of order 1 not containing y_1, no variable of order 1 occurs in p immediately before $\in$, and $x_0, \cdots, z_0$ are k variables ($k \geqslant 1$) of order 0, then the principles of the form

$$(\exists y_1)(x_0)\cdots(z_0)(\langle x_0, \cdots, z_0\rangle \in y_1 \equiv p) \tag{1}$$

are derivable from the following special cases:

(i) $(\exists y_1)(x_0)(\langle x_0, y_0\rangle \in y_1 \equiv x_0 \in y_0)$.

(ii) $(\exists y_1)(x_0)[x_0 \in y_1 \equiv (x_0 \in x_1 \,\&\, x_0 \in z_1)]$.

$(\exists y_1)(x_0)(x_0 \in y_1 \equiv \neg x_0 \in x_1)$.

(iii) $(\exists y_1)(x_0)[x_0 \in y_1 \equiv (\exists y_0)(\langle y_0, x_0\rangle \in x_1)]$.

$(\exists y_1)(x_0)(y_0)(x_0 \in y_1 \equiv \langle y_0, x_0\rangle \in x_1)$.

(iv) $(\exists y_1)(x_0)(y_0)(z_0)(\langle x_0, y_0, z_0\rangle \in y_1 \equiv \langle y_0, z_0, x_0\rangle \in x_1)$.

$(\exists y_1)(x_0)(y_0)(z_0)(\langle x_0, y_0, z_0\rangle \in y_1 \equiv \langle x_0, z_0, y_0\rangle \in x_1)$.

The proof of *T*3.2 is almost exactly the same as that of Bernays 1937 and Gödel 1940. There is no need to repeat the proof.

It is easily seen that (1) is equivalent to the principle:

(2) $(\exists y_1)(w_0)(w_0 \in y_1 \equiv q)$, which covers those cases of *T*3.2 (or *Ax*IV) where q is a sentence of order 1. Thus, by *Ax*VII we can disregard cases where variables of order 1 appear before $\in$; e.g., $x_1 \in y_0$ and $x_1 \in y_1$ can be replaced respectively by $(\exists x_0)(x_0 = x_1 \,\&\, x_0 \in y_0)$ and $(\exists x_0)(x_0 = x_1 \,\&\, x_0 \in y_1)$. Once we disregard these cases, (2) is seen to be literally contained in (1). On the other hand, given (2), we can get (1) by substituting $(\exists x_0)\cdots(\exists z_0)(w_0 = \langle x_0, \cdots, z_0\rangle \,\&\, p)$ for q.

Since (2) or its corresponding part in *Ax*IV seems to be the only principle for generating sets of order 1 (in other words, members of V_1), the considerations also render highly plausible that V_1 contains all and only the sets generated by (i)—(iv) of *T*3.2. This will be formulated as an axiom of limitation and proved to be consistent later on.

The next problem is to enumerate all sets of order n, for an arbitrary positive integer n. This can be got by a straightforward extension of the case for sets of order 1. It will be proved that all sets of order n get enumerated by a set in Σ_{n+2}. This depends on a generalization of *T*3.2:

*T*3.3. If p is a sentence of order $n+1$ (a positive integer) not containing y_{n+1}, no variable of order $n+1$ occurs in p immediately preceding $\in$, and $x_i, \cdots, z_j$ are k variables ($k \geqslant 1$) of orders $\leqslant n$, then the principles of the following form

$$(\exists y_{n+1})(x_i)\cdots(z_j)(\langle x_i, \cdots, z_j\rangle \in y_{n+1} \equiv p)$$

are derivable from the following special cases:

(A) $(\exists y_{n+1})(x_n)(z_n)(\langle x_n, z_n\rangle \in y_{n+1} \equiv x_n \in z_n)$;

(B) For each $y_i (i = 0, 1, \cdots, n)$, $(\exists y_{n+1})(x_n)(x_n \in y_{n+1} \equiv x_n \in y_i)$;

(C) Given two sets x_{n+1} and z_{n+1}:

$$(\exists y_{n+1})(x_n)[x_n \in y_{n+1} \equiv (x_n \in x_{n+1} \,\&\, x_n \in z_{n+1})],$$

$$(\exists y_{n+1})(x_n)(x_n \in y_{n+1} \equiv \neg x_n \in z_{n+1}),$$

$$(\exists y_{n+1})(x_n)(y_n)(\langle x_n, y_n\rangle \in y_{n+1} \equiv y_n \in z_{n+1}),$$

$$(\exists y_{n+1})(x_n)(y_n)(w_n)(\langle x_n, y_n, w_n\rangle \in y_{n+1} \equiv \langle y_n, w_n, x_n\rangle \in z_{n+1}),$$

$$(\exists y_{n+1})(x_n)(y_n)(w_n)(\langle x_n, y_n, w_n\rangle \in y_{n+1} \equiv \langle y_n, x_n, w_n\rangle \in z_{n+1}),$$

$$(\exists y_{n+1})(y_n)[y_n \in y_{n+1} \equiv (\exists x_i)(\langle x_i, y_n\rangle \in x_{n+1})] \quad (i=0, 1, \cdots, n).$$

The proof of *T*3.3 is similar to that of *T*3.2. Sentences of the form $x_i \in z_j (i < n)$ can be replaced by $(\exists x_n)(x_n = x_i \,\&\, x_n \in z_j)$, sentences of the form $x_n \in z_j (j < n+1)$ can be replaced by $x_n \in y_{n+1}$ for a suitable y_{n+1} (on account of (B)). Therefore, the above $(2n+8)$ special cases are adequate.

Here again, it seems plausible that V_{n+1} contains (all and) only the sets generated by the $(2n+8)$ axioms in $T3.3$. This will be formulated as an axiom of limitation and proved consistent.

For later use, we insert a few customary definitions:

*D*3.10. $x_\alpha \subseteq y_\beta =_D (z_\alpha)(z_\alpha \in x_\alpha \supset z_\alpha \in y_\alpha)$.

*D*3.11. $x_\alpha \subset y_\beta =_D (x_\alpha \subseteq y_\beta \ \&\ x_\alpha \neq y_\beta)$.

*D*3.12. $D(x_\alpha) =_D \hat{y}_\alpha (\exists z_\alpha)(\langle z_\alpha, y_\alpha\rangle \in x_\alpha)$ (α of the nonsuccessor kind).
$D(x_{\beta+1}) =_D \hat{y}_\beta (\exists z_\beta)(\langle z_\beta, y_\beta\rangle \in x_{\beta+1})$.

*D*3.13. $W(x_\alpha) =_D \hat{y}_\alpha (\exists z_\alpha)(\langle y_\alpha, z_\alpha\rangle \in x_\alpha)$ (α of the nonsuccessor kind).
$W(x_{\beta+1}) =_D \hat{y}_\beta (\exists z_\beta)(\langle y_\beta, z_\beta\rangle \in x_{\beta+1})$.

*D*3.14. $x_\alpha \in \hat{y}_\beta(z_\gamma) =_D (\exists w_\beta)[x_\alpha \in w_\beta \ \&\ (u_\beta)(\langle u_\beta, z_\gamma\rangle \in y_\beta \equiv u_\beta = w_\beta)]$.

If y_β is a function, then $y_\beta(z_\gamma)$ is the value of the function when the argument takes the value z_γ.

*D*3.15. $\hat{x}_\alpha \hat{y}_\alpha F(x_\alpha, y_\alpha) =_D \hat{z}_\alpha (\exists x_\alpha)(\exists y_\alpha)[z_\alpha = \langle x_\alpha, y_\alpha\rangle \ \&\ F(x_\alpha, y_\alpha)]$.

*D*3.16. $\hat{x}_\alpha \hat{y}_\alpha \hat{z}_\alpha F(x_\alpha, y_\alpha, z_\alpha) =_D \hat{w}_\alpha (\exists x_\alpha)(\exists y_\alpha)(\exists z_\alpha)[w_\alpha = \langle x_\alpha, y_\alpha, z_\alpha\rangle \ \&\ F(x_\alpha, y_\alpha, z_\alpha)]$.

§ 4. The Theory of Non-negative Integers

It is convenient to adapt to the system Σ the theory of transfinite ordinals and that of nonnegative integers developed by von Neumann and Bernays in a different framework (see especially Bernays 1941, *J. Symbolic Logic*, vol. **6**). The modifications needed are few. A few details are included to ensure completeness of presentation. The longer proofs are omitted on the ground that similar proofs are available in the literature.

The definitions of ordinals and cardinals used below are not the only possible ones in the system. We could as well have adopted the more traditional definitions given by Cantor and his successors (including Whitehead and Russell). Since the different approaches yield substantially the same amount of theory in the present system, there is no need to compare them here.

*D*4.1. A set x_α is said to be transitive if and only if $(y_\alpha)(z_\alpha)[(y_\alpha \in z_\alpha \ \&\ z_\alpha \in x_\alpha) \supset y_\alpha \in x_\alpha]$.

*D*4.2. A set x_α is said to be an ordinal number (in short, ord (x_α)) if it satisfies the following two conditions: (1) x_α is transitive; (2) the relation $\in$ is connex in x_α, i.e., $(y_\alpha)(z_\alpha)[(y_\alpha \in x_\alpha \& z_\alpha \in x_\alpha) \supset (y_\alpha \in z \vee y_\alpha = z_\alpha \vee z_\alpha \in y_\alpha)]$.

*D*4.3. The letters $\alpha, \beta, \gamma, \delta$ will be used as variables ranging over sets which are ordinal numbers in the system. For example α_a or β_a

is a variable ranging over all sets of order α which are ordinals.

The following theorems can be proved in the system Σ.

*T*4.1. If y_β is a nonempty set of ordinals and $u_{\beta+1}=\hat{x}_\beta(z_\beta)(z_\beta \in y_\beta \supset x_\beta \in z_\beta)$ (i.e., $u_{\beta+1}$ is the intersection of all elements of y_β), then $u_{\beta+1} \in y_\beta$.

The proof for this theorem is completely analogous to that for Theorem 2 on p. 7 of Bernays 1941.

*D*4.4. If γ_α and δ_β are two ordinals of orders α and β, then $\gamma_\alpha < \delta_\beta$ if and only if $\gamma_\alpha \subset \delta_\beta$; $\gamma_\alpha \leqslant \delta_\beta$ if and only if $\gamma_\alpha < \delta_\beta$ or $\gamma_\alpha = \delta_\beta$.

*T*4.2. $(\gamma_\alpha)(\delta_\beta)(\gamma_\alpha < \delta_\beta \vee \gamma_\alpha = \delta_\beta \vee \delta_\beta < \gamma_\alpha)$.

Proof. Consider the set $\{\gamma_\alpha, \delta_\beta\}$. By *T*4.1, the intersection of γ_α and δ_β belongs to the set and is therefore either γ_α or δ_β. If the intersection is γ_α, then $\gamma_\alpha \leqslant \delta_\beta$, if the intersection is δ_β, then $\delta_\beta \subseteq \gamma_\alpha$. Hence, by *D*4.4, the theorem is proved.

*T*4.3. Every set of ordinal numbers has a lowest member; in other words,

$$(x_\alpha)\{(y_\alpha)[y_\alpha \in x_\alpha \supset \text{Ord}(y_\alpha)] \supset (\exists z_\alpha)$$
$$[z_\alpha \in x_\alpha \,\&\, (y_\alpha)(y_\alpha \in x_\alpha \supset z_\alpha \leqslant y_\alpha)]\}.$$

Proof. By *T*4.1, the intersection of all members of x_α again belongs to x_α. It is, by *D*4.4, the lowest member of x_α.

The theory of nonnegative integers can now be developed.

*D*4.5. The successor x'_α of a set x_α is the set $\hat{y}_\alpha(y_\alpha \in x_\alpha \vee y_\alpha = x_\alpha)$.

*D*4.6. The set x is a finite ordinal or a nonnegative integer (in short, $Nn(x_\alpha)$) if and only if $Ord(x_\alpha)$ and

$$(\beta_\alpha)[\beta_\alpha \leqslant x_\alpha \supset \{\beta_\alpha = 0 \vee (\exists y_\alpha)(\beta_\alpha = y'_\alpha)\}].$$

The Dedekind-Peano axioms are immediate consequences:

*T*4.4. $Nn(0)$.

Proof. It is easily verified that the empty set 0 satisfies all the conditions of *D*4.2 and *D*4.6.

*T*4.5. $Nn(x_\alpha) \supset Nn(x'_\alpha)$.

*T*4.6. $(x_\alpha)[Nn(x_\alpha) \supset x'_\alpha \neq 0]$.

*T*4.7. $(x_\alpha)(y_\beta)\{[Nn(x_\alpha) \,\&\, Nn(y_\beta) \,\&\, x'_\alpha = y'_\beta] \supset x_\alpha = y_\beta\}$.

*T*4.8. Principle of mathematical induction.

$$(x_\alpha)\{[0 \in x_\alpha \,\&\, (y_\alpha)([Nn(y_\alpha) \,\&\, y_\alpha \in x_\alpha] \supset y'_\alpha \in x_\alpha)] \supset [(y_\alpha)(Nn(y_\alpha) \supset y_\alpha \in x_\alpha)]\}.$$

Proof. If there is a z_α, $Nn(z_\alpha)$ but $\neg z_\alpha \in x_\alpha$. Consider the set $w_{\alpha+1}$ of all such z_α. By *T*4.3, $w_{\alpha+1}$ has a lowest member w_α. By *D*4.6, either $w_\alpha=0$ or $(\exists y_\alpha)(w_\alpha=y'_\alpha)$. If $w_\alpha=0$, then $w_\alpha \in x_\alpha$ by hypothesis, a contradiction. If $w_\alpha=y'_\alpha$, then, by *D*4.6, $Nn(y_\alpha)$. Either $y_\alpha \in x_\alpha$, then, by hypothesis y'_α or $w_\alpha \in x_\alpha$, a contradiction. If $\neg y_\alpha \in x_\alpha$, then $y_\alpha \in w_{\alpha+1}$ and w_α is no longer the lowest member of $w_{\alpha+1}$, again a contradiction. Hence, $w_{\alpha+1}$ is empty and for all z_α, $Nn(z_\alpha) \supset z_\alpha \in x_\alpha$.

It can also be proved that all nonnegative integers are sets of order 0:

*T*4.9. $(x_\alpha)[Nn(x_\alpha) \supset (\exists y_0)(y_0=x_\alpha)]$.

Proof. Consider $x_{\alpha+1}=\hat{x}_\alpha[(\exists y_0)(y_0=x_\alpha)]$. By *D*3.6, $0 \in x_{\alpha+1}$. Assume $Nn(y_\alpha)$ and $y_\alpha \in x_{\alpha+1}$. By *Ax*V and *D*4.5, $y'_\alpha \in x_{\alpha+1}$. Hence, by *T*4.8, theorem is proved.

*D*4.7. Let m, n, k, i, j, be used as variables ranging over sets which are nonnegative integers. By *T*4.9, there is no need to attach order indices to these variables since all nonnegative integers are sets of order 0 and therefore of any order.

*D*4.8. $1=0', 2=1', 3=2'$, etc. as usual.

Using the variables introduced in *D*4.7, the theorems *T*4.5—*T*4.8 can be stated more briefly:

*T*4.5. $Nn(m')$.

*T*4.6. $m' \neq 0$.

*T*4.7. $m'=n' \supset m=n$.

*T*4.8. Principle of mathematical induction.

$$(x_\alpha)[0 \in x_\alpha \,\&\, (m)(m \in x \supset m' \in x_\alpha)] \supset (n) n \in x_\alpha.$$

Justification of recursive functions from the set-theoretic point of view was first given in Dedekind 1888. For our purpose, it is convenient to introduce a generalization of Dedekind's result which applies to different kinds of inductive definition:

*T*4.10. (Generalized Dedekind theorem on inductive definitions).

Assume that an arbitrary set M is introduced by an induction schema

$$(D) \begin{cases} \langle x_i, \cdots, z_j, 0\rangle \in M \equiv H(x_i, \cdots, z_j), \\ \langle x_i, \cdots, z_j, n'\rangle \in M \equiv G(x_i, \cdots, z_j, n, M), \end{cases}$$

where $x_i, \cdots, z_j$ are $k(k \geqslant 0)$ arbitrary variables of orders $\leqslant \alpha$, H and G are formulas of orders $\leqslant \alpha+1$ (if M is replaced by a set variable of order $\alpha+1$), and M occurs in G only in contexts of the form

$\langle a_i, \cdots, a_j, b\rangle \in M$, where the value of $b<n$. Then we can define a set $x_{\alpha+2}$ of order $\alpha+2$ in the system $\Sigma_{\alpha+2}$ such that the results of replacing M by $x_{\alpha+2}$ in (D) become theorems of the system $\Sigma_{\alpha+2}$.

A proof of this theorem is quite immediate from the literature. Roughly speaking, for each m, there is a set $y_{\alpha+1}$ of order $\alpha+1$ which, when substituted for M in (D), makes all the cases of (D) up to $n=m$ theorems in $\Sigma_{\alpha+1}$. The union or sum of these sets $y_{\alpha+1}$ for $m=0, 1, 2, \cdots$ is the required set $x_{\alpha+2}$ of order $\alpha+2$.

In particular, if M happens to be a function, we can also rewrite (D) in the form

$$\begin{cases} x_i = M(\cdots, z_j, 0) \equiv x_i = H(\cdots, z_j), \\ x_i = M(\cdots, z_j, n') \equiv x_i = G(\cdots, z_i, n, M). \end{cases}$$

Hence, it follows from $T4.10$ as a corollary:

*T*4.11. Assume that an arbitrary function f is defined by an induction schema

$$\begin{cases} f(w_m, \cdots, z_i, 0) = h(w_m, \cdots, z_i), \\ f(w_m, \cdots, z_i, n') = g(w_m, \cdots, z_i, n, f), \end{cases}$$

which satisfies conditions corresponding to those in *T*4.10. Then we can define a set $x_{\alpha+2}$ of order $\alpha+2$ which satisfies the definition for f.

In both *T*4.10 and *T*4.11, if α happens to be 0, $h(w_m, \cdots, z_i)$ defines a set of order 0, and $g(w_m, \cdots, z_i, n, c)$ defines a set of order 0 for any set c of order 0 (similarly for G and H), then a stronger theorem holds on account of the definition of terms of order 0. In short, we need only a set x_1 of order 1 because, for each given m, a set y_0 of order 0, when substituted for f, is already sufficient to make all the cases up to $n=m$ theorems in Σ_0. A discussion of the relevant points can be found in Bernays 1941 (especially p. 12). From this, it follows that all primitive recursive functions (in particular, addition and multiplication) can be defined in Σ_1 and, by *T*4.4—*T*4.8, the usual elementary number theory (e.g., the system in Hilbert-Bernays) can be developed in Σ_1.

As a matter of fact, if we make use of schemata, elementary number theory can even be got in Σ_0. This is possible because each definite set x_1 of order 1 is introduced in Σ_1 by a defining sentence $F(y_0)$ (say) of order 1 which contains no free variables and therefore only variables of order 0. Since in elementary number theory it is always possible to speak of the defining sentence of a set of nonnegative integers instead of the set itself, a reformulation of elementary number theory in Σ_0 is possible.

This known fact may be stated as a theorem:

*T*4.12. Elementary number theory is obtainable in the system Σ_0.

In particular, if we take the following simple case of *T*4.10

$$\begin{cases}\langle x_0, 0\rangle \in M \equiv x_0 = 0, \\ \langle x_0, n'\rangle \in M \equiv (\exists y_0)(x_0 = \hat{z}_0(z_0 = y_0 \vee z_0 \in y_0) \;\&\; \langle y, n\rangle \in M),\end{cases}$$

we can find a set Nn of order 1 such that

$$(x_a)\,[Nn\,(x_a) \equiv (\exists y_0)(y_0 = x_a \;\&\; y_0 \in Nn)].$$

*D*4.9. The set Nn of order 1 which is thus determined is said to be the set of nonnegative integers (finite ordinals).

It may be of interest to note that there is no unique set of ordinals which corresponds to the predicate *Ord*, because for any α, there are ordinal numbers of order higher than α. For any given α, however, it is possible to define a set On_α (of order $\alpha+1$) consisting of all and only the sets of order α which are ordinal numbers. Thus, by *Ax*VI, we can define On_α:

*D*4.10. For all x_a, $x_a \in On_a$ if and only if x_a is transitive and $\in$ is connex in x_a. (Compare *D*4.2).

It is also possible to define functions over On_a by means of transfinite induction, i.e. to find a function F in the system such that $F(0)$ gets a preassigned value and for each $\beta \leqslant \alpha$, the value of $F(\beta)$ depends in a definite way on the values of F for ordinal numbers less than β. The method is similar to the usual one (cf. Gödel 1940, 7.5), but special attention has to be paid to the orders of the sets involved.

We note incidentally that in general we can define in each system Σ_a more ordinal numbers than those which are $\leqslant \alpha$. Nonetheless, it does not follow that there exists some β which can be defined in Σ (i.e. in some system Σ_a) but which is not used as an order index. Indeed, we want to use all the ordinal numbers definable in Σ as order indices of the sets and variables. This is of course nothing objectionable. It is like saying that for each natural number n, we can define $10n$ to $10n+9$ in the n-th system, that there is a 0-th system, and that for each natural number i definable in some j-th system, there is also an i-th system.

§ 5. The Enumerability of All Sets

In this section, we illustrate how the following two theorems can be proved by applying *T*4.10:

*T*5.1. For each α, we can find a function E_α of order $\alpha+2$, such that E_α enumerates all sets of order α; in other words, $D(E_\alpha)=Nn$ and $W(E_\alpha)=V_\alpha$.

*T*5.2. For each α, we can define a model of Σ_α in $\Sigma_{\alpha+2}$ and formalize a consistency proof of Σ_α in $\Sigma_{\alpha+2}$ (i.e., prove an arithmetic sentence $Con(\Sigma_\alpha)$ in $\Sigma_{\alpha+2}$).

The considerations for proving both theorems are similar. We confine our discussions to *T*5.1 and assert *T*5.2 as provable analogously. For *T*5.2, the reader is, in addition, referred to Ch. XVIII. We note merely that since unrestricted mathematical induction is available in the system Σ, the difficulties about formalizing consistency proofs, as discussed in Ch. XVIII, do not arise here.

It is easy to find a function which enumerates all the sets of order 0 generated by *Ax*V. Thus, let $a(n)$ be the smallest m such that $(\exists k)(n=m+2^k)$ where m is an even multiple of 2^k, and $b(n)$ be the number k such that $n=a(n)+2^k$. Our problem is to find a function M such that:

$$\begin{cases}\langle x_0, 0\rangle \in M \equiv x_0 = \hat{y}_0(y_0 \neq y_0),\\ \langle x_0, n'\rangle \in M \equiv x_0 = \hat{y}_0[y_0 \in M(a(n')) \vee y_0 = M(b(n'))].\end{cases}$$

By *T*4.10, there exists a function of order 2 which satisfies these conditions. Actually, however, on account of *Ax*V, we can find a set of order 1 which, when substituted for M in the above sentences, already make the results theorems of the system Σ_1. This enumerating set will be referred to as E_0. The function E_0 enumerates the set V_0 of all sets of order 0 required to exist by the axioms of the system Σ.

Assume that V_1 consists of all and only those sets which satisfy the following conditions (compare *T*3.2):

(i) $\hat{x}_0\hat{y}_0(x_0 \in y_0) \in V_1$;

(ii) if $x_1 \in V_1$ and $z_1 \in V_1$, then $\hat{x}_0(x_0 \in x_1 \;\&\; x_0 \in z_1) \in V_1$;

if $x_1 \in V_1$, then $\hat{x}_0(\neg\, x_0 \in x_1) \in V_1$;

(iii) if $x_1 \in V_1$, then $\hat{x}_0(\exists y_0)(\langle y_0, x_0\rangle \in x_1) \in V_1$;

if $x_1 \in V_1$, then $\hat{x}_0\hat{y}_0(y_0 \in x_1) \in V_1$;

(iv) if $x_1 \in V_1$, then $\hat{x}_0\hat{y}_0\hat{z}_0(\langle y_0, z_0, x_0\rangle \in x_1) \in V_1$;

if $x_1 \in V_1$, then $\hat{x}_0\hat{y}_0\hat{z}_0(\langle y_0, x_0, z_0\rangle \in x_1) \in V_1$.

Let us try to find a set of order 3 which enumerates all members of V_1 (Compare Gödel 1940).

Consider all the ordered triples $\langle i, m, n\rangle$ of positive integers such that $0<i<8$. It is clearly quite easy to order all these triples and define a function (of order 1) which enumerates them:

*D*4.12. $\langle i_1, m_1, n_1\rangle$ precedes $\langle i_2, m_2, n_2\rangle$ if and only if either $i_1 < i_2$, or $i_1 = i_2$ but $m_1 + n_1 < m_2 + n_2$, or $i_1 = i_2, m_1 + n_1 = m_2 + n_2$, but $m_1 < m_2$.

*D*4.13. $J(m)$ is the m-th triple $\langle i, m, n\rangle$ $(0 < i < 8)$ under the ordering relation defined by *D*4.12.

It is also easy to define functions $K_1(m), K_2(m), K_3(m)$ (again of order 1), such that:

*D*4.14. $K_j(m)$ is the j-th member of $J(m)$.

To enumerate all sets of V_1, we define now a set M by the following schema:

$$\begin{cases} \langle x_1, 1\rangle \in M \equiv x_1 = \hat{w}_0\hat{z}_0(w_0 \in z_0) \\ \langle x_1, n'\rangle \in M \equiv \{[K_1(n') = 1 \;\&\; x_1 = M(1)] \lor [K_1(n') = 2 \;\&\; \\ \quad x_1 = \hat{w}_0(w_0 \in M[K_2(n')] \;\&\; w_0 \in M[K_3(n')] \lor [K_1(n') = 3 \;\&\; \\ \quad x_1 = \hat{w}_0(\neg\, w_0 \in M[K_2(n')])] \lor [K_1(n') = 4 \;\&\; x_1 = \\ \quad = \hat{x}_0(\exists y_0)(\langle y_0, x_0\rangle \in M[K_2(n')])] \lor [K_1(n') = 5 \;\&\; x_1 = \\ \quad = \hat{x}_0\hat{y}_0(y_0 \in M[K_2(n')])] \lor [K_1(n') = 6 \;\&\; x_1 = \hat{x}_0\hat{y}_0\hat{z}_0 \\ \quad (\langle y_0, z_0, x_0\rangle \in M[K_2(n')])] \lor [K_1(n') = 7 \;\&\; x_1 = \hat{x}_0\hat{y}_0\hat{z}_0 \\ \quad (\langle y_0, x_0, z_0\rangle \in M[K_2(n')])]\}. \end{cases}$$

It follows from *T*4.10 that there exists a set x_3 of order 3 such that when x_3 is substituted for M in the above sentences, the results become theorems of Σ_3. In what follows we shall denote the function thus defined by E_1. Thus, the enumerating function of V_1 is the function E_1 of order 3.

Similarly, for every positive integer n, we can define an enumerating function E_n of order $n+2$ which enumerates the set V_n of all sets of order n as given by *T*3.3. To fix our attention, let us assume that we have got enumerating functions E_0, E_1, E_2, E_3 for the sets V_0, V_1, V_2, V_3 respectively, and try to define E_4.

By *T*3.3, the sets of V_4 are determined by the following conditions:

(A) $\hat{x}_3\hat{z}_3(x_3 \in z_3) \in V_4$,

(B) If $x_4 \in V_3$, then $x_4 \in V_4$.

(C) If $x_4 \in V_4$ and $z_4 \in V_4$, then $\hat{x}_3(x_3 \in x_4 \;\&\; x_3 \in z_4) \in V_4, \cdots, \hat{x}_3\hat{y}_3\hat{z}_3(\langle y_3, x_3, z_3\rangle \in x_4) \in V_4$ (9 clauses corresponding to cases in (C) of *T*3.3).

We can view the sets V_4 as defined by an induction schema consisting of: (A) a finite number of clauses each stating that a certain given set of order $\leqslant 4$ belongs to V_4; (B) a finite number of clauses each stating that members of a certain enumerated set of order $\leqslant 5$ belongs to V_4; (C) a finite number of clauses each stating that a function of order $\leqslant 5$ (e.g. the function 'complement of') maps members of V_4 again to members of V_4.

In order to find an enumerating function for V_4, we can proceed similarly as with V_4. Since there are only finitely many clauses of the kind (C), there is a maximum positive integer such that the number of arguments for each function is $\leqslant n$. Suppose there are m_1 clauses of kind (A), m_2 clauses of order (B), m_3 clauses of kind (C), and $m = m_1 + m_2 + m_3$. Consider all the $(n+1)$-tuples $\langle i_1, \cdots, i_{n+1}\rangle$ of positive integers with $1 \leqslant i_1 \leqslant m$. These can be enumerated (by a set of order 1). All members of the set V_4 can be represented by these $(n+1)$-tuples in the following manner: for each i_1, $1 \leqslant i_1 \leqslant m_1$, all $(n+1)$-tuples $\langle i_1, \cdots, i_{n+1}\rangle$ represent one and only one set given by a clause of kind (A); for each given i_1, $m_1 + 1 \leqslant i_1 \leqslant m_1 + m_2$, and each given i_{n+1}, all $(n+1)$-tuples $\langle i_1, \cdots, i_{n+1}\rangle$ represent the i_{n+1}-th member of the $(i_1 - m_1)$-th set given by clauses of kind (B); for each given i_1, $m_1 + m_2 + 1 \leqslant i_1 \leqslant m$, all the $(n+1)$-tuples $\langle i_1, \cdots, i_{n+1}\rangle$ represent the value of the $(i_1 - m_1 - m_2)$-th function when the argument values are represented respectively by the i_2-th, $\cdots$, i_{n+1}-th $(n+1)$-tuples (If the function has less than n argument places, say j, use just the numbers $i_2, \cdots, i_{j+1}$). It is possible to represent the correlation between the $(n+1)$-tuples and the members of V_4 by a set of order 6. It is also possible to enumerate all the $(n+1)$-tuples by a set of order 1. Therefore, it is possible to enumerate V_4 by a set of order 6.

A comparison with the definition of E_1 should make it clear how V_4 and, for each positive integer n, V_n can be enumerated by a function E_n of order $n+2$.

The problem of enumerating V_ω is somewhat different because a theorem answering to *T*3.3 for sentences p of order ω would call for infinitely many clauses answering to (A)—(C) of *T*3.3. To apply the above method of enumeration, we would need something like an alternation of infinitely many clauses.

We recall that in our intuitive model, V_ω contains all and only the sets belonging to some of the sets $V_0, V_1, V_2, \cdots$; in other words, that V_ω is just the union of the sets V_i for all nonnegative integers i.

To find an enumerating function E_ω of V_ω, we introduce first an enumeration of the sets $V_0, V_1, V_2, \cdots$ by the following condition.

$$\begin{cases} \langle x_\omega, 0\rangle \in M \equiv x_\omega = V_0, \\ \langle x_\omega, n'\rangle \in M \equiv x_\omega = \hat{y}_\omega[y_\omega \subseteq M(n)]. \end{cases}$$

By *T*4.10, there is a function of order $\omega + 2$ which satisfies these conditions. Since, for each given m, a set of finite order is already enough to satisfy the sentences for all cases up to m, we can find a function of order $\omega + 1$ which, when substituted for M in these sentences, already make the results theorems of the system $\Sigma_{\omega+1}$. This enumerating function will be referred to as U_ω. Thus, for each n, $U_\omega(n) = V_n$. This enables us, in a sense, to make induction on the order indices and reduce infinitely many clauses to a finite number.

Moreover, we can also define a function T_ω of order $\omega + 2$ such that for every n, $T_\omega(n) = E_n$. This depends essentially on the fact that for each n, given E_n, we can construct E_{n+1} from E_n, using U_ω, by a finite number of clauses. (In fact, eight clauses). Thus, T is defined by these conditions:

(A) $\langle x_\omega, 0 \rangle \in T_\omega \equiv x_\omega = E_0$.

(B) $\langle x_\omega, n' \rangle \in T_\omega$ if and only if all the following eight conditions hold:

(i) $(m)\,\{K_1(m)=1 \supset x_\omega(m)=\hat{y}_\omega\hat{z}_\omega[y_\omega \in U_\omega(n) \ \& \ z_\omega \in U_\omega(n) \ \& \ y_\omega \in z_\omega]\}$;

(ii) $(m)\,\{K_1(m) = 2 \supset x_\omega(m) = [T_\omega(n)]\,[K_2(m)]\}$;

(iii) $(m)\,\{K_1(m) = 3 \supset x_\omega(m) = \hat{y}_\omega(y_\omega \in U_\omega(n) \ \& \ y_\omega \in [T_\omega(n)]\,[K_2(m)]$

$\& \ y_\omega \in [T_\omega(n)]\,[K_3(m)])\}$;

$\cdots\cdots\cdots\cdots\cdots\cdots\cdots\cdots\cdots\cdots\cdots\cdots\cdots\cdots\cdots\cdots$

(viii) $(m)\,\{K_1(m) = 8 \supset x_\omega(m) = \hat{y}_\omega[y_\omega \in U_\omega(n) \ \& \ (\exists z_\omega)(z \in U_\omega[f(n, m)]$

$\& \ \langle z_\omega, y_\omega \rangle \in [T'(n)]\,[K_2(m)])]\}$.

In clause (viii), the function f is such that $f(n, m)$ is the remainder of dividing $K_3(m)$ by $n + 1$. Clearly f can be defined by a set of order 1, and (viii) covers all the cases $\hat{z}_n(\exists w_i)(\langle w_i, z_n \rangle \in x_{n+1})$ for $i = 0, 1, \cdots, n$.

It follows from $T4.10$ that the conditions defining T_ω are satisfied by a function of order $\omega + 2$ in the system $\Sigma_{\omega+2}$.

Given T_ω, the enumeration E_ω of the set V_ω can be defined in some usual manner:

E_0: $a_{01}, \ \longrightarrow \ a_{02}, \ a_{03}, \ \longrightarrow \ a_{04}, \ \cdots$

E_1: $a_{11}, \ \ a_{12}, \ a_{13}, \ \ a_{14}, \ \cdots$

E_2: $a_{21}, \ \ a_{22}, \ a_{23}, \ \ a_{24}, \ \cdots$

$\cdots\cdots\cdots$

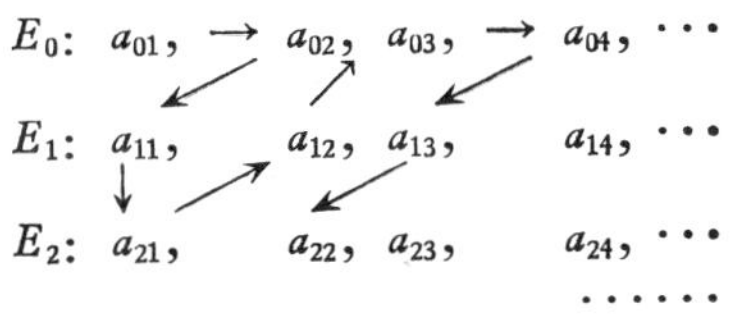

It is easy to define a function $g(m, n)$ such that $a_{m,n}$ is the $g(m, n)$-th in the above enumeration, and also two functions g_1 and g_2 such that $g_1(k)$ and $g_2(k)$ are respectively m and n if $g(m, n)$ is k. Using g_1 and g_2, we can define E_ω:

$$E_\omega(n) = E g_1(n)[g_2(n)] = [T_\omega(g_1(n))]\,[g_2(n)].$$

Since T_ω is of order $\omega+2$, E_ω is also of order $\omega+2$.

Given these discussions, it should appear plausible that, in general, V_α can be enumerated by a set E_α of order $\alpha+2$, and that $T5.1$ and $T5.2$ are true. In fact, for $\alpha=\omega+n$ and $\alpha=\omega\cdot n$, it is not hard to find E by considerations very similar to those used above. As we get to higher ordinals, the matter becomes more complex. We do not discuss these complications but assume that $T5.1$ and $T5.2$ have been established in their full generality.

§ 6. Consequences of the Enumerations

Given the enumerating functions E_α (of order $\alpha+2$), we can now formulate the axioms of limitation:

*Ax*VIII. For each α, $(x_\alpha)(\exists m)[E_\alpha(m)=x_\alpha]$.

The axioms of choice follow as immediate consequences from the enumerability of all sets:

CI. For every set x_α of nonempty sets y_α, there exists a set $z_{\alpha+2}$ which contains one and only one member from each set y_α in x_α. More exactly, if α is $\beta+1$ for some β, then there exists already such a set $z_{\alpha+1}$; if α is $\beta+2$ for some β, then there exists already such a set z_α.

For instance, let $x_{\beta+2}$ be a set of nonempty sets $y_{\beta+1}$ of order $\beta+1$. By E_β, all sets of order β can be enumerated. Let $\mu y_{\beta+1}$ be the first member of $y_{\beta+1}$ in the enumeration. Then the desired set $z_{\beta+2}$ is just the set $\hat{w}_\beta(\exists y_{\beta+1})(y_{\beta+1}\epsilon x_{\beta+2} \,\&\, w_\beta=\mu y_{\beta+1})$.

To prove *CI* formally in Σ, we have to use *Ax*VIII and mathematical induction. Details are omitted.

Similarly, forms of the continuum hypothesis also follow as consequences. Thus, since for each α, V_α is enumerable, the set On_α of all ordinals of order α, being a subset of V_α is also enumerable. From the enumerating function E_α (of order $\alpha+2$), it is easy to define an enumerating function E'_α (also of order $\alpha+2$) for On_α.

CII. For each α, there is a one-to-one correspondence (in $\Sigma_{\alpha+2}$) between all sets of order α and all ordinal numbers of order α.

In terms of E_α and E'_α, the correspondence is easily given by

$$\langle x_\alpha, y_\alpha\rangle \epsilon C \equiv (\exists m)[x_\alpha = E_\alpha(m) \,\&\, y_\alpha = E'_\alpha(m)].$$

By Gödel's theorem, for each system Σ_α, there is an arithmetic sentence of Σ_α, not decidable in Σ_α. By $T5.2$, $Con(\Sigma_\alpha)$ is provable in $\Sigma_{\alpha+2}$. Therefore, by the proof of Gödel's second theorem, undecidable sentence of Σ_α in Gödel's first theorem is also decidable in $\Sigma_{\alpha+2}$. It follows that Gödel undecidable sentence for any system Σ_α is decidable in the whole system Σ.

Of course, it does not follow that there are no undecidable sentences in the system Σ. This seems to be an open question.

Nevertheless, the system Σ seems to provide a sort of reply to Gödel's theorems. Among other things, *T*5.2 makes it quite clear that Gödel's second theorem does not imply that a consistency proof must be an argument which is intuitively less reliable than the methods used in the system thus proved consistent. For each α, $\Sigma_{\alpha+2}$ is intuitively quite as reliable as Σ_α.

The problem of proving the consistency of a given system is quite different from that of formalizing given proofs of consistency. It is perhaps more important to produce conviction. There are, to a surprisingly large extent, general agreements as to what kind of systems are known to be consistent, what are not. The reasons for such agreements may be harder to express and discuss.

The presence of *Ax*VIII leads to the question whether each system Σ_α is categorical relative to the theory of nonnegative integers contained in it, i.e., whether a unique interpretation for Σ_α is determined by each given interpretation for its theory of nonnegative integers. In a sense, the answer is obviously positive, since any relation between two sets can be treated as a relation between their corresponding integers in the enumerations, and the relation is fixed if we know all about the positive integers.

On the other hand, if we take the theory of integers as strictly those theorems of Σ_α which correspond to the theorems of ordinary elementary theory of nonnegative integers the answer is by no means easy to get.

The idea of axioms of limitation is rather natural and not new. Given a system of set theory, there are axioms which say categorically that such and such sets exist, and axioms which say that such and such sets exist provided such and such other sets exist. An axiom of limitation tries to say that we admit only those sets which are actually required to exist by the axioms for existence and no more.

For example, Fraenkel (1922) proposes to add to Zermelo's system the axiom: no other sets exist besides those which are required to exist by the explicitly stated axioms. Such an axiom is not satisfactory since it is not actually expressed by symbols available in the system. There is, therefore, the problem of translating it into a formula expressible in the given set theory (Zermelo's, in the particular case). When the system contains, as Zermelo's theory does, infinitely many axioms of existence, such a formulation is not known to be always possible. Even in cases where a formulation is possible, it is no trivial matter to give a formulation.

A second difficulty noted first by von Neumann (1925), concerns the matter of categoricalness. Take again Zermelo's set theory and assume that an axiom is formulated to the effect that there are only the sets required to exist. It might happen that the system has different and overlapping models but no smallest model. In particular, the intersection of all models for the system need not be a model for the system. In such a situation, at least two things can happen.

Either the supposed axiom of limitation does not give the desired effect and yields a contradiction. This would be the case when, for example, we give an exact restriction which, roughly, excludes all sets having no names in the system, and yet every model calls for some sets with no names in the system. In other words, sometimes an axiom explicitly requires just such and such sets, while in order to get a model for the axiom, we need more sets "to fill the gaps", because of the presence of impredicative definitions or circular references.

Or, if the axiom is formulated just loosely, then we do not get a contradiction but the interpretation of the axiom becomes ambiguous because it is no longer clear what are the sets which are required to exist. Take, for example, two overlapping models which have no common part that is again a model, there are sets which occur in one model but not in the other, are they sets strictly required to exist by the axioms or are they not?

These difficulties are closely connected with the presence of impredicative sets and definitions in the standard systems of set theory. We do not run into these obstacles with regard to our theory Σ because we admit no impredicative sets, no nonenumerable sets.

In a sense, the proposition '$V=L$' in Gödel 1940 can be viewed as an axiom of limitation for a standard set theory with impredicative sets. This task Gödel achieves by using transfinite ordinal numbers extensively.

§7. The Theory of Real Numbers

On the basis of the theory of nonnegative integers, it is quite easy to develop (already in Σ_1) ordinary theory of rational numbers, for example, by the method of Bernays 1942 (taking fraction triplets instead of rational numbers). Thus it is possible to identify fractions with certain sets of order 0, define the usual ordering relation among fractions, define a set *Fr* of order 1 which contains all and only the fractions, and introduce variables r, s, t (of order 0) which range over the fractions.

Real numbers can be defined as usual:

*D*7.1. For each α, x_α is a real number (of order α), or, more briefly, $Rn(x_\alpha)$, if and only if: (1) $x_\alpha \subset Fr$ and x_α is not empty; (2) $(s)(t)[(t \epsilon x_\alpha \,\&\, s \leqslant t) \supset s \epsilon x_\alpha]$; (3) $(s)[s \epsilon x_\alpha \supset (\exists t)(t > s \,\&\, t \epsilon x_\alpha)]$.

Clearly no set of order 0, being finite, can be a real number. However, for every $\alpha > 0$, there are real numbers of order α.

*D*7.2. For each $\alpha(\alpha > 0)$, there is a set Rn_α of order $\alpha + 1$ which consists of all and only the real numbers of order α.

From *D*7.1, for any two real numbers x_α and y_β either

$$x_\alpha \subset y_\beta \text{ or } y_\beta \subset x_\alpha \text{ or } x_\alpha = y_\beta.$$

*D*7.3. A real number x_α is said to be less than y_β if and only if $x_\alpha \subset y_\beta$. A set of real numbers is bounded above (resp. below) for which there exists a real number lower (resp. higher) than no member of the set.

The theorem of least upper bound is immediate.

*T*7.1. (Least upper bound). Every set of real numbers bounded above has a least upper bound; more exactly, for every $z_{\beta+1}$, if $z_{\beta+1} \subset Rn_\beta$ and $(\exists y_\beta)[y_\beta \epsilon Rn_\beta \,\&\, (x_\beta)(x_\beta \epsilon z_{\beta+1} \supset x_\beta \leqslant y_\beta)$, then there exists a real number $w_{\beta+1}$ which is the least upper bound of $z_{\beta+1}$; if α is an infinite ordinal of the nonsuccessor kind (a limiting number) and z_α is a set of real numbers, then there is a least upper bound of order α.

Proof. Given $z_{\beta+1}$, let $w_{\beta+1} = \hat{t}(\exists y_\beta)(y_\beta \epsilon z_{\beta+1} \,\&\, t \epsilon y_\beta)$. Then $w_{\beta+1}$ is easily seen to be a real number and the least upper bound of $z_{\beta+1}$. In case α is a limiting number, the least upper bound $\hat{t}(\exists y_\alpha)(y_\alpha \epsilon z_\alpha \,\&\, t \epsilon y_\alpha)$ of z_α is by definition of order $\alpha + 1$. Nonetheless, by the intuitive model, there is some $w_\beta, \beta < \alpha$ and $z_\alpha = w_\beta$. Therefore, the least upper bound is of order α (indeed, $< \alpha$, if we so desire). These can be proved in the system by the axiom of limitation. A related case will be discussed later on.

*D*7.4. A set x_α is finite or, more briefly, $Fin(x_\alpha)$, if and only if there is a set y_α of order α such that $(\exists n)(D(y_\alpha) = n)$ (notice n is the same as the set of all nonnegative integers $< n$) and $W(y_\alpha) = x_\alpha$ and y_α is one-to-one. The set x_α is infinite if it is not finite.

To justify this definition, we notice that if α is finite and contains the members $y^0, \cdots, y^k$, then the set $\hat{w}_\alpha(w_\alpha = \langle y^0, 0\rangle \vee \cdots \vee w_\alpha = \langle y^k, k\rangle)$ is a set of order $\leqslant \alpha$, because $y^0, \cdots, y^k$ are all of order $< \alpha$ (The exceptional case of $\alpha = 0$ is easily handled).

D7.5. A fraction t is less than a real number x if and only if $t \in x_a$; t is greater than x_a if and only if $(\exists s)(s<t \,\&\, \neg s \in x_a)$. A real number x_a is a limit point of a set of real numbers y_a if and only if, for every $t<x_a$ and $s>x_a$, there are infinitely many real numbers y_a, $t<y_a$ and $s>y_a$.

T7.2. The limit point theorem (Bolzano-Weierstrass). Given a bounded infinite set of real numbers (i.e. a set bounded above and bounded below), it has a limit point; more exactly, if x_a is a given bounded infinite set of real numbers, there is a real number y_{a+1} which is a limit point of x_a.

Proof. Define

$$y_{a+1} = \hat{t}(\exists w_a)(\exists z_a)[\mathrm{Fin}\,(z_a) \,\&\, z_a = \hat{u}_a(u_a \in x_a \,\&\, u_a < w_a) \,\&\, t \in w_a].$$

It can be proved by the usual argument that y_{a+1} is a real number and a limit point of x_a.

D7.6. A set x_a of real numbers is said to be a closed or open interval if there are two real numbers y_{a-1} and z_{a-1} (or y_a and z_a if α is a limiting ordinal number), $x_a = \hat{w}_{a-1}(w_{a-1} \in Rn_{a-1} \,\&\, y_{a-1} \leqslant w_{a-1} \,\&\, w_{a-1} \leqslant z_{a-1})$ or $x_a = \hat{w}_{a-1}(w_{a-1} \in Rn_{a-1} \,\&\, y_a < w_{a-1} \,\&\, w_{a-1} < z_{a-1})$. y_{a-1} and z_{a-1} are said to be the end points of the interval.

D7.7. A set y_β of intervals covers a set x_a of real numbers if every member of x_a belongs to at least one interval in y_β.

T7.3. The covering theorem (Heine-Borel). If x_a is a set of open intervals and x_a covers a closed interval y_β, then there is a finite subset z_a of x_a which also covers y_β.

Proof. Suppose $\alpha=\gamma+2$ and $\beta=\delta+1$. The left endpoint of y_β must lie within some interval $z_{\gamma+1}$ in x_a, with endpoints z_γ and w_γ. To fix our attention, let us keep $z_{\gamma+1}$ and z_γ fixed. Consider now the following set of one-one correlations between subsets of x_a and subsets of Nn: $M_{a+1} = \hat{w}_a[(w_a$ is a one to one correlation$) \,\&\, D(w_a) \subseteq Nn \,\&\, W(w_a) \subseteq x_a \,\&\, w_a(1) = z_{\gamma+1} \,\&\, (n)(f[w_a(n)] \in w_a(n')))]$, where $f[w_a(n)]$ is an easily definable function which gives the right endpoint of $w_a(n)$.

Either there is a member w_a of M_{a+1} such that $Fin(w_a)$ and the right endpoint of y_β belongs to a member of the range of w_a, then the theorem is proved.

Or, for every w_a of M_{a+1}, if $Fin\,(w_a)$, then for no m, does $w_a(m)$ include the right endpoint of y_β. The task is to prove this impossible. Let us consider the set $K_{a+1} = \hat{x}_\delta\{x_\delta \in y_\beta \,\&\, (\exists w_a)(\exists n)[w_a \in M_{a+1} \,\&\, x_\delta \in w_a(n)]\}$. It can be proved that $K_{a+1} = y_\beta$. For if not, there are members y_δ of y_β which do not belong to K_{a+1}. Either there is a smallest such y_δ or there is a limit point y_δ of such points. Neither is possible because y_δ, by hypothesis, belongs to some interval $u_{\gamma+1}$ of x_a, and therefore the left endpoint of $u_{\gamma+1}$ belongs to

$K_{\alpha+1}$ but the right endpoint does not. But this is impossible because $u_{\gamma+1}$ can be taken as the next interval.

Hence, $(\exists w_\alpha)(\exists n)[w_\alpha \epsilon M_{\alpha+1}$ and the right endpoint of y_β belongs to $w_\alpha(n)]$. In other words, there is a finite subset w_α of x_α which covers the interval y_β.

When either $\alpha \neq \gamma + 2$, or $\beta \neq \delta + 1$, the considerations are similar.

It should be noted that it is not surprising that we can derive *T*7.1, *T*7.2, *T*7.3, because we do not hesitate to use, when necessary, real numbers of higher orders.

§ 8. Intuitive Models

The transparent character of the systems Σ_α can best be seen by a more exact examination of the step by step construction of sentences and terms. Indeed, the systems Σ_α are set up in such a way that it is possible to interpret the variables as ranging over formal expressions. As a result, it is possible to well-order the expressions, and, in particular, the sentences of the system Σ_α so that intuitively acceptable models for the axiom systems are obtained. The nature of the systems Σ_α, as well as the justification of the axioms (including the axioms of limitation) can be grasped more easily through an understanding of the intuitive models for the systems Σ_α.

To facilitate considerations, we confine ourselves to sentences of Σ in which no free variables occur. This does not affect the generality because, for example, $F(x_\alpha)$ and $(x_\alpha)F(x_\alpha)$ are equivalent and we can afterwards give $F(x_\alpha)$ the same truth value as $(x_\alpha)F(x_\alpha)$.

*D*8.1. $Aj(a, b) =_D \hat{x}_0(x_0 \epsilon a \vee x_0 = b)$.

As before, let us refer to all terms of Σ_α which contain only 0 (the empty set) and Aj or are obtained from such by substituting free variables of order 0 for constants, as the basic terms. In general, when b is a constant basic term, we shall evaluate $a \epsilon b$ directly rather than first eliminating ϵ by *Ax*IV. This is an important difference between basic terms and others.

*D*8.2. All sentences of an arbitrary system Σ_α which do not contain free variables can be well-ordered by the following principles:

Assume an enumeration of all these sentences so that each sentence is correlated with a positive integer. Let p be an arbitrary sentence of Σ_α which is thus correlated to n_0. Let n_1 be the number of occurrences in p (counting all repetitions) of primitive symbols, n_2 be the number of occurrences (counting all repetitions) of symbols in p within basic terms, n_3 be the number of occurrences (counting all repetitions) of variables of order 0 in p but not within basic terms, $n_{2k+2}(k=1,2,\cdots)$ be the number of occurrences in p (counting all repetitions) of variables of order k, n_{2k+3} be the occurrences in p (counting all repetitions) of variables of order k in some term which occurs in a context of the form $b \in c$, where the order of $b \geqslant c$. Similarly, for each infinite ordinal $\beta+n$ (n a nonnegative integer), let $n_{\beta+2n}$ be the number of occurrences in p (counting all repetitions) of variables of order $\beta+n$, and $n_{\beta+2n+1}$ be the number of those in some term b which occurs in a context of the form $b \in c$, where the order of $b \geqslant c$. Since p is of finite length, only finitely many kinds of variable can occur. Therefore, each p is associated with a finite number of positive integers n_γ. If, for instance, the numbers are $n_{\alpha_1}, \cdots, n_{\alpha_k}, n_1, n_0 (\alpha_1 > \cdots > \alpha_k > 1 > 0)$, then we associate with p the ordinal number $\omega^{\alpha_1} \cdot n_{\alpha_1} + \cdots + \omega^{\alpha_k} \cdot n_{\alpha_k} + \cdots + \omega \cdot n_1 + n_0$. In this way each sentence gets an ordinal number and no two sentences get the same ordinal number. A sentence p is said to be prior to q if and only if the ordinal number of p is smaller than the ordinal number of q.

Given the well-ordering D8.2 of the sentences of Σ_α, we can now define a model of Σ_α in the following manner: a group of sentences with small ordinal numbers are to begin with called true or false according to intuitive interpretation, the truth and falsity of more complex sentences are determined completely by their relation to and the truth values of prior sentences.

Before giving details, we observe the following characters of the well-ordering:

*T*8.1. According to the well-ordering given in *D*8.2: (1) p and q both precede $p \vee q$; (2) p precedes $\neg p$; (3) if b is a term of order β or less, then $F(b)$ precedes $(\exists x_\beta)F(x_\beta)$; (4) if b is a term of order $\beta(\beta>0)$ or less $F(b)$ precedes $b \in \hat{x}_\beta F(x_\beta)$; (5) if a is of lower order than b and b is of no higher order than c, then $a \in b$ comes before $c \in b$; (6) if b is a constant basic term, $F(b)$ precedes $(\exists x_0)F(x_0)$.

The model or truth definition for Σ_α can be defined as follows:

Enumerate all constant basic terms of Σ_α in such a way that when a term b is a part of a term c, b comes before c. Let a, b, c, d be any constant term of this kind:

*D*8.3. (1) For every c, $c \in 0$ is false; (2) for every c and every d, $d \in c$ is false if c comes before d; (3) if the truth and falsity of sentences of the form $b \in d$, where both b and d precede $A_i(a, c)$, are all decided, then $b \in A_i(a, c)$ is true if either $b \in a$ is true or, for all d before b, $d \in c$ is true when and only when $d \in b$ is; $b \in A_i(a, c)$ is false if it is not true.

Clearly this merely makes more exact our intuitive notion about relations between finite sets made up of 0. For example, $0 \in \{0\}$, but not $0 \in \{\{\{0\}\}\}$, etc.

To complete the description of the model for Σ_α, we add only:

*D*8.4. (1) For every sentence p, $\neg p$ is true or false according as p is false or true; (2) $p \vee q$ is true or false according as whether or not at least one of p and q is true; (3) $(\exists x_\beta)F(x_\beta)$ is true or false according as whether or not there is some term b of order β or less such that $F(b)$ is true; (4) $b \in \hat{y}_\beta F(y_\beta)$, where b is of order β and $\hat{y}_\beta F(y_\beta)$ is not a basic term, is true or false according as whether or not $F(b)$ is true; (5) if the order of c is no higher than that of b, then $b \in c$ is true or false according as whether or not: there is some term a of order lower than that of b such that $a \in c$ is true and for every term d of order lower than that of b, $d \in b$ is true when and only when $d \in a$ is; (6) $(\exists x_0) F(x_0)$ is true or false according as whether or not there is some basic term b such that $F(b)$ is true.

It is quite easy to see from these descriptions that for every sentence p in a system Σ_α, p is either true or false, but cannot be both true and false. Thus, if b and c are two constant basic terms, then $b \in c$ is true or false but not both, according to *D*8.3. If p is a more complex sentence, by *T*8.1 and *D*8.4, we see by induction that p is again either true or false but not both.

The next problem is to verify that all theorems of each system Σ_α are true. For this, it is, as usual, sufficient to show that all axioms are true and rules of inference carry true sentences to true sentences. This is similar to the analogous problem handled in Fitch 1938.

Clearly all the rules of inference *Ri*1—*Ri*8 which concern only truth functions and quantification carry true sentences to true sentences, by dint of the clauses (1)—(3) in *D*8.4. Similarly the law of excluded middle *Ax*I is true.

By (1)—(3) of *D*8.4, *Ax*III is true.

By (1)—(4) of *D*8.4 (especially (4), of course), *Ax*IV is true.

*Ax*VIII is true because the model is, so to speak taylored to suit these axioms. Thus, on the bottom level, there are only the sets built up from 0 by repeated applications of *Aj*. On higher levels (orders), there exist only sets which are denoted by the set terms specified in describing the formalism. A comparison with the next section may make it clearer that *Ax*VIII is true in the model. By remarks on *Ax*V in §7, it follows rather directly that *Ax*V is true.

*Ax*VII is true on account of (5) of *D*8.4.

*Ax*VI is also true because the model excludes queer sets.

The hardest to verify is $AxII$. It is necessary and sufficient to verify $T2.4$: for any two constant terms b and c, $[b_\alpha = c_\beta \,\&\, F(b_\alpha)] \supset F(c_\beta)$, where $F(b_\alpha)$ is any sentence containing no free variables.

If $\alpha = \beta = 0$ (i.e., b and c are constant basic terms), and $F(b)$ is either $b \in d$ or $d \in b$, where d is another constant basic term, then $T2.4$ is true by $D5.3$.

Assume that $\alpha > 0$.

If $b_\alpha = c_\beta$ and $b_\alpha = d_0$ are true, then $c_\beta = d_0$ is also true. Thus, if $\alpha \geqslant \beta$, since all sets of order β are also of order α, then the assertion is true by definitions of $=$. If $\alpha < \beta$, $b_\alpha = d_0$ is equivalent to $(x_\beta)[x_\beta \in b_\alpha \equiv x_\beta \in d_0]$ by $AxVIII$. Hence, the assertion is again true.

If $b_\alpha = c_\beta$ and $b_\alpha \in d$ are true, where d is of order 0, then by $AxVII$, there is a term d_0 such that $b_\alpha = d_0$ is true. Hence, $c_\beta = d_0$ is true. If $b_\alpha \in d$ is true, by (5) of $D8.4$, $d_0 \in d$ is true. Hence, $c_\beta = d_0$ is true, by (5) of $D8.4$ again. $c_\beta \in d$ is also true. Hence, $T2.4$ is true for any α and β, if $F(b_\alpha)$ is $b_\alpha \in d$, where d is of order 0.

If $F(b_\alpha)$ is of the form $b_\alpha \in \hat{x}_\alpha G(x_\alpha)$, where $\hat{x}_\alpha F(x_\alpha)$ is not a basic term, then the case is reduced to the previous case where $F(b_\alpha)$ is $G(b_\alpha)$.

If $F(b_\alpha)$ is of the form $\neg G(b_\alpha)$, then the case is reduced to the previous case: $[c_\beta = b_\alpha \,\&\, G(c_\beta)] \supset G(b_\alpha)$.

If $F(b_\alpha)$ is of the form $G(b_\alpha) \vee H(b_\alpha)$, then the case is reduced to the cases where $F(b_\alpha)$ is $G(b_\alpha)$ and $H(b_\alpha)$ respectively. Similarly, if $F(b_\alpha)$ is of the form $(\exists x_\gamma) G(x_\gamma, b_\alpha)$.

Taking together these cases by inductive reasoning, it is established that $AxII$ is true.

Hence, all theorems of each system Σ_α are true. Since, for each p, p and $\neg p$ cannot both be true, the systems are proved to be consistent.

A more constructive proof of consistency will be presented in the next section.

§9. Proofs of Consistency

The system Σ or rather each system Σ_α for a given α can be proved consistent by a proof along the line of Lorenzen 1951 and Schütte 1952.

Our purpose is to prove that AxI—$AxVIII$ and $Ri1$—$Ri8$ taken together do not lead to contradictions.

Roughly speaking, we use an auxiliary system which is easily seen to be consistent and then prove that all theorems of Σ are also theorems in L.

The auxiliary system L may be described as follows:

*L*1. If a, b are basic set terms (i.e. set terms constructed from 0 solely by Aj), $a \in b$ or $\neg a \in b$ is a theorem according as $a \in b$ is true or false by the intuitive meaning.

*L*2. If $p_1 \vee \cdots \vee p_n$ is a theorem, then the results obtained by omitting repetitious terms, grouping terms, permuting terms remain theorems.

*L*3. (i) $p \rightarrow p \vee q$; (ii) $p \vee q \rightarrow p \vee \neg\neg q$; (iii) $\neg p \vee r$, $\neg q \vee r \rightarrow \neg(p \vee q) \vee r$; (iv) *Ri*7; (v) *Ri*8.

*L*4. $\neg(\exists x_0)F(x_0)$ is a theorem if for every basic set term b, $\neg F(b)$ is a theorem.

*L*5. $\neg(\exists x_\alpha)F(x_\alpha)$ is a theorem if for every set term b of order α or less, $\neg F(b)$ is a theorem.

*L*6. If p is a theorem containing $F(b)$ as part, b is a set term of any order, and $\hat{y}_\beta F(y_\beta)$ is a set term but not a basic one, then the result of substituting $b \in \hat{y}_\beta F(y_\beta)$ for $F(b)$ in p is also a theorem.

*L*7. Suppose b, c are basic terms, $\alpha > 0$, and $d_\alpha = b$ is a theorem. Then, if $b \in c$ is a theorem $d_\alpha \in c$ is a theorem; if $\neg b \in c$ is a theorem, $\neg d_\alpha \in c$ is also.

It is easy to see that this system L is consistent. For example, $0 \in 0$ is not a theorem in the system. Thus, by intuitive meaning, *L*1 does not make $0 \in 0$ a theorem. None of the other rules *L*2—*L*6 could make $0 \in 0$ a theorem either. Roughly speaking, *L*2 carries a theorem to another of the same length or complexity, *L*3—*L*6 carry shorter or less complex theorems to longer or more complex ones. *L*7 cannot yield $0 \in 0$ as conclusion since it cannot lead to conclusions of the form $d_\alpha \in c$, where $\alpha = 0$. Hence, none could have $0 \in 0$ as a consequent which is of the simplest kind of sentence in the system.

It is a little harder to verify that all theorems of each system Σ_α are also theorems of the above auxiliary system.

*Ri*1—*Ri*3 are cases of *L*2.

*Ri*4, *Ri*5, *Ri*7, *Ri*8 are cases of *L*3.

Hence, we need only consider the axioms and *Ri*6 (modus ponens, Schnittsregel).

To prove that *Ax*I is a theorem, we consider the various possible forms of p. If p is $a \in b$ where a, b are constant basic terms, then, by *L*1, either $a \in b$ or $\neg a \in b$ is a theorem of the system L. Hence, by (i) of *L*3 and *L*2, $\neg p \vee p$ is a theorem.

Given that $\neg p \vee p$ and $\neg q \vee q$ are theorems of L, it is easy to show by $L3$ and $L2$, that $\neg\neg p \vee \neg p$ and $\neg(p \vee q) \vee (p \vee q)$ are theorems of L.

Similarly, if b is of order β and $\neg F(b) \vee F(b)$ is a theorem of L, then $\neg b \in \hat{y}_\beta\ F(y_\beta) \vee b \in y\ F(y_\beta)$ is also a theorem of L by $L6$.

If for some b of order $\beta, \neg F(b) \vee F(b)$ is a theorem of L, then $\neg(\exists x_\beta)\ F(x_\beta) \vee (\exists x_\beta)\ F(x_\beta)$ is a theorem of L by (iv) and (v) of $L3$, and $L2$.

Therefore, for every $p, \neg p \vee p$ is a theorem of L. In other words, all cases of *Ax*I are theorems of L.

The most difficult step is to prove that the application of *Ri*6 (Schnittsregel, cut), leads from theorems of L to theorems of L. This can be treated in the manner of Schütte 1952.

We observe first that from any proof in L of $\neg(p \vee q) \vee r$, we can find a proof of $\neg p \vee r$ and a proof of $\neg q \vee r$. This is obvious because (iii) of $L3$ is the only rule which would have a sentence of the form $\neg(p \vee q) \vee r$ as consequent. Similarly, from a proof in L of $p \vee \neg\neg q$, we can find one for $p \vee q$, since (ii) of $L3$ is the only rule having a sentence of the form $p \vee \neg\neg q$ as consequent. From a proof of $\neg(\exists x_\alpha)\ F(x_\alpha) \vee p$ in L, we can find a proof of $\neg F(b) \vee p$ for each term b of order α or less; if $\alpha=0$, we can find a proof of $\neg F(b) \vee p$ for each constant basic term b.

Suppose that $p \vee q$ and $\neg q \vee r$ both are theorems of L. We want to show that $p \vee r$ is also a theorem of L.

For this purpose, let us, as before, disregard formulas with free variables, and assume that all formulas of L are correlated with ordinal numbers as in *D*9.2. We prove the result by an induction on the ordinal number correlated with the eliminated formula q: the result holds when q is of the simplest form; if the result is true for all crucial formulas with ordinal numbers less than that of q, then the result is true when the eliminated formula is q.

(I) q is a formula $b \in c$, where b and c contain no free variables.

(Ia) b and c are constant basic terms. By $L1$, either $b \in c$ or $\neg b \in c$ is a theorem of L. By the consistency of L, either $b \in c$ or $\neg b \in c$ is not a theorem of L. If $b \in c$ is not a theorem, then, in the proof of $p \vee b \in c$, $b \in c$ could have been introduced only by (i) of $L3$. Hence, p is already a theorem of L. Therefore, by (i) of $L3$, $p \vee r$ is also a theorem. Similarly, if $\neg b \in c$ is not a theorem of L, then r is already a theorem of L and therefore $p \vee r$ is also a theorem.

(Ib) If c is a constant term but b is not. Consider first the proof of $p \vee b \in c$ in L. Either $b \in c$ is introduced by (i) of $L3$, then by striking $b \epsilon c$ out all through, we get a proof of p. By applying again (i) of $L3$, we get $p \vee r$. Or if $b \epsilon c$ is not introduced by (i) of $L3$, it can only be introduced at first by $L7$, because no other rule which does not contain $b \epsilon c$ in the antecedent can contain $b \epsilon c$ in the consequent. Therefore, there is a basic term d such that $d=b$ and $d \epsilon c$ are two lines in the proof for $p \vee b \epsilon c$. Then in the proof of $\neg b \epsilon c \vee r, \neg b \epsilon c$ can only be introduced by (i) of $L3$. Otherwise, $\neg b \epsilon c$ can only be introduced at first by $L7$ because no other rule which does not contain $\neg b \epsilon c$ in the antecedent can contain it in the consequent. Then we would have for a certain basic term e, $e=b$ and $\neg e \epsilon c$ are two lines in the proof of $\neg b \epsilon c \vee r$. This is not possible, if d and e are the same, because then $d \epsilon c$ and $\neg e \epsilon c$ cannot both be theorems. Hence, if $\neg b \epsilon c$ is not introduced by (i) of $L3$, then there must be two distinct basic terms d and e such that $d=b$ and $e=b$ both are theorems of L. We want to prove this can never happen. Since d and e are distinct, there is a basic term a such that either $a \epsilon d$ and $\neg a \epsilon e$ are both theorems or $\neg a \epsilon d$ and $a \epsilon e$ are both theorems. Either $a \epsilon b$ or $\neg a \epsilon b$ is theorem. In either case, we cannot have both $d=b$ and $e=b$ as theorems. Therefore, in the proof of $\neg b \epsilon c \vee r$, $\neg b \epsilon c$ can only be introduced by (i) of $L3$. But then, by striking out $\neg b \epsilon c$ throughout the proof, we get a proof of r. Hence, applying (i) of $L3$ again, we get $p \vee r$.

(Ic) If c is not a basic term. Suppose c is $\hat{x}_a F(x_a)$. Reduce the case to the simpler case where q is $F(b)$.

(II) q has the form $p_1 \vee p_2$. By the preliminary remarks, from the proof of $\neg(p_1 \vee p_2) \vee r$, we can find proofs for $\neg p_1 \vee r$ and $\neg p_2 \vee r$. Hence, we can reduce the use of the Schnittsregel to simpler cases:

$$\begin{aligned} p \vee p_1 \vee p_2, \neg p_2 \vee r &\rightarrow p \vee p_1 \vee r, \\ &\rightarrow p \vee r \vee p_1 \\ p \vee r \vee p_1, \neg p_1 \vee r &\rightarrow p \vee r \vee r \\ &\rightarrow p \vee r. \end{aligned}$$

(III) q has the form $\neg p_1$. From the proof of $\neg\neg p_1 \vee r$, we can get a proof of $p_1 \vee r$. Therefore, we can reduce the case to the simpler one:

$$\begin{aligned} p_1 \vee r, p \vee \neg p_1 &\rightarrow r \vee p_1, p_1 \vee p \\ &\rightarrow r \vee p \\ &\rightarrow p \vee r. \end{aligned}$$

(IV) q has the form $(\exists x_a) F(x_a)$. From the proof of $p \vee (\exists x_a) F(x_a)$, we obtain for some b_a and some p_1, a proof of $p_1 \vee F(b_a)$, and also from the proof of $\neg(\exists x_\alpha) F(x_\alpha) \vee r$ a proof of $\neg F(b_\alpha) \vee r$. Hence, we can reduce the case to the simpler one:

$$p_1 \vee F(b_\alpha),\ F(b_\alpha) \vee r \rightarrow p_1 \vee r.$$

Now in the derivation of $p \vee (\exists x_\alpha) F(x_\alpha)$ from $p_1 \vee F(b_\alpha)$, if we replace $F(b_1)$ and $(\exists x_\alpha) F(x_\alpha)$ both by r, we get again a derivation whose last line is:

$$p_1 \vee r \rightarrow p \vee r.$$

This completes the proof that if $p \vee q$ and $\neg q \vee r$ are theorems of L, then $p \vee r$ is also. As a result, we are justified in using the Schnittsregel in L, if we want to.

The problem now remaining is to prove that *Ax*II—*Ax*VIII are theorems of L.

By $L6$ and $L1$, all cases of *Ax*IV are theorems of L.

Cases of *Ax*III are theorems of L by (iv) of $L3$ (viz., *Ri*7) and $L5$.

Cases of *Ax*V are theorems of L by $L5$, because every set term of order α (α a limit number) is also of some order less than α.

*Ax*VIII and *Ax*VI can be seen to be theorems of L by reflection on the meaning of the relevant formulas. For example, for each term b_α, we can find some definite n_0 such that $E_\alpha(n_0)=b_\alpha$ is a theorem of L if we break up E_α according to its definition.

To prove *Ax*II and *Ax*VII in L is a complex affair. We make the following general observation. By definition of $=$, it is possible to prove in L that $b_0=c_1$ (or $c_1=b_0$), for suitable terms b_0 and c_1. For suitable c_1 and c_2, it is also possible to prove that $c_1=c_2$, because $c_1=c_2$ is equivalent to

$$(x_0)[x_0 \in c_1 \equiv x_0 \in c_2] \;\&\; (x_1)[x_1 \in c_2 \supset (\exists y_0)(y_0 = x_1)].$$

And so on. This is how it is possible to prove $a_\alpha=b_\beta$ when $\alpha\neq\beta$.

To justify *Ax*II, we prove that for any given terms a_α and b_β,

$$a_\alpha = b_\beta \supset [F(a_\alpha) \equiv F(b_\beta)] \qquad \text{(i)}$$

is a theorem of L. If $\alpha=\beta=0$ and $F(a_\alpha)$ is $a_\alpha \in c_\gamma$ or $c_\gamma \in a_\alpha$, then $F(a_\alpha)$ and $F(b_\beta)$ are the same because no two basic terms denote the same set. If $\alpha=0$ or $\beta=0$ but not both and $F(a_\alpha)$ is $a_\alpha \in c_0$, then (i) is a theorem of L by $L7$. If $\alpha=0$ or $\beta=0$ but not both, $F(a_\alpha)$ is $c_\gamma \in a_\alpha$, and $a_\alpha=b_\beta$ is a theorem of L, then (i) is a theorem by definition of $=$ if there is a d_0, $d_0=c_\gamma$, and (i) is also a theorem if otherwise because both $\neg c_\gamma \in a_\alpha$ and $\neg c_\gamma \in b_\beta$ are then theorems. Similarly, if $\alpha \neq 0$, $\beta \neq 0$ but $F(a_\alpha)$ is $a_\alpha \in c_0$, then (i) is again a theorem. When $\alpha \neq 0$, $\beta \neq 0$, and $F(a_\alpha)$ is $c_\gamma \in a_\alpha$, we can eliminate a_α and b_β by *L6*. The cases where $F(a_\alpha)$ contain logical operators can easily be established by induction, because the Schnittsregel is, as we have shown, derivable in *L*. For example, it is easy to show:

$$p \supset [q \equiv r], p \supset [q_1 \equiv r_1] \rightarrow p \supset [(q \,\&\, q_1) \equiv (r \,\&\, r_1)].$$

The proof of *Ax*VII in *L* depends on the fact that, for example, in order to prove $a_\alpha \in b_{\beta+1} (\alpha > \beta)$ in *L*, we have to use *L7* at some stage and be able to prove for some term c_β, $a_\alpha = c_\beta$. Details for the argument are omitted.

§ 10. The System *R*

To facilitate comparison with the theory of types, we describe a system *R* which is closely related to the system Σ_ω.

10.1. *Levels, Types, Orders*

In *R*, non-negative integers are the individuals or, in other words, objects of the 0-th or bottom level. Sets and relations of them constitute objects of the first level. Sets and relations of these sets and relations of individuals make up objects of the second level. And so on, ad infinitum.

All sets and relations are introduced by abstraction from propositional formulas with free variables. Each set or relation is assigned a positive integer for its order, in accordance with the complexity of its definition. Thus, the order 1 is assigned to a set or relation which is introduced by using notions expressible in elementary number theory and whose definition, therefore, involves no other totalities than that of the non-negative integers. A set or relation whose definition in the system *R* involves no totalities other than those of the non-negative integers and the sets and relations of order 1 is of order 2. The definition of a set or relation of order 2 does not have to involve both kinds of totality; every set or relation of order 1 is also one of order 2. Similarly, a set or relation whose definition involves no totalities of order higher than 2 (counting the totality of non-negative integers as of order 0) is of order 3. And so on, ad infinitum.

Besides a level and an order, each set or relation has also a type which is determined partly by its order and partly by the types of its members. For example, a set of non-negative integers of order 5 is of type 5(0), a triadic relation of non-negative integers of order 8 is of type 8(0,0,0), a set of order 12 of sets of type 5(0) is of type

12(5(0)), a dyadic relation of order 9 between non-negative integers and relations of type 8(0,0,0) is of type 9(0,8(0,0,0)), and so on. Given the type of a set or relation, we know not only its order, but also its level.

More exactly, the type signs are defined in the following manner. The symbol 0 is the only type sign of order 0 and level 0. If $t_1, \cdots, t_n$ are any type signs each of order lower than $m(m>0)$ and the maximum level of $t_1, \cdots, t_n$ is k, then $m(t_1, \cdots, t_n)$ is a type sign of order m and level $k+1$. Moreover, for the same $t_1, \cdots t_n$, the sign $(t_1, \cdots, t_n)$ is a general type sign of level $k+1$ (and of order ω, if we wish). But we forbid the use of these general type signs as components for building up new type signs. When we speak of type signs we shall usually mean the type signs of finite orders. It will be observed that the characterization of type signs is by recursion. For example, 0, 1(0), 1(0,0), 2(0), 2(0,0), 3(0), 4(0,0,0), 15(0,0) are type signs of level 1, 2(1(0)), 3(0,1(0)) are type signs of level 2, 4(0,3(2(1(0),0))), 7(4(1(0), 2(1(0),0))) are type signs of level 4, 9(6(5(3(2(0))))) is a type sign of level 5, and so on. It follows from the characterization of type signs that the level of a type sign t is, roughly speaking, the number of the longest occurring succession of pairs of parentheses in t such that each non-extreme pair is enclosed in its predecessor and encloses its successor.

Moreover, since the definition of any set (or relation) must involve the totality of its members (or that of the members filling each of its places), the order of each set or relation is always higher (at least by 1) than the order of its members. Hence, the order of each type sign is always at least as large as its level. For example, there can never be a type sign of order 4 and level 5, although there can be one of order 5 and level 4 or one of order 5 and level 5.

10.2. *Expressions of the System R*

The principal expressions of the system R are the terms and the sentences. Among terms are those for non-negative integers, and those for sets and relations, obtained from sentences by abstraction. Sentences are obtained either from terms by using the identity sign = or the membership sign ϵ, or from other sentences by truth-functional operations or by quantification.

More exactly, the expressions of R are as follows:

10.2.1. Basic units: | (neither-nor), = (identity), ϵ (membership), ^(abstraction), 0(zero), 1(one), + (addition), · (multiplication), $w, x, y, z, \cdots$, , (comma), ((left parenthesis),) (right parenthesis).

10.2.2. The numerals 2,3,4, and so on, are introduced as abbreviations for $1+1$, $2+1$, $3+1$, and so on.

10.2.3. Type signs are defined as in 10.1.

10.2.4. Variables (of finite orders): When t is a type sign, $w^t, x^t, y^t, z^t, x_1^t, y_1^t$, and so on, are variables of type t. The variables m, n, k, i, j, and so on will often, when convenient, be used in place of the variables $w^0, x^0, y^0, z^0, w_1^0$, and so on. The level of a variable is the level of its type sign.

10.2.5. Terms of order 0 and level 0: the variables m, n, k, i, j, and so on, are; the numerals 0 and 1 are; if a and b are, then $a+b$ and $a \cdot b$ are.

10.2.6. Sentences of order m (m a positive integer): (1) if a and b are terms of order 0, then $a=b$ is a sentence of order m; (2) if t is $k(t_1, \cdots, t_n)$, $k \leqslant m$, $a_1, \cdots, a_n$ are terms respectively of types $t_1, \cdots, t_n$, and b is a term of type t, then $(a_1, \cdots, a_n) \in b$ is a sentence of order m (for example, $(j, 0) \in x^{n(0,0)}$ is of order n); (3) if p, q, $F(x^t)$ are sentences of order m and the order of t is smaller than m, then $p|q$, $(x^t)\, F(x^t)$ are sentences of order m.

10.2.7. Terms of type $k(t_1, \cdots, t_n)$ (k finite): (1) if t is $j(t_1, \cdots, t_n)$ and $j \leqslant k$, the variable w^t, x^t, y^t, and so on, are; (2) if $F(x_1^{t_1}, \cdots, x^{t_n})$ is a sentence of order k, then $\hat{x}_1^{t_1} \cdots \hat{x}_n^{t_n} F(x_1^{t_1}, \cdots, x_n^{t_n})$ is a term of type $k(t_1, \cdots, t_n)$. Hence a term obtained from a sentence by abstraction is of the same order as the sentence. From this and 10.2.6, it follows that in general, if $j \leqslant k$, a term of type $j(t_1, \cdots, t_n)$ is also one of order $k(t_1, \cdots, t_n)$.

10.2.8. General variables or variables of order ω (of infinite order): If t is $(t_1, \cdots, t_n)$ where $t_1, \cdots, t_n$ are any type signs (of finite orders), $w^t, x^t, y^t, z^t, x_1^t$, and so on, are variables of type t and order ω. Here, as with ordinary variables, the level of a variable is that of its type sign. Later we shall realize that free general variables actually serve the purpose of variables of indefinite order rather than those of infinite order.

10.2.9. Sentences of order ω: (1) if t is $(t_1, \cdots, t_n)$, $a_1, \cdots, a_n$ are terms respectively of types $t_1, \cdots, t_n$, and b is a term of type t, then $(a_1, \cdots, a_n) \in b$ is a sentence of order ω; (2) if a and b are terms of types $k(t_1, \cdots, t_n)$ and $(t_1, \cdots, t_n)$ respectively, or both of the type $(t_1, \cdots, t_n)$, then $a=b$, $b=a$ are sentences of order ω; (3) if p, q, $F(x^t)$ are sentences of order ω and the order of t is finite, then $p|q$ and $(x^t)\, F(x^t)$ are sentences of order ω; (4) Every sentence of a finite order is also one of order ω.

10.2.10. Terms of type $(t_1, \cdots, t_n)$ (and of order ω): (1) if t is $(t_1, \cdots, t_n)$ or $k(t_1, \cdots, t_n)$ (for some k), every variable w^t, x^t, y^t, and so on, is also a term of type $(t_1, \cdots, t_n)$; (2) if $F(x_1^{t_1}, \cdots, x_n^{t_n})$ is a sentence of order ω, then $\hat{x}_1^{t_1} \cdots \hat{x}_n^{t_n}\, F(x_1^{t_1}, \cdots, x_n^{t_n})$ is a term of type $(t_1, \cdots, t_n)$. From this and 11.2.9, it follows that every term of the type $k(t_1, \cdots, t_n)$, where k is any positive integer, is also a term of the type $(t_1, \cdots, t_n)$.

10.2.11. Sentences of order $\omega+1$: (1) A sentence of order ω is also one of order $\omega+1$; (2) if $p, q, F(x^t)$ are sentences of order $\omega+1$, where t may be of order ω, then $p|q$ and $(x^t)\ F(x^t)$ are sentences of order $\omega+1$. In other words, sentences of order $\omega+1$ may contain bound general variables; i.e. they may involve reference to certain totalities of sets or relations of all types $k(t_1, \cdots, t_n)$ ($k = 1, 2, 3, \cdots$).

It is important that we admit no terms which would contain bound general variables. In conformity with the general constructivistic approach, such terms would have to be of order $\omega+1$. Since in R we want to confine ourselves to objects of finite orders and therewith terms of order no greater than ω, we refrain from introducing either constant terms or variables of order $\omega+1$. Allowing bound general variables in defining terms and treating these terms as of order ω(i.e., as values of the general variables) would of course mean the employment of impredicative definitions which we have decided to forbid.

10.3. *Fundamental Definitions and Axioms of R*

From the basic signs | and ( ), we can define in usual manner the signs $\supset$ (if $\cdots$ then), & (and), $\equiv$ (if and only if), $\neg$ (not), $\vee$ (or), $\exists$ (for some). As usual, $a \neq b$ stands for $\neg\ a = b$.

The axioms and rules of inference of R are similar to those of Σ_ω, with certain necessary adjustments of course. For example, axioms of elementary number theory are included as axioms for the individuals (i.e. objects of the lowest level).

In the theory R, we have no idea whether formulas of the form

$$(\exists y(t_i, \cdots, t_n))(x^{t_i})\cdots(w^{t_n})[(x^{t_i}, \cdots, w^{t_n}) \in y(t_i, \cdots, t_n) \equiv p],$$

where p contains general variables, are true or false. If we could prove that all such sentences are true, we would be able to add them as axioms and get a system essentially equivalent to the simple theory of types. Indeed, in such a system, we could omit all the formulas and axioms involving anything but the general variables, and the result would be exactly the simple theory of types. On the other hand, in the simple theory of types we could also introduce by contextual definitions the variables of finite orders.

In the theory R, we can, if we wish to, dispense with relations altogether in the usual manner. Indeed, on account of the presence of elementary number theory at the bottom, we can identify relations with suitable sets of the same level.

For certain purposes, it may be useful to add also to *R* sets of order $\omega+1$ for each type. These would roughly serve the purpose of the classes or II–things in the von Neumann-Bernays set theory.

CHAPTER XXV

ORDINAL NUMBERS AND PREDICATIVE SET THEORY*

The Poincaré-Russell notion of predicativity seems to deserve renewed study in view of recent works by Lorenzen and others which appear to give hope of a predicative basis for ordinary mathematics. Gödel's predicative model of classical set theory relative to classical ordinals and more recent works by many logicians on hyperarithmetic sets produce the impression that the question of making the philosophical notion of predicativity more exact has become more nearly manageable. In what follows some highly tentative attempts at answering this question will be described. It is thought that some of the vague ideas described below might lead to more definite results in more capable hands. In particular, reasons are given for believing that the highly attractive domain of hyperarithmetic set theory does not provide us with a conclusive framework for dealing with all predicative sets. Some further extensions seem to require closer examination. Meanwhile, a rather simple axiom system H will be given which seems to codify hyperarithmetic sets just as well as usual formal systems do the notion of natural numbers and the notion of arbitrary sets.

In order to consider the detailed structure of definitions and proofs, ordinal numbers are of central importance. Ordinals seem indispensable in devising measures of complexity and the problem of determining the acceptable ordinals is usually a major step. For this reason, much space will be devoted to different systems of ordinals. Besides the famous class of recursive ordinals, narrower systems which are called strongly effective, as well as broader systems which appear to remain in some vague domain of the "constructive", will be discussed.

The notion of an inductive definition is also not entirely clear once we go beyond the familiar examples and try to get an exact general definition. Some of the difficulties will be stated, and a tentative general characterization will be given.

---

* This chapter appeared in *Zeitsch. f. math. Logik u. Grundlagen der Math.*, vol. 5, 1959.

§ 1. Systems of Notation for Ordinal Numbers

We shall study the representation of ordinals by positive or non-negative integers. This restriction to integers means that we are concerned only with systems of notation for Cantor's (first number class and) second number class. As is well-known, any well-ordering of a class of positive integers (its domain) determines a section of the second number class but need not be acceptable as a system of notation for ordinals since we may have no effective way of telling, e.g., whether a given integer in the domain represents the ordinal 0, a successor, or a limit.

If we use x^* to denote the ordinal represented by x, it seems possible to state some minimum requirements for a well-ordering V with domain D_V (a class of positive integers) to be a system of ordinal notation:

Definition 1. *A well-ordering V is a system of ordinal notation if:*

(1) $x \neq y$ if $x^* \neq y^*$, i.e., no two ordinals are represented by the same integer;

(2) there is an effective method to determine, for all x, $D_V(x)$, whether x^* is 0, a successor, or a limit;

(3) there is an effective method to determine, for all x, x^* being a successor, a y such that y^* is the predecessor of x^*;

(4) there is an effective method to determine, for every x, $D_V(x)$, a y such that y^* is the successor of x^*.

Remark 1. It may be objected that by using positive integers rather than numerals to represent ordinals, we may get into difficulty because there may be different numerical terms such that we cannot decide effectively whether they represent the same integer. In practice, we shall only use numerical terms whose corresponding numerals can be found effectively, thereby avoiding this difficulty. All the same, it will, in what follows, often be clearer if we think in terms of numerical expressions. In each system, we generally use a class of numerical expressions no two of which stand for the same integer and it is often convenient to use syntactical properties of the expressions.

Remark 2. Of course, as is well-known, no system of notation, being enumerable, could represent the whole second number class.

Remark 3. For the sake of definiteness, we shall assume the Church-Turing hypothesis: a function or predicate defined over a set D of positive integers is effectively calculable or decidable if and only if it is general recursive relative to D.

Remark 4. Given a system V of notation, V being a well-ordering, there usually exists an enumerable class of functions $f_1, f_2, \cdots$ such that (1) $D_V(f_n(m))$ if $D_V(m)$, and $V(f_n(m), f_n(k))$ if $V(m, k)$; (2) every limit ordinal x^* has, for each notation x, a function $f_x(n)$, $x^* = \lim(f_x(n))^*$. In general, we may either extract the class of functions from the well-ordering V or introduce it explicitly to begin with.

If we are interested in effective systems of notation, we would naturally impose more conditions (cf. Church 1938 and Kleene 1938):

Definition 2. *A well-ordering V is an effectively calculable system of notation for ordinals if there are partial recursive functions g_1, g_2, g_3, g_4, g_5 such that: (1) $x^* = y^*$ if $x = y$; (2) if $D_V(x)$, $g_1(x)$ is 1, 2, 3 according as x^* is 0, x^* is a successor, x^* is a limit; (3) if $D_V(x)$ and $g_1(x)$ is 2, $(g_2(x))^*$ is the predecessor of x^*; (4) if $D_V(x)$, $(g_3(x))^*$ is the successor of x^*; (5) if $D_V(x)$ and $g_1(x) = 3$, $g_4(x)$ is (a Gödel number of) a recursive function $f(n)$ such that $D_V(n) \rightarrow D_V(f(n))$, $V(m,n) \rightarrow V(f(m), f(n))$, and $\lim(f(n))^* = x^*$; (6) if x is a recursive function $f(n)$ satisfying the first two conditions and if $D_V(g_5(x))$, then $(g_5(x))^* = \lim(f(n))^*$.*

Remark 5. Since we are usually concerned with systems in which if an ordinal is represented, its successor is also, we have made no provisions in conditions (4) of definitions 1 and 2 that there might be a highest ordinal representable in some system of notation. In contrast, the clause "if $D_V(g_5(x))$" in condition (6) can be dropped only in exceptionally rich effective systems.

Remark 6. Since $D_V(x)$ if and only if $g_1(x) = 1$ or $V(\mu x(g_1(x) = 1), x)$, if g_1 is general recursive, then D_V is general recursive in V and functions general recursive in D_V are general recursive in V.

If we use functions $g_1, \cdots, g_5$ general recursive in D_V in the above definition, we get a different class of effective systems.

Quite often we are interested in systems which possess additional attractive properties.

Definition 3. *A well-ordering V is a maximal effective system if it satisfies the above definition when the hypothesis "if $D_V(g_5(x))$" is deleted from (6), i.e., when all increasing recursive sequences have limits.*

To justify this definition, we state the following theorem (Kleene 1938, p. 154):

1.1. If V is a maximal effective system and V' is an arbitrary effective system, every ordinal representable in V' is also representable in V.

The class of ordinals representable in maximal effective systems enjoys, therefore, a measure of stability and is conveniently referred to as the class of recursive ordinals. The least ordinal not in the class is often called ω_1 which is of course smaller than the minimum of the classical third number class.

The most widely used maximal effective system is Kleene's $<_0$.

Definition 4. *The relation $x <_0 y$ holds when $V(x,y)$ holds for all V satisfying the following conditions*: (1) $V(1,2)$; (2) $V(1,x) \rightarrow V(x,2x)$; (3) *if* $V(x,y)$ *and* $V(y,z)$, *then* $V(x,z)$; (4) *if* $(x)\ (Ey)\ T(e,x,y)$ *and* $(x)\ V(e(x),\ e(x+1))$, *then* $V(e(y),3^e)$. $O(x)$ *if and only if* $V(1,2x)$.

Remark 7. There are several minor differences between this and Kleene's original formulation: Kleene uses 2^x instead of $2x$, $3 \cdot 5^e$ instead of 3^e, sequences over all positive integers representing finite ordinals instead of all positive integers, i.e. (4′) if $(x)\ (Ey)\ T(e,2^x,y)$ and $(x)\ V(e(2^x),\ e(2^{x+1}))$, then $V(e(2^y),3^e)$. These inessential modifications seem desirable in view of the wide application of the system since the new formulation simplifies somewhat the notation. The last change requires some comment. If $e(n)$ gives a limit ordinal represented by 3^e by (4′), then $3^{e'}$ represents the same ordinal by (4), where $e'(n)=e(2^n)$; conversely, if 3^e represents an ordinal by (4), $3^{e'}$ represents the same ordinal by (4′) where $e'(n)=e(g(n))$, $g(1)=1$, $g(n+1)=2^{\mu k(2k>n)}$.

A more basic formal difference from Kleene's original definition is the separation of O from $<_0$. As a result, there is no problem here of converting an involved inductive definition to an explicit one. This formulation was introduced in Wang 1957.

Given an effective system, we may wish to require further that there be an effective method for deciding whether two integers represent the same ordinal, and, if not, which represents a greater ordinal. We are led to the following definition:

Definition 5. *A well-ordering V is a strongly effective system of notation for ordinals if it is an effective system and*: (7) *there is a general recursive function $g_6(x,y)$ such that for any x and y, $g_6(x,y)$ is $1,2,3,4,5,6$ according as $x^*=y^*$, $V(x,y)$, $x^*<y^*$, $y^*<x^*$, $V(y,x)$, or either $-D_V(x)$ or $-D_V(y)$.*

§ 2. Strongly Effective Systems

Two other desirable properties are uniqueness of representation and recursiveness of V and D_V. How are they related to condition (7) in the above definition?

2.1. A well-ordering V is a strongly effective system only if it is an effective system such that both V and D_V are general recursive.

Since $D_V(x) \equiv g_6(x,x)=1$ and $V(x,y) \equiv g_6(x,y)=2$.

2.2. If V is a strongly effective system, there is a recursive subset of D_V which contains one and only one representation for each ordinal represented in D_V.

We need only take those members a of D_V such that no integer smaller than a represents the same ordinal as a.

2.3. If V is an effective system and D_V is general recursive, V is recursively enumerable.

Since D_V is general recursive, so are g_1, g_2, g_4, if we give a common new value to all x, $-D_V(x)$. Hence, we can find a (primitive) recursive $P(x,y,n)$ which holds if and only if $D_V(x)$, $D_V(y)$, and (i) $g_1(x)=1$, but $g_1(y) \neq 1$, or (ii) $g_1(y)=2$, $g_2(y)=(n)_0$, and $P(x,(n)_0, (n)_1)$ or $x=(n)_0$, or (iii) $g_1(x)=3$, $g_4(x)=(n)_0$, $\{(n)_0\}(x)_2=(n)_3$, and $P(x,(n)_3,(n)_1)$. But $V(x,y)$ if and only if $(En)\ P(x,y,n)$.

2.4. If V is an effective system such that D_V is general recursive, and no two integers represent the same ordinal, then it is strongly effective.

By Df. 5, we need only find a general recursive $g_6(x,y)$ which is $1,2,5,6$ according as $x^*=y^*$, $V(x,y)$, $V(y,x)$, $-D_V(x)$ or $-D_V(y)$. The definition can be given by cases: $g_6(x,y)=1 \equiv (D_V(x)$ and $D_V(y)$ and $x=y)$, $g_6(x,y)=4 \equiv (-D_V(x) \vee -D_V(y))$; if neither holds, $g_6(x,y)=2$ or 5 according as $(En)\ P(x,y,n)$ or $(En)\ P(y,x,n)$ which is recursive since we can test $P(x,y,1)$, $P(y,x,1)$, $P(x,y,2)$, $P(y,x,2), \cdots$ and always come to a conclusion.

Example 1. A strongly effective system in which $x^*=y^*$ does not imply $x=y$. $1^*=0$, $3^*=0$, $(2x)^*=x^*+1$.

Example 2. An effective system which is not strongly effective but satisfies a weaker condition: (7′) there is a general recursive $g_7(x,y)$ which is $1,2,3$ or 4 according as $x^*=y^*$, $x^*<y^*$, $y^*<x^*$, or either $-D_V(x)$ or $-D_V(y)$. Thus, $1^*=0$, $(2x)^*=x^*+1$, $(3^i)^*=\omega$, $(5^i)^*=\omega 2$, the sequences for 3^i and 5^i be $f(3^i,1)=2i$, $f(3^i,n+1)=2f(3^i,n)$, $f(5^i,1)=3^i, f(5^i,n+1)=2f(5^i,n)$, but $V(2^n 3^i, 5^i)$ holds only when, for all $n, \{i\}\ (n)$ is defined if and only if $\{j\}\ (n)$ is defined. Hence V is not recursive because otherwise we would be able to decide whether a recursive definition defines a general recursive function. This incidentally also is an effective system which has a general recursive D_V but is not strongly effective.

2.5. Given a strongly effective system V, there exists a strongly effective system V' which contains representations for more ordinals.

Define $f(1)=\mu_x D_V(x)$, $f(n+1)=\mu_x(f(n)<x$ and $V(f(n),x))$, we have a recursive sequence whose limit represents an ordinal which

has no representation in D_V. We can then easily define V' by, e.g., taking as $D_{V'}$ the set of numbers x such that there exists y, $D_V(y)$ and $x=3^y$, or $x=2^n$, for any positive n. We can let 2^* be the new limit ordinal and $(2^{n+1})^*$ be 2^*+n.

This last theorem excludes the possibility of a maximum among strongly effective systems of notation for ordinals. This situation contrasts with the class of effective systems which do have maxima containing representations for all and only the recursive ordinals.

It may be thought that a maximal effective system with unique representation for every ordinal must be more complex than $<_0$. It is shown in Spector (1955) (Corollary 3 to Theorem 4) that such a system exists which is recursive in $<_0$ and therefore, in a definite sense, not more complex. We give here a slightly different example with an additional property.

2.6. There is a maximal effective system U such that (i) U is recursive in $<_0$, (ii) every ordinal $\dot{<}\omega_1$, has a unique representation in D_U; (iii) $O(a)\equiv(Ey)(D_U(y)$ and $D_U(y+_0a))$ (for definition of $+_0$, see Kleene 1955a).

An immediate corollary is:

2.7. There is an effective system which has one representation for each ordinal that is represented at all but is not a strongly effective system.

To prove 2.6, we set $a_1=b_1=1$, $a_{n+1}=\mu x(O(x)$ and $a_n<x)$, $b_{n+1}=b_n+_0a_{n+1}$, $D_U(a)\equiv(En)(a<_0b_n)$, $U(x,y)\equiv(D_U(y)$ and $x<_0y)$. By Theorems II and I of Kleene 1955a, $D_U(a)$ is recursive in O and U is recursive in $<_0$. But Kleene has proved: $a<_0a+_0b$ if $O(a)$ and $1<_0b$. Hence, $b_n<_0b_{n+1}$; and no two integers in D_U represent the same ordinal. Obviously, $O(x)\equiv(En)(x=a_n)$ and $\lim a_n^*=\omega_1$. Since $b^*\leqslant(a+_0b)^*$, $a^*\leqslant b^*$, $\lim b_n^*=\omega_1$. Since every member of O is some a_n and D_U is included in O, (iii) follows easily.

By combining 2.6 with Theorem I, Kleene 1955a, a rather arbitrary measure of the complexity of predicates and propositions of the forms $(\alpha)(Ex)R(a,\bar{\alpha}(x))$ and $(\alpha)(Ex)R(\bar{\alpha}(x))$ can be introduced. Thus, for each such predicate $A(a)$, we can find a primitive recursive ξ, $A(a)\equiv O(\xi(a))$.

Define now:

$i(x)=\mu_y(D_U(y)\ \&\ D_U(y+_0x))$,

$j(\hat{a}A(a),a)=i(\xi(a))$,

$j(\hat{a}A(a))=$ (the least upper bound in the ordering U of all values of $j(\hat{a}A(a),a)$).

$j(B)=j(\hat{a}(B\ \&\ a=a),1)$.

In these definitions B is any proposition of the required form, and we arbitrarily take 5 as a notation for ω_1, so that $j(\hat{a}A(a))$ may sometimes get the value 5.

If now we take a second-order predicate calculus based on the natural numbers and include sufficient rules for transforming quantifiers to ensure that every predicate gets a uniform normal form in the analytic hierarchy, we can get an "ordinal logic" by adding an "oracle" rule according to which for each given n, $D_U(n)$ can be written down as a theorem if it happens to be true. In such a "system", all true arithmetical and hyperarithmetical propositions become provable. Thus, for every such proposition B, in normal form, we can prove: $B \equiv D_U(j(B))$. But the right half, if true, is a theorem by the "oracle". In contrast with the cases studied by Turing 1939, invariance with respect to different representations of the same ordinal becomes trivially true, since every B has an order in D_U and every ordinal ω_1 has a unique notation in D_U.

Similarly, we can also give a rather artificial measure of the complexity of general recursive definitions according to the complexity of the proposition stating that the definition does define a general recursive definition, which is always of the form $(x)(Ey)\,R(x,y)$, R recursive. Or alternatively, we can change the definition into an ordinal recursion and consider the member of D_U which corresponds, by some standard correlation, to the recursive well-ordering needed. For example, it has been shown by Myhill 1953 and Routledge 1953 that ordinal recursions with different well-orderings of the order type ω suffice to give all general recursive functions. If we take a customary one-one image, say a, in O of each of the well-orderings, then $i(a)$ may be taken as a measure for the original general recursive definition.

In this connection it may be of interest to remark that we can also introduce directly a system of unique notations for all the recursive ordinals.

Definition 4′. *The system L is the intersection of all transitive relations V such that:* (1) $V(1,2)$; (2) $V(1,x) \rightarrow V(x,2x)$; (3) *if* $(x)(Ey)\,T(e,x,y)$, $(x)\,V(e(x), e(x+1))$, *and for no* f, $f<e$, *is it true that* $V(1,3^f)$ *and* $(m)(En)(Ek)\,V(e(m), f(k))$ *and* $V(f(m),e(n))$, *then* $V(e(z), 3^e)$.

We conclude this section by a few examples of strongly effective systems of notation for ordinals.

Example 3. A system of notation for all ordinals α, $\alpha<\omega^\omega$. $1^*=0$, $(2x)^* = x^* + 1$, $3^* = \lim (2^n)^* = \omega$, $(3^{2x})^* = \lim (2^n 3^x)^* = (3^x)^* + \omega$, if $(3^y)^* = \lim (f(n))^*$, then $(3^{(3y)})^* = \lim (3^{f(n)})^*$. Alternatively, V_3 is the minimal transitive relation satisfying the following conditions:

(1) $V_3(1,2)$, $V_3(1,3)$, (2) if $V_3(x,y)$, then $V_3(y,2y)$, (3) if $V_3(x,3^y)$, then $V_3(2x,3^y)$, (4) if $V_3(x,y)$, then $V_3(3^x,3^y)$. The domain D_3 is defined as $\hat{x}V_3(1,2x)$ or the smallest class satisfying: (1)$D_3(1)$, (2) $D_3(x)\rightarrow D_3(2x)$, (3)$D_3(x)\rightarrow D_3(3^x)$. It can be verified that if an expression x in D_3 contains only occurrences of 3, $(3^{(3^x)})^*=(3^x)^*\omega$. If we prefer a one-dimensional notation, we can write (m,n) instead of 2^m3^n, then 3^3 is $3^{(0,1)}$ or $(0,(0,1))$, $3^{(3^3)}$ is $(0,(0,(0,1)))$. If we verify first $(0,(0,(0,1)))^*=\omega^3$, we see then: $(n,(0,(0,1)))^*=\omega^3+n$, $(0,(n,(0,1)))^*=\omega^3+\omega n$, $(0,(0,(n,1)))^*=\omega^3+\omega^2 n$, $(0,(0,(0,n)))=\omega^3+\omega^3 n$, $(0,(0,(0,(0,1))))^*=\omega^4$.

Example 4. A system of notation for all ordinals α, $\alpha\dot{<}\omega^{(\omega^\omega)}$. The domain D_4 of V_4 is the smallest class satisfying: (1) D_4 (1), $D_4(p_n)$, p_n being the n-th prime, with $p_0=2$, (2) if $D_4(x)$, then D_4 $(2x)$, (3) if $a_1,\cdots,a_n$ are all in D_4 and for every j, a_j contains no part that is a prime greater than p_{i_j}, $0<i_1<\cdots<i_n$, then $D_4(p_{i_1}^{a_1}\cdots p_{i_n}^{a_n})$. $V_4(x,y)$ is the minimal transitive relation satisfying: if $x=2^jp_{r_1}^{a_1}\cdots p_{r_n}^{a_n}$, $y=2^kp_{s_1}^{b_1}\cdots p_{s_m}^{b_m}$, $j,k\geqslant 0$, $m,n\geqslant 0$, $0<r_1<\cdots<r_n$, $0<s_1<\cdots<s_m$, $a_i>0$, $b_i>0$, $D_4(x)$, $D_4(y)$, then $V_4(x,y)$ if either (1) $m=n$, $a_i=b_i$, $r_i=s_i$, and $j<k$, or (2) there exists t, $0\leqslant t<m$, $r_n=s_m$, $a_n=b_m,\cdots,r_{n-t+1}=s_{m-t+1}$, $a_{n-t+1}=b_{m-t+1}$, and (i) $r_{n-t}<s_{m-t}$ or (ii) $r_{n-t}=s_{m-t}$ but $V_4(a_{n-t},b_{n-t})$, or (iii) $t=n$.

Example 5. An extension V_5 of V_4 which uses all positive integers. The domain D_5 is the smallest class such that: (1) $D_5(1)$, (2) if $D_5(x)$, then $D_5(2x)$, (3) $D_5(p_n)$, for $n\geqslant 0$, (4) if $a_1,\cdots,a_n$ are all in D_5, $0<i_1<\cdots<i_n$, then $D_5(p_{i_1}^{a_1}\cdots p_{i_n}^{a_n})$. Different ways of extending V_4 to a V_5 over D_5 are open. The one we choose is as follows. $V_5(x,y)$ is the minimal transitive relation satisfying: (1) if $V_4(x,y)$, then $V_5(x,y)$; (2) if $D_4(x)$ but $-D_4(y)$, then $V_5(x,y)$; (3) if $x=2^jp_r^a$, $y=2^kp_s^b$, then $V_5(x,y)$ if and only if either (i) $p_r^a=p_s^b$, but $j<k$, or (ii) $b=p_r^a$ or $V_5(p_r^a,b)$ or (iii) $V_5(b,p_r^a)$, $a\neq p_s^b$, $-V(p_s^b,a)$, but $r<s$, or $r=s$ and $V_5(a,b)$; (4) if $x'=p_{r_1}^{a_1}\cdots p_{r_n}^{a_n}$, $y'=p_{s_1}^{b_1}\cdots p_{s_m}^{b_m}$, $x=2^jx'$, $y=2^ky'$, $V_5(p_{r_i}^{a_i},p_{r_{i+1}}^{a_{i+1}})$, $V_5(p_{r_i}^{b_i},p_{r_{i+1}}^{b_{i+1}})$, then $V_5(x,y)$ if and only if either (i) $x'=y'$, $j<k$, or (ii) there is an i, $0\leqslant i<m$, $a_n=b_m$, $r_n=s_m,\cdots$, $a_{n-i+1}=b_{m-i+1}$, $r_{n-i+1}=s_{m-i+1}$ and $V_5(p_{r_{n-i}}^{a_{n-i}},p_{s_{n-i}}^{b_{n-i}})$ or $i=n$.

Example 6. A system of notation for all ordinals α, $\alpha<\varepsilon_0$. The domain D_6 and the ordering V_6 are such that: $1^*=0$, $2^*=1$. $(2^2)^*=\omega$, $a^*+1=(3^b)^*$ if $a=2^b$, $a^*=(2^{a_1})^*+1+\cdots+(2^{a_m})^*$ if $a=p_1^{a_1}\cdots p_m^{a_m}$ and $-V_6(a_i,a_{i+1})$, $a^*+1=(ap_{m+1})^*$ if $a=p_1^{a_1}\cdots p_m^{a_m}$, $(2^b)^*=(2^a)^*\omega$ if $b^*=a^*+1$, hence, $(2^{(2^2)})^*=\omega^\omega$, etc. More exactly, D_6 and V_6 are the smallest set and transitive relation such that: (1) $D_6(1)$, $V_6(1,2)$; (2) if $D_6(a)$, then $D_6(2^a)$; (3) if, for every i, $D_6(a_i)$ and $-V_6(a_i,a_{i+1})$, then $D_6(p_1^{a_1}\cdots p_n^{a_n})$ and $V_6(2^{a_1},p_1^{a_1}\cdots p_n^{a_n})$; (4) if $D_6(p_1^{a_1}\cdots p_n^{a_n})$ and $D_6(p_1^{b_1}\cdots p_m^{b_m})$, then $V_6(p_1^{a_1}\cdots p_n^{a_n},p_1^{b_1}\cdots p_m^{b_m})$ if and only if there exists

$i, 0 \leqslant i < m$, $a_1 = b_1, \cdots, a_i = b_i$, and either $i = n$ or $V_6(a_{i+1}, b_{i+1})$; (5) if $V_6(a_1, b)$ and $D_6(p_1^{a_1} \cdots p_n^{a_n})$, then $V_6(p^{a_1} \cdots p^{a_n}, 2^b)$. In this system, by (3) and (5), if $V_6(a, b)$, then $V_5(2^a, 2^b)$; by (3), $p_1^{a_1} \cdots p_n^{a_n}$ represents an ordinal only if every a_i is a notation of 1 or a limit ordinal.

Example 7. If we use, for limit ordinals, not only powers of 2, but powers of all p_{2n}, $n \geqslant 0$, we get a system essentially the same as the representation studied in Ackermann 1951 and Schütte 1954. We have again: $1^* = 0$, $2^* = 1$. But $(p_1^{b_1} \cdots p_m^{b_m})^* = b_1^* + 1 + b_2^* + b_3^* + \cdots + b_m^*$, $(3^a)^* = a^* + 1$ if a^* is 1 or a limit ordinal, $(ap_{2m+1}^2)^* = a^* + 1$ if $a = p_1^{b_1} \cdots p_{2m-1}^{b_m}$, $(2^b p_{2t_2}^{a_2} \cdots p_{2t_n}^{a_n})^* = c^* \omega$, if $c = 2^{a_1} p_{2t_2}^{a_2} \cdots p_{2t_n}^{a_n}$ and $c^* = b^* + 1$. The additional complication is to order the notations for limit ordinals. The domain D_7 and the ordering V_7 are the smallest set and transitive relation such that: (1) $D_7(1)$, $V_7(1,2)$; (2) if $D_7(a_1), \cdots, D_7(a_n)$, $n > 0$, $t_i < t_{i+1}$, then $D_7(p_{2t_1}^{a_1} \cdots p_{2t_n}^{a_n})$; (3) if $b_1, \cdots, b_m$ are in D_7 each of the form in (2), and $-V_7(b_i, b_{i+1})$, then $V_7(b_i, p_1^{b_1} \cdots p_{2m-1}^{b_m})$, for every j; (4) if $D_7(p_1^{a_1} \cdots p_{2m-1}^{a_m})$ and $D_7(p_1^{b_1} \cdots p_{2n-1}^{b_n})$, then $V_7(p_1^{a_1} \cdots p_{2m-1}^{a_m}, p_1^{b_1} \cdots p_{2n-1}^{b_n})$ if and only if there exists an i, $0 \leqslant i < n$, $a_1 = b_1, \cdots, a_i = b_i$, and either $i = m$ or $V_7(a_{i+1}, b_{i+1})$; (5) if $D_7(c)$, $D_7(d)$, $c = p_1^{a_1} \cdots p_{2m-1}^{a_m}$, and $d = p_{2t_1}^{b_1} \cdots p_{2t_n}^{b_n}$, then $V_7(c, d)$ if and only if $V_7(a_1, d)$; (6) if $c = p_{2s_1}^{a_1} \cdots p_{2s_n}^{a_n}$, $d = p_{2t_1}^{b_1} \cdots p_{2t_m}^{b_m}$, $D_7(c)$, $D_7(d)$, then $V_7(c, d)$ if and only if either (i) there exists an i, $1 \leqslant i \leqslant m$, $b_i = c$ or $V_7(c, b_i)$, or (ii) there exists no i, $a_i = d$ or $V_7(d, a_i)$, but there exists j, $0 \leqslant j < m$, such that $t_m = s_n$, $b_m = a_n, \cdots, t_{m-j+1} = s_{n-j+1}$, $b_{m-j+1} = a_{n-j+1}$, and either (iia) $s_{n-j} < t_{m-j}$, or (iib) $s_{n-j} = t_{m-j}$ but $V_7(a_{n-j}, b_{m-j})$, or (iic) $j = n$.

§ 3. The Church-Kleene Class B and a New Class C

The system O of notation by Church and Kleene suggests a general pattern relative to any enumerable class of functions from positive integers to positive integers.

Definition 6. *A normal system of notation for ordinals based on an enumerable class of functions $f_1, f_2, \cdots$ from positive integers to positive integers is a well-ordering V which is the smallest transitive relation such that (1) $V(1,2)$, (2) if $V(1,x)$ then $V(x,2x)$, (3) if $(n)(Em)\, f_i(n) = m$ and $(n)\, V(f_i(n), f_i(n+1))$, then $(n)\, V(f_i(n), 3^i)$. Or alternatively, (1) $1^* = 0$, (2) $(2x)^* = x^* + 1$, (3) if $f_i(n)$ is defined for every n, and $V(f_i(n), f_i(n+1))$, then $(3^i)^* = \lim(f_i(n))^*$.*

For example, the class of functions could be all analytic functions in the sense of Kleene 1955b, or all functions from positive integers to positive integers expressible in Zermelo's set theory, or all functions general recursive in a given set A of positive integers, or all Herbrand recursive functions.

Similarly, we can also generalize the class of well-orderings studied by Turing, Markwald and Spector to define, for any class of functions $f_1(x,y)$, $f_2(x,y)$,$\cdots$ from positive integers to positive integers, the subclass of those f_i's which are well-orderings. For example, one can define the class of all well-orderings of the form $(\alpha)(Ex)\ R(a,b,\alpha,x)$, that of the form $(\alpha)\ (E\beta)\ (x)\ R(a,b,\alpha,\beta,x)$, and so on. Gödel numbers of these well-orderings form of course again sets of integers, the predicate forms of which might be of interest.

As an analogue to the identification of effectively calculable with general recursive functions we may wish to identify the Herbrand recursive (Gödel 1934, p. 26) with the effectively *definable* functions. The Herbrand recursive functions agree with the general recursive functions in that they are all defined by finite sets of equations of the same abstract form. They differ from the latter in that we merely require the existence of a unique function satisfying the equations but there is no demand that the value for each constant argument be derivable or calculable from the equations.

For example, $f(x)=2f(x+1)$ is an Herbrand recursive definition but not a general recursive definition, although the function defined is simply the constant function $f(x)=0$. The following definition by Kreisel defines an Herbrand recursive function f which is not general recursive, since $f(m,0)=0$ if and only if $(x)-T(m,m,x)$.

$$\begin{cases} f(m,n) = g(m,n,f(m,n+1)), \\ g(m,n,k) = 1 \equiv (Ex)(x \leqslant n \,\&\, T(m,m,x)), \\ g(m,n,k) = 2k \equiv -(Ex)(x \leqslant n \,\&\, T(m,m,x)). \end{cases}$$

One can also add parameters and reiterate this definition to show that all arithmetic functions are Herbrand recursive. Indeed, Addison, Gregorczyk-Mostowski-Ryll-Nardzewski, Kuznekov all prove that much more is true:

3.1. A function is Herbrand recursive if and only if it is represented by a hyperarithmetic predicate.

Hence, by Spector 1955, Theorem 6, it is possible to prove:

3.2. If in the definition of O and ω, we use Herbrand recursive functions instead of general recursive functions, we obtain the same upper bound ω_1.

Given, for example, the system O of ordinal notations, it would seem that we can further extend it by considering recursive functions which represent increasing sequences of order type ω_1 and get new systems of ordinal notations without appeal to the unrestricted notion of "all" possible sequences of a given ordinal type such as is common in the development of classical ordinals. The difficulty is to find natural stopping places in such further extensions.

The general pattern of extending a given system V with domain D_V (call it the a-th number class) to the next number class is exhibited in the following definition:

Definition 7. *The well-ordering P for the next number class is the minimum transitive relation such that:* (i) $V(x,y) \rightarrow P(x,y)$; (ii) $P(1,x) \rightarrow P(x,2x)$; (iii) *if* $V(c, 2a)$, D_c *is the c-th number class defined by* V_c, *for all x in* D_c, $(Ey)(f_i(x)=y)$ *and for all x, y in* D_c, $V_c(x,y) \rightarrow P(f_i(x), f_i(y))$, *then for all x in* D_c, $P(f_i(x), 3^i 5^c 7^a)$.

In particular, if we take $<_0$ as the given V, we can replace both i and f_i by e, an arbitrary (Gödel number of a) general recursive function.

Clearly the extension can be continued and we can even take union after making an infinite number of such extensions. There, however, has to be some control over the procedure of taking unions because we may fail to notice certain infinite sequences of extensions and we obtain no definiteness unless we have some preassigned way of keeping track of our extensions. If we use an analogue with Cantor's classical number classes and speak of F (the ordering of integers 2^n), O, P respectively as the first, second, and third number classes, we see that we can introduce an a-th constructive number class for any constructive ordinal notation a already introduced. Every constructive number class is, however, enumerable, and we could speak of their having different cardinalities only if we were to redefine cardinalities by restricting one-one correlations to suitable special kinds.

By appeal to the classical second number class, Church and Kleene define in their paper of 1937 (pp. 20—21), by induction, a class B of constructive ordinals. If we use general recursive functions instead of the λ-symbolism, their definition can be stated as follows.

We define by transfinite induction over the classical second number class a set of rules of representation:

Rule 0: (i) 1 represents the ordinal 0; (ii) if a represents the ordinal α, then $2a$ represents the successor of α.

Given Rule γ, for every γ, $\gamma \in \alpha$, we have:

Rule α: (i), (ii) and (iiiα): If (1) ι_α is the least ordinal a positive integer to represent which is not assigned by any Rule $\gamma (\gamma < \alpha)$; (2) $e(x)$ is a general recursive function (with Gödel number e), such that for all x and y, if the ordinal represented by x is less than that by y (according to any Rule γ_1, $(\gamma_1 < \alpha)$), the ordinal represented by $e(x)$ is less than that represented by $e(y)$ (according to any Rule γ, $\gamma < \alpha$ or $\gamma = \alpha$); and (3) a, c represent, α, γ_1 by some Rule γ, $(\gamma < \alpha)$:

then $3^e5^c7^a$ represents the limit β of the sequence of order type ι_{γ_1} represented by the function $e(x)$.

3.3. The class R of rules is given by: (1) Rule 0 belongs to R; (2) for every α, if for all $\gamma, \gamma < \alpha$, Rule γ belongs to R, then Rule α belongs to R; (3) for all α, Rule α belongs to R only as required by (1) and (2).

Definition 8. *A positive integer a belongs to the class B of ordinal notations if and only if there exist two ordinals β and α such that a represents β by Rule α and Rule α belongs to R.*

By the rules in R, a same ordinal may, in general, get infinitely many different representations. Although here we have one rule for each ordinal, when we define the class B without appeal to classical ordinals, we get one rule for each notation. Since one of our purposes is to increase our understanding of classical ordinals by constructive ordinals, it seems desirable to define the class B without explicit use of classical ordinals.

For this purpose, we use an inductive definition of B which deals only with positive integers and their classes. At the same time, if in Definition 7, we replace not only i and f_i by e, but (Ey) $(f_i(x)=y)$ by (Ey) $T^{D_e}(e,x,y)$, then we get a method of extension which would lead to the class C.

We introduce a few simple abbreviations.

3.5. $L(b,e,X,P)$ is the conjunction of:

3.5.1. $(x)(Ey)(X(b,1,2x) \rightarrow e(x)=y)$.

3.5.2. $(x)(y)(X(b,x,y) \rightarrow P(e(x),e(y)))$.

3.6. $N(u,X,P)$ is the conjunction of:

3.6.1. $(y)(P(1,y) \rightarrow P(y,2y))$.

3.6.2. P is transitive.

3.6.3. $(x)(y)(X([u/2],x,y) \rightarrow P(x,y))$.

3.6.4. $(b)(e)(x)((X([u/2],b,u)$ & $L(b,e,X,P)) \rightarrow P(e(x), 3^e5^b7^u))$.

3.7. $K(u,X,P)$ is the conjunction of 3.6.1, 3.6.2, and:

3.7.3. $(b)(d)(k)((X((u)_1,k,2k)$ & $X((u)_0(k),b,d)) \rightarrow P(b,d))$.

3.7.4. $(b)(e)(x)((X((u)_2,b,u)$ & $L(b,e,X,P,)) \rightarrow P(e(x),3^e5^b7^u))$.

3.8. $F(x,y)$ is the natural ordering of all positive integers which are powers of 2 (i.e., all notations of finite ordinals).

Definition 9. *The class B is $\hat{y}(Eu)D(u,1,2y)$, where $D(u,v,w)$ is true if and only if $X(u,v,w)$ holds for all X which satisfy the following conditions:*

$B1.\quad (u)(v)(w)(u=1\rightarrow(X(u,v,w)\equiv F(v,w)))$.

$B2.\quad (u)(v)(w)(a)(u=2a\rightarrow(X(u,v,w)\equiv(P)(N(u,X,P)\rightarrow P(v,w))))$.

$B3.\quad (u)(v)(w)(f)(c)(a)(u=3^f5^c7^a\rightarrow(X(u,v,w)\equiv(P)(K(u,X,P)\rightarrow P(v,w))))$.

From this definition, one arrives immediately at the following theorem by standard methods of transforming quantifiers.

Theorem 1. *There exists a primitive recursive predicate R such that* $B(a)\equiv(\alpha)(E\beta)(x)R(a,\bar{\alpha}(x),\bar{\beta}(x))$.

Except for one difference, the above definition and theorem were given in Wang 1957. The difference is that $B3$ was replaced there by a simpler condition:

$B3'.\quad x=3^f5^c7^a\rightarrow(X(x,y,z)\equiv(Ek)(X(c,k,2k)\ \&\ X(f(k),y,z)))$.

In classical analogy, the simpler definition confines one to ordinals which precede the least ordinal α such that $\alpha=$aleph α. The present definition is more faithful to the original Church-Kleene definition. This fact was recently pointed out by Kreider and Rogers in correspondence. They have examined the matter further, given and justified two related definitions rigorously, and proved a stronger theorem to the effect that B is also expressible in the form $(E\beta)(\alpha)(Ex)$ $S(a,\bar{\beta}(x),\bar{\alpha}(x))$. The writer does not know a proof that B cannot be expressed in the form $(\alpha)(Ex)R(a,\bar{\alpha}(x))$. Indeed, the writer had at first an erroneous proof that B can be so expressed. It was argued that $\equiv$ can be replaced by $\leftarrow$ in $B2$ and $B3$. Rogers pointed out that in such a definition, the intersection need no longer satisfy the conditions.

The class C with relative recursiveness can be treated similarly as B.

3.9. $L^*(b,e,X,P)$ is the conjunction of $L(b,e,X,P)$ and:

3.9.3. $(M)((z)(M(z)\equiv X(b,(z)_1,(z)_2))\rightarrow(x)(y)(T^M(e,x,y)\equiv e(x)=y))$.

3.10. $N^*(u,X,P)$ is obtained from $N(u,X,P)$ by dropping 3.6.3 and replacing $L(b,e,X,P)$ in 3.6.4 by $L^*(b,e,X,P)$.

3.11. $K^*(u,X,P)$ is obtained from $K(u,X,P)$ by substituting L^* for L in 3.7.4.

Definition 10. *The class C is* $\hat{y}(Eu)\,D^*(u,1,2y)$, *where* D^* *is defined as D with* N^* *and* K^* *replacing N and K in B2 and B3.*

It will be clear that the additional quantifier (M) can be combined with the quantifier (P) at both places in the new definition. Hence, one again has a similar theorem.

Theorem 2. *There exists a primitive recursive predicate S such that* $C(a) \equiv (\alpha)(E\beta)(x) S(a, \bar{\alpha}(x), \bar{\beta}(x))$.

§ 4. Partial Herbrand Recursive Functions

An Herbrand recursive definition is essentially a recursive condition $R(\bar{\alpha}(n))$ such that there is a unique function α_0 which satisfies R for all n. Naturally, we can also use, instead of a recursive condition, say an arithmetic or hyperarithmetic condition, and speak of Herbrand arithmetic and Herbrand hyperarithmetic definitions. Since, however, on account of the equivalence of hyperarithmetic with Herbrand recursive, a predicate is Herbrand recursive if and only if it is of both 1 function-quantifier forms, the class of Herbrand arithmetic or of hyperarithmetic predicates is the same as that of Herbrand recursive ones. In general, we can easily prove the following statement:

4.1. If an arbitrary quantifier-free condition $C(\bar{\alpha}(n))$ with a unique solution α_0 contains only predicates expressible in both n function-quantifier forms, then the predicate $\alpha_0(a)=0$ is also expressible in both n function-quantifier forms.

Proof. By choosing suitable forms for all predicates in C and then taking quantifiers to the beginning and contracting, the condition can also be expressed in both n function-quantifier forms. But

$$\alpha_0(a) = 0 \equiv (E\alpha)((n)C(\bar{\alpha}(n)) \,\&\, \alpha(a) = 0)$$
$$\equiv (\alpha)((n)C(\bar{\alpha}(n)) \rightarrow \alpha(a) = 0).$$

The gap between general recursive and Herbrand recursive functions is big. One may wonder whether there are natural intermediate classes of functions not based on the hyperarithmetic hierarchy. The following notion of semi-recursive seems not unnatural.

4.2. Let $B(e,x,y)$ be $(w)A(e,x,y,w)$ and $A(e,x,y,w)$ be an abbreviation of the recursive condition that e is a set of recursive equations containing a function variable f, y is $x+1$ equations

$$f(0) = a_0, \cdots, f(x) = a_x,$$

$a_0, \cdots, a_x$ being numerals, and if w is a derivation (as in general recursive definitions) from e plus y, then the conclusion is not an equality between two distinct numerals.

Definition 11. *A set of equations e is a semi-recursive definition if for every x, there exists a y such that* (i) $B(e,x,y)$; (ii) *for all z distinct from y, if* $B(e,x,z)$, *then there exist u greater than x and v an extension of z with* $u+1$ *equations* $f(0)=b_0, \cdots, f(u)=b_u$ *such that* $B(e,u,v)$ *does not hold. A function is semi-recursive if it is definable by a finite number of semi-recursive definitions. The notion of "semi-recursive in" can also be intro-*

duced in a similar manner as "recursive in", except that one has to require explicitly that any finite number of successive applications of the scheme is permissible.

It can be verified that the predicate "e is semi-recursive" is of the form $(x)(Ey)(z)(Ew)R(e, x, y, z, w)$, with R recursive.

Theorem 3. *Every semi-recursive definition has a unique solution.*

Proof. Condition (ii) assures uniqueness. By (i) and (ii) together, there is for every x a unique segment up to x which is indefinitely expandable. The union of these segments must be a solution, i.e., $(n)R(\bar{f}_0(n))$ is true where R is the given set of equations and f_0 is the union. If $R(\bar{f}_0(n_0))$ is not true, then since it can be changed into a numerical formula merely by substitutions, an equality between two distinct numerals must be derivable from it and therefore from $(n)R(\bar{f}(n))$ plus the auxiliary equations for $f(0)$ to $f(n_0)$.

Observe that (i) alone is not sufficient to assure existence of solution. For example, $f(n)=2f(n+1)$, $f(0)\neq 0$ together satisfy (i) but have no solution.

4.3. Every general recursive function is semi-recursive. Every semi-recursive definition is a partial recursive definition but not conversely.

The first assertion is obvious. The two halves of the second assertion are seen as follows: the solution of a semi-recursive definition must include all actually derivable values so that consistency is assured; e.g., the partial recursive definition $f(0)=1$, $f(x+2)=2f(x)$ is not semi-recursive.

The more interesting notion for studying predicative definitions is partial Herbrand recursive functions. For example, the predicates O and $<_0$ are partial Herbrand recursive. Indeed, the very notion is introduced with a view to characterize such predicates and their definitions.

Definition 12. *An arbitrary recursive condition $R(\bar{\alpha}(n))$ is a partial Herbrand recursive definition if the partial function α_0 such that*

$$\alpha_0(a) = b \equiv (\alpha)((n)\ R(\bar{\alpha}(n)) \rightarrow \alpha(a) = b)$$

satisfies the condition, i.e., $(n)R(\bar{\alpha}_0(n))$ is true. This is the function defined by the definition. A function is partial Herbrand recursive if it is defined by a partial Herbrand recursive definition or by a succession of partial Herbrand recursive definitions. The notion of "partial Herbrand recursive in" can also be defined by allowing function variables to occur in the defining conditions.

Thus, since every arithmetic predicate or hyperarithmetic predicate is partial Herbrand recursive, we can use arithmetic or hyperarithmetic, instead of recursive conditions. Hence, for example, $<_0$ is partial Herband recursive, and all predicates of the form $(\alpha)(Ex)R(a, \bar{\alpha}(x))$ are partial Herbrand recursive. Given a quantifier-free condition in which all predicates are of both 2 function-quantifier forms, the condition itself is also of both forms. But $(\alpha)((n)(\beta)C \to D)$ may be changed to $(\alpha)(En)(E\beta)(C \to D)$. Hence, by Addison-Kleene 1957, formula (1), we have:

4.4. Every partial Herbrand recursive predicate is of both 2 function-quantifier forms.

It is also possible to use examples of Addison-Kleene to show that there are partial Herbrand recursive predicates which are of higher hyperdegree than O. This also shows that, unlike partial recursive functions, not every succession of partial Herbrand recursive definitions can be replaced by a single one.

The interest of partial Herbrand predicates for the study of predicative definitions comes from a belief that if predicates occurring explicitly in an inductive definition are predicative, then the predicate determined by the inductive definition is also predicative. Yet the simplest way to characterize those conditions which are indeed inductive definitions seems precisely the requirement that the intersection of all sets satisfying the condition also satisfies the condition and is in fact the desired set. Thus, an inductive definition is nothing but a condition with the stipulation that all objects satisfying the condition belongs to the set and that an object belongs to the set only if it is positively required to do so by the condition.

This would seem to lead us to the conclusion that all partial Herbrand recursive predicates are predicative. Yet there may be other arguments against the assumption that inductive definitions from given material are always predicatively acceptable. There is also the problem of iterating the partial recursive schema an infinite number of times. We turn to these questions in connection with a general discussion of the notion of predicativity.

§ 5. Predicative Set Theory

Richard's solution of the Richard paradox led Poincaré to a statement of the vicious-circle principle which was heavily used by Russell. Their rather inexact general explanation of the apparently natural principle is open to various interpretations. It, therefore, seems necessary to make explicit the many conflicting choices which one is able to make without contradicting the basic vicious-circle principle.

5.1. The vicious-circle principle: if, provided a certain collection had a total, it would have members only definable in terms of that total, then the said collection has no total (Whitehead and Russell, p. 37); or, briefly, no totality can contain members definable only in terms of this totality.

Instead of the phrase "definable only in terms of", Russell also speaks of "involving" and "presupposing". It is pointed out in Gödel 1944 that these different versions are not equivalent for one who thinks of classes as pluralities existing independently of our knowledge and definitions. He would say that there are acceptable definitions which, though violating 5.1, do not violate the alternative formulations. It seems, however, clear that the original intention is to deal with definitions (intensions) rather than entities (like Cantor) or proofs (like Brouwer). That is why Russell regarded the different formulations as equivalent. For our present purpose, it seems best to adhere to 5.1.

On the other hand, there is also a sense in which one is concerned with objects rather than definitions. This is seen from the qualification of "in terms of" by "only". In other words, the principle is directed to the introduction of new objects. Once a range has been satisfactorily introduced, there is no objection against using an impredicative characterization to identify or select an object in the domain. For example, if we assume the totality of all positive integers given, there is no objection against using the least number operator to specify a principle of selection from the given totality; or, if we assume a class of real numbers given, there is no objection against speaking of a maximum of the class.

Impredicative characterizations are objected to not just as such but only as a means for initially introducing an object. One does not object to using in a proposed characterization bound variables whose predetermined range contains any object which may satisfy the characterization, but only to conditions which propose to introduce new objects and yet make use of bound variables which contain the objects to be introduced. In the latter case, the range of the variables are not yet determined at the time and may be affected by the definition itself or others, yet to be introduced, which depend on it. There is then a circle involved in the process of determining the range of the variable: the range of the variable depends on the constitution of the object (usually a set) to be introduced by the condition, but the structure of the object in turn depends on the range of the variables. Principle 5.1 rejects certain uses of bound variables, viz., those whose range contains members which are definable only by using these bound variables. This is equivalent to saying that bound variables can only be used in the introduction of some new object when their range is already determined at the time. That means, the range must not change with the introduction of new objects. In other words, new objects are only to be introduced stage by stage without disturbing the arrangement of things already introduced or depending for determinedness on objects yet to be introduced at a later stage.

Recently Hintikka 1956 suggests that there are two nonequivalent vicious-circle principles, a weaker one by Russell and a stronger one by Poincaré. The weaker one is interpreted to mean that bound variables are permissible in a condition introducing a new object x as long as x itself does not belong to their range. This amusing interpretation seems to be based on a strenuous misunderstanding. According to the literally quoted 5.1 given above, it is clear that if the constitution of x depends on the range, then not only the range must not contain x itself, but it must not contain anything definable only in terms of x either. Thus, in Hintikka's proposed theory, any condition Fy can define a set x of all objects distinct from x and satisfying Fy, provided only all bound variables in Fy are restricted by the clause "distinct from x". Hintikka himself and others have since shown the inconsistency of the principle. The following simple argument would both establish the inconsistency and bring out the point that his principle does violate the vicious-circle principle. Let ιy be the unit class of y, $\breve{\iota} y$ be z if ιz is y and the empty class otherwise. Then the set K defined by:

$$y \neq K \rightarrow (y \epsilon K \equiv (z)(z \neq K \rightarrow (y = \iota z \rightarrow y \notin \breve{\iota} z)))$$

leads to the contradiction $\iota\iota K \epsilon K \equiv \iota\iota K \notin K$. The source of the trouble is that, although z cannot be K itself, it can be, for example, ιK which is definable only in terms of K.

There, however, remains the basic question as to how ranges are to be used, what kind of definition is permissible in introducing ranges or totalities, what the basic stuff are, and how we are to put new objects together into an acceptable new range. Poincaré, Weyl, Lorenzen do not hesitate to use the God-given natural numbers and definitions by mathematical induction, while Russell persisted in his desire to get numbers out of sets even after he had adopted the "no class theory" towards sets. Before turning to the central question of permissible definitions, a brief review of the positive attempts to build mathematics on a predicative basis is in order.

Russell's well-known theory of types is a complex mixture of doctrines from various sources. Even though the axiom of infinity is only very reluctantly made use of and then as a hypothesis only, and natural numbers must be defined as complicated sets, yet Russell felt no hesitation in using numbers as indices of types and orders. Mixing of types is forbidden on the ground that otherwise we would get meaningless propositions. This does not follow from the vicious-circle principle since given a total of objects and a total of sets of these objects, the vicious-circle is not violated if we merge the two totals into one and use variables ranging over the larger new total. What Russell does is to stipulate a usage of the word "meaningful" so that, e.g., "the set of all positive integers is a positive integer" is not false (though meaningful) but meaningless. The arguments "from direct inspection" (Whitehead-Russell, p. 48) seems to be based on a confusion between ϕx and $\phi \hat{x}$. The former has an ambiguity to be eliminated and cannot meaningfully be used as the subject of a proposition, but not the latter. Thus, it seems there are at least two points on which one need not follow Russell in using the predicative approach: we are assuming natural numbers when we employ them as indices and if we have obtained other ordinal numbers as well, there is no conclusive logical reason why we should stop at natural number indices; if it turns out to be more convenient to mix types, neither the vicious-circle principle nor the matter of "functional ambiguity" is in a position to prevent this.

In Russell 1925, an attempt is made to derive mathematical induction from his ramified type theory. An error in the derivation is pointed out in Gödel 1944. Indeed, it is easy to give a proof that what Russell tried to do cannot be done since induction with regard to higher order sets can characterize lower order sets completely and therefore no finite number of orders can give the induction principle for all orders. But one can get mathematical induction with the help of an axiom of groundedness (the Fundierungsaxiom) which ought to be true for the predicative sets anyhow.

One thing quite definite in Russell's construction is that he is always willing to accept what might be called "immediate predicative extensions". Given any set of objects and any set of predicates of the objects, he is willing to accept all sets $\hat{x}Fx$ where x ranges over the given domain of objects and F is any formula obtained from the given predicates by truth-functional combinations and bound variables ranging over the domain of the given objects.

In Weyl 1918, natural numbers are taken as initially given and sets of them, sets of sets of them are introduced in the same manner up to every finite level. But Weyl permits only bound variables over natural numbers but none over sets. Weyl argues that otherwise one would get real numbers of different orders and the resulting analysis would be "artificial and impracticable", it would "lose sight of its proper object of inquiry, namely natural numbers". It seems highly plausible that Weyl's choice was a wise one. If the alternatives are to use either Weyl's theory or the wider theory permitting bound variables over sets, Weyl's would appear to use a more natural stopping place. For example, the least upper bound gets a natural weakened version dealing with all sequences of real numbers rather than sets of them, while the alternative approach would immediately give a feeling of unfinished structure and invite further extensions.

Such an extension is carried out in Lorenzen 1951 with the interesting remark that, for example, if we take the union of all real numbers of finite orders and the union of all sets of finite orders of them, then the least upper bound of any bounded set in the second union is always in the first union. This appears at first sight to solve the main difficulties in developing classical analysis from a predicative approach, but in fact it raises many inevitable new questions. Lorenzen's treatment is presented in an "operative" framework containing many stimulating facets which the writer finds hard to evaluate. In Wang 1954, a related development is sketched as an independent approach to foundations obtained more or less entirely from the tradition of axiomatic set theory. Kreisel and Schütte have remarked that the two developments are essentially similar, while others have found the more conventional scheme of the latter work more congenial. Perhaps on account of the radical differences in formal details, no thorough comparison of the two related ways has been made. Perhaps such a comparison is not necessary, especially since both seem to face yet unsolved central problems which appear to be fundamentally difficult.

The main difference from Russell's theory is the willingness to use transfinite indices of orders and levels. But there is then naturally the question how far one is permitted to go. It will not do tc say that we do not care on the ground that any limit ordinal would more or less suffice to leave classical analysis intact, and we are very much at home with a number of small limit ordinals. In so far as the choice of ordinals remains arbitrary, there is yet no theory to speak of. Non-conclusive discussions of this question are included in Wang 1954, Lorenzen 1955, and Lorenzen 1958.

In Wang 1954 (p. 261), it is suggested that certainly all the Church-Kleene recursive ordinals are permissible so that one can begin with the empty set or the set of natural numbers, make immediate predicative extension at every successor recursive ordinal, take union at every limit recursive ordinal. It is then suggested that we should also permit all ordinals which are order types of relations in the theory thus obtained which happen to be well-orderings and that this process can be reiterated. The writer believed at that time that in this way one must get much more than the recursive ordinals. This turns out to be wrong since Theorem 6 of Spector 1955 gives the surprising result that no ordinals beyond the recursive ones are obtained in this way. Hence, in so far as this particular way of extension is concerned, the question is settled. But the writer now feels that there are other ways of extension which cannot be excluded on the basis of the vicious-circle principle alone and therefore prefers to call the theory of ramified types with all and only recursive ordinals as indices the "hyperarithmetic set theory". There are many other attractive features in this theory and we shall return to it later on.

There is a distinction between free and bound variables, familiar today through the interest in recursive functions and proof theory, which seems to have been overlooked in the classical explanation of the vicious-circle principle. Thus, the distinction between a recursive and an arithmetic predicate is conspicuous today. According to Russell, a predicate presupposes the range of its argument values so that a recursive and an arbitrary arithmetic predicate equally presuppose the totality of natural numbers. Yet one would feel inclined to say nowadays that recursive predicates do not presuppose the totality of all natural numbers or at least do not presuppose it in the same way as nonrecursive predicates. Even if one's notion of predicativity is so narrow that there is no way of proving the set of natural numbers predicative, it still seems natural to suppose that recursive sets of arbitrary objects obtained from some finite number of simple objects such as the Eiffel Tower or the empty set by recursive procedures, are predicative. But the writer believes that this distinction is quite foreign to the spirit of the vicious-circle principle, it is a refinement that can only be brought out by more strongly constructive notions. Attempts to assimilate predicativity with computability at the present stage are more likely to generate confusion than assist synthesis. After all, the set of natural numbers can easily be got from one object by one effective operation, and then what is there in the vicious-circle principle to prevent us from quantifying over all natural numbers?

In striving for purity, we may wish to begin with the empty set and build up all finite sets based on it by the principle that given x and y, we can take the union of x with the unit set of y. We would wish to say that all these finite sets are predicative. But how do we continue to get infinite sets? Indeed, how do we see at once that we can get all these finite sets as against just some finite number of them, unless we are willing to accept some form of inductive characterization? Poincaré, Weyl, Lorenzen are quite explicit in their readiness to use inductive definitions while Russell's reluctance lands him into the artificial difficulty of the axiom of infinity. But when inductive definitions are converted into explicit ones by the Frege-Dedekind method, the results are definitely impredicative. The methods of Zermelo, Grelling, and Bernays avoid the axiom of infinity, that is, uses only the assumption there are infinitely many sets but not the assumption there is an infinite set, or uses quantification over all finite sets but not quantification over all infinite sets of these finite sets. Still the totality of all finite sets has to be presupposed. Since we have no wish to confine ourselves to some fixed number of finite sets, there seems no escape from accepting inductive definitions as a legitimate means of introducing new ranges and new sets.

This relaxation can be achieved in two verbally different ways. We may either restrict ourselves to the use of explicit definitions only and supplement 5.1 by a positive principle to permit inductive definitions, or, since there is no stated commitment to explicit definitions in the vicious-circle principle, we may permit implicit definitions which can be seen to be unobjectionable by our "light of nature" no matter what they become when turned into explicit definitions. There then remains the problem of characterizing the class of acceptable implicit definitions. Or, if we make bold to identify it with the class of inductive definitions, we should give an exact determination of this latter class.

We are now faced with a choice from at least the following classes: the primitive recursive definitions, the general recursive ones, the Herbrand recursive or Herbrand arithmetic ones, and the partial Herbrand recursive ones. It happens that if we use any of the first three classes and permit to use as indices any ordinal which is the order type of an acceptable relation which happens to be a well-ordering, we get the same theory, viz., the hyperarithmetic set theory. We can therefore confine ourselves to compare the merits and demerits of using the Herbrand arithmetic definitions versus the use of the partial Herbrand recursive definitions. As was observed above, successive applications of the latter type of definition give a broader class of predicates. If now we use any arithmetic conditions but allow each time only a single application of the partial Herbrand schema, then we get a class broader than the Herbrand arithmetic but narrower than the partial Herbrand recursive, containing exactly the predicates expressible in the form $(\alpha)(Ex)R(a,\bar{\alpha}(x))$, R recursive, in particular O and $<_0$. Let us call this class the semi-Herbrand arithmetic predicates.

Lorenzen 1958 seems to suggest identifying inductive sets with semi-Herbrand arithmetic sets, but perhaps his concept of "reflexion" actually serves to confine inductive sets to Herbrand arithmetic sets. In defence of the restriction to Herbrand arithmetic definitions, one may argue that an implicit definition should determine completely all members as well as non-members of the set defined, in this case from the accepted totality of natural numbers and its intended interpretation. This is true of the Herbrand arithmetic definitions but not of the semi-Herbrand arithmetic ones which only determine all members in a straightforward manner but not the non-members. (Compare Kreisel 1959). It is not easy to make this argument more exact without introducing additional principles of preference such as singling out attractive properties of hyperarithmetic sets and observing that other sets such as O do not have these nice properties. Since O is a complete predicate for all semi-Herbrand arithmetic predicates and since O can be got from $<_0$ in a quite determined manner, we may confine our attention to the definition of $<_0$. Here it seems clear that the set is determined stage by stage from the definition, provided we assume the totality of natural numbers and the intended interpretation of it and some specific recursive functions. The determination seems to apply both to members and non-members.

In any case, the argument is not to reject that semi-Herbrand arithmetic definitions are inductive but that such inductively defined predicates are acceptable in all contexts. This seems to represent a fundamental departure from the original intentions of people who try to develop the notion of predicativity, and a different criterion of acceptable implicit definitions must be used. Apart from the partly terminological and partly historical question as to what the "true" notion of predicativity is, such criteria will undoubtedly help to stabilize further the highly attractive domain constituting the hyperarithmetic set theory.

If one is willing to accept inductive definitions, it seems rather arbitrary to stop at the semi-Herbrand arithmetic sets. One argument would seem to be the anthropological centrality of natural numbers. No matter how one wishes to get the natural numbers, they are clearly what we want; once we have them, we cannot stop until we have exploited what we can do by quantifying over them and using inductive definitions. But we need not indulge ourselves in more extensions such as combining inductive definitions and quantifying over all members of the new totality O. Logically this argument is not entirely satisfactory since in further extensions we seem to be doing the same kind of thing as before. If, however, the wish is to obtain some theory adequate to developing the major portion of classical mathematics and having some measure of completeness, there are understandable reasons for stopping at better developed narrower domains, such as the semi-Herbrand arithmetic sets and Herbrand arithmetic sets.

But if we use the principle 5.1 with the proviso that all inductive definitions containing explicitly only notions already introduced, we seem to be led to the following theory:

5.2. The predicative sets satisfy the following conditions:

(1) The empty set is a predicative set.

(2) The procedure of getting the union of x and the unit set of y from given sets x and y is predicative.

(3) The procedure of getting an immediate predicative extension is predicative.

(4) The procedure of getting the union of a sequence of predicative sets with indices which have as limit a predicative ordinal number is predicative.

(5) Any set obtained from given predicative sets by a predicative procedure is predicative.

(6) An ordinal which is the order type of a predicative relation which happens to be a well-ordering is a predicative ordinal.

(7) An inductive definition containing explicitly only predicative notions defines a predicative set.

(8) Given any predicative ordinal, the result of iterating an inductive definition scheme as many times as the ordinal yields again a predicative set.

(9) The predicative sets satisfy the usual axioms of extensionality and groundedness.

A more formal description is made difficult on account of the need to specify more exactly the inductive definitions and their reiterated application. If possible, it is clearly desirable to describe the totality of predicative sets with a minimum appeal to classical set theory. Since however, it seems easier to pursue the matter with free use of classical set theory, an attempt will be made to describe predicative sets within the standard system codified, in particular, in Gödel 1940.

§ 6. Two Tentative Definitions of Predicative Sets

If we take the set theory of Gödel 1940 and add the axiom $V=L$, then we may say simply that a set in the theory is predicative if its order as defined there is a predicative ordinal. This does not quite help since we would presumably wish to define a predicative ordinal as any predicative set which is an ordinal. The complication is essentially that beyond the usual principles involved in the immediate predicative extensions one requires also the principle of extension by inductive definitions. Thus, given the set of all sets of a given order, we can get the sets of the next order by using not only the operations embodied in the axioms of group B but also by inductive operations over the given sets. This can be formulated exactly in the broader theory so that we get a somewhat more complicated model in which we still use the ordinals as indices but the procedure of going from one order to the next is more complex.

What is needed is an enumeration of all conditions $C(x)$ where all variables in C, apart from the unrestricted set variable x, are restricted to the set of all sets of a given order. These can be enumerated by a set in the following manner. Let V_a be the given set of all sets of order a, and P be its power set. Then each condition $C(x)$ defines a set of members x all in P, or a subset of P, i.e., a member of the power set Q of P. If we use the subscripts, a, p, q for variables ranging over V_a, P, Q respectively, then the conditions $C(x_p)$ and the sets defined by them are given by the following clauses:

$$(Ez_q)(x_p)(y_a)(\langle x_p, y_a\rangle \in z_q \equiv y_a \in x_p).$$

$$(u_q)(v_q)(Ez_q)(y_a)(x_p)(\langle x_p, y_a\rangle \in z_q \equiv (\langle x_p, y_a\rangle \notin u_q \,\&\, \langle x_p, y_a\rangle \notin v_q)).$$

$$(u_q)(Ez_q)(x_p)(y_a)(\langle x_p, y_a\rangle \in z_q \equiv (Ew_a)\langle x_p, w_a, y_a\rangle \in u_q).$$

$$(u_q)(Ez_q)(x_p)(y_a)(w_a)(\langle x_p, y_a, w_a\rangle \in z_q \equiv \langle x_p, w_a\rangle \in u_q).$$

$$(u_q)(Ez_q)(x_p)(y_a)(w_a)(t_a)(\langle x_p, y_a, w_a, t_a\rangle \in z_q \equiv \langle x_p, w_a, y_a, t_a\rangle \in u_q).$$

$$(u_q)(Ez_q)(x_p)(y_a)(w_a)(t_a)(\langle x_p, y_a, w_a, t_a\rangle \in z_q \equiv \langle x_p, w_a, t_a, y_a\rangle \in u_q).$$

Hence, it is possible to define a function $g(a, m)$ in classical set theory such that for every classical ordinal $a, g(a, m)$ is the set defined by the m-th condition $C(x_p)$ for that a.

In this way, it is possible to modify the definition of F (Gödel 1940, p. 37) to embody a clause that for each a, the next order includes also those sets y_p such that there is an m, y_p is the intersection of all members of $g(a, m)$ and y_p itself belongs to $g(a, m)$. Slight caution can also be taken to ensure that every order includes all sets of lower orders. Thus, to make things explicit, one may wish to use a function $F(\alpha, \beta, m)$ where $\beta \leqslant \alpha$, giving for each α, the m-th new set introduced at order β. For each α, this would give all sets of order α.

Now we may continue to say that a set is predicative if it is of an order that is a predicative ordinal. And an ordinal is predicative if it is (i) a finite set, (ii) the first infinite ordinal ω, or (iii) there exists a predicative set y well-ordered by a predicative set z such that it is isomorphic with y with respect to the natural ordering relation $\in$ and z (compare the formal definition on Gödel 1940, p. 22).

This completes the sketch of the first proposed definition of predicativity. One might feel this is still too narrow since, for example, it is not obvious that the sets B and C would be predicative by this definition, and, in general, there may be acceptable ways of extension which are not adequately anticipated by us. This leads to a second proposal which depends even more heavily on classical set theory.

We take again the system of Gödel 1940 and add a new predicate P with the single new axiom that for arbitrary sets x and y, if x is well-ordered by y and all proper y-sections of x have the property P then x has the property P. A set is predicative if it has the property P. (For formal definitions of the notions involved, see Gödel 1940, p. 21.) Thus the empty set trivially has the property P, all finite ordinals has the property P by iteration, then the first infinite ordinal has the property P, and so on. There is no apparent way to define a class in the original set theory which satisfies the axiom for P but contains no extraneous members, for such an explicit definition would need a bound class variable. Since the predicate P is not permitted in defining sets, we can not, for example, define the set of all enumerable predicative well-orderings and get some contradiction that way. With this definition, it is very easy to define relative predicativity to a given set: we need only add that it has the property P^*, all its members, members of its members, etc., have P^*, P^* satisfies the axiom for P, and a set is predicative relative to the given set if it has P^*. A class is predicative if all its members, all members of its members, etc., have the property P.

§ 7. System H: The Hyperarithmetic Set Theory

The fact that hyperarithmetic sets coincide with the Herbrand arithmetic sets and Spector's surprising result that no hyperarithmetic well-orderings can give more than the recursive ordinals both tend to stress the stability of the hyperarithmetic sets. While the major works on hyperarithmetic sets are only concerned with sets of non-negative integers, it seems natural to consider also a simultaneous increase in levels. It is in this latter sense that hyperarithmetic set theory is understood here. In Wang 1954, a scheme was given for which no decision was reached as to exactly what class of ordinals is used, although it was suggested that at least the recursive ordinals should be used. If one decides further that exactly the recursive ordinals are used, then that paper may be viewed as an attempt to develop hyperarithmetic set theory. A more elegant development is outlined in Spector 1957 with indication of a powerful method which can be used to prove a number of interesting closure properties about hyperarithmetic sets. Additional closure properties are given in Kreisel 1959.

If we wish to treat the matter purely set-theoretically, we seem to be led to a formal system H obtainable from the classical set theory by fairly simple modifications. For this purpose, it is more convenient to take the system of Bernays 1937 and 1941. The axioms of H are simply the axioms I—VII given there with axiom V_a (the Aussonderungsaxiom) and axiom V_d (the power set axiom) respectively replaced by their predicative counterparts:

$V_a h$. The immediately predicative subclasses of each set is again a set; in other words, if in the axioms of group III, all the set variables are restricted to range over members of a set, then the class variables can be replaced by set variables (not independent, see below).

$V_d h$. For every set, the class of all its immediate predicative subsets is again a set.

To arrive at a measure of natural completeness, we add also:

VIII. The axiom of categoricalness: the counterpart of Gödel's $V=L$.

While in classical set theory, there is some doubt as to whether the axiom is true according to the intuitive meaning of the set concept, here it seems to be something which we would naturally want.

In system H, most of the standard development of classical mathematics such as given by Bernays can be taken over with little modification except that higher infinities are no longer available. In particular, it appears plausible that the development of classical analysis by Lorenzen can be formalized in the system.

It may also be noted that the set of recursive ordinals is in this theory a class but not a set.

7.1. The set O is a class in system H; in other words, it can be defined by quantification over all hyperarithmetic sets. To prove this, we modify the definition of $<_0$ by considering all its proper sections and take union.

7.2. Let $C(m, x)$ be the conjunction of: (i) $\langle 1, 2\rangle \in x$; (ii) x is transitive; (iii) for all y, if $\langle 1, y\rangle \in x$ and $2y \neq m$, then $\langle y, 2y\rangle \in x$; (iv) if $(y)(Ez)\, T(e, y, z)$, $(y)(\langle e(y), e(y+1)\rangle \in x)$, and $m \neq 3^e$, then $\langle e(z), 3^e\rangle \in x$.

7.3. For all m, $m \in O$ if and only if $(Ey)\, C(m, y)$ and $(x)(C(m, x) \rightarrow m \in x)$.

For this class O, the principle of transfinite induction can be proved in H.

In the system H, the axiom II gives the finite sets and the axiom of infinity IV with the axiom of replacement V_b enable us to get infinite ordinals. Axiom $V_a h$ and axiom $V_d h$ enable us to get the immediate predicative extension at each stage. Actually, $V_d h$ is redundant, since every class belonging to some class or set is again a set and all the sets required by the axiom can be obtained. To obtain union at a limit ordinal, the axiom of replacement and the sum set axiom V_c can be used. Nevertheless, the system H is, like standard formulations of number theory and classical set theory, incomplete, and only complete by intention. And the incompleteness, as with number theory, can be characterized quite clearly by an infinite rule:

XI. The ω_1-rule: if a set happens to be an ordinal, we can take as an axiom the statement that it is an ordinal; or, if a set happens to be a well-ordering, we can take as an axiom that the set is a well-ordering.

It seems desirable to develop the system H without the infinite rule which may be of interest when one considers the interpretation of H.

References

[1] W. Ackermann, *Math. Z.*, **53** (1951), 403—413.
[2] J. W. Addison and S. C. Kleene, *Proc. Am. Math. Soc.*, **8** (1957), 1002—1006.
[3] P. Bernays, *Jour. Symbolic Logic*, **2** (1937), 65—77; **6** (1941), 1—17.
[4] A. Church, *Bull. Am. Math. Soc.*, **44** (1938), 224—232.
[5] A. Church and C. Kleene, *Fund. Math.*, **28** (1937), 11—21.
[6] M. Davis, Computability and Unsolvability, 1958, New York.
[7] K. Gödel, On Undecidable Propositions of Formal Mathematical Systems, mimeographed, Princeton, 1934.
[8] K. Gödel, Consistency of the Continuum Hypothesis, Princeton, 1940.
[9] K. Gödel, The Philosophy of Bertrand Russell, 123—153, 1944.
[10] K. J. J. Hintikka, *Jour. Symbolic Logic*, **21** (1956), 225—245.
[11] S. C. Kleene, *Jour. Symbolic Logic*, **3** (1938), 150—155.
[12] S. C. Kleene, *Am. Jour. Math.*, **77** (1955a), 405—428.
[13] S. C. Kleene, *Trans. Am. Math. Soc.*, **79** (1955b), 312—340.
[14] G. Kreisel, Predicative Analysis, mimeographed, Stanford, 1959.
[15] P. Lorenzen, *Math. Z.*, **54** (1951), 1—24.
[16] P. Lorenzen, Einführung in die Operative Logik und Mathematik, Berlin, 1955.
[17] P. Lorenzen, *Jour. Symbolic Logic*, **23** (1958), 110—111.
[18] J. Myhill, *Jour. Symbolic Logic*, **18** (1953), 190—191.
[19] N. A. Routledge, *Proc. Camb. Philos. Soc.*, **49** (1953), 175—182.
[20] B. Russell, Appendix B to Principia Mathematica, 1925.
[21] K. Schütte, *Math. Ann.*, **127** (1954), 15—32.
[22] C. Spector, *Jour. Symbolic Logic*, **20** (1955), 151—163.
[23] C. Spector, Summaries of Talks Summer Inst. Symb. Log., mimeographed, 377—382, Cornell, 1957.
[24] A. M. Turing, *Proc. London Math. Soc.*, **45** (1939), 161—228.
[25] H. Wang, *Jour. Symbolic Logic*, **19** (1954), 241—266.
[26] H. Wang, Summaries of Talks Summer Inst. Symb. Log., mimeographed, 383—390, Cornell, 1957.

[27] H. Weyl, Das Kontinuum, 1918, reprint, New York, 1960.
[28] A. N. Whitehead and B. Russell, Principia Mathematica, vol. 1, 1910.
[29] G. Kreisel, J. Shoenfield, Hao Wang, Number-theoretic concepts and recursive well-orderings, *Archiv für mathematische Logik und Grundlagenforschung*, **5** (December, 1959), 42—64.

THEORIE DES OPERATIONS LINEAIRES

By S. BANACH

—1933-63. xii + 250 pp. 5⅜x8. 8284-0110-1. **$4.95**

DIFFERENTIAL EQUATIONS

By H. BATEMAN

CHAPTER HEADINGS: I. Differential Equations and their Solutions. II. Integrating Factors. III. Transformations. IV. Geometrical Applications. V. Diff. Eqs. with Particular Solutions of a Specified Type. VI. Partial Diff. Eqs. VII. Total Diff. Eqs. VIII. Partial Diff. Eqs. of the Second Order. IX. Integration in Series. X. The Solution of Linear Diff. Eqs. by Means of Definite Integrals. XI. The Mechanical Integration of Diff. Eqs.

—1917-67. xi + 306 pp. 5⅜x8. 8284-0190-X. **$4.95**

MEASURE AND INTEGRATION

By S. K. BERBERIAN

A highly flexible graduate level text. Part I is designed for a one-semester introductory course; the book as a whole is suitable for a full-year course. Numerous exercises.

Partial Contents: PART ONE: I. Measures. II. Measurable Functions. III. Sequences of Measurable Functions. IV. Integrable Functions. V. Convergence Theorems. VI. Product Measures. VII. Finite Signed Measures. PART TWO: VIII. Integration over Locally compact Spaces (. . . The Riesz-Markoff Representation Theorem, . . .). IX. Integration over Locally Compact Groups (Topological Groups, . . . , Haar Integral, Convolution, The Group Algebra, . . .). BIBLIOGRAPHY. INDEX.

—1965-70. xx + 312 pp. 6x9. 8284-0241-8. **$7.95**

L'APPROXIMATION

By S. BERNSTEIN and CH. de LA VALLÉE POUSSIN

TWO VOLUMES IN ONE:

Leçons sur les Propriétés Extrémales et la Meilleure Approximation des Fonctions Analytiques d'une Variable Réelle, *by Bernstein.*

Leçons sur l'approximation des Fonctions d'une Variable Réelle, *by Vallée Poussin.*

—1925/19-69. 363 pp. 6x9. 8284-0198-5. 2 v. in 1. **$7.95**

CALCUL DES PROBABILITES

By J. BERTRAND

A well-known work.

—2nd ed. 1907-71. lvii + 322 pp. 5⅜x8. **In prep.**

ABHANDLUNGEN

By F. W. BESSEL

—1875-1971. 1,354 pp. 6x9. Three vols. in one. **In prep.**

OPERE MATEMATICHE

By E. BETTI

—1903/13-71. Approx. 1,100 pp. 6x9. **In prep.**

INTEGRALGEOMETRIE

By W. BLASCHKE and E. KÄHLER

THREE VOLUMES IN ONE.

VORLESUNGEN UEBER INTEGRALGEOMETRIE, Vols. I and II, by *W. Blaschke.*

EINFUEHRUNG IN DIE THEORIE DER SYSTEME VON DIFFERENTIALGLEICHUNGEN, by *E. Kähler.*

—1936/37/34-49. 222 pp. 5½x8½. 8284-0064-4. Three vols. in one. **$6.00**

FUNDAMENTAL EXISTENCE THEOREMS,

by G. A. BLISS. See EVANS

THEORY AND APPLICATIONS OF DISTANCE GEOMETRY

By L. M. BLUMENTHAL

"Clearly written and self-contained. The reader is well provided with exercises of various degrees of difficulty."—*Bulletin of A.M.S.*

—2nd (c.) ed. 1953-71. 359 pp. 5⅜x8. 8284-0242-6. **$7.95**

A HISTORY OF FORMAL LOGIC

By I. M. BOCHENSKI

Translated and edited by PROFESSOR IVO THOMAS.

A history and source book, by one of the world's leading authorities. Generous selections, from the Greeks to Peano, Russell, Frege, and Gödel, threaded together by explanatory comment. Within schools, the arrangement is by subject.

"Covers the whole period from pre-Socrates to Gödel . . . It sets such a high standard of excellence that one may doubt whether it will have any serious rivals for a long time to come."—*The Journal of Symbolic Logic.*

—2nd (c.) ed. 1970. xxii + 567 pp. 5⅜x8. 8284-0238-8. **$11.50**

VORLESUNGEN UEBER FOURIERSCHE INTEGRALE

By S. BOCHNER

—1932-48. vi + 229 pp. 5½x8½. 8284-0042-3. **$4.95**

ALMOST PERIODIC FUNCTIONS

By H. BOHR

Translated by H. COHN. From the famous series *Ergebnisse der Mathematik und ihrer Grenzgebiete,* a beautiful exposition of the theory of Almost Periodic Functions written by the creator of that theory.

—1951-66. 120 pp. 6x9. Lithotyped. 8284-0027-X. **$3.50**

WISSENSCHAFTLICHE ABHANDLUNGEN

By L. BOLTZMANN

—1909-68. 1,976 pp. 5⅜x8. 8284-0215-9.
Three vol. set. **Prob. $39.50**

LECTURES ON THE CALCULUS OF VARIATIONS

By O. BOLZA

A standard text by a major contributor to the theory. Suitable for individual study by anyone with a good background in the Calculus and the elements of Real Variables.

—2nd (corr.) ed. 1961. 280 pp. 5⅜x8. 8284-0145-4. Cloth **$4.50**
8284-0152-7. Paper **$1.19**

VORLESUNGEN UEBER VARIATIONSRECHNUNG

By O. BOLZA

A standard text and reference work, by one of the major contributors to the theory.

—1909-63. ix + 715 pp. 5⅜x8. 8284-0160-8. **$9.50**

THEORIE DER KONVEXEN KOERPER

By T. BONNESEN and W. FENCHEL

"Remarkable monograph."
—*J. D. Tamarkin, Bulletin of the A. M. S.*

—1934. 171 pp. 5½x8½. 8284-0054-7. **$4.50**

THE CALCULUS OF FINITE DIFFERENCES

By G. BOOLE

A standard work on the subject of finite differences and difference equations by one of the seminal minds in the field of finite mathematics.

Numerous exercises with answers.

—5th ed. 1970. 341 pp. 5⅜x8. 8284-1121-2. Cloth **$4.95**
—4th ed. 1958. 336 pp. 5⅜x8. 8284-0148-9. Paper **$1.39**

A TREATISE ON DIFFERENTIAL EQUATIONS

By G. BOOLE

Including the Supplementary Volume.

—5th ed. 1959. xxiv + 735 pp. 5⅜x8. 8284-0128-4. **$6.95**

HISTORY OF SLIDE RULE, *By F. CAJORI. See* BALL

INTRODUCTORY TREATISE ON LIE'S THEORY OF FINITE CONTINUOUS TRANSFORMATION GROUPS

By J. E. CAMPBELL

Partial Contents: CHAP. I. Definitions and Simple Examples of Groups. II. Elementary Illustrations of Principle of Extended Point Transformations. III. Generation of Group from Its Infinitesimal Transformations. V. Structure Constants. VI. Complete Systems of Differential Equations. VII. Diff. Eqs. Admitting Known Transf. Groups. VIII. Invariant Theory of Groups . . . XIV. Pfaff's Equation . . . XXI-XXV. Certain Linear Groups.

—1903-66. xx + 416 pp. 5⅜x8. 8284-0183-7. **$6.50**

THEORY OF FUNCTIONS

By C. CARATHÉODORY

Translated by F. STEINHARDT.

Partial Contents: **Part One.** Chap. I. Algebra of Complex Numbers. II. Geometry of Complex Numbers. III. Euclidean, Spherical, and Non-Euclidean Geometry. **Part Two.** Theorems from Point Set Theory and Topology. Chap. I. Sequences and Continuous Complex Functions. II. Curves and Regions. III. Line Integrals. **Part Three.** Analytic Functions. Chap. I. Foundations. II. The Maximum-modulus principle. III. Poisson Integral and Harmonic Functions. IV. Meromorphic Functions. **Part Four.** Generation of Analytic Functions by Limiting Processes. Chap. I. Uniform Convergence. II. Normal Families of Meromorphic Functions. III. Power Series. IV. Partial Fraction Decomposition and the Calculus of Residues. **Part Five.** Special Functions. Chap. I. The Exponential Function and the Trigonometric Functions. II. Logarithmic Function. III. Bernoulli Numbers and the Gamma Function.

Vol. II.: **Part Six.** Foundations of Geometric Function Theory. Chap. I. Bounded Functions. II. Conformal Mapping. III. The Mapping of the Boundary. **Part Seven.** The Triangle Function and Picard's Theorem. Chap. I. Functions of Several Complex Variables. II. Conformal Mapping of Circular-Arc Triangles. III. The Schwarz Triangle Functions and the Modular Function. IV. Essential Singularities and Picard's Theorems.

"A book by a master . . . Carathéodory himself regarded [it] as his finest achievement . . . written from a catholic point of view."—*Bulletin of A.M.S.*

—Vol. I. 2nd ed. 1958. 310 pp. 6x9. 8284-0097-0. **$6.50**

—Vol. II. 2nd ed. 1960. 220 pp. 6x9. 8284-0106-3. **$5.50**

ALGEBRAIC THEORY OF MEASURE AND INTEGRATION

By C. CARATHÉODORY

Translated from the German by FRED E. J. LINTON. By generalizing the concept of point function to that of a function over a Boolean ring ("soma" function), Prof. Carathéodory gives an algebraic treatment of measure and integration.

—1963. 378 pp. 6x9. 8284-0161-6. **$8.00**

VORLESUNGEN UBER REELLE FUNKTIONEN

By C. CARATHÉODORY

This great classic is at once a book for the beginner, a reference work for the advanced scholar and a source of inspiration for the research worker.

—3rd ed. (c.r. of 2nd). 1968. 728 pp. 5⅜x8. 8284-0038-5. **$12.00**

NON-EUCLIDEAN GEOMETRY, *by H. S. CARSLAW.*
See BALL

FORMULAS AND THEOREMS IN PURE MATHEMATICS

By G. S. CARR

Second edition, with an introduction by Jacques Dutka.

Over 6,000 formulas and results, systematically arranged, with indications or outlines of proofs, and references to the original periodical literature. Elementary through advanced results are covered, including even some quite esoteric topics (e.g., linkages and link-works). There is a most extensive and detailed index.

Partial Contents: PART I. Mathematical Tables. II. Algebra. III. Theory of Equations. IV. Plane Trigonometry. V. Spherical Trigonometry. VI. Elementary Geometry. VIII. Differential Calculus. IX. Integral Calculus. X. Calculus of Variations. XI. Differential Equations. XII. Calculus of Finite Differences. XIII. Analytic Geometry of the Plane. XIV. Analytic Geometry of Space. INDEX. FOLD-OUT PLATES.

It was the first edition of this work that inspired Ramanujan: "Through the new world opened to him [by Carr's book] Ramanujan went raging with delight. It was this book that awakened his genius."—*The Collected Papers of S. Ramanujan.*

—2nd ed. 1970. xxxvi + 935 pp. 5⅜x8. 8284-0239-6. **$12.50**

COLLECTED PAPERS (OEUVRES)

By P. L. CHEBYSHEV

One of Russia's greatest mathematicians, Chebyshev (Tchebycheff) did work of the highest importance in the Theory of Probability, Number Theory, and other subjects. The present work contains his post-doctoral papers (sixty in number) and miscellaneous writings. The language is French, in which most of his work was originally published; those papers originally published in Russian are here presented in French translation.

—1962. Repr. of 1st ed. 1,480 pp. 5½x8¼. 8284-0157-8.
Two vol. set. **$27.50**

THEORIE DER CONGRUENZEN

By P. L. CHEBYSHEV

This work, subtitled *Elemente der Zahlentheorie*, is the only of Chebyshev's writings not included in his Oeuvres (see above).

—1889-1970. xvii + 313 + 31 pp. 5⅜x8. **In prep.**

TEXTBOOK OF ALGEBRA

By G. CHRYSTAL

In addition to the standard topics, Chrystal's *Algebra* contains many topics not often found in an Algebra book: inequalities, the elements of substitution theory, and so forth. Especially extensive is Chrystal's treatment of infinite series, infinite products, and (finite and infinite) continued fractions.

OVER 2,400 EXERCISES (with solutions).

—7th ed. 1964. 2 vols. xxiv + 584 pp.; xxiv + 626 pp. 5⅜x8.
8284-0084-9. Cloth. Each vol. **$4.95**
8284-0181-0. Paper. Each vol. **$2.35**

MATHEMATICAL PAPERS

By W. K. CLIFFORD

One of the world's major mathematicians, Clifford's papers cover only a 15-year span, for he died at age 34. [Included in this volume is Clifford's English translation of an important paper of Riemann.]

—1882-67. 70 + 658 pp. 5⅜x8. 8284-0210-8. **$15.00**

ESSAI SUR L'APPLICATION DE L'ANALYSE AUX PROBABILITES

By M. J. CONDORCET

A photographic reproduction of a very rare and historically important work in the Theory of Probability. An original copy brings many hundreds of dollars in the rare book market.

—1785. Repr. 1971. 191 + 304 pp. 6x9. **In prep.**

MODERN PURE SOLID GEOMETRY

By N. A. COURT

In this second edition of this well-known book on synthetic solid geometry, the author has supplemented several of the chapters with an account of recent results.

—2nd ed. 1964. xiv + 353 pp. 5½x8¼. 8284-0147-0. **$7.50**

SPINNING TOPS AND GYROSCOPIC MOTION

By H. CRABTREE

Partial Contents: Introductory Chapter. CHAP. I. Rotation about a Fixed Axis. II. Representation of Angular Velocity. Precession. III. Discussion of the Phenomena Described in the Introductory Chapter. IV. Oscillations. V. Practical Applications. VI-VII. Motion of Top. VIII. Moving Axes. IX. Stability of Rotation. Periods of Oscillation. APPENDICES: I. Precession. II. Swerving of "sliced" golf ball. III. Drifting of Projectiles. IV. The Rising of a Top. V. The Gyro-compass. ANSWERS TO EXAMPLES.

—2nd ed. 1914-67. 203 pp. 6x9. 8284-0204-3. **$4.95**

THEORIE GENERALE DES SURFACES

By G. DARBOUX

One of the great works of the mathematical literature.

An unabridged reprint of the latest edition of *Leçons sur la Théorie générale des surfaces et les applications géométriques du Calcul infinitésimal.*

—Vol. I (2nd ed.) xii+630 pp. Vol. II (2nd ed.) xvii+584 pp. Vol. III (1st ed.) xvi+518 pp. Vol. IV. (1st ed.) xvi+537 pp. 8284-0216-7. **In prep.**

GESAMMELTE MATHEMATISCHE WERKE

By R. DEDEKIND

"The re-issue of these volumes . . . is a mark of the enormous importance to modern mathematical thought of Dedekind's great work."—*Mathematical Gazette.*

Three vols. in two. **$25.00**

THE DOCTRINE OF CHANCES

By A. DE MOIVRE

In the year 1716 Abraham de Moivre published his *Doctrine of Chances*, in which the subject of Mathematical Probability took several long strides forward. A few years later came his *Treatise of Annuities*. When the third (and final) edition of the *Doctrine* was published in 1756 it appeared in one volume together with a revised edition of the work on Annuities. It is this latter two-volumes-in-one that is here presented in an exact photographic reprint.

—3rd ed. 1756-1967. xi + 348 pp. 6x9. 8284-0200-0. **$7.95**

DE MORGAN. *See* D. E. SMITH

COLLECTED MATHEMATICAL PAPERS

By L. E. DICKSON

—1969. 4 vols. Approx. 3,400 pp. 6½x9¼. **In prep.**

HISTORY OF THE THEORY OF NUMBERS

By L. E. DICKSON

"**A monumental work** . . . Dickson always has in mind the needs of the investigator . . . The author has [often] expressed in a nut-shell the main results of a long and involved paper *in a much clearer way than the writer of the article did himself*. The ability to reduce complicated mathematical arguments to simple and elementary terms is highly developed in Dickson."—*Bulletin of A. M. S.*

—Vol. I (Divisibility and Primality) xii + 486 pp. Vol. II (Diophantine Analysis) xxv + 803 pp. Vol. III (Quadratic and Higher Forms) v + 313 pp. 5⅜x8. 8284-0086-5.
Three vol. set. **$22.50**

STUDIES IN THE THEORY OF NUMBERS

By L. E. DICKSON

—1930-62. viii + 230 pp. 5⅜x8. 8284-0151-9. **$4.95**

ALGEBRAIC NUMBERS

By L. E. DICKSON, et al.

TWO VOLUMES IN ONE.

Both volumes of the *Report of the Committee on Algebraic Numbers* are here included, the authors being L. E. Dickson, R. Fueter, H. H. Mitchell, H. S. Vandiver, and G. E. Wahlen.

Partial Contents: CHAP. I. Algebraic Numbers. II. Cyclotomy. III. Hensel's p-adic Numbers. IV. Fields of Functions. I′. The Class Number in the Algebraic Number Field. II′. Irregular Cyclotomic Fields and Fermat's Last Theorem.

—1923/28-67. ii + 211 pp. 5⅜x9. 8284-0211-6.
Two vols. in one. **$4.95**

PLANE TRIGONOMETRY

By L. E. DICKSON

In all his books, advanced and elementary, Professor Dickson is noted for the extraordinary clarity of his writing. This very elementary book is no exception.

"This book introduces at an early stage concrete applications . . . We thereby obtain an abundance of simple problems whose importance is so convincing that they cannot fail to arouse real interest. Actual experience with classes has firmly convinced the author that these practical applications offer the best means to drive home the principles of trigonometry and to make the subject truly vital."—*From Prof. Dickson's Preface.*

—1922-70. xii + 211 pp. 5⅜x8. 8284-0230-2. **$3.95**

INTRODUCTION TO THE THEORY OF ALGEBRAIC EQUATIONS, *by L. E. DICKSON. See* SIERPINSKI

VORLESUNGEN UEBER ZAHLENTHEORIE

By P. G. L. DIRICHLET and R. DEDEKIND

The fourth (last) edition of this great work contains, in its final form, the epoch-making "Eleventh Supplement," in which Dedekind outlines his theory of algebraic numbers.

"Gauss' *Disquisitiones Arithmeticae* has been called a 'book of seven seals.' It is hard reading, even for experts, but the treasures it contains (and partly conceals) in its concise, synthetic demonstrations are now available to all who wish to share them, largely the result of the labors of Gauss' friend and disciple, Peter Gustav Lejeune Dirichlet (1805-1859), who first broke the seven seals . . . [He] summarized his personal studies and his recasting of the *Disquisitiones* in his *Zahlentheorie.* The successive editions (1863, 1871, 1879, 1893) of this text . . . made the classical arithmetic of Gauss accessible to all without undue labor."—*E. T. Bell,* in *Men of Mathematics* and *Development of Mathematics.*

—4th ed. 1893-1968. xv + 657 pp. 5⅜x8. 8284-0213-2. **$13.50**

WERKE

By P. G. L. DIRICHLET

The mathematical works of P. G. Lejeune Dirichlet, edited by L. Kronecker.

—1889/97-1969. 1,086 pp. 6½x9¼. 8284-0225-6.
Two vols. in one. **$23.50**

THE INTEGRAL CALCULUS

By J. EDWARDS

A leisurely, immensely detailed, textbook of over 1,900 pages, rich in illustrative examples and manipulative techniques and containing much interesting material that must of necessity be omitted from less comprehensive works.

There are forty large chapters in all. The earlier cover a leisurely and a more-than-usually-detailed treatment of all the elementary standard topics. Later chapters include: Jacobian Elliptic Functions, Weierstrassian Elliptic Functions, Evaluation of Definite Integrals, Harmonic Analysis, Calculus of Variations, etc. Every chapter contains many exercises (with solutions).

—2 vols. 1921/22-55. 1,922 pp. 5x8.
8284-0102-0; 8284-0105-5. Each volume **$9.50**

TRANSFORMATIONS OF SURFACES

By L. P. EISENHART

Many of the advances in the differential geometry of surfaces in the present century have had to do with transformations of surfaces of a given type into surfaces of the same type. The present book studies two types of transformation to which many, if not all, such transformations can be reduced.

—2nd (Corr.) ed. 1962. ix + 379 pp. 5⅜x8.
8284-0167-5. **$6.50**

MATHEMATISCHE ABHANDLUNGEN

By G. EISENSTEIN

—Repr. of edition of 1847. iv+336 pp. 6½x9¼. **In prep.**

INTRODUCTION TO THE ALGEBRA OF QUANTICS

By E. B. ELLIOTT

—Repr. of 2nd ed. 1913-64. xvi + 416 pp. 5⅜x8.
8284-0184-5. **$6.00**

ELLIPTISCHE FUNCTIONEN

By A. ENNEPER

—2nd ed. 1890-1971. xix + 598 pp. 5⅜x8. **In prep.**

LOGARITHMIC POTENTIAL, and Other Monographs

By G. C. EVANS and G. A. BLISS

TWO VOLUMES IN ONE.

THE LOGARITHMIC POTENTIAL, by *G. C. Evans.*

FUNDAMENTAL EXISTENCE THEOREMS, by *G. A. Bliss.*

—1927/1934-68. viii + 150 + iv + 107 pp. 5⅜x8. **In prep.**

ASYMPTOTIC SERIES

By W. B. FORD

TWO VOLUMES IN ONE: *Studies on Divergent Series and Summability* and *The Asymptotic Developments of Functions Defined by MacLaurin Series.*

—1916/36-60. 341 pp. 6x9. 8284-0143-8. 2 v. in 1. **$6.50**

AUTOMORPHIC FUNCTIONS

By L. R. FORD

"Comprehensive . . . remarkably clear and explicit."—*Bulletin of the A. M. S.*

—2nd ed. (Corr. repr.) 1929-51. x + 333 pp. 5⅜x8.
8284-0085-7. **$6.50**

THE CALCULUS OF EXTENSION

By H. G. FORDER

—1941-60. xvi + 490 pp. 5⅜x8. 8284-0135-7. **$6.50**

GRUNDGESETZE DER ARITHMETIK

By G. FREGE

TWO VOLUMES IN ONE.

—1893/1903-69. xxvi + 253 + xvi + 266 pp. 5⅜x8.
Two vols. in one. **In prep.**

A SHORT HISTORY OF GREEK MATHEMATICS

By J. GOW

A standard work on the history of Greek mathematics, with special emphasis on the Alexandrian school of mathematics.

—1884-68. xii + 325 pp. 5⅜x8. 8284-0218-3. **$6.50**

THE ALGEBRA OF INVARIANTS

By J. H. GRACE and A. YOUNG

An introductory account.

Partial Contents: I. Introduction. II. The Fundamental Theorem. III. Transvectants. V. Elementary Complete Systems. VI. Gordan's Theorem. VII. The Quintic. VIII. Simultaneous Systems. IX. Hilbert's Theorem. XI. Apolarity. XII. Ternary Forms. XV. Types of Covariants. XVI. General Theorems on Quantics. APPENDICES.

—1903-65. vii + 384 pp. 5⅜x8. 8284-0180-2. **$4.95**

DIE AUSDEHNUNGSLEHRE

By H. G. GRASSMANN

The *Ausdehnungslehre* appeared in two different versions, that of 1844 and that of 1862. This work is the first version [with the interpolatory material added by Grassmann in 1878], in a fourth edition.

—4th ed. 1969. xii + 435 pp. 6x9. 8284-0222-1. **$12.50**

DIE AUSDEHNUNGSLEHRE VON 1862

By H. G. GRASSMANN

This work is the third edition of the 1862 *Ausdehnungslehre.* [See above for the 1844/78 version.]

—1971. vii + 511 pp. 6x9. 8284-0236-1. **In prep.**

GESAMMELTE MATHEMATISCHE UND PHYSIKALISCHE WERKE

By H. G. GRASSMANN

Volumes Two and Three of Grassmann's collected works. Volume One, part 1 and Volume One, part 2 are the two versions of the *Ausdehnungslehre* [see above].

—1971. 1,495 pp. 6x9. 8284-0236-1. Vols. 2 and 3. **In prep.**

A TREATISE ON DYNAMICS

By A. GRAY

—1911-71. xv + 626 pp. 5⅜x8. **In prep.**

LORD KELVIN: An Account of His Scientific Life and Works

By A. GRAY

—1908-71. ix + 309 pp. 5x7⅛. **Prob. $3.95**

MATHEMATICAL PAPERS

By G. GREEN

The collected papers of a celebrated mathematical physicist.

—1871-1970. xii + 336 pp. 5⅜x8. 8284-0229-9. **$8.50**

GYROSCOPIC THEORY

By G. GREENHILL

This work is intended to serve as a collection in one place of the various methods of the theoretical explanation of the motion of a spinning body, and as a reference for mathematical formulas required in practical work.

—1914-67. vi + 277 pp. + Fold-out Plates. 6½x10¾. 8284-0205-1. **$9.50**

LES INTEGRALES DE STIELTJES et leurs Applications aux Problèmes de la Physique Mathématique

By N. GUNTHER

The present work is a reprint of Vol. I of the publications of the V. A. Steklov Institute of Mathematics, in Moscow. The text is in French.

—1932-49. 498 pp. 5⅜x8. 8284-0063-6. **$6.95**

ONDES: Leçons sur la Propagation des Ondes et les Equations de l'Hydrodynamique

By J. HADAMARD

"[Hadamard's] unusual analytic proficiency enables him to connect in a wonderful manner the physical problem of propagation of waves and the mathematical problem of Cauchy concerning the characteristics of partial differential equations of the second order."—*Bulletin of the A. M. S.*

—Repr. 1949. viii + 375 pp. 5½x8½. 8284-0058-X. **$6.00**

REELLE FUNKTIONEN. Punktfunktionen

By H. HAHN

—1932-48. xi + 415 pp. 5½x8½. 8284-0052-0. **$6.00**

ALGEBRAIC LOGIC

By P. R. HALMOS

"Algebraic Logic is a modern approach to some of the problems of mathematical logic, and the theory of polyadic Boolean algebras, with which this volume is mostly concerned, is intended to be an efficient way of treating algebraic logic in a unified manner.

"[The material] is accessible to a general mathematical audience; no vast knowledge of algebra or logic is required . . . Except for a slight Boolean foundation, the volume is essentially self-contained."—*From the Preface.*

—1962. 271 pp. 6x9. 8284-0154-3. **$4.95**

INTRODUCTION TO HILBERT SPACE AND THE THEORY OF SPECTRAL MULTIPLICITY

By P. R. HALMOS

A clear, readable introductory treatment of Hilbert Space.

—2nd ed. 1957. 120 pp. 6x9. 8284-0082-2. **$3.50**

LECTURES ON ERGODIC THEORY

By P. R. HALMOS

CONTENTS: Introduction. Recurrence. Mean Convergence. Pointwise Convergence. Ergodicity. Mixing. Measure Algebras. Discrete Spectrum. Automorphisms of Compact Groups. Generalized Proper Values. Weak Topology. Weak Approximation. Uniform Topology. Uniform Approximation. Category. Invariant Measures. Generalized Ergodic Theorems. Unsolved Problems.

"Written in the pleasant, relaxed, and clear style usually associated with the author. The material is organized very well and painlessly presented."
—*Bulletin of the A.M.S.*

—1956-60. viii + 101 pp. 5⅜x8. 8284-0142-X. **$3.25**

ELEMENTS OF QUATERNIONS

By W. R. HAMILTON

Sir William Rowan Hamilton's last major work, and the second of his two treatises on quaternions.

—3rd ed. 1899/1901-68. 1,185 pp. 6x9. 8284-0219-1.
Two vol. set. **$29.50**

RAMANUJAN:
Twelve Lectures on His Life and Works

By G. H. HARDY

The book is somewhat more than an account of the mathematical work and personality of Ramanujan; it is one of the very few full-length books of "shop talk" by an important mathematician.

—1940-59. viii + 236 pp. 6x9. 8284-0136-5. **$4.95**

GRUNDZUEGE DER MENGENLEHRE

By F. HAUSDORFF

The original, 1914 edition of this famous work contains many topics that had to be omitted from later editions, notably, the theories of content, measure, and discussion of the Lebesgue integral. Also, general topological spaces, Euclidean spaces, special methods applicable in the Euclidean plane, the algebra of sets, partially ordered sets, etc.

—1914-49. 484 pp. 5⅜x8. 8284-0061-X. **$7.50**

SET THEORY

By F. HAUSDORFF

Hausdorff's classic text-book is an inspiration and a delight. The translation is from the Third (latest) German edition.

"We wish to state without qualification that this is an indispensable book for all those interested in the theory of sets and the allied branches of real variable theory."—*Bulletin of A. M. S.*

—2nd ed. 1962. 352 pp. 6x9. 8284-0119-5. **$7.50**

ELECTRICAL PAPERS

By O. HEAVISIDE

Heaviside's collected works are in five volumes: The two volumes of his *Electrical Papers* and the three volumes of his *Electromagnetic Theory.*

"The [forthcoming publication of my *Electromagnetic Theory*] brought the question of a reprint of the earlier papers to a crisis. For, as the later work grows out of the earlier, it seemed an absurdity to leave the earlier work behind. [It possesses] sufficient continuity of subject-matter and treatment, and even regularity of notation, to justify its presentation in the original form . . . It might be regarded . . . as an educational work for students of theoretical electricity."—*From the Preface.*

—2nd (c.) ed. 1892-1970. 1,183 pp. 5⅜x8. 8284-0235-3. Two vol. set. **$29.50**

ELECTROMAGNETIC THEORY

By O. HEAVISIDE

Third edition, with an Introduction by B. A. Behrend and with added notes on Heaviside's unpublished writings. A classic since its original publication in 1894-1912.

—3rd ed. 1970. 1,610 pp. 5⅜x8. 8284-0237-X. Three vol. set **$29.50**

VORLESUNGEN UEBER DIE THEORIE DER ALGEBRAISCHEN ZAHLEN

By E. HECKE

"An elegant and comprehensive account of the modern theory of algebraic numbers."
—*Bulletin of the A. M. S.*

—2nd ed. 1970. viii + 274 pp. 5⅜x8. 8284-0046-6. **$6.50**

INTEGRALGLEICHUNGEN UND GLEICHUNGEN MIT UNENDLICHVIELEN UNBEKANNTEN

By E. HELLINGER and O. TOEPLITZ

"Indispensable to anybody who desires to penetrate deeply into this subject."—*Bulletin of A.M.S.*

—1928-53. 286 pp. 5⅜x8. 8284-0089-X. **$4.95**

THEORIE DER ALGEBRAISCHE FUNKTIONEN EINER VARIABELN

By K. HENSEL and G. LANDSBERG

Partial Contents: PART ONE (Chaps. 1-8): Algebraic Functions on a Riemann Surface. PART TWO (Chaps. 9-13): The Field of Algebraic Functions. PART THREE (Chaps. 14-22): Algebraic Divisors and the Riemann-Roch Theorem. PART FOUR (Chaps. 23-27): Algebraic Curves. PART FIVE (Chaps. 28-31): The Classes of Algebraic Curves. PART SIX (Chaps. 32-37): Algebraic Relations among Abelian Integrals. APPENDIX: Historical Development. Geometrical Methods. Arithmetical Methods.

—1902-65. xvi + 707 pp. 6x9. 8284-0179-9. **$9.50**

Grundzüge Einer Allgemeinen Theorie der LINEAREN INTEGRALGLEICHUNGEN

By D. HILBERT

—1912-53. 306 pp. 5½x8¼. 8284-0091-1. **$4.95**

GEOMETRY AND THE IMAGINATION

By D. HILBERT and S. COHN-VOSSEN

Translated from the German by P. NEMENYI.

"A fascinating tour of the 20th century mathematical zoo. . . . Anyone who would like to see proof of the fact that a sphere with a hole can always be bent (no matter how small the hole), learn the theorems about Klein's bottle—a bottle with no edges, no inside, and no outside—and meet other strange creatures of modern geometry will be delighted with Hilbert and Cohn-Vossen's book."
—*Scientific American.*

"Should provided stimulus and inspiration to every student and teacher of geometry."—*Nature.*

"A mathematical classic. . . . The purpose is to make the reader *see* and *feel* the proofs. . . . readers can penetrate into higher mathematics with . . . pleasure instead of the usual laborious study."
—*American Scientist.*

"Students, particularly, would benefit very much by reading this book . . . they will experience the sensation of being taken into the friendly confidence of a great mathematician and being shown the real significance of things."—*Science Progress.*

"A person with a minimum of formal training can follow the reasoning. . . . an important [book]."
—*The Mathematics Teacher.*

—1952. 358 pp. 6x9. 8284-0087-3. **$7.50**

GESAMMELTE ABHANDLUNGEN (Collected Papers)

By D. HILBERT

Volume I (Number Theory) contains Hilbert's papers on Number Theory, including his long paper on Algebraic Numbers. Volume II (Algebra, Invariant Theory, Geometry) covers not only the topics indicated in the sub-title but also papers on Diophantine Equations. Volume III carries the sub-title: Analysis, Foundation of Mathematics, Physics, and Miscellaneous Papers.

—1932/35-66. 1,457 pp. 6x9. 8284-0195-0. Each vol. **$8.95**
Three vol. set **$23.50**

PRINCIPLES OF MATHEMATICAL LOGIC

By D. HILBERT and W. ACKERMANN

"As a text the book has become a classic . . . the best introduction for the student who seriously wants to master the technique. Some of the features which give it this status are as follows:

"The first feature is its extraordinary lucidity. A second is the intuitive approach, with the introduction of formalization only after a full discussion of motivation. Again, the argument is rigorous and exact . . . A fourth feature is the emphasis on general extra-formal principles . . . Finally, the work is relatively free from bias . . . All together, the book still bears the stamp of the genius of one of the great mathematicians of modern times."—*Bulletin of the A.M.S.*

—1959. xii + 172 pp. 6x9. 8284-0069-5. **$3.95**

SQUARING THE CIRCLE, and other Monographs

By HOBSON, HUDSON, SINGH, and KEMPE

FOUR VOLUMES IN ONE.

SQUARING THE CIRCLE, by *Hobson*. A fascinating account of one of the three famous problems of antiquity, its significance, its history, the mathematical work it inspired in modern times, and its eventual solution in the closing years of the last century.

RULER AND COMPASSES, by *Hudson*. "An analytical and geometrical investigation of how far Euclidean constructions can take us. It is as thoroughgoing as it is constructive."—*Sci. Monthly*.

THE THEORY AND CONSTRUCTION OF NON-DIFFERENTIABLE FUNCTIONS, by *Singh*. I. Functions Defined by Series. II. Functions Defined Geometrically. III. Functions Defined Arithmetically. IV. Properties of Non-Differentiable Functions.

HOW TO DRAW A STRAIGHT LINE, by *Kempe*. An intriguing monograph on linkages. Describes, among other things, a linkage that will trisect any angle.

"Intriguing, meaty."—*Scientific American*.

—388 pp. 4½x7½. 8284-0095-4. Four vols. in one. **$4.95**

SPHERICAL AND ELLIPSOIDAL HARMONICS

By E. W. HOBSON

"A comprehensive treatise . . . and the standard reference in its field."—*Bulletin of the A. M. S.*

—1931-65. xi + 500 pp. 5⅜x8. 8284-0104-7. **$7.50**

ELASTOKINETIK: Die Methoden zur Angenäherten Lösung von Eigenwertproblemen in der Elastokinetik

By K. HOHENEMSER

—(Erg. der Math.) 1932-49. 89 pp. 5½x8½. 8284-0055-5. **$2.75**

RULER AND COMPASSES, *by H. P. HUDSON*. See HOBSON

PHYSIKALISCH-MATHEMATISCHE MONOGRAPHIEN

By W. v. IGNATOWSKY, et al.

THREE VOLUMES IN ONE.

CONTENTS: 1. *Untersuchungen einiger Integrale mit Besselschen Funktionen und ihre Anwendung auf Beugungserscheinungen*, by Ignatowsky. 2. *Kreisscheibenkondensator*, by Ignatowsky. 3. *Table of a Special Function*, by Bursian and Fock.

—1932-66. 16 + 232 pp. 6¼x9¼. 8284-0201-9. Three vols. in one. **$5.50**

VORLESUNGEN UEBER DYNAMIK

By C. G. J. JACOBI

This is Volume 8 of the *Gesammelte Werke*.

—2nd ed. 1884-68. viii + 300 pp. 6½x9¼. 8284-0227-2. **$7.50**

GESAMMELTE WERKE

By C. G. J. JACOBI

The complete collected works of the renowned mathematician, edited by Karl Weierstrass (Vols. 2-7), C. W. Borchardt (Vol. 1), and A. Clebsch (Vol. 8). The second edition is a corrected reprint of Vols. 1-7 of the first edition (1881/91) and an unaltered reprint of Vol. 8.

—2nd ed. 1968. 4,032 pp. 6½x9¼.
8284-0226-4. Volumes 1-7. **$99.50**
8284-0227-2. Volume 8. **$7.50**

A TREATISE ON THE LINE COMPLEX

By C. M. JESSOP

"The best introduction to the subject."—*Virgil Snyder.*

—1903-68. xv + 364 pp. 5⅜x8. 8284-0223-X. **$7.95**

THE CALCULUS OF FINITE DIFFERENCES

By CHARLES JORDAN

"... destined to remain the classic treatment of the subject . . . for many years to come."—*Harry C. Carver, Founder and formerly Editor of the* ANNALS OF MATHEMATICAL STATISTICS.

—3rd ed. 1965. xxi + 655 pp. 5⅜x8. 8284-0033-4. **$7.50**

THEORIE DER ORTHOGONALREIHEN

By S. KACZMARZ and H. STEINHAUS

—1935-51. viii + 294 pp. 6x9. 8284-0083-0. **$4.95**

DIFFERENTIALGLEICHUNGEN: LOESUNGSMETHODEN UND LOESUNGEN

By E. KAMKE

Everything possible that can be of use when one has a given differential equation to solve, or when one wishes to investigate that solution thoroughly.

PART A: General Methods of Solution and the Properties of the Solutions.

PART B: Boundary and Characteristic Value Problems.

PART C: Dictionary of some 1600 Equations in Lexicographical Order, with solution, techniques for solving, and references.

"A reference work of outstanding importance which should be in every mathematical library."
—*Mathematical Gazette.*

—3rd ed. 1944. 692 pp. 6x9. 8284-0044-X. **$12.50**

DIFFERENTIALGLEICHUNGEN, *by KAEHLER.*
See BLASCHKE

HOW TO DRAW A STRAIGHT LINE, *by KEMPE.*
See HOBSON

ASYMPTOTISCHE GESETZE DER WAHRSCHEINLICHKEITSRECHNUNG

By A. A, KHINTCHINE

—1933-48. 82 pp. 5½x8½. 8284-0036-9. Paper **$2.00**

THE MATHEMATICAL THEORY OF THE TOP,
by F. KLEIN. See SIERPINSKI

FAMOUS PROBLEMS, and other monographs
By KLEIN, SHEPPARD, MacMAHON, and MORDELL

FOUR VOLUMES IN ONE.

FAMOUS PROBLEMS OF ELEMENTARY GEOMETRY, by *Klein*. A fascinating little book. A simple, easily understandable, account of the famous problems of Geometry—The Duplication of the Cube, Trisection of the Angle, Squaring of the Circle—and the proofs that these cannot be solved by ruler and compass—presentable, say, before an undergraduate math club (no calculus required). Also, the modern problems about transcendental numbers, the existence of such numbers, and proofs of the transcendence of *e*.

FROM DETERMINANT TO TENSOR, by *Sheppard*. A novel and charming introduction. Written with the utmost simplicity. PT I. Origin of Determinants. II. Properties of Determinants. III. Solution of Simultaneous Equations. IV. Properties. V. Tensor Notation. PT II. VI. Sets. VII. Cogredience, etc. VIII. Examples from Statistics. IX. Tensors in Theory of Relativity.

INTRODUCTION TO COMBINATORY ANALYSIS, by *MacMahon*. A concise introduction to this field. Written as introduction to the author's two-volume work.

THREE LECTURES ON FERMAT'S LAST THEOREM, by *Mordell*. This famous problem is so easy that a high-school student might not unreasonably hope to solve it; it is so difficult that tens of thousands of amateur and professional mathematicians, Euler and Gauss among them, have failed to find a complete solution. Mordell's very small book begins with an impartial investigation of whether Fermat himself had a solution (as he said he did) and explains what has been accomplished. This is one of the masterpieces of mathematical exposition.

—2nd ed. 1962. 350 pp. 5⅜x8. Four vols. in one.
8284-0108-X. Cloth **$4.95**
8284-0166-7. Paper **$1.95**

VORLESUNGEN UEBER NICHT-EUKLIDISCHE GEOMETRIE
By F. KLEIN

—1928-59. xii + 326 pp. 5x8. 8284-0129-2. **$6.00**

ENTWICKLUNG DER MATHEMATIK IM 19. JAHRHUNDERT
By F. KLEIN

TWO VOLUMES IN ONE.

Vol. I treats of the various branches of advanced mathematics of the prolific 19th century; Klein himself was in the forefront of the mathematical activity of latter part of the 19th and early part of the 20th centuries.

Vol. II deals with the mathematics of relativity theory.

—1926/27-67. 616 pp. 5¼x8. 8284-0074-1. Two vols. in one. **$8.95**

LEHRBUCH DER THETAFUNKTIONEN

By A. KRAZER

"Dr. Krazer has succeeded in the difficult task of giving a clear deductive account of the complicated formal theory of multiple theta-functions within the compass of a moderate sized text-book . . . Distinguished by clearness of style and general elegance of form."—*Mathematical Gazette.*

—1903-71. xxiv + 509 pp. 5⅜x8. 8284-0244-2. **$12.50**

WERKE

By L. KRONECKER

—6 vols. in 5. 1895/97/99/1929/30/31-68. 2,530 pp. 6½x8½.
Five vol. set. **$59.50**

GROUP THEORY

By A. KUROSH

Translated from the second Russian edition and with added notes by PROFESSOR K. A. HIRSCH.

Partial Contents: PART ONE: The Elements of Group Theory. Chap. I. Definition. II. Subgroups (Systems, Cyclic Groups, Ascending Sequences of Groups). III. Normal Subgroups. IV. Endomorphisms and Automorphisms. Groups with Operators. V. Series of Subgroups. Direct Products. Defining Relations, etc. PART TWO: Abelian Groups. VI. Foundations of the Theory of Abelian Groups (Finite Abelian Groups, Rings of Endomorphisms, Abelian Groups with Operators). VII. Primary and Mixed Abelian Groups. VIII. Torsion-Free Abelian Groups. Editor's Notes. Bibliography.

Vol. II. PART THREE: Group-Theoretical Constructions. IX. Free Products and Free Groups (Free Products with Amalgamated Subgroup, Fully Invariant Subgroups). X. Finitely Generated Groups. XI. Direct Products. Lattices (Modular, Complete Modular, etc.). XII. Extensions of Groups (of Abelian Groups, of Non-commutative Groups, Cohomology Groups). PART FOUR: Solvable and Nilpotent Groups. XIII. Finiteness Conditions, Sylow Subgroups, etc. XIV. Solvable Groups (Solvable and Generalized Solvable Groups, Local Theorems). XV. Nilpotent Groups (Generalized, Complete, Locally Nilpotent Torsion-Free, etc.). Editor's Notes. Bibliography.

—Vol. I. 2nd ed. 1959. 271 pp. 6x9. 8284-0107-1. **$6.00**
—Vol. II. 2nd ed. 1960. 308 pp. 6x9. 8284-0109-8. **$6.00**
—Vol. III. Approx. 200 pp. 6x9. **In prep.**

LECTURES ON GENERAL ALGEBRA

By A. G. KUROSH

Translated from the Russian by PROFESSOR K. A. HIRSCH, with a special preface for this edition by PROFESSOR KUROSH.

Partial Contents: CHAP. I. Relations. II. Groups and Rings (Groupoids, Semigroups, Groups, Rings, Fields, . . . , Gaussian rings, Dedekind rings). III. Universal Algebras. Groups with Multioperators (. . . Free universal algebras, Free products of groups). IV. Lattices (Complete lattices, Modular lattice, Schmidt-Ore Theorem, . . . , Distributive lattices). V. Operator Groups and Rings. Modules. Linear Algebras (. . . Free modules, Vector spaces over fields, Rings of linear transformations, . . . , Derivations, Differential rings). VI. Ordered and Topological Groups and Rings. Rings with a Valuation. BIBLIOGRAPHY.

—1970. 335 pp. 6x9. 8284-0168-3. **$6.95**

OEUVRES (Collected Works)

By E. LAGUERRE

With a preface by H. POINCARE.

—1898/1905-71. 1,202 pp. 5⅜x8. Two vol. set. **In prep.**

DIFFERENTIAL AND INTEGRAL CALCULUS

By E. LANDAU

A masterpiece of rigor and clarity.

"And what a book it is! The marks of Landau's thoroughness and elegance, and of his undoubted authority, impress themselves on the reader at every turn, from the opening of the preface . . . to the closing of the final chapter.

"It is a book that all analysts . . . should possess . . . to see how a master of his craft like Landau presented the calculus when he was at the height of his power and reputation."

—*Mathematical Gazette.*

—3rd ed. 1965. 372 pp. 6x9. 8284-0078-4. **$6.95**

HANDBUCH DER LEHRE VON DER VERTEILUNG DER PRIMZAHLEN

By E. LANDAU

TWO VOLUMES IN ONE.

To Landau's monumental work on prime-number theory there has been added, in this edition, two of Landau's papers and an up-to-date guide to the work: an Appendix by Prof. Paul T. Bateman.

—2nd ed. 1953. 1,028 pp. 5⅜x8. 8284-0096-2.
Two vols. in one. **$16.50**

VORLESUNGEN UEBER ZAHLENTHEORIE

By E. LANDAU

—Vol. I, Pt. 2. *(Additive Number Theory) xii + 180 pp. Vol. II. (Analytical Number Theory and Geometrical Number Theory) viii + 308 pp. Vol. III. (Algebraic Number Theory and Fermat's Last Theorem) viii + 341 pp. 5¼x8¼. *(Vol. I, Pt. 1 is issued as **Elementare Zahlentheorie** (in German) or as **Elementary Number Theory** (in English).) 8284-0032-6.
Three vols. in one. **$16.50**

GRUNDLAGEN DER ANALYSIS

By E. LANDAU

The student who wishes to study mathematical German will find Landau's famous *Grundlagen der Analysis* ideally suited to his needs.

Only a few score of German words will enable him to read the entire book with only an occasional glance at the Vocabulary! [A COMPLETE German-English vocabulary, prepared with the novice especially in mind, has been appended to the book.]

—4th ed. 1965. 173 pp. 5½x8½. 8284-0024-5. Cloth **$3.95**
8284-0141-1. Paper **$1.95**

FOUNDATIONS OF ANALYSIS

By E. LANDAU

"Certainly no clearer treatment of the foundations of the number system can be offered. . . . One can only be thankful to the author for this fundamental piece of exposition, which is alive with his vitality and genius."—*J. F. Ritt, Amer. Math. Monthly.*

—2nd ed. 1960. xiv + 136 pp. 6x9. 8284-0079-2. **$3.95**

ELEMENTARE ZAHLENTHEORIE

By E. LANDAU

"Interest is enlisted at once and sustained by the accuracy, skill, and enthusiasm with which Landau marshals . . . facts and simplifies . . . details."

—*G. D. Birkhoff, Bulletin of the A. M. S.*

—1927-50. vii + 180 + iv pp. 5½x8½. 8284-0026-1. **$4.50**

ELEMENTARY NUMBER THEORY

By E. LANDAU

The present work is a translation of Prof. Landau's famous *Elementare Zahlentheorie,* with added exercises by Prof. Paul T. Bateman.

—2nd ed. 1966. 256 pp. 6x9. 8284-0125-X. **$4.95**

Einführung in die Elementare und Analytische Theorie der ALGEBRAISCHE ZAHLEN

By E. LANDAU

—2nd ed. 1927-49. vii + 147 pp. 5⅜x8. 8284-0062-8 **$2.95**

NEUERE FUNKTIONENTHEORIE, *by E. LANDAU.*
See WEYL

Mémoires sur la Théorie des SYSTEMES DES EQUATIONS DIFFERENTIELLES LINEAIRES, Vols. I, II, III

By J. A. LAPPO-DANILEVSKII

THREE VOLUMES IN ONE.

A reprint, in one volume, of Volumes 6, 7, and 8 of the monographs of the Steklov Institute of Mathematics in Moscow.

"The theory of [systems of linear differential equations] is treated with elegance and generality by the author, and his contributions constitute an important addition to the field of differential equations."—*Applied Mechanics Reviews.*

—1934/5/6-53. 689 pp. 5⅜x8. 8284-0094-6.
Three vols. in one. **$12.50**

KURVENTHEORIE

By K. MENGER

Partial Contents: CHAP. I. The Old Concept of a Curve. II. The New Concept of a Curve . . . IV. The Sum of Curves. V. Properties under Deformation, etc. VI. Fundamental Theorem of Curve-Theoretical Concept of Order . . . VIII. Regular Curves. IX. Rational Curves . . . XII. The Universal Curve.

—2nd ed. 1932-67. vi + 376 pp. 6½x9¼. 8284-0172-1. **$12.00**

DIMENSIONSTHEORIE

By K. MENGER

—1928-72. iv + 318 pp. 6x9. **Tent.**

THE DEVELOPMENT OF MATHEMATICS IN CHINA AND JAPAN

By Y. MIKAMI

"Filled with valuable information. Mikami's [account of the mathematicians he knew personally] is an attractive features."

—*Scientific American.*

—1913-62. x + 347 pp. 5⅜x8. 8284-0149-7. **$6.00**

GESAMMELTE ABHANDLUNGEN

By H. MINKOWSKI

TWO VOLUMES IN ONE.

Minkowski's Collected Works are issued under the editorship of David Hilbert, with the assistance of Andreas Speiser and Hermann Weyl.

—1911-67. 871 pp. 6x9. 8284-0208-6. Two vols. in one. **$17.50**

GEOMETRIE DER ZAHLEN

By H. MINKOWSKI

—1896-53. viii + 256 pp. 5⅜x8. 8284-0093-8. **$4.95**

DIOPHANTISCHE APPROXIMATIONEN

By H. MINKOWSKI

—1907-57. viii + 235 pp. 5⅜x8. 8284-0118-7. **$4.95**

ESSAI D'ANALYSE SUR LES JEUX DE HAZARD

By R. de MONTMORT

A photographic reprint of one of the great works in the history of Probability.

The original work commands many hundreds of dollars on the rare book market.

—2nd ed. 1714. Repr. 1971. 468 pp. 6x9. **In prep.**

FERMAT'S LAST THEOREM, *by L. J. MORDELL.*
See KLEIN

INVERSIVE GEOMETRY

By F. MORLEY and F. V. MORLEY

—1937-54. xi + 273 pp. 5⅜x8. 8284-0101-2. **$3.95**

INTRODUCTION TO NUMBER THEORY

By T. NAGELL

A special feature of Nagell's well-known text is the rather extensive treatment of Diophantine equations of second and higher degree. A large number of non-routine problems are given.

—2nd ed. 1964. 309 pp. 5⅜x8. 8284-0163-2. **$5.50**

LEHRBUCH DER KOMBINATORIK

By E. NETTO

A standard work on the fascinating subject of Combinatory Analysis.

—2nd ed. 1927-58. viii + 348 pp. 5⅜x8. 8284-0123-3. **$6.00**

THE THEORY OF SUBSTITUTIONS

By E. NETTO

—2nd ed. (C.r. of 1st ed.) 1964. 304 pp. 5⅜x8. 8284-0165-9. **$4.95**

DIE GAMMAFUNKTION

By N. NIELSEN

TWO VOLUMES IN ONE.

HANDBUCH DER THEORIE DER GAMMAFUNKTION, by *N. Nielsen.* A standard, and very clearly written treatise on the gamma function and allied topics.

THEORIE DES INTEGRALLOGARITHMUS UND VERWANDTER TRANSZENDENTEN, by *N. Nielsen.* A treatise on certain transcendental functions. There are numerous references to the *Handbuch.*

—1906-65. 448 pp. 6x9. 8284-0188-8. Two vols. in one. **$7.50**

Vorlesungen über DIFFERENZENRECHNUNG

By N. H. NÖRLUND

—1924-54. ix + 551 pp. 5⅜x8. 8284-0100-4. **$6.50**

FUNCTIONS OF REAL VARIABLES
FUNCTIONS OF A COMPLEX VARIABLE

By W. F. OSGOOD

TWO VOLUMES IN ONE.

"*Well-organized courses, systematic, lucid, fundamental,* with many brief sets of appropriate exercises, and occasional suggestions for more extensive reading. The technical terms have been kept to a minimum, and have been clearly explained. The aim has been to develop the student's power and to furnish him with a substantial body of classic theorems, whose proofs illustrate the methods and whose results provide equipment for further progress."—*Bulletin of A. M. S*

—1936-58. 676 pp. 5x8. 8284-0124-1. Two vols. in one. **$6.50**

LEHRBUCH DER FUNKTIONENTHEORIE

By W. F. OSGOOD

THREE VOLUMES IN TWO.

Partial Contents: CHAP. I. The Calculus. II. Functions of Real Variables. III. Uniform Convergence. IV. Line Integrals and Multiply-Connected Regions. V. Set Theory. VI. Complex Numbers. Analytic Functions. Linear Transformations. VII. Rational Functions. VIII. Multiple-Valued Functions; Riemann Surfaces. IX. Analytic Continuation. X. Periodic Functions. XI. Infinite Series, Infinite Product Development . . . XIII. Logarithmic Potential. XIV. Conformal Mapping and Uniformization.

Vol. II: CHAPS. I-III. The Theory of Functions of Several Complex Variables. IV. Algebraic Functions and Abelian Integrals . . . VI. Abel's Theorem; Riemann-Roch Theorem; etc. VII. Periodic Functions of Several Complex Variables. VIII. Applications.

—Vol. I. 5th ed. 1928-65. 818 pp. 5⅜x8. 8284-0193-4. **$8.50**
—Vol. II. 2nd ed. 1932-65. 686 pp. 5⅜x8. 8284-0182-9. **$8.50**

IRRATIONALZAHLEN

By O. PERRON

—2nd ed. 1939-51. 207 pp. 5⅜x8. 8284-0047-4. Cloth **$3.75**
8284-0113-6. Paper **$1.50**

DIE LEHRE VON DEN KETTENBRUECHEN

By O. PERRON

Both the Arithmetic Theory and the Analytic Theory are treated fully.

"An indispensable work . . . Perron remains the best guide for the novice. The style is simple and precise and presents no difficulties."

—*Mathematical Gazette.*

—2nd ed. 1929-50. xii + 524 pp. 5⅜x8. 8284-0073-3. **$6.95**

EIGHT-PLACE TABLES OF TRIGONOMETRIC FUNCTIONS

By J. PETERS

Eight-place tables of natural trigonometric functions for every second of arc, with an appendix on the computation to twenty decimal places.

MAIN TABLE: The values of sine, cosine, tangent, and cotangent are given to 8 decimal places for every second of arc, from 0°0′0″ to 90°0′0″. For example, it can be read off directly from the table (without the need of interpolation) that the value of Cos 83°19′33″ is 0.11622293.

TABLE II (*Supplementary Table*)*:* 21-Place Tables of Sine and Cosine for every 10′ from 0°0′ to 90°0′.

TABLE III (*Supplementary Table*)*:* 21-Place Tables of Sine and Cosine and their Differences, for every second from 0′0″ to 10′0″.

Several other supplementary tables are given.

"Peters' table is considered to be the standard (i.e., the best) 8-place trigonometric table."

—*Mathematics of Computation*

—Fourth printing. 1968. xii + 956 pp. 8284-0174-8.
Regular edition **$25.00**
9294-0185-3. Thumb-indexed **$29.50**

METHODS FOR GEOMETRICAL CONSTRUCTION,
by J. PETERSEN. See BALL

GRAPHICAL METHODS, by RUNGE. *See* SIERPINSKI

EUCLIDES VINDICATUS

By G. SACCHERI

—2nd ed. 1971. Approx. 300 pp. 5⅜x8. 8284-0212-4. **In prep.**

ANALYTIC GEOMETRY OF THREE DIMENSIONS

By G. SALMON

A rich and detailed treatment by the author of *Conic Sections, Higher Plane Curves,* etc.

Partial Contents: Chap. I. Coordinates. III. Plane and Line. IV-VI. Quadrics. VIII. Foci and Focal Surfaces. IX. Invariants and Covariants of Systems of Quadrics. XI. General Theory of Surfaces. XII. Curves and Developables (Projective properties, non-projective properties, . . .).

Vol. II. Chap. XIII. Partial Differential Equations of Families of Surfaces. XIII (a). Complexes, Congruences, Ruled Surfaces. XIII (b). Triply Orthogonal Systems of Surfaces, Normal Congruences of Curves. XIV. The Wave Surface, The Centro-surface, etc. XV. Surfaces of Third Degree. XVI. Surfaces of Fourth Degree. XVII. General Theory of Surfaces. XVIII. Reciprocal Surfaces.

—Vol. I. 7th ed. 1927-58. xxiv + 470 pp. 5x8. 8284-0122-5. **$4.95**

—Vol. II. 5th ed. 1928-65. xvi + 334 pp. 5x8. 8284-0196-9. **$4.95**

CONIC SECTIONS

By G. SALMON

"The classic book on the subject, covering the whole ground and full of touches of genius."

—*Mathematical Association.*

—6th ed. xv + 400 pp. 5⅜x8. 8284-0099-7. Cloth **$4.95**
8284-0098-9. Paper **$1.95**

HIGHER PLANE CURVES

By G. SALMON

Chapter Headings: I. Coordinates. II. General Properties of Algebraic Curves. III. Envelopes. IV. Metrical Properties. V. Cubics. VI. Quartics. VII. Transcendental Curves. VIII. Transformation of Curves. IX. General Theory of Curves.

—3rd ed. 1879-1960. xix + 395 pp. 5⅜x8. 8284-0138-1. **$4.95**

LESSONS INTRODUCTORY TO THE MODERN HIGHER ALGEBRA

By G. SALMON

A classical account of the theory of Determinants and Invariants.

—5th ed. 1887-1964. xv + 376 pp. 5¼x8. 8284-0150-0. **$4.95**

MEHRDIMENSIONALE GEOMETRIE

By P. H. SCHOUTE

VOL. I: Die linearen Räume. VOL. II: Die Polytope.

—1902/05-71. 638 pp. 4½x7. Two vol. set. **In prep.**

PFAFF'S PROBLEM AND ITS GENERALIZATIONS

By J. A. SCHOUTEN and W. v. d. KULK

Partial Contents: CHAP. III. The Outer Problem. IV. Classification of Covariant Vector Fields and Pfaffians . . . VI. Contact Transformations. VII. Theory of Vector Manifolds and Element Manifolds . . . X. Solution of Systems of Differential Equations.

—1949-69. xvi + 542 pp. 5⅜x8. 8284-0221-3. **$12.00**

INTRODUCTION TO MODERN ALGEBRA AND MATRIX THEORY

By O. SCHREIER and E. SPERNER

An English translation of the revolutionary work, *Einführung in die Analytische Geometrie und Algebra.* Chapter Headings: I. Affine Space. Linear Equations. (Vector Spaces). II. Euclidean Space. Theory of Determinants. III. The Theory of Fields. Fundamental Theorem of Algebra. IV. Elements of Group Theory. V. Matrices and Linear Transformations. **The treatment of matrices is especially extensive.**

"Outstanding . . . good introduction . . . well suited for use as a text . . . Self-contained and each topic is painstakingly developed."

—*Mathematics Teacher.*

—2nd ed. 1959. viii + 378 pp. 6x9. 8284-0080-6. **$6.95**

PROJECTIVE GEOMETRY OF *n* DIMENSIONS

By O. SCHREIER and E. SPERNER

Translated from the German by CALVIN A. ROGERS.

Suitable for a one-semester course on the senior undergraduate or first-year graduate level. The background required is minimal: The definition and simplest properties of vector spaces and the elements of matrix theory.

There are exercises at the end of each chapter to enable the student to test his mastery of the material.

CHAPTER HEADINGS: I. n-Dimensional Projective Space. II. General Projective Coordinates. III. Hyperplane Coordinates. The Duality Principle. IV. The Cross Ratio. V. Projectivities. VI. Linear Projectivities of P_n onto Itself. VII. Correlations. VIII. Hypersurfaces of the Second Order. IX. Projective Classification of Hypersurfaces of the Second Order. X. Projective Properties of Hypersurfaces of the Second Order. XI. The Affine Classification of Hypersurfaces of the Second Order. XII. The Metric Classification of Hypersurfaces of the Second Order.

—1961. 208 pp. 6x9. 8284-0126-8. **$4.95**

VORLESUNGEN UEBER DIE ALGEBRA DER LOGIK

By E. SCHRÖDER

One of the classics of logic.

The present edition includes, as an addendum to the third volume, the complete text of the short two-volume work *Abriss der Algebra der Logik.*

—2nd ed. 1966. (1st ed.: 1890-1905; 1909/10.) 2,192 pp. 6x9. 5 vols. in 3. 8284-0171-3. Three vol. set. **$35.00**

GESAMMELTE MATHEMATISCHE ABHANDLUNGEN

By H. A. SCHWARZ

—1890-1971. 726 pp. 6x9. Two vols. in one. **In prep.**

AN INTRODUCTION TO THE OPERATIONS WITH SERIES

By I. J. SCHWATT

Many useful methods for operations on series, methods for expansions of functions, methods for the summation of many types of series, and a wealth of explicit results are contained in this book. The only prerequisite is knowledge of the Calculus.

—1924-62. x + 287 pp. 5⅜x8. 8284-0158-6. **$4.95**

PROJECTIVE METHODS IN PLANE ANALYTICAL GEOMETRY

By C. A. SCOTT

Chapter Headings: I. Point and Line Coordinates. II. Infinity. Transformation of Coordinates. III. Figures Determined by Four Elements. IV. The Principle of Duality. V. Descriptive Properties of Curves. VI. Metric Properties of Curves; Line at Infinity. VII. Metric Properties of Curves; Circular Points. VIII. Unicursal (Rational) Curves. Tracing of Curves. IX. Cross-Ratio, Homography, and Involution. X. Projection and Linear Transformation. XI. Theory of Correspondence. XII. The Absolute. XIII. Invariants and Covariants.

—3rd ed. 1923-61. xii + 290 pp. 5⅜x8. 8284-0146-2. **$3.95**

LEHRBUCH DER TOPOLOGIE

By H. SEIFERT and W. THRELFALL

This famous book is a modern work on *combinatorial topology* addressed to the student as well as to the specialist. It is almost indispensable to the mathematician who wishes to gain a knowledge of this important field.

"The exposition proceeds by easy stages **with examples and illustrations at every turn.**"

—*Bulletin of the A. M. S.*

—1934-68. vii + 353 pp. 5⅜x8. 8284-0031-8. **$6.00**

TEXTBOOK OF TOPOLOGY

By H. SEIFERT and W. THRELFALL

A translation of the above.

—Approx. 380 pp. 6x9. **In prep.**

TABLES OF ARC LENGTH

By E. G. SEWOSTER

Full title: EIGHT-PLACE TABLES OF LENGTHS OF CIRCULAR ARCS. The tabulation is for every second of arc, 0° to 45°.

—3rd ed. 1971. 270 pp. 7x10. 8284-0240-X. **Prob. $10.00**

FROM DETERMINANT TO TENSOR,

by W. F. SHEPPARD. See KLEIN

HYPOTHESE DU CONTINU

By W. SIERPINSKI

"One sees how deeply this postulate cuts through all phases of the foundations of mathematics, how intimately many fundamental questions of analysis and geometry are connected with it . . . a most excellent addition to our mathematical literature."

—*Bulletin of A. M. S.*

—2nd ed. 1957. xvii + 274 pp. 5⅜x8. 8284-0117-9. **$4.95**

CONGRUENCE OF SETS,
and other monographs

By SIERPINSKI, KLEIN, RUNGE, and DICKSON

FOUR VOLUMES IN ONE.

ON THE CONGRUENCE OF SETS AND THEIR EQUIVALENCE BY FINITE DECOMPOSITION, by *W. Sierpinski.* 1. Congr. of Sets. 2. Translation of Sets. 3. Equiv. of Sets by Finite Decomposition. 4. D. into Two Parts. . . . 7. Paradoxical D's. . . . 10. The Hausdorff Paradox. 11. Paradox of Banach and Tarski. 12. Banach Measure. The General Problem of Measure. 13. Absolute Measure. 14. Paradox of J. von Neumann.

THE MATHEMATICAL THEORY OF THE TOP, by *F. Klein.* Well-known lectures on the analytical formulas relating to the motion of the top.

GRAPHICAL METHODS, by *C. Runge.*

INTRODUCTION TO THE THEORY OF ALGEBRAIC EQUATIONS, by *L. E. Dickson.* Dickson's earliest (1903) account of the subject, substantially less abstract than his later exposition. *From Dickson's Preface:* "The subject is here presented in the historical order of its development. The First Part (Chaps. I-IV) is devoted to the Lagrange-Cauchy-Abel theory of general algebraic equations. The Second Part (Chaps. V-XI) is devoted to Galois' theory of algebraic equations . . . The aim has been to make the presentation strictly elementary, with practically no dependence upon any branch of mathematics beyond elementary algebra. There occur numerous illustrative examples, as well as sets of elementary exercises."

—1954/1897/1912/1903-1967. 461 pp. 5¼x8. 8284-0209-4.
Four vols. in one. **$6.50**

ELEMENTS DE LA THEORIE DES FONCTIONS ELLIPTIQUES

By J. TANNERY and J. MOLK

FOUR VOLUMES IN TWO.

—2nd ed. 1893/1902-71. 1,146 pp. 5⅜x8. **In prep.**

A HISTORY OF THE MATHEMATICAL THEORY OF PROBABILITY

By I. TODHUNTER

Introduces the reader to *almost every process and every species of problem which the literature of the subject can furnish.* Hundreds of problems are solved in detail.

—1865-1965. xvi + 624 pp. 5⅜x8. 8284-0057-1. **$7.50**

A HISTORY OF THE CALCULUS OF VARIATIONS IN THE 19th CENTURY

By I. TODHUNTER

A critical account of the various works on the Calculus of Variations published during the early part of the nineteenth century. Of the seventeen chapters, fourteen are devoted to the Calculus of Variations proper, two to various memoirs that touch upon the subject, and the seventeenth is a history of the conditions of integrability. Chapter Nine contains a translation in full of Jacobi's memoir.

—1862-1961. xii + 532 pp. 5⅜x8. 8284-0164-0. **$7.50**

SET TOPOLOGY

By R. VAIDYANATHASWAMY

In this text on Topology, the first edition of which was published in India, the concept of partial order has been made the unifying theme.

Over 500 exercises for the reader enrich the text.

CHAPTER HEADINGS: I. Algebra of Subsets of a Set. II. Rings and Fields of Sets. III. Algebra of Partial Order. IV. The Closure Function. V. Neighborhood Topology. VI. Open and Closed Sets. VII. Topological Maps. VIII. The Derived Set in T_1 Space. IX. The Topological Product. X. Convergence in Metrical Space. XI. Convergence Topology.

—2nd ed. 1960. vi + 305 pp. 6x9. 8284-0139-X. **$6.95**

LECTURES ON THE GENERAL THEORY OF INTEGRAL FUNCTIONS

By G. VALIRON

—1923-49. xii + 208 pp. 5¼x8. 8284-0056-3. **$3.95**

L'APPROXIMATION, *by VALLÉE POUSSIN.*
See BERNSTEIN

GRUPPEN VON LINEAREN TRANSFORMATIONEN

By B. L. VAN DER WAERDEN

—Ergeb. der Math. 1935-48. 94 pp. 8284-0045-8. **$2.95**

SYMBOLIC LOGIC

By J. VENN

A classic.

—2nd ed. 1894-1971. xxviii + 540 pp. 5⅜x8. **Prob. $8.50**

THE LOGIC OF CHANCE

By J. VENN

One of the classics of the theory of probability. Venn's book remains unsurpassed for clarity, readability, and sheer charm of exposition. No mathematics is required.

CONTENTS: PART ONE: Physical Foundations of the Science of Probability. CHAP. I. The Series of Probability. II. Formation of the Series, III. Origin, or Causation, of the Series. IV. How to Discover and Prove the Series. V. The Concept of Randomness. PART TWO: Logical Superstructure on the Above Physical Foundations. VI. Gradations of Belief. VII. The Rules of Inference in Probability. VIII. The Rule of Succession. IX. Induction. X. Causation and Design. XI. Material and Formal Logic . . . XIV. Fallacies. PART THREE: Applications. XV. Insurance and Gambling. XVI. Application to Testimony. XVII. Credibility of Extraordinary Stories. XVIII. The Nature and Use of an Average as a Means of Approximation to the Truth.

—4th ed. (Repr. of 3rd ed.) xxix + 508 pp. 5⅜x8.
8284-0173-X. Cloth **$6.00**
8284-0169-1. Paper **$2.25**

DIE GESCHICHTE DER TRIGONOMETRIE

By A. VON BRAUNMUEHL

A scholarly history of Trigonometry.

—1900/03. 535 pp. 5⅜x8. Two vols. in one. **In prep.**

STATISTICAL DECISION FUNCTIONS

By A. WALD

"A remarkable application to statistical theory of the methods and spirit of modern mathematics . . . makes effective use of the modern theory of measure and integration, and operates at a high level of rigor and abstraction . . . Its ultimate liberating effect on statistical theory will be great. It is to be hoped that so rich and stimulating a book as this will reach an audience among mathematicians."—*Bulletin of A.M.S.*

—1950-71. ix + 179 pp. 5⅜x8. 8284-0243-4. **$3.95**

ANALYTIC THEORY OF CONTINUED FRACTIONS

By H. S. WALL

Partial Contents: CHAP. I. The c. f. as a Product of Linear Fractional Transformations. II. Convergence Theorems. IV. Positive-Definite c. f. VI. Stieltjes Type c. f. VIII. Value-Region Problem. IX. J-Fraction Expansions. X. Theory of Equations. XII. Matrix Theory of c. f. XIII. C. f. and Definite Integrals. XIV. Moment Problem. XVI. Hausdorff Summability. XIX. Stieltjes Summability. XX. The Padé Table.

—1948-67. xiv + 433 pp. 5⅜x8. 8284-0207-8. **$7.50**

LOGIC, COMPUTERS, AND SETS

By H. WANG

Partial Contents: GENERAL (EXPOSITORY) SKETCHES (*Chaps. I-VI*) : I. The Axiomatic Method (§ 2. The problem of adequacy, . . . , §6. Gödel's Theorems, . . .). II. Eighty Years of Foundational Studies. III. The Axiomatization of Arithmetic (§2. Grassmann's calculus, . . . , § 6. Dedekind and Frege). V. Computation (§ 1. Concept of computability, . . . , § 6. Control of errors in calculating machines). CALCULATING MACHINES (*Chaps. VI-X*) : VI. A Variant to Turing's Theory. VII. Universal Turing Machines. VIII. The Logic of Automata. IX. Toward Mechanical Mathematics. FORMAL NUMBER THEORY (*Chaps. XI-XV*) : XII. Many-Sorted Predicate Calculi. XIII. Arithmetization of Metamathematics (§ 1. Gödel numbering, . . . , § 4. Arithmetic translations of axiom systems). XIV. Ackermann's Consistency Proof. . . . IMPREDICATIVE SET THEORY (*Chaps. XVI-XX*) : XVI. Different Axiom Systems . . . XVIII. Truth Definitions and Consistency Proofs . . . PREDICATIVE SET THEORY (*Chaps. XXI-XXV*) : XXII. Undecidable Sentences. XXIII. Formalization of Mathematics. . . .

Originally published under the title: *A Survey of Mathematical Logic.*

—1962-71. x + 651 pp. 6x9. 8284-0245-0. **$9.95**

LEHRBUCH DER ALGEBRA

By H. WEBER

The bible of classical algebra, still unsurpassed for its clarity and completeness. Much of the material on elliptic functions is not available elsewhere in connected form.

PARTIAL CONTENTS: *VOL. I.* CHAP. I. Rational Functions. II. Determinants. III. Roots of Algebraic Equations. V. Symmetric Functions. V. Linear Transformations. Invariants. VI. Tchirnhaus Transformation. VII. Reality of Roots. VIII. Sturm's Theorem. X. Limits on Roots. X. Approximate Computation of Roots. XI. Continued Fractions. XII. Roots of Unity. XIII. Galois Theory. XIV. Applications of Permutation Group to Equations. XV. Cyclic Equations. XVI. Kreisteilung. XVII. Algebraic Solution of Equations. XVIII. Roots of Metacyclic Equations.

VOL. II. CHAPS. I.-V. Group Theory. VI.-X. Theory of Linear Groups. XI.-XVI. Applications of Group Theory (General Equation of Fifth Degree. The Group G_{168} and Equations of Seventh Degree . . .). XVII.-XXIV. Algebraic Numbers. XXV. Transcendental Numbers.

VOL. III. CHAP. I. Elliptic Integral. II. Theta Functions. III. Transformation of Theta Functions. IV. Elliptic Functions. V. Modular Function. V. Multiplication of Elliptic Functions. Division. VII. Equations of Transformation. VIII. Groups of the Transformation Equations and the Equation of Fifth Degree... XI.-XVI. Quadratic Fields. XVII. Elliptic Functions and Quadratic Forms. XVIII. Galois Group of Class Equation. XIX. Computation of Class Invariant . . . XII. Cayley's Development of Modular Function. XXIII. Class Fields. XXIV.-XXVI. Algebraic Functions. XXVII. Algebraic and Abelian Differentials.

—3rd ed. 1908-62. 2,345 pp. 5⅜x8. 8284-0144-6.
Each vol. **$9.50**
Three vol. set. **$22.50**

FESTSCHRIFT HEINRICH WEBER

By R. H. WEBER, et al.

Twenty-nine memoirs by leading mathematicians, including: O. BLUMENTHAL, R. DEDEKIND, R. GANS, H. HAHN, D. HILBERT, A. KNESER, A. KRAZER, R. v. MISES, T. REYE, F. SCHUR, A. SOMMERFELD, A. SPEISER, P. STACKEL, E. STUDY, R. H. WEBER, J. WELLSTEIN.

—1912-71. viii + 500 pp. 5⅜ x 8. 8284-0246-9. **Prob. $12.50**

DAS KONTINUUM, und andere Monographien

By H. WEYL, E. LANDAU, and B. RIEMANN

FOUR VOLUMES IN ONE.

DAS KONTINUUM (Kritische Untersuchungen ueber die Grundlagen der Analysis), by *H. Weyl.* Reprint of 2nd edition.

MATHEMATISCHE ANALYSE DES RAUMPROBLEMS, by *H. Weyl.*

DARSTELLUNG UND BEGRUENDUNG EINIGER NEURER ERGEBNISSE DER FUNKTIONENTHEORIE, by *E. Landau.* Reprint of 2nd edition.

UEBER DIE HYPOTHESEN, WELCHE DER GEOMETRIE ZU GRUNDE LIEGEN, by *B. Riemann.* Reprint of 3rd edition, edited and with comments by H. Weyl.

—1917/1923/1929/1854-1960. 368 pp. 5⅜x8. 8284-0134-9.
Four vols. in one. **$6.50**

THE PELL EQUATION

By E. E. WHITFORD and H. KONEN

TWO VOLUMES IN ONE: *The Pell Equation,* by Edward E. Whitford; and *Geschichte der Pellsche Gleichung,* by Heinrich Konen.

—1912/01-71. 193 + 132 pp. 5⅜x8. **In prep.**

PROJECTIVE DIFFERENTIAL GEOMETRY OF CURVES AND RULED SURFACES

By E. J. WILCZYNSKI

An unabridged reprint, with correction of errata, of a standard work.

—1906-61. viii + 298 pp. 5⅜x8. 8284-0155-1. **$4.95**

A HISTORY OF THE CALCULUS OF VARIATIONS IN THE 18th CENTURY

By R. WOODHOUSE

"Those interested in the beginnings of the Calculus of Variations should read the book by Lagrange and the—unfortunately, very rare—book by Woodhouse. Euler's masterpiece [*Methodus . . .*] will then offer him very little difficulty. This work of Euler's is distinguished by the abundance of its examples and is, to this day, one of the most interesting books that the mathematical literature has to offer."—C. CARATHEODORY, in *Variationsrechnung und Partielle Differentialgleichungen erster Ordnung.*

—I. TODHUNTER

—1811-1965. ix + x + 154 pp. 5x8⅜. 8284-0177-2. **$3.95**

BEGINNER'S BOOK OF GEOMETRY

By G. C. YOUNG and W. H. YOUNG

An elementary beginner's book by two distinguished mathematicians. Unlike Birkhoff's *Basic Geometry,* which is intended for teenagers, this book is truly for young children.

"The right one from a psychological point of view . . . Its main object is to awaken the pupil's mind to the ideas by which we classify the properties of space; this is done by directions in paper-folding, in dissection of areas, in the construction of solid models, and the like. At the same time, various theorems are stated and proved."—*Nature.*

—2nd ed. 1905-70. xvi + 222 pp. 4⅝x6⅜. 8284-0231-0. **$4.50**

THE THEORY OF SETS OF POINTS

By W. H. YOUNG and G. C. YOUNG

—1906-71. Appr. 402 pp. 5⅜x8. **In prep.**

THE THEORY OF GROUPS

By H. J. ZASSENHAUS

In this considerably augmented second edition of his famous work, Prof. Zassenhaus puts the original text in a lattice-theoretical framework. This has been done by the addition of new material as appendixes, so that the book can also continue to be read, as before, on a strictly group-theoretical level.

"A wealth of material in compact form."

—*Bulletin of A. M. S.*

—2nd ed. 1958. viii + 265 pp. 6x9. 8284-0053-9. **$6.50**